S0-CBM-979

Magill's Cinema Annual 2007

Magill's Cinema Annual 2007

26th Edition
A Survey of the Films of 2006

Hilary White, Editor

A VideoHound® Reference

Detroit • New York • San Francisco • New Haven, Conn. • Waterville, Maine • London

Magill's Cinema Annual 2007
Hilary White, Editor

Project Editor
Michael J. Tyrkus

Editorial
Beverly Baer, Tom Burns, Jim Craddock, Kristen A. Dorsch, Kathleen D. Meek, Kathleen Lopez Nolan, Joseph Palmisano, Marie Toft

Editorial Support Services
Wayne Fong

Composition and Electronic Prepress
Gary Leach

Manufacturing
Rhonda Dover, Evi Seoud

For more information contact
Thomson Gale
27500 Drake Rd.
Farmington Hills, MI 48331-3535
Or you can visit our Internet site at
http://www.gale.com

ISBN-13: 978-1-55862-578-5
ISBN-10: 1-55862-578-X
ISSN: 0739-2141

Printed in the United States of America
10 9 8 7 6 5 4 3 2 1

Contents

Preface	VII
Introduction	IX
Contributing Reviewers	XV
User's Guide	XVII
The Films of 2006	1
List of Awards	453
Obituaries	455
Selected Film Books of 2006	467
Director Index	473
Screenwriter Index	477
Cinematographer Index	483
Editor Index	487
Art Director Index	493
Music Director Index	497
Performer Index	501
Subject Index	533
Title Index	547

Preface

Magill's Cinema Annual 2007 continues the fine film reference tradition that defines the VideoHound® series of entertainment industry products published by Thomson Gale. The twenty-sixth annual volume in a series that developed from the twenty-one-volume core set, *Magill's Survey of Cinema,* the *Annual* was formerly published by Salem Press. Thomson Gale's thirteenth volume, as with the previous Salem volumes, contains essay-reviews of significant domestic and foreign films released in the United States during the preceding year.

The *Magill's* editorial staff at Thomson Gale, comprising the VideoHound® team and a host of *Magill's* contributors, continues to provide the enhancements that were added to the *Annual* when Thomson Gale acquired the line. These features include:

- More essay-length reviews of significant films released during the year
- Obituaries and book review sections
- Trivia and "fun facts" about the reviewed movies, their stars, the crew, and production
- Quotes and dialogue "soundbites" from reviewed movies, or from stars and crew about the film
- More complete awards and nominations listings, including the American Academy Awards®, Golden Globe, New York Critics Awards, Los Angeles Film Critics Awards, and others (see the User's Guide for more information on awards coverage)
- Box office grosses, including year-end and other significant totals
- Publicity taglines featured in film reviews and advertisements

In addition to these elements, the *Magill's Cinema Annual 2007* still features:

- An obituaries section profiling major contributors to the film industry who died in 2006
- An annotated list of selected film books published in 2006

- Nine indexes: Director, Screenwriter, Cinematographer, Editor, Art Director, Music Director, Performer, Subject, and Title (now cumulative)

COMPILATION METHODS

The *Magill's* editorial staff reviews a variety of entertainment industry publications, including trade magazines and newspapers, as well as online sources, on a daily and weekly basis to select significant films for review in *Magill's Cinema Annual. Magill's* staff and other contributing reviewers, including film scholars and university faculty, write the reviews included in the *Annual.*

MAGILL'S CINEMA ANNUAL: A VIDEOHOUND® REFERENCE

The *Magill's Survey of Cinema* series, now supplemented by the *Annual,* is the recipient of the Reference Book of the Year Award in Fine Arts by the American Library Association. Thomson Gale, an award-winning publisher of reference products, is proud to offer *Magill's Cinema Annual* as part of its popular VideoHound® product line, which includes *VideoHound®'s Golden Movie Retriever* and *The Video Source Book.* Other Thomson Gale film-related products include the four-volume *International Dictionary of Films and Filmmakers, Women Filmmakers & Their Films,* the *Contemporary Theatre, Film, and Television* series, and the four-volume *Schirmer Encyclopedia of Film.*

ACKNOWLEDGMENTS

Thank you to Gary Leach for his typesetting expertise, and Wayne Fong for his invaluable technical assistance. The VideoHound® staff is thanked for its contributions to this project. For their invaluable assistance, *Magill's* would also like to thank Susan Norget at Susan Norget Film Promotion; Jeanne R. Birney at the Press Office of the New York Film Festival; Tammi Rosen at the Press Office of the Tribeca Film Festival; and Nancy Gerstman at Zeitgeist Films.

The Year in Film: An Introduction

Two thousand and six was a banner year for domestic and international films. Hollywood brought back favorites, including Disney's unstoppable *Pirates of the Caribbean* series as well as the animated animals of *Ice Age*. The year also marked the triumphant return of Superman after a twenty-year hiatus and ushered in a better-than-ever James Bond in *Casino Royale*. Even Rocky made a comeback this year. Dan Brown's controversial bestselling novel *The Da Vinci Code* turned into a controversial summer blockbuster in the hands of Ron Howard. While the war continued in Iraq, it was also much on the minds of filmmakers who offered the post 9/11 ruminations *United 93* and *World Trade Center*. American icon Clint Eastwood brought both *Flags of Our Fathers* and the companion film, the much-lauded *Letters from Iwo Jima* to the war film genre. Another critical favorite, *Babel,* featured an international cast and was filmed on three continents. British offerings included *The Queen* and *The Last King of Scotland,* both featuring Academy Award® winning performances by their lead actors. Former U.S. Vice President Al Gore starred in the Academy Award® winning documentary *An Inconvenient Truth,* which illuminated the topic of global warming. Lighter fare, such as the dark comedy *Little Miss Sunshine* and the silly but serious social commentary comedy of Sacha Baron Cohen's *Borat: Cultural Learnings of America for Make Benefit Glorious Nation of Kazakhstan* were also taken seriously and nominated for a host of awards as well. After a total of eight nominations for directing and screenwriting, legendary director Martin Scorsese finally won an Academy Award® for directing his Irish mafia drama *The Departed,* which also won Best Picture.

The movie industry looked bright in 2006, taking in $9.1 billion in receipts, up from $8.9 billion the previous year. *Pirates of the Caribbean: Dead Man's Chest* continued the franchise's siege, raiding the box office to become number one with $423 million domestically and over $1 billion worldwide and paving the way for the third installment in 2007. Coming in a distant second with $244 million was *Cars,* Disney/Pixar's heart-warming, animated tale of a hot rod who takes an unexpected detour in Anytown, USA. Another family friendly comedy, Fox's *Night at the Museum,* a surprise, late-year hit starring Ben Stiller, wasn't far behind, grossing $241 million. Fox also had the number four film, *X-Men: The Last Stand,* the final and highest-grossing X-Men film to date, pulling in $234 million. In fifth place was director Ron Howard and star Tom Hanks' critically-panned *The Da Vinci Code* which nonetheless had viewers intrigued to the tune of $217 million. Faring much better critically was the number six film of 2006 with $200 million in receipts, *Superman Returns,* directed by superhero specialist Bryan Singer and starring newcomer Brandon Routh as the Man of Steel, who was last seen on the big-screen some twenty years prior. Rounding out the top ten highest-grossing films of the year was the animated sequel *Ice Age: The Meltdown* ($195 million); the Academy Award® winning animated children's hit *Happy Feet* ($206 million); Daniel Craig's lauded blonde Bond of *Casino Royale* ($167 million); and Will Smith's Academy Award® nominated performance in the true story *The Pursuit of Happyness* ($162 million).

The Academy of Motion Picture Arts and Sciences boasted a particularly diverse and international spirit in 2006. Among the Best Picture nominees, Mexican director Alejandro Gonzalez Inarritu's *Babel,* filmed on three continents, illustrates the problems of communication shared by people worldwide. A France/USA/Mexico production, *Babel* was filmed in a host of languages including English, Spanish, Arabic, and Japanese Sign Language. Inarritu's friends and fellow countrymen, filmmakers Alfonso Cuaron and Guillermo del Toro all appeared at the Academy Awards® as nominees; Cuaron's dystopic drama *Children of Men* was nominated for Best Adapted Screenplay, Best Cinematography, and Best Editing while del Toro's dark fantasy/horror *Pan's Labyrinth* garnered six Oscar® nominations, including Best Foreign Language Film and eventually winning for Best Cinematography, Art Direction, and Makeup. Fellow Best Picture nominee *Letters from Iwo Jima* was significant as a mainly Japanese language film from the quintessentially American director Eastwood, who chronicles the Battle of Iwo Jima, as he also did in *Flags of Our Fathers,* from the point of view of the Japanese.

British director Stephen Frears' biographical drama *The Queen* focusing on Queen Elizabeth was a quiet, character-driven piece made memorable by the uncanny performance of Helen Mirren, who won every award for which she was nominated, including the Oscar®. *The Queen* received six Academy Award® nominations, including Best Picture and Best Original Screenplay.

The independent, dysfunctional family roadtrip comedy *Little Miss Sunshine* surprised many with its phenomenal success. The film won the Independent Spirit Award for Best Feature as well as garnering several Golden Globe and Academy Award® nominations, including Best Picture, Best Supporting Actress for the film's young star Abigail Breslin and Best Supporting Actor for Alan Arkin, who won the Oscar® over favored contender Eddie Murphy, who had won nearly every other award for his memorable performance in the musical *Dreamgirls.*

It was Martin Scorsese's year to take home Oscar® gold. After winning the Golden Globe, Directors Guild Award, and New York Film Critics Circle Awards for Best Director, his critically acclaimed *The Departed* took the Best Picture Oscar® as well as the long-awaited Best Director Award for Scorsese. The film also won Best Adapted Screenplay for writer William Monahan, Best Editing for Thelma Schoonmaker, and a Best Supporting Actor nomination for actor Mark Wahlberg.

African American actors had a great year in 2006. Winning the Best Actor Oscar® this year was Forest Whitaker for his powerful portrait of Ugandan dictator Idi Amin in Kevin Macdonald's *The Last King of Scotland,* beating out such actors as Peter O'Toole (*Venus*), Leonardo DiCaprio (*Blood Diamond*), Ryan Gosling (*Half Nelson*), and Will Smith (*The Pursuit of Happyness*). Although Arkin took the Best Supporting Actor Oscar®, nominees in that category also included African American actors Eddie Murphy (*Dreamgirls*) and Djimon Hounsou (*Blood Diamond*). Jackie Earle Haley (*Little Children*) and Mark Wahlberg (*The Departed*) were fellow nominees.

Women of a certain age also had a fine year for a change. Mirren competed for her Best Actress Academy Award® with the likes of acting powerhouse Meryl Streep, playing a fashionista boss from hell in *The Devil Wears Prada* and British legend Judi Dench, playing a twisted schoolteacher in *Notes on a Scandal.* The other Best Actress contenders included the most nominated actress of her generation, Kate Winslet, playing a philandering housewife in *Little Children,* and Penelope Cruz's best performance to date in Pedro Almodovar's *Volver.* The Best Supporting Actress category also reflected Oscar®'s international spirit, with Mexico's Adriana Barraza and Japan's Rinko Kikuchi nominated for their performances in *Babel.* Cate Blanchett was a nominee for *Notes on a Scandal* along with Abigail Breslin for *Little Miss Sunshine.* The Best Supporting Actress Oscar® ultimately went to former American Idol contestant Jennifer Hudson for her performance as Effie White in *Dreamgirls,* Bill Condon's acclaimed musical that won the Golden Globe for Best Musical Picture Musical or Comedy.

Sequels and remade classics continued to have a significant place in contemporary film. Along with box office leaders *Pirates of the Caribbean, Ice Age,* and *X-Men, Mission: Impossible III* and its high profile star Tom Cruise proved to be as popular as ever, with moviegoers forking over $134 million to see the latest mission. Combining sequel with horror and comedy, the fourth installment of the *Scary Movie* franchise grossed a whopping $90 million. Viewers apparently could not get enough of Tim Allen as Santa, with *The Santa Clause 3: The Escape Clause* taking $84 million home for Christmas. Horror darling *Saw III* saw $80 million in grosses while the appropriately titled *Jackass Number Two* retained both its lowbrow, homegrown image and its giant $72 million in box office receipts. Both Tyler Perry's "Madea" and *Big Momma's House* returned to big box office in 2006. With original creator and star Sylvester Stallone, Rocky got a minor facelift, dubbed *Rocky Balboa,* and was warmly welcomed by most critics and audiences with a healthy $70 million gross. Audiences were not quite as welcoming of the slick new *Miami Vice,* largely taking place outside Miami, which only recouped $63 million of its bloated $135 million budget. Directed by *Das Boot*'s Wolfgang Petersen, the remake of the 1970s classic disaster film *The Poseidon Adventure, Poseidon* seemed a shoe-in, but was ultimately doomed by a $160 budget, so-so script, and middling acting. At the bottom of the sequel and remake barrel was *Basic Instinct 2,* which was critically panned and shunned by audiences.

With the box office strength of *X-Men: The Last Stand* and *Superman Returns,* comic book fare and superheroes continued to fly high in 2006. *V for Vendetta,* starring Natalie Portman and Hugo Weaving, earned $70 million and critical acclaim. The tragic story of real-life Superman, George Reeves, also revived Ben Affleck's career with his notable performance in the drama *Hollywoodland.* Uma Thurman's turn as a crazed superhero in *My Super Ex-Girlfriend* garnered less than stellar reviews. The usual less-than-worthy additions to the genre included a lackluster *Ultraviolet* and the dismal *Zoom.*

Documentaries reflected prevalent environmental issues, led by the Academy Award® winning *An Inconvenient Truth,* which detailed the hazards of global warming and called for change worldwide. Similarly, the intriguing *Who Killed the Electric Car?* showed a social and environmental conscience. On the more whimsical side was *Wordplay,* featuring the world of crosswords and their eccentric inhabitants and the plethora of concert documentaries, including *Neil Young: Heart of Gold, Dave Chappelle's Block Party,* and the Beastie Boys' *Awesome...I F***in' Shot That!.*

Led by Guillermo del Toro's lauded *Pan's Labyrinth,* foreign films flourished. Pedro Almodovar triumphed again with *Volver,* which boasted a Golden Globe nomination for Best Foreign Language Film among its many honors. Other notable foreign films included Australia's *The Proposition,* an unforgettable, uber-violent western set in the outback directed by John Hillcoat; French director Andre Techine's *Changing Times,* a complex love story which reunited stars Gerard Depardieu and Catherine Deneuve; the Turkish/French drama *Climates*; Belgium's Dardenne borthers' *L'Enfant*; the Academy Award® nominated Indian drama *Water*; the touching Romanian drama *The Death of Mr. Lazarescu*; Italian writer/director Cristina Comencini's *Don't Tell*; Zhang Yimou's *The Curse of the Golden Flower*; and Jean-Pierre Melville's 1969 World War II war drama just released in the United States, *Army in the Shadows.*

Perhaps the biggest surprise hit of the year was *Borat: Cultural Learnings of America for Make Benefit Glorious Nation of Kazakhstan,* a comedy which was co-written by and starred British comedian Sacha Baron Cohen as a Kazakh journalist which grossed $128 million. With little fanfare ushering in the massive hit, *Borat* was surprisingly acclaimed and at the top of many notable critics lists of the year's best films. Baron Cohen received a Golden Globe Award for Best Actor for his performance in *Borat,* which also garnered an Academy Award® nomination for Best Adapted Screenplay. Another comedy, *Talladega Nights: The Ballad of Ricky Bobby,* starring the bankable and busy Will Ferrell (who also appeared in this year's *Stranger Than Fiction* and *Curious George*) proved popular with audiences, taking in $148 million. Magic proved profitable as well, especially period films featuring magicians. Christopher Nolan's *The Prestige* starred Christian Bale and Hugh Jackman as rival illusionists and kept co-star Michael Caine busy as usual (he also appeared in *Children of Men*), while the Edward Norton-starring *The Illusionist* was equally well-liked. Outstanding independent films included critical favorite *Thank You for Smoking, Old Joy,* and *Friends with Money.*

Surprise misses of the year included *All the King's Men,* which boasted an Oscar® winning writer/director (Steven Zaillian), a stellar cast including Sean Penn and Kate Winslet, and a Pulitzer Prize-winning story but was critically panned and made a disappointing $7 million at the box office. Darren Aronofsky's long-suffering project *The Fountain* with its time-traveling love story arrived in theaters with a resounding thud. The same was true of M. Night Shyamalan's *Lady in the Water,* Neil LaBute's cult horror remake *The Wicker Man* starring Nicolas Cage, and Terry Gilliam's gruesome *Tideland.* The biggest disappointment of the year may have been the Samuel L. Jackson vehicle, *Snakes on a Plane,* which became an Internet phenomenon prior to its release. The unprecedented buzz did not translate into either box office or critical acclaim, however.

Horror fans had much to celebrate, reveling in the gore offered up in such favorites as the aforementioned *Saw III, Hostel, The Descent,* and *Slither.* Alexandre Aja's remake of Wes Craven's 1977 classic *The Hills Have Eyes* did well at the box office, as did a remake of Richard Donner's 1976 *The Omen,* a faithful retelling conveniently released on 6/6/06. The fine people of *The Texas Chainsaw Massacre* franchise trotted out a middling prequel/regurgitation of its previous incarnations. Lesser efforts in the genre included *An American Haunting, When a Stranger Calls, See No Evil, BloodRayne,* and *Silent Hill.*

Although children would have a year between Harry Potter films, they had a plethora of other quality entertainment at their disposal, led by the hugely popular animated animal extravaganzas *Ice Age: The Meltdown* and penguin-fest *Happy Feet.* It appeared filmmakers could not get enough of animated critters, which also populated *Barnyard, Flushed Away, The Ant Bully, Curious George, Garfield: A Tail of Two Kitties,* and *Over the Hedge.* Both visually amazing and entertaining were the hits *Cars* and *Monster House.* Many were delighted with the release of E.B. White's children's classic *Charlotte's Web,* which finally made it to the big screen aided by a host of A-list celebrity voices and grossing a respectable $81 million. Children and adults alike could find inspiration in the wonderful *Akeelah and the Bee,* featuring newcomer Keke Palmer and Laurence Fishburne. Lesser kid pics included the disappointing action-adventure film *Zoom,* which was panned by critics and grossed a dismal $11 million at the box office.

Sadly, the world lost legendary filmmaker Robert Altman, who completed his final film, *A Prairie Home Companion,* in 2006. Hollywood also mourned the deaths of longtime screen favorites June Allyson, Glenn Ford, Maureen Stapleton, Shelley Winters, Red Buttons, Don Knotts, Jack Palance, Peter Boyle, Bruno Kirby, Christopher Penn, Robert Donner, Moira Shearer, Arthur Hill, Jane Wyatt, Mickey Hargitay, and Philippe Noiret. The film community also lost such behind-the-screen talents as producer/director Richard Fleischer; sound re-recording mixer Robert "Buzz" Knudson; production designer/art director Henry Bumstead; Hannah Barbera co-founder, animator Joseph Barbera; composer Akira Ifukube; fashion and costume designer Oleg Cassini; and cinematographer Sven Nykvist. These and other celebrated talents who passed away in 2006 are profiled in the Obituaries section of this book.

We at *Magill's* look forward to another exciting year in film and preparing the next edition of *Magill's Cinema Annual.* As always, we invite your comments, questions, and suggestions. Please direct them to:

Hilary White, Editor
Magill's Cinema Annual
Thomson Gale
27500 Drake Road
Farmington Hills, MI 48331-3535
Phone: (248) 699-4253
Toll-Free: (800) 347-GALE (4253)
Fax: (248) 699-8865

Contributing Reviewers

Laura Abraham
Freelance Reviewer

Michael Adams
Graduate School, City University of New York

Vivek Adarkar
Long Island University

Kjerstine Anderson
Freelance Reviewer

Richard Baird
Freelance Reviewer

Michael Betzold
Freelance Reviewer

John Boaz
Freelance Reviewer

David L. Boxerbaum
Freelance Reviewer

Beverley Bare Buehrer
Freelance Reviewer

Tom Burns
Freelance Reviewer

David E. Chapple
Freelance Reviewer

Peter N. Chumo II
Freelance Reviewer

David Flanagin
Freelance Reviewer

Jill Hamilton
Freelance Reviewer

Nick Kennedy
Freelance Reviewer

Eric Monder
Freelance Reviewer

David Metz Roberts
Freelance Reviewer

John C. Tibbetts
Freelance Reviewer

Christine Tomassini
Freelance Reviewer

Michael J. Tyrkus
Freelance Reviewer

James M. Welsh
Salisbury State University

Michael White
Freelance Reviewer

User's Guide

ALPHABETIZATION

Film titles and reviews are arranged on a word-by-word basis, including articles and prepositions. English leading articles (A, An, The) are ignored, as are foreign leading articles (El, Il, La, Las, Le, Les, Los). Other considerations:

- Acronyms appear alphabetically as if regular words.
- Common abbreviations in titles file as if they are spelled out, so *Mr. Death* will be found as if it was spelled *Mister Death.*
- Proper names in titles are alphabetized beginning with the individual's first name, for instance, *Gloria* will be found under "G."
- Titles with numbers, for instance, *200 Cigarettes,* are alphabetized as if the numbers were spelled out, in this case, "Two-Hundred." When numeric titles gather in close proximity to each other, the titles will be arranged in a low-to-high numeric sequence.

SPECIAL SECTIONS

The folowing sections that are designed to enhance the reader's examination of film are arranged alphabetically, they include:

- *List of Awards.* An annual list of awards bestowed upon the year's films by the following associations: Academy of Motion Picture Arts and Sciences, Directors Guild of America Award, Golden Globe Awards, Los Angeles Film Critics Awards, National Board of Review Awards, National Society of Film Critics Awards, New York Film Critics Awards, the Screen Actors Guild Awards, and the Writer's Guild Awards.
- *Obituaries.* Profiles major contributors to the film industry who died in 2006.
- *Selected Film Books of 2006.* An annotated list of selected film books published in 2006.

INDEXES

Film titles and artists are arranged into nine indexes, allowing the reader to effectively approach a film from any one of several directions, including not only its credits but its subject matter.

- *Director, Screenwriter, Cinematographer, Editor, Art Director, Music Director,* and *Performer* indexes are arranged alphabetically according to artists appearing in this volume, followed by a list of the films on which they worked. In the *Performer* index, a (V) beside a movie title indicates voice-only work.
- *Subject Index.* Films may be categorized under several of the subject terms arranged alphabetically in this section.
- *Title Index.* The title index is a cumulative alphabetical list of films covered in the twenty-six volumes of the *Magill's Cinema Annual,* including the films covered in this volume. Films reviewed in past volumes are cited with the year in which the film appeared in the *Annual*; films reviewed in this volume are cited with the film title in bold with a bolded Arabic numeral indicating the page number on which the review begins. Original and alternate titles are cross-referenced to the American release title in the Title Index. Titles of retrospective films are followed by the year, in brackets, of their original release.

SAMPLE REVIEW

Each *Magill's* review contains up to sixteen items of information. A fictionalized composite sample review containing all the elements of information that may be included in a full-length review follows the outline on the facing page. The circled number following each element in the sample review designates an item of information that is explained in the outline.

1. **Title:** Film title as it was released in the United States.
2. **Foreign or alternate title(s):** The film's original title or titles as released outside the United States, or alternate film title or titles. Foreign and alternate titles also appear in the Title Index to facilitate user access.
3. **Taglines:** Up to ten publicity taglines for the film from advertisements or reviews.
4. **Box office information:** Year-end or other box office domestic revenues for the film.
5. **Film review:** A signed review of the film, including an analytic overview of the film and its critical reception.
6. **Reviewer byline:** The name of the reviewer who wrote the full-length review. A complete list of this volume's contributors appears in the "Contributing Reviewers" section which follows the Introduction.
7. **Principal characters:** Listings of the film's principal characters and the names of the actors who play them in the film.
8. **Country of origin:** The film's country or countries of origin.
9. **Release date:** The year of the film's first general release.
10. **Production information:** This section typically includes the name(s) of the film's producer(s), production company, and distributor; director(s); screenwriter(s); cinematographer(s) (if the film is animated, this will be replaced with Animation or Animation direction, or it will not be listed); editor(s); art director(s); production designer(s); music composer(s); and other credits such as visual effects, sound, costume design, and song(s) and songwriter(s).
11. **MPAA rating:** The film's rating by the Motion Picture Association of America. If there is no rating given, the line will read, "Unrated."
12. **Running time:** The film's running time in minutes.
13. **Reviews:** A list of brief citations of major newspaper and journal reviews of the film, including publication title, date of review, and page number (when available).
14. **Film quotes:** Memorable dialogue directly from the film, attributed to the character who spoke it, or comment from cast or crew members or reviewers about the film.
15. **Film trivia:** Interesting tidbits about the film, its cast, or production crew.
16. **Awards information:** Awards won by the film, followed by category and name of winning cast or crew member. Listings of the film's nominations follow the wins on a separate line for each award. Awards are arranged alphabetically. Information is listed for films that won or were nominated for the following awards: American Academy Awards®, British Academy of Film and Television Arts, Directors Guild of America, Golden Globe, Los Angeles Critics Association Awards, National Board of Review Awards, National Society of Film Critics Awards, New York Critics Awards, Writers Guild of America, and others.

THE GUMP DIARIES ①

(Los Diarios del Gump) ②

Love means never having to say you're stupid.
—Movie tagline ③

Box Office: $10 million ④

In writer/director Robert Zemeckis' *Back to the Future* trilogy (1985, 1989, 1990), Marty McFly (Michael J. Fox) and his scientist sidekick Doc Brown (Christopher Lloyd) journey backward and forward in time, attempting to smooth over some rough spots in their personal histories in order to remain true to their individual destinies. Throughout their time-travel adventures, Doc Brown insists that neither he nor Marty influence any major historical events, believing that to do so would result in catastrophic changes in humankind's ultimate destiny. By the end of the trilogy, however, Doc Brown has revised his thinking and tells Marty that, "Your future hasn't been written yet. No one's has. Your future is whatever you make it. So make it a good one."

In *Forrest Gump,* Zemeckis once again explores the theme of personal destiny and how an individual's life affects and is affected by his historical time period. This time, however, Zemeckis and screenwriter Eric Roth chronicle the life of a character who does nothing but meddle in the historical events of his time without even trying to do so. By the film's conclusion, however, it has become apparent that Zemeckis' main concern is something more than merely having fun with four decades of American history. In the process of re-creating significant moments in time, he has captured on celluloid something eternal and timeless—the soul of humanity personified by a nondescript simpleton from the deep South.

The film begins following the flight of a seemingly insignificant feather as it floats down from the sky and brushes against various objects and people before finally coming to rest at the feet of Forrest Gump (Tom Hanks). Forrest, who is sitting on a bus-stop bench, reaches down and picks up the feather, smooths it out, then opens his traveling case and carefully places the feather between the pages of his favorite book, *Curious George.*

In this simple but hauntingly beautiful opening scene, the filmmakers illustrate the film's principal concern: Is life a series of random events over which a person has no control, or is there an underlying order to things that leads to the fulfillment of an individual's destiny? The rest of the film is a humorous and moving attempt to prove that, underlying the random, chaotic events that make up a person's life, there exists a benign and simple order.

Forrest sits on the bench throughout most of the film, talking about various events of his life to others who happen to sit down next to him. It does not take long, however, for the audience to realize that Forrest's seemingly random chatter to a parade of strangers has a perfect chronological order to it. He tells his first story after looking down at the feet of his first bench partner and observing, "Mama always said that you can tell a lot about a person by the shoes they wear." Then, in a voice-over narration, Forrest begins the story of his life, first by telling about the first pair of shoes he can remember wearing.

The action shifts to the mid-1950s with Forrest as a young boy (Michael Humphreys) being fitted with leg braces to correct a curvature in his spine. Despite this traumatic handicap, Forrest remains unaffected, thanks to his mother (Sally Field) who reminds him on more than one occasion that he is no different from anyone else. Although this and most of Mrs. Gump's other words of advice are in the form of hackneyed cliches, Forrest, whose intelligence quotient is below normal, sincerely believes every one of them, namely because he instinctively knows they are sincere expressions of his mother's love and fierce devotion. ⑤

John Byline ⑥

CREDITS ⑦

Forrest Gump: Tom Hanks
Forrest's Mother: Sally Field
Young Forrest: Michael Humphreys
Origin: United States ⑧
Language: English, Spanish
Released: 1994 ⑨
Production: Liz Heller, John Manulis; New Line Cinema; released by Island Pictures ⑩
Directed by: Robert Zemeckis
Written by: Eric Roth
Cinematography by: David Phillips
Music by: Graeme Revell
Editing: Dana Congdon
Production Design: Danny Nowak
Sound: David Sarnoff
Costumes: David Robinson
MPAA rating: R ⑪
Running time: 102 minutes ⑫

REVIEWS (13)

Entertainment Weekly. July 15, 1994, p. 42.
Hollywood Reporter. June 29, 1994, p. 7.
Los Angeles Times. July 6, 1994, p. F1.
New York Times Online. July 15, 1994.

QUOTES (14)

Forrest Gump (Tom Hanks): "The state of existence may be likened unto a receptacle containing cocoa-based confections, in that one may never predict that which one may receive."

TRIVIA (15)

Hanks was the first actor since Spencer Tracy to win back-to-back Oscars® for Best Actor. Hanks received the award in 1993 for his performance in *Philadelphia.* Tracy won Oscars® in 1937 for *Captains Courageous* and in 1938 for *Boys Town.*

AWARDS (16)

Academy Awards 1994: Film, Actor (Hanks), Special Effects, Cinematography

Nomination:

Golden Globes 1994: Film, Actor (Hanks), Supporting Actress (Field), Music

A

ACCEPTED

When every college turned them down...they made one up.
—Movie tagline

Reject rejection.
—Movie tagline

Box Office: $36.3 million

Accepted follows in the footsteps of a long line of comedies about teenage students rebelling against the higher education system. Nathan Lee of the *New York Times* called it "that most oxymoronic of genres, the Hollywood comedy about sticking it to the man." In said genre, there must be large parties, a band of lovable losers, and stiff authority figures who get taken down in the end.

In this film, the lovable losers are led by Bartleby Gaines (Justin Long), who is known as "B." A smart guy who cannot seem to apply his intellectual skills, B is rejected by every college he applies to. This news does not go over well with his overbearing father (Mark Derwin), so B has to come up with a Plan B. He invents a fictitious college, the South Harmon Institute of Technology. That the acronym created by this name spells an obscenity is one joke that screenwriters Adam Cooper, Bill Collage, and Mark Perez never get tired of belaboring.

B creates a fake acceptance letter for himself and even has his best friend, the nerdy and plump Schrader (Jonah Hill), create a nice looking website for the school. Things get complicated when B's parents insist on visiting the school and he is forced to come up with some sort of campus. He and his fellow rejects—smart girl Rory (Maria Thayer), weird guy Glen (Adam Herschman), and injured athlete Hands (Columbus Short)—rent an abandoned psychiatric facility. Demonstrating the skills of a world-class construction crew, they miraculously transform the creepy old building into something that could pass for a college.

B and his friends' not terribly well-thought-out plan to lounge around all year at South Harmon is upset one morning when five hundred students show up at the school. Apparently Schrader's website has been spewing out acceptance letters to anyone who applies to the school. B's first reaction is to turn them away but when he sees their eager gratitude at being accepted (plus their $10,000 tuition checks), he decides he will let them stay.

The school adopts a student-driven curriculum with classes such as "Foreign Affairs: Hooking Up Overseas," "How to Blow Up Stuff With Your Mind," and the popular "Doing Nothing." The kids create a sort of educational utopia, but unfortunately for them, the third act looms and an additional complication must be thrown their way. Said complication comes in the form of the preppy elite. In this case, it is the stuffy Dean Van Horne of the prestigious Harmon College (Anthony Heald) and his young henchman, frat boy Hoyt Ambrose (Travis Van Winkle). The dean is mad because South Harmon is making a mockery of education and, perhaps more importantly, he also wants to buy South Harmon's land to create a grand entrance to his college.

The biggest misstep of the film, besides those repetitive acronym jokes, is the climactic scene when Harmon and South Harmon meet before scowling board members at an accreditation hearing. A film like this does not need B emoting, "You rob these kids of their creativity and their passion—that's the real crime!" Still, the film hits most of its marks and does what it sets out to do. There are some laughs, some nubile girls, and some comeuppance for snooty types. Steve Pink, who wrote *Grosse Pointe Blank* (1997) and *High Fidelity* (2000), makes his directorial debut here. Perhaps his writing background helped because the banter in the film is slightly quicker and wittier than in most films of this ilk. While it is not *The Thin Man* (1934), neither is it *PCU* (1994).

Critics did not seem to realize the inherent absurdity of reviewing such a film and took their jobs quite seriously. Stephen Willliams of *Newsday* was quite disturbed by the "idea put forward that self-indulgence is a substitute for structured education, or, more to the point, that it's a substitute for life." Michael Phillips of the *Chicago Tribune* called the film "a mildly funny PG-13 effort that is just dying to release an R or unrated DVD version of itself." Peter Hartlaub of the *San Francisco Chronicle* wrote: "Much of *Accepted* is ludicrous, but even when the screenwriters and actors are insulting your intelligence, they have the courtesy to be consistently funny." Finally, Ty Burr of the *Boston Globe* wrote: "Low of brow and pure of heart, the movie plays like *Animal House* extra-lite, and as such it's decent indecent fun."

Jill Hamilton

CREDITS

Bartleby Gaines: Justin Long
Monica: Blake Lively
Jack Gaines: Mark Derwin
Dean Van Horne: Anthony Heald
Glen: Adam Herschman
Sherman Schrader: Jonah Hill
Hands: Columbus Short
Rory: Maria Thayer
Uncle Ben: Lewis Black
Hoyt Ambrose: Travis Van Winkle
Diane Gaines: Ann Cusack
Origin: USA
Language: English
Released: 2006
Production: Tom Shadyac, Michael Bostick; Shady Acres; released by Universal Pictures
Directed by: Steve Pink
Written by: Mark Perez, Adam Cooper, Bill Collage
Cinematography by: Matthew F. Leonetti
Music by: David Schommer
Sound: Steve Cantamessa, John Halaby
Editing: Scott Hill
Art Direction: Denise Hudson
Costumes: Genevieve Tyrrell
Production Design: Rusty Smith
MPAA rating: PG-13
Running time: 92 minutes

REVIEWS

Chicago Sun-Times Online. August 18, 2006.
Entertainment Weekly. August 25, 2006, p. 64.
Los Angeles Times Online. August 18, 2006.
New York Times Online. August 18, 2006.
San Francisco Chronicle. August 18, 2006, p. E5.
Variety Online. August 10, 2006.
Washington Post. August 18, 2006, p. C4.

AKEELAH AND THE BEE

Changing the world...one word at a time.
—Movie tagline

Box Office: $18.8 million

While learning to spell words like "xanthosis," "soliterraneous," and "logorrhea," a little girl on the wrong side of the tracks in Los Angeles learns a powerful lesson: "Our greatest fear is not that we are inadequate; our greatest fear is that we are powerful beyond measure...we ask ourselves, who am I to be brilliant, gorgeous, handsome, talented, and fabulous? Actually, who are you not to be?" (This quote is unattributed in the film and often credited to Nelson Mandela but is actually from Marianne Williamson and her book, *A Return To Love: Reflections on the Principles of A Course in Miracles.*) Directed by Doug Atchison from his Nicholl Fellowship-winning screenplay, *Akeelah and the Bee* is the first film produced by Starbucks Entertainment. Shot in thirty-one days for a mere $6 million, the film grossed a disappointing $19 million but received accolades from critics and audiences alike. Chronicling Akeelah Anderson's road from South Central Los Angeles to the Scripps National Spelling Bee in Washington DC, the film follows in the footsteps of the documentary *Spellbound* (2003) and the psychological drama *Bee Season* (2005). Inspirational and extremely family friendly, *Akeelah* also occasionally indulges in formulaic, feel-good moments and cheap sentiment.

Keke Palmer, in her first big screen lead role, plays Akeelah, a bright eleven-year-old whose father has died and whose mother Tanya (Angela Bassett) has too much to worry about with Akeelah's gangbanger brother and full-time nursing job to pay any attention to her. Like any normal girl her age, Akeelah likes to hang out with her friends and go to the mall. Unlike any of her friends, however, Akeelah also enjoys studying the dictionary to learn to spell new words. Because this singles her out as a "brainiac," Akeelah hides her light under a bushel, so to speak, only being coaxed into entering Crenshaw Middle School's first spelling bee after she is threatened with detention for her frequent absences.

Akeelah breezes through the undemanding competition, prompting her principal Mr. Welch (Curtis Armstrong) to seek a top-notch coach to guide her in the district competition while garnering exposure for his school in the process. Despite the fact that Professor Joshua Larabee (Laurence Fishburne) was himself a finalist at the national spelling bee, he is currently on a leave of absence after the death of his nine-year-old daughter and not sure he wants to take on the sassy, unmotivated Akeelah. The two clash after their initial meeting at Larabee's well-appointed home and Akeelah decides to go to the district competition alone.

At the district bee, Akeelah gets a taste of what serious business spelling bees are. After dodging some of the more difficult words, she somehow manages to qualify for the regionals. She gets unexpected help at the district competition from fellow contestant Javier (J.R. Villarreal), who gives her some friendly advice along with his phone number. She also meets the driven, spelling prodigy Dylan Chiu (Sean Michael Afable), an Asian American, who, like Javier, lives in the posh suburban Woodland Hills neighborhood.

Akeelah accepts Javier's invitation to join their spelling club, making the long trek to the other side of Los Angeles on several buses, where he then asks her to attend his birthday party. The party turns into a heated game of Scrabble, with Dylan taking on all the guests at once. When Akeelah nearly wins, she overhears Dylan's demanding father (Tzi Ma), who is also his spelling coach, angrily admonishing the boy for nearly being bested by "a little black girl." The party has its moments too, as when Javier plants a kiss on Akeelah's cheek, then jokingly ask her if she plans to sue him for sexual harassment. When Akeelah's well-meaning but misguided mother learns of her trip to Woodland Hills along with her involvement in the spelling bees—which she deems a waste of time—she bans Akeelah from participating. The resourceful girl then forges her mother's signature in order to proceed with the regional bee.

Enjoying her success and new friends, Akeelah finds she wants a shot at winning at the regionals in order to proceed to the national bee and enlists Larabee, after agreeing to his strict conditions. Some of his rules include being on time, never missing a daily session, and refraining from "street talk" while in his presence. Despite the occasional slip, Akeelah becomes a model student, and soaks up the Latin, Greek, and French that Larabee knows she must study in order to win against the far more advantaged and experienced spellers from better school districts. Akeelah's mother, innocently tipped off by Javier's mom who offers her a ride to the bee, barges in near the end of the regional competition and demands her daughter leave the stage. However, after talking with Larabee she is able to understand her daughter's determination and Tanya finally gets on board and lets her finish the regionals. Akeelah triumphs, along with Dylan and Javier, and qualifies for the national bee.

Larabee, whose tragedy conveniently mirrors Akeelah's, is quickly sinking into his own despair and brushes off the distraught finalist as the nationals grow closer by giving her 5,000 flashcards to study on her own. It is here the movie indulges in a little too much sentiment. Looking for help from her mother, Tanya encouragingly tells her she has thousands of coaches all around her and suddenly the whole neighborhood is pitching in to coach one of their own on to victory—from her best friend Georgia (Sahara Garey) to shopkeepers to the head gangbanger. Triumphantly plunking down the heavy boxes of cards and announcing she's memorized them all, Akeelah also confronts a surprised Larabee about his daughter, which he has never mentioned. He quickly comes to terms with her death and soon he's back on board as Akeelah's coach for the trip to the nationals.

The drama at the national bee plays out nicely, providing a rousing finish for the film. Javier finishes well but it is Akeelah and Dylan who end up in a head to head battle for the win. During a break, Akeelah again overhears Mr. Chiu berating Dylan and decides to throw the competition as this is Dylan's final year to compete in the national bee while Akeelah has several years ahead of her. She misspells a word that Dylan knows for a fact she can spell—he corrected her on it at their first acquaintance—and understands what she is doing and why. He counters by missing a word he can easily spell as well. During a short break in the competition, the two competitors have a heart to heart and decide to team up to try to win the bee together—something that has never occurred in bee history. Together, they spell the remainder of the words and become co-winners.

The extremely well-spoken Fishburne, who also produced the film, played a similar mentor role in *Searching for Bobby Fischer* (1993) and is completely convincing here as Akeelah's spelling guru. Their burgeoning respect and affection for one another is the heart of the film and both these appealing stars convey absolute realism. Villarreal and Afable are well cast as the affable Javier and more serious Dylan and the film nicely reflects the multicultural reality of Los Angeles, although it could have done without the stereotypical Mr. Chiu.

Hilary White

CREDITS

Dr. Larabee: Laurence Fishburne
Tanya: Angela Bassett
Akeelah: Keke Palmer
Mr. Welch: Curtis Armstrong
Georgia: Sahara Garey
Javier: J.R. Villarreal
Dylan Chiu: Sean Michael Afable
Mr. Chiu: Tzi Ma
Devon: Lee Thompson Young
Origin: USA
Language: English
Released: 2006
Production: Sid Ganis, Laurence Fishburne, Nancy Hult Ganis, Michael Romersa, Danny Llewelyn; Lionsgate, 2929 Entertainment, Out of the Blue Entertainment, Reactor Films Production, Cinema Gypsy Prods; released by Starbucks Entertainment
Directed by: Doug Atchison
Written by: Doug Atchison
Cinematography by: M. David Mullen
Music by: Aaron Zigman
Editing: Glenn Farr
Costumes: Sharen CQ Davis
Production Design: Warren Alan Young
MPAA rating: PG
Running time: 107 minutes

REVIEWS

Boxoffice Online. April 28, 2006.
Chicago Sun-Times Online. April 28, 2006.
Entertainment Weekly. April 28, 2006, p. 118.
Los Angeles Times Online. April 28, 2006.
New York Times Online. April 28, 2006.
San Francisco Chronicle. April 28, 2006, p. E5.
Variety Online. March 20, 2006.
Village Voice Online. April 25, 2006.
Washington Post. April 28, 2006, p. C1.

ALL THE KING'S MEN

Time brings all things to light.
—Movie tagline

Box Office: $7.2 million

Hurricane Katrina hit New Orleans on August 29, 2005, with a greater impact than expected, an awe-inspiring, deadly meteorological milestone few will forget. *All the King's Men* now has the distinction of being the last major motion picture to film there before the area's devastation, having wrapped principal photography the previous April. Surely it was hoped, however, that the production would be of note for its merit and not just its timing. The film is based upon one of the most revered American novels ever written (it won the Pulitzer Prize), and is a remake of one of the most memorable motion pictures in the history of American cinema (it won multiple Oscars®, including Best Picture). So hopes for it were high, especially with an impressive cast, including Sean Penn, Jude Law, Anthony Hopkins, Kate Winslet, James Gandolfini, Patricia Clarkson, and Mark Ruffalo. However, the film that was shot before the potent storm is, despite an unexpected additional year of re-editing, a highly disappointing, turgid, all-too-impotent presentation of the material.

When the previous adaptation of Robert Penn Warren's 1946 masterpiece hit theaters in 1949, longtime *New York Times* film critic Bosley Crowther praised it as "a rip-roaring film" due to its "quality of turbulence and vitality." In crafting the material for a cinematic presentation, producer/director/screenwriter Robert Rossen decided to boost the emphasis on the powerful, vibrant, riveting presence of mere "redneck hick" turned fearsome demagogue Willie Stark. This shifts focus somewhat away from the book's narrator (and arguably its protagonist), grad student turned journalist turned political trouble-shooter Jack Burden. Rossen thought that this would make for a more gripping filmic dramatization. Indeed, Broderick Crawford's portrayal of the character (who Warren based at least in part on Louisiana's legendary Huey Long) is a grabber of a performance worthy of the Academy Award® it received.

In preparing to make his *All the King's Men*, however, director/screenwriter/co-producer Steven Zaillian (Oscar®-winner for penning 1993's *Schindler's List*) insisted on steering clear of viewing Rossen's work in a vocal, steadfast determination to be truer to the source material, which inspired both filmmakers. Thus the story is told with the emphasis tipped back toward the man relating Willie's saga, with more of Jack's inner thoughts and turmoil, which supposedly lead to transformative, eye-opening life lessons. This sets the stage for one of the film's many problems, as Law's Jack is anything but mesmerizing.

Zaillian's presentation does a great deal of hopping around in time, which can get irritating. In the first few minutes of the film, he shows Jack traveling through the night on an apparently vital mission with Willie (Penn).

When they arrive at an old secluded mansion surrounded by ancient trees laden with Spanish moss, the men are about to enter when the director cuts away. Viewers are transported to five years earlier, when detached, cynical newspaperman Jack first met Willie, a non-drinking humble son of a poor farmer who enters politics because he has legitimate concerns, and truly cares about his fellow forgotten, downtrodden little people. As county treasurer, Willie's warnings about some shady dealings behind a schoolhouse construction contract go unheeded. A fire escape collapses, and children die.

Soon after the tragedy, burly, sweaty, sleazy politico Tiny Duffy (Gandolfini) shows up and cunningly entices this heretofore virtual unknown to take what seems like an oversized leap and run for governor. On the campaign trail, Willie sits on a train with Jack and Sadie Burke (Clarkson), the candidate's press secretary (and, shortly thereafter, mistress) and learns that he had only been lured into running so he would split the hick vote and assure victory for the man backed by the state machine. Willie washes down this demoralizing, disillusioning (but nonetheless instructive) bitter pill with a great deal of booze, hours later regaining both consciousness and his fighting spirit. He shoves the speech Duffy had prepared for him into the fat man's fat hands, sends the man flying down appropriately into some mud, and gives a defiant, rousing declaration of his independence. Willie has truly connected with his public for the first time, and viewers will notice how the crowds start to grow.

How audiences react to the eminently talented Penn's portrayal of Willie Stark will largely determine whether they find merit in *All the King's Men*. His Willie impressively bellows out steadfast promises of food, roads, bridges, schoolhouses if his people band together at the polls against the callous, monied, powerful protectors of the status quo. As for anyone who gets in the way of change, he exhorts his followers to "nail 'em up!" With hair askew and reminding one of a rooster's comb, Penn looks like a semi-crazed entrant in a cockfight. However, his performance increasingly seems like scenery-chewing, over-the-top bombast, a lot of blasting away but not enough drawing in audiences. Also, at low or high decibels, Penn's thickly-accented words are often so indistinct that many viewers wished for subtitles.

In stark contrast to Penn's Stark is Law's aforementioned wan Jack, who ponderously ponders throughout the film in a dreamy, dreary, monotonous voiceover narration. Especially when juxtaposed with Penn's often fevered, roaring energy, Law's colorless characterization seems all the more dull, and in turn he only serves to make Penn seem more unbridled and excessive.

In wielding his power on behalf of the powerless, Willie has made many equally powerful enemies. In battling them, he has come to decide that the end justifies the means, and those means have seemingly gotten increasingly underhanded and ugly. However, the film is crippled by way too much talking about what Willie has been up to and a glaring lack of scenes, which dramatically chronicle and palpably illustrate the well-intentioned character's gradual corruption and unsettling rise to fascist dictatorship. Multiple reviewers decried these unfortunate omissions in story presentation and character development. For instance, *Newsweek*'s David Ansen wrote of "crucial chunks" which "seem to have been left on the cutting-room floor." It is like the old nursery rhyme all over again, except that now *All the King's Men* is as fragmented and unsuccessfully put together as Humpty Dumpty.

Zaillian does provide one example of Willie at work when he finally lets the nocturnal car trip play out after having repeatedly revisited and then darted away from it. Jack has gone to work for now-Governor Stark, who won in a landslide. Willie and Jack proceed into the majestic old plantation house to pressure the latter's father figure, elderly Judge Irwin (Hopkins), to use his influence to "call off the dogs," referring to the stuffy, entrenched lawmen barking vociferously for the governor's removal from office. (Jack's fadingly-aristocratic family and friends have been decrying what they consider to be Willie's outrageous, hostile Robin Hood mentality.) The judge refuses to be bullied. Even though the man has been so good for so long to him, Jack nonetheless accepts an assignment from his new mentor to dig up dirt with which to blackmail this apparently principled old pillar.

Jack's vaguely intriguing, if repugnant, investigation uncovers facts that the judge took a bribe years before, part of some dirty dealings which led to a man's suicide. (The book makes it clear that Irwin's decision to do so was forced upon him.) After Jack takes damning evidence to the venerable gentleman, the latter's clearly foreshadowed choice of suicide over doing business with the Devil is rather moving. When a shocked (but, as played by Law, never distinctly shattered) Jack learns that the man these strong-armed, repellent tactics just drove to the grave was actually his father, few will sympathize with him.

Increasingly interspersed throughout these events are nostalgic snippets of when Jack was best friends with Adam Stanton (Ruffalo, in an especially underwritten role) and filled with ardor for his one true love, Adam's sister, Anne (Winslet). These remembrances of simpler, more serene times are highly bromidic detours. Willie wreaks more havoc on Jack's psyche by having one of his affairs (which Jack was previously blase about) with

Anne. High-minded Adam, now a doctor whom Jack has pressured at his boss' behest to head the fraud-tainted Willie Stark Medical Center, is tormented upon learning that he and his sister have now both been defiled. Although Willie survives impeachment, he fares less well after Adam guns him down in a statehouse hallway crammed with onlookers. The assassin is immediately felled by Willie's bodyguard/driver, Sugar Boy (Jackie Earle Haley), a chilling, ominous, heat-packing creature whom Zaillian's camera has repeatedly paused to linger upon throughout the film in a case of heavy-handed foreshadowing. The shot that follows is also overdone, looking down on the two dying men sprawled side by side and then zeroing in on the commingling of their slowly seeping blood in the crevices of the state seal imprinted in the floor beneath them.

Made on an estimated budget of $55 million, *All the King's Men* was only able to gross $7.2 million. Overall critical reaction was not positive, although some forecasted an Oscar® nomination for Penn due to his intense immersion into character. The remake was originally the brainchild of well-known political consultant and commentator James Carville. There are even more problems and curiosities to mention about *All The King's Men*, such as the actors' widely-varying success with the required accent (Hopkins, for example, does not even try) and Zaillian's bumping-up of the time period two decades to the 1950s because, according to the film's production notes, "any period before World War II seemed less contemporary and more 'nostalgic.'" "Nothing in the picture works," is what current *New York Times* reviewer A.O. Scott had to say about this latest adaptation, which is quite a comedown from Crowther's comments.

David L. Boxerbaum

CREDITS

Willie Stark: Sean Penn
Jack Burden: Jude Law
Anne Stanton: Kate Winslet
Tiny Duffy: James Gandolfini
Adam Stanton: Mark Ruffalo
Sadie Burke: Patricia Clarkson
Mrs. Burden: Kathy Baker
Sugar Boy: Jackie Earle Haley
Judge Irwin: Anthony Hopkins
Alex: Kevin Dunn
Willie's father: Frederic Forrest
Lucy Stark: Talia Balsam
Origin: USA
Language: English
Released: 2006
Production: Mike Medavoy, Ken Lemberger, Arnold W. Messer, Steven Zaillian; Rising Star, Relativity, Phoenix Pictures, Columbia Pictures; released by Sony Pictures
Directed by: Steven Zaillian
Written by: Steven Zaillian
Cinematography by: Pawel Edelman
Music by: James Horner
Sound: Drew Kunin
Editing: Wayne Wahrman
Art Direction: Gary Baugh
Costumes: Marit Allen
Production Design: Patrizia Von Brandenstein
MPAA rating: PG-13
Running time: 128 minutes

REVIEWS

Boxoffice Online. September 22, 2006.
Entertainment Weekly. September 29, 2006, p. 53.
Hollywood Reporter Online. September 21, 2006.
Los Angeles Times Online. September 22, 2006.
New York Times Online. September 22, 2006.
San Francisco Chronicle. September 22, 2006, p. E1.
Variety Online. September 10, 2006.
Washington Post. September 22, 2006, p. C1.

QUOTES

Jack Burden: "Graft is what you call it when who's doing it doesn't know what fork to use."

AMERICAN DREAMZ

Imagine a country where more people vote for a pop idol than their next president.
—Movie tagline

Box Office: $7.2 million

Paul Weitz's directorial resume now stretches from *American Pie* (1999) to *American Dreamz*, from the risque harpooning of baked goods to the satiric lampooning of our society's half-baked ideas about what is truly consequential. Clearly Weitz thinks there is a certain lack of discernment on the public's part when, as the film's poster states, "more people vote for a pop idol than their next president," referring to television ratings juggernaut *American Idol*, one of his latest film's targets. If characters in his teen sex comedy had only one thing on their minds, *American Dreamz* has too many on its, ranging from *Idol*, the questionable policies and intellect of President George W. Bush, and the ever-lurking threat of Arab terrorism. Instead of weaving quite so much together, some plot threads should probably have been snipped to improve the film's focus. Also, despite having all sorts of fakes and pretenders flashing big, utterly phony smiles, the satire itself could have used more or sharper teeth. There is more good-natured, if pointed ribbing here than truly angry, illuminating social commentary, more farce than real force.

Weitz's film simultaneously proceeds along three main paths, which it will attempt to merge down the road. On *American Dreamz*, a televised singing competition with ardent fans around the world, contestants are not only continually cut, but also cut to the quick by grinning, heartless, caustically clever judge Martin Tweed. (Think *Idol*'s Simon Cowell.) He is played by Hugh Grant, once again displaying an aptitude for retaining a charming appeal while acting like an utter louse. When first seen onscreen, Martin is so enthralled with a fax trumpeting his latest stunning ratings that his girlfriend's announcement that she is exiting his life barely registers. He then bemoans how being blithely happy about such things as his good news is impinged upon by the seemingly onerous burden of having to worry about how anyone else is feeling. "You make me feel like being a better person," he tells her, and apparently really resents it. "I'm not a better person," he points out. "I'm me." Martin is a peevishly unsettled mixture of egotism and self-loathing, and especially when he relates that his own mother said nobody would ever love him and declared him talentless, one cannot help feeling a tad sorry for the cad.

In a brief, telling moment alone, Martin fervently prays that the current season of *American Dreamz* will be the last, apparently finding the prospect of sifting through (and even just sitting through) performances by another throng of often self-deluded pop star wannabes to be an excruciating drag. So, perhaps for his own churlish amusement, Martin announces to his staff that he wants to shake things up a little, sending them on a hunt for some truly and interestingly flawed contestants. "Bring me some freaks!" he declares.

Speaking of people with defects, newly reelected dim-bulb President Staton (Dennis Quaid), looking for a change of pace, decides to read one of those newspapers he has heard so much about. Up to this point in time, he has been a mere marionette controlled by his crafty chief of staff (an unrecognizable, bald-pated Willem Dafoe, looking like a cross between Dick Cheney and Karl Rove). The chief of staff seems warily disturbed by the president's sudden determination to have a thought of his own, but also somewhat doubtful that much will come of the effort. For weeks on end, Staton pores over the papers in the bedroom he shares with his "happy pill"-popping, ultra-serene First Lady (Marcia Gay Harden). The president is simply flabbergasted by all the fascinating "stuff" he is at least temporarily absorbing. This prolonged absence from public view soon brings on rumors that Staton has had some sort of nervous collapse, and the country's confidence in him plummets. His chief of staff comes up with a solution (besides some of those pills): have the President rehabilitate his image by making a crowd-pleasing appearance as guest judge on the ultra-popular *American Dreamz*.

One place where opinions of Staton are especially low is in the Al-Qaeda-esque terrorist training camps where fervent Middle Eastern Muslim recruits shoot round after round into cardboard cutouts of the president. Amongst these fearsome fighters is Omer Obeidi (Sam Golzari), but the only thing he especially wants to conquer is Broadway due to his passionate love of show tunes. Omer's disgusted comrades break the highlights record he sings and dances to in his tent at night, and ship him off (and out of the way) to his wealthy relatives in California's Orange County. One is his flamingly gay cousin Iqbal Riza (Tony Yalda), who is certain he would triumph on *American Dreamz* if given the chance. He has sent in his audition tape and zealously practices in his private basement studio while awaiting word. Not surprisingly, the search for intriguing, entertaining, idiosyncratic pieces of work leads Martin's staff to Iqbal's doorstep. When they stumble instead upon Omer's blissful, belting karaoke singing while his cousin is at the mall, he gets the gig instead. (Iqbal's wholly expected hissy fit soon follows.)

The most interesting of the contestants is soulless Sally Kendoo (Mandy Moore), a blonde, curvy, Midwestern version of Martin. The pretty, scarily-driven young woman has every intention of crushing her competition, smiling sweetly all the while. Sally badly wants to be a star and can sing fairly well, but her most arresting performances are those in which she purposefully masquerades as a sincere, humane human being. Fakery is her true forte. When the *American Dreamz* crew that arrives at her door has camera trouble and initially fails to capture her surprise and jubilation, she waits for the problem to be solved and gives them some skillfully reproduced spontaneity.

Certain she is destined for greatness, Sally cannot allow what passes for her heart to be shackled to mundane smitten boyfriend, William Williams (Chris Klein), who goes off to Iraq after she breaks up with him and promptly gets shot in his pathetically-cherished Sally tattoo. She is genuinely sick to death of him, but when her canny agent (Seth Meyers) points out that a patriotic public would respond well to a contestant with a wounded soldier beau, Sally's cold aloofness instantly transforms into unsettling, calculated effusiveness. (Will proposes, but it is requested that he redo it on the show—and with a bigger, showier ring.) The minute

Martin lays eyes on Sally he is simultaneously smitten and repelled. "I look at you and see my own reflection," he says, characterizing what he observes as "revolting!" She senses he is a kindred unkind spirit, but narcissistically states that she is simply "not attracted to other people."

All these storylines and all these characters eventually coalesce during the competition's finale. The president arrives, secretly augmented with an earpiece through which his chief of staff will tell him what to say during this all-important appearance. Of course there are problems with the device, and Staton initially sounds particularly peculiar. He must finally endeavor, honestly if awkwardly, to speak for himself, rendering his Svengali obsolete. Omer, ordered by his comrades to become a suicide bomber and assassinate the president live on the air, has too much love and gratitude in his heart for the wonderfully supportive American people to follow through. (The sight of the terrorists incongruously luxuriating in a California hot tub and sipping cooling beverages with Omer is quite humorous.) Meanwhile, Will spies Sally and Martin having sex in her dressing room and reacts badly, strapping on the bomb Omer has ditched in a backstage bathroom and then heads onstage. Martin thinks this dramatic moment makes for such great television that he personally moves the camera forward, inadvertently detonating Will. Both men are blown to smithereens, but the show gets killer ratings. The next season, a synthetically sorrowful Sally takes the stage as the new host of *American Dreamz.*

Made on a budget of approximately $19 million, *American Dreamz* only managed to gross $7.3 million. Critical reaction was mixed. There are numerous inside jokes here which *American Idol* fans will enjoy. Those viewers who find President Bush lacking will undoubtedly find enjoyment in this latest parody. However, Weitz paired more memorably with Grant in *About a Boy* (2002) and with Quaid in *In Good Company* (2004). Still, *American Dreamz*'s satire is likely to elicit smiles and knowing nods, if not provoke much discussion or changes in attitude.

David L. Boxerbaum

CREDITS

Martin Tweed: Hugh Grant
President Staton: Dennis Quaid
Sally Kendoo: Mandy Moore
Chief of Staff: Willem Dafoe
William Williams: Chris Klein
Martha Kendoo: Jennifer Coolidge
First Lady: Marcia Gay Harden
Ittles: John Cho
Omer Obeidi: Sam Golzari
Chet Krogl: Seth Meyers
Iqbal Riza: Tony Yalda
Jessica: Marley Shelton
Accordo: Judy Greer
Nazneen Riza: Shohreh Aghdashloo
Agha Babur: Bernard White
Origin: USA
Language: English
Released: 2006
Production: Paul Weitz, Rodney Liber, Andrew Miano; Depth of Field; released by Universal
Directed by: Paul Weitz
Written by: Paul Weitz
Cinematography by: Robert Elswit
Music by: Stephen Trask
Sound: David Wyman
Music Supervisor: Kathy Nelson
Editing: Myron Kerstein
Art Direction: Sue Chan
Costumes: Molly Maginnis
Production Design: William Arnold
MPAA rating: PG-13
Running time: 107 minutes

REVIEWS

Boxoffice Online. April 21, 2006.
Chicago Sun-Times Online. April 21, 2006.
Entertainment Weekly. April 28, 2006, p. 115.
Los Angeles Times Online. April 21, 2006.
New York Times Online. April 21, 2006.
San Francisco Chronicle. April 21, 2006, p. E1.
USA Today Online. April 20, 2006.
Variety Online. March 21, 2006.
Washington Post. April 21, 2006, p. C1.

QUOTES

Martin to his ex-girlfriend: "You make me feel like I should be a better person. And—I'm not a better person!"

AN AMERICAN HAUNTING

Possession Knows No Bounds.
—Movie tagline

Box Office: $16.3 million

An American Haunting is what happens when you remove all intrigue and terror from *The Exorcist* (1973), *The Ring* (2002), and *Sleepy Hollow* (1999) and throw the remnants in a blender. The only scary thing about this film is that it was released at all. It takes about five minutes before it becomes apparent that the script is so lifeless and banal that even fine actors like Donald Sutherland (the patriarch, Mr. John Bell) and Sissy Spacek (Mrs. Lucy Bell) can't save it.

The story, based on actual events, takes place in Red River, Tennessee, at the beginning of the nineteenth century. The Bell family enjoys post-Revolutionary domestic bliss complete with a large drafty house and pleasantly compliant slaves with their four ruddy-faced children. Betsy Bell (Rachel Hurd-Wood), the eldest daughter, is a precocious, beautiful teenager beloved by all. It is all too cute and rustic to last, however. Enter Kathe Batts (played by Kathy Bates look-alike Gaye Brown), the witch-like hermit living the next farm over from the Bells. She has been cheated out of some land by John Bell, and wants revenge. She vows to destroy Mr. Bell (and his "precious daughter, too") with her dark and magical powers.

Suddenly, an unnecessarily thick fog befalls the town (one character even marvels at the prevalent mist). Mysterious rabid wolves are seen prowling about the town at night, and rotten-faced girls begin appearing in mirrors. It is all very formulaic. Crosses are seen flying off walls. Fireplaces become infernos. The Bells even assume (incorrectly of course) that slaves are responsible for the supernatural pranks.

Hurd-Wood's Betsy does her best Linda Blair impression by flailing around, panting incessantly, and screaming bloody murder. Spacek plays motherly concern convincingly, but it's hard to tell when her bangs are hanging in her eyes. Sutherland plays the benevolent daddy role well, and his performance is flawless stoicism. It's a shame the director chooses to have his character playing checkers while his daughter is being raped by a ghost night after night upstairs. That's just the beginning of the nonsensical choices made by writer/director Courtney Solomon. There are two young Bell children that disappear from the story for the majority of the film only to be revealed sleeping soundly three quarters of the way through.

James Johnston (played like an alcoholic lunatic by Matthew Marsh), a neighbor and friend of the family who, according to historical fact, did live with the Bells for a time during the haunting, ends up running around the house screaming scripture while the rest of the family looks on. Eventually, the hunky schoolmaster moves in as well, only to reveal to Mrs. Bell his latent romantic desires for the possessed young thing. Events such as these are not only ridiculous, but haphazardly executed, and every twist of the story stalls before it has a chance to develop.

The writers (Brent Monahan and Solomon) do blessedly leave out one point of fact in the story; Andrew Jackson, the seventh president of the United States, visited the Bell family when the famous story spread beyond the confines of Red River. He is famed to have said "I'd rather fight the entire British Army than to deal with the Bell Witch." It may have been interesting to see what nonsense could be made of this alleged occurrence, but with this particular incarnation, the shorter, the better.

The most embarrassing moments in the film, however, include the apparition point-of-view sequences. The audience has several chances to enjoy the viewpoint of the floating phantom, complete with cheesy close up reactions of the characters to the repeated, un-scary whisperings of "Betsyyyyyyy! Betsyyyyyyy!" and "You're gonna die!" It's not even funny-bad. It's just bad. And after floating around for a while, there are some terrible, confusing dream sequences in which the director cuts right back to reality, leaving the audience wondering if what transpired really happened, or if it was just more of the specter's psychological tricks. This happens more than once as the film careens toward one of the most idiotic resolutions of all time. Finally, the story is bookended by two poorly-acted scenes set in the present day in which the ghost delivers the moral of the story. This movie is, at best, a reminder that *The Exorcist* can withstand repeated viewings and remain terrifying, while some films can't even scare the first time.

Kjerstine Anderson

CREDITS

John Bell: Donald Sutherland

Lucy Bell: Sissy Spacek

Betsy Bell: Rachel Hurd-Wood

Richard Powell: James D'Arcy

James Johnston: Matthew Marsh

John Bell Jr.: Thom Fell

Kathe Batts: Gaye Brown

Origin: USA

Language: English

Released: 2005

Production: Andre Rouleau, Courtney Solomon, Christopher Milburn; Remstar, Midsummer Films, SC MediaPro Pictures, After Dark Films; released by Freestyle Releasing

Directed by: Courtney Solomon

Written by: Courtney Solomon, Brent Monahan

Cinematography by: Adrian Biddle

Music by: Caine Davidson

Sound: Ed Douglas

Editing: Richard Comeau
Costumes: Jane Petrie
Production Design: Humphrey Jaeger
MPAA rating: PG-13
Running time: 82 minutes

REVIEWS

Boxoffice Online. May 5, 2006.
Entertainment Weekly Online. May 3, 2006.
Los Angeles Times Online. May 5, 2006.
New York Times Online. May 5, 2006.
Variety Online. November 16, 2005.
Washington Post. May 6, 2006, p. C1.

QUOTES

Betsy: "I am tired. Our house makes strange noises at night."

ANNAPOLIS

50,000 Apply. 1,200 Are Accepted. Only The Best Survive.
—Movie tagline

Where Heroes Are Born And Legends Are Made.
—Movie tagline

Box Office: $17.1 million

Annapolis is a film any regular moviegoer has probably seen several times before, along the lines of *An Officer and a Gentleman* (1982) and *Top Gun* (1986). Despite utilizing such a familiar formula, director Justin Lin and writer Dave Collard still don't quite get it, apparently not realizing that all it takes is to simply show up and make sure to hit all the right moments. There needs to be a handsome young recruit who faces self-doubt, a hard-nosed drill sergeant-type and the rigors of the military to become a stronger, better person. Also, said recruit will find love with a beautiful woman. Lin and Collard get all this in and even include the mandatory scene in which the recruit has to get down on the ground and do an excessive number of push-ups. But then the movie veers disastrously off course and fails to work on many levels, despite the omnipresent swelling music informing audience members of the emotions they should be experiencing. Perhaps Lin, who directed the promising indie film *Better Luck Tomorrow* (2002) about a group of criminal Asian kids, could not quite stomach making such a trite film. It is hard to imagine that he enjoyed the fact that the one Asian character is the cliched "good" student who tells on the others when they break the rules.

Part of the problem is the main character, Jake Huard (James Franco). Jake works on a shipbuilding team with his foreman father, Bill (Brian Goodman). But he longs to attend the United States Naval Academy that lies across the river. His late mother had dreamed of him attending the academy, but his father and group of friends think he should just be happy working on ships. Jake gets a last minute opportunity to attend and is soon across the river meeting the stereotypical characters he will be spending his time with. There is the hard-nosed commander, Cole (Tyrese Gibson), the scrappy love interest, Ali (Jordana Brewster), and the weakling who cannot quite handle the military's obstacle course, Twins (Vicellous Shannon). Instead of rising to the occasion and becoming a better person, Jake remains ambivalent about the academy. He is not a good student and does not seem up for the academic rigors. He can box, however, and he sees his only hope as being successful in the annual brigade boxing championship. The boxing match would also give him the tantalizing possibility of a chance to punch out Cole. But it is not easy to root for someone who wants to get out of the regular work by winning a boxing match. It seems like he should have to work as hard as the other recruits. When Richard Gere's character in *An Officer and a Gentlemen* struggled, viewers wanted him to succeed. After all, as his character so memorably put it, "I got nowhere else to go!" But when Jake considers quitting, it seems like it might not be such a bad idea. After all, he is an indifferent student, does not seem terribly inspired by the school and does not appear to care much whether he succeeds. As Gregory Kirschling of *Entertainment Weekly*, who gave the film a C+, wrote: "Compellingly reserved and inscrutable at the start, Franco starts to lose us by the second hour, when his character's still not showing up for roll call on time, and isn't charismatic enough to bring us over to his side."

The whole movie is similarly tepid. Jake and Ali are romantically paired, but only share one chaste kiss. The relationship between Jake and Cole is similarly weak. Cole is a tough leader who demands a lot from his recruit, and Jake ends up punching him on two occasions. The punches are not the victorious comeuppance they should be, though, because Cole does not do anything unduly cruel. In fact, he keeps giving Jake extra breaks. Jake just looks like an undisciplined live wire—and not in a good way.

Robert Abele of the *Los Angeles Times* wrote that "neither lagging military recruitment nor movie attendance is likely to be helped by *Annapolis*, a by-the-numbers underdog drama." Christy Lemire of the *Associated Press* wrote: "This rousing, crowd-pleasing drama crams in every underdog cliche and military-movie cliche. Surely one of these alone would have been sufficient." Roger Ebert of the *Chicago Sun-Times* wrote that *Annapolis* "is the anti-Sundance film, an exhausted wheeze of bankrupt cliches and cardboard characters, the kind of film that has no visible reason for existing, except that everybody got paid." Finally, Stephen Holden of the *New York Times* wrote: "*Annapolis* is so gung-ho about the United States Naval Academy's ability to turn boys into fighting men and and rebels into scrappy team players that it could easily be confused with a military recruiting film."

Jill Hamilton

CREDITS

Jake Huard: James Franco
Cole: Tyrese Gibson
Ali: Jordana Brewster
Lt. Burton: Donnie Wahlberg
Twins: Vicellous Shannon
Bill Huard: Brian Goodman
Loo: Roger Fan
McNally: Chi McBride
Origin: USA
Language: English
Released: 2006
Production: Damien Saccani, Mark Vahradian; Touchstone Pictures; released by Buena Vista
Directed by: Justin Lin
Written by: Dave Collard
Cinematography by: Phil Abraham
Music by: Brian Tyler
Sound: Danny Mitchell
Editing: Fred Raskin
Art Direction: Christopher Tandon
Costumes: Gloria Gresham
Production Design: Patti Podesta
MPAA rating: PG-13
Running time: 108 minutes

REVIEWS

Boxoffice Online. January 27, 2006.
Chicago Sun-Times Online. January 27, 2006.
Entertainment Weekly Online. January 25, 2006.
Los Angeles Times Online. January 27, 2006.
New York Times Online. January 27, 2006.
Premiere Magazine Online. January 2006.
Variety Online. January 26, 2006.
Washington Post Online. January 27, 2006.

TRIVIA

The film was made without the support of the Navy or the Department of Defense.

THE ANT BULLY

The battle for the lawn is on.
—Movie tagline

This Summer It's Crunch Time.
—Movie tagline

Box Office: $28.1 million

The Ant Bully is the computer animated feature film based on the children's book by John Nickle and directed by John A. Davis. The film boasts a stellar cast, including Julia Roberts, Nicolas Cage, Bruce Campbell, Paul Giamatti, Ricardo Montalban, and Meryl Streep. Mostly overlooked amid the crowded field of animated fare at the time of its opening, it is a refreshingly optimistic and entertaining story about accepting the differences in others, teamwork, and gaining self-confidence. It is a invigorating break from the cynicism that has been creeping into the realm of animated films of recent years, while at the same time not going too far in the other direction, which has resulted in such bland fare as *Curious George* (2006). And unlike that film, there is enough enjoyment here for adults as well as children.

Lucas (voice of Zach Tyler Eisen) is a ten-year-old boy who lives in constant fear of the chubby neighborhood bully who towers over him and brags that he can do nothing to stop him "because I'm big and you're small." Too afraid to fight back and frustrated, he takes out his anger on a colony of ants in his yard by kicking the ant hill and spraying it with his squirt gun. To the ants he is known as the Destroyer and they live in constant fear that he will one day completely annihilate their home. When Lucas floods the colony with a garden hose the ants decide they must take action before it is too late. They get the ant wizard Zoc (voice of Nicolas Cage) to create a potion that will shrink Lucas down to their size so they can put the Destroyer on trial for crimes against the colony.

A small band of ants led by Zoc sneaks into Lucas' bedroom and pours the potion in his ear. Lucas wakes to find that he has been shrunk down to ant size and is soon taken by the group of ants to their colony. They bring him before the Queen (voice of Meryl Streep) where she sentences him to live and work in the colony until he learns what it means to be an ant. He is mentored by Hova (voice of Julia Roberts) who takes him under her mandible, much to the chagrin of Zoc, who has no love for the human.

It's tough going at first for Lucas as he learns to be a team player in the colony, as many ants don't trust him, especially Zoc. But when he inadvertently saves the colony from an attack by a swarm of wasps, he is suddenly hailed as a hero. Zoc, of course is not happy about this and his blind hatred and mistrust of humans prevents him from accepting that someone different from himself can be good.

But he loves Hova and she trusts Lucas so Zoc tries to understand why they accept the Destroyer so easily after all that he has done to them. When he has a conversation with Lucas telling him that humans destroy what they don't understand, he suddenly realizes that he is guilty of the same perception. Lucas has learned what it means to be an ant and now Zoc has to change his perspective on his perception of humans. He realizes that they are not so different after all.

When the exterminator Stan Beals (voice of Paul Giamatti) arrives to gas the colony, Lucas admits to the entire colony that he was the one that ordered him the day before, when he hadn't yet met them. He wants to help stop the exterminator, but the Head of Council (voice of Ricardo Montalban) doesn't trust him. Zoc vouches for Lucas and they hatch a plan to save the colony from the Cloudbreather. They form a fragile alliance with the wasps and convince them that they are fighting a common enemy, culminating in an aerial assault of military precision that is the ultimate big versus little battle. After defeating the exterminator, Lucas is brought before the queen mother again and rewarded for his bravery as she "knights" him with the ant name Rokai, as she doesn't see a human anymore but one of the colony.

He says goodbye to the colony and drinks the potion that will make him human size again, unfortunately that means he grows to full size naked in his front yard. Later the bully and his group show up and threaten Lucas again, but Lucas stands up to him and the group backs Lucas, who reiterates the film's theme "I'm small, but together we're big." The bully backs down and runs away. Full of self-confidence and with new friends, Lucas returns to the anthill and floods it—with Jelly Bellys, which are known to the ants as sweet rocks.

In fleshing out the story, writer/director John A. Davis has created an ant world with a diverse culture, its own religion, and values that are common to every being. It is a great fantasy adventure that can be viewed on many levels. And it is perhaps the first family film that is able to teach children and adults that "size doesn't matter."

David E. Chapple

CREDITS

Lucas Nickle: Zach Tyler Eisen (Voice)
Nicky: Jake T. Austin (Voice)
Zoc: Nicolas Cage (Voice)
Fugax: Bruce Campbell (Voice)
Queen Ant: Meryl Streep (Voice)
Hova: Julia Roberts (Voice)
Stan Beals: Paul Giamatti (Voice)
Steve: Myles Jeffrey (Voice)
Kreela: Regina King (Voice)
Doreen Nickle: Cheri Oteri (Voice)
Mommo: Lily Tomlin (Voice)
Beetle: Rob Paulsen (Voice)
Tiffany Nickle: Allison Mack (Voice)
Head of Council: Ricardo Montalban (Voice)
Fred Nickle: Larry Miller (Voice)
Blue Teammmate: Austin Majors (Voice)
Fly: Mark DeCarlo (Voice)
Spindle/Frog/Caterpillar: Frank Welker (Voice)
Ant #9: Nicole Sullivan (Voice)
Head Nurse: Vernee Watson-Johnson (Voice)
Origin: USA
Language: English
Released: 2006
Production: Tom Hanks, Gary Goetzman, John A. Davis; Playtone Picture; released by Warner Bros.
Directed by: John A. Davis
Written by: John A. Davis
Music by: John Debney
Sound: Christopher T. Welch
Editing: Jon Michael Price
Art Direction: Chris Consani
Production Design: Barry Jackson
MPAA rating: PG
Running time: 88 minutes

REVIEWS

Boxoffice Online. July 28, 2006.
Chicago Sun-Times Online. July 28, 2006.
Entertainment Weekly. August 4, 2006, p. 47.
Los Angeles Times Online. July 28, 2006.
New York Times Online. July 28, 2006.
San Francisco Chronicle. July 28, 2006, p. E7.
Variety Online. July 23, 2006.
Washington Post. July 28, 2006, p. C1.

QUOTES

Hova tells Lucas: "You just need to discover the ant within."

APOCALYPTO

No one can outrun their destiny.
—Movie tagline

When the end comes, not everyone is ready to go.
—Movie tagline

Box Office: $50.8 million

Mel Gibson delivered yet another violent action spectacle for the 2006 season, excavating and exploiting Mayan culture this time, and setting himself up for even more criticism: "Gibson's Gory Action Film Sacrifices a Noble Civilization to Hollywood," read the sub-title in the *Washington Post* for William Booth's feature headlined "Maya Mistake." In *The Nation,* an article by Earl Shorris entitled "Mad Mel and the Maya" was offered presumably so that readers could "grasp what a racist act Gibson has committed in the making of his new film." Reactions rose to increasingly shrill levels as if offering payback to Gibson for his anti-Semitic rants in public and the alleged insults to the Jews implicit in Gibson's last blockbuster, *The Passion of the Christ* (2004).

In the beginning of the picture, set in (barely) pre-Columbian time (with voyages of discovery apparently in transit to the New World), life was peaceful and idyllic for a Mayan village populated by innocent forest people until it was invaded by a rampaging tribe of warriors intent upon slaughtering almost everyone. The survivors of this mindless preemptive strike are led away on a long trek to a slave camp that services the bloodthirsty rulers of the area. Blood sacrifices are in order, due to famine and disease that is raging on all sides of a civilization in decline. The captives are hauled up to the top of a pyramid where they are laid out on a slab, their hearts plucked out, and their heads decapitated. But just as our hero, "Almost" (Rudy Youngblood, so named "Almost" by his captor back in the village, since as son of the tribal chief, his life was spared only at the last moment), is hauled to the sacrificial slab, a convenient eclipse saves him. He and some of the others are released. But the horrors are just beginning. They are forced to run a kind of gauntlet of thrown spears, slings, and arrows until they are killed. But "Almost," despite the spear in his gut, miraculously recovers enough to kill his pursuer. And for the rest of the film he runs and runs, and runs, with the slave traders, led by the imposing Zero Wolf (Raoul Trujillo), in hot pursuit.

Tracking shot after tracking shot captures his hurdles and gallops and slips and slides. That wound in his side appears to be healing mighty fast, because he keeps on running. For a while, he's up a tree. Then, a pursuing jaguar joins him and manages to dispatch one of the pursuers. Now, renamed "Jaguar Paw," our hero keeps running…all the way to a gigantic cataract. He dives to the bottom, survives, and keeps running. The pursuers follow suit. Those that live keep up the chase. Finally, our hero turns the tables and dispatches one of them with darts poisoned from the blood of a frog and another with a hatchet-like weapon. His confrontation with the leader culminates in a standoff, wherein the bad guy is gutted by a booby trap.

At the end of the long run, it starts to rain. Jaguar Paw and the two remaining pursuers are stopped dead in their tracks by the sight of arriving ships out in the harbor. White men have arrived, complete with armored soldiers and a priest holding a crucifix. Jaguar Paw reaches the deep cave where his wife (Dalia Hernandez), young son, and newly-born baby have been trapped all this time, arriving just in time to save them as the water rises. In an epilogue, Jaguar Paw and his family leave the area, the ships now empty in the harbor. "We are going to a new beginning," he tells his wife and children. They disappear into the forest. Jaguar Paw's story dominates the film: From a young man first learning fear (despite wise counsel from his stalwart father) to his epic journey toward manhood and survival. Despite the improbabilities, it's undoubtedly an impressive achievement. *Washington Post* reviewer Stephen Hunter described the film as a "sinewy, taut poem of action." But not everyone fully appreciated the poetry.

This is not the first time Mel Gibson has directed, of course: he indulged in Celtic barbarism in *Braveheart* (1995) long before his gruesome rendering of *The Passion of the Christ*, which grossed just under $500 million, thanks largely to the full-fledged support of evangelical Christians. Gibson not only directed but also co-wrote the script for *Apocalypto* with Farhad Safinia, resulting in an effective scare-machine that *Entertainment Weekly* called "the weirdest, most violent movie of the year." The dialogue (what little there is of it) is in the meso-American dialect of Yucatec. The cast includes mostly non-professional indigenous peoples, but they are not really present-day survivors of Mayan civilization. The locations are in Central America, adapting settings and subject matter that has rarely been depicted on screen. The costumes appear to be straight out of the *Mad Max* movies (1979-1985). The make-up consists of earplugs, nose-plugs, weird masks and headdresses, patterned tattooing, etc. At times you feel like you're on another planet with an alien race (which is no doubt the intended point).

Anthropologists were horrified at the impression Gibson created of the most sophisticated and subtle civilization of the New World: "It's a shocking movie to us," Brown University anthropology professor Stephen Houston told the *Washington Post*. "For millions of people this might be their first glimpse of the Maya. This is the impression that is going to last. But this is Mel Gibson's Maya. This is Mel Gibson's sadism. This is not the Maya we know." In fact, Mayan civilization peaked about 900 A.D., about six hundred years before Gibson's film is set. Then there is the matter of mass human sacrifice, not unknown to the Maya, but far more prevalent with the Aztec. Anthropologist Richard Hanson of Idaho State University defended Gibson's film, claiming that "for the most part it is very accurate." But, then, Professor Hanson was Gibson's paid consultant on the project, so he had better believe in the film's accuracy.

Earl Shorris expressed outrage in *The Nation* over Gibson's casting for the film. Rudy Youngblood, in the lead role as Jaguar Paw turns out to be a dancer from Oklahoma; in fact, none of the four lead roles went to true Maya, and "other featured players are either from Mexico City or Oaxaca." And yet, there are "more than a million Maya in Mexico, and more than 100,000 of them are monolingual Yucatecan Maya speakers." It is baffling to think that Mel Gibson would not have drawn on this natural resource pool, but, then, as Shorris points out: "Culture doesn't sell tickets. Violence does. Gibson has made what he calls 'a chase movie.' As we saw his Scot disemboweled and his Jesus battered into bloody meat, we will now see a young Maya running through the jungle to escape having his still beating heart torn from his chest." That's the excitement served up by this brutal movie.

Interviewed by Allison Hope Weiner for *Entertainment Weekly,* Gibson was rudely asked if he was making a "liberal" film in order "to get back into the good graces of Hollywood," after his drunken anti-Semitic comments in public and his television confession to Diane Sawyer of ABC Television. Gibson denied that and also denied that he was a Republican. But his latest film was alienating to *The Nation*, the premiere liberal standard-bearer among American periodicals. "For the title of his movie Gibson chose a Greek word related to the ideas in the Book of Revelation: apocalypse," according to Shorris. "Gibson has tried to sell the move as an allegory, using the fall of Maya civilization to limn the war in Iraq. But it is not about Iraq, and the end of the Maya classic period took place many centuries before the period Gibson chose for his film." Less thoughtful viewers will trivialize *Apocalypto* as merely an exciting chase movie with an exotic Central American setting, or, as Stephen Hunter called it, "bloody fun" that "really goes like hell."

James M. Welsh and John C. Tibbetts

CREDITS

Jaguar Paw: Rudy Youngblood
Seven: Dalia Hernandez
Blunted: Jonathan Brewer
Flint Sky: Morris Birdyellowhead
Turtles Run: Carlos Emilio Baez
Zero Wolf: Raoul Trujillo
Snake Ink: Rodolfo Palacios
Origin: USA
Language: English, Maya
Released: 2006
Production: Mel Gibson, Bruce Davey; Icon Productions, Touchstone Pictures; released by Buena Vista
Directed by: Mel Gibson
Written by: Mel Gibson, Farhad Safinia
Cinematography by: Dean Semler
Music by: James Horner
Sound: Fernando Camara
Editing: John Wright
Art Direction: Naaman Marshall, Roberto Bonelli
Costumes: Mayes C. Rubeo
Production Design: Tom Sanders
MPAA rating: R
Running time: 137 minutes

REVIEWS

Boxoffice Online. December 8, 2006.
Chicago Sun-Times Online. December 8, 2006.
Entertainment Weekly. December 15, 2006, p. 61.
Hollywood Reporter Online. December 1, 2006.
Los Angeles Times Online. December 8, 2006.
New York Times Online. December 8, 2006.
Newsweek Online. December 11, 2006.
Rolling Stone Online. November 21, 2006.
San Francisco Chronicle. December 8, 2006, p. E1.
Variety Online. December 1, 2006.
Washington Post. December 8, 2006, p. C1.

QUOTES

Jaguar Paw: "I am Jaguar Paw, son of Flint Sky. My Father hunted this forest before me. My name is Jaguar Paw. I am a hunter. This is my forest. And my sons will hunt it with their sons after I am gone."

TRIVIA

Gibson donated money to rebuild local housing destroyed by floods.

AWARDS

Nomination:
Oscars 2006: Makeup, Sound, Sound FX Editing
British Acad. 2006: Foreign Film
Golden Globes 2007: Foreign Film

AQUAMARINE

A Fish-Out-Of-Water Comedy.
—Movie tagline

Box Office: $18.6 million

Aquamarine is based on a book by Alice Hoffman that details a mermaid's visit to the human world, or at least the human world that exists in a small Florida resort town. Far more interesting to the film's desired audience of preteen girls, though, will be the parts about friendship and cute boys. The movie features one cute boy in particular, Raymond (Jake McDorman), a lifeguard at the beach club run by Claire's (Emma Roberts) grandparents. Claire and her best friend Hailey (Joanna "JoJo" Levesque) have spent the summer studying Jake and mooning over him. By reading numerous articles in girl magazines, they feel that have become experts on boys, including how to read their body language. They have deduced that Raymond is not only good-looking, blonde and often shirtless, but that he is a genuinely nice guy. They also suspect that he may like Cecilia (Arielle Kebbel), the local overly tan mean and rich girl.

But Cecilia is not their biggest problem. The big problem is that Hailey's mother has received a long-awaited job offer to study sea life in Australia. Hailey is going to have to move, and Claire will be without her only friend. This proves especially hard for Claire, since she has already lost her parents in a boat accident.

A possible answer to their problems arrives after a big storm when Claire and Hailey assess the damage and discover a mermaid (Sara Paxton) in their pool. The mermaid reports that her name is Aquamarine and that she has only three days to find true love. It seems that her father, Neptune, who does not believe in love, has arranged a marriage for her. If Aquamarine can find a boy to declare his love for her within three days, Aquamarine will escape her marriage. Claire and Hailey are chagrined that Aqua sets her sights on Raymond, but gamely agree to help her when they find out that Aqua will grant them a wish if her plan succeeds. A wish would allow them to stop Hailey from moving.

They instruct Aqua in the ways of attracting boys, including the techniques of calling and hanging up and walking by a boy and pretending to ignore him. Despite Aqua's strict adherence to their techniques, she manages to attract Raymond and indeed get him to like her. There are still some hurdles to overcome, such as the fact that Aqua has human legs during the day and fins at night. And although Raymond certainly likes Aqua, it is not at all certain that he loves her. Also, Hailey starts feeling guilty about her wish. Is it really right of her to make a wish that would ruin her mother's lifelong dream?

Aquamarine is a trifle, but to its intended audience, the movie may seem deep. It covers many of the basic concerns of preteen girls, including, in a fleeting way at least, the issues of broken families, parental death, being unpopular, finding a true friend, and attracting boys. The actresses who play the girls are well cast and their performances ring true. Paxton's mermaid is less appealing. She gets through the majority of her role with a perky, but equally vacant smile. Although Raymond seems like a nice, smart guy, given Aqua's absent personality, it is hard to believe that his attraction to her is based on anything but her lovely appearance.

Critics were fairly kind to the film. Wesley Morris of the *Boston Globe* did not like the movie himself but understood that there were others outside of his demographic who might like it quite a bit. He wrote that "*Aquamarine* is part *Splash* and part *Clueless* (when that dressing-room montage comes hurtling toward you, duck). But girls will know *Aquamarine* is unique because it's the rare movie that fiercely respects the altruistic loyalty that bonds girls to one another." Ruthe Stein of the *San Francisco Chronicle* wrote that "the movie has a sweetness and innocence that makes it near perfect entertainment for its target audience." Lisa Schwarzbaum of *Entertainment Weekly* gave the film a C+ grade and called it "a filmy pool of tropes and tchotchkes stereotypically associated with Girls of Today." Finally, Roger Ebert of the *Chicago Sun-Times* wrote: "*Aquamarine* is another movie where an event of earth-shaking astonishment takes place, and is safely contained within a sitcom plot...and yet—well, the movie is awfully sweet."

Jill Hamilton

CREDITS

Aquamarine: Sara Paxton
Claire: Emma Roberts
Cecilia: Arielle Kebbel
Ginny: Claudia Karvan
Hailey: Joanna "JoJo" Levesque
Raymond: Jake McDorman
Leonard: Bruce Spence
Grandpa Bob: Roy Billing
Marjorie: Tammin Sursok
Grandma Maggie: Julia Blake
Storm Banks: Shaun Micallef
Origin: USA
Language: English
Released: 2006
Production: Susan Carsonis; Fox 2000 Pictures, Storefront Pictures; released by 20th Century Fox
Directed by: Elizabeth Allen
Written by: Jessica Bendinger, John Quaintance
Cinematography by: Brian J. Breheny
Music by: David Hirschfelder
Sound: Craig Walmsley
Music Supervisor: Dana Sano, Anton Monsted, Jason Lamont

Editing: Jane Moran
Art Direction: Bill Booth
Costumes: Sally Sharpe
Production Design: Nelson Coates
MPAA rating: PG
Running time: 109 minutes

REVIEWS

Boxoffice Online. March 3, 2006.
Chicago Sun-Times Online. March 3, 2006.
Entertainment Weekly Online. March 1, 2006.
Los Angeles Times Online. March 3, 2006.
New York Times Online. March 3, 2006.
Variety Online. March 2, 2006.

QUOTES

Aquamarine regarding her mermaid status: "We are not fictional. We're discreet."

TRIVIA

The role of Aquamarine was originally offered to Jessica Simpson.

ARMY OF SHADOWS
(L'Armee des ombres)
(Army in the Shadows)
(The Shadow Army)

Since his death in 1973, Jean-Pierre Melville's reputation has increased as more and more of his rarely seen films have reached American theaters and become available on DVD. The essence of cool, especially in crime films such as *Bob le Flambeur* (1955), Melville has influenced directors as varied as Walter Hill, Quentin Tarantino, Neil Jordan, and Olivier Marchal. The long-awaited release of the World War II film *Army of Shadows* (1969) offers a glimpse of his work beyond the world of crime.

Army of Shadows is one of several older films lovingly restored and distributed by Rialto Pictures. Cinematographer Pierre Lhomme, whose impressive credits include *The Mother and the Whore* (1973), participated in the restoration to ensure that his moody lighting is displayed to its best advantage. *Army of Shadows* has muted tones, becoming as close to black-and-white as a color film can. This look is perfect for exploring the cloudy moral ambiguities and fatalism of war.

Set in 1942, *Army of Shadows,* based on a book by Joseph Kessel, opens with the arrival of civil engineer Philippe Gerbier (Lino Ventura) in a prison camp. The irony in this frequently ironic film is that the French built the camp to house German officers, but with the Nazi occupation of their country, the French collaborators imprison those opposing the Germans. Gerbier is involved in the Resistance and has been betrayed. Just as he is about to try to escape, he is taken to Gestapo headquarters. With one plan scuttled, he improvises another and escapes.

Gerbier then rounds up a team of operatives: Felix (Paul Crauchet), Claude le Masque (Claude Mann), Mathilde (Simone Signoret), Jean Francois (Jean-Pierre Cassel), and Le Bison (Christian Barbier). All operate under the command of Luc Jardie (Paul Meurisse), Jean-Francois' older brother. (That the younger Jardie knows Luc only as a stuffy intellectual holed up in his Paris apartment furthers the film's ironical tone.) In Marseille, Gerbier and his men capture and execute the traitor (Alain Libolt) who betrayed him.

On the Mediterranean coast, the operatives hide downed British and Canadian pilots. Gerbier and Luc board a submarine for London, where Luc is decorated by General de Gaulle. After Felix is arrested, Gerbier, who has never used a parachute, is dropped back into France and finds refuge in the chateau of a baron (Jean-Marie Robain). Jean-Francois gets himself arrested so that he can help Felix. Not knowing of his actions, Mathilde devises a plan to rescue Felix with Claude and Le Bison. After Gerbier is arrested, Mathilde comes up with another plan and saves him from a firing squad.

Best known for the writing *Belle de jour* (1928), the source of Luis Bunuel's 1967 film, Joseph Kessel was involved in the Resistance. After fleeing to England in 1942, he wrote *L'Armee des ombres: Chronique de la resistance* (1943) at the request of General Charles de Gaulle, based on his experiences and those of French exiles he met in England. According to Kessel, everything in the book happened to him or someone he knew. He joined the Royal Air Force in 1944 and flew reconnaissance missions as preparation for the D-Day invasion of France.

Melville, born Jean-Pierre Grumbach, was also in the Resistance, borrowing one of his cover names from the author of *Moby-Dick* (1951) and keeping it when he became a director. Attempting to reach England via Algiers, Melville was jailed in Spain for two months in 1942. By 1943, he was in the Free French artillery in Tunisia and took part in the liberations of Italy and France.

While in the Resistance, Melville read Kessel's book, as well as *Le Silence de la Mer* (1942) by Vercors, a pseudonym for Jean Bruller. This story of a German officer living in a small French village became Melville's first film in 1949. Another novel about France during the Occupation, *Leon Morin, Pretre* (1952), by Beatrix Beck, became the second of Melville's three World War II films in 1961.

Army of Shadows was made when Melville was at the height of his powers, sandwiched between his two best films, *Le Samourai* (1967) and *Le Cercle Rouge* (1970). *Army of Shadows* is not quite as good as those two masterpieces but may be a more personal film, a subtle but provocative look at how war leads ordinary people to carry out desperate acts.

The film had no U.S. release because American distributors saw no audience for a subtitled film about the French Resistance. At the height of the Vietnam War, many Americans, especially those in the much-sought-after youth audience, were tired of films about the glorious days of World War II. Ironically, this did not stop Hollywood from turning out poorly conceived and executed war films such as *Hornets' Nest* (1970) and *Tora! Tora! Tora!* (1970). Coming after the anti-de Gaulle riots of 1968, *Army of Shadows* was also seen as outdated in France.

Even if *Army of Shadows* had been released during this era, it would not have received the same acclaim as it has in 2006 because Melville was not yet generally perceived to be the genius he is today. Critics at the time trumpeted the styles of New Wave directors like Jean-Luc Godard and Francois Truffaut and the seeming artlessness of Robert Bresson and Eric Rohmer. In contrast, Melville, like Claude Chabrol, appeared merely to give Gallic spins to American genre films.

This tendency is less apparent in *Army of Shadows* than in Melville's crime films. He takes cliches of war films and re-imagines them within an existential context. Asked to kill the traitor, Claude trembles more than his intended victim. Claude begs to be released from this duty, but Gerbier is resolute that he must share responsibility for the death. Melville makes the ensuing strangulation uncomfortable for the audience to give some idea of the torment his characters are going through. The rescue of Felix, with Mathilde dressed as a nurse and Claude and Le Bison in German uniforms, is another war-film cliche offset when the attempt is called off because Felix is near death. Melville dramatically builds up the tension of the scene only to deflate it with the banality of reality.

Gerbier's rescue is more conventionally exciting, yet it has unforeseen consequences when one of the team has to be killed to protect the others. More irony comes with an epilogue describing the fates of the protagonists. Melville makes clear that in war there are no heroes, only survivors.

Beyond Nicole Stephane's relatively histrionic work in *Les Enfants Terribles* (1950), the performances in Melville's film are generally as understated as his overall style. Most of the actors in *Army of Shadows* are merely competent. The Italian-born Ventura was a beloved French star, often called the successor to Jean Gabin or the French Robert Mitchum. (Ventura and Meurisse co-star in Melville's 1966 noir *Le Deuxieme Souffle.*) Though Ventura commands the screen through the force of his authoritative bulk, he is not very expressive. An important scene with Gerbier in London watching young, uniformed Britons dancing does not have the necessary impact because Ventura is limited in exhibiting the character's feelings. Signoret is almost as stoic but conveys considerable emotions with her haunting eyes. Shots of her walking along with her middle-aged heft balanced precariously on spindly legs makes Mathilde even more poignant. Cassel, father of Vincent Cassel, moves with the self-conscious grace associated with American stars.

Finally, however, it may be just as well that American audiences had to wait thirty-seven years to see *Army of Shadows.* Viewers approaching it as just another French film would not have been alert to the nuances that become apparent when placed within the context of Melville's entire oeuvre. At 145 minutes, it is his longest film and moves slowly. In hiding after his escape, Gerbier is shown struggling to find something to do with his time and even resorts to reading the mathematical texts written by Luc. Melville conveys the unglamorous side of war with meticulous precision.

Michael Adams

CREDITS

Philippe Gerbier: Lino Ventura
Mathilde: Simone Signoret
Luc Jardie: Paul Meurisse
Jean Francois Jardie: Jean-Pierre Cassel
Claude le Masque: Claude Mann
Felix: Paul Crauchet
Le Bison: Christian Barbier
Paul Dounat: Alain Libolt
Baron de Ferte Talloire: Jean-Marie Robain
Origin: France, Italy
Language: French
Released: 1969
Production: Jacques Dorfmann; released by Rialto Pictures
Directed by: Jean-Pierre Melville
Written by: Jean-Pierre Melville
Cinematography by: Pierre Lhomme

Music by: Eric De Marsen
Editing: Francoise Bonnot
Costumes: Theo Meurisse
MPAA rating: Unrated
Running time: 140 minutes

REVIEWS

Boxoffice Online. April 28, 2006.
Chicago Sun-Times Online. May 21, 2006.
Entertainment Weekly Online. May 17, 2006.
Los Angeles Times Online. May 12, 2006.
New York Times Online. April 28, 2006.
San Francisco Chronicle. June 23, 2006, p. E5.
Washington Post. May 12, 2006, p. C5.

QUOTES

Jean Francois Jardie: "She said five minutes, but she'll wait a lifetime."

TRIVIA

The shot depicting German soldiers marching down the Champs Elysees was originally the last in the film and prints were sent to theaters as such. After the first showings, director Jean-Pierre Melville decided the scene should be placed at the start of the film and it was physically spliced into the new position, apparently resulting in several missing frames in the negative. These frames were restored from another source when the 2005 digital restoration was accomplished under the supervision of cinematographer Pierre Lhomme. The 2k resolution, digital restoration of the film took place at the Eclair Laboratories in Paris.

ART SCHOOL CONFIDENTIAL

Box Office: $3.3 million

Inspired by a four-page piece that appeared in Daniel Clowes' comic book *Eightball* (Issue #7, 1991), *Art School Confidential* is the second collaboration between director Terry Zwigoff and Clowes, who first got together to make the wonderful, bittersweet *Ghost World* (2001), which earned them an Academy Award® nomination for the screenplay. In one of that film's many brilliant sequences, the teenage heroine, Enid (Thora Birch), takes a remedial art class and has to face the foolishness, pretension, and insufferable political correctness that informs such training. *Art School Confidential* takes this essential premise and expands it to the length of a feature film, which, unfortunately, does not rise to the brilliance of *Ghost World*. While some of the situations and observations about art school are funny, the satire and plot line are not very sharp, and the objects of scorn are pretty obvious targets of ridicule.

We see the art school experience through the eyes of young Jerome Platz (Max Minghella), who gets accepted into Strathmore Institute, which does not live up to his noble vision of what art can be and whose very name, a reference to the famous paper company, cries commercialism. An admirer of Picasso, Jerome is, at heart, an innocent and idealist who finds himself surrounded by weirdos and immersed in a hypocritical world that has more to do with stringing students along than producing artists with practical skills or an appreciation of aesthetics. As Clowes, an art school graduate himself, writes in the comic, he wants to expose "the shocking truth about the biggest scam of the century!"

Clowes' screenplay is filled with an assortment of amusing oddballs, from pompous students who throw around jargon-laden critiques obviously meant to disguise the fact that they have no idea what goes into good art to the smug Professor Sandiford (a very funny John Malkovich), whose own twenty-five-year stint in the art world has gotten him no further than drawing triangles. Then there are Jerome's roommates—Matthew (Nick Swardson), a fashion major having a difficult time admitting that he is gay, and Vince (Ethan Suplee), a budding filmmaker whose grandfather is financing his student movie based on a string of real-life, unsolved murders plaguing the campus. The project ultimately becomes so abstract and experimental that the old man cannot figure out what precisely he is bankrolling. Steve Buscemi has a great cameo as the perpetually irritated Broadway Bob, the proprietor of a local cafe that showcases the best student work, and Jim Broadbent provides some caustic barbs as Jimmy, a bitter graduate of Strathmore and a failed artist living in a dingy apartment and who has nothing but contempt for the whole art school scene.

But while the characters have plenty of attitude, the story is rather thin. The film's main plot line revolves around Jerome's pursuit of Audrey (Sophia Myles), the beautiful art school model with whom he becomes entranced even before he arrives (in a great marketing move, her picture is featured in the school's brochure). A neophyte with women, Jerome approaches her very cautiously, but begins to develop a rapport until another student, Jonah (Matt Keeslar), whose mundane artwork is wildly overpraised by the class, becomes a rival, both for Audrey and for distinction in the school. Myles is a lovely actress, and it is not hard to see why Jerome would fall for such a beauty as Audrey, but because the characters are not very well developed and their connection is not very deep, it is hard to feel a real rooting interest in Jerome getting the girl.

Jerome's journey is one of increasing disillusionment as he navigates a crazy world in which his passion for great art is not shared. In a pointed shot at political correctness, a history professor (Anjelica Huston), one of the film's most sensible characters, lectures on the timelessness of art and has to field an inane student query about all the artists in the syllabus being dead, white men. When Jerome offers intelligent criticism of a student's art in class, he is unfairly seen as a bully, yet other fatuous students put down his fine work for a variety of pseudo-intellectual reasons. Worst of all, he begins to lose Audrey to the vapid Jonah and finally resorts to acquiring artwork from Jimmy to pass off as his own.

Unfortunately, Jimmy is the campus killer, and his paintings are of his victims and incorporate objects found on their bodies, which prompts authorities to arrest Jerome. The big irony is that, as a suspected murderer, all of a sudden Jerome is hailed as a major talent (although there is the added irony that no one seems to notice that the art he now produces from his jail cell looks nothing like the work that gained him notoriety in the first place), and, even though his lawyer could easily prove Jerome's innocence, his art dealer wants to wait because there is money to be made. The whole serial killer plot is a bit contrived and not very compelling until the very end, and, even then, it is an easy joke that Jerome becomes a celebrity only because of an unfair murder rap. But it is nonetheless a fitting and satisfying conclusion in a world where merit and aesthetics count for nothing and making money trumps everything. In the film's final scene, Audrey visits Jerome in jail—his supposed infamy has also enabled him to win the girl, although it helps that Jonah was really an undercover policeman investigating the murders, a revelation that destroys his reputation as an artist.

If *Art School Confidential* falls short of expectations, it is because Zwigoff and Clowes have already set the bar so high with the inspired wistfulness and satiric vision of *Ghost World*. The problem with their new film is that, while they are very smart at skewering art school dilettantes and their milieu, the filmmakers are not as interested in developing the protagonist, the narrative, or even an especially original setting. Beyond some general desire to be a great artist and to win Audrey, there is very little to distinguish Minghella's bland Jerome, whose struggle feels rather commonplace. While, in *Ghost World*, Birch's complex portrayal of the sardonic, melancholy Enid anchored a brilliant film whose stark, yet heartfelt, vision of outsiders in an increasingly desolate environment achieved a rare pop culture transcendence.

Peter N. Chumo II

CREDITS

Jerome Platz: Max Minghella
Audrey: Sophia Myles
Professor Sandiford: John Malkovich
Jimmy: Jim Broadbent
Matthew: Nick Swardson
Broadway Bob: Steve Buscemi (uncredited)
Jonah: Matt Keeslar
Vince: Ethan Suplee
Sophie: Anjelica Huston
Bardo: Joel David Moore
Origin: USA
Language: English
Released: 2006
Production: Lianne Halfon, John Malkovich, Russell Smith; United Artists, Mr. Mudd; released by Sony Pictures Classics
Directed by: Terry Zwigoff
Written by: Daniel Clowes
Cinematography by: Jamie Anderson
Music by: David Kitay
Sound: Marc Weingarten
Editing: Robert Hoffman
Art Direction: Peter Borck
Costumes: Betsy Heimann
Production Design: Howard Cummings
MPAA rating: R
Running time: 102 minutes

REVIEWS

Boxoffice Online. May 5, 2006.
Chicago Sun-Times Online. May 12, 2006.
Entertainment Weekly Online. May 3, 2006.
Los Angeles Times Online. May 5, 2006.
New York Times Online. May 5, 2006.
Variety Online. January 23, 2006.
Washington Post. May 12, 2006, p. WE33.

QUOTES

Nympho (to Jerome): "I just want you to know I definitely don't have AIDS. I mean, I've been tested like forty times so I know for a fact."

TRIVIA

Steve Buscemi is uncredited as trendy restaurant owner Broadway Bob.

ASK THE DUST

Robert Towne is best known as the screenwriter of two classic American films, *Chinatown* (1974) and *Shampoo*

(1975). Because of these films, other credits such as *The Last Detail* (1973), and uncredited work on films such as *Bonnie and Clyde* (1967) and *The Godfather* (1972), Towne is considered amongst the best screenwriters ever.

A Los Angeles native, Towne has considered an adaptation of *Ask the Dust*, a 1939 novel by John Fante, as his dream project since he first read it in 1971 while researching *Chinatown*. The novel focuses on an outsider, the usual Towne hero, struggling in the Los Angeles of the 1930s, when Towne was born. A native of Colorado who moved to Los Angeles to become a writer, Fante wrote a handful of books, of which *Ask the Dust* is the best known, that earned him a cult following, especially among writers such as Charles Bukowski, for their vivid characters and strong settings.

Because his books sold poorly (4,800 copies of *Ask the Dust*), Fante supported himself for several decades as a screenwriter. His best-known credit is the steamy-for-its-time *Walk on the Wild Side* (1962), though most of his work was for tripe like *My Six Loves* (1963). Fante was nominated for an Academy Award® for *Full of Life* (1957), based on his 1952 novel, but the film is a heavy-handed family comedy.

Towne was obviously attracted to Fante because of their similar backgrounds, and he befriended the older writer before Fante's death in 1983. Like Fante, Towne has written big-budget studio films, including *Days of Thunder* (1990) and *Mission: Impossible* (1996), to pay the bills. After failing to obtain financing for many years, Towne's dream project was finally realized when Colin Farrell expressed interest. The result, however, is a bit of a bore.

Arturo Bandini (Farrell) arrives in Los Angeles during the Depression intent upon becoming a famous writer. He has already published a story in the prestigious *American Mercury* and has a photograph of its famed editor, H. L. Mencken, his idol, on the wall of his room. (*Time* film critic Richard Schickel performs Mencken's voiceover narration.) Yet Arturo has writer's block until he meets sultry waitress Camilla Lopez (Salma Hayek). The two initially despise each other but soon become lovers. They bond in part because of prejudice. Arturo was constantly ridiculed back in Colorado for being Italian, and Camilla is made to feel an outsider in Los Angeles. When they go to a film, a woman Camilla sits next to moves rather than sit beside a Mexican. It is clear, however, that Arturo, like most of the realistic writers of the period, is preoccupied with looking for experiences he can transform into art.

Arturo, the hero of three other Fante novels, also has encounters with his landlady (Eileen Atkins), who refuses to give rooms to Jews or Mexicans, Hellfrick (Donald Sutherland), a down-on-his-luck neighbor, and Vera Rivkin (Idina Menzel), a fan who feels she cannot be loved after her body has been scarred by fire. Then Arturo and Camilla adopt a dog and take off for the desert.

It is difficult to make films about writing interesting because writers are essentially thinking or writing—not high drama. In the best ones, some other element has to enter the picture: murder dogs the screenwriter hero of *In a Lonely Place* (1950), and gender-bending romance enlivens *Shakespeare in Love* (1998). *Ask the Dust* perks up only during Vera's scenes because the character is a bit unbalanced and therefore dangerous. All the other characters are almost sleepwalkers. Except for a skinny-dipping episode, beautifully photographed by Caleb Deschanel, not much happens.

Screenwriting skills do not necessarily translate into directing ability. *Ask the Dust* is only Towne's fourth directorial effort. The others, *Personal Best* (1982), *Tequila Sunrise* (1988), and *Without Limits* (1998), are competent but show little visual flair or talent for handling actors. *Ask the Dust* is painfully slow and non-cinematic, more like an adaptation of a play than a film. This staginess is accentuated through Towne's having, because of financial restraints, to make *Ask the Dust* on a set in South Africa instead of on location in California, wrecking any chance at verisimilitude. *Ask the Dust* has an arid, vacant, lifeless feel, as authentic as the obviously transplanted palm trees.

Farrell, at his best playing bad boys, as in *Intermission* (2003), seems tentative, as if he has no idea who Arturo is. Farrell and the equally adrift Hayek, who took the part eight years before the film was made, have no chemistry, a major weakness for what is supposed to be a passionate love affair. Towne has written good love/sex scenes for other films, but the bedroom scenes in *Ask the Dust* are especially mechanical, despite the nudity. While Atkins and Sutherland are also at a loss in underwritten roles, Menzel steals the few scenes she is in, making Vera's desperate need for love indelible. Vera's stunted attempt to embrace life is the only true emotion in *Ask the Dust*.

Michael Adams

CREDITS

Arturo Bandini: Colin Farrell
Camilla Lopez: Salma Hayek
Hellfrick: Donald Sutherland
Mrs. Hargraves: Eileen Atkins
Vera Rivkin: Idina Menzel
Sammy: Justin Kirk
Soloman: Jeremy Crutchley

Voice of Mencken: Richard Schickel
Origin: USA
Language: English
Released: 2006
Production: Tom Cruise, Paula Wagner, Jonas McCord, Don Granger; Capitol Films, Cruise-Wagner Productions, VIP Medienfonds 3, Ascendant Production; released by Paramount Classics
Directed by: Robert Towne
Written by: Robert Towne
Cinematography by: Caleb Deschanel
Music by: Ramin Djawadi, Heitor Pereira
Sound: Nico Louw
Editing: Robert K. Lambert
Art Direction: Tom Hannam
Costumes: Albert Wolsky
Production Design: Dennis Gassner
MPAA rating: R
Running time: 117 minutes

REVIEWS

Boxoffice Online. March 10, 2006.
Chicago Sun-Times Online. March 17, 2006.
Entertainment Weekly Online. March 8, 2006.
Los Angeles Times Online. March 10, 2006.
New York Times Online. March 10, 2006.
Variety Online. February 2, 2006.

QUOTES

Camilla: "You call me beautiful at home, then you are ashamed to be seen with me in public. You are ashamed of beauty you recognize that no one else does. You are ashamed to love me!"

TRIVIA

Val Kilmer was once attached to the project but dropped out due to unspecified reasons.

ATL

A New American Story.
—Movie tagline

Box Office: $21.1 million

The narrative of *ATL* surrounds Rashad Swann (Tip Harris a.k.a. T.I.) and his circle of friends as they endure various challenges that result in major alterations in their identities. Rashad lives in a house in a poor neighborhood of Atlanta, Georgia with his Uncle George (Mykelti Williamson) and his younger brother, Antwone "Ant" Swann (Evan Ross). He has become the "man of the house" as his parents have passed away and Uncle George's janitorial duties prohibit him from assuming the effective parental role that Rashad knows Antwone requires. Rashad's circle of friends includes Esquire (Jackie Long), a kid from the South Side who attends a private high school and will attend an Ivy League college; Brooklyn (Albert Daniels), a sarcastic, verbal wit from New York City; and Teddy (Jason Weaver), a twenty-one year old high school senior who loves a party. Conditions in their area of town, while not destitute or squalid, cannot be considered privileged. Every Sunday night, all the youth from the area convene at the Cascade, a roller-skating rink. Attendance ensures that an individual is part of something bigger than one's self. The music, the lights, the motion, and the emotion keep the youth transfixed. It is a positive environment where small cliques could form and advance their skating skills as a team. Rashad feels like he is "floating above it all." At the Cascade, where Rashad works at the shoe rental counter, "problems didn't exist" and he has "no beefs." However, such a dream cannot last and the individual choices of Rashad's circle of friends and family have cataclysmic results.

Rashad meets a girl named New New (Lauren London) at the Cascade. They commiserate with each other and develop a relationship. At about the same time, Ant is lured by the materialistic aspects of a drug dealer's life and begins selling narcotics for Marcus (Antwan Andre Patton a.k.a. Big Boi). Finally, Esquire, who works at a country club, meets John Garnett (Keith David), a wealthy entrepreneur from the same area of Atlanta as Rashad and his crew. It is these relationships that engender the strife that writer Antwone Fisher utilizes to teach a few very simple lessons. After playing golf with John Garnett and lying to him about what part of Atlanta he is from, Esquire goes to Garnett's house to request a letter of recommendation. There, he discovers that New New, whose name is actually Erin, is Garnett's daughter. Esquire and Erin agree to hide each other's identity. One Sunday night, Erin's friend tells her parents about Erin's secret. Rashad also discovers the charade. When Erin comes to Rashad's house to apologize, Rashad seizes the necklace he had given her as a gift and rejects her as a phony. Esquire reveals to Garnett his own true identity and returns the letter of recommendation. Garnett shuns him but Esquire does not leave without accusing Garnett of turning his back on his own identity. On the "Last Sunday Night," Ant is robbed on a corner where he sells drugs. Marcus confronts him about the money and Ant runs away into an alley. Marcus pursues him but Rashad fortuitously arrives as well. Marcus ends up shooting Ant, who does not die, but learns a lesson. Esquire ends up getting a "mysterious" letter of recommendation, Rashad and Erin get back together, and Rashad finally gets the comic strips he's been working on published in a newspaper.

This is obviously a tale meant for young adults and painted with broad strokes. The lessons are incredibly simplistic. If you get involved with drugs, you will be arrested, beaten, robbed, and possibly shot. If you lie, you will not be trusted in the future. Be honest with yourself about who you are. Follow your dreams and you will be rewarded. These trite morals form the undercarriage of the narrative.

There is no element of society's underbelly in *ATL*. Unfortunately, there is also no drama in *ATL* either. The film is incredibly boring and predictable. The dialogue seems rather pointless on the whole. Most of it is composed of what plays like improvised one-liners. The supposedly scripted elements range from pedestrian, commonplace drivel to over-emphasized, over-inflected three word phrases. Also, there didn't seem to be a single shot that utilized more than about ten seconds of film. Remember, though, this is obviously not a film for adults or mature individuals. If you love MTV, this is the movie for you. The moral lessons imbedded in the story are conveyed implicitly and its messages are clear, though not explicit.

Nick Kennedy

CREDITS

Priscilla Garnett: Lonette McKee
Uncle George: Mykelti Williamson
John Garnett: Keith David
Teddy: Jason Weaver
Rashad: Tip Harris
New New: Lauren London
Ant: Evan Ross
Marcus: Antwan Andre Patton
Esquire: Jackie Long
Brooklyn: Albert Daniels
Star: Malika Khadijah
DJ Drama: Tyree Simmons
Origin: USA
Language: English
Released: 2006
Production: James Lassiter, Will Smith; Overbrook Entertainment; released by Warner Bros.
Directed by: Chris Robinson
Written by: Tina Gordon Chism, Antwone Fisher (story)
Music by: Aaron Zigman
Sound: Mary H. Ellis
Editing: David Blackburn
Art Direction: Jonathan Short
Costumes: Shawn Barton
Production Design: Robb Buono
MPAA rating: PG-13
Running time: 105 minutes

REVIEWS

Chicago Sun-Times Online. March 31, 2006.
Entertainment Weekly Online. March 31, 2006.
Los Angeles Times Online. March 31, 2006.
New York Times Online. March 31, 2006.
San Francisco Chronicle Online. March 31, 2006.
USA Today Online. March 31, 2006.
Variety Online. March 30, 2006.
Village Voice Online. March 28, 2006.
Washington Post. March 31, 2006, p. C5.

TRIVIA

Evan Ross, who plays Ant, is the son of Diana Ross.

THE AURA

Most reviewers of *Nine Queens* (2000), Fabian Bielinsky's debut as a feature-film director, called attention to its debt to David Mamet. Like *House of Games* (1987), Mamet's first film as a director, *Nine Queens* focuses on confidence tricksters and has twists within twists in its convoluted plot. Unlike *House of Games*, however, *Nine Queens* is primarily an entertainment, with little thematic weight, as with Mamet's *Heist* (2001). Bielinsky's second and, sadly, final film (he passed away in June 2006), *The Aura* (*El Aura*) has superficial similarities to *Heist*, but the Argentine director has something on his mind this time out. *The Aura* is compelling as a character study and as an examination of the ways chance rules lives.

Esteban Espinosa (Ricardo Darin) is a taxidermist in Buenos Aires, one of those people who escape from the harsh realities of the outside world by devoting himself to the painstaking details of his work. Taxidermy, for Esteban, whose name is never mentioned, is both a job and therapy. Esteban also enjoys fantasizing about committing a perfect crime. Waiting to pick up their checks at a natural history museum, he tells his colleague Sontag (Alejandro Awada) how he would rob the payroll office. When the pair travels to a remote hunting lodge in Patagonia, a locale reflecting his emotional isolation, Esteban discovers that the owner and guide (Manuel Rodal) is involved in some shady activities. Esteban, who has a photographic memory, stumbles into a plan to rob a gambling casino and impulsively, yet slowly, injects himself into the scheme. As with the structure of *Nine Queens*, unexpected things happen, and our hero adjusts his plans accordingly. Bielinsky gets considerable irony from the contrast between the taxidermist's desire for a smooth operation and the bumbling reality, with mistakes compounded by more mistakes.

The film's title refers to the protagonist's epilepsy. In the moments before having a seizure, Esteban experiences a sense of disorientation, which physicians call an aura. Not knowing when this condition will arise only intensifies the suspense of *The Aura.*

Esteban initially rejects Sontag's request that he accompany his friend on the trip because he does not want to kill animals. He changes his mind after returning to his apartment to discover his wife has left him. Bielinsky never explains why, but reveals two more deeply flawed marriages as the film progresses. The writer-director's two films suggest considerable sympathy for women trapped in a male-dominated world.

The Aura is much more than a heist film because of the fascinating way Bielinsky presents it. The film unravels almost in slow motion, as if to reflect Esteban's perplexed mental state. There are several driving scenes, especially one with Esteban trailing a wounded thief (Rafael Castejon), that seem to owe a debt to the stately rhythms of James Stewart following Kim Novak through the streets of San Francisco in Alfred Hitchcock's *Vertigo* (1958), another dreamlike film. Esteban never responds quickly to any development, carefully thinking matters through before taking any action, even when an immediate decision is needed.

Bielinsky's mastery is established with the opening shot. The film begins with Esteban sprawled on a marble floor, and Bielinsky lingers on him, forcing the viewer to ponder who he is and what has happened for some time before the camera pulls back to reveal he has passed out in front of a bank's ATM. The director's use of the Patagonian forest is also striking, making it both a solitary refuge and a repository of danger and evil.

Just as Joe Mantegna is essential to Mamet's early films, so is Darin to Bielinsky. Darin bears a strong resemblance to Mantegna and plays the con man in *Nine Queens* with an edgy cockiness similar to that of the American actor. His Esteban is a much less frenetic character, full of loneliness and quiet desperation. It is remarkable that an actor could be so convincing, so totally right, for two such emotional opposites.

Large portions of the film consist of shots of Esteban's staring at something and trying to make sense of it. Darin gives him more of a hangdog expression than with his *Nine Queens* character. Presenting Esteban as an everyman reacting to the chaos around him underscores the universality of *The Aura.* A wonderful touch by Bielinsky is having Esteban establish a rapport with a wolf-like dog with intense, pale eyes. Their relationship leads to an immensely satisfying way of concluding the film.

Watching *The Aura* is a somewhat melancholy experience. Before making *Nine Queens*, Americanized as *Criminal* (2004), Bielinsky worked as assistant director, second-unit director, and screenwriter on several films. His considerable skills in devising compelling plots, handling actors, and matching the rhythms of his films to the situations depicted indicate, together with his offbeat humor, he would have had much more success. *The Aura* illustrates his diversity as an almost silent film compared to the talky *Nine Queens.* But while in Brazil to shoot a television commercial, he died of a heart attack on June 28, 2006. He was only forty-seven. *Nine Queens* and *The Aura* constitute a considerable legacy for this marvelous storyteller.

Michael Adams

CREDITS

Esteban Espinosa: Ricardo Darin
Diana Dietrich: Dolores Fonzi
Sontag: Alejandro Awada
Sosa: Pablo Cedron
Urien: Jorge d'Elia
Julio: Nahuel Perez
Montero: Walter Reyno
Carlos Dietrich: Manuel Rodal
Vega: Rafael Castejon
Origin: Argentina, France, Spain
Language: Spanish
Released: 2005
Production: Pablo Bossi, Gerardo Herrero, Mariela Besuievski, Samuel Hadida; Patagonik Film Group, Tornasol Films SA, Davis Films; released by IFC First Take
Directed by: Fabian Bielinsky
Written by: Fabian Bielinsky
Cinematography by: Checco Varese
Music by: Lucio Godoy
Sound: Carlos Abbate, Jose Luis Diaz Ouzande
Editing: Alejandro Carrillo Penovi, Fernando Pardo
Art Direction: Mercedes Alfonsin
MPAA rating: Unrated
Running time: 138 minutes

REVIEWS

New York Times Online. November 17, 2006.
Variety Online. September 19, 2005.
Village Voice Online. November 14, 2006.

AWESOME! I F***IN' SHOT THAT!

Finally, Hornblower is taking back what's his.
—Movie tagline

As its iconoclastic complete title would signify, *Awesome! I F***in' Shot That!*, aspires to generate as much hysteria through its filmic and video coverage of a pop music event as the event itself. Its director Adam Yauch in competing with the real thing, ends up with a form of cinematic overkill, the chaotic nature of the overall filmic style canceling out the chaos on stage, which he no doubt seeks to glorify. The event is an October 9, 2004 Madison Square Garden concert by the Beastie Boys, stalwarts of a musical subgenre that could be called "white rap." The film's coverage has been compiled from over a hundred videos of the event, each the work of a Beastie fan given a camera for this very purpose.

On one level, Yauch aspires to turn film history on its head, his effort implying that filmic truth, be it of a concert or a war, can best be derived from those participating in it, and not from the objective standpoint of a documentarian. In this conviction, his film has a ready soul mate in the far more humble undertaking, *The War Tapes* (2006), which focuses on the Iraqi Occupation as captured by a group of National Guardsmen or Citizen Soldiers.

Awesome opens with a view of our planet lit up at night so as to support the grandiose assertion that millions will be watching what follows. The film then careens to a fast-motion sequence of the concert venue filling up. Backstage, the hundred-odd Beastie fans-cum-videographers are briefed: "Just keep shooting! Twenty years from now you'll be saying 'I f***ing shot that!'" As the parade of the Beasties' greatest hits gets under way, it becomes clear that the future will find nothing memorable in this jerky hodgepodge of professionally filmed footage and amateurish video digressions. As the screen splits into sixty mini-screens, as a tribute to the raucous Beasties, the one troubling characteristic that emerges, from the concert and it's filming, is that of insularity, especially on an ethnic plane. The only African American glimpsed in the audience is a security guard. Moreover, there's no effort to woo those not familiar with the music by, say, having the protest lyrics appear as subtitles.

An outsider to the scene would look on each of the numbers the Beasties bark out as an incitement to hostility. Even when they sing their "Song for New York City," all that comes across is distortion, both in the audio and the visuals that fill the stage. Then again, as pop phenomena go, no one could hear the Beatles either when they performed live. But the comparison stops there. The Beastie fans we see, in relation to those of the early Beatles, are much older. Typical amongst them is Hollywood star Ben Stiller, to whom the film keeps cutting without identifying him, as he mouths the Beastie lyrics. Consequently, despite the belligerence being enacted on stage, the Beastie audience, except for isolated instances of body slamming, seems to keep its adulation under control. So much so that at one point the Beasties have to plead: "Everybody get real excited for the DVD!"

True, the democratization of the proceedings through the video footage by fans has resulted in moments never before seen in a concert film, such as a shot of urination followed by flushing, as the Beasties sing, "We have to keep the party going on!" However, most of the personalized video doesn't appear to embody any personal vision at all, which leads to a more disturbing conclusion. For this generation of Beastie fans, access to the latest technology has only blinded them into using it to distort and disfigure. Thus, after a year spent by the filmmakers editing the footage, the result is nothing more than cinematic graffiti.

Had the Beastie concert been captured in the manner of a traditional concert film (such as this year's *Neil Young: Heart of Gold* by Jonathan Demme), the film, and the Beasties, would have fared much better. This is because the Beasties' beat is infectious and their voicing of protest feels genuine and the group shows a disarming talent for ironic comment. In the middle of the concert, the lights go off and the Beasties appear on a float, dressed in white suits, like decorations on a cake. The retro music they perform, unmelodic and lackluster, is a mere interlude. They soon return to give the people what they want: hostile diatribes.

It should therefore come as a shock to anyone who values youthful rebellion that at 10:18 p.m., the Beasties announce that "It's getting late!" To establish a communal rapport with their fans, the Beasties sing a number of songs that seem to blend with the audience. They are then shown scampering down hallways, into an elevator and back on stage. Their last song, they claim, is dedicated to George W. Bush and is called "Sabotage." Yet one can decipher little more than its title. As if to make up for all the inverted conformity, the film's final image is that of a fan blowing what is, presumably, illegal smoke into the lens of the camera.

Vivek Adarkar

CREDITS

Origin: USA

Language: English

Released: 2006

Production: John Doran, Adam Yauch; Oscilloscope Films; released by ThinkFilm

Directed by: Adam "MCA" Yauch

Cinematography by: Alexis Boling

Music by: Adam "MCA" Yauch, Adam Horovitz, Mike D

Sound: Jon Weiner

Editing: Neal Usatin
MPAA rating: R
Running time: 90 minutes

REVIEWS

Entertainment Weekly Online. March 29, 2006.
Hollywood Reporter Online. March 30, 2006.

B

BABEL

If you want to be understood...listen.
—Movie tagline

Box Office: $33.8 million

Babel is a complex film about the paradox of the human condition, of the simultaneous alienation and interconnectedness of people. *Babel*'s title, of course, is drawn from the biblical story of the Tower of Babel in which humanity, united by a common language, attempts to build a tower to heaven. God intervenes, confuses human language, and humanity scatters across the globe and abandons the tower, forever to be separated by distance and incapable of simple, direct communication. All of the characters in *Babel* are divided by language and culture, and are physically removed from one another by great distances, yet they are undeniably linked. Directed by Alejandro Gonzalez Inarritu, with a screenplay by Guillermo Arriaga, this story is told on both a grand scale and on an interpersonal level. Though the plot unfolds on an international stage, it is the individual stories, which emphasize familial relationships that drive the main action.

Babel's plot unfolds in essentially three locales (Morocco, San Diego/Mexico, and Tokyo), and is not strictly arranged in chronological order but is designed specifically to heighten the tension, the threat of danger. The film opens in Morocco with a shepherd, Abdullah (Mustapha Rachidi), buying a gun from a local tracker, Hassan (Abdelkader Bara) so that his sons can kill the jackals that are preying on the family's flock. When the boys test the gun with a little target practice, it is clear that Yussef (Boubker Ait El Caid) is a better shot than his brother Ahmed (Said Tarchani), which sets up an inadvertently deadly sibling rivalry. As the boys watch over the flock, they take turns trying to hit various targets, including a tour bus. Yussef takes aim at the bus and appears to miss. When the bus stops, the boys realize they must have hit it, and they run off in terror. The tension from this scene carries over in to the next when the film cuts abruptly to San Diego, where housekeeper and nanny Amelia (Adriana Barraza) is watching over Mike (Nathan Gamble) and Debbie (Elle Fanning), the children of Richard (Brad Pitt) and Susan (Cate Blanchett). This inter-cutting between multiple locales and storylines is the hallmark of *Babel.* Mike and Debbie are nervous about sleeping in the dark for fear that they will die as, apparently, their infant sibling recently did. Amelia makes no quarrel when the children ask her to stay with them and to keep the light on. The following morning, however, Amelia needs to go to Mexico to attend her son's wedding, but must wait for Susan's sister to arrive so that someone will be around to watch the children. When it becomes evident that Susan is not coming, and Amelia can find no one else to watch Mike and Debbie, she resolves to take them to Mexico with her. In these first two scenes alone, Inarritu establishes a sense of impending dread, and the potential for tragedy.

We cut back to Morocco, to find Richard and Susan having a very tense lunch in a Moroccan eatery. She throws out the ice in their drinks because she does not trust that the Moroccan water is safe to drink. They seem very out of place here—it appears that they have come to Morocco in the wake of their baby's death to be alone, to retreat from their lives, from themselves. It is not long before they are traveling on a bus, the very same bus we saw Yussef shoot at earlier. Susan sleeps against one of the windows. The scene is almost unbearably tense, because the audience knows what must be coming—the window breaks and Susan slumps over. The scene abruptly cuts to an auditorium in Tokyo in which deaf teenage girls are playing volleyball. One of them, Chieko (Rinko Kikuchi) is picked up by her father, Yasujiro (Koji Yakusho). They are having trouble connecting—Cheiko's mother has recently died, and it has created a gulf between father and daughter. Yasujiro drops Chieko off at J-Pop, an all-ages club/arcade/diner, and reminds her that she has an appointment with the dentist later that day. In the club, Chieko and her friend flirt with some boys but are quickly ostracized when it becomes clear that the girls are deaf. Chieko's separation from the world of sound and her feelings of longing for and alienation from that world reinforce the near impossibility of communication between different groups of people, a major theme in *Babel.* Chieko flashes one of the boys as retaliation for the rejection, showing her awareness of her own potential sexual power and underscoring her impotence to wield it in a way that might allow her to meaningfully connect with another human being.

The rest of the film unfolds along similar lines. Back in Morocco, when Abdullah arrives home late, he says that the police had closed his usual road and that the cause was rumored to be a dead American tourist. That night, Yussef and Ahmed cannot sleep out of guilt and fear. That sense of fear carries over when the film jumps back to the Mexican border where Amelia and her nephew, Santiago (Gael Garcia Bernal), cross into Mexico with Mike and Debbie in Santiago's derelict car. The children are visibly apprehensive about being in this alien world, and the differences between Mexico and their comparatively controlled California home can be seen both in the Mexican street life and in the obvious laissez faire attitude toward children at the wedding celebration. The children come close to settling in and having fun at the wedding, when they partake in a very disturbing game—Santiago twists the head off a live chicken and all the children except Mike and Debbie chase its still-moving headless body. Piggybacking on the horror of this scene, *Babel* shifts back to Morocco, where Richard tries to stop Susan's bleeding from an apparent gunshot wound. It will take too long, the tour guide tells Richard, to get to the nearest hospital. Susan's bleeding requires immediate attention, so they drive to the nearest town, which is barely more than a collection of hovels. Susan is taken to the residence of the town's doctor, where she waits for him. Richard leaves Susan briefly to make a call to Susan's sister to implore her to contact the U.S. Embassy in Morocco for help. He returns to find that Susan must be stitched up because she has lost a lot of blood. As Susan screams, the action jarringly cuts to Tokyo and the silent world of Chieko. Seated in the dentist's chair, she keeps attempting to kiss the dentist until he has her leave the office. She goes home to her apartment building and finds the police in the lobby questioning the concierge about her father. The police opt not to talk to Chieko when the concierge informs them that she is a deaf-mute. She clearly finds one of the policemen attractive. On a television, a news broadcast reports the shooting of an American tourist in Morocco, one of a few instances of *Babel*'s worlds being connected by more than just film editing. The world of *Babel*, though large and unwieldy, is linked.

Back in Morocco, the police investigate Susan's shooting by searching for whoever owns the rifle that was used. They interrogate Hassan, and Hassan says that he sold the rifle to Abdullah. When the police come to question Abdullah, Yussef and Ahmed say that the gun's owner actually lives far away, over the next mountain. The police leave reluctantly, suspicious that the boys are lying. In another nice detail which shows how unconsciously interwoven the world of *Babel* (and the world) is, the Moroccan police drive Toyotas, which are of course made in Japan. The film cuts back to Mexico and Amelia's son's wedding, which is becoming more and more raucous as the celebrants become increasingly intoxicated. At one point, Santiago shoots a pistol into the air in celebration, scaring Mike and Debbie. The scene is especially menacing, given that their mother has been shot half a world away. In Morocco, tension builds between Richard and the other tourists on the bus. They are pushing to leave, as many of them are elderly and need to get back to the hotel. The film cuts to Tokyo, and Chieko goes out on the town with her friend, her friend's cousin, and several of his friends. The boys ply the girls with whiskey and pills. When the group enters a club, the film's soundtrack cuts back and forth between the loud world of the club and Chieko's world of silence, emphasizing again a sense of disconnect. When Chieko finds her friend kissing one of the boys, she signals to her friend that she is going to leave. She returns to her apartment and asks the doorman to call one of the detectives, the one she likes, who was there earlier in the day.

From this point, the stories become more intense. Abdulah discovers that Yussef and Hassan shot the American tourist. They all go on the run and are pursued by the police. When the police shoot Hassan, Yussef picks up the rifle and shoots at the police. Back in Mexico, Santiago's car is searched by the border patrol. When it appears that they might arrest him, Santiago speeds away from the border crossing into the States. The children are terrified. Santiago drives into the desert and has Amelia and the children get out of the car. He promises to return for them later. The film cuts back to

Morocco, where Richard and the tour guide talk briefly about their children. When Richard is informed that an ambulance will not be coming for his wife, he leaves to call the U.S. Embassy. As he calls, the tour bus leaves them stranded.

In Japan, the police detective arrives at Chieko's apartment. Chieko brings him tea and proceeds to tell him that Yasujiro had nothing to do with her mother's death. The detective says that he is not there investigating her mother's death, but a rifle used in the shooting of an American tourist in Morocco which has been traced back to her father. The policeman says he has to leave, but Chieko asks him to stay and excuses herself momentarily. When she returns to the living room, she is naked. The policeman refuses her advances, but holds her while she cries. The movie shifts to Amelia, Mike, and Debbie lost in the desert. Santiago never returned for them. Amelia leaves the children to go search for help. When she comes across a border patrol agent, she implores him to come with her to look for the children. At first, it seems that they cannot locate the children, but they are ultimately found. In Morocco, Richard and Susan are airlifted to a hospital; she is operated on and survives. In Tokyo, the police lieutenant leaves the apartment and encounters her father, Yasujiro, in the hallway. He asks about the rifle and Yasujiro confirms that he visited Morocco on a hunting trip after his wife died and gave the rifle to Hassan for being a good tracker. The policeman leaves and Yasujiro enters the apartment. A Japanese news broadcast shown on a television in the apartment reveals that Susan has survived her gunshot wound. Yasujiro finds his daughter standing naked on the balcony. He goes to her and she cries as he holds her.

The final shot of the film, of Yasujiro holding his naked daughter on their balcony, captures perfectly what appears to be the central thesis of the film: that despite the barriers of language and culture that separate people, humanity is united in its pain and loneliness, and in wanting the best for one's own family. Appropriately, the camera pulls back slowly from Chieko and Yasujiro, gradually creating greater distance between the audience and the image of father and daughter, leaving the audience with the impression of the gulf between these characters on the one hand, and their connection via the bigger picture on the other. In this way, *Babel*'s content and form inform its function—by shifting back and forth between characters locked in their own personal struggles, the audience is allowed to see how the characters' actions and reactions unfold in a wider context. *Babel* makes the case that one's individual choices are not isolated, but are part of a much larger narrative. The effect is to powerfully remind the viewer that all of humanity experiences loss, hardship, and loneliness, as well as misunderstanding and prejudice, and that experiencing these things actually unites people, as does love of family.

John Boaz

CREDITS

Richard: Brad Pitt
Susan: Cate Blanchett
Santiago: Gael Garcia Bernal
Amelia: Adriana Barraza
Debbie: Elle Fanning
Yasujiro: Koji Yakusho
Mike: Nathan Gamble
Chieko: Rinko Kikuchi
Ahmed: Said Tarchani
Yussef: Boubker Ait El Caid
Abdullah: Mustapha Rachidi
Hassan: Abdelkader Bara
Origin: USA
Language: English, French, Japanese, Spanish
Released: 2006
Production: Jon Kilik, Steve Golin, Alejandro Gonzalez Inarritu; Zeta Films, Anonymous Content, Central Films; released by Paramont Vantage
Directed by: Alejandro Gonzalez Inarritu
Written by: Guillermo Arriaga
Cinematography by: Rodrigo Prieto
Music by: Gustavo Santaolalla
Sound: Jose Antonio Garcia
Editing: Stephen Mirrione, Douglas Crise
Production Design: Brigitte Broch
MPAA rating: R
Running time: 142 minutes

REVIEWS

Boxoffice Online. October 27, 2006.
Entertainment Weekly. November 3, 2006, p. 49.
Hollywood Reporter Online. May 24, 2006.
Los Angeles Times Online. October 27, 2006.
New York Times Online. October 27, 2006.
Rolling Stone Online. October 20, 2006.
Time Online. October 22, 2006.
USA Today Online. October 26, 2006.
Variety Online. May 23, 2006.
Village Voice Online. May 30, 2006.

AWARDS

Oscars 2006: Orig. Score
British Acad. 2006: Orig. Score
Golden Globes 2007: Film—Drama

Nomination:

Oscars 2006: Director (Inarritu), Film, Film Editing, Orig. Screenplay, Support. Actress (Barraza, Kikuchi)

British Acad. 2006: Cinematog., Director (Inarritu), Film, Film Editing, Orig. Screenplay, Sound

Directors Guild 2006: Director (Inarritu)

Golden Globes 2007: Director (Inarritu), Screenplay, Support. Actor (Pitt), Support. Actress (Kikuchi, Barraza), Orig. Score

Screen Actors Guild 2006: Support. Actress (Barraza), Support. Actress (Kikuchi), Cast

Writers Guild 2006: Orig. Screenplay

BARNYARD

The Original Party Animals.
—Movie tagline

What happens in the barn, stays in the barn.
—Movie tagline

Box Office: $72.6 million

In a summer filled with far too many computer animated children's films involving talking animals, *Barnyard*'s one way of standing out was being the film that made the biologically-incorrect and strangely unsettling artistic decision to create a male cow. There are some that may not know male cattle are not cows, but rather bulls. Most people will likely realize there is something terribly wrong with these creatures, especially one sporting prominent udders and speaking in the deep voice of Sam Elliott. As Manohla Dargis of the *New York Times* wrote: "The udder looks a lot like the base of a plumber's plunger and the teats look exceptionally friendly, like chubby little fingers waving toodle-oo. They're so friendly that it's hard not to stare at them." The udders gave other reviewers pause, as well. Carina Chocano of the *Los Angeles Times* wrote: "The image would be plenty disturbing enough if the characters didn't compound the shock by going about on hind legs and engaging in lots of bouncy physical activity. Reader, there were times when I felt compelled to avert my eyes and pray for pants."

Gender confusion aside, the story is pretty conventional and resembles a lesser *The Lion King* (1994). Otis (voice of Kevin James) is a young male cow who lives to have fun. He lives with his adoptive father, Ben (voice of Elliott), the no-nonsense leader of the barnyard animals. The animals, owned by a vegan farmer, like to hold big dance parties at night and play pranks on the humans. Ben, a serious cow, wishes for his son to take on some responsibility, but Otis only wants to dance and make mischief. "A strong man stands up for himself. A stronger man stands up for others," Ben advises his son gravely. One night, while filling in for Otis and guarding the farm, Ben is attacked by coyotes and killed. Otis has reached the point in his life in which he needs to become a man, that is, a bull, or rather a male cow.

Otis is surrounded by barnyard cohorts who stick with their gender and/or ethnic stereotypes. Good girl cow Daisy (voice of Courteney Cox) may well be the sweet cow that convinces Otis to settle down and start a family. Her best friend, brown cow Bessy (voice of Wanda Sykes), is none-too-surprisingly a sassy, no-nonsense type. Miles (voice of Danny Glover) is a wise old mule who dispenses the proper advice at the right time and mouse Pip (voice of Jeffrey Garcia) is the Mexican-accented sidekick.

There are some things that are very good about *Barnyard*. One of these was the casting decision that landed Elliott the role of Ben. Even though his character looks completely ridiculous, Elliott's somber Southern drawl adds a surprising gravitas to the character. That the actor could give such a silly-looking character such grace and dignity is a fine acting feat. The musical numbers are another highlight. Before Otis is forced to get responsible, there are some nice scenes of the animals dancing the night away. Director Steve Oedekerk makes the music and dancing so infectious that the animals are swept away with the sheer fun of it all. As Ty Burr of the *Boston Globe* put it, the numbers are "bizarrely catchy." The film has some funny bits in it, too. There is a farm dog named Duke (voice of Dom Irrera) who wants to be the leader of the barn, but cannot seem to shake his urge to chase any ball thrown at him. And there is a nice extended sequence in which Otis and some tough Jersey cows get back at a bratty human kid who goes cow tipping.

Critics, perhaps weary of so many similar films in such a short time span gave the movie a collective shrug. Burr of the *Boston Globe* called the film "nothing so much as *The Lion King* chewed in cud and digitally regurgitated." Michael Phillips of the *Chicago Tribune* objected to what he saw as excessive violence in the film, but wrote that "*Barnyard* can at least hold its head up as a sharply scripted effort that, while assembled from familiar elements, does not feel focus-grouped and committed to death." Bill Zwecker of the *Chicago Sun-Times* wrote: "Maybe I've just seen too many of these pictures, but the basically good—though not very inspired—*Barnyard* just stirred up a lot of 'been there, done that' feelings in me as I watched this film."

Jill Hamilton

CREDITS

Otis the Cow: Kevin James (Voice)

Daisy the Cow: Courteney Cox (Voice)

Ben the Cow: Sam Elliott (Voice)
Miles the Mule: Danny Glover (Voice)
Etta the Hen: Andie MacDowell (Voice)
Bessy the Cow: Wanda Sykes (Voice)
Dag the Coyote: David Koechner (Voice)
Mr. Beady/Snotty Boy/Snotty Boy's Father: Steve Oedekerk (Voice)
Peck the Rooster/Skunk: Rob Paulsen (Voice)
Duke the Dog: Dom Irrera (Voice)
Mrs. Beady: Maria Bamford (Voice)
Snotty Boy's Friend: Laraine Newman (Voice)
Igg the Cow: Maurice LaMarche (Voice)
Pip the Mouse: Jeffrey Garcia (Voice)
Origin: USA
Language: English
Released: 2006
Production: Steve Oedekerk, Paul Marshall; Nickelodeon Movies, O Entertainment; released by Paramount Pictures
Directed by: Steve Oedekerk
Written by: Steve Oedekerk
Music by: John Debney
Sound: Michael Hilkene, Philip A. Cruden
MPAA rating: PG
Running time: 89 minutes

REVIEWS

Boxoffice Online. August 4, 2006.
Chicago Sun-Times Online. August 4, 2006.
Entertainment Weekly. August 11, 2006, p. 51.
Los Angeles Times Online. August 4, 2006.
New York Times Online. August 4, 2006.
San Francisco Chronicle. August 4, 2006, p. E5.
Variety Online. August 3, 2006.
Washington Post. August 4, 2006, p. C2.

QUOTES

Ben (to son Otis): "A strong man stands up for himself. A stronger man stands up for others."

BASIC INSTINCT 2

Everything interesting begins in the mind.
—Movie tagline

Box Office: $5.8 million

When *Basic Instinct* came out in 1992, the overheated film propelled Sharon Stone to fame as the sexual and possibly homicidal, Catherine Tramell. The actress then spent years trying to overcome her potent image as the femme fatale. So, when *Basic Instinct 2* finally came out fourteen years later, it seemed to indicate that Stone had failed to become a serious actress. Thus, the film has the pallor of failure over it. It is somehow embarrassing watching Stone having to again vamp, tease, and flash the audience. The issue is not that a woman of her age is not able to be alluring—though some critics did seem oddly concerned by such a prospect. It is more that, since it is widely known that Stone did not want to repeat the role, the audience is, in a sense, bearing witness to her humiliation.

Of course, all of this could be overcome if the film was good, or at least pleasantly campy. But alas it is not. The film starts off promisingly with a jolt of adrenaline. Stone's Tramell is zipping though London city streets with a barely conscious famous soccer star (Stan Collymore) in the passenger seat. As she expertly maneuvers her sleek sports car, she is simultaneously involved in a sex act with the star. Apparently, this is not particularly safe, because the car plunges into a river and the soccer star is killed.

Stone is put on trial for the death and is assigned a court-appointed psychiatrist, Dr. Michael Glass (David Morrissey). Glass is a buttoned-down British fellow who is not nearly a match for Tramell. As Owen Gleiberman of *Entertainment Weekly* put it, Glass is "lured in a way that's so abstract that we're not quite sure if he wants to go to bed with her or write a thesis about her." In one of the many tiresome decisions made by screenwriters Leora Barish and Henry Bean, Tramell is diagnosed with a big case of "risk addiction." If there is anything that instantly takes the fun out of a dangerous, unpredictable character, it is slapping a label on them and diagnosing them with a pathology.

Dr. Glass is reasonably handsome, but he is pretty dull and does not seem to have a plethora of woman vying for his attention. Tramell could probably capture his interest with a pleasant smile and maybe an invitation to dinner. It seems like a bunch of extra work, then, that she goes to so much trouble to lure him. She hires him as her psychiatrist so that she can work him into a mental frenzy, she dons her vampiest clothes and insinuates herself into his inner circle of confidants. Glass is driven by sexual desire for Tramell coupled with fear and confusion. What exactly is Tramell's relationship with his ex-wife (Indira Varma)? And why do people around Glass keep dying suspiciously? In the hands of more skilled screenwriters, these could have been more interesting questions.

Although she suffered the most fallout, the fault of the film does not lie with Stone. She is impressively well preserved and expertly plays her character. She looks terrific in her dramatic, well-tailored outfits and wears a contemptuous sneer equally well. No, the fault lies in many other areas. It is in the casting decision that paired her with the buttoned-down and weak-seeming Morrissey. It is in the screenwriters insistence on wringing the excitement out of the film by placing the action in tastefully decorated doctor's offices and muted London streets. It is in having the gall to diagnose a famous movie character with a psychological illness instead of just letting her be free to wreck havoc.

Film critics pretty unanimously despised the film. Owen Gleiberman of *Entertainment Weekly* was the kindest of the lot, writing that "*Basic Instinct 2* isn't bad, exactly, but it lacks the entertaining vulgarity of the first film; it's *Basic Instinct* redone with more 'class' and less thrust." Manohla Dargis of the *New York Times* wrote that the film was "a disaster of the highest or perhaps lowest order." Ty Burr of the *Boston Globe* wrote: "Absurdly overheated and unforgivably dull, *Basic Instinct 2* is the accidental comedy sensation of the year to date." Of Stone's performance he wrote that she "appears to have had so much work done that her face resembles a tautly made bed, and her unchanging expression of smoldering arrogance seems less an acting decision and more the result of neurotoxins."

Jill Hamilton

CREDITS

Catherine Tramell: Sharon Stone
Dr. Michael Glass: David Morrissey
Det. Roy Washburn: David Thewlis
Dr. Milena Gardosh: Charlotte Rampling
Adam Tower: Hugh Dancy
Michelle Broadwin: Flora Montgomery
Peter Ristedes: Iain Robertson
Denise Glass: Indira Varma
Laney Ward: Anne Caillon
Kevin Franks: Stan Collymore
Dr. Jakob Gerst: Heathcote Williams
Origin: USA
Language: English
Released: 2006
Production: Mario Kassar, Andrew G. Vajna, Joel B. Michaels; Metro-Goldwyn-Mayer Pictures, IMF, C2/Intermedia; released by Sony Pictures Entertainment
Directed by: Michael Caton-Jones
Written by: Leora Barish, Henry Bean
Cinematography by: Gyula Pados
Music by: John Murphy
Sound: Rosie Straker
Editing: John Scott, Istvan Kiraly
Art Direction: Paul Inglis, James Foster
Costumes: Beatrix Aruna Pasztor
Production Design: Norman Garwood
MPAA rating: R
Running time: 114 minutes

REVIEWS

Chicago Sun-Times Online. March 31, 2006.
Entertainment Weekly Online. March 31, 2006.
Los Angeles Times Online. March 31, 2006.
New York Times Online. March 31, 2006.
San Francisco Chronicle Online. March 31, 2006.
USA Today Online. March 31, 2006.
Variety Online. March 29, 2006.
Washington Post. March 31, 2006, p. C1.

QUOTES

Catherine to Dr. Glass: "Do I make you uncomfortable?"

AWARDS

Golden Raspberries 2006: Worst Picture, Worst Actress (Stone), Worst Screenplay, Worst Sequel/Prequel

Nomination:

Golden Raspberries 2006: Director (Caton-Jones), Support. Actor (Thewlis)

BEERFEST

Comedy on tap.
—Movie tagline

Bring on the beer. They've got the nuts.
—Movie tagline

Prepare for the ultimate chug of war.
—Movie tagline

Box Office: $19.1 million

The Broken Lizard comedy troupe was formed in the 1990s at Colgate University's Beta Theta Pi fraternity. Since then, the group, with all of their frat boy humor unchanged by the ravages of time, has made a couple of films—*Club Dread* (2004) and *Super Troopers* (2001)—that put them at the periphery of moviegoers' consciousness. *Beerfest* did not propel the group to widespread fame and fortune, but did add another decent entry to their oeuvre of smart dumb humor. Or perhaps the correct term is dumb smart humor.

In this outing, brothers Todd and Jan Wolfhouse (Erik Stolhanske and Paul Soter), are sent to Germany to spread their grandfather's ashes. While there, they come upon a sort of *Fight Club*-like (1999) underground beer-drinking Olympics called Beerfest. The surly Germans accuse them of stealing an old family beer-making recipe and inform them that their dear beloved

Great Gam Gam (Cloris Leachman) was once a popular woman of the evening. How to deal with this? The brothers decide that the sensible solution is to spend a year in training so that they can come back the following year and win Beerfest.

They recruit their old college buddies, Fink (Steve Lemme), Landfill (Kevin Heffernan), and Barry Badrinath (Jay Chandrasekhar, who also directed the film). Fink is the resident nerd, who figures out all things that involve calculations and such. Landfill is a John Belushi type of character—a large man with large appetites who is comprised almost solely of id. The funniest of the characters is Barry, a one-time Ping-Pong champion who is now turning tricks in the street. All the best laughs in the film come from Chandrasekhar, an actor not afraid of absurdity or looking dumb. There is a scene in which he drunkenly picks up a woman in a bar (Mo'Nique). First the audience sees how Barry perceives his actions—that is, he is suavely luring this beautiful woman into his bed. Then the audience sees the reality of the situation—that is, Barry slurring and drooling messily over an extremely obese woman. Yes, it is crass to make fun of an overweight person, and yes, this exact gag was already done (and done better) on *The Simpsons,* but the way Chandrasekhar throws himself wholeheartedly into the scene makes it all work. *Salon.com* critic Andrew O'Hehir wrote that Chandrasekhar "seems to be in a different (and funnier movie) from the other four Lizards."

Although there are some funny moments, the movie never quite gets the momentum it needs to become a comedy classic. It is funny to see old drinking games like Thumper or Quarters exhumed and put up on the screen, but not so funny to see *Saturday Night Live*'s Will Forte doing a tired version of that show's Hans and Franz characters. How can a film that has a funny/touching scene featuring a bicycle built for five also have way too many lame jokes about a big beer stein, Das Boot? The members of the Broken Lizard troupe have a very average look about them—like they might be some of the guys from accounting who work in the cubicles down the hall. That alone is refreshing, and makes them seem like they might be especially subversive comedians. That they decide to trot out gags involving Leachman demonstrating lewd acts with a German sausage is kind of disappointing.

Critics disagreed on the merits, or lack thereof, of the film. Jeannette Catsoulis of the *New York Times* wrote: "In *Beerfest,* a gaseous celebration of binge drinking and family honor, the five comedians known collectively as Broken Lizard have created a frat-house staple for the ages." But Ty Burr of the *Boston Globe* called the film "brutally unfunny." Peter Hartlaub of the *San Francisco Chronicle* wrote that it's "an acquired taste that you won't know you possess until you pay $10 for a ticket.... Whether or not you have a good time watching *Beerfest,* it's clear the actors had a good time making it." Jeff Strickler of the *Minneapolis Star-Tribune* wrote that "fans of the group's earlier movies...know what to expect: cleverly construed bad taste." Andrew O'Hehir of *Salon.com* wrote: "Something about the [Broken Lizard] group dynamic just isn't working for me. They expend too much time on big, dumb, obvious jokes—like making all the German villains in *Beerfest* wear lederhosen and talk like girly-men versions of Arnold Schwarzenegger—and toss off much funnier material in two seconds."

Jill Hamilton

CREDITS

Barry Badrinath: Jay Chandrasekhar
Landfill: Kevin Heffernan
Fink: Steve Lemme
Jan Wolfhouse: Paul Soter
Todd Wolfhouse: Erik Stolhanske
Gunter: Eric Christian Olsen
Great Gam Gam: Cloris Leachman
Johann von Wolfhaus: Donald Sutherland (uncredited)
Cherry: Mo'Nique
Baron von Wolfhausen: Juergen Prochnow
Priest: M.C. Gainey
Otto: Will Forte
Origin: USA
Language: English
Released: 2006
Production: Bill Gerber, Richard Perello; Gerber Pictures, Legendary Pictures, Cataland Films, Broken Lizard; released by Warner Bros.
Directed by: Jay Chandrasekhar
Written by: Jay Chandrasekhar, Kevin Heffernan, Steve Lemme, Paul Soter, Erik Stolhanske
Cinematography by: Frank DeMarco
Music by: Nathan Barr
Sound: David Alvarez
Music Supervisor: Stephen Baker
Editing: Lee Haxall
Art Direction: David Baca
Costumes: Tricia Gray
Production Design: Clark Hunter
MPAA rating: R
Running time: 111 minutes

REVIEWS

Boxoffice Online. August 25, 2006.
Chicago Sun-Times Online. August 25, 2006.

Entertainment Weekly. September 1, 2006, p. 54.
Los Angeles Times Online. August 25, 2006.
New York Times Online. August 25, 2006.
San Francisco Chronicle Online. August 25, 2006.
Variety Online. August 24, 2006.
Washington Post. August 25, 2006, p. C6.

TRIVIA

Donald Sutherland is uncredited in the role of Jan and Todd's grandfather.

THE BENCHWARMERS

It's never too late to take a stand.
—Movie tagline

3 older dudes should be able to beat 9 young jocks...Right?
—Movie tagline

Box Office: $57.6 million

Anyone who does not possess a strong movie-going constitution is familiar with the experience of covering one's eyes during the more intense parts of horror movies. With *The Benchwarmers,* the eye-covering technique transcends its horror roots and moves over to the comedy genre. The usefulness of the technique becomes readily apparent during the opening minutes of the film. By not looking at the screen, one can avoid seeing Clark (Jon Heder), in an extended nose-picking sequence, or a bully sit on a young victim in order to pass gas on his face. The nose picking, for example, is no mere quick pick. It is long and much discussed, giving plenty of time to ruminate on what exactly what was going on. The movie is filled with, perhaps even fundamentally held together by, such cringe-inducing moments. There is projectile vomit, sprays of spit, a toxic portable potty, and characters who pass gas into one another's mouth. These are the sorts of images that need not be imbedded into one's long-term memory.

The story, written by longtime Adam Sandler cohorts Allen Covert and Nick Swardson, is, in its own way, almost equally offensive. Despite what some might consider plenty of star power, as well as the near constant spewing of various bodily fluids, the plot manages to drag. And it is not like the writers were working with complex plotting like that of *Memento* (2000), but they barely bothered to try to have the movie make sense.

Gus (Rob Schneider) is, by the standards of the movie, a cool guy. He is married to a beautiful woman, Liz (Molly Sims), who wants to start a family with him. How he managed his tastefully appointed house on his salary as a lawnmower is not fully explained. It is also not clear why he is so interested in hanging out with Clark, a paper boy who never takes off his helmet, and Richie (David Spade), a thirty-nine-year-old virgin who sports a Prince Valiant haircut and works in a video store.

Due to various plot permutations, the three team up to play baseball as a team called the Benchwarmers. These grown men play various teams of twelve-year-olds, and the audience is supposed to root for the men. Mel (Jon Lovitz) is an eccentric billionaire who offers to build a stadium for the team that wins a big championship. The whole thing has something to do with nerds getting revenge on the bullies that have tormented them. How three men beating teams of young boys will accomplish this goal is not satisfactorily explained.

Within the wreckage of the film, it is possible to see how the movie might have been at least slightly better. Heder, as he was in *Napoleon Dynamite* (2004), is somewhat of a genius of nerddom. Just seeing him feebly throw a baseball is a wonder to behold. But too much emphasis on nose picking makes his character less interesting, and just gross. Similarly, Spade gets in a few good lines, but his character is ill-formed. He excels at playing the smart-mouthed hipster, and whenever he tries something else, he just seems like that same character but wearing a bad wig. Surely someone as sharp-tongued as Spade's character would realize his own nerdiness and make a few personal styling adjustments.

The movie is filled with plugs for Sony PlayStation, Pepsi, and Pizza Hut. Pizza Hut must have paid a lot of money in product placement because at least two scenes take place in the restaurant. It is difficult to fathom why some Pepsi marketing manager thought it would be a good idea to have Spade's loser character constantly swigging Diet Pepsi, but they must have.

Critics were not, as a lot, big fans of *The Benchwarmers'* gross-out humor. Bill Muller of the *Arizona Republic* wrote that the film "is a crass collection of flatulence jokes, nose picking and potty-humor that's repetitive, poorly acted and ludicrous. It's so bad, it should be viewed only through a pinhole in a shoebox, much like an eclipse." Manohla Dargis of the *New York Times* wrote: "Filled with sprays of vomit, fountains of spit and enough hot body air to launch a flotilla of passenger balloons, *The Benchwarmers* is the sort of trash that Hollywood does really well." Roger Moore of the *Orlando Sentinel* gave the film an F grade and wrote that "if flatulence, crotch-kicks, tequila benders and nerd revenge are your thing, by all means, get to a multiplex." James Parker of the *Boston Globe* was the rare critic who wrote a semi-kind review of the film. "The movie as a whole is a more-than-acceptable addition to the genre of shameless and hastily made American comedy."

Jill Hamilton

CREDITS

Gus: Rob Schneider
Richie: David Spade
Clark: Jon Heder
Mel: Jon Lovitz
Liz: Molly Sims
Jerry: Craig Kilborn
Wayne: Tim Meadows
Howie: Nick Swardson
Carlos: Amaury Nolasco
Coach Bellows: Dennis Dugan
Sarah the Salad Girl: Erinn Bartlett
Nelson: Max Prado
Kathy Dobson: Brooke Langton
Ultimate Home Remodel Host: Lochlyn Munro
Mrs. Ellwood: Mary Jo Catlett
Umpire: Blake Clark
Poker guy: Terry Crews
Himself: Reggie Jackson (Cameo)
Voice of Darth Vader: James Earl Jones (Voice)
Origin: USA
Language: English
Released: 2006
Production: Adam Sandler, Jack Giarraputo; Columbia Pictures, Revolution Studios, Happy Madison Productions; released by Sony Pictures Entertainment
Directed by: Dennis Dugan
Written by: Nick Swardson, Allen Covert
Cinematography by: Thomas Ackerman
Music by: Waddy Wachtel
Sound: Thomas Causey
Editing: Peck Prior, Sandy Solowitz
Costumes: Mary Jane Fort
Production Design: Perry Andelin Blake
MPAA rating: PG-13
Running time: 81 minutes

REVIEWS

Boxoffice Online. April 7, 2006.
Hollywood Reporter Online. April 7, 2006.
Los Angeles Times Online. April 10, 2006.
New York Times Online. April 8, 2006.
Variety Online. April 7, 2006.

QUOTES

Mel: "If you build it, nerds will come."

AWARDS

Nomination:

Golden Raspberries 2006: Worst Actor (Schneider)

BEOWULF & GRENDEL

Heads Will Roll.
—Movie tagline

Beneath the Legend Lies the Tale.
—Movie tagline

A visually stunning U.K./Canada/Iceland production, *Beowulf & Grendel* is a modern revisionist telling of the epic Anglo-Saxon poem, "Beowulf," which many literary scholars concur is English literature's first classic. The film begins sometime in sixth century A.D. Daneland (now Denmark) with a hirsute, hulking figure walking along a grassy cliff with his hairy Aryan-Nordic looking son who appears to have hit puberty as a furry blond toddler. The elder troll picks up the scent of a band of Danish warriors mounted on Icelandic ponies rapidly galloping towards them. He picks up his son, the young Grendel, and lumbers off with him towards the high cliff overlooking the sea and black-sand beach. With the boy clinging to the cliff's edge, the brutish man-beast faces his attackers who quickly shoot his massive torso with arrows and toss a viscous flammable fluid at his feet and ignite him. The father stumbles back and falls off the cliff in a slow motion plummet to the black beach below. The Danish king, Hrothgar (Stellan Skarsgard), looks down the cliff to assure the giant's demise and makes eye contact with the boy who utters a low growl. He both spares the feral child and leaves him on his own. Grendel makes his way down to the beach and, unable to drag the massive corpse, takes a sword, which dwarfs him, and cuts off his father's head in order to carry it home.

Decades pass and the adult Grendel who traded his blond fuzz for a Neanderthal's forehead (performed with passionate vigor by Ingvar Sigurdsson whose four-year-old son played the younger Grendel) is staring up at the decomposed, mummified head of his father and seems to sing out a guttural eulogy. Hrothgar and his clan have prospered in this green, cold terrain. To honor this preeminence on coastal Iceland, where the film was shot, the aging king had a luxurious mead hall constructed out of sticks (more likely to be driftwood as the land is barren of trees) and named it Heorot. High above, Grendel observes this and pounds a rock against his forehead and shouts an unintelligible battle cry against his father's murderers.

The next day, Hrothgar discovers twenty of his warriors slaughtered in the hall except for one, the cowardly

Unferth (Olafur Darri Olafsson) who can only attribute his survival to passing out. "I had some beers," he explains to Hrothgar. A broken and soused Hrothgar sits upon a rock and contemplates his people's fate. He is greeted by a zealous Christian monk, frothing at the mouth, who has approached the boozy monarch to offer his service as a protective agent of providence to this archaic Danish "kingdom." After hearing the monk's pitch, Hrothgar morosely replies, "Christ, eh.... Heard of him. You ever have much luck with trolls?" Much of the movie's humor is derived from a cynical regard for the proliferation of Christianity. Later in the film as the monk beseeches Heaven on his knees outside of the mead hall, Grendel mimics his impassioned prayer with another chain of syllables. Whether Grendel is employing a dialect of his own or is simply imitating others is not explored.

In neighboring Geatland (now Sweden) a powerful Germanic warrior serving under Hygelac (Mark Lewis), Beowulf (portrayed by Scotland's Gerard Butler) entreats Hygelac to allow him to aid Hrothgar and his people by engaging and destroying the monster plaguing the Danes. Hygelac gives him his blessing and Beowulf along with thirteen other soldiers embarks to Daneland. Beowulf and his men are initially met with reservation but are put at ease by Hrothgar's enthusiastic greeting as he rushes out of Heorot drunk at midday and scantily robed (against an Icelandic wind). As is described in the ancient poem, Hrothgar advocated for Beowulf's father thus settling what would have evolved into a bloody feud. Having quelled the dispute, Beowulf feels a familial loyalty and indebtedness to Hrothgar. The natural rapport of the two men, as played by Skarsgard and Butler, has a polished, harmonious feel to it; one more extemporaneous than rehearsed.

Grendel approaches the hall's main entrance and smells the strangers' scents. Instead of attacking, Grendel switches tactics and expels a deluge of troll urine against the door that results in an overwhelming stench that the armored Geats succumb to. After a series of mishaps, Beowulf decides to go at it alone and plays detective by seeking the counsel of the local hermetic witch, Selma (Sarah Polley) who has been banished from the Danish community due to her power of prognostication. Selma tells Beowulf of a visitation Grendel once made to her where he entered her hut and raped her.

Beowulf is not a glory-seeking warrior and is conflicted with the ways of war. He does not find glamour in it, nor does he deny its necessity. He simply accepts it, but not without discretion. He is able to evoke a confession from Hrothgar, who admits to killing Grendel's father. Grendel is acting out of vengeance, not blind murderous ardor. The sentient "troll" is no more monstrous than his human prey and also abides to a personal code by not killing Hrothgar. This is either due to responding in kind to the king, as Hrothgar spared Grendel as an underling or as a method of emotional torture as he helplessly watches his people get slaughtered and live in constant fear. Hrothgar has attempted to fight Grendel, but the troll denies him a martyr's death.

Grendel returns to Heorot that night and snaps the neck of a single Geat—the one who destroyed his father's consecrated head when the group of soldiers found his cave—whom he susses out with his powerful sense of smell. Beowulf wrestles Grendel to the ground and entraps him by tying his wrist to a rope attached to an overhanging pulley. Leaping to escape, Grendel is instead suspended in the rafters above Heorot. Rather than be killed by his captors, he opts to severe his arm at the shoulder with a spear's head and escapes to the sea where the clawed hand of the Sea Hag (Elva Osk Olafsdottir) pulls him maternally home. (In the poem, Beowulf himself rips Grendel's arm out of its socket). The Sea Hag turns out to be Grendel's mother and in a fit of vengeance, kills many more Danes. Beowulf returns to Grendel's boggy lair and delivers a deadly slash to her with the same giant sword Grendel used to cut his father's head off of his corpse.

The film's Canadian director, Iceland native Sturla Gunnarsson seems to abide with the school of thought that less is more in that Grendel seems more humanoid than a troll from Norse mythology. The script seems to follow the logic that legends grow from real events and as time wears on, the legends evolve into the grandiose and supernatural (although the Sea Hag is definitely a preternatural creature). Grendel and his father could very well be just another offshoot of mankind rather than one of the cursed descendents of Cain as the poem describes them. Beowulf himself is described in the epic to be a warrior bearing the strength of thirty men. Gunnarsson's Beowulf is definitely bestowed with formidable fighting skills and a strong individual fortitude, but he is portrayed as being nothing more than a man complete with doubts and frailties as well as contrasting qualities such as compassion (as when he buries and honors Grendel in front of the troll's son and Selma) and vanity when he recounts before an inebriated audience at Heorot of the past battles he fought and emerged as victor.

Another characteristic of the film that is not found in the tributary poem is the polarization of the expanding Christian world and that of pagan culture. Beowulf observes Hrothgar's Christian baptism with silent contempt. Hrothgar, facing mortality, survivor's guilt, and continued existential ennui, has converted out of desperation. When Hrothgar inquires about Beowulf's thoughts on a possible afterlife in that the Christian faith offers Heaven, the Geat responds by saying that he will go where he is sent. Not quite a nihilist but far from a man of deity worship at least not in accord with this monotheistic belief system canvassing Scandinavia. In the poem, both Christianity and paganism are compatible and coexist without contention. But Beowulf's eternal destination will not come into question until after his fatal fight with the dragon, the last battle in the ancient saga of this Celt hero.

David Metz Roberts

CREDITS

Beowulf: Gerard Butler
Hrothgar: Stellan Skarsgard
Selma: Sarah Polley
Brendan the Celt: Eddie Marsan
Grendel: Ingvar Sigurdsson
Hondscioh: Tony Curran
Breca: Rory McCann
Thorkel: Ronan Vilbert
Thorfinn: Martin Delaney
Unferth: Olafur Darri Olafsson
Hygelac: Mark Lewis
Sea Hag: Elva Osk Olafsdottir
Origin: Great Britain, Canada, Iceland
Language: English
Released: 2006
Production: Paul Stephens, Eric Jordan, Jason Piette, Michael Cowan, Sturla Gunnarsson; Telefilm Canada, Astral Media, Harold Greenberg Fund, Icelandic Fim Center; released by Equinox Films
Directed by: Sturla Gunnarsson
Written by: Andrew Rai Berzins
Cinematography by: Jan Kiesser
Music by: Hilmar Orn Hilmarsson
Sound: Simon Okin
Editing: Jeff Warren
Art Direction: Einar Unnsteinsson
Costumes: Debra Hanson
Production Design: Arni Pall Johannsson
MPAA rating: R
Running time: 102 minutes

REVIEWS

Boxoffice Online. July 28, 2006.
Hollywood Reporter Online. July 12, 2006.
Los Angeles Times Online. July 28, 2006.
New York Times Online. July 7, 2006.
Variety Online. October 12, 2005.
Village Voice Online. July 5, 2006.

BIG MOMMA'S HOUSE 2

The Momma of all comedies is back.
—Movie tagline

Box Office: $70.1 million

Theoretically, writer Don Rhymer had six years to come up with new ideas for the second *Big Momma* film. What he came up with is pretty much the same thing as the original, which is basically: put Martin Lawrence in a fat suit and wait for comedy to ensue. The idea works to a certain extent. There are a few chuckles sprinkled throughout the film, but Rhymer and director John Whitesell seem equally concerned with having Big Momma be a good person who can dispense valuable Life Lessons. Fine, except whenever a life lesson is being learned, the movie is not being funny.

For those not educated in things pertaining to *Big Momma,* the first film had Malcolm Turner (Lawrence) go undercover as a large, old woman, Big Momma, to catch some bad guys. He also wooed and won Sherrie (Nia Long). In the sequel, Malcolm has married Sherrie and, per her request, has taken a less dangerous job teaching safety to kids. But when he hears of a big case involving a dangerous computer hacking plan to control the world, Malcolm decides to take a vacation and go undercover as Big Momma. He installs himself as a nanny in the lovely Southern California house of computer company owner Tom Fuller (Mark Moses). Tom's wife, Leah (Emily Proctor) is a tightly-wound woman who uses a color-coded system of pegs to organize her three children's overbooked schedules. Teenage Molly (Kat Dennings) has taken to the goth look and is dating a bad-news older boy. Carrie (Chloe Grace Moretz) is a cheerleader who needs help developing her moves. Toddler Andrew (Preston and Trevor Shores) likes to dive from high spots onto the floor. And Tom, for his part, is so busy with his taking-over-the-world hacking plan that he is not spending enough time with his family. Big Momma assesses the situation and decides that not only must he/she foil the hacking plot, but also help solve this family's emotional problems.

Big Momma's brand of knowledge is accurate and sometimes quite funny. After observing the toddler eating Brillo pads, she comments that the boy need not worry about making plans for Harvard. But there is a problem. While Big Momma is preaching to Tom about spending time with his family, Big Momma/Malcolm has completely abandoned his own family. He lies to Sherrie and says that he is at a safety conference and she begins to suspect that he is having an affair.

Not only is Big Momma a better person than Malcolm, she is also a lot more fun to watch. In the past few years, Lawrence has given lackluster performances in a slew of equally indifferent films. Something about donning that Big Momma gear seems to bring out whatever zest and comedic timing he still has left.

Critics—that is, those who even bothered to review the film—had few kind words. Kathy Cano Murillo of the *Arizona Republic* wrote that "there's only one reason to buy a ticket to *Big Momma's House 2*: Martin Lawrence in drag in a fat suit. Don't expect a morsel more of substance or wit." Lisa Rose of the *Newark Star-Ledger* wrote: "Watching the picture, you may forget that Lawrence was once [one] of the comedy scene's provocateurs. Raw talk and sublimated anger have been replaced with bland burlesque and derivative storytelling." Robert Abele of the *Los Angeles Times* was able to dredge up at least one compliment for the film, writing: "Taking in the bulbous, dimpled totality of Martin Lawrence's plus-size get-up in *Big Momma's House 2*—whether in a high-riding one-piece bathing suit or the customary flower print dress—it's hard not to marvel at the advances in drag technology since Fatty Arbuckle, *Some Like It Hot* (1959), and Monty Python." And Christy Lemire of the *Associated Press* wrote that "while Lawrence is in disguise, he manages to be grotesque and vaguely endearing at the same time, to make you squirm and occasionally laugh in spite of yourself."

Jill Hamilton

CREDITS

Malcolm/Big Momma: Martin Lawrence
Sherrie: Nia Long
Leah Fuller: Emily Procter
Tom Fuller: Mark Moses
Molly: Kat Dennings
Carrie: Chloe Grace Moretz
Andrew: Preston Shores/Trevor Shores
Liliana Morales: Marisol Nichols
Stewart: Josh Flitter
Crawford: Dan Lauria
Kevin: Zachary Levi
Origin: USA
Language: English
Released: 2006
Production: David T. Friendly, Michael Green; Deep River, 20th Century Fox, New Regency Pictures, Runteldat Entertainment; released by 20th Century Fox
Directed by: John Whitesell
Written by: Don Rhymer
Cinematography by: Mark Irwin
Music by: George S. Clinton
Music Supervisor: Jennifer Hawks
Editing: Priscilla Nedd Friendly
Art Direction: James E. Tocci, Craig Stearns
Costumes: Debrae Little
MPAA rating: PG-13
Running time: 98 minutes

REVIEWS

Entertainment Weekly Online. January 25, 2006.
Los Angeles Times Online. January 27, 2006.
New York Times Online. January 27, 2006.
Premiere Magazine Online. January 27, 2006.
Variety Online. January 27, 2006.

AWARDS

Nomination:

Golden Raspberries 2006: Worst Sequel/Prequel

BLACK CHRISTMAS

This holiday season, the slay ride begins.
—Movie tagline

Box Office: $16.2 million

Writer/director Glen Morgan is no stranger to remaking cheesy horror films from the 1970s for modern audiences. He did it in with his bland take on *Willard* (2003), and now he presents us with a new *Black Christmas.* A seminal film in the beginning days of the slasher genre, the original 1974 film was centered around a mysterious and unseen presence stalking a sorority house full of girls on Christmas Eve. They would get creepy calls on the phone before being picked off one by one. While not classic cinema by any means, it had the virtue of freshness. Thirty years later it just seems stale. Morgan's choice to make the killer known to the audience takes away the pseudo-voyeuristic identification of the viewer with the girls. If you cannot identify with the killer you cannot make the fear go away.

Here though, as with a lot of remakes, the theory of "more is better" applies. The filmmakers, apparently to justify their fees, decided to give the stalker a full backstory. This humanizes him, which leads to the audience pitying him, and ultimately takes away all the mysteriousness and horror of the film.

Another thing that the original had going for it was that it spent a lot of time establishing the characters in the sorority house. They were all different entities and as the audience got to know them they felt for them and rooted with them as they struggled to survive. Not so in this film. Because the killing starts almost immediately, there is no time to invest emotionally in the characters. To the audience, all of the girls in the house could be the same person. To be fair, they do have perfunctory wants and needs. But we don't care what happens to them, so it just becomes a slasher-by-numbers game. It's not who gets killed it's how they get killed, and they do get killed in ingeniously seasonal ways: stabbed with a candy-cane, Christmas lights, and ice-skates to name just a few.

The victims in this film are familiar faces to television viewers. The faceless sorority girls are haphazardly played by Kristen Cloke, Michelle Trachtenberg, Katie Cassidy, and Lacey Chabert to name a few. Andrea Martin, who was in the original, returns here as a different character, that of the house mother Ms. Mac to add a bit of undeserved legitimacy to the project.

The psycho stalker is named Billy (Robert Mann) and he had a really screwed up childhood. He murdered his family in this house years ago and now lives in an insane asylum. He has escaped and apparently wants to spend Christmas taunting and then killing helpless and clueless sorority girls for kicks. But is he the actual killer or is it someone else trying to make it look like him? This mystery is so underdone and telegraphed that one cannot help but think there was not enough time for rewrites of the script before going to camera.

The original, while taking itself seriously, had a touch of humor to ease the tension, but the remake doesn't have any at all. But it needn't have, because there was no tension to be relieved from in the first place. It's a sad state that one of the best writers and directors from television's *The X-Files* is now regurgitating the same schlock that that show so famously shunned and shied away from. The film was never screened for critics at the time of its release and for good reason. Whereas the original *Black Christmas* created a new genre of horror cinema conventions and style, the remake just spews them back out like a recycled glass of sour milk.

David E. Chapple

CREDITS

Melissa: Michelle Trachtenberg
Dana: Lacey Chabert
Heather: Mary Elizabeth Winstead
Mrs. Mac: Andrea Martin
Kelli: Katie Cassidy
Billy Lenz: Robert Mann
Kyle: Oliver Hudson
Lauren: Chris Lowe
Leigh: Kristen Cloke
Megan: Jessica Harmon
Agnes: Dean Friss
Origin: USA, Canada
Language: English
Released: 2006
Production: Marty Adelstein, Dawn Parouse; Hard Eight Pictures, 2929 Productions, Copper Heart Entertainment; released by Dimension Films
Directed by: Glen Morgan
Written by: Glen Morgan
Cinematography by: Robert McLachlan
Music by: Shirley Walker
Sound: Patrick Ramsay
Music Supervisor: Dave Jordan, JoJo Villanueva
Editing: Chris Willingham
Production Design: Mark Freeborn
MPAA rating: R
Running time: 84 minutes

REVIEWS

Boston Globe Online. December 26, 2006.
The Guardian Online. December 15, 2006.
Los Angeles Times Online. December 26, 2006.
New York Times Online. December 27, 2006.
The Observer Online. December 17, 2006.
Variety Online. December 26, 2006.
Washington Post. December 26, 2006, p. C1.

TRIVIA

Andrea Martin, who plays house mother Mrs. Mac, played sorority sister Phyllis in the original 1974 release.

THE BLACK DAHLIA

Inspired by the most notorious unsolved murder in California history.
—Movie tagline

Box Office: $22.5 million

James Ellroy's crime novels are some of the finest ever written by an American. Not content with being tough and noirish, Ellroy whips his narratives into a feverish, paranoid frenzy, in which even the most unusual occurrences possess an odd logic. Adapting Ellroy for the screen is daunting. The makers of *Cop* (1988), from the novel *Blood on the Moon* (1984), polished away most of the rough edges and were left with a slick but empty thriller. With *L.A. Confidential* (1997), however, director Curtis Hanson and co-writer Brian Helgeland captured the themes and tabloid style of Ellroy's 1990 novel perfectly. Brian De Palma's *The Black Dahlia* fails by trying too hard, perhaps, to be faithful to its source.

Ellroy's 1987 novel was inspired by the famous Black Dahlia murder case of 1947, in which Elizabeth "Betty" Short's brutally mutilated corpse was found in a vacant lot in Los Angeles on January 15. Because of the gruesomeness of the crime—her body was cut in half—and because her killer was never found, the case gained mythic stature. Ellroy has a particular interest in this crime because his mother was murdered in a similar unsolved case, as recounted in *My Dark Pages: An L.A. Crime Memoir* (1996).

Ellroy uses the facts of the Black Dahlia case, so called because of the popular 1946 film noir *The Blue*

Dahlia, only as a starting point, composing an elaborate picture of the varied social levels of 1940s Los Angeles, adding his typical antiheroes. Police detectives Dwight "Bucky" Bleichert (Josh Hartnett) and Lee Blanchard (Aaron Eckhart) are thrown together as partners because of their boxing prowess and soon become close friends. The friendship is strained a bit because of Bucky's attraction to Lee's live-in girlfriend, Kay Lake (Scarlett Johansson). While Josh Friedman's screenplay shifts the actions of Bucky and Lee between several cases, jumping about awkwardly at times, their main investigation is the death of Elizabeth "Betty" Short (Mia Kirshner), whose body is found a few yards from where the protagonists have just survived a bloody shootout. This proximity is fitting since coincidence is central to the plot.

Looking at footage of Betty's screen tests, Bucky, the much more sensitive of the cops, finds himself becoming infatuated by the murder victim's vulnerability and sexuality. When the investigation leads him to a lesbian nightclub frequented by Betty and her friend Lorna Mertz (Jemima Rooper), Bucky meets Madeleine Linscott (Hilary Swank). He is soon having an affair with the wealthy young woman who copies Betty's smoldering, black-clad look. Even after meeting Madeleine's eccentric parents (John Kavanagh and Fiona Shaw), Bucky finds himself torn between bad-girl Madeleine, good-girl Kay, and Betty's ghost.

Bucky eventually discovers that Madeleine, Kay, and Lee are not exactly what they seem, as his innocence is slowly stripped away. While Friedman and De Palma litter the narrative with both solid clues and red herrings, the discovery of the culprit(s) is not quite as shocking as they intend. *The Black Dahlia* is not entirely the inept travesty most of its reviewers claim, primarily because of the intrinsic strength of the material, the moody evocation of 1940s Los Angeles, and the likeability of the lead actors.

Yet it does seem to lurch wildly at times from point A to point C, while completely ignoring point B. It is difficult to determine if Friedman is striving valiantly to replicate Ellroy's distinctively manic style or is flailing away in a losing effort to keep up. Nevertheless, by the time *The Black Dahlia* reaches its denouement, it has gone well past the boundaries of logic and, some might say, taste. The revelation of the primary villain is a doozy that must be seen to be believed.

Some reviewers may have had problems with *The Black Dahlia* because of their enmity with De Palma, often dismissed as a talented hack and inept imitator of Alfred Hitchcock. Despite some respect for *Carrie* (1976), *Dressed to Kill* (1980), *Scarface* (1983), *The Untouchables* (1987), and *Carlito's Way* (1993), De Palma's films have not fared well with both critics and audiences. *Snake Eyes* (1998), *Mission to Mars* (2000), and *Femme Fatale* (2002), his films prior to *The Black Dahlia*, were particularly ridiculed by reviewers and ignored by audiences.

The Black Dahlia, though somewhat better than the director's recent efforts, has its share of overwrought moments, dull patches, incoherence, and sloppiness. Central to the plot are images of Conrad Veidt from Paul Leni's *The Man Who Laughs* (1928), a screening of which Kay, Lee, and Bucky attend. Were silent classics shown outside classrooms and museums in 1946 Los Angeles? Bucky keeps viewing Betty's screen tests, all shot by the same director (the off-camera voice of De Palma himself). Why would this director give her more than one test?

The connections to the Leni film, a pornographic film featuring Betty and Lorna, a painting in the Linscott mansion, and Linscott's old friend George Tilden (William Finley) all suddenly come together for Bucky in a way that strains credulity. While Los Angeles noirs are traditionally complex, as with *The Big Sleep* (1946) and *Chinatown* (1974), *The Black Dahlia* becomes almost ridiculous as it rampages toward a conclusion.

With the exception of Shaw, whose excessiveness is in keeping with De Palma's vision, most of the actors perform rather well. Hartnett, shifting gears from the boyish charm he displays in the first half of *Lucky Number Slevin* (2006), gives Bucky an intense earnestness. Several reviewers complained that Eckhart overacts, but Lee is strung out on amphetamines. Eckhart ably conveys the character's twisted loyalties.

As she has shown in *The Man Who Wasn't There* (2001) and *Girl with a Pearl Earring* (2003), Johansson has a face and manner adaptable to multiple periods. As Kay, she exudes a compellingly corroded innocence. As the sultry Madeleine, Swank is miles away from the androgyny of her Oscar® performances in *Boys Don't Cry* (1999) and *Million Dollar Baby* (2004). Swank adopts the husky voice of noir star Lizabeth Scott, but it seems to disappear when Madeleine is feeling stress. Both Johansson and Swank, however, are on screen surprisingly little. Kirshner makes Betty an amalgam of the other female characters, sensual yet desperate. The terrific Finley, star of De Palma's *Phantom of the Paradise* (1974), makes a welcome return after a thirteen-year absence from the screen.

Despite considerable lunacy on display, *The Black Dahlia* looks wonderful because of Jenny Beavan's excellent period costumes, especially Kay's sophisticated outfits, and production designer Dante Ferretti, whose credits include *Interview with the Vampire* (1993) and *The Aviator* (2004), brings his distinctive touch to everything, ranging from the police station to the Linscott mansion to the scene of Betty's demise. Legendary cinematographer Vilmos Zsigmond, working with De Palma for the first time since the disastrous *The Bonfire of the Vanities* (1990), does perhaps his best work since the similar *The Two Jakes* (1990). Going well beyond the noir cliche of the Venetian-blind shadows, Zsigmond lights the film to help underscore the characters' tangled emotions.

With its swooping crane shots and slow-motion violence, *The Black Dahlia* is clearly a De Palma film and is interesting, if deeply flawed. It had the misfortune of being in release at the same time as the much better *Hollywoodland* (2006). While *Hollywoodland* is far from perfect, it blends mystery, mood, period, and character more effectively. The similarities between the two may account in part for the box office failure of *The Black Dahlia*, together with bad word-of-mouth because of its overly complicated plot.

Michael Adams

CREDITS

Dwight "Bucky" Bleichert: Josh Hartnett
Kay Lake: Scarlett Johansson
Lee Blanchard: Aaron Eckhart
Madeleine Linscott: Hilary Swank
Russ Millard: Mike Starr
Ramona Linscott: Fiona Shaw
Emmet Linscott: John Kavanagh
Martha Linscott: Rachel Miner
Elizabeth "Betty" Short: Mia Kirshner
Lorna Mertz: Jemima Rooper
George Tilden: William Finley
Chief Green: Troy Evans
Pete Lukins: Gregg Henry
Sheryl Saddon: Rose McGowan
Coroner: Ian McNeice
Elizabeth Short's Father: Kevin Dunn
Origin: USA
Language: English
Released: 2006
Production: Art Linson, Avi Lerner, Moshe Diamant, Rudy Cohen; Millenium Films, Signature Pictures; released by Universal Pictures
Directed by: Brian De Palma
Written by: Josh Friedman
Cinematography by: Vilmos Zsigmond
Music by: Mark Isham
Sound: Jean-Paul Mugel
Editing: Bill Pankow
Art Direction: Christopher Tandon
Costumes: Jenny Beavan
Production Design: Dante Ferretti
MPAA rating: R
Running time: 121 minutes

REVIEWS

Boxoffice Online. September 15, 2006.
Chicago Sun-Times Online. September 15, 2006.
Entertainment Weekly. September 22, 2006, p. 69.
Hollywood Reporter Online. August 31, 2006.
Los Angeles Times Online. September 15, 2006.
New York Times Online. September 15, 2006.
Premiere Magazine Online. September 14, 2006.
San Francisco Chronicle. September 15, 2006, p. E1.
Variety Online. August 30, 2006.
Washington Post. September 15, 2006, p. C1.

TRIVIA

The off-screen voice heard in Betty Short's audition tape is that of director Brian De Palma.

AWARDS

Nomination:

Oscars 2006: Cinematog.

BLOOD DIAMOND

Truth...Fortune...Freedom...It will cost you everything.
—Movie tagline

Box Office: $56.2 million

All diamonds are supposed to be eye-catching, but *Blood Diamond* also hopes to be eye-opening. Along with offering up lovely shots of nature's awesome beauty and even more stunning views of man's appalling savagery and cutthroat avariciousness, the film also gives audiences an admonishing and most likely illuminating lecture on the possible connection between their baubles and some truly horrific bloodshed. Most powerful when its storytelling takes precedence over its well-intentioned pontificating, *Blood Diamond* is a flawed but estimable gem, featuring two noteworthy performances and a great deal of intense, ear-splitting, heart-breaking drama.

Set at the end of the 1990s amidst the nightmarish chaos of Sierra Leone's civil war, the film aims to alert diamond purchasers (the largest percentage of whom reside in the United States) that buying expensive jewels originally plucked from such strife-torn countries can be extremely costly to the locations' poverty-stricken populace. In this case, brutal warring factions in the northwestern African nation obtained more arms by selling diamonds mined with forced labor to profiteering middlemen. These outside exploiters of a bad situation then supplied the highly prosperous but also deficiently principled European diamond merchants. Coffer-busting sums of blood money could be made dealing in these prized but tainted gems (often called "conflict diamonds"), and so continued demand kept up an unconscionable fueling of unimaginable violence. The Kimberley Process, an international agreement struck in 2002, has made it harder but not impossible to traffic in this particular type of diamond. The makers of *Blood Diamond* were clearly betting that moviegoers, while largely unfamiliar with the problem, would not be unsympathetic.

Besides the juxtaposition created by the sight of lush, green landscapes with chirping birds which are suddenly disturbed by truckloads of menacing, marauding gunmen, there is also the decided contrast between two exceedingly dissimilar African natives who are both on a quest to find the same object but for very different reasons at the film's core. Introduced first is black fisherman Solomon Vandy (Djimon Hounsou), a solidly noble and selfless man who cares deeply about his family. They live in a village hut and appear to have little, yet Solomon seems as placid as the waters he fishes in his small boat. However, he dreams of a bright, promising future for his son, Dia (a well-cast Kagiso Kuypers), beaming with pride as he speaks of the boy someday becoming a doctor. Solomon warmly puts his arm around his son as the latter talks of their homeland's founding as a Utopian paradise.

Whatever the area's past, the present's calm is instantly shattered by the gleeful gunfire of rebel forces, who decimate the village in short order. During a chaotic scene of graphic slaughter, Solomon screams for his family to run for their lives as members of the arbitrarily and endlessly vicious Revolutionary United Front hold him down. Particularly ruthless and chilling is the imposing leader known as Captain Poison (an excellent David Harewood), who laughs as the remaining villagers line up to lose limbs or lives. At the last second, powerfully-built Solomon is spared, deemed useful to labor in the diamond fields.

It is there that Solomon finds a large, pink diamond, and daringly hides it between his toes despite having seen a fellow worker shot on the spot for having concealed a jewel within his cheek. There is excruciating suspense as Poison suspiciously searches Solomon's body, stopping just short of his feet. Solomon, however, is discovered trying to bury the stone for safekeeping, and just as Poison demands it, government troops wound the rebel and cart everyone off to jail.

The other African protagonist is Danny Archer (Leonardo DiCaprio), a white native of Zimbabwe (then Rhodesia) who was once a mercenary soldier and is now a soldier of fortune. A jewel smuggler who is as gutsy as he is jaded, Danny swoops down in a small plane into Sierra Leone's increasing instability to trade guns for diamonds he will secrete to neighboring Liberia, all the while stoking misery for profit without a detectable quiver or qualm. His attempt to surreptitiously transport his latest haul beneath the skin of a goat to mercenary/mentor Colonel Coetzee (Arnold Vosloo) is unsuccessful, but this bad luck appears to turn when Danny lands in the same jail as Solomon and Poison and overhears the latter threatening the former to learn the whereabouts of the singularly valuable diamond. There does not seem to be sympathy in Danny's eyes, only dollar signs.

Once Danny gets himself released, he pays to get Solomon out so that he can get in good with the fisherman. Danny presumptuously and purposefully refers to a partnership that now exists between them, a yoking which the highly suspicious Solomon makes clear he wants no part of. Danny, however, once again shows he knows how to work a deal, proposing that they split the profits from the diamond's sale in exchange for reuniting Solomon with what he values most: his family.

Before Solomon can answer, the two are desperately scurrying for cover amidst carnage and chaos as the capital city of Freetown suddenly erupts around them. Featuring a hand-held, kinetic camera searching anxiously along with the two men for safety, the scene is effectively nerve-wracking with its bloody mayhem, roaring gunfire, booming, fiery explosions, and unsettling sense of entrapment. Under this intense fire, an uneasy alliance is forged which both Danny and Solomon hope will get them what they want.

What fetching, crusading, American journalist Maddy Bowen (Jennifer Connelly) wants is information on exactly how people like Danny get their goods to the unscrupulous diamond market. Danny finds her annoyingly judgmental and pesky (when he is not making eyes at her), and he wishes she would go away—until he and Solomon desperately need her help to proceed. Unfortunately, while Connelly is fine in the role, the forward thrust of the action decelerates somewhat whenever she rattles off more facts and statistics in doing the film's most overt preaching. The character does, however, create some excitement for Danny when she tries to dirty dance the facts out of him. An amorphous, only partly convincing romantic attachment ensues.

Helping/using each other in order to obtain their own objectives, the three embark on an eventful, dangerous, sometimes contentious, and often quite gripping endeavor. While most of Solomon's family is located in a refugee camp, he is anguished to learn that Dia has been taken by the rebels. This development sets the stage for what are unquestionably the most dreadful and disturbing scenes in *Blood Diamond.* The film shows how Sierra Leone's rebel forces turned kids like Dia into cold-blooded killers, young boys stripped first of familial connections and then their innocence, humanity, morality, and, finally, their souls. As the youngsters' reeling, impressionable minds are carefully manipulated, viewers watch with intense discomfiture as wide-eyed children initially forced to be executioners become dead-eyed, forceful assassins. In one alarming instance, a wonderful teacher (Basil Wallace) who devotes his life to repairing these lost boys is shot point blank while talking kindly to a foulmouthed young thug. Even more disconcerting is the scene in which Solomon, having located Dia's encampment along with Danny, daringly sneaks up to his son and looks into the angry eyes of an absolute stranger. Perhaps the most memorable moment, however, comes when Danny and Solomon, having finally retrieved the all-important diamond, learn the depths of Dia's indoctrination when the recently-rescued boy aims a gun at his own father. Solomon's taking-down of, and breaking through to, his son is suspenseful and particularly moving.

Throughout *Blood Diamond*, the most powerful, magnetic presence is the superb Hounsou's admirable Solomon. The character is strong, caring, resolute, morally upright, and steeped in a deep, palpable sadness and guilt over his inability to protect his loved ones. DiCaprio is also a standout as the film's cynical, accurately-accented antihero who covets the exceptional diamond as his yearned-for "ticket out of this God-forsaken continent." The question hangs in the air throughout the film as to whether he will steal the diamond from Solomon in the end, and one senses that Danny is as unsure as the audience of the answer. Viewers learn that he carries inside the loss of his parents to hideous torture, and this painful knowledge of how malevolence can destroy a family may have created sympathy in him for the Vandys' plight. In the end, a mortally-wounded Danny hands off to Solomon and Dia that gleaming ticket to a better life and nobly urges them on to go meet his plane, finally bleeding to death upon naturally red soils once again made redder.

Blood Diamond received many positive reviews and earned five Oscar® nominations, including nods for Hounsou (Best Supporting Actor) and DiCaprio (Best Actor). Made on a reported budget of $100 million, it earned just over half that much in its initial release. In an interesting development, a highly apprehensive diamond industry increased their advertising budget by 22 percent for fear the film would hurt holiday season sales. However, those behind this production stressed that they were solely decrying the sale of conflict diamonds, and hoping that people's consciences would trump even the most alluring color, cut, clarity, and carat weight.

David L. Boxerbaum

CREDITS

Danny Archer: Leonardo DiCaprio
Solomon Vandy: Djimon Hounsou
Maddy Bowen: Jennifer Connelly
Colonel Coetzee: Arnold Vosloo
Dia Vandy: Kagiso Kuypers
Simmons: Michael Sheen
Nabi: Jimi Mistry
Ambassador Walker: Stephen Collins
Captain Poison: David Harewood
Benjamin Kapanay: Basil Wallace
Cordell Brown: Anthony Coleman
Jassie Vandy: Benu Mabhena
Origin: USA
Language: English
Released: 2006
Production: Paula Weinstein, Edward Zwick, Marshall Herskovitz, Graham King; Virtual Studios, Spring Creek Productions, Bedford Falls; released by Warner Bros.
Directed by: Edward Zwick
Written by: Charles Leavitt
Cinematography by: Eduardo Serra
Music by: James Newton Howard
Sound: Ivan Sharrock
Editing: Steven Rosenblum
Art Direction: Daran Fulham
Costumes: Ngila Dickson
Production Design: Dan Weil
MPAA rating: R
Running time: 143 minutes

REVIEWS

Chicago Sun-Times Online. December 8, 2006.
Entertainment Weekly. December 15, 2006, p. 69.
Hollywood Reporter Online. December 1, 2006.
Los Angeles Times Online. December 8, 2006.
New York Times Online. December 8, 2006.
Premiere Magazine. December 2006, p. 39.
San Francisco Chronicle. December 8, 2006, p. E1.
Variety Online. November 30, 2006.
Washington Post. December 8, 2006, p. C6.

QUOTES

Danny (to Maddy): "Now in America, it's bling-bling. But out here, it's bling-bang."

AWARDS

Nomination:

Oscars 2006: Actor (DiCaprio), Film Editing, Sound, Sound FX Editing, Support. Actor (Hounsou)

Golden Globes 2007: Actor—Drama (DiCaprio)
Screen Actors Guild 2006: Actor (DiCaprio), Support. Actor (Hounsou)

BLOODRAYNE

Driven by revenge.
—Movie tagline

Box Office: $2.4 million

German director Uwe Boll is certainly developing a niche for himself as a filmmaker. But what he might want to consider is whether it is a niche he really wants to fill. In 2003, he released a horrendous film based on a video game called *House of the Dead*, followed in 2005 by another video game adaptation, *Alone in the Dark*, which boasted the particularly hideous casting choice of Tara Reid as a scientist. *BloodRayne*, Boll's third game-based feature whose title is even cringe-worthy, also boasts the same pathetic quality and another notably poor casting choice. In this case, it is Sir Ben Kingsley, who won an Academy Award® for playing the title role in *Gandhi* (1982), cast as the most powerful vampire in the world, Kagan. Kingsley might be okay as the most powerful vampire in the world if the rankings were based on something like intelligence or emotional intensity. But if physical strength is a factor at all, it is hard to believe that the aging actor would even be in the top fifty. This is especially apparent in a climatic sword fight at the end of the film where Kingsley does not seem to have the slightest idea of what to do with a sword. He is, however, able to stand stiffly with one hand behind his back while thrusting the sword forward with the other. Boll capitalizes on this by using lots of quick-cut angles to give the impression that Kingsley is actually fighting, or for that matter, actually moving. Wesley Morris of the *Boston Globe* described Kingsley's performance as being "mechanical…like a coin-operated Dracula."

Much of the movie is similarly off. As a whole, *BloodRayne* is almost bad enough to be funny in a campy sort of way. But, at some point, the sheer laziness of the direction, writing, and acting becomes simply too overwhelming and any feelings of kindness toward the film get weighted down by the never-ending badness of it all. The movie is supposed to take place in eighteenth-century Romania, yet the females all wear leather low-rider pants and midriff-baring tops, and everyone speaks in a combination of modern slang and a curiously stilted English that sounds somewhat akin to the way Yoda phrases things. To quote one character: "If they want a fight, a fight they will get."

The story focuses on Rayne (Kristanna Loken), who is a dhampir, a half-vampire, half-human hybrid. She sucks blood, but can live on non-human blood. She is seeking vengeance against Kagan, her father, who raped and killed her mother. To defeat him, she needs to locate a magic eye and other various magical body parts, which are scattered across the globe.

In between wearing lots of tight clothing and taking off her shirt for no particular reason, Rayne interacts with a series of strange casting choices. Michael Madsen and Michelle Rodriguez are part of The Brimstone Society, a group of fighters who want to defeat Kagan too. Rodriguez's performance is notable only for her especially bad, Madonna-esque British accent. Also on-board are Billy Zane and Meat Loaf, who is so bad in his one scene that his overacting stands out over bloody fighting, hordes of writhing topless women, and corpses hanging from the ceiling like cured hams.

Oddly, this mishmash was written by Guinevere Turner, best known for her work on the relatively acclaimed television show *The L Word*, and the films *Go Fish* (1994) and *American Psycho* (2000). Unfortunately, if there was any shred of cleverness in her original screenplay, it has been obliterated by Boll's careless direction.

Movie critics, already embittered over having to review *Grandma's Boy* in the same weekend, had no kind words for *BloodRayne*. Gregory Kirschling of *Entertainment Weekly* gave the film an F grade and commented: "As you might expect from any movie that begins with the promise of 'special appearance by Billy Zane' and features Meat Loaf Aday decked out in a Spinal Tap wig and writhing around with naked women, *BloodRayne* is ghastly-bad. But not ghastly-bad enough." In the *Los Angeles Times*, John Anderson wrote that "the only thing left unsliced is the ham in *BloodRayne*." Elizabeth Weitzman of the *New York Daily News* had about the nicest thing to say about the film, stating that "in the domain of bad taste, Boll has become an acknowledged master. By those standards, *BloodRayne*, with its riotously atrocious performances, boldly gratuitous nudity and laugh-out-loud hairpieces, is his finest work yet."

Jill Hamilton

CREDITS

Rayne: Kristanna Loken
Vladmir: Michael Madsen
Sebastian: Matthew Davis
Katarin: Michelle Rodriguez
Kagan: Ben Kingsley
Domastir: Will Sanderson
Regal Monk: Udo Kier

Leonid: Meat Loaf Aday
Inacu: Michael Pare
Elrich: Billy Zane
Fortune Teller: Geraldine Chaplin
Origin: Germany, USA
Language: English
Released: 2006
Production: Shawn Williamson, Daniel Clarke; Boll KG Prods., Herold Prods, Pitchback Pictures; released by Romar Entertainment
Directed by: Uwe Boll
Written by: Guinevere Turner
Cinematography by: Mathias Neumann
Music by: Henning Lohner
Sound: Michael Bartylak
Editing: David Richardson
Art Direction: Christian Corvin, Vieru Vlad
Costumes: Carla Baer
Production Design: James Steuart
MPAA rating: R
Running time: 95 minutes

REVIEWS

Boxoffice Online. January 6, 2006.
Entertainment Weekly Online. January 11, 2006.
Premiere Magazine Online. January 6, 2006.
Variety Online. January 6, 2006.

QUOTES

Elrich: "Would you stop throwing things at me?!"

TRIVIA

The prostitutes in the scene with Leonid are actual Romanian prostitutes.

AWARDS

Nomination:

Golden Raspberries 2006: Worst Picture, Worst Actress (Loken), Worst Support. Actor (Kingsley), Worst Support. Actress (Rodriguez), Worst Director (Boll), Worst Screenplay

BOBBY

He saw wrong and tried to right it. He saw suffering and tried to heal it. He saw war and tried to stop it.
—Movie tagline

Box Office: $11.2 million

Shortly after being declared the winner of the California primary of June 5, 1968, and becoming the favorite to win the Democratic Party presidential nomination, Robert Kennedy was killed in the kitchen of the Ambassador Hotel in Los Angeles by Sirhan Sirhan. Coming just two months after the assassination of Rev. Martin Luther King Jr., and less than five years after the murder of President John Kennedy, the slaying was the final blow to the hopes of many Americans that a national leader could bridge the racial conflicts in the nation's cities and the deep divisions over the war in Vietnam. Kennedy's brief, quixotic campaign captured the imagination of a nation; his motorcades through cities and rural areas were inspiring scenes in which he touched thousands of supporters of all races. That this candidate of the people was risking his life by campaigning without much protection was one thing that set him apart, and so were his heartfelt, if somewhat convoluted, speeches about bringing people together.

The film clips of these campaign stops, and the closing-credits' still photographs of Robert Kennedy with his family and constituents, are the most powerful sequences in Emilio Estevez's muddled, misconceived film *Bobby.* Despite the name, the movie isn't an intimate look at the complicated legendary politician, unless you believe that hero worship from afar constitutes intimacy. Kennedy's words and images hover above the film, and the final scene of his assassination is both moving and powerful, though only in a contrived rub-our-noses-in-tragedy way, but the movie isn't about Kennedy. It's about rounding up a cast of celebrities, spinning them around in a stereotypical ensemble just like you see in almost every current television drama, and having them spout banalities and enact scenes whose connection to Kennedy are, at best, tenuous and, at worst, inane.

Estevez grew up with Kennedy hero worship; his father, Martin Sheen, who appears in the movie as a stockbroker who has seen the light of antimaterialism, is a big fan of the Kennedys, and Estevez was weaned on tales of the heady 1960s. He appears to be trying to make a movie not just about Bobby Kennedy, but also about the spirit of the 1960s that his campaign arguably epitomized. But he fails miserably to capture the era in any meaningful way.

His idea, hardly an inspired one, is to track the day leading up to the assassination through the experiences of a huge cast of characters staying in and working at the hotel. Early on, in an exchange between Harry Belafonte, who plays an old man with no discernible backstory, and Anthony Hopkins, who plays John Casey, a riff on a man who actually worked at the hotel from the 1920s to the 1960s, Estevez clumsily telegraphs his intent with a reference to *Grand Hotel,* the 1930s Greta

Garbo film about a Berlin hotel filled with celebrities. In *Bobby,* however, the hotel and the film are filled mostly with a weird cross-section of supposedly common people, and the intent is to illustrate that these are the people whose divisions Kennedy is going to overcome. That's an absurd notion. Even the Kennedy speeches we hear in *Bobby* don't make any claims that we shall overcome philandering, alcoholism, recreational drug use, obsessions with shopping, creeping senility, overly competitive chess playing, adolescent irresponsibility, and the other issues plaguing Estevez's motley cast of characters.

Estevez, giving himself the most put-upon role, plays an unhappy man managing the singing career of his alcoholic wife, Virginia Fallon, played by Demi Moore in a rather lame imitation of a dissipating career, perhaps inspired by her own downward celebrity spiral. She has trouble staying sober, but why are audiences expected to care? The hotel manager, Paul Ebbers, played by William H. Macy in a style indistinguishable from many other Macy roles, is having an affair with a hotel switchboard operator (Heather Graham, all weepy after an unspecified tawdry or abusive or failed sexual encounter with her big boss—we're not sure which, because Estevez doesn't bother to show what happens). He eventually gets his comeuppance from his wife Miriam, the hotel hair stylist, played in a surprisingly effective low key by Sharon Stone, barely recognizable under heavy mascara and a ratted blonde hairdo. Miriam is tipped off by an assistant manager (Christian Slater), whom her husband fired earlier in the day for refusing to let his mostly Mexican kitchen staff take time off to vote. This is Estevez's extremely forced idea of a great racial injustice: the dishwashers are made to work a double shift because of the busy night ahead that will include Kennedy's post-election party.

The gravest injustice is that Jose (Freddy Rodriguez), a busboy with a puzzling halo of sanctity and a heart of gold, won't be able to use the tickets he bought to go with his dad to the Dodgers game to watch Don Drysdale try to pitch a record sixth consecutive shutout that night (an event that really occurred, as certified by Kennedy's reference to it in remarks from the hotel ballroom's podium). Jose's chagrin at working a double shift becomes the excuse to whip up a conflict between Miguel (Jacob Vargas), who is seething about the exploitation of his race, and chef Edward Robinson (Laurence Fishburne). Robinson uses his struggles to find the right level of sweetness for his blueberry cobbler recipe as the basis for lecturing Miguel about anger management, explaining that nobody finds a sour and raging Miguel very tasty. If there were a screenwriting award for worst extended metaphor, Estevez's efforts here should win hands-down. Even Fishburne is smirking as he gives the speech, as if he's trying to make the awful lines more digestible. His character is a stereotype: the savvy, wise black man who has learned how to parlay his rage into better treatment. The trick, he tells the Mexican workers, is to let the white man think he's come up with the idea of civil rights.

If such a notion were played out with irony or purpose, it might have been worth exploring, but it passes quickly. Estevez's reference to the rage that followed King's assassination is just that: a half-knowing nod. Ditto his superficial way of noting the wrenching tragedy of Vietnam: Lindsay Lohan marrying Elijah Wood to keep him out of the draft. When Lohan decides to make the marriage of political purpose into something romantic, the pair fall into a kiss and then down into a horizontal embrace with all the chemistry of two marionettes. Estevez also believes it is important to note that some young people were doing drugs in the 1960s, and so we are treated to the diversion of Ashton Kutcher in a headband, seeking God through LSD, and turning on two straight-laced campaign workers (Shia LaBeouf and Brian Geraghty) in a couple of scenes played for goofy laughs. Apparently this has some relationship in Estevez's mind to Kennedy's campaign: perhaps the fact that both the campaign and rampant LSD usage occurred in the same decade.

The soundtrack seems to have the same tenuous link to the era. After an irritating sound motif that resembles ringing doorbells and continues through the first part of the film, as Estevez introduces us to all the characters in rapid fashion, the background becomes a near-continuous soundtrack of 1960s music, almost all either of the Motown or psychedelic variety, as if unseen radios were playing the tunes (at a few spots you can barely hear a deejay between songs). Probably few people now will care that almost all of the songs Estevez uses predated 1968, in some cases by as much as six years, and that no radio stations of the era played songs of even a year or two earlier: they only played current hits. The music is emblematic of the sort of false authenticity that plagues the entire movie.

With the female characters, Estevez seems to be reaching for some kind of emerging feminist sentiment; the closest he comes is when Moore's character suddenly blurts out to Stone's hair stylist: "We are all whores, it's just that some of us get paid for it," and then apologizes. Helen Hunt, playing Sheen's fashion-obsessed wife, is a victim of indoctrination, liberated when her husband, who has been battling depression, tells her that they are more than all the stuff they've accumulated; the scene is as contrived as a greeting card. Graham's switchboard operator is obviously in need of counseling too: she gets it from a fellow worker, Patricia (Joy Bryant), who later makes a move on the Kennedy staff's one black worker,

Dwayne (Nick Cannon). Everyone in the film seems to have expertise in psychology: Hopkins, beating Belafonte at chess while they talk about getting old, knows a hotel is not a home. Also among the less relevant characters is a reporter for a Czechoslovakian radio station (Svetlana Metkina, who is the most energetic and riveting member of the cast), who is upbraided by a Kennedy campaign manager for daring to seek an interview while being from a Communist country.

If Estevez is implying that Kennedy was the hope for curing most of these characters' difficulties, the film is ludicrous. But if instead he is simply laying out his version of a 1960s canvas, the movie suffers from acute meaninglessness. Some reviewers compared the film, unfavorably, to Robert Altman's *Nashville* (1975), a movie you shouldn't even mention in the same breath. Estevez doesn't understand that just having an ensemble cast doesn't mean you have interesting characters. To present a lot of vignettes is not to tell a coherent story, as *Nashville* did. It's supremely difficult to care about any of the characters in *Bobby*, because their stories are all so superficial and movie-of-the-week. It's as if the film was conceived by some sort of social critic, who demanded "let's have one of these, and these, and these"—an alcoholic celebrity, a betrayed wife, a philanderer, a stoned hippie, a couple of old men, some illegal Mexican workers, a black sage, a do-gooder, a couple of hypocrites, a Communist, a stockbroker doubling as a sensitive trainer, a smart waitress from Ohio, and on and on. Nobody told Estevez that a writer should kill off some of his favorite characters in revising his script; he seems to have kept everyone around, even if they represent even a glimmer of an idea.

The doleful earnestness of *Bobby* is reflected in its writer-director's hangdog countenance as he plays the manager-husband of the celebrity from hell. It's fitting, because Estevez has made his own celebrity hell here, gathering a cast of notables and then spinning them all around in a sort of screenwriting blender. The method spits out no story at all, just a series of barely coherent (and in many cases wrongheaded or trite) observations on an era Estevez clearly doesn't understand as more than a set of platitudes. The film is no fitting tribute to Robert Kennedy, but merely an excuse to have some of the big cast rolling around on the kitchen floor with their own survivable bloody wounds. It's like a big Hollywood orgy of vicarious victimhood, a wish that we were there too, we were the people Kennedy was going to save and we ended up emotionally tattered too. Hardly. The real people surely had more interesting lives and things to say than the cardboard cutouts Estevez concocted.

Michael Betzold

CREDITS

John Casey: Anthony Hopkins
Nelson: Harry Belafonte
Paul Ebbers: William H. Macy
Miriam Ebbers: Sharon Stone
Timmons: Christian Slater
Jose: Freddy Rodriguez
Edward Robinson: Laurence Fishburne
Virginia Fallon: Demi Moore
Jack Stevens: Martin Sheen
Samantha Stevens: Helen Hunt
Diane: Lindsay Lohan
William: Elijah Wood
Dwayne: Nick Cannon
Angela: Heather Graham
Fisher: Ashton Kutcher
Cooper: Shia LaBeouf
Jimmy: Brian Geraghty
Wade: Joshua Jackson
Miguel: Jacob Vargas
Patricia: Joy Bryant
Lenka Janacek: Svetlana Metkina
Agent Phil: David Krumholtz
Tim Fallon: Emilio Estevez
Susan Taylor: Mary Elizabeth Winstead
Origin: USA
Language: English
Released: 2006
Production: Michael Litvak, Edward Bass, Holly Wiersma; Bold Films; released by Weinstein Co.
Directed by: Emilio Estevez
Written by: Emilio Estevez
Cinematography by: Michael Barrett
Music by: Mark Isham
Sound: Glenn Moore, Michael Minkler
Editing: Richard Chew
Costumes: Julie Weiss
Production Design: Patti Podesta
MPAA rating: R
Running time: 119 minutes

REVIEWS

Boxoffice Online. November 17, 2006.
Entertainment Weekly. November 24, 2006, p. 84.
Hollywood Reporter Online. November 15, 2006.
Los Angeles Times Online. November 17, 2006.
New York Times Online. November 17, 2006.
Premiere Magazine Online. November 16, 2006.
USA Today Online. November 17, 2006.
Variety Online. September 5, 2006.

AWARDS

Nomination:

Golden Globes 2007: Film—Drama, Song ("Never Gonna Break My Faith")

Screen Actors Guild 2006: Cast

BORAT: CULTURAL LEARNINGS OF AMERICA FOR MAKE BENEFIT GLORIOUS NATION OF KAZAKHSTAN

High Five!
—Movie tagline

Box Office: $128.4 million

The eponymously titled *Borat: Cultural Learnings of America for Make Benefit Glorious Nation of Kazakhstan* chronicles the misadventures of Borat (British satirist Sacha Baron Cohen) and his corpulent sidekick, Kazakh television producer, Azamat Bagatov (Ken Davitian). The misogynistic, anti-Semitic character (who resembles an overgrown Charlie Chaplin in a gray suit and clashing brown shoes) originally sprang into America's living rooms as one of Cohen's various alter egos from HBO's *Da Ali G Show.*

Borat's cinematic introduction takes place in his decrepit third world hometown of Kuczek (credited as being shot in Romania). It is there that he engages in a long amorous lip lock with his sister who he proclaims with pride to be "number four prostitute in all of Kazakhstan." There is a revered community tradition in Kuczek called the running of the Jew in which local children chase and taunt a huge papier-mached Jewish caricature through the village's worn out dirt roads.

Borat's mission is an irony in and of itself and is as shoddy as the film's content and "mockumentary" style camera work. Kazakhstan's Ministry of Information has commissioned Borat to study the "U.S. and A." in order to acquire knowledge that could assist his own country. As clarified by Borat: "Although Kazakhstan a glorious country, it have a problem, too: economic, social, and Jew." As with the modus operandi of such television shows as *Punk'd, The Jamie Kennedy Project,* and the classic (non-toxic) *Candid Camera,* Cohen employs his own staple of guerilla theater when interviewing a bi-coastal cross-section of the seemingly typical American citizen. Only a few of the scenes were scripted.

In his New York hotel room Borat catches a rerun of *Baywatch* and becomes smitten with Pamela Anderson. Upon hearing of his wife's death, he heads to Los Angeles in a dilapidated ice cream truck in pursuit of Anderson's "vazhin." During his cross country survey he interacts with young African American men playing the dice game Cee-lo. He also sings his unique version of Kazakhstan's National Anthem (whose lyrics just happen to match the music of "The Star-Spangled Banner") before an audience at a rodeo in Salem, Virginia: "Kazakhstan greatest country in the world/All other countries are run by little girls...Filtration system a marvel to behold/It remove 80 percent/Of human solid waste." He meets with gay rights advocates and claims to be homophobic yet does not realize that much of his overtures to other men would be construed as homosexual behavior. He continues on his odyssey and rents a room from an elderly Jewish couple that run a bed and breakfast. Later, he mistakes two roaches in his room to be the couple metamorphasized. He throws dollar bills at them and races headlong to his ice cream truck for a hasty getaway. He has dinner with members of the genteel south and defecates in a clear plastic bag and brings it back to the table.

He catches his producer stimulating himself to a picture of Anderson, flies into a jealous rage, and the two engage in a disturbingly smutty and excruciatingly long, naked wrestling match after which they decide to end their relationship. A drunken interlude with a group of University of South Carolina frat boys ensues in which they show him Pamela and Tommy Lee's famous show-all video with Borat becoming moody and despondent. Seeking guidance and counsel, Borat attends a Pentecostal rally where he meets a Supreme Court Chief Justice from Mississippi (James W. Smith) along with Congressman Chip Pickering representing Mississippi's third district. Meanwhile, he learns the power of forgiveness and returns to his quest.

Upon being reunited with his producer, Borat finds his bombshell icon at a book signing event and boldly attempts to shove the *Baywatch* star inside the Kazakhi marriage sack, chasing her out into the bookstore parking lot where he is restrained by security. He finally decides that Luenell (played by the comedienne of the same name), a kind black prostitute he earlier befriended, would make a more suitable wife. They are married and he brings her back to his hometown, along with many other American gifts for his fellow countrymen (including a dildo which he offers to a neighbor as a prosthetic limb).

Although lauded as a comedic genius by the majority of critics, many strayed from Cohen's vitriolic tribute to America. Cohen misrepresents the United States by manipulating his victims into giving him the responses he is fishing for in order to bolster this feature length work of propaganda. He also fashions his fictitious Kazakhstan into a distorted reflection of America; a reflection showing only its arrogance, bigotry, racism and suggestive of widespread ignorance. Duncan Shepherd of the *San Diego Reader* provided this insight about Borat's unrehearsed bits: "They give rise to moral concerns—to say nothing of legal ones—that far overshadow artistic ones. Can, as an example, an Alabama minister's wife—bluntly insulted for her dearth of pulchritude—be safely assumed to be less of a human being than our guerilla artiste, or has the latter's sexism perhaps crossed over, there, from fiction into reality?"

David Metz Roberts

CREDITS

Borat Sagdiyev: Sacha Baron Cohen
Herself: Pamela Anderson
Azamat Bagatov: Ken Davitian
Luenell: Luenell
Himself: Pat Haggerty
Himself: Alan Keyes
Origin: USA
Language: English
Released: 2006
Production: Jay Roach, Sacha Baron Cohen; Everyman Pictures, Dune Entertainment, Major Studio Partners, Four by Two; released by 20th Century Fox
Directed by: Larry Charles
Written by: Peter Baynham, Dan Mazer, Anthony Hines, Sacha Baron Cohen
Cinematography by: Luke Geissbuhler, Anthony Hardwick
Music by: Erran Baron Cohen
Sound: Scott Harber
Music Supervisor: Richard Henderson
Editing: Craig Alpert
Art Direction: David Saenz de Maturana
Costumes: Jason Alpert
MPAA rating: R
Running time: 82 minutes

REVIEWS

Boxoffice Online. November 3, 2006.
Chicago Sun-Times Online. November 3, 2006.
Entertainment Weekly. November 10, 2006, p. 53.
Hollywood Reporter Online. November 1, 2006.
Los Angeles Times Online. November 3, 2006.
New York Times Online. November 3, 2006.
San Francisco Chronicle. November 3, 2006, p. E1.
Variety Online. September 10, 2006.
Village Voice Online. October 31, 2006.
Washington Post. November 3, 2006, p. C1.

QUOTES

Borat: "Kazakhstan is the great country in the world—all other countries are run by little girls."

AWARDS

Golden Globes 2007: Actor—Mus./Comedy (Cohen)
Nomination:
Oscars 2006: Adapt. Screenplay
Golden Globes 2007: Film—Mus./Comedy

THE BOYNTON BEACH CLUB

(The Boynton Beach Bereavement Club)

Box Office: $3.1 million

Susan Seidelman's film gets off to an interesting start when a retiree in South Florida gets ready to take out the trash and then goes jogging and dancing down the street. He puts a favorite CD into his portable player, and, while dancing down the street to the jumpy rhythms of "Poppa Loves Mambo," gets run over and killed by a careless old lady (Renee Taylor) who is backing her car out of her garage while jabbering on her cell phone. Is this funny, or what? Is it supposed to be funny? The film is decidedly unconventional (hence a slow release campaign, in hopes that it may develop strong buzz via word-of-mouth, for there is a potential target audience for this picture of senior citizens nationwide). The result of this opening sequence is to catch the audience off guard, and certainly to put the viewers in sympathy with the man's widow, Marilyn (Brenda Vaccaro). Her husband did everything for her. He helped with the housework. He emptied the trash. He balanced the checkbook. Marilyn had even been able to let her driver's license expire. This movie mainly (but not wholly) concerns her spiritual recovery; after all, it begins and ends with her. As Chris Kaltenbach correctly observed in the *Baltimore Sun*, "this movie takes chances that few others would dare, with an audience in mind that most of Hollywood seems to have forgotten." And that's courageous.

Certainly, Marilyn is front and center, and with a vivacious Vaccaro in the role, one can easily understand why; but there are other troubled and lovable geezers also thrashing about in a sea of love. Almost equally important is Lois, the spunky and energetic decorator played by Dyan Cannon, swept off her feet by a handsome devil named Donald (Michael Nouri), who seems to be a real estate developer but, in fact, turns out to be merely a bug exterminator. (Deceptions abound in this movie, and that's what gives it much of its charm.) Donald looks a little like a more mature George Clooney and is apparently far more charming than one might expect, say, paradigm bugman Tom DeLay, to be. At least Lois is impressed. She befriends Marilyn in Marilyn's hour of need and she is far more understanding than Marilyn's children, who come to Florida for the funeral and then leave her with a dog that she doesn't really want. Pathos is always potentially waiting around the next corner to be turned, but the plot never quite turns utterly bathetic or pathetic (though, indeed, it comes close: vide the blushing incident Jack [Len Cariou] has with a female pharmacist, who loudly explains how to ingest a Viagra-like drug for maximum effect, then directs him to where the condoms are, while three older ladies giggle like teenagers).

Sally Kellerman plays Sandy, another apparent widow, who uses the Bereavement Club at Boynton Beach to meet eligible suitors, and soon has plans for Jack a widower whose wife recently died. (Yes, the working title was *The Boynton Beach Bereavement Club*, but for obvious reasons the publicity department put the kibosh on that title, accurate though the description might have been.) The mixture of death and hotsy-totsy relationships could well constitute a violation of taste, but Seidelman generally keeps the tone upbeat and reasonably well balanced and good-humored, though sometimes a bit too cutesy. Joseph Bologna plays Harry, a widower happy to be a bouncing bachelor in a field of withering peaches. His ploy is Internet dating, but he gets a babe who is more than he bargained for, and a hooker to boot. Fortunately, Harry has enough sense to know when to say, "Enough!" And that gets the plot out of a potentially sleazy corner. Harry is an over-the-hill make-out artist, cast in a teen sex comedy way past his prime. To listen to Harry talk, one might imagine that all the old boys have to talk about is sex. They display no apparent interest in other topics, such as sports, television, or politics, though Harry does have a sort of enthusiasm for cooking.

The story, by the way, was inspired by the experiences of Florence Seidelman, the mother of the director, who well understands life in a very upscale Florida retirement "community." Florence gets credit for the story and also for being the co-producer (with her daughter) of the movie. The screenplay was written by Susan Seidelman and Shelly Gitlow. Director Susan Seidelman established her credentials twenty years ago in 1985 with a benchmark film entitled *Desperately Seeking Susan*, which was both edgy and interesting and turned a singer called Madonna into a facsimile of a movie star, helping to establish the singer's career. *Washington Post* reviewer Stephen Hunter claimed that *Desperately Seeking Susan* was the only good movie Madonna ever made. *The Boynton Beach Club* is not as likely to shift the earth on its axis. It's a late-Boomer generation comedy that will find its niche, sure enough, but it falls a bit short of the director's earlier brilliance.

Hunter praised this film about oldsters "desperately seeking reentry" for its "generally gentle wit" and the "superb performances" Seidelman pulls from her "brilliant cast." Carina Chocano of the *Los Angeles Times* was impressed by the wealth of solid performances and by the picture's optimism. *New York Post* reviewer Lou Lumenick believed he had watched a "rare movie that doesn't caricature senior citizens." Anyone in that age bracket might conclude otherwise, but the caricatures are by and large good natured and tolerable for viewers possessed of a sense of humor. See Jack try to cook, for example, after being given a few lessons by the self-sufficient Harry. Watch his romantic dinner go up in flames, and wonder about what happened to all that smoke that came pouring out of the oven. But how many erectile dysfunction jokes can any reasonable viewer tolerate? Watching Jack and listening to Harry, one might suppose that sex is what senior citizens crave most, rather than companionship to offset bereavement. The movie may often seem trivial and silly to anyone who has thought seriously about grief and loss, and that is a bit of a problem. Ruthe Stein of the *San Francisco Chronicle* opined that such topics combined with sex and romance are "practically unprecedented on the big screen." Discounting the tricky diction of the so-called "big screen," the *Chronicle* reviewer should have to watch *The Mother* (2003), first released in Britain, then exported to the United States in 2004, starring Anne Reid as a woman whose husband dies early in the first reel and slowly (and painfully) attempts to rebuild her life. *The Boynton Beach Club* is also about rebuilding, but within the framework of a romantic comedy here, a fantasy world almost totally exempt from suffering, pain, and true bereavement. In *The Mother,* Hanif Kureishi offered a grimly imagined and humorless story. Florence Seidelman, who has walked the streets of those retirement neighborhoods in paradise is far more optimistic; even if she too often courts the ridiculous and the absurd, she gives the film the feeling of a lived story. As Stephen Hunter noted in the conclusion of his review, the film "won't make anyone happy to grow old, but it sure works hard at providing the counterintuitive lesson to our youth-nuts culture: It's okay to age."

One of the real pleasures of *The Boynton Beach Club* is that it represents a nostalgic reunion for geezer voyeurs. If the memory still works, for example, Sally Kellerman may be recognized as Hot Lips from Robert Altman's *M*A*S*H* (1970), cuddling with Len Cariou from *The Four Seasons* (1981), Brenda Vaccaro from

Midnight Cowboy (1969), and Dyan Cannon from *Bob & Carol & Ted & Alice* (1969) being courted by Michael Nouri, the guy from *Flashdance* (1983). Even if these memorial associations do not immediately come to mind, there will still be echoes of subconscious resonance of temps perdu. Once viewers come to the realization that Seidelman's film is "a rose-colored fantasy of aging," Stephen Holden advised in his *New York Times* review, they will then be able "to relax and enjoy the bittersweet comic performances." Stephen Hunter hit the right chord in his *Washington Post* review when he wrote that "there are plenty of reasons to like the movie," most especially the casting and the gentle wit. As the film audience ages, watch for more such features; but don't expect them all to be as amusing as Seidelman's *The Boynton Beach Club.*

James M. Welsh

CREDITS

Lois: Dyan Cannon
Marilyn: Brenda Vaccaro
Sandy: Sally Kellerman
Harry: Joseph Bologna
Jack: Len Cariou
Donald: Michael Nouri
Platinum Blond: Renee Taylor
Origin: USA
Language: English
Released: 2005
Production: Susan Seidelman, Florence Siedelman; Snowbird Films; released by Samuel Goldwyn Films
Directed by: Susan Seidelman
Written by: Susan Seidelman, Shelly Gitlow
Cinematography by: Eric Moynier
Music by: Marcelo Zarvos
Sound: Jon Tendrich
Editing: Keiko Deguchi
Costumes: Sarah Beers
Production Design: Kevin Kropp
MPAA rating: R
Running time: 105 minutes

REVIEWS

Chicago Sun-Times Online. August 18, 2006.
Los Angeles Times Online. August 4, 2006.
New York Times Online. August 4, 2006.
San Francisco Chronicle. August 18, 2006, p. E5.
Variety Online. October 26, 2005.
Washington Post. August 18, 2006, p. C1.

TRIVIA

Director Susan Seidelman got the idea for the movie from her mother Florence, who received a producer's credit.

THE BREAK-UP

...pick a side.
—Movie tagline

Box Office: $118.7 million

As its title suggests, *The Break-Up* chronicles the split between a couple who, we are led to believe, once loved each other very much. Woody Allen mined similar territory to great comic effect in the wistful and hilarious *Annie Hall* (1977), still the benchmark for films of this type and proof that a romantic comedy can end unhappily and still be very funny and wise. But *The Break-Up,* directed by Peyton Reed, is also billed as a romantic comedy and, unfortunately, is not much of one. In the opening scene, Gary (Vince Vaughn) and Brooke (Jennifer Aniston) meet at a Chicago Cubs game, where he tries desperately to get a date with her despite the fact that she is with another man. Because he is aggressive and even somewhat boorish and she is standoffish, it may be surprising that they get together in the first place, but, as is so often the case in the movies, opposites attract, and a cute title sequence swiftly carries us through the fun times via a series of silly snapshots of the happy couple.

Vaughn gets a story credit on *The Break-Up,* along with Jeremy Garelick and Jay Lavender, who wrote the screenplay. And it is the screenplay that proves to be the film's downfall. For while the costars are quite likeable, the script leaves Gary and Brooke very little to do but fight and get even with each other in a series of confrontations and shouting matches that grow tiring and more irritating as the movie progresses.

The film has a compelling premise in that Gary and Brooke have reached the point many couples get to, where little issues become exacerbated through carelessness and thoughtlessness. But *The Break-Up* does not paint them as equally culpable. An overgrown child who would rather watch sports on TV than do the household chores that fall on Brooke's shoulders, Gary takes for granted all the things she does to make their lives run smoothly. When she tells him off in their big fight, her anguish and frustration are very real, epitomizing someone who does not really want to break up but feels that taking a stand is the only way to get her partner to change. Since neither will leave their prized condo, however, they still must put up with each other on a daily basis—a situation leading to stunts like Gary buying the pool table Brooke has long denied him and

Brooke trying to make Gary jealous by dating other men. There are, admittedly, some entertaining moments along the way, such as Brooke getting Gary ousted from the bowling team, which leaves him exiting the bowling alley hurt and shirtless. And, in a funny sequence, a good-looking date for Brooke ends up bonding with Gary over video games and taking little interest in her.

Vaughn and Aniston do their best to bring to life characters that are not very well developed. Gary and his two brothers own a bus company that takes visitors on tours of Chicago, and Vaughn, not surprisingly, is perfect as the motormouth comedian of a guide. He also has some poignant moments when he reveals, with just a look or a few words, the vulnerability behind Gary's confident facade. And Aniston brings a genuine depth to Brooke's disappointment with a relationship that she has invested so much in and expected to be different.

Indeed, the actors dig deep to find the core of this bruised relationship. But after a while, the skirmishes become repetitive, and the honest emotions are undercut by slack comedy bits, such as Gary getting his brother to recruit a bevy of young hotties for a night of strip poker—resulting in a very clumsy and unfunny scene—just because Brooke is out on a date.

The Break-Up not only neglects to tell a compelling story but also skimps on believable characters. Jon Favreau, Vaughn's buddy from *Swingers* (1996) and *Made* (2001), is wildly inconsistent as Gary's friend, Johnny O. At first, he is the supportive bartender sympathizing with Gary when he is dumped, but near the end, Johnny O levels with his friend and upbraids him for his selfishness, in essence pointing out why Brooke left him. These tough-love words inspire Gary to try to win Brooke back, but there is no authentic motivation for Johnny O to make Gary see his negative side beyond the need to wrap up the film and force a change in Gary. In Johnny O's last scene, in yet another shift in character that comes out of nowhere, he is intimating to Gary that they should kill the man they think is Brooke's new suitor.

Most of the other characters are relatively flat, generally embodying a single trait and not doing much to enliven the film. Addie (Joey Lauren Adams), Brooke's best friend and confidante, rarely rises above dispensing self-help advice and support-group cliches. Judy Davis is only sporadically amusing as the haughty, diva-like Marilyn Dean, owner of the art gallery where Brooke works, and Christopher (Justin Long), the effeminate receptionist there, is an annoying gay stereotype. The big question about Richard (John Michael Higgins), Brooke's brother, is whether or not he is gay, but he definitely rubs Gary the wrong way as the perky lead singer of an a cappella group and is more tiresome than funny. Ann-Margret makes a very brief appearance as Brooke's mother, begging the question why such a major talent would take a small role just about any actress could have played. Jason Bateman's Riggleman, a realtor and friend, has one of the film's few sharp scenes as he lays out the plan for selling the condo, acting as a pal concerned for his friends but also looking out for his own financial interests.

Despite Gary's last-minute efforts to be a better man and reform his ways—even cleaning the condo and cooking a dinner to show he cares—Brooke goes through with the split, but the film ends with a coda in which the former lovers bump into each other on the street and the hint of a spark suggests that they may have a second chance together. The final scene, however, rings false and feels tacked on. After a full-length movie of constant bickering and no evidence of the good times Gary and Brooke may have once shared, we have no rooting interest in seeing this couple reunited. It would be better for them to admit their incompatibility and just leave it at that.

Peter N. Chumo II

CREDITS

Brooke Meyers: Jennifer Aniston
Gary Grobowski: Vince Vaughn
Addie: Joey Lauren Adams
Marilyn Dean: Judy Davis
Lupus Grobowski: Cole Hauser
Johnny O: Jon Favreau
Wendy Meyers: Ann-Margret
Christopher: Justin Long
Dennis Grobowski: Vincent D'Onofrio
Riggleman: Jason Bateman
Andrew: Peter Billingsley
Richard Meyers: John Michael Higgins
Carson Wigham: Ivan Sergei
Origin: USA
Language: English
Released: 2006
Production: Vince Vaughn, Scott Stuber; Wild West Productions; released by Universal Pictures
Directed by: Peyton Reed
Written by: Jeremy Garelick, Jay Lavender
Cinematography by: Eric Alan Edwards
Music by: Jon Brion
Sound: John Pritchett
Editing: David Rosenbloom, Dan Lebental
Art Direction: David Sandefur
Costumes: Carol Oditz
Production Design: Andrew Laws

MPAA rating: PG-13
Running time: 106 minutes

REVIEWS

Boxoffice Online. June 2, 2006.
Chicago Sun-Times Online. June 2, 2006.
Entertainment Weekly Online. May 31, 2006.
Los Angeles Times Online. June 2, 2006.
New York Times Online. June 2, 2006.
Premiere Magazine Online. June 2, 2006.
Variety Online. March 25, 2006.
Washington Post. June 2, 2006, p. C1.

QUOTES

Gary: "Is that how you want to play it, Brooke? Because I can play it like that. I'll play it like Lionel Richie, 'All Night Long,' lady."

TRIVIA

Jennifer Aniston's character Brooke gets a "Telly Savalas" wax job during the movie. Savalas was Jennifer Aniston's real-life godfather.

BRICK

A detective story.
—Movie tagline

Box Office: $2 million

Taking its inspiration from classic hard-boiled detective films such as *The Maltese Falcon* (1941), *The Big Sleep* (1946), and *Chinatown* (1974), writer-director Rian Johnson's smart and sophisticated *Brick* is a twisty, often convoluted mystery. It's main innovations are plunging a neo-noir story in a suburban high school setting and creating a tough-guy patois all its own, some of it real and some of it invented, to create a hip world that also conveys a genuine sense of danger and the constant threat of violence. Yet the movie is so stylized that its distance from real school life is about as great as that of the typical teenage sex comedy. Like David Mamet and Quentin Tarantino, whose distinctive dialogue can be both real and artificial at the same time, Johnson's language helps create a world that somehow borders on our own but is clearly a hyperrealist version of it. Lines such as "bulls would gum it," which translates as "cops would mess things up," may be hard to follow at first, but only contribute to the film's pleasure. Add to the mix Johnson's dashes of humor and unpredictable character quirks, and the result is a unique movie experience and one of the most auspicious feature-film debuts in quite some time.

Audiences should not be misled by the high school setting. We never see a classroom or meet a teacher, although we make visits to the parking lot, library, football field, and assistant vice principal's office. For *Brick* is not interested in high school life per se, but rather the setting itself as an alienating place where the self-appointed gumshoe, Brendan (Joseph Gordon-Levitt), must negotiate the school's underworld, composed of shady characters, stoners, and femmes fatale, who seem to have their own social order apart from normal adult supervision.

The film begins with Brendan staring at the body of Emily (Emilie de Ravin), his former girlfriend, who has been killed and whose body has been left at a drainage tunnel, and then we flash back two days to see the events leading up to her demise. Emily is obviously in trouble and contacts Brendan for help, uttering words on the phone in a jumble that send Brendan on a labyrinthine journey populated by an array of odd and sometimes scary characters. There is Kara (Meagan Good), the imperious drama student who obviously has a past with Brendan, but whose elliptic answers are of little help. A mysterious invitation leads Brendan to a party at Laura's (Nora Zehetner) house. Laura, the seductive rich girl in a red Chinese dress, is the high school answer to the femme fatale, mysterious in the way she toys with Brendan and dangles clues before him as she leads him into more danger. Dode (Noah Segan) is a stoner who hangs out with the other stoners behind the coffee shop. Tugger (Noah Fleiss) is the muscle behind the local drug operation, while Brad (Brian White) is the obnoxious football player who is always ranting about how, if the coach would only put him in the game, things would be different. He is a minor character, but his angry outbursts are comical because, in any other teen film, they might be taken seriously and his hostility to Brendan would be a real threat, but, in the criminal world laid out in *Brick*, Brad's hotheadedness is a pretty minor concern.

Brendan's staunch ally, his only one, really, is the Brain (Matt O'Leary), an apt nickname for a stereotypical nerd in thick glasses who can solve a Rubik's Cube in a matter of seconds. If he is not in the library, then he is sitting by the school building all alone, and yet, despite his solitary existence, seems to have the inside scoop on what is going on.

Once the film works its way back to Emily's corpse, Brendan is determined to find out who is responsible and infiltrates the high school's version of a crime syndicate, ruled over by the Pin (Lukas Haas), who, at twenty-six, is older than everyone else but still lives with his mother. Scenes of his clueless mom serving cereal and juice to his friends as if they were a wholesome group and not a gang overseeing drug operations in the basement are very funny. And when the Pin rides around in the back of a van lit by a table lamp, the strange detail stands out but is never mentioned. Despite such bits of humor, however, the screenplay does not devolve into camp or parody. The Pin, who uses a cane and treats Brendan well, is actually a sympathetic character with a soft spot for Tolkien, and Brendan's quest to solve the mystery is taken seriously, not as a pretext for laughs.

The story follows noir conventions, to be sure, as the protagonist constantly struggles to make sense of the clues, runs into trouble, and is beaten up repeatedly, but Johnson puts his own unique signature on the material. For as detailed and circuitous as the plot may be, the quirky touches and offbeat scenes make the film memorable. For example, while the story is set in the contemporary world where the Brain uses his mom's cell phone, the screenplay also tips its hat to old-school detectives by having Brendan communicate mainly via pay phone, as if young people relied on such devices, let alone could easily find one when they need to. Brendan's meeting with Assistant Vice Principal Gary Trueman (Richard Roundtree), the closest we get to an adult authority figure, is a small gem and plays like a private detective maintaining an uneasy truce with the local police department, while working as an informant on his own terms. There is also a chase around the school grounds that ends comically when Brendan outsmarts his pursuer by luring him into crashing into a pole. And Johnson brings his own visual style to the genre, thanks to his longtime friend and director of photography, Steve Yedlin, who often shoots scenes at odd angles, especially Emily's corpse at the drainage tunnel, and has one great shot, in which a speeding car races by Brendan and narrowly misses hitting him.

The more Brendan investigates, the more complicated the scenario becomes, and it would be disingenuous to claim that it is always an easy story to follow, but part of the fun is trying to keep up. The film climaxes with a showdown between Tugger and the Pin, which turns into a drug deal gone awry over a missing brick of heroin and culminates in Tugger killing the Pin and a police raid, orchestrated by Brendan, that leaves Tugger dead.

But in the film's final scene, Brendan, like many private eyes before him, lays out the real plot, which shows that the duplicitous Laura framed Emily for a bad brick of heroin and essentially sent her to her death at the hands of Tugger. Laura also stole the last brick that precipitated the catastrophic standoff between Tugger and the Pin, leading to the slaughter that Brendan narrowly escaped. The hero puts all the pieces together, although it must be acknowledged that Brendan's detailed recap of events and the revelation of Laura's machinations are so complex that it is a bit difficult to follow in just one viewing. It is implied that Laura will get her comeuppance (with Brendan's help, Trueman finds the missing brick in Laura's locker), but, true to the noir tradition, Brendan realizes just how sordid the world is and how he has, in a sense, been defeated even after restoring a semblance of order: he must live with the knowledge that Emily was carrying his unborn child when she was killed.

Brick was a true labor of love for Rian Johnson, who spent six years struggling to get his film made and sought financing from family and friends. By the time he shot the movie over a quick twenty-day schedule in San Clemente and at the high school he attended, Johnson knew exactly what he wanted, and the result is one of the most entertaining and audacious movies of the year. The recipient of the Special Jury Prize for Originality of Vision at the 2005 Sundance Film Festival, *Brick* illustrates the way that an old, familiar genre can be reinvented and reinvigorated by creating a bold verbal and visual style that immerses the audience in a world we have never seen before. Perhaps it could be called high school noir. For despite Johnson's obvious debt to the classics for the broad outlines of his narrative, he does not merely mimic familiar conventions but rather carves out his own niche from the incongruity of high schoolers playing at being adults.

Even more remarkable, perhaps, is the fact that he accomplishes this feat without condescending to his generic forebears or lampooning them. *Brick* may have a streak of dark comedy running through it, but the drama is not played for laughs, and the performances from a mainly young cast, particularly Joseph Gordon-Levitt's as the stubborn and determined detective, are uniformly excellent.

Peter N. Chumo II

CREDITS

Brendan: Joseph Gordon-Levitt
The Pin: Lukas Haas
Tugger: Noah Fleiss
The Brain: Matt O'Leary
Laura: Nora Zehetner
Dode: Noah Segan
Kara: Meagan Good
Emily: Emilie de Ravin
Brad Bramish: Brian White
Assistant Vice Principal Gary Trueman: Richard Roundtree
Big Stoner: Lucas Babin

Origin: USA
Language: English
Released: 2006
Production: Ram Bergman, Mark G. Mathis, Johnson Communications, Norman Dreyfuss; Bergman/Lustig
Directed by: Rian Johnson
Written by: Rian Johnson
Cinematography by: Steve Yedlin
Music by: Nathan Johnson
Sound: Dennis Grzesik
Costumes: Michele Posch
Production Design: Jodie Tillen
MPAA rating: R
Running time: 110 minutes

REVIEWS

Chicago Sun-Times Online. April 7, 2006.
Los Angeles Times Online. March 31, 2006.
New York Times Online. March 31, 2006.
San Francisco Chronicle. January 28, 2005.
USA Today Online. March 31, 2006.
Variety Online. January 28, 2005.
Village Voice Online. March 28, 2006, E5.

QUOTES

Brendan: "I've got knives in my eyes, I'm going home sick."

THE BRIDESMAID
(La Demoiselle d'honneur)

After more than fifty features to his name, master French filmmaker Claude Chabrol demonstrates through his 2004 effort, *The Bridesmaid* (released in 2006 in the U.S.), that he has reached the consummate phase of his long, diversified and prolific career. No other filmmaker of renown can boast as varied an output, one that spans the most detailed social realism, feverish commercially oriented pulp for the global market and what he is most famous for, sophisticated suspense thrillers for the art house circuit. As *The Flower of Evil* (2003) made clear, Chabrol, during this late creative phase, not only aspires to reflect the socio-political tumult of our time through the most unoriginal and even pedestrian plot elements, but to extend that distillation into the very use of his camera. Thus, *The Bridesmaid,* along with his other later works, stands to be dismissed (as many critics have) as a fall from artistic grace. Yet it is precisely this ambivalence that Chabrol, with the self-assurance of a veteran, seems to thrive upon.

Chabrol was one of the founders of the French New Wave (c. 1958), a polemical school of filmmaking centered on the notion of cinematic purity, using the camera as a fountain pen. With its other co-founders, Francois Truffaut dead and Jean-Luc Godard retreating into video, Chabrol remains holding the fort by himself. In *The Bridesmaid,* at significant moments, Chabrol uses his camera to evoke a transcendental force, hovering over the lives of his two amoral lovers. Like puppets that cannot perceive the puppeteer, his protagonists are too much in love to see what is goading them on, as if it were from a parallel universe. Thus, for a viewer willing to make the effort to decipher this near-perfect marriage of form and content, *The Bridesmaid* emerges as a fruitful meditation on, as a minor character in the film puts it, a "world falling apart."

Chabrol's glamorous couple—Philippe Tardieu (Benoit Magimel), a handsome yuppie of a sales agent and Stephanie or Senta, a part-time actress and model, played by Laura Smet, who resembles a colder version of Renee Zellweger—find themselves overcome by the need to kill for revenge, as well as to prove a love beyond moral law. One ends up actually killing, and the other only acquiescing, but both serve as a displacement for that most feared archetype of our time: the self-destructive religious terrorist. Strangely, it is not religion that seems to animate their lives, but mythology from a timeless past that guides their danse macabre. What allows for such a mystically-oriented filmic narrative (based on a mystery novel by the American Ruth Rendell) to work is Chabrol's icy cool mode of filmmaking, which keeps us as much at a distance from the horrendous deeds the film gravitates towards as from the mythological substratum that provides the film with its ideological thrust.

As could be said to be his trademark, Chabrol begins by painstakingly constructing a veneer of normalcy, a mode of exposition that began with his first feature, *Le Beau Serge* (1958), in which he used the actual inhabitants of a French village. Here, it is the port region of the Pays de Loire. The film thus opens with a prolonged track of a bleached out industrial wasteland. Like that of Orson Welles in the classic *Citizen Kane* (1941), Chabrol's camera starts telling its story before introducing its principals, thereby rendering the setting and inanimate objects as important. Docks give way to apartment buildings, which segue into residential houses. The camera then makes a turn on an elite suburban street and comes to a stop in front of a house where a kidnapping has taken place, an event being reported on the local TV news.

That coverage is being viewed in the Tardieu's cramped living room by the beautiful Sophie (Solene Bouton) and her younger sister, the rebellious Patricia (Anna Mihalcea), who listen agog for news of the victim, who was in their school. We soon learn that Sophie is about to be married to Jacky (Eric Seigne), a well-meaning simpleton who is employed as a clerk at City Hall, while Philippe, the eldest, has no matrimonial plans in mind. In fact, he has just broken up with a girlfriend and doesn't seem to miss one. Christine (Aurore Clement), their graying but still attractive widowed mother, looks much too kind to be able to control her disparate flock.

Two plot elements are soon pulled into this domestic fold. The first is Gerard (Bernard Le Coq), a prosperous though emotionally aloof businessman, with whom Christine plans to start life afresh. The second is more mysterious: a marble bust of Flora, the mythological goddess of flowers, but whom no one identifies as such, which stands on a pedestal in the Tardieu garden, and which Christine wants to present to Gerard. Thus, for us, Flora embodies a purity stemming from a timeless past, her beauty soon to take on an uncanny dimension. When Christine takes her offspring to dine with Gerard, neither the girls nor Philippe take to him. Patricia finds him "tripped out," an expression Christine doesn't understand, while Philippe ends up missing Flora as he looks at her bare pedestal that night.

In the midst of the wedding preparations, Philippe dutifully goes about his work, selling plumbing fixtures for the rotund avuncular Nadeau (Pierre-Francois Dumeniaud), a boss much pleased with the young man's persuasive skills. On one such outing, Philippe spots Flora in the courtyard of a client's neighbor. He finds out that Gerard had to "sell and move" to Italy. That night, Philippe leaps over a gate and steals Flora, wrapping her in a newspaper and stashing her in his closet. Gerard, it turns out, hasn't bothered to call Christine. "He's a creep!" Philippe says, as he tries to console his mother. A subplot has Christine worried that she may be losing Patricia to drugs. Philippe agrees to talk to her.

At the wedding, the group portrait presents a curious sight. Jacky and Sophie look well matched and happy beyond words. At the far side, however, looking somewhat sullen, stands the eponymous bridesmaid. Philippe, strolling around like an outsider himself, is spurred to inquire from Patricia as to who she is. When she tells him, the first thing he says is: "Doesn't she look like Flora?" Chabrol's camera quickly pans to Flora's vacant pedestal as the scene fades out.

That evening, Stephanie appears on Philippe's doorstep, rain-soaked in her bridesmaid gown. She dries herself using Philippe's bathrobe. When he offers her a fresh set of clothes, she drops the robe and embraces him, half-naked. She then makes him repeat her name over and over, that is, the name she wants to be known by: Senta, the heroine of *The Flying Dutchman.* Philippe looks clearly aroused though taken aback by the light domination she has started practicing on him.

In the scenes that follow, Senta represents the profligate sexuality missing from Philippe's life. She forces him to take her to the beach at dawn and there, by the waves, unravels her past. Slyly, she admits to having been an actress, thereby making him doubt everything she says. When he corroborates her account with Jacky, her cousin, he finds he does have one thing in common with Senta: they both have been without a father.

In bed, Senta says that she has been waiting for Philippe all her life, and that she knew this at first sight. She is now prepared to bestow on him everything she owns, mainly her villa. Philippe laps it all up, which in turn undercuts any dramatic conflict between them. On one level, we can see that Philippe is venting his repressed emotions, given his hi-tech lifestyle, just as Stephanie, as Senta, is invoking homespun mysticism when she spouts: "You are my destiny! You are my karma!" Combining her spiritual hunger with her physical needs, it is Senta who initiates the loveplay when she takes him down to her basement dwelling.

Philippe's behavior soon becomes quixotic. He retrieves Flora from the closet and places her on his desk. As if too distracted to work, he closes his laptop and kisses Flora. He even takes her to bed. When he then rings Senta (and she doesn't pick up), things get murky. It isn't clear whether Philippe's unnatural attachment to Flora is the result of Senta awakening in him a sense of the occult, or the other way around.

Chabrol thus ends up portraying Flora as a go-between who brings Philippe and Senta together. This would have been fine had he not, in the plot twists that follow, used Flora to add a mystical dimension to his tale, evoking one of his favorite themes, that of the elite trapped by murderous passion.

We can see that Philippe has somersaulted into a romantic relationship with Senta, yet he detects cracks in her story, and tells her as such. If she's a stage actress, shouldn't she have playscripts lying around? This results in her flying into a rage, which he tries to assuage by affirming his love. She demands proof in four ways: he should plant a tree, write a poem, make love to someone of his gender, and lastly, kill someone, anyone. Philippe laughingly agrees to the first two, but as far as the other two, he admits it's not his "cup of Nescafe." She promptly casts him out.

When she returns, Philippe makes it clear that he cannot live without her, and for the first time we see them naked in the throes of lovemaking. Philippe assumes she has forgotten about her crazy demands, then is tempted to pose as a killer when he learns that the

Tramp (Michel Duchaussoy) who has been squatting on her estate has been murdered on the docks. With a bottle of wine, Philippe presents her with the newspaper turned to the story. The next morning Philippe wakes up in her bed to be told by her that she has been up since four in the morning, taken a bus to a nearby town, walked two miles, to make sure she wasn't followed, and murdered Gerard, in revenge for what he has done to Philippe's family. From all Philippe told her, she was able to trace his whereabouts. Philippe looks shaken, but half-doubtful. It is only when he finds Gerard alive and well that he laughs it all off.

Wishing to leave all thoughts of killing behind them, Philippe presents her with a bust of Flora and a proposal of marriage, which she readily accepts. Ironically, it is just then that he's called away on a police matter. Sophie has been arrested with stolen loot. While at the station, Philippe is questioned on a quite unrelated matter: his having been spotted near the scene of a murder, that of Gerard's houseguest, who was found killed exactly in the manner Senta described. Philippe clears himself to the satisfaction of the authorities, but is left shattered. His first response is to break off with Senta, at least for a while. But this, it is now clear, is no longer an option. Almost coincidentally, he runs into the Tramp he claimed to have murdered. It seems the newspaper report was erroneous. Philippe gives the Tramp all the cash he has and tells him to move to a far off neighborhood.

This sets the stage for the film's climax. To make up for her blunder (in killing Gerard's houseguest), Senta tells Philippe that she has murdered the woman who tried to steal her first love from her. This time, we are shown the bloodied corpse in her closet, which takes us and Philippe by shock. She then presses Philippe to help her bury it in the woods. But it is too late, as policemen's feet, glimpsed through her basement skylight, along with hard knocks on the door make clear. Senta now pleads with Philippe not to leave her. He promises undying attachment. Chabrol dissolves to the bust of Flora, now in Senta's basement, a beatific smile on her face, as the end credits roll over her.

Vivek Adarkar

CREDITS

Philippe Tardieu: Benoit Magimel
Stephanie/Senta: Laura Smet
Christine: Aurore Clement
Gerard Courtois: Bernard Le Coq
Sophie Tardieu: Solene Bouten
Patricia Tardieu: Anna Mihalcea
The Tramp: Michel Duchaussoy
Jacky: Eric Seigne
Nadeau: Pierre-Francois Dumeniaud
Origin: France
Language: French
Released: 2004
Production: Antonio Passalia, Patrick Godeau; Alicelio; released by First Run Features
Directed by: Claude Chabrol
Written by: Claude Chabrol, Peter Leccia
Cinematography by: Eduardo Serra
Music by: Matthieu Chabrol
Sound: Monique Fardoulis
Editing: Monique Fardoulis
Costumes: Mic Cheminal
Production Design: Francoise Benoit-Fresco
MPAA rating: Unrated
Running time: 111 minutes

REVIEWS

Hollywood Reporter Online. September 9, 2004.
Los Angeles Times Online. September 8, 2006.
New York Times Online. August 4, 2006.
San Francisco Chronicle. August 1, 2006, p. E7.
Variety Online. September 19, 2004.
Village Voice Online. August 1, 2006.

QUOTES

Senta (to Philippe): "You are my destiny and I am yours."

TRIVIA

The Bridesmaid is Claude Chabrol's fifty-fourth feature film.

BUBBLE

Another Steven Soderbergh Experience.
—Movie tagline

Steven Soderbergh likes to try new things while making money off the tried and true. In between making commercial blockbusters like those in the *Ocean's Eleven* franchise (beginning in 2001), Soderbergh, who redefined indie film success with his groundbreaking debut *sex, lies, and videotape* (1989), dabbles on the experimental frontier. His last attempt at such unorthodoxy, *Full Frontal* (2002), was a complex and confusing but rewarding effort to explore the intersection of creative fantasy and reality. His newest venture, *Bubble,* is much different: a bare-bones depiction of working-class jealousy that's about as far from Hollywood as it's possible to be (and that would be West Virginia).

Soderbergh ventured into one of the most economically depressed areas of the country to shoot a simple story about factory workers. What's more, he further turned his back on Hollywood not just by going extremely low-budget but by using non-actors in the film as well. Most notably, he found lead actress Debbie Doebereiner working behind the drive-through window of a burger joint. Plump, unglamorous, and middle-aged, the red-haired Doebereiner is not someone most casting directors would go near, much less cast for a central role.

Just as iconoclastic as the casting, setting, budget, and story line was Soderbergh's much-noted decision to release *Bubble* on video on the same date as its theatrical release. This was a bold move at a time when Hollywood was fighting furiously to promote the virtues of going to the cinema rather than renting, following a year (2005) of falling box-office receipts. In essence, Soderbergh was admitting that there is no fighting the power of rentals, but he must have been counting on his own notoriety to help the film succeed in theaters. That strategy seemed to fail; with the film coming out on video, even art houses had little incentive to book it, and *Bubble* had minuscule box-office impact.

It certainly is a film suited to the small screen. Written by Coleman Hough, who proved he could handle more complex material with his screenplay for *Full Frontal, Bubble* is essentially a three-person character play with a ridiculously thin plot. Martha (Doebereiner) is a veteran worker at a doll factory who lives with her aged and ailing father and spends her spare time sewing doll clothes for a little extra pay. As the film opens, it's clear she is smitten with Kyle (Dustin Ashley), a young man who is a bit aimless and has drifted into a factory job. Kyle lives with his mother and, since he has no car, often calls on Martha for rides. He works a night job sweeping up at another factory. Martha is glad to be of service. They are friends despite their age difference—Martha is old enough to be Kyle's mother—and though there is no romantic behavior between the two, it's clear Kyle is very important in Martha's dull life.

Enter Rose (Misty Wilkins), a new hire at the doll factory. Soderbergh doesn't waste any time telegraphing the plot: as the boss introduces Rose, we see her eyes meeting Kyle's, and Kyle smiling back, and Martha looking from one to the other, catching their stares, and registering alarm. From this point, the plot plays out predictably. In lunchroom conversations, Rose comes off as a bit too wild, earning Martha's disapproval. When she asks Martha to drive her to a housecleaning job, Martha finds her taking a luxurious bubble bath in her employers' rub. Then Rose asks her to baby-sit for her two-year-old daughter so Rose can go out on a date. When Kyle shows up as her date, Martha is the only one surprised; we're not. And when events turn tragic, no further surprises await.

At first blush *Bubble* offers its own charms. It's great to see a story set in the real heartland of America, and characters who are struggling with low-wage jobs and no prospects for anything better. These characters aren't salt-of-the-earth types, however; there's nothing noble about their lives, and nothing attractive about their personalities.

What is at first refreshingly real and uncluttered dialogue, entirely free of Hollywood cliche, soon becomes tiresome. It's painfully obvious that Hough is laboring mightily to scrub the interchanges of anything clever that diminish their authenticity. But realism for its own sake isn't laudatory. The very reason we like fiction and especially movies is that they provide not just a way to take us out of our lives, but to reach new perspectives that might shed some light on human foibles.

Bubble is all hyperrealism to no effect. The casual complaints of the three factory workers, and the awful mediocrity of their lives, are neither telling nor tragic. *Bubble* doesn't take a political or personal stand; it just situates the most common of fictional devices—a love triangle—in a pedestrian setting, and with characters that are flat and unappealing.

Even more annoyingly, Soderbergh seems obsessed with shooting most of the conversations between the characters in long or medium shots. You see Martha and Kyle walking into the factory, tiny dots of humanity in the parking lot, but you hear them talking as if you were right beside them. In much of the film, the principals are situated as barely recognizable beings within a blank industrial landscape. The point is obvious, and belabored: these folks are prisoners of their own environment.

But what the flat dialogue and the equally flat filmmaking technique produce is no revelation. *Bubble* moves ploddingly, and there's nothing much to this Soderbergh experiment except a too-obvious attempt to be anti-glamorous. Nothing crackles in the movie, nothing sparkles, but neither do the dullness nor the darkness give us relief or revelation. Life's a boring grind.

Compare this slice-of-life in the backwoods of America to 2005's *Junebug*, and you'll see the contrast. Soderbergh's film has characters who are real but of no interest; *Junebug* is bursting with energy and sass, though the characters are equally realistic. *Bubble* comes dangerously close to looking like a studied attempt by a Hollywood insider to be defiantly proletarian. Soderbergh's purpose is hard to grasp: a director who can make films bursting with fascinating characters and complex plots, whether they are caper films, political films (*Traffic* [2000]) or romantic labyrinths *(sex, lies, and videotape)* here seems to be trying to prove that even a pro can make a low-budget film that looks like the work of an amateur.

Doebereiner is largely responsible for any emotional impact left by this deliberately unemotional film. When Soderbergh places her in church and then isolates and bathes her face with a heavenly glow, it's not clear why he's doing it, but he's clearly taken with her. Standing in for an entire class of ordinary, overlooked people seems to be Martha's role, so Doebereiner has a heavy load to carry, but she manages to pull it off almost effortlessly. While the other actors simply mumble and recede, Doebereiner has a barely capped fire burning inside the ennui of her exterior and her life. We tend to believe in the pain of her loneliness even when the script and direction turn her story into something of a burlesque of pity. She is perfectly cast for this role, but *Bubble* is mired in its own insistence on being some sort of anti-Hollywood statement and there's simply not much there.

Michael Betzold

CREDITS

Martha: Debbie Doebereiner
Kyle: Dustin Ashley
Rose: Misty Wilkins
Jake: K. Smith
Origin: USA
Language: English
Released: 2006
Production: Gregory Jacobs; Section Eight, Magnolia Pictures, 2929 Entertainment, HDNet Film
Directed by: Steven Soderbergh
Written by: Coleman Hough
Cinematography by: Steven Soderbergh
Music by: Robert Pollard
Sound: Larry Blake
Editing: Mary Ann Bernard
MPAA rating: R
Running time: 73 minutes

REVIEWS

Boxoffice Online. January 27, 2006.
Chicago Sun-Times Online. January 27, 2006.
Entertainment Weekly Online. January 25, 2006.
Los Angeles Times Online. January 27, 2006.
New York Times Online. January 27, 2006.
Variety Online. September 3, 2005.
Washington Post Online. January 27, 2006, p. WE38.

QUOTES

Martha about Rose: "I'm not too sure about her. She scares me a little."

TRIVIA

The first film to be simultaneously released on cable, DVD, and in theaters.

AWARDS

Nomination:
Ind. Spirit 2007: Director (Soderbergh)

C

CACHE
(Hidden)

Box Office: $3.6 million

Celebrated German writer-director Michael Haneke's timely suspense thriller from France, *Cache* (*Hidden*), shows the quiet face of terror in relation to the hyperkinetic modalities in which we lead our lives. What terror as an ever-widening global means of achieving sociopolitical ends does, the film seems to say, is to turn our hi-tech lifestyle against ourselves. In its current manifestation, this collective nightmare conceals a xenophobic aspect as well. Like Haneke's Parisian intellectual elite, we fear the outsider as well as the fact that through the cyberworld and its extensions, the terrorist's identity becomes indistinguishable from those whom we have always trusted. Thus, the fear spawned by this cloak of normalcy, which terror necessarily needs in order to breed, ends up with our terrorizing ourselves. It is Haneke's skill as a filmmaker that he can concretize such an abstract notion to demonstrate that the unreality at the root of a nightmare, while we are experiencing it, does not make it any less real.

From its very first shot, *Cache* asserts the notion of film and its extensions as comprising the invisible technofabric of our time, one that veils not only the content of the films we see, but their form as well. Unlike in other thrillers, we are forced to watch spellbound as Haneke takes film storytelling back to its origins. As a child of the Industrial Revolution, cinema served to point out how people were trapped within the urban worlds of their own making. The fixed, unwavering gaze of the very first Lumiere films was not a mere window into the world; it became a means of trapping the world, almost as if the medium itself was the puppeteer that no one saw or, more importantly, cared to think about. It is this ethos that Haneke brilliantly revives.

An unbearably prolonged shot of a street in an upscale neighborhood on a quiet sunny morning opens the film. Even the titles are inconspicuously superimposed over it in a linear form, as if they were mere data. It is only when we hear voiceovers and the inconsequential action in the shot is reversed that we become aware that we have been watching a videotape. But this is no formal filmic digression, we come to learn, but an intrusion into the private lives of Haneke's protagonists. Georges (Daniel Auteuil), a handsome erudite host of a literary TV talk show, and Anne (Juliette Binoche), his attractive wife who works in publishing, are at a loss to understand why someone would make a two hour video of the street in front of their town house and then leave it on their doorstep in a shopping bag. The ambivalent nature of what they perceive as a threat to their security then begins to unravel.

Georges, Anne, and their pre-teen son Pierrot (Lester Makedonsky), comprise a happy family. Into scenes of their everyday life, which include Pierrot's energetic swimming class, Haneke suddenly interjects the next disturbing video, a fixed camera from the same vantage point, taking in the same scene, except at night. This time, the tape comes wrapped in a strange drawing, the kind a small child would draw, of a face with a streak of red streaming from the mouth. The video is intercut with a brief shot of a boy of Middle Eastern descent peeking from behind a window with a frightened expression. Haneke's point-of-view shot that follows is identical to the video we have been watching.

The menace that has targeted Georges and his family increases in slight degrees. Anne receives a phone call where the male caller wants to talk to Georges but refuses to identify himself. Georges receives a postcard of the same strange drawing in his office mail, while Pierrot gets one at school. Haneke's camera then stealthily glides inside a dingy, dark apartment that night to show the boy seen earlier by the window coughing blood into his hands. That night, as Georges and Anne are entertaining their close friends, the doorbell rings. Georges excuses himself, but there is no one there. He then steps out and screams into the night: "Show yourself you coward!" Then, as he is about to close the door, he finds a third video at his feet, this time wrapped in a drawing of what looks like a rooster with a streak of red around its neck. This proves particularly uncanny, since one of his guests had just finished recounting a story about a neck wound. Calmly, Georges puts the video away and returns to the cozy ambiance of walls covered from floor to ceiling with books. But when Anne tells their guests about the stalker, Georges plays the video he has just received. Unlike the others, this is a shot taken from behind the windshield of a car being driven along a country road on a rainy day. The car comes to a stop in front of a villa that Georges identifies as the house he grew up in.

This puts Georges, and the film's narrative, on an altogether different track as Haneke introduces the theme of post-colonial guilt in western society. When Georges explores his childhood past, with the help of his bed-ridden mother (the veteran Annie Girardot in an affecting cameo), he unleashes a nightmare revolving around the mysterious figure of Majid, an Algerian boy his parents had planned to adopt. The last drawing now begins to make sense as Georges dwells on a childhood memory of little Majid slaughtering a rooster and then scaring Georges with the bloody axe. The incident was a mere prank, but one which Georges reported to his father, thereby resulting in Majid not being adopted.

From here on it becomes clear that interwoven with the film's thriller plot is Georges's attempt to come to terms with his long-buried guilt. If there is a weakness in Haneke's dramatic exposition, it would be that he is forced to abandon even his few omniscient glimpses of the underclass in order to get us to side with Georges as he struggles with his private demons.

Georges's inner conflict drives a wedge between him and Anne. The two fight over what Georges is hesitant to reveal, and which Anne feels is of the utmost concern to her and Pierrot. The next video to arrive shows an immigrant neighborhood and a hallway leading to an apartment door. Georges follows the clues and tracks down the now middle-aged Majid (Maurice Benichou), a very simple, humble man who, even when Georges bombards him with accusations, claims to have no knowledge of the videos. Unbeknownst to Georges, however, he is being videographed as he threatens the innocent Majid. This video will later make its way to Georges's producer at the TV station, who becomes alarmed at how it might damage Georges's career.

Anne's fears about Pierrot's vulnerability come alive when he doesn't return from school and cannot be found at his friend's place. Her emotional distress at being left out of Georges's hunt for their stalker worsens. Georges has Majid and his son (Walid Afkir), who is in his twenties, arrested as suspects in Pierrot's kidnapping, even though Georges knows that without evidence, they will soon be let go. For both Anne and Georges, this night is the dramatic low point of their ordeal. When he is alone in the kitchen, Georges breaks down weeping. Haneke captures this in an unwavering medium shot. We begin to see Pierrot's absence as foregrounding the helplessness of this elite couple behind the veneer of their intellectual savoir faire.

Given the film's ideological thrust, it would have been a surprise if any harm were to have come to Pierrot; he is brought home by a classmate's mother the next morning. Haneke instead saves his film's shocker for the next sequence which, after all the non-events that have preceded it, results in a twist so unexpected and horrifying that it has to rank as amongst the most chilling jolts in movies.

Georges visits Majid when the latter invites him to his apartment. As Georges walks in, Majid closes the door and says, "I want you to be present for this." He then removes a long razor from his pocket, flips it open and slashes his own throat, sending a streak of blood against the wall as he collapses lifeless. Georges, with his back to the camera, can only look on petrified before he is racked by sobs. Again, Haneke captures the entire scene in a fixed medium shot.

Majid's suicide serves as a denouement, but on a deeper plane, resolves nothing. In an epilogue of sorts, Majid's son visits Georges in his office. The latter is convinced that it was he who prepared the videos, even though the son denies having done so. His intent in confronting Georges, he claims, is merely to point out to him that it was because of Georges that Majid was deprived of an education and a decent life. Georges retorts that he feels not a shred of guilt and sends the young man on his way. We, as the audience, take leave of the film disturbed by the fact that neither Georges and his family, or us for that matter, can feel any safer.

Vivek Adarkar

CREDITS

Georges: Daniel Auteuil
Anne: Juliette Binoche
Georges's Mother: Annie Girardot
Majid: Maurice Benichou
Georges's editor: Bernard Le Coq
Pierrot: Lester Makedonsky
Majid's son: Walid Afkir
Origin: France, Austria, Germany, Italy
Language: French
Released: 2005
Production: Margaret Menegoz, Veit Heiduschka; Les Films du Losange, Wega-Film, Bavaria Films, Bim Distribuzione; released by Sony Pictures Classics
Directed by: Michael Haneke
Written by: Michael Haneke
Cinematography by: Christian Berger
Sound: Jean-Paul Mugel, Jean-Pierre Laforce
Editing: Nadine Muse, Michael Hudecek
Costumes: Lisy Christl
Production Design: Emmanuel de Chauvigny, Christoph Kanter
MPAA rating: R
Running time: 121 minutes

REVIEWS

Boxoffice Online. December 23, 2005.
Los Angeles Times Online. December 23, 2005.
New York Times Online. December 23, 2005.
Variety Online. May 14, 2005.

AWARDS

L.A. Film Critics 2005: Foreign Film

CARS

Ahhh...it's got that new movie smell.
—Movie tagline

Our Cars Speak For Themselves.
—Movie tagline

Life is a journey. Enjoy the trip.
—Movie tagline

Gear up.
—Movie tagline

The All-New 2006.
—Movie tagline

Box Office: $244 million

Pixar has been using computer graphics to conquer new frontiers in animation since the enormously successful *Toy Story* (1995) showed audiences how sophisticated animation could be coupled with a delightful story line to match or eclipse anything that Disney was doing in its heyday. The studio followed with *A Bug's Life* (1998), *Toy Story 2* (1999), *Monsters Inc.* (2001), *Finding Nemo* (2003), and *The Incredibles* (2004). It seemed that there was no concept or creature that Pixar could not turn into a family blockbuster.

Now that Pixar has been bought by Disney, it is not unreasonable to wonder if the company can keep its reputation as a pioneer? In its latest feature, *Cars,* Pixar retains its bold vision, but does seem to have lost its edge. *Cars* is as remarkable a piece of animation as its predecessors. It looks great, and is full of wonderfully detailed scenes, vivid color, and fanciful touches. Particularly appealing are its landscapes: beautifully rendered Western panoramas that prove computer animation can be as artistic as traditional methods.

This time around, though, Pixar has tackled a subject that is problematic, rendering an imagined world totally inhabited by cars. The principal characters are racing cars competing for the so-called Piston Cup (an obvious play on NASCAR's Winston Cup). The movie opens with a big race at a track in the South, introducing us, through an announcer's narration, to the three main competitors—a respected veteran in his last season, the perennial also-ran, and an exciting rookie named Lightning McQueen (voice of Owen Wilson). The stands are filled with fans, who are also cars. The announcers are cars. The pit crew personnel are cars. Everyone is a car.

This concept, whipped into shape by no less than six screenwriters including director John Lasseter (who helmed the two *Toy Story* movies), presents the filmmakers with a formidable set of problems. For one thing, in a world with only cars, there are no animals, and as McQueen travels across country to a second showdown race, he travels through a strangely vacant landscape. The one attempt at solving this dilemma gives us insects that are miniature flying Volkswagen bugs, but that is as far as the concept stretches. Another problem is that cars are not easy to make humanoid; they have no arms or legs, so their actions are limited. The animators use windshields to make eyes and faces, rather than the grilles customarily used to anthropomorphize automobiles; they do as much as they can with wheels to simulate movements and expressions, and the result is intriguing but ultimately unsatisfying. It's not that the cars are not distinct or expressive enough, but their variety is limited (the filmmakers cheat a bit by including other types of vehicles including tractors, trucks, and vans). What they are capable of doing and experiencing is also limited, and the car-world translation does not quite work adeptly. There is a running subplot gag, for example, about a couple who are lost and the man continually refuses to ask directions, but the pair travel side by side and you wonder why the woman just doesn't go off on her own.

Lightning McQueen is not a very sympathetic protagonist, either. He follows a familiar moralistic cartoon hero's character arc—he is cocky and conceited and has to learn that there is more to life than winning. There's also a limit to which the animated expressiveness of cars can make us feel emotionally attached to the characters, especially McQueen. Rather than becoming involved in the characters, as millions did with the stars of *Toy Story,* even kids may feel more like they are watching a clever exercise rather than being consumed by a gripping story. It also doesn't help that Wilson is the voice of McQueen: his smart-aleck, off-putting manner does not let us inside the character, and when he reaches for sympathy, he lands mostly in the gee-whiz register. Wilson is so good at being insincere his efforts at legitimate sincerity do not register.

But the real weaknesses of the film are that the action is sparse, the plot is thin and predictable, and the ideas are incongruous. The movie is bookended by nearly identical race scenes that come complete with promotional fantasies that seem to have arisen out of the mind of a two-year-old boy. NASCAR racing is the country's most popular sport, and obviously the filmmakers are confident they have hitched their conceptual wagon to a winner. But it's a stretch to put over the notion that winning is not central to auto racing, that somehow this most commercialized and technological of all sports has traditions that connect to slower, humanistic values. But that is what *Cars* tries to say, and the effort comes off as Hollywood's liberal, pro-environmental take on NASCAR, a sort of phony populism.

The film's central proposition is a doubtful one: even cars long for a day when cars did not rule the world. The movie focuses its energy on what happens after its hero, McQueen, gets lost on his way out to California and ends up in Radiator Springs, a town on Route 66 that is an echo of its former self due to a traffic-diverting freeway. So this movie, which is ostensibly aimed at kids, is steeped in nostalgia for an era that passed away in these kids' grandparents' youth. Most of the film takes place in the aforementioned Radiator Springs, but not much happens there. McQueen is sentenced to repaving the main drag as community service after a speeding rampage. The town is filled with characters that are based on stereotypes and half-developed ideas. There's Mater, a tow truck (his name a play on the Texan pronunciation of "tomato") that is a dim yokel with a heart of gold (voice of Larry the Cable Guy). There is a rather perfunctory love interest, a cute little blue car named Sally (voice of Bonnie Hunt), who has a strange backstory; she's an attorney who dropped out of the fast lane in Los Angeles and ended up staying and loving the boondocks and running the local hotel. There is Doc Hudson (voice of Paul Newman), the town's leading citizen; who has a secret that helps teach a lesson. We also have a hippie VW bus (voice of George Carlin), a military type, a sheriff, and an embarrassing bunch of Italian and Mexican ethnic stereotypes (filled by the likes of Tony Shalhoub and Cheech Marin). All these characters are ultimately little more than cliches.

The filmmakers have plenty of fun joking around with these characters and getting the maximum mileage out of a plot that meanders and then runs head-on into preachiness. They do a lot of moaning and groaning about how life has passed by Route 66, imagining a time when style mattered more than getting there, as if the freeway system were a recent defilement. You have the suspicion—and the roster of a half-dozen scriptwriters confirms it—that studio marketers loved the potential demographic gold mine of coupling a NASCAR-themed story with nostalgia for small-town life, which might make more sense if auto racing was not the commercialized spectacle it is. This is not Pixar at its snappiest, and it looks suspiciously like an enterprise whose idea machines are running low on fuel.

Watching *Cars* is a generic experience; the movie has its own brand and logo. The title itself suggests a premise rather than a story. The redemptive moment at the film's climax has absolutely nothing to do with the rest of the movie. In short, this is a movie long on "high concept" and short on story and memorable characters and, no matter how snazzy the exterior, it is still story and characters that make any entertainment vehicle run like a winner.

Michael Betzold

CREDITS

Lightning McQueen: Owen Wilson (Voice)
Doc Hudson: Paul Newman (Voice)
Mater: Larry the Cable Guy (Voice)
Sally Carrera: Bonnie Hunt (Voice)
Sarge: Paul Dooley (Voice)
Red: Joe Ranft (Voice)
Fillmore: George Carlin (Voice)
Lizzie: Katherine Helmond (Voice)
Chick Hicks: Michael Keaton (Voice)
Ramone: Richard "Cheech" Marin (Voice)
Mack: John Ratzenberger (Voice)
Luigi: Tony Shalhoub (Voice)
The King: Richard Petty (Voice)

Guido: Guido Quaroni (Voice)
Flo: Jenifer Lewis (Voice)
Sheriff: Michael Wallis (Voice)
Origin: USA
Language: English
Released: 2006
Production: Darla K. Anderson; Walt Disney Pictures, Pixar; released by Buena Vista
Directed by: John Lasseter
Written by: Joe Ranft, John Lasseter, Dan Fogelman, Kiel Murray, Phil Lorin, Jorgen Klubien
Cinematography by: Jean-Claude Kalache
Music by: Randy Newman
Editing: Ken Schretzmann
Production Design: Bill Cone, Bob Pauley
MPAA rating: G
Running time: 118 minutes

REVIEWS

Boxoffice Online. June 9, 2006.
Chicago Sun-Times Online. June 9, 2006.
Entertainment Weekly Online. June 7, 2006.
Los Angeles Times Online. June 9, 2006.
New York Times Online. June 9, 2006.
Premiere Magazine Online. June 8, 2006.
Variety Online. June 4, 2006.
Washington Post. June 9, 2006, p. C1.

QUOTES

Minny: "Oh, for the love of Chrysler!"

TRIVIA

Originally titled *Route 66,* the film's name was changed so as not to imply a connection with the TV show *Route 66* (1960).

AWARDS

Golden Globes 2007: Animated Film
Nomination:
Oscars 2006: Animated Film, Song ("Our Town")
British Acad. 2006: Animated Film

CASINO ROYALE

Box Office: $167 million

Critics of the venerable James Bond franchise have been saying for years that it is past time for 007 to hang up his Walther PPK. The anti-Bond brigade has claimed that Ian Fleming's superspy, born near the beginning of the Cold War, has become an anachronism and the films have become increasingly unrealistic, relying more and more upon big explosions and other special effects. Faced with the decision of whether to let Bond die painfully or reinvent him, producers Barbara Broccoli and Michael G. Wilson have surprised many observers by returning Bond to his gritty roots with *Casino Royale.*

Casino Royale (1953) is the first of Fleming's thirteen Bond novels and was also the first to be dramatized, on the American television anthology series *Climax!* in 1954, with Barry Nelson as Jimmy Bond and Peter Lorre as the villain, Le Chiffre. When producer Albert R. Broccoli acquired the rights to Fleming's novels, *Casino Royale* was not part of the package. As a result, it was filmed in 1967 as a spoof, with David Niven, Peter Sellers, and Woody Allen as various incarnations of 007 and Orson Welles as Le Chiffre. This *Casino Royale* has become legendary as an incoherent mess, with too many directors (at least five, including John Huston) and screenwriters, with uncredited contributions reportedly by Ben Hecht, Joseph Heller, Terry Southern, and Billy Wilder, as well as Allen and Sellers. Except for the card game between Bond and Le Chiffre, it has little to do with its source.

Casino Royale is far from a spoof, striving to remain rooted in the violent, morally ambiguous post 9/11 world and trying to match the realism of the seemingly more relevant spy films, *The Bourne Identity* (2002) and *The Bourne Supremacy* (2004). The grittiest Bond since 007 married, only for his wife to die, in *On Her Majesty's Secret Service* (1969), *Casino Royale* has been called by many reviewers the best in the series since Sean Connery's heyday with *From Russia with Love* (1963) and *Goldfinger* (1964). It is also notable for introducing a new Bond, Daniel Craig, following Connery, George Lazenby, Roger Moore, Timothy Dalton, and Pierce Brosnan.

Casino Royale begins with a black-and-white pretitle sequence with Bond brutally beating a man to death in a restroom. Soon afterward, he is in Uganda, chasing a suspected terrorist, Mollaka (Sebastien Foucan), and what a chase it is. The two men hurl themselves through a construction site, bounding over and bouncing between various dangerous obstacles. With these two sequences, director Martin Campbell, who also made *GoldenEye* (1995) with Brosnan, sets the tone for the rest of the film, with Bond narrowly escaping death innumerable times, and establishes that this will be a darker, more sadistic 007. The Uganda scene, overseen by stunt coordinator Gary Powell, whose father, uncle, and older brother performed stunts in earlier Bond films, shows the influence of Asian action films, though the characters never unrealistically defy gravity.

Casino Royale, reflecting its source, is meant to be the story of how Bond launched his legendary career, showing how he earns his license-to-kill status in the pre-title sequence. For the rest of the film, Bond must prove himself worthy of the trust of his boss, M (Judi Dench), who assigns him to nab Le Chiffre (Mads Mikkelsen), a slimy figure who bankrolls terrorist organizations around the world. Bond goes to Montenegro and Le Casino Royale, where Le Chiffre plans to raise money through a high-stakes poker game requiring a $10 million deposit. Vesper Lynd (Eva Green) is assigned by the Chancellor of the Exchequer to keep an eye on Bond and her majesty's cash. Bond is also assisted by Mathis (Giancarlo Giannini), MI6's local field agent, and, later, by Felix Leiter (Jeffrey Wright) of the CIA.

To show a more human side of 007, Bond frequently makes mistakes. He grows too cocky during the poker game, allowing Le Chiffre to trick him into losing his stake. Coming after Denise Richards as film history's least-convincing scientist in *The World Is Not Enough* (1999), the Bond woman was also due for updating. As a result, Vesper becomes the hero's equal at quick thinking, as when she saves his life. Sleek and efficient when she meets Bond, Vesper eventually descends into despair.

Casino Royale strikes a good balance between the action scenes, the interplay between Bond and his colleagues, and the poker game. While the Bond films have often been attacked for cartoonish violence, believable characters endure real pain here, especially when a nude Bond is tortured. Early in his career on British television, Campbell made two outstanding miniseries, the espionage saga *Reilly: Ace of Spies* (1983) and the political thriller *Edge of Darkness* (1985), in which the actions of the protagonists have considerable human consequences, paving the way for his work on *Casino Royale.*

The film is written by Bond veterans Neal Purvis and Robert Wade, *The World Is Not Enough* and *Die Another Day* (2002), and Paul Haggis, who wrote *Million Dollar Baby* (2004), *Crash* (2005), and *Flags of Our Fathers* (2006). These credits lead to expectations of superficiality, combined with heavy-handed social commentary, but somehow, the three created the screenplay as sophisticated entertainment for the age of terrorism without grinding any political or sociological axes or undercutting the seriousness of Bond's dilemma.

David Arnold's score has occasional echoes of John Barry's famous music for earlier Bonds but is generally more dramatic and romantic than is usual, with a possible reference to Barry's *Hanover Street* (1979). Cinematographer Phil Meheux, who worked with Campbell on *GoldenEye*, offers darker, muted, more noirish lighting, similar to his excellent work on *The Long Good Friday* (1980). A tiny flaw is Stuart Baird's editing of a Venice sequence, with continuity errors as he cuts back and forth between a collapsing building and the characters inside.

Another notable contributor is Daniel Kleinman, who designed the opening credits. Jettisoning the usual nude or seminude women behind the titles, Kleinman, inspired by the cover of the first edition of the novel, a playing card bordered by eight red hearts dripping blood, uses a card-and-gun motif, mixing images of Bond with animation, much like the credits of Hollywood films from the mid-1960s. These credits, coming after the violent opening, signal again that this is a new Bond. Similarly, the film does not end with Bond embracing a woman but with 007 holding a gun in his hand.

Mikkelsen, best known for the Danish drug thriller *Pusher* (1996), is suitably creepy as the scarfaced Le Chiffre. That he is not the usual Bond supervillain, aiming for world domination but just a greedy murderer, makes Le Chiffre even more frightening when he finally confronts the seemingly overmatched Bond. As she showed in Bernardo Bertolucci's *The Dreamers* (2003), Green combines sexiness, brains, and vulnerability, though Vesper perhaps becomes too vulnerable too quickly toward the end of the film. She is the most poignant of Bond's women since Diana Rigg's Tracy Di Vicenzo in *On Her Majesty's Secret Service.*

The biggest question, of course, about *Casino Royale* is how Craig stacks up against his predecessors. Brosnan is a sturdy 007, much better than the plots he was given. The underrated Dalton is good in *The Living Daylights* (1987), but unfortunately had to take some of the blame for *License to Kill* (1989), easily the worst Bond. Lazenby is adequate in his one shot: *On Her Majesty's Secret Service.* Moore, despite a few good moments, especially in *The Spy Who Loved Me* (1977), is too much of a dandy to fit the image most have of Bond. Connery, who played the character seven times, including the non-Broccoli *Never Say Never Again* (1983), defined the role with his distinctive blend of physicality, charm, and humor, always rising above the pulp level of the material.

Several actors were rumored to be in consideration to succeed Brosnan, including Orlando Bloom, Colin Farrell, Hugh Jackman, and Ewan McGregor, with Clive Owen the frontrunner. The British press was not enthusiastic about Craig's selection, with one headline blaring: "The Name's Bland...James Bland." Other journalists called the actor Mr. Potato Head because his ears stick out somewhat. Hostile Web sites such as craignotbond.com appeared. In an interview in *Esquire* (September 2006), Craig said his response to this controversy was "to work twice as hard to get it right. Get it beyond right."

Craig, who joins Moore as the only Bonds actually born in England, comes the closest to matching Connery's ideal. Though some have criticized his working-class looks and his boxer's swagger, Craig is an arresting presence, a combination of Steve McQueen's cool and James Cagney's energy. He is an excellent actor who has appeared mostly in supporting roles in flawed or obscure films, exceptions being his evil clergyman in *Elizabeth* (1998) and his charismatic gangster in *Layer Cake* (2004). Most of the early naysayers retreated when confronted by the cruel efficiency of Craig's 007. Even the actor's supporters could not have expected him to be this good, this definitive, so quickly. Craig, the smooth direction, and the intelligent screenplay combine to make *Casino Royale* the best Bond ever.

Michael Adams

CREDITS

James Bond: Daniel Craig
Vesper Lynd: Eva Green
Le Chiffre: Mads Mikkelsen
M: Judi Dench
Felix Leiter: Jeffrey Wright
Mathis: Giancarlo Giannini
Solange: Caterina Murino
Steven Obanno: Isaach de Bankole
Alex Dimitrios: Simon Abkarian
Valenka: Ivana Milicevic
Villiers: Tobias Menzies
Carlos: Claudio Santamaria
Mollaka: Sebastien Foucan
Mr. White: Jesper Christensen
Origin: Great Britain, USA, Czech Republic, Germany
Language: English
Released: 2006
Production: Michael G. Wilson, Barbara Broccoli; Eon Productions, MGM, Columbia Pictures; released by Sony Pictures
Directed by: Martin Campbell
Written by: Paul Haggis, Neal Purvis, Robert Wade
Cinematography by: Phil Meheux
Music by: David Arnold
Sound: Chris Munro
Editing: Stuart Baird
Art Direction: Simon Lamont
Costumes: Lindy Hemming
Production Design: Peter Lamont
MPAA rating: PG-13
Running time: 144 minutes

REVIEWS

Boxoffice Online. November 17, 2006.
Chicago Sun-Times Online. November 15, 2006.
The Daily Mirror Online. November 4, 2006.
Entertainment Weekly. November 24, 2006, p. 79.
The Guardian Online. November 10, 2006.
Hollywood Reporter Online. November 9, 2006.
Los Angeles Times Online. November 17, 2006.
New York Times Online. November 17, 2006.
Rolling Stone Online. November 13, 2006.
San Francisco Chronicle. November 16, 2006, p. E1.
Variety Online. November 9, 2006.
Washington Post. November 17, 2006, p. C1.

QUOTES

Vesper: "It doesn't bother you, killing those people?"
Bond replies: "Well, I wouldn't be very good at my job if it did."

AWARDS

British Acad. 2006: Sound

Nomination:

British Acad. 2006: Actor (Craig), Adapt. Screenplay, Cinematog., Film Editing, Visual FX, Orig. Score

CATCH A FIRE

The spark that ignites us, unites us.
—Movie tagline

Box Office: $4.3 million

In 1980, the workers at the Sasol oil refinery in Secunda (located in the former province Transvaal) are subjected to ruthless segregation. Even the use of a "white" restroom might put the native population at risk of being arrested. Worse, if they are suspected in a recent series of terrorist actions against the refinery, they could be caught and hanged. *Catch a Fire* is based upon the true story of foreman Patrick Chamusso (Derek Luke) and his wife and children, who are all living as good a life as might be expected under these circumstances, but the father is subjected daily to these depredations. Although he is innocent, Patrick will ultimately be accused of fighting with a rebel army of terrorists for social and political change. He comes under suspicion from Boer Security Chief Nic Vos (Tim Robbins) when his whereabouts are under question during the night of one such terrorist action. Now, Patrick is not a terrorist; he's been doing his best to toe the line for the sake of his family. But Patrick harbors a secret that he's reluctant to divulge to Nic: during the night in question he was visiting a woman with whom he had had a child. He's fearful that this revelation will ruin his marriage. Ironically, when he does confess this to Nic, he's not believed. He's subjected to torture and finally released. Nic is convinced that whatever Patrick is, he's not a terrorist.

After his release, Patrick is a changed man. Angered by his treatment, he decides to join the military wing (MK) of the African National Congress (ANC) camp in Mozambique, even though it means he must leave his family. Training goes on in the camp and Patrick draws upon his experience at the refinery to help plan an assault on it. These plans are momentarily interrupted when Nic and his men raid the terrorist compound. Patrick escapes. Armed with bombs, he makes his way back to the refinery. But his plan is thwarted when Nic follows him and disarms the bomb. Patrick is wounded in the melee but escapes. However, his whereabouts are betrayed by his wife Precious (Bonnie Henna), who is angered by the news of his infidelity. He is captured and sentenced to the Robben Island prison. He remains there until 1991 when Nelson Mandela is restored and apartheid banished. Chamusso served ten years of a twenty-four-year sentence.

The film ends with a celebration, an unabashed tribute to the spirit of the freedom fighters. There are also images of the real Chamusso talking into the camera and horsing around with the actor who represented him and shots at his Two Sisters orphanage, named for two AIDS orphans he brought home. According to the *New York Times*, Chamusso intends to use money earned from the sale of his story to finance his Two Sisters organization. The genesis of Noyce's film began when Joe Slavo, the white chief of staff of the military wing of the African National Congress, suggested to his daughter, Shawn, that she should write a screenplay depicting Patrick Chamusso as an unlikely political activist.

Slowly, inexorably, the film accumulates vignettes of apartheid life in the huddled townships and the almost casual daily incursions of the Boer police. None of the characters are portrayed as cardboard saints or villains. Patrick has his secrets. And Nic, while pretty despicable, is nonetheless portrayed as somebody who has his own family to protect (he compels his daughters to learn how to shoot at the local firing range, for example). He seems to have moments of compassion and tolerance, but usually, as the script suggests, he is bound in the service of his job. When, for example, he invites Patrick to a Sunday dinner, the true motive behind the invitation turns out to be a not-so-thinly veiled interrogation. He reunites Patrick with his wife in a jail cell, but then sits back and remorselessly watches it on a TV monitor. As Claudia Puig noted in her *USA Today* review, the film's "wan attempt to humanize" this thoroughly "malicious character" is not at all convincing.

Among the film's powerful instances of parallel editing is the scene where the almost celebratory burial of slain freedom fighters is contrasted with a more stiffly formal burial of several security police. As *New York Times* reviewer Manohla Dargis pointed out, the Australian director Phillip Noyce "knows how to keep the action in high gear," but the problem is, Dargis added, that in this film "the action doesn't just move; it rushes with such chaotic speed that the scenes don't have time to develop." On the other hand, Noyce is hardly an "action" director. From his breakthrough film, *Newsfront* (the surprise hit of the 1978 Cannes Film Festival, later called by the British Film Institute "one of the finest achievements of the New Australian Cinema") to the extraordinary *Rabbit-Proof Fence* (2002), Noyce's track record depends more on thought-challenging films rather than on action. Although he has done hack work on pictures like *The Saint* (1997) and *Clear and Present Danger* (1994), his career is redeemed by several better and more substantive films, such as his remake of Graham Greene's *The Quiet American* (2002).

One would expect Noyce's reputation to carry this picture, but reviews were oddly mixed. Puig claimed the movie "vibrantly captures African life with a rousing musical score." Though the film may be "preachy at times," it's a "well constructed action thriller elevated by Luke's performance." That said, she then only gives the picture two-and-a-half stars. *The New York Times* review carped that "Mr. Luke's and Mr. Robbins's performances nonetheless suggest a more interesting story than the one here." The *Baltimore Sun* thought that Robbins was "less effective" in character than Derek Luke, because his character is not so likable by nature. According to a *New York Times* feature by Kristin Hohenadel, Noyce wanted the Robbins character to be "three dimensional, because the film would not be worthy of being watched if the policeman was just a caricature of a racist." Noyce therefore hired an ex-policeman named Hentie Botha to serve as an on-location technical adviser. Botha explained that out of zeal to do right for his country, "your methods became more extreme, and the more extreme, the more success you had, the more acknowledgement" would be forthcoming, even though superiors "might have suspected you're overstepping the bounds." Noyce arrived in Johannesburg nine months before the shooting was to commence in order to study and internalize the social tensions, so as better to understand the context. As actress Bonnie Henna explained to the *New York Times*: "It's the kind of story that picks at scabs. It's picking at the scabs of even those who are telling it." Another consultant on the project was one of Chamusso's fellow prisoners on Robben Island, Napthali Manana, who now works for the African National Congress in Johannesburg.

Reviews were more interestingly mixed in evaluating the film's political message, which was of utmost importance to the director. "South Africa's recent history is a beacon to the rest of the world in terms of the peaceful resolution of bitter interracial conflict," Noyce explained, "keeping the infrastructure of the country intact, preserving the rights of citizens on all sides. The movie really is about the South African miracle." For Noyce, the "moral consequences of that struggle to all the participants, and then how in this society they've managed to move beyond that struggle" was crucial. "They live with it, they don't deny it, but they live together."

Despite elegance of that level, for *New York Times* reviewer Dargis, the film was simply borderline incoherent. The cross-cutting that was intended to link the performances of Luke and Robbins threaten to rip the film apart, according to Dargis, making parallel scenes "play like commercials for a film that never materializes." On the other hand, Chris Kaltenbach of the *Baltimore Sun* wrote that although Noyce's "main objective is to praise the bravery and dedication of the black South Africans who fought to end apartheid," the film is also clearly a warning "against the inhuman treatment of one's adversaries, and the parallels with what's happening in Guantanamo and Abu Ghraib are chilling." The film is potentially thoughtful and political in a way that most American films are not, and that may be reason for encouragement and applause.

James M. Welsh and John C. Tibbetts

CREDITS

Patrick Chamusso: Derek Luke
Nic Vos: Tim Robbins
Precious Chamusso: Bonnie Henna
Zuko September: Mncedisi Shabangu
Joe Slovo: Malcolm Purkey
Origin: USA, Great Britain, South Africa
Language: English
Released: 2006
Production: Tim Bevan, Eric Fellner, Anthony Minghella, Robin Slovo; Working Title Productions, Mirage Enterprises, StudioCanal; released by Focus Features
Directed by: Phillip Noyce
Written by: Shawn Slovo
Cinematography by: Ron Fortunato, Garry Phillips
Music by: Philip Miller
Sound: Derek Mannsvelt
Music Supervisor: Nick Angel
Editing: Jill Bilcock
Art Direction: Delarey Wagener
Costumes: Reza Levy
Production Design: Johnny Breedt
MPAA rating: PG-13
Running time: 101 minutes

REVIEWS

Chicago Sun-Times Online. October 27, 2006.
Entertainment Weekly. November 3, 2006, p. 52.
Hollywood Reporter Online. September 11, 2006.
Los Angeles Times Online. October 27, 2006.
New York Times Online. October 27, 2006.
San Francisco Chronicle. October 27, 2006, p. E1.
USA Today Online. October 26, 2006.
Variety Online. September 10, 2006.
Washington Post. October 27, 2006, p. C6.

QUOTES

Patrick Chamusso: "My family was punished for nothing. So let it be for something now."

CHANGING TIMES

(Les temps qui changent)

Can your first love also be your last?
—Movie tagline

Influential French director Andre Techine (*Strayed* [2003], *The Wild Reeds* [1994]) takes the beautiful idea of timeless, unrequited love and skillfully weaves it into a complicated and rich character-driven drama about opposites colliding: ideas, cultures, and people's very natures. Reuniting French legends Catherine Deneuve and Gerard Depardieu, *Changing Times* (*Les temps qui changent*) marks their seventh collaboration and their first film together since 1980 when they starred in Francois Truffaut's *The Last Metro.* Co-written by Techine, Laurent Guyot, and Pascal Bonitzer, *Changing Times* subtly and effectively explores the mysteries of the human heart.

Depardieu plays Antoine, a wealthy construction supervisor based in Paris, who is currently in the northern Moroccan city of Tangier to oversee the building of a large communications complex in the Free Trade Zone that includes a TV station to rival Al Jazeera. When we first see Antoine, inspecting one of the digs on his site, he is completely engulfed by a sudden avalanche. The film then flashes back to his arrival in Morocco and events leading up to the disaster.

It turns out Antoine's presence in Tangier is not purely business related. He gives instructions to his social director Nabila (Nabila Baraka) to regularly send roses to an unknown recipient. The mystery woman turns out to be Cecile (Deneuve), the host of a French-Moroccan radio show who lives in Tangier with her much younger, doctor husband Natan (Gilbert Melki). When she receives the anonymous bouquet, she unsentimentally dumps it in the trash can.

It is revealed that Antoine and Cecile were each others first loves, and their strikingly opposite natures is then immediately apparent. Some thirty years have passed since they parted and in that time, Cecile has gone with the flow, albeit rather testily, marrying twice and having children, while for Antoine, who has carried a torch for Cecile and never married, time has virtually stood still. Initially, he follows her around unseen, carrying a timeworn black-and-white photo of them as young lovers. Antoine's perpetual clumsiness causes them to finally meet, walking into a plate glass window after watching her at the grocery store. He badly bumps his nose, which turns even more embarrassing as he is also forced to admit to the doctor who comes to his aid that he has also "emptied [his] bowels." Even more humiliating, his rescuer turns out to be Cecile's husband. After a brief conversation, a busy and distracted Cecile offhandedly rebuffs several of his requests to meet again.

Cecile is currently busy with her son Sami (Malik Zidi) who has shown up unexpectedly from his home in Paris with his live-in girlfriend, Nadia (Lubna Azabal), and Said (Jabir Elomri), her nine-year-old son by another man. The chilly Cecile tries to warm up to the girl and young child she has never met, while Sami disappears for days at a time. Making matters worse, Natan has discovered that Nadia, who has stolen his prescription pad, is addicted to tranquilizers.

Drug addiction aside, there is something off about Sami and Nadia's relationship, akin to having an unspoken understanding that binds neither of them. It becomes apparent why, when we see that Sami has been dashing off for trysts with his old flame: a young Moroccan man named Bilal (Nadem Rachati). A study in opposites, Sami is a strawberry blonde covered in freckles, while Bilal is a swarthy Moroccan. They met in Paris, but Bilal grew weary of being a poor outsider there and is now back in Morocco, happily taking care of a posh estate overlooking the sea for its absent owners. Bilal has a carefree attitude toward his sexuality, unlike the more conflicted Sami who refuses to leave the drug-adled Nadia—who knows all about Sami and Bilal and approves—even though it is clear he prefers sex with men. Bilal succinctly encapsulates his friend's dilemma: "You're half Moroccan, half French, half man, half woman. It must be difficult knowing who you are."

Nadia has her own sub-drama going on. She came to Tangier with Sami in the hopes of meeting up with her identical twin sister, Aicha (also played by Azabal). Another study in extremes, Aicha is a devout Muslim who takes her job at McDonald's seriously and has no interest in men. As with Cecile and Antoine, Aicha keeps putting off Nadia's requests to meet, finally admitting to her sister that although she loves her, she won't meet with her because she is a bad influence. With Sami's consent, Nadia and Said return to Paris, where he will follow; their relationship both platonic and deep.

The heart of the film, however, is Antoine's obsession with Cecile and after several rebuffs, he finally just shows up at her house. It's an idyllic scene with Cecile's family gathered, romping in the pool, while she is busy inside working with her friend from the station, Rachel (Tanya Lopert). "It's usually women who get worked up and carry the torch like that," Cecile's clearly impressed coworker remarks about Antoine's slavish devotion. Cecile is still unmoved by Antoine's dedication, however, driving him to more desperate measures. Antoine knows that Nabila, a local North African, is probably familiar with voodoo and asks her for a love spell. Nabila replies that most spells just lead to trouble, but gives him a voodoo video to watch anyway. He falls short of ritually sacrificing live poultry, but does place the photograph of he and Cecile under her bed when briefly at her home. Later, while she takes him to tour a home he might be interested in renting, he clumsily declares his undying love for her, prompting her to order him never to see her again.

Back at home, Cecile's marriage is unraveling. She knows Natan has affairs but he is also drinking more than ever, unhappy that his business is waning. He wants them to move back to Casablanca but Cecile wants to stay in Tangier for her job. They disagree on their treatment of Sami as well; Cecile knows he "likes boys" and wants the three of them to have a frank discussion about it, something the surprised Natan thinks is none of their business. After Sami leaves for Paris, an unhappy Cecile takes an unexpected tack by taking Antoine up on his offer with one caveat: she won't stay with him forever, as he'd like, but she'll simply use him as an opportunity to take a little holiday away from her normal life. He quickly agrees and they unceremoniously bed down in his posh hotel room. As she awaits a subsequent meeting, she is annoyed that he is late only to discover from the hotel desk clerk that he has been in an accident; the one shown at the beginning of the film.

As a now shorter-haired Cecile leans over Antoine's bedside, it is clear some months have passed. Natan has moved back to Casablanca without her. Antoine, in a coma from the accident, lays motionless as Cecile recounts events of her daily life, and it is clear that it took his near-death for her to realize she loved him as well. He opens his eyes to see her smiling over him.

Techine's devotion to detail, together with Depardieu's acting excellence, allow for a wonderfully, painfully human Antoine, who drops a large pile of money at a casino in front of the cash poor Natan, walks smack into a glass door, and climbs down into a hole on a construction site, only to have it cave in on him. Deneuve shows admirable restraint as Cecile, making her uptight but still likable. The costars familiarity comes through while never feeling overly sentimental. On the contrary, their interactions do seem to lack a certain grand passion that is supposedly driving Antoine and later Cecile.

As well as creating a rich, emotional landscape, Techine also successfully details the sights and sounds of Tangier, with its delicate, tension-filled mix of cultures somehow coexisting, just as the varied characters in the film. Angelique Kidjo provides the amazing vocals that add to the international flavor with the songs, "Tumba," "Okanbale," and "Les petits Riens."

Hilary White

CREDITS

Cecile: Catherine Deneuve
Antoine Lavau: Gerard Depardieu
Natan: Gilbert Melki
Sami: Malik Zidi
Nadia/Aicha: Lubna Azabal
Rachel Meyer: Tanya Lopert
Nabila: Nabila Baraka
Said: Idir Elomri
Bilal: Nadem Rachati
Said: Jabir Elomri
Origin: France
Language: French
Released: 2004
Production: Paulo Branco; France 2 Cinema, Canal Plus, CNC; released by Gemini Film
Directed by: Andre Techine
Written by: Andre Techine, Pascal Bonitzer, Laurent Guyot
Cinematography by: Julien Hirsch
Music by: Juliette Garrigues
Sound: Thierry Delo
Editing: Martine Giordano
Art Direction: Ze Branco
Costumes: Christian Gasc, Catherine Leterrier
Production Design: Ze Branco
MPAA rating: Unrated
Running time: 98 minutes

REVIEWS

Hollywood Reporter Online. February 13, 2005.
Los Angeles Times Online. August 4, 2006.
New York Times Online. July 14, 2006.
Premiere. July 13, 2006.
San Francisco Chronicle. July 21, 2006, p. E5.
Variety Online. December 16, 2004.
Village Voice Online. July 11, 2006.

QUOTES

Bilal (to lover Sami): "You're too indecisive, but I guess that's normal. You're half Moroccan, half French, half man, half woman. It must be difficult knowing who you are."

TRIVIA

Changing Times is the fourth film that Andre Techine and Catherine Denueve have made together and the seventh for Denueve and Gerard Depardieu.

CHARLOTTE'S WEB

Pig Tales.
—Movie tagline
Help Is Coming From Above.
—Movie tagline

Box Office: $81 million

The E.B. White children's classic *Charlotte's Web* has been animated or filmed before, most notably in 1973 in a cartoon version. It's a sure winner, and with the latest advances in computer graphics and animatronics, it's no surprise it's been brought to the screen again, in a technically marvelous but somewhat underwhelming version from Nickelodeon Movies.

Director Gary Winick knows not to meddle too much with White's timeless story that, improbably and marvelously, wrings true and heartfelt lessons about life and death from a tale about a friendship between a barnyard pig and a spider. Dakota Fanning is a natural for the lead human role as Fern, the girl whose belief in a pig inspires the story. Not so natural are the choices of Julia Roberts as the voice of Charlotte the spider, Steve Buscemi as Templeton the rat, John Cleese as Samuel the sheep, and Oprah Winfrey as Gussy the cow. Robert Redford and Cedric the Entertainer are also in the voice cast, and Dominic Scott Kay provides the gee-whiz little-boy's voice for Wilbur the pig. Among this casting are some puzzling celebrity choices that bespeak a project where stars drive the casting rather than the requirements of the script.

Danny Elfman, a veteran of musical scores for family films, is on hand to provide a swelling, but not overly ham-handed score that remains in the service of the story. Cinematographer Seamus McGarvey is similarly restrained, giving us sweeping idyllic rural panoramas that perfectly capture the vibrant open spaces of rural and small-town life in Maine—even though the film was inexplicably shot in Australia. And veritable legions of computer animators are on hand—the film's credits, listing them all, take up a full ten minutes of the movie's running time—yet the movie still feels a little overly long and padded.

Technically, it's a triumph. The best scenes are those in which Charlotte is first spinning the words in her web that she hopes will save Wilbur from the slaughter awaiting all pigs raised on farms. The cameras take us on a dizzying tightwire act that perfectly captures the exhilarating skill of the spider and the essence of the wonder of life that is a central motif of the story. As rendered for this movie, Charlotte is a strange but appealing creature—she looks like a little old man with whiskers. That the other barnyard animals pronounce her at first to be disgusting doesn't make sense the way she is depicted; she's just much too cute to be disgusting.

Even cuter is Wilbur, a pink and puckish little pig that looks more like a toy than a real animal. You can do wonders with CGI (computer-generated imagery) these days, and the animators capture the look and gait of all the barnyard animals. But, with Kay's voice drenched with cute precociousness and Wilbur's body rendered more like a Disney cartoon, the filmmakers start to stray from the essence of White's theme of wonderful ordinariness and give us a realm of too-perfect preciousness.

They go even farther with Templeton, who is a serviceable enough rat as far as his looks. But Buscemi pegs Templeton's scruffy orneriness with a sort of wise-guy hard-heartedness that seems more Buscemi than E.B. White. And whether we need to see Templeton's underground lair as a labyrinth of discarded junk is debatable—certainly the added excitement of Templeton being chased by a hen's egg down his tunnel is not something White thought essential.

There is an odd sort of conceptual compromise in the film: on the one hand, the story and characters are treated with a degree of reverence, but the filmmakers can't resist the temptation to make even *Charlotte's Web* into a Nickelodeon-style feature. Therefore, audiences must endure the addition of a pair of stupid crows who talk about their fear of a scarecrow, and there is even a fart joke that is the definition of egregious. Farting in *Charlotte's Web*? Don't these people get it? It's as if they wanted to hedge their bets against their belief that something as beautiful and superbly crafted as this story doesn't need fashionable tinkering.

In the end, despite some beautifully sentimental scenes, it's clear that the connection with White's unabashed but simple sentiment is strained. When the narrator talks about how the people of the county have been changed by the miracles that have occurred, you're left to wonder what that means. Either the filmmaker succeeds in showing the change so that it doesn't need to be talked about, or the movie fails.

Fanning is superb, casual, and extremely natural. Close to becoming a teenager, Fanning is such a veteran that she has an ease that colors every scene she's in. She resists every temptation to be precocious, even when the script eggs her on, and never calls attention to herself. She's comfortable letting the animatronic animals be the stars, and they are. If only the screenwriters, Susannah Grant and Karey Kirkpatrick, had showed a consistently similar restraint. Faithful to the original in most spots, they can't resist the temptation to shout out morals and to provide unwelcome diversions and detours.

Roberts makes Charlotte a monotone creature, mistaking the spider's penchant for a somewhat formal vocabulary for an absence of personality. Her Charlotte sounds too much like a sweet but courageous mom, and too little like a revolutionary free spirit. The celebrities voicing the other animals provide a bunch of barely palatable banter. The human actors playing the farmers come off as dimwitted rubes. Generally, the movie plays it safe, shying away from memorable characters and personalities and mistaking White's celebration of the splendors of ordinary life for a lack of inventiveness. *Charlotte's Web,* this time around, manages to make one of the most expertly and economically crafted tales ever written into something almost trite.

Michael Betzold

CREDITS

Fern: Dakota Fanning
Charlotte: Julia Roberts
Templeton: Steve Buscemi
Samuel: John Cleese
Wilbur: Dominic Scott Kay
Gussy: Oprah Winfrey
Golly: Cedric the Entertainer
Bitsy: Kathy Bates
Betsy: Reba McEntire
Ike: Robert Redford
Brooks: Thomas Haden Church
Elwyn: Andre Benjamin
Mr. Arable: Kevin Anderson
Mrs. Arable: Essie Davis
Homer Zuckerman: Gary Basaraba
Mrs. Zuckerman: Siobhan Fallon
Dr. Dorian: Beau Bridges
Narrator: Sam Shepard (Voice)

Origin: USA
Language: English
Released: 2006
Production: Jordan Kerner; Walden Media, Nickelodeon Movies, Kerner Entertainment Company; released by Paramount Pictures
Directed by: Gary Winick
Written by: Susannah Grant, Karey Kirkpatrick
Cinematography by: Seamus McGarvey
Music by: Danny Elfman
Sound: Ben Osmo
Editing: Susan Littenberg, Sabrina Pilsco
Art Direction: Tom Nursey
Costumes: Rita Ryack
Production Design: Stuart Wurtzel
MPAA rating: G
Running time: 96 minutes

REVIEWS

Boxoffice Online. December 15, 2006.
Chicago Sun-Times Online. December 15, 2006.
Entertainment Weekly. December 22, 2006, p. 60.
Hollywood Reporter Online. December 11, 2006.
Los Angeles Times Online. December 15, 2006.
New York Times Online. December 15, 2006.
San Francisco Chronicle. December 15, 2006, p. E1.
Variety Online. December 10, 2006.
Washington Post. December 15, 2006, p. C1.

THE CHILD
(L'Enfant)

Written and directed by brothers Luc and Jean-Pierre Dardenne, *The Child* (*L'Enfant*), which won the Golden Palm at Cannes in 2005, follows in the footsteps of their 2002 masterpiece, *The Son,* with a straightforward yet incredibly moving tale of man and morality. From the beginning credits, which roll bleakly without music, the film is striking in the fact that it contains no soundtrack, leaving only the camera to tell the story of the film's main character, Bruno.

Bruno (Jeremie Renier) is a young, low-level thief and drug dealer who spends his money as fast as he can steal it, although not always on himself. He buys a fancy pram for his nine-day-old son Jimmy as well as a snazzy leather jacket for his teenage girlfriend Sonia (Deborah Francois). Sonia has just left the hospital with their newborn son when she tracks down her wayward boyfriend and learns that they are temporarily homeless as the always-enterprising Bruno has sublet Sonia's apartment for a few days for extra cash. She spends her first night away from the hospital in a homeless shelter with a boyfriend who thinks work is for suckers. Nothing can dim her affection for Bruno, however, and when he rents a convertible for the day, they take Jimmy for a drive while they coo and cuddle and chase each other around like children in the park.

Their familial bliss is short-lived, however. Although Sonia dotes on Jimmy, Bruno views his child as just another opportunity to make a quick buck and when one of his fences casually mentions that they could make a bundle from couples wishing to adopt, it isn't long before Bruno takes her up on the offer. He finds the opportunity when Sonia asks him to take Jimmy for a walk as she stands in the long welfare line. A chilling scene depicts Bruno talking on a payphone, being directed where to go to make the exchange. A short bus ride later, Bruno takes the baby up a few flights of stairs to an empty room where he gently lays the child down on his leather jacket on the floor. His cell phone rings and he goes into the empty room next door and awaits further orders. The faceless transaction is complete when, after another call, he finds a wad of money where the child once lay. An utterly unremorseful Bruno then returns with the empty stroller and casually tells Sonia he has sold their child. Sonia passes out in shock and Bruno carries her to the hospital. Bruno has done the one thing that Sonia cannot forgive. She notifies hospital staff, launching an investigation while Bruno quickly realizes he must get the child back or face serious consequences. Telling the authorities that Sonia is just gunning for revenge, he makes the necessary calls and is quickly able to return the money and retrieve the child unharmed. Not without a hitch, however, as a man appears who informs him that they have lost a great deal of money in the transaction and Bruno must pay them back double the money—what they lost on the deal.

Although Sonia is reunited with her child, she refuses to forgive the still unrepentant Bruno—who more than once gives her the excuse that he thought they would eventually have another child—and kicks him out of her apartment. He seems lost without her but has no time to wallow in self-pity as he looks for his next easy dollar, which he finds when he sells the baby's pram and Sonia's leather jacket, which she jettisoned along with Bruno. The baby sellers have tracked him down and remind him of his still steep debt he can work off by stealing for them. He quickly gets to work, assembling his gang, which consists of two pre-adolescent boys who provide a motorbike and get a small cut for helping him. Bruno and one of the boys hop on the bike and snatch a woman's purse. He is chased by a witness. Bruno and the boy initially give them the slip but are stuck when one of the bike's tires catches on some wire fencing. They are forced to hide in the river until the pursuers pass, leaving the boy freezing and unable to continue on foot. Bruno leaves him in an abandoned building to retrieve the bike, but sees the authorities have caught up to them and discovered the boy, whom they take away.

Although Bruno knows he will get away with yet another crime, he undergoes a radical change. Unwilling to let the boy take the fall, he turns himself in, saying the whole thing was his idea. Bruno is next seen as he emerges from his prison cell to greet a visitor. It is Sonia, and in the moving final scene, the two have a tender reunion as Bruno breaks down in a flood of tears. Our knowledge of Bruno comes solely from the events onscreen, with no backstory or history offered save an awkward interaction with his estranged mother (Mireille Bailly) that suggests a troubled upbringing. His immorality seems a consequence of a harsh life, but the film's end hints at redemption.

The Dardennes never try to elicit sympathy for or justify the actions of their main character, rather they simply observe his actions in a completely nonjudgmental style to stunning effect. Renier's realistic portrayal and the simple, straightforward manner in which the story unfolds is aided by the capable cinematography of Alain Marcoen and seamless editing of the sometimes impressively long cuts by Marie-Helene Dozo.

Hilary White

CREDITS

Bruno: Jeremie Renier
Young Thug: Fabrizio Rongione
Plainclothes Officer: Olivier Gourmet
Sonia: Deborah Francois
Steve: Jeremie Segard
Thomas: Samuel de Ryck
Mere Bruno: Mireille Bailly
Origin: Belgium, France
Language: French
Released: 2005
Production: Jean-Pierre Dardenne, Luc Dardenne, Dennis Freyd; Les Films du Fleuve, Archipel 35
Directed by: Jean-Pierre Dardenne, Luc Dardenne
Written by: Jean-Pierre Dardenne, Luc Dardenne
Cinematography by: Alain Marcoen
Sound: Thomas Gauder
Editing: Marie-Helene Dozo
Costumes: Monic Parelle
MPAA rating: R
Running time: 95 minutes

REVIEWS

Boxoffice Online. March 24, 2006.
Entertainment Weekly. March 31, 2006, p. 41.
Los Angeles Times Online. March 24, 2006.
New York Times Online. March 24, 2006.
Variety Online. May 17, 2005.
Village Voice Online. March 21, 2006.

QUOTES

Bruno: "I find money, so there is no need to hang onto it."

TRIVIA

Jeremie Renier made his film debut in the Dardennes' film *La Promesse* (1996).

CHILDREN OF MEN

No children. No future. No hope.
—Movie tagline
The last one to die please turn out the light.
—Movie tagline
The future's a thing of the past.
—Movie tagline

Box Office: $34.9 million

The human race is heading towards the finish line in *Children of Men*, on its last lap and about to lapse due to universal infertility, ferocious instability, and nightmarish inhumanity. Ground down by underlying anxieties and an overwhelming sense of despair, the Earth's disconsolate final generations live out their lives amidst sudden, fiery eruptions of violent discontent in an otherwise grey, deadened world. In the middle of all this doom and suffocating gloom, a character is asked how he can remain so calm, seemingly unaware of the oblivion looming on the horizon. The man's solution is to simply not think about what might lie ahead, something the film's director and co-writer Alfonso Cuaron is unwilling to do. Many people comfort themselves with the reassuring notion that what truly frightens us is either unlikely or far off, but what makes this cautionary tale, loosely based upon best-selling author P.D. James's 1992 detour from mystery into dystopic science fiction, so potently unsettling is that it takes place a mere twenty-one years away in a world appearing not quite far enough removed from our own to allow for a consoling sense of detachment. Cuaron's almost ceaselessly somber, thoughtful and thought-provoking film is a riveting, suspenseful stunner, filled with thoroughly chilling images of decay and uniformly bleak, chilly skies.

Both James's novel and Cuaron's adaptation begin with the death of a teenager who was humanity's last successful birth, a celebrity due to his significance who was murdered upon refusing to sign an autograph. The hopeful sound of a newborn's cry has not been heard since his birth eighteen years before, due perhaps to environmental changes and pollutants or some insidious, destructive virus—worries not unfamiliar to current audiences. This mysterious and dispiriting development has apparently brought out the worst in people and exacerbated existing tensions. Terror and chaos reign throughout much of the world, with England preserving some semblance of order by clamping down on its society with dictatorial muscle.

The film's first scenes take place in the London of 2027, still with recognizable landmarks, familiar double-decker bus-dotted traffic, and an abundance of its popular pubs and coffeehouses, one of which is destroyed by a startling, concussive blast mere moments into the film. Narrowly avoiding ending up like (or even worse than) the hysterical woman grasping her severed arm is the film's haggard, world-weary and decidedly reluctant hero, Theo Faron (well-cast Clive Owen). The deafening explosion is a shocking, impossible-to-ignore manifestation of people's uneasiness. The city streets are carelessly littered with trash and purposefully defiled with graffiti. One cannot help but notice the people who angrily pelt passing trains with rocks, and even more disturbing are the sidewalk cages crammed with refugees who have been rounded up by the suspicious, omnipresent armed policemen and their snarling dogs. This inhumanely confined humanity, often begging for mercy through the fencing, reminds one of Jewish suffering during the Nazi Holocaust, especially since these people are also being transported to camps. A subversive group called the Fishes is fighting an upstream battle against such oppression. Formerly politically active Theo might now be joining them if he had not lost his only child to the flu pandemic of 2008 and since escaped into self-protective apathy.

With cigarettes and a flask to assist him, Theo works at the Ministry of Energy, ironic since he seems particularly drained of it himself. For some solace, he ventures far out into the countryside, where his vibrant and eccentric old friend, Jasper (a memorable, long-haired, air-guitar-playing Michael Caine), provides much-needed comic relief and, along with the forests which surround his secluded home, a welcome bit of color. Jasper, a former political cartoonist and still something of a hippie, finds comfort in 1960s music and homegrown hallucinogens as his beloved wife, a photojournalist tortured out of her career and her mind, stares blankly from a wheelchair.

Back in the city, Theo is abruptly thrown into a passing van by some masked men and spirited off to meet with Julian Taylor (Julianne Moore), the leader of the Fishes and the mother of his little boy, whose death apparently tore their relationship apart. She offers him a hefty 5,000 pounds sterling if he will use his connections to secure vital transport papers, which will get a certain girl past multiple security checkpoints on her way to the coast. Julian stresses the money, apparently knowing what is likely nowadays to motivate Theo. It seems to work, as he goes off to see his wealthy, elite cousin, Nigel (Danny Huston) who high-mindedly rescues some of the world's greatest works of art for a collection no one will soon be around to see. Theo is only able to obtain papers that will require him to accompany the traveler. He agrees, but only in exchange for more money.

The person to be transported turns out to be an initially surly black girl named Kee (Clare-Hope Ashitey), who does indeed turn out to be the key to everything, as she is pregnant. It is a seemingly miraculous development but, viewers learn, far from another Immaculate Conception. Still, it is undoubtedly no accident that more than one character, staring with astonished awe and near reverence at her big belly, utters the words "Jesus Christ!" If Kee is gotten safely to the mysterious and ultra-secret Human Project, mankind will be saved. (It was especially hard to miss these religious undertones since the film opened in the U.S. on Christmas Day.)

The fact that Kee may go into labor at any moment makes her safe passage through treacherous territory seem all the more pressing and perilous, generating apprehension and anxious anticipation in those watching. There are numerous surprising and often quite harrowing events along the way, including double-crosses and reversals of fortune, which ratchet-up the tension as the plot races thrillingly forward.

As Theo sets out with Kee, Julian, and fellow Fishes Luke (Chiwetel Ejiofor) and midwife Miriam (Pam Ferris), some initial, lighthearted playfulness is shattered when they are suddenly attacked and pursued. Julian, her throat just filled with laughter but now pierced by a gunshot wound, dies bloodily in her seat as the speeding car races to outdistance those chasing it, which eventually include the police. A unique camera rig was created to swivel around and view all the occupants inside as well as what is transpiring outside without having to resort to any cutting. Thus, this highly laudable, twelve-minute-long continuous take seems especially realistic and acutely alarming for those watching, as if they too are surrounded and imperiled. That the car is not only tiny but cramped and traveling on a narrow road with tall, dense woods on either side only adds to this feeling of entrapment.

Other memorable scenes in *Children of Men* include Miriam's eerie and poignant recollection within an obsolete schoolhouse of when the sounds of children disappeared, and Jasper's paying with his life for the indispensable help he courageously provides. With the death of Jasper and that of Julian, a clearly-affected Theo has now lost everyone who has meant anything to him, and his outrage shatters his apathy and spurs him on to assertive, resolute action. Kee informs him of Julian's assertion that he was the only person who could be trusted implicitly. Theo will neither let down the woman he loved nor Kee and the world's last hope.

The film's most powerfully disconcerting sequence takes place during the thunderous, cataclysmic uprising in the coastal refugee camp where Theo has just helped Kee deliver her baby girl. Further use of extended shots and George Richmond's roving handheld camera make viewers feel as if they too are in a desperate, terrifying search for safety amongst all the bullets and blasts.

Children of Men began with the end of the world in sight but ends with what appears to be a hopeful new beginning. Theo rows Kee and her tiny girl to a buoy in foggy waters nearby, where they hope to rendezvous with the Human Project. The two still do not know if the group even actually exists. While waiting expectantly, Kee is horrified to see that she is filling the small, bobbing boat with blood, but it is actually coming from a wounded Theo. Having valiantly done all he could for her, and now offering some kind reassurance and almost fatherly advice, he is rewarded with Kee's heartwarming naming of her daughter after his son. With a contented smile, Theo slumps over and dies just as a ship becomes visible through the mist. The Human Project's vessel, slicing through the gloom to the rescue, bears the name Tomorrow, symbolism which seems meant to convey the hopeful notion that tomorrow will bring good things. Another apparently positive sign: as the film's title appears onscreen before the credits roll, it is accompanied by the sound of children's laughter.

Made on a budget of approximately $72 million, *Children of Men* struggled to gross half of that despite glowing reviews. It justly earned a number of nominations and awards, including Oscar® nominations for its adapted screenplay, cinematography, and editing. Besides Cuaron, kudos go especially to director of photography Emmanuel Lubezki and production designers Jim Clay and Geoffrey Kirkland. Work on the script for *Children of Men* continued over nine years in which the world became a much more uncertain and uneasy place. War, stunning new levels of terrorism, increasingly obvious global warming, and the challenges brought on by significant geographic shifts in population are just some of the things which have made the planet more turbulent and toxic. Such developments informed the writing of a story which ends up seeming all too plausible, hitting uncomfortably close to home. With his film, Cuaron said he hoped to make people face "the circumstances today that are crafting our future."

David L. Boxerbaum

CREDITS

Theo Faron: Clive Owen
Julian Taylor: Julianne Moore
Jasper: Michael Caine
Luke: Chiwetel Ejiofor
Patric: Charlie Hunnam
Miriam: Pam Ferris
Nigel: Danny Huston
Syd: Peter Mullan
Kee: Clare-Hope Ashitey
Origin: USA
Language: English
Released: 2006
Production: Marc Abraham, Eric Newman, Hilary Shor; Hit and Run Music, Strike Entertainment, Ingenious Media Partners, Toho-Towa; released by Universal Pictures
Directed by: Alfonso Cuaron
Written by: Alfonso Cuaron, Timothy J. Sexton
Cinematography by: Emmanuel Lubezki
Sound: David Evans
Editing: Alfonso Cuaron, Alex Rodriguez
Art Direction: Gary Freeman, Malcolm Middleton
Costumes: Jany Temime
Production Design: Jim Clay, Geoffrey Kirkland
MPAA rating: R
Running time: 108 minutes

REVIEWS

Boston Globe Online. December 25, 2006.
Boxoffice Online. December 25, 2006.
Hollywood Reporter Online. September 4, 2006.
Los Angeles Times Online. December 22, 2006.
New York Times Online. December 25, 2006.
Premiere Magazine Online. December 27, 2006.
San Francisco Chronicle. December 25, 2006, p. C2.
Variety Online. September 3, 2006.
Village Voice Online. December 19, 2006.
Washington Post. December 25, 2006, p. C1.

AWARDS

British Acad. 2006: Cinematog
Nomination:
Oscars 2006: Adapt. Screenplay, Cinematog., Film Editing
British Acad. 2006: Visual FX

CLERKS II

No Experience Necessary.
—Movie tagline

No Missions, No Mutants, No Man of Steel, No Money, and No Bullshit Catchphrases.
—Movie tagline

Standing for Truth. Standing for Justice. Standing Around.
—Movie tagline

They Still Don't Like You. In Fact, They Like You Even Less.
—Movie tagline

With no power comes no responsibility.
—Movie tagline

Box Office: $24.1 million

Clerks (1994), the black-and-white, micro-budget cult hit that launched writer/director Kevin Smith's career, gets a slick, color update with the sequel, *Clerks II*, a dozen years later. The four main characters reprise their roles and Smith retains the original's love affair with hilarious pop culture patter, raunchy sex jokes, and the angst of growing older in the world of the minimum-wage register jockey. With the apt working title *The Passion of the Clerks*, within this sequel actually lurks a romantic comedy, with the thirty-something protagonists Dante Hicks and Randal Graves also managing to find careers they can be passionate about. Some early scenes fall flat with forced dialogue and wooden delivery and it takes a while to build up steam, but once it does *Clerks II* surely won't disappoint any of Smith's die-hard fans.

Fans of *Clerk*'s will remember New Jersey's Dante (Brian O'Halloran) and Randal (Jeff Anderson) are the titular clerks, biding time at the Quick Stop convenience mart and the video store next door, respectively. The sequel cleverly begins in black-and-white as Dante drives up to the Quick Stop to open its familiar roll-up steel door revealing a raging, colorized fire behind it. The boys are then forced into flipping burgers at nearby bovine-themed fast food joint Mooby's. Little else changes, however, with the somewhat more ambitious Dante and his obnoxious, customer-harassing pal Randal, engaging in a lot of meaningless dissection of life, sex, and the world in general. Dante, however, is looking forward to finally getting a fresh start with his controlling fiancee, a sort of Martha Stewart on speed, Emma Bunting (played by Smith's real-life wife, Jennifer Schwalbach Smith), who has planned jobs and a new life for them in Florida.

Dante, however, is not immune to the considerable charms of Mooby's manager Becky Scott (Rosario Dawson), an independent, free-spirited Latin beauty. Becky, rather inexplicably, likes Dante too, and in-between toenail-painting sessions (hers), they refer to a night of passion they had on the restaurant's prep table after closing. Dawson's presence is refreshing, bringing a much-needed seriousness and respectability to the otherwise silly proceedings.

Randal, meanwhile, enjoys torturing their nineteen-year-old co-worker and rabid *Lord of the Rings* fan Elias (Trevor Fehrman). Coming from a strict Evangelical Christian family, the ridiculously naive virgin that is Elias couldn't be any more ripe for the cynical Randal's barbs and the two make wonderfully comedic foils. One particularly creative exchange revealing Elias's utter lack of basic sexual knowledge leaves the never-at-a-loss-for-words Randal utterly speechless.

Of course, no *Clerks* film would be complete with drug dealer Jay (Jason Mewes) and his mute sidekick Silent Bob (director Smith). Smith provides a delicious twist on the characters, imagining they were court-ordered to rehab where they converted to Christianity. Jay wears a Jesus t-shirt while Silent Bob is able to produce a Bible on command. Just as they stood watch outside the Quick Stop trying to scare up business, they stand sentinel outside Mooby's, proffering drugs and religious advice; A. O. Scott, of the *New York Times*, noting their dual "function as Greek chorus and comic relief."

The bare bones plot has Dante impregnating Becky and being forced to choose between his likeable but clearly mismatched fiancee and the boss he's actually in love with. Randal's miffed that Dante wants to leave him and sad because he has no other friends or anything at all to occupy his time. The donkey show he hires for Dante's going away party lands the boys in jail where they decide that Dante should stay and marry Becky and that Randal and he should buy the burned out Quick Stop and run it themselves with money borrowed from Jay and Silent Bob.

Some of the film's best and most enjoyable scenes involve heated geek-speak debates on such topics as: Which trilogy is better, *The Lord of the Rings* or *Star Wars*? Randal offers his pro-*Star Wars* view on the *Rings* films: "They're three movies about walking!" While Smith never provides the definitive answer, he vehemently portrays Randal as the superior debater, his homoerotic thoughts on Frodo and Sam causing the rival Hobbit Lover (Kevin Weisman) to "refund" his milkshake. Dante is forced to explain the difference between Anne Frank and Helen Keller to a clueless Randal, who nonetheless makes reference to the "deaf" Anne Frank until the film's end. *Entertainment Weekly*'s Owen Gleiberman says that the film's characteristic talkiness is "so smart about being stupid that the characters' verbosity becomes, in every sense their saving grace." Other highlights include the boys go-carting to the tune of "Raindrops Keep Fallin' on My Head." And a surprisingly fun musical number erupts, utilizing the

Jackson 5's "ABC" while Becky teaches Dante how to dance on the restaurant's roof.

There are several, especially tasteless, belabored gags. The grueling and offensive scene of "interspecies erotica" with a donkey and his skinhead handler being the most obvious. There is an unsuccessful attempt to make it somewhat more palatable with a heartfelt speech from the handler. Also, a reference to a particular oral sex act is a running gag mentioned at least a dozen times.

While the focus is on the main characters, Smith still parades a string of colorful customers to add passing interest. Jason Lee has the largest of these as an obnoxious former classmate of Dante and Randal's, who shows up to rub his millionaire status in their blue-collar noses. Ben Affleck wears a moustache in his blink-and-you'll miss it walk-on. Wanda Sykes' outraged customer, incensed into leaving by Randal's "porch monkey" comment, is the film's funniest, however.

For those who think it's all superficial nonsense, Smith does tackle such topics as misspent youth, true love, lasting friendship, the definition of success, and religion, among others. He also brings the franchise to a nice close. Coming full circle, the director bookends the film with a black-and-white final scene with Dante and Randal at their beloved Quick Stop.

Hilary White

CREDITS

Dante Hicks: Brian O'Halloran
Randal Graves: Jeff Anderson
Jay: Jason Mewes
Becky Scott: Rosario Dawson
Silent Bob: Kevin Smith
Emma Bunting: Jennifer Schwalbach Smith
Lance Dowds: Jason Lee
Teen #2: Ethan Suplee
Elias Grover: Trevor Fehrman
Hobbit Lover: Kevin Weisman
Wife: Wanda Sykes
Gawking guy: Ben Affleck (Cameo)
Origin: USA
Language: English
Released: 2006
Production: Kevin Smith, Scott Mosier; View Askew; released by Weinstein Co.
Directed by: Kevin Smith
Written by: Kevin Smith
Cinematography by: David Klein
Music by: James L. Venable
Sound: Whit Norris
Editing: Kevin Smith
Art Direction: Marc Fisichella
Costumes: Roseanne Fiedler
Production Design: Robert Holtzman
MPAA rating: R
Running time: 98 minutes

REVIEWS

Associated Press Online. July 17, 2006.
Boxoffice Online. July 21, 2006.
Chicago Sun-Times Online. July 21, 2006.
Entertainment Weekly. July 28, 2006, p. 44.
Los Angeles Times Online. July 21, 2006.
New York Times Online. July 21, 2006.
San Francisco Chronicle. July 21, 2006, p. E5.
Variety Online. May 28, 2006.
Village Voice Online. July 18, 2006.
Washington Post. July 21, 2006, p. C1.

QUOTES

Randal: "Hey, there is only one 'Return' and it's not 'of the King,' it's 'of the Jedi.'"

CLICK

What If You Had A Universal Remote...That Controlled Your Universe?
—Movie tagline

Box Office: $137.3 million

Imagine a remake of *It's a Wonderful Life* (1946) in which Adam Sandler takes on the James Stewart role of George Bailey. In this new version, however, the hero is not a thwarted adventurer whose communal obligations prevent him from living the life he wants but rather a workaholic whose career and family responsibilities are constantly in conflict. *Click*, directed by Frank Coraci from a script by Steve Koren and Mark O'Keefe, is not a direct remake of the Frank Capra classic, but it does bear a strong resemblance in its plot and theme, if not its sensibility—an update of sorts for multitasking professionals being pulled in too many directions at once. *Click* was produced by Sandler's company, and it bears the stamp of his adolescent high jinks, flatulence humor, and raunch, but it also tries to say something serious about leading a worthwhile life. And ultimately the two sides, the juvenile and the adult, clash in a very awkward, unsettling, and unsatisfying way.

Sandler has been at his most adult in films that he did not have a hand in producing, namely *Punch-Drunk Love* (2002) and *Spanglish* (2004), but perhaps, as he advances into middle age the purely childish shtick needs to be tempered with some maturity. The combination in *Click*, however, never quite works. Just as it was a stretch to see Sandler as a world-class chef in *Spanglish*, it is hard to see him as a successful architect in *Click*. But even though his Michael Newman has a good job, loving parents (Henry Winkler and Julie Kavner), a beautiful wife named Donna (Kate Beckinsale), and two adorable children, his life seems to be in chaos. Working long hours to impress his smarmy boss, John Ammer (David Hasselhoff), Michael is constantly chasing after a promotion that always seems just out of reach.

The symbols of his constant frustration are the array of remote controls that clutter his living room and only add to his confusion when he wants to turn on the TV and inadvertently turns on something else. Seeking a universal remote to simplify his life, he goes to Bed Bath & Beyond and stumbles upon a back room presided over by a mysterious fellow named Morty (Christopher Walken in mad scientist garb that seems to be an homage to Christopher Lloyd's Doc from the *Back to the Future* films [1985, 1989, and 1990]). He introduces the hapless Michael to a one-of-a-kind universal remote free of charge with the stipulation that it can never be returned. The remote, however, is not a regular household gadget but rather a magical device that, Michael soon discovers, enables him to take control of his environment in a variety of ways, including muting the noise around him, visiting key moments from his past as if they were chapters on a DVD, freezing time, and fast-forwarding through life's tough moments, such as fights with his wife.

The scenario allows Sandler to engage in all the buffoonery we might expect from this overgrown kid, including freezing his boss and hitting him repeatedly so he has a big headache and farting in his face after he delays Michael's big promotion. Such lowbrow humor is indicative of Sandler's style, and the movie also has running jokes about the family dog humping a stuffed animal and Michael racing through sex only to leave his wife unsatisfied. But all of the vulgarity plays uneasily against the serious story of a man trying to be a model employee while agonizing over the time he is missing with his family.

The remote, of course, in allowing him to control time, only makes him miss out on the small joys of family life. And eventually the fantasy of control turns into a nightmare when Michael, desperate for the promotion, has the remote fast-forward to the big day, resulting in the loss of more than a year. Then the device goes on autopilot and fast-forwards at will according to the preferences Michael has already indicated. He loses whole chunks of his life; his children grow up without him really knowing them, his wife leaves him and remarries, and his father passes away without Michael appreciating him near the end. Morty, it turns out, is not some wacky scientist but rather the angel of death (the root of his name should have been a clue).

The scenes of an older Michael facing not only morbid obesity (Sandler in a gross fat suit), illness, and even death but also the realization that he drifted away from the people he loved most are, at times, very moving. But these sequences are also such a bizarre, even disturbing turn from Sandler's sophomoric antics in the first part of the movie that it is almost hard to take them seriously. It is as if the film were designed to cater to Sandler's adolescent base while giving him a chance to flex some dramatic muscle at the end with some dark and depressing material lodged into an otherwise goofball film, but the result is not persuasive or coherent. The film's moral—enjoy life and the people you love while you can instead of living your life on autopilot—is hard to argue with but is undercut by the silliness and crudeness that precede it.

If *Click* leads the audience through so many cliches and a trite message, it ends on one of the stalest of narrative devices, the cop-out that it was all a dream. Michael dreamed everything when he fell asleep on a bed at Bed Bath & Beyond, which means that he still has time to mend his ways, which he does. Like George Bailey before him, Michael had to learn that he really did have a wonderful life all along.

Sandler delivers what we would expect from his man-child persona, but he needs a strong director like *Punch-Drunk Love*'s Paul Thomas Anderson to bring out his more poignant side. Beckinsale is beautiful—even in Donna's older years, she is stunning—but does not have much to do beyond grow more and more frustrated with a marriage that is not what she had hoped it would be. Walken, however, brings a bit of his menacing charm to the otherwise familiar mad scientist role.

The most salient aspect of *Click* may be that it is an attempt, albeit a very flawed one, to cast Sandler in a role in which he can indulge the anarchic impulses that have made him a bankable star while giving his character genuine adult responsibilities and issues. The screenplay cannot master this tough balancing act, but perhaps successfully mixing the two is nearly impossible. The end result finally makes us wonder if Sandler can segue into more mature roles after building a screen persona on bratty, childish behavior. If he does, it will take far more accomplished than the sloppy if well-meaning *Click*.

Peter N. Chumo II

CREDITS

Michael Newman: Adam Sandler
Donna Newman: Kate Beckinsale

Morty: Christopher Walken
Bill: Sean Astin
John Ammer: David Hasselhoff
Ted: Henry Winkler
Trudy: Julie Kavner
Janine: Jennifer Coolidge
Origin: USA
Language: English
Released: 2006
Production: Adam Sandler, Jack Giarraputo, Neal H. Moritz, Steve Koren, Mark O'Keefe; Columbia Pictures, Revolution Studios, Happy Madison Productions, Original Film; released by Sony Pictures Entertainment
Directed by: Frank Coraci
Written by: Mark O'Keefe, Steve Koren
Cinematography by: Dean Semler
Music by: Rupert Gregson-Williams
Sound: Jeffrey J. Haboush, Bill W. Benton
Editing: Jeff Gourson
Art Direction: Alan Au, Jeff Mossa
Costumes: Ellen Lutter
Production Design: Perry Andelin Blake
MPAA rating: PG-13
Running time: 98 minutes

REVIEWS

Boxoffice Online. June 23, 2006.
Chicago Sun-Times Online. June 23, 2006.
Entertainment Weekly Online. July 5, 2006.
Los Angeles Times Online. June 23, 2006.
New York Times Online. June 23, 2006.
Premiere Magazine Online. June 21, 2006.
Variety Online. June 22, 2006.
Washington Post. June 23, 2006, p. C1.

QUOTES

Morty (about Michael): "He's always chasing the pot of gold, but when he gets there, at the end of the day, it's just corn flakes."

TRIVIA

The lead singer of the Cranberries, Dolores O'Riordan, cameos as the singer who sings "Linger" at Ben's wedding.

AWARDS

Nomination:

Oscars 2006: Makeup

CLIMATES

(Iklimler)

Celebrated Turkish filmmaker Nuri Bilge Ceylan's serious depiction of the breakup of a contemporary romance, *Climates* (*Iklimler*), proves that in the arena of global filmic realism, silences are indeed golden. On a flippant level, one could argue that there are less subtitles to read; on a deeper level, however, in Ceylan's expert hands, we can see that these are not momentary breakdowns in communication, but silences that trap their victims.

The silences between the craggy-faced Isa (Ceylan), who is in his forties, and the childlike Bahar (Ebru Ceylan, his wife), who is much younger, reflect a plane of stasis, a floundering of an intimacy that at one time must have generated a bond of psycho-sexual compatibility. They are both successful in what they do: he as a professor of architecture and she as an art director working in television; it is just their emotional life that we see falling apart.

We first see them in the midst of historical ruins as Isa is photographing the colonnades and Bahar is standing a good distance away, looking at him pensively. It is only later that we come to know that what is plaguing her is Isa's disloyalty. In the harsh sunlight of their summer vacation, it hangs over them like a metaphysical cloud. As Bahar gazes at Isa, a tear spreads across her cheek, possibly out of self-pity.

While dining al fresco at a friend's summer retreat, Bahar remains sullen. The next day, while she's sunbathing on a beach, Isa suggests that it would be better if they lived apart for some time; they could still be friends. Bahar answers that she wouldn't mind that, as long as they didn't have to be friends. Isa then apologizes for a "meaningless" fling he had with Serap, someone we know only by name at this stage. But for Bahar it is clearly a festering wound. Isa is even prepared to allow her the license he has enjoyed: "You're young. You're attractive. You can get all the men you want." But Bahar only smirks.

This resentment simmering inside Bahar, expressed more through her silences than in what she says, can be seen as part indignance and part frustration. It explodes when she is riding pinion on a scooter on a scenic stretch of a hill road. She suddenly blinds Isa by putting her hands over his eyes, which sends them both veering off. Neither is hurt, but it causes Isa to rage that if she wants to kill herself, he will gladly throw her off the precipice, which he almost does. After shoving him away, Bahar walks off, sobbing. At a bus station Isa hands her a ticket to Istanbul and mentions that they could get together in the big city. She however rejects this option, clearly wanting nothing more to do with him.

Isa returns to the temple ruins, with their majestic columns, lies down, looking almost defeated by the past. The ruins could be representing his lost ideal of a love life. In Istanbul, Isa puts on a cheerful face at work. At a multistoried bookstore, a symbol of Turkey's glitzy consumer culture, he bumps into a friend whose girlfriend turns out to be Serap (Nazan Kirilmis). His friend clearly knows nothing about their liaison. That night we see Isa waiting in the shadows outside her building. Serap sees him as she is about to enter her apartment. She walks in, closes the door behind her, bolts it shut but remains frozen in indecision, as if contemplating the gravity of the situation. When she does open the door at last, Isa is right there.

Isa's cool demeanor doesn't last long. In the film's only erotic scene, he abandons it for a macho-style, almost Neanderthal overpowering of the worldly-wise Serap in an act that borders on rape. As if to drive home his domination, in the throes of love play, he forces into her mouth a nut that has fallen on the floor, which she had earlier refused to eat.

The scenes that follow, Isa with his parents, colleagues, and a friend, only serve to sketch further the background to Isa's life. They do nothing for the film's dramatic quotient, nor do they lift Isa out of the doldrums he is clearly experiencing after losing Bahar. It is only when he decides to fly to a wintry town, where she is shooting, that the film picks up its emotional thread.

Isa and Bahar reunite in the middle of a snowy street outside her hotel. Isa's pleading smile is all it takes for Bahar to smile back. Her new busy life without him seems to have cleansed her of the bitterness she had been harboring when we last saw her. This is an all-new Bahar, who looks the same but with a life of her own, in which the only time she can spare for Isa, even though he has traveled all that distance to see her, is for a quick coffee. Isa wanders through the town by himself, as forlorn as the landscape, either unable to accept the change in Bahar or having seen through it.

When he barges into her van on location, she is sitting by herself, sobbing, as if his mere presence has wiped out the freedom she had been enjoying the four months they had been apart. On his part, he confesses that he has changed completely and so, wants her to quit her job and fly back with him to Istanbul. This makes her weep. Isa speaks of making a fresh start, of getting married and having kids. For Bahar, it seems, it is more of the past. She then snaps out of it to ask him pointedly if he has seen Serap again. He lies that he hasn't. She clearly doesn't believe him. As he leaves, he looks back to see her laughing to herself.

Then, as if in the throes of indecision, she visits Isa in his hotel room. She says nothing as she enters, but proceeds to lie down on the bed. Isa kneels down in silence, his head at her feet. Without exchanging a word, they lie beside each other, both finding an unspoken bond as victims of a fate neither can change, and one that will require them to part ways, maybe forever.

Vivek Adarkar

CREDITS

Isa: Nuri Bilge Ceylan
Bahar: Ebru Ceylan
Serap: Nazan Kirilmis
Mehmet: Mehmet Eryilmaz
Arif: Arif Asci
Guven: Can Ozbatur
Origin: France, Turkey
Language: Turkish
Released: 2006
Production: Zeybeo Ozbatur, CO Production; Pyramide Productions; released by Zeitgeist Films
Directed by: Nuri Bilge Ceylan
Written by: Nuri Bilge Ceylan
Cinematography by: Gokhan Tiryaki
Sound: Olivier Do Huu, Ismail Karades, Thomas Robert
Editing: Nuri Bilge Ceylan, Ayhan Ergursel
MPAA rating: Unrated
Running time: 97 minutes

REVIEWS

Hollywood Reporter Online. May 22, 2006.
Los Angeles Times Online. November 10, 2006.
New York Times Online. October 27, 2006.
Variety Online. May 21, 2006.
Village Voice Online. October 24, 2006.

THE COVENANT

In 1692, five families with untold power formed a covenant of silence. One family, lusting for more, was banished, their bloodline disappearing without a trace. Until now.
—Movie tagline

Box Office: $23.3 million

Renny Harlin's *The Covenant* was the third post-Labor Day release in September of 2006 to deny special screenings for reviewers. Both the *Washington Post* and the *New York Times* exacted payback for this critical slight by sniping ridicule after paying the price of admission. Desson Thomson's *Washington Post* review, for example, bore the title "Pecs Bad Boys" because all of the "Covenant" insiders were teen heartthrobs sporting "six-pack abs, gel-glopped hair, major pec definition, and ivory-perfect teeth." The movie was obviously designed for an audience of randy teenagers out for thrills and chills. It starts out with the boys having fun at a roadhouse somewhere in New England before the plot takes several improbable (and unconvincing) turns. The plot supposedly concerns witchcraft carried over from the seventeenth century. So the movie is a would-be supernatural thriller. All the boys of the Covenant are possessed of supernatural powers. That's the good news; the bad news is that the more they exercise their powers, the more rapidly they age, and using their powers, they have discovered, can be seductive.

Lead warlock Caleb Danvers (Steven Strait), therefore, constantly argues restraint, even though, early in the film, the boys use their combined powers foolishly to levitate their Humvee in order to elude a police chase. This makes no sense whatsoever, of course, other than to demonstrate to the viewers what the boys are presumably capable of doing, and to alert the audience that when the power is exercised, the boy's eyes turn red and light up in a distinctive and potentially disturbing way. Caleb inherited the power from his father, now old and worn out way before his time at the age of forty-four, living the life of a vegetative prune in a spooky house on the outskirts of town. Some of Caleb's young friends are reckless and irresponsible. Their inherited power is traced back to five families from colonial New England, all involved in the famous Salem witch-hunts. Since there are only four boys in the Covenant, the viewer can see trouble coming. It comes in the person of new student Chase Collins (Sebastian Stan), whose abuse of power disturbs the universe. Caleb first suspects his colleagues, Tyler Sims (Chace Crawford), Reid Garwin (Toby Hemingway), and Pogue Parry (Taylor Kitsch). However, when Pogue is injured in a mysterious motorcycle accident, Caleb begins to search for other solutions. All the boys are enrolled in a prep school, the Spenser Academy, which physically resembles the school of wizardry in the Harry Potter films. In fact, the shadow of Harry Potter looms large over this whole intellectually stunted enterprise.

All the boys except Caleb live on campus. Caleb lives at home to look after his mother (Wendy Crewson), who is a lush but means well. Caleb finds a new friend in Sarah Wenham (Laura Ramsey), who eventually becomes a pawn in Chase's scheme to blackmail Caleb. Chase methodically goes after all of Caleb's friends. Pogue is hospitalized because he attempted to help his friend and Sarah's roommate, Kate Tunney (Jessica Lucas), has a "spider spell" cast on her by wicked Chase. Chase first uses his power against Caleb when the two of them are competing in a freestyle swimming contest, causing Caleb to knock himself unconscious by hitting his head on the side of the swimming pool.

A showdown is therefore inevitable. Chase demands that Caleb surrender his power when he "ascends" to it on his eighteenth birthday (whatever that means); otherwise, Chase threatens to kill Sarah, Caleb's mom, and his three Covenant friends. Caleb refuses, of course, and the two do battle at the end, attacking each other with what appear to be toxic jellyfish. Caleb is just about defeated when his mom goes to his father and begs him to "will" Caleb his power, even though to do so may kill the father. The father makes this sacrifice, and Caleb defeats Chase, who probably escapes to fight another day (and to make a sequel). As Desson Thomson described it, "Nothing hurts them. They can fly. And the music never stops."

The reviews were laughable. Nathan Lee wrote a parody of a review in teenspeak that appeared in the *New York Times* the day after the film opened. This review refused to summarize the plot, choosing instead to describe the ridiculous action, including the "super cheesy" effects, "like at the end, when Caleb is fighting the evil transfer student, they fly around a barn and throw magic Jell-O at each other." Or how about "where these spiders crawl all over this girl and go in her nose and stuff." *The Washington Post* was not at all inclined to take the film seriously, either. Reviewer Desson Thomson at least made a half-hearted attempt to describe the framework as an "uninspired composite of X-Men and the Harry Potter series." J. S. Cardone wrote the uninspired, imitative screenplay. Director Renny Harlin is best known as an action director, after making *Cliffhanger* (1993) and *Die Hard 2: Die Harder* (1990). *The Covenant,* then, was a summer release that just wasn't quite good enough to be a summer release, but not quite bad enough to go directly to video. The irony was that it was good enough to be the top-grossing film the weekend it opened. Even so, its weekend total was only a puny $8.9 million. Casting a basically unknown cast can't have been expensive, so a sequel is probably inevitable by Hollywood logic, but it will be nothing to look forward to.

James M. Welsh

CREDITS

Caleb Danvers: Steven Strait
Sarah Wenham: Laura Ramsey
Evelyn Danvers: Wendy Crewson
Chase Collins: Sebastian Stan
Pogue Parry: Taylor Kitsch
Reid Garwin: Toby Hemingway
Kate Tunney: Jessica Lucas
Tyler Sims: Chace Crawford
Origin: USA

Language: English
Released: 2006
Production: Tom Rosenberg, Gary Lucchesi; Lakeshore Entertainment, Screen Gems; released by Sony Pictures
Directed by: Renny Harlin
Written by: J.S. Cardone
Cinematography by: Pierre Gill
Music by: Tomandandy
Sound: Claude Letessier
Music Supervisor: Michael Friedman
Editing: Nicolas De Toth
Art Direction: Pierre Perrault
Costumes: April Napier
Production Design: Anne Pritchard
MPAA rating: PG-13
Running time: 97 minutes

REVIEWS

Boston Globe Online. September 9, 2006.
Entertainment Weekly. September 22, 2006, p. 72.
Hollywood Reporter Online. September 11, 2006.
New York Times Online. September 9, 2006.
Variety Online. September 8, 2006.
Washington Post. September 9, 2006, p. C6.

CRANK

Poison in his veins, Vengeance in his heart.
—Movie tagline

There are a thousand ways to raise your adrenaline. Today, Chev Chelios will need every single one.
—Movie tagline

Box Office: $27.8 million

Catering to the modern ADD filmgoer, *Crank* (2006) is an adrenaline-rush chase film, revenge-thriller cocktail mixed with equal parts *Speed* (1994) and *D.O.A.* (1950) with a little of *The Blues Brothers* (1980) thrown in for extra flavor. Written and directed by Mark Neveldine and Brian Taylor, *Crank* has a breakneck pace reminiscent of the coked-up urgency in the last twenty minutes of Martin Scorsese's *GoodFellas* (1990). A fun adrenaline-pumping actioner that revels in its video game roots rather than denying them, the film starts with a video-game scoreboard on screen even before the opening credits roll. In fact the music, which includes such rock anthems as Quiet Riot's "Metal Health," and Loverboy's "Turn Me Loose" could almost be used as a video-game soundtrack. Unlike overwrought video game films such as *Doom* (2005) and *Resident Evil* (2002), *Crank* constantly reminds the audience that they are essentially watching a video game come to life. Neveldine and Taylor make no bones about it. There is something refreshing about that honesty and forthrightness that endears itself to the audience right away.

Jason Statham is Chev Chelios, a mafia hitman who wakes up in his Los Angeles apartment the morning after carrying out an assigned hit on Chinese mob boss Dom Kim. His vision is blurred and he is having a hard time keeping his balance. He stumbles into his living room where he finds his television on and a DVD in front of it with the hand-written words "F**k You." He plays the DVD, which reveals the face of rival gang leader Verona (Jose Pablo Cantillo), who informs him that he has injected him with a poison called a Beijing Cocktail that will kill him in one hour.

Chev speeds through the streets of Los Angeles and calls his girlfriend Eve (Amy Smart), but as usual she is not answering, so he leaves an exasperated message. He then tries to contact his quirky underworld doctor friend Miles (a perfectly cast Dwight Yoakam) but the doctor is not in and his service doesn't know where he is. A quick cut-away shows that Doc Miles is in Las Vegas. He calls his androgynous friend Kaylo (Efren Ramirez) to put the word out that he is looking for Verona.

He then goes to meet another gang leader, Orlando (Reno Wilson), to see if he knows where Verona is, but Orlando doesn't know. His heart ebbing, Chev buys some cocaine from Orlando but finds that it is not working fast enough. To jump-start his heart he proceeds to start a fight with Orlando's entire gang before jumping back into his car and speeding off.

With the police now chasing after him, Chev tries to lose them by driving through an indoor mall. While driving he gets a call from Doc Miles. He tells Chev that keeping his adrenaline flowing is the only way to slow the effects of the poison, emphasizing that "If you stop, you die."

When his car ends up stuck on an escalator, he runs out of the mall and takes a taxi to Beverly Hills, where he finds his boss Carlito (Carlos Sanz) having a pool party. Spotting Carlito in the pool, Chev dives in and explains the situation, but suspiciously Carlito offers him no help. As Chev speeds down Los Angeles streets downing several cans of Red Bull and energy packets, Doc Miles calls back to let him know that there really is no antidote for him. But he can delay the effects for some time if he goes to the hospital and gets himself an injection of epinephrine, an artificial form of adrenaline given to heart patients. But Miles tells him to be careful to only use a fifth of the syringe.

Kaylo calls back and tells him Verona's brother has been spotted at a restaurant. Chev confronts the brother in an alleyway behind the restaurant, chops off his gun-hand with a cleaver, shoots him in the head with his own gun, rips the gold chain from his neck, and uses his cell phone to call Verona to let him know that he will be coming to kill him next.

At the hospital the pharmacist finds Chev's agitated behavior suspicious and refuses to give him any epinephrine and instead calls the police. A chase with police through the hospital corridors ensues. Inexplicably he sneaks into a patient's room and changes into a hospital gown. At gunpoint, Chev then forces an orderly pushing a medicine cart to give him a syringe of the epinephrine while the cops are holding guns on him. He is given the syringe and he demands that the orderly "juice him" with the defibrillator pads. The shock sends him flying backward into an elevator where he injects himself with the full load of the syringe, sending him into a frenzy. He is soon running down the street at breakneck speed in a hospital gown. He steals a police motorcycle, riding it until he crashes into an open-air cafe.

He heads to Eve's apartment and they have a nice domestic scene in which she begins to bring up issues that in light of his situation, don't really matter to Chev. Bored, his heart starts to fade, and the only thing he can do to stay awake is burn his hand in a waffle iron in the kitchen where she cannot see. Chev convinces Eve that they should go to Chinatown for lunch and have a talk. As they are leaving Chev notices a couple of thugs from Verona's gang who have been sent there to kill her. While Eve's back is turned Chev knocks them out. In the restaurant, Chev confesses to Eve that he is not a computer game programmer, but a professional hitman. He refused carry out the killing of Dom Kim last night and secretly let him go.

Eve doesn't believe his story and storms out of the restaurant. As he follows her out into a crowded area, he feels his heart start to slow again. He grabs her and has sex with her in full view of a crowd of onlookers and a bus filled with Korean schoolgirls who cheer them on. He gets a call from Kaylo who informs Chev that he knows where Verona is. As Chev hangs up it is revealed that Verona is holding Kaylo in a warehouse. At the warehouse Chev discovers Kaylo's lifeless body and that his boss Carlito, working with Verona, set him up. A gun battle breaks out and Chev shields himself with Kaylo's body; he is surprised to see Eve in the elevator watching. As they speed away, Eve comes to realize the story that Chev told is true. They escape the thugs and head for Doc Miles's office.

There the doctor tells him that the damage is too extensive, and that there is no way that he can prevent his death. Chev tells the doctor to give him just enough time to kill Verona and Carlito. Chev sets up a meeting with Verona to exchange his brother's necklace for an antidote to the poison.

The meeting takes place on the roof of an absurdly trendy high-rise hotel. Chev demands the antidote but Verona and Carlito tell him that there is none. As they laugh at him, Chev points his fingers in the shape of a gun at one of the bodyguards and "pulls the trigger." A gunshot is heard and the bodyguard falls backward with a bullet hole in his head. Dom Kim and his gang are standing behind Chev and they are soon engaged in a gun battle with Carlito and Verona's gang. Meanwhile Chev chases after Verona who is about to escape in a helicopter. Chev jumps on the helicopter as it rises and he and Verona battle high above Los Angeles. Eventually, Chev pulls Verona out of the copter and as they free-fall Chev breaks Verona's neck. As Chev floats to his death he makes a last call to Eve on his cell phone. As usual he gets her answering machine. He leaves her a last message, hanging up just seconds before he smashes down on a car parked on the street below.

David E. Chapple

CREDITS

Ricky Verona: Jose Pablo Cantillo
Chev Chelios: Jason Statham
Eve: Amy Smart
Kaylo: Efren Ramirez
Doc Miles: Dwight Yoakam
Orlando: Reno Wilson
Carlito: Carlos Sanz
Origin: USA
Language: English
Released: 2006
Production: Tom Rosenberg, Gary Lucchesi, Richard Wright, Skip Williamson; GreenStreet Films, Radical Media, Lakeshore Entertainment; released by Lionsgate
Directed by: Mark Neveldine, Brian Taylor
Written by: Mark Neveldine, Brian Taylor
Cinematography by: Adam Biddle
Music by: Paul Haslinger
Sound: Steve Morrow
Music Supervisor: Brian Lawrence
Editing: Brian Berdan
Art Direction: Chris Cornwell
Costumes: Christopher Lawrence
Production Design: Jerry Fleming
MPAA rating: R
Running time: 87 minutes

REVIEWS

Boxoffice Online. September 1, 2006.
Entertainment Weekly. September 15, 2006, p. 54.

Hollywood Reporter Online. September 9, 2006.
Los Angeles Times Online. September 4, 2006.
New York Times Online. September 2, 2006.
Variety Online. September 1, 2006.

QUOTES

Doc Miles (to Chev): "You stop, you die."

CURIOUS GEORGE

Welcome to the world of Curious George!
—Movie tagline
Show Me The Monkey!
—Movie tagline

Box Office: $58.3 million

Curious George is a sweet lullaby of a film based on the classic characters created in a series of books written and drawn by the husband and wife team of H. A. Rey and Margaret Rey. They follow the adventures of a monkey named George and his human friend. Considered by some to be harmless children's books and sometimes noted by others for its social satire, the books and characters have been around since 1941 and have finally made it to the big screen, primarily using traditional 2-D animation with a little bit of the computer kind to help out. Directed by Matthew O'Callaghan, the film, long in development limbo, finally materialized with the help of Ron Howard's Imagine Entertainment and several writers. Unfortunately, children and their parents may find themselves bored with the whole thing and their own curiosity dulled by the meandering story and hackneyed plot. It is nice to look at but lacking any substance. There are plenty of pretty colors and high jinks to keep very young children entertained, but the thin storyline, slow pacing and the plethora of bland Jack Johnson songs will leave older kids and adults wanting more.

In the jungles of Africa, George (voice of Frank Welker) is an active and precocious monkey who plays with other animals and lives a carefree life. Meanwhile, Ted (voice of Will Ferrell) is the curator of the Bloomsberry Museum in New York, which is in financial trouble. The museum's owner, Mr. Bloomsberry (voice of Dick Van Dyke) tells Ted that because they don't have a new exhibit to bring customers in, he will have to sell the museum to a company that wants to tear it down and make it a parking lot. Bloomsberry's son Junior (voice of David Cross), who never liked the museum and never had his father's support, prefers the parking lot. Waxing nostalgic, Mr. Bloomsberry tells Ted the story of the one missed opportunity in his life, not finding the Lost Shrine of Zagawa, which contains a giant forty-foot ruby idol of a monkey. He regrets not having been there to find it due to the untimely birth of Junior, and now that Junior is all grown up, he's too old to do it. Ted, realizing that the Lost Shrine of Zagawa could be the key exhibit that brings the people back and thus save the museum, volunteers to go to Africa. This doesn't sit too well with Junior and he attempts to sabotage the mission by burning half the map to the lost Shrine.

Ted goes to a safari clothing shop to get the appropriate attire and is tricked into buying a yellow safari suit and matching hat. The two New Yorkers behind the counter (with fake Australian accents) convince him that "yellow is the new khaki." Dressed in his new outfit, Ted boards a ship (named the *H.A. Rey* in honor of the author of the books) to Africa amid the laughter of the crew.

Soon after arriving in Africa, Ted and his group find themselves hopelessly lost in the jungle. A despondent Ted wanders off by himself, where he draws the attention of George who charms him with a game of peek-a-boo with his hat. Eventually Ted and his group find what they think is the Lost Shrine of Zagawa, only to realize that the idol is only three inches tall, not the giant that they were hoping for. Ted calls Mr. Bloomsberry in New York to break the news, but when Ted sends him a picture of the idol with his cell phone, because of the low angle of the shot, Bloomsberry mistakes the picture as the giant idol of his dreams.

Differing slightly from the book, Ted does not purposefully bring George back with him; instead George secretly stows away on the ship carrying Ted back to New York. Once the ship arrives in New York Harbor the fun begins. George follows Ted to his apartment building, which has strict no pets allowed policy, which is overseen by a ruthless doorman named Ivan (voice of Ed O'Ross) with a superhuman sense of smell. This of course leads to some generic hide-and-seek antics between Ivan, Ted, and George that ultimately leaves Ted with an eviction notice.

Ted and George then make their way to the museum, where a massive advertising campaign for the Lost Idol Of Zagawa has begun, complete with a giant banner hanging in the front of the building, while a crowd eagerly awaits outside. Ted arrives and confesses to Mr. Bloomsberry that the idol is not what they expected, much to the delight of Junior, who lets the crowd in hoping to embarrass Ted. This leads to an accident involving George and a destroyed dinosaur skeleton and Ted's firing. Blaming George for all his troubles, Ted calls animal control and tells them that there is a vicious monkey attacking him, but they are too busy and can't come right now.

With no place to stay, Ted and George find themselves sleeping on a park bench in Central Park, where they form a bond eating fireflies and sticking out their tongues at each other. Leaving no detail unturned and having already explained to the audience the Man in the Yellow Hat's origin, the writers next tackle the final unnecessary detail: the origin of George's name. The next morning Ted and George come upon a group of kids in a small zoo who want to know the name of the monkey. Ted names him George after a statue of George Washington standing nearby.

Ted finds that the kids are all students from Miss Maggie's (voice of Drew Barrymore) class and he begins to tell her his woes. Suddenly he sees the iconic image of George floating away with a bunch of balloons. Ted chases after him floating on his own set of balloons. He catches up to George just in time as George's balloons are popped. They float together through the city until they come upon the Bloomsberry museum.

Ted gets an idea and contacts his inventor friend Clovis (voice of Eugene Levy). Together they devise a hologram device that will turn the three-inch idol into a forty-foot hologram. As they race to the museum, George accidentally activates the hologram, projecting a forty-foot version of himself in the streets, sending everyone outside into a panic. Inside, Bloomsberry agrees to give the device a try, but Junior sabotages the plan by making it look like George poured coffee into the machine.

The museum now closed, Ted and George walk the streets when animal control suddenly shows up to send George back to Africa. Ted rationalizes that he has done the right thing, but quickly has a change of heart and decides to rescue George. He finds him caged in the hold with the only source of light being the single shaft of sunlight beaming through a porthole. He holds the idol above his head where the beam catches it. It then turns out that when sunlight shines through the idol it creates a map of the real location of the Lost Shrine of Zagawa, the saving grace of the museum. Together, they take the ship to Africa where they find the giant idol and bring it back to the museum.

David E. Chapple

CREDITS

Ted, the Man in the Yellow Hat: Will Ferrell (Voice)
Maggie: Drew Barrymore (Voice)
Bloomsberry Jr.: David Cross (Voice)
Clovis: Eugene Levy (Voice)
Bloomsberry: Dick Van Dyke (Voice)
George: Frank Welker (Voice)
Miss Plushbottom: Joan Plowright (Voice)
Ivan: Ed O'Ross (Voice)
Balloon Man: Clint Howard (Voice)
Origin: USA
Language: English
Released: 2006
Production: Ron Howard, David Kirschner, Jon Shapiro; Universal Pictures, Imagine Entertainment; released by Universal
Directed by: Matthew O'Callaghan
Written by: Ken Kaufman
Cinematography by: Julie Rogers
Music by: Heitor Pereira
Sound: Cheryl Murphy
Production Design: Yarrow Cheney
MPAA rating: G
Running time: 86 minutes

REVIEWS

Boxoffice Online. February 10, 2006.
Chicago Sun-Times Online. February 10, 2006.
Entertainment Weekly Online. February 8, 2006.
Los Angeles Times Online. February 10, 2006.
New York Times Online. February 10, 2006.
Variety Online. February 4, 2006.
Washington Post Online. February 10, 2006, p. C01.

QUOTES

Ted, the Man in the Yellow Hat: "You don't give a monkey a latte!"

TRIVIA

The *H.A. Rey,* the ship that brings George to America, was named in honor of the books' author.

CURSE OF THE GOLDEN FLOWER

(Man cheng jin dai huang jin jia)

Unspeakable secrets are hidden within the Forbidden City.
—Movie tagline

Box Office: $6.5 million

In *Curse of the Golden Flower* (*Man cheng jin dai huang jin jia*), director Zhang Yimou reunites with actress Gong Li eleven years after their last collaboration for a sweeping epic of Shakespearean proportions amid the backdrop of the later Tang Dynasty of tenth century China. It is a twisting tale of royal intrigue, loyalty, incest, and murder surrounded by the vibrant, primary-color-filled cinematography of Xiaoding Zhao, the lavish production design by Huo Tingxiao, and a stirring score by Shigeru Umebayashi.

Chow Yun Fat is Emperor Ping, a ruthless leader and the even more ruthless husband of Empress Phoenix (Gong Li). Their marriage is a loveless one; he having left his first wife imprisoned many years before in order to marry the daughter of the king of Liang (Gong Li). Having found out that she has been having an affair with her stepson Prince Wan (Liu Ye), he has been secretly and slowly poisoning her with the help of the Imperial Physician (Ni Dahong). Soon she will lose her mind and then her life. Wan feels guilty and ashamed about the affair and is actually having a second affair with the physician's daughter and palace servant, Jiang Chan (Man Li).

Soon the Empress's oldest son Prince Jai (Jay Chou) returns home for the annual Crysanthemum Festival. The empress takes the opportunity to enlist Prince Jai in plotting a coup to remove the emperor and install Jai on the throne, meanwhile the palace grounds fill with golden crysthanemums.

Later, when a mysterious masked woman approaches Empress Phoenix to tell her that she is being poisoned, the Emperor sees her and demands she take her mask off. She turns out to be his first wife—now married to the Royal Physician and the mother of Wan's secret lover Chan. The Physician is sent to live outside the palace grounds by the Emperor.

When Wan is meeting with Chan at the Physician's home, the mother demands that Wan leave. Chan chases after Wan and the emperor's soldiers go to the house and kill the doctor but end up instead in a battle with the Empress's loyal soldiers, giving the wife time to escape and head for the palace. Upon arriving she confesses that she is Emperor Ping's first wife and Wan's mother. Horrified by the incestual implications, Chan runs out into the courtyard with her mother chasing after her. The Emperor has them killed. Suddenly, a group of soldiers in golden armor enter the compound killing the Emperor's guards. They are lead by Jai and, as they approach the palace, the Emperor's youngest son, Prince Yu—disgusted by his family's scheming and backed by several soldiers—impulsively demands that his father abdicate the thrown to him. The emperor doesn't take kindly to this and soon has Yu's soldiers killed while he proceeds to beat Yu to death for his disloyalty.

Meanwhile, a giant army of silver armored warriors surrounds the palace and fills the courtyard. A brutal and bloody battle ensues between the gold and silver armored warriors, eventually leaving Jai the only "golden" soldier to fight against the entire army of silver. He does his best but knows he cannot win. As does his mother, Empress Phoenix, who finally orders Jai to stop; the coup has failed.

The blood-soaked compound is tended to by several workers who efficiently clear away the deads bodies and replace the blood-soaked flowers with fresh ones so the Festival can go on as planned. Inside the palace the Emperor gloats, revealing to the Empress and Jai that he knew about the coup for a long time and that now Jai must do whatever he is told if he wants his life to be spared. The Emperor then demands that Jai personally administer the poison to the Empress every day. Jai refuses the order by killing himself with his sword, leaving the Emperor and Empress without any offspring. The consequences of their actions are not felt until it is too late.

While vastly different in tone from *Crouching Tiger, Hidden Dragon* (2003), and *Hero* (2002), but no less colorful and dynamic, this is Zhang Yimou's most lurid film to date. The fight choreography and brutal battle scenes are a lyrical mix of swordplay and wirework that is a bloody and poetic ballet.

David E. Chapple

CREDITS

Empress Phoenix: Gong Li
Crown Prince Wan: Liu Ye
Emperor Ping: Chow Yun Fat
Prince Jai: Jay Chou
Prince Yu: Qin Junjie
Jiang Chan: Man Li
Imperial Physician: Ni Dahong
Imperial Physician's Wife: Chen Jin
Origin: China
Language: Chinese
Released: 2006
Production: Bill Kong, Zhang Weiping; Edko Films, Beijing New Picture Film Company, Film Partner International; released by Sony Pictures Classics
Directed by: Zhang Yimou
Written by: Zhang Yimou, Wu Nan, Bian Zhihong
Cinematography by: Xiaoding Zhao
Music by: Shigeru Umebayashi
Sound: Tao Jing
Editing: Cheng Long
Art Direction: Zhao Bin
Costumes: Yee Chung Man
Production Design: Huo Tingxiao

MPAA rating: R
Running time: 114 minutes

REVIEWS

Boxoffice Online. December 22, 2006.
Chicago Sun-Times Online. December 22, 2006.
Los Angeles Times Online. December 22, 2006.
New York Times Online. December 21, 2006.
San Francisco Chronicle. December 22, 2006, p. E6.
USA Today Online. December 22, 2006.
Variety Online. December 12, 2006.
Washington Post. December 22, 2006, p. C5.

AWARDS

Nomination:
Oscars 2006: Costume Des.

D

THE DA VINCI CODE

Seek the truth, seek the codes.
—Movie tagline

So Dark the Con of Man.
—Movie tagline

Break the codes.
—Movie tagline

Box Office: $217.5 million

Anyone who read Dan Brown's page-turner novel *The Da Vinci Code* (2003) just knew it would be made into a movie. It had all the ingredients: a great hook, an engaging mystery, fascinating locales, cerebral heroes, unusual villains, and action. The question for its loyal readers was how true to the book would the moviemakers be. For them the news is good. Director Ron Howard and screenwriter Akiva Goldsman (who won an Oscar® for his script for another collaboration with Howard, 2001's *A Beautiful Mind*) have created a film that is a paradigm of how to adapt a much-loved novel to the screen. *The Da Vinci Code,* the movie, may be a streamlined version of *The Da Vinci Code,* the book, but it retains all the novel's major characters, plot points, and most importantly, its feel and style.

This, however, is not good news for those who felt that Dan Brown's novel was nothing more than a web of lies used to attack the Catholic Church. Most vocal in their condemnation was the Catholic organization that ends up being behind the evil plot of Brown's story, Opus Dei. Calling the novel "libelous and blasphemous," Opus Dei and the Catholic Church didn't go so far as call for a boycott of the movie, but their condemnations created enough controversy—and therefore publicity—to ensure a big opening weekend for the film, attracting both the loyal and the curious.

What some of these critics fail to comprehend is that *The Da Vinci Code*, in either version, is fiction and readers and audiences know it. Oh sure, Brown gives his premise a lot of conjectured historical background to "prove" his points—causing a minor hiccup for the movie's release when Brown was charged with plagiarism but subsequently cleared in London courts—but that's half the fun. The other half is how the mystery plays out. Conspiracies are often in the eye of the beholder, and in this case it may be an overly-sensitive church that sees attacks where there's really nothing more than entertainment. To Howard's credit, he does throw the church a few crumbs in his movie, emphasizing the importance of belief in Jesus even in today's world. As one character states at the end of the film, "the only thing that matters is what you believe."

For the few people left who haven't read the book, the plot is as follows. One dark night the curator of the Louvre in Paris, Jacque Sauniere (Jean-Pierre Marielle), is found dead in the museum's Grand Gallery. He is nude and spread-eagled on the floor with a diagram and messages written around him in his own blood. The inspector in charge of the investigation, Bezu Fache (Jean Reno) brings in an American author and professor of religious symbiology, Robert Langdon (Tom Hanks), to see the crime scene for two reasons: to interpret the symbols and because Langdon knew and was supposed to meet with Sauniere while Robert was guest lecturing in Paris. Langdon recognizes that the curator has positioned himself exactly like Da Vinci's sketch, the

Vitruvian Man. While Robert ruminates on the meaning of the numbers and the words written around the body ("O, Draconian devil"), they are interrupted by Officer Sophie Neveu (Audrey Tatou), a police cryptologist, and, as it turns out, Sauniere's estranged granddaughter. Sophie lets Langdon know that the police suspect him in the murder, have placed a GPS chip in his coat jacket, and that they need to escape as soon as possible.

As the police get sidetracked chasing the positioning device that has been thrown on a garbage truck, Sophie and Robert begin to solve the puzzle before them. The devil phrase is an anagram for Leonardo Da Vinci, which leads them to his famous painting, the *Mona Lisa*, where they find another message, "So dark the con of man," and eventually are led to a key, which is attached to a cross that is the symbol of the Priory of Sion. The Priory traces its roots to the crusades and the Knights Templar. Their purpose was to protect the source of God's power on Earth, to protect the Holy Grail. However the Templars, the military arm of the Priory, were declared Satanists and butchered by the church in 1307. But what became of the Grail?

The key eventually leads Sophie and Robert to a bank where they find a wooden box containing a cryptex, five dials that must be arranged correctly to spell out the word that will open the box without destroying the parchment inside. But the police close in and they escape only with the help of bank representative Vernet (Jurgen Prochnow), who, it turns out, is not helping them escape, as much as he is desirous of obtaining the cryptex for himself and will kill them to get it.

Sophie and Robert manage to outwit Vernet and make their way to Chateau Villette where Sir Leigh Teabing (Ian McKellen) lives. Teabing is an old friend of Robert's and an expert on the history of the Holy Grail. He gives the duo a lecture on Emperor Constantine and the Council of Nicea, Da Vinci and *The Last Supper*, and tells them that the Grail may not be a cup but a person and that Jesus' line lives on because he married Mary Magdalene and they had a daughter. Their descendents carry the blood of Christ and protecting them is the job of the Priory of Sion. The reason they need protecting is that the Church refuses to admit this happened and has actually actively suppressed anything that might attest to it. Hence the destruction of the Templars.

This brings us to Jacques Sauniere's murderer. He is an albino monk named Silas (Paul Bettany). Silas is a member of the secretive Catholic group Opus Dei and is under the control of Bishop Aringarosa (Alfred Molina) and a mysterious person referred to only as "The Teacher." Silas has been ordered to interrogate and murder the grand masters of the Priory in search of the keystone, the map to the Grail. All tell him it is under the rose line in the church of Saint Sulpice in Paris, but it is a ruse. Now Silas knows that Robert and Sophie are also chasing after the keystone, and he goes after them. He, and the police, find themselves at the chateau and our daring duo manage to escape in the nick of time using Teabing's jet, with Teabing and his butler along for the ride, of course. Clues lead them to the Temple Church in London then to Westminster Abbey and eventually to a chapel in Scotland, where the mystery is finally resolved, but not before several more people die and a few other twists are revealed.

Some critics have claimed that Tom Hanks is not well cast as the action hero in this murder mystery, but perhaps they didn't read the book. What's needed in *The Da Vinci Code* is a cerebral Sherlock Holmes, not a muscular Arnold Schwarzenegger, and Hanks does a highly credible job. He is by turns smart, caring, funny, and appealing. He has a definite chemistry with Audrey Tatou, even if it isn't necessarily a romantic one.

Tatou is also aptly cast. She is more than the passive sidekick or bland female love interest since she eventually becomes a piece of the puzzle herself. Tatou radiates both vulnerability and strength. She seems to be both a mystery and an open book and that makes her very interesting to watch as the story unfolds.

The best casting choice, however, may be Jean Reno as the hard-nosed Inspector Bezu Fache, but then author Brown admits he wrote the character with Reno in mind. Reno keeps the viewer off balance because we never know if he's a good guy or a bad one. Is he working for the police or the church? Is he really looking for the murderer or trying to cover everything up, using Robert as a scapegoat? And speaking of hiding a character's true colors, no one can do that better than Ian McKellen.

Paul Bettany as the albino monk, Silas, is more puzzling. In the book he is looming and sinister, but Bettany portrays him as just weird. His Silas seems more tormented than terrifying, more of a tortured pawn than a malevolent villain. Alfred Molina's Bishop Aringarosa is actually a scarier villain. Even though he doesn't directly commit murder or mayhem, he comes across as premeditated evil.

Keeping the reader/viewer guessing, causing them to challenge their preconceptions and use their brains to solve this fascinating puzzle is one of the main reasons the book and the movie were successful. Fast-moving, smart, engaging, and great looking, *The Da Vinci Code* was a hotly anticipated movie that delivered on its promise. It is a mental scavenger hunt that is appealing and intriguing, and told in a style that should entertain all but the most intellectually lazy of viewers or those who will not abide their faith or church challenged in any way for any reason.

Beverley Bare Buehrer

CREDITS

Dr. Robert Langdon: Tom Hanks
Sophie Neveu: Audrey Tautou
Sir Leigh Teabing: Ian McKellen
Bishop Manuel Aringarosa: Alfred Molina
Silas: Paul Bettany
Capt. Bezu Fache: Jean Reno
Andre Vernet: Jurgen Prochnow
Lt. Collet: Etienne Chicot
Jacques Sauniere: Jean-Pierre Marielle
Origin: USA
Language: English, French, Latin
Released: 2006
Production: John Calley, Brian Grazer; Imagine Entertainment, Columbia Pictures; released by Sony Pictures
Directed by: Ron Howard
Written by: Akiva Goldsman
Cinematography by: Salvatore Totino
Music by: Hans Zimmer
Sound: Daniel Pagan
Music Supervisor: Bob Badami
Editing: Dan Hanley, Mike Hill
Art Direction: Giles Masters, Anthony Reading
Costumes: Daniel Orlandi
Production Design: Allan Cameron
MPAA rating: PG-13
Running time: 149 minutes

REVIEWS

Boston Globe Online. May 19, 2006.
Chicago Sun-Times Online. May 18, 2006.
Los Angeles Times Online. May 17, 2006.
New York Times Online. May 18, 2006.
Variety Online. May 16, 2006.

AWARDS

Nomination:

Golden Globes 2007: Orig. Score
Golden Raspberries 2006: Worst Director (Howard)

DATE MOVIE

Everyone wants a happy ending.
—Movie tagline

For people who LOVE date movies and people who HATE them.
—Movie tagline

The Feel-You-Up Movie Of The Year.
—Movie tagline

An Unprotected Comedy.
—Movie tagline

Get Your Date To Come This February.
—Movie tagline

Box Office: $48.5 million

In a seemingly desperate attempt at avoiding the inevitable, 20th Century Fox stalled the box office death of this senseless and inane romantic comedy by withholding it from critics prior to its belated Valentine's Day release. At a mere seventy minutes in length, it is simply sixty-seven minutes too long and would have been better off had it been relegated to the music video industry. *Date Movie* trudges along in a swampy, repetitive death crawl into cinematic purgatory. Never mind the straight to video route, *Date Movie* should have gone straight to a Monday matinee on the USA Network.

Maintaining the formula that made for a successful *Scary Movie* franchise, screenwriters Jason Friedberg and Aaron Seltzer (who also served as the film's director) take a stab at parodying a long line of romantic comedy films. Fans of the abundant genre will note obvious satires of such releases as *Pretty Woman* (1990), *The Wedding Planner* (2001), *Wedding Crashers* (2005), *My Best Friend's Wedding* (1997), *Shallow Hal* (2001), as well as a catalogue of others. However, the main sources of parody used repeatedly throughout the boggy plot, as well as serving as a distorted template, are *Bridget Jones's Diary* (2001), *My Big Fat Greek Wedding* (2002), and both *Meet the Parents* (2000) and its sequel, *Meet the Fockers* (2004)

The film's rotund heroine is Julia Jones (bravely played by Alyson Hannigan), who is love-starved to the extent that she shamelessly serenades a group of repulsed construction workers. This courtship dance is complete with a send-up of the iconoclastic Marilyn Monroe moment in *The Seven Year Itch* (1955) when she steps upon a sidewalk grating and her dress flies up revealing enormous deposits of cellulite. Julia works at a restaurant run by her African American father Frank (Eddie Griffin) who disapproves of her adulation of a customer whom she shares sparks with. Adam Campbell plays the British knight-in-shining-armor-of-camp, Grant Funkyerdoder. Unbearably frustrated, Julia seeks out the professional assistance of none other than Hitch (Tony Cox). Only the stature of this alternate version of the title character played by Will Smith from *Hitch* (2005) is diminutive. He endeavors to give Julia an extensive makeover by employing the use of an auto body shop where she undergoes an interesting liposuction job as well as some detailed body work. The result is Hannigan sans the fat suit.

Grant and Julia's initial romance takes them to A Restaurant (the establishment's actual name) where Grant borrows a page from *When Harry Met Sally* (1989) and mimics an orgasm that is no match for Meg Ryan's convincing performance. After Julia wins over her Hugh Grant caricature, the couple must now deal with her father's objection as well as coping with introducing him to Grant's parents. The film's closest *Brokeback Mountain* (2005) moment is when the Funkyerdoder's Latino manservant is introduced as Grant's first lover. Jennifer Coolidge engages in a fun spoof of Barbra Streisand's character in *Meet the Fockers* that briefly redeems the film. Another obstacle the couple must hurdle is the interfering schemes of a former nubile love and gorgeous best friend of Grant's, Andy (Sophie Monk).

Andy is introduced by provocatively handling two mega size cheeseburgers a la Paris Hilton style in her Burger King commercial. This causes a brief rift in Grant and Julia's budding relationship but the couple is determined to overcome all barriers that would stymie their efforts to enter marital bliss. They meander on their crooked course and consult a wedding consultant (a Jennifer Lopez analogue who bears a Jurassic derriere), aptly named Jell-O (Valery Ortiz). Eventually the couple perseveres, secures the bonds of matrimony, and lives happily ever after; realizing there probably isn't a sequel in their horizon.

In addition to obvious nods to *Say Anything* (1989) and *Sleepless in Seattle* (1993), *Date Movie* goes off trajectory and aims at films outside of romantic comedy bilge and briefly lampoons *Kill Bill* (2003/2004), *King Kong* (2005), and even *Napoleon Dynamite* (2004). With very few exceptions, *Date Movie* is a labored effort that grossly misses its mark at being an entertaining comedy. By padding the film's structure with a collage of romantic comedy hits, along with a celebrity jab at Michael Jackson (shown trying to seduce a child with a plush bumblebee before being clobbered by the boy's mother), the film's cohesiveness is compromised rendering it unoriginal and ultimately, forgettable.

David Metz Roberts

CREDITS

Julia Jones: Alyson Hannigan
Frank Jones: Eddie Griffin
Bernie Funkyerdoder: Fred Willard
Roz Funkyerdoder: Jennifer Coolidge
Grant Funkyerdoder: Adam Campbell
Andy: Sophie Monk
Linda: Meera Simhan
Betty: Marie Matiko
Nicky: Judah Friedlander
Anne: Carmen Electra
Hitch: Tony Cox
Jell-O: Valery Ortiz
Origin: USA
Language: English
Released: 2006
Production: Paul Schiff, Jason Friedberg; Regency Enterprises, New Regency; released by 20th Century Fox
Directed by: Aaron Seltzer
Written by: Aaron Seltzer, Jason Friedberg
Cinematography by: Shawn Maurer
Music by: David Kitay
Sound: Robert Janiger
Editing: Paul Hirsch
Art Direction: Daniel A. Lomino
Production Design: William Elliott
MPAA rating: PG-13
Running time: 83 minutes

REVIEWS

Boxoffice Online. February 17, 2006.
Entertainment Weekly Online. February 22, 2006.
Los Angeles Times Online. February 20, 2006.
Premiere Magazine Online. February 2006.
Variety Online. February 17, 2006.
Washington Post Online. February 18, 2006, p. C01.

QUOTES

Julia Jones: "You had me at hello."
Grant Funkyerdoder: "I'm just a girl. Standing in front of a boy. Asking him to love me."

AWARDS

Golden Raspberries 2006: Worst Support. Actress (Electra)

DAVE CHAPPELLE'S BLOCK PARTY

You're invited to the party of the decade!
—Movie tagline

Box Office: $11.7 million

Dave Chappelle's Block Party (alternately referred to simply as *Block Party*) is an unusual film. Composed of interviews as well as travel- and concert-footage, yet not quite a documentary and not entirely a concert film, it is more than the sum of its parts: it serves as a unique testament to what appears to have been a very fun project to plan and implement. Although the seemingly haphazard arrangement of events in the film may at first seem to be the result of overly self-aware editing for its own sake, a closer examination of the content and form of the film makes it clear that the intent is to give the audience a fun, memorable experience while emphasizing the uniqueness of that experience.

Taking its inspiration from *Wattstax* (1973), the concert documentary filmed in Watts and the Los Angeles Coliseum, *Dave Chappelle's Block Party* is, ostensibly, about Dave Chappelle putting together a concert with various rap performers in the Bedford-Stuyvesant neighborhood of Brooklyn, New York. But from the very first shot of Chappelle himself hilariously trying to assist two men who are trying to start a car, it is clear that this is to be something more than a simple concert film. Chappelle, bullhorn in hand, stands in front of a park in New York, a marching band practicing in the background, and announces the acts who will be performing in *Block Party*: Kanye West, Mos Def, Talib Kweli, Common, the Fugees, Dead Prez, Erykah Badu, Jill Scott, and the Roots. These superstars were chosen, Chappelle says, because he is a fan of all of them and, though he never clearly articulates his motives for putting *Block Party* together, it is clear that his intent was to throw Brooklyn an unforgettable party.

The film jumps from Chappelle in Brooklyn to Chappelle wandering the streets of Dayton, Ohio, where he lives. Chappelle gives out passes to the locals, Willy Wonka-style. Chappelle does not only target Dayton's African American population with passes to the concert, but he also makes sure to offer them to the elderly white lady that owns the store where he buys his cigarettes, and other denizens of his neighborhood. This is interspersed with occasional footage from the concert, which both adds to the anticipation of the performances to come as well as creating a funny juxtaposition—imagining the locals of Dayton in Brooklyn for a massive hip-hop block party. Eventually, Chappelle comes across Ohio's Central State University marching band and asks them if they will play his block party in Brooklyn. After some bureaucratic shuffling with the University's administration, the band is given the go-ahead to perform at the block party and their excitement is palpable.

Block Party is full of these wonderful surprises. The main location for the party is in front of the Broken Angel building in Bedford-Stuyvesant, Brooklyn. The building is little more than a dilapidated shell, occupied by perhaps the most bizarre elderly couple in America. The lady of the house does not care for rap music because of its emphasis on foul language and, though she hopes to marry Sergei Rachmaninoff when she dies, she is more than happy to let Chappelle use the front as the building as the main performance space. Chappelle himself, aware of the humor in the situation, says privately that if a film crew were scouting a location for a crack house, he might recommend the Broken Angel building. Chappelle also tours the local Salvation Army to find furniture for the crew and performers to use when they are resting between performances. While there, he comes across a piano, and plays some of the composition "'Round About Midnight" by Thelonius Monk. This is interspersed with rehearsal footage, showing the Roots' drummer, ?uestlove, saying that Chappelle, not a trained musician, has devoted his entire musical education to this piece. Chappelle says that comedians are sticklers for timing and that he finds Monk's timing worth studying, emphasizing the mutual appreciation between comics and musicians. Perhaps the most moving segment in this location-scout vein is Chappelle's visit to the local day care center in Bed-Stuy which, apparently, produced many of the hip-hop artists who perform at the block party. He has wonderful chemistry with the children, asking them to address him as "Mr. Black Bush," one of his characters from his popular *Chappelle's Show*. When they do, Chappelle is clearly touched. He plays pool with the children, and even challenges one of them to a footrace. The effect of all of these encounters is to convey Chappelle's personal investment in this party, and it allows the audience to invest in it as well.

The concert itself is absolutely electric. From the opening performance of Kanye West's "Jesus Walks," backed by the full Central State University marching band, to the surprise reunion of the Fugees and Lauryn Hill's powerful performance of the Roberta Flack classic "Killing Me Softly," all of the acts seem to pour as much of themselves into this endeavor as Chappelle himself. And the forum, as shown by both the rehearsal footage interspersed with the songs themselves, lends itself to really cutting loose. Erykah Badu, her afro weave buffeted by unforgiving winds, sheds it at one point, and later dives into the crowd. Badu joins Jill Scott during her set. Rapper Big Daddy Kane makes a surprise appearance and does a song or two backed by the Roots. Chairman Fred Hampton of the Black Panthers addresses the crowd and adds some social consciousness to the mix. Chappelle himself, not to be outdone, keeps the proceedings moving like a comic hip-hop version of the diabolical emcee from *Cabaret* (1972). When rain threatens to shut the show down, Chappelle does some hilarious spoken word to his own bongo accompaniment in order to raise the concertgoers' spirits. He does some old-time call and response comedy shtick with Mos Def and the band, he does a bit of the James Brown "Hit me!"

routine, trying to see if he can trick the band into missing a cue, and he even pulls a guy out of the crowd to have a rap battle with him (both participants end up somewhat bruised, metaphorically). When it finally comes time to close out the show and for everyone to go home, Chappelle says: "We shook up the world! Let's leave here and do something good." Through his love of the music and his comic craft, *Dave Chappelle's Block Party* leaves the viewer wanting to do just that.

Much of the power in *Dave Chappelle's Block Party*, though, is the result not only of the force-of-nature artistry of performer and producer Chappelle and the various musicians who lend their talents to the project, but also of the mind and talent of the director and co-producer, Michel Gondry. Unlikely collaborators, Chappelle and Gondry completely eschew linear narrative in presenting this concert. Other concert films that do this, such as Martin Scorsese's documentary of the Band's final concerts, *The Last Waltz* (1978), tend to intersperse songs with pertinent documentary footage, like interviews with the band about the song about to be performed, reminiscences about other performances, and so forth. The form of *Dave Chappelle's Block Party*, however, is much more impressionistic, like a memory or a dream of the event rather than a straightforward retelling of the event itself, a style befitting Gondry, the director of films that explore the secret lives of dreams, such as *Eternal Sunshine of the Spotless Mind* (2004). The lead character in that film, Joel Barish, learns that memories are associated with emotions, and that the emotions that go into a memory dictate how that memory is mapped in the brain. Gondry, through his editing, seeks to implant in the mind of the audience a concert memorable not only for its star-power and artistry, but also for all of the heart and soul that go into its inception and execution.

John Boaz

CREDITS

Himself: Dave Chappelle
Origin: USA
Language: English
Released: 2006
Production: Bob Yari, Mustafa Abuelhija, Julie Fong; Rogue Pictures, Bob Yari Production, Partizan Films, Pilot Boy, Kabuki Brothers Films Production; released by Rogue Pictures
Directed by: Michel Gondry
Cinematography by: Ellen Kuras
Sound: William Tzouris
Music Supervisor: Corey Smyth
Editing: Sarah Flack, Jeff Buchanan
Production Design: Lauri Faggioni
MPAA rating: R
Running time: 100 minutes

REVIEWS

Boxoffice Online. March 3, 2006.
Chicago Sun-Times Online. March 3, 2006.
Entertainment Weekly Online. March 1, 2006.
Los Angeles Times Online. March 3, 2006.
New York Times Online. March 3, 2006.
Variety Online. February 27, 2006.
Washington Post Online. March 3, 2006.

QUOTES

Dave Chapple regarding music and comedy: "I'm mediocre at both and yet have managed to talk my way into a fortune."

TRIVIA

Dave Chappelle self-financed this project.

THE DEATH OF MR. LAZARESCU

(Moartea domnului Lazarescu)

One of the best films released domestically in 2006, *The Death of Mr. Lazarescu* (*Moartea domnului Lazarescu*) is a truly great tragicomedy. Director Cristi Puiu's sophomore feature, the ostensibly simple tale of a sick man's journey through a maze of hospital bureaucracy during one hellish night, becomes a fascinating and profound masterwork—and a powerful statement about modern society. What is even more damning is that the story is based on fact—a real-life case of a man turned down by five hospitals and left for dead on the streets of Romania in 1997.

In the screenplay by Puiu and Razvan Radulescu, a sixty-two-year-old alcoholic widower, Dante Remus Lazarescu (Ion Fiscuteanu), lives in squalor in his Budapest apartment. Feeling sick to his stomach, he calls an ambulance to take him to the hospital. After waiting awhile, he asks his neighbors, Mr. and Mrs. Sterian (Doru Ana and Dana Dogaru), for help; they also try to help expedite the ambulance service. When the emergency vehicle finally arrives, the medic Mioara Avram (Luminta Gheorghiu) and driver Leo (Gabriel Spahiu) move Mr. Lazarescu down his apartment steps, but his condition makes the job difficult. On the way out the door, Mr. Lazarescu asks Mr. Sterian to take care of his cats while he is away and call his sister, who lives nearby, and his daughter, who lives in Canada.

The nightmare begins in earnest as Ms. Avram escorts Mr. Lazarescu to the closest emergency room, where they discover that victims of a major bus accident have filled up all of the city's hospitals. Moreover, Mr. Lazarescu is badgered and bullied by an arrogant doctor who is annoyed that his latest patient is a hopeless drunk, and therefore not worthy of treatment. Soon enough, Ms. Avram must take Mr. Lazarescu to another hospital, but she is misinformed about which hospital is the correct one. Again, Mr. Lazarescu must be transferred. In the meantime, he is feeling worse and getting little treatment (only several misdiagnoses). Finally, Mr. Lazarescu lands in a hospital where tests can be performed to determine his exact illness, but even for this to happen, some special favors and behind-the-scenes maneuvering occurs just so he can be placed at the top of the list for x-rays. Unfortunately, the news is very bad. Mr. Lazarescu is terminally ill and the doctors believe that he may not last the night. So, what started as almost a routine matter becomes instantly tragic and Ms. Avram, who has taken to the elderly man despite her own family and health troubles, worries that Mr. Lazarescu does not fully grasp the gravity of the situation (and, ironically, she had guessed the severity of the illness early on, before any of the doctors). In the last sequence, Mr. Lazarescu is being readied for surgery, which is both necessary to keep him alive and futile because it won't help for very long.

The actual denouement adds a surprising and unexpected spiritual element after two-and-a-half hours of ultra-earthbound realism (though a few of the character names might be a tip-off for some). The film would have been exceptional even without this transcendental moment, but it reframes the entire text in a subtly provocative, self-reflexive way.

The critics were suitably impressed by this remarkable feature. During a time when the film was finding favor on the festival circuit, Jay Weissberg wrote that the film's "dour take on the dehumanizing process of medical treatment is leavened by black humor and dialogue that always rings true." Later, in the *Chicago Sun-Times,* Roger Ebert wrote that the film "lives entirely in the moment, seeing what happens as it happens, drawing no conclusions, making no speeches, creating no artificial dramatic conflicts, just showing people living one moment after another, as they must." The documentary-style approach (with shaky, hand-held camerawork by Oleg Mutu and cinema verite "staging") benefits immeasurably a film that would otherwise seem like nothing more than a slick satire (such as Arthur Hiller's *The Hospital* [1971]).

Clearly, director Puiu has more on his mind than merely criticizing the medical establishment (though his digs alone are worth the price of admission—e.g. the snotty doctors acting with god-like superiority over the patients). As Kenneth Turan noted in the *Los Angeles Times,* "this striking, singular film…is really about life. A mordant parable of and about our time as well as a poem of personal urban decay, *Lazarescu* investigates how we treat one another, how we interact with the world. Puiu was inspired by Eric Rohmer's *Six Moral Tales* (1963-1972) to make this the first of a projected six studies of love, in this case love for one's neighbor that is indicated by its ghost." *The Death of Mr. Lazarescu* speaks universally about many things and deserves wide attention. Hopefully, the oft-putting title and seemingly bleak subject matter won't dissuade those who really should see it.

Eric Monder

CREDITS

Mioara Avram: Luminata Gheorghiu
Dante Remus Lazarescu: Ion Fiscuteanu
Leo: Gabriel Spahiu
Sandu Sterian: Doru Ana
Miki Sterian: Dana Dogaru
Dr. Ardelean: Florin Zamfirescu
Origin: Romania
Language: Romanian
Released: 2005
Production: Alexandru Munteanu; Mandragora Production
Directed by: Cristi Puiu
Written by: Cristi Puiu, Razvan Radulescu
Cinematography by: Oleg Mutu
Music by: Andreea Paduraru
Sound: Cristian Tamovetchi, Constantin Fleancu
Editing: Dana Bunescu
Art Direction: Christina Barbu
Costumes: Christina Barbu
MPAA rating: R
Running time: 154 minutes

REVIEWS

Boxoffice Online. April 28, 2006.
Chicago Sun-Times Online. May 12, 2006.
Entertainment Weekly Online. April 19, 2006.
Los Angeles Times Online. May 5, 2006.
New York Times Online. April 26, 2006.
Premiere Magazine Online. April 26, 2006.
Variety Online. May 17, 2005.

TRIVIA

This is the first in a series of six feature films that Cristi Puiu will direct, called "Stories from the Suburbs of Bucharest."

DECK THE HALLS

There glows the neighborhood.
—Movie tagline

Box Office: $35 million

Since fruitcake has fallen out of favor, the new unwanted Christmas tradition has become the annual trotting out of the unfunny Christmas movie. The idea behind such movies is that Christmas is a staid, institutionalized holiday, ripe for mockery. Maybe that was true years ago, when happy, picture-perfect families ruled the holiday movie screen, but now the need is just not there. Part of what makes comedy funny is an element of surprise and these movies have forgotten that. Every man, woman, and child in America knows that any holiday comedy is going to contain one or more of the following elements: tasteless bodily function jokes, family fights, problematic decorations, a fire, and a ruined holiday dinner. *Deck the Halls* contains many of these elements, which director John Whitesell regurgitates as humorlessly as they were penned by Matt Corman, Chris Ord, and Don Rhymer.

It is hard to believe that it took a team of writers to come up with this hour and thirty-three minute screenplay because *Deck the Halls* is the type of movie that practically writes itself. It stars Danny DeVito and Matthew Broderick playing, respectively, a crass, loudmouth type and an uptight, fussy sort of fellow. The casting alone shows the lack of inspiration in this film as it would have been a much more interesting movie had their roles been reversed.

Steve Finch (Broderick), a prim optometrist in the cute small town of Cloverdale, Massachusetts, considers himself the resident "Christmas Guy." Because he never had "good" Christmases growing up, he is determined that his family will have festive Christmases, with plenty of traditions and fun. Unfortunately for Steve's family, he focuses much more on the traditions than the fun. Steve forces his family to wear hideous matching sweaters for the annual Christmas photo and he is so lacking in spontaneity that he has the next five years of Christmas trees already growing at a local tree farm. It is obvious that all of Steve's carefully laid plans will be torn asunder when Buddy Hall (DeVito) moves in across the street. Buddy is a brash car salesman with a buxom wife, Tia (Kristin Chenoweth), and two blonde, scantily-clad daughters, Emily (Sabrina Aldridge) and Ashley (Kelly Aldridge). Buddy is apparently a wonderful salesman, but he is unable to stick with a job. When one of his dim daughters shows him a website with which you can see your house from space, Buddy is horrified to learn that his house is not visible. He decides to make it his life's mission to make his house appear on the site. The way to achieve this goal, he decides, is to put up voluminous Christmas decorations.

Buddy irks Steve on many levels. He was already going to dislike Buddy simply because Buddy is untidy and uncouth. But when Buddy's lights and the subsequent traffic they bring start keeping Steve up at night, Steve's distaste turns to hate. He is especially horrified to realize that his position as the town's "Christmas guy" is being usurped by Buddy. Because this is a Christmas movie, the two men will, of course, make amends. But in the meantime, the audience must sit through not one, but two Christmas tree fires, an unfortunate run-in with camel excrement and, perhaps worst of all, trite lines from the movie wives about Christmas really being about family.

Kyle Smith of the *New York Post* was the rare critic who enjoyed the film, writing that "*Deck the Halls* does the job fine, and although Aunt Mabel is going to warm to its macrame and Jell-O-mold spirit a lot more than nose-pierced Nikki, it is a better option than the third *Santa Clause*." Other critics did not care for it at all. A.O. Scott of the *New York Times* wrote: "Mr. Broderick and Mr. DeVito look tired and out of sorts, and you can hardly blame them, given the picture's inept, curdled mixture of sappiness and crude humor." Richard Roeper of the *Chicago Sun-Times* wrote: "You cannot believe how excruciatingly awful this movie is. It is bad in a way that will cause unfortunate viewers to huddle in the lobby afterward, hugging in small groups, consoling one another with the knowledge that it's over, it's over—thank God, it's over." Ty Burr of the *Boston Globe* wrote that the film "is just one more complacent, sold-out Christmas product, a thin layer of Hallmark sentimentality surrounding a cynical core." Finally, Sam Adams of the *Los Angeles Times* wrote that "like a fatally snarled string of Christmas lights, *Deck the Halls* promises holiday cheer but delivers only frustration."

Jill Hamilton

CREDITS

Buddy Hall: Danny DeVito
Steve Finch: Matthew Broderick
Kelly Finch: Kristen Davis
Tia Hall: Kristin Chenoweth
Madison Finch: Alia Shawkat
Wallace: Jorge Garcia

Carter Finch: Dylan Blue
Ashley Hall: Kelly Aldridge
Emily Hall: Sabrina Aldridge
Origin: USA
Language: English
Released: 2006
Production: Arnon Milchan, Michael Costigan, John Whitesell; New Regency, Regency Enterprises, Corduroy Films; released by 20th Century Fox
Directed by: John Whitesell
Written by: Don Rhymer, Matt Corman, Chris Ord
Cinematography by: Mark Irwin
Music by: George S. Clinton
Sound: Patrick Ramsay
Music Supervisor: Patrick Houlihan
Editing: Paul Hirsch
Art Direction: Dan Hermansen
Costumes: Carol Ramsey
Production Design: Bill Brzeski
MPAA rating: PG
Running time: 93 minutes

REVIEWS

Chicago Sun-Times Online. November 22, 2006.
Hollywood Reporter Online. November 22, 2006.
Los Angeles Times Online. November 22, 2006.
San Francisco Chronicle. November 22, 2006, p. E1.
Variety Online. November 21, 2006.
Village Voice Online. November 21, 2006.
Washington Post. November 22, 2006, p. C1.

AWARDS

Nomination:

Golden Raspberries 2006: Worst Support. Actor (DeVito), Worst Support. Actress (Chenoweth)

DEJA VU

If you thought it was just a trick of the mind, prepare yourself for the truth.
—Movie tagline

Box Office: $64 million

Director Tony Scott wastes little time getting things moving in his latest film, *Deja Vu.* He gives us quick, personal glimpses into a few moments in the lives of those traveling aboard a New Orleans ferry on their way to celebrate Mardi Gras. There is a teacher with her class of young children, a grandfather playing with his grandchild, young couples, and a lot of sailors on leave. They're all so happy and eager...and then they all blow up. Only a few minutes into his film, Scott has started his roller coaster of a movie on its fascinating and fast-paced journey.

Now we watch as the survivors are cared for on land and the bodies are retrieved from the water. We are told 543 people have been killed. Why and how could this have happened, and who did it? These are the questions Doug Carlin (Denzel Washington) of the U.S. Bureau of Alcohol, Tobacco, and Firearms will try to answer. A veteran of the Oklahoma City bombing, Carlin is smart, careful, and observant. While some investigate the ferry and its debris, he's climbing around on the Crescent City Bridge looking for clues. He obviously thinks outside the proverbial box.

But then he is told about a body that has washed up on shore that appears to be a ferry victim, but she died an hour before the explosion. He goes to the morgue and investigates and is immediately captivated by the body of the beautiful young woman. Her name is Claire Kuchever (Paula Patton) and Doug notices that she's missing an earring and has had the fingers of her right hand cut off. He also notices a gummy residue around her mouth, which indicates that she has had it taped. Although Claire obviously wasn't a victim of the explosion, Doug is sure that she is indirectly involved with it. Doug investigates Claire's home and finds a few interesting things. There are bloody bandages in her bathroom, the magnets on her refrigerator spell out "U can save her," and, to his astonishment, there is a message on her answering machine...from him!

Doug's expert investigative abilities are noticed by FBI agent Andrew Pryzwarra (Val Kilmer) who convinces Doug to join the team involved in a special, top-secret project run by Dr. Alexander Denny (Adam Goldberg). Przywarra tells Doug that the team has access to seven surveillance cameras, hence the project's name Snow White, and with them they can digitally re-create the past. There are a few limitations, though. They can only go exactly four days and six hours into the past, but they can go anywhere their "machinery" is near, even through walls.

While it would seem as if they should be staking out the ferry, Doug immediately tells them to follow the past activities of mystery woman Claire. So the satellites lock onto Claire's apartment and they watch as the woman Doug has just seen dead in the morgue is happily doing her daily activities, feeding her cat, talking on the phone, and showering for a date. Like voyeurs, the team can't take their eyes off this phantom woman, and it also becomes quickly obvious that Doug has started to fall in love with her. (More than one critic has compared this aspect of the film to the classic film noir *Laura* [1944].) It's not long before watching Claire pays off and they discover who has murdered her and blown up the ferry. He is a disgruntled, psychotic "patriot," Carroll Oerstadt (Jim Caviezel). Doug interviews Carroll but the madman prattles on about destiny and how "human collateral is the cost of freedom."

Meanwhile back at Snow White headquarters, imagine Doug's surprise when he finally figures out what the others knew all along: what he thought was nothing more than a "movie" of the past, turns out to be real. Somehow Snow White doesn't just look four days and six hours into a past that has come and gone, they are actually watching the present in what can only be explained as an alternate universe. Doug now begins to wonder if instead of just looking into this present/past why not try to communicate with it. And if they can send messages back, why not people. And if they can go back in time in any capacity, then why not change the group's mission from trying to discover who blew up the ferry to stopping the explosion from happening at all. And we know that Doug would like nothing more than to save Claire, too (after all didn't the fridge tell him that "U can save her"?).

Obviously *Deja Vu* is not the usual crime thriller/ mystery, sci-fi love story. It has a lot of action including many, perhaps too many, car chases, but the one in which Doug chases Carroll at night four days and six hours in the past with the help of a special pair of time-travel goggles while in reality he is actually traveling on roads in the daytime in the present is especially fascinating. But what is even more absorbing is that screenwriters Bill Marsilii and Terry Rossio (best known for *Shrek* [2001] and the *Pirates of the Caribbean* series [2003-2007]) have put together a mystery that truly requires that the viewer engage his/her brain. This story, while never cheating on the action or suspense, challenges one's every assumption. Clues that seem at first hardly worth noting turn out to be of major importance because of the manipulation of time-space.

For some, putting this much science into their fiction makes their heads hurt—and that may have been a problem for some less-than-scientific-minded reviewers—but *Deja Vu* does a highly credible job of weaving current theories into its plot. A part of this reliability comes from the fact that the filmmakers have enlisted the talents of populist scientist Dr. Brian Greene, expert on string theory and professor of physics at Columbia University. The author of the highly readable *The Fabric of the Cosmos* and *The Elegant Universe*, Greene has kept the story grounded in theory while still allowing for flights of fantasy. Also helping to ground the film is actor Denzel Washington whose ease in front of the camera gives him an everyman quality. Washington's presence and intelligence help to create a believability for Agent Carlin even as he undertakes some incredibly unbelievable actions.

Several other films recently have played with the idea of a rift in the space-time continuum. This year it was *The Lake House* and Caviezel did it before in *Frequency* (2001). But this current entry is a techno-thriller that really wants you to wonder what are time, reality, and destiny. The result is not only a compelling mystery packed with action, it is also filled with engrossing metaphysical questions. Even if a viewer isn't well-informed about all the latest theories of quantum physics, superstrings, parallel universes, and the space-time continuum, if one is willing to suspend one's natural belief that time is linear, then one will enjoy a truly suspenseful and fun mystery that leaves one with a lot to talk about later.

Beverley Bare Buehrer

CREDITS

Doug Carlin: Denzel Washington
Agent Pryzwarra: Val Kilmer
Claire Kuchever: Paula Patton
Jack McCready: Bruce Greenwood
Alexander Denny: Adam Goldberg
Carroll Oerstadt: Jim Caviezel
Gunnars: Elden (Ratliff) Henson
Shanti: Erika Alexander
Origin: USA
Language: English
Released: 2006
Production: Jerry Bruckheimer; Touchstone Pictures, Scott Free; released by Buena Vista
Directed by: Tony Scott
Written by: Terry Rossio, Bill Marsilii
Cinematography by: Paul Cameron
Music by: Harry Gregson-Williams
Sound: Art Rochester
Music Supervisor: Bob Badami
Editing: Chris Lebenzon, Jason Hellmann
Art Direction: Scott Plauche
Costumes: Ellen Mirojnick
Production Design: Chris Seagers
MPAA rating: PG-13
Running time: 126 minutes

REVIEWS

Boston Globe Online. November 22, 2006.
Chicago Sun-Times Online. November 22, 2006.
Hollywood Reporter Online. November 20, 2006.
Los Angeles Times Online. November 22, 2006.
New York Times Online. November 22, 2006.

Premiere Magazine Online. November 20, 2006.
San Francisco Chronicle. November 22, 2006, p. E1.
Variety Online. November 17, 2006.
Washington Post. November 22, 2006, p. C1.

QUOTES

Oerstadt (to Carlin): "You think you know what's coming? You don't have a clue."

THE DEPARTED

Lies. Betrayal. Sacrifice. How far will you take it?
—Movie tagline

Cops or Criminals. When you're facing a loaded gun, what's the difference?
—Movie tagline

Box Office: $132 million

Martin Scorsese established his reputation as one of the most distinctive American filmmakers with *Mean Streets* (1973), *Taxi Driver* (1976), and *Raging Bull* (1980), examining again and again what it means to be a man in a violent world. Since *GoodFellas* (1990), most of his output has disappointed critics, who long for the director to abandon period pieces such as *The Age of Innocence* (1993) and spiritual quests like *Kundun* (1997). While two more period films, *The Gangs of New York* (2002) and *The Aviator* (2004), found many supporters, others implored Scorsese to return to the modern urban setting he knows best. He does just that with *The Departed.*

The Departed is closely based upon *Infernal Affairs* (2002), one of the most stylish and internationally successful Hong Kong films. It tells the parallel stories of two young Massachusetts state policemen, Billy Costigan (Leonardo DiCaprio) and Colin Sullivan (Matt Damon). While Billy is asked by his superiors, Queenan (Martin Sheen) and Dignam (Mark Wahlberg), to go undercover to infiltrate the gang of Frank Costello (Jack Nicholson), Colin is already acting as Frank's double agent on the police force.

The Departed alternates between the two spies, with Billy and Colin not crossing paths until late in the film. Both the cops and the crooks, however, learn that they have been compromised, and Colin, ironically, is assigned to find the mole. William Monahan's screenplay explores how living two lives at once changes the protagonists, with Billy becoming especially rattled. If Colin makes a mistake, he will be arrested. If Billy does, he will die.

Infernal Affairs focuses on the two protagonists with the gang leader constantly lurking in the background. *The Departed* differs from its source primarily in greatly expanding the criminal's role, as befits an actor of Nicholson's stature. Making Frank a more formidable presence increases the danger Billy faces. Nicholson, who reportedly enhanced the screenplay, makes Frank larger than life. He told *Time*, "I just thought my guy was written a little too classy." He wears a devilish beard, recalling his character in *The Witches of Eastwick* (1987), and while he does not resort to his patented raised eyebrows and giant smile as much as he might, he does chew the scenery, throwing off the film's rhythms, according to some commentators. Nicholson seems to be striving to match Joe Pesci's over-the-top villain from *GoodFellas,* though he does less shouting.

In addition to a much bloodier conclusion, the other major difference between *Infernal Affairs* and *The Departed* is in making the police psychiatrist, Madolyn (Vera Farmiga), who acts as the undercover officer's confessor in the original, Colin's live-in girlfriend as well as Billy's lover. While this triangle makes an already tense situation even more complicated, Madolyn is underwritten and falls for both men too easily. One important aspect of these relationships seems to point toward a revelation that never transpires.

Though his role is not quite as complex as that of Howard Hughes in *The Aviator*, DiCaprio brings his usual intensity to Billy. Because the character spends most of the film nervously anticipating discovery, the role lacks needed diversity. Billy's scenes with Madolyn carry the same unease as those with Frank. The great Tony Leung finds more nuances with this character in *Infernal Affairs.* Damon is also good but limited by a one-note role, except when Colin is initially charming Madolyn.

The supporting cast is uniformly excellent. Sheen gives Queenan a quiet authority, in contrast with the cocky bluster of his President Bartlett on *West Wing* (1999-2006). Wahlberg, in his best work since *Boogie Nights* (1997), makes the profane, hot-heated Dignam compelling. Although Wahlberg, the only Massachusetts native among the leads, and Alec Baldwin, terrific as Colin's supervisor, have no scenes with Nicholson, they seem to be competing with his outrageousness, as when Baldwin ends a scene by plunging his face into a bowl of ice water.

Though surprisingly few reviews noted it, the best supporting performance is by Ray Winstone as Frank's main henchman, known as Mr. French, a perverse allusion to the Sebastian Cabot character, a butler, in the bland situation comedy *Family Affair* (1966-1971). While Frank seems to play at being evil, Mr. French is the real thing. Obviously having learned a thing or two about stealing scenes from Ben Kingsley in *Sexy Beast*

(2000), Winstone, slovenly and greasy-haired, commands the screen.

Monahan, another Bostonian whose only previous credit is the quite different Crusades epic *Kingdom of Heaven* (2005), gives *The Departed* the same kind of distinctive tough-guy dialogue Mardik Martin, Paul Schrader, and Nicholas Pileggi have for earlier Scorsese films. When Billy tells Queenan that he understands deception, Dignam explodes: "No, you don't know. Because if someone like you knew what we did, that would make us cunts. Are you calling us cunts?" As Mr. French explains to Billy, "There's guys you can hit and guys you can't hit. Now he's not a guy you can't hit, but he's pretty close to a guy you can't hit."

Scorsese's other urban films are set in New York, New Jersey, and Las Vegas and center around Italian-Americans. Yet the Boston Irish of *The Departed* are close kin to these characters. Like Harvey Keitel's Charley Cappa in *Mean Streets*, they are torn between bad and honorable behavior, tormented by Catholic guilt. To make clear that the Church has failed its mission, Scorsese shows a nun smoking and drinking a beer in a diner. In this same scene, Frank lambastes a priest as a pederast and proclaims, "In this archdiocese, God don't run the bingo."

The dual nature of the *Infernal Affairs* protagonists is a metaphor for the schizophrenic nature of Hong Kong, moving uneasily from capitalism to socialism. Similar dichotomies haunt the characters in *The Departed*: law vs. order, faith vs. secularism, and friendship vs. betrayal. Scorsese includes a shot on a television screen of John Ford's *The Informer* (1935), in which an Irish rebel informs on his friends, not only as an acknowledgment of a master but as a reminder of the complexities of and divisions within Irish loyalties. Scorsese underscores the theme of guilt and responsibility with an homage to the conclusion of Carol Reed's *The Third Man* (1949). What does it mean to be a man in Scorsese's violent universe: loss, regret, sacrifice, uncertain identity, and death.

While Scorsese handles several set pieces with great verve, too many of the dialogue scenes are shot rather conventionally, with standard two-shots and close-ups, slowing the film's energy considerably. A major scene, with Billy and Colin secretively communicating with Queenan and Frank by cell phone, is not as imaginatively handled as co-directors Andrew Lau and Alan Mak did in *Infernal Affairs*. A few other scenes, as with a pivotal shootout, lack the dramatic tension of the original.

Cinematographer Michael Ballhaus, a frequent Scorsese collaborator, gives the film a gray, grainy, overcast look appropriate to the characters' forlorn natures. While Thelma Schoonmaker is usually acclaimed for her editing of Scorsese's more extreme scenes, the standout here is her cutting of a love scene between Billy and Madolyn to Van Morrison's version of Pink Floyd's "Comfortably Numb." Known for his pioneering use of pop music in serious dramas, Scorsese also employs songs by the Rolling Stones, the Allman Brothers Band, Badfinger, the Beach Boys, and LaVern Baker. Patsy Cline's "Sweet Dreams" appears several times, including the closing credits, as a wistful comment on the film's tangled romances.

Scorsese makes a major blunder by ending *The Departed* with a lame visual joke that undercuts the emotional impact of what he has so painstakingly achieved. While the film may not quite be a return to the form of the director's glory days and lacks the existential depth of *Infernal Affairs*, it is always engrossing and frequently entertaining.

Michael Adams

CREDITS

Billy Costigan: Leonardo DiCaprio
Colin Sullivan: Matt Damon
Frank Costello: Jack Nicholson
Sgt. Dignam: Mark Wahlberg
Capt. Queenan: Martin Sheen
Mr. French: Ray Winstone
Madolyn: Vera Farmiga
Brown: Anthony Anderson
Capt. Ellerby: Alec Baldwin
Barrigan: James Dale
Fitzy: Mark Rolston
Cousin Sean: Kevin Corrigan
Barrigan: James Dale
Gwen: Kristen Dalton
Origin: USA
Language: English
Released: 2006
Production: Brad Grey, Graham King, Brad Pitt; Plan B Entertainment, Initial Entertainment Group, Vertigo Entertainment; released by Warner Bros.
Directed by: Martin Scorsese
Written by: William Monahan
Cinematography by: Michael Ballhaus
Music by: Howard Shore
Sound: Danny Michael
Editing: Thelma Schoonmaker
Art Direction: Nicholas Lundy, Terri Cariiker-Thayer
Costumes: Sandy Powell
Production Design: Kristi Zea
MPAA rating: R
Running time: 150 minutes

REVIEWS

Boxoffice Online. October 6, 2006.
Chicago Sun-Times Online. October 6, 2006.

Entertainment Weekly. October 13, 2006, p. 107.
Hollywood Reporter Online. October 2, 2006.
Los Angeles Times Online. October 6, 2006.
New York Times Online. October 6, 2006.
Newsweek Online. October 9, 2006.
Premiere Magazine Online. October 3, 2006.
Rolling Stone Online. September 28, 2006.
San Francisco Chronicle. October 6, 2006, p. E1.
Variety Online. September 29, 2006.
Washington Post. October 6, 2006, p. C1.

QUOTES

Mob boss Frank Costello: "I say—kill everybody."

AWARDS

Oscars 2006: Adapt. Screenplay, Director (Scorsese), Film, Film Editing
Directors Guild 2006: Director (Scorsese)
Golden Globes 2007: Director (Scorsese)
Writers Guild 2006: Adapt. Screenplay

Nomination:

Oscars 2006: Support. Actor (Wahlberg)
British Acad. 2006: Actor (DiCaprio), Adapt. Screenplay, Director (Scorsese), Film, Film Editing, Support. Actor (Nicholson)
Golden Globes 2007: Actor—Drama (DiCaprio), Film—Drama, Screenplay, Support. Actor (Nicholson, Wahlberg)
Screen Actors Guild 2006: Support. Actor (DiCaprio), Cast

THE DESCENT

Afraid of the dark? You will be.
—Movie tagline

Face Your Deepest Fear.
—Movie tagline

Scream Your Last Breath.
—Movie tagline

Box Office: $26 million

Violent and gory but also intelligent and suspenseful, *The Descent* is one of the most effective horror films to be released in some time. A group of women embarks on a hiking expedition through a series of uncharted caves in the Appalachian Mountains only to discover a race of primitive, flesh-eating creatures living below the surface. These human-like "crawlers," as they are called in the credits, are a savage species that have developed an acute sense of hearing to compensate for their blindness from living below the earth's surface. But elevating *The Descent* beyond common horror fare is its old-school approach; the ghoulish creatures and shocks may be requisites for the genre, but the movie, written and directed by British filmmaker Neil Marshall, does not skimp on character development, especially with its protagonist, Sarah (Shauna Macdonald), whose "descent" is as psychological as it is physical.

The core group of six spelunkers consists of three women whom we meet on a white-water rafting trip in the film's opening scenes. Sarah is best friends with Beth (Alex Reid) and Juno (Natalie Mendoza), but we can sense a rift—Juno is having an affair with Sarah's husband, and Beth is suspicious. The film jolts us with its first surprise only a few minutes into the action when Sarah is injured and her husband and daughter are killed in a freak auto accident. The memory of her shattered family, especially her daughter's demise, haunts Sarah, who suffers from a mental breakdown. A year later, the women go on the cave expedition and are joined by three other women: Holly (Nora-Jane Noone), Juno's protege and the toughest of the group; Sam (MyAnna Buring), a medical student; and Rebecca (Saskia Mulder), her older sister.

Juno is the de facto leader of the group but is not completely trustworthy. Without telling anyone, she purposely guides the expedition on a trip through undocumented caves because she thinks that it will be a great adventure discovering a new cave system together. Marshall skillfully develops the tension between the women, especially Juno and Beth, and allows his characters to interact with each other for quite a while before giving us a glimpse of the creatures that will prey on them. At the same time, he establishes a sense of genuine dread of the environment, the claustrophobia of the caves, the struggle to move through darkness and enclosed spaces, and the desperation to find a way out when none is readily apparent.

The crawlers themselves, who, in their facial features, call to mind a more primitive Lord Voldemort from *Harry Potter and the Goblet of Fire* (2005), are creepy, slimy creatures whose instinct is simply to survive. There are some truly scary sequences involving the crawlers (including one genuine jump-out-of-your-seat moment), but what gives the film an added dimension is the largely unspoken conflict between some of the women, an uneasiness that is only exacerbated once the crawlers attack. At the conclusion of one fight with the creatures, Juno inadvertently wields a pick into Beth's throat and, in a panic, flees. When Sarah later finds the wounded Beth, she reveals what Juno did as well as proof (in the form of a necklace that she ripped off Juno's neck) that Juno had an affair with Sarah's husband. The suffering Beth begs for death, and Sarah puts her out of her misery.

As flawed as she is, however, Juno is, in some ways, the heart of the film—the most adventurous of the women, the most cunning, and the most complicated in her motives. Surely the guilt she feels over the affair is part of the reason for organizing the trip in the first place, a way to raise Sarah's spirits and put the past behind them. Fighting the hardest to save her friends from the crawlers, Juno is never the villain, and Mendoza, giving the most physical, complex, and charismatic performance, makes her a nuanced character.

The Descent occasionally flirts with repetition as the women trek through uncharted caves, squeeze through tight passages, traverse wide chasms, and alternate between fighting off attacks from the hideous creatures and hiding from them. But despite hewing fairly closely to the horror formula of a group of people who get picked off by monsters one-by-one, the film maintains suspense and a sense of foreboding. Ridley Scott's *Alien* (1979) is the closest precursor to the film's narrative structure, but Marshall also peppers his thriller with visual homages to a slew of other classics, including *The Shining* (1980), *Apocalypse Now* (1979), and *Carrie* (1976).

Holly, Sam, and Rebecca fall prey to the crawlers, leaving Sarah and Juno to try to make their way out of the caves. Given their history, however, the final confrontation is more about them than their adversaries. Knowing what Juno did to Beth but not that it was an accident, Sarah ultimately attacks Juno and leaves her to be devoured by the crawlers. Sarah then makes her way out, climbing up a mountain of bones and bursting through the earth to the world above.

Throughout the film, Marshall plays with the idea that the descent of the title is not just physical but emotional as well, especially for Sarah, who finds her already tenuous grip on sanity increasingly in jeopardy. At one point, her primal screams are even mistaken for those of the crawlers, and, by the end, she is covered in blood, thus denoting her own descent into the animal world. In the film's startling final scene, after she has gotten away, she has a vision of Juno's ghost, thus suggesting that Sarah may always be haunted.

The Descent does not break new ground in the horror genre, but it is an intense, suspenseful execution of the monster-movie formula, and the principal characters have enough of a backstory to make their plight more involving than we would find in most fright films. Writer/director Marshall has made that rare character-driven horror movie that grabs the audience not only with scary monsters and an eerie environment but with humans whose own conflicts make them just as intriguing.

Peter N. Chumo II

CREDITS

Sarah: Shauna Macdonald
Juno: Natalie Mendoza
Beth: Alex Reid
Holly: Nora-Jane Noone
Rebecca: Saskia Mulder
Paul: Oliver Milburn
Sam: MyAnna Buring
Jessica: Molly Kayall
Origin: Great Britain
Language: English
Released: 2005
Production: Christian Colson; Celador Films, Northern Prods.; released by Lionsgate
Directed by: Neil Marshall
Written by: Neil Marshall
Cinematography by: Sam McCurdy
Music by: David Julyan
Sound: Nick Thermes, Nigel Heath, Michael Maroussas
Editing: Jon Harris
Art Direction: Jason Knox-Johnston
Costumes: Nancy Thompson
Production Design: Simon Bowles
MPAA rating: R
Running time: 99 minutes

REVIEWS

Boxoffice Online. August 4, 2006.
Chicago Sun-Times Online. August 4, 2006.
Chicago Tribune Online. August 4, 2006.
Entertainment Weekly. August 11, 2006, p. 49.
New York Times Online. August 4, 2006.
San Francisco Chronicle. August 4, 2006, p. E5.
Variety Online. July 11, 2005.
Washington Post. August 4, 2006, p. C2.

TRIVIA

The original ending shown in the film's U.K. version was slightly changed for its U.S. release. The director had already shot alternate endings.

THE DEVIL AND DANIEL JOHNSTON

Intensely moving, *The Devil and Daniel Johnston* documents the story of artist and musician, Daniel Johnston. By turns haunting, disturbing, charming, and dreadful, the events of his life are related by family and friends.

Born into a devoutly Christian family, Daniel was a precocious youth in grammar school. His mother reports, however, that upon entrance into middle school, Daniel "lost confidence in himself." He began to express himself through art and became known as "The Eyeball Guy" because of his obsession with drawing and painting images of eyeballs anywhere he could. Daniel became fascinated with John Lennon and his thoughts on art. Art became necessity for Daniel, who expressed himself through painting, drawing, making films, playing music, recording songs, and acting.

After Daniel finished high school, his parents became concerned that because of his art he had become a "laughing stock." Also, because he could not hold a job and therefore donate to the church, he had become "an unprofitable servant of the Lord." Daniel's personal faith, however, was strong and he began to attend Abilene Christian College. Unfortunately, he immediately complained of fierce pain in his arms, hands, feet and fingers (an early warning sign of manic depression) and left college to recuperate at home. He then attended the Kent State Art School where he met Laurie Allen, whom Daniel describes as the love of his life. Though his love was unrequited and she married an undertaker, her presence would haunt Daniel's art for decades. Of her, he explains, "She inspired a thousand songs, and then I knew I was an artist." When she married, Daniel became immensely depressed and obsessed with the piano. His parents took him out of school and sent him to his brother in Houston. He worked at Astroworld while trying to get his life in order. At this time, he obtained a synthesizer and transformed his brother's garage into a recording studio, where he would stay up all night long recording his thoughts and music. Daniel would continue to record his most intimate feelings and opinions for decades. Daniel then moved in with his sister, but eventually ran away with the carnival. That's right: the carnival. In 1985, while with the carnival in Austin, Texas, Daniel was in a portable restroom and—presumably because he had taken too long—was physically attacked upon exiting by a large man who had been waiting. Distraught, Daniel fled to a local Church of Christ. The carnival pulled out of town, leaving him in downtown Austin.

Daniel began to attend shows and network within the burgeoning Austin music scene while also obtaining a job cleaning tables at McDonald's, of which he was very proud. He became known as the "crazy kid with the weird music" and when MTV rolled into town to film a show called *Cutting Edge*, Daniel maneuvered his way onto the show and his performance was broadcast. It had always been a dream of his to be on MTV. Though record companies began calling McDonald's to contact Daniel, he withdrew, smoking marijuana and refusing to play live. After a particularly frightening experience at a Butthole Surfers' show—the first time he took LSD—Daniel entered a destructive period. LSD became a habit with Daniel who began to experience manic episodes, during which he became violent, attacking his manager and brother. He became obsessed with the devil and had visions of reforming the wrongs that plague humans. Very late one cold night in 1986, while on LSD, Daniel waded into the shallow creek next to the Winship Drama Building on the campus of the University of Texas and attempted to baptize his friends. They became frightened and eventually the police arrived. He was placed in the Austin State Hospital, in a mental ward. There, his obsession with the devil intensified. He started discarding his possessions and spoke of "dying to live forever." Figures, numbers and symbols possessed special meaning to Daniel. The number nine, what he called the "human number," Daniel drew wherever he could.

In 1987, Daniel began to take medication to treat his manic depression. Throughout the year, he tried many different drugs which began to stifle his creativity. In April 1988, Daniel was invited to New York City to work with Sonic Youth. He was arrested at the Statue of Liberty for drawing Christian fish on the monument passages. His comrades tried to get him out of New York and back home but Daniel believed that he was born to be famous and that he was on a religious mission to defeat the devil's attempts to remove him from New York. He was again hospitalized.

After recording with Jad Fair in Maryland, where he began dressing all in white, he went off his medication and got off of his bus back to West Virginia a few towns too early. He wandered around thinking everyone was "possessed by Satan." When an old woman told him to be quiet, Daniel ran up to her second story apartment and scared her to the point where she jumped out of her window and broke both of her ankles.

After being hospitalized again, Daniel was invited to play some large, reputable shows in Austin. The trip was highly successful. On the flight home, in his father's personal aircraft, Daniel began to state that he was Casper the Friendly Ghost. He pulled the keys from the ignition and threw them out the window, forcing the plane into a spin. After his father regained the controls, he safely landed the plane in some trees. During his next hospitalization, Daniel felt that he had lost his soul to the devil, who had made him famous.

When Kurt Cobain, the lead singer of Nirvana, began to wear a shirt featuring the cover artwork for Daniel's *Hi, How Are You?* album at all of his photo shoots, it brought surprising interest in Daniel and his work. Immediately, Elektra and Atlantic records began a bidding war over his major debut. Daniel believed Elektra was Satanic since they hired Metallica. Suddenly,

Daniel dropped his manager and longtime friend, Jeff Tartakov. He then signed with Atlantic Records and released the album *Fun*. It sold only 5,000 copies and he was dropped from the label in 1996.

Daniel went back to live in Waller, Texas with his parents, on whom, in his medicated state, he relied heavily. Overweight from years of medication, he enjoyed shopping at the local department stores and started playing with a band called *Danny and the Nightmares*. Much of his artwork is in demand and some has toured internationally. By 2003, Daniel's reputation had also grown internationally and he began to tour around the world.

Both tragic and hope-inspiring, Daniel Johnston's story has elements to which we can all relate. Like John Lennon, he believes in "love" and that "art has always been inspired by beauty."

Nick Kennedy

CREDITS

Origin: USA
Language: English
Released: 2005
Production: Henry S. Rosenthal; A This Is That, Complex Corporation; released by Sony Pictures Classics
Directed by: Jeff Feuerzeig
Written by: Jeff Feuerzeig
Cinematography by: Fortunato Procopio
Music by: Daniel Johnston
Sound: James LeBrecht
Editing: Tyler Hubby
MPAA rating: PG-13
Running time: 110 minutes

REVIEWS

Chicago Sun-Times Online. April 14, 2006.
Los Angeles Times Online. March 31, 2006.
New York Times Online. March 31, 2006.
Rolling Stone Online. March 30, 2006.
San Francisco Chronicle. April 7, 2006, p. E5.
Variety Online. February 1, 2005.
Village Voice Online. March 28, 2006.

THE DEVIL WEARS PRADA

Hell on Heels.
—Movie tagline

Box Office: $124.7

The Devil Wears Prada tells a familiar coming-of-age story: a fresh-faced college graduate moves to the Big City, lands a job with the boss from hell, meets the challenge head-on and grows in the process. Based on the best-selling novel of the same name by Lauren Weisberger, which in turn is allegedly based on her experience working as an assistant for *Vogue* Editor-in-Chief Anna Wintour, *The Devil Wears Prada* has a lot in common with another, though much darker, film in this genre, *Swimming With Sharks* (1996). Both are about recent college graduates who land in careers parallel to the ones they really want, and both films depict their protagonists becoming gradually more and more immersed in the wants and needs of their unreasonably demanding bosses. But where *Swimming With Sharks* fully embraces dark comedy to the point of being almost morbidly cynical, director Dave Frankel keeps things in *The Devil Wears Prada* pretty light and appropriately glamorous, but shallow.

Andrea "Andy" Sachs (Anne Hathaway), just out of journalism school, is sent to interview for the position of second assistant to Miranda Priestly (Meryl Streep) the editor-in-chief of *Runway* magazine, a premiere fashion publication in the world of *The Devil Wears Prada*. Andy is very plain and no-nonsense, so she is of course immediately a target for ridicule at the obsessively image-conscious *Runway*. Emily (Emily Blunt), Miranda's first assistant—someone as important as Miranda must, of course, have two assistants—says upon seeing Andy that the human resources department certainly has "a sense of humor." When Miranda shows up in the office unexpectedly early, she rattles off an incredible list of instructions to Emily, the last of which is to send Andy in for an interview. Miranda points out that Andy is absolutely wrong for *Runway*, as she has no sense of style or fashion. Andy gives an impassioned speech that impresses Miranda, and she gets the job.

So begins Andy's descent into the fashion world. At first, Andy simply does not see what all the fuss is about when it comes to both fashion and her job. During a run-through for the next issue of the magazine, an assistant holds up two very similar-looking belts for Miranda to choose from and says that they look "so different." Andy snickers and is treated to a withering lecture from Miranda on how the very color of the sweater she is wearing was actually selected by the people at *Runway*, so her own tastes have been shaped by the fashion industry, the very thing she feels apart from. Andy, aware that working as Miranda's assistant for a year will probably enable her to get any job she wants in publishing, vows to stick with the job for a year. A montage follows of Andy working the job from hell, emphasized by various shots of Miranda slamming her coat and bag down on Andy's desk for her to hang up.

And so goes the structure of *The Devil Wears Prada*: Andy has a setback, overcomes obstacles, and comes out the other end tougher for it. Things appear to be going quite well for Andy, until she cannot get Miranda a last-minute flight out of a hurricane-beset Miami. When Miranda admonishes Andy severely, Andy despondently turns to *Runway*'s fashion director, Nigel (Stanley Tucci), for advice. Nigel is unsypathetic and points out that she is going through the motions of her job, but is not really in it. "Fashion," Nigel says, "is greater than art because you live your life in it." Andy vows to make an effort to dive into the fashion world and, appropriately, Nigel gives her a makeover. That is largely the message of *The Devil Wears Prada*: all it takes to improve one's station is some glib career advice and a wardrobe change.

Ultimately, Andy becomes so involved in doing her job that she can no longer separate herself from it. She becomes the image of the perfect assistant. Every challenge thrown at her is met with aplomb, but it all comes with a cost. She loses her friends and eventually her boyfriend, she usurps Emily's place at Miranda's side for *Runway*'s fashion week in Paris, and she finds herself constantly at Miranda's beck and call. In justifying these actions to others and herself, her response is, unfailingly, "I don't have a choice." In Paris, faced with the possibility that Miranda is about to be fired, Andy does everything she possibly can to warn Miranda. But Miranda, always the political animal, is not only aware of her imminent ousting, but she has already foiled it through her own machinations: she saves her job by manipulating her rival into taking another job, one she had originally procured for Nigel. When Miranda compares her betrayal of Nigel to Andy's betrayal of Emily, Andy finally sees that if she stays on this path, she will become just like Miranda, and that she, in fact, does have a choice: to quit. She does, and pursues a career in journalism.

The Devil Wears Prada, certainly designed to be fluff, is pathologically shallow. One of the major weaknesses of the film is Andy's relationships with her apparently old friends, and especially with her boyfriend, Nate (Adrian Grenier). While they were perhaps written in as an attempt to deepen the sense that Andy has a life outside of work or to raise the stakes for her, giving her something to lose, Andy's extra-office relationships only serve to heighten the film's sense of superficiality. Neither she nor they seem to be particularly invested in one another: her friends seem more than happy to accept the trinkets and perks that she provides them with, but they also berate her for changing, not in a way caring friends would, but in a self-righteous way designed to call attention to the direction in which the plot must inevitably move. The friends are essentially props whose function is to serve as benchmarks for exactly where Andy is in the story: they go from toasting the new job and accepting the filthy lucre of the fashion industry, to being flummoxed that Andy is constantly answering Miranda's calls and being vocal about not liking who she is becoming. Andy's boyfriend does not fare much better here. In fact, when their relationship falls apart, Andy very quickly goes on the rebound while in Paris with a writer she admires and has formed a bond with but barely knows, Christian Thompson (Simon Baker).

The Devil Wears Prada makes a few attempts at trawling for insight and pathos. Miranda's and Nigel's speeches about the reach and meaning of fashion, and by extension the fashion industry, is about as deep as the film gets. Also, Nigel's monologue to Andy about really investing oneself in one's work certainly has the feel of authenticity, as he has clearly embraced this philosophy himself, but it is obvious that this path has more than damaged him a bit, and by the end of the film, it is clear that Andy, though she has overcome obstacles and attained a place for herself in her chosen profession, has not escaped unscathed. Given the evidence, the audience is justified in questioning whether exposure to these beliefs (that the long arm of fashion affects everyone and that immersion in work is worthwhile) warrants the nearly two hours of sadism it has just witnessed. The only moment in the film that comes close to true emotional gravity is when Andy discovers a shaken Miranda in her hotel room, on the verge of another divorce, worried about what horrible things her children will have to read in the tabloids about her. But this too is glossed over, and the brief peek into Miranda's emotional life only serves to subvert her as a truly powerful object of either admiration or loathing. And when the most vile character in a movie is given the most human moment in the story, one wonders if Andy, the person the audience is asked to root for, is really worth its sympathy.

John Boaz

CREDITS

Andy Sachs: Anne Hathaway

Miranda Priestly: Meryl Streep

Nate: Adrian Grenier

Christian Thompson: Simon Baker

Nigel: Stanley Tucci

Emily: Emily Blunt

Lilly: Tracie Thoms

Richard Barnes: David Marshall Grant

Stephen: James Naughton

James Holt: Daniel Sunjata

Jocelyn: Rebecca Mader

Doug: Rich Sommer
Origin: USA
Language: English
Released: 2006
Production: Wendy Finerman; Fox 2000 Pictures; released by 20th Century Fox
Directed by: David Frankel
Written by: Aline Brosh McKenna
Cinematography by: Florian Ballhaus
Music by: Theodore Shapiro
Sound: T.J. O'Mara
Editing: Mark Livolsi
Art Direction: Tom Warren
Costumes: Patricia Field
Production Design: Jess Gonchor
MPAA rating: PG-13
Running time: 106 minutes

REVIEWS

Boxoffice Online. June 30, 2006.
Chicago Sun-Times Online. June 30, 2006.
Entertainment Weekly Online. June 21, 2006.
Los Angeles Times Online. June 30, 2006.
New York Times Online. June 30, 2006.
Premiere Magazine Online. June 29, 2006.
Variety Online. June 22, 2006.
Washington Post. June 30, 2006, p. C1.

QUOTES

Miranda Priestly: "The details of your incompetence do not interest me."

AWARDS

Golden Globes 2007: Actress—Mus./Comedy (Streep)
Nomination:
Oscars 2006: Actress (Streep), Costume Des.
British Acad. 2006: Actress (Streep), Adapt. Screenplay, Costume Des., Makeup, Support. Actress (Blunt)
Golden Globes 2007: Film—Mus./Comedy, Support. Actress (Blunt)
Screen Actors Guild 2006: Actress (Streep)
Writers Guild 2006: Adapt. Screenplay

DON'T COME KNOCKING

A new kind of road movie.
—Movie tagline

Directed by Wim Wenders from a screenplay written by Sam Shepard, *Don't Come Knocking* stars Shepard as Howard Spence, a disaffected, burned-out movie actor who one day rides off on horseback from the Utah set where he is filming a Western. While we do not know his precise motivations, we gather that he is suffering from a general malaise; even his last name, an obvious pun on "spent," seems to sum up his situation. He leaves the film crew in disarray (they are forced to shoot around him as best they can) and ends up discovering his family, some of whom he has never met before. *Don't Come Knocking* is a slow-moving, often labored piece of art house cinema whose script lacks any sense of momentum and whose themes of family and connection feel half-baked and even trite. Nonetheless, the performances, especially those by the actresses who play the women in Howard's orbit, lend the film a much-needed credibility and even glimmers of poignancy.

Howard's first step brings him to his mother (Eva Marie Saint), who, unbelievably enough, welcomes him back without probing him about his thirty-year absence. She is curious about all the gossip surrounding his wild movie-star ways—a career punctuated by an abundance of women, drugs, and alcohol—but her offhand question about his child takes him by surprise. He did not know that he was a father, and the revelation sends him from his mother's home in Elko, Nevada, to Butte, Montana, where he made a film many years ago and had an affair with a local waitress.

Butte is depicted in an odd way—as a sleepy town where the streets are generally deserted but the bars are overflowing with customers and everyone Howard needs to meet are somehow always easy to find, especially Doreen (Jessica Lange), the waitress with whom he produced a son, Earl (Gabriel Mann), who is now an adult and just happens to play guitar and sing in a local bar. Hovering at the periphery of the action is Sky (Sarah Polley), a solitary young woman whose mother just passed away and who walks around with the urn containing her ashes.

Doreen is very gracious with Howard, especially considering the fact that she had to raise their son without him. But Howard is at a loss as to how to connect with Earl, who is angry from the outset at discovering the father he never knew, and the film essentially has nowhere to go with this relationship. Earl, so flummoxed at meeting Howard, goes on a tirade during which he throws practically all of his possessions out of his apartment onto the street below. Howard, meanwhile, spends his time in Butte looking grim and melancholy, full of regret for the things he might have done differently. In a rather far-fetched plot turn, Sky turns out to be Howard's daughter, and attempts to bond with this man who does not seem to know what he wants.

While the story itself is static, at least many of the performances are engaging. Lange finds the right balance between Doreen's warmth and toughness. When Howard hits on the idea that he and Doreen should get married and admits that not marrying her was the big mistake of his life, she unleashes all the passion, rage, and frustration buried inside her for so many years. Fairuza Balk brings some spunk and offbeat humor to Amber, Earl's oddball girlfriend, making her slightly spacey and weird yet endearing at the same time. She has a bizarre scene where she dances on Earl's sofa in the middle of the street while he plays his guitar. It is completely random and goofy but also a bit surreal in a David Lynch kind of way.

And Sarah Polley is simply luminous as Sky. Despite the tragedy and apparent suddenness of her mother's death, Sky has an almost otherworldly calmness and serenity about her, which anchors the film. With an unflappable sense of composure and the touching way she pursues a father who continually resists her and a half brother who cannot let go of his hostility, Polley's Sky is the story's emotional heart. She raises the film's big themes when she speculates about Earl's fear of being related and suggests to Howard that he settle down in Butte; the search for family and home is, after all, what the film is about.

Unfortunately, these themes are never explored with any depth, the tone is inconsistent, and the characters, at heart, rarely rise above being mere types. Moreover, the sheer coincidence of how everyone connected to Howard could converge at the same time and at the exact same place strains credulity. Indeed, it is not clear to what extent we are to read the film as realism or as an off-kilter fable where chance encounters are simply accepted as the norm.

Despite its narrative shortcomings, *Don't Come Knocking* is quite stunning visually, with cinematographer Franz Lustig capturing the grandeur of the wide-open West, the starkness of the lonely road, and the beautiful nuances of daylight and nighttime in a small town. Some shots, however, veer toward pretentiousness. Howard's dislocation from life, for example, is communicated twice with a spinning camera, first when he enters a casino in Elko and is bombarded with bright lights all around him and later when an exhausted Howard sits in the sofa in the middle of the street and the camera circles around him, obviously symbolizing the confusion in his mind regarding the new relationships he has had to sort through.

But the screenplay does not come to terms with these newfound family ties beyond a series of overwrought confrontations and fights and ultimately meanders to a conclusion that resolves nothing. Throughout the film, a stoic investigator named Sutter (Tim Roth) is on Howard's trail with the charge to bring him back to the movie set. (Sutter, incidentally, represents the antithesis of Howard's situation—a man who is not only unencumbered by any family but likes it that way—yet the screenplay does nothing insightful with this dichotomy.) Finally catching up with Howard, Sutter allows him to say his good-byes to his children, during which Sky reflects on all the times she used to look at his photographs and ponder their possible kinship.

But because the characters are poorly developed and the plot is both plodding and often implausible, even Sky's haunting, mesmerizing farewell does not quite have the emotional pull that it should. We are supposed to feel the great weight of missed opportunities and the sadness of lost years, but the actors, as good as they are, can only do so much to create an inner life that has not been written. At the end, it is hard to say if Howard has been redeemed or even changed by his journey. The movie he returns to make is called *Phantom of the West*, which may as well be a description of Howard himself, as elusive at the end as he is at the beginning.

Peter N. Chumo II

CREDITS

Howard Spence: Sam Shepard
Doreen: Jessica Lange
Sky: Sarah Polley
Earl: Gabriel Mann
Sutter: Tim Roth
Amber: Fairuza Balk
Howard's Mother: Eva Marie Saint
Old Ranch Hand: James Gammon
Director: George Kennedy
Starlet: Marley Shelton
Wild Eye: Rodney A. Grant
Producer #1: Tim Matheson
Producer #2: Julia Sweeney
Mr. Daily: Kurt Fuller
First Assistant Director: James Roday
Origin: USA
Language: English
Released: 2005
Production: In-Ah Lee, Peter Schwartzkopff, Karsten Brunig; HanWay, Reverse Angle Intl.; released by Sony Classics Pictures
Directed by: Wim Wenders
Written by: Sam Shepard, Wim Wenders (story)
Cinematography by: Franz Lustig
Music by: T-Bone Burnett

Sound: Matthew Nicolay
Editing: Peter Przygodda, Oli Weiss
Art Direction: William Budge, Nicole Lobart
Costumes: Caroline Eselin
Production Design: Nathan Amondson
MPAA rating: R
Running time: 110 minutes

REVIEWS

Boxoffice Online. March 17, 2006.
Los Angeles Times Online. March 17, 2006.
New York Times Online. March 17, 2006.
San Francisco Chronicle Online. March 24, 2006.
Seattle Post-Intelligencer Online. March 24, 2006.
Variety Online. May 19, 2005.
Village Voice Online. March 14, 2006.

QUOTES

Howard Spence to his mother: "I don't know what to do with myself anymore."

TRIVIA

Sam Shepard and Wim Wenders previously worked together on *Paris, Texas* (1984).

DON'T TELL
(La Bestia nel cuore)
(The Beast in the Heart)

Nominated for an Academy Award® for Best Foreign Language Film in 2006, *Don't Tell* (*La Bestia nel cuore*) is a beautiful and powerfully moving Italian drama focusing on the child molestation of a brother and sister and the secret inner-workings of families. Writer/director Cristina Comencini is a veteran of family drama and she is at her best here, adapting yet another of her popular novels for the screen along with writers Francesca Marciano and Giulia Calenda.

Sabina (Giovanna Mezzogiorno) is a beautiful actress who has happily resigned herself to dubbing television movies for a steady paycheck while her handsome live-in boyfriend Franco (Alessio Boni), a die-hard theater actor, is less satisfied with the prospects of finding gainful employment in a cheesy television hospital drama. They are happy together though, sharing a passionate and loving relationship. Boni—so wonderful as Matteo in the U.S. release of *The Best of Youth* (2005)—and Mezzogiorno share significant on-screen chemistry with the brooding artistic Franco nicely offsetting Sabina's pragmatism and sunniness.

Both Sabina's parents are some years deceased and she is unexpectedly summoned to approve the moving of their remains. This event stirs up buried memories as well and she has a nightmare about her father (Valerio Binasco) that hints at molestation. She begins to question the events she remembers as a child and calls on a childhood friend whom she visits from time to time for clarification. Emilia (Stefania Rocca), now a blind recluse, used to come to Sabina's and her older brother Daniele's house to study and with warm fondness, recalls her parents, both teachers, quietly grading papers in the next room and doting on their children. Sabina reveals nothing of her dream to Emilia, Franco, or her other close friend and dubbing director, Maria (Angela Finocchiaro). Maria, however is not shy about unburdening herself to Sabina. The middle-aged Maria is devastated over her husband having recently left her for their daughter's best friend. She tells only Sabina the real reason her husband left and when asked why she is so afraid to tell others, Maria brings up one of the themes of the film: no one wants to admit to the outside world that someone in their family is a monster. You are still a family no matter what has been done. Accordingly, Sabina decides the only person she can talk to about her disturbing dreams is her brother, now a college professor who is married and living in the States. Preparing for her trip to Charlottesville, Virginia, the once happy Sabina continues the unraveling process started by the dream. Thinking about Maria's wandering husband, she snaps at Franco and predicts he will be unfaithful during her trip and her irrational behavior begins to put a strain on their relationship.

Luigi Lo Cascio, who played Boni's older brother in *The Best of Youth,* plays the adult Daniele who, on the surface, seems to have a good relationship with his wife and two children but which definitely show undercurrents of strain. Sabina particularly notices his reluctance to show physical affection to his older son Giovanni (Lewis Lemperuer Palmer) while he is somewhat more comfortable around his younger son Bill (Jeke-Omer Boyayanlar). After receiving some cryptic hints from his wife Anne (Lucy Akhurst), including the revelation that Daniele has been much better since all the therapy, Sabina is able to convince Daniele to talk frankly about what happened to them as children. Daniele shockingly reveals that he was the victim of sexual abuse by their father with their mother's knowledge. He did his best to protect Sabina but his father admitted on his deathbed he abused Sabina twice when she was very young.

In one of the film's two amusing subplots taking place back in Italy, Emilia, a lesbian who pines for Sabina, has now fallen in love with Maria, whom Sabina sent to keep an eye on Emilia in her absence. Though far-fetched, their mutual attraction is quite touching as the sensitive young blind woman is drawn out by the frank and gently wizened Maria, who, in turn, is made to feel beautiful again by the adoring and sensual Emilia. But refusing to let love be simple, Comencini soon shines the cold light of reality upon their relationship and the one-time lovebirds become the jealous and argumentative source of much of the film's comedy.

Another comic subplot involves Franco's budding relationship with his very funny TV director Andrea (talented comic actor Giuseppe Battiston). Although Andrea is invested in doing bad TV for a living, he was once a promising theater director, as Franco points out on their first meeting. As they work together, though, Andrea reveals his secret passion to do a film about two attractive garbage-people who fall in love after they rescue a baby they find in the trash. Over dinner, he suggests Franco for the part, along with an eager young actress who works on the set and has a crush on Franco named Anita (Francesca Inaudi).

Going back to Italy, Sabina now has two secrets from Franco as she also learns she is pregnant with his child. Franco harbors a dangerous secret as well, having given in to Anita's frequent and bold advances, the two slept together one night. With tension rife within the household, Sabina reveals she's pregnant but that she no longer wants to be with Franco as he comes clean about his one night stand. All the main characters gather at Andrea's house in the last reel and while Emilia and Maria bicker and Franco and Andrea discuss their film, Sabina wanders off into in a surreal scene and boards an empty bus where she goes into labor. The group split up to find her and they all meet up again at the hospital where Sabina has given birth to a boy whom she names after her brother and she happily reunites with Franco. Ending on a humorous note, Andrea tells the newborn that he will be the "star" of his film: "I'm going to put you in the garbage!"

Franco Piersanti's score meshes well with the action in this gracefully filmed effort that highlights the wonderful performances of the fine ensemble cast and a story that lingers long after the credits have rolled.

Hilary White

CREDITS

Sabina: Giovanna Mezzogiorno
Emilia: Stefania Rocca
Maria: Angela Finocchiaro
Franco: Alessio Boni
Daniele: Luigi Lo Cascio
Father: Valerio Binasco
Giovanni: Lewis Lemperuer Palmer
Bill: Jeke-Omer Boyayanlar
Anne: Lucy Akhurst
Andrea: Giuseppe Battiston
Anita: Francesca Inaudi
Origin: Italy
Language: Italian
Released: 2005
Production: Riccardo Tozzi, Giovanni Stabilini, Marco Chimenz; RAI Cinema, Cattleya (Italy), Beast in the Heart Films (U.K.), Alquimia Cinema (Spain), Babe; released by A 01 Distribution
Directed by: Cristina Comencini
Written by: Francesca Marciano, Giulia Calenda, Cristina Comencini
Cinematography by: Fabio Cianchetti
Music by: Franco Piersanti
Sound: Bruno Pupparo
Editing: Cecilia Zanuso
Costumes: Antonella Berardi
Production Design: Paola Comencini
MPAA rating: R
Running time: 120 minutes

REVIEWS

Los Angeles Times Online. March 17, 2006.
New York Times Online. March 17, 2006.
San Francisco Chronicle Online. March 17, 2006.
Variety Online. September 13, 2005.
Village Voice Online. March 14, 2006.

AWARDS

Nomination:

Oscars 2006: Best Foreign Language Film

DOWN IN THE VALLEY

Sometimes it's hard to find your way.
—Movie tagline

David Jacobson's flawed neo-Western showcases a stunning performance by co-producer Edward Norton as a delusional, self-styled cowboy aimlessly wandering Los Angeles's San Fernando Valley. Jacobson, whose previous directorial outings include *Dahmer* (2002) and *Criminal* (1994), is clearly at home fleshing out the disturbed persona to the exclusion of many of the supporting characters, and allowing the overly long and ambitious storyline to lose it's way among inane situations and a surfeit of symbolism. Hailing from Van Nuys, Jacobson does achieve just the right look of the bleak, sun-bleached Los Angeles landscapes contrasted with idyllic grassy oases miraculously appearing just outside the city.

Played by Evan Rachel Wood, October is a typical So-Cal teen who lives in a modest, retro-looking ranch in the Valley with her stern, corrections officer father Wade (David Morse) and shy little brother Lonnie (Rory Culkin). Pretty and spirited, Tobe, as she is more commonly known, looks to quell her boredom by cruising in cars with friends and hitting the beach. It is during one of these sojourns that she comes across the thirty-something Harlan Caruthers (Norton), who, like the full-service gas station he works in, seems highly anachronistic. Polite Harlan wears a broken-in cowboy hat and an aw-shucks aura that makes the other kids laugh, but which Tobe finds charming. When he tells her he's a ranch hand from South Dakota and that he's never seen the ocean, she takes the opportunity to ask the shy cowpoke to come along with them to the beach. When Harlan quits his job on the spot to do so, Tobe is completely taken in by his inner-bad boy as well. They spend the long day together on the beach, frolicking in the waves and are soon making love in a motel room. Although he is at least twice her age and looks it, Harlan radiates an innocence that makes it seem almost as if Tobe is a city-dwelling Lolita corrupting this pure-hearted country boy.

This, however, is not actually the case in this tale of loneliness and longing in the Valley. Back at the seedy room Harlan temporarily calls home, we see a very different person than the laid-back cowboy we have come to know thus far. Instead of oozing well-mannered charm and backwoods wisdom, Harlan is smoking pot and swearing at his loud neighbors in a voice that has lost its amiable country twang and suddenly sounds suspiciously like everyone else in Los Angeles. The brilliance of Norton's performance is that, although this moment comes fairly early in the film, he still is able to convince the audience, as well as himself, that who he pretends to be is who he desperately wants to be at heart. It also harkens back to his foreshadowing advice to Tobe on their first date, when he told her, in so many words, that you can be whatever you want to be.

Although Harlan, back in character, comes calling on Tobe the next day, Wade makes it clear that he is less than thrilled with his young daughter's choice of beau. Lonnie, though, like Tobe, finds Harlan charming and attentive—something Wade, who openly disdains Lonnie's shy ways, is definitely not. Harlan goes right along romancing Tobe, sometimes taking Lonnie along for the ride. Harlan and Tobe climb aboard a bus which is their only means of transport, and travel to a friend's gorgeous ranch outside the city where they ride a white horse together. When they return, Harlan's "friend," ranch owner Charlie (a wonderful but underused Bruce Dern), greets them with a shotgun in a quite unfriendly manner, claiming not to know Harlan. Harlan protests his innocence, claiming the elderly Charlie must be off his medication. The police are called in and a steaming Wade picks them up, warning Tobe not to see her cowboy lover again.

The cracks in Harlan's fragile psyche start to show when Tobe goes out of town for the weekend, leaving the needy Harlan to lurk around her house.. There he finds the equally needy Lonnie and busies himself by taking the boy out on his horse and teaching him how to shoot. Harlan finds himself on the wrong side of Wade, who forbids him to see Lonnie or Tobe again. Even Tobe starts to second-guess her relationship with Harlan after his behavior begins to grow odder and more desperate and she begins to distance herself from him.

Harlan's obsession with Tobe won't be quelled, however, and he shows up unexpectedly in her house begging her to run off with him, adding that they can send for Lonnie later. When Tobe's enthusiastic greeting eventually turn to protests that grow quite nasty, the gun Harlan has in hand "accidentally" fires straight into Tobe's stomach. A distraught Harlan flees the scene, leaving her for dead when her father comes home and discovers her. He rushes her to the hospital. While Wade holds vigil at Tobe's bedside, however, the opportunistic Harlan returns to the house where Lonnie has been virtually abandoned by his father. The conniving sociopath shot himself after leaving the crime scene in an effort to convince Lonnie that Wade shot Tobe and himself. Lonnie buys Harlan's story and the two go off on the white horse Harlan has stolen.

The final reel sinks into ridiculousness as the two runaways find they have squatted on the movie set of a western, where Harlan feels right at home mingling with the extras. It is here that the inevitable Old West-style "shoot-out" takes place, with Wade, who has now found out about Harlan's troubled and criminal past in juvenile facilities and foster homes, and another officer chasing the two down. Harlan shoots down the officer and wounds Wade before Lonnie and a wounded Harlan escape on horseback. Even though it now must be achingly clear to Lonnie that Harlan is psychotic, he remains loyal to him to the end, even as Wade limps in to finish Harlan off. With Tobe now completely healed from the seemingly fatal wound, Wade drives her and Lonnie to the ranch to lovingly scatter Harlan's ashes and fondly remember their misguided friend.

Tobe and her family seem one-dimensional and patly cliched—restless, misunderstood teen; heavy-handed, misguided father; neglected younger brother—and the characters and backstory are woefully underdeveloped. Culkin's character, especially, could have been fleshed out further as his performance certainly merits it. Despite this and the sometimes tortuous pacing, the film is a tour-de-force for Norton, whose pitch-perfect performance is fascinating to watch in a piece that might have succeeded as a character study rather than a romantic drama cum modern day western.

Hilary White

CREDITS

Harlan: Edward Norton
Tobe: Evan Rachel Wood
Wade: David Morse
Lonnie: Rory Culkin
Steve: John Diehl
April: Kat Dennings
Kris: Hunter Parrish
Charlie: Bruce Dern
Bill Sr.: Muse Watson
Sheridan: Geoffrey Lewis
Sherri: Aviva
Jeremy: Aaron Fors
Shell: Heather Ashleigh
Origin: USA
Language: English
Released: 2005
Production: Holly Wiersma, Adam Rosenfelt, Edward Norton; Holly Wiersma/Element Films
Directed by: David Jacobson
Written by: David Jacobson
Cinematography by: Enrique Chediak
Sound: Steve Morrow
Music Supervisor: Matt Aberly, Jay Faires
Editing: Lynzee Klingman, Michael Hofacre
Art Direction: Michael Atwell
Costumes: Jacqueline West
Production Design: Franco-Giacomo Carbone
MPAA rating: R
Running time: 114 minutes

REVIEWS

Boxoffice Online. May 5, 2006.
Chicago Sun-Times Online. May 19, 2006.
Entertainment Weekly Online. May 10, 2006.
Los Angeles Times Online. May 12, 2006.
New York Times Online. May 5, 2006.
Premiere Online. May 2, 2006.
Variety Online. May 14, 2005.
Washington Post. May 12, 2006, p. C1.

QUOTES

Harlan (to Tobe): "You can do anything you wanna do. You can be anybody you wanna be. You just have to decide on it."

TRIVIA

The film's $8 million budget was wholly financed by producer-financier Sam Nazarian of Element Films.

DREAMGIRLS

Fame comes and goes, stars rise and fall, but dreams live forever.
—Movie tagline
One Dream Will Change Everything.
—Movie tagline
All you have to do is dream.
—Movie tagline

Box Office: $101.2 million

The Motown Sound is one of the most distinctive types of American popular music, blending aspects of rhythm and blues, soul, gospel, rock, and jazz into a slick, heavily melodic style. *Dreamgirls*, adapted from the 1981 Broadway musical, with book and lyrics by Tom Eyen and music by Henry Krieger, is supposedly a thinly veiled version of the beginnings of Motown, but suffers from dramatic cliches, poorly developed characters, and bland music.

Dreamgirls is the story of how a three-woman Detroit singing group, originally named the Dreamettes and later the Dreams, gets its big break and deals with the turmoil of success. The group is clearly inspired by the Supremes, composed of Diana Ross, Mary Wilson, and Flo Ballard and Motown's most successful act during the 1960s. Just as Motown founder Berry Gordy, Jr., created the group's sound, replacing Ballard as lead singer with Ross, *Dreamgirls* depicts the discovery of the Dreamettes by Curtis Taylor, Jr. (Jamie Foxx), a Detroit automobile dealer, and his slow grooming of the group for stardom.

The Dreamettes go from amateur performances with Effie White (Jennifer Hudson) as lead singer and Deena Jones (Beyonce Knowles) and Lorrell Robinson (Anika Noni Rose) as backups to lending support for soul singer James "Thunder" Early (Eddie Murphy). Later, even though Effie is Curtis's lover, he makes the more beautiful, and therefore more commercial, Deena the heart of the Dreams.

The backstage infighting of show business has always been fascinating, with *All About Eve* (1950) and *A Star Is Born* (1937, 1954, 1976) among the more prominent film examples. The dramatic tension in *Dreamgirls* comes from Curtis's ruthless ambition and his cruel manipulation of those around him. He steals Early away from longtime manager Marty Madison (Danny Glover) only to try to change his style, with tragic results. He marries Deena but sees her only as a product, never as a person. A poorly developed subplot is Early's longtime affair with Lorrell. Curtis's dumping of Effie leads to her estrangement from her brother, C. C. (Keith Robinson), who writes all the group's songs. While Effie and Early evoke some sympathy as victims, they remain sketchily drawn characters.

One of the problems with many musicals is that already thin plots are stretched to fill in the gaps between the songs. This flaw would be less bothersome in *Dreamgirls* if the songs were remotely entertaining, but they are all a pale imitation of the Motown Sound. At the opening of the film, fragments of four performances are seen, and except for a blues song performed in the style of B. B. King, all sound exactly the same. For the rest of *Dreamgirls*, the blandness continues, undercutting the premise of the immense popularity of the Dreams, who appear on the cover of *Time*. Even though Early is modeled after such robust artists as James Brown, Otis Redding, and Marvin Gaye, his songs also lack distinction. For the first half hour of *Dreamgirls*, all the numbers are performed on stage. When they suddenly appear off stage, performed in character to express the thoughts of the protagonists, the effect is jarring. *Dreamgirls* has not initially seemed that kind of musical.

While Foxx is a good actor when he has a good script, as in *Collateral* (2004) and *Ray* (2004), he is underwhelming otherwise. Foxx approaches Curtis tentatively, as if he does not want this obvious villain to be too unlikable. Knowles, the popular singer of tunes almost as undistinguished as those in *Dreamgirls*, strives to sound like Ross but comes off as a weak imitator. While Ross has a reputation as a pushy diva, the screenplay by Bill Condon, who also directs, makes Deena a Pollyanna with no spunk. Even reviewers who liked *Dreamgirls*, and the majority did, found fault with Knowles, but she is given too little to work with to determine if she has any acting talent.

Then there is the much-acclaimed performance of Hudson. Effie is the emotional soul of *Dreamgirls*, yet the character consists of only a few broad strokes. Hudson has a powerful voice, but so have numerous other *American Idol* contestants, which she once was. As Etta James and Aretha Franklin have shown, soul is about nuance and phrasing, not just volume. When not singing, Hudson resorts to sassy-fat-black-woman cliches. Her big number, "And I'm Telling You I'm Not Going," which reportedly elicits applause from most audiences, is musically no different from her other songs. Rather than an anthem of defiance, as it seems at first, the song is about a woman's capitulation to humiliation.

Murphy's equally praised performance at first also seems overrated, but he kicks things into gear in the second half of the film by staring down C. C., who objects to Early's drug use, and by defying expectations at a televised tribute to Curtis. More than the other actors, Murphy takes an obvious delight in performing and is not afraid to expose his character's dark side. Glover effortlessly imbues Marty with more complexity than the script allows, becoming a moral force through the authority of his performance more than the script's preachiness. The best musical moment comes courtesy of Loretta Devine, who originated the role of Lorell. As a Detroit nightclub singer performing at a wake, she gives "I Miss You, Old Friend" a depth of feeling missing elsewhere.

While Condon showed some visual flair in his earlier films, such as *Gods and Monsters* (1998) and *Kinsey* (2004), *Dreamgirls* lumbers from one scene to the next as unimaginatively as a made-for-television film. There is little to distinguish it from predecessors dealing with similar material, except that *The Five Heartbeats* (1991), *What's Love Got to Do with It* (1993), *Why Do Fools Fall in Love* (1998), and *Ray* have better music. Even *Sparkle* (1976), the campy first fictional treatment of the Supremes, has a certain trashy vitality lacking in *Dreamgirls*. Condon has apparently studied the films of Steven Spielberg carefully, however, and he works valiantly to manipulate the audience's emotions to hide the flaws of *Dreamgirls*. Those willing to give in to the film's simplistic emotionality will be rewarded.

Like many period films, *Dreamgirls* makes a few factual errors. White singers are condemned for stealing the songs of black performers and making them bigger hits for an audience resistance to so-called race music. This practice was rampant with people like Elvis Presley and Pat Boone in the 1950s but had dissipated by the period of *Dreamgirls*. The film shows such an act performing on *American Bandstand* (1952-1989) while teenagers dance in front of the singers, but Dick Clark always had the kids sit during such guest appearances. During a scene in the mid-1960s, legendary Beatles producer is referred to as Sir George Martin, a title he did not earn until 1996. Condon mixes in footage of the 1967 Detroit riots, only to show a sign announcing a performance by the Dreams on New Year's Eve 1966.

Motown is the Supremes singing "Where Did Our Love Go," Marvin Gaye performing "I Heard It through the Grapevine," and Smokey Robinson doing "The Tracks of My Tears." Such songs have the style and grace and emotional impact missing from *Dreamgirls*.

Michael Adams

CREDITS

Curtis Taylor Jr.: Jamie Foxx
James "Thunder" Early: Eddie Murphy

Deena Jones: Beyonce Knowles
Lorrell Robinson: Anika Noni Rose
Effie White: Jennifer Hudson
Marty Madison: Danny Glover
Michelle: Sharon Leal
C.C. White: Keith Robinson
Jazz Singer: Loretta Devine
Origin: USA
Language: English
Released: 2006
Production: Laurence Mark; DreamWorks Pictures; released by Paramount Pictures
Directed by: Bill Condon
Written by: Bill Condon
Cinematography by: Tobias Schliessler
Music by: Henry Krieger
Sound: Willie Burton
Music Supervisor: Matt Sullivan, Randy Speedlove
Editing: Virginia Katz
Art Direction: Thomas Voth
Costumes: Sharen CQ Davis
Production Design: John Myhre
MPAA rating: PG-13
Running time: 130 minutes

REVIEWS

Chicago Sun-Times Online. December 22, 2006.
Entertainment Weekly. December 22, 2006, p. 54.
Hollywood Reporter Online. December 1, 2006.
Los Angeles Times Online. December 15, 2006.
New York Times Online. December 15, 2006.
Newsweek Online. December 11, 2006.
Rolling Stone Online. November 21, 2006.
San Francisco Chronicle. December 15, 2006, p. E1.
Variety Online. November 30, 2006.

TRIVIA

Film is dedicated to Michael Bennett, the director/choreographer of the original Broadway production, who died in 1987.

AWARDS

Oscars 2006: Sound, Support. Actress (Hudson)
British Acad. 2006: Support. Actress (Hudson)
Golden Globes 2007: Film—Mus./Comedy, Support. Actor (Murphy), Support. Actress (Hudson)
Screen Actors Guild 2006: Support. Actor (Murphy), Support. Actress (Hudson)

Nomination:

Oscars 2006: Art Dir./Set Dec., Costume Des., Song ("Listen," "Love You I Do," and "Patience"), Support. Actor (Murphy)
British Acad. 2006: Orig. Score
Directors Guild 2006: Director (Condon)
Golden Globes 2007: Actress—Mus./Comedy (Knowles), Song ("Listen")
Screen Actors Guild 2006: Cast

DUCK SEASON
(Temporada de patos)

Adulthood is a moving target.
—Movie tagline

Although *Duck Season* (originally titled *Temporada de patos,* directed in Mexico by Fernando Eimbcke, starring Diego Catano as Moko, Daniel Miranda as Flama, Danny Perea as Rita, and Enrique Arreola as Ulises) was made in 2004, it was not destined to reach North American markets until 2006. This independent film comedy certainly has much to recommend it, including several nominations and awards from international film festivals. In 2006, for example, it was nominated for the Independent Spirit Award for Best Foreign film after two years of climbing the Awards ladder. In 2005 it won the Special Jury Prize at the Paris Film Festival, as well as a nomination for the Grand Prize. It also won the MTV Movie Award in 2005 for Favorite Actress for Perea. In 2004 it won the Grand Jury Prize at the AFI Fest, the Mayahuel Award for Best Film at the Guadalajara Mexican Film Festival. That same year Eimbcke won the Best Director award at the Thessaloniki Film Festival and was nominated for the Best First Work—Fiction Award at the Golden Ariel Awards in Mexico. Alfonso Cuaron (arguably Mexico's most commercially successful director working in the United States), who served as Executive Producer, helped the production along.

The story of *Duck Season* can be told quickly. Ducks fly in a "V" formation because one duck paves the way for the one behind, who in turn leads another, and is the rest are swept up in the trajectory. They take turns leading the flock—one, then another, so that when the leader is tired, another can quickly take his place. And so on, until they all fly away toward the horizon and their instinctual destination.

But the movie *Duck Season* is not simply about migrating ducks. Set in a tenth-floor high-rise apartment in Mexico City, it's a comedy about four young people who find themselves hanging out one long Sunday afternoon in Mexico City. There is a painting over their couch of ducks in flight, which gives the film its quirky title. The painting can be hypnotic: When you look at it, you can almost hear the lapping of the water, and the distant quacks of the ducks. And you start to imagine the picture is actually moving. Which is only part of the magic of this movie from Mexico by newcomer Eimbcke, who directed the film and also collaborated on the original screenplay with Paula Markovitch. (Some European reviewers found the duck painting "horrible," and also protested that the film moves slowly and that nothing much seems to happen.)

We almost feel sorry for those who come to this film already alerted to its strange and unexpected and moving qualities. As Roger Ebert wrote in the *Chicago Sun-Times*, to describe the film's plot would be a mistake for two reasons, because the story should unfold "to you in your own time, and because the movie isn't about what happens, but about how it happens." For those who must read on, however, here's the deal: Two fourteen-year old boys, Moko (Diego Catano) and Flama (Daniel Miranda), are left behind in the apartment when Moko's mother goes out for the day. The kids, described as "selfish brats" by *London Observer* reviewer Philip French, sit around and play video games ("Bush vs. Bin Laden," for example) and drink Coke and munch chips. They order a pizza. The deliveryman, ironically named Ulises (Enrique Arreola), comes around, tired and bedraggled after climbing ten flights of stairs of the urban high-rise apartment building. Claiming he's late by thirty seconds, the boys refuse to pay for the pizza. The delivery guy stages a sit-down while the boys hungrily regard the unopened pizza. Meanwhile, Rita (Danny Perea), a sixteen-year old girl next door, neglected and left by herself on her birthday, comes in to borrow the oven to make herself a birthday cake. While Rita putters about the kitchen, the boys engage the pizza man in a game of video soccer. At the deciding moment of victory, however, the game shuts off because of a power failure. Over the next few hours, these four characters simply hang out. One of the boys engages in some harmless kissing with the girl. Both boys experiment innocently with their own homoerotic moment. One of them wonders why his red hair isn't common to anyone else in his family, and he begins to doubt his parentage, to the amusement of his friends. And they all eat the brownies Rita has prepared. But because there's marijuana in the brownies, everybody gets stoned. Be warned, however: this meager summary tends to undercut this film's magic because it foreshadows its strange and unexpected, quirky and moving qualities that would best be experienced firsthand.

At this point the film takes off. Accompanied by the wonderful music from Beethoven's Fourth Piano Concerto, viewers are treated to a prolonged series of static shots and uneventful moments that yields to a lyrically surreal sequence in which everyone enjoys a high. Slow-motion shots follow close-ups of water dripping and mouths munching and line dancing. It's an intoxicating sequence signaling more surreal moments to come, when, for example, Ulises grows increasingly absorbed with the duck painting on the wall. He grows so preoccupied with it he slips into the bathtub and regards it hanging on the opposite wall of the bathroom (as a rubber ducky floats beside him in the tub). He dreams he's standing stark naked on the seashore, surrounded by skies and ducks while taking a phone call from his irate boss. He tells off the boss and quits his job. In another sequence the boys stage their own tiny rebellion against the system: They take potshots at all the furniture and bric-a-brac that's been forever the subject of dispute between one of the kid's perpetually quarreling parents. That's the way it is in duck season, you take wing and head south. But this comedy never "goes south."

At the end, after more lounging about and indulging in a game of "Guess-the-Color of the Freske Chocolate" piece (which the girl loses every time), Rita leaves. The boys decide they're going to Acapulco. And the delivery guy rides away down the street, the duck painting strapped to his back, fading into the distance. Seldom will you see a film that seems to show so little while implying so much. The unexpected intersections of these characters are like the quirky trajectory that brings the unsuspecting viewer to this little gem. Roger Ebert thought it was "the meandering quality of the material that [made] it feel real."

So this would seem to be an independent film comedy, tinged with (or perhaps influenced by) "magic realism." *Village Voice* reviewer J. Hoberman called it "a kind of *Cat in the Hat* [comedy] without the cat." In England, *The Guardian* reviewer Peter Bradshaw described it as a "stagey chamber piece" that succeeds because of its "gentle, quirky humour." Hoberman was a bit more guarded: "Like the power that flickers on and off," he wrote, "this slight conceit is intermittent in its humor—but it's consistently well acted, especially by the kids." Less tolerant was *London Times* reviewer Wendy Ide: "There is not a whole lot going on," she complained of the "banal activities" captured by the film, there's "a cursory attempt at French kissing in the kitchen" before they all "get stoned on hash brownies and giggle a lot." *London Observer* film critic Philip French came closer to getting it right, however, when he praised *Duck Season* as "the confident debut of a young Mexican director." Although it took the film two years to get to the United States, it was probably worth the wait. Yes, it's shot mainly in black-and-white (except for three short flashbacks). And yes, for quite awhile it seems the rather amateurish work of a filmmaker who doesn't know how to move his camera or how to stage action. But, gradually, one realizes every shot counts; and when the tightly composed, static shots begin to yield to a more lyrical, even fantastic mode, the viewer gradually takes wing, just as these characters are doing.

James M. Welsh and John C. Tibbetts

CREDITS

Ulises: Enrique Arreola
Moko: Diego Catano
Flama: Daniel Miranda
Rita: Danny Perea
Origin: Mexico
Language: Spanish
Released: 2004
Production: Christian Valdelievre; released by Warner Independent Pictures
Directed by: Fernando Eimbcke
Written by: Fernando Eimbcke, Paula Markovitch
Cinematography by: Alexis Zabe
Music by: Alejandro Rosso
Editing: Maria Rodriguez
Production Design: Diana Quiroz
MPAA rating: R
Running time: 90 minutes

REVIEWS

Chicago Sun-Times Online. March 17, 2006.
Entertainment Weekly Online. March 8, 2006.
Los Angeles Times Online. March 10, 2006.
New York Times Online. March 10, 2006.
Premiere Magazine Online. March 9, 2006.
Village Voice Online. March 7, 2006.

QUOTES

Rita to Moko: "Memory can be exercised. Of course you have to care about things to remember them."

E

EIGHT BELOW

The Most Amazing Story Of Survival, Friendship, And Adventure Ever Told.
—Movie tagline

Box Office: $81.6 million

Eight Below is a heart-rending story about a team of sled dogs stranded in the brutal glacial terrain of Antarctica. Released by Walt Disney Pictures, *Eight Below* gives a "suggested by" credit to the 1983 Japanese film, *Nankyoku Monogatari,* which was reportedly based on true events that occurred during a Japanese expedition in 1958. According to that film, of the fifteen Sakahalin huskies used on the mission, only two survived. These two canine brothers, Taro and Jiro, have been preserved at the National Science Museum at Ueno, Tokyo. In the Disney version of the tale, director Frank Marshall (who directed another cold-defying survival film, *Alive,* in 1993) teamed up with screenwriter David DiGilio and crafted a script that is an amalgam of elements from the true account, portions of the Japanese film, and a bit of creative license.

Terrain guide Jerry Shepard (Paul Walker) is employed at a research base in Antarctica which is utilized by the National Science Foundation. An intellectual hotshot from UCLA, Dr. Davis McClaren (Bruce Greenwood) convinces Shepard to take him to a crater formed by a meteor, which is believed to have originated from the planet Mercury. Instead of snowmobiles, Jerry opts for the team of dogs to pull them along the hazardous course to the site. Despite being called back by the base due to a massive snowstorm threatening the area, Jerry allows himself to be swayed against his better judgment by the professor and ignores the order to abort. Once McClaren obtains a fragment that he believes will propel him to fame among his colleagues, the two head back.

During the trek back, McClaren falls through a thin portion of ice. Fighting against the approaching cataclysmic storm, Jerry's frostbite, and the doctor's hypothermia, the team of eight dogs successfully brings the duo back, sparing them from a certain frigid demise. The turbulent storm forces the base to evacuate and Jerry is forced to leave the dogs behind because the pilot, his former love Katie (Moon Bloodgood), informed him that the plane cannot fly with the additional weight of the canines. She promises to take him back once the storm subsides. Of course, for Disney's requisite drama to occur this is unlikely to happen anytime soon and the storm escalates in its savagery. The dogs are left alone with only their ingenuity and cunning, obviously a nascent trait in the two Alaskan Malamutes and six Siberian Huskies.

The dogs survive by eating various fowl as well as a the frozen carcass of a killer whale and even manage to dodge the deadly territorial behavior of a leopard seal which manages to bite and consequently almost kill Maya, who serves as the pack's matriarch. Meanwhile, Jerry is fighting an uphill battle against egos and bureaucracy in order to retrieve his dogs. McClaren is struck with a moment of empathy when he views a drawing his son Eric (Connor Christopher Levins) made of the dogs with the loving scrawl: "My hero is the dogs who saved my Daddy." With that, the Professor provides the financing for a rescue mission.

Although a touching story with an effective theme of domestic dog vs. nature, it has not gained unanimous praise from all critics. Jeff Strickler of the *Minneapolis Star Tribune* enjoyed the canine plot considerably more than the human component and admits that Paul Walker's casting did not work for him. "Walker," he writes, "best known for *The Fast and the Furious* movies, is an action star who fares best in the early scenes when his character is adventuring. Sitting around, moping about his inability to save the dogs that saved him, is not the actor's strong suit."

David Metz Roberts

CREDITS

Jerry Shepard: Paul Walker
Davis McClaren: Bruce Greenwood
Charlie Cooper: Jason Biggs
Dr. Andy Harrison: Gerard Plunkett
Mindo: August Schellenberg
Eve McClaren: Wendy Crewson
Eric McClaren: Connor Christopher Levins
Katie: Moon Bloodgood
Rosemary: Belinda Metz
Origin: USA
Language: English
Released: 2006
Production: David Hoberman, Patrick Crowley; Walt Disney Pictures, Spyglass Entertainment, Mandeville Films; released by Buena Vista
Directed by: Frank Marshall
Written by: Dave DiGilio
Cinematography by: Don Burgess
Music by: Mark Isham
Sound: Kirk Francis
Editing: Christopher Rouse
Art Direction: Jeremy Stanbridge
Costumes: Jori Woodman
Production Design: John Willett
MPAA rating: PG
Running time: 120 minutes

REVIEWS

Boxoffice Online. February 17, 2006.
Chicago Sun-Times Online. February 17, 2006.
Entertainment Weekly Online. February 15, 2006.
Los Angeles Times Online. February 17, 2006.
New York Times Online. February 17, 2006.
Premiere Magazine Online. February 16, 2006.
Variety Online. February 8, 2006.
Washington Post Online. February 2006.

QUOTES

Jerry Shepard to Maya: "How's my best girl doing?"

TRIVIA

The borrowed snow tractor in the film is named "Mare Biscotti," which translates to "Sea Biscuit," a film director Frank Marshall produced.

EMPLOYEE OF THE MONTH

In order to get the girl, he's gotta get his shift together.
—Movie tagline

Box Office: $28.4 million

It was not lack of publicity that was the downfall of *Employee of the Month*. In the weeks prior to its release, costar Jessica Simpson was a regular feature in the tabloids. Speculation about whether or not she had an affair with costar Dane Cook gave the film pages and pages of publicity. Unfortunately, few of these pages were devoted to extolling the virtues of the film.

The film is pretty much an Adam Sandler film, except that Sandler had nothing to do with it. In the man-child role that is a de rigueur for such movies is popular comedian Dane Cook. Zack (Cook) is coasting along in his job as a box boy at Super Club, a Costco-like megastore. He does the minimum required at his job and spends his downtime on the job—that would be pretty much all day—in a secret spot he and his buddies, Lon (Andy Dick) and Russell (Harland Williams), have set up within a tall stack of boxes. Only in a movie with this level of maturity would the main hero be someone who hangs out in a secret fort at age thirty-four. When Zack is not playing cards in this version of a tree house, he spends his time racing a little mini-bike around the store and whizzing though the wide aisles on his Heelys roller shoes: what the film considers the epitome of cool.

Zack's days behaving as a sub-par Chevy Chase are over when a new cashier, Amy (Jessica Simpson), arrives at the store. Amy is gorgeous and rumor has it that she only likes guys who win the store's employee of the month award. Zack knows that he must win the award if he hopes to get the girl.

Zack's big problem (besides the fact that he works as a box boy at Super Club) is that Vince (Dax Shepard) is a shoo-in for the award. Vince is a favorite of managers and customers alike. He is a friend to old ladies, a sly flirt with young female customers, and a model employee to his gushing boss, Glen Gary (Tim Bagley). Vince, who has won the award for seventeen straight months, is especially anxious to win the award this particular month because the prize is a newish Chevy Nova.

There is something depressing and small about a contest that has Simpson and a Nova as the prizes. That does not have to be a bad thing. *Office Space* (1999) and TV's *The Office* have created wonderful comedy from uninspired workplaces. But *Employee of the Month* only comes up with uninspired comedy. Wesley Morris of the *Boston Globe* wrote that this is "a movie about adults whose lives revolve entirely around a New Mexico superstore. And no matter how many times a character gets whacked in the head, hit in the groin, or called lame, slutty, stupid, or gassy, the whole thing feels like a tragedy."

Cook, as Zack, does not have much in the way of charisma, despite the film's insistence to the contrary. Yes, Zack is indeed the alpha male of the story, but writers Greg Coolidge (who also directed), Don Calame, and Chris Conroy do not exactly give him much in the way of competition. Vince is a petty, snippy man who thinks that possessing the key to the cashier's lounge is the definition of success. And with friends played by nebbishy Dick and Williams, even Pat Sajak would seem manly and cool. Simpson's Amy is similar to Simpson's Daisy Duke—a character whose main personality trait is that she smiles a lot. Perhaps with different actors and a zippier script, *Employee of the Month* could have been a lot better. But then, the same could be true of any lackluster movie.

Neither critics nor the general moviegoing public cared much for the film. Ruthe Stein of the *San Francisco Chronicle* wrote: "This will never be the movie of the month, but you could do a lot worse at the multiplex." Jeannette Catsoulis of the *New York Times* wrote: "Replete with loser buddies, limp subplots and a dwarf named Glen Ross (Danny Woodburn), *Employee of the Month* is more tired than a Wal-Mart greeter at the end of a Saturday shift." Mark Olsen of the *Los Angeles Times* thought Cook floundered in his role. "Stripped of his usual delivery," Olsen wrote, "he struggles to convey regular-guy likability, coming across instead as alternately flat or arrogant." Finally, Ann Hornaday of the *Washington Post* objected to Simpson, writing that "rarely has an actress exuded such blank nothingness as Simpson, a one-woman vapid delivery system who sucks the energy and joy out of every scene she's in, like some freakishly well-endowed black hole."

Jill Hamilton

CREDITS

Zack: Dane Cook
Amy: Jessica Simpson
Vince: Dax Shepard
Lon: Andy Dick
Glen Gary: Tim Bagley
Glen Ross: Danny Woodburn
Russell: Harland Williams
Jorge: Efren Ramirez
Origin: USA
Language: English
Released: 2006
Production: Andrew Panay, Peter Abrams, Robert Levy, Joe Simpson; Tapestry Films; released by Lionsgate
Directed by: Greg Coolidge
Written by: Greg Coolidge, Dan Calame, Chris Conroy
Cinematography by: Anthony B. Richmond
Music by: John Swihart
Sound: Steve Morrow
Music Supervisor: Jay Faires
Editing: Kimberly A. Ray, Tom Lewis
Art Direction: Guy Barnes
Costumes: Denise Wingate
Production Design: Jon Gary Steele
MPAA rating: PG-13
Running time: 103 minutes

REVIEWS

Entertainment Weekly. October 20, 2006, p. 60.
Hollywood Reporter Online. September 29, 2006.
Los Angeles Times Online. October 6, 2006.
New York Times Online. October 6, 2006.
San Francisco Chronicle. October 6, 2006, p. E5.
Variety Online. September 29, 2006.
Washington Post. October 6, 2006, p. C5.

AWARDS

Nomination:

Golden Raspberries 2006: Worst Actress (Simpson)

END OF THE SPEAR

Dare to Make Contact.
—Movie tagline

Box Office: $11.7 million

End of the Spear is a film based on the real life 1956 slayings of five male missionaries by Waodani tribesmen in the Ecuadorian jungle. At least a basic understanding of Evangelical Christianity is important when deciding whether someone would like or dislike this film. Understanding of religious doctrines or the movement of Christianity in South America is not necessary, but a basic understanding might help make sense of a questionable script.

The film is primarily a drama with a serious moral undertone. Nate Saint (Chad Allen) is the husband of Marj Saint (Cara Stoner) and father of Steve (Chase Ellison). Nate, a pilot, also has his spiritual duty: He is convinced he must find and eventually convert to Christianity the isolated Ecuadorian tribe called the Waodani. It is a well-documented fact that the Waodani are a very violent culture whose warfare threatens to exterminate them. By spreading the word of God to the natives, Nate and his four-member team hope to save the Waodani. Nate's exact plan in not clear, which perhaps is not even an important point. The real crux of the story lies with what happens after Nate's plan goes awry.

Some people have argued that this film is nothing more than another attempt by white Christians to force their religion onto others. Some argue that the producers were using the film as a vehicle to show the Waodani tribe as a group of ignorant and violent people in need of salvation. Others have a more sympathetic yet equally pessimistic argument when they write that this is nothing more than a film filling the Christian void in Hollywood. Although there are a number of films with overt as well as covert religious leanings, many still argue that there is a serious lack of religious films coming out of Hollywood. Still others argue that this film is nothing more than a historical, familial drama. As with many debates, there is probably some truth in all of these theories. Regardless of what motives the filmmakers had, what most audience members and critics alike agree upon is that it is not a subtle film. If nothing else, *End of the Spear* will make you think and possibly ponder individual choices.

End of the Spear is a weighty movie. The dialogue is wooden in parts and the acting uneven. The film drags and bores until finally the news of the missionaries' deaths reaches their families. When the wives and children of the missionaries move in with the inhospitable tribespeople, the real movie starts.

It is important to note the amazing aerial photography by Robert Driskell, however. Even though most of the filming was done in Panama and not Ecuador's Amazon, the views are breathtaking.

Although *End of the Spear* is an unevenly acted film, filled with poor dialogue, horrible music, and dreadfully tacky costumes, there is something intriguing in the general story. This story may not have created a big stir when the original tragedy was first reported in the international news, but this movie will have you glued to the screen.

There is something fascinating with a film which makes us wonder what we, as individuals, would do if faced with the type of personal tragedy we see onscreen. While it may seem idiotic to many of us the way the missionaries ignored the propensity to violence which the Waodani clearly had, one would have to have a heart of steel not to be touched by this film. In fact, although the film is extremely violent in parts, it is important to the story and not over the top. The basic premise of forgiveness is intoxicating and people will question their own ability to do so. Only if one can ignore the film's obvious faults will the true moral of the story unfold. With all the problems in this film, it is still one which evokes thoughts and discussion among the people who watch it, which is what a solid film should always do.

Laura Abraham

CREDITS

Nate Saint/Steve Saint: Chad Allen
Young Steve Saint: Chase Ellison
Mincayani: Louie Leonardo
Rachel Saint: Sara Kathryn Bakker
Marj Saint: Cara Stoner
Kimo: Jack Guzman
Dayumae: Christina Souza
Origin: USA
Language: English, Spanish
Released: 2006
Production: Bob Ewing, Mart Green, Tom Newman, Bart Gavigan; Every Tribe Entertainment; released by M. Power
Directed by: Jim Hanon
Written by: Bart Gavigan, Jim Hanon, Bill Ewing
Cinematography by: Robert Driskell
Music by: Ronald Owen
Sound: Robert Marts
Editing: Miles Hanon
Art Direction: Jeff LeGore
Costumes: Mari-An Ceo
Production Design: Clarence L. Major
MPAA rating: PG-13
Running time: 112 minutes

REVIEWS

Entertainment Weekly Online. January 18, 2006.
Los Angeles Times Online. January 20, 2006.
New York Times Online. January 20, 2006.
Variety Online. January 19, 2006.
Washington Post Online. January 20, 2006, p. WE39.

QUOTES

Nate Saint: "Do you know how far away the sun is?"

Young Steve Saint: "Ninety-three million miles."

Nate Saint: "Do you know that that's just a fraction of how much I love you?"

ERAGON

You are stronger than you realize. Wiser than you know. What was once your life is now your legend.

—Movie tagline

Box Office: $74.5 million

One of 2003's bestsellers was a fantasy novel written by a home-schooled teenager, Christopher Paolini. He started it when he was fifteen, had it published by his family, and three years later, it was picked up by Knopf publishers. The book, *Eragon* is part one of what Paiolini calls his Inheritance Trilogy. While the book shows remarkable accomplishment for a teenager, it does have its problems. Mainly, *Eragon* is incredibly derivative of other fantasy stories. One can't help but notice the similarities between it and the Star Wars films and, of course, the Lord of the Rings Trilogy. Unfortunately, when director Stefan Fangmeier, who comes from a visual effects background and makes his directorial debut with Eragon, translated the book to the screen the book's shortcomings were magnified.

The story begins, as these stories usually do, with an establishing shot of a downtrodden and dismal village in the land of Alagaesia, while a voiceover gives us all the historical mythology we need to know to make sense of the story to come. Many years ago, society only existed due to the protection of dragon riders. Then King Galbatorix (John Malkovich) kills off all the dragon riders and, with the help of his army of Urgals and his evil sorcerer Durza (Robert Carlyle) who controls some sort of super-human (but made-of-bugs Ra'zacs), they set out to control the world.

When a dragon's egg is stolen from Galbatorix by the warrior elf princess Arya (Sienna Guillory), he sends Durza out to get it back. Should it make its way to its future rider, those dragon-riding Jedi Knights would be reborn and the rebels of his empire would be given hope. Arya is captured by Durza, but not before she casts a magic spell and sends the egg off to find its potential rider. It appears at the feet of seventeen-year-old Eragon (Ed Speleers). Of course a dragon's egg just looks like a beautiful blue stone and Eragon tries unsuccessfully to trade it for food. Galbatorix seems to know where the egg is and sends out his men to bring it back and get rid of the rider.

Eragon, however, doesn't know he's the rider and neither does his family. Consequently the boy is quite surprised when the egg hatches, revealing the female dragon Saphira (voice of Rachel Weisz), and when his Uncle Garrow (Alun Armstrong) is murdered. Eventually Eragon hooks up with this story's version of Obi-Wan, Brom (Jeremy Irons), who tutors him in magic, fighting, and dragon riding. Together the two, along with Saphira, travel to the Varden to join the rebels.

Of course this will not be an easy trip. As Eragon perfects his skills (learning, for example, that he can communicate telepathically with Saphira), they are pursued by Galbatorix's men. Then there is the side trip Eragon makes because he keeps seeing Arya in his dreams. He knows she is being held captive and desperately needs help, so against Brom's orders he sets out on Saphira to save her. He also finds, at one point, that he's being followed by a mysterious young man named Murtagh (Garrett Hedlund), who rescues Eragon more than once.

Eventually Eragon will make it to the Varden who are led by Ajihad (Djimon Hounsou) and there will be an all-out battle at Farthen Dur (built in an abandoned rock quarry and crater at a volcano in Hungary) and the audience is set up for the sequel, part two of the trilogy (the book is titled *Eldest*).

Screenwriter Peter Buchman had a huge task before him. He had to take a book of more than five hundred pages and cut it down to a one hundred-minute movie. He also had to keep the book's legion of fans happy, while not alienating non-fans. Unfortunately, he ends up cutting the material so severely that relationships are not developed and many characters are only minimally drawn. Amazingly, with all that cutting, the movie ends up being ponderously slow. It lumbers along from special effect to special effect with little momentum and creates even less interest.

While the special effects are good—although some might have trouble with a feminine dragon—and the location shots beautiful and dramatic (it was filmed in Hungary and Slovakia), the human characters are not compelling and some aren't even likeable. Worst of all is the alleged hero, Eragon. It's amazing to think that after a worldwide search—which the filmmakers claim they performed—the best they could come up with is newcomer Ed Speelers. He is bland, his acting wooden, and the Eragon he portrays is bratty, petulant, reckless, and utterly annoying. This hardly makes for a hero worth investing one's time and emotions in. Other characters become an unfortunate mix of over-the-top cardboard cutouts, having to deliver stilted and mannered dialogue. It would be laughable if one weren't already lulled into somnolence by the leaden story.

There are other, maybe even better, dragon movies out there, *Dragonheart* (1996) and *Reign of Fire* (2002) come to mind. Even the studio must have realized the film wasn't all they hoped it would be because they gave it very little publicity. In the end, *Eragon* has the feel of a blockbuster fantasy but seems incredibly empty. It is as if this complex world of dragons and magic and good and evil has been hollowed out, an intriguing shell with no heart or soul.

Beverley Bare Buehrer

CREDITS

Brom: Jeremy Irons
Arya: Sienna Guillory
Durza: Robert Carlyle
Galbatorix: John Malkovich
Eragon: Ed Speleers
Ajihad: Djimon Hounsou
Murtagh: Garrett Hedlund
Angela: Joss Stone
Saphira: Rachel Weisz (Voice)
Uncle Garrow: Alun Armstrong
Origin: USA
Language: English
Released: 2006
Production: John Davis, Wyck Godfrey; Ingenious Film Partners, Davis Entertainment Company, Fox 2000 Pictures; released by 20th Century Fox
Directed by: Stefan Fangmeier
Written by: Peter Buchman
Cinematography by: Hugh Johnson
Music by: Patrick Doyle
Sound: Mac Ruth
Editing: Roger Barton
Art Direction: Jonathan McKinstry
Costumes: Kym Barrett
Production Design: Wolf Kroeger
MPAA rating: PG
Running time: 104 minutes

REVIEWS

Chicago Sun-Times Online. December 15, 2006.
Hollywood Reporter Online. December 14, 2006.
Los Angeles Times Online. December 15, 2006.
New York Times Online. December 15, 2006.
San Francisco Chronicle. December 15, 2006, p. E9.
Variety Online. December 14, 2006.
Washington Post. December 15, 2006, p. C1.

EVERYONE'S HERO

No matter where life takes you, always keep swinging.
—Movie tagline

Box Office: $14.5 million

In the way Christopher Reeve pressed on with life after his devastating 1995 spinal cord injury, the paralyzed former Superman made spirits soar and became everyone's hero. Recalling his amazing optimism and dauntless determination, it is not at all hard to understand what would have drawn Reeve to this project about perseverance in the face of seemingly insurmountable odds. He had already begun work as the animated film's director (and an executive producer) when he died in 2004 at age fifty-two. Reeve's devoted wife, Dana, also a part of the project, urged that it continue on to fruition. Before the film reached theaters she was gone as well, a forty-four year old non-smoking victim of lung cancer. *Everyone's Hero* is dedicated to them both. Knowledge of their tragic deaths adds a definite poignancy to the proceedings, and makes one feel like a heel in criticizing it. It is wished, however, that the work were noteworthy for reasons other than being a sad swan song, that it was something remarkable, captivating, and likely to endure. Unfortunately, the film is otherwise unmemorable, merely modestly appealing, slight, and bland as it delivers admittedly meaningful and laudatory messages to never give up for the youngest of filmgoers.

Produced by IDT Entertainment, *Everyone's Hero* was originally a bedtime story created by its founder and chairman, Howard Jonas, for his own children. The film's focus is ten-year-old Yankee Irving (agreeably voiced by Jake T. Austin), who is as well known for striking out amongst the other kids in his New York City neighborhood as his idol Babe Ruth is for swatting home runs. When Yankee whiffs he does so with a lot of heart and spectacular ineptitude, smashing himself in the back of the head with his follow-through and winding up on the ground in a humiliated heap. None of the other kids want Yankee on their team, and they let him know it. One day, Yankee finds an old baseball under a dilapidated car abandoned on the sandlot. Upon taking it home with him, he is shocked to learn that it can talk. None of the other people in the film can hear the ball, and they very well might consider themselves lucky since Screwie (voice of Rob Reiner) is a rather irritating, cantankerous complainer. Screwie is so annoying because he was fouled out of the park the first time he was used in a major league game, and was never retrieved. It was apparently thought that the bitter ball would keep viewers in stitches, but many will want to tan his hide.

The film takes place in 1932, when the country was as depressed in its own way as poor Yankee is in his. The boy's parents, Stanley (voice of Mandy Patinkin) and Emily (voice of Dana Reeve), are concerned but busy. Yankee's father can ill afford to lose his job as a janitor at the glorious "House that Ruth Built," but that is what happens after the dejected boy visits his father there one evening. Following a pep talk about how even the greatest ballplayers have slumps but "just keep swinging," Stanley tries to cheer up his son by taking the wide-eyed little superfan into the Yankees' locker room, where he is awed to see Ruth's beloved custom-made bat, nicknamed Darlin' (voice of Whoopi Goldberg, sounding like a diva Southern belle). It is the eve of the World Series, in which the Yankees will face the Cubs, and the latter team's unscrupulous owner, Napoleon Cross (voice of an unbilled, but enjoyable Robin Williams) has ordered equally unscrupulous pitcher Lefty Maginnis (voice of William H. Macy) to neutralize the Babe by sneaking in dressed as a security guard and swiping his bat. (The idea is apparently that Babe without his Darlin' is like Samson without his hair.) Since Yankee and his father were the last ones known to be near the bat, they are blamed and Stanley is fired, pending Darlin's return. Once Yankee recognizes Lefty as the guard he saw in the locker room, the boy works up his courage and heads off with Screwie on a quest to help his baseball hero and, even more importantly, his dad.

Everyone's Hero becomes a buddy road picture of sorts as the boy and his peevish traveling partner battle Lefty for possession of Darlin' all the way to Chicago, where the Series' final, deciding game will be played. In one of the film's more involving scenes, Yankee must leap between moving trains to evade his nemesis. Kids will probably enjoy watching the bumbling, stinky-footed, booger-laden villain bash spread-eagled into a signpost, get electrocuted during a storm, and generally suffer enough goofy mishaps to get anyone placed permanently on the disabled list. Less comical is the continued friction between the ball and the bat, as the quarrelsome equipment's self-centered, sniping quickly grows tiresome.

During Yankee's selfless, thousand-mile mission to get a hold of Darlin', he also acquires skills and, in turn, confidence he previously did not possess. As he is pelted with apples by a couple of bullies along the way, Marti (voice of Raven-Symone), the daughter of Negro Leaguer Lonnie Brewster (voice of Forest Whitaker) teaches him how to keep his eye on the ball. On Lonnie's team bus heading toward Chicago, the ebullient players fine-tune the inept young hitter's stance. While these African American characters are vital to Yankee's success, the filmmakers, perhaps trying to keep things light and as cheerful as the film's overall color palette, steer clear of elucidating tots in any way about segregation and the pre-Jackie Robinson color barrier. Yankee also meets some good-natured hobos who stress the importance of bouncing back from hardship. When Darlin' sweetly and sappily consoles a homesick Yankee, Screwie's critical comment may seem rather apropos: "Oh Brother, you could pour this stuff on pancakes!"

When Yankee successfully reaches the ballpark where the decisive game is in progress, he is confined to the owner's box, overlooking the proceedings but unable to affect them. "I'm just a kid," he says forlornly. "I should've just quit." However, the bat and ball come together to convince him not to give up hope, and with a can-do attitude, the three find a way to get Darlin' down to Babe. For his heroic efforts, Yankee Irving is deemed deserving of an at bat with the entire Series on the line. Lefty is on the mound. After some bolstering words from Babe himself (voice of Brian Dennehy), Yankee, armed with Darlin' and his new adroitness and self-assurance, hits a delighted Screwie for an inside the park home run. The Yankee players and fans erupt joyously, and the boy's recently arrived parents proudly shout, "that's my boy!" and envelope him in their loving arms. Listening on the radio back home, the kids who once teased Yankee now fanatically chant his name. The film's finale, satisfying if only marginally affecting, repetitively hammers home *Everyone's Hero*'s uplifting mantra of perseverance.

Made on a budget estimated at between $30 and $50 million, *Everyone's Hero* struggled at the box office. The film's overall agreeable but unexceptional nature includes its CGI (computer-generated imagery) animation, with characters' movements sometimes noticeably lacking in fluidity. It's heart, however, is unquestionably, squarely in the right place. So while Yankee overcame great obstacles and got his happy ending, the makers of *Everyone's Hero* pressed past the unexpected deaths of both Reeves to garner reviews which were, for the most part, respectfully dismissive.

David L. Boxerbaum

CREDITS

Yankee Irving: Jake T. Austin (Voice)
Screwie: Rob Reiner (Voice)
Darlin': Whoopi Goldberg (Voice)
Lefty Maginnis: William H. Macy (Voice)
Mandy Patinkin: Stanley Irving (Voice)
Marti Brewster: Raven-Symone (Voice)
Mr. Robinson: Robert Wagner (Voice)
Lonnie Brewster: Forest Whitaker (Voice)
Babe Ruth: Brian Dennehy (Voice)
Napoleon Cross: Robin Williams (Voice, uncredited)
Yankees' Manager: Joe Torre (Voice)
Emily Irving: Dana Reeve (Voice)
Origin: USA
Language: English
Released: 2006
Production: Ron Tippe, Igor Khait; IDT Entertainment; released by 20th Century Fox

Directed by: Christopher Reeve, Daniel St. Pierre, Colin Brady
Written by: Robert Kurtz, Jeff Hand
Cinematography by: Andy Wang, Jan Carlee
Music by: John Debney
Sound: Sean Garnhart
Music Supervisor: Dawn Soler
Editing: John Bryant
Art Direction: Kevin R. Adams
MPAA rating: G
Running time: 88 minutes

REVIEWS

Boxoffice Online. September 15, 2006.
Chicago Sun-Times Online. September 15, 2006.
Entertainment Weekly. September 22, 2006, p. 76.
Hollywood Reporter Online. September 15, 2006.
Los Angeles Times Online. September 15, 2006.
New York Times Online. September 15, 2006.
San Francisco Chronicle. September 15, 2006, p. E15.
Variety Online. September 14, 2006.
Washington Post. September 15, 2006, p. C4.

F

FACTOTUM

Never get out of bed before noon.
—Movie tagline

What matters most is how well you walk through the fire.
—Movie tagline

n. A man who never had a job he liked; and never kept a job he had.
—Movie tagline

Charles Bukowski was a controversial American writer whose most notable work spanned the period from the Beat Generation of the 1950s through the 1970s. A disaffected and antisocial alcoholic, Bukowski wrote novels, short stories, and poetry that shared the perspective of a cynical, misogynist observer of daily working-class life. Something of a cult figure, Bukowski is hailed by some critics for his forceful, blunt perspective on the American underclass and is dismissed by others as somewhat shallow and limited.

Bukowski also wrote a number of screenplays, the most celebrated being *Barfly* (1987), a drama about a violent alcoholic couple played by Mickey Rourke and Faye Dunaway. The movie *Tales of Ordinary Madness* (1981) is also adapted from his work. Now comes *Factotum,* based on Bukowski's 1975 book of the same name. It's directed by Norwegian Bent Hamer, following up on his debut *Kitchen Stories* (2003), which garnered some critical praise but negligible box office receipts. Hamer co-wrote the screenplay for *Factotum* with Jim Stark.

Factotum is a thinly disguised autobiographical story in which Bukowski represents himself as Henry Chinaski, an alcoholic, gambler, and master of odd jobs. Matt Dillon plays Chinaski as a very soft-spoken, emotionally vacant hulk of a writer trying to get one of his works published. The casting of Dillon is what gave this film some resonance among some critics; a few of whom hailed this as Dillon's best performance yet.

But though Dillon does succeed in making the Chinaski character as compelling and memorable as he can be, it is like trying to inhabit a rotting, empty vessel. Hamer's approach is to make the film into something resembling the cinematic equivalent of a Bukowski story—spare and nearly plotless, a series of vignettes and scenes that revel in their own weightlessness.

Hamer's movie is deadpan in the extreme, with an amazing number of scenes that go nowhere and play out without cinematic flourishes. Many of the scenes are filmed with a static camera from a medium range, as if you were a fly on a wall of the seedy apartments and small factories and taverns that make up the protagonist's rather paltry world. The combined effect of Dillon's understated, semicomatose performance and Hamer's flat, deliberately unprovocative filmmaking is to create a calculated opposite of the moviegoing experience most Americans are accustomed to, much as Bukowski's own writing brought readers into a place where the usual literary goals and devices were muted or absent.

The idea is to strip us of our expectations about dramatic tension, character development, plot, and even visual perspective and give us a chance to get into this muted world of the perpetually medicated soul. The problem is that Hamer's refusal to provide us any points of access or to concede to even the barest expectations of a movie experience is that we are being browbeaten by omission into submission. Just like a movie that hits audiences over the head by shouting at us with unsubtle style, a film and story that refuses to touch us in any meaningful way is shouting at us in its own way, as if we can be conquered by the excess of rhetorical vacancy.

There's nothing wrong with subtlety in a film, but *Factotum* isn't subtle, it's empty. Chinaski gains and loses a number of jobs, and he goes in and out of a relationship with another alcoholic, Jan (Lili Taylor), a love affair that is defined mainly by the frequency of loveless-looking couplings and by the inability of these two wrecks to communicate with each other beyond sexual intercourse. Meanwhile, he writes, and his narrator's voice tells us that he writes only for himself and doesn't care about what critics or audiences think, which begs the question of why he continues to submit manuscripts to various publications in hopes one will get published.

Clearly, Chinaski as a character is something of a Bukowski fraud: he is Bukowski himself boasting of how uncaring a loner he is, how much he refuses to play by society's rules, and how meaningless life is. He's practically shouting: look at me and how little I care for pretense and success, how much I refuse to make my ordinary working and drinking and gambling life into something more dramatic and attractive than it is. Hamer and Dillon are playing along with this conceit of the antisocial antihero.

Along the way, a few comments are thrown in that are supposed to make us see Chinaski as a friend of the workingman and a foe of the rich bosses, but in the absence of any sentiment for anyone but himself (and even little of that), the lines seem stilted and phony, especially a scene in which a rich usurper takes Chinaski and Jan's favorite seat at the racetrack and, at Jan's urging, Chinaski pummels him with his fists.

Of course, in a film such as this the protagonist has no character arc: he is static, moving through various jobs (a pickle factory, a bicycle repair shop, and others) and passing through the lives of several women (one is played by Marisa Tomei, in a nearly incomprehensible sequence of scenes that involve a rich yachtsman and several younger women). We learn next to nothing about the stories and poems he is writing, but there is a climax of sorts when one of them gets accepted.

No insight is gained into this artist of the underclass, because insight is presumably a corrupt bourgeois conceit. No concession is made to political correctness, either: Chinaski, like Bukowski, is an unapologetic user and degrader of women, but not in a vicious way. It's just that every person in his world is disposable. He doesn't flaunt his greatness, but clearly he has a high opinion of himself as some sort of prince of the common man, more princely because he never boasts and rarely even talks.

Dillon's performance is dead-on: he is precisely like the image Bukowski wants to convey, the man who believes in nothing and seemingly aspires to nothing, the man with little to say but a desire to let words flow through him, the man with observations that are often as mundane as the subjects and people he observes.

The film seems to be as rootless as its material, existing largely outside of identifiable time and place. If the milieu is meant to be Los Angeles in the 1950s or 1960s, anachronisms abound, but Hamer doesn't seem to care. When the yachtsman takes his friends for a ride on what looks to be a lake, it's referred to as an ocean. But why would anyone bother to care about such things? To care would be to demand a respect for convention that *Factotum* despises. But its unconventionality has no purpose beyond being unconventional, as if that in itself is enough to constitute art.

Michael Betzold

CREDITS

Henry Chinaski: Matt Dillon
Jan: Lili Taylor
Laura: Marisa Tomei
Manny: Fisher Stevens
Pierre: Didier Flamand
Jerry: Adrienne Shelly
Grace: Karen Young
Tony: Tom Lyons
Origin: USA, Germany, Norway
Language: English
Released: 2006
Production: Jim Stark, Bent Hamer; BulBul Film, StarkSales Inc.; released by IFC Films
Directed by: Bent Hamer
Written by: Bent Hamer, Jim Stark
Cinematography by: John Christian Rosenlund
Music by: Kristin Asbjornsen
Sound: John L. Sims Jr.
Editing: Pal Gengenbach
Costumes: Tere Duncan
Production Design: Eve Cauley Turner
MPAA rating: R
Running time: 94 minutes

REVIEWS

Boxoffice Online. August 18, 2006.
Chicago Sun-Times Online. August 25, 2006.
Entertainment Weekly. August 25, 2006, p. 66.

Los Angeles Times Online. August 18, 2006.
New York Times Online. August 18, 2006.
San Francisco Chronicle. August 25, 2006, p. E1.
Variety Online. May 14, 2005.
Village Voice Online. August 15, 2006.
Washington Post. August 255, 2006, p. C7.

QUOTES

Henry: "All I want to do is get my check and get drunk. Now, that may not sound noble, but it's my choice."

FAILURE TO LAUNCH

To leave the nest, some men just need a little push.
—Movie tagline

Box Office: $88.6 million

Tom Dey has directed high profile actors in mediocre comedies before, including Robert De Niro in *Showtime* (2002) and Jackie Chan and Owen Wilson in *Shanghai Noon* (2000), so there is nothing surprising that his latest directorial effort starring Sarah Jessica Parker and Matthew McConaughey fails to impress. The movie's box office success ($88 million) was mainly due to the appeal and chemistry of its stars, along with fine support performances by the eclectic cast, including Kathy Bates, Terry Bradshaw, and Zooey Deschanel. Exhibiting an uneasy balance between comedy and drama, incongruous slapstick sequences, and inexplicable editing, Carina Chocano of the *Los Angeles Times* noted the significant difference between the charm of the lead actors versus the strength of the film: "I found myself wishing they were in a different movie, maybe one as sophisticated as *The Philadelphia Story* (1940), which the movie references, but doesn't remotely live up to."

The high-concept comedy features thirty-something bachelor buddies—the blithely-named Tripp (McConaughey), Ace (Justin Bartha), and Demo (Bradley Cooper)—still living at home with their parents. Although Dey cites the prevalence of the trend to delay leaving the nest, the fact that the buff and handsome Tripp does quite well as a high-end boat salesman, Ace is a wealthy computer geek, and Demo a rakish adventurer, makes this premise seem all the more unlikely. The boyhood friends exhibit symptoms of their arrested development by frequently engaging in activities, such as mountain biking, rock climbing, and playing paintball, while having clean sheets and a home-cooked meal awaiting them apres play. Tripp's parents, Sue (Bates) and Al (Bradshaw), however, think its time that their thirty-five-year-old son had a place of his own and, inspired by a success story from a couple within their circle, decide to follow suit and hire "transition consultant" Paula (Parker) who guarantees to fix Tripp's "failure to launch."

Paula's technique is simple: look good, find out what he's interested in and pretend to be interested in it too, have him share a sad experience with her, and have him teach her something. This accomplished, the guy automatically falls for her, which supposedly makes him more amenable to getting a place of his own, whereupon she dumps the newly propped-up sad sack who now has enough self-esteem not to care. And she accomplishes it all without ever sleeping with the guy. The fact that Paula tricks men into falling in love with her and dumping them for a living belies the fact that Paula may have some issues herself, which is humorously pointed out by her eccentric roommate Kit (Deschanel). Even the obsessive and bad-tempered Kit is able to snag a real, viable boyfriend before the smart, funny, and attractive Paula.

Paula knows better than anyone that boys just want to have fun so she rolls with the good times, which includes joining Tripp and his friends in a testosterone-filled paintball battle. Paula wins, proving she's more than worthy of being able to hang with the guys and ensuring another date. She enlists the help of a friend who works in a veterinary office in order to get Tripp to share a sad experience with her, pretending a strange dog there for a teeth cleaning is actually her dog about to be put to sleep. Next, when Tripp teaches her how to sail, her work is nearly done. The only trouble is, she actually had a great time sailing with Tripp. And then there's the fact she finds him so attractive. Even though Paula is still in denial, Kit recognizes the signs and calls her on the fact that she has fallen for Tripp.

Whenever one of Tripp's "relationships" threatens to get serious, Tripp inevitably invites the woman home—his parent's home, that is. Once they get a load of mom and dad the "relationship" is over and Tripp is free to start another doomed relationship with a new woman. When he invites Paula home, however, he's surprised that she is so welcoming of the arrangement. They proceed upstairs to his room where Paula breaks her cardinal rule about never sleeping with a client.

When Ace catches her out with another client, she confesses that she's just been pretending to be Tripp's girlfriend for professional reasons and he blackmails her into setting him up with Kit. Up until this point, quirky Kit's only interest was in getting rid of an annoying mockingbird living outside her window and driving her crazy. When she hooks up with Ace, she essentially kills two birds with one stone—getting Ace to shoot the pest with his BB gun, while simultaneously falling in love with him. The bird, of course, doesn't die and they both immediately regret their actions to the point where Ace rushes the bird inside to try and revive him by performing mouth-to-beak resuscitation with zany results. There are several instances of incongruous slapstick zaniness with wildlife, although it is usually Tripp on the receiving end of an angry animatronic animal.

Ace spills the beans about Paula to Tripp who then makes an announcement to Paula and his family, who are gathered for dinner, that he's on to their scheme and he is indeed moving out, no thanks to the treacherous Paula. A minor crisis of conscience ensues and Paula decides to leave her job and move home herself only to have Tripp's friends come to the rescue to keep the lovebirds together. Naturally, they accomplish this by tying Tripp to a chair, gagging him, and locking him in a room with Paula, their every move monitored by Ace's multitude of webcams set up around the room. Their happy reunion is broadcast via Ace's laptop onto the big screen at a cafe for the enjoyment of friends and patrons alike.

Although Dey assembles a likeable and talented cast, the film boasts a predictable plot, marred by implausible events and uneven mix of comedy and ill-fitting drama best illustrated by the film's big "reveal," the eye-rolling information that Tripp is the way he is due to the fact an ex-girlfriend died leaving him permanently heartbroken and practically raising her son with another man. Of the technical merits of the film, Roger Ebert of the *Chicago Sun-Times* noted that "there's unusually jerky cutting on lines of dialogue, back and forth, as if the film is unwilling to hold the characters in the same shot while they talk to each other.... Perhaps because [Dey] couldn't stand to look at any one shot for very long? That's the way I felt."

Hilary White

CREDITS

Tripp: Matthew McConaughey
Paula: Sarah Jessica Parker
Kit: Zooey Deschanel
Ace: Justin Bartha
Demo: Bradley Cooper
Al: Terry Bradshaw
Sue: Kathy Bates
Melissa: Katheryn Winnick
Jeffrey: Tyrell Jackson Williams
Techie Guy: Patton Oswalt
Bud: Stephen Tobolowsky
Boatyard Couple: Peter Jacobson
Origin: USA
Language: English
Released: 2006
Production: Scott Rudin, Scott Aversano; Aversano Films Production; released by Paramount
Directed by: Tom Dey
Written by: Tom J. Astle, Matt Ember
Music by: Rolfe Kent
Sound: Steve Aaron
Editing: Steven Rosenblum
Art Direction: Kevin Constant
Costumes: Ellen Mirojnick
Production Design: Jeremy Conway
MPAA rating: PG-13
Running time: 97 minutes

REVIEWS

Boxoffice Online. March 10, 2006.
Chicago Sun-Times Online. March 10, 2006.
Entertainment Weekly Online. March 8, 2006.
Los Angeles Times Online. March 10, 2006.
New York Times Online. March 10, 2006.
Premiere Magazine Online. March 10, 2006.
Variety Online. March 5, 2006.
Washington Post Online. March 10, 2006.

THE FAST AND THE FURIOUS: TOKYO DRIFT

If You Ain't Outta Control, You Ain't In Control.
—Movie tagline

Speed Needs No Translation.
—Movie tagline

Box Office: $62.5 million

What do you do when your film series has run out of gas? Go to Japan. Following in the footsteps of such cinematic masterpieces as *Bad News Bears Go to Japan* (1978) and *Teenage Mutant Ninja Turtles III* (1993), the makers of the *Fast and Furious* franchise take their show on the road to the land of the rising sun for the third, and hopefully last, installment, *The Fast and The Furious: Tokyo Drift*. A modern day Eastern "western" that presents an unlikable lead character, fun racing sequences, attractive girls, and even a cameo by Vin Diesel.

A selfish go-nowhere high-school punk named Sean Boswell (Lucas Black), who has a problem keeping his eyes off other guys' girlfriends and an even bigger problem with authority is the "hero" of this installment. He considers himself a good driver, even though he seems to wreck every car he drives, starting with the one he uses to race against the jock boyfriend of the latest girl he can't ignore. The offending boyfriend Clay (Zachery Ty Bryan) races Sean through an unfinished housing construction site where the two racers literally destroy property values before flipping their cars and ending up in the local police station. At the police station Sean's exasperated mother is told that he will likely be sent to Juvenile Hall due to the Three-Strikes rule. The only way he can avoid jail is if he's sent to live with his father (Brian Goodman), who is in the military in Tokyo, and will surely straighten him out.

Major Boswell lays down the law to Sean about going to school during the day, coming right home right after, and then it's lights out by ten; a set of rules that Sean quickly sees as optional. On his first day of school Sean immediately feels out of place. He feels embarrassed about dressing in a traditional Japanese school uniform and not understanding his Japanese teacher. He also finds the Japanese food in the cafeteria a little scary. If only there was something that he could find in common with these people, maybe he could adapt to his new life.

Enter Twinkie (Bow Wow), an American hustler who is part of the Japanese street racing underground. After school Twinkie takes Sean to a parking structure that is apparently ground zero for the racing culture. Sean immediately sets his eyes on Neela (Nathalie Kelley) who just happens to be the girlfriend of Takashi (Brian Tee), known as the Drift King (DK), and the nephew of a yakuza mob boss. Full of bravado and lacking any common sense whatsoever, Sean challenges Takashi to a race. There is only one problem: Sean doesn't have a car. Han (Sung Kang), a member of Takashi's gang, sees something in Sean that no one else does, and throws him the keys to one of his cars. As he races Takashi to the top of the circular structure, Sean proves to the crowd that he has never crashed a car he didn't drive. He hasn't quite got the gist of "drifting," the art of breaking and shifting to make your car slide or drift to one side while rounding corners.

By the time he reaches the top, Sean's ego and Han's ride are totaled, and he becomes Han's employee to pay off the debt. His first job is to collect a late payment from a sumo wrestler at a bathhouse, resulting in a cultural clash that ends with Sean being thrown onto the sidewalk with the payment in hand. One night Han confesses to Sean that he likes him because he is Takashi's "kryptonite" and he agrees to train Sean in the "ways of drifting." They spend their days racing around mountain roads that look suspiciously like those in Southern California, until several cars later, Sean is getting pretty good. He begins to win races on the underground circuit, to the increasing annoyance of Takashi, who spends most of the film brooding and scowling, especially about the fact that his girlfriend is getting too close to Sean.

Enter Uncle Kamata (Sonny Chiba, bringing a real sense of menace to the proceedings) the yakuza boss and uncle of Takashi. He comes to inform his nephew that Han has been stealing from him and that he wants the problem taken care of or else. Takashi goes to Han's hideout, where he also finds Neela and Sean. He pulls a gun on Han and is about to shoot him when Twinkie distracts him, allowing Han to jump in his car and speed away. What follows next is one of the film's set-pieces: a race through the surprisingly traffic-free streets of Tokyo that puts everybody's drifting skills to the test, but ultimately leaves Han dead in his burning car.

With nowhere else to go, Sean and Neela go to Sean's father's house for help, but before the father can open the door, Takashi shows up and threatens to blow their heads off. Luckily, Sean's father didn't answer the front door, and surprises Takashi from behind with his own gun. He orders Takashi to leave and never come back and then he gives his son a stern look and goes inside.

Knowing that Takashi wants to kill him, Sean goes to Kamata's hideout to apologize to him for embarrassing his family name by fighting with his nephew. Impressed by his bravery and audacity Kamata allows him to speak. Sean figures there can be a peaceful way out of this predicament and offers to race Takashi, with the loser agreeing to leave Tokyo forever, terms which Kamata has no problem with, much to Takashi's surprise.

Given his father's '67 Mustang to drive, Sean races Takashi down a treacherous winding mountain road while spectators track the race with their video cell phones, while Chiba earns his day-player rate waiting in his dapper attire at the bottom of the mountain. The final race is actually quite fun, not because of a rooting interest in the main character, but for the vicarious experience the filmmakers provide for the audience. Director Justin Lin puts the audience in the race by placing his camera inside the cars for a driver's-eye view as they careen through the mountain curves allowing the audience to experience a real sense of vertigo whenever the cars swerve too close to the edge. It is an interactive roller coaster; a *Bullitt* (1968) for a new generation.

In the end Sean wins the race, is set free by Kamata, gets the girl, becomes the newest Drift King in Tokyo, and is challenged to a race in a cameo by Vin Diesel.

David E. Chapple

CREDITS

Sean Boswell: Lucas Black
Twinkie: Bow Wow

Han: Sung Kang
Earl: Jason J. Tobin
Clay: Zachery Ty Bryan
Twinkie: Bow Bow
Morimoto: Leonardo Nam
DK (Takashi): Brian Tee
Neela: Nathalie Kelley
Major Boswell: Brian Goodman
Uncle Kamata: Sonny Chiba
Cindy (Clay's girlfriend): Nikki Griffin
Ms. Boswell: Lynda Boyd
Reiko: Keiko Kitagawa
Case Worker: Vincent Laresca
Dominic Toretto: Vin Diesel (uncredited)
Origin: USA
Language: English
Released: 2006
Production: Neal H. Moritz; Relativity; released by Universal
Directed by: Justin Lin
Written by: Chris Morgan
Cinematography by: Stephen Windon
Music by: Brian Tyler
Sound: Peter J. Devlin
Editing: Fred Raskin, Kelly Matsumoto
Art Direction: Tom Reta
Costumes: Sanja Milkovic Hays
Production Design: Ida Random
MPAA rating: PG-13
Running time: 105 minutes

REVIEWS

Boxoffice Online. June 16, 2006.
Chicago Sun-Times Online. Jun 16, 2006.
Entertainment Weekly Online. June 14, 2006.
Los Angeles Times Online. June 16, 2006.
New York Times Online. June 16, 2006.
Premiere Magazine Online. June 15, 2006.
Variety Online. June 13, 2006.
Washington Post Online. June, 2006.

QUOTES

Sean Boswell to Drift King: "You're like the Justin Timberlake of Japan."

TRIVIA

Volkswagen donated four prototype R32s, which appear in the film, and four Touran minivans to fulfill its agreement with Universal to plug each other's products. Toyo donated 4,000 tires for the movie, of which roughly half were used. Additionally, Volk Racing donated 170 wheels.

FINAL DESTINATION 3

This Ride Will Be The Death Of You.
—Movie tagline

Box Office: $54.1 million

Final Destination 3, the latest installment in the series which share the same name but different numbers, continues in the tradition of its predecessors in that it contains the franchise's two stand-out elements. All three films begin with a fast-paced, opening disaster segment that has the viewer white-knuckled and holding their breath until it is played out. Secondly, all three offer some of the most creative deaths ever filmed. That being said, there is also the standard complaint about sequels at work here: the law of diminishing returns. With each film the novelty wears a bit thinner and knuckles are a little less white.

In *Final Destination 3*, the opening sequence takes place in an amusement park where McKinley High's Grand Night Out is taking place. Among those celebrating is Wendy Christensen (Mary Elizabeth Winstead) who is there to take pictures for the school's yearbook. She's accompanied by her boyfriend Jason (Jesse Moss), his best friend Kevin (Ryan Merriman), and Kevin's girlfriend Carrie (Gina Holden). Wendy, a serious control-freak is a bit upset by two things. She does not get along with her boyfriend's friend, jokester jock Kevin and she is really nervous about riding the roller coaster, "Devil's Flight." In fact, Wendy is so upset about the thought of being out of control on the coaster that she refuses to sit in the front with her boyfriend and instead ends up sitting next to Kevin towards the back. Although a fellow student assures her that the odds of dying on a roller coaster are 1 in 150 million, Wendy still doesn't feel safe enough and wants off. But it's too late.

In a technically wonderful sequence we experience excruciating close-ups of the mechanics of death taking control of the ride. Restraints come loose, camera straps wrap around rails, wheels come off, sparks fly, cars and kids go flying. We then realize it was nothing more than a premonition that Wendy is having. She quickly jumps off the coaster before it starts up, arguments ensue, others chime in and soon the coaster is sent down the track with ten riders left standing on the platform. The events foreseen by Wendy then come true, and McKinley High School now mourns some students as it graduates others.

While Wendy suffers through survivor's guilt, Kevin tells her about two other occurrences he knows of in which people survived an encounter with death only to find that death comes looking for them. (Basically he recounts the plots of *Final Destination* and its sequel.) And that's when Wendy shows him the pictures she took that fated night in which she believes there might be clues to upcoming tragedies. These are revelations that will come too late for Ashley (Chelan Simmons) and Ashlyn (Crystal Lowe) who meet their grisly doom being fricasseed in tanning booths while listening to "Roller Coaster of Love" on their headsets. The next to meet his fate is self-proclaimed ladies' man Frankie

Cheeks (Sam Easton) who gets killed by a runaway truck while waiting in his car at a fast food drive-thru. Frankie is followed by the athlete Lewis (Texas Battle) who probably shouldn't have been in the gym working out on the day Wendy and Kevin try to warn him of his impending doom which has something to do with a sultan and crossed scimitars. Goth girl Erin (Alexz Johnson) and her boyfriend Ian (Kris Lemche) are next to be dispatched. And who are the two riders no one seems to remember and whose picture is too obscured to figure out? Because when these four are gone, it's Kevin and Wendy's turn.

If the deaths described above sound a bit unusual but not that odd, then you are not familiar with the *Final Destination* movies. A large part of the dark and perverse humor of the series does not come from trying to guess who is going to die next or even if they're going to die. The suspense is in how they're going to die, how much Rube Goldberg inventiveness will be involved, how many red herrings will be offered, and how long will it take.

This third installment does benefit from having the original director, James Wong, who also collaborates with the first film's scriptwriter, Glen Morgan, and the original film's director of photography Rob McLachlan, but even this may not be enough to revive the novelty of the first film released in 2000. The second installment, released in 2002, suffered from familiarity but still offered enough suspense and action to be worth the price of a ticket. The same may be true of the third film. It still contains that wonderful sense of menace and an intriguing view of events as if being viewed by death or fate itself. It also retains its sense of humor (the only actor to appear in all three films is Tony Todd who is the voice of the billboard devil at the roller coaster entrance saying, prophetically, "You can run but you can't hide") and the original's sense of homage (watch for characters with names that refer to other horror directors: Romero, Freund, Halperin).

By now the novelty may be wearing a little thin in this series of supernatural thrillers, the dialogue may be getting a little stiff and the plot predictable, but they're still good looking movies with spectacularly filmed death sequences and a heck of a lot more fun to watch than a lot of other recent horror films.

Beverley Bare Buehrer

CREDITS

Wendy Christensen: Mary Elizabeth Winstead
Kevin Fischer: Ryan Merriman
Ian McKinley: Kris Lemche
Lewis Romero: Texas Battle
Jason Wise: Jesse Moss
Ashlyn Halperin: Crystal Lowe
Ashley Freund: Chelan Simmons
Erin: Alexz Johnson
Carrie Dreyer: Gina Holden
Frankie Cheeks: Sam Easton
Julie Christensen: Amanda Crew
Origin: USA
Language: English
Released: 2006
Production: Craig Perry, Warren Zide, Glen Morgan, James Wong; Hard Eight Pictures, Pratical Pictures, Matinee Pictures; released by New Line Cinema
Directed by: James Wong
Written by: James Wong, Glen Morgan
Cinematography by: Robert McLachlan
Music by: Shirley Walker
Sound: Rob Young
Editing: Chris Willingham
Art Direction: Tony Wohlgemuth
Costumes: Gregory Mah
Production Design: Mark Freeborn
MPAA rating: R
Running time: 92 minutes

REVIEWS

Boxoffice Online. February 10, 2006.
Chicago Sun-Times Online. February 10, 2006.
Entertainment Weekly Online. February 8, 2006.
Los Angeles Times Online. February 10, 2006.
New York Times Online. February 10, 2006.
Variety Online. February 8, 2006.

QUOTES

Erin: "So going by your theory, from this picture I'm going to OD on nail varnish and Ian's going to die of embarrassment!"

TRIVIA

Reportedly due to unfavorable reactions at preview screenings, the ending was re-shot, which was also the case with the two previous films in the series.

FIND ME GUILTY

Sometimes the best defense…is a wiseguy.
—Movie tagline

Box Office: $1.1 million

Veteran director Sidney Lumet tried something a little different in *Find Me Guilty.* Fascinated by the longest criminal trial in U.S. history, the federal government's racketeering case against the Lucchese crime family of New Jersey, he wrote and directed a feature based largely on actual trial transcripts and cast Vin Diesel, of all people, in the starring role.

It has been a long time since Lumet made a movie with much impact, as he's dallied in all manner of unsuccessful projects. Lumet's always been uneven, but this is the man who gave us the wondrous *Dog Day Afternoon* (1975) and showed he knew how to make tense courtroom drama with the compelling films *The Verdict* (1982) and, way back in the 1950s, *Twelve Angry Men* (1957). This project doesn't yield that kind of drama, but it is curious and fascinating because of its authenticity. Yet Lumet, now in his eighties, shows he no longer has firm command of his storytelling elements even though, as always, he gets effective performances out of his cast.

The film opens with Jackie DiNorscio (Diesel) being shot in his bedroom at point-blank range by his cousin Tony Compagna (Raul Esparza). "Why are you doing this?" he asks. "I love you." That is DiNorscio's mantra: he and his family and friends are bonded by love, not murderous intent. Somehow, Tony fails to end Jackie's life, and when he gets out of the hospital, Jackie is immediately arrested during a drug deal engineered by a government agent who entraps him. He is sentenced to thirty years in prison.

But soon he is courted by a powerful district attorney, Sean Kierney (Linus Roache), who offers him a deal. He will get his sentence cut if he agrees to testify against the other members of the Lucchese family in an upcoming RICO trial. DiNorscio rejects the offer, because he's not the kind of guy who rats on his friends and relations.

Kierney has assembled a massive case against the family: seventy-six counts covering twenty defendants. It is the result of years of investigation, and he's got a huge cast of witnesses, some of them informants, including Jackie's cousin Tony. While the other defendants, his associates, come to trial with their own well-heeled attorneys, Jackie is incarcerated throughout the two-year ordeal, serving the drug sentence. Because he felt he was let down by his former lawyer, DiNorscio insists on representing himself.

His decision rubs the other defendants the wrong way, and goes against the strong advice of their lead counsel, Ben Klandis (Peter Dinklage). It also angers Kierney and flummoxes the judge (Ron Silver). In his opening statement, DiNorscio plays the clown, insisting "I'm not a gangster. I'm a gagster" and putting on a fedora to demonstrate that it might just be the way a gangster's supposed to look that makes him a suspect. He also admits he doesn't know the law and has only a sixth-grade education, but promises the jury he will speak from the heart.

Soon he is endangering the entire case. He makes crude jokes and badgers the defendants, and at one point challenges the authority of the judge. The judge threatens to separate him from the other defendants. The prosecution team, worried about the impact of a loose cannon in the courtroom, tries to find a way to get him to self-destruct, including taking away his easy chair from his cell—a chair that Jackie, who has a bad back, says is absolutely necessary for him to have in order to get any sleep.

Diesel plays DiNorscio as a big-hearted, rough-edged, sentimental clown. In DiNorscio's view, government harassment is responsible for the death of his brother, an alcoholic, and for the long prison terms served by him and his father. During the trial, Jackie's mother dies, but he isn't released to go to the funeral, and he has an impassioned scene with his ex-wife (Annabella Sciorra), who visits him. DiNorscio insists that his motivation is always love for his friends and family, and acts as if he doesn't have a bad bone in his body. He is generous to a fault: the title of the movie comes from his closing summation, where he asks the jury to convict him but find his cohorts innocent.

During testimony, however, there are allusions to DiNorscio's habits of using cocaine and prostitutes, and of various other criminal activities. These are glossed over as the mistakes of a confused man. Lumet, using Diesel's lunkheaded charms to perfection, paints DiNorscio as a victim, not to say a martyr: the fall guy for the gangsters. Were this not based on an actual story the audience might think this a ludicrous set-up, but just because Lumet has used actual trial transcripts to craft the story, it's not clear he's gotten the big picture accurate.

Lumet does try to balance the sympathy he's cooked up for Diesel's character by having Kierney rant about how much these mobsters cost the average citizen, represented by the men and women of the jury, by adding to the costs of their goods and transactions. But Roache plays the prosecutor as a zealot who is stressed near to the breaking point by the demands of his make-or-break case. On the other hand, Dinklage is dignified and authoritative as the hard-nosed but reasonable lead counsel for the defendants. Casting him is another odd choice, but effective: the fact that he is small in stature works in a reverse way to confer extra gravitas on him.

The film suffers, however, from a lack of curiosity about the government's case. Why would the feds save as their last witness Jackie's cousin Tony, who is a hopeless drug addict and who has confessed to attempting to kill his cousin? How did the government put together a case that seemed, at least according to the trial excerpts selected here, to depend so heavily on compromised witnesses and on hearsay?

Another problem is that *Find Me Guilty* suffers from a lack of focus. Staying true to life, the film must skip around among the over six hundred days of testimony, and at times the centerpiece of the plot, DiNorscio's role, gets lost in fascination with the other notable points of the trial: one of the defendants suffers a heart attack and the trial resumes after a few days with him attending on a hospital gurney. We're not sure, either, whether mob boss Nick Calabrese (Alex Rocco) has other reasons to despise Jackie besides his clownish courtroom performance. In the end, our understanding of the case and the principal figures involved is too superficial.

Lumet seems also to be fascinated simply by the spectacle of the trial and the courtroom's accommodations. He shoots a lot of scenes from long range, situating DiNorscio at the far end of a cellblock or as a tiny speck in the middle of the huge trial. This technique serves to distance the audience from what's happening on the screen. Overlong at more than two hours and suffering from a lack of dramatic tension, the film is only mildly entertaining and doesn't show the master's touch that Lumet used to have. Diesel's performance is surprisingly credible, however, but the entertainment value of his trial antics diminishes as he eventually toes the line before the judge, and his speeches do not end up being compelling enough to merit this kind of attention. Overall, the material doesn't support the weight of a feature-film treatment, as Lumet doesn't really take us inside what happened, but merely makes us spectators who dip in and out of the long ordeal.

Michael Betzold

CREDITS

Jackie DiNorscio: Vin Diesel
Ben Klandis: Peter Dinklage
Sean Kierney: Linus Roache
Judge Finestein: Ron Silver
Nick Calabrese: Alex Rocco
Bella DiNorscio: Annabella Sciorra
Max Novardes: Richard Portnow
Chris Newberger: Robert Stanton
Tony Compagna: Raul Esparza
Jerry McQueen: Domenick Lombardozzi
Gino Mascarpone: Paul Borghese
DiNorscio's Lawyer: Jerry Adler
Sara Stiles: Marcia Jean Kurtz
Origin: USA
Language: English
Released: 2006
Production: Bob Yari, Robert Greenhut, George Zakk, T.J. Mancini, Bob Debrino; One Race Films, Zweite Academy, Yari Film Group, Three Wolves Productions; released by Freestyle Releasing
Directed by: Sidney Lumet
Written by: Sidney Lumet, T.J. Mancini, Robert J. McCrea
Cinematography by: Ron Fortunato
Music by: Richard Glasser
Sound: Coll Anderson
Editing: Tom Swartwout
Art Direction: Emily Beck
Costumes: Tina Nigro
Production Design: Christopher Nowak
MPAA rating: R
Running time: 125 minutes

REVIEWS

Chicago Sun-Times Online. March 17, 2006.
Los Angeles Times Online. March 17, 2006.
New York Times Online. March 17, 2006.
San Francisco Chronicle Online. March 17, 2006.
Variety Online. February 16, 2006.
Village Voice Online. March 14, 2006.

QUOTES

Jackie DiNorscio: "I'm not a gangster. I'm a gagster."

FIREWALL

Everything He loves Is About To Be Used Against Him.
—Movie tagline

They're Already Inside.
—Movie tagline

Nothing Is More Dangerous Than A Man With Everything To Lose.
—Movie tagline

Box Office: $48.7 million

Firewall is a lackluster, derivative thriller with an overly complicated and lengthy set-up that leads to a ridiculous denouement and a lot of loose ends. Harrison Ford stars in his first movie since the equally unsuccessful *Hollywood Homicide* (2003). Here he plays Jack Stanfield, an authoritative suit-and-tie family man with a smart, attractive wife named Beth (Virginia Madsen), two kids—fourteen-year-old Sarah (Carly Schroeder) and eight-year-old Andy (Jimmy Bennett)—and an adorable dog named Rusty that likes to bark and hates wearing his collar.

Stanfield and his family are under surveillance. Jack is the head of network security at Seattle's Landrock Pacific Bank, which is in the midst of a big merger that has him butting heads with Accuwest's security chief Gary Mitchell (Robert Patrick). Jack has a very loyal secretary named Janet (Mary Lynn Rajskub) and a longtime associate named Harry (Robert Forster). Jack's world is about to be turned upside down. He discovers his identity has been compromised when a debt collector shows up at the bank, loudly declaring that Jack has been gambling online and owes $95,000; Gary, who already doesn't trust Jack, overhears this unpleasant information.

Jack joins Harry for a drink to meet an investment manager named Bill Cox (Paul Bettany) who is apparently trying to headhunt the two men to work for him. While Bill is schmoozing, four men break into the Stanfield home, hold the family hostage, and begin setting up elaborate surveillance equipment. When Jack gets into his car after the meeting, Bill climbs in too, pulls a gun, and tells Jack to drive home. Jack tries to reassure his terrified family; he figures Bill wants to rob the bank but Bill isn't too quick to explain his scheme.

The next morning, Jack is outfitted with audio and video surveillance and sent off to work. He tries ineffectually to alert those around him that something is wrong but they merely think he's tenser than usual. Bill shows up posing as a federal banking official and gets a tour of the vault and the online network. Jack learns that Bill wants him to transfer $100 million to an offshore account ($10,000 each from the bank's 10,000 richest customers) using the computer system. Only the system has been changed because of the merger. (Bill had this long and elaborate surveillance on Jack for months but is surprised by the merger—one of many unbelievable circumstances.)

They return home and Bill shows he means business by shooting fellow crook Willy (Vincent Gale), who screwed up. Bill gives Jack twelve hours to come up with a new plan to get the money transferred. Since he originally designed the software, Bill is sure that Jack can get around the firewall. Jack screws up their home security in an effort to have his family escape but they get caught and further anger the crooks. Jack comes up with a plan to access the accounts using a scanner from his fax machine and his daughter's iPod. Bill accompanies Jack to the bank the next day and forces him to fire Janet because she seems suspicious. Then Gary gets suspicious when Jack begins accessing accounts, deleting security footage, and crashing the bank's network. (However, Jack has managed to use a coworker's camera phone to photograph the needed account information.) Jack transfers the money and Bill leaves. Jack attacks Gary when he tries to stop him leaving the bank and Gary calls the cops but nothing comes of this.

When Jack returns home, everyone is gone and all the equipment has been removed. Bad guy Liam (Nikolaj Coster Waldau) is waiting to kill him but Jack gets rid of Liam (using a glass coffee pot) and takes his cell phone. Jack calls Harry for help (he's not home) and then decides to break into his apartment to wait for him. For some reason, Jack decides to play Harry's phone messages and hears a call Beth was forced to make; she says she loves Harry and has finally found the courage to leave Jack. Harry enters his apartment with Bill (Jack is hiding); Bill kills Harry with Jack's gun and then leaves. Jack realizes he's been set-up to seem like a jealous, unstable husband who is in debt, has stolen from the bank, and is going to disappear. He takes the gun and runs out.

Jack then goes to Janet's apartment, tells her what's been happening and begs for her help. She gets the phone that has the account information from her coworker and takes Jack to the airport so he can use the wireless transfer at the bank's branch office. Jack transfers the money out of Cox's overseas account. Jack then calls Cox on Liam's cell and tells him what he's done: "You get the money when I get my family." The family, along with the dog, are in a van with computer geek Vel (Kett Turton) and thuggish Pim (Vince Vieluf) while Bill is driving Beth's car.

Jack, who's been using Janet's laptop, realizes that Rusty's dog collar contains a GPS chip and he can use it to track him. They start after the thugs (who are headed out of town) until Rusty is thrown out of the van for barking too much. But when Jack finds Rusty it just so happens that he can see Beth's car parked by an abandoned lake house. He leaves Janet (and Rusty) behind and tells her to call the cops. Bill kills Vel for letting Jack's daughter Sarah escape and Jack kills Pim when he goes after Sarah. That leaves Bill alone with Beth and young Andy. Jack breaks into the house, allowing the two to run, while he gets into a window-breaking, pummeling brawl with Bill. Jack kills Bill, reunites with his family, and the police show up.

Ford is now in his early sixties (he was born in 1942) and has been successful a long time; he's also played this sort of role many times before. He's handsomely weathered and in good shape and there's no particular reason that his character couldn't have a wife who's twenty years younger as well as a young family. Bettany is thirty years younger than Ford but he's a weedy English guy so you don't expect him to be tough enough to get the better of Ford's character. Bettany is not particularly believable as a psychopathic bad guy, maybe because he doesn't seem menacing. Madsen is wasted in a supportive/protective role and only Rajskub makes any kind of impression in her secondary part as Forster, Patrick, and Alan Arkin (as another bank exec) have little screen time.

According to an interview with Ford and director Richard Loncraine, they and the studio were concerned about the script even while shooting (it's Joe Forte's first produced screenplay). They had reason to be; maybe production should have been delayed until the problems, whatever they might have specifically been, could have been worked out. Thrillers are destined to have their implausible aspects and plot holes but *Firewall*'s faults are glaring because it's cliched and generally boring. The characters are two-dimensional ciphers except for Ford, who's a generic hero. Maybe, at this stage in his career, Ford is unwilling to take chances on something out of the ordinary or maybe Hollywood has him typecast. *Firewall* makes little impression and is destined to be a footnote among the actor's much better roles.

Christine Tomassini

CREDITS

Jack Stanfield: Harrison Ford
Bill Cox: Paul Bettany
Beth Stanfield: Virginia Madsen
Janet Stone: Mary Lynn Rajskub
Gary Mitchell: Robert Patrick
Harry Romano: Robert Forster
Arlin Forester: Alan Arkin
Sarah Stanfield: Carly Schroeder
Andy Stanfield: Jimmy Bennett
Pim: Vince Vieluf
Vel: Kett Turton
Willy: Vincent Gale
Liam: Nikolaj Coster Waldau
Origin: USA
Language: English
Released: 2006
Production: Armyan Bernstein, Jonathan Shestack, Basil Iwanyk; Village Roadshow Pictures, Beacon Pictures, Thunder Road Productions; released by Warner Bros.
Directed by: Richard Loncraine
Written by: Joe Forte
Cinematography by: Marco Pontecorvo
Music by: Alexandre Desplat
Sound: Patrick Ramsay
Editing: Jim Page
Art Direction: Helen Jarvis
Costumes: Shuna Harwood
Production Design: Brian Morris
MPAA rating: PG-13
Running time: 120 minutes

REVIEWS

Boxoffice Online. February 10, 2006.
Chicago Sun-Times Online. February 10, 2006.
Entertainment Weekly Online. February 8, 2006.
Los Angeles Times Online. February 10, 2006.
New York Times Online. February 10, 2006.
Premiere Magazine Online. February 10, 2006.
Variety Online. February 4, 2006.
Washington Post Online. February 10, 2006.

QUOTES

Jack Stanfield: "You'll get the money, when I get my family."

TRIVIA

When Harrison Ford called Virginia Madsen, leaving a message on her answering machine offering her a part in the movie, Madsen initially thought it was a practical joke.

FLAGS OF OUR FATHERS

A single shot can end the war.
—Movie tagline

Box Office: $33.6 million

Joe Rosenthal's stirring photograph of Old Glory being hoisted atop Mount Suribachi on Iwo Jima in 1945 instantly became indelible in the national consciousness, helping to convince war-weary Americans that the arduous battle in the Pacific was being won. However, despite its still-undiminished power, the image's potency and permanence cannot trump the harrowing, gore-drenched ones lodged stubbornly and painfully in the memories of those who witnessed such nightmarish loss there. One starts to understand the terrifying experience these men, so many still in their teens, were able to survive upon learning that more than a quarter of all the Medals of Honor awarded during World War II were for conduct in this one battle for strategic Iwo. It is no wonder that so many who made it back intact did not want to talk during the years that followed about all they had seen, pretending to be unable to recall what they could no longer hope to forget.

One such man was John "Doc" Bradley, a Navy Corpsman depicted in Rosenthal's hurriedly-snapped and now iconic picture. Even until his death in 1994, Bradley had remained tightlipped about it all, even to his family, although the haunting dreams and hallucinations he suffered revealed what he could only imperfectly tamp down. It was after his passing that Bradley's son,

James, tried to fill in the blanks in the story of his father's place in history, resulting in the deeply affecting, heartily-hailed bestseller, *Flags of Our Fathers*, written with Ron Powers and published in 2000.

The faces of the six men in the famous photo are obscured, but Bradley's book reveals more than was ever known before about them and the task depicted, allowing the public to not only see who they were but also understand how the three who survived the war saw themselves. The trio had been plucked from the filth and stench of combat to come back home, uncomfortably leaving their brothers in arms behind to be trotted around a newly-buoyed and grateful country as exceptionally useful tools for a vital government war bond drive. They expressed varying degrees of unease while being lauded, wined, and dined as others died, particularly since what had so inspired the nation was actually the dramatic-looking erection of a replacement flag, one of the least hazardous things they and their fellow troops had done. Despite the courage in battle, the memorable kindness he exhibited in tending to the injured, the wounds he himself suffered, and the medal he earned, Bradley, like the others, still emphasized that those deserving the most gratitude are "the guys who didn't come back."

Now director Clint Eastwood has brought the book to the screen, creating a powerful, poignant look at the heroism and hurt, fortitude and frailty, fact and propaganda. Just as many people have asserted that its source material is the best book ever written about Iwo Jima, Eastwood's examination of the subject surpasses John Wayne's fictionalized *The Sands of Iwo Jima* (1949) and Tony Curtis' *The Outsider* (1961), which focused on Pima Indian and Marine Ira Hayes, the most tortured and tragic member of the surviving flag-raisers.

Flags of Our Fathers begins with the elderly John Bradley's (George Grizzard) tormented nocturnal reliving of his past, later crawling upon a staircase in a desperate, delusional search for a comrade he knows died on Iwo Jima almost a half century ago. The film then proceeds on three fronts, intercutting between James Bradley's (Tom McCarthy) pursuit of his father's story, the invasion of Iwo Jima, and the lives afterward of a younger John Bradley (Ryan Phillippe), Hayes (Adam Beach), and Marine Rene Gagnon (Jesse Bradford).

In scenes leading up to their departure for the island, Eastwood clearly seeks to emphasize the youthful exuberance, excited anticipation, and even gung-ho cockiness of those who have yet to visit hell. The troops enjoy listening to music, playing cards, smoking cigarettes, and playing practical jokes on the most callow amongst them like Franklin Sousley (Joseph Cross). As throngs of men gather on the decks of a parade of ships, the sun shines brightly upon them as they jubilantly go off to give the enemy an enthusiastic comeuppance. Their cheeriness is quickly tempered, however, by the harsh realization that none of the ships can stop to pick up an unfortunate, screaming man who has fallen overboard. "So much for no man left behind," Bradley says grimly.

The mood darkens ever further once the sea of troops lands in wave upon wave on silent beaches, which are suddenly pounded by a horrific, ear-splitting, and decimating onslaught. Eastwood chose to shoot the Iwo Jima scenes in Iceland, which has similar black sand beaches. The bloody, chaotic, cacophonous action sequences seem all too unsettlingly real, reminiscent of the much-talked-about D-Day landing sequence in *Saving Private Ryan* (1998), directed by *Flags of Our Fathers*' co-producer, Steven Spielberg. In contrast to the earlier scenes, Eastwood and his veteran director of photography, Tom Stern, desaturate these images except for their grisly red highlights, draining the life out of the visuals as the same is being done to the men.

On the fifth day of a battle that would rage for over a month, U.S. forces reached the top of the crucial mountain and planted their flag. Since the Secretary of the Navy ordered it be given to him as a souvenir, a second one had to be run up Suribachi by Gagnon to take its place. Rosenthal happened to be in the right place at the right time, and the photo caused a seismic burst of optimism and patriotism after being plastered on the front page of virtually every newspaper in the country. Soon afterward, President Franklin D. Roosevelt directed that the men in the picture be identified, and the three still living, full of mixed emotions, were ordered home.

Especially interesting is the way each man reacts to and copes with this overwhelming, unexpected turn of events. Whether at a reenactment of the flag raising before 50,000 roaring, worshipful fans at Soldier Field in Chicago; a fancy dinner with military bigwigs which includes an ice cream sculpture of the event (inappropriately and sickeningly topped with a bright red sauce); or during any of their other appearances on the successful bond drive, Bradley is kind, soft-spoken, levelheaded, and humble; Gagnon quite enjoys basking in the adulation (excitedly collecting job offers thrown his way); while emotionally-charged Hayes is wracked with guilt. He feels like a fraud, asserting that what they are being honored for was nothing extraordinary, especially compared to the men who gave their lives. Hayes also feels like a shirker, someone who has deserted those who had expected him to watch their backs. He is especially troubled by the cover-up needed to save the military embarrassment over its misidentification of one of the now-deceased men in the photograph. (Shortly after being told of this while in Washington for a visit to meet President Truman, Hayes stares glumly and with great significance at a bust of Abraham Lincoln.) Racism adds to Hayes' burden, incongruously present even amidst his country's deep appreciation. He frequently uses alcohol to anaesthetize and loses control, eventually getting his wish to be shipped back into combat, but with the label of being "an embarrassment to his uniform." Beach is achingly affecting, a standout in a uniformly well-acted production which also lets viewers get to know the other worthy young men who did not make it back alive.

As the three get the star treatment while helping the war effort stateside, the minds of Bradley and Hayes in particular are continuously, drawn back to dreadful, disquieting, and heartbreaking memories which will not go away. What can fade away surprisingly quickly, as *Flags of Our Fathers* shows, is even the most intense fame. Once the war was over and the country moved on, the men were virtual has-beens almost as swiftly as they had become heroes. Gagnon's propitious employment opportunities evaporated. Bitter and disillusioned, he worked menial jobs for the rest of his life, which also featured an unhappy marriage. Hayes was often in the bottle, in jail, or both, passing away on a reservation at the age of thirty-two. This tormented, wholly reluctant celebrity died, ironically enough, from exposure. Only Bradley was able to carve out a successful, satisfactory life, but there was always that "wall of silence" about his wartime experiences.

While *Flags of Our Fathers* deservedly found itself on many lists of the best films of 2006, it was not quite as triumphant at the box office. Made on a budget of approximately $55 million, it grossed just over $33 million during its initial release. Bradley's book was exceptionally adapted by William Broyles, Jr. (Oscar® nominated for *Apollo 13* [1995]) and Paul Haggis (Oscar®-winner for *Crash* [2004]). Fascinatingly, Eastwood was so absorbed by his subject that he decided to do a companion film, the already-acclaimed *Letters From Iwo Jima* (2006), which looks at the battle from the point of view of the Japanese.

David L. Boxerbaum

CREDITS

John "Doc" Bradley: Ryan Phillippe
Rene Gagnon: Jesse Bradford
Ira Hayes: Adam Beach
Sgt. Mike Strank: Barry Pepper
Keyes Beech: John Benjamin Hickey
Bud Gerber: John Slattery
Ralph Ignatowski: Jamie Bell
Hank Hansen: Paul Walker
Col. Chandler Johnson: Robert Patrick
Capt. Severance: Neal McDonough
James Bradley: Tom McCarthy
Pauline Harnois: Melanie Lynskey
Franklin Sousley: Joseph Cross
Belle Block: Judith Ivey
Commandant Vandegrift: Chris Bauer
Dave Severance: Harve Presnell
John Bradley: George Grizzard
Mr. Beech: Len Cariou
Origin: USA
Language: English
Released: 2006
Production: Clint Eastwood, Steven Spielberg, Robert Lorenz; Amblin Entertainment, Warner Bros., DreamWorks Pictures, Mapaso; released by Paramount Pictures
Directed by: Clint Eastwood
Written by: William Broyles Jr., Paul Haggis
Cinematography by: Tom Stern
Music by: Clint Eastwood
Sound: Walt Martin
Editing: Joel Cox
Art Direction: Jack G. Taylor Jr., Adrian Gorton
Costumes: Deborah Hopper
Production Design: Henry Bumstead
MPAA rating: R
Running time: 131 minutes

REVIEWS

Boxoffice Online. October 20, 2006.
Chicago Sun-Times Online. October 20, 2006.
Entertainment Weekly. October 27, 2006, p. 49.
Hollywood Reporter Online. October 10, 2006.
Los Angeles Times Online. October 20, 2006.
New York Times Online. October 20, 2006.
Rolling Stone Online. October 16, 2006.
San Francisco Chronicle. October 20, 2006, p. E1.
Time Online. October 15, 2006.
Variety Online. October 9, 2006.
Washington Post. October 20, 2006, p. C1.

QUOTES

Sgt. Strank: "I told my men I'd bring them all home to their mothers. Which means I already lied to half of them."

Dave Severance: "If you can get a picture, the right picture, you can win a war."

TRIVIA

The film is dedicated to production designer Henry Bumstead, casting director Phyllis Huffman, and photographer Joe Rosenthal, who all died during production.

AWARDS

Nomination:

Oscars 2006: Sound, Sound FX Editing

Golden Globes 2007: Director (Eastwood)

FLICKA

Box Office: $20.9 million

Flicka is the 2006 version of the 1940 Mary O'Hara classic book *My Friend Flicka.* The elementary school staple spawned a movie version in 1943, starring a young Roddy McDowell, which became a popular favorite. For this version, the name has been shortened to the more aerodynamic *Flicka.*

In *Flicka*, lead character Ken has become Katy McLaughlin (Alison Lohman). Katy is returning for the summer to her family's picturesque Wyoming horse ranch. Her family does not yet know that the headmaster of Katy's pricey private school is going to be sending a letter home requesting that the girl repeat a grade. The headmaster is displeased that Katy's habit of daydreaming about horses is getting in the way of her filling out her exams.

Katy is a born rancher and the perfect person to take over as second-in-command for her dad, Rob (country singer Tim McGraw). Rob, however, is oblivious to his daughter's talents and has already decided that his son, Howard (Ryan Kwanten), should be in charge of the ranch. Howard, meanwhile, does not particularly like ranching and wants to leave to go to college. A family meeting might help straighten things out, but it would knock about an hour and half of screen time off the film.

Throughout the summer, Katy finds herself clashing with her father because, as the story ham-fistedly keeps pointing out, she is so much like him. "When are you going to look at your daughter and realize she's you?" says Rob's wife Nell (Maria Bello), in one of the film's typically overwrought dramatic moments. Although the screenplay, written by Mark Rosenthal and Lawrence Konner, says Katy is her dad, she is simultaneously compared to a wild horse, Flicka. Flicka is a black mustang, who, like Katy, cannot be tamed. Pretty girl Katy dubs the horse Flicka, after a nickname the Swedes apparently use for a pretty girl.

Katy wants to bring the horse home; her father does not. Katy wants to tame the horse so she can ride it; her father thinks she should not. Katy wants to keep the horse at the ranch; her father sells the horse to a rodeo owner. Through every conflict, Katy defies her father's wishes and does what she wants. The idea is supposed to be that she is so dedicated to Flicka that she will do anything to have her. Often, however, it just looks like Katy is a disobedient kid. Her defiance almost kills her and her beloved horse.

Still, *Flicka* has some things to recommend it. Top on that list is the scenery. The green rolling hills and picturesque Wyoming mountains on the McLaughlin ranch look like they might be just around the corner from Brokeback Mountain. The performances are good, too. McGraw brings an old-fashioned Hollywood masculinity to his role as the protective dad. Lohman is good enough, even if only for the fact that she is a twenty-seven-year-old actress convincingly playing a teenager. Kwanten has the right kind of non-threatening handsomeness that is right for the twelve-year-old girl demographic that the film is aimed toward. And Bello is nice to watch, just to see her Hollywood version of a ranch wife. As Manohla Dargis of the *New York Times* points out, this is a woman who "has rustled up wild gooseberry pancakes with creme fraiche for breakfast or is gardening in the afternoon sun with a flashing grin and an impeccably coiffed fall of hair." On the clean and charmingly decorated ranch that this wife lives on, surely there is never the unpleasant stench of horse manure.

Critics were split about whether *Flicka* was a good film or not. Michael Wilmington of the *Chicago Tribune* wrote: "In this *Flicka*, everything is a little too big, grandiose and commercially beautiful." Wesley Morris of the *Boston Globe* wrote that "the best parts of *Flicka* are its pinch-me optimism and its old-fashioned-movie flourishes." Peter Hautlaub of the *San Francisco Chronicle* wrote: "There are some nice moments and beautiful scenery, but the film is often slow and the dialogue is overwrought. And the apparent lesson of the movie? Keep disobeying your parents and you'll eventually get your way." Finally, Manohla Dargis of the *New York Times* called the film "an entertainingly ridiculous update." Wrote Dargis: "*Flicka* is padded with minor incident and a wealth of beauty shots that inspire intense vacation-home envy, but the parts never cohere dramatically."

Jill Hamilton

CREDITS

Katy McLaughlin: Alison Lohman

Rob McLaughlin: Tim McGraw

Nell McLaughlin: Maria Bello

Howard McLaughlin: Ryan Kwanten

Gus: Dallas Roberts

Norbert Rye: Nick Searcy

Rick Koop: Jeffrey Nordling
Jack: Danny Pino
Origin: USA
Language: English
Released: 2006
Production: Gil Netter; Fox 2000 Pictures; released by 20th Century Fox
Directed by: Michael Mayer
Written by: Mark Rosenthal, Lawrence Konner
Cinematography by: J. Michael Muro
Music by: Aaron Zigman
Sound: Richard Van Dyke
Editing: Andrew Marcus
Art Direction: Peter Borck
Costumes: Molly Maginnis
Production Design: Sharon Seymour
MPAA rating: PG
Running time: 94 minutes

REVIEWS

Chicago Sun-Times Online. October 20, 2006.
Entertainment Weekly. October 27, 2006, p. 55.
Hollywood Reporter Online. October 19, 2006.
New York Times Online. October 20, 2006.
Premiere Magazine. November 2006, p. 45.
San Francisco Chronicle. October 20, 2006, p. E5.
Variety Online. October 17, 2006.
Washington Post. October 20, 2006, p. C5.

QUOTES

Nell (to her husband Rob): "When are you going to look at your daughter and realize she's you?"

FLUSHED AWAY

Someone's Going Down.
—Movie tagline

Box Office: $64.4 million

Aardman Animation is known for its claymation stop-motion films, for which the studio has won several Oscars®. Probably the most well-known works produced by Aardman are the Wallace and Gromit films (the duo eventually appeared in their own feature-length production in 2005) and *Chicken Run* (2000), distributed by DreamWorks Animation SKG. The latest co-venture between Aardman and DreamWorks, *Flushed Away* is unique because it is animated with computer-generated imagery (CGI) instead of stop-motion. Interestingly, though, the characters and settings in the film look distinctly like Aardman creations, i.e., they look like characters from Wallace and Gromit. Like the most popular Aardman productions, *Flushed Away* features many humorous moments, often in the form of sight gags, witty one-liners, and random pop culture references. Fortunately, such humor is frequent enough in the movie to help keep the pace going, but is not overdone to the point that it becomes tiresome. Also, the main characters in the story are appealing and interesting enough to minimize the lack of a well-developed plot, which is one of the film's weaknesses. Though the story moves along quickly enough to hold the viewer's attention, it tends at times to progress too swiftly, turning major developments into sudden leaps. Still, it is a fun, entertaining movie even if it is short on substance.

Flushed Away tells the story of Roddy (voice of Hugh Jackman), a mouse who enjoys an upscale, posh life as a beloved pet in a Kensington flat. When his owner Tabitha (voice of Rachel Rawlinson) and her family leave for vacation, Roddy leaves his cage and has free reign in the house. Since he is alone, he has no one to interact with, so Roddy plays with Tabitha's toys—cars, dolls, balls, etc.—and seems to have a lot of imaginative fun, among other things, playing volleyball, going to the beach, and attending a movie premiere. However, his organized fun is interrupted when another mouse—a grungy, crude fellow named Sid (voice of Shane Richie)—arrives through the sink, having come from the sewer. Sid is impressed with the surroundings and declares that he is going to stay in this home forever, much to the horror of Roddy, who concocts the idea of telling Sid the toilet is a Jacuzzi so he can flush the uninvited guest back to where he came from. Sid's not as ignorant as Roddy believes, though, and promptly Roddy finds himself being pushed into the toilet and flushed away.

In the sewer, Roddy discovers a busy, well-populated mouse city. Searching for someone who can help him find his way back home, he meets Rita (voice of Kate Winslet), a spunky scavenger who captains a boat called the Jammy Dodger. Before the two have a chance to talk, a group of apparent thugs led by nasty Spike (voice of Andy Serkis) shows up demanding that Rita turn over a ruby. Rita insists the ruby belonged to her father but claims she doesn't have it. However, Roddy sees it in her back pocket and, to protect himself, tells Spike where it is. Still, even though they have the ruby, Spike and gang take Rita and Roddy to their leader, the Toad (voice of Ian McKellen), who is obsessed with the world "up top" and has a large collection of items from beyond the sewer. The Toad is initially impressed to learn that Roddy comes from Kensington, considering him an individual of "quality," until Roddy calls his collection "amusing" and then accidentally destroys some of it, which infuriates the Toad. Rita and Roddy manage to retake the ruby and escape being "iced"; in the process of getting away, Rita takes an electrical cable from a console, which the Toad calls the master cable. This upsets the amphibian more than having lost the ruby.

The bulk of the movie details the adventures of Roddy and Rita as they get to know each other and flee from the Toad's minions. After Roddy proves to Rita that the ruby is actually a fake, he promises her that he can give her real rubies, emeralds, and diamonds to help her family if she will take him up top and back to his home in Kensington. She agrees and they set out on the journey. Meanwhile, the Toad turns to his cousin LeFrog (voice of Jean Reno) to pursue the mice and reclaim the master cable.

After Roddy makes it back to Kensington, he soon realizes that, despite how luxurious his life might have seemed, he is lonely and misses having a family like Rita's. He ultimately returns to the sewer to stop the Toad when he discovers the villain's true plot. Once he and Rita save the day, the mouse decides to stay among his new friends.

Many of the most humorous moments in *Flushed Away* come from somewhat irreverent comic situations and witty one-liners. For example, at one point, when Rita is hanging by a line as she and Roddy escape from the Toad's minions, Roddy latches onto her legs and is carried along beneath her; afraid he is going to fall, he cries, "There are things I want to do, things I want to see!" At that point, his weight pulls Rita's pants down to reveal her underclothes. "That wasn't one of them," he intones. The movie also includes numerous amusing pop culture references, though some of them would go over the heads of the youngest audiences. Some of the funnier characters in the movie are the slugs that inhabit the sewers in numbers approaching that of the mice. They sing (often incomprehensibly) and provide comic sound effects such as creepy, sinister humming when Roddy enters a potentially frightening area of the sewer.

While Roddy and Rita are very likeable characters, their relationship seems to jump rather quickly from one of somewhat amiable conflict to one of a budding romance. Of course, since this is an animated film, and one that does not take itself too seriously at that, one should not expect much realism in the development of characters. *Flushed Away* is intelligent enough to poke fun at itself while poking fun at many other things, and in that way it succeeds as an entertaining and amusing film. It does not try to tackle social issues or develop significant themes, but it succeeds in what it attempts to do: tell a fast-paced, fun story with enough smart, irreverent humor to hold the attention of both children and adults.

David Flanagin

CREDITS

Roddy St. James: Hugh Jackman (Voice)
Rita: Kate Winslet (Voice)
The Toad: Ian McKellen (Voice)
Le Frog: Jean Reno (Voice)
Whitey: Bill Nighy (Voice)
Spike: Andy Serkis (Voice)
Rita's Mum: Kathy Burke (Voice)
Rita's Dad: David Suchet (Voice)
Sid: Shane Richie (Voice)
Rita's Grandma: Miriam Margolyes (Voice)
Tabitha: Rachel Rawlinson (Voice)
Origin: USA, Great Britain
Language: English
Released: 2006
Production: Peter Lord, David Sproxton, Cecil Kramer; DreamWorks Animation, Aardman Features; released by Paramount Pictures
Directed by: David Bowers, Sam Fell
Written by: Dick Clement, Ian La Frenais, Chris Lloyd, Joe Keenan, William Davies
Music by: Harry Gregson-Williams
Sound: Andy Nelson, Jim Bolt
Editing: John Venzon
Production Design: David A.S. James
MPAA rating: PG
Running time: 84 minutes

REVIEWS

Boxoffice Online. November 3, 2006.
Chicago Sun-Times Online. November 3, 2006.
Entertainment Weekly. November 10, 2006, p. 58.
Hollywood Reporter Online. October 17, 2006.
Los Angeles Times Online. November 3, 2006.
New York Times Online. November 3, 2006.
San Francisco Chronicle Online. November 3, 2006.
Variety Online. October 15, 2006.
Washington Post. November 3, 2006, p. C1.

AWARDS

Nomination:
British Acad. 2006: Animated Film

FLYBOYS

Box Office: $13 million

It should come as a warning—or perhaps an enticement—that a *Flyboys* video game was made available to coincide with the movie's release. It makes sense—*Flyboys'* script is at about video-game level in sophistication. There are airplane fight sequences, a pretty French romantic interest, and a crew of green pilots just waiting to experience a rite of passage.

It is too bad that *Flyboys* is such a rote exercise, because its inspiration is an interesting story. The movie is based on the real-life Lafayette Escadrille. In World War I, a group of Americans headed over to French soil to join in the fight against the Germans. This was before America had entered the war. Airplanes were only newly invented, but they were already being used in combat. The duty of the pilots in the Lafayette Escadrille was to shoot down Germans. The life expectancy of the pilots performing this task was only a few weeks. A successful mission meant that more of your men came back than did not.

The first, and perhaps biggest, flaw in the film was the casting of James Franco as hero Blaine Rawlings. Franco's one-note acting only makes it all the more clear just how similar this character is to the other boy-becomes-a-man-through-military-service character he played in *Annapolis* (2006). Blaine, who comes from a family of Texas ranchers, enlisted because his family ranch has been foreclosed upon. No matter, though, because everyone here is playing a stereotype. There is the portly rich kid, Briggs Lowry (Tyler Labine), who enlisted because his father made him. There is the handsome William Jensen (Philip Winchester), with the pretty girlfriend back home. (Naturally, there is a scene in which she runs beside his train as he sets off overseas.) Eddie Beagle (David Ellison) claims to be a Wisconsin farm boy, but may just be a German spy. And there's the religious guy, Higgins (Christien Anholt), who wears the standard issue round glasses and soft face donned by many other war movie characters of this ilk.

More interesting is hardened squadron leader, Reed Cassidy (Martin Henderson), who has lost all his friends to war. He keeps a pet lion and gives Rawlings well-timed, sage advice. It is easy to see that he is doomed so that the story arc can accommodate Rawlings coming to manhood. Eugene Skinner (Abdul Salis) is a black boxer who wants to fly planes because, while he is in the air, no one can see what color he is. The racial issues brought up by his character are interesting, but it is difficult to tell which aspects are historically accurate and which are the product of a contemporary mindset.

Flyboys is a very mannerly film. For one thing, it looks quite nice. Directory of photography Henry Braham does a nice job lighting the scenes. The bar where the pilots go after their battles is so wonderfully lit it seems a tad self-conscious. Briggs is a polite hero who is idealistic, caring and loves children. He meets his love interest, Lucienne (Jennifer Decker), in a brothel, but is relieved to hear that she is not one of the employees there. The two share chaste attempts at overcoming their language barrier.

The aerial scenes are terrifically filmed. Director Tony Bill uses his computer-generated images effectively to give a sense of immediacy to the dogfight scenes. It helps that he used some actual planes from that time. Bill also does a good job of conveying the idea that these guys were piloting something no more stable than a sort of flying go-cart. If their machine guns failed, for example, the men were issued a small hammer to give the gun a good whack.

Most movie critics felt like they had seen it all before. Michael Phillips of the *Chicago Tribune*, who fully realized why people attend such a movie—as he put it, "They go for the eeeeerrrrroooww and the rat-a-tat-tat"—nevertheless felt that the film came up short. "Just about everything in the video-gamey World War I picture *Flyboys* rings false," he wrote. Walter Addiego of the *San Francisco Chronicle* wrote: "Besides some fine dogfight sequences, it often feels threadbare, just an exercise in recycling." Finally, Mario Tarradell of the *Dallas Morning News* questioned the decision to release a war movie during an actual war and wrote: "When *Flyboys* finally ends, a too-long 139 minutes later, there's a sense of emptiness, perhaps even disgust. It's bad enough to endure a movie while we watch the never-ending conflict in Iraq. It's even worse to sit through one that's ultimately a waste of time."

Jill Hamilton

CREDITS

Blaine Rawlings: James Franco
Reed Cassidy: Martin Henderson
Capt. Thenault: Jean Reno
William Jensen: Philip Winchester
Eddie Beagle: David Ellison
Lucienne: Jennifer Decker
Briggs Lowry: Tyler Labine
Eugene Skinner: Abdul Salis
Higgins: Christien Anholt
Origin: France, USA
Language: English
Released: 2006
Production: Dean Devlin, Mark Frydman; Ingenious Film Partners, Electric Entertainment, Skydance Prods.; released by MGM
Directed by: Tony Bill
Written by: Blake T. Evans, David S. Ward, Phil Sears
Cinematography by: Henry Braham

Music by: Trevor Rabin
Sound: Ian Voight
Music Supervisor: Peter Afterman, Margaret Yen
Editing: Christopher Blunden, Ron Rosen
Art Direction: Matthew Gray
Costumes: Nic Ede
Production Design: Charles Wood
MPAA rating: PG-13
Running time: 139 minutes

REVIEWS

Boxoffice Online. September 22, 2006.
Entertainment Weekly. September 29, 2006, p. 58.
Hollywood Reporter Online. September 22, 2006.
Los Angeles Times Online. September 22, 2006.
New York Times Online. September 22, 2006.
Premiere Magazine. October 2006, p. 43.
San Francisco Chronicle. September 22, 2006, p. E9.
Variety Online. September 21, 2006.
Washington Post Online. September 22, 2006.

QUOTES

Cassidy (to new recruits): "Let me guess. You're here because you thought it'd be fun to fly airplanes."

FOR YOUR CONSIDERATION

Box Office: $5.5 million

For Your Consideration comes from a prominent comedy pedigree: it was put together by the same team that created the classic *This Is Spinal Tap* (1984), as well as the hilarious *Waiting for Guffman* (1996), *Best in Show* (2000), and *A Mighty Wind* (2003). A prominent star of all five and the director of the three latter films, Christopher Guest directs *For Your Consideration* and brings the same sharp insight into the behind-the-scenes workings of the entertainment industry to this skewering of the Academy Awards® process as he did to the music industry (*This Is Spinal Tap*), community theatre (*Waiting for Guffman*), dog shows (*Best in Show*), and the PBS obsession with 1960s folk group reunions (*A Mighty Wind*), and does so with effective, if not quite funny, results.

Marilyn Hack (Catherine O'Hara) is a working Hollywood actress for whom stardom eludes, until she finds herself playing a matriarch with a terminal illness in *For Your Consideration*'s movie-within-the-movie, *Home for Purim.* Buzz begins to build on the Internet that Marilyn could be nominated for an Academy Award® for her performance. This send ripples throughout the entire set of *Home for Purim.* Her fellow actors seem to be genuinely happy for her, but they also find themselves swept up in Oscar® fever. Victor Allan Miller (Harry Shearer), known in the world of *For Your Consideration* mostly for his commercial work, is happy to be participating in *Home for Purim,* insofar as it will probably land him better commercials (possibly without having to audition). When he appears with Marilyn on a morning television show, *Wake Up L.A.*, and the hosts mention that he, too, is the subject of Oscar® speculation, Victor hopes that he might not have to do commercials anymore. Thus far untouched by nomination rumors, fellow cast members Callie Webb (Parker Posey) and Brian Chubb (Christopher Moynihan) claim that the work is what is important and not awards or nominations. They play siblings in *Home for Purim*, but are lovers off the set. When the head of the studio, Martin Gibb (Ricky Gervais), reads aloud to the entire set from an article in *Variety* that Callie, too, has received some Oscar® attention, it begins to erode her relationship with Brian, and *Home for Purim* begins to crumble under the pressure of its own potential bonanza at the Academy Awards®.

Martin, aware that the film is now getting unexpected publicity, seeks to make it more appealing to a wider audience. He fears that its emphasis on Jewish culture will not play in middle America, and he asks writers Philip Koontz (Bob Balaban) and Lane Iverson (Michael McKean) to "tone down the Jewishness." Callie eventually has a breakdown on the set after an argument with Brian over her obsession with the possibility of being nominated, when prior to the *Variety* article she did not seem to care about awards. *Home for Purim* is eventually re-named *Home for Thanksgiving*, and critical buzz seems to favor the film as a major Oscar® contender. Marilyn and Callie are the two most obviously affected by their apparent impending nominations: Marilyn, in preparation for her ascendancy into the Hollywood A-list, does what so many aging Hollywood actresses do and gets a makeover complete with appropriately hideous plastic surgery; Callie allows her relationship with Brian to disintegrate.

The night before the nominations are announced, all of the principal players, minus Brian, gather at a party thrown by Martin, who toasts "the future nominees of *Home for Thanksgiving.*" When the nominations come down the next day, however, the only one to be nominated is Brian, the sole principal actor who received no advance praise. Victor, Callie, and especially Marilyn are devastated. A quick follow-up sequence reveals all of them to be working as variations of themselves prior to their brief flirtation with Oscar® glory: Victor continues with his commercial work; Callie, in an attempt to return to the roots of her artistry, does a horrifyingly bad one-woman show at a small theatre in Los Angeles; and Marilyn, apparently fed up with the constant disappointment of acting professionally, opts for the one career that her skill-set and ego will tolerate—acting coach.

What makes *For Your Consideration* both work as a satire and perhaps fail as pure comedy is its details. The title of the film, "For Your Consideration," is itself a phrase that appears on ads for various would-be Oscar® contenders in trade magazines such as *Variety* and *The Hollywood Reporter,* as well as on the videocassettes and DVDs sent to the thousand of Academy Awards® voters during Oscar® season. The film within *For Your Consideration, Home for Purim,* though an exaggeration of an independent film in both content and scale, is exactly the kind of movie one might plausibly expect to receive early Oscar® buzz. It is a period piece about a family reunion, featuring a dying matriarch with a lesbian daughter who brings her lover home to meet the family—exactly the sort of ensemble, dysfunctional minority family, low-budget piece avid Oscar®-speculators might reasonably expect to see nominated for acting and screenplay awards. These specifics all serve to pointedly indict the publicity component of the Oscar® process, but they are played at such an exaggerated level that they lose a bit of their authenticity and tend to be alienating rather than compelling. For instance, *Hollywood Now* is an *Entertainment Tonight/Extra*-style show co-anchored by Chuck Porter (Fred Willard) and Cindy Martin (Jane Lynch) and, while it is mostly a dead-on send-up of *Entertainment Tonight*, Fred Willard's completely over-the-top performance, normally welcome in this type of movie, only serves to pull the audience out of the world of *For Your Consideration* by practically screaming, "this is an exaggeration of this kind of show." Were this the only talk-show lampoon in *For Your Consideration,* one might wonder if it were intended to be a screwball spoof rather than humorous criticism, but when contrasted with the perfectly pitched *Charlie Rose* parody (whose anchor asks rhetorical questions of *Home for Purim*'s writers, only to answer them himself) or any of the other recognizable talk-show types portrayed—morning talk radio, late night Letterman-style talk variety, and a particularly embarrassing depiction of an MTV *TRL*-like show—it is unclear why *Hollywood Now* gets so much emphasis.

Significantly, unlike the other films this group of actors has become associated with, *For Your Consideration* is not done in the faux-documentary, or "mockumentary" style of its predecessors. By opting for an objective narrative style, the audience is allowed to remain voyeurs, and the public's worship of the cult of celebrity from afar is most certainly a voyeuristic act. This has the effect of making the audience part of the thing criticized rather than an accomplice in the criticism, strengthening the film's point perhaps but weakening the joke. No one goes to a comedy to be indicted. The mockumentary form would allow the audience a sense of entering the world of these characters, while *For Your Consideration*'s objectivity keeps the audience on the outside looking in, and the act of watching the film takes on the dimension of gawking at a celebrity train wreck. In this light, the phrase "For Your Consideration" itself takes on an almost pedantic tone. Whatever the intention of the filmmakers, the style certainly hinders this particular troupe, who have made the mockumentary form their forte.

John Boaz

CREDITS

Marilyn Hack: Catherine O'Hara
Victor Allan Miller: Harry Shearer
Callie Webb: Parker Posey
Corey Taft: John Michael Higgins
Brian Chubb: Christopher Moynihan
Whitney Taylor Brown: Jennifer Coolidge
Chuck Porter: Fred Willard
Cindy Martin: Jane Lynch
Martin Gibb: Ricky Gervais
Philip Koontz: Bob Balaban
Lane Iverson: Michael McKean
Sandy Lane: Ed Begley Jr.
Simon Whitset: Jim Piddock
Mary Pat Hooligan: Rachel Harris
Morley Orfkin: Eugene Levy
Jay Berman: Christopher Guest
Pam Campanella: Carrie Aizley
Origin: USA
Language: English
Released: 2006
Production: Karen Murphy; Shangri-La Entertainment, Castle Rock Entertainment; released by Warner Independent Pictures
Directed by: Christopher Guest
Written by: Eugene Levy, Christopher Guest
Cinematography by: Roberto Schaefer
Music by: C.J. Vanston
Sound: Hamilton Sterling
Editing: Robert Leighton
Art Direction: Pat Tagliaferro
Costumes: Durinda Wood
Production Design: Joseph T. Garrity
MPAA rating: PG-13
Running time: 86 minutes

REVIEWS

Boxoffice Online. November 17, 2006.
Chicago Sun-Times Online. November 17, 2006.

Entertainment Weekly. November 24, 2006, p. 81.
Hollywood Reporter Online. November 16, 2006.
Los Angeles Times Online. November 17, 2006.
New York Times Online. November 17, 2006.
Rolling Stone Online. November 13, 2006.
Variety Online. September 11, 2006.
Village Voice Online. November 14, 2006.
Washington Post. November 17, 2006, p. C4.

QUOTES

Corey Taft: "In every actor there lives a tiger, a pig, an ass, and a nightingale, and you never know which one's gonna show up."

Victor: "Oscar® is the backbone of this industry, an industry not known for backbone."

AWARDS

Nomination:

Ind. Spirit 2007: Actress (O'Hara)

THE FOUNTAIN

What if you could live forever?
—Movie tagline

Box Office: $10.1 million

Refusing to simply accept death and let go, a man embarks on a long, passionate, and often painful struggle for triumphant rebirth. This description applies to Darren Aronofsky, the writer and director of *The Fountain,* as well as the film's dauntless hero-in-triplicate, Tomas/Tommy/Tom Creo. After Aronofsky grabbed attention with his first two films, *Pi* (1998) and *Requiem for a Dream* (2000), the director next began work on what aimed to be a uniquely presented, stirring, thought-provoking, and highly romantic rumination on mankind's never-ending quest for immortality. Aronofsky's thoughts about the finite nature of life, born of his turning thirty and his parents' battles with serious illness, his old friend Ari Handel's neuroscientific research on primates, and books on Spanish conquistadors and various religious beliefs were all swirled together to create a highly unusual, highly ambitious, psychedelic sci-fi concoction which will undoubtedly not be to many people's tastes.

When Brad Pitt originally signed on to the project six years ago, plans for Aronofsky's latest modestly-budgeted, artsy creation swelled into a star vehicle. Cate Blanchett was attracted to join the project, crews were hired, and construction began on large-scale sets in Australia. As the budget continued to balloon up to $70 million, Warner Bros. got a bad case of the financial fidgets: either Aronofsky and producer Eric Watson would secure a supplemental source of financing, or their film would not get made. Dogged attempts to do so were eventually successful, crews were re-hired, and went back to work in 2002—just in time for Pitt to back out. Unable to attract Russell Crowe or other big names to take Pitt's place, the plug was pulled, and the production perished. With all hope for his film seemingly, suddenly down the drain, Aronofsky went into a protracted career-stalling funk.

Unable to shake his desire to see the project to fruition, Aronofsky was ready to press on in 2004, scaling down the production as much as possible, revising his script, and presenting it once more to the studio. Despite being surprised to see *The Fountain* again, the company took it back. The $35 million proposal was greenlighted, and would now star Hugh Jackman and Aronofsky's girlfriend, Rachel Weisz.

If only the story of rebirth in the film itself were as easy to follow. *The Fountain*'s epic, thousand-year love story takes place during three separate time periods which remain anything but. The film spends a great deal of time hopping between them, sometimes for a full scene, many times for fleeting images, and occasionally combining eras within a single frame. This chronic, abrupt zigzagging between the 16th, 21st, and 26th centuries, meant to be an illuminating intertwining of ultimately-connected strands, will feel to some like Attention Deficit Disorder storytelling. A good way to orient oneself is to take note of how much hair is currently sprouting about Jackman's head at any given time.

The main portion of *The Fountain* takes place in our current century where driven scientific researcher Tommy (Jackman with a full head of hair, but no beard) is engaged in an agonized race against time to save his beloved dying wife Izzi (Weisz). Although she looks marvelous, viewers learn that she is slowly being dragged into the grave by brain cancer. Dressed predominantly in white and lit in an angelic fashion, Izzi has made peace with her prognosis, and wants to help her tortured husband toward serene acceptance during the time she has left. However, Tommy desperately clings to the belief that death is something that can be cured, and feverishly labors in a dimly-lit basement laboratory on a single-minded search for a miracle within the tumor-studded grey matter of monkeys. His research appears to have come up with a thrilling, landmark discovery to stop aging in its tracks, but since it will do nothing to eradicate Izzi's particular problem, Tommy could not care less and keeps his eyes on the prize. Straining mightily, the man is willing to blot out anything that threatens to sidetrack him from his endeavor to hang on to the one he holds dear—including the one he is trying to save. Tommy cannot bear to lose Izzi and thus sometimes becomes rather unbearable, barking at her when she interrupts his work with the idea that they take a pleasurable stroll through the first snow of what will likely be her last winter. In Tommy's mind, there is no time to take the time, and he tragically misses out on simply enjoying their last days together. By toiling instead in his dark, subterranean lab, Tommy fails to see the light.

Izzi busies herself with the writing of a manuscript entitled "The Fountain" about Spanish conquistadors sent amongst the Maya by an Inquisition-threatened Queen Isabel to locate the legendary Tree of Life. Just a sip of the sap supposedly makes one live indefinitely. Scenes jumping back five hundred years make her story come alive, as heroic Tomas (Jackman, full head of hair and thick mustache and beard) confronts brutal native warriors in a murky, eerie, claustrophobic jungle sequence, seemingly taking place in either the middle of the night or the middle of a nightmare. Tomas would apparently do anything for his radiant, ethereally-beautiful queen (Weisz, looking particularly fetching), who gives him a ring and a promise that upon his success: "I shall be your Eve, and together we shall live forever." Tomas does indeed find the immense, gnarled Tree, drinks from a hole he cuts in its trunk, and suddenly sprouts vegetation which covers his entire body. The terminally ill woman's tome has one more chapter to be written. Izzi tells Tommy about Mayan beliefs pertaining to life after death which she hopes will give him some comfort, and implores him to take the old-fashioned pen and ink she uses to write her book and cathartically "finish it."

The final incarnation of these two soul mates is five hundred years into the future, where Tom (a baldheaded, clean-shaven Jackman) sits in the lotus position and drifts upwards through outer space in what looks like a gigantic soap bubble. Those watching should realize that this is still Tommy because he bears a ring tattoo he had given himself all those years before with Izzi's pen and ink. With him is a massive old tree, which he lovingly whispers to and nuzzles when not nibbling on its bark. If viewers are paying close attention to Aronofsky's tortuous, tangled, and irksomely-redundant presentation, they can assume that the seed pod Izzi had given her husband to plant upon her grave had since flourished, sucking up her remains and thus making her once again amongst the living as the Maya believed. The waving little hairs which reach out from its trunk as Tom tenderly kisses it mirror repeated shots showing hairs on the back of Izzi's neck as Tommy cuddles with her. Having felt guilty and crushed upon her death, it seems he aims to transport them, arm-in-branch, to Xibalba, the distant, golden nebula she had told him about from which the Maya believed the dead would be reborn in a massive explosion. Visions of Izzi, at one point complete with hospital bed, appear to Creo (incidentally, Spanish for "I believe"), and her voice incessantly urges him to "finish it," which apparently means to cease his fearful fighting of the end and liberate himself by placidly embracing what is to come. Long before viewers witness Xibalba's destruction, gloriously creating light and, supposedly, new life, many will find themselves impatiently echoing her words.

When *The Fountain* was premiered at the Venice Film Festival, it was reportedly "roundly booed," leaving audience members "perplexed." Many critics panned Aronofsky's work outright (more than one used the term "mess"), while others were able to respect and even enjoy his daring creativity despite the film's problems. The box office take was minimal. Creating a captivating sense of awed wonderment in viewers is different from making them wonder in frustration or befuddlement exactly what in the world is going on. *The Fountain* succeeds (if that is the right word) in eliciting both reactions. It is visually arresting, pretentious, thoughtful, maddeningly convoluted, endlessly repetitive, thoroughly romantic, periodically touching, and, particularly in the portion involving that far-off nebula, challengingly and confoundingly lofty. Still, one cannot help but think of how Tommy's desperate endeavor to buy more time with Izzi supplanted much of the precious time they had left. True, his efforts can be viewed as folly, but one cannot help but admire his attempt. The same will be said by some of Aronofsky's *The Fountain.*

David L. Boxerbaum

CREDITS

Tomas/Tommy/Tom Creo: Hugh Jackman

Isabel/Izzi Creo: Rachel Weisz

Dr. Lillian Guzetti: Ellen Burstyn

Conquistador: Clifford Curtis

Father Avila: Mark Margolis

Origin: USA

Language: English

Released: 2006

Production: Eric Watson, Arnon Milchan, Iain Smith; Protozoa Pictures, New Regency Pictures, Regency Enterprises; released by Warner Bros.

Directed by: Darren Aronofsky

Written by: Darren Aronofsky

Cinematography by: Matthew Libatique

Music by: Clint Mansell

Sound: Brian Emrich

Editing: Jay Rabinowitz

Art Direction: Isabelle Guay, Michele Laliberte

Costumes: Renee April
Production Design: James Chinlund
MPAA rating: PG-13
Running time: 95 minutes

REVIEWS

Boxoffice Online. November 22, 2006.
Chicago Sun-Times Online. November 22, 2006.
Hollywood Reporter Online. September 5, 2006.
Los Angeles Times Online. November 22, 2006.
New York Times Online. November 22, 2006.
Premiere Magazine. November 2006, p. 41.
Rolling Stone Online. November 13, p. 206.
San Francisco Chronicle. November 22, 2006, p. E5.
Variety Online. September 4, 2006.
Washington Post. November 22, 2006, p. C4.

QUOTES

Tommy: "Death is a disease, and there's a cure. And I will find it!"

AWARDS

Nomination:

Golden Globes 2007: Orig. Score

FREEDOMLAND

The Truth Is Hiding Where No One Dares To Look.
—Movie tagline

Box Office: $12.5 million

If *Freedomland* is not, to borrow from the Bard, "full of sound and fury, signifying nothing," it comes all too close. It certainly is a letdown for those who admired Richard Price's 1998 bestselling novel, especially since it was the author himself who distilled his lengthy tome (the paperback version released to coincide with the film's release runs 655 pages) into the screenplay for this disappointing cinematic offering. On that latest edition's cover, reviewers use superlatives to trumpet the source material as a significant achievement. One critic calls it "heartbreaking," an adjective that, in a less complimentary sense, may very well be used by those who had high hopes for this adaptation. If Price's book was thought to be a compelling, powerful, socially relevant, and generally-well-done page-turner, the film is overdone in some ways, underdone in others, and, in short, undone by a poor presentation.

Freedomland was misdirected by Joe Roth (predominantly a studio executive and producer), perhaps seeing if he could fare better with knitted-brow-serious material after faltering with *Christmas with the Kranks* (2004). With Roth at the helm, and with important characters and elements already excised by Price, there are only two scenes here that truly intrigue. There are performances of dour colorlessness and blank, near-catatonia, as well as those which are feverishly overwrought and rabid, painfully devoid of much-needed, subtle shadings. One of the leads actually manages to hit both extremes. There are parts of the film which confound, exasperate, strain one's credulity, or simply fail to impress, let alone involve. No wonder it was released in that stretch of the studios' release schedule when hobbled productions are dumped into theaters. It may have been too frigid in February to do much outside in some parts of the country, but a snug auditorium showing *Freedomland* was forbidding in its own right.

The film begins in promising fashion with one of the aforementioned sequences, which successfully grasp viewers' attention. Brenda Martin (Julianne Moore) is seen walking along dimly lit inner-city streets in an intriguing, trance-like fashion. Slowly and silently, she makes her way to a medical center's emergency room, revealing a dazed, tear-stained face and bloodstained hands. Detective Lorenzo Council (Samuel L. Jackson) arrives to hear Brenda's story of being carjacked by a black man while taking a shortcut through the Armstrong projects of Dempsey, New Jersey, on her way home to neighboring blue-collar suburban Gannon. Flashbacks show what she says transpired. Lorenzo wonders why this white woman would have ventured alone into such a tough neighborhood, but Brenda, a former addict with a generally troubled past, assures him that it was not to score drugs. Actually, she works at an after-school program there, and is known, liked, and respected by the community's minority residents.

While telling her tale, Brenda starts hitting herself in the head over and over again, as if in excruciating torment. Then she suddenly gets around to revealing a startling fact she had amazingly left out of her initial account: the car had sped away with her four-year-old son Cody still inside. Upon hearing Brenda's horrific omission, viewers immediately understand her overwhelming agony, but sympathy will be almost instantly mixed with suspicion. After all, one would expect the imperiled child to have been the first thing out of most terrified parents' lips. Naturally (but mistakenly), those watching now anticipate a suspenseful race to rescue the tyke, and Lorenzo, who knows Dempsey and its people like the back of his hand, seems like the ideal person to track the culprit down and save the day. Audiences will also expect him to soothe this poor woman (who seems, after all, to be teetering dangerously upon the brink of complete emotional collapse) before heading out on his desperate mission. Instead, Lorenzo inexplicably becomes nearly as overcome as Brenda. He rushes around swearing and bellowing questions at her, failing to absorb bits of information she has already provided. He begins gasping for air and has what appears to be an anxiety-induced asthma attack, grappling for an inhaler as the camera-work becomes equally agitated and vertiginous. This decidedly unhelpful and unprofessional eruption and subsequent near-swoon is quite curious and does not inspire confidence. It also continues what quickly seems like a "Can you top this?" contest of hysterics and scenery chewing.

Added to the delirium is Brenda's brother Danny (Ron Eldard), who also goes ballistic and cannot wait to aggressively descend upon the projects and perhaps break a skull or two. With much jockeying for jurisdiction, the white police from Gannon move in to seal off the black neighborhood. The unsettled residents are vocal in their understandable outrage. The response, they say, has never been so zealous when the victim was a minority. One character states that the place "is ticking like a time bomb," which strikes one as being an apt description of just about every person viewers have met so far.

As Brenda continues to enthusiastically bash various parts of her body, swear up a storm, say a cryptic little thing here and then gush with tortured exposition there, the character frankly grows tiresome, and most will lose patience with her along with their initial sympathy. It is not at all hard for Lorenzo and those watching *Freedomland* to question whether they have heard the whole truth from her.

The locked-down residents and riot gear-laden police grow increasingly agitated as truculence heads toward tumult. As a black policeman, Lorenzo is caught in the middle and gets heat from both sides as he tries to solve the case. (He hears both cries of "Uncle Tom!" as well as charges of "protecting your own.") The way Lorenzo goes about getting to the bottom of things seems to stray unreasonably from accepted police procedure, just one of the things which will likely make viewers scratch their heads even more than Brenda beats hers. He suddenly seems sure she killed her son, but it is unclear exactly what facts exist to convince him. Out of the blue, Lorenzo expresses a "gut feeling" to search the ruins of Freedomland, an old, abandoned foundling asylum, asserting it would be the choicest place for a "child to hide." Either a person believes Brenda's car-jacking story or suspects that she herself did something to Cody, but in which scenario is he a runaway? Also, since Brenda is supposedly so universally well thought of and accepted amongst the blacks of Armstrong, and is, as far as anyone knows, a pitiable, innocent victim of horrific circumstances, it is curious when a woman on the street barks, "You stay away from my child!" Then, during a talk Lorenzo has with Brenda at her place, the camera holds expectantly on the two of them gazing at each other, their faces so very close together. Those watching will brace with incredulous certitude: they are going to kiss! It is a weird, pregnant pause, which leads to nothing.

Chances are, no one was hoping for lust to enter into the already overheated proceedings, but there are numerous things which do indeed lead to a feeling of being let down. When the wholly-expected riot finally erupts, it is cliche-ridden, poorly executed, and packs little punch. It also turns out that Cody had died quietly at home, when he swallowed too much of the cough syrup his mom had left in the apartment to make him sleepy, while she irresponsibly popped out to rendezvous with her black lover. They then buried the child in the woods to avoid charges of negligence. To that undramatic fizzle, add a list of underwritten peripheral characters, too many plot lines of too little interest (including one about Lorenzo and his imprisoned son), and nothing new to say.

With a budget of around $35 million, *Freedomland* was only able to gross $12.5 million. Critical reaction was negative, with the *New York Times'* Manohla Dargis calling it "an early candidate for worst film of the year." Most reviewers tended to agree that the best scene the film has to offer is that in which Karen Collucci (Edie Falco) finally gets the truth out of Brenda. The mother of a murdered child and now the leader of a group which helps hunt for missing youngsters, Karen is able to quietly, gently but purposefully use her own pain to connect with Brenda's and release the truth, one shattered mom to another.

David L. Boxerbaum

CREDITS

Lorenzo Council: Samuel L. Jackson
Brenda Martin: Julianne Moore
Karen Collucci: Edie Falco
Danny Martin: Ron Eldard
Boyle: William Forsythe
Felicia: Aunjanue Ellis
Billy Williams: Anthony Mackie
Marie: LaTanya Richardson Jackson
Reverend Longway: Clarke Peters
Origin: USA
Language: English
Released: 2006
Production: Scott Rudin; Revolution Studios; released by Sony Pictures Entertainment

Directed by: Joe Roth
Written by: Richard Price
Cinematography by: Anastas Michos
Music by: James Newton Howard
Sound: Tom Fleischman, Myron Nettinga
Editing: Nick Moore
Art Direction: Patricia Woodbridge
Costumes: Ann Roth, Michelle Matland
Production Design: David Wasco
MPAA rating: R
Running time: 113 minutes

REVIEWS

Boxoffice Online. February 17, 2006.
Chicago Sun-Times Online. February 17, 2006.
Entertainment Weekly Online. February 15, 2006.
Los Angeles Times Online. February 17, 2006.
New York Times Online. February 17, 2006.
Premiere Magazine Online. February 15, 2006.
Variety Online. February 9, 2006.
Washington Post Online. February 17, 2006.

QUOTES

Leo Sullivan: "Let go and let God."

FRIENDS WITH MONEY

Box Office: $13.3 million

The aptly titled *Friends with Money* is an episodic journey into the world of four friends whose lives and relationships are, to a large degree, informed by money—specifically, either the possession or the lack of it. Money affects how the characters perceive those around them, and colors how other characters perceive them. Written and directed by Nicole Holofcener, this film is more about subtle character study than it is about plot—it uses a vignette structure, with occasionally overlapping storylines, to examine the lives of four women who have apparently been friends for a long time and are now entering middle age. The separate stories of these women, though thematically connected, ultimately serve to isolate them and to dissipate the film's impact and energy, as does its languid pace (its eighty-eight minute running time feels considerably longer).

The friends with money in this film are Franny (Joan Cusack), Jane (Frances McDormand), and Christine (Catherine Keener), all of whom are also married, which makes Olivia (Jennifer Aniston), the poor, unmarried friend who is working as a maid the object of much concern and unsolicited advice. Olivia is a maid at least partly by circumstance. She once was a teacher who taught at a very well-to-do prep school, and the rich students teased her because she drove an old car and gave her quarters for food, so she quit. Interestingly, Olivia seems to allow this sort of condescension, which may be a contributing factor to her poverty. She certainly is unable to stand up for herself in her relationships with men. When Marty (Bob Stephenson), an unkempt-looking man, hires Olivia to clean his filthy, small house, he talks her down from her usual asking price. When Franny hooks Olivia up with her womanizing personal trainer, not only does the trainer have the nerve to invite himself along to Olivia's housecleaning appointments, mostly in order to have sex with her, but he also insists on compensation for helping her clean when he does nothing. Throughout the film, Olivia also places phone calls to a former married lover of hers and she always hangs up when he answers. Ultimately, the lover's wife answers and tells Olivia to get her own man and hangs up. Olivia screams, "I would if I could!" into the disconnected line, which is both an admission of her situation, as well as an abdication of responsibility for it. Ironically, her passivity pays off because it turns out that slovenly Marty, who finally asks Olivia out, is actually rich and living off inherited wealth. Olivia, then, is allowed to forego the pain of transformation for the safety of stasis, with the added benefit of shedding a horrible job.

Olivia's antithesis is Franny, the friend that all the others consider to be the very picture of wealth. In fact, she has so much money that she has difficulty deciding to whom she and her husband Matt (Greg Germann) should donate two million dollars. Significantly, less screen time is devoted to Franny than to the other friends—she has the least amount of conflict in her life. All of her friends attribute her great life to her wealth, including the fact that she and Matt still have a very active sex life, regardless of the fact that, with the exception of Olivia, they are very well off themselves. Franny spends her screen time either talking about wanting to help Olivia, but not actually doing it, or talking to her husband about how they should spend their money. She sets Olivia up with her personal trainer, even though he tells her a story about having sex with a woman in public—apparently any man, to Franny, is better than no man at all. This is because, for Franny, satisfying her own need to intervene in Olivia's life is more important than serving Olivia's best interests. At one point, Franny foregoes discretion entirely and attempts to discuss, in front of Christine, loaning Olivia money which embarrasses Olivia to the point that she squelches the conversation, even though she needs the money. Overall, Franny serves as the "ultimate" that the others view as one end of the happiness spectrum for their own lives, in contrast to the downtrodden Olivia.

The two remaining friends, Jane and Christine, serve as a pairing of opposites in much the same way as Franny and Olivia. Jane, a well-off clothing designer, is obsessed with the tiny injustices she feels are being done to her, and she inveighs against them loudly. When Jane is tailgated, passed and flipped off, she later throws an insult at the driver when he passes her on foot in a crowd. She berates a woman who takes her parking spot, the same woman whose son had a play date with her son recently, and the woman did not have the decency to say hello to Jane the next day. She yells at two people who cut in line in front of her at Old Navy and is asked to leave the store for making a scene. She later tells her son that those small injustices, like cutting in line or stealing a parking spot add up to make the world an uglier place. Ultimately, Jane's sense of disappointment in people comes from the aging process itself. Despite her wealth and good marriage, she feels the end coming. She says that she feels tired, and laments that there is no more wondering "what my fabulous life is going to be like." The life she has is it, as though a privileged life otherwise well-lived is not enough.

The foil for Jane's persistent awareness of injustice is Christine's almost willful obliviousness to things and events around her. It appears that her heretofore-comfortable life as a Hollywood screenwriter has closed her off and allowed her to turn inward, though she maintains a facade of involved concern. Though her marriage is falling apart, she cannot see it. The addition she and her husband are putting on their house is ruining the view for the entire neighborhood, but when confronted by a neighbor, she claims not to have known that was the case—this despite being told outright of the addition's scale by the contractor at the beginning of the film. That is only the most glaring, egregious example of Christine's self-absorption, but many small ones are evident as well. She is constantly bumping into things in her own home. When she notices something different about her husband, he remarks that he shaved his beard weeks before. That this lack of vision is deliberate and not due to mere carelessness is clear in her constant insistence that Jane's husband, Aaron (Simon McBurney), is gay. While Aaron is, in fact, a sensitive man, concerned with his appearance and who occasionally does attract gay men, he is devoted to and ostensibly very much in love with his wife. What Aaron really is for Christine is an opposite of her own husband, David, who is an insensitive bully. Christine's inability to engage her husband, though, makes her project her negativity onto Jane and Aaron's marriage: if Aaron is gay, then perhaps someone on earth will be having a worse marriage than she is.

The title *Friends with Money* suggests, beyond simple summary of the film's content, that the story is supposed to articulate the feelings of the outsider, or anyone who feels like an outsider. This is a movie about attitudes toward both life and wealth, or at least perceived abundance, and as such is also about the "other"—those that have what one feels one lacks, or someone who seems to be lacking compared to oneself—and the alienating effect money can have on relationships. The upshot of all this rankling over money, aging, and happiness, however, is that the film practically exalts self-involvement. The structure is compartmentalized into separate stories, and all of the women in those stories spend a very long time measuring themselves against the lives of their friends. Frankly, not much else happens. It may be argued that *Friends with Money* should be commended for artistically wrestling with the feelings most people have about life. That an audience should be subjected to the woes and complaints of the privileged for an hour and a half because they do it in a slightly funnier, more philosophical way than most people, however, does not justify the exultation of navel-gazing. Detailed character exploration is laudable, but if the best argument for the film's success as art is, "I really see myself in these people," then it is likely that the film in question has done little more than pander to the ego of the viewer.

John Boaz

CREDITS

Olivia: Jennifer Aniston
Franny: Joan Cusack
Christine: Catherine Keener
Jane: Frances McDormand
David: Jason Isaacs
Mike: Scott Caan
Aaron: Simon McBurney
Matt: Greg Germann
Other Aaron: Ty Burrell
Marty: Bob Stephenson
Origin: USA
Language: English
Released: 2006
Production: Anthony Bregman; This Is That; released by Sony Pictures Classics
Directed by: Nicole Holofcener
Written by: Nicole Holofcener
Cinematography by: Terry Stacey
Music by: Craig Richey, Rickie Lee Jones
Sound: Pud Cusack
Music Supervisor: Tracy McKnight

Editing: Rob Frazen
Art Direction: G. Victoria Ruskin, Stephen Carter
Costumes: Michael Wilkinson
Production Design: Amy Ancona
MPAA rating: R
Running time: 88 minutes

REVIEWS

Boxoffice Online. April 7, 2006.
Chicago Sun-Times Online. April 7, 2006.
Entertainment Weekly. April 14, 2006, p. 59.
Los Angeles Times Online. April 7, 2006.
New York Times Online. April 7, 2006.
People. April 17, 2006, p. 37.
San Francisco Chronicle. April 7, 2006, p. E5.
USA Today Online. April 6, 2006.
Variety Online. January 20, 2006.
Village Voice Online. April 4, 2006.

TRIVIA

Actress Catherine Keener and director/writer Nicole Holofcener previously worked together on *Walking and Talking* (1996) and *Lovely and Amazing* (2001).

AWARDS

Ind. Spirit 2007: Support. Actress (McDormand)
Nomination:
Ind. Spirit 2007: Screenplay

G

GABRIELLE

Channeling Ingmar Bergman with endless shots, relentless close-ups, and dramatic lighting, French director Patrice Chereau creates an intense, almost theatrical portrait of a crumbling marriage. It is a beautiful and artistically done piece that at times is also extremely difficult to watch, due to the harsh, emotional intensity and sometimes claustrophobic feel, but ultimately rewarding in its brutal honesty. Adapted by Chereau and Anne-Louise Trividic, who also collaborated on Chereau's *Intimacy* (2001) and *His Brother* (2003), from the short story "The Return" by Joseph Conrad. While Conrad's story takes the point of view of the husband, quickly unraveling after his wife leaves him for another man, Chereau expands the female role to accommodate his talented star Isabelle Huppert, in what is, surprisingly, their first collaboration.

Chereau, who also directs theatre and opera, utilizes a variety of filmic techniques to dramatically convey his message, including titles appearing onscreen similar to those used in silent films, and scenes in black-and-white, lusciously shot by cinematographer Eric Gautier, to bookend the piece. Swelling violins may be heard in the sometimes melodramatic yet thoroughly modern score by Fabio Vacchi. A costume drama set in Paris of 1912, the film nonetheless has a timeless feel, with the dialogue, more formal at the film's start, gradually loosening as the film progresses.

Pascal Greggory, whom Chereau has worked with several times, stars in the complex role of Jean Hervey. Jean walks through a bustling train station on his way home from work, his narrated thoughts conveying contentment with his comfortable position. Life has always been good to the affluent Jean: a stately home filled with fine art paintings and sculpture, a bevy of interesting friends, and the perfect wife—all effortlessly acquired—are among the things he credits for his enviable stature in society. As he enters his impeccable home, the uniformed maids scurry to clean the dirt from beneath his feet as he confidently climbs the tall staircase to greet his wife. Instead, however, his safe, secure world comes crashing in on him when he instead finds a note on his dressing table from her saying she has left him for another man.

In that wonderful scene, Greggory perfectly conveys Jean's dazed disbelief while Chereau emphasizes the importance of the note's discovery, presenting multiple takes of Jean spying the letter through the mirror and at various angles. Before even opening it, he immediately senses that a letter addressed to him in his wife's hand could only mean one thing. He steadies himself with a drink that comes crashing down as he reads it; Jean's confident facade shattered forever as well.

The plot twist is that his wife of ten years, Gabrielle (Huppert), comes back before Jean even has a chance to comprehend her leaving. While this serves to throw Jean even further off balance at first, he quickly regains his composure, realizing that with her return, he has not lost. Despite annoying gossip that surely will spread like wildfire via the servants, Jean believes things can go on as usual; insisting she dress for dinner and refusing to discuss the details of her aborted attempt at abandoning their life together.

At first Gabrielle is strangely silent while Jean haughtily lectures and admonishes. Then, slowly, over dinner, as the servers rush in and out carrying plates, the facts of Gabrielle's disappearance emerge. She fell in love, for the first time, she explains, with an editor-in-chief, played by Thierry Hancisse, who works for a publication Jean finances and one among a group of bohemian types that gather each Thursday evening at the Hervey's for dinner parties. Jean openly detests the man, and watching his face as Gabrielle explains in detail the intimate acts she begged him to perform is painful to watch. The shocking details of their marriage are also revealed. Gabrielle and Jean did not fall in love and get married; rather she was "chosen" by him for a wife. The couple only engaged in intercourse during the first few months of their marriage, after which Gabrielle insisted on separate beds. Jean, who finds emotion "revolting" was happy to comply.

In the intimate scenes where Gabrielle confides in her devious young maid Yvonne (Claudia Coli), she reveals she has only been happy twice in her life. The first was when she fell in love; the second, when she left the note. She tells Jean she has returned because she couldn't bear the reality of living in social obscurity and poverty and prefers to live a comfortable, loveless life with him. There is a moment when he asks her if she came back because she knew Jean loved her and she says witheringly, that she came back only because she was sure that he did not. It would be unbearable to her if he did love her. He is devastated and the absolute irony of the story is although she has known love and can now live without it, Jean, who has lived without love his entire life, realizes he now cannot go on knowing she does not love him; can no longer wear the pretense of the happy couple. During their usual Thursday soiree, her former lover's presence drives Jean to further madness and he leaves the house, never to return.

Greggory's transformation from self-satisfied stuffed shirt to passionate lover driven mad during the course of the film is astonishing. He is matched by the cool, reserved but nonetheless perfectly effective performance of the fascinating Huppert, whose silences reveal as much about her character as the dialogue.

Hilary White

CREDITS

Gabrielle Hervey: Isabelle Huppert
Jean Hervey: Pascal Greggory
Madeleine: Chantal Neuwirth
Yvonne: Claudia Coli
The Editor-in-Chief: Thierry Hancisse
Guest: Thierry Fortineau
Guest: Louise Vincent
Guest: Clement Hervieu-Leger
Origin: France, Germany, Italy
Language: French
Released: 2005
Production: Joseph Strub, Serge Catoire, Ferdinanda Frangipane; Arte France Cinema, StudioCanal, Azor Films, Love Streams Production
Directed by: Patrice Chereau
Written by: Patrice Chereau, Anne-Louise Trividic
Cinematography by: Eric Gautier
Music by: Fabio Vacchi
Sound: Guillaume Sciama, Benoit Hillebrant, Olivier Do Huu
Editing: Francois Gedigier
Art Direction: Olivier Radot
Costumes: Caroline De Vivaise
MPAA rating: Unrated
Running time: 90 minutes

REVIEWS

Boston Globe Online. July 28, 2006.
Hollywood Reporter Online. September 2, 2005.
Los Angeles Times Online. August 4, 2006.
New York Times Online. July 14, 2006.
Variety Online. September 6 2005.
Village Voice Online. July 11, 2006.

QUOTES

Jean: "Emotions are revolting."

GAME 6

Where were "you" on that night?
—Movie tagline

One of the most highly regarded contemporary American novelists, Don DeLillo examines language, technology, chaos, and violence in such novels as *White Noise* (1985), *Libra* (1988), and *Underworld* (1997). *Game 6,* his first screenplay, resembles DeLillo's fiction through its treatment of the paranoia of urban America.

Nicky Rogan (Michael Keaton) is a New York playwright with one big hit. He is hoping his new play will be a success but fears the reaction of critic Steven Schwimmer (Robert Downey, Jr.), known for his vicious reviews. Rogan's life is further complicated by his separation from his wife, Lillian (Catherine O'Hara), the hostility of his daughter, Laurel (Ari Graynor), and the declining mental faculties of his father, Michael (Tom Aldredge). His play's leading man (Harris Yulin) has picked up a parasite in his brain on a film location and suffers from short-term memory loss, making it difficult for him to recall his lines.

Then there are the Boston Red Sox. Although a native New Yorker, Rogan is a lifelong Red Sox fan, and the night his play opens, his team will play the New York Mets in the sixth game of the 1986 World Series. With a three-to-two lead in the best-of-seven series, the Red Sox are one win away from their first World Series victory since 1918. Does Rogan think they will win? Well, they never have in his lifetime. His Red Sox fandom becomes a metaphor for his general pessimism.

Rogan's fear of Schwimmer is ironic because the critic is even more paranoid. He lives in an empty building, stealing electricity from an outside source. Schwimmer practices Buddhist chants but finds little peace. He wears disguises whenever he must venture outside and carries a huge handgun. His reclusiveness and power have earned Schwimmer a cover story in *New York* magazine. His omnipresent visage on buses and the tops of taxis stares at Rogan wherever he goes, recalling the haunting eyes on the billboard for the oculist in F. Scott Fitzgerald's *The Great Gatsby* (1925), the most famous literary exploration of American success and failure.

Rogan's playwright friend Elliot Litvak (Griffin Dunne) has become a shambling nervous wreck after Schwimmer attacked one of his plays. The episodic film also gives Rogan encounters with Joanna Bourne (Bebe Neuwirth), a producer and his occasional sexual partner, and Paisley Porter (Shalom Harlow), a waitress in his favorite bar. Porter is also an actress, having appeared in Litvak's disastrous play.

Before becoming a successful writer, Rogan supported himself as a cab driver, and he enjoys talking to cabbies, all but one refugees from other countries, asking where they take restroom breaks. (His favorite spot was under the Manhattan Bridge.) The lone American driver is Toyota (Lillias White), a philosophical African American accompanied by her young grandson, who does his homework while riding around the city. Toyota accompanies Rogan to a bar to watch the aforementioned baseball game, trying to encourage him to abandon his negativity and believe in people.

The potential sappiness of this portion of *Game 6* is diminished by the game itself. Within one strike of victory, the Red Sox find a dramatic way to lose, culminating with Mookie Wilson's grounder between Bill Buckner's legs. (The Red Sox lost the seventh and deciding game the following night.)

Several of those critics harshly reviewing *Game 6* claimed that the film has lost considerable impetus through the Red Sox's finally ending their World Series drought, formerly known as the Curse of the Bambino, in winning the 2004 championship. *Game 6* was made before then, appearing less than three months later at the 2005 Sundance Film Festival. Perhaps the delay in its theatrical release until March 2006 was intended to establish some distance from Boston's recent heroics.

Finally, however, the baseball history does not matter that much. DeLillo uses baseball as a metaphor in *Underworld* and football as the same in *End Zone* (1972). What matters is that Rogan feels unworthy of love and success and uses the Red Sox in part for self-flagellation. Like the baseball team, he feels he is capable of success only up to a point. The implication is that America makes the struggle for success too difficult, especially for artists. Sports teams have only other teams to contend with. Artists have personal demons, as well as critics, who have no one to answer to for their convoluted motives, unrealistic standards, and deep-rooted neuroses. Or at least, that is how the Rogans of the world interpret matters. *Game 6* implies that Rogan is foolish for caring what Schwimmer thinks. He should trust his own judgment in determining whether his work is good.

Game 6 is the kind of film that actors enjoy making because they have lots of dialogue and get to express complicated emotions. Director Michael Hoffman, whose credits include *One Fine Day* (1996), gives his actors free reign, but the film's talkiness and visual sluggishness may be tiresome for some viewers. The film is especially ugly. Production designer Bill Groom creates a dirty, graffiti-splattered New York that seems to belong more to the 1970s than the 1980s and David M. Dunlap's cinematography complements this look through graininess and dim lighting.

The actors, however, are appealing. Keaton, who has not had a good film role since he played ATF agent Ray Nicolette in both *Jackie Brown* (1997) and *Out of Sight* (1998), ably conveys the contradictions raging within Rogan, his self-loathing at war with his need to believe in his abilities. Rogan is a picaresque hero like Sebastian Dangerfield in J. P. Donleavy's *The Ginger Man* (1955). He has to keep moving to survive. In his mostly silent role, Downey, who worked with Hoffman in *Soapdish* (1990) and *Restoration* (1995), makes the critic a cracked mirror image of the playwright. Neither man can truly be happy in his work.

Game 6 builds to a showdown between the playwright and the critic that resembles the confrontation between Humbert Humbert and Clare Quilty near the end of Vladimir Nabokov's *Lolita* (1955). *Game 6* is a meandering, slowly paced film that seems to be losing its way several times only to redeem itself with a sweet, upbeat conclusion.

Michael Adams

CREDITS

Nicky Rogan: Michael Keaton
Steven Schwimmer: Robert Downey Jr.

Elliot Litvak: Griffin Dunne
Lilian Rogan: Catherine O'Hara
Joanna Bourne: Bebe Neuwirth
Paisley Porter: Shalom Harlow
Jack Haskins: Roger Rees
Laurel Rogan: Ari Graynor
Renee Simons: Nadia Dajani
Peter Redmond: Harris Yulin
Michael Rogan: Tom Aldredge
Toyota Moseby: Lillias White
Matthew: Amir Ali Said
Origin: USA
Language: English
Released: 2005
Production: Amy Robinson, Griffin Dunne, Leslie Urdang, Christine Weiss Lurie; Shadowcatcher Entertainment, Serenade Films, Double Play, VOX3 Films
Directed by: Michael Hoffman
Written by: Don DeLillo
Cinematography by: David M. Dunlap
Music by: Yo La Tengo
Sound: Joshua Anderson
Editing: Camilla Toniolo
Art Direction: Kate Aronsson Brown
Costumes: Renee Ehrlich Kalfus, Elizabeth Shelton
Production Design: Bill Groom
MPAA rating: R
Running time: 87 minutes

REVIEWS

Chicago Sun-Times Online. March 24, 2006.
New York Times Online. March 10, 2006.
Premiere Magazine Online. March 7, 2006.
Variety Online. January 26, 2005.

TRIVIA

Michael Keaton, Robert Downey Jr., and Bebe Neuwirth all worked on this film for a hugely reduced salary of $100 per day.

GARFIELD: A TAIL OF TWO KITTIES

The Ego Has Landed.
—Movie tagline

Box Office: $28.4 million

As with the first mostly live-action *Garfield* (2004), based on Jim Davis' comic strip, one should not expect *Garfield: A Tail of Two Kitties* to be any more sophisticated than the comic itself. The first film was meagerly adequate as a translation of the comic, but also a fairly forgettable movie with appeal primarily for children and, perhaps, fans of the strip. The second movie is more of the same, though it attempts a "bigger" plot that is less inspired by the comic strip. Where the first movie loosely borrowed some of its plot from the strip, adding in a requisite villain, apparently the producers of *Garfield: A Tail of Two Kitties* decided the sequel needed a storyline with a larger scope than most of the simple plots characteristic of the comic. So, instead of borrowing ideas from the comic, the filmmakers borrowed (very broadly) from Mark Twain's 1882 *The Prince and the Pauper* (as opposed to Charles Dickens' classic, as the title implies), sending chubby cat Garfield (voice of Bill Murray) to London where he could meet up with a royal doppelganger to trade places with. The result is a movie that is marginally better than the first, adequate but not inspired. *Garfield: A Tail of Two Kitties* has its amusing moments and is entertaining on an elementary level, but it probably would not be on anyone's list for best family film of the year.

The set-up for Garfield's journey to London is rather simple. Garfield's owner Jon (Breckin Meyer) is ready to propose to his veterinarian girlfriend Liz (Jennifer Love Hewitt), but Liz unknowingly throws a wrench in his plan when she announces that she is going to London to speak at a fundraiser. Jon then decides to make the most of the situation and follow her to England to surprise her, where he can then propose. On his way to the airport, Jon drops off Garfield and dog Odie at the kennel, but of course the two animals escape and hide in Jon's clothes bag. Jon meets up with Liz in London, and he actually seems pleasantly surprised to learn that Garfield and Odie have accompanied him. Liz warns, however, that they need to be careful because the animals could be deported if they were discovered.

Meanwhile, not far from London at Carlyle Castle, Lady Eleanor has just passed away and left the estate to her beloved, pampered cat Prince, who just happens to be Garfield's double. This does not go over well with the Lady's nearest relative, Lord Dargis (Billy Connolly), who quickly decides to make the cat disappear. After putting Prince in a basket and throwing him in the river, Dargis embarks on a plan to rid the estate of its many barnyard animals and develop the land with exclusive condominiums.

Confined to Jon's hotel room, Garfield promptly finds himself bored, so he and Odie set out to find Jon. The two animals' tour of London is cut short, however, when the estate's butler Smithee (Ian Abercrombie), who has been searching for Prince, sees Garfield and mistakes him for the missing feline. Smithee grabs Garfield and takes him back to the castle. Shortly thereafter, Prince shows up on the same street, climbing out of the sewer, and meets Odie. In yet another chance-defying coincidence, Jon presently appears and thinks Prince is Garfield. Vowing to keep close watch on the two animals lest they get lost in the city, Jon takes Prince back to the hotel.

Back at the castle, Garfield is welcomed by bulldog Winston (voice of Bob Hoskins) and a host of barnyard animals, all of whom realize very quickly that the cat is not Prince. Winston wants Garfield to take Prince's place, though, to save them all and stop Dargis' plans. This leads to a series of humorous fish-out-of-water scenes in which Garfield enjoys being pampered and catered to by Smithee and the other animals, who find him a bit crude for their tastes yet are grateful for his presence. At one point, when Garfield complains about British cuisine and proclaims that he just wants a big plate of lasagna, the animals find a lasagna recipe and make it from scratch (making a huge mess in the process). In London, Prince is first amazed by the unsophisticated life led by Jon and Liz...until he has his first taste of lasagna, which he declares is the best thing he has ever tasted. Soon he is spending his time much like Garfield did, lazily eating, napping, and watching television. However, when Odie shows him a flyer with a local map, Prince sees Carlyle Castle and remembers that he needs to get back to the estate to help his friends. He says goodbye and heads out to make his way back home.

At the castle, hijinks and slapstick humor abound as Dargis attempts various methods of killing Garfield, which backfire and result in pain to himself. When Prince returns and meets Garfield, the two cats plot to foil Dargis once and for all. The plot culminates in a confrontation that pits everyone—Garfield, Prince, Odie, and finally Jon—against the baffled and disheveled Dargis.

There are some genuinely funny moments in *Garfield: A Tail of Two Kitties,* though many of the jokes and hijinks have been seen before, and overall the film adequately brings the comic cat to life. In general, the film seems to be aimed more at children, yet many of the jokes are clearly for an older audience, often including allusions to pop culture or literature that may escape notice by young crowds—Garfield, for example, alludes to *Silence of the Lambs* (1991), the television series *The Jeffersons,* and *Oliver Twist.* The special effects, particularly the blending of the CGI (computer-generated imagery) Garfield with live action, are mostly effective and interesting to watch, though it remains a bit odd that Garfield is obviously CGI while all the other animals are real. Practically speaking, it may have been too expensive to make all the animals CGI, but doing so would have made the film seem more consistent. Also, it is interesting that all of the animals speak (to each other) except Odie. Evidently, he really is not a very bright dog. Still, *Garfield* does not aspire to be a family classic—it is content to be an entertaining, funny children's movie, and as such, those inconsistencies are probably not that significant.

David Flanagin

CREDITS

Liz: Jennifer Love Hewitt
Jon Arbuckle: Breckin Meyer
Lord Dargis: Billy Connolly
Abby: Lucy Davis
Smithee: Ian Abercrombie
Mr. Hobbs: Roger Rees
Abby: Lucy Davis
Garfield: Bill Murray (Voice)
Prince: Tim Curry (Voice)
Winston: Bob Hoskins (Voice)
Eenie: Jane Leeves (Voice)
Meenie: Jane Horrocks (Voice)
Christophe: Sharon Osbourne (Voice)
Preston: Richard E. Grant (Voice)
Rommel: Vinnie Jones (Voice)
McBunny: Rhys Ifans (Voice)
Narrator: Roscoe Lee Browne (Voice)
Origin: USA
Language: English
Released: 2006
Production: John Davis; Davis Entertainment Company; released by 20th Century Fox
Directed by: Tim Hill
Written by: Joel Cohen, Alec Sokolow
Cinematography by: Peter Lyons Collister
Music by: Christophe Beck
Sound: David MacMillan
Editing: Peter S. Elliott
Art Direction: Louis M. Mann
Costumes: Francine Jamison-Tanchuck
Production Design: Tony Burrough
MPAA rating: PG
Running time: 80 minutes

REVIEWS

Boxoffice Online. June 16, 2006.
Chicago Sun-Times Online. June 16, 2006.
Entertainment Weekly Online. June 14, 2006.
Los Angeles Times Online. June 16, 2006.
New York Times Online. June 16, 2006.
Variety Online. June 15, 2006.

QUOTES

Garfield to Odie: "Time to grab some chow before I eat your liver, with some fava beans and a nice Chianti."

AWARDS

Nomination:

Golden Raspberries 2006: Worst Sequel/Prequel

GLORY ROAD

Winning changes everything.
—Movie tagline

The incredible story of the team that changed the game forever.
—Movie tagline

Box Office: $42.6 million

Feel-good, inspirational sports movies face the challenge of not seeming too much like other great films in the genre. Most stories about underdog teams (or players), struggling against the odds to finally become victorious, are logically going to share similarities, so the trick in making such a film unique is finding a way to make it stand out, whether through characterization, technique, underlying theme, or some other element that can be fully developed to heighten the importance of the story. *Glory Road* manages to accomplish what is necessary to tell a truly moving, meaningful sports-centered story, even though its basic plot may seem to echo that of similar movies. It achieves its success by using the sport as context for well-developed character exploration that also delves into significant social issues.

Glory Road tells the true story of how coach Don Haskins (Josh Lucas) helped make NCAA history by fielding a team of mostly African American players who then went on to become the first all African American team to win the national championship in 1966. Haskins heads to Texas Western College in El Paso, Texas, after being a high school girls' basketball coach in Fort Worth. Texas Western is a very small school with almost no budget, so in order to find the best possible players willing to come to the college, Haskins defies convention and courts controversy by recruiting seven African American players for the team, promising them that they will be starters and not spend most of the season on the bench. Initially there are some minor tensions between the white team members and the new black players, but soon they begin warming up to each other. More importantly, when the "Mighty Miners" begin training for the season and face Haskins' strict discipline, not all of the players are happy, but as the coach tells player Bobby Joe Hill (Derek Luke), "If you quit right now, you quit every day for the rest of your life."

After the team fails to win the first game, Bobby Joe urges Coach Haskins to let the players loose to play "their way." Haskins relents to some degree and says, "Play your way and my way." The strategy works, because the team starts winning, much to the surprise of everyone. The Miners become the talk of the division, inspiring both support and hatred. One player, Nevil Shed (Al Shearer), is beaten up in a public restroom, and later, after winning a very close game, the boys find blood splattered all over their motel room and racist epithets written on the walls in blood. The racism and hatred they encounter discourages them, and at their next game, the African American players seem to lose their touch, failing to play as a team and, as the announcer describes it, seem to give up. They lose the game, breaking their winning streak, a failure that astounds and infuriates the coach. The boys explain that he and the white players cannot understand what it is like, facing the prejudice and the constant threats. The more they win, the worse it gets, they explain. "They're trying to take our dignity away from us," says player Willie Cager (Damaine Radcliff). "It's inside you," the coach counters. "No one can take away what you don't give them…Hold your heads up!" Haskins urges. "Shut them up! Win!"

The Miners make it to the Midwest Regional Finals, where they narrowly defeat Kansas after going into two overtimes. This victory leads them next to the NCAA National Championship game against Kentucky, coached by the legendary Adolph Rupp (Jon Voight), who has led the Kentucky Wildcats to previous national championships. The night before the game, Coach Haskins makes a decision to play only the African American team members to make a statement and end once and for all the claims that his black players cannot handle the pressure and are not an intelligent enough team to be championship winners. In one of the movie's many emotionally moving scenes, Haskins explains his decision and insists that he does not want to hurt anyone, and player Jerry Armstrong (Austin Nichols) stands up to affirm the decision, expressing support and understanding. At this point, it has all become much more than a game; it has become an important struggle against ignorance and hatred. When the Miners go on to beat Kentucky, it is an event that is deemed the "greatest upset in NCAA history"—and, in retrospect, it has been called one of the most important moments in the history of college basketball.

By the end of *Glory Road,* it is not simply the Miners' victory in the national championship game that makes the climax powerfully inspirational. Coach Haskins and the players love the sport of basketball, something they repeat often throughout the story, but this struggle became more than just a matter of an underdog rising to meet seemingly unbeatable odds in a game of skill. Bolstered by strong performances from the cast, these characters, their relationships, and their struggles are developed well over the course of the film, drawing the audience in to identify with them and care about their difficult journey—both the journey as great players of the sport and the journey in standing up against social oppression.

The filmmakers did take some liberties with the historical facts in *Glory Road* (for example, Haskins did not take the Miners to the national championship the first year he was at TWC, and many of the games during their winning season were not as close as depicted in the movie). However, these differences do not detract from the authenticity of the story or hurt it in any way—the filmmakers obviously took liberties simply to tighten up the story and to add more drama by making some of the games closer than they really were. The most important elements of the story are true, and that makes the film even more inspiring. Indeed, stories about the kind of human victory seen in *Glory Road* cannot be told too often.

David Flanagin

CREDITS

Don Haskins: Josh Lucas
Bobby Joe Hill: Derek Luke
Jerry Armstrong: Austin Nichols
Adolph Rupp: Jon Voight
Moe Iba: Evan Jones
Orsten Artis: Alphonso McAuley
Willie Worsley: Sam Jones III
Mary Haskins: Emily Deschanel
Nevil Shed: Alan Shearer
David Lattin: Schin A.S. Kerr
Harry Flournoy: Mehcad Brooks
Willie "Scoops" Cager: Damaine Radcliff
Origin: USA
Language: English
Released: 2006
Production: Jerry Bruckheimer; Walt Disney Pictures; released by Buena Vista
Directed by: James Gartner
Written by: Chris Cleveland, Bettina Gilois
Cinematography by: John Toon, Jeffrey L. Kimball
Music by: Trevor Rabin
Sound: Kathleen Cusack
Music Supervisor: Bob Badami
Editing: John Wright
Art Direction: Kevin Constant
Costumes: Alix Friedberg
Production Design: Geoffrey Kirkland
MPAA rating: PG
Running time: 106 minutes

REVIEWS

Boxoffice Online. January 13, 2006.
Chicago Sun-Times Online. January 13, 2006.
Entertainment Weekly Online. January 11, 2006.
Los Angeles Times Online. January 13, 2006.
New York Times Online. January 13, 2006.
Premiere Magazine Online. January 12, 2006.
Variety Online. January 6, 2006.
Washington Post Online. January 13, 2006.

QUOTES

Coach Don Haskins: "You'll play basketball my way. My way is hard."

TRIVIA

The real-life Don Haskins was cast as an extra in the film as the gas station attendant.

GOAL! THE DREAM BEGINS

Every Dream Has A Beginning.
—Movie tagline

Box Office: $4.2 million

Touchtone Pictures, the studio behind *Goal! The Dream Begins,* had a lot of faith in their project. *Goal!* is the first in a planned series of three movies dealing with soccer, or football as it is called outside of the United States. The second installment, *Goal! 2: Living the Dream,* which deals with hero, Santiago Munez (Kuno Becker, a well-known Mexican actor) joining the Real Madrid team, has already been shot and will be released in 2007. *Goal! 3* will be in theaters in 2008.

The strategy had several things going for it. Before it was released in the United States, *Goal!* was already a hit in England. And, when the film was released in the United States, soccer was becoming a national obsession as Americans became fascinated by the World Cup. The movie also deals lightly with issues of illegal immigration, which was also a hot news topic at the time of the film's release. Add to that that the film is well-made, inspirational and not nearly as cloying as sports films can be, and *Goal!* seemed well on its way to becoming a success. Despite this, *Goal!* was only playing in six theaters after nine weeks in release.

The movie deals with the rise of Santiago, an illegal Mexican immigrant who lives with his little brother (Jorge Cervera), saintly grandmother (Miriam Colon) and brusque father (Tony Plana) in a tiny house in Los Angeles. When Santiago is not busy working at a Chinese restaurant and his father's lawn care company, he plays soccer with a local underfunded team. During a weekend game, Glen (Stephen Dillane), a former player for Newcastle United, notices Santiago's skill and invites him to England to try out for his old team. Santiago's father is not only against the idea, he seems offended that Santiago would even consider it. For Santiago to dream of a different life is an insult to his father's entire system of values. "Keep your feet on the ground and not your head in the sky," is one of his father's typically gruff comments.

Much of the rest of the movie involves Santiago being presented with obstacles and overcoming them. Santiago's father steals Santiago's airfare money. Santiago gets his chance to try out for the team but finds himself flailing around gracelessly on the field when confronted by the unfamiliar wet British weather conditions. Santiago gets another big chance on the field but is sidelined by an asthma attack. What makes Santiago an appealing character is that he not only succeeds, but he manages to be a good guy in the process. When the United's star player and playboy, Gavin Harris (Alessandro Nivola), tries to get the handsome Santiago involved in his partying lifestyle, Santiago decides he would be better off with his steady girl, team nurse, Roz (Anna Friel). Since television and tabloids are filled with reports of handsome young men getting into trouble with fame, it is nice to see one, albeit a fictional one, who decides that he will stay on the straight-and-narrow.

Overall, the performances are topnotch. Becker is appealing as the eager would-be star who needs more than just one lucky break to propel him to his dream. Dillane is also good as the weary former player who is willing to put himself out to help someone else follow the dream of playing professional soccer. And Colon has an understated power as the grandmother who is willing to sacrifice her own savings and go against her son's wishes to help her talented grandson follow his dream. And those who follow the sport will be pleased to spot players David Beckham, Zinedine Zidane, and Alan Shearer in cameos.

Most critics agreed that the film was a pretty much by-the-numbers sports film, but they varied on whether the film was nevertheless enjoyable. Roger Ebert of the *Chicago Sun-Times* wrote that "*Goal! The Dream Begins* is a rags-to-riches sports saga containing all the usual elements, arranged in all the usual ways, and yet it's surprisingly effective." Ty Burr of the *Boston Globe* wrote: "Handsomely shot and with a likable lead in Kuno Becker, it also suffers from a script so outrageously generic you could buy it at Costco." G. Allen Johnson of the *San Francisco Chronicle* wrote: "It is the best American-made sports film since *Miracle*. It's a pitch-perfect achievement by director Danny Gannon, a skilled professional not known for his artistry." Finally, Michael Phillips of the *Chicago Tribune* wrote: "*Goal! The Dream Begins* is an inspirational sports movie, but I liked it anyway."

Jill Hamilton

CREDITS

Santiago Munez: Kuno Becker
Gavin Harris: Alessandro Nivola
Erik Doenheim: Marcel Iures
Glen Foy: Stephen Dillane
Roz Harmison: Anna Friel
Hughie McGowan: Kieran O'Brien
Barry Rankin: Sean Pertwee
Mal Braithwaite: Gary Lewis
Christina: Cassandra Bell
Hernan Munez: Tony Plana
Mercedes: Miriam Colon
Cesar: Jorge Cervera
Himself: Kieron Dyer
Himself: David Beckham
Himself: Zinedine Zidane
Himself: Alan Shearer
Bluto: Lee Ross
Carl Francis: Ashley Walters
Carol Harmison: Frances Barber
Jamie Drew: Kevin Knapman
Origin: USA
Language: English
Released: 2006
Production: Mark Huffam, Mike Jefferies, Matt Barrelle; Walt Disney Pictures, Milkshake Films; released by Buena Vista
Directed by: Danny Cannon
Written by: Dick Clement, Ian La Frenais, Adrian Butchart
Cinematography by: Michael Barrett
Music by: Graeme Revell, Graeme Revell
Editing: Chris Dickens
Art Direction: Thomas T. Taylor
Costumes: Stuart Rose
Production Design: Laurence Dorman
MPAA rating: PG
Running time: 118 minutes

REVIEWS

Boxoffice Online. May 12, 2006.
Chicago Sun-Times Online. May 12, 2006.

Entertainment Weekly Online. May 10, 2006.
Los Angeles Times Online. May 12, 2006.
New York Times Online. May 12, 2006.
Variety Online. September 9, 2005.
Washington Post. May 12, 2006, p. C1.

QUOTES

Santiago (referring to his father): "Maybe the old man is right. You dare to dream, you lose."

TRIVIA

The role of Santiago was originally going to be played by Gael Garcia Bernal.

THE GOOD GERMAN

If war is hell, then what comes after?
—Movie tagline

Every heart has its secrets, some more dangerous than others.
—Movie tagline

Box Office: $1.2 million

Steven Soderbergh is definitely a difficult director to categorize. His credits include sensitive low-budget films such as *sex, lies, and videotape* (1989) and *King of the Hill* (1993), big-budget commercial projects like *Ocean's Eleven* (2001), somewhat pretentious Academy Award® favorites like *Erin Brockovich* (2000) and *Traffic* (2000), and low-budget, offbeat oddities such as *Schizopolis* (1996), *Full Frontal* (2002), and *Bubble* (2006). What Soderbergh does best, however, is crime. After stumbling a bit with his first film noir, *Underneath* (1995), he recovered with two vastly entertaining efforts, *Out of Sight* (1998) and *The Limey* (1999). *The Good German* is a tribute to, and deconstruction of, the films noir that appeared right after World War II.

Adapted by Paul Attanasio from Joseph Kanon's 2001 novel, *The Good German* focuses on war correspondent Jake Geismer (George Clooney), who arrives in Berlin in July 1945 to cover the Potsdam Conference for the *New Republic.* At Potsdam, just outside Berlin, Harry S. Truman, Winston Churchill, and Joseph Stalin met to decide how to govern Germany, which had surrendered on May 8. Jake never actually witnesses any of the conference, becoming embroiled in a complicated plot involving Germany's polluted moral climate.

Jake, also an army captain, is assigned an army driver, Patrick Tully (Tobey Maguire), who talks about his mom's apple pie and his back-home girlfriend's 4-H projects. Tully's boyish charm, however, is a cover for his real, more malevolent personality. Tully runs a successful black-market operation, stealing whatever he can from the army and selling to whoever can meet his price. He is also involved with a German prostitute, Lena Brandt (Cate Blanchett), whom he hopes to transport to the United States. Some of the characters' motivations are a bit murky, and it is not clear why Tully wants to help Lena. Vicious and cynical, Tully does not care for her or anyone else.

Complicating matters is the question of the fate of Lena's husband, Emil (Christian Oliver), whom she claims is dead, and why the army is looking for him. Then there is Jake, who employed Lena before the war when he ran the Associate Press's Berlin office. They were lovers then, and he still loves her.

Though he sees himself as a tough newspaperman, Jake represents a naive, somewhat idealistic America. He thinks Lena can forget about her husband, about what she has experienced in the war, and renew their affair. He doesn't understand that she has changed, that the world is a different place, that mom's apple pie is just a myth. Like Europe itself, Lena is a survivor and will do whatever she can to save herself. Jake is forced to face up to reality when someone thrusts into his hands the army newspaper *Stars and Stripes* with its headline announcing that the United States has dropped the atomic bomb on Japan.

What is most striking about *The Good German* is its visual style. Not only has Soderbergh shot it in black and white, as most films of the 1940s were, but he has striven to make it look like a film from this period. Soderbergh told the *New York Times* that he would have been happy to be Michael Curtiz, the longtime Warner Brothers contract director best known for *Casablanca* (1942) and *Mildred Pierce* (1945), because Curtiz, like Soderbergh, made lots of films in numerous genres.

With *The Good German*, the director tries to emulate Curtiz's mastery of the studio style. Under the pseudonym Peter Andrews, Soderbergh serves as his own cinematographer, and he decided to use the types of lenses available to Curtiz. These provide a wider range, allowing more characters to appear realistically within a frame. Soderbergh's delight in this technique can be seen with a shot of Jake alone at the end of a bar. Jake appears in the lower left corner of the frame, with the bar extending endlessly across the rest of the screen in apparent tribute to a similar shot in Billy Wilder's *The Lost Weekend* (1945). As Mary Ann Bernard, Soderbergh also edits his films, employing here the wipes and dissolves typical of the 1940s.

Production designer Philip Messina recreated postwar Berlin on a Burbank sound stage by modeling his sets in part on those in Wilder's Berlin-set *A Foreign*

Affair (1948). Costume designer Louise Frogley assembled some of the wardrobe from the costume warehouses at Warner Brothers.

The most direct influence on *The Good German* is Carol Reed and Graham Greene's *The Third Man* (1949), set in the rubble of postwar Vienna. In both films, an American protagonist loses much of his native innocence while stumbling across a convoluted mystery involving an old friend, a mysterious woman, the black market, and the military. Soderbergh uses his locales, often crumbling buildings, in much the same way as Reed, and there is shadowy, atmospheric lighting like Robert Krasker's. But his visual style eschews Reed's tilted angles for the most part in favor of Curtiz's more conservative style, with the occasional smoothly flowing tracking shot for which Curtiz was famous.

Clooney is good as the man who understands the complexities of matters much less than he thinks he does. Jake is conflicted by wanting to find the truth while realizing he may not like what he finds. Blanchett's Lena is a decidedly unsentimental whore. Beautifully photographed, Blanchett, resembling here Alida Valli in *The Third Man*, conveys Lena's weariness economically. Some reviewers protested that Maguire was miscast, but it is this casting against type that makes Tully so creepy. Soderbergh's lighting makes Maguire's twisted smirk look like the mask of an evil clown.

Also delivering outstanding supporting performances are Beau Bridges as a no-nonsense army officer, Jack Thompson as a sleazy Congressman, Tony Curran as Jake's sympathetic bartender, Ravil Isaynov as a Russian general, Robin Weigert as another prostitute, Leland Orser as a duplicitous officer, and Don Pugsley as a silent assassin. Soderbergh had his actors watch *Mildred Pierce* and *The Third Man* to understand what he was trying to achieve.

Many reviewers were annoyed at the disparity between the classical visual style of *The Good German*, inviting expectations of bittersweet romance and uplifting emotions in the manner of *Casablanca*, and its harsh reality. Soderbergh and Attanasio, who wrote the brilliant screenplay for *Donnie Brasco* (1997), include sex, brutal violence, and considerable profanity. The point, of course, is that there was a wide gap between the world according to Warner Brothers and the way things really were in 1945. This dichotomy is exactly what makes *The Good German* stylish and compelling, if emotionally distant.

The film's cynicism is in keeping with its noir roots. While the films noir of the early 1940s, such as *The Maltese Falcon* (1941), have cynical elements, they weren't truly dark until Wilder's *Double Indemnity* (1944). After the war, noir became even darker and more psychological acute, as with Jacques Tourneur's *Out of the Past* (1947) and Robert Siodmak's *Criss Cross* (1949), the source of Soderbergh's *Underneath*.

For some, the final scene, which visually copies that of *Casablanca*, is somewhat jarring. In addition to being an homage to Curtiz, the scene reinforces the filmmakers' point that the world has changed. Jake is not a romantic figure like Humphrey Bogart's Rick Blaine, but a lost soul. Lena is not a noble sacrificer like Ingrid Bergman's Ilsa Lund, but a war criminal. Jake can never be the same as he was before returning to Berlin, just as America and Europe would never recover the innocent optimism destroyed by the war.

Michael Adams

CREDITS

Jake Geismer: George Clooney
Lena Brandt: Cate Blanchett
Patrick Tully: Tobey Maguire
Colonel Muller: Beau Bridges
Danny: Tony Curran
Bernie Teitel: Leland Orser
Congressman Breimer: Jack Thompson
Hannelore: Robin Weigert
Emil Brandt: Christian Oliver
General Sikorsky: Ravil Isayanov
Gunther Behn: Don Pugsley
Origin: USA
Language: English
Released: 2006
Production: Ben Cosgrove, Gregory Jacobs; Section Eight, Virtual Studios; released by Warner Bros.
Directed by: Steven Soderbergh
Written by: Paul Attanasio
Cinematography by: Steven Soderbergh (as Peter Andrews)
Music by: Thomas Newman
Sound: Paul Ledford
Editing: Steven Soderbergh (as Mary Ann Bernard)
Art Direction: Doug J. Meerdink
Costumes: Louise Frogley
Production Design: Philip Messina
MPAA rating: R
Running time: 107 minutes

REVIEWS

Chicago Sun-Times Online. December 22, 2006.
Entertainment Weekly. December 22, 2006, p. 62.
Hollywood Reporter Online. December 11, 2006.
Los Angeles Times Online. December 15, 2006.
New York Times Online. December 15, 2006.

Premiere Magazine. January/February 2007, p. 44.
Rolling Stone Online. November 21, 2006.
San Francisco Chronicle. December 22, 2006, p. E1.
Variety Online. November 30, 2006.
Washington Post. December 22, 2006, p. C1.

AWARDS

Nomination:

Oscars 2006: Orig. Score

THE GOOD SHEPHERD

The true story of the birth of the CIA through the eyes of a man who never existed.
—Movie tagline

Edward Wilson believed in America, and he would sacrifice everything he loved to protect it.
—Movie tagline

Box Office: $59.9 million

With the approach of World War II, the United States government created the Office of Strategic Services (OSS) to conduct foreign intelligence operations. When the OSS was disbanded at the end of the war, it became clear that a fulltime espionage unit was needed because of the unstable international political situation and the possible threat posed by the Soviet Union. Thus, the Central Intelligence Agency was formed in 1947. *The Good Shepherd* traces the history of the OSS and the CIA from 1939 to 1961 through the experiences of one man, questioning many of the underlying assumptions of foreign intelligence as it goes. The ironic title refers to Jesus' statement that "The good shepherd lays down his life for the sheep" and indicates the protagonist's self-delusion.

The Good Shepherd opens in 1961 with the failure of the Bay of Pigs invasion, a CIA operation designed to remove the Fidel Castro regime from power. CIA agent Edward Wilson (Matt Damon) then receives a blurry photograph of a couple in bed accompanied by an audio tape of fragments of the pair's conversation, apparent evidence related to the identity of someone who compromised the Bay of Pigs operation. The film returns frequently to this evidence until Wilson uncovers the shocking truth. *The Good Shepherd* then flashes back to 1939 and the recruitment of young Edward as an agent while an undergraduate at Yale University. The film cuts back and forth between chronological events and those of 1961.

The Good Shepherd is a critique of the upper-middle-class mid-twentieth-century American male as a conformist, what came to be known, after the title of William H. Whyte's influential 1956 study of bureaucracies, as the organization man. Eric Roth's brilliant screenplay reveals little about Edward other than his privileged background and the suicide of his father (Timothy Hutton) when he was six. Edward is not a naive idealist compromised by his work but a blank slate ready for the imprint of others. It is this quality that attracts his recruiter, FBI agent Sam Murach (Alec Baldwin).

A significant part of Edward's development, or lack thereof, is his being elected to Skull and Bones, the notorious Yale secret society, founded in 1832, whose members have included Presidents William Howard Taft, George H. W. Bush, and George W. Bush, as well as McGeorge Bundy, national security advisor under John F. Kennedy and Lyndon B. Johnson, Senator John Kerry, conservative pundit William F. Buckley, Jr. More importantly, members of Bones were heavily involved in the OSS and the CIA. Edward tries to walk away from the society during a humiliating initiation, but when he allows himself to be talked into going back, his fate is sealed, his soul lost forever.

Edward first proves his value as a spy by betraying his mentor, Dr. Fredericks (Michael Gambon), a literature professor, as a Nazi sympathizer. This betrayal is made easier by his repugnance for Fredericks's homosexuality: read nonconformity. Edward also betrays his girlfriend, Laura (Tammy Blanchard), a deaf student, with a tryst with Clover Russell (Angelina Jolie), the flamboyant sister of a classmate (Gabriel Macht) and daughter of a United States senator (Keir Dullea). When Clover's pregnancy requires Edward to marry her, Laura must be left behind. Edward then also leaves Clover and their unborn son for six years while serving with the OSS in London. After the war, Clover is willing to begin again but finds Edward's taciturn behavior unbearable.

Edward is the epitome of the man married to his work, and this aspect of *The Good Shepherd* provides considerable universality. Through Edward's failures as husband, father, and even lover, Roth and director Robert De Niro try to expose an entire generation (or two or three) that gave over their emotional and even intellectual lives in the pursuit of profit, power, and the approval of others like themselves.

The Good Shepherd subtly suggests that the American government overreacted to the Soviet menace as a means of solidifying power in the hands of a few and that the Soviets, depicted here as even more duplicitous than their counterparts in the West, did the same. The CIA is presented as a paranoid organization wanting less to diminish the threat of foreign powers than to perpetuate this threat to justify its existence. Always lurking in the background is the sense of entitlement of the Bones-dominated CIA. A particularly chilling moment comes when General Bill Sullivan (De Niro), a character based on Wild Bill Donovan, founder of both the OSS and the CIA, tells Edward that he will exclude Jews and Negroes from the postwar agency and include as few Catholics as possible, even though he is Catholic himself. Women, of course, never enter the equation.

In addition to the reactionary, thematically confused *Forrest Gump* (1994), Roth wrote *The Insider* (1999) and *Munich* (2005), addressing big, morally complex issues similar to those in *The Good Shepherd.* Roth's CIA screenplay has been around for over a decade, earning legendary status as one of the best films never made, with directors such as Francis Ford Coppola, Wayne Wang, Philip Kaufman, and John Frankenheimer attached to the project. Matters always fell apart for various reasons, including Frankenheimer's death. De Niro, the star of Frankenheimer's *Ronin* (1998), took over.

Having De Niro direct a film of such epic scale is a bit of a surprise, because his one previous film as a director, *A Bronx Tale* (1993), tells a much more modest story. As an actor, De Niro has an affinity for confident, manipulative, yet somewhat repressed characters, especially the corrupt priest of *True Confessions* (1981), the master thief in *Heat* (1995), and the political advisor in *Wag the Dog* (1997). His identification with his conflicted protagonist may contribute to the excellence of *The Good Shepherd* as a character study.

The most surprising aspect of *The Good Shepherd* is how assured De Niro's direction is. The camera always seems to be in the right place, and scenes seem to last just the right length. Editor Tariq Anwar helps give the film a magisterial pace. Cinematographer Robert Richardson's work here is similar to his moody, claustrophobic lighting for Oliver Stone's *Nixon* (1995). A standout scene is the moral turning point for Edward, shot in bleached-out, gray tones in a winding London street to underscore the theme of moral ambiguity.

Like many actors-turned-directors, De Niro relies too much on close-ups, but he does get uniformly excellent performances from his large cast. Leonardo DiCaprio was originally set to play Edward, but reportedly backed out in favor of *Blood Diamond* (2006). Damon does not have DiCaprio's range or charisma, but he may be a better choice for the repressed, essentially timid Edward. The character has some of the singleminded focus of Damon's characters in *The Departed* (2006) and, especially, *Syriana* (2005). Though Edward strives to shut out any doubts about his actions, Damon occasionally displays the character's qualms by dipping his head or eyes.

Clover could have been a cliched neglected wife, but Jolie imbues her with considerable strength. Jolie's startling resemblance to Loretta Young is fitting for a well-dressed, independent-minded woman from this period. Blanchard gives a nuanced performance as the only person who loves Edward and is willing to forgive him. Martina Gedeck gives a subtle, moving performance as another woman ill used by Edward.

Billy Crudup is suitably creepy as Edward's British mirror image, a character inspired by double agent Kim Philby. The best of the many excellent performances is that of Gambon, who conveys an amazing range of emotions in a scene in which Fredericks seems to accuse Edward and forgive him at the same time.

De Niro has said in interviews that he consulted with his mentor, Martin Scorsese, in preparing and editing *The Good Shepherd.* Possible Scorsese influences can be seen, particularly when a suspected Russian double agent (Mark Ivanir) is tortured by Edward's gruesomely intense assistant (the outstanding John Turturro). The film's operatic tone also recalls Scorsese, as it does Coppola. The similarity between Edward's and Michael Corleone's descent from innocence to evil in Coppola's *The Godfather* (1972) and *The Godfather: Part II* (1974) has been noted by several reviewers. Yet the flawed hero of *The Good Shepherd* is actually more like Gene Hackman's morally blind surveillance expert in Coppola's *The Conversation* (1974). Edward is even closer to the protagonist of Bernardo Bertolucci's *The Conformist* (1970). Both characters will do anything to fit in. Both also have their destinies set in motion in part by misunderstanding pivotal early experiences.

While David Denby of the *New Yorker* called it "one of the most impressive movies ever made about espionage," *The Good Shepherd* received mixed reviews, with many critics complaining of its length and deliberate pace. Others said it is both too muddled and too literal. For it to work as well as it does, however, and for viewers to appreciate its complexities, *The Good Shepherd* must accrue Edward's sins slowly, the better to savor them.

Michael Adams

CREDITS

Edward Wilson: Matt Damon
Margaret "Clover" Russell Wilson: Angelina Jolie
Sam Murach: Alec Baldwin
Laura: Tammy Blanchard
Arch Cummings: Billy Crudup
Dr. Fredericks: Michael Gambon
Philip Allen: William Hurt
Thomas Wilson: Timothy Hutton

Senator John Russell Sr.: Keir Dullea
Ray Brocco: John Turturro
Joseph Palmi: Joe Pesci
John Russell Jr.: Gabriel Macht
Hanna Schiller: Martina Gedeck
Edward Wilson Jr.: Eddie Redmayne
Richard Hayes: Lee Pace
Yuri Modin: John Sessions
Bill Sullivan: Robert De Niro
Valentin Mironov #2: Mark Ivanir
Origin: USA
Language: English
Released: 2006
Production: James G. Robinson, Jane Rosenthal, Robert De Niro; Morgan Creek Productions, Tribeca Productions, American Zoetrope; released by Universal
Directed by: Robert De Niro
Written by: Eric Roth
Cinematography by: Robert Richardson
Music by: Marcelo Zarvos, Bruce Fowler
Sound: Tom Nelson
Music Supervisor: Kathy Nelson
Editing: Tariq Anwar
Art Direction: Robert Guerra
Costumes: Ann Roth
Production Design: Jeannine Oppewall
MPAA rating: R
Running time: 160 minutes

REVIEWS

Chicago Sun-Times Online. December 22, 2006.
Entertainment Weekly. December 22, 2006, p. 56.
Hollywood Reporter Online. December 11, 2006.
Los Angeles Times Online. December 22, 2006.
New York Times Online. December 22, 2006.
San Francisco Chronicle. December 22, 2006, p. E1.
Variety Online. December 8, 2006.
Washington Post. December 22, 2006, p. C1.

QUOTES

Edward Wilson: "It isn't about dedication and loyalty, it's about belief in what we do."

AWARDS

Nomination:
Oscars 2006: Art Dir./Set Dec

A GOOD WOMAN

Seduction. Sex. Scandal. She's the talk of the town.
—Movie tagline

Every saint has a past. Every sinner has a future.
—Movie tagline

Although Oscar Wilde wrote only nine plays, one novel, and a few short stories, there have been over a hundred film and television adaptations of his works. The reasons are obvious: vivid characters, witty, timeless dialogue, and gentle tweaking of society's pretensions. While *An Ideal Husband* (1895) and *The Importance of Being Earnest* (1895) have been successfully transferred to the big screen, Wilde's other plays have not been so fortunate. The previous major adaptation of his 1893 play *Lady Windermere's Fan* is Otto Preminger's *The Fan* (1949), a rather flat interpretation despite a screenplay co-written by Dorothy Parker and a reasonably good cast: Jeanne Crain, Madeleine Carroll, and George Sanders. *A Good Woman*, the latest attempt, is also deeply flawed.

Director Mike Barker and screenwriter Howard Himelstein move Wilde's social satire from Victorian England to the Italian Riviera of the early 1930s. Mrs. Erlynne (Helen Hunt) is notorious for having affairs with married men and is almost broke. When she sees a photograph in a society magazine of a young American couple living in Italy, she leaves London for the Amalfi coast with a gleam in her eye. She soon intrudes into the lives of Robert Windermere (Mark Umbers), a wealthy investment banker, and his wife, Meg (Scarlett Johansson).

Soon, everyone in Amalfi except Meg is gossiping about Robert and the much older Mrs. Erlynne. Meanwhile, young Lord Darlington (Stephen Campbell Moore) has fallen for Meg, and a middle-aged English aristocrat known as Tuppy (Tom Wilkinson) gazes longingly at Mrs. Erlynne. When Meg finds evidence that Robert has been giving checks regularly to Mrs. Erlynne, she is crushed by his betrayal. As Wilde would do much more elegantly in his masterpiece, *The Importance of Being Earnest* there is much confusion about who is doing what to or with whom until a mildly surprising revelation leads to a sorting of the characters' relationships.

Reviewers of *A Good Woman* were puzzled by the change in locale and period, but adaptations of novels and plays, especially those of Shakespeare, alter the original setting all the time. Without the change, the film could not end with a lovely shot of one couple flying off in a plane. Hunt and Johansson are also more credible in 1930s fashions than they would be as Victorian ladies, though the costumes by John Bloomfield, who also worked on the very similar *Being Julia* (2004), cannot overcome the miscasting of the two stars.

As with Jennifer Aniston in *Derailed* (2005), Hunt is just not a femme fatale. Not only does she look at least a decade older, except for one shot, than her actual age, Hunt does not exude the sexy danger central to Mrs. Erlynne. When a character late in the film describes Mrs. Erlynne as old, this observation seems crueler to Hunt than to the character. While Johansson is believable as an adult in Woody Allen's *Match Point* (2005), here she seems like a teenager pretending to be an adult. She seems to have no understanding of the character. Umbers' stiff, blank performance doesn't help, but Moore is excellent as Lord Darlington shifts between suavity and desperation. Even better is Wilkinson at conveying Tuppy's sensitivity and decency. His is a lovely, subtle performance. Hunt is much livelier in her scenes with Wilkinson, just as Johansson is more assured in her exchanges with Moore.

As he showed in *Best Laid Plans* (1999) and the 1996 television version of Anne Bronte's *The Tenant of Wildfell Hall,* Barker knows how to frame shots and pace a film. There is an excellent series of shots, well edited by Neil Farrell, cutting back and forth to a woman dressing while concealing her identity, that helps elucidate the film's themes. The cinematography by Ben Seresin, who also shot *Best Laid Plans,* is seductive, especially a night shot of Mrs. Erlynne and Tuppy framed against an enormous blue-gray sky.

A Good Woman improves in its second half and is not quite as awful as some reviewers indicated, but there is no obvious reason for its existence. Like many recent British period films such as *Up at the Villa* (2000), *Being Julia,* and *Ladies in Lavender* (2004), it just lies there quietly, charming now and then, and then going back to sleep.

Michael Adams

CREDITS

Mrs. Erlynne: Helen Hunt
Meg Windermere: Scarlett Johansson
Robert Windermere: Mark Umbers
Lord Darlington: Stephen Campbell Moore
Tuppy: Tom Wilkinson
Origin: USA, Great Britain, Italy, Spain
Language: English, Italian
Released: 2004
Production: Jonathan English, Alan Greenspan, Howard Himelstein; Meltemi Entertainment, Thema Productions, Beyond Films, Magic Hour Media; released by Lionsgate Films
Directed by: Mike Barker
Written by: Howard Himelstein
Cinematography by: Ben Seresin
Music by: Richard G. Mitchell
Sound: Maurizio Argentieri
Editing: Neil Farrell
Art Direction: Pier Luigi Basile
Costumes: John Bloomfield
Production Design: Ben Scott
MPAA rating: PG
Running time: 99 minutes

REVIEWS

Entertainment Weekly Online. February 1, 2006.
Los Angeles Times Online. February 3, 2006.
New York Times Online. February 3, 2006.
Variety Online. September 19, 2004.
Washington Post. February 3, 2006, p. C1.

QUOTES

Lord Darlington: "I can resist everything except temptation."

TRIVIA

The role of Lord Darlington was originally offered to Joseph Fiennes who instead turned it down for the role of Bassanio in Michael Radford's adaptation of *The Merchant of Venice* (2004).

A GOOD YEAR

Everything matures...eventually.
—Movie tagline

Box Office: $7.4 million

There are exquisite world-class wines, indelibly memorable for the way they surprise and delight the palate, and there are paltry potables one would rather spit out than swallow. *A Good Year*, largely set amongst the vineyards of Provence, is comparable to something in between: going down easily, boasting beautiful colors, and yet inescapably wanting.

Six years after their Oscar®-winning *Gladiator* (2000), Russell Crowe and director Ridley Scott were looking to reteam. Scott came up the idea of bringing Peter Mayle's 2004 novel to the screen, a book which was actually Scott's idea in the first place. "I was looking for an excuse to come back to France to shoot a film," remembers the director, who has had a getaway home and vineyard there for fifteen years. Over a bottle of wine, he pitched an idea to friend and neighbor Mayle, who had escaped to the South of France to become a highly successful extoller of Provence's charms and virtues. "I said, 'You write the book, then I'll get the film rights,'" the director recalls.

So that is how Scott and Crowe got to spend a pleasurable shoot in what has been called "the most enticing place this side of Paradise," on a sort of working vacation. In the wake of legal ramifications resulting from his infamous New York phone-hurling incident, Crowe was in particular need of a lighthearted, charming role to offset his well-publicized loutishness. However, what grew from the men's enjoyable toil is merely a middling film. The film, made on a budget of approximately $35 million, withered on the vine, failing to gross even a fifth of that. Reviews were mixed, but no one was overwhelmed.

As *A Good Year* begins "a few vintages ago," young Max Skinner (Freddie Highmore) is spending yet another frolicsome summer at La Siroque, the lovely Provencal estate of his Uncle Henry (Albert Finney). Henry, a buoyant bon vivant with a lust for life, among other things, is, trying to pour all sorts of wisdom into his nephew. As Max is played by the winning Highmore, one is initially taken with the boy, excusing clear signs of cockiness as darling self-confidence. Jump ahead to Max as an adult (Crowe), however, and it is revealed that his self-satisfaction has grown, and the adjective of assured may now be shortened to merely the first three letters.

Max is an obnoxious, avaricious London bonds trader. Max's devoted assistant, Gemma (Archie Panjabi), repeatedly endeavors to cut him down to size with sweetly delivered slams like, "They should bury you face down Max, because that's the way you're headed." Breaking a gentleman's agreement and apparently coming within a hair's-breadth of breaking laws, Max's cunning brings in an astonishing $77 million in one day. "Winning is not everything," he declares, basking in the approbation of his colleagues. "It is the only thing." These people may marvel at Max, but, like the rivals who bitterly damn him, they seem fairly certain that there is hollowness where a heart should be within that puffed-up chest.

Max does, indeed, seem rather heartless upon learning that his supposedly-beloved uncle has died and the old man's cherished house and vineyards are now his. He can barely tear himself away from gloating over his financial coup to go off to France, and then only does so to see how much money he might rake in by selling his new acquisition. It is certainly a far cry from expressions of wistful nostalgia. The two men had been estranged for some time, as Henry had, understandably, not liked what Max had become.

While Max's single-minded pursuit of the dollar has been chronicled almost exclusively with interior shots dimly lit in cool shades of blue, subsequent scenes in the fresh open air of the French countryside are bathed in a bright, golden light. Even in these divine surroundings, however, Max is as yet a jerk, giving the finger to a group of local bicyclists he passes on the road, and then spitefully invoking the name of non-native Tour de France winner Lance Armstrong for good measure. Later, his obliviousness to others is further underscored when he is nearly runs down lovely restaurateur Fanny Chenal (Marion Cotillard). Shortly after his arrival at La Siroque, Max alienates Francis Duflot (Didier Bourdon), the longtime caretaker of the property's vineyards, who loves them as deeply and passionately as did Henry. Duflot is incensed that Max would even think of selling what Henry had hoped his next of kin would treasure.

As Max surveys the grounds, he accidentally falls into a swimming pool devoid of water but not of muck, and tries to extricate himself in a seemingly endless scene almost completely devoid of successful humor. When a scornful, vengeful Fanny appears on the scene to turn on gushing water that sends him flying, this fall becomes a sort of comeuppance for Max. His suspension, pending investigation of his recent triumph, is another.

At liberty to make improvements around La Siroque to impress potential buyers, the time is now ripe for this experience to improve Max. Each day he spends amidst extraordinary surroundings at once stirring and soothing, and each time something triggers yet another warm memory of long-ago closeness and fun with Henry, one knows that fundamental reevaluation and transformation are dead ahead. Anyone who has not wholly anticipated this healing (or perhaps restoring) of Max's soul should first shrink with embarrassment and then get out to see more films. The same goes for those who are at all surprised when the initial friction between Max and Fanny melts away her icy reserve until love is in the air. The conventions of this genre really leave the two with no choice whatsoever but to fall into bed together before the credits roll, although her unresponsiveness does vanish with startling abruptness.

There are subplots that arise, like the complicating arrival of an enticing young Californian (Abbie Cornish) who may or may not be Henry's illegitimate daughter and rightful heir. However, everything leads up to Max's eventual choice between his old, hard-charging life in bustling London and this new, more relaxed, and ultimately more satisfying one with Fanny in Provence. It is sweet when they end up together, remembering that they had met at La Siroque as children and guessing that fate has engineered their reunification, but this love story is rather sketchy and flat. The film's comedy is also never particularly potent. Crowe succeeds at being cheerful but only fleetingly charming, in a role many could see being played by Hugh Grant. He tries awfully hard to be captivating, as this mediocre film does as a whole. Still, if viewers are in an undemanding mood for something pleasantly innocuous, all those vibrant shots of Provence go a fair distance toward making one forget about everything else that fails to intoxicate in *A Good Year.*

David L. Boxerbaum

CREDITS

Max Skinner: Russell Crowe
Uncle Henry: Albert Finney
Fanny Chenal: Marion Cotillard
Christie Roberts: Abbie Cornish
Charlie Willis: Tom Hollander
Young Max: Freddie Highmore
Sir Nigel: Kenneth Cranham
Gemma: Archie Panjabi
Francis Duflot: Didier Bourdon
Ludivine Duflot: Isabelle Candelier
Origin: USA
Language: English
Released: 2006
Production: Ridley Scott; Ingenious Film Partners, Scott Free, Fox 2000 Pictures; released by 20th Century Fox
Directed by: Ridley Scott
Written by: Marc Klein
Cinematography by: Philippe Le Sourd
Music by: Marc Streitenfeld
Sound: Jean-Paul Mugel
Editing: Dody Dorn
Art Direction: Freddy Evard, Robert Cowper
Costumes: Catherine Leterrier
Production Design: Sonja Klaus
MPAA rating: PG-13
Running time: 118 minutes

REVIEWS

Boxoffice Online. November 10, 2006.
Chicago Sun-Times Online. November 10, 2006.
Entertainment Weekly. November 17, 2006, p. 95.
Los Angeles Times Online. November 10, 2006.
New York Times Online. November 10, 2006.
San Francisco Chronicle. November 10, 2006, p. E1.
Variety Online. September 10, 2006.
Washington Post. November 10, 2006, p. C5.

QUOTES

Max: "This place just doesn't suit my life." Fanny replies: "It is your life that doesn't suit this place."

TRIVIA

Peter Mayle's novel *A Good Year* is dedicated to Ridley Scott, who suggested the idea to the author.

GRANDMA'S BOY

Sex. Drugs. Nakedness. Rude language... And proud of it!
—Movie tagline

Box Office: $6 million

Grandma's Boy stars Allen Covert and is directed by Nicholaus Goossen, but the salient information for moviegoers is that the film was produced by Adam Sandler. The Happy Madison logo (the symbol of Sandler's production company) at the beginning of the film connotes several things, but mostly it portends that the following eighty or so minutes of the film will be spent detailing the unlikely adventures of an affable man-child.

In *Grandma's Boy,* said man-child is Alex (frequent Sandler costar Covert). Alex is a thirty-five-year-old video game tester who is lauded by his young and nerdy coworkers for his amazing video game prowess. Alex enjoys basking in their admiration. After all, as an aging video game tester, he is probably not getting much admiration elsewhere. When Alex is kicked out of his friend's parents' house for some unplanned lewdness, he has nowhere to live. His grandmother, Lilly (Doris Roberts), invites him to stay with her and her two elderly friends. Grace (Shirley Jones) is a randy woman who boasts of her sexual conquests of old-time stars like Charlie Chaplin. (In one of the film's many discomforting moments, she boasts something along the lines of "He wasn't silent after being with me!") Bea (Shirley Knight) is suffering from some sort of dementia and her dotty behavior is considered by writers Covert, Barry Wernick, and Nick Swardson to be ample comedy fodder. Alex, wanting to remain the Alpha male among his coworkers, brags that he is living with three women and implies that he is having hot relations with all of them. He does not mention their age or that one of them is his grandmother.

There is not much in the way of big plot developments. The company gets a lovely new supervisor, Samantha (Linda Cardellini), who seems like she might be interested in Alex. And there is some trouble with J.P. (Joel David Moore), a genius video game developer who talks in a robotic voice and imagines himself to be some sort of superior alien being. There is also, none too surprisingly, a big house party, in which the older women eat pot brownies and act goofy.

Grandma's Boy is not void of merit. It offers an inside look into the world of video game companies, or what we might imagine them to be like. The nerd culture seems accurately observed and, from an anthropological standpoint, it is quite interesting. Covert, who looks vaguely like Mel Gibson, is a more palatable boy-hero than Sandler. He seems, for lack of better word, cooler than Sandler. Sandler is more of a clown while Covert is more of an everyman. A thirty-five year old who lives with his grandma and seeks only to have parties and play video games would be many people's definition of a loser, but Covert has enough charm to make his extended adolescence seem like a well-thought out lifestyle choice. And with so many jokes being tossed out, there are bound to be a few that hit the mark.

Other aspects of the film are not so on the mark. The tasteless jokes that the writers put into the mouths of these veteran female actors are embarrassing for all concerned. The frank sexuality of Jones' character is so over-the-top that it is hard not to feel shame on the actress's behalf. And then there are the, by now, overly predictable cameos by Kevin Nealon and Rob Schneider. If they were funny, they could be excused, but both actors seem to be afflicted by a complete lack of comedic inspiration. Maybe their stuff was funny when they were hanging out with the writers, but it does not show up on the screen.

Critics, who are rarely fans of Sandler in comedy mode, did not like the film. Jami Bernard of the *New York Daily News* wrote: "There is no drug potent enough to make *Grandma's Boy* worth eighty-seven minutes of your life." Gregory Kirschling of *Entertainment Weekly* gave the film a D grade and wrote: "*Grandma's Boy*, a low-gas frat comedy...does a very thorough job of reducing every recognizable member of the cast to probably career lows." Peter Hartlaub of the *San Francisco Chronicle* called the film "amusing at times but mostly bad." Lisa Rose of the *Newark Star-Ledger* wrote: "While Sandler has diversified his acting portfolio, as a producer, he remains a sultan of stupidity, funding movies that are likely a party to make, but are a death march to watch." Finally, Roger Moore of the *Los Angeles Times* wrote that "the best thing going for this stoner comedy is that its target audience won't remember it."

Jill Hamilton

CREDITS

Alex: Allen Covert
Grandma Lilly: Doris Roberts
Grace: Shirley Jones
Bea: Shirley Knight
Samantha: Linda Cardellini
J.P.: Joel David Moore
Mr. Cheezle: Kevin Nealon
Yuri: Rob Schneider
Dante: Peter Dante
Jeff: Nick Swardson
Shiloh: David Spade
Origin: USA
Language: English
Released: 2006
Production: Allen Covert; Wilshire 1, Happy Madison Productions, Level 1 Entertainment; released by 20th Centruy Fox
Directed by: Nicholaus Goossen
Written by: Barry Wernick, Allen Covert, Nick Swardson
Cinematography by: Mark Irwin
Music by: Waddy Wachtel
Sound: Kami Asgar
Editing: Tom Costain
Art Direction: Alan Au, Jeffrey Mossa
Costumes: Maya Lieberman
Production Design: Perry Andelin Blake
MPAA rating: R
Running time: 96 minutes

REVIEWS

Entertainment Weekly Online. January 11, 2006.
Variety Online. January 6, 2006.

QUOTES

Alex: "My Grandma drank all my pot."

THE GROOMSMEN

There's a difference between getting older and growing up.
—Movie tagline

Anyone choosing Edward Burns' latest film *The Groomsmen* based solely on the DVD cover will be sorely disappointed. "TIL DEATH DO WE PARTY" leers the cover blurb, with the PARTY written in an especially lurid red. Brittany Murphy is pictured wearing a bridal gown and a sultry smile, as she gets a piggyback ride from Burns. In the background, costars John Leguizamo, Matthew Lillard, Jay Mohr, and Donal Logue look like they are, indeed, partying 'til death.

But besides accurately showing who stars in the film, the cover does little to portray what the movie is actually like. A more accurate cover blurb might be, "More of the same from Edward Burns!" Beginning with his breakout film, *The Brothers McMullen* (1995), Burns has been making pretty much the same film over and over. The films tell stories about men, generally men who live in nice-looking, working class towns on the east coast, near New York. There is usually an impending commitment with a woman, which throws one of the men into a period of doubt. And there are male bonding scenes, perhaps over drinking or a manly sport like fishing, where the men talk a lot more than men generally do in Hollywood films. The saving grace for Burns' career is that the film he keeps making is enjoyable enough.

The Groomsmen is an especially good version. Perhaps it works in the film's favor that, after more than ten years of similar fare, no one expects Burns to have any new tricks up his sleeve. Also, on this outing, Burns has a particularly good cast. His costars are like a who's who of underappreciated actors of a certain age. The weakest link in the ensemble is Burns himself. He casts himself as Paulie, a thoroughly decent guy who is thirty-three years old and facing the prospect of marriage. Paulie may well love his fiancee, Sue (Murphy), but the primary reason he is marrying her is because she is pregnant. Paulie's dilemma is interesting, but neither Burns' writing nor his acting make the situation spark. Paulie is such a nice guy that is seems like whether he and his wife are a good match or not, it will be okay. Paulie will either be quietly happy or quietly unhappy. It is not exactly the kind of dire stakes that make for a compelling film.

More interesting is Paulie's group of friends. His brother, Jimbo (Logue) is in some sort of emotional tailspin. He is cold to his wife, getting in fights with his friends and spending his days drinking at a strip club. Paulie's cousin, Mike (Mohr), still lives at home with his dad. Mike thinks he still lives at home so that he can take care of his father, but in reality, he is not ready to leave. Mohr plays Mike with a sweetness that is appealing. T.C. (Leguizamo) was a popular member of the group who abruptly left for New York City eight years earlier. Here, again, Burns drops an opportunity for drama. T.C. left because he was gay, but when he returns and announces this, his friends react with a shrug. Their reaction is good for social progressiveness, but not for dramatic tension. The most well-adjusted of the group is Dez (Lillard). He has a job, a strong marriage and some kids. Lillard is a wonderful actor (even his portrayal of Shaggy in the wretched *Scooby-Doo* movies was oddly good) and it is nice to see him cast as something other that the wild and crazy types he usually plays.

For creating a strong sense of place and creating realistic characters, Burns should earn an A for *The Groomsmen.* But as far as creating an interesting story, and for his own acting, Burns only ranks about a C. And for those expecting a movie about a bunch of guys partying 'til death—and instead getting a movie about a bunch of guys having sincere talks—the movie would probably rank about an F.

Most critics made mention of the similarity between Burns' films. Ty Burr of the *Boston Globe* called *The Groomsmen* "one of the better variations." "That's not to say it's a great movie" continued Burr, "Just honest and unpretentious (as well as pat, talky, and predictable) about the difficulties of being a middle-aged boy in the outer boroughs of New York." Gene Seymour of *Newsday* wrote that "*The Groomsmen's* set-up is so ready-to-wear for Burns' roughneck-weepie aesthetic that you almost think he's used it before." Mick LaSalle of the *San Francisco Chronicle* wrote: "Really, in every way, this is like any other Edward Burns film, except for one thing. It's unmistakably better. This is the movie I believe Burns has been trying to make since *The Brothers McMullen*, eleven years ago."

Jill Hamilton

CREDITS

Paulie: Edward Burns
Jimbo: Donal Logue
Mike Sullivan: Jay Mohr
T.C.: John Leguizamo
Dez Howard: Matthew Lillard
Tina Howard: Shari Albert
Jack: Spencer Fox
Matt: John A. Russo
Julianna: Heather Burns
Jen: Jessica Capshaw
Sue: Brittany Murphy
Mr. B: Arthur J. Nascarelli
Paulie's Mom: Marion McCorry
Top Cat: Joe Pistone
Pops Sullivan: John F. O'Donohue
T.C's Dad: Jamie Tirelli
Barfight Patron: Kevin Kash
Dez's Mom: Catharine Bolz
Krystal: Amy Leonard
Origin: USA
Language: English
Released: 2006
Production: Edward Burns, Margot Bridger, Philippe Martinez, Aaron Lubin; Marboro Road Gang; released by Bauer Martinez Distribution
Directed by: Edward Burns
Written by: Edward Burns
Cinematography by: William Rexer
Music by: Robert Gray, P.T. Walkley
Sound: Ben Cheah
Editing: Jamie Kirkpatrick
Costumes: Catherine Thomas
Production Design: Dina Goldman
MPAA rating: R
Running time: 99 minutes

REVIEWS

Boxoffice Online. July 14, 2006.
Entertainment Weekly. July 28, 2006, p. 45.

Hollywood Reporter Online. July 13, 2006.
New York Times Online. July 14, 2006.
Variety Online. May 3, 2006.
Village Voice Online. July 11, 2006.

THE GRUDGE 2

Two Years Ago, A Door Was Opened.
—Movie tagline
What Was Once Trapped, Will Now Be Unleashed.
—Movie tagline

Box Office: $39.1 million

The Grudge 2 is the sixth installment in director Takashi Shimizu's series of haunted house horror films in what is seemingly becoming his life's work. It seems that the cursed characters in his film series are not the only ones who can't let go of a grudge. The sequel to his own American remake to the Japanese *Ju-on* films, *The Grudge* (2004), comes two years too early for an audience that didn't need another rehash of the same plot. It almost seems that once a viewer enters the movie theater for a screening of one the *Grudge* films, a curse is cast upon the viewer who will be terrorized every two years with the same plot over and over again. This time, though, the filmmakers decided to tell three different stories, while still relying heavily on the previous entry's staple of disjointed timelines.

For those who don't know the backstory, there is a house in Tokyo where a horrible murder took place and anyone that enters the house will be cursed, terrorized, driven crazy, and eventually killed by the ghostly victims of the crime. In the 2004 *Grudge*, cursed Karen Davis (Sarah Michelle Gellar) had burned down the Japanese house holding the evil spirits of the murdered Kayako (Takako Fuji) and her son Toshio (Yuya Ozeki) at the hands of the jealous husband and father Takeo Saeki (Takashi Matsuyama), in an attempt to end the curse once and for all. It didn't work.

Because of the fire, the curse that had been contained in the house has now been released. It has gone global, reaching all the way to Chicago where the movie opens with a creepy scene involving a stepmother named Trish (Jennifer Beals) killing her verbally abusive husband with a sizzling frying pan to the head. In another storyline that slightly lifts from his second film from the Japanese series, *Ju-on 2* (2003), a shy exchange student Allison (Arielle Kebbel) is brought to the Saeki house by two of her classmates Vanessa (Teresa Palmer) and Miyuki (Misako Uno) who force her to go inside with them.

Karen, who is in a Tokyo hospital, gets a visit from her sister Aubrey (Amber Tamblyn) who has been sent by her sick mother to bring her back home. The hospital staff is worried that Karen is a danger to herself and others and so she is tied down in restraints. Karen has just enough time to explain the curse to Aubrey and warn her not to go into the house before she is sedated. When an apparition confronts her behind her bed, Karen escapes her restraints and runs to the roof of the hospital, where she faces her demon, who promptly pulls her off the building to her death. Aubrey and a reporter named Eason (Edison Chen) decide to investigate, eventually learning the secrets of the past events surrounding the murders of Kayako and Toshio.

As the film progresses, the focus shifts ping-pong style between the three plotlines that merely exist to provide Shimuzu opportunities for cheap scares, to steal from his previous films, and to provide more victims to be terrorized and dispatched by Toshio and his mother.

There is, it has to be said, some genuine creepiness in the film as in one scene where a schoolgirl blindly reaches under her desk to pet a cat, only to find little Toshio hugging her legs. There are some new details, such as the backstory of Kayako and the introduction of her mother, but is all very useless and unnecessary padding to the basic story once it is clear where it is all leading.

Director Shimizu and American screenwriter Stephen Susco bring nothing new to the series in the way of scares, opting to rehash elements of previous entries. Like a carnival ride through a haunted house, the scares never change, just the names and faces of the people exposed to them. Not surprisingly, a third film is in the works, as well as another Japanese sequel. You have been warned.

David E. Chapple

CREDITS

Aubrey: Amber Tamblyn
Allison: Arielle Kebbel
Karen: Sarah Michelle Gellar
Trish: Jennifer Beals
Bill: Christopher Cousins
Eason: Edison Chen
Vanessa: Teresa Palmer
Miyuki: Misako Uno
Kayako: Takako Fuji
Itako: Kim Miyori
Toshio: Oga Tanaka
Toshio Saeki: Yuya Ozeki (unconfirmed)
Origin: USA
Language: English

Released: 2006
Production: Sam Raimi, Robert Tapert, Taka Ichise; Ghost House Pictures, Columbia Pictures; released by Sony Pictures
Directed by: Takashi Shimizu
Written by: Stephen Susco
Cinematography by: Katsumi Yanagijima
Music by: Christopher Young
Sound: Kiyoshi Kakizawa
Editing: Jeff Betancourt
Art Direction: Akio Kikuchi, Tomoko Kotakemori
Costumes: Kristen M. Burke
Production Design: Iwao Saito
MPAA rating: PG-13
Running time: 95 minutes

REVIEWS

Boston Globe Online. October 14, 2006.
Entertainment Weekly. October 27, 2006, p. 55.
Los Angeles Times Online. October 16, 2006.
New York Times Online. October 14, 2006.
San Francisco Chronicle. October 13, 2006, p. E1.
Variety Online. October 13, 2006.
Washington Post. October 14, 2006, p. C1.

QUOTES

Itako: "There can be no end to what has started."

THE GUARDIAN

When lives are on the line, sacrifice everything.
—Movie tagline
How do you decide who lives or dies?
—Movie tagline
Risk Everything.
—Movie tagline

Box Office: $55 million

The Guardian is the type of movie that has a little something for everyone. That is because its parts are seemingly cobbled together from movies gone before. It has a little romance, some adventure, a bit of comedy and some family drama. It is a credit to the considerable charms of stars Ashton Kutcher and Kevin Costner, as well as the skill of director Andrew Davis, that the film is more pleasant diversion than hideous mishmash.

Ben Randall (Costner) is a veteran Coast Guard Rescue Swimmer. He is based in Kodiak, Alaska, and goes out on dangerous missions rescuing swimmers from the frigid Bering Sea. Randall has become legendary among Coast Guard Swimmers for the amount of people he has saved, as well as his unwavering devotion to saving lives. His long-suffering wife, Helen (Sela Ward), is in the process of leaving him because of this focus on his job. "I need to rescue myself," she tells him.

During one perilous nighttime rescue, Randall risks the lives of his team when he goes against orders and tries to save just one more person. It is a fatal miscalculation and the rescue helicopter plunges into the sea and catches fire. Randall is the only survivor.

To let him/force him to process his grief, Randall is sent to teach aspiring rescue swimmers at an elite Florida training facility. The most promising student in his class is Jake Fischer (Kutcher), a former star high school swimmer. Fischer is cocky and primarily interested in breaking all of Randall's swimming and rescue records.

In predictable fashion, Randall knows that he must teach Fischer that teamwork, not personal glory, is what is important. Randall must suffer at the hands of his superiors for his unorthodox teaching methods, like having his students experience hypothermia by plopping them in ice-cold water. Fischer finds romance with a local teacher, Maggie McGlone (Bonnie Bramlett), who insists that she wants to keep things casual. There will be that one person in the Coast Guard class who will not be able to meet his goals—unless the team can pull together to help him. And, of course, after their initial rivalry, Fischer and Randall will come to respect and admire each other.

None of these plot points are new, or particularly surprising, but they come together in a pleasing fashion. Director Davis is known for his action films such as *The Fugitive* (1993) and *Under Siege* (1992), so it is no surprise that the action sequences are well done. The rescues, with their quickly sinking boats, crashing waves, and helicopters running low on fuel are harrowing and exciting. But the stuff between the action scenes—that is, the relationships—works well, too. Fischer and his girlfriend have an easy banter that seems real enough, especially for this type of film. And Costner and Ward do a good job underplaying the breakup of their marriage. Most of the emotions in their split go unsaid, which spares the audience the pain of sitting through an overwrought breakup scene, but also echoes the unexpressed emotions that must have helped bring down their marriage. The training school sequences work well, too. It is always somewhat interesting to see what sorts of trials—such as treading water for an hour—that such folks must endure.

More critics disliked the film than liked it. Richard Roeper of the *Chicago Sun-Times* hated the film and wrote: "A part of me wants you to endure *The Guardian* just so we can bond over the howler of an ending." Wesley Morris of the *Boston Globe* called the film "emotionally runny." A.O. Scott of the *New York Times* wrote that *The Guardian* "is an action movie, a basic training movie, a swaggering sea adventure, a home front melodrama and an inspiring tough-love heroic teacher fable. If the aggregate of all these movies is exhausting and occasionally overwrought, some of the parts are stirring and effective, though not exactly fresh." Stephanie Zacharek of *Salon.com* liked seeing the fifty-one-year-old Costner playing a man his own age. She wrote that "it feels like a blessing to see a fiftyish face in the movies that hasn't been pruned and planed and polished."

Jill Hamilton

CREDITS

Ben Randall: Kevin Costner
Jake Fischer: Ashton Kutcher
Emily Thomas: Melissa Sagemiller
Capt. William Handley: Clancy Brown
Maggie McGlone: Bonnie Bramlett
Helen Randall: Sela Ward
Jack Skinner: Neal McDonough
Frank Larson: John Heard
Hodge: Brian Geraghty
Ken Weatherly: Dule Hill
Cate Lindsey: Shelby Fenner
Wild Bill: Alex Daniels
Origin: USA
Language: English
Released: 2006
Production: Beau Flynn, Tripp Vinson; Firm Films, Beacon Pictures, Touchstone Pictures, Contrafilm; released by Buena Vista
Directed by: Andrew Davis
Written by: Ron L. Brinkerhoff
Cinematography by: Stephen St. John
Music by: Trevor Rabin
Sound: Richard Goodman
Editing: Dennis Virkler, Tom Nordberg
Art Direction: Andrew Max Cahn, Austin Gorg
Costumes: Mark Peterson
Production Design: Maher Ahmad
MPAA rating: PG-13
Running time: 139 minutes

REVIEWS

Boxoffice Online. September 29, 2006.
Chicago Sun-Times Online. September 29, 2006.
Entertainment Weekly Online. September 27, 2006.
Hollywood Reporter Online. September 18, 2006.
Los Angeles Times Online. September 29, 2006.
New York Times Online. September 29, 2006.
Premiere Magazine Online. September 28, 2006.
San Francisco Chronicle. September 29, 2006, p. E1.
Variety Online. September 17, 2006.
Washington Post. September 29, 2006, p. C1.

QUOTES

Ben Randall: "I ask myself every day why I was the one to survive."

TRIVIA

The rescue sequences were filmed in a 750,000 water tank constructed in Shreveport, Louisiana.

H

HAPPY FEET

WARNING: May Cause Toe-Tapping.
—Movie tagline

Box Office: $195.6 million

Happy Feet may not rank with the very best animated films (whether computer or traditionally animated) that have been produced to date—that distinction can be claimed almost exclusively by films made by Disney and Pixar—yet in numerous ways it still manages to achieve levels of sophistication and uniqueness that raise it above average paint-by-the-numbers animated fare. Visually, the film unveils a stunning, often beautiful landscape of natural wonders, characters, and movements that are eerily realistic at the same time that they are clear evidence of an elaborate, painstaking artistry possible only through the use of today's computer technology. Storywise, *Happy Feet* follows an uncommon path for its genre, starting with the introduction of a young character who faces a familiar struggle—a sort of "oddball" who does not fit in with the crowd—and taking unexpected turns as it ventures into darker social, political, and psychological themes not usually treated so directly or frankly in animated films.

Happy Feet opens with sprawling, intricately detailed vistas of Antarctica that look as if they could be in a beautifully photographed live-action film. The world of the emperor penguins—revealed later to be dubbed Emperor Land by its residents—is introduced and immediately the audience learns that these penguins cherish the ability to sing. In fact, all the emperor penguins sing, and most often they sing popular tunes modified slightly to relate to their penguin lives. As the story opens, two particular lovebirds—Memphis (voice of Hugh Jackman) and Norma Jean (voice of Nicole Kidman)—become swept up in song to express their love for each other on the eve of the females' long trek to find food. When Norma Jean leaves with all the other females, Memphis becomes the guardian of their egg. Unfortunately, he fails to be as careful as he should be, and while singing of his yearning for his absent spouse, he accidentally lets go of the egg, which tumbles away across the snow. The penguin makes a panicking, mad dash to recover the egg, which he does, but a narrator explains the seriousness of Memphis' carelessness: letting an egg get away from the father's protection, even for a moment, could have dire consequences for the little one inside.

When the eggs all start to hatch, Memphis' egg is the last one to crack open. Right away, it is obvious that something is different about the little emperor penguin that comes out. The baby penguin seems to have a life of his own, pattering so quickly that the penguin barely seems to be able to control himself. When asked what's wrong, little Mumble (adult voiced by Elijah Wood) simply says that he is "happy."

As he grows, Mumble's peculiarities become more obvious and more troublesome for his father and the other penguins around them. Most importantly, Mumble cannot sing well—he can only screech. The fact that Mumble cannot find or does not have a "heart song" distresses Memphis and promptly Mumble finds himself sadly alone while his peers hone and perfect their vocal skills. However, Mumble soon discovers that he does have a peculiar ability to express his joy with his feet—through dancing. The penguin elders, however, consider

Mumble's dancing an aberration; when Mumble has grown into a young adult and eventually encourages some of the other young penguins to try out their own dancing skills, the elders warn them all that this "aberration" has led to the food shortage they have been experiencing. The Great Penguin, claims Noah the Elder (voice of Hugo Weaving), is unhappy with their deviant ways and is punishing them by reducing their food supply. Ultimately, Mumble is instructed to leave Emperor Land, and he vows to find the real cause of the food shortage.

His journey leads him to meet five smaller, carefree penguins (all of whom have Mexican accents); the most outspoken of them, Ramon (voice of Robin Williams), calls Mumble "Big Guy" and proclaims that Mumble is cool. "You have moves...charisma," Ramon says. The penguins become a team and head off to uncover the mystery of where all the food has gone. After seeing a strange, "alien" machine under the water, they visit Lovelace (also voice of Robin Williams), an older, chief-like penguin who supposedly has all the answers. In time, Lovelace leads them to the Forbidden Shore, where they discover alien structures and an alien ship. In his desperation to uncover the truth and take it back to his homeland, Mumble follows the ship out to sea and eventually washes up on a shore far away, where he is taken by humans and placed in a zoo.

After several months in the zoo, during which time Mumble falls into depression and eventually a kind of psychotic trance induced by being trapped inside a confined area, a little human girl makes a visual connection with Mumble that inspires him to dance for her. The humans are amazed by his ability to dance, of course. Soon, Mumble finds himself back in Antarctica, returning to Emperor Land, but he has not come back alone. An expedition of humans has followed him. Upon seeing the humans, the elders accuse Mumble of betraying them, but when they realize that the humans want to see them dance, even Noah starts to dance. The film moves toward a happy ending, then, as the world sees the dancing penguins as a sign that the animals are trying to communicate with them. The humans decide to leave Antarctica alone and the penguin food supply returns.

Although some of the characters in *Happy Feet* are included for their comic value—Ramon, for instance—most are complex in their development. Mumble is a likeable character who faces a struggle that has been depicted onscreen many times—someone who is "different," facing the pain of being left out and ostracized, looking desperately for a way to be accepted and embraced for who he is—but he is not as dynamic as some of the other penguins. Beautiful voiced Gloria (voice of Brittany Murphy), for example, has always shown some level of affinity for Mumble but keeps her distance until she realizes that there is something wonderful and "joyful" about his dancing. She becomes a friend who stands up for him, so it is almost surprising that when she follows after Mumble to join him on his quest, he pretends to not care for her and sends her back because he is concerned for her safety, adding a level of psychological realism that comes unexpectedly. Mumble's father Memphis is also a fairly round character who shows some psychological depth. He is not merely a disappointed father who eventually comes around to accepting his son's differences. His own guilt over his failure before Mumble hatched combines with guilt over not embracing and defending his son, and as a result he loses the ability to sing. He does, however, learn to dance when Mumble returns home.

Happy Feet has its share of unexpectedly dark moments. Lovelace's gradual choking from a plastic six-pack can wrapper around his neck is emphasized so much that it can be painful to watch. Mumble's descent into despair and a mind-numbing, apathetic stupor while in captivity also takes the story into a stark kind of psychological complexity that is not common for animated films. Additionally, while other animated films have dealt with characters being treated differently or left out of the group because of some peculiar quality or characteristic, the extent to which Mumble is ostracized, blamed for the society's woes, and finally exiled to live on his own seems a bit more gritty and painful than what is typically shown. The environmental issues underlying the real threat to the penguin world are not unlike similar issues addressed in some other animated films, but in *Happy Feet* the consequences of human intrusion into a previously untouched ecosystem somehow seem drearier and less likely to be realistically solved, despite the turn the story takes at the end. In fact, the happy ending of the film almost seems too contrived and forced. As the plot takes its dark turns, and especially as Mumble finds himself locked up in captivity, the mood of the film suggests that it could potentially spiral downward to a darker, sadder ending. Darker elements such as this make the film more complex and layered in meaning and depth.

At the same time, the shifts in mood from joyous singing to sad realism occasionally seem awkward, tending toward the impression that the film has some difficulty deciding what its primary focus should be. The fact that live-action footage of human beings is incorporated into the latter scenes of the film contributes to this impression. The further *Happy Feet* shifts from the tone established early in the film, the less consistent it seems, yet overall the artistry of the detail with which this animated world is rendered, combined with strong character development and meaningful underlying themes, helps elevate the film above its tonal shortcomings.

David Flanagin

CREDITS

Mumble: Elijah Wood (Voice)
Ramon/Lovelace: Robin Williams (Voice)
Gloria: Brittany Murphy (Voice)
Memphis: Hugh Jackman (Voice)
Norma Jean: Nicole Kidman (Voice)
Noah: Hugo Weaving (Voice)
Boss Skua: Anthony LaPaglia (Voice)
Miss Viola: Magda Szubanski (Voice)
Baby Mumble: E.J. Daily (Voice)
Trev: Steve Irwin (Voice)
Mrs. Astrakhan: Miriam Margoyles (Voice)
Origin: USA
Language: English
Released: 2006
Production: Doug Mitchell, George Miller, Bill Miller; Village Roadshow Pictures, Kennedy Miller, Animal Logic Film; released by Warner Bros.
Directed by: George Miller
Written by: George Miller, John Collee, Judy Morris, Warren Coleman
Music by: John Powell
Sound: Wayne Pashley
Music Supervisor: Christine Woodruff
Editing: Margaret Sixel, Christian Gazal
Art Direction: Simon Whiteley
Production Design: Mark Sexton
MPAA rating: PG
Running time: 87 minutes

REVIEWS

Boxoffice Online. November 17, 2006.
Chicago Sun-Times Online. November 17, 2006.
Entertainment Weekly. November 24, 2006, p. 84.
Hollywood Reporter Online. November 3, 2006.
Los Angeles Times Online. November 17, 2006.
New York Times Online. November 17, 2006.
Variety Online. November 10, 2006.
Washington Post Online. November 16, 2006.

QUOTES

Memphis (about son Mumble's tap-dancing): "It just ain't penguin."

TRIVIA

The end credits of the movie list more than 1,000 names.

AWARDS

Oscars 2006: Animated Film
British Acad. 2006: Animated Film
Golden Globes 2007: Song ("The Song of the Heart")

Nomination:

British Acad. 2006: Orig. Score
Golden Globes 2007: Animated Film

HARD CANDY

Strangers should never talk to little girls.
—Movie tagline

Box Office: $1.0 million

Hard Candy is a daring movie. Even the most superficial description of the plot shows how risky the subject matter is: a meeting between a fourteen-year-old girl and a thirty-two-year-old photographer who have been flirting on the Internet. But that doesn't begin to delineate the unnerving territory this intense drama covers.

Sparsely shot from the opening credits to the conclusion, *Hard Candy* might induce a kind of claustrophobia in an unsuspecting viewer. Working from a brilliantly unorthodox script by Brian Nelson, first-time director David Slade does not waste time with preliminaries. He starts with a computer screen full of inappropriately flirtatious chat messages between the two strangers, who quickly agree to meet for the first time after a couple weeks' acquaintance online.

At the rendezvous, the young girl has short hair, an attitude that combines tomboyish innocence and clumsy attempts at flirtation, and an obvious intelligence and self-assurance. Hayley (Ellen Page) meets Jeff (Patrick Wilson) in a public place; immediately they circle, predator and prey, and pronounce each other more exceptional than each had expected. Indeed, Jeff is no stereotypical troller: he is handsome and witty and shows no hint of being desperate, dull, or dangerous. Hayley alternates between shy coquettishness and immature teasing.

When Jeff invites her back to his house, it's on the pretense of sharing a bootlegged concert tape. In the car on the way, Slade captures both parties in this odd pair smiling at each other but also looking the other way, their faces revealing something dangerous and unspoken. At this point the moviegoer is already screaming in discomfort: are we really expected to watch a seduction of an underage girl by an immoral man? But as Hayley and Jeff engage in an awkward verbal dance, it doesn't seem that outright lust has overcome their judgments.

Unconventionally plotted, *Hard Candy* takes a turn less than a half-hour through that upsets all expectations. It's better not to know what's coming, but it's impossible to describe the movie without revealing the early twist. After Hayley asks Jeff to take photos of her while she performs a perfunctory striptease, Jeff passes out and awakens bound to a chair with rope. The hunter has been captured by the game.

It's now clear this isn't going to be a movie about exploitation, but about comeuppance. A large measure of suspension of disbelief is required: one would think Jeff wouldn't be so easily overpowered, and in the few scenes where he attempts or makes an escape you wonder why he hadn't done so earlier. But *Hard Candy* isn't a complete stretch. It's increasingly clear that the online world is full of sexual predators and young victims, and it's a growing societal problem. This movie simply asks us to imagine what would happen if one brave and cunning teenager turned the tables.

The movie quickly descends into treacherous territory. This is not going to be a politically motivated feminist lecture, and neither is it going to be a sweet little caper. Hayley is burning with a desire for vengeance—though the plot skimps on making it clear why—but she's not consumed by her need. She exacts the kind of investigation and punishment that challenges our sense of power relationships. The film's suggestion that the powerless can, through courage and cunning, exact justice on their victimizers can be exhilarating. But this candy is indeed hard to swallow, as Nelson and Slade take our natural rooting interest for Hayley and test it severely, by making her taste for violent, sick retribution both graphic and disturbing. But this, too, is not really egregious, because that's often what happens when those who are abused gain power.

Thanks to some very adept screenwriting and an amazing performance by Page, *Hard Candy* takes on a disorienting quality as we wade through some emotional quicksand. Jeff is a monster, but Hayley is a nightmare: a precocious teenager who uses words as weapons and whose idea of morality is sophomoric. Hayley's inquisition is dripping with sarcasm, irony, and the power of the awakened oppressed—and these, as much as her cruelties are what ultimately humiliate Jeff. At times Jeff seeks to assert the upper hand by patronizing Hayley or posing as someone who knows more than she simply because of his age. That only infuriates Hayley more, and rightly so.

Hard Candy is not exactly a cat-and-mouse game, because the balance of power, once established, does not ever shift significantly. It is more like a street-rules trial, in which Hayley serves as detective, prosecutor, judge, and executioner: she gathers evidence, indicts the accused, and decides what punishment to mete out.

With a searing central idea, *Hard Candy* doesn't bother with window dressing. Almost the entire film is a two-person showdown, shot in the sparse settings of Jeff's home and with little background music—just a constant low hum of household electrical appliances, a buzzing that suggests a world where nature has been vanquished. Where the film stumbles is in clarifying the nuances of both characters' motivations, especially Hayley's. Is a missing girl that she accuses Jeff of abducting a friend of Hayley's, or is Hayley just an anonymous avenger? Why is Hayley so intent on exploiting Jeff's still-burning passion for his first love? Certainly the girl does everything she can to ensnare Jeff in the traps he has set for himself in his own life, but is she doing so as a stand-in for everyone who is an exploited child, as she claims in the film's one preachy moment? The film might have worked more powerfully if its two characters were not so symbolic of predator and prey-turned-avenger, but characters with better fleshed-out backstories. On the other hand, the murkiness of Hayley's motivations adds to the nightmarish quality of Jeff's experience as her captive. Someone as smooth and practiced as he is does not expect to be snared, and Hayley keeps exceeding all expectations.

Most Hollywood movies manipulate emotions so that audiences cheer for their protagonist. This one avoids that easy identification, drawing us in but distancing us from easy emotional connections. Slade eschews the tricks that would make audiences cheer Hayley on. One imagines her lonely and haunted, like true heroes are, and her exploits will go unknown. Her purposes, after all, are at conflict with decent society's solutions to these problems. *Hard Candy* has no sugarcoating.

Wilson, who was effective in *The Alamo* (2004), pulls off a difficult role with strength and cunning. We have to at first believe in his normalcy and then in his utter depravity, and he makes us do so. Page, a relative newcomer, is even more amazing: we know from the start she is not completely sane but she convinces us that that doesn't matter: and that her character's purpose is, at least arguably, noble even if depraved. Working fluidly with the sharp dialogue Nelson has written for her, Page gives a riveting, sad, heartening, heroic, tragic, and extremely intense performance. *Hard Candy* is not for the faint of heart, but it provides plenty of rewards for those with the stomach for probing deeply into dark corners of human relationships. Even at 103 minutes, however, this punchy film seems unnecessarily drawn out, and it loses steam when it draws out the most excruciating scene. Fiction can powerfully uncover truth and power, and *Hard Candy* succeeds in doing so. Its primary purpose is to provoke thought, not to casually entertain, but Hayley's running commentary is superb black comedy at times, though terrifying at others.

Michael Betzold

CREDITS

Hayley Stark: Ellen Page
Jeff Kohlver: Patrick Wilson

Judy Tokuda: Sandra Oh
Janelle Rogers: Jennifer Holmes
Nighthawks Clerk: Gilbert John
Origin: USA
Language: English
Released: 2006
Production: David W. Higgins, Richard Hutton, Michael Caldwell; Vulcan Productions, Launchpad Productions; released by Lionsgate Films
Directed by: David Slade
Written by: Brian Nelson
Cinematography by: Jo Willems
Music by: Molly Nyman, Harry Esscott
Sound: Dennis Grzesik
Music Supervisor: Hans Ritter
Editing: Art Jones
Art Direction: Felicity Nove
Costumes: Jennifer Johnson
Production Design: Jeremy Reed
MPAA rating: R
Running time: 103 minutes

REVIEWS

Boxoffice Online. April 14, 2006.
Entertainment Weekly. April 21, 2006, p. 57.
Hollywood Reporter Online. April 13, 2006.
Los Angeles Times Online. April 14, 2006.
New York Times Online. April 14, 2006.
USA Today Online. April 13, 2006.
Variety Online. January 26, 2005.
Village Voice Online. April 11, 2006.

QUOTES

Hayley to Jeff: "Just because a girl knows how to imitate a woman doesn't mean she's ready to do what a woman does."

THE HEART OF THE GAME

It's your life. Make every shot count.
—Movie tagline

For seven years, first time feature writer/director Ward Serrill dutifully followed Seattle's Roosevelt High School girls basketball team and their Coach William M. Resler's quest for a Washington State championship. The result is *The Heart of the Game,* a documentary whose story is on par with anything a Hollywood screenwriter could dream up, complete with a great sports rivalry, a star player battling life on and off the court, and an eccentric coach whose methods seem, at times, to defy logic. Although this is Serrill's first theatrical release, he has long created films for corporations and non-profits.

Resler is a University of Washington tax professor who applies for the job of girls basketball coach at Roosevelt High. He is a man in his fifties with three grown daughters and no coaching experience. Resler brings a "defense first and last" philosophy to the team, employing a full court press from the start of each game until the last second. His team has no offensive strategy, just the mantra, "Run, run, run. Run like hell." Along with his unusual on-court strategy, he employs a wide range of motivational and confidence-building techniques. He encourages his girls to think of themselves as a blood-thirsty pack of wolves, driving them with phrases like, "Sink your teeth into their necks" and directing them to break the opponent "like a twig." His techniques generate rapid results and soon Roosevelt is among the state's elite.

As interesting as Resler's story and coaching philosophy are, it is the introduction of Darnellia Russell, an underprivileged African American girl who comes to Roosevelt to "do better" that drives the film. Darnellia is a basketball phenomenon, but she feels a bit out of place at the predominantly white Roosevelt, claiming at one point, "I've never been around so many white people before." Her uneasiness leads her to skip practice and struggle in the classroom. It is up to Resler to convince her "how smart she is," so that she can make the most of herself in the classroom and on the court.

Fate deals a cruel blow to Darnellia when she gets pregnant by her longtime boyfriend before her senior year. She is forced to drop out of school, but with her mother and grandmother's support, she comes back to school for her senior year. The Washington Interscholastic Activities Association (WIAA) declares Darnellia ineligible, claiming that her pregnancy did not qualify as a "hardship," which would have allowed her another year of play, because "she made her own choice." A protracted legal battle ensues, with the WIAA threatening forfeiture of all Roosevelt games. In a bold sign of team unity, the players vow to play on regardless of the consequences. Lawyer Kenyon E. Luce steps in to volunteer his services and fight for Darnellia's reinstatement, claiming that the WIAA policy is discriminatory against pregnant women.

With the court case still pending an appeal by the WIAA after Luce's victory, The Roughriders face off against their formidable inner-city rival Garfield, coached by former Harlem Globetrotter Joyce Walker. Ironically enough, Garfield is the school Darnellia would have played for if she had not opted to go to Roosevelt. Resler, in a feel-good moment straight out of Hollywood, vows that every player will see action in the championship game regardless of the score, since every player put their neck on the line for Darnellia. In spite of her many obstacles, Darnellia manages to make the school's honor roll and is voted Player of the Year.

The Heart of the Game was often compared to the Academy Award®-nominated documentary *Hoop Dreams* (1995), which followed two inner city Chicago-area basketball phenoms in their quest for glory, and the similarities are hard to ignore. This film does a fine job of tackling the issues of race and class struggle along with the sexism that is built into the high school sports system. Ward Serrill does a fine job juggling the many storylines but leaves the viewer longing for more, perhaps expanding on the inherently dramatic contrasting coaching styles of the eccentric Resler and basketball legend Joyce Walker. And while Darnellia's story is the movie, Serrill never really seems to connect with the youth and it is the Kris Kringle-like Resler who comes across as the movie's star.

Although high school girls' basketball is certainly not one of America's most popular sports, even seemingly obscure sports—like the wheelchair rugby depicted in *Murderball* (2005)—take on an almost universal appeal and larger significance when we are introduced to the individuals involved in them and given proper filmic treatment by a capable director. This is certainly true of *The Heart of the Game.*

Michael White

CREDITS

Origin: USA
Language: English
Released: 2005
Production: Ward Serrill, Liz Manne; Woody Creek Prods.; released by Miramax Films
Directed by: Ward Serrill
Written by: Ward Serrill
Cinematography by: Ward Serrill
Sound: David Howe, Mike McAuliffe
Editing: Eric Firth
MPAA rating: PG-13
Running time: 97 minutes

REVIEWS

Boxoffice Online. June 9, 2006.
Chicago Sun-Times Online. June 16, 2006.
Entertainment Weekly Online. June 7, 2006.
Los Angeles Times Online. June 9, 2006.
New York Times Online. June 9, 2006.
Variety Online. October 5, 2005.
Washington Post. June 16, 2006, p. C1.

QUOTES

Bill Resler: "Devour the moose!"

THE HILLS HAVE EYES

The lucky ones die first.
—Movie tagline

Box Office: $41.8 million

"A work of art is never finished, only abandoned."
—Anonymous

Sometimes abandonment is a good thing. *The Hills Have Eyes* should have been permanently banished to the year 1977. But in the era of regurgitated horror flicks, Papa Jupiter makes a comeback, following the river of remakes flooding American cinema in recent years: *The Texas Chainsaw Massacre* (1974, 2003), *The Fog* (1980, 2005), *House of Wax* (1953, 2005), *The Omen* (1976, 2006), and *The Amityville Horror* (1979, 2005) are examples of the trend toward repeating old plotlines. Wes Craven, the author of the original, stands by this 2006 work, directed by Alexandre Aja, as producer.

The beginning of the film provides this backdrop for the story: "Between 1945 and 1962, the United States conducted 331 atmospheric nuclear tests. Today, the government still denies the genetic effects caused by the radioactive fallout."

The Carter Family is on vacation en route to San Diego traveling through the New Mexico desert in an SUV towing a trailer. Ethel Carter is played by Kathleen Quinlan, whose character in *Breakdown* (1997) disappeared following the mechanical failure of the couple's SUV in the middle of the desert.

Ethel and her husband, Bob (Ted Levine) plan to celebrate their twenty-fifth anniversary with their daughter, Lynn (Vinessa Shaw), son-in-law Doug (Aaron Stanford), their baby, Catherine, teens Brenda (Emilie de Ravin) and Bobby (Dan Carter), and two German shepherds, Beauty and Beast. Bob is an ex-cop who transitions to the compulsory post-retirement career of security guard and shows little restraint in showing his disdain for the liberal Doug. They stop at the Gas Haven to refuel and are given directions for a short cut by a yellow-toothed degenerate.

The short cut takes the family to an area inhabited by the descendants of miners who refused to evacuate their desert homes. The SUV sustains blowouts from spikes placed on the neglected road and they split up. Bob heads back to the Gas Haven and Doug goes in the opposite direction to seek help. The family is stalked and preyed upon by the aforementioned descendants, who have mutated into radioactively deformed cannibals who survive by murdering and consuming naive travelers. Craven purportedly loosely modeled this story after the legend of Alexander Sawney Beane, who led a large brood of killers that cannibalized over 1,000 unsuspecting travelers in sixteenth century Scotland.

Bob is bound to a tree and burned alive by the clan's patriarch, Papa Jupiter (Billy Drago), after discovering that the gas attendant has been baiting tourists into the nefarious clutches of the multi-generational nuclear family. Bobby chases off after Beauty, who he later finds gutted, and is befriended by a ravaged, DNA-damaged Little Red Riding Hood-like mutant called Ruby (Laura Ortiz). Meanwhile back at the trailer, Lizard (Robert Joy) rapes the helpless Lynn, who has been left alone with the baby as the rest of the family runs in the direction of Bob's execution site. Unable to save Bob, the family returns to find Lynn dying of a gunshot wound to the head and the baby missing.

Doug, now endowed with paternal courage, switches into predator mode and discovers a military testing village complete with 1950s-style architecture and mannequins bearing radiation burns. After numerous bloody fight scenes with Lizard, the sole benevolent mutant, Ruby, sacrifices herself by hurling herself against Lizard, sending them both to their deaths over a cliff. Following a gritty tooth-and-nail fight with Jupiter, who was found noshing on Ethel's heart, Brenda plunges a mining pick through his skull. Brenda and Bobby are reunited with Catherine, Doug, and Beast. A sequel is suggested as the family survivors are observed through a pair of binocular lenses. The original had its own sequel, the aptly titled *The Hills Have Eyes 2* (1985).

Many critics viewed the abundant gore as a boring overkill. Richard Roeper of the *Chicago Sun-Times* had this comment: "I appreciate a quality kill and a good jolt of the senses as well as anybody, but this is an ugly slice of splatter porn that simply wore me out."

David Metz Roberts

CREDITS

Doug: Aaron Stanford
Ethel: Kathleen Quinlan
Brenda: Emilie de Ravin
Lynn: Vinessa Shaw
Bob: Ted Levine
Ruby: Laura Ortiz
Big Brain: Desmond Askew
Bobby: Dan Byrd
Gas Station Attendant: Tom Bower
Papa Jupiter: Billy Drago
Lizard: Robert Joy
Pluto: Michael Bailey Smith
Origin: USA
Language: English
Released: 2006
Production: Wes Craven, Marianne Maddalena, Peter Locke; Fox Searchlight, Craven/Maddalena Films, Peter Locke Production, Dune Entertainment, Major Studio Partners; released by 20th Century Fox
Directed by: Alexandre Aja
Written by: Gregory Levasseur
Cinematography by: Maxime Alexandre
Music by: Tomandandy
Sound: Albert Bailey
Editing: Baxter
Art Direction: Gregory Levasseur, Tamara Marini
Costumes: Danny Glicker
Production Design: Joseph C. Nemec III
MPAA rating: R
Running time: 107 minutes

REVIEWS

Boxoffice Online. March 3, 2006.
Chicago Sun-Times Online. March 10, 2006.
Entertainment Weekly Online. March 8, 2006.
Los Angeles Times Online. March 10, 2006.
New York Times Online. March 10, 2006.
Premiere Magazine Online. March 9, 2006.
Variety Online. March 2, 2006.
Washington Post Online. March 2006.

QUOTES

Little Girl: "Mister, will you play with us?"

THE HISTORY BOYS

History. It's just one bloody thing after another.
—Movie tagline

Box Office: $2.7 million

Alan Bennett's 2004 play *The History Boys* has been a huge hit around the world. In London, it won an Olivier Award as best new play and then toured Australia and Japan before doing almost capacity business on Broadway in 2006 and winning six Tonys, including best play and best direction (Nicholas Hytner). Those unlucky enough to miss the stage production are unlikely to grasp what all the excitement was about when they see Hytner's screen adaptation. Even with the same cast and director, and with Bennett doing the screenplay, the film version has little of the dazzle of the play.

Set in Yorkshire in 1983, *The History Boys* focuses on eight students from humble origins who have shots at attending university at Cambridge or Oxford. A new teacher, Irwin (Stephen Campbell Moore), is brought in to coach the boys for their essay examinations and their interviews with the officials who decide who will attend the United Kingdom's most prestigious universities. (Bennett is an Oxford man, while Hytner went to Cambridge.)

The essence of *The History Boys* is a conflict in educational philosophy. Irwin wants the students to stand out by challenging conventional wisdom about such topics as medieval history. Whether the views they espouse are their own or whether they even firmly grasp the ideas is irrelevant. What matters is making an impression. Meanwhile, the history teacher Mrs. Lintott (Frances de la Tour) offers the conventional approach of actually expecting her students to learn something. At the other extreme from Irwin is Hector (Richard Griffiths), who teaches general studies, bombarding the boys with poems and music in hopes that something will stick. For Bennett, Mrs. Lintott represents the practical, Irwin the cynical, and Hector knowledge for knowledge's sake. It slowly becomes clear that Hector and his style are on the way out and Irwin on the ascent in Margaret Thatcher's Britain.

Then there are the boys themselves. Posner (Samuel Barnett) is a Jewish homosexual with singing talent. Dakin (Dominic Cooper) is a ladies' man upon whom Posner has a crush. Akhtar (Sacha Dhawan) is a Muslim. Crowther (Samuel Anderson) is black. Timms (James Corden) is the fat class clown. Rudge (Russell Tovey) is the seemingly dumb jock. Lockwood (Andrew Knott) is impulsive. Scripps (Jamie Parker) is the most rational and reflective. Even reviewers of the play observed that all this smacks of the cliches of World War II films, in which every soldier had to have a defining characteristic and little else. Posner and Dakin, the acknowledged leader of the pack, are the only reasonably developed of the boys, with clear strength and weaknesses, and Barnett and Cooper give standout performances.

The oddest aspect of the film adaptation is that the play itself may be more cinematic. As transitions between scenes, Hytner projected filmed bits of business involving the boys cavorting around their school. These mini-films had a style and energy missing from the film. Hytner previously directed *The Madness of King George* (1994), also from a Bennett play, with more panache.

The worst aspects of *The History Boys* are the unimaginative compositions of the shots, a sluggish pacing, and unusually ugly cinematography. Andrew Dunn shot *The Madness of King George*, *Gosford Park* (2001), and *Stage Beauty* (2004) with meticulous attention to the emotional tone of scenes. His work here resembles those washed-out British films of the 1970s in which the monochromatic colors reflect the characters' despair. Apparently, no one told Dunn that *The History Boys* is essentially a comedy.

Bennett the screenwriter fleshes out his original material by adding an art history teacher (Penelope Wilton) and a physical education instructor (Adrian Scarborough) for no apparent reason. Their scenes are deadly dull. An architectural field trip is also added, as are journeys to Oxford and Cambridge. One of the play's points is that the students are being suffocated by their lack of opportunity. Taking them outside diminishes this effect.

Another pointless change involves Dakin. In the play, he brags about his relationship with the secretary of the dim-witted headmaster (Clive Merrison), but she is glimpsed only in one of the transition films as a tall, blonde goddess (Georgia Taylor) who seems clearly out of Dakin's league, eliciting a laugh from the audience. For the film, Bennett makes her a central character, and the romance with Dakin is too mundane.

Also problematic is the subplot involving Hector's getting into trouble for fondling the students while giving them a ride home on the back of his motorcycle. The play is essentially a vaudeville, with songs, jokes, and celebrity impressions. Everything moves at such a fast pace that it's easy to overlook the moral implications of a teacher sexually harassing a student. What is meant to be just another example of Hector's eccentricity becomes more bothersome within the much more realistic context of the film.

Moore is good as the conflicted Irwin, making the character less pedantic than he is in the play. Griffiths and de la Tour deservedly won Tonys for their Broadway performances, but they seem somewhat muted here. Mrs. Lintott's one-liners seem less funny because of Hytner's clumsy pacing, and Hector has become more pathetic. Griffiths, who memorably plays a similar character in the cult classic *Withnail & I* (1987), and de la Tour play well off each other. Yet their timing, like everything else about the film, seems less effective than it does in the play.

Michael Adams

CREDITS

Hector: Richard Griffiths
Dorothy Lintott: Frances de la Tour
Timms: James Corden
Crowther: Sam Anderson
Irwin: Stephan Campbell Moore
Posner: Samuel Barnett
Dakin: Dominic Cooper
Scripps: Jamie Parker
Akthar: Sacha Dhawan
Rudge: Russell Tovey
Fiona: Georgia Taylor
Lockwood: Andrew Knott
Headmaster: Clive Merrison
Mrs. Bibby: Penelope Wilton
Wilkes: Adrian Scarborough
Origin: USA, Great Britain
Language: English
Released: 2006
Production: Kevin Loader, Damian Jones, Nicholas Hytner; DNA Films Ltd., BBC Two Films; released by Fox Searchlight Pictures
Directed by: Nicholas Hytner
Written by: Alan Bennett
Cinematography by: Andrew Dunn
Music by: George Fenton
Sound: John Midgley
Music Supervisor: Ian Neil
Editing: John D. Wilson
Costumes: Justine Luxton
Production Design: John Beard
MPAA rating: R
Running time: 109 minutes

REVIEWS

The Guardian Online. October 13, 2006.
Hollywood Reporter Online. November 2, 2006.
Los Angeles Times Online. November 21, 2006.
New York Times Online. November 21, 2006.
The Observer Online. October 15, 2006.
Premiere Magazine. December 2006, p. 43.
Rolling Stone Online. November 13, 2006.
San Francisco Chronicle. November 21, 2006, p. F1.
Variety Online. October 11, 2006.
Village Voice Online. November 14, 2006.

QUOTES

Irwin: "History nowadays is not a matter of conviction, it's a performance. It's entertainment."

AWARDS

Nomination:

British Acad. 2006: Actor (Griffiths), Support. Actress (De la Tour)

THE HOLIDAY

Box Office: $63.2 million

Throughout *The Holiday*, written and directed by Nancy Meyers, the lovelorn Iris (Kate Winslet), who is spending Christmas in Los Angeles, watches classic films under the tutelage of an elderly neighbor and retired screenwriter named Arthur (Eli Wallach). The idea is that watching the cinematic heroines of Hollywood's golden age will make her a stronger woman and better able to have a fulfilling love life. She raves about Irene Dunne, stares transfixed at Rosalind Russell in *His Girl Friday* (1940), and discusses *The Lady Eve* (1941) with Arthur. While *The Holiday* does not belabor the point, Iris eventually learns to exhibit the "gumption," as Arthur calls it, of these leading ladies and to put her romantic life in order. The irony, however, is that other lessons from these comedies seem lost on Meyers herself, whose film demonstrates very little of the snap and verve, lively dialogue, and fast pace of the screwball era. *The Holiday* is not without its pleasantries, but the romantic relationships are rather flat, and, as she did in *Something's Gotta Give* (2003), Meyers stretches scenes way too long; ultimately, it is impossible to justify a running time of two hours and sixteen minutes for what is a fairly simple, straightforward romantic comedy.

When we first meet newspaperwoman Iris, she is a clueless doormat, pining for ex-boyfriend Jasper (Rufus Sewell), who, unbeknownst to her, is set to announce his engagement to another woman at the company holiday party. Meanwhile, in Los Angeles, Amanda (Cameron Diaz), a successful producer of movie trailers, is throwing out her two-timing boyfriend, Ethan (Edward Burns). Because both women are at a low point and neither wants to be at home during the holiday season, they trade residences through an Internet arrangement. The well-to-do Amanda gets to spend time in Iris's quaint but small cottage, while Iris gets to enjoy the high life in Amanda's Southern California mansion complete with a swimming pool.

True to the formula, each woman trying to escape romantic entanglements soon finds a new man in her life. Iris's brother, Graham (Jude Law), arrives at Amanda's door, and they promptly fall into bed together. But despite Diaz and Law's attractiveness, there is not a great deal of chemistry between them, no essential pull that would make us root for them to get together, other than the fact that they are the stars and are supposed to fall in love. It is a fairly bland, by-the-book romance. The most intriguing aspect of their relationship, in fact, comes when Amanda discovers that this supposed playboy is actually a widower and devoted father to two small daughters. The little girls are an absolute delight, and bring to the relationship a charm that does not exist between Amanda and Graham.

Half a world away, Iris starts a friendship with Miles (Jack Black), a film composer, with the possibility that it may become something more after his beautiful actress girlfriend, Maggie (Shannyn Sossamon), cheats on him. Iris's story is more fascinating than Amanda's, not just because Winslet is a more inventive actress than Diaz, but because Iris is given a sweet subplot with Arthur the screenwriter, whose advice for becoming the leading lady of her own life through classic movies is an enchanting notion. It would have been better if we saw more of a connection between the films Iris watches and how she evolves. The big turning point occurs when Jasper, who is still engaged, comes running to her, and she exhibits the resolve finally to reject him for good, something that, by this time, should be a matter of common sense and not something that has to be learned from the silver screen.

The fun aspect of this story is that Iris gently brings Arthur out of his shell, persuading him to accept a lifetime achievement award from the Writers Guild of America and helping him to get in shape so that he can walk to the stage on his own. Their rapport feels like the least formulaic aspect of the story, although their relationship eventually becomes too big a part of the shapeless screenplay. Indeed, it says something about *The Holiday* as a romantic comedy that their platonic bond is more fully realized and emotionally satisfying than the supposedly romantic one slowly developing between Iris and Miles. Although Miles is amusing and nice, there is no spark between them that would make Iris fall so quickly for this guy. Indeed, the normally clownish Black is fairly subdued and seems a bit out of place in the world of romantic comedy. Despite the fact that everyone is eventually paired off for a happy ending, the Iris-Miles coupling feels perfunctory, since they still seem more like friends than lovers.

In addition to Iris empowering herself through intensive movie watching, *The Holiday* introduces other cute touches, such as Amanda periodically imagining her own life as material for movie trailers and Miles rhapsodizing about the magic of the Santa Ana winds. But such elements feel half formed, as if Meyers were trying out some interesting ideas but not following through or adequately developing any of them. A certain predictability plagues the film as well. For example, when we learn that Amanda has not cried since she was fifteen and her parents divorced—a detail that feels more like a character quirk than a real definition of who she is—we can be sure that, once she realizes her love for Graham, tears will come to her eyes. And, of course, the successful, beautiful woman who cannot find love despite all of her other accomplishments is itself a cliche.

Most disappointing is that Meyers seems unwilling to take any risks with the conventions of romantic comedy or challenge the audience with a fresh spin on the genre. Moreover, given the film's premise—transplanting an Englishwoman to Los Angeles and a Southern California gal to Surrey—the possibilities for culture clash could have been entertaining, but the film is content with easy jokes, such as Amanda struggling to drive on the left side of the road. *The Holiday* is good-natured and elicits smiles based on the appeal of its stars, especially Winslet, whose warmth and exuberance demonstrate that she can excel in just about any genre. Weighed down by its slow pace and lackluster rhythm, however, the movie itself will never enter the list of essential, life-changing masterpieces that Arthur gives to Iris.

Peter N. Chumo II

CREDITS

Amanda: Cameron Diaz
Iris: Kate Winslet
Graham: Jude Law
Miles: Jack Black
Arthur: Eli Wallach
Ethan: Edward Burns
Jasper: Rufus Sewell
Maggie: Shannyn Sossamon
Ernie: Bill Macy
Norman: Shelley Berman
Bristol: Kathryn Hahn
Ben: John Krasinski
Origin: USA
Language: English
Released: 2006
Production: Nancy Meyers, Bruce A. Block; Relativity, Waverly Films, Universal Pictures, Columbia Pictures; released by Sony Pictures
Directed by: Nancy Meyers
Written by: Nancy Meyers
Cinematography by: Dean Cundey
Music by: Hans Zimmer
Sound: Petur Hliddal
Editing: Joe Hutshing
Art Direction: Dan Webster
Costumes: Marlene Stewart
Production Design: Jon Hutman
MPAA rating: PG-13
Running time: 135 minutes

REVIEWS

Boxoffice Online. December 8, 2006.
Chicago Sun-Times Online. December 8, 2006.

Entertainment Weekly. December 15, 2006, p. 67.
Hollywood Reporter Online. December 1, 2006.
Los Angeles Times Online. December 8, 2006.
New York Times Online. December 8, 2006.
San Francisco Chronicle. December 8, 2006, p. E5.
Variety Online. November 30, 2006.
Washington Post. December 8, 2006, p. C1.

QUOTES

Amanda: "You know, Graham, I just broke up with someone and considering that you showed up and you're insanely good-looking and probably won't remember me anyway, I'm thinking we should have sex—if you want."

Graham replies: "Is that a trick question?"

HOLLYWOODLAND

Living in Hollywood can make you famous. Dying in Hollywood can make you a legend.
—Movie tagline

In a town full of fiction, everyone has a version of the truth.
—Movie tagline

Everyone has secrets. Everyone has motives.
—Movie tagline

Box Office: $14.4 million

In 1950, actor George Reeves (Ben Affleck) brought comic book hero Superman to life, and before the decade's end, Superman apparently took the life of George Reeves. Having shot to fame by encasing his beefy build within a skintight, caped costume to boldly defend truth, justice and the American way, the frustratingly typecast star eventually put a loaded Lugar to his head.

Or did he? Reeves' death was ruled a suicide, the act of a depressed actor whose career had started quite promisingly with *Gone with the Wind* (1939), then faltered, and finally rose to its greatest heights as the Man of Steel on a "kiddie show" millions embraced but he himself dismissed. The actor was after a more serious, more respectable brand of achievement and fame on the big screen, and Reeves' immense success on the small screen not only failed to catapult him upward, but tied him down, snuffing out any real chance of attaining what he yearned for.

There have always been nagging questions surrounding Reeves' demise, curiously ill-fitting evidentiary pieces to the puzzle, including the absence of fingerprints on the gun, the forty-five minutes it took for others in the house to call police, and the two additional bullet holes found around the room. Such things have led to speculation, suspicion, and an enduring Hollywood mystery involving something more sinister. Perhaps Reeves was shot during an argument with his tempestuous fiance, Leonore Lemmon (Robin Tunney) who made him feel less over-the-hill. Maybe he was murdered by Toni Mannix (Diane Lane), his long-time married lover whom he had recently dumped for Lemmon. Then again, it could have been Toni's husband, Eddie Mannix (Bob Hoskins), MGM's mob-connected second-in-command, whose displeasure was not with his wife's liaisons outside of their open marriage, but with anyone who made her unhappy. Any of these people might have been put out enough to do Reeves in at the age of forty-five. No one has ever been able to nail down exactly what transpired in the wee hours of June 16, 1959, and the absorbing, well-acted *Hollywoodland* does not even try, presenting a number of theories.

The way *Hollywoodland* unites the actor's troubled story with that of fictitious, sleazy gumshoe Louis Simo (Adrien Brody), intent on making a name for himself investigating Reeves' death, is rather detrimental—but far from fatal—for the film. Beginning just after Reeves' demise, it comes alive, and is far more captivating, during segments flashing back to pivotal and often painful points in the actor's life. Indeed the first such scene, in which a dapper Reeves and a vivacious Toni first meet at a party, springs from one of Simo at the morgue. In this initial flashback, Reeves is trying hard to get noticed and calculatingly positioning himself so as to be included in a press photographer's shot of Rita Hayworth. Toni, no longer a Ziegfeld girl but still beautiful, is one person who definitely notices him, sidling up to him and pouring on the seductive charm. They begin an affair after she explains that her powerful husband is fine with her openly extramarital couplings. In fact, a subsequent shot shows Reeves, Toni, Eddie, and his Asian mistress dining shoulder to shoulder.

Soon Reeves finds himself living in a nice house purchased by Toni. This does not seem to make him especially uncomfortable. He also soon finds himself being considered for the starring role in a "dirt-cheap" production aimed at children. This he does find humiliating. Reeves takes the job for the money, dons the now-famous Superman outfit, and, gazing into a mirror, decides that he looks "like a damn fool." Toni tries to bolster his spirits and ego by declaring him charming in the role. Reeves is sure, however, that it is all a "waste of time," and that "no one with a lick of sense would watch that show." However, a huge number of pint-sized viewers began racing home faithfully to watch Superman's endeavors—often with their approving parents—and Reeves is shocked to find himself a sensation.

One scene signals the problem ahead, in which Reeves is advised to put out his cigarette as some fresh-faced, impressionable Boy Scouts gawk: Superman does not smoke, and the children seem unable to distinguish between the character and his portrayer. More disturbing is the public appearance where a gun-toting tyke with real bullets aims to test whether they will really bounce off the superhero's mighty chest.

The casting of Affleck was interesting, as he, like Reeves, knows a thing or two about the glare of the spotlight and how it can burn. Affleck was thus able to bring a compassionate understanding to the portrayal of Reeves, a palpable, ultimately poignant depth and complexity beneath and beyond mere handsome amiability. Watch him in the scene where Reeves, connected to wires so his character can appear to fly, uses humor to try to gloss over a humiliating, unexpected plummet to the floor. After a thrilled Reeves won a part in the prestigious, star-studded *From Here to Eternity* (1953), an opportunity which could reveal Superman as a worthwhile steppingstone, watch the mortified discomfort on Affleck's face as his character sits at a screening and endures the laughter and belittling jeers of those who cannot accept the actor in any other role. In a subsequent memorable moment, in which Reeves is lost in thought, one clearly senses that a terrible realization is sinking in, that he can almost hear doors slamming shut. Finally, there is the dispirited, far-off gaze and air of resignation in his final moments. It is an affecting and effective portrait Affleck paints, an upswing in his career, deserving of the critical acclaim and award nominations coming his way.

Lane is also a standout. She is quite captivating, whether playing vibrant or vulnerable, and in the scene where Toni explodes at Reeves for taking up with Leonore, she does both at once. Lane was also rather courageous in allowing herself to appear older than her forty-one years, proclaiming the experience "liberating!" Hoskins nicely shows off his skill as the tough man who hates to see his wife cry.

Hollywoodland suffers moderately during the scenes focusing on Simo, the other man whose life has not panned out the way he had hoped, who fails to truly value the good things that have come his way. Brody is a fine actor, and his character's investigation into Reeves' death is intriguing, but when the film deals with Simo's relationships with his girlfriend, ex-wife, and son, not to mention his other cases, most viewers will find themselves yearning for the next flashback. Toward the end of the film, a weary, stymied Simo gazes with regret at old home movies of happier times. Finally facing some hard facts about his life, he chooses to redirect his energies, taking the hopeful path of reconnecting with his family instead of surrendering like Reeves to despair. "It's as though Reeves had to die just so this guy could understand what really matters," lamented critic Leah Rozen.

Still, *Hollywoodland* is a well-acted and often quite engrossing look at the darker side of the limelight. The feature film debut for both screenwriter Paul Bernbaum and director Allen Coulter, it grossed almost $14.5 million. Most critics had good things to say about it, particularly the performances. In one scene, Reeves' mother (Lois Smith), who was always adamant in her belief that her son was murdered, snaps at well-wishers who were sorry for her "loss." "My son was not lost," she declares. "He was taken." No one will probably ever know if the latter is true, but it seems fairly certain after watching *Hollywoodland* that the former was.

David L. Boxerbaum

CREDITS

Louis Simo: Adrien Brody
Toni Mannix: Diane Lane
George Reeves: Ben Affleck
Eddie Mannix: Bob Hoskins
Helen Bessolo: Lois Smith
Leonore Lemmon: Robin Tunney
Art Weissman: Jeffrey DeMunn
Russ Taylor: Brad William Henke
Jack Patterson: Dash Mihok
Laurie Simo: Molly Parker
Carol: Kathleen Robertson
Howard Strickling: Joe Spano
Origin: USA
Language: English
Released: 2006
Production: Glenn Williamson; Miramax Films, Back Lot Pictures; released by Focus Features
Directed by: Allen Coulter
Written by: Paul Bernbaum
Cinematography by: Jonathan Freeman
Music by: Marcelo Zarvos
Sound: Glen Gauthier
Music Supervisor: Dan Lieberstein
Editing: Michael Berenbaum
Art Direction: Patrick Banister
Costumes: Julie Weiss
Production Design: Leslie McDonald
MPAA rating: R
Running time: 126 minutes

REVIEWS

Boxoffice Online. September 8, 2006.
Chicago Sun-Times Online. September 8, 2006.

Entertainment Weekly. September 15, 2006, p. 51.
Los Angeles Times Online. September 8, 2006.
New York Times Online. September 8, 2006.
Premiere Magazine. September 2006, p. 34.
San Francisco Chronicle. September 8, 2006, p. E1.
Variety Online. August 17, 2006.
Washington Post. September 8, 2006, p. C1.

AWARDS

Nomination:

Golden Globes 2007: Support. Actor (Affleck)

HOODWINKED

Trouble In The Hood.
—Movie tagline

Armed And Dangerously Dumb.
—Movie tagline

Red Riding Hood, The Woodsman, Granny, The Wolf. Not Your Typical Crime. Not Your Usual Suspects.
—Movie tagline

Box Office: $51.4

The story of Little Red Riding Hood gets a postmodern spin in the delightful and energetic *Hoodwinked,* which takes its cues from such unlikely sources as Akira Kurosawa's *Rashomon* (1950) and classic detective fiction. It all adds up to a radical retelling of a familiar story with great wit, a fresh perspective, catchy musical numbers, and unpredictable characters. As in many films that begin with an intriguing premise, sustaining a clever idea to the very end proves a bit difficult as the filmmakers resort to a familiar action finale, and the animation is not as sophisticated as we are used to seeing in other computer-animated features. Nonetheless, the sheer inventiveness more than makes up for the movie's minor shortcomings.

Directed by Cory Edwards from a screenplay he wrote with Todd Edwards and Tony Leech, who both served as co-directors, the movie begins with the sassy but endearing Red (voice of Anne Hathaway) arriving at her grandmother's house and meeting up with the Wolf (voice of Patrick Warburton), dressed in Granny's clothes. The banter is sharp and very funny—"Are we just gonna sit around here, talk about how big I'm gettin'?" the Wolf retorts when Red rattles off all his big features, as she is known to do in the fairy tale. Soon Red exposes the Wolf, a bound and gagged Granny Puckett (voice of Glenn Close) comes bursting out of the closet, and a Woodsman (voice of James Belushi) wielding an ax charges through the window of Granny's cottage. Police arrive, and Chief Grizzly (voice of Xzibit) ropes off the crime scene because the incident may be related to a rash of goody robberies plaguing the forest. The investigation begins in earnest when a shrewd frog detective named Nicky Flippers (voice of David Ogden Stiers) arrives on the scene and decides to question each of the four involved.

Thus are we treated to four stories of the incidents leading up to the meeting in the house. As each character tells his or her story, we become aware of overlap and how characters cross paths with each other at various points in their narratives and how a minor character in one story can become the star of another. What ties everything together is the sly sense of humor, often revolving around secret identities. The Wolf, for example, is not out to eat Red; he is really a newspaper reporter investigating the notorious Goody Bandit, whose robberies have put so many goody shops out of business (apparently goodies are a staple of the forest's economy) and who may be targeting Granny next. The Woodsman is not really a lumberjack but rather a struggling actor named Kirk trying to get a job playing a lumberjack in a commercial for Paul's Bunion Cream. His feeble attempts at getting into character by chopping trees leads to a giant tree coming down and rolling after him all the way to Granny's home. Granny has the most bizarre story of all as an award-winning Xtreme athlete who was skiing on the slopes against a fierce, underhanded European team. Her identity is even a secret from Red, who feels betrayed that Granny leads such an exciting life while the sheltered Red, like so many animated heroines, longs to see the world.

The main achievements of *Hoodwinked* are twofold. First is the off-kilter comic sensibility, which transforms a classic fairy tale into a madcap mystery with bright gags and silly puns. The cops are the three little pigs, Red busts some karate moves on the Wolf when he confronts her in the forest, and the Wolf, disguised in sheep's clothing, pays off a sheep informant and has a hyper squirrel photographer named Twitchy (voice of Cory Edwards), who talks rapidly but claims never to drink coffee. Even throwaway one-liners cannot help but bring a smile, as when Nicky asks Red what she is called when she is not wearing the red hood and she deadpans, "I usually wear it."

The second innovation is structure—audiences today have grown used to movies that splinter chronology and employ multiple points of view a la *Pulp Fiction* (1994) and *The Usual Suspects* (1995), but the audacity of bringing such a labyrinth to a family-friendly animated feature is nonetheless refreshing. As each version of the story is revealed, we not only view the events from different perspectives but see the bigger narrative gradually filled in, often to our surprise. When Red, during a high-speed chase in a mine car, finds herself going off the track and in freefall, she sees Granny in the sky urging her to use her hood, which doubles as a makeshift parachute. We might think this is a vision on Red's part, akin to Luke Skywalker hearing Ben Kenobi admonishing him to use the Force. But when we see Granny's story, we understand that it really is Granny flying through the air during her ski jump. The pieces all interlock to create one story that may have been cute if told in linear fashion but would not have been nearly as engaging.

If the resolution does not quite live up to what has gone before, that is probably because the villain is not very exciting and his grand scheme feels random. A rabbit named Boingo (voice of Andy Dick) has figured in everyone's story, if sometimes only briefly, leading Nicky to conclude that this seemingly benign, furry creature is the Goody Bandit. It turns out that Boingo is really an evil mastermind who is stealing goody recipes so that he can inject an ingredient that will make them more addictive and thus create a fortune for himself. Red follows him and is captured but breaks free to help her new-found friends capture Boingo and his accomplices. It is a somewhat conventional ending for a movie that has been anything but, although even here there are some inventive touches. Kirk, for example, gets to infiltrate the bad guys' hideout by pretending to be an evil henchman and thus fulfill his dream as an actor. And the Wolf goes undercover impersonating a building inspector making sure the evil lair is up to code, as if evil lairs had their own governmental guidelines.

As a fractured fairy tale, *Hoodwinked* is hip and smart like its feisty heroine, but it does not wear its coolness as a badge of honor or distance the audience with its ironic edge. Instead, it creates offbeat, sometimes goofy, versions of familiar characters and places them in a fast-moving, spunky little tale that may be outrageous and nontraditional but never loses its heart and sense of good cheer.

Peter N. Chumo II

CREDITS

Red: Anne Hathaway (Voice)
Granny: Glenn Close (Voice)
The Woodsman: James Belushi (Voice)
The Wolf: Patrick Warburton (Voice)
Det. Bill Stork: Anthony Anderson (Voice)
Nicky Flippers: David Ogden Stiers (Voice)
Chief Grizzly: Xzibit (Voice)
Woolworth: Chazz Palminteri (Voice)
Boingo: Andy Dick (Voice)
Twitchy: Cory Edwards (Voice)
Japeth the Goat: Benjy Gaither (Voice)
Origin: USA
Language: English
Released: 2005
Production: Maurice Kanbar, Sue Bea Montgomery, Preston Stutzman, David K. Lovegren; Kanbar Entertainment, Kanbar Animation, Blue Yonder Films; released by Weinstein Co.
Directed by: Cory Edwards
Written by: Cory Edwards, Todd Edwards, Tony Leech
Music by: Todd Edwards
Sound: Tom Myers, Mark Keefer
Music Supervisor: John McCullough
Editing: Tony Leech
MPAA rating: PG
Running time: 89 minutes

REVIEWS

Boxoffice Online. January 13, 2006.
Entertainment Weekly Online. January 11, 2006.
Los Angeles Times Online. January 14, 2006.
New York Times Online. January 13, 2006.
Variety Online. December 15, 2005.
Washington Post Online. January 13, 2006, p. C05.

QUOTES

Red: "What big ears you have."
The Wolf: "All the better to hear your petty insults with!"

TRIVIA

Andy Dick ad-libbed the line where Boingo tells his henchman Keith to change his name because it's "not very scary sounding" and embarrassing to say.

HOOT

It's time to stand up for the little guys.
—Movie tagline

Box Office: $8.1 million

Released in the same year as the documentary *An Inconvenient Truth* (2006) and the animated children's hit *Happy Feet* (2006), *Hoot,* aimed at children and teenagers, also addresses the timely issue of environmental protection in a rapidly changing world. Its pleasures are simple: clear blue Florida seas; steel drum Jimmy Buffet songs; and spunky kids saving cute, innocent burrowing owls. Notable for directing multiple episodes of popular television series, including *Frasier* and *Becker,*

Wil Shriner, who adapted the screenplay from Carl Hiaasen's novel, makes his big screen directorial debut. It's solid but bland family fare with its humor painted in big broad strokes atop a serious message.

Pre-teen protagonist Roy Eberhardt (Logan Lerman) is a perpetual outsider, forced to move from the idyllic wilds of Montana to stupid, sunny Florida—his sixth such move in eight years. It's no surprise to Roy, then, when he finds trouble right off the bat while riding the school bus in the form of big bully Dana Matherson (Eric Phillips), who has a penchant for choking new kids. While physically menacing Roy, Dana also gives him the nickname "Cowgirl," which, unfortunately for Roy, sticks. What is a surprise to Roy and everyone on the bus, happens when Roy—distracted by a strange, barefoot, running boy he sees for a second time out the window—turns around and punches Dana in the face, breaking his nose. He hurries off the bus to try and catch the feral boy when he runs into more trouble: a soccer player dubbed Beatrice the Bear (Brie Larson) due to her large stature and aggressive behavior. She also threatens to knock his block off, but he still manages to follow the boy to a golf course before losing him. Then he's promptly plunked in the head by a stray ball. (Lerman is forced to relive the timeworn gag later in the film).

His oblivious, stock-issue parents (Neil Flynn and Kiersten Warren) have no idea why Roy is getting into so much trouble at his new school and force him to write a letter of apology to the bully who was choking him on a daily basis. He grudgingly does so, but of course, Dana will give no quarter. Still trying to track down the barefoot boy, Roy instead finds Beatrice, who warns him to stop nosing around and mind his own business. He wants her to deliver some shoes to the boy, and sensing that he's just trying to help, Beatrice warms to Cowgirl. She quickly reveals their secret: the barefoot boy, whom she calls Mullet Fingers (must everyone have a cutesy nickname?), is her half-brother, a sort of cross between Huck Finn and Henry David Thoreau. He's hell-bent on saving a bunch of burrowing owls being threatened by the construction of a Mrs. Paula's Pancake House in their neighborhood. Mullet Fingers (Cody Linley) has seen too much of this kind of reckless development in his community and is determined to stop it anyway he can. He's even made the papers with his bulldozer-stopping antics, which catches Roy's eye.

Roy likes the way Mullet thinks, and soon he's on board with the plan to halt the construction and save the owls. They are adorable animatronic creations too, innocently peeking out every now and then from their tiny burrows. Of course, not everyone thinks so. Namely, one Curly Branitt (Tim Blake Nelson), whose job is to get construction underway. He is thwarted at every turn by the two wily boys and by soulless corporate executive Chuck Muckle (Clark Gregg), who is constantly on the phone to Branitt threatening to fly down to the site if he doesn't get things going. Curly enlists the help of inept local policeman, Officer David Delinko (Luke Wilson) to catch the perpetrators. Delinko's first order of business is to stake out the site at night where he promptly falls asleep in his cruiser and wakes in the morning to find someone has painted all the windows black and vandalized the site right under his nose, once again. This enrages his Central Casting superior (John Archie), under pressure from the mayor to get that pancake hut built pronto, who takes away his cruiser and supplies him instead with a golf cart. The humiliated but earnestly determined officer continues on his mission unabated.

While Mullet does things the hard way, Roy uses his smarts to find a better way to bring the owl slaughter to a halt. Roy simply asks his dad, a G-man who works for the Justice Department, how he catches the bad guys at work. "The key is to catch 'em in their paperwork," Mr. Eberhardt replies. Soon, Roy's at the County Clerk's office (manned by Kin Shriner, director Wil's twin brother) rummaging through construction permits and finds a page suspiciously missing from the environmental reports. In the final reel, the three kids stage a coup, with Mullet capturing and hog-tying the evil Muckle, while the others invite Mayor Grandy (Robert Wagner) and the press to the "groundbreaking ceremony" for Mrs. Paula's where they instead reveal to the whole community the evidence they discovered that the owls are legally protected. Even the actress playing Mrs. Paula (Jessica Cauffiel) gets in on the feel-good vibes, announcing, in character, that Mrs. Paula wants to donate the land to be used as an owl sanctuary. Mission accomplished.

Lerman and Larson are attractive, likeable and proficient in their roles and actually have believable on-screen chemistry, while the good-looking Linley seems a bit outmatched in the acting department. Overall, Shriner does a decent job but shamelessly "borrows" a memorable scene from *Caddyshack* (1980), as he has an enraged Muckle spraying a fire extinguisher directly into the owl's holes while gleefully muttering anti-owl epithets. Thankfully, the film does not end with a triumphant owl emerging from it's burrow dancing to Kenny Loggins' "I'm Alright."

Hilary White

CREDITS

Officer David Delinko: Luke Wilson
Roy Eberhardt: Logan Lerman

Curly Branitt: Tim Blake Nelson
Beatrice Leep: Brie Larson
Mullet Fingers: Cody Linley
Mr. Eberhardt: Neil Flynn
Chuck Muckle: Clark Gregg
Mrs. Eberhardt: Kiersten Warren
Mother Paula/Kimberly: Jessica Cauffiel
Garrett: Dean Collins
Mayor Grandy: Robert Wagner
Captain: John Archie
City Clerk: Kin Shriner
Dana Matherson: Eric Phillips
Jimmy Buffett: Mr. Ryan
Origin: USA
Language: English
Released: 2006
Production: Frank Marshall, Jimmy Buffett; New Line Cinema, Walden Media, Kennedy/Marshall; released by New Line Cinema
Directed by: Will Shriner
Written by: Will Shriner
Cinematography by: Michael Chapman
Music by: Phil Marshall, Michael Utley, Mac McAnally
Sound: Walter Anderson
Editing: Alan Edward Bell
Costumes: Christopher Lawrence
Production Design: Steven Lineweaver
MPAA rating: PG
Running time: 90 minutes

REVIEWS

Boxoffice Online. May 5, 2006.
Chicago Sun-Times Online. May 5, 2006.
Entertainment Weekly Online. May 3, 2006.
Los Angeles Times Online. May 5, 2006.
New York Times Online. May 5, 2006.
Variety Online. May 3, 2006.
Washington Post. May 5, 2006, p. C5.

QUOTES

Roy Eberhardt: "We've got to stop this construction once and for all."
Mullet Fingers: "We're the only ones who care."
Roy: "We're the only ones that know!"

TRIVIA

Singer-songwriter Jimmy Buffet not only contributed to the soundtrack, he co-produced and cameos as science teacher Mr. Ryan.

HOSTEL

Welcome To Your Worst Nightmare.
—Movie tagline

Box Office: $47.3 million

Writer/director Eli Roth follows up *Cabin Fever* (2003) with another, more stylish gorefest, the fairly well-received *Hostel,* presented by none other than Quentin Tarantino. Roth reportedly also tripled the amount of blood used in *Cabin Fever,* with *Hostel* boasting an impressive 150 gallons. *Variety*'s John Anderson assessed, "*Hostel* may become something of a classic among *Fangoria* magazine's readership, acolytes of George Romero and audiences who thought *Saw II* (2005) was for babies."

Roth reportedly was inspired to make *Hostel* after reading about a Thai Internet business that charged $10,000 for the opportunity to kill another human being. The intended victims were poverty-stricken enough that they were driven to offer up their lives in exchange for money given to their surviving relatives.

Roth moves the tale to Europe, where backpacking college pals Josh (Derek Richardson) and Paxton (Jay Hernandez) along with the newly-befriended Icelander Oli (Eythor Gudjonsson) are naturally drawn to Amsterdam, where they are free to drink, smoke and debauch with abandon. So much so that they are kicked out of both a club and their hotel. They meet a young man, Alex (Lubomir Bukovy), who regales them with tales of a hostel in Bratislava where the all the women literally love Americans. Oli, the self-professed "king of the swing" and the other randy boys can't resist and hop the next train. In a bit of foreshadowing, they encounter a bizarre Dutch businessman (Jan Vlasak) who likes to eat with his hands and who makes a move on Josh, to the others' amusement.

At the hostel they meet the beautiful Natalya (Barbara Nedeljakova) and Svetlana (Jana Kaderabkova) who invite them to join them at a nude spa and a night out on the town, the end of which finds the girls coupling with Americans Paxton and Josh as Alex had promised. Meanwhile, Oli and his newfound friend and fellow hostel guest Yuki (Keiko Seiko) mysteriously disappear, leaving Josh and Paxton to search for them. Yuki's friend Kana (Jennifer Lim) shows the boys a chilling picture she received on her cell phone which depicts Oli and Yuki in front of a factory smokestack with the message: "Sayonara." While Oli and Yuki have, in fact, been taken to an abandoned factory used for torture, the boys disregard the message.

Paxton then receives another eerie cell phone picture message of Oli's bodyless head with the message, "I go home." They are sufficiently creeped out enough to think about leaving Bratislava with Kana, but not before they decide to party with their European vixens at a nightclub. Josh falls ill and heads back to the hostel, while a drunken Paxton passes out in the club's storage room.

Josh wakes to find that he is handcuffed and in his underwear in a strange room, being tortured by the Dutch businessman from the train. After brutally drilling Josh about the legs and body, the Dutchman cuts his Achilles tendons. Josh flounders on the floor for awhile before the man finally kills him offscreen.

Meanwhile, Paxton find his way out of the storage room the next day and finds that Josh and Kana are missing. He contacts the police to no avail and attempts to find the smokestack in the cell phone photo, but his phone is stolen by a gang of vicious children. He runs into Svetlana and Natalya, who tell him Josh and Oli are at an art show.

Natalya brings Paxton to the factory, where he spies the man from the train hovering over Josh's body. Natalya laughs as two large men drag him down the hall to a cell, passing gruesome scenes in the other rooms. His torturer, a German (Petr Janis), soon arrives, Ignoring Paxton's pleas. Trying to bite the man's fingers, Paxton is accidentally set free as the man cuts through the handcuffs with the chainsaw he's been wielding, taking off two of Paxton's fingers. Paxton manages to kill the torturer, shooting him in the head with his own pistol, and escapes the room with his severed fingers.

Fleeing through the factory, Paxton hides in a cart loaded up with bodies being delivered to a butcher (Josef Bradna), whom he knocks out with a hammer. Raiding a locker to disguise his mangled hand, he finds a business card for Elite Hunting with prices written on it: American $25,000, European $10,000, Russian $5,000.

Paxton meets a visiting American (Rick Hoffman) who, mistaking Paxton for a fellow killer, talks to him about the $50,000 he paid for a little something extra. Paxton steals the man's pistol and continues to flee, but turns back when he reconizes Kana's screams. The American has a blowtorch to Kana's eye when Paxton shoots him.

They flee in a stolen car pursued by the guards, and mow down Natalya and Alex, who was also in on the operation. Paxton then bribes the vicious children, the Bubble Gum Gang, with gum that he found in the car and instruct them to kill the guards upon arrival. However, when Paxton and Kana get to the train station, the other guards are already there, along with police. Kana, sickened by glimpsing her disfigured face, jumps in front of a passing train, effectively creating a diversion for Paxton, who hops on a train to freedom.

On the train, Paxton recognizes the voice of Josh's torturer and follows him into a restroom in Prague. Finally able to exact revenge, Paxton tortures him before finally slitting his throat, then hops another train out.

Hilary White

CREDITS

Paxton: Jay Hernandez
Josh: Derek Richardson
Dutch Businessman: Jan Vlasak
Oli: Eythor Gudjonsson
Natalya: Barbara Nedeljakova
Svetlana: Jana Kaderabkova
Alex: Lubomir Bukovy
German Surgeon: Petr Janis
The Butcher: Josef Bradna
Yuki: Keiko Seiko
Kana: Jennifer Lim
American Client: Rick Hoffman
Origin: USA
Language: English, Czechoslovakian, Dutch, German, Icelandic, Italian, Japanese
Released: 2006
Production: Eli Roth, Mike Fleiss, Chris Briggs; Screen Gems, Lionsgate, Next Entertainment, Quentin Tarantino, Raw Nerve Production; released by Lionsgate Films
Directed by: Eli Roth
Written by: Eli Roth
Cinematography by: Milan Chadima
Music by: Nathan Barr
Sound: Tomas Belohradsky
Editing: George Folsey Jr.
Art Direction: David Baxa
Costumes: Franco-Giacomo Carbone
Production Design: Franco-Giacomo Carbone
MPAA rating: R
Running time: 95 minutes

REVIEWS

Boxoffice Online. January 6, 2006.
Entertainment Weekly Online. January 4, 2006.
Los Angeles Times Online. January 6, 2006.
New York Times Online. January 6, 2006.
Premiere Magazine Online. January 6, 2006.
Variety Online. January 4, 2006.

QUOTES

Oli: "I am the king of the swing!"

TRIVIA

Director Eli Roth issued a formal apology to the Icelandic Minister of Culture, for all the damage this film may cause to Iceland's reputation.

HOW TO EAT FRIED WORMS

New town. New friends. New menu.
—Movie tagline
It's Global Worming!
—Movie tagline

Box Office: $13 million

How to Eat Fried Worms is a Bob Dolman adaptation based on the 1973 children's book written by Thomas Rockwell. It comes as no surprise that, as with many adaptations, the book features a more basic, and certainly more reasonable, scenario than the movie. It seems that watching a film about eating worms is not nearly as appealing as reading a book about the same thing. This is clearly a movie made with fans of the book in mind, so for them, it works. But for the rest, it is a gross-out that fades quickly from memory. There is not enough substance to keep audiences entertained for all ninety-eight minutes, unless one is a young boy between the ages of eight to eleven. The same story, told as a short, would be acceptable and cute.

The film's main character is eleven-year-old Billy Forrester (Luke Benward), who must eat ten worms in one day. Even a kid's movie needs a motive to make it seem believable. Billy is the new kid in school and knows what happens to new kids at school, so he is not surprised when he becomes the target for abuse. He immediately runs into the fifth grade bully Joe Guire (Adam Hicks) on his first day of school. Joe and his evil sidekicks have put worms in Billy's lunchbox.

Billy throws a worm at Joe, who calls Billy names and both of them make a disgusting bet in which Billy agrees to swallow ten creepy crawlies in a row without vomiting. There will be a group of witnesses to make sure things go as planned and no one tries to back out of the dare.

When Saturday rolls around the group of kids begin their daylong journey around the city looking for various ways to prepare the worms. There are some very genuinely creative ways to cook worms demonstrated here. But even more interesting is Billy, initially portrayed as having a weak stomach, clearly able to stand up to the bullies, gobbling down the worms apparently without trouble. He refuses to back down and although the behavior is utterly disgusting it is impossible not to gain some respect for Billy.

The feel-good nature of the film is evident but the "gross" factor is just too strong. It's clear why this film was popular with the elementary school crowd; because it does make adults squirm. *How to Eat Fried Worms* could appeal to adults, as well as kids, because of the basic moral premise of the story, which says bullies are bad and friendships take time to develop.

Laura Abraham

CREDITS

Billy Forrester: Luke Benward
Erika: Hallie Kate Eisenberg
Twitch: Alexander Gould
Principal Burdock: James Rebhorn
Joe Guire: Adam Hicks
Adam: Austin Rogers
Dad: Tom Cavanagh
Mom: Kimberly Williams-Paisley
Origin: USA
Language: English
Released: 2006
Production: Mark Johnson, Philip Steuer; Walden Media; released by New Line Cinema
Directed by: Bob Dolman
Written by: Bob Dolman
Cinematography by: Richard Rutkowski
Music by: Mark Mothersbaugh, Bob Mothersbaugh
Sound: Ethan Andrus
Music Supervisor: Lindsay Fellows
Editing: Janice Hampton
Art Direction: John Frick
Costumes: Kathleen Kiatta
Production Design: Caty Maxey
MPAA rating: PG
Running time: 98 minutes

REVIEWS

Boxoffice Online. August 25, 2006.
Chicago Sun-Times Online. August 25, 2006.
Entertainment Weekly. September 1, 2006, p. 53.
Los Angeles Times Online. August 25, 2006.
New York Times Online. August 25, 2006.
San Francisco Chronicle. August 25, 2006, p. E5.
Variety Online. August 21, 2006.
Washington Post Online. August 25, 2006.

QUOTES

Erika: "Boys are so weird."

TRIVIA

The book's author, Thomas Rockwell, is the son of famed artist Norman Rockwell.

I

ICE AGE: THE MELTDOWN

Kiss Your Ice Goodbye.
—Movie tagline

The Pack Is Back.
—Movie tagline

The Chill Is Gone.
—Movie tagline

Box Office: $195.3 million

Ice Age: The Meltdown improves on its predecessor (2002's *Ice Age*) in several ways, a rare thing for a sequel to accomplish. While the computer animated *Ice Age* was successful at the box office, it was an average family film, based on an interesting premise but mired in mediocre humor and a simplistic, uninspired plot. *The Meltdown* improves the areas that were weakest in the first movie. The plot is not a very complex one at a basic level, yet the episodic scenes that make up the storyline are more interesting and serve to develop characterization. The main characters are more endearing, partially due to their relationships with new characters that allow them to develop and become more dynamic. The film is colorful, energetic, and amusing, achieving a memorable charm that may be appealing to children and adults alike.

A mammoth named Manny (voice of Ray Romano), a sloth named Sid (voice of John Leguizamo), and a saber-toothed tiger named Diego (voice of Denis Leary) have settled down among other animals in a vast valley surrounded by high walls of ice. When conniving Fast Tony (voice of Jay Leno) warns that doomsday is coming, Manny tells him to stop scaring everyone, but before long it becomes apparent that Fast Tony was unknowingly speaking the truth. The ice is melting, and Manny points out that when the ice walls around the valley melt, the valley will flood. The animals learn from a vulture (voice of Will Arnett) that a boat awaits them at the other end of the valley, if they can survive the trek there.

Manny, Sid, and Diego set out on the journey and soon meet two hyperactive, playful possums named Crash (voice of Seann William Scott) and Eddie (voice of Josh Peck) with a "sister" named Ellie (voice of Queen Latifah). But Ellie is not a possum; she's a mammoth. Manny is initially excited to meet Ellie because he has been sadly contemplating the depressing thought that he was the only mammoth left. Unfortunately, Ellie believes she is a possum, even going so far as to try to hang from tree branches by her tail. Ellie and her brothers decide to join Manny, Sid, and Diego on their trek across the valley.

The middle portion of the movie follows their adventures along the way. Manny and Ellie do not get along very well at first, but Manny develops a fondness for Ellie even though he thinks she is stubborn and perhaps a little crazy. Eventually, Ellie realizes that she is in fact a mammoth when she comes across a familiar setting from her childhood and recalls memories long forgotten. Manny tries clumsily to talk to her about the necessity of keeping their species alive, but she is at first offended. Meanwhile, Sid encounters a group of mini-sloths who worship him as the "fire king" but want to sacrifice him to a river of lava in the hope that it will save them, while Diego has the least interesting adventures as he battles a crippling fear of water.

When they come within sight of the other end of the valley, they see that the "boat" is an enormous hollowed-out tree trunk sitting atop a lone mountain. However, a field of erupting geysers lay between them and the mountain, and Ellie thinks it is too dangerous to cross, so she proposes going back and finding a way around the field. Manny insists that they do not have the time to go back, but Ellie stubbornly decides to do so anyway. Manny, Sid, and Diego keep going straight forward, despite the dangerous geysers. Not surprisingly, Ellie ends up in trouble, as the waters start rushing in toward this end of the valley, so it is up to Manny to save her.

In the end, when the waters recede and everyone is safe on dry land, the ice walls split and reveal a huge herd of mammoths heading into the valley. Ellie and Manny are astounded to learn that they are not, in fact, the last mammoths alive. Ellie starts to follow the herd to be with her own kind, but Manny plans on staying with Sid and Diego…that is, until the latter two tell him that he should go after Ellie. When Manny does in fact run after Ellie, she turns around and comes back to him happily. "I don't want us to be together because we have to; I want us to be together because we want to," Manny says. "And I want to be with you." In a touching conclusion, all of the friends decide to stay together as they realize that they are a family and are their own "herd."

One reason *The Meltdown* is more colorful than the original is because it is more visually interesting, as the characters get to inhabit landscapes that are not formed purely of ice. Beyond that the characters are rounder, more interesting, and more fun to watch. The relationship between Manny and Ellie is particularly enjoyable, while Crash and Eddie are delightful and endearing when they could have been annoying. Sid, who tended toward the annoying side in the first movie, is more genuinely amusing, and his scene with the mini-sloths, who return at the end, is one of the highlights of the film, even though it is rather brief. Diego suffers the most in the movie; he is an interesting character, but he does not have much to do.

Ice Age: The Meltdown falls into a rare category as a sequel that succeeds where its processor was weak. It should be applauded for not simply staying with a formula that proved profitable for *Ice Age*. Even standing on its own, without comparison to the first movie, *The Meltdown* succeeds as a better-than-average family film. If there are any future sequels, they would do well to follow the example set by this film, or even take the improvement a step further and explore a bit more complex storyline.

David Flanagin

CREDITS

Manny: Ray Romano (Voice)
Sid: John Leguizamo (Voice)
Diego: Denis Leary (Voice)
Crash: Seann William Scott (Voice)
Eddie: Josh Peck (Voice)
Ellie: Queen Latifah (Voice)
Lone Gunslinger Vulture: Will Arnett (Voice)
Fast Tony: Jay Leno (Voice)
Mr. Start: Joseph Bologna (Voice)
Mrs. Start: Renee Taylor (Voice)
Aardvark dad: Stephen (Steve) Root (Voice)
Female Ox: Mindy Sterling (Voice)
Cholly: Alan Tudyk (Voice)
Female Mini Sloth: Clea Lewis (Voice)
Origin: USA
Language: English
Released: 2006
Production: Lori Forte; 20th Century Fox Animation, Blue Sky Studios; released by 20th Century Fox
Directed by: Carlos Saldanha
Written by: Peter Gaulke, Gerry Swallow, Jim Hecht
Cinematography by: Harry Hitner
Music by: John Powell
Sound: Randy Thom
Art Direction: Thomas Cardone
MPAA rating: PG
Running time: 90 minutes

REVIEWS

Chicago Sun-Times Online. March 31, 2006.
Entertainment Weekly Online. March 31, 2006.
Los Angeles Times Online. March 31, 2006.
New York Times Online. March 31, 2006.
San Francisco Chronicle Online. March 31, 2006.
USA Today Online. March 31, 2006.
Variety Online. March 30, 2006.
Washington Post. March 31, 2006, p. C5.

IDIOCRACY

How can one man have so much success on television and so little success on the big screen? That's the question that hounds Mike Judge. Judge shot to fame as the creator of MTV's *Beavis & Butthead*, a subversively lowbrow animated series that quickly became an international sensation and spawned a successful movie spin-off, *Beavis & Butthead Do America* (1996). Given the popularity of the Beavis franchise and Judge's acclaimed animated sitcom for the Fox Network, *King of the Hill*, which debuted in 1997, it wasn't surprising when Fox greenlit Judge's first live-action film, *Office Space* (1999), a satire on the inanity of the modern workplace and a box office failure. However, the film found a devoted following thanks to multiple airings on television, and slowly became a cult favorite. Subsequently, many of the movie's catch phrases have worked their way into the cultural lexicon, a variety of tie-in merchandising emerged, and *Office Space* has become one of Twentieth Century Fox's best-selling DVDs of all time.

With *Office Space*'s underground success, it again wasn't surprising that Fox would eventually give Judge another shot at directing a live-action comedy. What was surprising was the ultimate result: *Idiocracy*. Originally titled *3001,* this futuristic comedy had one of the most unusual releases of any recent feature from a major studio. Fox, apparently unhappy with Judge's final result, delayed the movie's premiere for almost two years after its completion and, when they eventually did release *Idiocracy* in September 2006, they only opened the movie in seven cities (avoiding major markets like New York City) with absolutely no publicity. In fact, if moviegoers wanted to find showtimes on Moviefone.com for *Idiocracy* during its limited release, the film was derisively listed as *Untitled Mike Judge Comedy.* And, while we may never know the financial or political reasons why Fox chose to release the film as they did, the whole situation begs the question: was *Idiocracy* bad enough to deserve such an obscure, unpublicized release?

The short answer is no, although the final product is far from Judge's best work. Perhaps the funniest thing about *Idiocracy* is its central conceit—that mankind's future will not be populated by our best and brightest, but rather by those who procreate the most. This point is made abundantly clear by one of the film's most inspired sequences in which we cut between a yuppie couple who keep putting off having a baby for a variety of reasons (focusing on their careers, the stock market is down, etc.) and a white-trash redneck couple who keep having unprotected sex. As the childless yuppie couple gets older and older, we watch a graphic of the rednecks' family tree growing at an exponential rate. A narrator tells the audience, "while most science fiction of the day predicted a future that was more civilized and more intelligent...all signs indicated that the human race was heading in the opposite direction—a dumbing down." Mike Judge's future is not the brave new world of Asimov or Clarke. It's a moronic Jerry Springer hell where the lowest common denominator has become the status quo. In a review in *The Onion A.V. Club*, Nathan Rabin commented that, "There's a good chance that Judge's smartly lowbrow *Idiocracy* will be mistaken for what it's satirizing, but good satire always runs the risk—to borrow a phrase from a poster-boy for the reverse meritocracy—of being misunderestimated."

The main plot of *Idiocracy* follows Joe Bauers (Luke Wilson), an Army librarian who revels in being average and only wants to fade into the background until he can finally start drawing his government pension. Against his will, Joe is drafted into a military hibernation program that will place him in cryogenic sleep for a year. Because no female soldiers were average or expendable enough for the project, the Army hires a prostitute, Rita (Maya Rudolph), to act as Joe's counterpart. One of the film's recurring jokes is Joe's steadfast inability to realize what Rita really does for a living. Joe and Rita are placed into hibernation pods, and the project commences. However, thanks to a bureaucratic snafu, the program is cancelled by the Army and quickly forgotten. Eventually, the hibernation pods are hauled off to a landfill, with Joe and Rita still sleeping inside. They sleep for almost a thousand years until their pods are accidentally rediscovered in the year 2974.

When Joe awakens in the future, he discovers an America covered with mountains of garbage and advertisements on every possible surface. It's a world where people can live their entire lives within the walls of Costco and where the U.S. government is a subsidiary of "AOL-Time-Warner-Starbucks." People eat a goo-like substance out of a jar labelled "Food" and the two most popular television networks are the Violence and Masturbation Channels. There's a terrifically filthy joke about watching the name of the restaurant Fuddruckers evolve throughout time into its eventual lowbrow zenith. A garbage landslide unearths Joe's pod, which crashes into the apartment of Frito (Dax Shepard), a grunting slovenly futuristic everyman, who rarely leaves his La-Z-Boy with its built-in toilet. Because language has deteriorated throughout the centuries, when Joe speaks, Frito can barely understand him. Disoriented from his hibernation, Joe stumbles across the hellish garbage-covered city to a hospital, still somehow convinced that he's just hallucinating. Joe finds that hospitals are now set up like Jiffy Lubes—you stand in line until a technician hooks you into a machine that loudly offers a pre-recorded diagnosis ("You've got hepatitis!"). When Joe finally gets to see a doctor, who offers the diagnosis that Joe might be "retarded," he begins to realize what's happened. His panic is interrupted when the doctor notices that Joe is "unscannable"—everyone in the future has a UPC tattoo on their hands—and sets off an alarm calling the authorities. Joe flees the hospital, confused but determined to find Rita, the only person he knows that might still be alive.

Rita's pod was unearthed in the same landslide, but when Joe finds her, it's clear that she's been handling the future-shock much better than he has. When the government authorities finally apprehend Joe and Rita, President Camacho—a professional wrestler who wears a special "president" costume—gives Joe a startling piece of information. Even though Joe was considered painfully average in his own time, in the future, he is the smartest man on the planet and the world needs him to solve their most pressing problems. If Joe can't help, he'll be sent to the ominous-sounding "Rehabilitation." But if he can, he'll become the Secretary of the Interior and have a chance to find a rumored government time machine that could take him back to his own time.

Everything about the concept behind *Idiocracy* is sublime. Judge's vision of the future is a scarily plausible extension of our modern society, where Paris Hilton and Donald Trump dominate the airwaves and families gladly sign up to be humiliated on network reality shows. However, even though Mike Judge the writer has a scathing comedic voice, Mike Judge the director is simply (and sadly) not talented enough to make that voice work on-screen. Perhaps the scope of the film was too ambitious, and Judge is more comfortable within the mundanity of an office cubicle, but almost everything about *Idiocracy* falls flat in its final execution. Sight gags are poorly staged, jokes are trampled on by indifferent actors, and the overall look of the film looks thrown together and cheap. Not that setting your movie in a dystopian future is easy on a production designer, but earlier films like Woody Allen's *Sleeper* (1973) and Andrew Niccol's *Gattaca* (1997) created similar worlds on a limited budget that looked infinitely better. There are inspired moments of design sprinkled throughout *Idiocracy*—giant, city-sized Costco stores, fast-food vending machines that deduct funds directly from your welfare account—but they are so poorly filmed that we're only allowed quick, frustrating glances.

The characters of *Idiocracy* are similarly infuriating. As much as we want to like Luke Wilson's affable everyman protagonist, he's just too blandly ingratiating to really care about. Maya Rudolph, who's proven time and time again that she's an extremely talented comedienne on *Saturday Night Live*, is given a one-note (and practically one-joke) character to play, which is unfortunate, particularly since Rita needed to be a more lively foil to Joe's overwhelming averageness. The citizens of *Idiocracy*'s futuristic confederacy of dunces have a hard time as well, trying to sell Judge's concept of an irritating, grating future without being irritating and grating themselves. The results are mixed, with Dax Shepard underplaying his role until you almost ignore him, and a variety of gifted comedians (Justin Long, Thomas Haden Church, and Stephen Root, among others) delivering a series of over-the-top cameos. In the end, with *Idiocracy*'s limitless potential so apparent, you can see why Fox originally greenlit the film and, sadly, after viewing Judge's execution of said potential, you can also see why the studio wasn't too quick to release it.

Tom Burns

CREDITS

Joe Bauers: Luke Wilson
Rita: Maya Rudolph
Frito: Dax Shepard
President Camacho: Terry Crews
Secretary of State: David Herman
Narrator: Earl Mann
Doctor: Justin Long
CEO of Brawndo: Thomas Haden Church
Judge Hank "The Hangman" BMW: Stephen Root (uncredited)
Origin: USA
Language: English
Released: 2006
Production: Mike Judge, Elysa Koplovitz; Ternion; released by 20th Century Fox
Directed by: Mike Judge
Written by: Mike Judge, Etan Cohen
Cinematography by: Tim Suhrstedt
Music by: Theodore Shapiro
Sound: Mack Melson
Editing: David Rennie
Art Direction: William Ladd Skinner
Costumes: Debra McGuire
Production Design: Darren Golford
MPAA rating: R
Running time: 84 minutes

REVIEWS

Boxoffice Online. September 1, 2006.
Entertainment Weekly. September 15, 2006, p. 56.
LA Weekly Online. August 30, 2006.
Los Angeles Times Online. September 4, 2006.
Variety Online. September 1, 2006.

IDLEWILD

Box Office: $12.6 million

Idlewild was one of the most audacious films to come out in 2006. It was a flashy, creative, wild musical that was like nothing else in the multiplex. In a way, audacity was expected, considering the source of the film: that is, Andre Benjamin and Antwan A. Patton, better known as Andre 3000 and Big Boi of the innovative and popular duo OutKast. There was much anticipation over the film, mostly from people anticipating that the duo had the same magic touch with film that they had with music.

Idlewild's momentum died down quite a bit when the film's release was delayed by several months. Benjamin and Patton explained that they were tinkering with the music for the film, but delays usually signal trouble for a movie, and the news cast a pall over *Idlewild*. In retrospect, tinkering with the music seems like a plausible enough reason because, despite the duo's musical background, the visuals are the standout feature of the film. This is a film in which music notes literally dance on the page and a rooster embossed on a whiskey flask talks to its owner. It is as if writer and director Bryan Barber, who directed the OutKast videos "Hey Ya" and "Roses," had a lifetime of visual ideas and decided to pack them all into one film, just in case he never had another chance to use them.

The film revolves around two denizens of Church, a rollicking nightclub in Idlewild, Georgia. Rooster (Patton), who grew up running moonshine for his father, has a bunch of kids and a wife, Zora (Malinda Williams), who wishes he would stop bedding chorus girls and move the family to the country. Rooster helps his uncle, Spats (Ving Rhames), in running Church and is also on hand to take the stage when need be. His longtime best friend, Percival (Benjamin), is a piano player whose quiet demeanor belies the creativity and passion brewing inside. Percival is content enough playing piano at night and working at the family funeral home with his unsmiling widowed father, Percival Sr. (Ben Vereen), until a beautiful lady singer, Angel (Paula Patton), arrives in town. Add to this a slick gangster, Trumpy (Terrence Howard), and you have love, crime and music.

Of these, the most interesting thing is the music. *Idlewild* takes place in the 1930s, but the music played inside is a mash-up of 1930s jazz and modern hip-hop. For a small-town speakeasy, Church has a lot of talent inside. Macy Gray appears as one of the singers, Taffy, and the raucous musical dance numbers were choreographed by Tony award winner, Hinton Battle. The dance sequences are truly stunning. Less stunning is the plotline, which seems cobbled together from various gangster movies and musicals. After seeing another amazing dance sequence, it is difficult to go back and care about the rest of the movie's reality.

Of the two main players, it is Benjamin who seems to have true movie star talent. His brooding face expresses much more than the lines Barber's script gives him to say. And Benjamin gets the best sequence in the film. It shows him waking up with a song in a bedroom filled with clocks. As the clocks strike, the cuckoos pop out and join in the surreal number.

Critics seemed dazzled enough. Owen Gleiberman of *Entertainment Weekly* gave the film an A- and called it "madly soulful and enjoyable." "I'm not sure what OutKast fans, let alone the *Snakes on a Plane* (2006) crowd will make of it, but *Idlewild* is a film of spiky delights—a vision of African American pop culture rising above the heartache and sin that has nurtured it," he wrote. Teresa Wiltz of the *Washington Post* wrote: "In many ways it's a two-hour music video, except that for all its fluffiness, its impact lingers long after the Busby Berkeleyesque credit sequence rolls, thanks to the filmmaker's visual innovations and OutKast's funkily eccentric sensibility." Stephanie Zacharek of *Salon* wrote: "Barber has made a movie that's so big, and so visually and aurally enveloping, that there's no way you can look at it and say you've seen it all before." But Ann Powers of the *New York Times* wrote: "Patton and Benjamin can both hold the screen and are great in their musical sequences, but sorry, they aren't actors."

Jill Hamilton

CREDITS

Percival: Andre Benjamin
Rooster: Antwan Andre Patton
Angel: Paula Patton
Trumpy: Terrence Howard
Zora: Malinda Williams
Taffy: Macy Gray
Percy Sr.: Ben Vereen
Spats: Ving Rhames
Sunshine Ace: Faizon Love
Origin: USA
Language: English
Released: 2006
Production: Charles Roven, Robert Guralnick; Mosaic Media Group, Forensic Films, HBO Films; released by Universal Pictures
Directed by: Bryan Barber
Written by: Bryan Barber
Cinematography by: Pascal Rabaud
Music by: John Debney
Sound: David M. Kelson, Larry Long
Music Supervisor: Andre Benjamin, Antwan Andre Patton
Editing: Anne Goursaud

Art Direction: Gary Diamond
Costumes: Shawn Barton
Production Design: Charles Breen
MPAA rating: R
Running time: 120 minutes

REVIEWS

Boxoffice Online. August 25, 2006.
Chicago Sun-Times Online. August 25, 2006.
Entertainment Weekly. September 1, 2006, p. 49.
Los Angeles Times Online. August 25, 2006.
New York Times Online. August 25, 2006.
San Francisco Chronicle. August 25, 2006, p. E5.
Variety Online. August 20, 2006.
Washington Post. August 25, 2006, p. C1.

TRIVIA

Andre Benjamin is Andre 3000 and Antwan A. Patton is Big Boi from the hip-hop group OutKast

THE ILLUSIONIST

Nothing is what it seems.
—Movie tagline

Box Office: $39.9 million

Two films involving magic were reasonably well received during the year: Neil Burger's *The Illusionist* appeared first in August, at the end of the summer market, followed by Christopher Nolan's *The Prestige* (2006), in October. Both films depended on illusory, deceptive, and misleading plots. Nolan's film centered on the rivalry between two magicians to perfect the ultimate illusion. Burger's film, on the other hand, wraps a romantic plot around a master "illusionist" practicing in Vienna in 1900. Writer/director Neil Burger's film adaptation of Steven Millhauser's short story "Eisenheim the Illusionist," transports viewers back a hundred years to Viennese music halls and the palatial apartments of Crown Prince Leopold (Rufus Sewell).

The Crown Prince is betrothed to Sophie von Teschen (Jessica Biel), whose backstory is gradually and eventually revealed. The aristocratic Sophie, it turns out, was infatuated with young Eisenheim (Aaron Johnson), the humble son of a simple carpenter separated by class from Sophie. Once their affair is discovered, her parents forcefully part the young lovers. Young Eisenheim becomes an apprentice to an itinerant sorcerer. When the youngsters are about to be separated, Sophie begs Eisenheim to make them disappear, a trick then beyond his powers.

For the next fifteen years, Eisenheim (Edward Norton) works to perfect his powers before returning to Vienna and becoming a celebrity performer. He will eventually work his magic in the presence of Crown Prince Leopold, who is even more obsessive than Chief Inspector Uhl (Paul Giamatti) about discovering the magician's secrets. He has, in fact, instructed Uhl to spy on Eisenheim. Unwittingly, the Crown Prince reunites Eisenheim with his childhood sweetheart, as Sophie volunteers to serve as the magician's stage assistant.

Eisenheim's nightly performances are closely monitored by the Vienna Police. Uhl—a role the gifted Giamatti was born to play—is very watchful of fraud, but also driven by obsessive curiosity. He really wants to unlock the mysteries of the illusions created on stage. Eisenheim had been content with floating oranges, a mysteriously growing orange tree, and butterflies arriving on the scene carrying a woman's handkerchief, but is now dealing with life and death. Lately, Eisenheim has been materializing a young woman, Sophie, on stage. Sophie had been carrying on an affair with Eisenheim, right under Leopold's nose. She had apparently been murdered earlier by Leopold—the details are visually obscured so that viewers cannot see exactly what happened and are therefore left guessing. When Sophie materializes on stage, the crowd divines that Leopold is her murderer. Before the police can arrest Eisenheim, he disappears, along with Sophie. It's only later that the Inspector learns the truth—that, indeed, Leopold had murdered her. Faced with reprisals, Leopold turns a revolver on himself. But, then, nothing is quite what it seems.

In a series of revelatory moments suffered by the Inspector on a train platform, we learn that Eisenheim had faked Sophie's death and planted clues that led the Inspector to Leopold's guilt. This leaves Eisenheim and Sophie, both presumed dead, or at least missing, to reunite happily somewhere in the countryside.

Steven Millhauser, who wrote the original story, won the Pulitzer Prize in 1997, and Neil Burger was more than a little embarrassed by the wholesale changes he made to the plot and characters, frustrated by a story he considered cinematic, lyrical, transcendent, and, unfilmable. Burger's solution was "to create a narrative structure for the story that preserved its spirit while making it more palatable to financiers. A trick," Burger confessed, "to get the movie made. In the short story, Eisenheim becomes a threat to the powers-that-be because he's 'crossing boundaries'—blurring the distinction between illusion and reality, art and life." Burger wanted "to maintain this theme but also to make it more concrete," and for that reason he "invented a love interest for Eisenheim and a rival who is also a political leader. I expanded the role of a police inspector, briefly mentioned in the short story, and made him the narrator of the film." When Burger finally wrote to Millhauser from Prague, a week before shooting was to commence, he did so reluctantly; but Millhauser then wrote him back to say that he was not disturbed by the changes because he understood that "re-invention was inevitable" in this case.

Although famous for the intensity he has brought to his film roles, Edward Norton is very restrained in his performance here, and, as a consequence, his stage magic scenes are quiet and elegant. *Entertainment Weekly* praised Neil Burger for being able to capitalize on Norton's strengths so well. Playing Norton's powerful screen rival, Rufus Sewell is the very soul of sinister elegance and arrogance. No stranger to aristocratic roles, he would have preferred to play the police inspector, but is perfect as the Crown Prince. *New York Times* writer Sarah Lyall described Sewell's Leopold in *The Illusionist* as "superior, funny and intermittently terrifying." Regardless of how effective these actors may be, Paul Giamatti is really the star here, since he dominates screen time as narrator and since it is his revelation at the end that turns the story. Both Giamatti and Sewell are striking enough as character actors to challenge Norton, perhaps bringing out the best of his abilities. The Prague locations stand in reasonably well for turn-of-the-century Vienna, and Dick Pope's cinematography makes good use of the Czech cityscape. *The Illusionist* is a beautiful film, and the plot is tricky enough to suggest that a second viewing might be in order.

Not all the reviewers were totally enchanted by this picture. Ann Hornaday wrote in her *Washington Post* review that *The Illusionist* is "as tasteful and pedigreed as a movie comes," that it "glows with visual opulence and intellectual high-mindedness"; she respected "its themes of art, truth, history and romance," and yet, she found the movie somehow "disappointing." She clearly wanted to like the film, but the magic acts are obviously staged with camera trickery, which takes away from the intended ambiguity of the story. "The film's final few moments, which reveal delectable twists and turns, feel unearned, as if the audience has been cheated of being let in on the scheme," Hornaday complained. Rather like one of Eisenheim's stage routines, the film "tantalizes viewers with the promise of an engrossing tale, leads them on and then—poof—disappears." Still, the film was a refreshing treat for mid-August in the midst of the silly season and did manage to showcase the talents of at least two—and arguably three—of the most accomplished actors currently working on screen.

James M. Welsh and John C. Tibbetts

CREDITS

Eisenheim: Edward Norton
Sophie: Jessica Biel
Crown Prince Leopold: Rufus Sewell
Inspector Uhl: Paul Giamatti
Josef Fischer: Eddie Marsan
Young Eisenheim: Aaron Johnson
Origin: USA
Language: English
Released: 2006
Production: Michael London, Brian Koppelman, David Levien, Bob Yari; Bull's Eye Entertainment, Contagious Entertainment; released by Yari Film Group
Directed by: Neil Burger
Written by: Neil Burger
Cinematography by: Dick Pope
Music by: Philip Glass
Sound: Petr Forejt
Editing: Naomi Geraghty
Art Direction: Vlasta Svobodova, Stefan Kovacik
Costumes: Ngila Dickson
Production Design: Ondrej Nekvasil
MPAA rating: PG-13
Running time: 110 minutes

REVIEWS

Boxoffice Online. August 8, 2006.
Entertainment Weekly. August 9, 2006.
Hollywood Reporter Online. December 29, 2005.
Los Angeles Times Online. August 18, 2006.
New York Times Online. August 18, 2006.
Washington Post Online. August 18, 2006.

AWARDS

Nomination:

Oscars 2006: Cinematog.
Ind. Spirit 2007: Screenplay

IMAGINE ME & YOU

There Goes The Bride.
—Movie tagline

In her review of *Imagine Me & You*, Allison Bendikt of the *Chicago Tribune*, wrote, "I guess there's something progressive going on when a lesbian love story gets to be just as dreadful and tacky as most straight ones." She makes a good point. In the past, gay-themed films, usually relegated to the art house circuit, had something to prove. They either had to be terribly clever, groundbreaking, or in the case of *Brokeback Mountain* (2005), awfully important. *Brokeback*, for example, did not just come to theaters, it made an entrance. There was a furious flurry of controversy, countless op-ed pieces devoted to it and an equally endless number of lame jokes made about it. It is not good for the backers of *Imagine Me & You* that the film came to theaters with nary a peep from the general public, but it is good for the general acceptance of homosexual love.

The movie is not a breakthrough event for moviegoers either. *Imagine Me & You* is indeed a by-the-book romantic comedy. It even has the obligatory race to the airport at the end of the film, accompanied by shouted public declarations of love. In the film, Rachel (Piper Perabo) is a lovely British girl set to marry an equally lovely British guy, Heck (Matthew Goode). The two have been friends forever and are finally getting around to formalizing their relationship. As she walks down the aisle, Rachel locks eyes with their comely florist, Luce (Lena Headey), and realizes, right then and there, that it is "love." (As is usual in such films, there is not much attention to detail. In this case, there is no explanation as to why the florist is lingering around at the wedding.) In other handy plot contrivances, Luce makes fast friends with Rachel's precocious little sister, Beth (Sharon Horgan), guaranteeing that there will be plenty of opportunities for her to show up at various family functions.

Writer/director Ol Parker, in his directorial debut, fails to imbue the wedding eye-contact moment with enough punch, and it is hard to see that such a powerful connection has been made. It could equally be the fault of the acting, but it is difficult to realize that Rachel has been fundamentally changed by the encounter. Soon she is tortured by romantic longings for Luce and giving Heck cold glances. However, Rachel feels the best route is to squelch her feelings and stick with the kind, witty husband. After all, he is her best friend. But what with the various chance meetings (once, poor Heck even asks Luce to escort his wife for the evening), Rachel finds her feelings becoming more and more pressing. For her part, Luce is equally attracted to Rachel but does not want to contribute to the dissolution of a couple.

All of this could be more engaging, but somehow it never clicks. The movie starts out promisingly. The British director and London setting give hope that the film might veer into *Notting Hill* (1999) territory. And Goode, who starred in *Match Point* (2005), has the amiable wit of Hugh Grant. But it is not enough. Yes, the plot contrivances, the lackluster chemistry, and the foregone conclusion bring the film down but the turning point is when Goode's character starts noticing something is amiss. When Heck is basking in Rachel's love, he has a jaunty attitude and a playful air. Single-handedly, he gives the film a similar jauntiness. After he feels Rachel pulling away from him, he stops being funny and the film dies a slow death. The poor audience is left only with a stale romantic comedy and the wait for that airport car chase.

Imagine Me & You almost universally received the same response from critics. In short, that it was basically a gay version of the usual trite romantic comedy. Colin Covert of the *Minneapolis Star Tribune* wrote: "The film is as formulaic as a trigonometry textbook." Mick LaSalle of the *San Francisco Chronicle* wrote: "Aside from the gay element, it's exactly the kind of likable, enjoyable and fundamentally dishonest romantic comedy that people have been making for years." Manohla Dargis of the *New York Times* wrote: "En route to the obvious clinch there are long walks, awkward pauses, family dysfunction and fireworks, though not from the visibly uncomfortable leads." Finally, Roger Ebert of the *Chicago Sun-Times* wrote: "Here is a movie that begins with a tired romantic formula, and tries to redeem it with lesbianism."

Jill Hamilton

CREDITS

Rachel: Piper Perabo
Luce: Lena Headey
Heck: Matthew Goode
Tessa: Celia Imrie
Ned: Anthony Head
Cooper: Darren Boyd
Edie: Eva Birthistle
Beth: Sharon Horgan
H: Boo Jackson
Ella: Sue Johnston
Origin: USA
Language: English
Released: 2006
Production: Barnaby Thompson, Sophie Balhetchet, Lynda LaPlante, James Spring; BBC Films, Cougar Films, Fragile Films, X Filme, Focus Features; released by Fox Searchlight
Directed by: Ol Parker
Written by: Ol Parker
Cinematography by: Benjamin Davis
Music by: Alex Heffes
Sound: Max Hoskins
Editing: Alex Mackie
Costumes: Consolata Boyle
Production Design: Eve Mavrakis
MPAA rating: R
Running time: 93 minutes

REVIEWS

Boxoffice Online. January 27, 2006.
Chicago Sun-Times Online. February 3, 2006.

Entertainment Weekly Online. January 25, 2006.
New York Times Online. January 27, 2006.
Washington Post Online. February 3, 2006, p. WE43.

QUOTES

Rachel: "Everyone promises you happily ever after...but life turns into a different kind of fairy tale."

AN INCONVENIENT TRUTH

A Global Warning.
—Movie tagline

Nothing is scarier than the truth.
—Movie tagline

Box Office: $24.1 million

This documentary raises concerns about the world's drastic rise in atmospheric carbon dioxide, which contributes to global warming. Its narrator is former Vice President of the United States and one-time presidential candidate, Al Gore. Directed by Davis Guggenheim, *An Inconvenient Truth* has the distinction of being the third highest grossing documentary in U.S. history.

Guggenheim humanizes the highly technical nature of the documentary by intercutting scientific data with segments from Gore's personal life and political career. The former VP presents the empirical evidence for global warming and the difficult interplay between foreign governments, domestic policies, and the global economy. From this evidence, Gore theorizes that humanity will be grossly affected if rapid, unilateral change is not forthcoming. Examining annual temperatures and carbon dioxide levels for the past 600,000 years in desolate Antarctica, he notes a recent—in geographic terms—significant escalation during a relatively short period of time. He suggests that Hurricane Katrina could be a harbinger of greater disasters to come.

Gore's message is not one of doom and gloom. Rather, he believes the world can reverse its course. However, he does suggest that change must be imminent, before the planet's dire condition reaches a point of no return. In a personal analogy to this, he talks about his sister, a heavy smoker who eventually succumbed to the ravages of lung cancer. He makes the point that had she quit at some point, this disease could have been prevented, pointing out that successful action can be made by reducing carbon dioxide output and replenishing forests, he encourages his audience at large to take personal initiative and learn how to aid in this enterprise.

While attending Harvard, Gore first became aware of global warming when he took a course taught by Roger Revelle, one of the pioneers in measuring carbon dioxide levels. He sponsored the first congressional hearing on the matter as the Representative for Tennessee's fourth district. Bringing in authorities on the issue at the time, he believed he could sway his fellow congressman to pursue the appropriate legislation. He was disappointed to see that the wheels of bureaucracy were not necessarily in league with the health of the planet.

During the Clinton years, Gore devised a plan that would radically reduce greenhouse gases. By initiating a carbon tax, motivation to decrease the consumption of fossil fuels would grow, thus meeting the plan's objective; it was moderately carried out in 1993. He then interceded on behalf of the Kyoto Protocol implemented in 1997. This international treaty was designed to limit the concentration of greenhouse emissions in the atmosphere and to increase atmospheric stability. By December 2006, 169 nations had signed the treaty. A notable exception is the United States. During his run for President as the Democratic Party's nominee, Gore vowed that as President he would strive to ratify the Kyoto Protocol.

Following his defeat by George W. Bush, Gore spent more time on fighting global warming and less on politics. Editing a slideshow he made several years previously, Gore began a national and international tour. By the time the film was made, Gore disclosed that he gave approximately 1,000 presentations on the matter.

If no action is taken within ten years, the planet may hit the "tipping point" and begin an exponential slide into the destruction of civilization, as well as the majority of plant and animal life. "There is no controversy about these facts," he says in his filmed lecture. "Out of 925 recent articles in peer-review scientific journals about global warming, there is no disagreement. Zero." Despite this universal agreement among scientists, a database search shows that 57 percent of periodicals are skeptical of the reality of global warming and that an alarming 43 percent support it.

So alarmed by the content of the movie, Roger Ebert of the *Chicago Sun-Times* wrote this compelling statement in his review of the film: "In thirty-nine years, I have never written these words in a movie review, but here they are: You owe it to yourself to see this film. If you do not, and you have grandchildren, you should explain to them why you decided not to."

David Metz Roberts

CREDITS

Origin: USA
Language: English

Released: 2006
Production: Lawrence Bender, Laurie David, Scott Z. Burns; Participant Production
Directed by: Davis Guggenheim
Cinematography by: Davis Guggenheim, Bob Richman
Music by: Michael Brook
Editing: Jay Cassidy, Dan Swietlik
MPAA rating: PG
Running time: 100 minutes

REVIEWS

Boxoffice Online. May 26, 2006.
Chicago Sun-Times Online. June 2, 2006.
Entertainment Weekly Online. May 24, 2006.
Los Angeles Times Online. May 24, 2006.
New York Times Online. May 24, 2006.
Premiere Magazine Online. May 23, 2006.
Variety Online. January 30, 2006.

QUOTES

Al Gore: "I'm Al Gore, and I used to be the next President of the United States."

AWARDS

Oscars 2006: Feature Doc., Song ("I Need to Wake Up")

INFAMOUS

There's more to the story than you know.
—Movie tagline

Box Office: $1.2 million

The release of *Infamous* was held back a year to avoid competition with the award-winning *Capote* (2005), but the two movies were still released in such close succession and are so similar in content and theme that critics could not help but view the later film in comparison to *Capote*. Both movies explore the same period of Truman Capote's life, when the diminutive, eccentric writer traveled to Holcomb, Kansas to research and write an article about the violent slaying of a farm family by two men, an experience that led to the writing of a "nonfiction novel" called *In Cold Blood*. Both films present the same premise—that while the publication of *In Cold Blood* was in one way the high point of Capote's writing career, it also ruined him personally. However, while *Capote* was a thoughtful, compelling, and sometimes mysterious film featuring a virtuoso performance by its lead actor, *Infamous* is less consistent in tone and more superficial in its execution of the darker elements of the story. Divorced from a comparison to the earlier film, this version of Capote's story is a generally well-made and intriguing look at the events that lead to the author's downfall, but realistically it cannot be evaluated without seeing it in the shadow of its superior predecessor.

Director and writer Douglas McGrath presents roughly the first half of the film with a large dose of light-hearted frivolity as Truman Capote (Toby Jones) spends his spare time in Manhattan in 1959 associating with various flashy matrons of high society. When he reads a story about the murder of a family in rural Kansas, Capote heads to Holcomb, accompanied by friend Nelle Harper Lee (Sandra Bullock). The humor continues upon Capote's arrival in Holcomb, where he initially has a difficult time fitting in with the locals, who repeatedly call him "lady." However, the tone of the film changes significantly after the author meets and begins to get to know one of the two killers, Perry Smith (Daniel Craig). The earlier merriment and comedy are replaced by somber developments as Capote gets close to Smith to encourage the killer to open up and share the truth about himself. The two gradually form a bond, and Capote finds himself attracted to Smith even while needing an "ending" to his book in the form of Smith's execution. The film attempts a more intimate exploration of the relationship between Capote and Smith than was developed in *Capote*, yet the relationship seems to be superficially rendered, presented very matter-of-factly; this could be partially due to the awkwardness of Craig's casting. As a muscular, taller man, Craig's Smith seems mismatched with the small Truman—and, in fact, the real Smith was reported to be physically similar to Capote, which could help explain some of the kinship they felt with one another.

Interestingly, one of the most fascinating characters in the film is Harper Lee. Bullock's performance is sensitive and finely-tuned in a nuanced portrayal that offers an insightful glimpse into the wearied character of the woman who failed to write anything after the huge success of *To Kill a Mockingbird*. On the other hand, McGrath uses some of Capote's other friends in an unusual technique that tends to be distracting rather than genuinely helpful, interrupting the chronological flow of the story to interject "interviews" with some of the writer's acquaintances later in life. These brief segments, which are meant to shed more light onto the path that Truman's life took, generally seem a bit awkward and out of place, giving the film a documentary feel that, again, often contrasts with the tone of the film as a whole.

Toby Jones gives an entertaining performance in mimicking the mannerisms and cartoonish voice of Capote; physically, he more closely resembles the author than does Philip Seymour Hoffman in *Capote*. Yet, more often than not, his portrayal seems to be just that—a mimicking of Truman Capote, lacking the depth of a fully realized, complex character. Overall, the performance echoes the strengths and weaknesses of the film: both are emotionally involving at times and interesting to watch, but both seem to struggle to find their deeper complexities.

David Flanagin

CREDITS

Truman Capote: Toby Jones
Harper Lee: Sandra Bullock
Perry Smith: Daniel Craig
Dick Hickock: Lee Pace
Bennett Cerf: Peter Bogdanovich
Alvin Dewey: Jeff Daniels
Slim Keith: Hope Davis
Babe Paley: Sigourney Weaver
Marcella Angelli: Isabella Rossellini
Diana Vreeland: Juliet Stevenson
Kitty Dean: Gwyneth Paltrow
Jack Dunphy: John Benjamin Hickey
Origin: USA
Language: English
Released: 2006
Production: Christine Vachon, Anne Walker-McBay, Jocelyn Hayes; Killer Films; released by Warner Independent Pictures
Directed by: Douglas McGrath
Written by: Douglas McGrath
Cinematography by: Bruno Delbonnel
Music by: Rachel Portman
Sound: Ethan Andrus
Editing: Camilla Toniolo
Art Direction: Laura Ballinger Gardner
Costumes: Ruth Myers
Production Design: Judy Becker
MPAA rating: R
Running time: 118 minutes

REVIEWS

Boxoffice Online. October 13, 2006.
Chicago Sun-Times Online. October 13, 2006.
Entertainment Weekly. October 20, 2006, p. 55.
Los Angeles Times Online. October 13, 2006.
New York Times Online. October 13, 2006.
Premiere Magazine. October 2006, p. 43.
San Francisco Chronicle. October 13, 2006, p. E5.
Variety Online. August 31, 2006.
Washington Post. October 13, 2006, p. C1.

AWARDS

Nomination:

Ind. Spirit 2007: Support. Actor (Craig)

INLAND EMPIRE

A Woman In Trouble.
—Movie tagline

What to make of David Lynch's *Inland Empire*? Certainly viewing it in hopes of being told a story will be a sorely disappointing experience. That will become clear about the time a group of people dressed in rabbit suits appears on a minimalist sitcom stage. The female rabbit grimly irons, then says, "What time is it?" The canned laugh track erupts in laughter and applause. As if this were not odd and eerie enough, the set is lit in such a way that the rabbits look about as creepy as folks in rabbit suits can. Around this point it becomes abundantly clear that one is watching an art film, with a capital "A."

This, of course, is not a bad thing, it is just uncommon to come upon such a challenging art film. The mind wants to piece together the fragments of story because it seems as if they all might suddenly add up to form some sort of coherent whole. It does not happen. As in a dream, where a childhood home suddenly becomes the local supermarket, things in *Inland Empire* take big and nonlinear leaps. Initially, it appears as though the movie is about an aging actress, Nikki Grace (Laura Dern), who is happy to have scored a lead role in a movie, a Southern melodrama called *On High in Blue Tomorrows*. Her happiness is diminished somewhat when a creepy old Polish woman claiming to be a neighbor (Grace Zabriskie) comes to Nikki's house and proceeds to tell her an old folk tale about murder.

Nikki and her young, handsome costar, Devon Berk (Justin Theroux), begin table readings with their acclaimed director, Kingsley Stewart (Jeremy Irons). They are upset to hear that the film is actually a remake of a film that was never finished. They would probably be more upset if they knew that the film was cursed and that an alternate universe version of Nikki is lurking around their set. But that will come later (or will it?). As the actors film scenes of their characters Susan Blue and Billy Side falling in love with each other, the actors start falling for each other, too.

It is perhaps normal for an actress to become very involved with her character, but Nikki seems to actually transform into her character for real. Is Nikki really a wealthy actress or is she a poor woman living in a dark apartment? Or perhaps she is a prostitute working in 1930s Poland, or is it current-day Hollywood Boulevard?

Who is the prostitute who nervously watches a static-filled television? And finally, what exactly are those rabbits supposed to mean? Despite the film's three hour running time, none of this ever becomes clear.

Critics were generally baffled by the film, and the ratings they gave depended on their tolerance for such bafflement. Ty Burr of the *Boston Globe* wrote: "It's useless to judge the new movie as a movie when in fact it's cubism, relentlessly applied to celluloid like thick smears of oil on a canvas." Manohla Dargis of the *New York Times* called it "one of the few films…that deserves to be called art," then went on to say, "*Inland Empire* isn't a film to love. It is a work to admire, to puzzle through, to wrestle with. Its pleasures are fugitive, even frustrating." "I can't totally recommend *Inland Empire*," wrote Gene Seymour of *Newsday*, "but something tells me I'd be a fool to totally dismiss it." Owen Gleiberman of *Entertainment Weekly* gave the film a C and wrote: "The best defense I can muster for David Lynch's *Inland Empire*, a three-hour, shot-on-video head-trip experiment in how to leave an audience baffled to the point of numbness is that there's no director I'd rather watch disappear up his own posterior." Finally, Carina Chocano of the *Los Angeles Times* wrote: "It's a dreamlike state of altered conscientiousness that lasts for hours. It's a piece of music in which a theme is repeated above and below its first statement. It's a tough movie to sit though."

Jill Hamilton

CREDITS

Nikki/Susan: Laura Dern
Devon/Billy: Justin Theroux
Kingsley Stewart: Jeremy Irons
Freddie Howard: Harry Dean Stanton
Visitor: Grace Zabriskie
Piotrek: Peter J. Lucas
Marilyn: Diane Ladd
Doris: Julia Ormond
Henry the Butler: Ian Abercrombie
Rabbit: Scott Coffey (Voice)
Rabbit: Naomi Watts (Voice)
Origin: USA, Poland, France
Language: English
Released: 2006
Production: Mary Sweeney, David Lynch; StudioCanal, Asymmetrical Productions, Camerimage 2; released by 518 Media Inc./Absurda
Directed by: David Lynch
Written by: David Lynch
Cinematography by: Odd Geir Saether
Sound: David Lynch
Editing: David Lynch
Art Direction: Christina Wilson
Costumes: Heidi Birens, Karen Baird
MPAA rating: R
Running time: 172 minutes

REVIEWS

Los Angeles Times Online. December 15, 2006.
New York Times Online. December 6, 2006.
Premiere Magazine Online. December 7, 2006.
Rolling Stone Online. November 21, 2006.
Variety Online. September 6, 2006.
Village Voice Online. December 5, 2006.

INSIDE MAN

It looked like the perfect bank robbery. But you can't judge a crime by its cover.
—Movie tagline

Box Office: $88.5 million

Directed by Spike Lee from a script by first-time screenwriter Russell Gewirtz, *Inside Man* is a taut, clever thriller that hearkens back to one of Lee's personal favorites, the classic *Dog Day Afternoon* (1975), but, at the same time, feels wholly of this moment, presenting a post-9/11 New York City fraught with racial and ethnic tensions that are always bubbling just under the surface. *Inside Man* is a genre piece, a bank robbery/heist film propelled by witty dialogue, first-rate performances from the entire cast (especially the three leads), and a well-paced plot that keeps our attention to the very end. The risk of taking on such a mainstream production is that the independent-minded, socially conscious Lee could be seen as selling out by making a studio product. The irony is that Lee has not only made one of his best films and an accomplished thriller, but imbued it with a subtext that, for all its subtlety and nuance, says more about our contemporary mind-set and race relations than many of his other films that are far more obvious and even heavy-handed about their politics.

Clive Owen plays Dalton Russell, the ringleader behind an elaborate bank heist in New York City's financial district. Despite acting for much of the film with a mask on his face, Owen is able to convey the menace, humor, and intelligence of this mastermind and even make him a sympathetic character. Dressed as painters, Russell and a team of three others enter a bank and proceed to take the employees and customers hostage, forcing them to don painters' uniforms so that no one will be able to distinguish them from the criminals. A detective named Keith Frazier (Denzel

Washington) and his partner, Bill Mitchell (Chiwetel Ejiofor), are called in to head up the team dealing with the crisis. It is a tremendous opportunity since a cloud of suspicion hangs over Frazier over some missing money in an earlier case, and his promotion to detective first grade has stalled. Washington walks a fine line as a man in charge and yet vulnerable if things do not go well. Like his antagonist, Washington's Frazier has a funny side that makes for some great exchanges between these smart adversaries.

Complicating an already tense situation is the fact that the debonair founder and president of the bank, Arthur Case (Christopher Plummer), is very worried about something personal in the vault that, if exposed, could ruin him. He summons Madeline White (Jodie Foster), a savvy power broker whose precise job is unclear but who has entree to the highest echelons of society. Through her connections with the mayor, she gains access to the crime scene, thus beginning a very contentious relationship with Frazier. Foster is coolly elegant and sexy, playing a shrewd businesswoman who never has to raise her voice to exert her influence, but who is also proud to show off her gorgeous legs.

Much of the film is a three-way cat-and-mouse game between the robbers, law enforcement, and Madeline, but what lifts the script above the typical heist flick is the subtext of racial and ethnic strife that animates many of the interactions. The bank hostages form a broad, multicultural group that we would expect in New York City, and, when one, Vikram Walia (Waris Ahluwalia), is released to the police, his turban leads a cop to misidentify him as an Arab and, it is implied, a possible terrorist—in reality, he is a Sikh. But even in the midst of Vikram's complaints about racial profiling, Frazier jokes, "I bet you can get a cab though," thus defusing the hostile situation.

The multicultural stew is played for more fun when the police bug the bank and think that the robbers are speaking in a foreign tongue, possibly from Central Europe but one that nevertheless they cannot recognize. Frazier pipes the broadcast out into the street because he just assumes that the city is so diverse that any ethnicity can be found at a moment's notice. Sure enough, a man immediately knows that the language is Albanian because he used to be married to an Albanian. While it turns out that the robbers have outsmarted the police and were merely playing an old recording to throw them off track and stall for time, the offhand ethnic detail nevertheless resonates and amuses.

But the subtext that connects the film's characters goes beyond race to a broader statement about the human condition and is best articulated by a little boy, Brian (Amir Ali Said), whose words are more profound than he realizes. Sitting with Russell in the bank's vault, Brian looks around at all the money and declares, "You're trying to get paid too," a line that, it turns out, applies to just about everyone in the film. And when he is being questioned by the police—the film periodically flashes forward to interrogations taking place after the hostage crisis is over—it is impossible for him to tell the robbers from the hostages. "With the masks, they look all the same," Brian observes. These guileless statements, taken together, cut to the core of human relationships, for, in this cross section of society, everyone really is the same. That is to say, trying to get paid. From a minor character such as the Albanian ex-wife, who expects the police to fix her parking tickets as a price for her help, to Madeline who, in working for Case, is helping a man cover his Nazi past, everyone indeed has their price. Case is the most venal of all, a man who, in betraying Jews to the Nazis during World War II, made a fortune in blood money that enabled him to start his first bank and enjoy a career of respectability cloaking a shameful past. Even Frazier, an upstanding character who is ultimately cleared of suspicion involving the missing money, declares, "Everybody's getting theirs. I'm gonna get mine," as he looks forward to his overdue promotion. No one, not even the hero, is immune from looking out for himself.

Lest it seem that *Inside Man* is weighed down by heavy social issues, it works beautifully as a suspenseful thriller and hostage tale. The standoffs between Russell and Frazier are edgy yet playful; during their one in-person meeting, when Russell learns that Frazier has cold feet about marrying his girlfriend because of a lack of money, Russell admonishes him that love should trump financial concerns, as if relationship advice were normal banter between a criminal and detective.

When the police finally make their move to storm the bank—at a certain point, Frazier loses command of the situation to Captain Darius (Willem Dafoe)—the hostages and the robbers (also dressed as hostages) flee, but Russell stays behind, secure in a little cell he and his cohorts have constructed for him behind the bank's storage room. With no hostages harmed and nothing apparently missing form the vault, the police are ultimately stumped. Only Frazier continues to investigate and discovers a safe-deposit box with no official record, one belonging to Case. The diamonds in the box have been cleaned out, but Russell has left behind a ring that allows Frazier to trace Case's war crimes. Visiting Case and then Madeline, Frazier makes it clear that he has the upper hand, although it is not clear what, if any, action he will take.

Frazier receives the promotion he coveted, which, it is implied, Madeline helped push along to reciprocate for getting access to Russell during the siege. However,

Frazier receives something from Russell as well—a diamond. In a coincidence that could only happen in the movies, after hiding in his makeshift room for several days, Russell is leaving the bank at the precise moment when Frazier is coming in to investigate the safe-deposit box. Russell brushes up against Frazier and slips the diamond in his pocket. The implication, of course, is that now Frazier can marry his girlfriend, thus following up on their previous conversation about love and marriage. It is not only a funny ending but also a final detail of moral ambiguity that makes Frazier himself just a bit complicit in the crime he was investigating.

Inside Man is especially exciting because, on its face, it looks like a conventional genre movie. And yet, in casting an eye on a city where ethnic divisions are ever present and where just about everyone is out to get theirs, Lee and Gewirtz use the genre for ironic commentary about where we are today; as fractured as we may sometimes be as a country, what unites us, it seems, is self-interest, whether it takes the form of major crimes or petty greed. It is a view of human nature that might be depressing were it not leavened with a wicked sense of humor and packaged so slyly in such a great popular entertainment.

Peter N. Chumo II

CREDITS

Detective Keith Frazier: Denzel Washington
Dalton Russell: Clive Owen
Madeline White: Jodie Foster
Arthur Case: Christopher Plummer
Captain John Darius: Willem Dafoe
Detective Bill Mitchell: Chiwetel Ejiofor
Captain Coughlin: Peter Gerety
Mobile Command Officer Rourke: Daryl (Chill) Mitchell
Stevie: Kim Director
Miriam Douglas: Marcia Jean Kurtz
Vikram Walia: Waris Ahluwalia
Brian: Amir Ali Said
Origin: USA
Language: English
Released: 2006
Production: Brian Grazer; Universal Pictures, Imagine Entertainment, Brian Grazer Productions; released by Universal
Directed by: Spike Lee
Written by: Russell Gewirtz
Cinematography by: Matthew Libatique
Music by: Terence Blanchard
Sound: William Sarokin
Editing: Barry Alexander Brown
Art Direction: Chris Shriver
Costumes: Donna Berwick
Production Design: Wynn Thomas
MPAA rating: R
Running time: 129 minutes

REVIEWS

Boxoffice Online. March 24, 2006.
Chicago Sun-Times Online. March 24, 2006.
Entertainment Weekly. March 31, 2006, p. 40.
Los Angeles Times Online. March 24, 2006.
New York Times Online. March 24, 2006.
San Francisco Chronicle Online. March 24, 2006.
Variety Online. March 18, 2006.
Village Voice Online. March 24, 2006.
Washington Post. March 24, 2006, p. C1.

QUOTES

Dalton: "My name is Dalton Russell. Pay strict attention to what I say because I choose my words carefully and I never repeat myself."

INVINCIBLE

Dreams are not lived on the sidelines.
—Movie tagline

Box Office: $57.8 million

In South Philadelphia in the 1970s, football is more than a game. It's the very lifeblood of long-suffering working-class guys. The memory of a championship-winning touchdown kept one man going even through his wife's long illness and through years of hard factory labor. And it's his son who was brought up on these barely articulated hopes.

In *Invincible,* a true-to-life story of how South Philly bartender Vince Papale (Mark Wahlberg) lived every fan's dream, an underdog sports saga is nicely embedded in the specifics of a time and place. First-time director Ericson Core deftly opens the film with shots that both introduce characters and define lunch-bucket urban America. Not since *8 Mile* has a major U.S. city looked so authentically gritty and industrial as Philadelphia looks in this film.

After the brilliant opening credits sequence, which seem to promise a movie that will use sports to tackle social issues, *Invincible* settles quickly into a predictable yarn with few surprises. But the settings remain true to life and the soundtrack of popular music true to the era.

For Papale and his friends, days spent toiling at the Westinghouse plant or looking for work, nights in the bar or sitting on stoops and talking about friends lost to Vietnam, are redeemed in Friday night neighborhood football games in a scrubby vacant lot illuminated by the headlights of their parked cars. This is where these guys have their only real shot at winning anything.

From this vacant lot to the bleachers in Veterans Stadium is a small leap of imagination for these football fanatics. Just like boys, watching their heroes inspires their own fantasies on the gridiron. But what happens when their heroes no longer inspire? Frustration abounds.

Philadelphians are known as the toughest sports fans in the U.S., and this film makes a stab at explaining why. These men desperately need someone to live out their dreams, and they don't tolerate less than all-out effort, because that's the way they live their lives. They're knowledgeable about the game and appreciative of hard work, and disdainful of prima donnas. And that's why they're so angry and disappointed with their Eagles, whose proud history has been trashed by recent indifferent losing seasons.

Into the wreckage of this team comes a new coach, Dick Vermeil (Greg Kinnear), who's come from a California college into a crucible of football fervor. Vermeil's first step as Eagles head coach is to announce an open tryout—more to pump up fan enthusiasm than with any expectation of finding a useable player.

The film takes its time getting us to the point where Papale tries out, making it clear that his decision is more than a personal crisis of confidence, it's a test of the whole neighborhood's integrity. Like his friends, Papale has suffered plenty—he's first laid off from his part-time job as a substitute teacher, and then his wife of five years walks out on him, leaving only a note that says, in essence, you'll never amount to anything.

Down at Max's bar, Papale picks up more hours and an immediate love interest. Janet (Elizabeth Banks) suddenly appears as a new bartender (the owner's cousin from New York) almost immediately after Vince's wife leaves. The plot couldn't be more obvious—the new girl on the scene is not only pretty, perky, and kind, she's as big a football fanatic as the rest of the crew (though a fan of the hated rival New York Giants), trading trivia with the best of them. Also, she's the only female in Vince's world. None of these men seem to have wives or girlfriends or women they work with. The world of the film is overwhelmingly male, as if these folks are living in an alternate universe of long ago.

As his buddies urge him to go to the tryout, Vince borrows money from his father, establishing the paternal line of football-as-life inheritance as dad retells the story of that 1948 Eagles player's touchdown.

Wahlberg, as usual, plays the silent, brooding type well. He doesn't display much emotion and seems remarkably free of anger (except for the scene where his wife leaves him and he pounds the walls of their apartment). Wahlberg's is a repressed masculinity, and he's a saintly sort of martyr, and a reluctant hero. There's barely a trace of ego, and he makes Papale into an almost iconic sort of loyal, forgiving fan who can barely even entertain a dream of this magnitude, much less realize it.

Once the football begins, the film remains keenly observant, though its best moves seem to pick their way through a minefield of cliches. A remarkable number of quiet little moments move the film along, including several in which Kinnear, who seems miscast—too nice a guy to be a football coach—shares Papale's rookie jitters. Kinnear is almost playing the same character as Wahlberg—the innocent with a big heart who dares to dream. Kinnear, who plays besieged and bewildered better than macho, just sounds barely credible when he tries to be a tough-talking coach.

Insurmountable odds are one essential ingredient for a sports movie, and *Invincible* has them. It also has the requisite longing for a more innocent time. Thirty years ago, the idea that a fan could bridge the gap between rooting for and playing for a pro team was hard to imagine; today, it would be impossible. The filmmakers seem to regard the 1970s as the fading end of innocence, and the soundtrack speaks to the era as a time of idealism being crushed. But the movie goes light on the themes it brings up. Many of Vince's buddies go on strike at Westinghouse, but their battle is content-free and colorless. We don't even know what they're striking for, all we know is that this is another cross the workingmen have to bear.

Given the predictability of the plot, and the similarity to so many other underdog sports movies, *Invincible* is surprisingly watchable. It is restrained when other sports films might be loud and boisterous. While it seems to stretch to invent subplots—a running feud between Vince and a buddy named John is insufficiently explained—*Invincible* stays true to form and wants desperately to probe the heart of what it means to be a diehard fan. That it fails to move that explanation far beyond a cliche is the film's big disappointment, but the movie certainly possesses a pleasing attitude. It's straightforward if sometimes sappy, and it doesn't grandstand. And it seems to delight in itself, loving its own story so much we're won over despite the frequent cornball moments.

Core, a cinematographer by trade, indulges himself with too many slow-motion shots, but the football action is well staged, and it is when Wahlberg is on the field that he's most credible. He captures precisely the agony of an aging athlete in deep water, struggling to stay afloat. He betrays his emotions with tiny eye movements and head nods; he's a consummate actor of the understated. When he returns to the neighborhood alley game in the middle of a pelting rainstorm, the scenes of men wrestling and running in the mud seem to approach the essence of sports' appeal—the love of the game, the joy of striving for the sake of striving.

Michael Betzold

CREDITS

Vince Papale: Mark Wahlberg
Dick Vermeil: Greg Kinnear
Janet: Elizabeth Banks
Frank Papale: Kevin Conway
Max: Michael Rispoli
Tommy: Kirk Acevedo
Leonard Tose: Michael Nouri
Wade Chambers: Jack Kehler
Sharon Papale: Lola Glaudini
Carol Vermeil: Paige Turco
Pete: Michael Kelly
Origin: USA
Language: English
Released: 2006
Production: Gordon Gray, Mark Ciardi, Ken Mok; Mayhem Pictures, Walt Disney Pictures; released by Buena Vista
Directed by: Ericson Core
Written by: Brad Gann
Cinematography by: Ericson Core
Music by: Mark Isham
Sound: James Sabat
Editing: Jerry Greenberg
Art Direction: Charley Beal
Costumes: Susan Lyall
Production Design: Sarah Knowles
MPAA rating: PG
Running time: 104 minutes

REVIEWS

Boxoffice Online. August 25, 2006.
Chicago Sun-Times Online. August 25, 2006.
Entertainment Weekly. September 1, 2006, p. 51.
Los Angeles Times Online. August 25, 2006.
New York Times Online. August 25, 2006.
San Francisco Chronicle. August 25, 2006, p. E5.
Variety Online. August 22, 2006.
Washington Post. August 25, 2006, p. C6.

QUOTES

Frank (to son Vince): "A man can only take so much failure."

TRIVIA

The real Vince Papale is six foot two while actor Mark Wahlberg is about five foot eight.

J

JACKASS NUMBER TWO

When is the last time a movie made you beg for mercy?
—Movie tagline

Box Office: $72.7 million

When MTV first came out with the television show *Jackass,* as well as being a dynamic show for the producers, it was a breakthrough for immature boys everywhere. The show featured Johnny Knoxville and Bam Margera, regular guys who were pro skateboarders and all around adrenaline junkies. The secondary cast of "characters" were just as much fun as the "stars" and included Bam's parents, Steve-O and the classic and wonderful Wee Man. These guys would perform stunt after stunt that increasingly became not just more dangerous but more idiotic in nature. The show was widely popular amongst the MTV audience for its outrageousness style. The footage was poorly lit and jumpy at best. It always had an air of home movie making which felt like watching friends videotaping their own stunts. This type of "style" was its charm and one of the reasons young people around the world embraced it.

The show eventually went off the air, but not before MTV had made *Jackass: The Movie* (2002). One reason the film was better than the show was that the film was free from the restraints of television censorship. The boys were able to let loose and really pull out all the stops. The beauty of *Jackass: The Movie* was that it had pranks that made fun of themselves as well as other people. The similar, skit-driven movie *Borat* (2006), also brilliant in it's idiocy, is purely a vehicle for showing the stupidity of others It's simply a joyful, fly-on-the-wall look at one's craziest high school friends in action.

If you know either the original TV show or the first *Jackass* film, you will not be shocked to read that *Jackass Number Two* is much of the same. And if you are the kind of person who liked the first *Jackass,* and you know who you are, you will like this one just as much. To keep things fresh *Jackass Number Two* periodically features tricks that require serious makeup and prosthetics, transforming the now famous stars into people others may not recognize. Even if you find these guys disgusting, it's hard to dislike them because of the fun they seem to be having.

This reviewer's audience at *Jackass Number Two* screamed out loud and was not afraid to participate in the film, which can make for a highly enjoyable movie experience. Oftentimes, audience interaction takes away from the film, but in the case of *Jackass Number Two* it almost seems a necessary part of the film. The same can be said of the original, proving that both films are an interactive experience begging the audience to cringe, yell, scream while daring one to look away all at the same time.

Laura Abraham

CREDITS

Himself: Johnny Knoxville
Himself: Bam Margera
Himself: Chris Pontius
Himself: Ryan Dunn
Himself: Steve-O
Himself: Dave England

Himself: Preston Lacy
Himself: Ehren McGhehey
Origin: USA
Language: English
Released: 2006
Production: Spike Jonze, Jeff Tremaine, Johnny Knoxville; MTV Films, Lynch Siderow Prods., Dickhouse; released by Paramount Pictures
Directed by: Jeff Tremaine
Written by: Preston Lacy, Sean Cliver
Cinematography by: Dimitry Elyashkavich, Lance Bangs, Rick Kosick
Sound: Cordell Mansfield
Music Supervisor: Manish Raval
Editing: Seth Casriel, Matthew Probst, Scott Simmons
Art Direction: J.P. Blackmon
MPAA rating: R
Running time: 95 minutes

REVIEWS

Entertainment Weekly. September 29, 2006, p. 58.
Hollywood Reporter Online. September 22, 2006.
Los Angeles Times Online. September 22, 2006.
New York Times Online. September 22, 2006.
San Francisco Chronicle. September 22, 2006, p. E5.
Variety Online. September 21, 2006.
Washington Post. September 22, 2006, p. C1.

JET LI'S FEARLESS
(Fearless)
(Huo Yuan Jia)

Jet Li in his final martial arts epic.
—Movie tagline
"Mastering others is strength. Mastering yourself makes you fearless." Lao Tzu
—Movie tagline

Box Office: $24.6 million

Jet Li's Fearless (a.k.a *Fearless* and *Huo Yuan Jia*), Li's reported final Wushu (martial arts) film, chronicles the life of martial arts master Huo Yuanjia, a legendary figure in Chinese history who famously fought four foreign fighters in a single day in the early years of the twentieth century. It is a fitting that he should choose to play Huo Yuanjia in his last "fighting" film, as his connection to that name goes all the way back to one of his first and best films, *Fist of Legend* (1994), where his character was a student of Huo Yuanjia. Jet Li seems to have come full circle, now the same age as the master when he died and echoing the same philosophy of the virtues of martial arts: that it is not about winning or losing, but about spiritual and physical self-improvement. As with *Fist of Legend* and many times since, producer/star Li partners with fight choreographer Yuen Wo Ping to create some of the most exhilarating fight sequences, as fast as they are brutal, and a testament to the fact that Li still has his chops. From the opening shot, director Ronny Yu shows a China in a struggle for its identity

The film opens in 1910 Shanghai as western influences are invading the Chinese way of life and stealing its identity. It is in this backdrop that Huo battles three opponents representing three countries and three distinct fighting disciplines: a British boxer, a Spanish fencer, and a German spear fighter. Defeating them all one by one, he prepares for the fourth and final bout against Tanaka (Shido Nakamura), a Japanese karate expert. A flashback to thirty years ago, shows him as a child in his home town of Tianjin, China, watching others train with his father Huo Endi (Collin Chou). His father was a master who refused to train his son, so Yuanjia began to secretly watch his father teach, and trained himself. One day he watches his father fight another man in a public bout where his father loses. The son of the man teases Yuanjia to the point where he challenges him to a fight in the same arena, where he is quickly humiliated. Vowing to become the best martial artist ever, he spends several years training as hard as he can until he grows into a very formidable fighter.

After winning several bouts he quickly becomes known as one of the best fighters in China. With an undefeated record he becomes increasingly selfish and arrogant. He is a master now and quickly finds himself surrounded by eager students. A rival master named Chin arrives in town and starts causing problems, including injuring one of Yuanjia's students. Yuanjia confronts Chin to a fight in the middle of the restaurant owned by his friend Jinsun (Yong Dong) where Chin is with friends celebrating his birthday. After a brutal fight that destroys the restaurant, he kills Chin in a fit of pent up fury.

When Yuanjia arrives home he finds that his mother and daughter have been murdered out of revenge. When he goes to Chin's home that evening, Chin's son admits to murdering his family right before he slices open his own throat.

Devastated, Yuanjia leaves town and tries to drown himself in a river, but is saved by a blind village girl named Moon (Betty Sun). Along with her grandmother (Yun Qu) Moon slowly brings Yuanjia back to health. He is put to work in the village rice fields, where at first he doesn't do so well, but many years pass and he begins to adapt to his new life. He learns kindness and mercy and that winning at all costs is not as important as your spiritual well being.

One day he leaves the village to pay respects to his dead parents, promising to return to Moon as soon as he can. When he returns to Tianjing it is 1907 and he is surprised to see the town has changed. No longer is it the small town he remembered, but a busy city with western troops and shops. He visits his parents' graves and pays his respects and goes to see Master Chin's family and apologize to them.

He returns to his home to find it empty and deserted save for family friend Lai Foo, who has been taking care of it in his absence. He has barely managed to hold onto the property even though creditors came every day to collect their money and had taken everything piece by piece.

After he sees a newspaper headline about an American fighter named Hercules O'Brien (Nathan Jones) traveling the country bragging that he is defeating "the sick men of Asia" Yuanjia goes to see his former friend Jinsun to apologize and ask for money to go to Shanghai to fight Hercules. At first Jinsun doesn't think it is a good idea but, sensing a change in Yuanjia, loans him the money.

In Shanghai Yuanjia defeats O'Brien in a public match that gains the respect of the Chinese people and annoyance of the members of the Foreign Chamber of Commerce, who feel that Yuanjia is a threat to their colonial power. They decide to set up a public spectacle that will insure their victory: Four of the best foreign fighters against Yuanjia in one night. The Japanese member vowing that defeat is guaranteed and that after the bout China "will have nothing to brag about." For the future of his martial arts school and the pride of his people, Yuanjia agrees to the bout.

Back in 1910 he fights the fourth and final opponent Tanaka to a stalemate. During a break, the Japanese council member switches Yuanjia's tea with poison. Dizzy and spitting blood Yuanjia fights on, eventually defeating Tanaka and giving the Chinese people a sense of respect. As he dies in the hospital he has a vision of Moon on a hillside, where he is able to say goodbye.

David E. Chapple

CREDITS

Juo Yuanjia: Jet Li
Anno Tanaka: Shido Nakamura
Moon: Betty Sun
Nong Jinsun: Yong Dong
Hercules O'Brien: Nathan Jones
Huo Endi: Collin Chou
Grandma: Yun Qu
Origin: China, Hong Kong
Language: English, Chinese
Released: 2006
Production: Yang Buting, Jet Li; China Film, Elite Group Enterprises, Xing He Investment; released by Rogue Pictures
Directed by: Ronny Yu
Written by: Wang Bin, Chris Chow, Christine To, Li Feng
Cinematography by: Hang-Seng Poon
Music by: Mei Linmao
Sound: Wu Lala
Editing: Virginia Katz, Richard Learoyd
Art Direction: Kenneth Mak
Costumes: Thomas Chong
MPAA rating: PG-13
Running time: 103 minutes

REVIEWS

Boxoffice Online. September 22, 2006.
Hollywood Reporter Online. September 21, 2006.
Los Angeles Times Online. September 22, 2006.
New York Times Online. September 22, 2006.
Premiere Magazine Online. September 21, 2006.
San Francisco Chronicle. September 22, 2006, p. E5.
Variety Online. March 22, 2006.
Washington Post Online. September 22, 2006.

TRIVIA

Director Ronny Yu edited forty minutes out of the final release, thus cutting out the roles played by Michelle Yeoh and Thai boxer Somluck Kamsing.

JOHN TUCKER MUST DIE

Don't Get Mad, Get Even.
—Movie tagline

Box Office: $41 million

With no formal instruction on how the dating world works, teenage girls must turn to sources like books, friends and movies to figure out its mysteries. As long as there are teenage girls looking to date teenage boys, there will be films like *John Tucker Must Die.*

Director Betty Thomas, who showed a deft hand for comedy in *The Brady Bunch Movie* (1995) and Howard Stern's *Private Parts* (1997) keeps *John Tucker Must Die* moving along at a brisk pace. Parts of the story, written by Jeff Lowell, strains credibility, but Thomas keeps the proceedings moving along quickly enough so there is little time to dwell on the plot problems. She is also helped by a likable, professional cast, who inject whatever believability they can scrounge up into their underwritten parts.

The teen referred to in the title is John Tucker (Jesse Metcalfe), the all-around popular guy of the high school. When not leading the basketball team to victory, he dates three different high school girls: budding broadcaster Carrie (Arielle Kebbel); vegan activist Beth (Sophia Bush); and head cheerleader Heather (Ashanti). When the three find out about each other, they decide to get revenge on John. Instead of killing him, as the title would suggest, they decide on a fate worse than death—making him unpopular.

Unfortunately for the jealous girls, popularity seems to be inextricably wired into John's DNA. When the girls spike his muscle-building drink with estrogen, John starts getting very emotional on the basketball court. "He's being mean!" he shrieks to the referee. But instead of being shunned for his odd behavior, John finds a whole new level of popularity as a sensitive man who is not afraid to cry. When the girls spread the rumor that John has herpes, he takes the opportunity to become an activist for herpes education.

Finally, the girls bring out their most devious plan yet. They recruit new girl Kate (Brittany Snow), as bait for John. The idea is that they will get John to fall in love with Kate, then she will drop him so that he can get a taste of what it is like to be rejected. Kate is doubtful about the idea, but since she is so desperate to finally be accepted, she agrees. As she says in a voiceover, Kate is used to being invisible in high school. Her mother, Lori (Jenny McCarthy), is perennially choosing bad men to date. So predictable is this pattern that Kate has taken to calling them all Skip, because that is what they end up doing. Whenever a man breaks Lori's heart, she and Kate move to a different town.

Since the three girls do not consider Kate ready to snare John, they put her through some rigorous romance training, complete with such valuable tips as pausing for several seconds before answering a boy. The plan works, and soon John is indeed falling in love with Kate. But she might also be falling for him. This could make for some awkward plot problems, so another Tucker brother, Scott (Penn Badgley), is handily dropped into the story to help cauterize the loose plot ends. Viewers will know that Scott and Kate are destined for each other because they both like early Elvis Costello and Cheap Trick. Viewers might also notice that those pop culture references would be meaningful to someone, say, director Betty Thomas' age, rather than a teen in 2006. But such is the curse of the high school movie directed by someone who is well out of high school.

Nathan Rabin of *The Onion A.V. Club* was one who made fun of the film's dated pop culture references and wrote: "One of the unheralded guilty pleasures of inane teen sex comedies comes from watching middle-aged filmmakers haplessly attempt to gauge the pulse of teen America." Kyle Smith of the *New York Post* wrote: "As tasty as a quart of s'mores, *John Tucker Must Die* is a slumber-party that belongs of the same shelf as *Bring It On* (2000) and *10 Things I Hate About You* (1999)." Roger Ebert of the *Chicago Sun-Times* was well aware that he was not part of the film's demographic and wrote: "It's about two-fifths bad, mostly toward the incoherent ending, but the ratio is...well, not bad." Finally, Wesley Morris of the *Boston Globe* wrote that "the movie is as inconsequentially pleasant as its star, and far nicer than the title lets on, too."

Jill Hamilton

CREDITS

John Tucker: Jesse Metcalfe
Heather: Ashanti
Carrie: Arielle Kebbel
Kate: Brittany Snow
Beth: Sophia Bush
Lori: Jenny McCarthy
Chemistry Teacher: Fulvio Cecere
Scott: Penn Badgley
Origin: USA
Language: English
Released: 2006
Production: Bob Cooper, Michael Birnbaum; Landscape Entertainment; released by 20th Century Fox
Directed by: Betty Thomas
Written by: Jeff Lowell
Cinematography by: Anthony B. Richmond
Music by: Richard Gibbs
Sound: Patrick Ramsay
Music Supervisor: Alex Patsavas
Editing: Matthew Friedman
Art Direction: Bo Johnson
Costumes: Alexandra Welker
Production Design: Marcia Hinds
MPAA rating: PG-13
Running time: 82 minutes

REVIEWS

Chicago Sun-Times Online. July 28, 2006.
Hollywood Reporter Online. July 27, 2006.
Los Angeles Times Online. July 28, 2006.
New York Times Online. July 28, 2006.

San Francisco Chronicle. July 28, 2006, p. E7.
Variety Online. July 27, 2006.

QUOTES

Scott warns his brother John about Kate: "She likes old school Elvis Costello, listens to obscure podcasts, and she reads Dave Eggers. She's deep."

AWARDS

Nomination:

Golden Raspberries 2006: Worst Support. Actress (McCarthy)

JOYEUX NOEL

(Merry Christmas)

Christmas Eve, 1914. On a World War I battlefield, a Momentous Event changed the lives of soldiers from France, Germany and England.
—Movie tagline

Box Office: $1 million

As The Great War erupted across Europe in 1914, the requirements for joining the British Army included a minimum height of five feet eight inches for a potential recruit. By October of that same year, three inches were shaved from this prerequisite. Britain's casualty rate during the first three months of the war soared to a number almost equivalent to their army's original pre-war size. The height requirement was lowered once again to five foot three. In the Battle of Marne, French and British forces obstructed Germany's march to Paris. Both sides sustained a loss of half a million soldiers. Government propaganda in the United Kingdom obscured the true account of the ghastly carnage inflicted by machine gun fire which shredded bodies left littered in No Man's Land, that zone between opposing trenches occupied only by the unburied dead.

Author Erich Maria Remarque portrays similar events from a German perspective in perhaps the most celebrated novel about World War I, *All Quiet on the Western Front.* By the close of the "war to end all wars," ten million men were killed in battle. On Christmas Eve, 1914, a historical wartime anomaly occurred: French, Scottish, and German soldiers laid down their weapons and met in No Man's Land to celebrate the birth of the Messiah.

Writer/director Christian Carion addresses this stranger-than-fiction story, crafting the skillfully acted and directed *Joyeux Noel.* Despite Carion's melodramatic embellishments the story is a dramatic and powerful undertaking conveying an antiwar message by highlighting the humanity shared by enemies. Although pacifistic, it never loses momentum by becoming overbearingly didactic.

Among the characters Carion introduces are two brothers from a Scottish hamlet who are conscripted. One seems exuberantly enthusiastic about the prospect of leaving his tiny village, while his quiet, more vulnerable-looking brother does not carry the same elation. They are followed by the Anglican priest of their local parish, Father Palmer, who serves both as chaplain and stretcher-bearer in addition to being a proficient bagpipe player. Among the ranks of the French is Lt. Audebert (Guillaume Canet) who is in command of the regiment fighting alongside the Scots. He is a deeply burdened and conflicted young officer who is at odds with his father (Bernard Le Coq) who also serves as the general Audebert reports to. Prior to an attempt at building up troop morale by suggesting that they might soon be homebound before they combat their German counterparts nestled in trenches located within earshot of each other, he vomits.

Among the German troops is a famed opera tenor, Nikolaus Sprink (Benno Furman) who has been summoned to perform a night of duets with his Danish lover, Anna Sorensen (Diane Kruger) before a small congregation of high ranking officers. It is Anna who gained approval from the upper echelons to grant Sprink's temporary respite from trench duty. Their singing is initially stilted due to Sprink's battle fatigue, but the duo provide a successful performance although the actors are unable to conceal the fact that they are only lip synching to the true chorus of Rolando Villazon and Nathalie Dessay.

Sprink, loyal to his regiment, insists on returning in order to sing to them as well. Anna, in turn, refuses to remain behind and joins him. They arrive to find the German trenches full of tiny tannenbaums supplied by Berlin. Sprink and Anna sing "Silent Night" and "Adeste Fidelis" while the Germans place tiny fur trees above their bulwarks and their front is quickly lit up. Father Palmer accompanies Sprink with his bagpipes in an apparent move of spiritual conviction and Sprink blindly springs up into No Man's Land to continue his song as he approaches the allied force. He is not fired upon. Soldiers from both sides cautiously peek over their fortifications, hesitantly climb out, and lay down their arms as they slowly approach each other among the scattered corpses of their respective countrymen.

The three commanding officers form a triumvirate and agree to a temporary cease-fire for Christmas Eve. The men enjoy this unprecedented detente by sharing champagne and chocolate and exchanging letters they wish to have mailed to loved ones on the other side. Father Palmer facilitates an impromptu Mass in Latin; a language, which like music, is universally understood. This unofficial reconciliation is as ordinary as it is bizarre and it becomes blazingly clear that these men, sworn to kill each other in the name of God, carry the same traits and backgrounds. Most are tradesmiths or agrarians and are common men within their nations. An observation by Lieutenant Audebert provides a pervasive insight bearing no borders: "We have more in common with the German soldiers than with the French politicians that are sending us to war." This cessation of hostilities is extended into Christmas Day where soccer games are played and the dead are buried. The kinship experienced is so acute that both groups of men huddle in the same trenches in order to avoid artillery fire bombarding their ramparts at different forewarned intervals.

Once this fraternization is discovered by the powers that be, the soldiers are dealt with harshly and with disdain; placing their actions on par with treason. They are quickly withdrawn and reintegrated at other locations along the front lines and are replaced with soldiers untainted by humanitarian regard—pawns to state mandated warfare. The war continues for four more years and the event becomes only a reprieve from certain death for these men.

In perhaps the film's most poignant scene, Father Palmer questions his sanctimonious bishop's chastisement by informing him that he felt led by Christ to perform what he has come to believe to be the most important Mass he will ever deliver. The Bishop is in accord with allied martinets and rebukes Father Palmer's compassionate acts, equating patriotism with divinity and proceeds to deliver a sermon that takes a passage from the Gospel of Matthew out of context. Palmer removes his wooden crucifix and walks away. Whether this is an abandonment of his faith or the Anglican Church is not known.

Joyeux Noel is a tapestry of significant themes, diverse cultures, and both subtle and emblazoned ironies. One such irony involves the German commander, Horstmayer (Daniel Bruhl). Not only is he Jewish, but his wife is French. Sadly, the viewer can make a tragic guess as to Horstmayer's fate even if he survives this First World War under the Kaiser with Germany's upcoming Fuhrer of the Third Reich. In one of the film's lighter moments, Horstmayer and Audebert learn they are both "courting" the same tabby cat that has apparently traversed both sides with flagrant disregard for the line of demarcation (even the ravages of war cannot change the feline temperament). Horstmayer has named the cat Nestor and Audebert has named the animal Felix. This minor subplot is also based on true events and in reality; the cat in question was suspected of spying and consequently executed by the French military. Carion shot the scene, but eventually had it excised as it overstretched the realm of credibility.

Although ultimately tragic in its sentiment, *Joyeux Noel*'s message of tolerance and charity should resonate soundly for many Christmas seasons to come.

David Metz Roberts

CREDITS

Anna Sorensen: Diane Kruger
Nikolaus Sprink: Benno Furmann
Lieutenant Audebert: Guillaume Canet
Palmer: Gary Lewis
Horstmayer: Daniel Bruhl
Jonathan: Steven Robertson
Gueusselin: Lucas Belvaux
General Audebert: Bernard Le Coq
Bishop: Ian Richardson
William: Robin Laing
La Chatelaine: Suzanne Flon
Le Chatelain: Michel Serrault
Ponchel: Dany Boon
Gordon: Alex Ferns
Jorg: Frank Witter
Le Kronprinz: Thomas Schmauser
Zimmermann: Joachim Bissmeier
Origin: France, Germany, Great Britain, Belgium, Romania
Language: English, French, German, Latin
Released: 2005
Production: Christophe Rossignon; Nord-Ouest, TF-1 Films, Senator Films Produktion, Artemis Films Production, Media Pro Pictures; released by UGC
Directed by: Christian Carion
Written by: Christian Carion
Cinematography by: Walther Vanden Ende
Music by: Philippe Rombi
Sound: Pierre Mertens
Editing: Andrea Sedlackova
Art Direction: Jean-Michel Simonet
Costumes: Alison Forbes-Myer
MPAA rating: PG-13
Running time: 110 minutes

REVIEWS

Boxoffice Online. March 3, 2006.
Chicago Sun-Times Online. March 10, 2006.
Los Angeles Times Online. March 3, 2006.
New York Times Online. March 3, 2006.
Premiere Magazine Online. March 3, 2006.
Variety Online. May 16, 2005.

JUST MY LUCK

Good luck charm. Bad luck magnet.
—Movie tagline

Everything changed in the wink of an eye.
—Movie tagline

Box Office: $17.3 million

Just My Luck is a sweet-natured, supernatural romance of two strangers, one with extraordinarily good luck and one with extreme bad luck, who magically switch fates and suddenly experience the world from vastly different points of view. Lindsay Lohan stars as Ashley Albright, a public relations executive who seems to have been born under a lucky star. From having bad weather clear up for her when she steps out on the street to meeting a handsome, rich man in an elevator and immediately getting a date, everything seems to go her way. Jake Hardin (Chris Pine), on the other hand, a would-be music producer, can never get a break, from stepping in puddles on stormy days to failing in his tireless marketing efforts on behalf of a young pop band that could be his ticket to success.

Directed by Donald Petrie and written by I. Marlene King and Amy B. Harris, *Just My Luck* aims to be a modern-day Cinderella story, a light diversion targeted at Lohan's young fans. And while the starlet does not make an enormous stretch as an actress, she demonstrates that she can make the transition to an adult role and succeed as a romantic comedy lead. She is very refreshing, both as a young beauty and as a physical comedienne gamely engaging in lots of slapstick and pratfalls. While the film itself feels pedestrian at times—the screenplay hits all the familiar notes and reversals of fortune we would expect from this formula—*Just My Luck* still entertains on the appeal of its two stars and its fairy-tale trappings.

While Ashley lives a very privileged life (her Fifth Avenue apartment would be out of reach for most young professionals in New York), she gets her big chance when her colleagues are late for a meeting with a demanding big-time music mogul, Damon Phillips (Faizon Love), and she improvises her way through a pitch that wins him over. Her idea to throw a glamorous masquerade ball puts her on the fast track to success; it also provides Jake with the venue where he can sneak in and pass as one of the professional dancers to get his band's demo to Phillips. At the big gala, Ashley and Jake run into each other and share a dance where they kiss, which, unbeknownst to each of them, transfers his bad luck to her and her good luck to him. Jake saves Phillips from being hit by a cab, and he is so grateful that Jake's band, the real-life McFly, gets an audition and then a music contract.

Ashley, on the other hand, experiences one calamity after another—from breaking a heel to getting thrown in jail and fired after inadvertently setting up her imperious boss, Peggy Braden (Missi Pyle), with a male escort (Carlos Ponce) to facing a flooded apartment and having to move in with two friends, Maggie (Samaire Armstrong) and Dana (Bree Turner), to nearly being electrocuted by an out-of-control hairdryer. Ashley's misfortunes may be broadly comic, but Lohan acquits herself well with this outlandish shtick. And after a fortune teller (Tovah Feldshuh) clues Ashley in to what really happened, there is a cute and funny sequence in which she goes on a scavenger hunt of sorts to find all the dancers from the party and kiss each one to try to get her luck back.

When she finally meets Jake after a punishing day, he is very kind to her because he sees all the misfortune she has endured and relates to her as a kindred spirit. He even helps her get his old job at a bowling alley, which leads to more episodes of misfortune, such as Ashley struggling to work the lane buffer, being swallowed up by the pinsetter, and facing electrocution while changing a neon bulb. Once again, this is not inspired comedy, to say the least, but it is entertaining fluff that works because Ashley is so winning in her obliviousness, and, at her core, a good-hearted heroine to root for, even if she once took for granted all of her good fortune. Moreover, while Pine and Lohan may not be the most magnetic screen couple, they play off each other quite nicely and develop a sweet rapport.

Ashley finally figures out Jake's identity and kisses him to take her luck back, which results in disaster at McFly's big concert until she has a change of heart and races to kiss him before he is ruined. Sidestepping the seemingly no-win issue of which one will end up with a lucky future, the film ends on a note of good cheer when they both kiss Katy (Makenzie Vega), Jake's little cousin, who is a bright kid but also plagued by misfortune, and thus transfer the luck to her.

Just My Luck is a case where old-fashioned charm triumphs over a trite script. It is also a great boon that Lohan is very likeable and even adorable as Ashley, no small feat considering that she could have been insufferable in her lucky phase. Sadly, the screenplay itself bungles every opportunity to set up more compelling conflicts. A sexy employee at the record company, for example, is obviously interested in Jake but exists only so that Ashley will mistakenly think that he has a girlfriend and never poses a serious roadblock to the romance. And Ashley's two gal pals are merely sounding boards for her but do not have very distinctive personalities. Maggie is a budding songwriter, but a conflict near the end revolving around whether McFly will sing one of her tunes is a tepid subplot.

Just My Luck is a workmanlike romantic comedy that does not do anything especially original but does impart a moral lesson. Ashley is never mean-spirited, but she does not appreciate all of her good fortune. Only by being brought low and seeing that her luck can be stripped from her at any time does she learn empathy for her fellow man. The movie does not belabor the point, to be sure, in what is, first and foremost, a light romance, but Ashley grows and becomes a woman who sees that there is more to life than being lucky.

Peter N. Chumo II

CREDITS

Ashley Albright: Lindsay Lohan
Jake Hardin: Chris Pine
Maggie: Samaire Armstrong
Dana: Bree Turner
Damon Phillips: Faizon Love
Peggy Braden: Missi Pyle
Katy: Makenzie Vega
Madame Z: Tovah Feldshuh
Antonio: Carlos Ponce
Origin: USA
Language: English
Released: 2006
Production: Arnon Milchan, Arnold Rifkin, Donald Petrie; released by 20th Century Fox
Directed by: Donald Petrie
Written by: I. Marlene King, Amy Harris
Cinematography by: Dean Semler
Music by: Teddy Castellucci
Sound: Tom Nelson
Editing: Debra Neil-Fisher
Art Direction: Dennis Bradford
Costumes: Gary Jones
Production Design: Ray Kluga
MPAA rating: PG-13
Running time: 108 minutes

REVIEWS

Boxoffice Online. May 12, 2006.
Chicago Sun-Times Online. May 12, 2006.
Entertainment Weekly Online. May 17, 2006.
Los Angeles Times Online. May 12, 2006.
New York Times Online. May 12, 2006.
Variety Online. May 11, 2006.

QUOTES

Jake: "Is it just me or did I just get lucky?"

AWARDS

Nomination:
Golden Raspberries 2006: Worst Actress (Lohan)

K

KEEPING MUM

Some family secrets are best kept...buried.
—Movie tagline

They took her in. Now she's taking them out.
—Movie tagline

Box Office: $1.6 million

Writer/director Niall Johnson taps into a long-standing tradition of wickedly funny British comedy, so dark and droll that it might shock American viewers, as Charlie Chaplin found out when, late in his career, he released his murderous comedy, *Monsieur Verdoux* (1947). A cult picture now, it was a "film maudit"that was taken out of circulation for seventeen years after its initial release. Chaplin's famous little tramp persona was replaced by a spirit from the dark side. Likewise, in *Keeping Mum* the Rowan Atkinson character, Walter Goodfellow, a rural clergyman in the village of Little Wallop, is far removed from Mr. Bean, the voiceless comic character Atkinson perfected for British television. In his *New York Times* preview, Dave Kehr warned readers that in this picture Atkinson "tries to shake the kiddie image of the Mr. Bean films," but true Bean consumers will take offense, since a great many adults were secret Bean fans to begin with.

Atkinson plays a muddled lump of pastoral piety, a man in search of a spine and a soul. For no clear reason, the Rev. Goodfellow has been selected to be the keynote speaker at a forthcoming clerical conference, and he spends most of the movie attempting to write his "sermon." It gives evidence of turning into a dull speech, until the mysterious new housekeeper arrives, and serves as his muse. This little comic parable has allegorical potential. The fable presents people of different ages facing and overcoming problems. The only thing not quite lifelike is that the Good seem to have a sort of advantage here. Little Petey Goodfellow and his sister face coming-of-age decisions, and the Rev. Goodfellow needs to regain his marital equilibrium.

The housekeeper, Grace Hawkins (Maggie Smith), is a lady with strong notions of morality, but she also has a troubled past. Unbeknownst to her employer, she has served prison time for murder. Why she turns to this particular family for employment is not at all clear until the end, but it turns out she has her reasons. During her tenure there, she mothers the family and gives the Reverend both inspiration and confidence, no matter that some murderous intent may also be involved, since the plot development is loaded with perverse turns.

New York Times reviewer Stephen Holden likened this fable to an *Alfred Hitchcock Presents* package, but it operates within the tradition of the Ealing comedy classics, such as *Kind Hearts and Coronets* (1951) and, perhaps even more to the point here, *The Ladykillers* (1955). In these black comedies, things are not exactly what they seem.

Grace Hawkins is a cherubic and pleasantly angelic presence who suddenly materializes in Little Wallop. And just in the nick of time, since the vicar's wife, Gloria (Kristin Scott Thomas), is slowly going mad with sexual frustration and suffering from marital neglect. She is secretly being courted by a vulgar American golf pro appropriately named Lance (Patrick Swayze), who wants her to run off with him to Australia. The Goodfellow children are also dangerously dysfunctional. Young son Petey (Toby Parkes) is mercilessly terrorized and taunted by school bullies, and adolescent daughter Holly (Tamsin Egerton) shows clear signs of being boy crazy, signs that her father, of course, is too preoccupied to notice. Frustrated Gloria can't sleep at night because of a neighbor's constantly barking dog. Grace sees to it that the dog conveniently disappears. The school bullies who chase Petey on their bicycles are thwarted when their brakes fail to work as they are pedaling at full tilt, thanks to Grace and her wire-cutters. But her most amazing transformation here is the change that Grace brings about by suggesting that Walter study the Song of Solomon, helping him to recover not only his humanity, but also a badly-needed sense of humor. Revitalized, Walter becomes the hit of the clerical convention, dazzling the regional clergy with his wit and good humor.

The film begins by offering the audience privileged information about Grace's backstory. We see her as a young woman (played by Emilia Fox), aboard a train with an enormous—and bloody—trunk, filled, it turns out, with the chopped-up remains of her unfaithful husband and his mistress. Young Grace is saved from the death penalty because, at the time of her capture, she is pregnant. She comes to Little Wallop four decades later, carrying that same trunk.

The British cast is up to the challenge of bringing the stereotypes to life in an agreeable and nearly convincing way. Atkinson is perfect as the clueless clergyman. As Stephen Holden wrote in his *New York Times* review, Scott Thomas is more than capable as "the chilly English beauty with a volcanic libido," and Maggie Smith is truly memorable as the ever-smiling "genteel psychopath"; only the leaden Swayze stumbles as the oversexed, uncouth American jock. Otherwise, this picture is near perfect in its execution, a triumph of tone and nuance. To claim, as one reviewer did, that this role was an unusual one for Maggie Smith is to overlook the comic potential of the dangerously absurd Miss Jean Brodie in her prime, as imagined by Muriel Spark and Jay Presson Allen. In fact, *Keeping Mum* is probably a role better matched to Smith's talents than the role of Professor Minerva McGonagall flitting around Hogwarts on her broomstick. Unfortunately *Keeping Mum* was probably too perverse and esoteric for American viewers, but for those attuned to black comedy, it was delicious.

James M. Welsh

CREDITS

Grace Hawkins: Maggie Smith
Walter Goodfellow: Rowan Atkinson
Lance: Patrick Swayze
Gloria: Kristin Scott Thomas
Rosie: Emilia Fox
Mr. Brown: James Booth
Mrs. Parker: Liz Smith
Holly: Tamsin Egerton
Petey: Toby Parkes
Origin: Great Britain
Language: English
Released: 2005
Production: Julia Palau, Matthew Payne; Isle of Man, Summit Entertainment, Azure Films; released by ThinkFilm
Directed by: Niall Johnson
Written by: Niall Johnson, Richard Russo
Cinematography by: Gavin Finney
Music by: Dickon Hinchliffe
Sound: Martin Trevis
Editing: Robin Sales
Art Direction: Simon Lamont
Costumes: Vicki Russell
Production Design: Crispian Sallis
MPAA rating: R
Running time: 103 minutes

REVIEWS

Chicago Sun-Times Online. September 29, 2006.
Entertainment Weekly. September 29, 2006, p. 58.
New York Times Online. September 15, 2006.
San Francisco Chronicle. September 29, 2006, p. E5.
Variety Online. December 6, 2005.
Village Voice Online. September 12, 2006.

TRIVIA

Film is dedicated to actor James Booth (Mr. Brown), who died in August 2005.

KEEPING UP WITH THE STEINS

Something's not quite kosher.
—Movie tagline

Box Office: $4.3 million

Keeping Up with the Steins is an extremely warm-hearted comedy that simultaneously, and accurately, skewers the excess of Hollywood while it emphasizes the importance of religion, tracing a young Jewish boy's journey into manhood. Director Scott Marshall has a strong Hollywood pedigree to draw from, both for the observations made within the film and in making the film itself, as the son of Garry Marshall (who also stars as Grandpa Irwin) and nephew of Penny Marshall. Like Mike Meyers doing Linda Richman, the Yiddish flies fast and furious, mostly from Grandpa Irwin, but thankfully the film refuses to make caricatures of its funny, dimensional characters in a film that invokes *Little Miss Sunshine* (2006) with its portrayal of a dysfunctional family that sticks together through trials and tribulations.

The film is narrated by its wonderfully normal protagonist, Benjamin Fiedler (Daryl Sabara) who attends the bar mitzvah of one of his peers, Zachary Stein (Carter Jenkins), whose dad is powerful Hollywood agent Arnie Stein (Larry Miller). It is no ordinary affair but an absolute spectacle taking place aboard a cruise ship and featuring a *Titanic* theme with Zach dramatically making his entrance to the party atop the bow of a moving model of the ship, exulting, "I'm king of the Torah!" alongside a Kate Winslet lookalike in costume. No expense is spared, as evidenced by the trained killer whale wearing a yarmulke. It's a bar mitzvah that is brilliant in its horrific over-indulgence.

Glowering in the background is Benji's dad Adam (Jeremy Piven), also a big Hollywood agent. Adam and Arnie are rivals; former partners who now live to compete with one another. Partly driven by his own miserable bar mitzvah, Adam vows to plan a mitzvah for Benji that will not only rival the Steins in its excess, but knock it out of the park, so to speak, with an elaborate baseball-themed bash that will take place in Dodger Stadium. His understanding wife Joanne (Jamie Gertz) is happy to help, along with the Stein's party planner Casey Nudelman (a funny Cheryl Hines), whom they've recruited.

While Adam furiously busies himself trying to fill Dodger Stadium with some six hundred guests and A-list talent that may include Neil Diamond singing the national anthem, he fails to notice that his son has no interest in any of it. Benjamin is, in fact, (rightly) mortified by it all and trying to deal with the serious issues of understanding exactly what this whole ritual means and struggling to comprehend the Hebrew text he must read aloud from the Haftara during the ceremony. He cleverly manipulates the dilemma that arises involving his absentee grandfather Irwin (Garry Marshall) in an effort to take focus away from him and the grand affair. Adam is furious that Irwin abandoned himself and his mother Rose (a lovely and wise Doris Roberts) some twenty-five years ago and the two have not spoken in years. Benji takes it upon himself to send Irwin a "personalized" invitation that has him coming two weeks early. He figures all the drama with grandpa will get him off the proverbial hook.

Neo-hippie Irwin, his long gray hair in a ponytail, arrives with his much younger girlfriend Sacred Feather a.k.a. Sandy (Daryl Hannah) who blissfully live together in a trailer on an Indian reservation. Neophyte screenwriter Mark Zakarin and director Marshall delicately handle the scenes between Irwin, Rose, and Sandy, carefully avoiding any pat cliched reactions. Rose is calm and accepting of both Irwin's return and Sandy's presence, while Sandy tells Adam and Joanne she's "profoundly moved" by the strong chemistry that still exists between her boyfriend and his former wife.

Unfortunately for Benji, the far-out mitzvah plans proceed as planned even with the distractions Irwin and Sandy provide (including the two skinny-dipping in the pool). Irwin's visit has, however, provided unexpected benefits for the stressed out thirteen-year-old. Irwin throws his mom off the scent, literally, when Benji gets ill after an experiment with alcohol. Irwin also listens to the boy's worries about the bar mitzvah and sets up a meeting with the rabbi (Richard Benjamin) who explains to Benji, for the first time, in detail, what it really is supposed to be about. Benji and his grandpa bond, spending time talking, playing basketball, and yelling at road rage cases via the loudspeaker system in Irwin's rickety van.

Benji now has the self-confidence to tell his mom that he wants to change the bar mitzvah plans to something a little more personal. Adam, though heartbroken, agrees. Dodger Stadium and all the trimmings are cancelled. After Benji successfully chants the Hebrew passages required at the religious ceremony, the guests head to the Fiedlers own backyard for the party. A small folk band plays, prompting the suspicious Arnie, wondering why they would ever cancel Dodger Stadium, to wonder if the theme is now "Fiedler on the Roof. Very clever!" All is not perfect, however, with Adam and Irwin still at each others throats. In a nod to his reel-life namesake, Benji jumps into the pool and sits at the bottom to get some peace and quiet, ala *The Graduate* (1967). This causes the two squabbling elders to realize they need to make peace, if only for Benji's sake. The film ends on a warm note, with Neil Diamond showing up at the party to perform an appealing, unplugged version of "Hava Nagilah," while three generations of Fielders are hoisted into the air.

While it seems like Piven, who effortlessly oozes fast-talking agent through his pores, has been neatly typecast, this role actually predates *Entourage*. The cast, a wonderful blend of comedy veterans and talented young actors, is universally good. Zakarin's semi-autobiographical script is a well-balanced blend of comedy and drama that focuses on the importance of spirituality without getting preachy. There are some derivative moments, like the drinking scene with Benji and his friends that borrows some recognizable dialogue from *Fast Times at Ridgemont High* (1982, toned down for the younger set) and the comedy is all very wholesome in a non-threatening way. Still, Marshall's sophomore outing is entertaining family fare with substance and style.

Hilary White

CREDITS

Benjamin Fiedler: Daryl Sabara
Adam Fiedler: Jeremy Piven
Irwin Fiedler: Garry Marshall
Joanne Fiedler: Jami Gertz
Casey Nudelman: Cheryl Hines
Sacred Feather/Sandy: Daryl Hannah
Rose Fiedler: Doris Roberts
Arnie Stein: Larry Miller
Zachary Stein: Carter Jenkins
Rabbi Schulberg: Richard Benjamin
Karen Sussman: Miranda Cosgrove
Sandra Taylor: Raylene Stein
Himself: Neil Diamond (Cameo)
Origin: USA
Language: English, Hebrew
Released: 2006
Directed by: Scott Marshall
Written by: Mark Zakarin
Cinematography by: Charles Minsky
Music by: John Debney
Editing: Tara Timpone
Production Design: John Demeo
MPAA rating: PG-13
Running time: 99 minutes

REVIEWS

Boxoffice Online. May 12, 2006.
Chicago Sun-Times Online. May 12, 2006.
Entertainment Weekly Online. May 10, 2006.
Hollywood Reporter Online. May 12, 2006.
New York Times Online. May 12, 2006.
Variety Online. May 9, 2006.

THE KING

The devil made me do it.
—Movie tagline

With elements of Greek tragedy, biblical allegory and the surreal, *The King* weaves a dark tale of a troubled man's search for his real father that leads to one family's undoing. Directed by Britain's James Marsh and written by Marsh and producer Milo Addica, *The King* is a unique drama filled with complex characters whose actions commendably defy Hollywood convention, as well as viewers' expectations, and pose interesting philosophical and moral questions. With deliberate pacing and delicately beautiful score, the filmmakers create an appealing, almost hypnotic, microcosm filled with luscious details for the well-cast characters to unravel around. Although it is set in the modern day, this independent film further capitalizes on its appealingly timeless quality with costumes and other details looking distinctly mid-century.

The talented Gael Garcia Bernal stars as Elvis Valderez, a sailor who, at the start of the film, receives an honorable discharge from the Navy and embarks on his new life in the civilian world. Elvis buys a sharp 1969 Cougar and makes a quick stop at a brothel before checking into a cheap hotel in Corpus Christi, Texas. Donning his uniform, he immediately proceeds to an evangelical Christian church. Before he can locate the preacher however, he runs into Malerie (Pell James), an attractive young girl, to whom he is immediately attracted. Malerie, clearly intrigued by the handsome, outgoing stranger, tells him where he can locate pastor David Sandow (William Hurt). Elvis waits until the sermon is over and follows the pastor as he leaves church with his perfect family, including daughter Malerie, son Paul (Paul Dano) and wife Twyla (Laura Harring). David gets out of the car where the enthusiastic Elvis asks David for a hug, just like he saw the people in church doing during service. At first, thinking Elvis is merely an aspiring church member, David warmly embraces him and introduces him to his family before learning he truth. "My mother told me about you. Her name was Yolanda. She told me your name," Elvis tell him. David does admit that, yes, he knew Elvis' mom before he was "saved" but he wants nothing to do with anything from that sinful life now and warns him to stay away. He then tells his family to have nothing to do with Elvis. Twyla knows about David's past and takes Elvis' appearance as a sign of trouble to come.

Whether his motivation is true love or revenge is not clear, but Elvis has little trouble luring Malerie away from the house on the pretext of showing her his car. The two are soon whiling away the afternoons swimming, sharing walks along a favorite marshy area, and eventually, coupling in Elvis's motel. The two become so emboldened that Elvis even comes to the Sandow home in the middle of the night, sleeping with Malerie in her own room. Paul spots Elvis as he's leaving. A devout Christian and talented musician, Paul wants to be a preacher. Normally non-confrontational Paul drives to Elvis's motel room to square off with him. He warns Elvis to stay away from his sister and threatens to tell his father, who will ban him from ever seeing her again. Angry and frustrated at the possibility, Elvis impulsively grabs his dinner knife and stabs Paul in the stomach. "How does it feel," he spits as Paul crumbles to the floor, although Elvis seems surprised that Paul is dead and conflicted about what he's done. He cleans up and gets rid of the body in the marsh and clandestinely returns Paul's truck to the family home.

The police write off Paul's disappearance as merely the behavior of an impulsive teenager although Twyla, quickly unraveling, knows otherwise. Malerie seems unconcerned as well, but has bigger things to think about when she learns she's pregnant with Elvis's child. Elvis is happy when she confides in him, saying they will keep the baby, before driving her to the marsh to confess something much darker. Among the many surprises of the film is the calm acceptance with which Malerie greets the news of her brother's murder at the hands of her lover. Malerie leads Elvis in an improvised prayer service for Paul at the water's edge and things go on as if nothing happened.

It appears that David may suspect that Elvis is somehow responsible for his daughter's suddenly insubordinate behavior or Paul's disappearance as he stakes out the pizza place where Elvis works and then pays him a visit at his motel room. Elvis is reticent to agree to David's invitation to go for a ride with him until David echoes the challenge Elvis made when initially trying to get Malerie to go with him: "Are you afraid?" Instead of anything nefarious, David takes Elvis to an archery range to teach him bowhunting techniques. David has had a day of reckoning and decided he was wrong where Elvis was concerned and now brings his prodigal son fully into the fold. In an eerie scene, Elvis is ushered in by the family to live in Paul's now vacant room. He goes to church with the family where David publicly announces that Elvis is his son from a prior sinful relationship. Even Twyla, initially opposed to Elvis coming to live with them, seems to be warming up to the helpful, agreeable boy. Malerie, however, is rocked by the very public announcement that Elvis is, in fact, her brother. Elvis is elated by the public acceptance, however, and in a poignant scene with Malerie, makes a paper crown for himself as he finally feels loved by his father and his makeshift family, as she despairingly tells him they are going to hell.

Elvis's victory is short-lived, however, when Malerie's bedroom door is promptly locked and he is barred entry. The final blow comes when he sees Malerie in what appears to be a heartfelt confession to her mother. The next shot is an excruciating pan from the window in Elvis's room, which shows his rifle and spent shotgun shells, to the garden-like patio populated, around to the French doors in the back of the house, and back through the various rooms in the house to the bedroom where Elvis is laying the almost-dead Malerie next to her dead mother, putting a pillow to her face and pressing down. He sets the house aflame and heads to the church. During one of David's sermons earlier in the film, he had commanded his congregation to "get right with God." The statement eerily comes back to him as a blood-soaked Elvis speaks the film's last lines, pleading before a befuddled David, "I need to get right with God."

Bernal, who speaks with a flawless regional accent, is a tour-de-force as the unfathomable Elvis, mastering the ability to switch emotions on a dime: happy-go-lucky one minute, seething with inner rage the next. Hurt is equally brilliant as the charismatic preacher/suburban cowboy who sports a blond handlebar moustache, sideburns and a convincing Texas twang. James, who, apparently unbeknownst to the filmmakers, was in her late twenties when the film was shot, is completely convincing as Elvis's ill-fated teenage paramour who, ignored by her father and dismissed by her brother, finds him a sympathetic soul. Dano is excellent in the complicated role of a young man with an unwavering faith that is just starting to get tested as he explores his music and his newly emerging manhood. Harring is memorable and equally strong in a smaller role.

The focus of the film is always Elvis, whose motives largely remain a mystery. It appears that none of the killings were premeditated but the specter of revenge cannot be ignored. David finally acknowledges his own sins and attempts to atone for them, but whether Elvis truly wants to be forgiven for his sins and whether he can be forgiven for such heinous crimes are another matter that the film addresses but, wisely, does not attempt to answer.

Hilary White

CREDITS

Elvis Valderez: Gael Garcia Bernal

Malerie Sandow: Pell James

Paul Sandow: Paul Dano

Pastor David Sandow: William Hurt

Twyla Sandow: Laura Harring

Origin: USA

Language: English

Released: 2005

Production: Milo Addica, James Wilson; Content Film, Edward R. Pressman Film Corporation, FilmFour; released by ThinkFilm

Directed by: James Marsh

Written by: Milo Addica, James Marsh

Cinematography by: Eigil Bryld

Music by: Max Avery Lichtenstein

Sound: Rachel Chancey
Editing: Jinx Godfrey
Costumes: Lee Hunsaker
Production Design: Sharon Lomofsky
MPAA rating: R
Running time: 105 minutes

REVIEWS

Boxoffice Online. May 19, 2006.
Chicago Sun-Times Online. June 16, 2006.
Entertainment Weekly Online. May 24, 2006.
New York Times Online. May 19, 2006.
Variety Online. May 15, 2005.

KINKY BOOTS

How Far Would You Go To Save The Family Business?
—Movie tagline

Box Office: $1.8 million

"Please, God, tell me I have not inspired something burgundy," says the horrified drag queen Lola (Chiwetel Ejiofor) to her fledgling boot maker Charlie (Joel Edgerton). Red, of course, is the desired color, thigh-high the preferred length and boasting a sky-high stiletto heel. Despite the fact that Lola wears glitzy gowns and wants her footwear as flashy as any stereotypical drag queen, nothing else about her is typical of film drag queens. As embodied by Ejiofor, Lola is large and muscular and plays it straight, (well, nearly) using his own booming baritone voice and without a trace of femininity or affectation in his performance. *Chicago Sun-Times'* Roger Ebert marveled, "He plays the role not as a man pretending to be a woman, and not as a woman trapped in a man's body, and not as a parody of a woman, and not as a gay man, but as a *drag queen,* period..."

Inspired by a true story, the film introduces us to Charlie Price, who inherits Price & Sons shoe factory in Northampton from his father Harold (Robert Pugh), forcing Charlie and his reluctant fiancee Nicola (Jemima Rooper) back from exciting London. Charlie discovers that the factory, which crafts quality men's brogues, is facing bankruptcy after years of losses from being unable to compete with changing styles, cheap labor, and even cheaper shoes. The dejected heir is forced to lay off fifteen of the company's employees, most of whom he's known since childhood. Before he ousts worker Lauren (Sarah-Jane Potts), however, she forthrightly tells Charlie that perhaps he should find a way to make the business work instead of impotently firing en masse. He responds by going to London, where he spies Lola surrounded by a group of forbidding young men in an alley. Trying to rescue her, he instead gets a boot to the head...hers. He awakes in the dressing room of the drag club Lola works in, where, hobbling around on her broken heel, she complains that the women's shoes they are forced to wear can't hold the weight of a real man. The seed planted, Charlie, back in Northampton, grabs Lauren and takes her to The Angel Club where Lola performs and tells them both of his idea to save the factory: make durable, quality footwear that appeals to the "niche market" of drag queens.

Charlie's clumsy first attempt is a chunky-heeled, suede monstrosity the color of dried blood that is met with an angry reception and the aforementioned "burgundy" comment. Lola then comes to Northampton to design the line of footwear herself, aided by Charlie and the factory's master craftsmen. Among them is Don (Nick Frost), who is vocal in his homophobic comments directed towards Lola, despite that fact that she is now out of drag—looking thoroughly masculine—and going by her real name Simon. Simon reveals to Charlie that he was once a promising boxer—at his father's urging—until both realized it was futile as there were very few heavyweights that wore dresses. The opening scene depicting what looks like a little black girl dancing along the boardwalk in red, high-heeled women's shoes until her stern father calls her inside is recalled. Simon's father disowned him and eventually died without the two reconciling.

The factory gets busy building the new boots for a big show in Milan that could make or break the entire operation. Still at odds, Don and Lola finally resolve their issues in an arm-wrestling match. Lola lets Don win in front of the entire factory. He is well aware that she allowed him to win, and when he confronts her, she asks only that he "change someone's mind about something" in return for the favor. Despite Charlie (and the faithful Lauren) finally believing in himself, Nicola believes that turning the factory into condos is the most sensible plan. Undaunted, Charlie and the gang get the boots ready for Milan, but not before a few minor obstacles pop up. The fed-up footwear workers rebel against Charlie's newfound perfectionism and walk out before the job is finished. Don, making good on his promise to change someone's mind, overhears Charlie's impassioned speech to Nicola about saving the factory and convinces the workers to come back and finish the job. A rather contrived, last-minute fight has a drunken Charlie belittling Lola's penchant for wearing dresses in staid Northampton, leaving Lola in tears and Charlie in Milan without anyone to model the boots, as Lola and the rest of The Angel Club's performers were to strut the styles on the Italian catwalk. He leaves an apologetic plea on Lola's voicemail and then dons the impossibly tall, patent leather red boots himself, looking like so much runway roadkill. Lola and the Angels triumphantly take the stage and march around the dazed Charlie, performing a winning routine.

Apart from providing the film with a lurid title—and the new name of the factory—it really doesn't matter that Charlie's business makes boots. Regardless of the product, the important thing is the relationship that develops between two seemingly different characters who work together and find that they actually have a lot in common. It doesn't even matter that Charlie ends up with the right girl, only that he finds himself in the end. Some critics mentioned that Lola's sexuality was downplayed for mass consumption—she only fleetingly refers to her attraction to Charlie during a dance with Lauren near the end—but that is also beside the point. Refreshingly, it is a film that features someone of indeterminate sexuality that isn't all about discovering or coming to terms with that person's sexuality.

Television director Julian Jarrold makes his film debut, enmeshing drama and comedy to just the right effect. *Kinky Boots* also gets its savvy, modern sensibility from writer Geoffe Deane, a TV writer and former lead singer of the Brit pop band Modern Romance, and Tim Firth. Keeping things lively are the wonderfully appropriate songs and musical numbers, "Whatever Lola Wants," "My Heart Belongs to Daddy," and the show-stopping medley, "These Boots Were Made for Walkin'/In These Shoes/Cha Cha Heels/Going Back to My Roots/Yes Sir I Can Boogie" all winningly performed by Ejiofor.

Hilary White

CREDITS

Charlie Price: Joel Edgerton
Lola: Chiwetel Ejiofor
Lauren: Sarah-Jane Potts
Nicola: Jemima Rooper
Melanie: Linda Bassett
Don: Nick Frost
George: Ewan Hooper
Harold Price: Robert Pugh
Richard Bailey: Geoffrey Streatsfield
Origin: Great Britain
Language: English
Released: 2006
Production: Nick Barton, Suzanne Mackie, Peter Ettedgui; Miramax Films, Harbour Pictures, Price Productions; released by Miramax
Directed by: Julian Jarrold
Written by: Tim Firth, Geoff Deane
Cinematography by: Eigil Bryld
Music by: Adrian Johnston
Sound: Paul Davies, Tim Alban, Richard Davey
Music Supervisor: Liz Gallacher
Editing: Emma E. Hickox
Art Direction: Philip Elton
Costumes: Sammy Sheldon
Production Design: Alan Macdonald
MPAA rating: PG-13
Running time: 106 minutes

REVIEWS

Boxoffice Online. April 14, 2006.
Entertainment Weekly. April 21, 2006, p. 56.
Los Angeles Times Online. April 14, 2006.
New York Times Online. April 14, 2006.
San Francisco Chronicle. April 14, 2006, p. E5.
Variety Online. April 23, 2005.
Village Voice Online. April 11, 2006.

AWARDS

Nomination:

Golden Globes 2007: Actor—Mus./Comedy (Ejiofor)

L

LADY IN THE WATER

Time is running out for a happy ending.
—Movie tagline

A Bedtime Story.
—Movie tagline

Box Office: $42.2 million

M. Night Shyamalan is one of those writer/directors whose name alone is enough to bring people into the theater. His *Sixth Sense* (1999) took in $672 million worldwide and gave us a new cultural catchphrase: "I see dead people." His later movies, *Unbreakable* (2000), *Signs* (2002), and *The Village* (2004) didn't do quite as well, but well enough to keep the financing coming for his quirky and undeniably original projects. People have come to expect a mix of suspense and twists from his stories about ordinary people who find themselves in extraordinary situations. His latest effort, *Lady in the Water*—his first film for Warner Bros. after leaving Disney because of their seeming lack of support for this fairy tale—fits that profile, but only just barely.

The story takes place in a prosaic five-story, U-shaped apartment complex in Philadelphia called the Cove. As its caretaker, Cleveland Heep (Paul Giamatti) makes his rounds changing light bulbs, fixing leaks, killing cockroaches, and showing the newest tenant, cynical movie and book critic Mr. Farber (Bob Balaban) to his apartment, we are introduced to some of the complex's other quirky inhabitants. There's Reggie (Freddy Rodriguez) who is lifting weights to improve only one side of his body and Mrs. Bell (Mary Beth Hurt) who has an affinity for stray animals. In a book-lined apartment lives the quiet Mr. Leeds (Bill Irwin) who spends all day watching television, and living with his son, Joey (Noah Gray-Cabey), is the crossword puzzle maven Mr. Dury (Jeffrey Wright). There's also a Hispanic family with five daughters as well as a Korean mother with her semi-serious college student daughter Young-Soon Choi (Cindy Cheung). In a non-smoking apartment lives an assortment of smoking slackers (one of whom is Jared Harris) and in another lives frustrated writer Vick Ran (M. Night Shyamalan) and his sister Anna (Sarita Choudhury).

But by far the strangest "tenant" at the Cove is the sea nymph Story (a Narf), whom Cleveland discovers living in a secret world through the grate at the bottom of the apartment complex's swimming pool. Story (Bryce Dallas Howard) has come to the Cove to give inspiration to a writer whose work will inspire mankind and become the seeds of change. But there are a few problems. First of all, Story seems reluctant to tell Cleveland her purpose and how to achieve it so he ends up getting it piecemeal from Mrs. Choi as translated by her daughter in the form of a fairy tale with which she grew up. Secondly, she only has a few days in which to complete her mission before she is taken back to the Blue World by the giant eagle the Eatlon and she doesn't know who it is she's supposed to inspire. Oh, and one more glitch, she's being stalked by a Scrunt, a large, hyena-like creature that can disappear in the grass and who emits a poison called kii. But at least it can be stopped by three simian-like creatures called Tartutics who are the fearsome law keepers of the Blue World.

Luckily for Story she has some pre-placed helpers in the complex. There's a Symbolist who will interpret signs from the universe, a Guardian who will protect her, a Healer whose job is pretty obvious, and a group called the Guild whose purpose is much less clear. But she and they have no idea who they are. It is now up to Cleveland, who saved Story from the Scrunt once and is assumed to be the Guardian, to find out who the others are and help Story achieve her mission then return to the Blue World. To help him do this, Cleveland receives instruction in character foreshadowing as done in the movies from Mr. Farber and from this advice begins selecting from the complex's tenants.

Shyamalan has said that the story of *Lady in the Water* is based on an impromptu bedtime story he made up for his two daughters. Unfortunately, that off-the-cuff kind of storytelling still shows in the screenplay. For a viewer to buy into this kind of movie, there has to be an intrinsic logic and coherence to the elements of the plot, but Shyamalan has left far too many threads hanging from the fabric out of which he has sewn his fairytale.

From the start, when the movie opens with a voiceover (David Ogden Stiers) supplying the background of the Blue World, its characters and their relationship to men, we know we're in unfamiliar territory. Between the fact that we're unfamiliar with the mythology of this tale and Howard's maddeningly whispered dialogue obscuring many plot points, one often feels the "huh" factor as the movie unfolds. We never learn why the Scrunts are trying to kill Narfs. We keep hearing about the Blue World and Story does have a home of sorts under the apartment pool but where exactly is this Blue World and why do its inhabitants care about humans? The Tartutics are supposedly so evil they killed their parents on the night they were born so why are they put in charge of justice and law keeping in the Blue World? How is it that only an elderly Korean woman knows this myth? Doesn't Cleveland buy into Story's tale a little too easily? And what would most people really think if they found their apartment manager with a seemingly traumatized and half naked young girl in his cottage? But that never enters anyone's head at the Cove; they buy into the story just as easily as Cleveland does. But then again, faith is one of Shyamalan's favorite themes.

As a result of all this, it is difficult to suspend one's disbelief. However, it doesn't necessarily mean it's an unwatchable movie. *Lady in the Water* has its share of "boo" moments and atmospheric cinematography and as a story of redemption—another one of Shyamalan's favorite themes—and a coalescing of neighbors into a helping whole, it is at least uplifting. The characters are interesting and very well played, especially Giamatti's caretaker. A deeply wounded man, Cleveland is convincingly played by Giamatti and turns out to be the heart as well as the brains of the movie.

Of course there is the requisite Shyamalan plot twist although not what one might expect...but that makes it a good twist, right? Let's just say it involves the film's funniest bit, cranky critic Farber and his "isn't it obvious" advice.

Beverley Bare Buehrer

CREDITS

Story: Bryce Dallas Howard
Cleveland Heep: Paul Giamatti
Mr. Dury: Jeffrey Wright
Harry Farber: Bob Balaban
Reggie: Freddy Rodriguez
Anna Ran: Sarita Choudhury
Goateed Smoker: Jared Harris
Mr. Leeds: Bill Irwin
Mrs. Bell: Mary Beth Hurt
Mrs. Bubchik: Tovah Feldshuh
Vick Ran: M. Night Shyamalan
Young-Soon Choi: Cindy Cheung
Joey Dury: Noah Gray-Cabey
Narrator: David Ogden Stiers (uncredited)
Origin: USA
Language: English
Released: 2006
Production: M. Night Shyamalan, Sam Mercer; Blinding Edge Pictures, Legendary Pictures; released by Warner Bros.
Directed by: M. Night Shyamalan
Written by: M. Night Shyamalan
Cinematography by: Christopher Doyle
Music by: James Newton Howard
Sound: Charles Munro
Music Supervisor: Sue Jacobs
Editing: Barbara Tulliver
Art Direction: Christina Wilson, Stefan Dechant
Costumes: Betsy Heimann
Production Design: Martin Childs
MPAA rating: PG-13
Running time: 108 minutes

REVIEWS

Boxoffice Online. July 21, 2006.
Chicago Sun-Times Online. July 21, 2006.
Entertainment Weekly. July 28, 2006, p. 42.
Los Angeles Times Online. July 21, 2006.
New York Times Online. July 21, 2006.
San Francisco Chronicle. July 21, 2006, p. E5.
Variety Online. July 16, 2006.
Village Voice Online. July 18, 2006.
Washington Post. July 21, 2006, p. C1.

QUOTES

Story: "It's about to get very dangerous."

AWARDS

Golden Raspberries 2006: Worst Actor (Shyamalan), Worst Director (Shyamalan)

Nomination:

Golden Raspberries 2006: Worst Picture, Worst Screenplay

THE LAKE HOUSE

How do you hold on to someone you've never met?
—Movie tagline

What if you found the one you were meant for… but you lived 2 years apart?
—Movie tagline

Box Office: $52.3 million

The Lake House is a slow-paced romantic fantasy that reunites stars Keanu Reeves and Sandra Bullock for the first time since *Speed* (1994). It is directed by Argentinean Alejandro Agresti in his first Hollywood release and written by David Auburn (best-known for his play *Proof*). *The Lake House* is a remake of the South Korean film *Siworae* (2000) although it is better known by its international title, *Il Mare*, the name of the house in that movie.

The house in *The Lake House* doesn't have a name and is a series of glass boxes, set on stilts, over a lake in Illinois. As the movie opens, Dr. Kate Forster (Bullock) is packing up her things and moving out of the house with her dog, Jack. Kate has taken a job in Chicago and is moving into an apartment near the hospital. She places a note into the mailbox asking the next tenant to forward any stray mail, also mentioning there is a box in the attic that's not hers, and noting the painted paw prints on the walkway. While Kate is busy trying to adjust to her new job, architect Alex Wyler (Reeves) is busy at a condo construction site and moving into his home, which is the lake house in a much more dilapidated state. He finds Kate's note and wonders what is going on because he is obviously the first tenant the house has had in a long time, there are no paw prints, and no box in the attic. However, when Alex starts painting the walkway, a stray dog shows up and runs through the paint. Alex adopts the dog.

On Valentine's Day, 2006, Kate is having lunch with her mother (Willeke Van Ammelrooy) in Daley Plaza when she witnesses an accident. She tries to help an injured man but he dies in her arms. Her colleague and friend, Anna (Shohreh Aghdashloo), advises the depressed Kate that she should revisit a place that made her happy. Kate returns to the lake house and finds a note from Alex that's equally puzzling but she writes a reply. When we see Alex again it's in front of the architectural offices of his famous father, Simon Wyler (Christopher Plummer), an egocentric curmudgeon from whom he is estranged; Alex does reconnect with his younger brother, Henry (Ebon Moss-Bachrach). Alex later visits his father and learns that he is writing his memoirs. Alex decides to look up the address of Kate's apartment building and discovers that it is just being built. Alex and Kate reluctantly come to the conclusion that while she is living in 2006, he is living in 2004 but they can communicate through the mailbox.

The two start getting to know each other via old-fashioned correspondence. When Kate tells Alex she misses the trees around the lake house, he takes a sapling and plants it in front of her apartment building and it magically appears before her full-grown. Henry visits the lake house and urges his brother to stop wasting his talent; they had talked about opening their own firm called Visionary Vanguard. Alex is restoring the lake house but complains to Henry that "Dad knew how to build a house, not a home." Kate decides to see if they can somehow meet in 2004. She tells him she was at a train station on a certain day and left behind a book. Alex gets to the station and sees a couple kissing goodbye; Kate gets on the train and Alex notices the book on a bench. He rushes to give it to her but the train is gone. At least Alex knows what Kate looks like.

Kate's ex-boyfriend Morgan (Dylan Walsh) comes to Chicago and they try to have dinner at a restaurant called Il Mare but it's booked. Next, Jack is seen running away from Alex; by the time Alex finds the dog, he is at the house that Morgan owns. During a chat, Morgan learns about the lake house and mentions that his girlfriend has always wanted to live by a lake. Alex says she can rent the property when he moves. Morgan invites Alex to come to his girlfriend's surprise birthday party and since Alex now knows that Kate is the girlfriend, he agrees. Kate is not having a good time at the party and goes outside where Alex joins her. He asks if she ever read *Persuasion* and she replies that it is a favorite of hers. When Alex asks about the plot, Kate tells him that it is about two people who fall in love but the timing is wrong and they separate. The would-be lovers meet years later and wonder if it is too late for them to have a second chance. Kate tells Alex that she became a doctor because of her father, who died when she was a teenager. They kiss until Morgan interrupts them. On the same night in 2006, Kate is having a drink with Anna and telling her that "the one man I can never meet I would like to give my whole heart to."

Alex's father has a heart attack and Alex makes a hospital visit but is still bitter over the way he treated Alex's mother. He built the lake house for her but abandoned it when she left after his fame came between them. When Kate learns of Simon's death, she goes to the mailbox and leaves a copy of the now-published memoirs for Alex. Alex sees a photograph of himself and his father in front of the lake house. Alex insists that he and Kate arrange a meeting in 2006; per her suggestion, he goes to the Il Mare restaurant and makes a reservation two years in advance—Valentine's Day, 2006. Kate shows up but Alex never does. He insists something must have happened but Kate tells him that she can't live in a fantasy anymore and asks him to stop writing. Alex doesn't but Kate won't pick up any more of his letters. In 2006, Kate decides to give Morgan another chance and they move in together. Alex moves out of the lake house and packs up all their letters and leaves them in a box in the attic. Jack runs away from Alex again and is eventually found by Morgan. Alex also visits Morgan's law office and gives him the keys to the lake house to give to Kate.

Alex moves to Chicago and he and Henry go into business, calling their firm Visionary Vanguard Associates; Alex keeps tweaking the design of the lake house. Then the timeline gets even more confusing because it apparently jumps ahead from 2006 to 2008. Kate and Morgan meet with Henry on Valentine's Day to discuss renovating some property. She sees the lake house drawing and asks Henry about it. Kate then asks if she can meet Alex but Henry tells her that his brother was killed in an accident by Daley Plaza on Valentine's Day, 2006. Kate realizes that this is why Alex stood her up at the restaurant and that in her last letter to him she said she was having lunch in Daley Plaza on Valentine's Day. She races out to the lake house and leaves a note for Alex not to go anywhere near Daley Plaza but to be patient and meet her at the lake house. He does go to the Plaza and sees Kate but remembers her telling him to just wait and he doesn't cross the street. Instead they finally meet at the mailbox by the lake house. Kate thankfully tells Alex: "You waited."

Acceptance of the time warp premise is crucial to enjoyment of the movie. Some reviewers wondered why the duo didn't email or text message each other, but neither of them use a computer, and while Kate uses a cell phone, Alex apparently does not. So much is peculiar that it is best just to suspend rational thought. Reeves and Bullock still have an appealing chemistry together, though both their characters are depressed and lonely, with father issues. The supporting roles serve primarily as sounding boards, although Plummer seems happy chewing the scenery.

Students of architecture may find the house very familiar. It looks as if production designer Nathan Crowley was heavily influenced by Philip Johnson's 1949 Glass House. The lake house was built by the production crew on Maple Lake in Cook County, Illinois. Since the land is part of a forest preserve, the house had to be dismantled after filming ended and the property restored to its natural state. One of the better features of *The Lake House* is its use of the Chicago setting and over forty locations. The Il Mare restaurant in the movie is actually the Park Grill.

Christine Tomassini

CREDITS

Alex Wyler: Keanu Reeves
Kate Forster: Sandra Bullock
Anna: Shohreh Aghdashloo
Morgan: Dylan Walsh
Simon Wyler: Christopher Plummer
Henry Wyler: Ebon Moss-Bachrach
Kate's Mother: Willeke Van Ammelrooy
Mona: Lynn Collins
Origin: USA
Language: English
Released: 2006
Production: Roy Lee, Doug Davidson; Village Roadshow Pictures, Vertigo; released by Warner Bros.
Directed by: Alejandro Agresti
Written by: David Auburn
Cinematography by: Alar Kivilo
Music by: Rachel Portman
Sound: Scott D. Smith
Editing: Lynzee Klingman, Alejandro Brodersohn
Art Direction: Kevin Kavanaugh, Thomas Voth
Costumes: Deena Appel
Production Design: Nathan Crowley
MPAA rating: PG
Running time: 108 minutes

REVIEWS

Boxoffice Online. June 16, 2006.
Chicago Sun-Times Online. June 16, 2006.
Entertainment Weekly Online. June 14, 2006.
Los Angeles Times Online. June 16, 2006.
New York Times Online. June 16, 2006.
Premiere Magazine Online. June 16, 2006.
Variety Online. June 11, 2006.
Washington Post. June 16, 2006, p. C1.

QUOTES

Kate: "It's kind of a long-distance relationship."

TRIVIA

Kate's apartment, located at 1620 Racine, is the same address that Sean Connery's character lived at in *The Untouchables.*

LARRY THE CABLE GUY: HEALTH INSPECTOR

They'll Give Anyone A Badge.
—Movie tagline

Box Office: $15.6 million

As a public service, theaters should shut down their snack bars during screenings of *Larry the Cable Guy: Health Inspector*. After sitting through the numerous shots or descriptions of and sound effects from the backside of its star, it is the rare movie patron who will feel like finishing his bucket of popcorn. As an added convenience, theaters might want to provide viewers with antiseptic wipes for those suffering an overwhelming urge to scrub themselves clean of this film.

The opening montage of the film is a clear indication of what is to come. Larry (Larry the Cable Guy) is waking up and the camera focuses in on the part of his rear that is not covered by his pajamas. Larry scratches, urinates in the shower and steps onto a slice of pizza. It is not so much funny as merely extremely gross. The rest of the film is pretty much the same thing, plus a lot of flatulence, along with a plot tacked on to make it seem more movie-like.

Said plot has to do with the misleadingly named Larry the Cable Guy's job as a health inspector. In a twist on cop movies from time immemorial, Larry is a rogue inspector who does not play by the rules but is the best person on the force. He gets assigned a mismatched partner, in this case, a by-the-book female, Amy Butlin (Iris Bahr). Needless to say, writers Jonathan Bernstein and James Greer think that her last name alone is cause for hilarity.

Larry and Butlin are soon pursuing a big case. Someone is putting something in the food at local restaurants that causes patrons to vomit and/or have extremely loud gas. Naturally all of this is vividly shown, complete with realistic sound effects. There is a big cook-off coming up and the health inspectors suspect that someone is trying to knock out the competition.

There is also a subplot about Larry and a love interest, Jane (Megyn Price). Not since Courtney Thorne-Smith played Carrot Top's love interest has an actress had to work so hard to portray an inexplicable attraction. Larry's apparent bowel issues, his boorishness and slovenliness do not seem to matter to Jane, who simpers, "I feel so comfortable with you." To which he replies, "Other than my underbritches creepin' up on me, I feel pretty comfortable too."

Although the filmmakers made sure all things rear-end related are explored, then explored a few more times, they apparently needed additional gross-outs to fill screen time. So there is some extra material thrown in to stretch things out involving spittoons, cockroaches, and nasty bits in restaurant mayonnaise. Truly, this is probably the most nauseating movie ever made. For those who prefer more than a gross sight gag, the movie has jokes about gay people, wheelchair-bound folks and Larry's "semi-retarded" neighbor Donnie (David Koechner).

A quality cast surrounds Larry, but the movie is so obsessed with the emissions from Larry's body that the supporting players are not allowed to shine. Bruce Bruce is Big Shug, a very large fellow who runs a down-home restaurant that specializes in things deep-fried. Also on-board are Joe Pantoliano as Mayor M. T. Gunn, who may or may not be involved with the poisonings, and Joanna Cassidy as the owner of an upscale restaurant. Kid Rock and Jerry Mathers (forever known for his role as The Beaver on *Leave it to Beaver*) show up in halfhearted cameos.

Critics were not shown early screenings of the film, and most likely, they were not happy to see any screenings of the film. Christy Lemire of the *Associated Press* wrote: "*Larry the Cable Guy: Health Inspector* has a severe anal fixation, the sights and sounds of which are graphically ghastly. Worse yet, none of it is the slightest bit funny." Tom Maurstad of the *Dallas Morning News* wrote: "There's no mystery as to why *Larry the Cable Guy: Health Inspector* wasn't screened for the press prior to release." Ruthe Stein of the *San Francisco Chronicle* wrote: "This so-called comedy is so not funny, it makes *Deuce Bigalow: Male Gigolo* look like Chaplin." Lou Lumenick of the *New York Post* called the film, "virtually unwatchable and laugh-free." Finally, Jeannette Catsoulis of the *New York Times* called it "unpleasant, uncouth, and painfully unfunny."

Jill Hamilton

CREDITS

Larry: Larry the Cable Guy
Lily Micelli: Joanna Cassidy
Donnie: David Koechner
Art Tatlock: Thomas F. Wilson
Mayor M.T. Gunn: Joe Pantoliano
Amy Butlin: Iris Bahr
Big Shug: Bruce Bruce
Brenda: Brooke Dillman
Jack Dobbs: Tony Hale

Jane's Mom: Lisa Lampanelli
Jane Whitley: Megyn Price
Himself: Jerry Mathers (Cameo)
Himself: Kid Rock (Cameo)
Origin: USA
Language: English
Released: 2006
Production: Alan Blomquist, J.P. Williams; Lionsgate, Parallel Entertainment Pictures, Shala Entertainment, Samwilla; released by Lionsgate
Directed by: Trent Cooper
Written by: Jonathan Bernstein, James Greer
Cinematography by: Kim Marks
Music by: Steven R. Phillips, Tim P.
Sound: Billy Byers
Editing: Greg Featherman
Art Direction: Andrew White
Costumes: Beverly Safier
Production Design: Macie Vener
MPAA rating: PG-13
Running time: 89 minutes

REVIEWS

Los Angeles Times Online. March 26, 2006.
New York Times Online. March 28, 2006.
San Francisco Chronicle Online. March 27, 2006.
Variety Online. March 24, 2006.

AWARDS

Nomination:

Golden Raspberries 2006: Worst Actor (Larry the Cable Guy)

LASSIE

More Than A Hero. A Legend.
—Movie tagline

The image that comes to mind when most people hear the name Lassie is the miraculous canine of the TV series that began in 1954. That Lassie, set in the idealized TV version of the 1950s, forever had Lassie fending off wild animals, famously saving Timmy from the well, and generally doing everything but choosing stocks for the family portfolio. It is not surprising that that version of Lassie is so embedded in peoples' minds because the TV series ran for twenty years.

But the original Lassie was actually a bit different. The amazing dog first appeared in 1938 in an Eric Knight story. His subsequent book in 1940, *Lassie Come Home,* then the 1943 movie version of the book—starring Roddy McDowall and Elizabeth Taylor—proved that the story of the smart dog was as persistent as the dog itself. That original story was set in England before World War II and it had a darker tone than later incarnations. The 2006 *Lassie* returns the story to those grittier roots.

Lassie is about the only spot of brightness in little Joe Carraclough's (Jonathan Mason) life. He lives in the poor town of Greenhall where his mother, Sarah (Samantha Morton), spends her days doing the wash by hand and trying to make a home with the little money the family has. His father, Sam (John Lynch) works long hours in the village's mine.

When the mine closes, Joe's parents decide that the only way to get by is to accept the offer of the local rich man, the Duke of Rudling (Peter O'Toole), to buy Lassie. His granddaughter, Cilia (Hester Odgers), has taken a fancy to the dog and the Duke is happy to indulge her wishes. Little Joe is devastated and, as it turns out, so is Lassie. No sooner is Lassie placed in her new cage at the Duke's mansion then she digs a hole under the fence and finds her way back to Joe's flat. The Duke's evil dog keeper, Hynes (Steve Pemberton), captures Lassie, puts her back in the kennel and she promptly does the same thing, this time leaping over the fence, as shown in slo-mo detail. Like the original title suggests, the rest of the movie is about Lassie coming home.

Her big challenge, and the main dramatic action of the film, comes when the Duke and Cilia cart the dog off to yet another castle they have in Scotland. This time, Lassie does not have to leap a fence and run across town, but has to travel over five hundred miles, facing danger every paw step of the way. One of the more charming interludes of Lassie's journey is the portion she shares with a lonely puppeteer, Rowlie (Peter Dinklage). In movies like *The Station Agent* (2003), Dinklage has perfected the character of the lonely, soulful outsider.

This film is filled with similarly fine acting. Morton is stoic but hopeful as Joe's overburdened mother. Lynch conveys a quiet panic as his character realizes he is not going to be able to support his family. Mason is thankfully free of the cuteness and mugging of a lot of Hollywood child actors, and, by contrast, O'Toole's hamminess is delightfully welcome. Strangely, all the things that make this film good might be what would turn children away. For a demographic accustomed to brightly-colored talking animals, a dark film set in prewar England might not be horribly appealing.

It was, however, quite appealing to movie reviewers. This version of Lassie had more than a few critics reaching for their handkerchiefs. Michael Wilmington of the *Chicago Tribune* wrote that "the last twenty or so minutes of this film—a sequence with Rowlie and his little dog Toots (named after Knight's own pet) and an annihilating snow scene—had me, I confess, in tears." Gene Seymour of *Newsday* wrote: "Knight's story retains enough of its power to ensure, even in this modest rendering, that it never fails to make your eyes mist and your cheeks warm." Nancy Churnin of the *Dallas Morning News* wrote that "the collie that became a star back in 1943 can still make you cry and cheer in the all-new *Lassie.*" Finally, Jeannette Catsoulis of the *New York Times* wrote that this particular Lassie "exhibits a repertory of facial expressions that would put Jim Carrey to shame." For example, "when little Joe—in a scene that perfectly evokes the British school system's once-joyful embrace of corporal punishment—gets whacked on the wrist by a ruler-happy teacher, the sight of a sorrowful Lassie licking the welts is enough to bring even the most flint-hearted viewers to their knees."

Jill Hamilton

CREDITS

The Duke of Rudling: Peter O'Toole
Cilia: Hester Odgers
Sarah: Samantha Morton
Sam: John Lynch
Rowlie: Peter Dinklage
Joe: Jonathan Mason
Hynes: Steve Pemberton
Daisy: Jemma Redgrave
Colonel Hulton: Edward Fox
Colonel French: John Standing
Jeanie: Kelly Macdonald
Mr. Justice Murray: Robert Hardy
Origin: USA, Great Britain, Ireland, France
Language: English
Released: 2005
Production: Ed Guiney, Francesca Barra, Charles Sturridge; Odyssey Entertainment, Isle of Man, Classic Media, Firstsight Films; released by Samuel Goldwyn Company
Directed by: Charles Sturridge
Written by: Charles Sturridge
Cinematography by: Howard Atherton
Music by: Adrian Johnston
Sound: Mervyn Moore
Music Supervisor: Caitriona Walsh
Editing: Peter Coulson, Adam Green
Art Direction: Colman Corish, Irene O'Brien
Costumes: Charlotte Walter
Production Design: John Paul Kelly
MPAA rating: PG
Running time: 100 minutes

REVIEWS

Chicago Sun-Times Online. September 1, 2006.
Entertainment Weekly Online. August 30, 2006.
Los Angeles Times Online. September 1, 2006.
New York Times Online. September 1, 2006.
Variety Online. December 20, 2005.

TRIVIA

The movie was filmed in Scotland, Ireland, and the Isle of Man.

LAST HOLIDAY

She Always Thought She Was Somebody...And She Was.
—Movie tagline

Box Office: $38.4 million

In his review of *Last Holiday*, Roger Ebert of the *Chicago Sun-Times* wrote, "It is good to attend important cinema like *Syriana* (2005) and *Munich* (2005), but on occasion we must be open to movies that have more modest ambitions: They only want to amuse us, warm us, and make us feel good." In this way, *Last Holiday* plays like an old-fashioned Hollywood movie. (In fact, it is a remake of a 1950 film starring Alec Guinness.) *Last Holiday* boasts lovely locations, sumptuous clothes and a happily-ever-after ending.

Georgia Byrd (Queen Latifah) is a mild-mannered sales clerk in a large New Orleans department store. Instead of actually living the life she desires, she collects all her fantasies in a notebook she labels "Book of Possibilities." In it, she pastes her favorite recipes, travel plans, and photos of her good-looking and equally shy coworker, Sean Matthews (LL Cool J). At night she watches the cooking channel and cooks fabulous meals for her young neighbor. Meanwhile, she nibbles her nightly Lean Cuisine.

Georgia's life changes when she slips and falls at work. A CAT scan reveals that she has a terminal brain disease and only a few weeks to live. There is an operation with a small chance of curing her condition, but her HMO will not pay for it. Faced with this news, Georgia decides to cash in all her retirement savings and head on her dream trip to the Grandhotel Pupp in the Czech Republic. The kitchen there is run by her idol, Chef Didier (Gerard Depardieu). She has put off living her life thus far and is determined to make up for it.

Once there, Georgia throws herself into all that the hotel has to offer with great gusto. At dinner she orders the entire menu and immediately endears herself to Chef Didier. At a nearby table, some important guests look on enviously as the chef ignores them and courts Georgia's attention. For plot reasons, the guests at this other table happen to include the Type-A owner of Georgia's store, Matthew Kragen (Timothy Hutton); his mistress and employee, Ms. Burns (Alicia Witt); and a senator and a congressman (Giancarlo Esposito and Michael Nouri). They wonder about the mysterious and wealthy guest. Most of them are enchanted by her gusto and lust for life and clamor to add her to their circle. But Kragen is wary and suspects that she is from a rival firm out to discover his nefarious dealings with the senator and congressman.

But these plot issues do not matter much. Of greater importance is watching Georgia enjoy herself at the famous old hotel. She rolls blissfully in her soft, high-thread count sheets, tries lots of buttery foods and marvels at the detail in the intricate lobby ceiling. "Do you ever just want to cry looking at that ceiling?" she asks a hotel employee. She giggles to learn that the hotel's name is pronounced "poop." And in a *Pretty Woman* (1990) inspired sequence, she shops for fabulous gowns at an expensive shop. This is classic wish-fulfillment stuff and seems to be the main point of the movie. With such good feelings floating about, it does not seem that odd that Sean shows up to declare his love. And even Georgia's death sentence seems like something that will surely be cleared up by a quick plot device.

Most critics liked the film and credited it to the charms of Queen Latifah. Stephanie Zacharek of *Salon* wrote: "Watching *Last Holiday*, I kept waiting for the moment I could decree the movie truly terrible, the instant I could comfortably put my pen and notebook away and give it up for lost. But that moment never came, partly because I never fail to take pleasure in Latifah, and partly because I couldn't shake the eerie feeling that the movie I was watching was something of a ghost from another time." Jessica Reaves of the *Chicago Tribune* wrote that "although this is not exactly a profound film, and the message ('Live every day as if it's your last') is hardly new; it's testament to this movie's joyous energy that it doesn't matter in the least." Roger Ebert of the *Chicago Sun-Times* wrote: "*Last Holiday* is a movie that takes advantage of the great good nature and warmth of Queen Latifah, and uses it to transform a creaky old formula into a comedy that is just plain lovable." Finally, Manohla Dargis of the *New York Times*; who did not like the film, still had kind words for Latifah, and wrote: "Queen Latifah has a beautiful smile and the sort of relaxed screen presence that can take some performers decades to hone, but even this superflack for Wal-Mart can't gold-plate junk."

Jill Hamilton

CREDITS

Georgia Byrd: Queen Latifah
Sean Matthews: LL Cool J
Matthew Kragen: Timothy Hutton
Senator Dillings: Giancarlo Esposito
Ms. Burns: Alicia Witt
Chef Didier: Gerard Depardieu
Rochelle: Jane Adams
Ms. Gunther: Susan Kellerman
Darius: Jascha Washington
Adamian: Matt Ross
Dr. Gupta: Ranjit Chowdhry
Marlon: Mike Estime
Congressman Stewart: Michael Nouri
HMO Administrator: Julia Lashae
Reverend: Richmond Werner
Himself: Emeril Lagasse
Lady Moocher: Shirl Cieutat
Origin: USA
Language: English
Released: 2006
Production: Laurence Mark, Mark Rapke; Imagemovers; released by Paramount Pictures
Directed by: Wayne Wang
Written by: Jeffrey Price, Peter S. Seaman
Cinematography by: Geoffrey Simpson
Music by: George Fenton
Sound: Allan Byer
Music Supervisor: Deva Anderson
Editing: Deidre Slevin
Art Direction: Richard Johnson
Costumes: Daniel Orlandi
Production Design: William Arnold
MPAA rating: PG-13
Running time: 112 minutes

REVIEWS

Boxoffice Online. January 13, 2006.
Chicago Sun-Times Online. January 13, 2006.
Entertainment Weekly Online. January 11, 2006.
Los Angeles Times Online. January 13, 2006.
New York Times Online. January 13, 2006.
Variety Online. January 8, 2006.
Washington Post Online. January 13, 2006.

QUOTES

Georgia Byrd: "Next time...we will laugh more, we'll love more; we just won't be so afraid."

TRIVIA

The Food Network's chefs prepared all the dishes served in the movie, traveled with the crew to do the cooking, and taught Queen Latifah basic cooking techniques in order to look like a professional chef in the movie. The Food Network also featured the recipes used on their website.

THE LAST KING OF SCOTLAND

Charming. Magnetic. Murderous.
—Movie tagline

Box Office: $16.2 million

Just as Dame Helen Mirren's performance as Elizabeth II in *The Queen* (2006) was, for some, the year's breakaway performance for an actress, so Forest Whitaker's performance as one of the world's cruelest dictators, General Idi Amin Dada of Uganda, was, perhaps the year's breakaway performance for an actor. *Wall Street Journal* reviewer Joe Morgenstern was so enraptured by Whitaker's portrayal that he called it "one of the great performances of modern movie history." *Newsweek* reviewer David Ansen praised Whitaker for "uncorking the power that he usually holds in check" in this "bravura performance." Perhaps the reason for such hyperbole was that serious viewers had been waiting for months to see quality performances in quality films. No doubt the portrayal was extraordinary, and Whitaker's timing could not have been better.

The other main performance of note here is that of Scottish actor James McAvoy as Nicholas Garrigan, just out of medical school in Scotland, and whimsically in quest of exotic adventure in randomly picked Uganda. *The Last King of Scotland* is not exactly a biographical picture, however, of the dictator and his Scottish doctor, as Lisa Schwarzbaum explained in *Entertainment Weekly*: Although the film was shot in documentary style, and although Amin was in fact served by a Scots doctor, she wrote, "this one is a fabrication." The fabrication was ably scripted by Peter Morgan and Jeremy Brock who adapted the screenplay for director Kevin Macdonald from a 1998 novel by Giles Foden. Idi Amin presided over a reign of terror in Uganda during the 1970s. The treatment attempts to define the man behind the monster by mingling fact with fiction, a potentially dangerous trend these days. The easy way out, on the other hand, as one reviewer noted, would have been to play Idi Amin as purely evil rather than attempting a more nuanced and human performance. Macdonald, who shot the film on location in Uganda, told *Entertainment Weekly* that his picture was "a thriller with a Faustian pact at the center."

Idi Amin, whose modest titles included "Lord of All the Beasts of the Earth and Fishes of the Sea," was a larger-than-life figure who had a mad obsession with all things Scottish, even to the point of wearing kilts and Tam-o'-Shanters. The Scottish obsession resulted from Amin's training at Sandhurst, the British equivalent of West Point. As a young man, Amin had supported the British by fighting against the Mau Mau. As a reward, the British sent him to Sandhurst, then supported his rise to power back in Africa. After serving under Ugandan President Apollo Milton Obote, Amin usurped him and seized power in 1971, ruling for nearly the rest of the decade.

In order to understand Idi Amin, Whitaker went to Uganda to observe firsthand the province where Amin was born so he could learn the appropriate dialect and also to visit Amin's brother, Amule. This link was essential for the actor: "I needed to understand what it's like to be African, what it's like to be Ugandan," Whitaker told *Entertainment Weekly*. Fortunately, Whitaker and Macdonald had the permission and cooperation of current Ugandan president, Yoweri Museveni. Whitaker regarded the role as a remarkable opportunity: "On the technical side," he told journalists in New York (as reported by critic Marsha McCreadie), "I tried to lower the register of my voice, and on an emotional level, to access the spirit of the person from a place inside me."

Whitaker was not Macdonald's first choice to play Idi Amin, however, because the actor first impressed the director as being too gentle. But Whitaker won him over by reading the violent scene where Amin turns on Garrigan, his Scottish doctor, for the first time. "He was explosive," Macdonald told the *Washington Post*. "Really scary. You wanted to step back a bit." Whitaker is so over-the-top and overpowering in the finished film that, as Lisa Schwarzbaum wrote, the "balance of star power" should have been "off-kilter," but, she explained, "that disparity turns out to be the point on which the picture pivots." *New Yorker* critic David Denby was impressed by the character's "terrifying affability." Noting that "like many sociopaths, he can be surprisingly empathic," Denby states that "any check on his desires sends him into a rage, and, as Whitaker takes off into astonishing tirades, one eye opens wide, and the other droops viciously—even his vision is schizoid."

Research for the film was very impressive. Both Whitaker and Macdonald spent hours meeting with President Museveni and his cabinet in Kampala in order to get permission to film in Urganda and to use the Ugandan army. They both interviewed Ugandans who revered Amin's memory and his brand of nationalism, as well as former members of Amin's regime. Macdonald, who saw Dr. Garrigan as an immature, greedy and obviously "flawed white figure," conceived the film as being mainly "about colonial power, the Third World in general, and Uganda in specific." As a filmmaker grounded in documentary approaches, Macdonald insisted on shooting on location in Uganda in order to get the background details right, such as buildings from the 1950s and 1960s that are still standing. The realism helps to make the story convincing.

In her *Washington Times* review, Kelly Jane Torrance predicted that Forest Whitaker was "guaranteed an Oscar® nomination for his portrayal" and even went so far as to consider him the front-runner for the Best Actor Academy Award®, despite Sean Penn's crackerjack performance in *All the King's Men* (2006). But Whitaker's performance "does what *All the King's Men* failed to do," in the opinion of *Baltimore Sun* critic Michael Sragow, because "it expresses the visceral connection of a popular demagogue and his people." Lending support to Whitaker and McAvoy, though creating less of a stir, were Gillian Anderson as Sarah Merrit, a married doctor who attempts to give Dr. Garrigan advice and guidance, and Kerry Washington as Amin's wife Kay, with whom Dr. Garrigan gets dangerously friendly and intimate. When pregnancy results, Kay begs Garrigan to perform an abortion on her, but he considers himself unqualified to perform the procedure. Although he later reconsiders, by then it is too late, and Kay dies as a result of the sloppy work of a native abortionist. *Newsweek* reviewer David Ansen considered this plot turn a "dubious contrivance, as is the insertion of the famous Entebbe hijacking (which is not in Foden's book)." In the film, however, the latter makes for a very useful deus ex machina, quite literally.

Despite questionable plot contrivances, the film appears to have caught the spirit of the times and of one of the most remarkable dictators of the century. The viewer feels urgently distressed and ill at ease when Amin makes requests that quickly turn into demands on Dr. Garrigan. It is clear that the temperamental dictator will not be forgiving of bad judgment or mistakes. At the end, Amin knows that Garrigan has betrayed him and has his henchmen set a procedure of torture and punishment in motion. For mysterious reasons, the doctor who had been replaced by Garrigan as the dictator's personal physician takes pity and helps him to escape at the last moment, putting his own life in extreme jeopardy. The conclusion offers some emotional satisfaction, but is so deceptive that thoughtful viewers might feel shortchanged. The direction is so seamless, and the acting so powerful that they will also leave the theatre shaken by a powerful spectacle of cruelty and human misfortune. That, in the larger scheme of things, is the right message to be conveyed. Garrigan, a puerile and pampered British twit, is easily flattered and seduced by Amin's charm and by his own sense of power, until, finally, he is forced by the General to realize that he is deserving of nothing.

James M. Welsh

CREDITS

Idi Amin: Forest Whitaker
Nicholas Garrigan: James McAvoy
Kay Amin: Kerry Washington
Sarah Merrit: Gillian Anderson
Stone: Simon McBurney
Origin: Great Britain, Germany
Language: English
Released: 2006
Production: Andrea Calderwood, Lisa Bryer, Charles Steel; DNA Films Ltd., FilmFour, Fox Searchlight Pictures; released by 20th Century Fox
Directed by: Kevin Macdonald
Written by: Peter Morgan, Jeremy Brock
Cinematography by: Anthony Dod Mantle
Music by: Alex Heffes
Sound: Michael Wollmann
Editing: Justine Wright
Art Direction: Joannah Stutchbury
Production Design: Michael Carlin
MPAA rating: R
Running time: 121 minutes

REVIEWS

Boxoffice Online. September 27, 2006.
Entertainment Weekly Online. September 27, 2006.
Hollywood Reporter Online. September 4, 2006.
Los Angeles Times Online. September 27, 2006.
New York Times Online. September 27, 2006.
Premiere Magazine. October 2006, p. 42.
Rolling Stone Online. September 28, 2006.
Variety Online. September 6, 2006.

AWARDS

Oscars 2006: Actor (Whitaker)
British Acad. 2006: Actor (Whitaker), Adapt. Screenplay
Golden Globes 2007: Actor—Drama (Whitaker)
Screen Actors Guild 2006: Actor (Whitaker)

Nomination:

British Acad. 2006: Film, Support. Actor (McAvoy)

THE LAST KISS

We all make choices. What's yours?
—Movie tagline

Box Office: $11.6 million

The Last Kiss is a simply told story of love, temptation, and loss, about fearing the contentment of adulthood after the passion of youth and what it takes to commit to a relationship.

Michael (Zack Braff) seems to have it all: a good job as an architect, a lovely and pregnant girlfriend, Jenna (Jacinda Barrett), and a few really good friends. However, some of his friends have problems. His friend Chris (Casey Affleck) is in a troubled marriage with a nagging wife and a crying baby. He thought having a child would bring them closer together, but all it did was make them want to kill each other. His friend Izzy (Michael Weston) is despondent because he has been dumped by his girlfriend so he obsessively confronts her while planning a motorcycle trip to Terra del Fuego. Kenny (Eric Christian Olsen) is a bartender who can't seem to grow up and lives for lots of casual sex with whoever is handy.

Michael does indeed have a problem, even if he is just barely aware of it. He's turning thirty, it feels like a death sentence, and he is coming to the realization that everything seems so predictable. In his own words, "there are no more surprises" in his life, even though it has turned out just as he expected.

At the wedding of another friend, he is feeling a little depressed, and not quite knowing why. Into his boring and predictable life steps Kim (Rachel Bilson), a very attractive college sophomore. For some reason Kim is flirting with Michael. Now to give Michael credit he does tell Kim he has a girlfriend, he just fails to mention that she is pregnant. Kim, however, has no scruples about Michael's relationship and makes her play.

Based on the 2002 Italian film *L'Ultimo Bacio* by Gabriele Muccino, and adapted by screenwriter Paul Haggis, *The Last Kiss* features smart dialogue and a great ensemble cast.

As in his previous film *Garden State* (2004), Braff once again turns in a solid and likable performance even though his character may not always be so likable. Braff has a kind of nervous energy that can make his characters look guilty even when they haven't done anything, but this expressive face also makes him highly watchable, especially when a reaction shot is called for. He projects a warmth and humor that makes him everyone's idea of a good friend.

Unfortunately for Jacinda Barrett, not much is known about Jenna, except her reactions to Michael's actions. Because of this lopsided view, she mainly comes across as manipulating and bitchy. There is very little background on Rachel Bilson's Kim, as well, so her attraction to Michael is something of a mystery.

A more balanced portrait of a two-way relationship may be found with Jenna's mother, Anna (Blythe Danner), and her father, Stephen (Tom Wilkinson), although they, too, have problems. His emotionally distant psychologist and her emotionally over-reacting and cheating wife seem more well-rounded. Consequently, their relationship is more understandable.

The Last Kiss is a relatively quiet little film about male angst and how middle age panic now hits guys in their thirties. It takes a perceptive look at modern relationships, the choices we make, and whether or not we make them with the realization that our choices have consequences. The characters in *The Last Kiss* may not always choose to act ethically or admirably, but they do act in an understandable way. Part comedy and part drama, this film is just like life.

Beverley Bare Buehrer

CREDITS

Michael: Zach Braff
Jenna: Jacinda Barrett
Chris: Casey Affleck
Izzy: Michael Weston
Anna: Blythe Danner
Stephen: Tom Wilkinson
Lisa: Lauren Lee Smith
Arianna: Marley Shelton
Kim: Rachel Bilson
Kenny: Eric Christian Olsen
Professor Bowler: Harold Ramis
Origin: USA
Language: English
Released: 2006
Production: Tom Rosenberg, Gary Lucchesi, Andre Lamal, Marcus Viscidi; Lakeshore Entertainment; released by DreamWorks Pictures
Directed by: Tony Goldwyn
Written by: Paul Haggis
Cinematography by: Tom Stern
Music by: Michael Penn
Sound: David Giammarco
Editing: Lisa Zeno Chrugin
Art Direction: Gilles Aird
Costumes: Odette Gadoury
Production Design: Dan Leigh
MPAA rating: R
Running time: 105 minutes

REVIEWS

Boxoffice Online. September 15, 2006.
Chicago Sun-Times Online. September 15, 2006.
Entertainment Weekly. September 22, 2006, p. 73.
Hollywood Reporter Online. September 11, 2006.
New York Times Online. September 15, 2006.

San Francisco Chronicle. September 15, 2006, p. E9.
Variety Online. September 13, 2006.
Washington Post. September 15, 2006, p. C4.

LETTERS FROM IWO JIMA

Box Office: $13.5 million

In 2006, Clint Eastwood made his case against war in two films in two languages concerning the same battle in the Pacific Theatre of World War II, moving, in the words of *New York Times* critic A.O. Scott, "into territory that few Western directors have even tried to comprehend...with a calm mastery that provides fuel for endless reflection as well as overwhelming emotional impact." To say that *Letters from Iwo Jima* is the flip side of *Flags of Our Fathers* (2006) might trivialize this very serious film about patriotism, honor, and sacrifice in battle, but both films look at the same conflict over a relatively useless Pacific island of tremendous symbolic importance, since it was the first battle fought on Japanese soil in 1945. The Japanese forces were commanded by Lt. General Tadamichi Kuribayashi (played by Ken Watanabe), ready to die with honor for their Emperor. There is no logical question about the outcome of the invasion. The Japanese are outnumbered and outgunned. Their mission is suicidal and might be considered pointless were it not for the issue of national honor, also linked with religious devotion to Shintoism, worship of the island-nation's Emperor-God.

The film, scripted by Japanese American Iris Yamashita and Paul Haggis, begins with a prologue, set in the present, showing archaeologists uncovering a packet buried in the floor of a cave on Iwo Jima. The archaeologists marvel at the way the caves have been dug, as the frame of reference then shifts back sixty years to show Japanese soldiers in the caves. An outnumbered contingent of 20,000 Japanese soldiers are charged with defending a five-mile by two-and-a-half-mile strip of volcanic rock located five hundred miles south of Japan from the coming American invasion. Arriving officers and soldiers soon realize that they are on a suicide mission. Two of the new arrivals are General Kuriybayashi and Baron Nishi (Tsuyoshi Ihara), two aristocratic officers and gentlemen, the first a former commander of the Imperial Guard and the latter a champion equestrian in the 1932 Los Angeles Olympics. They bring a whiff of elegance to the waste and desperation of the place. Baron Nishi has had his horse flown in and surveys the island from horseback. Kuribayashi immediately suspends some of the brutal discipline imposed on the soldiers and orders cessation of the beach defenses in favor of entrenched weapons on higher ground, and the digging of the caves in the northern mountains. The water is bad and the food consists mainly of meager seaweed soup. Some of the soldiers speculate that they may be dead even before the Americans arrive, and arrive they do, in overwhelming numbers.

Fragments of the letters referenced in the title are read on the soundtrack, providing the audience with glimpses of past events in the lives of these men. As a civilian, Saigo (played by Japanese pop star Kaszunari Ninomiya) was a baker, conscripted from his domestic life and family to join the military. Both the General and the Baron had spent considerable time in America. The General was educated in America and the Baron had even once entertained Douglas Fairbanks and Mary Pickford in California, as he reminisces to a wounded American soldier from Oklahoma.

Eastwood provides intimations of the slaughter to come. First, airplanes appear out of nowhere to strafe the area. Then, a flotilla of ships from Saipan materializes in an instant out past the breakers, and the American landing begins on February 19, 1945. The Japanese allow the invaders to arrive in platoons on the beach, then, suddenly, after the beach is filled with soldiers, the battle is joined as Japanese artillery fire begins. Most of the second half of the film is set inside the vast network of mountain caves and tunnels as the soldiers make their various decisions to either retreat to another tunnel or blow themselves up with grenades. Communications break down. One of the men straps bombs to himself and wanders off toward the American entrenchments, positioning himself on the ground with the dead, waiting for an American tank that never arrives, undercutting the man's desperate courage. Eastwood was fascinated by the nihilistic nature of the subterranean Japanese bunker mentality: "They went there knowing they were going to die," Eastwood told Steve Daly of *Entertainment Weekly*. "What kind of a mind does that?"

Meanwhile, a Marine is captured and mercilessly beaten and bayoneted to death; but in a contrasting episode, when another wounded marine is brought to the camp, the Baron shares memories of America with him, which seems to comfort the soldier, who later dies of his wounds. Some of the Japanese see the island as sacred Japanese territory; others regard it merely as a desolate waste. Some defend the honor of their country; other merely try to survive. Some kill themselves without hesitation; others quail at the prospect and question the act. That's the way it is with this film, brutality mixed with mercy, horror mixed with tenderness. Eventually, the Baron is blinded and shoots himself with his rifle. The General is wounded and left with one of his men. Failing to order him to decapitate him with his sword, he shoots himself as well. His last request to Saigo, the baker: to be buried on a spit of land that has not yet fallen to the enemy and is therefore still symbolically the "homeland."

Eastwood's epilogue returns viewers to the present as the packet is unearthed. Spilling out are the undelivered letters, hundreds of letters, falling in slow motion to earth, each bearing a voice from the past, a remnant of fallen lives, voices that are heard echoing on the soundtrack, speaking of past glory, and misery, awaiting reception by a world still at war. The sparseness of the letters heard on the soundtrack is a little surprising. One could criticize the second half of the film for its numbing starkness, as it offers a potentially wearisome series of incidents and encounters in the seemingly endless tangle of Iwo Jima's claustrophobic tunnels as these warriors await the inevitable end. More tightly focused than *Flags of Our Fathers*, *Letters from Iwo Jima* both benefits and fails. It tells the story of a key battle of the war distinctively, though some will prefer the multi-layered structure and thematic complexity of the first film. It also documents a terrible human sacrifice. While 22,000 Japanese soldiers dug in to defend the island, only 1,083 survived.

According to Lisa Schwarzbaum of *Entertainment Weekly*, Eastwood originally intended to tell the story of the Battle for Iwo Jima twice, from both the American and from the Japanese perspectives. His first offering, *Flags of Our Fathers*, she wrote, was a "good, if earthbound, portrait of GI bravery overtaken by wartime hype," reflecting upon "image and reality in the service of patriotism." But, like most reviewers, Schwarzbaum was even more impressed by *Letters from Iwo Jima*, which she called a "soaring achievement, as Eastern in its appreciation of group discipline as *Flags* is Western in its contemplation of individual responsibility." So impressed was she that Schwarzbaum placed the film at the top of her list of best films of 2006, for she thought that by evoking a key battle of the Pacific Theatre in World War II, Eastwood was also evoking the current sacrifice of American soldiers in the Middle East: "With calm control and utmost respect, a quintessentially American director has made a war picture that honors every soldier (and soldier's mother) everywhere, with the superb care of an old moviemaking pro who continues to grow as an artist."

Following the Washington DC, opening of the film, *Washington Post* reviewer Stephen Hunter wrote a piece reflecting on the novelty of Eastwood's film in humanizing Japanese soldiers, who had been hideously stereotyped in films following World War II. Conceding that he might have missed a title or two, Hunter only found four films where they were not: *Beach Red*, starring Cornel Wilde and made during the height of the Vietnam war in 1967; *Hell to Eternity* (1960), starring Jeffrey Hunter and directed by Phil Karlson); *Hell in the Pacific* (1968), directed by John Boorman and starring Lee Marvin and the great Japanese actor Toshiro Mifune; and David Lean's *The Bridge on the River Kwai* (1957), starring Alec Guinness, Jack Hawkins, and Sessue Hayakawa as the Japanese officer, Colonel Saito. Michael Bay paid some attention to the Japanese perspective in *Pearl Harbor* (2001), but *Tora! Tora! Tora!* (1970) was a far better re-telling of the Pearl Harbor attack, however, as represented by a team of American and Japanese directors (Toshio Masuda and Kinji Fukasaku, working with Richard Fleischer, who began the project with Akira Kurosawa, Japan's famous director). *New York Times* critic Stephen Holden nailed down the film's importance more convincingly by describing it as a "classic anti-war movie that doesn't preach, editorialize or jerk tears," made, courageously, while our country is at war not with another nation, but with a conceptual dissident ideology, abstract, and difficult to grasp and comprehend, like the motives of the Japanese soldiers on Iwo Jima.

When the film opened in Kansas City on January 19, 2007, *Kansas City Star* reviewer Robert W. Butler found value in Eastwood's "unblinking look into the enemy [that] lets us see ourselves." *New York Times* reviewer A.O. Scott claimed the film was "close to perfect" and, in his opinion, the "best American movie of the year." *Time* magazine, the *Los Angeles Times*, and the National Board of Review agreed that it was the best film of the year, and it garnered two Golden Globe nominations for Best Foreign Language Film (which it won) and for Best Director. When the Oscar® nominations were finally announced, *Iwo Jima* was the Eastwood film that was placed in contention for the year's Best Picture and Director.

James M. Welsh and John C. Tibbetts

CREDITS

General Kuribayashi: Ken Watanabe
Baron Nishi: Tsuyoski Ihara
Lt. Ito: Shidou Nakamura
Saigo: Kazunari Ninomiya
Shimizu: Ryo Kase
Origin: USA
Language: Japanese
Released: 2006
Production: Clint Eastwood, Steven Spielberg, Robert Lorenz; Amblin Entertainment, Malpaso Productions, DreamWorks Pictures; released by Warner Bros.
Directed by: Clint Eastwood
Written by: Iris Yamashita, Paul Haggis (story)
Cinematography by: Tom Stern

Music by: Kyle Eastwood, Michael Stevens
Sound: Walt Martin
Editing: Joel Cox, Gary D. Raoch
Costumes: Deborah Hopper
Production Design: Henry Bumstead, James Murakami
MPAA rating: R
Running time: 145 minutes

REVIEWS

Boxoffice Online. December 20, 2006.
Entertainment Weekly. December 22, 2006, p. 59.
Hollywood Reporter Online. December 8, 2006.
Los Angeles Times Online. December 20, 2006.
New York Times Online. December 20, 2006.
Rolling Stone Online. December 12, 2006.
San Francisco Chronicle. December 20, 2006, p. E1.
USA Today Online. December 19, 2006.
Variety Online. December 7, 2006.

AWARDS

Oscars 2006: Sound FX Editing
Golden Globes 2007: Foreign Film
Nomination:
Oscars 2006: Director (Eastwood), Film, Orig. Screenplay
Golden Globes 2007: Director (Eastwood)

THE LIBERTINE

He didn't resist temptation. He pursued it.
—Movie tagline

Box Office: $4.8 million

"We have a pretty witty king, Whose word no man relies on; He never said a foolish thing, Nor ever did a wise one."—John Wilmot, 2nd Earl of Rochester

In candle-hued darkness, Johnny Depp's rakish John Wilmot, the Earl of Rochester leans forward to tell us, "You are not going to like me." Fans of Stephen Jeffrey's stage play will be pleased. As though watching the beginning of Laurence Olivier's *Richard III* (1955), we are transported inside the Earl's sex infused mind. He tells us that he is "always up for it. Always." The women will love him, and the men will hate him.

After a promising opening, the film has a tendency to dip and skip a few tracks, sinking the seventeenth century backdrop into a thick fog of browns, blacks, the occasional maidenly white and garbled dialogue.

One must admire Depp's performance, which trades in his Keith Richard-tinged Jack Sparrow for a snarling Johnny Rotten take on the Earl. The sense of deterioration is palpable in the performance, though one may yearn for a touch of pathos a bit sooner. As Ben Brantley of the *New York Times* states, when Rochester, "fingers his tresses, it's not split ends he's contemplating; it's the meaninglessness of life." We feel this a bit late in the film, as Depp hobbles about on two staves looking a bit like Michael Jackson crossed with Vincent D'Onofrio's outrageous portrayal of the drug dealer "Pooh-Bear" in *The Salton Sea* (2002).

The Libertine focuses mainly on this deterioration, as well as Rochester's relationship with his wife, his friends, King Charles II (John Malkovich), and the famous English stage actress Elizabeth Barry (Samantha Morton). There is much humor in his relationship with Charles II, who Rochester intends to annoy at every turn. The King wants a play, the Earl will give him smut. He will also become entangled with his leading lady, Barry. Though there is an historical account that proves beyond most doubts that Rochester was Barry's lover, there is no proof that he was her acting coach. The stage and film version play upon the myth written by Edmund Curll—known for his exaggerations—that Barry had been fired from the boards multiple times before going under the wing of Rochester. Or in this case under the sheets. Many of the film's delights take place in the darkened theatre between Rochester and Barry.

The stage version lost much of its panache in its translation to the screen. Much of the humor of the stage productions is nowhere to be seen. Instead the film at times feels a bit indulgent, and the existentialist nihilism is lost in a smoky forest orgy scene.

Laurence Dunmore makes his directorial film debut, providing sections of beautiful cinematography and slow movement. Apparently, Depp loved working with Dunmore on a commercial and suggested he direct the film. Halfway though the film are redundant scenes portraying the Earl's alcoholism and syphilis.

Dunmore also operated the camera for almost every shot in the film, most of which was lit using candles rather than conventional movie lights. In order to keep the candle effect but still get enough light, cinematographer Alexander Melman designed a special stand that held a bank of candles and a reflective backing. Set hands nicknamed these Birthday Cakes.

A strong supporting cast that is caught through a lens as dirty as Rochester's mind parade through London spewing riffs of poetic filth one moment, and in the next, such melodramatic lines as, "I cannot forgive you for teaching me to love life." The film ends with Rochester renouncing atheism, whispering to the audience, "do you like me now? Do you like me now?" The film ends as strongly as it began. The middle is a bit problematic.

Richard Baird

CREDITS

Earl of Rochester: Johnny Depp
Elizabeth Barry: Samantha Morton
King Charles II: John Malkovich
Elizabeth Malet: Rosamund Pike
Sir George Etherege: Tom Hollander
Jane: Kelly Reilly
Harris: Jack Davenport
Alcock: Richard Coyle
Countess: Francesca Annis
Downs: Rupert Friend
Molly Luscombe: Clare Higgins
Charles Sackville: Johnny Vegas
Origin: Great Britain
Language: English
Released: 2005
Production: Lianne Halfon, John Malkovich, Russell Smith; Odyssey Entertainment, Isle of Man, Cineville/Picture Entertainment; released by Entertainment Film Productions, Weinstein Co.
Directed by: Laurence Dunmore
Written by: Stephen Jeffreys
Cinematography by: Alexander Melman
Music by: Michael Nyman
Sound: John Hayes, Roger Savage
Editing: Jill Bilcock
Art Direction: Patrick Rolfe
Costumes: Dien van Straalen
Production Design: Ben van Os
MPAA rating: R
Running time: 130 minutes

REVIEWS

Boxoffice Online. March 17, 2005.
Entertainment Weekly Online. November 22, 2005.
Los Angeles Times Online. November 25, 2005.
Variety Online. November 13, 2005.

QUOTES

Rochester: "In my experince those who do not like you fall into two catagories: the stupid and the envious."

TRIVIA

The Stephen Jeffreys play on which the film is based was produced by the Steppenwolf Theatre Company and starred John Malkovich and Martha Plimpton.

LITTLE CHILDREN

Box Office: $5.3 million

Little Children, adapted from Tom Perrotta's novel of suburban angst and adultery by Perrotta himself and the film's director, Todd Field, is an ambitious project touching on adult issues few films routinely explore, namely, the dilemmas of middle-age people finding themselves at a dead end in life and struggling with the ramifications of their choices. This probing look at unhappy suburbanites is often funny and smart, which makes the movie all that more of a disappointment when it fails to live up to its initial promise. With the exception of a few notable departures, the screenplay is very faithful to the source material while sharing the novel's major flaws—a wobbly narrative spine, a lackluster final act, and an unsure resolution that does not bring to a coherent finish the various plot elements that are initially so compelling. As a result, this second feature from the director of *In the Bedroom* (2001), another overrated exploration of family dysfunction, offers some great individual moments but no profound insights into this familiar world.

Kate Winslet, in one of her best performances, leads a fine cast as Sarah Pierce, a frustrated housewife whose restlessness stems from the simple truth that she is not living the life she once envisioned for herself. A one-time Ph.D. candidate in English literature, she now takes her daughter, Lucy (Sadie Goldstein), to the playground, where Sarah sits with the other mothers, at once one of them and apart from them. The use of an omniscient narrator (Will Lyman) to key us in to the internal lives of the characters and provide wry commentary is a bold, sometimes effective touch, albeit one that functions to try to smooth over plot holes and telegraph character motivations and thoughts that the actors are capable of communicating on their own. When he intones that Sarah saw herself as an anthropologist studying the lives of suburban women as if they were a foreign tribe, it is a sardonic observation, but, just from her body language and the way she sets herself apart from the other women, we can immediately understand the isolation she feels.

The circle of women gets a bit of a jolt when a stay-at-home father visits the playground with his little son. Because of the dad's youthful good looks, they playfully dub him the Prom King, but, like a clique of teenage girls, are too scared to talk to him. On a dare, Sarah not only introduces herself but also gives him a hug and then a kiss for all of her companions to see. Her actions make her a pariah to the group, but her impulsiveness clearly has its roots in a yearning for something else, something that even she could not probably fully articulate.

The Prom King's name is Brad Adamson (Patrick Wilson), and, like Sarah, he is stuck in a life he despises. While Sarah is married to Richard (Gregg Edelman), a distant, older man whose obsession with Internet porn has alienated him from Sarah, Brad seemingly has a perfect marriage with the beautiful Kathy (Jennifer Connelly), a documentary filmmaker. But having failed the bar exam twice, he has let his family down and his life has come to a standstill. As Sarah shrewdly observes, "Maybe you just don't want to be a lawyer." The problem, however, is that what Brad does want is not clear, which makes him a handsome cipher, but his dream, amorphous as it is, seems to have something to do with recapturing his youth; instead of studying at the library at night, he watches teenage skateboarders doing stunts and wishes that he could be one of them.

When an acquaintance named Larry (Noah Emmerich) invites him to join a late-night football league, Brad is flattered and revels in the chance to relive his glory days. But Larry is really a bully, a self-appointed community watchdog with a mission to harass Ronnie J. McGorvey (Jackie Earle Haley), a convicted sex offender who exposed himself to a little girl and who, recently released from prison, has returned home to live with his elderly mother, May (Phyllis Somerville). While Larry's actions are extreme—posting flyers with Ronnie's picture, scrawling "EVIL" on the walkway to the McGorvey home, and waking the McGorveys with a bullhorn late at night—the town's parents are also gripped by fear of Ronnie. In one of the film's most stunning sequences, he appears at the local pool, looking ridiculous in a diving mask, snorkel, and flippers. In a chilling shot, we view the children in the pool from his underwater point of view. When the adults identify this supposed monster in their presence, the kids flee the water as if a shark had magically appeared.

What is most disturbing about Ronnie is that he is not only attracted to children but is indeed an overgrown child himself. In scenes with his mother, who desperately wants to believe in her son's goodness and has hopes for his future despite all evidence to the contrary, there is a genuine tenderness brought vividly to life by Haley and Somerville, who capture something very poignant about this sad relationship. It is a pure love that is almost tragic because, as one disastrous date through the personal ads seems to confirm, this is the only relationship he seems capable of—stuck as a little boy calling his mother "Mommy"—and yet, at the same time, he is conscious of his abnormal urges as he struggles against them.

But if Ronnie is stuck in a hellish, prolonged childhood, the point seems to be that he is an extreme form of the other characters, who long for their lost childhoods, a time before spouses, children, and middle-age responsibilities and disappointments began to weigh them down. The title ultimately refers not to literal children but rather adults such as Sarah, seeking escape through her afternoons with Brad at the community pool. Their meetings are platonic at first, but her red bathing suit hints at the passion just waiting to be unleashed, and we are not surprised when they begin an affair.

Winslet's natural beauty is downplayed in the first part of *Little Children* (the novel's Sarah is frumpier than Winslet could ever be), but, as Sarah spends more time with Brad, she becomes more radiant, as in one gorgeous shot in which she is backlit by the shimmering pool. But Winslet's achievement is more internal than external; she reveals Sarah's hopeful girlishness waiting to be recovered while illuminating the need and even the desperation for Sarah to find a world that makes sense to her apart from the one that she has struggled to fit in. Winslet delivers a complex, nuanced portrayal that is worthy of a better screenplay.

While Field and Perrotta set up these sympathetic characters, they do not seem to know what to do with all the simmering conflicts, and the story fizzles once the affair commences. The only suspense is whether Kathy will figure out what is going on (Richard, whose Internet fantasy life has been drastically diminished from the novel, hardly matters), but, once Kathy detects a genuine intimacy between Sarah and Brad in a well-played, funny dinner scene, the story has nowhere to go.

Because there seems to be no satisfying way to tie up the disparate plot strands, the screenplay tries to force a climax that brings the characters together. Sarah and Brad make a plan to run away, and the designated time just happens to be the night when Ronnie's mother passes away—she has a heart attack after Larry badgers her one time too many. Ronnie flies into a rage and ends up at the playground, where Sarah is awaiting her rendezvous with Brad. But Brad never shows up because he stalls watching the skateboarders and injures himself when they invite him to do a stunt. Sarah is left to confront Ronnie, who has castrated himself (a grotesque, shocking, and unbelievable character development), and Larry, of all people, ends up driving him to the hospital. (In the novel, Ronnie is a darker character who does not mutilate himself but instead confesses to the long-held community suspicion that he kidnapped and murdered a little girl—a backstory whose omission in the screenplay makes Ronnie more sympathetic.) The film's narrator leaves us with the impression that this evening supposedly provides a moment of redemption for Ronnie and Larry as well as a fresh start for Sarah with her family. When she gets a scare thinking for a moment that she has lost Lucy on the street, Sarah comes to realize how much she loves her daughter, as if this incident could suddenly erase all the anxiety she has felt at home. And Brad's newfound appreciation of his family, via a conk on the head literally knocking some sense into him, feels just as facile.

But these preposterous, contrived plot turns only illustrate the way the narrator is finally used as a crutch to give the audience a false feeling of hope and a hollow sense of closure. There is nothing to suggest that Sarah's home life will be any more fulfilling than it has been (or Brad's either, for that matter). Neither character has fundamentally changed, and the hunger for a different life will not simply disappear. The ending is ultimately one of failure, even if the narrator tries to convince us that the reality is more optimistic. Perhaps he is not omniscient after all.

Peter N. Chumo II

CREDITS

Sarah Pierce: Kate Winslet
Brad Adamson: Patrick Wilson
Ronnie J. McGorvey: Jackie Earle Haley
Larry Hedges: Noah Emmerich
Richard Pierce: Gregg Edelman
May McGorvey: Phyllis Somerville
Narrator: Will Lyman
Lucy Pierce: Sadie Goldstein
Kathy Adamson: Jennifer Connelly
Origin: USA
Language: English
Released: 2006
Production: Todd Field, Albert Berger, Ron Yerxa; Bona Fide, Standard Film Company; released by New Line Cinema
Directed by: Todd Field
Written by: Todd Field, Tom Perrotta
Cinematography by: Antonio Calvache
Music by: Thomas Newman
Sound: Edward Tise
Editing: Leo Trombetta
Art Direction: John J. Kasarda
Costumes: Melissaa Economy
Production Design: David Gropman
MPAA rating: R
Running time: 130 minutes

REVIEWS

Boxoffice Online. October 6, 2006.
Chicago Sun-Times Online. October 20, 2006.
Entertainment Weekly. October 13, 2006, p. 109.
Hollywood Reporter Online. September 13, 2006.
Los Angeles Times Online. October 6, 2006.
New York Times Online. September 29, 2006.
Newsweek Online. October 9, 2006.
Variety Online. September 4, 2006.
Washington Post. October 20, 2006, p. C5.

LITTLE MAN

Big things come in small packages.
—Movie tagline

Box Office: $58.6 million

The Wayans family has made a niche for themselves in film and silliness is pretty much the key tenet of their filmic creed. Whether or not the plots make sense or are even remotely believable, does not seem to matter. Indeed, Shawn and Marlon Wayans' last team effort, *White Chicks* (2004), had the brothers playing young, white blonde socialites. *Little Man* stretches believability even further. In this film, Marlon Wayans plays a pint-sized man. That Marlon is not actually a small person is solved by superimposing his face onto the body of a small person or in this case, two different small people, Linden Porco and Gabriel Pimental. The special effects are far superior to those in *White Chicks*. In that film, Marlon looked less like a perky blonde than some sort of freakish alien being. In *Little Man*, Marlon's face really does look like it is attached to the small body.

Calvin (Marlon Wayans) is a tiny thug just getting out of jail. His buddy Percy (Tracy Morgan) picks him up and the two immediately set out to steal a jumbo-sized diamond. They steal the jewel, but are chased by the police. A panicked Calvin drops the diamond into a woman's purse. That woman, Vanessa (Kerry Washington) is an upwardly mobile career woman whose husband, Darryl (Shawn Wayans), wants her to slow down and start having children.

Calvin and Percy use Darryl's parental ambitions against him in their plan by dressing Calvin in baby clothes and setting him at the couple's doorstep. Calvin, with his adult face, military tattoo and strangely buff body, does not look much like a baby, but that does not matter.

Calvin will play baby until he gets a chance to snatch Vanessa's purse and recover the diamond. Instead of just taking the purse and running, Calvin stays the whole weekend, creating enough time for many jokes about breast-feeding, and building a tender relationship between the would-be father and son.

The plot elements simply exist to service the jokes—and the bawdier, the better. Of course, there are numerous gags involving a hit to the groin. Also offered up for comedy is gastronomic distress, voyeurism, and a dog urinating on Calvin's face.

It would be easy to be offended by the humor found here, but the Wayanses have a genial way about them. Their films have an appealing eagerness to please.

Critics were not all that impressed with the film. Darel Jevens of the *Chicago Sun-Times* wrote: "The Wayanses rely on their usual tired jokes here—spit-takes, white people speaking jive, Marlon grimacing in gastrointestinal distress." Kevin Crust of the *Los Angeles Times* wrote that "the screenplay...is devoid of verbal wit, instead relying on a relentless stream of Looney Tunes-inspired violence." Wesley Morris of the *Boston Globe* wrote: "Frankly, the prospect of a movie starring Marlon Wayans as a thirty-six-inch-tall ex-con pretending to be a toddler did not excite me, but the film's enthusiasm for the lowest imaginable humor and Marlon's seemingly boundless skill at bringing it off are contagious." Finally, Keith Phillips of *The Onion A.V. Club* wrote: "The movies aren't exactly funny—let's not mince words; they're hardly funny at all—but at least they go for it."

Jill Hamilton

CREDITS

Calvin: Marlon Wayans
Darryl: Shawn Wayans
Vanessa: Kerry Washington
Percy: Tracy Morgan
Pops: John Witherspoon
Greg: Lochlyn Munro
Walken: Chazz Palminteri
Calvin Body: Linden Porco
Soccer Mom: Molly Shannon
Calvin Body: Gabriel Pimental
Dinosaur Rex: Paul DeMielche
Janet: Alex Borstein
Brittany: Brittany Daniel
Origin: USA
Language: English
Released: 2006
Production: Keenen Ivory Wayans, Marlon Wayans, Shawn Wayans, Lee R. Mayes, Rick Alvarez; Revolution Studios, Wayans Brothers Production; released by Sony Pictures Entertainment
Directed by: Keenen Ivory Wayans
Written by: Marlon Wayans, Shawn Wayans, Keenen Ivory Wayans
Cinematography by: Steven Bernstein
Music by: Teddy Castellucci
Sound: Eric J. Batut
Editing: Nick Moore, Mike Jackson
Art Direction: Gwen Margetson
Costumes: Jori Woodman
Production Design: Leslie Dilley
MPAA rating: PG-13
Running time: 97 minutes

REVIEWS

Boxoffice Online. July 14, 2006.
Los Angeles Times Online. July 14, 2006.
New York Times Online. July 14, 2006.
Premiere Magazine Online. July 13, 2006.
San Francisco Chronicle. July 14, 2006, p. E7.
Variety Online. July 13, 2006.
Washington Post. July 14, 2006, p. C5.

AWARDS

Golden Raspberries 2006: Worst Actor (Wayans), Worst Actor (Wayans), Worst Remake

Nomination:

Golden Raspberries 2006: Worst Picture, Worst Actor (Schneider), Worst Director (Wayans), Worst Screenplay

LITTLE MISS SUNSHINE

Where's Olive?
—Movie tagline

A family on the verge of a breakdown.
—Movie tagline

Everyone just pretend to be normal.
—Movie tagline

Box Office: $59.9 million

Dysfunctional family comedies are reliably appealing, and the family at the heart of *Little Miss Sunshine* is certainly a worthy addition to the wonderful eccentrics that populate films like *The Royal Tenenbaums* (2001) and *The Squid and the Whale* (2005). Piling into a rickety, yellow VW bus, the Hoover family journeys to the Golden State to fulfill the All-American dreams of the young Olive (Abigail Breslin), who yearns to win a beauty pageant's titular title. While seeking superficial validation, Olive and the filmmakers cleverly turn tradition on its head with her chutzpah and staunch belief in her unique abilities. In this way, the film illustrates the importance of family while honoring the spirit of individuality.

The married team of Jonathan Dayton and Valerie Faris are seasoned music-video and commercial directors who made their feature debut with *Little Miss Sunshine,* which was penned by first-time screenwriter Michael Arndt. The newcomers first try struck a nerve with audiences and critics alike, grossing nearly $60 million at the box office (it cost $8 million to produce) and garnering a host of awards and award nominations, including scoring Best Picture at The Producers Guild Awards (eleven of the past seventeen films that have won this award went on to win the Academy Award® for Best Picture). The film and its actors also boasted four Academy Award® nominations, including Best Picture, and two Golden Globe nominations.

Mom Sheryl (Toni Collette) has taken on the care of her suicidal, homosexual brother Frank (Steve Carell), a jilted Proust scholar. Moving in with the rest of her ragtag brood, Frank is introduced to son Dwayne (Paul Dano), a Nietzsche fan who has taken a vow of silence until he can become a pilot; dad Richard (Greg Kinnear), a struggling motivational speaker; the out-spoken, heroin-addicted Grandpa (Alan Arkin); and Olive, a cute little girl with huge glasses and even bigger ambition. Clearly these characters could have easily slipped into broad caricatures, but here they are safe in the capable hands of the filmmakers and the accomplished actors.

Olive, slavishly watching hours and hours of beauty pageant footage, has perfected her talent routine (which is not revealed until the film's final act) with the help of Grandpa and is thrilled when the family's answering machine reveals that she has qualified to compete in the Little Miss Sunshine pageant in California. Learning from her parents that she can do anything in life she puts her mind to, she still sometimes needs reassurance. Grandpa tells her she's the most beautiful girl in the world, which she questions with "You're just saying that." Grandpa endearingly protests, "No! I'm madly in love with you and it's not because of your brains or your personality." Despite everyone in the family having competing interests and not feeling particularly excited about seeing their special little Olive participate in the horror show that is the child beauty pageant, they somehow manage to put their own obsessive issues aside for the good of Olive and set out from their Albuquerque, New Mexico home to Redondo Beach, California.

The van proves as quirky as most of its denizens, and one of the film's running gags is that the whole family is forced to push start it, slowly running alongside, while Richard shoves it into gear. Crises big and small arise as we get to know the Hoovers on a new and deeper level. Richard and Sheryl bicker about his failing career, Dwayne is sullen, and Grandpa ribs Frank about his sexual orientation while reading porn. Olive, as always, is upbeat in her own offbeat way. In between the wry hilarity, some poignant moments appear. One particularly moving scene has Dwayne discover he is color blind and can never become a pilot, crushing his only dream in life. Frank, who was deeply in love with a grad student who left him heartbroken after ditching him for a rival Proust scholar, is able to help Dwayne through the crisis despite his own pain.

The wonderful ensemble, without exception, shows a multitude of levels and nuance within its characters while the script's uniquely funny situations and witty dialogue drive the film nicely along, even as it teeters toward slapstick near the end of the trip when Grandpa's journey is cut short by his unexpected death. With pageant time growing dangerously close, the family is forced to abscond from the hospital with Grandpa's body to make it on time. The dark humor is somehow made to work, and upon checking Olive in at the pageant, Richard asks, as casually as possible, if there is a funeral home nearby.

At the pageant, it's clear how out of place little Olive seems among the primped, teased, hair-sprayed, and made-up young contestants. A bit pudgy in the middle with waist-length, undone locks, ever-present spectacles, and amateur costume, Olive cheerily works on her much-practiced routine. When it is her turn on stage, she sweetly dedicates the performance to Grandpa, who she says showed her the moves. "Where is your Grandpa?" the MC innocently asks. "In the trunk of our car," Olive explains matter-of-factly. She ends up performing a hysterically raunchy dance to Rick James' "Super Freak" that appalls the judges and most of the audience. Her proud family, however, wildly applauds her unique style.

Hilary White

CREDITS

Richard: Greg Kinnear
Sheryl: Toni Collette
Olive: Abigail Breslin
Frank: Steven Carell
Grandpa: Alan Arkin
Dwayne: Paul Dano
Origin: USA
Language: English
Released: 2006
Production: Marc Turtletaub, Peter Saraf, Albert Berger, Ron Yerxa; Big Beach, Bona Fide; released by Fox Searchlight
Directed by: Jonathan Dayton, Valerie Faris
Written by: Michael Arndt
Cinematography by: Tim Suhrstedt
Music by: Mychael Danna
Sound: Steve Morrow
Editing: Pamela Martin
Art Direction: Alan E. Muraoka
Costumes: Nancy Steiner
Production Design: Kalina Ivanov
MPAA rating: R
Running time: 101 minutes

REVIEWS

Boxoffice Online. July 28, 2006.
Chicago Sun-Times Online. August 4, 2006.
Entertainment Weekly. August 4, 2006, p. 50.
Hollywood Reporter Online. January 23, 2006.
Los Angeles Times Online. July 26, 2006.

New York Times Online. July 26, 2006.
Premiere Magazine Online. July 26, 2006.
San Francisco Chronicle. August 4, 2006, p. E1.
Variety Online. January 21, 2006.
Village Voice Online. July 25, 2006.
Washington Post. August 4, 2006, p. C1.

AWARDS

Oscars 2006: Orig. Screenplay, Support. Actor (Arkin)
British Acad. 2006: Orig. Screenplay, Support. Actor (Arkin)
Ind. Spirit 2007: Director (Dayton), Director (Faris), Film, Support. Actor (Arkin), First Screenplay
Screen Actors Guild 2006: Cast
Writers Guild 2006: Orig. Screenplay
Nomination:
Oscars 2006: Film, Support. Actress (Breslin)
British Acad. 2006: Director (Dayton), Director (Faris), Film, Support. Actress (Collette, Breslin)
Directors Guild 2006: Director (Dayton), Director (Faris)
Golden Globes 2007: Actress—Mus./Comedy (Collette), Film—Mus./Comedy
Ind. Spirit 2007: Support. Actor (Dano)
Screen Actors Guild 2006: Support. Actor (Arkin), Support. Actress (Breslin)

LONESOME JIM

Change your outlook. Change your life.
—Movie tagline

In Steve Buscemi's indie-style feature *Lonesome Jim,* the title character, played diffidently by Casey Affleck, comes home to small-town Indiana at age twenty-seven after failing to make a successful life for himself in New York City. There he comes face-to-face with his dysfunctional parents and older brother. His mom, Sally (Mary Kay Place), is terminally perky; his dad, Don (Seymour Cassel), is a cauldron of barely repressed anger; his brother, Tim (Kevin Corrigan), is divorced, going nowhere, and suicidal.

If *Lonesome Jim* reminds you of more than a few other movies, it's because this theme of the prodigal child returning from the big city to a messed-up home has become a very popular one. It happens in *Garden State* (2004), a much more nuanced movie; *Junebug* (2005), *Transamerica* (2005), and many other features of recent years. But those films had characters with substance, whereas this script by first-time writer James Strouse gives us little but anguish.

Jim arrives home in a state of existential anxiety, and nearly collapses in the kitchen while shedding tears of deep despair. Jim, whose New York job consisted of walking dogs but who insists he was also a writer—though there is no palpable evidence of that—has completely given up on himself and is mired in tremendous self-doubt. But we never know exactly why. His personality is something of a blank, and Affleck plays him in a monotone, cherishing his own worthlessness.

Though it doesn't have an emo soundtrack, *Lonesome Jim* might be called an emo movie—awash in the kind of self-loathing and apathy that characterize that popular brand of music. Jim is sad because life is sad, but why life is sad seems unimportant to Strouse and Buscemi. It's just a given.

Could it be that Jim is messed up because his parents are terrors? That hardly seems the case. Place gives a standout performance—by far the best in the film—as an always-giving, never-asking-anything mother without any tinges of self-pity. Her cheerfulness and love for her sons seem ridiculous given the circumstances, but the movie wants to have it both ways: at first mocking her, and finally, in a paroxysm of mawkishness, adoring her. In either case, she doesn't seem like the kind of crazy-making mom we've seen in many other movies, though clearly her grip on reality is sometimes tenuous. The father, Don, apart from one fit of controlling rage, seems fairly inconsequential.

In a key scene, after Tim has attempted suicide and Jim has moped around the house doing nothing but looking pained for weeks, Sally asks Jim outright: What did we do as parents to make you boys so miserable? Jim's answer has no content to it, but is scathingly mean. Maybe some people just shouldn't be parents, he says.

The main trouble with *Lonesome Jim* is that it dispenses with any need to explain why its characters are what they are. Jim is depressed about life for no specific reason. The dreams he left Indiana to pursue in New York are unspoken ones. Yes, he has a wall full of posters of famous writers, all of whom committed suicide or drank themselves to death. But nowhere in the film do we see him writing, does he talk about what he's written, or does he give any indication of actually being a writer.

Jim says he came home to have a nervous breakdown, but his brother beat him to it. Jim helped that happen, by telling his older brother how bad Tim's life seems to be: divorced, living at his parents' house at age thirty-two in order to afford child support; and working in his parents' ladder-making factory, having given up his dream of becoming a CIA agent. Tim goes out and drives his car into a tree and ends up in a coma, and Jim feels guilty.

Life sucks for Jim, but it's hard to feel much sympathy for him, because he doesn't seem to try. He lacks a character so can't have a character flaw—he's just a blank. As played by Affleck, he's a slacker extraordinaire with a personality deficit. That makes it all the harder to believe that Liv Tyler, who plays a kind-hearted nurse named Anika, falls for him. That's also because Anika's character is underwritten too. She at first seems to crave sex for its own sake, then continues to express interest in Jim after his initial bedroom performance proves woefully inadequate, then seems to shift her attentions to Tim, then somehow falls in love with Jim. There is no rhyme or reason for these emotions and behaviors: Anika, who has a young son, Ben (Jack Rovello), is sweet but doesn't seem desperate. Tyler makes her an attractive character, a sort of earth mother figure, the kind of woman a man might want to settle down with. But there's no on-screen chemistry between Affleck and Tyler.

In fact, *Lonesome Jim* has a credo of anti-chemistry in all its interactions. People are mean to one another because that's the way people are. Jim and Tim are caustic towards each other and their parents. This allegiance to the idea of human beings as toxic makes the eventual sentimentalism of the plot all the more unbearable. In the disguise of an unconventional movie, *Lonesome Jim* becomes very conventional indeed. Ben takes to Jim, for reasons as unfathomable as his mother's. Jim takes over for Tim as the coach of Tim's daughter's basketball team, which hasn't scored a single point the entire season, and in the final game, Jim gives a tortured pep talk that is really a self-monologue. The basketball team is an obvious aphorism for Jim's life: is it worth trying one more time when all previous results have failed? Of course it is, and Ben, who has inexplicably been allowed to join a girls' league, gets the redemptive basket.

Along the way to this hokey resolution, there's some mildly entertaining wackiness, provided mostly by Mark Boone Jr. as Evil, Jim's dope-dealing uncle. It's a stretch of huge proportions to imagine Evil as Don's brother: in age, appearance, demeanor, and interests, there's no match. Boone, overweight and dissipated, at least gives the film a memorable minor character; he saves the movie from being completely dull. But Buscemi seems to shrink from outright satire, because that might ruin the dour mood he's going for.

As a film about existential despair, *Lonesome Jim* fails for lack of character delineation. The dialogue ranges from occasionally witty to often insipid, and Buscemi's direction is less than inspired. He shouldn't have resisted the impulse to make the film more comic, but that, too, would have shown signs of life among this cast of the half-dead.

It's hard to care about the people in *Lonesome Jim* because their characters are so lifeless. It's hard to invest much interest in people who don't seem to invest much in themselves. It's hard to feel sorry for depressed people who cannot even articulate a reason for their depression. The dilemma of a twenty-seven-year-old returning home because his life isn't working would resonate more if he had an actual life, but Affleck's Jim doesn't want to risk having one. The script doesn't risk much either, and neither does the director. Place, however, gives a wonderfully believable seriocomic performance that isn't self-mocking but is still genuinely funny. What Tyler is doing in this film is unclear: her talents are wasted. As for Affleck, he plays emo well, but then there's not much of a trick to playing an affectless guy with a whiny voice. And ultimately, the film doesn't have the courage of its convictions. If Jim is going to be saved from himself in the most conventional fashion, why go to such pains to make him appear so unsaveable? Jim isn't really depressed and he's not mentally ill: he just needs a reason for living. And Liv Tyler is certainly such a reason.

Michael Betzold

CREDITS

Jim: Casey Affleck
Anika: Liv Tyler
Sally: Mary Kay Place
Don: Seymour Cassel
Tim: Kevin Corrigan
Ben: Jack Rovello
Evil: Mark Boone Jr.
Origin: USA
Language: English
Released: 2006
Production: Galt Niederhoffer, Celine Rattray, Daniela Taplin Lundberg, Jake Abraham, Gary Winick; InDigEnt, Plum Pictures; released by IFC Films
Directed by: Steve Buscemi
Written by: James C. Strouse
Cinematography by: Phil Parmet
Sound: Warren Shaw
Music Supervisor: Alex Steyermark, Linda Cohen
Editing: Plummy Tucker
Costumes: Victoria Farrell
Production Design: Chuck Voelter
MPAA rating: R
Running time: 91 minutes

REVIEWS

Boxoffice Online. March 24, 2006.
Chicago Sun-Times Online. March 31, 2006.

Entertainment Weekly. March 31, 2006, p. 42.
New York Times Online. March 24, 2006.
Rolling Stone Online. March 21, 2006.
San Francisco Chronicle Online. March 31, 2006.
Variety Online. January 24, 2005.
Village Voice Online. March 21, 2006.

QUOTES

Jim to Anika: "There are so many fun and cheery people in the world. Don't you think you'd be better off with one of them?"

TRIVIA

Film is set, and was filmed around, screenwriter James C. Strause's hometown of Goshen, Indiana.

LOOKING FOR COMEDY IN THE MUSLIM WORLD

In *Looking for Comedy in the Muslim World*, writer/director Albert Brooks plays a version of himself, a comedian named Albert Brooks, who is thrust into a very awkward and often uncomfortable situation—just what we would expect from the man who escaped the rat race only to find disaster on the open road in *Lost in America* (1985) and who had to face a heavenly tribunal in *Defending Your Life* (1991). In Brooks's latest film, the United States government sends him on an overseas mission to find out what makes Muslims laugh. The hysterical premise is, given the delicate state of world affairs today (especially the West's relation to Islam), rife with comic possibilities. Unfortunately, the execution largely falls flat and is only intermittently entertaining. The comic bits are overly familiar rehashes of Brooks's shtick, and yet the film could have been very amusing if he wrote a satisfying screenplay on which to hang his comic episodes. Instead, he has cobbled together a shapeless story that goes nowhere and ends abruptly, without a satisfying comic payoff.

The movie begins on the funny, absurd note of Brooks trying to get the lead in a remake of *Harvey* (1950) and not impressing director Penny Marshall (playing herself), who does not even ask him for an audition. He knows that he is not a handsome James Stewart leading man and tries in vain to persuade her that this version could be different. But Brooks is in store for a bigger role when he gets summoned by a government commission formed to take a new strategy in understanding the Muslim world and presided over by real-life politician and actor Fred Dalton Thompson, who enlists him to go to India and Pakistan to see what makes the people laugh and then present his findings in a daunting five-hundred-page report. Although Brooks is initially reticent, when the Medal of Freedom is dangled before him as a possible reward, he cannot resist.

His mission seems hopeless from the start, with two bureaucrats assigned to assist him who are never as enthusiastic as he would like. Stuart (John Carroll Lynch) is at least supportive and friendly, but Mark (Jon Tenney) is critical of *Lost in America*, thus rubbing the insecure Brooks the wrong way almost immediately. Brooks hires a very pretty assistant, Maya (Sheetal Sheth), who does not understand American comedy but tries her best to get Brooks's deadpan sarcasm and takes great joy when she seems to be making progress. She is a lovely and delightful foil for Brooks's anxious, worrywart persona, and they share some cute interplay involving his attempt to get her to pad his report with historical research. Another running joke pokes fun at outsourcing as we periodically see banks of telephone operators answering calls for a variety of Western companies, even, in a great punch line, for the White House.

A potentially hilarious subplot involves Maya's Iranian boyfriend, Majeed (Homie Doroodian), growing jealous of Brooks when Maya seems to be getting too friendly. While this conflict goes nowhere, Majeed at least gets one great line; when Maya claims that he is not funny and he counters, "I was the funniest one in school and the funniest one in explosives training," it is the kind of politically incorrect zinger that the film could have used more of.

Much of the film, however, is very tame, consisting of Brooks asking common folk what makes them laugh or trying out jokes that people do not think are funny. To test out American humor on a bigger scale, Brooks decides to put on a live comedy show in New Delhi, which is the centerpiece of the movie. Longtime fans will enjoy Brooks's particular brand of stand-up, but it gains nothing fresh from being performed in an Indian context, and, while it is supposed to be funny to see Brooks squirm as his routines fall flat, the show is almost guaranteed to be an utter failure since no one in a foreign culture without a background in American humor could possibly comprehend his jokes—a ventriloquist who does not know the basics in handling a dummy, an improv sketch in which he skewers the very concept of improv by rejecting the audience's directions and instead doing what he wants. An episode in which Brooks gets smuggled across the border into Pakistan (he cannot get a visa and has to travel stealthily at night) results in him doing his show around a campfire for aspiring Pakistani comics as if they were in a Vegas nightclub. Unbelievably, they get all the jokes that bombed in India, although it is impossible to figure out why. Yet another half-baked subplot has the Arab network Al-Jazeera calling Brooks in for a meeting. Thinking that the network wants to help him with his project, he is dismayed when the executives offer him a TV sitcom called *That Darn Jew*, about an American Jew living in a Muslim apartment complex. Once again Brooks flirts with something politically incorrect and risky but does not develop the gag beyond the idea itself.

In terms of a plot, the only genuine intrigue revolves around Brooks's activities inadvertently leading to increased tension between India and Pakistan as his mere presence and words are misinterpreted by government officials, eventually bringing the two countries to the brink of war. The idea of the inept Brooks causing an international crisis is ingenious and could have been played for smart, sophisticated laughs, but, just as the global situation is heating up, the American embassy demands that all high-profile people return home. In a disappointing, arbitrary ending, all of the loose ends are tied up in a written postscript: the discord between India and Pakistan ends when Brooks is identified as the source of the problem, he submits a six-page report to the U.S. government, and the program to understand Muslims is suspended in favor of more military spending (presumably the traditional American way to deal with foreign affairs). The movie feels unfinished, as if Brooks had given up on the only real plot threads he had created. Narrative may not be Brooks's strong suit to begin with, but setting up conflicts only to dismiss them is essentially cheating the audience.

Looking for Comedy in the Muslim World is a huge disappointment, if only because the current social climate is perfect for cross-cultural shenanigans and satiric jabs at global affairs. All Brooks really proves is that comedy has a cultural basis and that, if an audience does not have the same background or references, it will not get the jokes, but the film says nothing specific about the Muslim world, which is supposedly the whole point of the movie. Brooks's dry humor is not crowd-pleasing to begin with and could even be considered an acquired taste, but the topic here is timely enough and provocative enough that a thoughtful, or even outlandish, treatment could have yielded rich comic rewards.

Peter N. Chumo II

CREDITS

Himself: Albert Brooks
Maya: Sheetal Sheth
Stuart: John Carroll Lynch
Mark: Jon Tenney
Himself: Fred Dalton Thompson
Herself: Penny Marshall
Emily: Amy Ryan
Majeed: Homie Doroodian
Stage Manager: Duncan Bravo
Laura: Emma Lockhart
Origin: USA
Language: English
Released: 2006
Production: Herb Nanas; Shangri-La Entertainment; released by Warner Independent Pictures
Directed by: Albert Brooks
Written by: Albert Brooks
Cinematography by: Thomas Ackerman
Music by: Michael Giacchino
Sound: Dan Wallin, Mike Aarvoid
Editing: Anita Brant Burgoyne
Costumes: Deborah Everton
Production Design: Stephen Altman
MPAA rating: PG-13
Running time: 98 minutes

REVIEWS

Boxoffice Online. January 20, 2006.
Chicago Sun-Times Online. January 20, 2006.
Entertainment Weekly Online. January 18, 2006.
Los Angeles Times Online. January 20, 2006.
New York Times Online. January 20, 2006.
Premiere Magazine Online. January 30, 2006.
Variety Online. December 16, 2005.
Washington Post Online. January 20, 2006, p. C01.

TRIVIA

Sony Pictures Classics was originally set to distribute the film in the U.S. but opted out due to the film's controversial title, which they wanted to change. Warner Independent Pictures then became the film's U.S. distributor.

THE LOST CITY

A place you leave is a place that lives forever.
—Movie tagline

Box Office: $2.4 million

The dream projects of many actors and directors often end up being too personal to have the desired effect on viewers. As with Francis Ford Coppola's *Tucker: The Man and the Dream* (1988), filmmakers sometimes get too emotionally entangled with their projects to see the flaws in their conceptions. Such, unfortunately, is the case with Andy Garcia, who spent sixteen years trying to get *The Lost City* on the screen. This look at the effect of events in Cuba during 1958-1959 on one family is clearly heartfelt but a bit flat.

Fico Fellove (Garcia) is relatively comfortable with his life as the owner of the El Tropico nightclub in Havana. His brothers, Luis (Nestor Carbonell) and Ricardo (Enrique Murciano), however, oppose the dictatorial regime of Fulgencio Batista (Juan Fernandez). Their professor father, Federico (Tomas Milian), wants political change through legislation, not the revolution espoused by Fidel Castro (Gonzalo Menendez). Events throw Fico and Luis' wife, Aurora (Ines Sastre) together, and they fall in love. After Batista flees Cuba and Castro assumes control, Aurora abandons Fico to serve the new leader.

Although *The Lost City* is defiantly anti-Castro, it does not shy away from the evils of Batista. The dictator is presented as a smug, arrogant, preening, ruthless monster who acts condescending to everyone, especially his loyal assistant Pizzi (Ruben Rabasa). If he doesn't care for Pizzi, how can he have any concern for his citizens?

Just as smug and evil, however, is rebel leader Ernesto "Che" Guevara (Jsu Garcia). A far cry from the heroic soldier-poet of leftist legend, this Che cares only for power. He even refuses to allow Fico to call him Che. But except for newsreel footage of executions and Che's arrogant behavior—he callously kills a wounded soldier—*The Lost City* is not actually that hard on the revolutionaries. They force Fico to fire his saxophone player because the instrument is a tool of colonialists. Much more unsettling is losing Aurora to the romantic allure of revolution.

As a young writer in Castro's Cuba, screenwriter G. Cabrera Infante held various positions in the government and edited a cultural and literary supplement to Revolucion, the semiofficial newspaper of the revolution. By 1961, however, Cabrera Infante, whose parents were founding members of the Cuban Communist Party, clashed with officials over the censorship of artists, and Castro shut down his publication. He finally gave up on the revolution and immigrated to England in 1966.

Cabrera Infante, who died in 2005, was fascinated by the Havana nightlife of the pre-Castro era, and it figures prominently in his fiction, especially his best-known novel, *Three Trapped Tigers* (1967). The first half of *The Lost City* is almost a musical, with much singing and dancing in El Tropico and other clubs. Like Humphrey Bogart's Rick Blaine in *Casablanca* (1943), an obvious major influence on the film, Fico strives to exist in a world he can control that shuts out nasty matters like politics. While Blaine moves from stoicism to heroism, the more mundane Fico merely becomes frustrated over his losses.

Within the context of *The Lost City*, the revolution seems the result primarily of Batista's thuggish behavior. The poverty and social inequalities that spurred Castro to overthrow the government are never depicted. As a result, the film comes off as being somewhat naive.

Cabrera Infante was also a film critic in Cuba, writing and lecturing about such classic Hollywood directors as Howard Hawks, Alfred Hitchcock, and Orson Welles. Though his previous major screenwriting credit is to the cult action film *Vanishing Point* (1970), Cabrera Infante aims for the romantic, epic scope of old Hollywood, especially the films of Vincente Minnelli. He fails, however, to make the characters more than shakily motivated sketches. The suicide of one has little emotional impact because he is so vague.

Though Garcia, directing his first feature-length film, stages most of his scenes well and makes some interesting choices in framing shots, the pace is deadly slow for most of the 143 minutes, and there are frequently jarring transitions from scene to scene. American gangster Meyer Lansky (Dustin Hoffman) wants Fico to introduce gambling to El Tropico, an odd suggestion given that the Batista regime is already in trouble at this point, and the club owner refuses. Soon afterward, a bomb goes off on stage, and a dancer is killed. Fico then goes on as if nothing has happened. The absurdity of this situation is only heightened by the failure of the dancer to shed blood or give any other sign of being mortally wounded.

The screenwriter's romantic intentions are well served by Garcia, who left Cuba when he was five, as the film's composer. Combining Cuban rhythms with the kind of lush score associated with Hollywood films of the 1950s, Garcia provides some essential emotional shading. As an actor, however, Garcia is oddly inexpressive. Except for his seedy journalist in Kenneth Branagh's *Dead Again* (1991), Garcia never conveys much emotion, always seems rather glum. He has one good moment in *The Lost City* when Fico gives an odd look to a character drinking coffee from a saucer.

Sastre, a former model, is beautiful and has some screen presence but is used primarily as an ornament. Milian, wonderful as the evil Mexican general in Steven Soderbergh's *Traffic* (2000), underplays what could have become a too sentimental part. Hoffman, who worked with Garcia in *Hero* (1992) and *Confidence* (2003), plays the legendary gangster as a senior citizen out for a Sunday stroll. His performance recalls that of Lee Strasberg playing a fictional version of Lansky in Coppola's *The Godfather, Part II* (1974). This association is unfortunate because Coppola, unlike Garcia, captures the glamour, danger, and chaos of 1959 Havana indelibly. Even Sydney Pollack's similar failure, *Havana* (1990), has more vitality than *The Lost City*.

What little life there is in *The Lost City* comes from its oddest element: the presence of Bill Murray as a nameless American known only as the Writer, though he never seems to do any writing. The Writer is Fico's friend and confidante, serving the same function as the fools attendant upon kings in the plays of William Shakespeare. Though Cabrera Infante intended the character to be a comic self-portrait, Murray, always dressed in coat, tie, and shorts, seems to be improvising his lines, assuming the wiseacre persona familiar from such films as *Ghostbusters* (1984). Much of what the Writer says is not that funny, as with confusing Meyer Lansky with Oscar Mayer of wiener fame, but Murray's deadpan delivery is vastly entertaining. His character's presence in Havana makes little sense and the tone of his scenes clashes with the rest of the film, but it is always a delight when he appears.

Michael Adams

CREDITS

Fulgencio Batista: Juan Fernandez
Fico Fellove: Andy Garcia
Luis Fellove: Nestor Carbonell
Ricardo Fellove: Enrique Murciano
Don Donoso Fellove: Richard Bradford
Captain Castel: Steven Bauer
Fidel Castro: Gonzalo Menendez
Meyer Lansky: Dustin Hoffman
Colonel Candela: Julio Oscar Mechoso
Don Federico Fellove: Tomas Milian
Rodney: William Marquez
The Writer: Bill Murray
Miliciana Munoz: Elizabeth Pena
Dona Cecilia Fellove: Millie Perkins
The Emcee: Tony Plana
Aurora Fellove: Ines Sastre
Pizzi: Ruben Rabasa
Che Guevara: Jsu Garcia
Origin: USA
Language: English
Released: 2005
Production: Frank Mancuso Jr., Andy Garcia; Cineson, Lionsgate, Crescent Drive Pictures
Directed by: Andy Garcia
Written by: G. Cabrera Infante
Cinematography by: Emmanuel Kadosh
Music by: Andy Garcia
Sound: Stephan Von Hase
Editing: Christopher Cibelli
Art Direction: Carlos Menendez, Sylvia Conde
Costumes: Deborah L. Scott
Production Design: Waldemar Kalinowski
MPAA rating: R
Running time: 143 minutes

REVIEWS

Boxoffice Online. April 28, 2006.
Hollywood Reporter Online. November 9, 2005.
Los Angeles Times Online. April 23, 2006.
Los Angeles Times Online. April 28, 2006.
New York Times Online. April 28, 2006.
Variety Online. September 7, 2005.
Village Voice Online. April 25, 2006.

LOVERBOY

Some mothers aren't meant to be moms.
—Movie tagline

Like his directorial debut, *Losing Chase* (1996), the ubiquitous actor Kevin Bacon's second effort is a testimony to several bad ideas: having an actor direct a movie, having that actor cast his wife in the starring role, and having their daughter also playing a major part.

If *Loverboy* is the vanity project it appears to be—giving Bacon's spouse Kyra Sedgwick a rare leading role—it's certainly an odd one. Neither Segdwick's character nor the minor character Bacon plays is in any way sympathetic. Bacon's bizarre attempts to make satirical comedy out of a strangely disturbing story about a mother's excessive love for her child result in a jarring clash of tones and styles

The novel, by Victoria Redel, was a best seller. The script by Hannah Shakespeare is something of a mess, at least as realized on the screen by Bacon. It starts with Emily (Sedgwick) pretending to teach her darling six-year-old child Paul (Dominic Scott Kay) how to drive a real car. It's one of the many fantasy games that the pair has been playing since Paul was born. Emily's character narrates the story of how the child was conceived. Having her act as narrator is problematic, given the film's conclusion.

Emily says that having a child was her greatest desire, though if true it's not clear why she waited until she was well over age thirty or why she wants to do so alone. True, her own parents (played by Bacon and Marisa Tomei) were so absorbed in each other that they neglected her as a child. Emily certainly wants to give her child all the attention she didn't get, and she distrusts anyone else to give it.

Her quest to conceive starts with a ridiculous plan to mix together the genetic contributions of several men. How sequential liaisons all over the country serve the purpose of a fantasized shared fatherhood is hard to fathom, and it immediately pegs Emily as a lunatic. It does give Bacon a chance to show Sedgwick in full seductive splendor. These scenes are played for laughs, but the light tone, with rather perky music, splashes over into a scene in which Emily miscarries. It is the first of many tonal clashes in this movie. The next is an abrupt shift into romantic mode with Emily's seduction by a nameless character (Campbell Scott), which results in a full-term pregnancy. Flash forward to Emily with the baby, and another absurd scene involving a nameless friend usurping Emily's breast-feeding rights.

It appears that *Loverboy* is going to be an offbeat comedy, but the rest of the film betrays that expectation. It consists of scenes with Emily as the doting mother with a six-year-old whom she insists on calling "Loverboy," and flashbacks to Emily's distressed youth, where at age ten she (played by Sosie Bacon, has to put up with the neglect from her parents. These flashback scenes are shot in a sort of tilted-camera funhouse fashion, with Bacon and Tomei vamping in loud, awful 1970s outfits. Other flashback scenes involving young Emily's adoration for a neighbor, Mrs. Harker (Sandra Bullock), who seems to be an ideal mother are shot in glowing golden sepia, as if they are staged in heaven, and these are not played for comic effect at all.

Sosie Bacon stumbles around in these flashbacks in a sullen style. It is not clear whether this is her attempt to play a saddened child or is simply her response to being forced into this movie by her actor parents. She does get to sing a David Bowie song.

Sedgwick's scenes with Kay are increasingly difficult to stomach. Her character's smothering niceness and total dedication to her privately shared fantasy with her son is played straight at times and comically at others. Kay does well depicting the son's normal reactions to opportunities to go to school, play with other kids, and go fishing with Mark (Matt Dillon), who then beds his mother in a go-nowhere subplot. These are all things Emily can't allow, setting up the inevitable awful ending, which has been telegraphed throughout the movie.

By all rights, *Loverboy* could have stood, or failed, as either a gloomy or over-the-top depiction of an excessively overprotective mother's quest for the perfect child-rearing experience. It could have been turned into a satire of the modern American obsession with a child-centered world that masks the narcissism of the parents who pursue it. Instead, this film is a mishmash of tones and themes. As a director, Bacon seems to be trying to go beyond any sort of broad comic treatment, and the film's attempts at making a serious emotional impact are badly undercut by its frivolity. You can't treat the material so flippantly and then expect audiences to take it seriously.

Child abuse in its various forms isn't a laughing matter, and Bacon alternates between comedy and soapy melodrama in a fashion that never rises above mediocre. It's no wonder *Loverboy* died a quick death at the box office.

Michael Betzold

CREDITS

Emily Stoll: Kyra Sedgwick
Marty Stoll: Kevin Bacon
Jeanette: Blair Brown
Mark: Matt Dillon
Mr. Pomeroy: Oliver Platt
Paul's father: Campbell Scott Kay
Sybil Stoll: Marisa Tomei
Allen Rawley: John Lafayette
Paul: Dominic Scott Kay
Emily as a child: Sosie Bacon
Anita Biddle: Jessica Stone
Miss Silken: Melissa Errico
Principal: Nancy Giles
Mrs. Harker: Sandra Bullock
Origin: USA
Language: English
Released: 2005
Production: Daniel Bigel, Michael Mailer, Avi Lerner, Kyra Sedgwick, Kevin Bacon; Mixed Breed Films; released by ThinkFilm
Directed by: Kevin Bacon
Written by: Hannah Shakespeare
Cinematography by: Nancy Schreiber
Music by: Michael Bacon
Sound: Joe Caterini
Music Supervisor: William Derella
Editing: David Ray
Art Direction: Chris Shriver
Costumes: John Dunn
MPAA rating: R
Running time: 86 minutes

REVIEWS

Boxoffice Online. June 16, 2006.
Entertainment Weekly Online. June 14, 2006.
Los Angeles Times Online. June 16, 2006.

New York Times Online. June 16, 2006.
Variety Online. February 2, 2005.

LUCKY NUMBER SLEVIN

Wrong Time. Wrong Place. Wrong Number.
—Movie tagline

Box Office: $22.4 million

Lucky Number Slevin is the cinematic equivalent of the latest diet beverage, fat-free product, or meat substitute. It tries awfully hard to duplicate something people have enjoyed in the past but is unable to hide the fact that it is not the real deal. The film clearly aimed to be Quentin Tarantino-esque, but falls into the less satisfying category of Tarantino-lite. It has the kind of plot and presentation that makes both contortionists and practitioners of sleight-of-hand sigh with contentment, a multitude of bullets, aren't-we-witty dialogue, and pop culture references from screenwriter Jason Smilovic in his feature film debut. The star-powered film comes off as a derivative, convoluted, mildly entertaining exercise in smug, strained cleverness, and as its smart-alecky protagonist breezes along as if the harrowing predicament in which he finds himself does not really matter, most viewers will likely remain similarly detached.

Enough people are slain in *Lucky Number Slevin* to bury a coroner in work for weeks. They are blown away, stabbed, beaned with killer fastballs, and slowly asphyxiated using plastic hoods secured tightly around their necks. Speaking of necks, one is expertly snapped early on by a wheelchair-bound Mr. Smith (Bruce Willis) after he rolls up to a dozing man in a terminal, wakes him, and tells him a horrific story shown in a series of flashbacks. Smith says he is in town for a "Kansas City Shuffle" that has been almost twenty years in the making. He tells of a man who had placed a large and seemingly sure-fire bet on the pharmaceutically-enhanced seventh horse in the tenth race at New York's Aqueduct in 1979. To the man's horror, his dreams of a big payday went down the drain when the horse suddenly went down on the track. As a result, he found himself hopelessly in debt to the kind of men who aim to collect—one way or the other. In short order, he was badly beaten and agonizingly suffocated to death, and his wife was shot while washing dishes. A firearm is then shown pointed at the head of their young son, Henry (Oliver Davis). Smith finishes his story by swiftly finishing off his unsuspecting listener. You cannot have a Kansas City Shuffle without a body, he points out, and wheels away the corpse in the chair he clearly never needed. So darker things were lurking undetected beneath Smith's casual manner and storytelling. The same is true of *Lucky Number Slevin*.

After a fade to black, viewers see a broken-nosed Slevin Kelevra (Josh Hartnett) shaving, clad only in a towel. Slevin has had a run of particularly bad luck. His apartment has been condemned, he caught his girlfriend in bed with another man, and he has been mugged. Slevin states that he has come to New York to stay as a guest of a friend named Nick Fisher, although Nick is nowhere to be found upon his arrival. Nick's genial, garrulous, live-wire of a neighbor, Lindsey (Lucy Liu), immediately shows a keen desire to uncover both Nick's whereabouts and what is under Slevin's towel. While some things about Slevin remain hidden, some viewers may detect a resemblance between him and young Henry, last glimpsed with a gun poised at the back of his skull. Some may also notice the similarity between his first name and the number of the horse which turned out to be so unlucky for Henry's father.

Strong suspicions that there is more going on here than meets the eye intensify when Slevin remains blithely smart-mouthed as two thugs mistake him for Nick and drag him off to see the Boss (Morgan Freeman). The Boss, calm, smooth, and dignified, informs this person he thinks is Nick that his debt of $96,000 is due in three days. An ice-covered corpse visible in a nearby freezer shows he means business. One would expect someone in such a tight spot to be shaken and cautiously tight-lipped, but Slevin is still blase and sassy in the face of an offer he cannot refuse: the debt will be forgiven if Slevin kills Yitzchok the Fairy (Michael Rubenfeld), the homosexual son of the crime lord's one-time friend but long-time rival, the Rabbi (Ben Kingsley), in retaliation for the Rabbi's killing of the Boss's son. "Why do they call him the Fairy?" asks Slevin. "What's he got, wings? He flies around sprinkling magic dust on people?" Slevin remains an amazingly unfazed wiseacre when the Rabbi's henchmen subsequently whisk him off to the treacherous Talmudic scholar's penthouse directly across the street from the Boss's lair. Due to their intense dread and mistrust of each other, neither crime boss ever ventures outside. "You must be Nick Fisher," the Rabbi states. "Must I be?" Slevin retorts, "because it hasn't been working out for me lately." The rambling rabbi demands payment of $33,000 that Nick owed. Smith, now revealed to be an ominous figure known as Goodkat, reappears sans wheelchair.

Despite the fact that the Boss, the Rabbi, a dogged detective named Brikowski (Stanley Tucci), Lindsey, and even the Fairy show an intense interest in Slevin, most of those watching the film will find Hartnett leaden and uninteresting. Viewers may be curious but not care about what lies ahead for him, and very few will find themselves anywhere close to the edge of their seats. References are made to Hitchcock's *North by Northwest* (1959), similar in its mistaken identity plot, but with an infinitely more captivating and skilled actor in Cary Grant. Reminders of this classic do *Slevin* no favors.

The tone suddenly grows more serious in the latter part of *Lucky Number Slevin*, as the screenplay stops endeavoring to slay viewers with clever quips and gets back to obliterating more characters. Slevin murders the Fairy. Then he kills the Boss and the Rabbi, tied back to back and desperately gasping for air under their clear plastic bags. Last to go is Brikowski. As the corpses start to pile up, so do all the talky explanations and revelations, many presented in the film's multitude of flashbacks. It turns out that Slevin is indeed Henry, and he has set all this in motion to exact revenge on the people who had anything to do with the slaughter of his parents. An unusual bleeding-heart of an assassin, Goodkat just could not bear to put a bullet in Henry's brain back then, raised him, and is now helping him settle old scores. So the mobsters, their sons, various underlings, bookies, a corrupt cop, the man with the catastrophic crick in his neck (actually Nick Fisher and used to make the Fairy's death look like a tryst gone wrong) are all wiped out, and the Kansas City Shuffle is complete. It looked for a time like Lindsey was among the deceased as Goodkat thought she knew too much, but it is revealed that, thanks to a tip from Slevin, she had donned a bulletproof vest. The film goes soft in the end, with Goodkat forgiving Slevin for going behind his back to warn Lindsey, and then kindly handing over Slevin's father's pocket watch to him.

Lucky Number Slevin turns out to be the kind of film one may have to see more than once to fully digest how it all fits together, but few will feel enough motivation to do so. Made on a budget of $27 million, it earned just under $25.5 million. More than one critic rightly used the phrase "too clever by half" to describe the film. Paul McGuigan previously directed Hartnett in *Wicker Park* (2004). To devotees of Quentin Tarantino, their latest effort will seem like a pretender.

David L. Boxerbaum

CREDITS

Slevin: Josh Hartnett
The Boss: Morgan Freeman
The Rabbi: Ben Kingsley
Lindsey: Lucy Liu
Brikowski: Stanley Tucci
Mr. Goodkat: Bruce Willis
Dumbrowski: Peter Outerbridge
Sloe: Mykelti Williamson
Roth: Danny Aiello
Henry: Oliver Davis
Yitzchok: Michael Rubenfeld
Detective Murphy: Robert Forster
Elvis: Dorian Missick
Slevin's Girlfriend: Jennifer Miller
Marty: Kevin Chamberlin
Origin: USA
Language: English
Released: 2006
Production: Chris Roberts, Anthony Rhulen, Christopher Eberts, Kia Jam, Andreas Grosch; Ascendant Pictures, FilmEngine, VIP 4 Production, Capitol Mitchell; released by Weinstein Co.
Directed by: Paul McGuigan
Written by: Jason Smilovic
Cinematography by: Peter Sova
Music by: J. Ralph
Sound: Louis Marion
Editing: Andrew Hulme
Art Direction: Pierre Perrault, Colombe Raby
Costumes: Odette Gadoury
Production Design: Francois Seguin
MPAA rating: R
Running time: 110 minutes

REVIEWS

Boxoffice Online. April 7, 2006.
Chicago Sun-Times Online. April 7, 2006.
Entertainment Weekly. April 14, 2006, p. 64.
Los Angeles Times Online. April 7, 2006.
New York Times Online. April 7, 2006.
People. April 17, 2006, p. 40.
San Francisco Chronicle. April 7, 2006, p. E1.
USA Today Online. April 7, 2006.
Variety Online. January 22, 2006.
Village Voice Online. April 4, 2006.
Washington Post. April 7, 2006, p. C1.

QUOTES

Lindsey to Slevin: "I just thought if you were still alive when I got back from work tonight…maybe we could go to dinner or something?"

Mr. Goodkat: "I'm a world-class assassin. Don't worry, I'm going to kill somebody."

M

MADEA'S FAMILY REUNION

Learn dignity. Demand respect.
—Movie tagline

There's nothing broken that can't be fixed with love.
—Movie tagline

This February, you're invited.
—Movie tagline

Come as you are. Leave different.
—Movie tagline

Box Office: $63.2 million

Tyler Perry's film, *Diary of a Mad Black Woman* (2005), was a surprise success, making almost $22 million in its opening weekend, despite bad reviews from critics. In *Madea's Family Reunion,* Perry, a successful playwright, sticks with the peculiar formula that has worked for him. The film has his usual lineup of women who have been done wrong, the idea that Christianity is the solution to problems, and plenty of off-color jokes, most of them involving flatulence. Perry not only wrote the film and directed it (his first outing behind the camera) but also plays three roles.

Perry spends most of his time on-screen as Madea, a long-running character from his stage shows, as well as *Diary of a Mad Black Woman.* Madea, a large woman attired in billowing housedresses, dispenses love, whippings and plenty of down-home sayings like "It's not what you're called, it's what you answer to." She lives with her brother, Joe (also Perry), the primary source of the aforementioned flatulence. Joe likes to leer at women and complain. He and Madea spend their spare time taking potshots at each other. Perry also plays Brian, an attorney and the representative of a black man stepping up to his role as a responsible Christian family man.

Also in the family is Lisa (Rochelle Aytes), a beautiful young woman set to marry Atlanta's most eligible bachelor, Carlos (Blair Underwood). The problem here is that Carlos beats Lisa and threatens to kill her if she leaves him. When Lisa finally gets up the courage to tell the truth about her situation to her mother, Victoria (Lynn Whitfield), she tells her daughter "You need to just stop doing what you're doing to make him angry." Victoria, a fading beauty with expensive tastes, knows that Carlos is the only chance she has for maintaining her pricey lifestyle.

Victoria is an equally bad mother to her other daughter, Vanessa (Lisa Arrindell Anderson). Victoria has always resented that Vanessa's father was poor and considers the young woman to be from bad stock. She allowed some horrific things to happen to Vanessa as a child and these events have colored Vanessa's adult relationships with men. When she meets nice guy Frankie (Boris Kodjoe), a bus driver who paints and loves children, she has a hard time learning to trust him.

Meanwhile, over at Madea's big house, a different sort of mothering is being practiced. After violating some terms of probation, Madea is assigned caregiving duties to a rebellious teen, Nikki (Keke Palmer). Madea handles the girl by paying attention to her schoolwork and doing plenty of spanking. In one scene that rankles, Madea gets out a belt and beats the child. That it is played for laughs casts a disturbing pallor over Perry's worldview. Still, Madea is a charming character and a crowd favorite. When Madea threatens violence on someone who has crossed her, audience members are inspired to shout at the screen with encouraging words like "He-ell, no" and "You go, Madea."

Madea's Family Reunion also boasts an illustrious cast of less violent elder females. Cicely Tyson and Maya Angelou show up as relatives, Myrtle and May, who are full of inspiring words to teach the younger generation about the big stuff like love and faith. Just having those two elders in the film adds some gravitas to the proceedings and Perry capitalizes on that well.

Critics were split on the film. Some found it to be a rollicking soap opera, while others found it to be poorly made and full of heavy-handed moralizing. Lisa Rose of the *Newark Star-Ledger* wrote that the film "is another helping of earnest but amateurish entertainment, an unwieldy hodgepodge of prayer, punchlines and *Mommie Dearest* (1981) histrionics." Ruthe Stein of the *San Francisco Chronicle* wrote: "*Family Reunion* doesn't know if it wants to be a comedy or a drama and ends up mostly a melodrama with scenes that would be embarrassing on a soap opera." Wesley Morris of the *Boston Globe* wrote: "Rather than push for sitcom nonsense, Perry spins a mean, satisfying soap opera out of his middle-class landscape." Finally, Anita Gates of the *New York Times* wrote that the film is "an unabashed chick flick with a painfully gaudy wedding that includes live angels hanging on wires from the ceiling. What the movie really needs is more of the fat lady throwing political correctness to the winds and slugging obnoxious adolescents."

Jill Hamilton

CREDITS

Madea/Joe/Brian: Tyler Perry
Carlos: Blair Underwood
Victoria: Lynn Whitfield
Frankie: Boris Kodjoe
Isaac: Henry Simmons
Vanessa: Lisa Arrindell Anderson
May: Maya Angelou
Lisa: Rochelle Aytes
Milay Jenay Lori: Jenifer Lewis
Myrtle: Cicely Tyson
Nikki: Keke Palmer
Origin: USA
Language: English
Released: 2006
Production: Reuben Cannon, Tyler Perry; Lionsgate, Tyler Perry Co.; released by Lionsgate
Directed by: Tyler Perry
Written by: Tyler Perry
Cinematography by: Toyomichi Kurita
Music by: Tyler Perry, Elvin D. Ross
Sound: Jim Hawkins
Editing: John Carter
Costumes: Keith Lewis
Production Design: Ina Mayhew
MPAA rating: PG-13
Running time: 107 minutes

REVIEWS

Boxoffice Online. February 24, 2006.
Entertainment Weekly Online. March 1, 2006.
Los Angeles Times Online. February 27, 2006.
Variety Online. February 24, 2006.
Washington Post Online. February 24, 2006.

TRIVIA

Tyler Perry was offered a seven-picture deal after the first week record-breaking release of his first "Madea" film from Lionsgate Home Entertainment.

MAN OF THE YEAR

Could this man be our next president?
—Movie tagline

Box Office: $37.3 million

Barry Levinson's election-year satire treads the line nimbly between politics and entertainment, with perhaps a touch of romance thrown in. What better topic these days, when news and "infotainment" are scrambled together in a hideous spectacle nightly on cable television and even on the network news as reinvented by the producers out to sell the persona of Katie Couric as a plausible news anchor? Certainly the media-savvy director Levinson and his star, Robin Williams, were making the talk-show rounds to hype this timely political comedy. On the evening before the film opened nationally, for example, they were brought before an audience of howling teenagers at Georgetown University in Washington DC, by Chris Matthews on his cable program *Hardball.* As big time celebrity guests they dominated the hour, with Williams cracking jokes and Levinson plugging the movie's thesis to a student audience who, when polled, revealed that very few of them cared enough about politics to register to vote. *Hardball,* which often seems like a parody of a serious political program itself, concluded that night with the Hoya marching band marching on stage playing the Hoya fight song. Little was learned, but the movie was duly promoted. This all becomes transparent when one sees Matthews as "News Anchor No. 1" in the film's credits. It's pure reciprocity.

In *Man of the Year* Robin Williams plays talk-show host Tom Dobbs, who works so much in the style of Jon Stewart that *Baltimore Sun* reviewer Michael Sragow suggested that the film could have been sold as *Jon Stewart Goes to Washington*. One night, while hosting his show, Dobbs is asked by a woman in the television audience why he shouldn't run for president. The audience applauds enthusiastically, as studio audiences are wont to do, and this leads to an Internet campaign that culminates in his becoming a candidate. Dobbs finally agrees to run because he thinks the campaign will give him a platform to discuss serious issues. But he soon discovers that he can only keep the attention of would-be voters if he resorts to his stand-up shtick.

There are two major movements in the film: 1) The candidacy and rise to power of Tom Dobbs, television comedian, and, 2) a failed election, spoiled by malfunctioning voting machines made by the Delacroy Corporation, and the programmer, Eleanor Green (Laura Linney), who attempted to report flaws in the system to her corporate head and who, after the flawed election results, is determined to tell President-elect Dobbs that he didn't really win the Presidency. Her mission is complicated, however, by a sinister corporate cover-up orchestrated by Alan Stewart (Jeff Goldblum), that not only gets Eleanor fired, but molested and shot-up with drugs to make her look completely irresponsible. None the less, after a nervous collapse at the corporate coffee-shop, Eleanor pulls herself together enough to fly to Washington DC, and then somehow manages to penetrate the President-elect's inner circle to tell him the truth. Of course, she falls in love with him immediately (this is a story made in Hollywood, after all), and he is obviously quite taken by her. His advisors want him to reject her as a nutcase once she has delivered her message, but when he discovers he is not really the elected president, he also comes to realize that he is not suited for the office.

Perhaps that is where the plot goes wrong. Is there any reason why a comedian should not be qualified to be president if he is seriously interested in the issues and cares about the good of the nation? After all, haberdashers and peanut-farmers and movie actors have now held the office, so why not a comedian? Dobbs is obviously literate, amusing, and popular, and his candidacy seems credible enough; but the screenplay stacks the deck against him. He wins the election not because the voters accept him but because of a software glitch in the computer voting machines. And that should be our worst nightmare. There were many skeptics going into the mid-term elections of 2006 who believed such a scenario might well be plausible.

On the other hand, Dobbs is a likable character, made all the more so by the fact that he seems humble enough to recognize his own limitations. Williams has proven himself both as a comedian and as an actor. One of his first movie roles was for director Levinson in *Good Morning, Vietnam* (1987), in which he played a flamboyant Saigon radio personality inspired by real-life DJ Adrian Cronauer. In this film, however, Williams is partly doing a star turn by performing the kind of spontaneous comedy that appears natural to him. Christopher Walken is effective as Dobbs's manager, Jack Menken, who narrates the story in flashback from his wheelchair. But Linney provides the most intense and effective performance of the film playing whistle-blower Eleanor Green, who struggles to maintain her integrity while being chased all over Washington by Delacroy goons who want to kidnap, institutionalize, discredit, and silence her.

The reviews were mixed, but mainly negative, and sometimes confused. *Premiere* magazine, for example, failed to explain the plot accurately when Sara Brady wrote that Dobbs "wins the Oval Office through a polling error," though perhaps she meant a voting-machine error, since elections are still won by votes being cast. The *Baltimore Sun* was more favorable and cited "many magic moments." Reviewer Michael Sragow found Levinson's "mingling of comedy and suspense with common decency" particularly "refreshing." In Washington DC, the reception was less warm. Jennifer Frey, in her review for the *Washington Post*, was a stern and humorless taskmistress. For her the picture "never really figures out what kind of movie it wants to be," internal evidence to the contrary. What that apparently means is that the reviewer had notions of what she wanted the movie to be, and, unfortunately, those notions did not coincide with what Levinson had in mind. But in a political atmosphere friendly neither towards Congress nor the White House, not word-of-mouth, the popularity of Williams, nor the media campaign launched by Levinson could save the picture.

Although *Wall Street Journal* reviewer Joe Morgenstern found the script "intriguing"—a candidate for president who is actually witty and spontaneous, an election gone awry because of a nationwide system of badly programmed and flawed electronic voting machines—Morgenstern concluded that the film "doesn't know what to make of its own hero—is he a demagogue, a truth-teller or an empty-headed sloganeer taking on empty suits?" In her *USA Today* review, Claudia Puig dismissed the movie as being "stuffed with stale, safe humor." And of course the conservative Republican *Washington Times* trashed the movie as "an awkward mix of satire and suspense."

In conclusion, *Man of the Year* could have turned out to be critic-proof and may have survived the negative reviews if Williams had been able to maintain a following of mature viewers who appreciate his comic quips and rapid repartee. *Entertainment Weekly* critic Lisa Schwarzbaum was arguably wrong in claiming that Williams "would never stand a chance, either as a presidential candidate or as a TV talk-show comic," if one considers the comedian's track record on the talk-show circuit. The film's publicity campaign included an interview with Williams that was the cover story of the November/December issue of *AARP The Magazine*, which claims to be the "World's Largest Circulation Magazine." In that interview Williams spoke of comedy as "acting out optimism," then went on to explain his motives in *Man of the Year* as follows: "It's not skewed to one party or the other; it's just basically saying that the system as it stands doesn't work. If you disagree, you are called unpatriotic." The movie is a satire, and it might have fared better with reviewers had they been able to get their minds around that concept. In his interview, Williams asked this rhetorical question: "Could it happen? A computer malfunction? No—not in Ohio!" There may be an object lesson here. The marketing strategy pulled the film through its opening weekend, when it grossed $12.6 million, placing third behind *The Grudge 2* (2006) and Martin Scorsese's *The Departed* (2006). Two weeks out of the gate it had grossed $22 million on its way to a final tally of just over $37 million.

So, Robin Williams has a political agenda suggesting that things could be better and gives neither political party the advantage of escaping dullness or stupidity. The allegory here is clear enough, as Eleanor is determined to speak the truth to power (that is, to the man who would be president). The Constitutional dilemma is resolved at the end, the Democrat who resumes power seems a little more human, and Dobbs is free to continue his successful television career, with Eleanor working as his producer. Though the mainline critics were not conceding the point, *Man of the Year* was just as timely as *Wag the Dog* had been in 1997, but it failed to carry through on its own premise. If American politics are to be governed by a media circus, then why shouldn't a clown be elected to the Presidency? It's not exactly unprecedented.

James M. Welsh

CREDITS

Tom Dobbs: Robin Williams
Eleanor Green: Laura Linney
Jack Menken: Christopher Walken
Eddie Langston: Lewis Black
Alan Stewart: Jeff Goldblum
Hemmings: Rick Roberts
Origin: USA
Language: English
Released: 2006
Production: James G. Robinson, David Robinson; Morgan Creek Productions; released by Universal Pictures
Directed by: Barry Levinson
Written by: Barry Levinson
Cinematography by: Dick Pope
Music by: Graeme Revell
Sound: Robert F. Scherer
Music Supervisor: Alan Mason
Editing: Steven Weisberg, Blair Daily
Art Direction: Joshu de Cartier
Costumes: Delphine White
Production Design: Stefania Cella
MPAA rating: PG-13
Running time: 108 minutes

REVIEWS

Chicago Sun-Times Online. October 13, 2006.
Entertainment Weekly. October 20, 2006, p. 59.
Hollywood Reporter Online. October 9, 2006.
Los Angeles Times Online. October 13, 2006.
New York Times Online. October 13, 2006.
San Francisco Chronicle. October 13, 2006, p. E1.
Variety Online. October 6, 2006.
Washington Post. October 13, 2006, p. C5.

QUOTES

Stewart: "The perception of legitimacy is more important than legitimacy itself."

MANDERLAY

Liberation. Whether They Want It Or Not.
—Movie tagline

Writer/director Lars von Trier receives a lot of flack for making films highly critical, even scornful, of the United States despite the fact that he has never set foot on American soil. (His extreme fear of flying, he claims, prevents him from traveling very far from his native Denmark.) But an outsider's view can be valuable, insightful, and challenging, as it was in *Dogville* (2004), an unflinching exploration of the dark heart at the center of a small town. It was the first part of a planned trilogy casting a cynical eye on American ideals, and now the second film, *Manderlay*, has arrived. It is, unfortunately, a huge disappointment, a plodding, dull, and disjointed film about race and slavery that feels as if von Trier were simply throwing on the screen all his unformed notions about America's racial history without fashioning a thoughtful narrative or compelling characters through which he can express his ideas.

Bryce Dallas Howard, the daughter of director Ron Howard, plays Grace, a role originated by Nicole Kidman in *Dogville*. Grace and her gangster father (formerly played by James Caan, now portrayed by Willem Dafoe), along with his entourage have fled the carnage they inflicted on the mining town of Dogville, Colorado, after the citizens there gave refuge to Grace and then heaped on her every kind of abuse. Heading south, Grace and the gangsters stumble upon a plantation in Alabama called Manderlay, where, in 1933, slavery continues despite its legal abolition seventy years earlier. Inexplicably still the do-gooder despite learning some harsh lessons about human nature in Dogville, Grace takes it upon herself to set right centuries of oppression and, using the force of her father's gun-toting henchmen, frees the slaves. She ends the reign of Mam (Lauren Bacall, playing a much smaller role than she had in *Dogville*), who dies suddenly, thus giving Grace the opportunity to take charge of the plantation.

The casting in *Manderlay* is the first big mistake. Kidman is a wonderful and far more expressive actress than the emotionally blank Howard, and Grace undergoes so many trials to which Howard cannot bring genuine conviction. Moreover, it is odd that a supposedly more experienced Grace, having suffered in Dogville, should be played by a younger actress who exudes such blinkered naivete. It is as if the Dogville experience taught Grace nothing. And Dafoe does not convey the menace and authority that Caan brought to the role of a ruthless gangster who is a doting father under the surface.

Stylistically, *Manderlay* is similar to *Dogville* in its minimalist aesthetic. Both films were shot on a huge soundstage with few props, and outlines drawn on the floor to denote the various buildings and fields. But what once felt bold and experimental now feels old and tiresome. Moreover, the scheme simply worked better in *Dogville*'s small-town setting, where the dynamics and interactions of the various households provided much of the tension as poor Grace had to navigate her way among the different families. But the geography of *Manderlay*'s plantation is not as clear, nor is it really very important where the slaves live in relation to their white masters, who are now being held prisoner by Grace's henchmen.

Whereas *Dogville* took the time to introduce the townspeople, von Trier does not delineate the characters very well in *Manderlay*. Aside from Mam, the white family is never more than a fairly nondescript group. Chloe Sevigny, one of the biggest names in the cast, hangs around the periphery with very little to do. The slaves, however, fare only marginally better. Danny Glover plays Wilhelm, the old house slave who is fearful that the former slaves may not be ready for freedom and thinks they have little chance in the world. He becomes a right-hand man to Grace in her experiment in democracy. Isaach De Bankole plays Timothy, the handsome, standoffish slave suspicious of Grace. But the slaves never rise above such designations as "clowning nigger" and "pleasing nigger," the kinds of descriptions found in *Mam's Law*, the pernicious guidebook that lists the various personae adopted by slaves and that spells out instructions for running the plantation. Hearing John Hurt, reprising his role as the unseen narrator, utter the word "nigger" with his sweet yet sarcastic tone, is probably meant to be shocking, but, after a while, the epithet loses its force. More importantly, weak characterizations tar the film with the same guilt von Trier thinks he is exposing. When Grace mistakes one black man for another, it is meant to be a jab at white society, for whom, as the cliche goes, all blacks look alike. But the episode, which leads nowhere, could just as easily apply to von Trier, who cannot see the black people as individuals any more than Grace can.

Bearing the burden of America's racial sins, Grace feels that it is her duty to help the downtrodden. But her efforts do not have the salutary effects she hoped they would. She teaches lessons in democracy, emphasizing the importance of the ballot, which leads to the absurdity of two factions disagreeing over what time it is and putting the question to a vote. In one sequence, Grace gives the whites their comeuppance by having them wear blackface and serve the former slaves, but this obvious bit of role reversal is just an isolated stunt that does not have any larger effect on the characters or the plot.

Because the homes have been neglected and repairs need to be made, Grace suggests cutting down the trees in the nearby woods, only to discover later that the trees served as a kind of defense. As a result, Grace's good intentions, coupled with a lack of knowledge of the local culture, produce unintended consequences when a dust storm arrives and ruins the cotton crop. With not enough food to go around, hard times hit the plantation, and, when a sick little girl dies because an old woman stole her food, the community votes to put her to death, a sentence that Grace must carry out, albeit reluctantly. It is not hard to see von Trier's political point (obviously directed at America's proclivity to try to spread democracy around the world) that, when an outsider comes to a community and tries to impose democracy, the results are disastrous. This idea could have been provocative if it flowed out of a well-constructed narrative, instead of being hammered home in incident after incident showcasing Grace's failures.

The only other major narrative thread is Grace's increasing sexual attraction to Timothy, who comes to haunt her thoughts and dreams, culminating in an encounter that may not be rape, but certainly looks painful and dehumanizing for Grace and makes us wonder if she is now receiving some kind of retribution for her fantasies. But the consequences are never dealt with because, shortly thereafter, it is discovered that Timothy stole the money from the harvest and gambled it away. In a confusing rush of events that is described instead of shown, it seems that the gangsters, whom Grace had dismissed, returned and killed several residents of Manderlay, both black and white, in a futile attempt to steal the money, which was already gone. It is frustrating, however, given the amount of time the film wastes on unimportant events, that such a crucial turning point is handled so carelessly that it is hard to figure out exactly what happened.

But the real surprise at the end is the revelation that Wilhelm wrote *Mam's Law*. Fearing what freedom would bring, he and Mam conspired to keep the old slave system in place, an arrangement that many of the slaves knew about, thus making themselves complicit in their bondage. They could have left Manderlay anytime they wanted but chose the security of slavery over the unknown of living in a free world. In a heavy-handed sequence, Wilhelm goes on to explain that America was not ready for their freedom and still is not ready, which comes across as a clumsy polemical critique but not something that has been demonstrated dramatically. Wilhelm and the others are intent on forcing Grace to take on Mam's role and reinstituting slavery, in essence keeping her prisoner as their master. It is, of course, an ironic reversal—the liberal emancipator becoming a master who ultimately whips Timothy for his theft. Grace finally escapes on foot from her would-be captors and runs east across a giant map of the United States.

After so many episodes that feel disconnected from each other, *Manderlay* ends on a dizzying set of plot twists and incendiary political statements, but they feel forced and tacked on to give the film a dramatic and philosophical weight that it has not earned. Von Trier has been very audacious in past films, both aesthetically and philosophically, but in *Manderlay*, he takes a very simplistic approach to the complex subject of race and slavery in America and serves up an inert drama that ends up saying nothing. It's good that we have such a filmmaker who takes chances, and, when his ideas and narrative come together (as they did in *Dogville*), the result can be stunning. But *Manderlay* is a dead end that makes one wonder if von Trier can possibly redeem the trilogy when he sets about filming its concluding chapter.

Peter N. Chumo II

CREDITS

Grace: Bryce Dallas Howard
Timothy: Isaach De Bankole
Wilhelm: Danny Glover
Grace's Father: Willem Dafoe
Mam: Lauren Bacall
Mr. Robinson: Jean-Marc Barr
Bertie: Geoffrey Bateman
Niels: Jeremy Davies
Thomas: Michael Abiteboul
Edvard: Virgile Bramly
Bingo: Ruben Brinkman
Venus: Dona Croll
Narrator: John Hurt
Dr. Hector: Zeljko Ivanek
Mr. Krispe: Udo Kier
Stanley Mays: Rik Launspach
Victoria: Llewella Gideon
Old Wilma: Mona Hammond
Elisabeth: Ginny Holder
Jim: Emmanuel Idowu
Joseph: Teddy Kempner
Flora: Suzette Llewellyn
Philomena: Chloe Sevigny
Bruno: Charles Maquignon
Mark: Joseph Mydell
Jack: Javone Pierce
Sammy: Clive Rowe
Rose: Nina Sosanya
Origin: Denmark, Sweden, Netherlands, France, Germany, Great Britain
Language: English
Released: 2005
Production: Vibeke Windelov; Zentropa Entertainment, Isabella Films International, Memfis Film Intl., Ognon Pictures, Manderlay Ltd.
Directed by: Lars von Trier
Written by: Lars von Trier
Cinematography by: Anthony Dod Mantle
Sound: A.D. Stoop, Marten Negenman
Editing: Molly Marlene Stensgard
Art Direction: Peter Grant
Costumes: Manon Rasmussen
MPAA rating: Unrated
Running time: 139 minutes

REVIEWS

Boxoffice Online. February 3, 2006.
Chicago Sun-Times Online. February 17, 2006.

Entertainment Weekly Online. February 1, 2006.
Los Angeles Times Online. February 3, 2006.
New York Times Online. January 27, 2006.
Premiere Magazine Online. January 30, 2006.
Variety Online. May 16, 2005.

QUOTES

Grace about the slaves: "We brought them here, we abused them, and made them what they are."

TRIVIA

A donkey was put to death while filming, and amid protests from animals rights groups, executive producer Peter Aalbaek Jensen told Swedish media that "people should not be upset—instead they should think about the situation of the Third World." The movie was filmed in Sweden, and Swedish law allows that animals can be put to death in movie productions if a veterinarian is the one carrying out the killing. However, director Lars von Trier later cut the scene from the film.

MARIE ANTOINETTE

Let Them Eat Cake.
—Movie tagline

Box Office: $15.9 million

A stunning visual achievement on par with Stanley Kubrick's *Barry Lyndon* (1975), director Sofia Coppola's *Marie Antoinette* bears her unique stamp, presenting her version of France's iconic queen in a modern way that includes a signature 1980s pop soundtrack that also seamlessly mixes with classical, and a dreamlike quality achieved, in part, by the moody ambient sound. Based on Antonia Fraser's biography *Marie Antoinette: The Journey,* the film admirably presents Marie's history from the perspective of the young girl herself—something rarely done in cinema and something that Coppola has shown she does remarkably well in films like *The Virgin Suicides* (1999) and *Lost in Translation* (2003).

Of course, along with Marie and Louis XVI, Versailles itself is a character as painstakingly rendered, as are the beautiful costumes. While Patrice Leconte's *Ridicule* (1996) arguably presents a more detailed portrait of life in the court of King Louis XVI, Coppola's vision focuses on Marie's private reality, purposefully ignoring the larger events of the time. A long way from its sole cinematic predecessor in 1938, Coppola's Marie also leaves out the storied "Let them eat cake" quote.

An effortlessly pitch-perfect Kirsten Dunst plays Marie Antoinette of Austria, the youngest daughter of Holy Roman Emperor Francis I and Empress Maria Theresa (a well-used Marianne Faithfull), who now rules Austria while securing a powerful political match for her daughter with France's shy Dauphin Louis-Auguste (Jason Schwartzman). A striking and effective early scene takes Marie away from her beloved family in a lavish coach. Upon reaching France's border, she is stripped, literally, of all things Austrian, her nakedness underscoring her absolute vulnerability.

She meets her intended, underplayed with subtle humor by Schwartzman, and is suitably crestfallen. Life as dauphine at the court of Versailles is no picnic for the newcomer, with *Variety*'s Todd McCarthy likening her to a "youngster moving to a new high school, with its environment of gossip and petty rivalries." After an elaborate wedding in Versailles' breathtaking cathedral, the two are expected to get down to the business of creating heirs. Historically, and in Coppola's version as well, Louis is challenged in the sexual arena and they remain childless for more than eight years.

In the interim, Louis fiddles with his locks and goes hunting while Marie learns the business of queen-in-training, mainly consisting of going to balls and picking out elaborate gowns, shoes, and hairstyles. She must also learn the endless royal protocol and etiquette, which she receives from Judy Davis' pushy and prim Comtesse de Noailles, who also provides more than a fair bit of the film's early humor. She also receives sage advice from the more relatable Count Mercy D'Argenteau (Steve Coogan). Marie is not without detractors, however, and two of the worst are Aunt Victoire (a clever Molly Shannon) and Aunt Sophie (Shirley Henderson) who refer to her in derogatory terms such as "that Austrian strudel." She is able to win a few good friends, including Princesse Lamballe (Mary Nighy) and the Duchesse de Polignac (Rose Byrne) who become part of her party posse. She has more of a problem with Madame Du Barry (Asia Argento), the much-hated mistress of lusty King Louis XV (Rip Torn). The decadent pair provides a wonderful contrast to the chaste younger couple.

Marie begins to blossom amid the tight-knit world of Versailles, indulging her love of fine food and gambling all night. It is however, her budding fashion savvy that wins over the court. With the help of her stylist, she introduces the iconic sky-high wigs, which begin to grow ever taller, featuring elaborate decor; a birdcage complete with peeping bird in one and her most famous wig with ensconced battleship atop.

Marie's life changes again in 1774 when King Louis XV dies of smallpox and Louis-Auguste is crowned King Louis XVI, making her Queen of France at nineteen. Louis famously remarks, "Dear God, guide and protect us. We are too young to reign."

Miles away, her mother, growing increasingly desperate with Marie's inability to produce a successor to the throne, sends Marie's beloved older brother Joseph (Danny Huston) to see to the matter. Joseph and Louis have a heart-to-heart in an amusing scene with a prominently featured elephant's trunk. Soon after, the couple repeatedly consummates the royal marriage, and in 1778 they produce a daughter, Marie Therese Charlotte (Lauriane Mascaro at age two; Florrie Betts at six), and later sons Louis-Joseph and Louis-Charles and the youngest, Sophie Beatrix.

Marie's favorite country getaway is a gift from Louis, a smaller chateau dubbed Le Petit Trianon. There, she plays with her adorable children, reads Rousseau, and contemplates the beauty of nature; her much lampooned shepherdess period. She also is free to frolic with her lover, the handsome Swedish soldier Count Fersen (Jamie Dornan). Feeling much at home, Marie is also at liberty to display her artistic talents, singing and performing in shows in the chateau's little theater and inviting Louis and some of the court to watch.

Thus, Marie whiles away the days in pleasant fantasy for much of the film's 123 minutes. France, however, is now sorely in debt due to royal excess and the financing of the American Revolution. Coppola in no way prepares the viewer for the eleventh-hour arrival of the angry mob outside the gates. A jarring scene shows the ransacked palace and the royals escaping in their carriage. Coppola carefully avoids any violence, ending the film before their imprisonment and inevitable beheadings several years later. In this way, she keeps the fantasy intact for both the viewer and Marie until nearly the end.

In discussing the film, there is perhaps no better place to begin than with the unique soundtrack. Coppola claims to have found inspiration in the New Romantic pop sound of the 1980s—which was, in turn, influenced by eighteenth century extravagance—that seems completely appropriate to Marie's 1780s life. The Gang of Four's "Natural's Not in It" plays like the royal couple's anthem with the lyrics "The problem of leisure/ What to do for pleasure." "I do like a new purchase" the song aptly continues. A scene depicting Marie and her friends presented with a dazzling array of candy-colored satin slippers, dresses and cakes plays out marvelously to Bow Wow Wow's "I Want Candy." Music supervisor Brian Reitzell explained: "It was all very organic. The story dictated the music, which follows the dramatic arc." New Order, Sioxsie and the Banshees, The Strokes, and Coppola's favorite French electronica duo, Air, mix with Antonio Vivaldi's classic violins, and the gorgeous harpsichord of Francois Couperin.

While reviews of the film were mixed, many high-profile critics gave praise. The *New York Times*' A. O. Scott called it "not so much a psychological portrait as a tableau of mood and atmosphere. Highly theatrical and yet also intimate and informal." *Rolling Stone*'s Peter Travers noted that while Internet buzz labeled the film for "girls and gays" only and conceded that the director left much out, "But what Coppola does focus on provokes and fascinates." *Marie* ranked among Roger Ebert's highest-rated films of 2006, decrying, "Every criticism I have read of this film would alter its fragile magic and reduce its romantic and tragic poignancy to the level of an instruction film." In the arena of official recognition, the film received a Golden Palm nomination at the Cannes Film Festival—where it was famously booed.

Hilary White

CREDITS

Marie Antoinette: Kirsten Dunst
Louis XVI: Jason Schwartzman
Comtesse de Noailles: Judy Davis
Louis XV: Rip Torn
Duchesse de Polignac: Rose Byrne
Princesse Lamballe: Mary Nighy
Madame Du Barry: Asia Argento
Aunt Victoire: Molly Shannon
Aunt Sophie: Shirley Henderson
Joseph: Danny Huston
Count Mercy D'Argenteau: Steve Coogan
Marie Therese (age 2): Lauriane Mascaro
Marie Therese (age 6): Florrie Betts
Empress Maria Teresa: Marianne Faithfull
Count Fersen: Jamie Dornan
Origin: USA
Language: English
Released: 2006
Production: Ross Katz, Sofia Coppola; American Zoetrope, Columbia Pictures, RK Films; released by Sony Pictures
Directed by: Sofia Coppola
Written by: Sofia Coppola
Cinematography by: Lance Acord
Sound: Stuart Wilson
Music Supervisor: Brian Reitzell
Editing: Sarah Flack
Art Direction: Anne Seibel
Costumes: Milena Canonero
Production Design: K.K. Barrett
MPAA rating: PG-13
Running time: 123 minutes

REVIEWS

Boxoffice Online. October 20, 2006.
Chicago Sun-Times Online. October 20, 2006.
Entertainment Weekly. October 27, 2006, p. 51.

Hollywood Reporter Online. May 25, 2006.
Los Angeles Times Online. October 20, 2006.
New York Times Online. October 13, 2006.
Premiere Magazine. October 2006, p. 40.
San Francisco Chronicle. October 20, 2006, p. E1.
Variety Online. May 24, 2006.
Washington Post. October 20, 2006, p. C1.

QUOTES

Marie Antoinette: "Letting everyone down would be my greatest unhappiness."

AWARDS

Oscars 2006: Costume Des.

Nomination:

British Acad. 2006: Costume Des., Makeup

THE MARINE

Box Office: $18.8 million

Few movies wholeheartedly embrace their essential B-movie selves. *The Marine* is a B-movie and it knows it. So, even though the movie is bad in myriad ways, it also redeems itself through its self-knowledge.

The first few moments of *The Marine* are indistinguishable from a Marine recruitment ad. In front of an American flag, a soldier dressed in a uniform stands erect and salutes the camera. The soldier is John Triton (John Cena). Cut to Triton in the midst of battle in an Al Qaeda terrorist compound. When a fellow solider asks the heavily muscled Triton how they can get around a group of enemies, Triton intones, "We don't. We go through them." Triton is ordered to wait for backup, but in what looks like some sort of steroidal rage, he single-handedly rescues some fellow Marines. For this, he is kicked out. This presents a career crisis since being a Marine seems to be Triton's only form of self-identification. "I'm a Marine," he says several times.

Against the wishes of his patient and loving wife, Kate (Kelly Carlson), Triton immediately accepts a job as a security guard at a downtown high-rise office building. He loses that job on the first day after he tosses an arrogant yuppie through the lobby windows.

Triton decides to go on a vacation with Kate to South Carolina. They stop at a gas station and things go awry. A group of jewel thieves, led by Rome (Robert Patrick), has also stopped for gas when a police car pulls up. The thieves panic and, in the ensuing melee, the gas station is blown up and Kate is kidnapped.

This sets in motion the sole storyline for the rest of the film. That is, Triton wants his wife back. Triton chases the bad guys, and things go boom. Triton's action is not all that interesting. Basically, he runs through the swampland looking determined. The villains are much more entertaining. Patrick, who makes a winking reference to *Terminator 2: Judgment Day* (1991), is the comic relief in the film. At one point, during a tense moment, he takes a cell phone call to firm up the terms of his cable service.

Cena is less successful. He is a lesson in the extremes that the human body can take. Other than passing anatomical interest, Cena does not have much to offer, however. He shows little to no flair for comedy, nor does he seem to have any dramatic instincts. Explosions can fill in a lot of the gaps, but they cannot do it all.

Critics seemed to give the film a little more slack than they would normally give such fare. Nathan Rabin of *The Onion A.V. Club* wrote: "John Bonito's directorial debut thankfully has a sense of humor about itself, even though Cena lacks the wry self-deprecation that allowed The Rock to escape the wrestling-actor ghetto." Peter Hartlaub of the *San Francisco Chronicle* wrote that "if everyone who sees it would just drink a six-pack of Pabst Blue Ribbon beforehand, the low-budget action film would get better reviews than *My Dinner With Andre* (1981)." Mark Olsen of the *Los Angeles Times* wrote: "It's not a good film by any practical standard, but *The Marine* is bad in just the right way, a mindless throwaway that's at least smart enough not to take itself too seriously." Wesley Morris of the *Boston Globe* wrote: "You want more for Cena than this."

Jill Hamilton

CREDITS

Rome: Robert Patrick
Kate Triton: Kelly Carlson
Morgan: Anthony Ray Parker
Van Buren: Jerome Ehlers
John Triton: John Cena
Angela: Abigail Bianca
Origin: USA
Language: English
Released: 2006
Production: Joel Simon, Kathryn Sommer Parry, Jonathan Winfrey; WWE Films; released by 20th Century Fox
Directed by: John Bonito
Written by: Alan B. McElroy, Michell Gallagher
Cinematography by: David Eggby
Music by: Don Davis
Sound: Paul Brincat
Music Supervisor: Randy Gerston
Editing: Dallas S. Puett
Art Direction: Daryl Porter

Costumes: Graham Purcell
Production Design: Herbert Pinter
MPAA rating: PG-13
Running time: 93 minutes

REVIEWS

Boston Globe Online. October 14, 2006.
Entertainment Weekly. October 27, 2006, p. 55.
Hollywood Reporter Online. October 16, 2006.
New York Times Online. October 14, 2006.
Variety Online. October 15, 2006.

QUOTES

Rome: "I think I can now add kidnapping to my list of atrocities."

THE MATADOR

A hitman and a salesman walk into a bar...
—Movie tagline

Box Office: $12.6 million

Pierce Brosnan's willingness to play against his suave James Bond image becomes very apparent in a scene from *The Matador*, when the actor, playing a scruffy, ill-mannered assassin, shuffles across a Mexico City hotel lobby, drunk and clad only in black cowboy boots and a tiny Speedo. Brosnan barely has a paunch, but what little he does have, he gamely pushes out to achieve the proper slovenliness.

The Matador is not a great movie, but what it does have is a sprightly spirit. Brosnan seems more than happy to be a man behaving badly and his delight translates to a certain zestiness in the film. It is also helped along by writer/director Richard Shepard and cinematographer David Tattersall, who filmed the whole movie—even scenes set in European cities—in vibrant Mexico City. The film is really a fairly traditional buddy comedy, but in a movie season bloated with big important films, *The Matador*, seems fresh by comparison.

Julian Noble (Brosnan) and Danny Wright (Greg Kinnear) first meet in a hotel bar in Mexico City. Julian is in town for a hit. Danny is there to close a deal. Since he and wife Bean's (Hope Davis) teenage son was killed a few years before, Danny has been riding a wave of bad luck in business. If he does not get this deal, he fears he may lose Bean. Danny is a boring, mild-mannered guy and that is exactly why he is attracted to the mysterious Julian. As the two talk, Julian reveals that he is a hit man or, as he puts it, "a facilitator of fatalities."

Julian is rough and boorish. When Danny tells him about the death of his son, Julian interrupts with a dirty joke. Danny is offended and somewhat frightened by Julian, but is also intrigued with his exotic lifestyle. In one scene, Julian takes Danny to a bull fight and explains that a skillful matador makes death more palatable for his victim by doing the killing quickly and neatly. He shows off his own skills to Danny when the two select a human victim in the arena. With a honed technique, Julian sets up a plan to kill. He selects a spot by the men's restroom, monitors the security guards, and figures out diversionary and escape plans. The killing is only theoretical, but Danny is thrilled.

For his part, Julian is just happy to have a friend. His life has been spent traveling the globe, drinking, frequenting brothels, and avoiding human connection. Now middle-aged, he is starting to lose his edge. He has botched a job, and when he messes up another, he will be a target for assassination himself.

Even though Danny and Julian have a friendship, it is a tenuous one. Danny is a friend to Julian, but he is offended when Julian asks for his help on a job. And it is hard to tell whether Julian truly considers Danny to be a friend or is just waiting to exploit him. With the amoral Julian, it could well be both. Months later, when Julian shows up in the middle of the night at Bean and Danny's doorstep, it is difficult to tell what is going to happen. Is Julian there to hide from his bosses, to seduce Bean, to enlist Danny in some of his dirty work? Whichever it is, Bean is thrilled to meet this man her husband has spoken so much about. She immediately asks to see Julian's gun and comments gleefully that she feels so "cosmopolitan" entertaining a hit man in their living room in the middle of the night.

Critics disagreed over the merits of the film, but most praised Brosnan's performance. David Denby of the *New Yorker* called Brosnan's performance "startling," but wrote, "*The Matador* teeters between comedy and moral inquiry but doesn't quite make it either way." Roger Ebert of the *Chicago Sun-Times* wrote: "Brosnan is so intriguing to watch in the movie. Unshaven, trembling, hung-over, fearful, charming, confiding, paranoid, trusting, he clings to Danny and Bean like a lost child at the zoo." Stephen Holden of the *New York Times* wrote: "Pithy remarks put into the mouth of a star playing against type impart a greasy sheen of sophistication to *The Matador*, a weightless, amoral romp about a professional hit man facing a mid-life crisis." Finally, Wesley Morris of the *Boston Globe* wrote that "the film has a vibrant pop style: The colors burst off the screen, the editing rhythms are precise and absorbing, and you could almost cha-cha with the camera's movement."

Jill Hamilton

CREDITS

Julian Noble: Pierce Brosnan
Danny Wright: Greg Kinnear
Carolyn "Bean" Wright: Hope Davis
Mr. Randy: Philip Baker Hall
Lovell: Dylan Baker
Phil Garrison: Adam Scott
Origin: USA
Language: English
Released: 2006
Production: Pierce Brosnan, Sean Furst, Beau St. Clair, Brian Furst; DEJ Productions, Equity Pictures Medienfonds GmbH & Co. KG II, Furst Films, Irish DreamTime; released by Miramax Films
Directed by: Richard Shepard
Written by: Richard Shepard
Cinematography by: David Tattersall
Music by: Rolfe Kent
Sound: Santiago Nunez
Editing: Carole Kravetz-Akyanian
Art Direction: Marcel Del Rio
Costumes: Catherine Thomas
Production Design: Rob Pearson
MPAA rating: R
Running time: 96 minutes

REVIEWS

Boxoffice Online. December 30, 2005.
Chicago Sun-Times Online. January 6, 2006.
Entertainment Weekly Online. January 4, 2006.
Los Angeles Times Online. December 30, 2005.
New York Times Online. December 30, 2005.
Premiere Magazine Online. December 22, 2005.
Variety Online. January 23, 2005.
Washington Post Online. January 6, 2006, p. C05.

QUOTES

Julian Noble: "I need a break. There's no retirement home for assassins is there? Archery at four. Riflery at five."

Bean: "Aren't we cosmopolitan having a trained assassin stay overnight."

MATERIAL GIRLS

It's a short trip from the penthouse to the poorhouse.
—Movie tagline

Box Office: $11.4 million

Sisters Tanzie and Ava Marchetta, played by real-life siblings Hilary and Haylie Duff, respectively, lead a carefree life of celebrity, privilege, and ritzy parties in the would-be comedy *Material Girls*, a misguided effort to put together two attractive, rising starlets that doesn't give them enough funny, engaging material to work with. Heiresses to a cosmetics dynasty, the Marchettas find themselves down on their luck when a company scandal forces them to learn the harsh realities of life. Even the lightest of comedies should have some grounding in reality that connects the outrageous events to our world, but the script for *Material Girls* is a hodgepodge of silly set pieces that rarely work on their own, let alone build a cohesive story. What makes *Material Girls* more of a disappointment is that it was directed by Martha Coolidge, whose *Valley Girl* (1983) was a quirky and sweet film revolving around a character similar to the Marchetta sisters.

The Marchettas may be spoiled and oblivious to how truly privileged they are, but they are not mean or obnoxious. Tanzie actually has a sentimental side and wants to follow in the footsteps of their late father, an innovator in the cosmetics field, while Ava is more immersed in the culture of celebrity and her shallow TV-actor boyfriend.

Tragedy strikes the girls when the Marchetta cosmetics line comes under attack for causing skin damage, a charge that transforms the Marchettas from A-list partygoers into instant pariahs. Protesters gather outside their mansion's gates and pelt the windows with eggs, as if the practices of a cosmetics company could spur so much immediate, organized outrage. But the action becomes more farfetched when an errant cigarette starts a fire. That the sisters do not call the fire department or take any serious measures to put out the fire makes the situation completely implausible. They simply flee the blaze and end up at the home of their loyal housekeeper, Inez (Maria Conchita Alonso), where they stay for a while, never even bothering to check on the condition of their home, which they assume has burned down.

Many of the jokes aimed at the Marchettas' insular life are funny, such as Tanzie identifying the Spice Girls as "classic rock" or the girls, assuming that valet parking is a universal aspect of life, give their car to guys in Inez's dicey neighborhood and never see it again. The pampered princesses' uneasy foray into public transportation also provides some cute jabs at their naivete and well-heeled existence.

Such light satire of the wealthy, while amusing, cannot compensate for the essential hollowness of the screenplay. The big conflict revolves around a rival cosmetics company headed by a mogul named Fabiella (Anjelica Huston, wasted in a meaningless role), who has been trying to acquire the Marchettas' company. In light of the scandal, however, she will now pay only sixty cents on the dollar, which means that the girls could walk away with $60 million each. While their reputation may be in jeopardy, their financial future is never at stake.

Believing in their father's innocence, the spunky heroines get into girl-detective mode and try to clear his good name. They enlist the aid of a lawyer, Henry Baines (Lukas Haas), who helps the girls even though he has contempt for their willful ignorance of real poverty. True to the formula that opposites must attract, by the end he and Ava fall in love. Tanzie carries on a flirtation with Rick (Marcus Coloma), a lab technician at the company who is eager to aid in their sleuthing. Like so much of *Material Girls*, these couplings feel trite and contrived—tacked-on romantic interests that supposedly show the girls appreciating good-hearted, decent guys after all their rich friends have deserted them. It is a cliched lesson and ultimately not a very persuasive one.

Likewise, the detective aspect of the story is not very convincing, although the plucky Tanzie donning a pushup bra and taking on an Erin Brockovich persona to obtain secret files is quite a funny sight. The girls do establish their father's innocence by discovering that he had changed the cosmetics formula and that one of the so-called victims had a skin condition before she used their merchandise. The big revelation is an arbitrary deus ex machine. Just about anything could have been produced to wrap up the mystery. Everything ends happily, but aside from the fact that Tanzie and Ava have fallen in love with men they would have once deemed beneath them, there is no sense that the girls have grown. They may have saved the company and restored its honor, but the methods they employ are so random that even their successful detective work seems more the result of good luck than keen intelligence or dogged determination.

The best that can be said of *Material Girls* is that the Duff sisters have a certain wholesome appeal and charm that makes the clunky plot occasionally entertaining. It is a minor tribute to them that the Marchettas are as likable as they are. The jury is still out on whether the Duffs have the talent to forge enduring careers in Hollywood, but a better script would allow for more fun.

Peter N. Chumo II

CREDITS

Ava Marchetta: Haylie Duff
Tanzie Marchetta: Hilary Duff
Fabiella: Anjelica Huston
Tommy Kazenbach: Brent Spiner
Henry Baines: Lukas Haas
Margo Thorness: Judy Tenuta
Inez: Maria Conchita Alonso
Craig: Obba Babatunde
Rick: Marcus Coloma
Origin: USA
Language: English
Released: 2006
Production: Guy Oseary, Milton Kim, Tim Wesley, Mark Morgan; Maverick Films, Patriot Pictures, Concept Entertainment, Rafter H Entertainment; released by MGM
Directed by: Martha Coolidge
Written by: Amy Rardin, John Quaintance, Jessica O'Toole
Cinematography by: Johnny E. Jensen
Music by: Jennie Muskett
Sound: David MacMillan
Music Supervisor: Dawn Soler
Editing: Steven Cohen
Art Direction: Ian Phillips
Costumes: Van Broughton Ramsey
Production Design: James H. Spencer
MPAA rating: PG
Running time: 100 minutes

REVIEWS

Boston Globe Online. August 19, 2006.
Entertainment Weekly. September 1, 2006, p. 53.
Hollywood Reporter Online. August 21, 2006.
Los Angeles Times Online. August 18, 2006.
New York Times Online. August 19, 2006.
Variety Online. August 20, 2006.

QUOTES

Henry (to Ava): "You're all frosting and no cupcake."

AWARDS

Nomination:

Golden Raspberries 2006: Worst Actress (Duff), Worst Actress (Duff)

MIAMI VICE

No Order. No Law. No Rules.
—Movie tagline

Box Office: $63.4 million

Because of such films as *The Last of the Mohicans* (1992), *Heat* (1995), *The Insider* (1999), and *Collateral* (2004), any film by director Michael Mann is worth anticipating. Before earning fame in films, Mann was best known as executive producer of the hit television series *Miami Vice* (1984-1989). He was reportedly given the directive of making "MTV cops" by an NBC executive and, with creator Anthony Yerkovich, devised a series featuring glamorous undercover detectives, fast cars, faster boats, drug-dealing scum, and a little sex—all dancing to the beat of the era's pop music. After actor Jamie Foxx suggested to Mann, whom he had worked with on *Ali* (2001) and *Collateral,* bring the series to the big screen, the director was inspired to create *Miami Vice.* The film is like a bigger, longer version of an episode of the series—and is, in fact, loosely based on one—and while it is moderately entertaining, it is a big disappointment by Mann's standards.

While the television series took the time to manufacture backstories for the heroes played by Don Johnson—rejected by his wife, seeing his partner killed—and Philip Michael Thomas—out to avenge his brother's murder—the film jumps right into the action without establishing the characters. Mann, who also wrote the screenplay, does little to develop Sonny Crockett (Colin Farrell) and Ricardo Tubbs (Jamie Foxx) until he introduces the women in their lives, and Tubbs' relationship with fellow cop Trudy Joplin (Naomie Harris) is more of a plot device than a romance.

Miami Vice opens with an undercover operation in a crowded nightclub, a scene staged much like one in *Collateral.* Crockett then learns that an informer (John Hawkes), who has infiltrated a white-supremacist drug gang, is in trouble. This leads to Crockett and Tubbs posing as drug dealers to get inside a massive Colombian operation headed by the ironically named Arcangel de Jesus Montoya (Luis Tosar). Before they can get to Montoya, they are confronted, in Haiti, by Montoya's suspicious lieutenant, Jose Yero (John Ortiz), and Crockett meets Isabella (Gong Li), who is half-Chinese and half-Cuban and is apparently Montoya's mistress. Crockett and Isabella are instantly attracted to one another, further complicating the undercover operation. Matters get messier when Trudy is kidnapped by the white supremacists, who are working with Yero. FBI agent Fujima (Ciaran Hinds), who initiated the sting, keeps trying to interfere with Crockett and Tubbs. All this builds to an explosive climax.

Miami Vice can be better appreciated by looking at its source, a 1985 episode of the series entitled "Smuggler's Blues," which serves as an outline for the film. The most direct parallel between the two is Trudy's kidnapping, with Mann adding embellishments, primarily Isabella and the white supremacists, to flesh out the story. The television series was criticized for being all style and no substance and the same can be said of the film. It looks terrific, and the plot is engrossing, if often unnecessarily difficult to follow, but it rarely connects emotionally.

While reviewers have blamed Foxx and, especially, Farrell for failing to instill much life into their characters, the fault lies with Mann who makes Crockett and Tubbs conceits more than characters. Crockett mumbles something about his father to Isabella, and that is essentially all we know about him. Foxx, so good in *Collateral* and *Ray* (2004), merely stands around glowering, while Farrell struggles to look intense. While Farrell can be effective in small doses, as in his supporting roles in *Minority Report* (2002) and *Intermission* (2003), he is generally dull in leading parts. He livens up a bit in his scenes with Li, with both ably conveying their characters' feelings of longing and regret.

Though many reviewers complained about being unable to understand much of what Li is saying, she is more intelligible than in her disastrous performance in *Memoirs of a Geisha* (2005). Li, who turned down the role played by Amy Brenneman in *Heat,* shows some of the spark she generates in films directed by Zhang Yimou, Chen Kaige, and Wong Kar Wai. While she is totally lost in *Memoirs of a Geisha,* here she gets across Isabella's conflicted emotions. Thanks in part to the cinematography of Dion Beebe, who also shot *Memoirs of a Geisha,* Li looks different from scene to scene and sometimes even within scenes, going from tormented and haggard to confidently beautiful seemingly at will.

Mann's failures as a screenwriter also undercut the efforts of such excellent performers as Hinds and Barry Shabaka Henley, in the role played by Edward James Olmos in the series, who have little to do. As cop Gina Calabrese, Elizabeth Rodriguez gets to deliver just one stirring speech. Harris, has more lines but no depth to her character. Why even cast such a quirky performer as Justin Theroux, as Zito, if all he gets to do is shoot an automatic weapon? The film's best performance comes from Ortiz, who gives Yero a sly furtiveness that transcends being a stock villain.

One of the elements for which the television series is best known is its pioneering use of popular music to help tell its stories. Popular 1980s acts such as Roxy Music, Tina Turner, Chaka Khan, Jackson Browne, and Phil Collins were heard throughout the series. The film features Moby, India.Arie, Mogwai, and others, closing with Nonpoint's hip-hop version of Collins' "In the Air Tonight." While Mann may have intended the constantly changing styles, with the emphasis on techno, to highlight the chaos into which his protagonists are thrown, the result is more tiring than illuminating.

As with *Collateral,* Beebe shot *Miami Vice* in high-definition video so that it looks much better in theaters with digital projection. The film seems a bit murky because all the scenes take place at night, on cloudy days, or in dimly lit rooms, as befitting the noir material, but it still looks like a conventionally shot film most of the time. The big exception is the raging gun battle at the end when the swirling handheld images look like something out of the reality program *Cops*, a dismal comparison Mann surely did not intend.

The sound during this shootout is unusually realistic, adding to the scene's intensity. William Goldenberg and Paul Rubell, both Mann veterans, edit the gunplay so fluidly that it is almost possible to know who is shooting at whom. While the action of *Miami Vice* is good, however, it never adds up to much. The best scenes come when Isabella takes Crockett to Cuba to reveal another side of herself. If only Mann had spent more time trying to enhance the humanity of his characters then perhaps the film would have done the television series justice.

Michael Adams

CREDITS

Sonny Crockett: Colin Farrell
Ricardo Tubbs: Jamie Foxx
Isabella: Gong Li
Trudy Joplin: Naomie Harris
Montoya: Luis Tosar
Jose Yero: John Ortiz
Castillo: Barry Shabaka Henley
FBI Agent Fujima: Ciaran Hinds
Alonzo Stevens: John Hawkes
Zito: Justin Theroux
Gina Callabrese: Elizabeth Rodriguez
Origin: USA
Language: English
Released: 2006
Production: Michael Mann, Pieter Jan Brugge; Forward Pass Productions, Motion Picture ETA Produktionsgesellschaft; released by Universal
Directed by: Michael Mann
Written by: Michael Mann
Cinematography by: Dion Beebe
Music by: John Murphy
Sound: David Ronne
Editing: William Goldenberg, Paul Rubell
Art Direction: Carlos Menendez
Costumes: Janty Yates, Michael Kaplan
Production Design: Victor Kempster
MPAA rating: R
Running time: 132 minutes

REVIEWS

Boxoffice Online. July 28, 2006.
Chicago Sun-Times Online. July 27, 2006.
Entertainment Weekly. August 4, 2006, p. 45.
Los Angeles Times Online. July 28, 2006.
New York Times Online. July 28, 2006.
San Francisco Chronicle. July 28, 2006, p. E1.
Variety Online. July 23, 2006.
Washington Post. July 28, 2006, p. C1.

QUOTES

Sonny Crockett: "Do you understand the meaning of the word 'foreboding,' as in badness is happening right now?"

MISSION: IMPOSSIBLE III

The mission begins.
—Movie tagline

Box Office: $134 million

Of the three *Mission: Impossible* films produced to date, *Mission: Impossible III* (*M:i:III*) most closely resembles the 1960s television series on which the film franchise is rather loosely based, at least insofar as its overall style and plot structure are concerned. Whereas the first, somewhat confusing film began with a secret agent team mission reminiscent of the television show and quickly shifted focus to one character (Ethan Hunt, played by Tom Cruise) bent on uncovering a traitor who betrayed the team, and whereas the second film played out as a typical action picture showcasing a series of stunts and relying even less on a team—resembling a James Bond movie even more than the original film—*M:i:III* is a slightly more character-driven movie that manages to maintain a fairly coherent story while it speeds through several plots twists and elaborate action sequences. The film still differs from the original television series in that it does not involve a complex, carefully plotted scheme to use intelligence and deception to outwit and bring the bad guy to justice. Ultimately, *M:i:III* is at its core an action film, but it does not aspire to be more than that and succeeds in its quest to tell a fast-paced story that is calculated to rapidly grab the audience's attention and not let go until the final credits roll.

Director J. J. Abrams, helming a big-screen film for the first time after finding success behind the small screen with the television series' *Alias* and *Lost*, chooses to open the film with a pivotal, intense scene from the climactic sequence of the story. Ethan Hunt, strapped to a chair, faces an icily low-key interrogator (Philip Seymour Hoffman) who informs him that an explosive charge has been inserted into his head and demands that Ethan tell him the location of the Rabbit's Foot. There is also someone else in the room—a young woman (Michelle Monaghan), also bound to a chair and silenced with duct tape—and Hunt's tormentor threatens to shoot her at the count of ten if he's not given the information he wants. Ethan vehemently protests that he thought he'd already given him the item and in distress begs the man to spare the woman. The interrogator keeps counting, while Ethan's protests grow more intense, and finally reaches the number ten…at which point he pulls the trigger. Abruptly the scene ends and the opening credits begin. Obviously calculated to invest the audience in the story, this opening sequence typifies the movie that follows. When the scene is revisited much later in the film, it should come as no surprise that all was not as it seemed the first time around. Still, as a gripping setup for the movie, the sequence turns much of the rest of the film into essentially a very long flashback as the audience anticipates the events that lead up to this confrontation and contemplates the outcome of the unfinished scene.

When the story begins (chronologically), the world seems more peaceful for Ethan Hunt. He has retired as an active agent for the Impossible Mission Force (IMF) and now works as a trainer and instructor for the agency. He is engaged to Julia (Monaghan), the woman who appeared to have been shot in the opening sequence, but he has not told Julia about his true occupation. During an engagement party, Ethan gets a call that leads him to a meeting with IMF supervisor Musgrave (Billy Crudup), who informs him that Lindsey Farris (Keri Russell), a former pupil of Ethan's, with whom he had a special bond, has been captured by a ruthless arms dealer named Owen Davian (Hoffman) and is being held in Berlin. Not surprisingly, Musgrave wants Ethan reenlist and rescue Lindsey. Ethan only briefly wrestles with the idea, coming up with an excuse to give Julia to explain his leaving town, then proceeds to assemble his team for the mission in Berlin. He joins familiar agent Luther Stickell (Ving Rhames) and new faces Declan Gormley (Jonathan Rhys Meyers) and Zhen Lei (Maggie Q) for the expedition to Germany, where they succeed in freeing Lindsey. The rescue sequence concludes with an exciting helicopter chase through a field densely populated with huge, dangerous windmills, but events take a tragic turn when Lindsey suddenly dies from an explosive charge the villains placed inside her head.

Quietly mourning Lindsey's loss but unable to share his sadness with his fiancee, Ethan resolves to bring Davian to justice. Having been informed by Musgrave and IMF boss Theodore Brassel (Laurence Fishburne) that Davian has always managed to elude capture, Ethan and his colleagues learn that Davian is planning on selling something called the "Rabbit's Foot" for $850 million. Speculating that the Rabbit's Foot could be a world-threatening weapon, Ethan's team sets out, without authorization, to apprehend the arms dealer. Their mission takes them to Vatican City and involves an enjoyable scheme in which Ethan disguises himself as Davian and briefly takes his place. The plot works and the team nabs the villain (and his briefcase), but unfortunately their victory is short-lived. While transporting Davian via truck, an IMF convoy comes under attack on the middle of a bridge. In one of the movie's most visually kinetic and pulse-pounding scenes, Ethan watches in bewilderment as an assault from the air turns the bridge into a scene of wrecked cars and explosions. Davian's people come to his rescue and Ethan only manages to destroy the assault drone before his nemesis is whisked away in a helicopter.

Of course the plot thickens as it twists once again. Davian kidnaps Julia and calls Ethan to threaten that he will kill her if Ethan does not obtain the Rabbit's Foot and deliver it within forty-eight hours. However, before he has a chance to contemplate his next action, Ethan is taken into custody by IMF and angrily chastised by Brassel, whom Ethan has suspected to be a dirty agent in league with Davian. Luckily for Ethan (it seems), Musgrave covertly helps him escape custody and lets him know that Julia is in Shanghai, where the Rabbit's Foot is also supposed to be. Ethan heads to Shanghai and there discovers his loyal team is waiting for him, determined to help. The team devises a scheme to retrieve the Rabbit's Foot, a mission that takes Ethan to the top of a skyscraper in downtown Shanghai. This actually turns out to be one of the more disappointing sequences in the movie simply because Ethan enters a building and then is next seen exiting it (through a window)—his adventure inside is completely left to the imagination, which comes as a surprise as all of Ethan's other exploits are detailed on screen.

Ethan informs his friends that he was successful in getting the Rabbit's Foot (though he still does not really know what it is), housed and protected in a canister, and he sets out to deliver the item and save Julia. He soon finds himself where the movie started: strapped to a chair, with Davian threatening to shoot Julia and set off a charge implanted in his head if he does not disclose the location of the Rabbit's Foot. As mentioned before, this time, as the scene continues, expectations are challenged as the plot twists again several times—the woman is in fact shot, but she is not really Julia, and an IMF supervisor is indeed in league with Davian, but it is not Brassel. Interestingly, as the film speeds toward its climax, Abrams infuses the story with a genuine sense of jeopardy, giving no assurances that Ethan or Julia will survive. Everything is indeed resolved happily, though, and the film concludes with Ethan and Julia preparing to leave for their honeymoon—but not before Ethan asks Brassel for an explanation of the Rabbit's Foot. Not surprisingly, no answer is provided, so the film ends with one puzzle unsolved.

Of course it does not really matter what the Rabbit's Foot is; the device is simply a classic MacGuffin, an element that helps move the story along but ultimately has no meaning. The plot wisely does not hinge completely on this particular MacGuffin; it exists to advance one level of the story—Davian's motivation—but its importance to the central conflicts of the film is only superficial. Thus, Abrams' teasing of the audience by refusing to explain the Rabbit's Foot is not meant to frustrate but to amuse, as if openly acknowledging that ultimately it is unimportant.

The quickly paced editing of the film and the visual style—frame compositions, coloring, and movement—may be reminiscent to viewers familiar with Abrams' television series, for much of the atmosphere, look, and energy of *M:i:III* shares similarities with the shows *Alias* and *Lost.* Fortunately, those qualities help the film rather than hinder it. The movie's score, by Abrams' composer of choice Michael Giacchino, frequently recalls themes from the original television series while also incorporating many mood-manipulating elements similar to Giacchino's work for the two aforementioned television series. Tom Cruise reportedly wanted Abrams to direct *Mission: Impossible III* after seeing *Alias* on DVD, and indeed, Abrams manages to imbue the movie with stylistic devices and elements that distinguish it as a J. J. Abrams film. The plot twists and pacing propel the movie forward and keep it interesting, but the story never becomes confusing, as was the tendency with the first *Mission: Impossible* (1996) film, and also avoids the stylistic excesses found in *Mission: Impossible II* (2000).

M:i:III also tackles character development more successfully than its predecessor. Ethan's relationship with Julia deepens his character psychologically and adds a layer of realism to his motivations. In a similar vein, while Julia is ultimately not a major character, her presence and her more important role at the end help give the film some emotional texture that is often missing from action-heavy movies. Ethan's relationship with his colleagues—especially Luther—is also developed a bit more than in the previous films. Luther's attitudes about Ethan getting involved in a relationship, to say nothing of his getting married, help to give his character more definition and also suggest that there is more to his friendship with Ethan than just the work they do together.

Overall, *Mission: Impossible III* does not attempt or pretend to explore significant themes nor does it try too hard to emphasize drama and psychological depth. It intends to be a smart, enjoyable action film that keeps the audience wondering. Thanks largely to Abrams' contributions as well as good performances from the cast, it manages to do just that.

David Flanagin

CREDITS

Ethan Hunt: Tom Cruise
Luther: Ving Rhames
Lindsey Farris: Keri Russell
Owen Davian: Philip Seymour Hoffman
Julia: Michelle Monaghan
Theodore Brassel: Laurence Fishburne
Musgrave: Billy Crudup
Benji: Simon Pegg
Declan: Jonathan Rhys Meyers
Melissa Meade: Sasha Alexander
Kevin: Greg Grunberg
Beth: Carla Gallo
Brownway: Eddie Marsan
IMF Agent Pete: Jose Zuniga
Zhen Lei: Maggie Q
Origin: Germany, USA
Language: English
Released: 2006
Production: Tom Cruise, Paula Wagner; Cruise-Wagner Productions; released by Paramount
Directed by: J.J. Abrams
Written by: J.J. Abrams, Alex Kurtzman, Roberto Orci
Cinematography by: Dan Mindel
Music by: Michael Giacchino
Sound: Jeff Wexler
Editing: Marianne Brandon, Mary Jo Markey
Art Direction: Daniel T. Dorrance
Costumes: Colleen Atwood
Production Design: Scott Chambliss
MPAA rating: PG-13
Running time: 126 minutes

REVIEWS

Boxoffice Online. May 5, 2006.
Chicago Sun-Times Online. May 4, 2006.
New York Times Online. May 5, 2006.
Time Magazine. May 4, 2006.
Variety Online. May 3, 2006.

MRS. PALFREY AT THE CLAREMONT

Life Is Just Waiting For You To Invite It In.
—Movie tagline

Box Office: $1.7 million

Joan Plowright plays the largest role of her career and undoubtedly one of her best as the title character in this simple, sentimental tale of an unlikely friendship between a struggling young writer and an elderly widow. Director Dan Ireland and screenwriter Ruth Sachs adapted British writer Elizabeth Taylor's 1971 novel, which was set in the 1950s, bringing it into the present day.

The recently-widowed Mrs. Sarah Palfrey (Plowright) arrives at London's Claremont Hotel, a long-term residence for the elderly, to find that nothing is as she expected. Rather than a stately, grand manor, the Claremont, with its flickering neon sign, is as tattered as its aged bellboy and most of its quirky guests. But other than the "Oh dear!" she utters when finally alone in her tiny room, Mrs. Palfrey puts on her best face, and dress, as she goes downstairs to dine in the common room.

Not wanting to be a bother to her daughter Elizabeth (Anna Carteret), who lives in Scotland, Mrs. Palfrey relocates to London with the hope of spending time with her twenty-six-year-old grandson Desmond (Lorcan O'Toole), who works in the British Museum Archives. Her phone calls ignored by the busy Desmond, she is forced to dine alone, night after night, fending off the intrusive questions and pitying looks of the long-time Claremont residents. Although a bit strange herself, Mrs. Arbuthnot (a wonderful Anna Massey) manages to make Mrs. Palfrey's first night there far more comfortable. As despressing and lonely as the Claremont may be, Mrs. Arbuthnot also wryly tells her, "No one is allowed to die here."

Her life takes an unexpected turn, however, when she trips and falls outside the basement apartment of the aspiring writer and street musician Ludovic Meyer (Rupert Friend). He rushes out to aid the distressed senior, inviting her in for a little first aid and tea. They find they have much in common, and form an immediate kinship that surpasses either's natural familial bonds. Mrs. Palfrey invites him to the Claremont for dinner to repay his kindness, boasting to the residents that she will have a guest for dinner on Saturday. When they naturally assume it must be the much talked about but never seen Desmond, Mrs. Palfrey doesn't deny it. She confesses her lie to Ludo, who cheerfully agrees to pass himself off as Mrs. Palfrey's grandson.

All of the Claremont residents fawn over Mrs. Palfrey's extremely handsome "grandson," which has the added benefit of raising her own stock among the gossipy guests. She's asked out to a "do" by the Claremont's Mr. Osborne (Robert Lang) who proffers a drunken but not insincere proposal of marriage. Mrs. Palfrey gently but firmly turns him down, saying she is beginning to enjoy her newfound independence and vowing she'll never marry again.

When the real Desmond finally turns up, Mrs. Palfrey is simply annoyed that he might ruin her charade with Ludo, telling him as she ushers him out of the dining room that the hotel doesn't allow family to visit while informing the inquisitive guests that he is merely her overzealous accountant. Meanwhile, her friendship deepens with Ludo as they share a common love of poetry, and music. One of the film's highlights is a poignant scene in which Ludo plays his guitar and sings a moving version of her favorite song "For All We Know."

When Sarah tells Ludo her favorite movie is the 1940s British romantic drama *Brief Encounter* (1945) he heads to the video store to check it out, only to find someone else reaching for it at the same time. Gwendolyn (Zoe Tapper) is like a younger version of Sarah—kind, intelligent, witty—and she and Ludo fall in love.

Just as Mrs. Palfrey is getting comfortable with her new life, she experiences some setbacks. Her memory seems to be going and she is growing irritable. Her daughter Elizabeth comes to visit for dinner and takes her to task for her rude treatment of Desmond. Mrs. Palfrey retorts that she has a life now—and a marriage proposal to boot—and that Desmond and Elizabeth both need to respect that. Mrs. Arbuthnot wanders over to their table but collapses in front of them. Mrs. Palfrey reads in the obituaries later that her friend has died. It isn't long before Mrs. Palfrey herself meets with an accident that lands her in the hospital with a broken hip. It is not her family but Ludo who is by her side throughout. Complications ensue, including pneumonia, and she passes away before Ludo can deliver the story he has finally completed in her honor.

While the material is thoughtfully and delicately handled, the film suffers from some editing and shot composition problems at times, haphazardly cutting from one scene to the next. Some critics complained of anachronisms caused by failing to wholly update all elements of the story, leaving Ludo to peck away on an archaic typewriter, as well as an obvious lack of modern conveniences anywhere. While Friend is charismatic and convincing in the role, he does seem almost too good to be true—eschewing friends his own age to spend time with Mrs. Palfrey. Occasional voiceovers nicely tell bits of the story would-be writer Ludo is penning about his aged friend. Thoughtful touches include Mrs. Palfrey wearing Celia Johnson's hat from *Brief Encounter* when she arrives at the Claremont.

Hilary White

CREDITS

Mrs. Sarah Palfrey: Joan Plowright
Ludovic Meyer: Rupert Friend

Elizabeth: Anna Carteret
Gwendolyn: Zoe Tapper
Mrs. Arbuthnot: Anna Massey
Mr. Osborne: Robert Lang
Mrs. Post: Marcia Warren
Mrs. Burton: Millicent Martin
Desmond: Lorcan O'Toole
Origin: Great Britain
Language: English
Released: 2005
Production: Lee Caplin, Zachary Matz, Carl-Jan Colpaert; Picture Entertainment; released by Cineville/Picture Entertainment
Directed by: Dan Ireland
Written by: Ruth Sacks
Cinematography by: Claudio Rocha
Music by: Stephen Barton
Sound: Jerry Gilbert
Editing: Nigel Galt, Virginia Katz
Art Direction: Fabrice Spelta
Costumes: Maja Meschede
Production Design: Julian Nagel
MPAA rating: Unrated
Running time: 108 minutes

REVIEWS

Boxoffice Online. December 2, 2006.
Chicago Sun-Times Online. May 5, 2006.
New York Times Online. November 25, 2005.
San Francisco Chronicle. May 19, 2006, p. E5.
Variety Online. November 27, 2005.
Village Voice Online. November 21, 2005.

QUOTES

Mrs. Palfrey: "Most of my life I've been somebody's daughter, somebody's wife, and somebody's mother. I would like to spend the rest of my time here being simply myself."

TRIVIA

Lorcan O'Toole, making his film debut as Desmond, is the son of actor Peter O'Toole.

MONSTER HOUSE

There goes the neighborhood.
—Movie tagline

Box Office: $73.6 million

The hyper-realistic CGI triumph *Monster House,* destined to become a children's Halloween staple, attests to its first-class genesis, executive produced by Steven Spielberg and Robert Zemeckis. Directed with visual flair by newcomer Gil Kenan, who was hired after of the producers saw his UCLA senior year short film *The Lark* (2002), a live-action/animated horror fantasy.

The film's crisply-rendered animation is nearly photo-quality when it comes to the landscapes and the animated children are full of unbelievably sophisticated facial expressions thanks to a technology first utilized in Zemeckis' *Polar Express* (2004) that digitally captures the movements of real actors. The filmmakers shot for forty-two days with live actors and sets before turning them into animated equivalents. The result is an extremely naturalistic look that behooves the talented cast. The script, by Dan Harmon, Rob Schrab, and Pamela Pettler from Harmon and Schrab's story, matches the high-quality animation, with smart and witty dialogue that offers something for adults as well as kids.

Lead character D.J. (voice of Mitchel Musso) is suspicious of a strange house that is directly across the street and its reviled denizen, Mr. Nebbercracker (voice of Steve Buscemi). In the beautifully shot opening scene, an intricately detailed autumn leaf falls to the ground and lands on a pig-tailed little girl's tricycle. She gets stuck on Nebbercracker's lawn, which has a tendency to "grab" things and he emerges from the creepy-looking house enraged, snatching the girl's trike and leaving her to run home crying.

D.J. and his chubby sidekick Chowder (voice of Sam Lerner) watch with a telescope from D.J.'s room and decide to stand up to the skinny, toothless old man. D.J. tries to reason with Nebbercracker, who proceeds to throttle him but then the old man collapses and appears to die, driven away in an ambulance. D.J. is wracked with guilt, thinking he has killed the man, unbeknownst to his happily oblivious parents, voiced by Fred Willard and Catherine O'Hara, who go away to a dental convention and leave him with babysitter Elizabeth. Zee, as she prefers to be called (voice of Maggie Gyllenhaal), is a punk rocker who has little use for the care and feeding of children, preferring to spend her time with her obnoxious boyfriend Bones (voice of Jason Lee). Neither Zee nor Bones believes the kids' tale of a "haunted" house that "eats" people and so, naturally, a curious Bones is promptly sucked in by the giant Persian rug that serves as the house's tongue. The blissfully unaware Zee wanders off to find him, never to be seen again...until the scene that plays during the end credits.

The incompetent cops voiced by Kevin James and Nick Cannon, doing their best Abbott and Costello routine, don't believe the kids either but that's much to do with the uncooperative house itself. Normally, when someone wanders onto the lawn, the house's top windows open up like giant eyes, while its porch and front doorway turn into a huge, fanged mouth that devours anyone in it's path. Even the surrounding lawn and trees grasp and suck in helpless animals and people. But, the clever house does its best Michigan J. Frog routine—standing frozen and unresponsive—when adults are around.

The boys team up with the savvy red-headed Jenny (voice of Spencer Locke) after they save her from nearly getting devoured by the hungry house. After consulting with pizza delivery boy/paranormal expert Skull (voice of Jon Heder), the three kids hatch a plan to get the house drunk on cold medicine but end up getting put in the back of a squad car by the police instead. Before they can take the kids downtown for booking, however, the cops are conveniently eaten by the house. The squad car also gets sucked in but the kids manage not to get digested and the sleeping house has no idea they are still inside of it. They then seek to find the "heart" of the house, the furnace they reckon, and destroy it.

In the basement, they come upon what turns out to be the key to the mystery of the house. Nebbercracker was rumored to have fattened up his hugely obese wife, Constance (voice of Kathleen Turner), so he could kill and eat her. They find Constance's corpse surrounded by a loving shrine proving that this was not the case. However, before they can do any more snooping, the house discovers them and seeks to snuff them out. Using the gag reflex of the house's uvula, which they discovered earlier, they are spit out onto the lawn.

Surprisingly, Nebbercracker isn't dead after all but instead comes back with his arm in a sling and as cranky as ever. The kids tell him of their macabre discovery of Constance and he confesses the truth. He rescued his beloved wife from the life of a circus freak and began building her dream house. Constantly harassed about her weight by the neighborhood kids, Constance works herself up into a murderous rage. Nebbercracker tried to restrain her but she fell to her death in the house's foundation. Her murderous spirit is now fueling the house's ravenous appetite for neighborhood kids. Nebbercracker knows they must stop Constance before Halloween comes—a death sentence for innocent trick-or-treaters.

The rest of the film becomes an action movie with the kids battling the dangerous, now-mobile house on a construction site. After some close calls, D.J. delivers the deathblow, stuffing a bundle of dynamite down the chimney, completely obliterating the evil house. Constance's spirit is released and everyone the house has devoured emerges, only slightly scathed, while the kids happily run off to enjoy their Halloween.

In addition to a wonderful cast and smart story, *New York Times* critic A.O. Scott appreciated the "moments of amusing, self-conscious auto-homage: a Wilson basketball with a human face smudged onto it; plumbing fixtures that come to life with the slinky movements of *Jurassic Park* (1993) dinosaurs; a suburban Halloween out of *E.T.* (1982)" Additionally, Scott notes that "the deeper imprint of Mr. Spielberg's influence, in particular, lies in the film's evocation of childhood as a state of wonder tinged with darkness."

Hilary White

CREDITS

Chowder: Sam Lerner (Voice)
Mr. Nebbercracker: Steve Buscemi (Voice)
Zee: Maggie Gyllenhaal (Voice)
Reginald "Skull" Skullinski: Jon Heder (Voice)
DJ: Mitchel Musso (Voice)
Jenny: Spencer Locke (Voice)
Officer Lister: Nick Cannon (Voice)
Officer Landers: Kevin James (Voice)
Bones: Jason Lee (Voice)
Mom: Catherine O'Hara (Voice)
Constance: Kathleen Turner (Voice)
Dad: Fred Willard (Voice)
Origin: USA
Language: English
Released: 2006
Production: Steve Starkey, Jack Rapke; Columbia Pictures, Robert Zemeckis, Steven Spielberg, Relativity, Imagemovers; released by Sony Pictures Entertainment
Directed by: Gil Kenan
Written by: Pamela Pettler, Dan Harmon, Rob Schrab
Cinematography by: Xavier Perez Grobet
Music by: Douglas Pipes
Sound: William B. Kaplan
Editing: Adam Scott
Art Direction: Greg Papalia, Norman Newberry
Costumes: Ruth Myers
Production Design: Ed Verreaux
MPAA rating: PG
Running time: 91 minutes

REVIEWS

Boxoffice Online. July 21, 2006.
Chicago Sun-Times Online. July 21, 2006.
Entertainment Weekly. July 28, 2006, p. 45.
Los Angeles Times Online. July 21, 2006.
New York Times Online. July 21, 2006.
San Francisco Chronicle. July 21, 2006, p. E1.
Variety Online. July 4, 2006.
Washington Post. July 21, 2006, p. WE36.

QUOTES

DJ: "I kissed a girl! I kissed a girl on the lips!"

AWARDS

Nomination:

Oscars 2006: Animated Film

Golden Globes 2007: Animated Film

MY SUPER EX-GIRLFRIEND

He broke her heart. She broke his everything.
—Movie tagline

Box Office: $22.5 million

Uma Thurman, flashing bits of her *Kill Bill* (2003) persona, stars as a super-jealous superhero who magnificently menaces her mild-mannered ex in this female revenge fantasy. While the film is not without its charms, writer Don Payne (*The Simpsons*) and the director Ivan Reitman (*Ghostbusters* [1984]), whose lesser, recent efforts include *Evolution* (2001) and *Father's Day* (1997), fail to make the most of a wonderful premise and talented cast in what could have been more than just a fun spoof of *Fatal Attraction* (1987) starring Supergirl.

Luke Wilson plays Matt Saunders, a pasty-skinned New York architect who secretly lusts after his pretty blond co-worker Hannah Lewis (the similar-sounding Anna Faris) who is, however, dating the swarthy, six-pack sporting male model Steve (Mark Consuelos). Matt's gleefully chauvinist colleague Vaughn (*The Office*'s Rainn Wilson) prods the woefully undersexed Matt into approaching a bespectacled, buttoned-down type brunette on the subway one evening on the premise that it's always the quiet ones who harbor an inner wild thing. Little do either of them know that while Jenny Johnson (Uma Thurman) is an assistant curator at an art gallery by day, by night she's G-Girl, a bone fide blonde, cape-wearing, sky-riding heroine. Despite being as single and socially awkward as most superhero alter egos, Jenny turns down Matt's invitation for a date. She changes her mind when shortly thereafter, a thug snatches her purse and Matt ineptly comes to her rescue—something Jenny can uniquely appreciate.

Jenny got her G-Girl powers in high school after coming into contact with a meteor but her neurotic, irrational, obsessive, and needy behavior are all God-given, and despite an epic, wall-shattering, bed-breaking roll in the hay, Matt begins to regret getting involved with Jenny. Dating G-Girl has its privileges, though, and when Jenny reveals her secret identity to Matt, he asks her to take him flying—something he's always wanted to do—which ends with a sexy romp in the sky.

When Matt and Hannah innocently visit a construction site on work business, Jenny unexpectedly shows up and, assuming the worst, blows her stack. Matt tries to diffuse the situation by suggesting they double date with Hannah and Steve. The date turns sour when Steve has to suddenly cancel, awkwardly leaving Matt alone with the two women. When the news reports a missile heading toward New York, Matt breathes a sigh of relief, knowing G-Girl will have to fly to the rescue, conveniently ending an uncomfortable dinner situation. Relcutantly, G-Girl does just that but returns in time to see Matt and Hannah embracing happily as the city is saved. After a scary ride home where Jenny destroys his passenger car window in a fit of rage, Matt thinks maybe she's not the one for him. He breaks the news to her the next night, where, predictably, she doesn't take the blow off very well, leaving Matt collapsed beneath the fridge where she throws him and a gaping hole in the ceiling when she flies off.

While G-Girl does use her powers to terrorize Matt in petty ways—including launching his car into space with the words "You suck" written on it, and even getting him fired—it turns out she had every reason to be jealous of Hannah. Steve has been cheating on Hannah and soon the consoling friend Matt and his coworker find themselves between the sheets, setting the stage for the film's set-piece: G-Girl throwing a live Great White Shark through Hannah's apartment window.

Matt responds by joining forces with supervillian Professor Bedlam (Eddie Izzard), G-Girl's arch-nemesis. The backstory is that Bedlam (a.k.a. Barry) and Jenny had a thing in high school and while making out in the back seat of his car, the aforementioned meteor hurtled to earth nearby. After Jenny wandered out to explore, the meteor exploded, leaving Jenny newly buxom and blonde. Barry eventually ended their budding relationship and devoted the rest of his life to foiling her. Matt agrees to Bedlam's plan that involves taking a piece of the meteor, which he has saved in his refrigerator, and luring G-Girl to touch it again which he explains will have the reverse effect this time, taking away her powers for good. In return, Bedlam agrees to retire from his life of knavery.

The third act has Matt going to the gallery to woo back Jenny, who happily agrees to a romantic rooftop dinner with him that night. He brings the meteor chunk in a large gift box but they are interrupted by a concerned Hannah who proceeds to get in a girlfight with Jenny who quickly turns into G-Girl. Vaughn stops by mid-fight, accidently opening the box and causing a now even angrier G-Girl to lose her powers just as

Bedlam and his henchman make their entrance. While Matt and Vaughn take on the nowhere near retired Bedlam and his men, G-Girl struggles to get back to the meteor to restore her powers while Hannah attempts to stop her. An explosion ensues, with Hannah disappearing from over the rooftop, only to return with red-hair and the ability to fly. The two superpowered females continue their aerial tussle throughout the city, eventually ending when they crash into a fashion show. Apparently, the meteor has restored some reason to G-Girl as she admits to Matt that she never really loved him but was in love with Bedlam all the time, who more than reciprocates her feelings.

Hannah and Matt go home together for a repeat of the wall-breaking sex he first experienced with his superhero-ex. They meet up with Jenny and Barry by Matt's destroyed car in the street, which Jenny promises to replace, when Jenny is suddenly called off to "work," hearing the cries of people in trouble. Hannah offers to help her out and the two fly off to the city's rescue, leaving their amused boyfriends holding their purses.

The film has some fun playing with gender roles and delivers some legitimate laughs. Thurman appears to have a great time, relishing the rare opportunity to play a comic, action hero role written for a woman while Luke Wilson's normally spot-on low-key performance gets a little lost in the shuffle. Izzard delivers in a small role, while the very funny Wanda Sykes, as Matt and Hannah's boss and Rainn Wilson steal their respective scenes. Many of the action scenes involving G-Girl's do-gooding are lackluster, as is Matt's milquetoast routine. The film is most enjoyable when we're watching Matt's psycho-ex do her thing.

Hilary White

CREDITS

Jenny Johnson/G-Girl: Uma Thurman
Matt Saunders: Luke Wilson
Hannah Lewis: Anna Faris
Steve: Mark Consuelos
Vaughn Haige: Rainn Wilson
Professor Bedlam/Barry: Eddie Izzard
Carla Dunkirk: Wanda Sykes
Origin: USA
Language: English
Released: 2006
Production: Arnon Milchan, Gavin Palone; Regency Enterprises, New Regency, Pariah Production; released by 20th Century Fox
Directed by: Ivan Reitman
Written by: Don Payne
Cinematography by: Don Burgess
Music by: Teddy Castellucci
Sound: Danny Michael
Editing: Sheldon Kahn
Art Direction: Patricia Woodbridge
Costumes: Laura Jean Shannon
Production Design: Jane Musky
MPAA rating: PG-13
Running time: 96 minutes

REVIEWS

Boxoffice Online. July 21, 2006.
Chicago Sun-Times Online. July 21, 2006.
Los Angeles Times Online. July 21, 2006.
New York Times Online. July 21, 2006.
San Francisco Chronicle. July 21, 2006, p. E5.
Variety Online. July 20, 2006.
Washington Post. July 21, 2006, p. C1.

QUOTES

Jenny: "You know, Matt, I have to help people every day, but nobody's ever helped me before you."

N

NACHO LIBRE

Don't you want a little taste of the glory?
—Movie tagline

Box Office: $80.2 million

Nacho Libre is built on an absurd premise: a monk, Ignacio or "Nacho" (Jack Black), becomes a luchador—a performer of lucha libre, Mexican professional wrestling—not only to realize his lifelong dream of becoming a wrestler, but also to win enough money to feed the children who live at Ignacio's monastery-supported orphanage. Fortunately, all of the potentially disastrous elements of *Nacho Libre* are marshaled expertly to uplifting and heartwarming, if implausible and somewhat ridiculous, results by writer/director Jared Hess and co-writer Jerusha Hess, who created the surprise cult smash juggernaut *Napoleon Dynamite* (2004), and collaborators-turned-producers Jack Black and Mike White. Like *Napoleon Dynamite*, *Nacho Libre*'s charm and ultimate triumph lies in the power of its enormous heart, in friends standing by one another to make things happen, and in trusting the determination of a quirky, bumbling underdog.

Frustrated that the other monks in his order will neither give him the money to buy fresh ingredients for the children's meals nor provide him with more important responsibilities in the monastery, Nacho resolves to fight in a lucha libre match to win the money. He enlists the help of a wiry thief, Esqueleto (Hector Jimenez), to be his wrestling partner. They fight with all they can muster, but lose anyway. When they are paid regardless of the loss, they become hooked, and Nacho is able to buy fresh food for the orphanage. Meanwhile, Nacho is taken with a new arrival at the orphanage, Sister Encarnacion (Ana de la Reguera), who has come to be a teacher. She has a very low opinion of luchadores (wrestlers), and Nacho keeps his nocturnal activities a secret from her.

Nacho's main relationships in the film—Esqueleto, the orphans, and Encarnacion—provide much of the emotional glue that holds *Nacho Libre* together and prevent it from becoming pure slapstick. When they stand side-by-side, Nacho and Esqueleto look like some sort of demented, Latin Laurel and Hardy. The pair plays off one another well. When the two are about to go into their first real match, Nacho expresses concern over Esqueleto's salvation, for Nacho is a man of the cloth, but Esqueleto only believes in science. One of the funniest moments of the film is Nacho's impromptu baptism of Esqueleto, which he accomplishes by sneaking up behind Esqueleto with a small bowl of water and dunking his head in it, face first. When the children, who know Nacho's secret, are caught wrestling in the yard at the orphanage, and Nacho has to admonish them because sister Encarnacion is standing right there, it is clear that he loves these kids and they love him. As for Encarnacion, Nacho is unsure of how to woo her. He is given an idea by Esqueleto: Nacho will take Encarnacion for a night-time walk, and Esqueleto and his friends will attack Nacho and let him win. The plan backfires when Nacho is attacked by real thugs and is beaten, but it is clear that Encarnacion feels something for him anyway.

The defeat at the hands of the street criminals shakes Nacho's confidence, and he determines to get real fighting skills. Esqueleto has a plan. He takes Nacho to a gypsy who knows where to find eagle eggs. The gypsy leads Nacho and Esqueleto to an eagle nest and promises that by ingesting the eggs, Nacho will receive "eagle powers." Nacho scales a cliff, cracks open an eagle egg, and ingests its disgusting-looking contents. That night, when he is defeated in the ring, he tells Esqueleto that those powers were a lie. Ever more desperate, they decide that their only chance to really be wrestlers is to get into the professional leagues. They form a plan to attend a party to which all of the wrestlers and the biggest promoter in town are going. When they are turned away at the door, Esqueleto hops the wall and Nacho sneaks in with the band. Inside, Esqueleto hears of a multi-fighter match, the "Battle Jam," the winner of which will fight Ramses, the champion, in an exhibition bout; while Nacho, presumed to be part of the band, is coerced into singing an extemporaneous and very funny song about Ramses. They are both thrown out of the party.

The next morning, Nacho suddenly realizes that he has forgotten to buy groceries for the orphans for breakfast. He has a confrontation with Encarnacion, and she tells him that it is only noble to fight for someone who needs help. She counsels him to pray for forgiveness. When he prays before the candles in the chapel, he accidentally sets fire to his robe revealing his wrestling clothes underneath. Exposed, he leaves the monastery, and vows to win the "Battle Jam." The match starts with seven wrestlers, but eventually it comes down to Nacho and a wrestler named Silencio. Silencio defeats Nacho handily, and Nacho must leave the monastery in disgrace. Following a montage of Nacho in the wilderness—which is really about two-hundred yards outside of town—Esqueleto comes to Nacho with news that Silencio cannot fight (a quick flashback reveals that Esqueleto ran over Silencio's foot when he threatened a child), and Nacho, as the second place winner, must fight Ramses in Silencio's stead. Nacho gives Esqueleto a letter to deliver to Encarnacion. He does, and she reads it. In the letter, Nacho reveals his plan to fight and to leave all the money for the orphans. He also reveals his love for Encarnacion.

As Nacho prepares for the match against Ramses, he tells Esqueleto he fears he will be hurt in the ring and that no one will ever hear the song he wrote for Encarnacion while he was in the wilderness. He sings it to Esqueleto, and it is hilarious: "To kiss your mouth/I break my vow/No no no, no no, no WAY JOSE." The song is cut short when Nacho is called to the ring. Ramses' entrance is appropriately over the top. He is enormous, and it seems clear that Nacho cannot possibly beat him. The fight is appropriately epic and ridiculous. Ramses unmasks Nacho in the ring (a great insult). As Nacho is being held to the floor, Ramses' boot to his throat, Encarnacion enters the stadium with the orphans, who are all dressed in variations of Nacho's lucha libre costume. Upon seeing her and the children, Nacho is imbued with superhuman strength and tosses Ramses out of the ring. His eagle powers manifest themselves as he soars over the crowd and pins Ramses, winning the match. The film then cuts to a school bus driving through the countryside. It is the bus Nacho has purchased for the orphans. He is driving, taking them on a field trip to Mayan pyramids and, of course, Encarnacion is with them.

Nacho Libre is a sweet and sporadically funny film. Overall, it is touching and uplifting, much like *Rocky*, another film about a fighting underdog. Nacho succeeds because he fights for love and the children who need him—they are what give him the strength he needs to defeat his opponent, which is the sort of underdog a comedy requires. The wrestling in *Nacho Libre* is physically proficient, well choreographed, and performed for maximum comedic effect. Some may gripe that Black's accent sounds fake or exaggerated, but there is no arguing that when he says, "Anyways," or when he grabs an opponent in the ring for the first time, bear-hugs him, and says "SQUEEZE," it is almost impossible not to laugh.

John Boaz

CREDITS

Ignacio/Nacho: Jack Black
Emperor: Peter Stormare
Sister Encarnacion: Ana de la Reguera
Esqueleto: Hector Jimenez
Guillermo: Richard Montoya
Chancho: Darius A. Rose
Juan Pablo: Moises Arias
Chuy: Diego Eduardo Gomez
Segundo Nunez: Carlos Maycotte
Ramses: Cesar Gonzalez
Origin: USA
Language: English
Released: 2006
Production: Michael White, Julia Pistor, Jack Black, David Klawards; Nickelodeon Movies, Black & White Prods; released by Paramount
Directed by: Jared Hess
Written by: Jared Hess, Jerusha Hess, Mike White
Cinematography by: Xavier Perez Grobet
Music by: Danny Elfman
Sound: Santiago Nunez
Editing: Billy Weber
Art Direction: Hania Robledo
Costumes: Graciela Mazon

Production Design: Gideon Ponte
MPAA rating: PG
Running time: 91 minutes

REVIEWS

Boxoffice Online. June 16, 2006.
Chicago Sun-Times Online. June 16, 2006.
Entertainment Weekly Online. June 14, 2006.
Los Angeles Times Online. June 16, 2006.
New York Times Online. June 16, 2006.
Premiere Magazine Online. June 16, 2006.
Variety Online. June 15, 2006.
Washington Post. June 16, 2006, p. C1.

QUOTES

Nacho: "Chancho, when you are a man, sometimes you wear stretchy pants in your room…just for fun."

TRIVIA

During one of the wrestling scenes, Jack Black jumped from the ring and struck his head on a chair, causing a gash above his right eye that required stitches.

NANNY McPHEE

You'll Learn To Love Her. Warts And All.
—Movie tagline
Behave or Beware.
—Movie tagline

Box Office: $47.1 million

The male lead of the fairy-tale *Nanny McPhee* is poor Mr. Brown (Colin Firth). His wife has died and left him with seven unruly children whose only virtue seems to be that they are quite adept at making nannies quit. In fact, nanny number seventeen has just left because she believed the six older children had cooked and eaten the baby. It was a record for the children since this nanny only lasted three days, eight hours and forty-three minutes. When Mr. Brown desperately returns to the nanny placement service, they just as desperately pretend to be closed. But just then a soft voice wafts its way to Mr. Brown's ears. "What you need is Nanny McPhee." Good advice, but who is she and how does one contact her?

This is not Mr. Brown's only problem. As an undertaker, he does not make much money—certainly not enough to support his large family—so he relies on the support of his half-blind Aunt Adelaide (Angela Lansbury). But Aunt Adelaide is a pragmatist and believes the children need a stepmother more than a nanny, so she has given Mr. Brown one month to find one or she'll cut him off. Unfortunately, the only single woman the shy and awkward Mr. Brown knows is the fashion-challenged and assertively aggressive Mrs. Quickly (Celia Imrie), who recently buried her third husband. While Mr. Brown figures out how to overcome his natural revulsion in order to propose to Mrs. Quickly, his children run amok in the kitchen while the cook, Mrs. Blatherwick (Imelda Staunton), is tied to the tabletop. Quite unexpectedly, there is a knock at the door. It is the mysterious Nanny McPhee (Emma Thompson). Dresssed all in black, imposing, snaggle-toothed, and bedecked with warts and a unibrow, Nanny McPhee introduces herself, states her terms of employment, and then makes her way past Mr. Brown and the scullery maid Evangeline (Kelly Macdonald) to the kitchen. There the children blatantly state that they plan on playing all night without stopping. They get their wish as Nanny McPhee gives a rap of her magic cane, time speeds up and the children play to the point of exhaustion. Finally, they relent and offer to go to bed. With another rap of her cane, the kitchen is cleaned up and the children tucked in their beds as if nothing had ever happened.

But the next day they are back plotting ways to rid themselves of their new nanny. They pretend to be sick and demand to stay in bed, but once again Nanny McPhee will hoist them on their own petard. With a rap of her cane, the children actually become sick, are really stuck in their beds, and have to take the most disgusting medicine ever created. Eventually the children again relent and come to respect Nanny McPhee—or, at least her magic—and, when that happens, her appearance begins to change.

When Aunt Adelaide makes a sudden visit for tea, the children are told to put their best clothes on, which they do, only they put them on the pig and the donkey and the chickens and the dog. The far-sighted Aunt Adelaide predictably mistakes the animals for the children and demands to take one of the girls home with her to teach her to become a proper lady. Mr. Brown, however, has no desire to let any of his children go, but cannot say no to Aunt Adelaide. Perhaps Nanny McPhee can figure some way around her. And so it is that when Aunt Adelaide leaves, one of the girls of the Brown household does go with her but it is not one of Mr. Brown's daughters. She leaves with Evangeline who, it is learned, has always dreamed of a better life and also has a crush on Mr. Brown. Nanny McPhee now has no moles. But even as Nanny McPhee civilizes the children, and the children slowly come to respect her, one has to wonder if even she is capable of dealing with the man-eating Mrs. Quickly and the incredibly colorful wedding she has planned for husband number four—Mr. Brown.

Nanny McPhee is a delightful children's story that, while it may not appeal to all adults, should appeal to the child in them. It is a pretty standard fairy tale with misbehaving children and a clueless father undergoing a few really close calls who, eventually all live happily ever after. Based on the Nurse Matilda series of children's books written in the 1960s and 1970s by Christianna Brand, Nanny McPhee evolved because American audiences do not realize that nurses in England are often called sister while it is the nanny who is called nurse. As for Matilda, it was changed to McPhee to avoid any confusion because of the Roald Dahl book and the film made from it that had already claimed that name. Actress/writer Emma Thompson shows an obvious affection for *Nanny McPhee*, both in the way she has written the script and the way she plays the character. Her deadpan delivery of the line "I did knock" every time she mysteriously appears in a room is a sly running joke, and the way Nanny nods respectfully to Mrs. Brown's empty chair is quite touching.

If the story is too traditional or childish for some adults, then surely they can appreciate the excellent British cast. Colin Firth's dithering and doting Cedric Brown is endearing in his cluelessness. His guilt over needing money to support his family and for having lost his wife is apparent. Kelly Macdonald's charming but timid scullery maid, who we know loves the children no matter how badly they behave, is similarly likeable. It is fun to hate the supercilious and painfully colorful Celia Imrie's Mrs. Quickly, and, speaking of colorful, there is probably nothing redder then Imelda Staunton's face as the cook. It is nice to see Angela Landsbury again in her first feature film role in twenty years, complete with a horrendous prosthetic nose and her first pie in the face.

Nanny McPhee is an imaginative visual feast combining Edwardian settings presented in saturated color to the point of being perhaps a bit overwhelming and garish. But the rich, fanciful colors are exactly what make the animals in the children's clothing and the penultimate wedding scenes so much fun. It is also what helps make the final wedding scene, all in white, so magical. *Nanny McPhee* is a sweet movie that should provide solid family entertainment.

Beverley Bare Buehrer

CREDITS

Nany McPhee: Emma Thompson
Mr. Brown: Colin Firth
Evangeline: Kelly Macdonald
Mr. Wheen: Derek Jacobi
Mr. Jowis: Pat Barlow
Mrs. Quickly: Celia Imrie
Mrs. Blatherwick: Imelda Staunton
Simon: Thomas Sangster
Aunt Adelaide: Angela Lansbury
Lily: Jenny Daykin
Tora: Eliza Bennett
Eric: Raphael Coleman
Sebastian: Samuel Honywood
Christianna: Holly Gibbs
Baby Agatha: Hebe Barnes
Baby Agatha: Zinnia Barnes
Origin: USA, Great Britain
Language: English
Released: 2006
Production: Lindsay Doran, Tim Bevan, Eric Feller; Universal Pictures, StudioCanal, Metro-Goldwyn-Mayer Pictures, Working Title Productions, Three Strange Angels; released by UIP, Universal
Directed by: Kirk Jones
Written by: Emma Thompson, Matt Robinson
Cinematography by: Henry Braham
Music by: Patrick Doyle
Sound: Simon Hayes
Editing: Justin Krish, Nick Moore
Costumes: Nic Ede
Production Design: Michael Howells
MPAA rating: PG
Running time: 97 minutes

REVIEWS

Boxoffice Online. January 27, 2006.
Chicago Sun-Times Online. January 27, 2006.
Entertainment Weekly Online. January 25, 2006.
Los Angeles Times Online. January 27, 2006.
New York Times Online. January 27, 2006.
Variety Online. October 24, 2005.
Washington Post Online. January 27, 2006.

QUOTES

Nanny McPhee: "When you need me, but do not want me, then I will stay. When you want me, but do not need me, then I have to go."

TRIVIA

The beach scene, filmed at Dorset's Durdle Door, features a huge climb both down to the beach and back up again, requiring that the six tons of filming equipment used be helicoptered down to the beach.

THE NATIVITY STORY

Her child would change the world.
—Movie tagline

One Couple. One Journey. One Child...who would change the world...forever.
—Movie tagline

Box Office: $37.6 million

Often referred to as the "weeping prophet," Jeremiah makes this Old Testament prophecy: "Behold, the days come, saith the Lord, that I will raise unto David a righteous branch, and a King shall reign and prosper, and shall execute judgment and justice in the earth" (Jer. 23:5). This is cause for alarm for King Herod the Great. The prominent Roman historian, Tacitus, confirmed that Herod was coronated as the minor ruler of Galilee following Mark Anthony's recommendation to the Roman Senate. Herod served under Caesar Augustus as a "gubernatorial" king over Galilee. In an effort to stymie this divine trajectory, Herod (played by Welsh actor Ciaran Hinds), who irritably storms about his palace with an ornately big, oily mane, devises a plan of infanticide for all males under the age of two years. The slaughter is executed upon the town of Bethlehem (the city of David), a settlement approximately five miles south of Jerusalem. It is the birthplace of both King David and his renowned descendent, Jesus of Nazareth. With his flamboyantly adorned son, Antipas (Alessandro Giuggioli) at his side, Herod personally oversees the bloodshed. The future tetrarch of Galilee, Antipas reluctantly decapitates the distant cousin of Jesus, John the Baptist, at the bidding of his stepdaughter, Salome.

Following the onset of this carnage, the film cuts back to a year where the elderly priest Zachariah (Stanley Townsend) was chosen by lot to enter the temple to burn incense. During this once in a lifetime communion, Zachariah is visited by the angel Gabriel (Alexander Siddig). The gospel according to Luke records Gabriel's visit as a true corporeal appearance. The film deviates from this in that Zachariah hears only the voice of the angel informing him that he and his wife, Elizabeth (Shohreh Aghdashloo) will bear a son to be named John, evidenced by the smoke from the incense that blows about by the angel's breath. Zachariah is doubtful of this as the couple is beyond the ripe years for bearing children. Chided by Gabriel for his doubt, Zachariah is told he will remain mute during the course of Elizabeth's pregnancy.

Concurrently in Nazareth, the movie introduces the teenage Mary, who aids in the agrarian community's labor. Mary (sixteen-year-old Maori actor, Keisha Castle-Hughes) is portrayed as a typical, almost anachronistic, teenage girl who is both playful and laughs with her peers, as well as being in conflict with her parents. It is of interest to note here the signature of director Catherine Hardwicke. Having cultivated a career as a production designer, creating much of the set design for the western *Tombstone* (1993), Hardwicke brings a characteristic sense of authenticity to the set by depicting the daily life of Nazarenes as being brutal and arduous. Barely subsisting on a Roman system of feudalism, these Jewish vassals are subjected to severe constraints (one villager is forced to allow Roman centurions to procure his daughter as he is financially indebted to the empire). The inhabitants are seen squashing grapes with their feet to make wine and baking goat milk to make cheese. She paints a raw rustic existence. Coupled with this style, Hardwicke highlights her forte for representing teen angst as seen in her previous directorial works *Thirteen* (2003) and *Lords of Dogtown* (2005). Similar to the latter feature, where coastal skate grommets are catapulted into sudden sub cultural fame, Mary evolves from a brooding young girl whining about her arranged marriage to a man she pouts about not being in love with, to the young lady whom Elizabeth declares as being "blessed among women." Her accelerated maturation begins once Gabriel appears to her in a revelation that she will give birth to the Son of God and that he will be conceived by the Holy Spirit.

Upon returning from an extended visit with Zachariah and Elizabeth, Mary finds the inhabitants of her small hamlet skeptical and somewhat apprehensive when they see her impregnated. Both her fiance, Joseph (played with heartfelt sincerity by Oscar Isaac) and her parents suspect her explanation of angelic visitation, divine conception, and intact virginity to be fabricated.

Joseph, a hardworking, able-bodied, yet soft-spoken young man is more heartbroken than astonished or angered and although he is within his right by Mosaic law to legally have her stoned to death, he tearfully decides to silently break the engagement. In another deviation from scripture, the screenplay shows a dark portion of Joseph's psyche as he dreams of "casting the first stone." This is perhaps an allusion to Christ's prevention of a harlot's execution when he responded to her sanctimonious accusers with this insight: "Let he who is without sin cast the first stone." In Joseph's dream, the stoning is interrupted by Gabriel who stands in his way and extinguishes any doubts he harbored regarding Mary's account.

By Caesar's decree, a census is mandated for taxation purposes and all subjects are required to return to the land of their ancestors for an accurate count. As Joseph is from Bethlehem, the couple embark on their journey to the town of his fathers with Mary being carried by donkey.

Artistic license is interwoven in this screenplay penned by Mike Rich. He skillfully threads elements of the Nativity story without negating from the source material found only in two of the four gospels. Of the two, Luke's version is longer and more fleshed out than the one written by Matthew, a former tax collector, who was one of the original twelve apostles. Luke, known to be a physician, was possibly the sole gentile author of the New Testament and foremost historian of the early Christian church. Only in his version does it record John the Baptist's birth and the gathering of shepherds around the savior's manger. The magi, however are only mentioned by Matthew.

Little is known of the magi. They traveled from the Far East and were able to foretell the birth of the "King of the Jews" by viewing his star in the east. Traditionally, they are depicted as being ethnically diverse kings (possibly based on presenting Jesus with three gifts of gold, frankincense, and myrrh). In the script's story arc, they are featured as a form of comic relief and are a wealthy, astute, eccentric trio wearing ostentatious clothing befitting an ancient glitterati. They view the foretelling event by noticing a particular alignment of stars from an oracle of water which reflects the cosmos. As they approach Bethlehem, they make inquiries to Herod. It is the magi who point Herod in the direction of Christ's impending birth and he instructs them to return upon finding the child, falsely adding that he too would like to worship him. They agree, but upon an emotional viewing of the Christ child with the shepherd folk, they realize that Herod is a charlatan and decide on an alternate route home.

Infusing well-known Christian elements to this synthesis, Rich shows Joseph buying a fish from a local fisherman during the couple's trek. Many of Christ's disciples were fishermen and Christ often made allegorical references to fishing to fortify his teachings. Also appearing throughout the story is a bird representing the Holy Spirit which occasionally flies over key scenes such as Mary's conception and the birth of Jesus. A dove is often displayed as a divine icon representing the Holy Ghost.

The Nativity Story is not as mysterious as its trailers conveyed but is a faithful telling of the first Christmas. It avoids the controversial, unlike *The Last Temptation of Christ* (1988), which provoked an uproar among the Christian community because it depicted Jesus fantasizing about marrying and having children with Mary Magdalene. Likewise it dodged the criticism given to Mel Gibson's *The Passion of the Christ* (2004) which many held offensive for its abundance of graphic violence and charges of anti-Semitism. Hardwicke presents a biblical story, sans the blood and scandal, that is as reverent as the regard held by the film's three Wise Men upon their witnessing the Messiah, and delivers a timely message of hope for a world which remains fraught with strife and despair.

David Metz Roberts

CREDITS

Mary: Keisha Castle-Hughes
Elizabeth: Shohreh Aghdashloo
Anna: Hiam Abbass
Joaquim: Shaun Toub
Joseph: Oscar Isaac
Zechariah: Stanley Townsend
Herod: Ciaran Hinds
The Angel Gabriel: Alexander Siddig
Antipas: Alessandro Giuggioli
Melchior: Nadim Sawalha
Balthasar: Eriq Ebouaney
Origin: USA
Language: English
Released: 2006
Production: Wyck Godfrey, Marty Bowen; Temple Hill; released by New Line Cinema
Directed by: Catherine Hardwicke
Written by: Mike Rich
Cinematography by: Elliot Davis
Music by: Mychael Danna
Sound: Ian Voight
Editing: Robert K. Lambert, Stuart Levy
Art Direction: Maria Teresa Barbasso, Antonio Tarolla
Costumes: Maurizio Millenotti
Production Design: Stefano Ortolani
MPAA rating: PG
Running time: 102 minutes

REVIEWS

Boxoffice Online. December 1, 2006.
Chicago Sun-Times Online. December 1, 2006.
Entertainment Weekly. December 8, 2006, p. 55.
Hollywood Reporter Online. November 22, 2006.
Los Angeles Times Online. December 1, 2006.
New York Times Online. December 1, 2006.
San Francisco Chronicle. December 1, 2006, p. E1.
Variety Online. November 21, 2006.
Washington Post. December 1, 2006, p. C1.

NEIL YOUNG: HEART OF GOLD

Box Office: $1.9 million

Neil Young: Heart of Gold is a stirring portrait of a vital veteran artist at a crucial time in his life. Filmed in late

2005 after the loss of his father and having nearly died himself of a brain aneurism, *Neil Young: Heart of Gold* is a straightforward concert film by director Jonathan Demme. Though most well-known for his Oscar®-winning films of the early 1990s, *Silence of the Lambs* (1991) and *Philadelphia* (1994), Demme is no stranger to filming live concerts, as he is also the director of the Talking Heads' seminal concert film *Stop Making Sense* (1984) and the film version of the late Spaulding Gray's monologue/performance art piece *Swimming to Cambodia* (1987). Demme brings the same techniques used in those movies to *Heart of Gold*, such as long takes and little to no audience footage. The album to be performed, Young's *Prairie Wind*, is both a meditation on life and an opportunity for giving thanks, and Demme's filmmaking serves these ends well.

The film opens with documentary footage of Neil Young and various members of the band traveling around Nashville, Tennessee, talking about the years that have passed. This footage provides some context for the concert, not only in terms of history, but also in terms of tone. *Prairie Wind,* in many ways, reflects the thoughts of an artist closer to the end of his journey than the beginning. In fact, many of the reminiscences recount Young's recent near-fatal aneurism. Even the chosen venue, The Ryman Auditorium in Nashville, former home of the Grand Ole Opry, seems to speak of homecoming after a long life's journey. The tone of the concert is perhaps best set by Young himself, who says just before the curtain goes up, "I just want to play well, share the stage with my friends, give the best that I can." It is the master craftsman of songs who is to be on display, and not the incendiary rock icon who inspired many of the grunge bands of the early 1990s.

The concert proper begins with a full-length performance of the *Prairie Wind* album. The concert in fact, it is announced, is the album's world premiere. Most of this portion of the concert is performed in front of a very warmly lit and colored backdrop of a North American prairie scene. Young is joined on stage by many people with whom he has previously performed, including Emmylou Harris and his wife, Pegi Young. The songs in the *Prairie Wind* section of the concert are remarkable, and all of the technical elements—the lighting, the staging, and the camerawork—enhance them. For instance, following the first two songs with the entire band illuminated, the third song, a somber ballad called "Falling Off the Face of the Earth," features Young seated on a chair in the center of the stage, illuminated by a small pool of white light, producing an effect that visually highlights the sense of isolation created by the song itself. Another song, "It's a Dream," features floating and extremely dream-like camerawork.

Young often prefaces a song with an anecdote, sometimes about the song at hand or about a feeling the song engenders in him. Before "It's a Dream," Young talks about his father's death, and how he suffered from dementia prior to passing. The sadness of that story carries over into the song that immediately follows "Prairie Wind," whose prominent refrain, "Prairie wind blowin' through my head," powerfully encapsulates the pain of loss, change, and forgetting. It also simultaneously invokes Young's father's lost mind and the singer's own fading memories. Similarly, when Young introduces the songs prior to "Here For You," Young talks about his daughter and goes so far as to call "Here For You" an "empty nester" song. The stage backdrop changes from the prairie to an interior scene of a cabin, but lit in the same warm tones that pervaded the opening, and the combined effect of Young's introduction, the slight change of scene, and the power of the song itself is one of transcendence. The same can be said of the next number, "This Old Guitar." To this point in the show, Young seems to have been both addressing his feelings regarding the approaching end of his life, while simultaneously giving thanks for all the blessings he has had. It is only fitting that Young should include his guitar, such a major part of his life's journey, in the list of things for which he is thankful. Young lets the audience know that the guitar was once owned by country great Hank Williams. The song, played by Young solo at first and then expanded to a duet with Emmylou Harris, has an unusual poignancy in the context of the concert: the guitar must have been in the Ryman before, as Hank Williams himself played there, and now it, like Young, has returned, older and wiser. The final song of the *Prairie Wind* set is the apt "When God Made Me," an openly meditative song about what God might have been thinking when he made the narrator of the song. "When God Made Me" is a fitting culmination to this half of the concert, as it carries Young's heretofore personal journey into a much wider context, exploring the meaning of culture and values. It is Young's prayer for tolerance.

The second half of the concert is essentially a very brief greatest hits set with particular emphasis on his *Harvest* and *Harvest Moon* albums. The same fine and thoughtful camerawork and lighting apply, and Young continues to imbue each song with all the emotion he can muster. He starts with a song he wrote in the late 1960s, "I Am a Child," cuts to "Harvest Moon" from the early 1990s, and then performs three straight from the mid-1970s, his peak period: "Heart of Gold," "Old Man," and "The Needle and the Damage Done." All of these songs, though chosen from a palette of different decades, are perfectly in line with the journey established in the rest of the concert: a survey of Young's life to this point, with an emphasis on thanksgiving. "I Am a Child" is a lovely ballad of the joys of the beginning of life, played on solo guitar, while "Harvest Moon" is about rekindling a love affair, and "Heart of Gold" is about the search for that perfect love. "Old Man," Young reveals, was written about the caretakers of the ranch where he lives to this day, while "Needle and the Damage Done" is a perennial song of loss. In the final songs of the show, Neil says goodbye to his favorite dog in "Old King," traces life's path in "Comes a Time," and pays homage to Ian Tyson, one of his greatest influences, by covering his song "Four Strong Winds," played to powerful effect by the entire band lining the front of the stage strumming guitars. The show closes with "One of These Days," which best expresses the driving force behind this concert film: "One of these days/I'm gonna sit down and write a long letter/To all the good friends I've known/And I'm gonna try and thank them all/For all the good times together." This concert is, indeed, Young's thank you letter to his friends and family, and to his fans. As the credits roll, Young is shown playing "The Old Laughing Lady" to an empty Ryman Auditorium, and that is what the viewer is left with after watching *Neil Young: Heart of Gold*: the sense of a man and his artistry.

John Boaz

CREDITS

Origin: USA
Language: English
Released: 2006
Directed by: Jonathan Demme
Cinematography by: Ellen Kuras
Music by: Neil Young
Editing: Andy Keir
MPAA rating: R
Running time: 103 minutes

REVIEWS

Boxoffice Online. February 10, 2006.
Entertainment Weekly Online. February 8, 2006.
Los Angeles Times Online. February 10, 2006.
New York Times Online. February 10, 2006.
Premiere Magazine Online. February 9, 2006.
Variety Online. January 26, 2006.
Washington Post Online. February 10, 2006.

QUOTES

Jonathan Demme on Young's music: "Neil's lyrics evoke images in my head."

NIGHT AT THE MUSEUM

Everything comes to life.
—Movie tagline

Box Office: $244.8 million

The overarching plot of the loser father who has to compete against his ex-wife's new, highly successful fiance in order to redeem himself in his son's eyes is a pretty hackneyed storyline. Similarly, the plot about a loser who has to prove himself to himself in order to take control of his life is also a little timeworn. So if one were to judge *Night at the Museum* strictly in terms of the story's originality, it would fail miserable. Fortunately, *Night at the Museum* has more to offer. But while it is slight and silly, it is perfect for family viewing.

Based on Milan Trenc's children's book, screenwriters Robert Ben Garant and Thomas Lennon have taken the original thirty-two pages of narrative and added jokes and sight gags, stirred in some great visual effects compliments of supervisor Jim Rygiel (*The Lord of the Rings* films) and some terrific CGI effects courtesy of Rhythm & Hues, rounded up a powerhouse cast, and delivered a lightweight, but nonetheless entertaining film.

Larry Daley (Ben Stiller) cannot hold on to a job, an apartment, or his son's admiration. He is a dreamer who, among other things, invented the unsuccessful Snapper, which turns things off and on with the snap of one's fingers. As he watches his son's respect dwindle away and with an eviction notice hanging over his head, Larry goes to an employment agency where Debbie (Stiller's real-life mother, Anne Meara) reluctantly tells him about a job at the Natural History Museum. Although it is not what he had in mind, Larry's desperate and goes to the interview.

Because the museum is losing money, the three older and experienced night guards Cecil (Dick Van Dyke), Gus (Mickey Rooney), and Reginald (Bill Cobbs) are retiring and will be replaced by one, younger, cheaper guard, Larry. Imagine Larry's surprise when he's basically tossed the keys and a few pages of instruction and left on his own on his first night. Imagine Larry's greater surprise when a huge Tyrannosaurus Rex skeleton disappears only to turn up later and chase him through the halls. Frantically checking his sheet, he reads: "Number 1: throw the bone." It turns out the dinosaur isn't trying to kill Larry but, like a playful puppy, wants to play fetch with him.

Larry quickly notices that other displays in the museum have also come to life, and he desperately checks his instruction sheet where "Number 2" tells him to "lock up the lions or they'll eat you." Unfortunately locking up the lions also has Larry trying to deal with a nasty capuchin monkey named Dexter. Dexter not only makes Larry's life miserable, he also steals his keys and instructions, the latter of which he tears up. Larry is now completely on his own.

The next day, in an attempt to figure out what's going on, Larry gets Cecil to tell him about the magical tablet of the Egyptian Pharaoh Ankmenrah (Rami Malek). Ever since it arrived at the museum in 1952, everything comes to life at night. But anything caught outside the museum come dawn will turn into dust. It is Larry's job not only to make sure that no one gets into the museum after it closes, but to also make sure nothing gets out. But with no instructions, Larry has to figure things out as he goes.

He starts by following one of the museum docents, Rebecca Hutman (Carla Gugino), as she leads some children on a tour. Rebecca is a history student who has been writing her dissertation on Sacajawea (Mizuo Peck) for four years and is up to nine-hundred pages but still is not satisfied. Then Larry begins reading everything he can find on the topics of his most trouble-making displays. Luckily for him, he gets additional help from Teddy Roosevelt (Robin Williams).

From warring dioramas with Lilliputian rebels—Jedediah (Owen Wilson) in a wild west railroad exhibit whose Manifest Destiny runs headlong into the Roman Emperor Octavius (Steve Coogan), who believes that the Romans must expand or die—to a colossal Easter Island head demanding bubble gum and a rampaging life-size Attila the Hun (Patrick Gallagher), not to mention the Neanderthals trying to light fires, Larry has his hands full. His inability the next morning to explain to the museum's director Dr. McPhee (Ricky Gervais) why some exhibits look as if they've been tampered with almost gets him fired, but the audience knows that Larry will not only keep his job but that eventually he will succeed in taming the exhibits, as well as redeem himself in his son's eyes.

Night at the Museum is one of those movies that may have viewers quoting one-liners ("I'm feeling a connection here," says Larry to the distant Debbie at the employment agency, which becomes an inside joke when one knows the actors are mother and son) and describing antics, such as the giant T-rex wagging its tail like a huge dog, to explain the fun. But some jokes must be seen to be understood. How else to explain Gervais' tongue-tied, nonsense-speaking museum director who can never finish a sentence or the antics of and relationship between Jedediah and Octavius?

Granted, director Shawn Levy does not have a great track record with comedies, and a better director might have turned what is a good movie into a much better one, but at least *Night at the Museum* redeems Levy's reputation to some extent. Although it is slight and silly, it is also good family fun.

Beverley Bare Buehrer

CREDITS

Larry Daley: Ben Stiller
Rebecca: Carla Gugino
Cecil: Dick Van Dyke
Gus: Mickey Rooney
Reginald: Bill Cobbs
Erica Daley: Kim Raver
Dr. McPhee: Ricky Gervais
Teddy Roosevelt: Robin Williams
Nick Daley: Jake Cherry
Jedidiah: Owen Wilson
Octavius: Steve Coogan
Attila: Patrick Gallagher
Ankmenrah: Rami Malek
Sacajawea: Mizuo Peck
Don: Paul Rudd
Debbie: Anne Meara
Origin: USA
Language: English
Released: 2006
Production: Shawn Levy, Chris Columbus, Michael Barnathan; 21 Laps, 1492 Pictures, Ingenious Film Partners; released by 20th Century Fox
Directed by: Shawn Levy
Written by: Robert Ben Garant, Thomas Lennon
Cinematography by: Guillermo Navarro
Music by: Alan Silvestri
Sound: Rob Young
Editing: Don Zimmerman
Art Direction: Helen Jarvis
Costumes: Renee April
Production Design: Claude Pare
MPAA rating: PG
Running time: 108 minutes

REVIEWS

Chicago Sun-Times Online. December 22, 2006.
Hollywood Reporter Online. December 22, 2006.
Los Angeles Times Online. December 22,2006.
New York Times Online. December 22, 2006.
San Francisco Chronicle. December 22, 2006, p. E1.
Variety Online. December 21, 2006.
Washington Post. December 22, 2006, p. C6.

THE NIGHT LISTENER

Listen for the truth.
—Movie tagline

Box Office: $7.8 million

Gabriel Noone (Robin Williams) is a storyteller who hypnotically spins his tales on his "Noone at Night" public radio show. He claims that as a storyteller he is like a magpie, taking the bright and shiny parts of his life and turning them into tales to read each night to his loyal listeners. One such tale is called "The Night Listener," and he claims it is a true story.

It begins with Gabriel's live-in boyfriend of eight years, Jess (Bobby Cannavale), walking out on him. Jess is doing well even though he has AIDS and feels he no longer needs Gabe to take care of him. Jess just wants "to live." This trauma not only leaves Gabe feeling rejected and alone, it also gives him a bad case of writer's block, which is disastrous as he has five shows a week to write. Then a publishing industry friend of his (Ashe, played by Joe Morton) gives him a soon to be published book to read; the author, a fourteen-year-old boy, is a big fan of Gabe's. The book is the terrible story of how this young boy was exploited for the sexual pleasure of adults, including his parents, and is now dying of AIDS.

Moved by his story—or perhaps sensing more trinkets for the magpie to pluck—Gabe calls the boy, Pete (Rory Culkin). The two begin a telephone friendship that also includes the social worker who adopted Pete, Donna (Toni Collette). Once while visiting Gabe, Jess hears both Pete and Donna's voice and he makes a startling suggestion: Pete's voice sounds an awful lot like Donna's and raises the possibility that perhaps there is no Pete and Donna is just scamming everyone. When Donna abruptly cancels an invitation for Gabe to come and spend Christmas with Pete in their Wisconsin home, Gabe voices Jess' observation to his editor friend. When Pete's book is cancelled, Gabe is concerned enough to go to Wisconsin anyway to try and ferret out the truth about Pete and Donna. It is not as easily done as one might expect.

The Night Listener is the product of author Armistead Maupin, who is best known for his serial novels that became the basis for the television miniseries *Tales of the City.* The film is based on something that really happened to Maupin. In 1992 a manuscript titled *Rock and a Hard Place: One Boy's Triumphant Story,* written by a sexually abused young boy named Anthony Godby Johnson, fell into Maupin's hands. Maupin was so touched by the story that he wrote a jacket blurb for it only to discover later, as in the movie, that the boy and his adoptive mother's identity were a bit questionable. Unlike the movie, however, Maupin never tried to unravel the mystery. Instead, like a magpie, he mined the incident for a novel that was published in 2000 and eventually became this movie, which Maupin himself adapted for the screen, along with Terry Anderson and director Patrick Stettner.

The result is a subtle, small film about storytelling, the truth, and how and why we connect with other human beings. It addresses the issues of identity and illusion and the psychology behind both. It moves at a very even pace, which may give it the appearance of being a mystery without much suspense, but this is not a typical crimed-based mystery. As Maupin states, the story is a mystery of the human heart and that is why it is a film focusing on characters and the plot while the mystery's resolution is secondary.

Comedian Robin Williams gives a very subdued performance as the radio story spinner Noone, but his character's pain and confusion is obvious. The one time when Noone actually explodes—at the Wisconsin police who arrest him and shock him with a cattle prod—the audience only views it in silence through a window. Williams's Noone is like *Good Morning Vietnam*'s (1987) Adrian Cronauer on sedatives, which may lead some viewers to feel his performance is lifeless or humorless. Cronauer and Noone, however, are totally distinct characters who just happen to have similar occupations and the same actor playing them.

Similarly, chameleon Toni Collette's Donna is a morphing character: Solidly protective of Pete, yet somehow not completely honest. Eventually she becomes an enigma; while she is obviously a badly wounded woman, she is also more than a bit creepy. While eagerly and hopefully trying on a sweater she knitted, we see a little girl looking for approval, but when Gabe doesn't describe it to her in glowing terms, she turns hostile within seconds, intimating how this woman may actually act.

The Night Listener is an even, well-crafted, and well-acted picture. But it is also a film in which the pacing may be slower than some will tolerate, the characters are more important than the plot and, although the plot is interesting, it may not be resolved to everyone's satisfaction.

Beverley Bare Buehrer

CREDITS

Gabriel Noone: Robin Williams
Donna Logand: Toni Collette
Jess: Bobby Cannavale
Ashe: Joe Morton
Pete Logand: Rory Culkin

Anna: Sandra Oh
Pap Noone: John Cullum
Origin: USA
Language: English
Released: 2006
Production: Robert Kessel, Jeffrey Sharp, John Hart, Jill Footlick; Fortissimo Films, Hart Sharp Entertainment; released by IFC Films
Directed by: Patrick Stettner
Written by: Patrick Stettner, Armistead Maupin, Terry Anderson
Cinematography by: Lisa Rinzler
Music by: Peter Nashel
Sound: Noah Vivekanand Timan
Music Supervisor: Linda Cohen
Editing: Andrew Keir
Art Direction: Eva Radke
Costumes: Marina Draghici
Production Design: Michael Shaw
MPAA Rating: R
Running time: 90 minutes

REVIEWS

Boxoffice Online. August 4, 2006.
Entertainment Weekly. August 2, 2006.
Hollywood Reporter Online. January 23, 2006.
Los Angeles Times Online. August 4, 2006.
New York Times Online. August 4, 2006.
Premiere Magazine. August 4, 2006.

NIGHT WATCH

(Nochnoi Dozor)

All That Stands Between Light And Darkness Is The Night Watch.
—Movie tagline

Box Office: $1.5 million

The first in a trilogy, *Night Watch* (*Nochnoy Dozor*) is a dark and gory fantasy horror film from Russian director Timur Bekmambetov and is based on a popular series of Russian novels by author Sergei Lukyanenko. A blockbuster hit in Russia, the entire trilogy has been picked up by Fox Searchlight. The second installment, *Day Watch* (2006) was recently released in Russia. The third as yet untitled film will be shot in America with an English speaking cast.

Night Watch boasts superb production values belying its $4 million budget, interesting actors, and plenty of visual panache, but is a little confusing on first viewing. It is a complicated and convoluted story, and the director promises that the second film will be more coherent and less dark in tone.

Many centuries ago the forces of light and dark met in bloody battle. They were known as the "Others." There were Light Others and Dark Others. Realizing both sides were too evenly matched and there could be no winner, a truce was agreed upon between the Lord of Light Geser (Vladimir Menshov) and the Lord of Darkness Zavulon (Viktor Verzhbitsky).

Two groups were created to ensure that the truce was not broken. The Night Watch was created to monitor the Dark Others, and Day Watch was created to keep an eye on the Light Others. The truce has lasted for many centuries, but there is a legend that one day a Great One will be born and choose one side over the other, tipping the balance and bringing about the final battle between the forces of light and dark, with the fate of mankind in the middle.

In 1992 Anton Gorodetsky (Konstantin Khabensky) has found out that his ex-girlfriend is now with another man and pregnant. In desperation, Anton seeks out a witch who promises that she can make her love him again for the right price. She also promises to kill the unborn baby. She warns him that he will have to live with the sin of murdering the child for the rest of his life. Not really believing her, he agrees to her terms.

Just as the witch is about to complete the spell, a man and woman appear and grab her. These two, Bear (Aleksandr Samojlenko) and Tiger Cub (Anna Slyusaryova), are members of the Night Watch and they have come to arrest the dark witch for using her powers for evil. Anton has been witnessing this from the corner of the room. Bear and Tiger Cub are surprised that he can see them and surmise that Anton is a newly awakened Other, telling him he must now choose a side, Light or Dark.

In 2004, he fights for the side of Light as a member of Night Watch, alongside Bear and Tiger Cub, hunting various violators of the truce and protecting mankind from unlicensed vampires, dark witches, and shapeshifters. They report to their leader Geser who hands them their next assignment.

Somewhere in Russia is a boy named Yegor (Dmitry Martynov) who needs to be protected from a couple of vampires, and Anton is assigned to find him before they do. The boy is more important to the big picture than the vampires or the thick-witted Anton had thought. Even up close, Anton doesn't see any family resemblance in the twelve-year-old boy. That would hasten the film to its obvious conclusion and get in the way of a convoluted and time-consuming side plot involving a desperate hunt for a blond girl, who may have a curse on her and could be the Great Other.

That it turns out not to be her but Anton's son Yegor will not come as a shock A rooftop battle between Anton and Zavulon for Yegor's soul ends with Yegor finding out that he was to be aborted by Anton's actions. This revelation causes him to reject his father and the Light. He chooses to join the side of Dark, thus setting the stage for the sequel.

The film, while not entirely original, does boast some interesting aspects. One of the most interesting innovations is the use of subtitles for something more than dialogue, adding an extra level of character to the drama. They sometimes fade from the screen as a hand waves them off or elegantly transform to bloody wisps when a vampire is speaking.

David E. Chapple

CREDITS

Geser: Vladimir Menshov
Zavulon: Viktor Verzhbitsky
Anton Gorodetsky: Konstantin Khabensky
Svetlana: Maria Poroshina
Olga: Galina Tyunina
Ignat: Gosha Kytsenko
Kostya: Alexsei Chadov
Alisa: Zhanna Friske
Andrei: Ilya Larutenko
Darya, Witch: Rimma Markova
Irina: Maria Mironova
Semyon: Alexei Maklakov
Bear: Aleksandr Samojlenko
Tiger Cub: Anna Slyusaryova
Yegor: Dmitry Martynov
Female Vampire: Anna Dubrovskaya
Origin: Russia
Language: Russian
Released: 2004
Production: Anatoly Maximov, Konstantin Ernst; Gemini Film, First Channel, Tabbak, Baselevs; released by Fox Searchlight
Directed by: Timur Bekmambetov
Written by: Timur Bekmambetov, Sergei Lukyanenko
Cinematography by: Sergei Trofimov
Music by: Yuri Potyeyenko, Valera Viktorov, Mukstar Mirzakeev
Sound: Sergei Karpenko
Editing: Dmitri Kiselev
Costumes: Ekaterina Diminskaya
Production Design: Vara Yavdyushko
MPAA rating: R
Running time: 114 minutes

REVIEWS

Boxoffice Online. February 17, 2006.
Chicago Sun-Times Online. February 24, 2006.
Entertainment Weekly Online. February 15, 2006.
Los Angeles Times Online. February 17, 2006.
New York Times Online. February 17, 2006.
Premiere Magazine Online. March 7, 2006.
Variety Online. August 24, 2004.
Washington Post Online. February 24, 2006.

QUOTES

Kostya and his father are in the meat locker at the butcher shop. After drinking pig's blood, Anton has just left Vampire, Kostya's father: "Why did you bring him?"

Kostya: "He became like us."

Father: "No, Kostya. He's a Light one. And Light ones only drink blood in one situation…when they're hunting those like us."

TRIVIA

A reproduction of Rembrandt's painting *Nightwatch* can be briefly seen in Anton's apartment reflected in a window.

NOTES ON A SCANDAL

One woman's mistake is another's opportunity.
—Movie tagline

Box Office: $17 million

In Richard Eyre's *Notes on a Scandal*, adapted by playwright Patrick Marber from Zoe Heller's novel *What Was She Thinking? Notes on a Scandal*, Barbara Covett (Judi Dench) lives a solitary existence as a secondary-school history teacher in a lower-class London district. Cynical about her profession and her students, skeptical of teachers who believe that they can make a difference, and unlucky in love, she faces a bleak existence that she spells out in detail in her diary through a funny, poignant, and biting voice-over narration. Barbara is the center of this highly entertaining and complex character study and psychological thriller. She embodies a range of qualities; she is tragic, scary, pathetic, manipulative, and moving, sometimes in the course of a single scene, and Dench's multilayered portrayal of a woman who can command a classroom with ease but cannot connect one-on-one with another person is one of the best performances of the year—a masterful characterization of a woman on the verge of madness.

The catalyst for the story is the arrival of a new art teacher, Sheba Hart (Cate Blanchett). Young and attractive, Sheba is a bit of a free spirit and a woman who can instantly captivate a room just by entering. The faculty members are drawn to her, as is a fifteen-year-old student named Steven Connolly (Andrew Simpson), with whom Sheba embarks on a torrid affair. Sheba's highly inappropriate, criminal behavior is complicated by the fact that she is married to an older man, Richard (Bill Nighy), and has two children, Polly (Juno Temple), a snarky teenage daughter, and Ben (Max Lewis), a sweet boy with Down's syndrome. When Barbara discovers the affair, she confronts Sheba and extracts a full confession. Barbara does not want to turn Sheba in to the authorities. Instead, she plays the sympathetic confidante and uses her knowledge to gain Sheba's goodwill and trust. As the story progresses, it becomes clear that Barbara has romantic illusions about a future with the novice teacher.

The kick of Heller's novel is that it is told through the first-person voice of Barbara, and all her avowals of friendship run counter to the self-serving way she manipulates Sheba's transgression to her own advantage. The novel invites us to read between the lines and realize that, on some level, the deluded Barbara really believes that she is looking out for Sheba's best interest. The film and its voice-over are more explicit in showing Barbara's real motives, sexual and psychological, and thus the adaptation loses some of the subtlety of the source material, in which Barbara can never admit to herself her true sexual nature. Moreover, the screenplay alludes several times to a friendship that Barbara had with another teacher—just hinted at in the novel—and how it went sour when that teacher did not reciprocate Barbara's feelings. The novel is more circumspect about Barbara's repressed lesbianism, yet it is understandable for the movie to punch up the story's more sensational aspect and zero in on Barbara's frustrated desires.

Blanchett is a more than worthy match for Dench and is very strong as a conflicted woman seduced by the thrill of being pursued by a student and teetering between a good, if dull, family life and the craving for something more. The film creates hints of a backstory for Sheba—a punk-rock past that alludes to a youth she may be trying to recapture—but, quite wisely, does not spell out her motivations.

Nighy is effective as Richard, who, in just a few scenes, fills out a man who knows his advanced age could be an obstacle to his wife, but who still feels the sting of betrayal when he learns of the affair. In one scene, though, when he rants at Sheba about the spell Barbara has on her, the outburst seems out of place for his character, especially since he does not seem fed up with Barbara at this point.

Enriching the film but never overtaking the central conflict is the class tension underlying the characters. The school serves a working-class demographic, and Barbara is clearly from this background. But Sheba is from the upper-middle class, what Barbara derisively calls "bourgeois bohemia," living a life of comfort but a bit of a hippie at the same time. It is a world of class privilege, of which Barbara is scornful and probably envious of as well; her attraction is not just to Sheba but also to the world she inhabits. It is easy to see, given her background, how Sheba falls from grace, seduced not only by the thrill of being wanted, but also by the idea of helping a working-class boy develop his artistic talent. Adding to the complexity of the characterizations, Steven himself turns out to be a shrewd deceiver, creating a sob story of a wretched home life because he instinctively knows that it will draw the sympathy of a bourgeois liberal such as Sheba. For all her supposed sophistication, Sheba is fairly naive and an easy read for those who would prey on her.

Barbara herself is oddly sympathetic, in that she is defined more by her loneliness than her thwarted sexual desire. This is a woman who yearns for the touch of another person more than she does a full-blown affair. One scene in which she strokes Sheba's arms is creepy and sad at the same time. Exhibiting no vanity in looking older than she ever has on screen, Dench balances the vulnerable and the chilling aspects of Barbara and shows that the two are connected. A subplot devoted to her dying cat—her only true companion apart from her diary—illustrates the point. When she returns from the veterinarian crying over her cat and does not receive what she deems the adequate response from Sheba, who chooses her son's school play over Barbara, her sudden emotional turn is frightening. In her mind, she really is a good friend, and to receive anything less than utter loyalty in return is a complete betrayal.

Barbara avenges this perceived slight by revealing the secret the first chance she gets, setting in motion the chain of events leading to Sheba's public disgrace and arrest. Barbara does not emerge unscathed; the school's headmaster, who thinks that Barbara knew all along about Sheba's affair, does not like Barbara's old-fashioned approach to education and essentially forces her to resign by threatening to expose her infatuation with a former teacher who did not appreciate her attention.

Just when it seems that Barbara has gotten what she wants, that is to say, Sheba leaving her family and staying with Barbara, Sheba finds the diary and learns that her supposed protector is not the friend she has pretended to be, which precipitates a physical confrontation between them. It is an intense tour de force scene for Blanchett, who unleashes all the fury and frustration that has built up in Sheba.

At this point, the film makes a key departure from the novel, which ends with Sheba forgiving Barbara and staying with her. The film ends on a happier note, at least in the sense that Sheba is no longer under the older women's influence. Sheba returns to her husband, who takes her back, and gets a ten-month sentence. In Barbara's last scene, she is retired and trying to get chummy with a stranger, obviously a possible replacement for Sheba. The message is clear—Barbara faces a life-goes-on ending in which she will continue to try to make a human connection, although her awkwardness makes her prospects pretty dim. The film's ending is a bit of a letdown; it is rather abrupt and also very conventional, leaving us with the sense that order has been restored, while the novel ends on an ambiguous but disturbing note.

The movie's major flaw is not the tepid ending, but the overdone, loud Philip Glass score, which threatens to overpower the actors. Even in relatively understated scenes such as Barbara walking up to Sheba's house for lunch, the music turns a small incident into a momentous occasion. In a subtle scene in which Barbara lovingly picks up a strand of hair that has fallen from Sheba's head—an early sign of infatuation—the music blares and builds to a crescendo to underscore a point that needs little musical accompaniment. The music not only loses its effectiveness, but detracts from the drama and suggests that Eyre lacked faith in his actors to touch us emotionally.

Notes on a Scandal is an incisive psychological drama with two of our best actresses taking real risks with complex, flawed characters. If some of the subtlety from the novel has been sacrificed in favor of a more conventional approach, that may be an unfortunate but a necessary consequence of moving from a first-person novel to a film. Nonetheless, the screenplay is an excellent adaptation that does justice to Barbara's point of view through the wicked voice-over while also expanding the other characters. *Notes on a Scandal* is a magnificent showcase for two actresses at the top of their craft doing some of the most daring work of the year.

Peter N. Chumo II

CREDITS

Barbara Covett: Judi Dench
Sheba Hart: Cate Blanchett
Richard Hart: Bill Nighy
Steven Connolly: Andrew Simpson
Polly Hart: Juno Temple
Ben Hart: Max Lewis
Origin: Great Britain, USA
Language: English
Released: 2006
Production: Scott Rudin, Robert Fox; DNA Films Ltd., Fox Searchlight Pictures, U.K. Film Council, BBC Films; released by 20th Century Fox
Directed by: Richard Eyre
Written by: Patrick Marber
Cinematography by: Chris Menges
Music by: Philip Glass
Sound: Jim Greenhorn
Editing: John Bloom, Antonia Van Drimmelen
Art Direction: Hannah Moseley
Costumes: Tim Hatley
Production Design: Tim Hatley
MPAA rating: R
Running time: 91 minutes

REVIEWS

Boston Globe Online. December 27, 2006.
Boxoffice Online. December 27, 2006.
Hollywood Reporter Online. December 11, 2006.
Los Angeles Times Online. December 27, 2006.
New York Times Online. December 27, 2006.
Newsweek Online. December 18, 2006.
Premiere Magazine. January/February 2007, p. 46.
Variety Online. December 8, 2006.
Village Voice Online. December 26, 2006.
Washington Post. December 27, 2006, p. C1.

QUOTES

Sheba (to Barbara): "Marriage and kids, it's wonderful, but it doesn't give you meaning."

TRIVIA

Richard Eyre previous directed Judi Dench in *Iris* (2001).

AWARDS

Nomination:

Oscars 2006: Actress (Dench), Adapt. Screenplay, Support. Actress (Blanchett), Orig. Score
British Acad. 2006: Actress (Dench), Adapt. Screenplay
Golden Globes 2007: Actress—Drama (Dench), Screenplay, Support. Actress (Blanchett)
Screen Actors Guild 2006: Actress (Dench), Support. Actress (Blanchett)

THE NOTORIOUS BETTIE PAGE

The Pin-Up Sensation That Shocked The Nation.
—Movie tagline
Show Some Restraint.
—Movie tagline

Good Girl. Bad Girl. Sinner. Saint. Who is...
—Movie tagline

Box Office: $1.4 million

In the 1950s, two women defined new frontiers of sexuality for masses of American men: Marilyn Monroe and Bettie Page. While Monroe was the sexpot who "va-voomed" her way into mainstream culture, defining female eroticism for a generation of newly loosened libidos, Page was the guilty pleasure of millions of men who sought out her pin-up images in less acceptable locations. Her leggy, busty, come-hither poses graced the covers and pages of the kind of magazines that now are openly displayed in bookstores worldwide, but in the 1950s were taboo. The dark-haired Page was the more daring, more forbidden counterpart to the lusty blonde Monroe. Page was the pin-up queen who never, despite her efforts, broke through to a legitimate acting or modeling career. And she also toyed with more explicit pornography that, in her day, could get those who peddled it prosecuted for breaking stringent anti-obscenity laws.

By herself, Page didn't pioneer the lingerie-clad pin-up poses that became a lasting obsession with male consumers, but in her heyday she epitomized the provocative look that teased and taunted near the boundary between acceptable femininity and forbidden indecency. She went further, too: posing for nude or seminude photos that took her persona one step further. And, while achieving a very successful career in all aspects of pin-up modeling, she crossed the bounds of acceptability by posing for photographs that suggested bondage, domination, and submission. In these photos and some films, she might be wielding a whip or wearing a gag, spanking another model or being trussed up herself—and these were the images that brought the wrath of the righteous down on her and on the people who took and sold these images.

In more recent days, Bettie Page has become an enduring cult figure, embraced by a new generation of sex-positive feminists who admire how she projected her powerful eroticism. In addition, her pin-up art is collected by connoisseurs, for whom her images are the quintessence of nostalgia for a style and attitude widely derided in the 1960s and 1970s as objectifying women, but now seen by some in a different light. In an era where, starting with Madonna, female performers, musicians, and actresses have vamped and posed with outfits that incorporate teasing lingerie and high heels and other pin-up-style outfits, Page has been hailed for a pioneering look and admired for her daring and attitude. In a time when light bondage, in Page's era derided as a dangerous psychological perversion, has become a more mainstream recreational practice for many couples, the furor over Page seems quaint but evocative.

You would think, given all this, that a biopic of Bettie Page would positively sizzle with attitude, while exploring how the ascent of modern pornography from an underground, semi-legal industry to a widely available commodity has helped define, for better or worse, new incarnations of fashion and feminine attitudes. To look closely at such an iconic figure through the lens of what has happened since should be a sure-fire recipe for a fascinating and wildly popular movie.

But writer/director Mary Harron has given us sanctimoniousness instead of sizzle, and blather instead of controversy, in her limpid and tepid *The Notorious Bettie Page*. This is a movie that asks its audience to buy an unbelievable character: a pioneering sexual rebel who is as naive and innocent as a babe in the woods. Instead of a notorious figure, Bettie Page is presented as someone so dim-witted she doesn't ever understand what she is doing, an unthinking body onto whom men are projecting fantasies about which she doesn't have a clue.

Gretchen Mol is well cast as Page—with her dark, thick hair and searching eyes, she bears a striking resemblance to the pin-up queen. And, especially in an opening prologue that shows how a Times Square magazine seller gets busted for selling her bondage photos, Harron and her crew accomplish a wonderful jump of setting the proceedings in a moody film noir atmosphere. Most of the film is shot in black and white, except for bursts of faded color as the plot moves into the mid-1950s, and the entire movie looks authentic as it bridges the world between uptight postwar convention and the coming of mainstream sexual liberation.

The film backs up from its fulcrum in the mid-1950s to show us a cursory backstory that establishes Page as the child of uptight Southern religious conservatives. One scene strongly suggests her father abused her, and another suggests she got joy by posing for photos even as a young teenager. These scenes in fact are played back to back, implying a connection between her teasing and her suffering, but that connection is never developed.

Instead of delineating a psychological motivation for Page, Harron simply shows her falling gradually into more risque modeling without any plan or awareness. She goes to New York to escape Tennessee after an extremely truncated sequence that shows her being wooed by a young man, marrying him, and then leaving him after he slaps her across the face. Like all subsequent scenes involving her relationships with men, the sequence seems scant and rushed, as if the film were uninterested in Page's relationships with men. Her own sexuality is given scant attention.

In fact, Page comes off as one of the least developed and most superficial central characters in any biopic ever. She is a blank slate, unmotivated, and almost without a personality. She thinks it is fun to show off her body, and obviously enjoys the attention, but Page's character does not seem to have any real reason to do what she does. She is all childish innocence, even as she ages through her twenties and into her thirties.

She is first "captured" by a photographer who spots her walking on a New York City beach and changes her hairstyle, giving her the trademark bangs she wore with her long hair. Eventually she falls in with Irving Klaw (Chris Bauer) and his sister Paula (Lili Taylor), who make a living doing commercial photography and short films that include more risque fare, and even private sessions for special clients who have various fetishes. Page sails through these shoots with little curiosity and even less understanding. She does not know a foot fetish from a manicure, thinks bondage is just posing with a bunch of props, and projects in these shoots the same superficial and incongruously contrived expressions that she uses in her other photo shoots.

Meanwhile, in scenes that are laughably overdone, Page studies Method acting, but doesn't seem to understand why it's not appropriate to disrobe when she is supposed to be projecting seething cauldrons of inner emotion. These scenes are stilted in their earnest suggestion that Page was a misunderstood thespian.

The Notorious Bettie Page is deadly straightforward and serious. When her latest in a series of live-in lovers illuminates her on how "sick" and shameful her bondage photos are, poor Bettie looks like an innocent girl slapped on the hand for swiping cookies from the jar. Later, while she waits outside a Congressional hearing room, she hears stories of how bondage is not only twisted but also potentially fatal. In an amusingly ironic twist (in fact, the only amusing thing in the movie), David Strathairn, Oscar®-nominated for playing Edward R. Murrow in *Good Night and Good Luck* (2005), plays Senator Estes Kefauver, the politician trying to make points by attacking the cancer of pornography that is eating away at American's body politic, Kefauver being the Joe McCarthy of porn. In fact, Strathairn's Kefauver suggests, pornography is worse than Communism, because it is attacking the country from within.

As an exploration of this confrontation over values, *The Notorious Bettie Page* is simple-minded and dull. We get neither a clear understanding of what makes Page tick nor a sense of what is at stake in the furor her photos have helped to raise. She is merely an innocent bystander at the epicenter of a cultural earthquake. It is as if she was a sleepwalker in a disaster movie. In the end, she is born again and turns into a sidewalk preacher, but even in this new incarnation, she does not condemn what she has done, continuing to see nakedness as innocence, so there is hardly a moral shift.

The real Page was religious and might have started out as a babe in the woods. To ask audiences to accept that Page never knew what she was doing is preposterous. There is nothing in her biography to prove the fact that she was an abuse victim who continued to be exploited by heartless pornographers, but Harron wants to insist she was victimized. If Harron's goal is to make Page seem sympathetic by casting her as a dupe of powerful, leering men, it backfires. Page is such a cipher in this film to the point that you do not care about her at all. We do not even see her being exploited financially; the economics of her career is another subject in which Harron is completely uninterested.

The men in the film are by turns silly and quasi-sinister, but mostly they, too, seem like barely grown-up little boys, tongues hanging out of their mouths. What is worse is that the notorious Bettie Page seems in every way non-threatening, not notorious at all. A woman who exercised tremendous power over countless men, who achieved great success in her underground career, and who represented part of a soon-to-be-widespread rebellion against the established order is reduced in this film to a powerless and uninteresting naif.

Harron has achieved what you might think would be impossible: The story of one of the raciest, most sexualized figures in our cultural history has been made into a film that is studiously non-erotic. Because Page is clueless and disconnected in this film, her photo shoots are not only contrived (as they undoubtedly were) but also lacking in any sexual power. Page is about as provocative as a toothpaste commercial, even in her more outrageous costumes and performances. Mol portrays her as vacant and fake in her sauciness; though the actress tries hard to give her some pizzazz, the script defeats her utterly. This Bettie Page is almost asexual.

If someone suggests doing a movie about the life and impact of Bettie Page on our culture, about how she managed to worm her way into the fantasies of millions while doing things that were perceived as dangerous to American society and family, about why and how she achieved what she did, a studio boss should greenlight the project immediately. Because that movie has yet to be made.

Michael Betzold

CREDITS

Bettie Page: Gretchen Mol

Irving Klaw: Chris Bauer

John Willie: Jared Harris
Bunny Yeager: Sarah Paulson
Maxie: Cara Seymour
Paula Klaw: Lili Taylor
Estes Kefauver: David Strathairn
Preacher in Nashville: John Cullum
Nervous Man: Matt McGrath
Teacher: Austin Pendleton
Billy Neal: Norman Reedus
Scotty: Dallas Roberts
Preacher in Miami: Victor Slezak
June: Tara Subkoff
Jerry Tibbs: Kevin Carroll
Edna Page: Ann Dowd
Mr. Gaughan: Michael Gaston
Little John: Jefferson Mays
Gengel: Peter McRobbie
Marvin: Jonathan M. Woodward
Origin: USA
Language: English
Released: 2006
Production: Pamela Koffler, Katie Roumel, Christine Vachon; Picturehouse, HBO Films, Killer Films, John Wells; released by Picturehouse
Directed by: Mary Harron
Written by: Mary Harron, Guinevere Turner
Cinematography by: W. Mott Hupfel III
Music by: Mark Suozzo
Sound: Brian Miksis
Editing: Tricia Cooke
Art Direction: Thomas Ambrose
Costumes: John Dunn
Production Design: Gideon Ponte
MPAA rating: R
Running time: 91 minutes

REVIEWS

Boxoffice Online. April 14, 2006.
Entertainment Weekly. April 21, 2006, p. 53.
Los Angeles Times Online. April 14, 2006.
New York Times Online. April 14, 2006.
San Francisco Chronicle. April 14, 2006, p. E1.
USA Today Online. April 13, 2006.
Variety Online. September 20, 2005.
Village Voice Online. April 11, 2006.

O

OLD JOY

A friendship gets a meaningful examination in *Old Joy*, a minimalist road picture with a lot to offer. Director Kelly Reichardt's long-awaited second feature is a small-scale but special piece of work, using very little in the way of narrative or film technique to create a deeply felt character piece.

Reichardt's screenplay, co-written with Jonathan Raymond, from a short story by Raymond, takes place in contemporary Portland, where two friends, Mark (Daniel London) and Kurt (Will Oldham), reunite for a hiking trip in the Cascade Mountains. Initially, Mark hesitates to go on the outing because his wife, Tanya (Tanya Smith), is expecting their first baby. But eventually, Mark and Kurt meet up and travel into the mountain range.

During the weekend, Mark and Kurt talk about the current state of their lives, one about to be a father, the other about to be evicted from his apartment, and Mark outwardly seems more content than Kurt about his lot. During a drinking session in the woods, Kurt starts to reveal some insecurity about the friendship, but Mark tries to reassure Kurt. As the men try to find their destination, Hot Springs, Kurt shows even more confusion and instability, but once they arrive, the mood changes and Kurt becomes calmer. After a soak in twin outdoor tubs, the friends decide to return home. Back in the city, they go their separate ways—Mark back to a life of snug domesticity and Kurt to a less certain existence, involving possible homelessness.

Old Joy joins a long tradition of buddy-buddy road pictures but differs from many in the genre. Typically, road pictures depend on action and melodrama to maintain momentum. For example, in Jerry Schatzberg's seminal and similar *Scarecrow* (1973) and the more recent *Sideways* (2004), the drifters have many adventures. Even the makers of European road pictures, including Manuel Poirier's *Western* (1997), seem to feel obligated to add twists and turns to the plot.

Old Joy goes in another direction altogether. Here, the story is much more minimal, almost imperceptible, but Reichardt neatly plays off of the earlier conventions by constantly threatening "something" will happen. That "something" generates from Kurt's nature—as the narrative progresses, viewers may well wonder if the man has "snapped" and might hurt his friend. The drinking scene is preceded by Kurt and Mark firing guns on a makeshift shooting range, and the image of the guns sets up audience expectations for a later, more significant use of the weapons. But this never happens—the guns are never seen again. Likewise, in the climactic hot tub scene, Kurt moves over to give Mark a backrub. Close-ups on Mark's face reveal unease and the ones on Kurt's face are more dubious: will he kill Mark by strangling or drowning him or will he act out a latent sexual desire with his old friend? Neither happens.

Thus, *Old Joy* does not become another *Brokeback Mountain* (2005), yet more than one critic found an inevitable comparison. For example, in *Variety*, Scott Foundas wrote, "Though it sounds on paper like a straight version of *Brokeback Mountain* or perhaps *Sideways* with granola substituted for wine, *Old Joy* is really a film about our inability to stop the hands of time, and about the search for sanctuary in an increasingly chaotic world."

A more appropriate contrast for *Old Joy* would be Alfonso Cuaron's *Y tu mama tambien* (2001), given that the latent homoerotic impulses of the latter film's protagonists are finally revealed in the climax but are not the primary focus. In fact, the films' political attitudes are more paramount, depicting the challenging social and economic conditions amidst a reactionary era. Both Reichardt and Cuaron use shots of gloomy environments outside the windows of the moving cars to reveal much more than can ever be said in dialogue, though Reichardt also has Mark listening to the griping of the host on the liberal radio network, Air America, at the beginning and end of the film.

J. Hoberman compared *Old Joy* to another recent film when he wrote in the *Village Voice*, "Coming in the same year as Andrew Bujalski's similarly understated and character-driven *Mutual Appreciation* (2005), it attests to a new strain in Amerindie production—literate but not literary, crafted without ostentation, rooted in a specific place and devoted to small sensations. If *Old Joy* is more laid-back and contemplative than *Mutual Appreciation*, it's because the characters are more weathered. Open-ended as it may appear, it has a crushing finality. For all the wool-gathering and guitar-noodling, this road movie is at least as tender as it is ironic."

Actually, to be fair, *Old Joy* stands on its own and the "guitar-noodling" is good stuff performed by Smokey Hormel, as are the other production elements, including Peter Sillen's pensive, widescreen cinematography, Reichardt's own thoughtful, measured editing, and, best of all, the performances by Oldham and London (Oldham, a musician in the indie scene, does an especially compelling job—part moving, part scary, and always watchable). As with Reichardt's first feature, *River of Grass* (1995), about a woman's effort to escape her surrounding, you may not entirely appreciate the director's spare approach, but there is no denying the film is an original.

The only genuine flaw to *Old Joy* is an early sequence between Mark and his wife. It is poorly played by Tanya Smith and not as well written as the rest of the film. Otherwise, one might argue another problem with *Old Joy* is that it would be nice to see and hear further episodes between the friends, Mark and Kurt, but isn't that what the friends—at least Kurt—themselves want and cannot really have? Besides, it is a testament to a film if it keeps you wanting more. *Old Joy* delivers that kind of experience.

Eric Monder

CREDITS

Kurt: Will Oldham
Mark: Daniel London
Tanya: Tanya Smith
Origin: USA
Language: English
Released: 2006
Production: Neil Kopp, Jay Van Hoy, Anish Savjani, Lars Knudsen; Film Science, Washington Square Films; released by Kino International
Directed by: Kelly Reichardt
Written by: Kelly Reichardt, Jonathan Raymond
Cinematography by: Peter Sillen
Sound: Eric Offin
Editing: Kelly Reichardt
MPAA rating: Unrated
Running time: 76 minutes

REVIEWS

New York Times Online. September 20, 2006.
San Francisco Chronicle. October 20, 2006, p. E5.
Variety Online. February 28, 2006.
Village Voice Online. September 19, 2006.

QUOTES

Kurt: "Sorrow is nothing but worn-out joy."

THE OMEN

His Day Will Come.
—Movie tagline

From the eternal sea he rises. Creating armies on either shore. Turning man against his brother. Until man exists no more.
—Movie tagline

The prophecy is clear. The signs are unmistakable. On the 6th day of the 6th month in the year 2006 his day will come.
—Movie tagline

Box Office: $54.6 million

In 1976 director Richard Donner made a little horror film that went on to become a classic. Heavy on atmosphere and story and easy on the special effects and graphic gore, *The Omen* was a box office hit that exploited that decade's paranoia and fears. Thirty years later, we still suffer from many of the same fears and with the ultimate marketing sign from Satan, a release date of June 6, 2006 (666: the sign of the beast), who wouldn't want to capitalize on this perfect calendar opportunity? Of course this meant releasing a movie on a Tuesday instead of the usual Friday, but Hollywood executives simply couldn't pass up this one-time only scheduling opportunity.

So in 2006 we have a remake of *The Omen*. To differentiate it from the original, sometimes the title is listed as *The Omen: 666*, but there is little else to distinguish the two. This latest version is almost a shot for shot, scene for scene, line by line remake of the original. There are no new characters, new storylines, or new insights. However, it does look good, thanks to cinematographer Jonathan Sela's use of light and dark (his cold, blue Rome is an interesting contrast to the usual warm, orange Italy of the cinema) and it actually contains some truly scary moments and persuasively sinister music.

Like the original, the story begins in the Vatican observatory where an astronomer notices a trio of comets creating a "star" over Rome. From there he makes the giant leap of revelation that the Antichrist has just been born and we're on the eve of Armageddon. He takes this news to the Pope who looks appropriately dismayed—and then the church pretty much disappears from the story. It appears that just knowing he's around is all that is required of them; heaven forbid they should actually try and do something about his presence!

Over at the maternity ward in a Rome hospital, Robert Thorn (Liev Schreiber), a secondary official at the American embassy rushes to the bedside of his pregnant wife Katherine (Julia Stiles). There he is told that their baby has died and that Katherine has suffered internal problems and will never get pregnant again. However, there is a small mercy, the priest tells him. Also in the hospital is an orphaned baby born on the same day. Why not let the delicate Katherine take him home as her own and not tell her? A crushed Robert agrees when he is told that "God will forgive this little deception."

Not long afterward, Robert's boss is made ambassador to Great Britain and Robert is to go with him as his deputy. But in a death worthy of the *Final Destination* movies (2000-2006), his boss dies and Robert, who by the way is the president's godson, is made ambassador and goes in his place.

Flash forward a few years and it is their son's birthday party. Damien (Seamus Davey-Fitzpatrick) is a quiet little boy, dark-haired and almost angelic in appearance. However, there's something not quite right about him. And there's something wrong with his nanny, too, as she's on the roof with a noose around her neck ready to jump, all for Damien's sake, or so she yells just before plunging to her death in front of the panic-stricken party guests. Naturally, Damien is totally unaffected by this horrible event, but the chaos that ensues delights the many paparazzi covering the high-profile social event.

Faced with finding another nanny, Katherine interviews many applicants and is just about out of steam when in walks an unexpected candidate, Mrs. Baylock (Mia Farrow). She is sweet, soft-spoken, and has years of experience. With an uncanny ability to say exactly the right things, she gets the position. It soon becomes apparent that she has more than just a hired hand's interest in the little boy.

Meanwhile, Robert suddenly finds himself faced with Father Brennan (Pete Postlethwaite), who seems like he has had more than his share of Communion wine. Totally lacking in tact, he proceeds to tell Robert that his son is the Antichrist and must be killed—a message any normal father would accept unquestioningly, right? Brennan is persistent and eventually Robert is persuaded to meet with him to find out more, rendezvousing outside in the midst of a violent storm. Shortly afterward, the unfortunate priest dies, skewered by a falling metal spike that was hit by lightening.

One of the swarm of photographers who surround the Thorns is Keith Jennings (David Thewlis), who was at Damien's birthday party and also caught Brennan leaving the embassy. What bothers Jennings is that in all his photos of the nanny there is a light shadow around her neck, just like the noose. Similarly, all his photos of Father Brennan show a light shadow about to pierce his body, just like the metal rod that killed him. What really worries him is that while taking pictures in Brennan's room he captures himself on film reflected in a mirror and there's a light shadow just about to sever his head from his neck. He might be the next to die if he can't figure this mystery out. (But just as one can't figure out why the Vatican is just sitting on its hands in this story, one can't help but wonder why Jennings is the only photographer with equipment with precognitive powers.)

Jennings now approaches Robert to help convince him that there's something evil at work, and the two set out for Rome to find the original priest who gave Damien to the Thorns and, through him, discover who Damien's real mother is. It's a trip that will take them to an island monastery, a spooky cemetery, and finally to Antichrist extermination expert Bugenhagen (Michael Gambon).

During all this Damien has been busy scaring the gorillas at the zoo, throwing fits rather than enter a church, and being hand-fed strawberries by his doting nanny who has also allowed Damien to adopt a vicious pet dog, much to the dismay of his increasingly suspicious and terrified mother. Katherine's suspicions are confirmed as he proceeds to intentionally ride his tricycle into her as she is precariously balanced on a chair on the upper floor, causing her to fall over a balcony railing, ending her pregnancy and putting her in the hospital.

Whether Damien truly is the Antichrist is not the mystery of this story. Whether the Thorns will figure it out in time is. One problem with the remake is that because most viewers probably already know the plot, many scenes—especially the talky, intimate ones between Robert and Katherine—really slow the movie down.

Schreiber and Stiles are intelligent actors and worthy successors to Gregory Peck and Lee Remick from the original. And young Seamus Davey-Fitzpatrick certainly scowls well, but more often than not here, what's most interesting and enjoyable about the film is not character development but simply getting to the next scary part. One bit of interesting character change, though, is Mia Farrow's Mrs. Baylock. In the original, Billie Whitelaw was almost evil incarnate right from the beginning, but with Farrow, the original mother of Satan's spawn in *Rosemary's Baby* (1968), we see sweetness before the sinisterness. A fun bit of stunt casting to accompany the stunt release date. But it works.

Beverley Bare Buehrer

CREDITS

Robert Thorn: Liev Schreiber
Katherine Thorn: Julia Stiles
Mrs. Baylock: Mia Farrow
Keith Jennings: David Thewlis
Father Brennan: Pete Postlethwaite
Bugenhagen: Michael Gambon
Damien: Seamus Davey-Fitzpatrick
Origin: USA
Language: English
Released: 2006
Production: Glenn Williamson, John Moore; released by 20th Century Fox
Directed by: John Moore
Written by: David Seltzer
Cinematography by: Jonathan Sela
Music by: Marco Beltrami
Sound: Ian Voigt
Editing: Don Zimmerman
Art Direction: Martin Kurel, Katerina Kopicova
Costumes: George L. Little
Production Design: Patrick Lumb
MPAA rating: R
Running time: 110 minutes

REVIEWS

Boxoffice Online. June 6, 2006.
Chicago Sun-Times Online. June 6, 2006.
Entertainment Weekly Online. June 7, 2006.
Los Angeles Times Online. June 6, 2006.
New York Times Online. June 6, 2006.
Variety Online. June 5, 2006.
Washington Post. June 6, 2006, p. C1.

QUOTES

Damien: "Did I scare you, Mommy? I didn't mean to."

OPEN SEASON

One Fur All And All Fur One.
—Movie tagline

Boyz 'n the Wood.
—Movie tagline

The Odd Are About To Get Even.
—Movie tagline

Box Office: $84.3 million

It is difficult to imagine just how many cutesy, computer-animated films featuring sassy, talking animals the human brain can actually process. In 2006, Hollywood seemed determined to find out. Movies like *Open Season* make it appealing to enact some sort of law that moviemakers must come up with an excellent, exciting new twist on the genre before they even draw up a storyboard. It would save everyone a lot of wasted hours. It is not that *Open Season* is particularly bad, it is just that this movie has already been done.

This film concerns a big bear named Boog (voice of Martin Lawrence). Boog lives a good, comfortable life with his friend and caretaker, forest ranger Beth (voice of Debra Messing). He performs with her in an animal show and she gives him plenty of food and a cozy garage to sleep in. Boog meets the requisite unwanted, talkative, annoying sidekick when he rescues a perky deer named Elliot (voice of Ashton Kutcher) from the hood of mean hunter Shaw's (voice of Gary Sinise) truck.

As sidekicks usually do, Elliot devises a madcap scheme that has Boog and Elliot break into a convenience store and gorge themselves on sugar-filled delicacies. This, and various other Elliot-induced misbehaving ends up with Boog being shipped off to the wild. Beth makes sure that Boog is dropped off in the part of the forest that is presumed to be relatively free of hunters.

In the short term, though, hunters are the least of Boog's worries. Since he was raised in captivity, he knows nothing about surviving in the wild. He does not know how to find food and he does not care for his fellow woodland creatures, such as a beaver called Reilly (voice of Jon Favreau); a deer named Ian (voice of Patrick Warburton); and a squirrel known as McSquizzy (voice of Billy Connolly). Of these, only McSquizzy, along with his fellow surly, brogue-accented squirrels is even remotely memorable.

Boog decides that the only reasonable solution to his plight is to find his way home. The obstacles to this quest include Elliot's alarming lack of a sense of direction and the pending start of hunting season. Along the way, tepid scatological humor, halfhearted attempts at excitement, and Boog's gradual acceptance of the idea that perhaps his home is in the wild after all fill-out the narrative.

There is nothing to point to in the film as being the single problem that its lacking. Lawrence and Kutcher read their lines in a perfectly acceptable fashion (though Lawrence's comedic talent is oddly not in evidence here). The animals are all well rendered. The soundtrack, which includes music by the Talking Heads and the Replacements' Paul Westerberg, is better than most. In many ways, *Open Season* is the quintessential kiddie flick. It has the right look, the correct style and types of jokes, and the suitably famous voices behind the characters. What the film does not have is the spark of passion or quirkiness that makes a film like this work. So many people were involved in the making of this film—seven writers for example—that perhaps the film suffered for the lack of a strong singular vision.

The complaints critics voiced about the mind-numbing familiarity of *Open Season* took on a similar monotonous quality themselves. Laura Kern of the *New York Times* wrote that "periodic bursts of cleverness and eye-popping imagery…can't disguise that this is just another movie full of jive-talking computer-generated animals with little new to say." Peter Hartlaub of the *San Francisco Chronicle* wrote "there are times when *Open Season* seems like a film that skipped its first installment—going straight to the uninspired money-making sequel." Bill Zwecker of the *Chicago Sun-Times* opined that "while the filmmakers here have provided us with a passable tale that is mildly humorous, *Open Season* breaks no new ground, from neither the animation nor the storytelling." Finally, Janice Page of the *Boston Globe* felt kindly toward the story, writing: "Even though its premise is embarrassingly tired…[the screenplay] has just enough spunk and giggles to occasionally win you over."

Jill Hamilton

CREDITS

Boog: Martin Lawrence (Voice)
Elliot: Ashton Kutcher (Voice)
Shaw: Gary Sinise (Voice)
Beth: Debra Messing (Voice)
McSquizzy: Billy Connolly (Voice)
Reilly: Jon Favreau (Voice)
Bobbie: Georgia Engel (Voice)
Giselle: Jane Krakowski (Voice)
Gordy: Gordon Tootoosis (Voice)
Ian: Patrick Warburton (Voice)
Origin: USA
Language: English
Released: 2006
Production: Michelle Murdocca; Columbia Pictures, Sony Pictures Animation; released by Sony Pictures
Directed by: Roger Allers, Jill Culton
Written by: Steve Bencich, Maurizio Merli, Nat Maudlin
Music by: Paul Westerberg, Ramin Djawadi
Sound: Tim Chau, Tateum Kohut
Editing: Pamela Ziegenhagen-Shefland
Art Direction: Andy Harkness
Production Design: Michael Humphries
MPAA rating: PG
Running time: 99 minutes

REVIEWS

Boxoffice Online. September 29, 2006.
Chicago Sun-Times Online. September 29, 2006.
Entertainment Weekly Online. September 27, 2006.
Hollywood Reporter Online. September 29, 2006.
Los Angeles Times Online. September 29, 2006.
New York Times Online. September 29, 2006.
San Francisco Chronicle. September 29, 2006, p. E4.
Variety Online. September 28, 2006.
Washington Post Online. September 29, 2006.

OVER THE HEDGE

Taking back the neighborhood…one snack at a time.
—Movie tagline

Box Office: $155 million

Over the Hedge is an amusing animated film that shares a valuable lesson about the real meaning and importance of family without becoming schmaltzy or targeting itself too narrowly toward children. At the same time, it does not attempt to be self-conscious or cynical in the vein of some other recent animated films such as *Shrek* (2001) or *Hoodwinked!* (2005). The setting is somewhat limited, of course, since all of the action takes place in a confined area of a suburban neighborhood, yet the rich and detailed animation makes the most of the locations and character renderings. More importantly, though, the characterizations are genuinely memorable, funny, and touching at times. *Over the Hedge* is not an epic, ambitious animated film, but it is a well-made and entertaining story that celebrates the value of simplicity.

The Film tells the story of RJ (voice of Bruce Willis), a raccoon who finds himself in trouble when he tries to steal food from the stash of a hibernating bear named Vincent (voice of Nick Nolte). When Vincent wakes up to discover RJ, the raccoon accidentally sends the bear's entire stash of food into the path of a truck. Vincent then demands that RJ replace everything within the next week.

In his search to find food, RJ comes across a group of forest animals who have just awakened from a winter of hibernation to find an enormous hedge surrounding them; on the other side of the hedge, a sprawling suburban neighborhood has sprung up over the winter. The animals, led by turtle Verne (voice of Garry Shandling), are amazed and bewildered by the hedge until RJ introduces himself and explains that it is "the gateway to the good life." He tries to convince them that the human neighborhood is a paradise that will enable them to gather more than enough food for themselves before the next winter. Verne, who spends a few unpleasant moments on the other side of the hedge, opposes the idea, but the others are quickly convinced that RJ is right, particularly after they taste cheese chips. Human life, RJ claims, centers around food. "We eat to live. They live to eat," he says. "For humans, enough is never enough."

The animals begin frequent expeditions into the neighborhood to steal food (and other items such as video games and even, at one point, a television). The humans are promptly alerted to their presence but cannot capture them. Most, however, do not seem as terribly disturbed by the animal intrusions as Gladys (voice of Allison Janney), the uptight president of the homeowners' association who is horrified to see the foragers invading her yard. She summons the exterminator Dwayne (voice of Thomas Haden Church), who calls himself the "verminator," to rid the neighborhood of the animals.

Meanwhile, the grateful animals express their thanks to RJ by constructing a "home" for him, consisting of a nice chair (a stolen carseat) and a television with a universal remote control. At this point, they consider RJ their leader, a fact that obviously bothers Verne. The turtle subsequently decides to pack up all the food they have stolen and return it to the humans, explaining to RJ that he just wants to save them all from getting killed. RJ tries to stop him, fearing that he will not be able to settle his debt with Vincent, but a series of missteps and freak accidents leaves all the food destroyed. Consequently, the rest of the animals are not too happy with Verne, and their resentment toward him only grows when he slips up and calls them too "stupid" to know better than to trust RJ.

While Verne regrets his careless words and the way he has hurt his friends (whom he considers his family), RJ struggles with feelings of guilt over the way he has deceived everybody, yet he also fears what will happen when Vincent wakes up and expects to see his stash replaced. When Verne tells him that he made a mistake in trying to return the food and that the animals now need RJ more than they needed him, the raccoon starts to tell him the truth—until he sees a deliveryman bringing an enormous amount of food to Gladys' house. Hoping he can still gather all the food he needs, RJ hatches a plan with Verne and the others to sneak into Gladys' house during the night to steal the food. Unfortunately, Dwayne has installed countless sophisticated traps—some of them illegal—all over the yard, so their plan requires a bit of derring-do and trickery, leading to an amusing scene in which smart-mouthed skunk Stella (voice of Wanda Sykes) disguises herself as a feline and woos Gladys' portly cat Tiger (voice of Omid Djalili). The animals manage to sneak into the house and gather all the food they can possibly transport, but things go awry and all of them except RJ end up as Dwayne's captives.

Of course RJ cannot handle the guilt of having betrayed his new friends, especially when Vincent says that the raccoon will one day wind up just like him. So, instead of turning the food over to the bear, RJ uses it to launch himself at Dwayne's truck so he can rescue his friends. The climactic scenes of the film follow the animals' rescue and happy reunion and then a final showdown that ultimately pits Vincent against Dwayne and Gladys. In the end, RJ decides to stay with his new friends, who invite him to be part of their family. In this way, RJ ultimately obtains everything he really needs and wants, even though it is not what he thought he needed.

David Flanagin

CREDITS

RJ: Bruce Willis (Voice)
Verne: Garry Shandling (Voice)
Hammy: Steven Carell (Voice)
Ozzie: William Shatner (Voice)
Penny: Catherine O'Hara (Voice)
Lou: Eugene Levy (Voice)
Stella: Wanda Sykes (Voice)
Vincent: Nick Nolte (Voice)

Dwayne: Thomas Haden Church (Voice)
Gladys: Allison Janney (Voice)
Heather: Avril Lavigne (Voice)
Tiger: Omid Djalili (Voice)
Bucky: Sami Kirkpatrick (Voice)
Spike: Shane Baumel (Voice)
Quillo: Madison Davenport (Voice)
Origin: USA
Language: English
Released: 2006
Production: Bonnie Arnold; DreamWorks Animation; released by Paramount
Directed by: Tim Johnson, Karey Kirkpatrick
Written by: Karey Kirkpatrick, Len Blum, Lorne Cameron, David Hoselton
Music by: Rupert Gregson-Williams
Editing: John Carr
Art Direction: Christian Schellewald, Paul Shardlow
Production Design: Kathy Altieri
MPAA rating: PG
Running time: 84 minutes

REVIEWS

Entertainment Weekly Online. May 17, 2006.
Los Angeles Times Online. May 19, 2006.
San Francisco Chronicle Online. May 19, 2006.
Washington Post Online. May 19, 2006, p. C01.

P

PAN'S LABYRINTH

(El Laberinto del Fauno)

Innocence has a power evil cannot imagine.
—Movie tagline

Box Office: $35.4 million

Mexican horror specialist Guillermo del Toro's latest effort to reach these shores, *Pan's Labyrinth*, succeeds in putting across a rare use of this film genre in order to reflect political realities, which mask the horror in the world we take to be normal. Not content to relegate his scare fest to a closed-off physical world, such as that found in tales of haunted houses, murderous psychopaths and half-human monsters, writer/director del Toro allows what is frightening to permeate the day-to-day world of his characters, so that what emerges is a study of how the blackest black, as embodied in the force of unrivalled militaristic power, can hopefully be kept in its place by the whitest white, an inner strength guiding each individual toward what is morally just.

If his *Labyrinth*, which he so painstakingly and ambitiously constructs, exhibits a drawback, it would have to be in the very cinematic form that binds him, which bestows a fast-paced, dazzling allure upon his unmistakably serious intent, thereby risking his earnest plea—on behalf of the supernatural having practical value—will be perceived as a comic book.

From the podium of the New York Film Festival, where his film was chosen for the coveted closing night slot, del Toro provided the historical basis for his period piece, set in the Spain of the mid-1940s, a time when the Spanish Civil War is supposed to have ended with the triumph of Franco's dictatorial regime. "In fact," del Toro pointed out, "the last member of the Resistance was executed in the sixties. That's exactly the point of the movie. This is not a war that was neatly framed by what the history books say. It is still alive today in some form or another."

Del Toro's remarks place his curious mix of politically-charged events and the parallel universe of otherworldly happenings within a contemporary context not spelled out in the film. However, the antinomy he sets up at the start sustains his engrossing brew of narrative events throughout.

His heroine, little Ofelia (Ivana Baquero), is first seen engrossed in a storybook about an underground realm, as she is taken to meet her stepfather, the ruthless Vidal (Sergi Lopez). He commands a military outpost in the forest that has been set up to decimate what is left of the Resistance. Through captivating digital effects, a primeval world comes alive as the setting for a tale of a princess, too pure for the earthly realm, who suffered and died, only to have her spirit search for another body through which she can return to her underground kingdom. In the back seat of a car with a military escort, Ofelia is forced to snap her book shut by her pregnant mother, Carmen (Ariadna Gil), who dismisses the fairy tale as nonsense. Overcome by an attack of nausea, Carmen orders the car to stop. This allows Ofelia to wander off by herself. It also allows the film to introduce its supernatural elements as part of the very fabric of Ofelia's real world.

Filled with a sense of curiosity and wonder, and believing the accidental stop was preordained, Ofelia picks up a magical stone. A grasshopper leads her to a sculpture of a stone head missing one eye. A repulsive spider crawls out of the eye cavity as Ofelia realizes the stone in her hand is the missing eye. Undeterred, she replaces the stone into the eye socket. This event foreshadows the role Ofelia's courage and belief will play in the secret underground kingdom. She has been chosen to perform tasks that may appear inconsequential, and even repellent, in relation to the real world, but become a matter of survival in a parallel universe. When Ofelia is called away, the film makes clear where it stands in this conflict between the two worlds. Del Toro's camera remains with the grasshopper, allowing it to fill the screen, as Ofelia is whisked away in the background.

At the military outpost, which is to be Ofelia's home, she is put under the care of Mercedes (Maribel Verdu), a kindly governess who will take on the role of a mother-figure, a substitute for the eventually bed-ridden Carmen. Mercedes will also play a role in the film's subplot as a collaborator in the Resistance, secretly helping the band of rebels in the hills led by Pedro (Roger Casamajor), her brother. She obtains medical supplies from Dr. Ferreiro (Alex Angulo) who has been called in to serve Carmen. Like a silent witness to Ofelia's plight in a world ruled by Vidal, the grasshopper reappears perched on bags of cement.

For all her otherworldly leanings, Ofelia remains close to her mother. When the two are in bed, Ofelia asks her why she had to marry someone like Vidal. Carmen answers that she had been lonely too long. To ease her pain, Carmen gets Ofelia to tell the baby a story. Ofelia puts her head to her mother's abdomen and starts on a fable about a rose whose scent could bestow eternal life. As she does so, digital effects allow us to enter the mother's womb and see the embryo bathed in red.

To counter this maternal domestic warmth, the film shifts gears to show Vidal's brutality. When two hunters, a father and a son, are brought before him, Vidal punishes them for being reds. Despite their claims that they were merely shooting rabbits, Vidal kills the son, repeatedly stabbing him in the face. He then shoots the father dead. When rabbits are indeed found in their bags, Vidal remains unrepentant.

In Carmen's bedroom, Carmen has fallen sleep, but Ofelia sits up in bed as she spots the flying grasshopper, who positions himself on her blanket. "Are you a fairy?" Ofelia asks. Again, digital magic allows the creature to sprout wings and lead Ofelia to a stone archway near the outpost, then down rocky steps into a well. After Ofelia fearlessly descends into this underground realm of stone, the wiry figure of the half-human Faun (Doug Jones) welcomes her. "I am the mountains, the woods and the earth!" he proclaims. He tells Ofelia that she is in fact Princess Moanna, but that she will have to perform three tasks to open the portals of her kingdom, where her subjects are waiting for her to once again rule over them. As her guide in this adventure, the Faun presents her with a Book of Secrets, that staple of the horror tale, the repository of ancient wisdom by which the monster can be destroyed. In del Toro's contemporary digital universe, however, its pages are blank.

The next morning in her bathtub, as Ofelia opens the magic Book, its pages start to drip red and words appear in a strange language. Carmen then tells her that she will live like a princess. What Carmen means, of course, is that she will be dressed in the best finery. Ofelia, next seen dressed in a frilly black dress, wants to milk a cow, like Mercedes. Ofelia confides in her about the Faun, but just then the governess is called away by Vidal. The storage barn has been burgled, without any evidence of a break-in. Vidal questions Mercedes, since she was supposed to have the only other key. Before Vidal can probe further, smoke is seen coming from the hills and Vidal and his men ride off in pursuit.

The words that take form in the Book tell Ofelia that the woods nearby are magical and home to strange creatures, and that there is a colossal fig tree that has been dying. Here and in the later episodes, what transpires in the magical world has its counterpart in Ofelia's real world; Carmen's health too will progressively worsen. As the Book orders, Ofelia steps into the bark of the Tree, leaving her black dress and the Book behind. As she proceeds, all kinds of repulsive, leech-like insects stick to her, but she continues fearlessly. The scene harkens back to similar moments in Steven Spielberg's *Indiana Jones and the Temple of Doom* (1984). Ofelia then confronts a gigantic Toad who resembles a digital reincarnation of Jabba the Hut. This creature extends his long tongue, spewing out all kinds of muck onto Ofelia, who flinches but does not back away from her task, which is to throw three magical stones into the Toad's mouth. The Toad then throws up more muck, along with the Key that Ofelia needs.

The film then gives Vidal a chance to voice his ideological leanings. As he entertains the Mayor and his wife, Vidal speaks of "a new, clean Spain." His stance is that of someone who believes his views to be right and just, allowing, as he sees it, his side to win the war. The moral thrust of his words is undercut by the rebels gaining in their assault against his deputies, owing to the ammo they have been receiving from Mercedes. It is only in the film's final section that Vidal suspects her, but by that time many of his men have been shot down in an ambush. When he then tortures Mercedes, she is able to slice his mouth with a hidden knife.

The Faun gives Ofelia the tasks she is to perform, some to cure Carmen and others to obtain magical objects from the underground realm. Like any mortal, Ofelia slips up, unable to save her mother, and also gives in to temptation, after her boldness has led to her triumph over a Cyclops-like creature. Her weakness at this stage would have been enough to confine her to the mortal realm. But after Carmen dies in childbirth, the Faun gives Ofelia one last chance to become the Princess: she has to bring her baby brother down into the labyrinth, which she will enter by tracing a door on the floor of her bedroom using a magic chalk. Before Ofelia can do so, Vidal spots her, so that Ofelia has no recourse but to run towards the cave, carrying her baby brother. Inside the cave, the Faun tests her by requesting the baby's blood in order to open the last Portal. When Ofelia refuses, the Faun retorts: "But you hardly know him!" The Faun then banishes her, resulting in Vidal snatching the baby from her and shooting her dead at point blank range. Once outside, Vidal is confronted by the rebels. Foreseeing his end, he hands the baby to Mercedes, who gets her revenge by vowing that his child will never even know his name.

Like all spinners of fantastic tales, del Toro saves his greatest flourish for the end. Ofelia's spirit rises from her dying body, and Ofelia finds herself in a palace hall, the center of a paradise kingdom ruled by her father and Carmen, the Princess's reward for not spilling her brother's blood.

Vivek Adarkar

CREDITS

Vidal: Sergi Lopez
Mercedes: Maribel Verdu
Faun/Pan/Pale Man: Doug Jones
Dr. Ferreiro: Alex Angulo
Ofelia: Ivana Baquero
Carmen: Ariadna Gil
Pedro: Roger Casamajor
Origin: Mexico, Spain
Language: Spanish
Released: 2006
Production: Bertha Navarro, Alfonso Cuaron, Guillermo del Toro; Telecino, Estudios Picasso, Tequila Gang, Esperanto Filmoj; released by Picturehouse
Directed by: Guillermo del Toro
Written by: Guillermo del Toro
Cinematography by: Guillermo Navarro
Music by: Javier Navarrete
Sound: Miguel Polo
Editing: Bernat Vilaplana
Costumes: Lala Huete
Production Design: Eugenio Caballero
MPAA rating: R
Running time: 112 minutes

REVIEWS

Boxoffice Online. December 29, 2006.
Hollywood Reporter Online. May 27, 2006.
Los Angeles Times Online. December 29, 2006.
New York Times Online. December 29, 2006.
Premiere Magazine. January/February 2007, p. 46.
San Francisco Chronicle. December 29, 2006, p. E1.
Variety Online. May 27, 2006.
Village Voice Online. December 26, 2006.

AWARDS

Oscars 2006: Art Dir./Set Dec., Cinematog., Makeup
British Acad. 2006: Costume Des., Foreign Film, Makeup
Ind. Spirit 2007: Cinematog
Nomination:
Oscars 2006: Foreign Film, Orig. Screenplay, Orig. Score
British Acad. 2006: Cinematog., Orig. Screenplay, Sound, Visual FX
Golden Globes 2007: Foreign Film
Ind. Spirit 2007: Film

PHAT GIRLZ

Her dreams are about to get a whole lot bigger.
—Movie tagline

Box Office: $7 million

As inside every fat woman, there is reportedly a lovely thin woman waiting to be revealed, *Phat Girlz* is an ungainly film with a lithe, graceful film hidden somewhere deep inside. The film is not exactly bad, but it could have been really quite good.

There are a few things working against *Phat Girlz.* The first is that the film lacked a decent budget, and it shows. It was originally given a $10 million budget before being slashed to $2.5 million. This prompted changes in the screenplay and, at one point, filming was stopped entirely. Production resumed six months later but this led to a slew of continuity errors including costume changes and the time switching inexplicably from day to night and back again. Another problem is the inexperience of first time writer/director Nnegest Likke. Her screenplay is not punchy or funny enough. It is awkwardly structured and does not flow well. For example, at the point between the second and third acts, Jazmin (Mo'Nique) hits bottom and ends up sobbing in her bed surrounded by half-eaten food. A brief shot of

Jazmin lolling about in bed hitting the Haagen-Dazs would have been enough to convey the message, but Likke lets Jazmin cry for several long minutes rather than making the point quickly.

Conversely, Likke's inexperience is also one of the best things about the film. Most directors have filmmaking down to such a science that a lot of the unpredictability of comedy is lost due to the routine way it is filmed. Likke does not know the meaning of a subtle shot, so there are some over-the-top reaction shots that are so ham-fistedly filmed that they become funny. Some of the reaction shots are reminiscent of the herky-jerky rhythm of silent comedies. Likke's lack of polish makes for a fresher look than most modern low-budget comedies. But the main asset of the film is star Mo'Nique. As, Jazmin, a plus-sized woman searching for love and success, Mo'Nique must be funny but believable, sympathetic but not pitiful and be able to play both drama and romance to carry this film. She does all of this and is a commanding screen presence.

Jazmin is a clerk in a large Los Angeles retail store. She and her plump, mousy friend Stacey (Kendra C. Johnson) watch morosely from the sidelines as Jazmin's thin cousin, Mia (Joyful Drake), gets all the dates. Jazmin dreams of presenting her clothing designs for large women to her store's big boss, Robert Myer (Eric Roberts), but her condescending, weasely boss, Dick Eckhard (Jack Noseworthy) continually blocks her way. Jazmin's luck starts to change when she wins a contest sponsored by a diet pill manufacturer. The prize is a trip to a five-star resort in Palm Springs. Jazmin does not relish the idea of going to a place where she will be surrounded by even more skinny women, in bathing suits, no less, but Mia forces her to go. At the resort, Jazmin and her friends meet a group of attractive Nigerian doctors. To Jazmin and Stacy's shock, the men are wildly attracted to their size. In their country, they say, the larger the woman, the higher her social status. Buff, alpha-male Tunde (Jimmy Jean-Louis), immediately falls for Jazmin. Jazmin is so conditioned to being ignored or teased, that she can not fathom that a man could really be attracted to her. Tunde's interest throws her world askew and she is unsure quite how to react. Is a man's love enough to boost a woman's self esteem and propel her to follow her dreams of success? Since this is a chick flick, that is indeed the case.

Critics mostly liked Mo'Nique's performance but found Likke's screenplay and direction lacking. Nathan Lee of the *New York Times* called the film "an undernourished comedy." Brian Orndorf of *FilmJerk.com* wrote: "Made on the cheap (shot with low-grade DV cameras), and unfortunately looking like it too, the picture is a mess of ideas looking for some type of dramatic form. First time writer/director Nnegest Likke has her heart in the right place, but the intensity of her inexperience blinds every scene." Kyle Smith of the *New York Post* wrote: "The film is amateurishly directed and sluggishly paced with an anorexic plot. Even the photography, sound and costumes are substandard. But ...Mo'Nique is largely, if not enormously, appealing." Wesley Morris of the *Boston Globe* wrote: "It's the sort of unvarnished personal journey picture that used to crop up back in the days of the true independent cinema movement of the early 1990s, when black women were telling positive stories about themselves." Finally, Kathy Cano Murillo of the *Arizona Republic* wrote: "Mo'Nique and her co-stars deliver an arsenal of laughs, and the overall message of triumphs and learning to accept one's self is admirable. Unfortunately, those elements are not strong enough to cleanse the *Phat Girlz* palate."

Jill Hamilton

CREDITS

Jazmin Biltmore: Mo'Nique
Tunde: Jimmy Jean-Louis
Akibo: Godfrey
Dick Eckhard: Jack Noseworthy
Stacey: Kendra C. Johnson
Mia: Joyful Drake
Robert Myer: Eric Roberts
Origin: USA
Language: English
Released: 2006
Production: Robert Newmyer, Steven J. Wolfe; Outlaw Productions, Sneak Preview Entertainment, Fox Searchlight Pictures, 10 Times Greater Productions; released by 20th Century Fox
Directed by: Nnegest Likke
Written by: Nnegest Likke
Cinematography by: Dean Lent, John Ndiaga Demps
Music by: Stephen Endelman
Sound: Monroe Cummings, Scott Stolz
Editing: Zack Arnold
Art Direction: Peggy Wang
Production Design: Warren Alan Young, Natasha Baumgardner
MPAA rating: PG-13
Running time: 99 minutes

REVIEWS

Boxoffice Online. April 7, 2006.
Los Angeles Times Online. April 10, 2006.
New York Times Online. April 8, 2006.

San Francisco Chronicle. April 8, 2006, p. E1.
Variety Online. April 9, 2006.

QUOTES

Jazmin: "I ain't fat. I'm sexy-succulent."

THE PIANO TUNER OF EARTHQUAKES

(L'Accordeur de tremblements de terre)

The Quay Brothers' second feature film blends horror, opera, animation, and New Age symbolism, but it never becomes anything more than a pretentious movie version of a coffee table tome. Over many years, Stephen and Timothy Quay have created quirky, fascinating animated shorts. But the brothers' highly anticipated first feature and first live-action film, *Institute Benjamenta* (1994), disappointed many. Sadly, *Piano Tuner of Earthquakes* is no better. While the classical score is enchanting and some of the images are gorgeous, the ninety-nine-minute film feels like ninety-nine hours.

The story by the Quay Brothers and Alan Passes centers around eighteenth-century opera diva, Malvina van Stille (Amira Casar), who, on the eve of her wedding to the heroic Adolpho (Cesar Sarachu), is killed by the dastardly Dr. Emmanuel Droz (Gottfried John). Malvina's corpse is then abducted by Droz, who takes her body to his fortress in a strange, supernatural underworld, where he commands his robotic underlings to resurrect Malvina from the grave. He then hires a naive piano tuner, Felisberto (also played by Sarachu), to help author an opera for Malvina about her death and subsequent rebirth.

When the revitalized Malvina notices the obvious physical resemblance between Felisberto and Adolpho, she slowly falls in love with the lithe, romantic piano tuner. Felisberto reciprocates her feelings and, consumed by his passion, he begins plotting to rescue Malvina and return with her to the real world. However, the evil doctor becomes aware of the escape plan and tries to use his sexy maid, Assumpta (Assumpta Serna), to seduce Felisberto away from Malvina. As the denouement nears, Felisberto's final presentation of his opera sparks the destruction of Droz's mythological kingdom, the demise of Dr. Droz, and a poignant parting between Felisberto and Malvina.

Now that film fans have so many new avenues to experience movies that reject mainstream values—art-house cinemas, specialty cable film channels, and boutique DVD box sets, among others—*The Piano Tuner of Earthquakes* may very well find an audience, albeit an atypical one, but even fans of the modernist classics of Peter Greenaway, Guy Maddin, and Jan Svankmajer may have problems with the Quays' latest piece of alternative cinema. What the filmmakers have seemingly failed to grasp is that there is a certain timeliness required in creating shocking or revolutionary film images. What is esoteric one day is expected the next. In their first feature, the Quays fail to conjure up any images that we haven't seen before. As such, *Piano Tuner* feels oddly dated, almost like a student film circa 2001. To make matters worse, in 2006, *Piano Tuner* had to compete with Darren Aronofsky's similarly heavy-going and dream-like *The Fountain* (2006). It's regrettable that the Quays—who are such a defining, vibrant force in animated shorts—can't seem to bring that same maverick verve to their live action debut.

There are rules that work for animation that simply don't translate to live action; this is perhaps most apparent in regards to the screenplay for *Piano Tuner* which contains dialogue that no flesh-and-blood human should ever have to speak. For example, Assumpta flirts with Felisberto by commenting "When I lace up my shoes, I notice only afterwards my toe, which I assumed was inside, is still hanging outside." Not even Trevor Duncan and Christopher Slaski's lush instrumentals can make dialogue that awkward and plodding sound lyrical and true. But even without its useless dialogue, *Piano Tuner* never escapes its uninspired roots, functioning as simply a soporific revision of such German Expressionist classics as *The Cabinet of Doctor Caligari* (1920) and *Nosferatu* (1922).

The critics were not unduly harsh toward *Piano Tuner*, acknowledging the skill behind the production, and some were even laudatory, including the *Hollywood Reporter*'s Ray Bennett: "The film is about vanity and pride, and the caging of beauty. Its elaborate fabrication has an intoxicating quality that captures the imagination like all good horror stories." Still, Leslie Felperin in *Variety* summed up the wider reaction: the "...accumulation of striking tableaux doesn't make for a satisfying narrative whole, and by time the final automata whirs into gear there's no traction to hold audience interest beyond the sheer pleasure of the imagery itself."

Eric Monder

CREDITS

Malvina van Stille: Amira Casar
Dr. Emmanuel Droz: Gottfried John
Assumpta: Assumpta Serna
Adolfo Blin/Don Felisberto Fernandez: Cesar Sarachu

Origin: France, Great Britain, Germany
Language: Portuguese, English
Released: 2005
Production: Hengameh Panahi; Mediopolis Film, Koninck Studios, Lumen Films; released by Zeitgeist Films
Directed by: Stephen Quay, Timothy Quay
Written by: Stephen Quay, Timothy Quay
Cinematography by: Nic Knowland
Music by: Christopher Slaski
Sound: Larry Sider
Editing: Simon Laurie
Costumes: Kandis Cook
Art Direction: Eric Veenstra
Production Design: Stephen Quay, Timothy Quay
MPAA rating: Unrated
Running time: 99 minutes

REVIEWS

Boxoffice Online. November 17, 2006.
Chicago Sun-Times Online. January 5, 2006.
Hollywood Reporter Online. August 11, 2006.
Los Angeles Times Online. December 1, 2006.

THE PINK PANTHER

Get a clue!
—Movie tagline
Pardon His French.
—Movie tagline
The Pink Panther diamond is missing...And the world's greatest detective is solving the case one mistake at a time.
—Movie tagline

Box Office: $82.2 million

Reviving the old *Pink Panther* franchise, with Steve Martin replacing Peter Sellers in the lead role as the bumbling Inspector Clouseau, seemed like a bankable idea when it was first conceived. *The Pink Panther*, when it was finally released early in 2006, briefly became the top box-office movie in the country, mostly for lack of competition in the bleak movie season of early February. Then it quickly faded because of poor reviews and unhappy word-of-mouth critiques.

This film was a long time coming. MGM first started making a new, tenth *Pink Panther* movie in the year 2000. The project went through the competent comedic hands of director Ivan Reitman and through a rumor mill of stars, including Kevin Spacey and Mike Myers, before Martin agreed to play the role. At that point Reitman was replaced by Shawn Levy, who had directed Martin in the newest *Cheaper by the Dozen* films. Still, the release date of the film, originally scheduled for Christmas 2004, was held up more than a year, reportedly because test audiences didn't find the film very funny.

It must have been a real dud before it went back to the studio for fixes, because what finally did appear on screen is one of Martin's worst movies. *The Pink Panther* is one of the most successful comedic franchises ever, catapulting Peter Sellers into stardom, proving the adeptness of director Blake Edwards, and spawning both an iconic and globally familiar theme song by Henry Mancini and a cartoon character recognizable by generations of audiences. Martin is certainly an improvement on the attempt in the 1990s to make Robert Benigni into Clouseau in a previous unfortunate attempt to revive the series. The veteran and talented comic does his best to make Clouseau a memorable idiot, but the film is so ploddingly written and so badly directed that it's just short of an embarrassment.

Screenwriter Len Blum and director Levy seem to know what the required elements of a Pink Panther movie are: physical slapstick, outrageous accidents, verbal buffoonery, and a spoofing kind of spy-movie intrigue. Neither knows how to put these together into a movie that works. The result is that *The Pink Panther* appears to be an amalgam of loosely connected short skits, whose themes are rather repetitive, with an attempt at times to make the action sweeping and meaningful. Thus, when the murder Clouseau must solve is depicted in the movie's prologue, the scene is shot like a commercial or music video, with swelling and pounding music and a phony "big-movie" perspective.

The mystery is who killed a soccer coach, on the field, at the close of a big game between France and China, and who stole the Pink Panther diamond, an outsized ring that the coach is wearing for reasons never explained. The head of the Paris police, Dreyfus (Kevin Kline), sees this as an opportunity to get himself the country's Medal of Honor and a fame he has always desired. His plan is to hire the bumbling small-town detective Clouseau to distract the press, while he secretly cracks open the case himself, making himself look good in comparison. This is, to say the least, a bizarre plot device—why a man who wants fame would seek refuge rather than attention from the media is hard to fathom.

The rest of the movie unfolds in predictable and ridiculous fashion. One by one, Clouseau interrogates the suspects, chief among them the dead coach's girlfriend, the singer Xania (played without a shred of intelligence, though plenty of wide-eyed enthusiasm by Beyonce Knowles). The script perfunctorily runs through a series of suspects (and it's immediately obvious who the killer is) before finding an excuse to send Clouseau to New York to pursue Xania. This provides the film's only really hilarious scene, one shown in the trailers almost in its entirety—Martin's Clouseau getting a voice lesson in how to say "I want a hamburger" in American English. Martin, who is adept at verbal play, mangles the lesson magnificently.

But that skit, successful as it is, only serves to highlight the rather ridiculous conceit that all the supposedly French people in the movie are speaking English with French accents while in France. There is a mocking moment when Kline corrects himself after mimicking one of Martin's overly accented words—Kline has an accent but a less ridiculous one. Martin makes hay of Clouseau's speech patterns, but it's a poor substitute for really comic moments.

Martin, who initially had reservations about trying to follow in the shoes of Sellers' signature character, should have heeded them. He bounces along obliviously above the wreckage of silly, unfunny visual gags; lame exchanges of stilted dialogue; and even a totally misplaced maudlin moment or two. There is no zing to the comic writing, and many of the scenes fall flat; the writing lacks all the deft subtlety of Martin's own scripts. The film is tone-deaf: we see a gag in which Clouseau parallel parks his tiny car in a huge space and rams both the police car behind him and another car in front of him. That's mildly amusing, but then he rams them twice more, just in case anyone was going out for popcorn the first time.

There's no plot to speak of—just a series of unconnected events that follow in linear fashion until the film's final revelations, which do not come out of a thoughtful script but simply out of thin air. There's nothing to prepare us for the notion that Clouseau has suddenly been transformed from idiot to idiot savant—he doesn't bumble into figuring out who the murderer is, he just suddenly becomes heroic, somehow.

Emily Mortimer is along for the ride as Clouseau's admiring secretary, Nicole, but we never know why she is attracted to the inspector—she's not mousy enough to be dying for attention, and she doesn't seem dumb enough to fall for his stupidity masquerading as cockiness. As Clouseau, Martin doesn't maintain a consistency in his character; when he is corrected by his assistant (Ponton played by Jean Reno), he sometimes ignores the information, and sometimes argues against it. Clive Owen appears in an uncredited cameo, and he's a breath of fresh air.

The idea, in one scene, that Clouseau could be playing both the good cop and the bad cop (not knowing they should be separate cops) is funny, and it's the kind of thing that fits with Martin's absurdist humor, but even this scene falls flat: it should have been played out to its illogical extreme. The same thing happens with a globe that Clouseau has unleashed from its moorings, and with a series of jokes about bicyclists crashing—both motifs should have kept going throughout the film. It's as if there's no confidence in the jokes here, so they don't get extended.

Sellers as Clouseau was endearing because he believed in himself, despite his incompetence. Martin plays Clouseau as a buffoon who is also arrogant and thus undeserving of anything but contempt. Kline is restrained but has nothing to do other than be the foil for Martin; he's too subtle a comic to work in this milieu. It's only the fact that, even in an off film, Martin is a very funny guy that saves this *Pink Panther* from the scrap heap. But Martin needs better material. This film has a paucity of ideas, and the ones it has are badly executed.

Michael Betzold

CREDITS

Clouseau: Steve Martin
Dreyfus: Kevin Kline
Ponton: Jean Reno
Nicole: Emily Mortimer
Yuri: Henry Czerny
Cherie: Kristin Chenoweth
Larocque: Roger Rees
Xania: Beyonce Knowles
Nigel Boswell: Clive Owen (Cameo, uncredited)
Origin: USA
Language: English
Released: 2006
Production: Robert Simonds; Metro-Goldwyn-Mayer Pictures, Columbia Pictures, Robert Simonds Production; released by Sony Pictures Entertainment
Directed by: Shawn Levy
Written by: Steve Martin, Len Blum
Cinematography by: Jonathan Brown, George Folsey Jr.
Music by: Christophe Beck, Randall Poster, Henry Mancini
Sound: Chris Carpenter, Andy Koyama
Editing: Brad E. White
Art Direction: Peter Rogness
Costumes: Joseph G. Aulisi
Production Design: Lily Kilvert
MPAA rating: PG
Running time: 92 minutes

REVIEWS

Boxoffice Online. February 10, 2006.
Chicago Sun-Times Online. February 10, 2006.

Entertainment Weekly Online. February 8, 2006.
Los Angeles Times Online. February 10, 2006.
New York Times Online. February 10, 2006.
Premiere Magazine Online. February 10, 2006.
Variety Online. February 4, 2006.
Washington Post Online. February 10, 2006.

QUOTES

Ponton: "You never cease to surprise me, sir."
Inspector Jacques Clouseau: "It's true. My surprises, they are rarely unexpected."

TRIVIA

Mike Myers and Kevin Spacey were both considered for the role of Inspector Clouseau, while Jackie Chan was considered for the part of Clouseau's assistant, Kato.

AWARDS

Nomination:

Golden Raspberries 2006: Worst Support. Actress (Chenoweth), Worst Remake

PIRATES OF THE CARIBBEAN: DEAD MAN'S CHEST

Captain Jack is back.
—Movie tagline

Box Office: $423.3 million

Taking in $55.5 million in ticket sales on its first day of release, *Pirates of the Caribbean: Dead Man's Chest* broke the opening day box office record previously held by *Star Wars III: Revenge of the Sith* (2005). By the end of the weekend, with $132.5 million in box office receipts, it had broken the three-day ticket sales record of *Spider-Man* (2002). It was pretty obvious that this sequel to *Pirates of the Caribbean: The Curse of the Black Pearl* (2003) had a built-in audience eager for the latest exploits of beautiful and spirited Elizabeth Swann (Keira Knightley), dashing young Will Turner (Orlando Bloom), and the foppishly funny Captain Jack Sparrow (Johnny Depp).

So what is the trio up to this time? Well, it may seem unnecessarily complicated, but it goes something like this. Captain Jack Sparrow has made a deal with Davy Jones, the Ruler of the Ocean Depths (Bill Nighy), and if he cannot get out of it he will be condemned to spend eternity serving Davy. The one way Jack can escape Davy's clutches is to find, naturally, Davy Jones' locker. Inside the locker is Davy's heart; put there because it was so badly broken by his love and he couldn't stand the pain. Because of this, however, Davy now feels nothing. It is said that whoever controls Davy Jones' heart controls Davy, and Davy controls the stealthiest and swiftest ship of the sea—the Flying Dutchman—and also the not-so-mythical, sea monster, the Kraken. However, in order to open the locker Jack first needs to find its key. To help him find the key, Jack uses a strange little compass that instead of pointing north always points in the direction of the holder's fondest desire. Unfortunately in the hands of the morally ambiguous Jack whose sole goal in life seems to be self-preservation and enrichment, the compass just flails about never offering Jack a heading for his ship, the Black Pearl, to set sail.

But there is someone else who is also on a Caribbean treasure hunt, Lord Cutler Beckett (Tom Hollander). Lord Beckett is in the employ of the powerful and exploitative East India Company and they know that if they could control the seas these prototype corporate raiders could reap more profit than any pirate ever dreamed of. Think how easy it would be to control the seas if there were no pirates, and how easy that would be if the Company controlled Davy Jones and the Kraken. Lord Beckett starts his search by trying to take possession of the one thing that will show him where Davy Jones's heart is, Jack's compass. Using his authority with the East India Company and backed by the power of the British crown, Beckett undertakes a truly underhanded tactic to acquire the compass: for what better way to locate the hard-to-find Jack than through his easy-to-find friends. Armed with warrants, Beckett has Will and Elizabeth arrested on their wedding day for their role in Jack's escape in the first movie. Their punishment is to be death unless Will helps Beckett find Jack and the compass.

While Elizabeth languishes in jail, Will goes in search of Jack while Jack is in search of the key, only to have Elizabeth escape from jail to go in search of Will. The hunt eventually takes the Black Pearl to an island inhabited by the Pelegostos, cannibals who mistake Jack for a god trapped in human form, and whom they plan to release from these bonds by roasting and eating Jack. But in the first of the movie's two great set pieces, his crew escapes from round cages made from the bones of previous meals that hang precariously over a gorge. Meanwhile, Jack makes his own escape even though he has been bound and suspended over a fire like a giant shish kebab.

After these escapes, and a slight side trip to visit the soothsayer Tia Dalma (Naomie Harris), Jack, Will, and the crew of the Black Pearl meet up with Davy Jones who has come to collect Jack's soul per their agreement.

But Jack offers a trade: one hundred souls in exchange for his one, beginning with Will's. Davy gives Jack three days to come up with the other ninety-nine and so the Black Pearl heads off to the lawless pirate port of Tortuga to enlist a few more "crew men" while Will acts as hostage on the Flying Dutchman. In port, Jack runs into Elizabeth and the disgraced, ex-Commodore Norrington (Jack Davenport) who was hopelessly in love with Elizabeth in the first film only to lose her to Will while also losing his prisoner Jack Sparrow. Norrington signs on with Jack and, along with Elizabeth, boards the Black Pearl. Elizabeth enlists in order to find Will, while Norrington is on a search of his own, for redemption, and he thinks he knows how to get it—bring the compass, key, or chest to the East India Company himself.

Meanwhile, back on the Flying Dutchman, Will has made two discoveries. The first is that his father, Bootstrap Bill Turner (Stellan Skarsgard), who was in Jack's crew in the original movie but never seen (he had been thrown overboard before the story started), is a crewmember on the Flying Dutchman and indentured to Davy Jones. The second discovery is where Davy keeps the key to his locker. With his father's help, Will steals the key and escapes. It is not long before everyone, including Davy's motley crew, is on the island where Davy's chest lay buried. Here we not only get multiple sword fights and chases, we get the film's second great set-piece, a sword fight atop and within a huge water wheel set loose from the mill to which it was attached that is now caroming around the island.

Unfortunately, there is no tidy wrap-up for *Pirates of the Caribbean: Dead Man's Chest*, but there is a double "ending" that is really a set up for *Pirates of the Caribbean: At World's End* (2007). In fact, *Dead Man's Chest* is barely a stand-alone movie. Without knowledge of the first film many of the characters and plot points may not be fully appreciated at best or may not make much sense at worst. Similarly, without the conclusion of the third film, one is left hanging at the end of this story. Although there are plenty of tantalizing questions left hanging, not the least of which is a kiss between Elizabeth and Jack that is witnessed by Will.

The first two parts of this trilogy—which was inspired by a ride at the Disney Amusement Parks that was in turn updated after the success of the first movie—have proven to be two genuine box office summer hits. After the incredible success of *Dead Man's Chest,* one can imagine Disney revamping the ride yet again, possibly to include a bungee drop in a round cage of bones. Its success also implies an eager first-weekend audience awaiting the release of the third installment, which was filmed concurrently with *Dead Man's Chest.*

While *Dead Man's Chest* is not as original as *The Curse of the Black Pearl,* and while it may have trouble standing on its own storywise, it still looks great, has a highly effective score, offers some very engaging characters doing lots of exciting things, and throws in some great special effects and some truly funny gags and quips. What more could one ask for in a summer movie?

Beverley Bare Buehrer

CREDITS

Jack Sparrow: Johnny Depp
Will Turner: Orlando Bloom
Elizabeth Swann: Keira Knightley
Bootstrap Bill Turner: Stellan Skarsgard
Davy Jones: Bill Nighy
Tia Dalma: Naomie Harris
Norrington: Jack Davenport
Gov. Weatherby Swann: Jonathan Pryce
Gibbs: Kevin McNally
Cutler Beckett: Tom Hollander
Ragetti: Mackenzie Crook
Pintel: Lee Arenberg
Captain Bellamy: Alex Norton
Cotton: David Bailie
Marty: Martin Klebba
Mercer: David Schofield
Origin: USA
Language: English
Released: 2006
Production: Jerry Bruckheimer; Walt Disney Pictures; released by Buena Vista
Directed by: Gore Verbinski
Written by: Ted Elliott, Terry Rossio
Cinematography by: Darius Wolski
Music by: Hans Zimmer
Sound: Lee Orloff
Editing: Craig Wood, Stephen E. Rivkin
Art Direction: William Ladd Skinner, Bruce Crone, William Hawkins
Costumes: Penny Rose
Production Design: Rick Heinrichs
MPAA rating: PG-13
Running time: 150 minutes

REVIEWS

Boxoffice Online. July 7, 2006.
Chicago Tribune Online. July 7, 2006.
Entertainment Weekly. July 14, 2006, p. 59.
Los Angeles Times Online. July 5, 2006.
New York Times Online. July 7, 2006.

Premiere Magazine Online. July 5, 2006.
San Francisco Chronicle. July 6, 2006, p. E1.
Variety Online. July 3, 2006.

QUOTES

Davy Jones to Jack Sparrow: "You owe me your soul. And it's time to pay up."

AWARDS

Oscars 2006: Visual FX
British Acad. 2006: Visual FX
Nomination:
Oscars 2006: Art Dir./Set Dec., Sound, Sound FX Editing
British Acad. 2006: Costume Des., Makeup, Sound
Golden Globes 2007: Actor—Mus./Comedy (Depp)

POSEIDON

Mayday...
—Movie tagline

Box Office: $60.6 million

New Year's Eve aboard the luxury cruise ship *Poseidon* will not mark the beginning of a happy year for almost all of its passengers and crew, for as the countdown begins and the traditional songs are sung, a 150-foot rogue wave is blocking out the midnight moon. The ship's crew desperately tries to swing the ship about to meet it head on, but there is not enough time. Soon the celebration turns to tragedy as the ship is pitched onto its port side and then turned completely upside down, lethally tossing about people and objects, large and small, like socks in a clothes dryer. When the panic subsides slightly, the *Poseidon*'s captain (Andre Braugher), who had been leading the toast in the ship's oddly small main ballroom, along with the nightclub singer Gloria (Black Eyed Peas' Stacy "Fergie" Ferguson, looking extremely out of place in an evening gown), assures his panicked passengers that an automatic distress and GPS system will soon have rescuers there.

But there are some who won't wait to be rescued and feel they must take action for themselves. These are the characters we will follow through the rest of the story. Unfortunately, these are also characters that director Wolfgang Petersen and screenwriter Mark Protosevich spend so little time and effort introducing that most people won't really care who makes it out and who won't. And this, of course, becomes a problem when one of the main reasons to watch this type of disaster movie is the game of trying to determine who will live, who will die, in what order, and how.

These characters are typical disaster film stereotypes and are introduced to us almost in code. We are offered a situation, a bit of dialogue, a piece of clothing that tells us immediately who this cardboard cutout is. In *Poseidon* we will travel to the bottom of the ship—all or part of the way—with the following characters. The reluctant leader is professional cruise ship gambler and ex-navy man Dylan Johns (Josh Lucas) who, obviously, will redeem himself by the end of the movie. Firmly attached to Dylan is nine-year-old Conor (Jimmy Bennett) who desperately demands that Dylan save him and his single mom Maggie (Jacinda Barrett) too. Predictably Conor will eventually disobey his mother, wander off, and put his own and other lives in jeopardy. (Why is it that the kids never die in these kinds of movies?) To help them navigate the ship's interior, they enlist the aid of crew member Valentin (Freddy Rodriguez). Tagging along is Richard Nelson (Richard Dreyfuss) a gay architect who has just been jilted by his long-time lover and was about to commit suicide by jumping over the ship's rail when he saw the wave coming and ran back inside. Why? So now they not only have a crew member to map out the ship, they have a navy man to explain how the ship works, and they've got an architect to tell them about the ship's structure. Could things get any more convenient for the plot?

Absolutely, because they are joined by Robert Ramsey (Kurt Russell) who is desperately trying to get to the floor below/above them to the disco where his nineteen-year-old daughter Jennifer (Emmy Rossum) and her boyfriend Christian (Mike Vogel) have been dancing in the New Year. And by the way, Robert is an ex-mayor of New York City who also just happens to be an ex-fireman, which is another incredibly convenient source of knowledge on a ship that is burning, as well as possibly sinking. Oh, and pretty predictably Jennifer and Christian are engaged but afraid to tell her overprotective father. The lovers' immediate problem before Daddy arrives, however, is that Christian is trapped under a heavy piece of metal that Jennifer can't budge and electrical wires all around them are zapping in the water and electrocuting people at random. Jennifer gets some help from Elena (Mia Maestro) who has been traveling as a stowaway with Valentin's help because she can't afford the cost of returning to New York to be with her hospitalized brother. But even these two women can't lift the debris until helped by Lucky Larry (Kevin Dillon), a gambler, drunk and all round unlikable and annoying guy and surely one of the first to die...we hope.

So now the cast of characters is complete and the game begins as we watch them fight the rising water, the sneaky fires, the floating bodies, the upside-down topography, the debris-clogged passageways, and the groans and shudders of the dying ship. We watch them fight panic and fear and claustrophobia. We see them rise to the occasion and fall, helping each other...and it's hard to care all that much about them. Even the special effects just wash over a viewer as just another event to passively observe.

Thankfully, this remake of the 1972 original *The Poseidon Adventure*—which actually isn't so much a remake as a superimposing of new characters onto the original situation—saves us from its predictability by tipping the ship over quickly and keeping to a short running time of ninety-nine minutes. This allows the story to move along at a steady pace while fear of boredom never sinks a basically cursory interest in the fate of the characters.

Beverley Bare Buehrer

CREDITS

Dylan Johns: Josh Lucas
Robert Ramsey: Kurt Russell
Jennifer Ramsey: Emmy Rossum
Maggie James: Jacinda Barrett
Conor James: Jimmy Bennett
Elena: Mia Maestro
Captain Bradford: Andre Braugher
Richard Nelson: Richard Dreyfuss
Christian: Mike Vogel
Lucky Larry: Kevin Dillon
Velentin: Freddy Rodriguez
Gloria: Stacy Ferguson
Origin: USA
Language: English
Released: 2006
Production: Wolfgang Petersen, Duncan Henderson, Mike Fleiss, Akiva Goldsman; Virtual Studios, Radiant/Next Entertainment/Irwin Allen Prods./Synthesis Entertainment; released by Warner Bros.
Directed by: Wolfgang Petersen
Written by: Mark Protosevich
Cinematography by: John Seale
Music by: Klaus Badelt
Sound: David M. Kelson
Editing: Peter Honess
Art Direction: Luke Freeborn, Desma Murphy
Costumes: Erica Edell Phillips
Production Design: William Sandell
MPAA rating: PG-13
Running time: 99 minutes

REVIEWS

Boxoffice Online. May 12, 2006.
Chicago Sun-Times Online. May 11, 2006.
Entertainment Weekly Online. May 10, 2006.
Los Angeles Times Online. May 12, 2006.
New York Times Online. May 12, 2006.
Premiere Magazine Online. May 11, 2006.
Variety Online. May 7, 2006.
Washington Post. May 12, 2006, p. C1.

QUOTES

Robert Ramsey: "There's nothing fair about who lives and who dies."

TRIVIA

Two separate sound stages at Warner Bros. studios were used to film the interior shots of the ship. One set had the ballroom built right-side-up, the other identical set was built upside-down. The upside-down set was built on top of a large water tank that allowed it to be filled with water and drained in a matter of hours.

AWARDS

Nomination:
Oscars 2006: Visual FX
Golden Raspberries 2006: Worst Remake

POSTER BOY

The Conservative Agenda Now Has a Gay Son.
—Movie tagline

Poster Boy is dedicated to Herbert Ross, who died in 2001, and who was originally slated to direct an earlier version of the film. Instead, this 2004 release slowly made its way through the festival circuit and is the directorial debut of film editor Zak Tucker. It is a diffuse story, filled with annoyingly jumpy, hand-held camerawork, whose message is dissipated by some extraneous characters and contrivances that take the focus off the Kray family.

It opens with journalist Jack Brauer (Sheff Stevens) arranging an interview in New York with Henry Kray (Matt Newton), the nineteen-year-old son of Jack Kray (Michael Lerner). Brauer wants Henry to tell him about the "incident" that happened six months earlier as his father, an arch-conservative senator from North Carolina, was in the midst of a too-close re-election campaign and expecting his son to be the poster child for his campaign. The film alternates between their interview and the events, with some connecting scenes that Henry could know nothing about. Henry explains that he is not doing the interview to get back at his father and that they have not spoken since that November.

Senator Kray and his long-suffering wife Eunice (Karen Allen) are in Manhattan to meet with Henry, who is a student at liberal Barken College. The Senator is giving a speech at the college to rally the youth vote and wants his son to introduce him. Why a speech at a New York college will help the re-election campaign of a North Carolina senator is anyone's guess—maybe the press coverage is intended to impress the folks back home. Eunice warns her bullying husband that Henry is "sensitive" and "doesn't have the taste for blood that you do." After being pressured by his father, Henry reluctantly agrees to do his bidding. When the Senator leaves the hotel, he runs into a gay activist protest and Anthony (Jack Noseworthy), who will soon figure into the story more prominently.

Anthony is in his late-twenties; he shares an apartment with best friend, Izzie (Valerie Geffner), who swallows anti-depressants like candy pills. She is HIV-positive from a boyfriend who has died. Anthony has turned to political activism to fill the loneliness in his own life. Meanwhile, Henry has skipped out of town and headed to the family's vacation house in Palm Springs. Eunice, who is not above manipulation herself, sends eager young Republican Skip (Ian Reed Kessler), a fellow student at Barken, to retrieve her errant son. When Henry refuses, Skip threatens him: "I will tell your father that you are a fag." A cynical Henry retaliates by taking the conservative young man to a gay nightclub but does return with him.

Anthony and Izzie go out for the evening and decide to crash a college party at Barken. Anthony sees Henry, thinks he's cute, and makes his move without knowing who he is. Henry, who's out at college, spends the night with him. Anthony discovers Henry's identity the next morning when he is confronted by a campus activist. The young man has a "booty chart" detailing Henry's campus conquests and wants to add Anthony's name. When Anthony meets up with Izzie, he tells her he wants to stay on campus: "What do you think Mr. Family Values would do if he knew his son was a friend of Dorothy's?" Izzie doesn't care and is angry that Anthony would cavalierly mess up someone else's life. Izzie wanders oblivious after their fight and walks in front of the Senator's limo. A concerned Eunice takes Izzie with them and looks after her.

Anthony meets with the campus protest group and tells them that in order to hurt the Senator, they need to attack what he cares most about, which he believes is Kray's family. Anthony tracks down Henry and appears sympathetic when Henry tells him that he "just wants to disappear." Henry tells the journalist (in regards to his father): "As long as I played the good son—went along—played invisible, then at least we had a relationship. Maybe not the best one, but I could pretend."

In the meantime, one of Kray's flunkies has discovered the protesters have placed copies of the booty chart around campus. After bringing the chart to the Senator's attention, he points out that the names Henry is linked to are all male. Henry and Anthony get drunk together and Henry tells Anthony to come with him to the speech. The journalist thinks Henry did this deliberately to end the charade but Henry, who has previously told Brauer that his father is addicted to politics, replies that everything in his father's life is "subservient to politics, even his own prejudices." That all that would matter to him was how the campaign would be affected if the fact that Henry was gay were revealed.

Izzie comes to the speech and sits next to Eunice while Henry insists that Anthony join him on the dais even as Anthony tries to tell Henry the truth about himself. Henry begins to read the introductory speech that has been written for him about his father's family values. Disgusted by the lies, Henry hesitates and abruptly ends his remarks. The Senator then takes over and announces that Henry is leaving school to join his political campaign. Furious with his father's high-handedness, Henry stands and pulls Anthony into a long kiss, which causes a media commotion. When they have all been hustled into a quieter location, Senator Kray is ready to spin the incident: "Jack Kray's gay son is part of the new American family." Henry refuses to follow his lead anymore. Later, Eunice is furious when her husband won't call Henry and walks out on him after stating "I hate this pathetic life of ours."

After conferring with Izzie, Anthony tracks Henry down and apologizes for his deception. Henry's more upset that he outed himself: "I was totally invisible.... What I blew, Anthony, was my cover." The next morning they part and the film ends with Henry and the journalist concluding their interview. His father squeaked out a campaign win: "I think the kiss put him over. His cronies probably felt really sorry for him." He hasn't kept in contact with Anthony but he does know that Izzie has died; Henry's mother attended the funeral. Finally, Henry tells Brauer: "Where does that leave my father and me? Well, I don't have to look over my shoulder anymore."

Poster Boy makes some valid points about the divisiveness of American politics. Henry reiterates to his interviewer that a cause cannot be just if it pits people against each other. He may be scared of his father but he also wants to be part of a family. Henry has managed to divide himself between being an out gay young man and being the "poster boy" his father wants. But he can't do it anymore; he doesn't trust anyone and his deceptions are destroying him. In the end, he loses his father but is at least trying to live honestly with himself. *Poster*

Boy has some good performances by Newton, Allen, and a scarily effective Lerner but loses momentum when it turns away from the family drama at its heart.

Christine Tomassini

CREDITS

Henry Kray: Matt Newton
Eunice Kray: Karen Allen
Jack Kray: Michael Lerner
Anthony: Jack Noseworthy
Izzie: Valerie Geffner
Skip: Ian Reed Kesler
Jack Brauer: Sheff Stevens
Origin: USA
Language: English
Released: 2004
Production: Stanley F. Buchtal, Dolly Hall, Rebecca Chaiklin, Jeff Campagna; Shallow Pictures; released by Regent Releasing
Directed by: Zak Tucker
Written by: Ryan Shiraki, Lecia Rosenthal
Cinematography by: Wolfgang Held
Music by: Mark Garcia
Sound: Dan Ferat
Music Supervisor: Jim Black
Editing: Pamela Scott Arnold
Art Direction: Miguel Alvarez
Costumes: Doug Hall
Production Design: Doug Hall
MPAA rating: R
Running time: 98 minutes

REVIEWS

Los Angeles Times Online. August 11, 2006.
New York Times Online. August 18, 2006.
San Francisco Chronicle. August 18, 2006, p. E5.
Variety Online. May 5, 2004.
Village Voice Online. August 15, 2006.
Washington Post Online. August 25, 2006.

QUOTES

Anthony (about Henry's conservative father): "What do you think 'Mr. Family Values' would do if he knew his son was a 'friend of Dorothy's'?"

A PRAIRIE HOME COMPANION

Radio like you've never seen it before.
—Movie tagline

Live every show like it's your last.
—Movie tagline

Box Office: $20.3 million

Director Robert Altman was eighty years old when he made this melancholy, folksy feature (his thirty-eighth), an adaptation of Garrison Keillor's public radio variety show that began airing in 1974. Altman shot it at the Fitzgerald Theater in St. Paul, Minnesota, where the actual show is produced. Besides Keillor as master of ceremonies, the film version features a number of the show's stock company, including the house band, singer Jearlyn Steele, sound effects man Tom Keith, Sue Scott (who plays the make-up lady), and Tim Russell (as the harried stage manager). Keillor's script also brings to visual life some of the characters that have been part of the program over the years. Viewers may get more out of the film if they are also fans of the radio show, or they may find it disconcerting to see pulp P.I. parody Guy Noir personified as Kevin Kline in 1940s attire.

Guy starts us off as the narrator, sitting in Mickey's Diner (an actual diner that frames the film) having dinner before crossing the street for his last night as the theater's security guard. He informs us that the show is shutting down and the theater has been sold to a Texas conglomerate that is turning the property into a parking lot. But no one really wants to admit that. It is a Midwestern attribute Guy believes: "If you ignore bad news, it might go away." Backstage everything is in chaos as the performers get ready, and Keillor (known as GK) works on his script, which he will frequently ignore much to the exasperation of very pregnant stage hand Molly (Maya Rudolph). GK, with his bulldog face, trademark suit, red tie, and sneakers, is so busy telling his yarns that he can barely make it onstage on time.

Everybody is busy reminiscing and planning what they will do this last night. Included are the Johnson Girls, Yolanda (Meryl Streep) and Rhonda (Lily Tomlin), middle-aged sisters who are the survivors of a four-sister act. Yolanda is sweet and ditzy while Rhonda is more practical—she is going to get through the trying night by sipping liquor from her coffee cup. Accompanying them is Lola (Lindsay Lohan), Yolanda's impatient daughter who writes poems about suicide. The sisters fondly invoke their hard-working mama, who only smiled when the girls sang, and what happened to poor sister Wanda, who was jailed for accidentally shoplifting a donut, which ruined their reputation in the Christian market and lead to the fatal heart attack of their father.

The program's other (unrelated) duo are cowboy singer/comedians Dusty (Woody Harrelson) and Lefty (John C. Reilly), who grumble about each other's personal habits and perform somewhat risque material to the horror of the stage manager. Then there is old-timer Chuck Akers (L.Q. Jones), a raffish fellow having a backstage romance with the cheerful sandwich lady (Marylouise Burke). Little does Chuck know that this will indeed be his last performance. It seems that the mysterious blonde in the white trench coat who has been wandering about backstage—much to Guy's consternation—is literally the angel of death (she is known in the credits as "Dangerous Woman" and played by Virginia Madsen). Unfortunately, this is one conceit that does not work well at all, especially since the angel is given to portentous pronouncements.

And so *A Prairie Home Companion* meanders along, cross-cutting between backstage and onstage dramas—missed cues, forgotten lyrics, dropped script pages. Chuck suffers a fatal heart attack, but GK, who does not want to tell the audience that this is the show's last performance, also does not want to acknowledge the singer's death on air: "I'm of an age when if I started to do eulogies, I'd be doing nothing else" (Keillor is sixty years old). The lovely Yolanda, with her girlish voice and mannerisms, is still upset that a brief romance with GK did not work out and is not afraid to mention the subject while onstage singing (the actors all do their own vocals). The angel sits with GK backstage, informing him that she was once a listener of the program who laughed so hard at a joke while driving that the car went off the road in a fatal accident. She has done her job by escorting Chuck from this mortal coil, but she sticks around to hear the rest of the program. This is a good thing, especially when the dour Axeman (Tommy Lee Jones) shows up near the close.

Axeman is the hatchet man for the Texas corporation that bought the theater. Guy thinks it would be nice if the angel happened to pay Axeman a little visit. She does, and Axeman dies in a car wreck. However, as Guy says, it did not change anything—the theater is still torn down. Before that happens, though, Lola is forced onstage to vamp a peculiar version of "Frankie and Johnny" (the show is short by six minutes) with everyone cheering her on. Viewers see a final scene in the diner with the Johnson sisters, GK, Lefty, Dusty, and possibly Guy all planning for a farewell tour: Yolanda has bought a bus and they will visit all the little towns where their faithful listeners reside. The angel watches from the doorway. While the credits roll, viewers return to the theater for a rousing send-off of "Red River Valley" by the entire group.

The characters of *A Prairie Home Companion* are nice people and it is relaxing to spend a couple of hours in their company listening to old songs, bad jokes, rambling stories, and commercials for such things as rhubarb pie, pickled herring, biscuits, and duct tape. Keillor has a soothing baritone voice made for the radio and is not afraid to take his time or repeat himself. The rest of the cast are equally relaxed and charming. What could be better on a rainy Saturday night than singing and storytelling amongst old friends?

Christine Tomassini

CREDITS

Yolanda Johnson: Meryl Streep
Rhonda Johnson: Lily Tomlin
Lola Johnson: Lindsay Lohan
Dusty: Woody Harrelson
Lefty: John C. Reilly
Guy Noir: Kevin Kline
Axeman: Tommy Lee Jones
Chuck Akers: L.Q. Jones
Dangerous Woman: Virginia Madsen
Molly: Maya Rudolph
Lunch Lady: Marylouise Burke
GK: Garrison Keillor
Origin: USA
Language: English
Released: 2006
Production: Robert Altman, Joshua Astrachan, Wren Arthur, David Levy, Tony Judge; GreeneStreet Films, River Road Productions, Sandcastle 5 Productions, Prairie Home Production; released by Picturehouse
Directed by: Robert Altman
Written by: Garrison Keillor
Cinematography by: Edward Lachman
Sound: Drew Kunin
Editing: Jacob Craycroft
Art Direction: Jeffrey Schoen
Costumes: Catherine Thomas
Production Design: Dina Goldman
MPAA rating: PG-13
Running time: 105 minutes

REVIEWS

Boxoffice Online. June 9, 2006.
Chicago Sun-Times Online. June 9, 2006.
Entertainment Weekly Online. June 7, 2006.
Los Angeles Times Online. June 9, 2006.
New York Times Online. June 9, 2006.
Premiere Magazine Online. June 5, 2006.
Variety Online. February 12, 2006.
Washington Post. June 9, 2006, p. C5.

QUOTES

Garrison Keillor: "We come from people who brought us up to believe that life is a struggle, and if you should feel really happy, be patient: this will pass."

TRIVIA

Tom Waits and Lyle Lovett were originally cast as singing cowboys Lefty and Dusty.

AWARDS

Nomination:

Ind. Spirit 2007: Director (Altman)

THE PRESTIGE

Are you watching closely?
—Movie tagline

Box Office: $53 million

Christopher Priest's *The Prestige* is a complex, sometimes challenging period novel employing multiple narrators, a modern-day framing device, and shifts back and forth in time to tell the story of a deadly feud between rival magicians in turn-of-the-century England. These are not mere entertainers passing time on the vaudeville circuit but rather serious artists committed to inventing new illusions that will push the art form into new realms. The film version embraces this vision of magic as a total way of life as well as the novel's enthralling mix of mystery, romance, and even science fiction yet deftly takes liberties with its overall conception.

Adapting the work with his brother Jonathan, director Christopher Nolan has streamlined and even reimagined the narrative, discarding the contemporary characters and drastically reworking the central plotline but retaining its playful, mysterious, and even macabre essence. It is a stunning example of how, by not being faithful to every plot device and ancillary character and by simplifying a sprawling work without dumbing it down, the result can be a suspenseful, entertaining thriller true to the spirit of its source.

The film simultaneously develops several timelines that, when taken together, tell one compelling tale. In the first narrative strand, Alfred Borden (Christian Bale) is on trial for the murder of fellow magician Robert Angier (Hugh Jackman), who drowned in a water tank during one of his shows, while Borden, who had infiltrated the performance space, looked on. The second strand takes place before the murder and focuses on Angier's journey to Colorado Springs in America to seek the help of maverick scientist and inventor Nikola Tesla (an unrecognizable, beguiling David Bowie). The final narrative piece takes us back to the beginning of the magicians' relationship, to a time when the two men were friends and worked together as apprentices to Milton (Ricky Jay, a real-life magician who also served as an advisor on the movie). When Julia (Piper Perabo), Milton's assistant and Angier's wife, dies in a freak accident onstage, Angier holds Borden responsible, thus beginning a lifelong feud, which becomes the film's central conflict.

While the rival magicians do their best to disrupt and sabotage each other's acts and even go so far as to hurt each other (Angier maims Borden's hand during a bullet trick), their main arena for one-upmanship becomes "The Transported Man," an illusion in which Borden enters a cabinet on one side of the stage, closes the door, and emerges almost instantaneously from a second cabinet just a few feet away. It is a highly acclaimed trick and one that Angier is desperate to discover the solution to. He goes so far as to send his lovely assistant, Olivia (Scarlett Johansson), to work for Borden as a spy. The ploy appears to pay off when Angier obtains Borden's journal and embarks on a journey to meet Tesla. His breakthroughs in electricity enable Angier to outdo Borden with an illusion called "The Real Transported Man," in which Angier seems to be able to move himself across the auditorium via this revolutionary source of power.

The screenplay freely moves among its timelines and requires the close attention of the viewer to keep the various plot strands in their proper place. Helping to unify the story is Cutter (Michael Caine), Angier's confidant, manager, and designer of illusions, who gives the audience a kind of entry point into this complicated world. Caine brings an avuncular sincerity to the part, which is crucial since the two main characters often allow their single-minded passion for magic and revenge to override their humanity.

Indeed, both men are driven to the point where they allow the people in their orbit, especially the women, to be hurt. Although Angier supposedly loves Olivia, he has no problem using her to get Borden's secrets. Johansson, incidentally, makes the most of the familiar part of the magician's assistant, caught in the middle but exhibiting her own spunk and sense of independence. And when Borden falls for Olivia, his devoted wife, Sarah (Rebecca Hall), ends up heartbroken, ultimately being driven to suicide.

Jackman is great as the debonair Angier, who seems to be touched with a bit of madness, especially in his overweening quest for vengeance and obsession to create the ultimate illusion. Bale matches him as the scrappier Borden, who is more aloof but just as devious. Both are committed to their art, but the magnetic Angier is the charming, dashing showman with an aristocratic bearing, while Borden comes across as a lower-class striver with a chip on his shoulder and something to prove. Borden may be the more challenging role because it is hard to pinpoint his motives, and only at the end can we appreciate the complexity of the part. For much of the film, he seems to be the villain, but Bale effectively balances the scoundrel and showman with the qualities of a loving father trying to protect the fate of his daughter, Jess (Samantha Mahurin), as he awaits his execution.

The denouement consists of a series of revelations and reversals that cast a new light on what we have already seen. Angier, we finally learn, is not dead and has a second identity as Lord Cordlow, the man who, working behind the scenes, has succeeded in buying Borden's magic equipment before he hangs. Angier also takes custody of Jess after Borden's execution, saving her from an orphanage but also getting revenge by taking the thing most dear to his adversary. The next big twist, however, is that Borden has a twin brother, who was the secret to "The Transported Man" and has been in disguise as Fallon, his loyal assistant. One brother loved Sarah, and the other loved Olivia, but they each had to live essentially half a life and keep their identities secret even to those they loved in order to maintain the integrity of their act. These magicians are, in some weird way, the original Method actors, assuming a role so completely that they live it even when they are not onstage.

The surviving Borden brother kills Angier, who has an even more shocking secret. Every time he performed "The Real Transported Man," the electrical apparatus made a copy of him so that, as a result of the trick, a duplicate Angier had to perish in the water tank. In a creepy ending, we see rows of tanks of Angiers, while Borden, on a happier note, is reunited with Jess. All of these disclosures are a lot to digest, especially since they come very rapidly, but, for the alert moviegoer, the delight is thinking back over the movie and figuring out how all of the pieces fit together.

The Prestige is especially suited to director Christopher Nolan, whose brooding films, from his art house puzzler *Memento* (2001) to his acclaimed blockbuster *Batman Begins* (2005), revolve around the slippery nature of identity and tortured souls seeking revenge. Nolan takes these dark themes into a mysterious, ultimately otherworldly place in *The Prestige* and does it with such style and panache, including stunning visuals by cinematographer Wally Pfister and gorgeous production design by Nathan Crowley, that being fooled at the hands of such a cinematic magician becomes a huge part of the fun.

Peter N. Chumo II

CREDITS

Alfred Borden: Christian Bale
Robert Angier: Hugh Jackman
Cutter: Michael Caine
Olivia: Scarlett Johansson
Julia: Piper Perabo
Sarah: Rebecca Hall
Nikola Tesla: David Bowie
Milton: Ricky Jay
Jess Borden: Samantha Mahurin
Alley: Andy Serkis
Owens: Roger Rees
Origin: Great Britain, USA
Language: English
Released: 2006
Production: Emma Thomas, Aaron Ryder, Christopher Nolan; Newmarket Films, Syncopy, Warner Bros., Touchstone Pictures; released by Buena Vista
Directed by: Christopher Nolan
Written by: Christopher Nolan, Jonathan Nolan
Cinematography by: Wally Pfister
Music by: David Julyan
Sound: Richard King
Editing: Lee Smith
Art Direction: Kevin Kavanaugh
Costumes: Joan Bergin
Production Design: Nathan Crowley
MPAA rating: PG-13
Running time: 128 minutes

REVIEWS

Boxoffice Online. October 20, 2006.
Chicago Sun-Times Online. October 20, 2006.
Detroit Free Press Online. October 20, 2006.
Detroit News. October 20, 2006, p. 5F.
Entertainment Weekly. October 27, 2006, p. 54.
Hollywood Reporter Online. October 16, 2006.
Los Angeles Times Online. October 20, 2006.
New York Times Online. October 20, 2006.
Premiere Magazine Online. October 19, 2006.
San Francisco Chronicle. October 20, 2006, p. E5.
USA Today Online. October 20, 2006.
Variety Online. October 13, 2006.
Village Voice Online. October 17, 2006.
Washington Post. October 20, 2006, p. C6.

QUOTES

Alfred: "A real magician invents something new."

Cutter (referring to Alfred): "He can do what magicians pretend to do."

TRIVIA

Christian Bale and Michael Caine were also co-stars in Christopher Nolan's *Batman Begins* (2005), while Hugh

Jackman and Scarlett Johansson co-starred in Woody Allen's *Scoop* (2006).

AWARDS

Nomination:

Oscars 2006: Art Dir./Set Dec., Cinematog

THE PROMISE
(Wu ji)
(Master of the Crimson Armor)

Since bursting onto the international film scene with *Farewell, My Concubine* (1993), Chinese writer-director Chen Kaige has struggled to match the critical and commercial success of his biggest hit. Chen has tried erotic romance with *Temptress Moon* (1996) and his ill-fated English-language debut, *Killing Me Softly* (2002), epic adventure with *The Emperor and the Assassin* (1999), and a smaller, more personal film with *Together* (2002).

While his more esteemed countryman Zhang Yimou is able to move back and forth with ease between intimate films and spectacles, Chen, with the notable exception of *Together*, seems to stumble a bit with each new effort. *The Promise* seems to be an attempt to match Zhang's wondrous *House of Flying Daggers* (2004), blending action, visual splendor, and romance, but what emerges seems ill-conceived and clumsily executed.

The Promise is a fable; it begins by introducing two of the protagonists as children, the only survivors of a massive battle. The girl, an orphan, is told by the Goddess Manshen (Chen Hong) that she will have a life of wealth and power but will not be able to love unless she learns how to bring the dead back to life by turning back time. Twenty years later, the girl has grown to be Qingcheng (Cecilia Cheung), who lives with a ruthless king (Cheng Qian). The king's enemy Wuhuan (Nicholas Tse) plans to assassinate him. General Guangming (Hiroyuki Sanada) is the only one who can save the king, but the general is injured and sends the slave Kunlun (Jang Dong-gun) in disguise. Kunlun sees the king about to throw Qingcheng off a roof and kills the ruler to save her. Thinking her masked rescuer is the general, Qingcheng falls for him.

The rest of *The Promise* deals with the consequences of the deception, with more confusions about identity. The general falls for Qingcheng and continues to let her believe he was her savior. Qingcheng, Kunlun, and Guangming take turns being the prisoner of the evil Wuhuan, who sends Snow Wolf (Liu Yeh) to kill the slave only for Kunlun to befriend his would-be assassin.

The Promise is a fantasy set in no definite period. Given the costumes, swords, and arrows, it seems to occur in the distant past, although Chen has said in interviews that it takes place three thousand years in the future. The plot serves merely as an excuse for Chen's visual embellishments, the real heart of the film. At $40 million, *The Promise* is the most expensive film ever made in China and was a hit there, trailing only *Titanic* (1997) and Zhang's *Hero* (2002) at the box office.

Less money appears to have been spent on sets and costumes than on special effects. Kunlun's greatest skill is his immense speed, and much of the film involves his running away from foes. In what should be a spectacular sequence which introduces the slave and the general, Wuhuan sends a tremendous herd of bulls to trample Guangming's soldiers. Kunlun runs in front of the rampaging beasts, turning them back into the enemy.

Alas, the computer-generated imagery (CGI) is not that realistic, and the entire episode, as well as several later scenes, is cartoonish. *The Promise* resembles a Japanese anime fantasy but lacks that genre's inventiveness, style, and charm. Anime master Hayao Miyazaki would never attempt a project with such a simplistic plot and poorly developed characters.

Every man she encounters goes crazy for Qingcheng, but it is difficult to see why. Cheung's performance consists of poses and coy glances. There is no passion or life of any sort in her character. A popular Korean singer, Jang, who resembles the great Yun-Fat Chow, star of *Crouching Tiger, Hidden Dragon* (2000), gives Kunlun two emotions: blank stoicism and quivering fear. Although used to life as a slave, Kunlun seems to cower when he doesn't need to. Sanada, so much better in James Ivory's *The White Countess* (2005), also makes the general a two-note character, either bold or confused. The actors, however, are mostly victims of Chen's screenplay, which allows for no nuances of characters. The one exception is Tse, whose father, Yin Tse, appears in *Temptress Moon.* He gives Wuhuan an unpredictable slyness.

Music is important in Chen's films: the opera of *Farewell, My Concubine*, the blind banjo player of *Life on a String* (1991), the violin prodigy of *Together,* and the folk songs of mountain villages in *Yellow Earth* (1984). While the score by Klaus Badelt includes some Chinese motifs, echoing *Yellow Earth,* especially toward the end, most of his music is big-budget Hollywood noise that punctuates the obvious. Badelt, fittingly, is the composer for *Pirates of the Caribbean: The Curse of the Black Pearl* (2003) and *Poseidon* (2006).

While the CGI of *The Promise* is often disappointing, the costumes, especially Snow Wolf's black feathered cloak, and sets of Tim Yip, art direction Oscar® winner for *Crouching Tiger, Hidden Dragon,* are the film's most striking qualities. Another *Crouching Tiger, Hidden Dragon* veteran, cinematographer Peter Pau, provides bright images, with lots of reds and greens. *The Promise* is the kind of film in which some viewers will find themselves admiring the flowers in the background of a scene more than on what they are supposed to be focusing.

Michael Adams

CREDITS

General Guangming: Hiroyuki Sanada
Kunlun: Jang Dong-gun
Qingcheng: Cecilia Cheung
Wuhuan: Nicholas Tse
Snow Wolf: Liu Yeh
Goddess Manshen: Chen Hong
One-eye: Qian Bo
Yeli: Yu Xiaowei
King: Cheng Qian
Origin: China, USA
Language: Chinese
Released: 2005
Production: Etchie Stroh, Chen Hong, Han San Ping; Moonstone Entertainment, Beijing 21st Century/Shengkai/China Film Group/Capgen Investment Group/Moonstone Prods.
Directed by: Chen Kaige, Zhang Tan
Written by: Chen Kaige
Cinematography by: Peter Pau
Music by: Klaus Badelt
Production Design: Tim Yip
MPAA rating: PG-13
Running time: 103 minutes

REVIEWS

Boxoffice Online. May 5, 2006.
Chicago Sun-Times Online. May 5, 2006.
Entertainment Weekly Online. May 3, 2006.
Los Angeles Times Online. May 5, 2006.
New York Times Online. May 5, 2006.
Variety Online. December 29, 2005.
Washington Post. May 5, 2006, p. C5.

QUOTES

Goddess Manchen: "Once you have accepted your destiny, nothing can alter it unless time flows backwards, snow falls in the spring, and the dead come back to life."

TRIVIA

Cost an estimated $40 million to produce, and is the biggest-budget Chinese film to date.

THE PROPOSITION

This land will be civilized.
—Movie tagline

Box Office: $1.9 million

The Australian western *The Proposition* is a gritty, tough, bloody, achingly beautiful, and unique motion picture. Not since the heyday of Sam Peckinpah has a director combined brutality and lyricism in such a compelling way, but unlike Peckinpah, director John Hillcoat isn't rubbing his audience's faces in gratuitous violence, and neither is he making the violence itself into an elegiac spectacle. The brutal scenes are simply part of the stark reality of the Australian outback in the 1880s and the battle for control taking place between British authorities, Irish outlaws, and aborigines.

Songwriter Nick Cave wrote the script, as well as providing a song that literally haunts the film, as its lyrics are whispered in the background of many scenes. Cave worked with Hillcoat once before, collaborating with him on the screenplay for the 1998 prison picture *Ghosts...of the Civil Dead.* But while that film garnered bad reviews, *The Proposition* was deservedly highly praised by critics, though it received only belated and limited theatrical release in the United States.

It is a work of great daring and craftsmanship, challenging but absolutely mesmerizing. It takes many of the motifs of American Westerns and makes them much more stark and unforgiving. The movie literally opens with a blast: the protagonist, Charlie Burns (Guy Pearce), is stumbling around a shack and fending off a storm of bullets coming through the windows and tin walls. Within a few seconds, two Chinese prostitutes lay dead, and Charlie's younger brother Mikey (Richard Wilson) is wounded. In the next scene, the two brothers are sitting at a table in the shack, with light streaming through dozens of bullet holes in the walls, as their attacker, Captain Morris Stanley (Ray Winstone), quietly and calmly makes Charlie a proposition. By Christmas Day, nine days hence, he vows to hang Mikey by the neck for his role in the slaughter of a pioneer family. The only way to prevent Mikey's death, Stanley says, is for Charlie to hunt down and kill his brother Arthur (Danny Huston), who is the monstrous mastermind of the gang of outlaws that until recently included all three brothers. Charlie, weary of bloodshed, has recently forsaken Arthur and taken Mikey with him to protect him from further violence.

Charlie doesn't like it, but he has little choice; he doesn't want his little brother to hang. Given a horse and a gun by Stanley, he sets off for the wild ridges where Arthur and the rest of the gang are hiding out. Meanwhile Mikey is imprisoned in the frontier town, which is nothing more than a few buildings stuck up in the desert. The spare set makes the typical frontier town of movie westerns look palatial; there are no sidewalks, streets, or connected buildings, just a structure here and there, all of them liable to blow down in a storm.

On the edge of town live Stanley and his genteel British wife Martha (Emily Watson). She is trying to make a home out of this godforsaken posting, and Captain Stanley is trying to tame the place so she has a chance at again living in civilization. Their home is surrounded by a fenced garden full of roses, and beyond that is a limited expanse of vacant, treeless frontier that stretches to the horizon. Martha's life has been shattered by the Burns gang's violence; the wife and mother killed in their nearby massacre was her closest friend. She gradually learns her husband has taken the law into his own hands, when she overhears wealthy landowner Eden Fletcher (David Wenham), who functions as Stanley's de facto boss, chew out Stanley for offering two of the Burns brothers amnesty if one of them kills Arthur. Then she is forced to witness the enactment of Fletcher's heartless order—Stanley's men giving Mikey one-hundred lashes—that places the teenage boy near death.

On his journey to the hills where Arthur has his hideout, Charlie visits the farm where the Burns brothers killed the settler family (though it's not clear whether Charlie was involved). Then he stumbles into a remote outpost where an erudite but racist British bounty hunter named Jellon Lamb, played to drunken and chilling perfection by John Hurt, shows he is a formidable rival. Lamb speaks of Arthur and his hideout in the same way Marlon Brando's Captain Kurtz is spoken of in *Apocalypse Now* (1979), as a mysterious powerful monster who is feared even by the natives.

When Charlie ventures up into the ridges, he is attacked by aborigines and speared through the chest; his life is saved by Arthur's gang. His brother's aboriginal mistress uses a poultice to heal him. On a ridge overlooking a splendid sunset, the brothers talk. Arthur is a contemplative lover of nature, an articulate brute who speaks of the bonds of family, insisting that his gang is the real nobility in this realm.

What Stanley's proposition has unleashed is a fury of unintended consequences that spins out of control, into bloody retributions by the British soldiers on the aborigines. The unrest sends Stanley and his wife into bunker mode, as he bars all the doors in their home. Inside, shut out from the alien surroundings, they try to celebrate Christmas as if they were back home. Meanwhile, the Burns brothers plot a daring rescue.

A mere plot summary doesn't do justice to the beauty and depth of this film. One could accuse John Hillcoat of overusing the achingly beautiful cinematography of Benoit Delhomme, but that would be like complaining about too much beauty: the land itself, empty and primeval and unforgiving and brilliant, is arguably the film's real protagonist. Arthur Burns, in particular, is taken with it. Cave's ghostly song speaks of arguments between the sun, moon, stars, and the land. Charlie Burns journeys through the frontier in the manner of epic quests. The Stanleys are trying to subdue the land enough to make a home. But it certainly does not seem hospitable.

Nature is a force by its mere presence and overriding stillness. Trapped in its unforgiving wilderness are the bitter and idiotic rivalries between the British authorities, the Irish outlaws, and the aborigines. Civilization has a tenuous hold, and lives hang in the balance, subject to whim or rage. Hillcoat never sugarcoats the conflicts nor the nature of the human beasts who are fighting it out, but he also manages to make every member of the cast, even the brutal Arthur, into a sympathetic character. All are people of some substance who have gone somewhat or completely mad.

Hillcoat is masterful at staging scenes in startlingly innovative and compelling ways. Take, for example, a scene in which Watson's Martha Stanley is recounting a disturbing nightmare for her husband. Martha is taking a bath, and her husband is standing in the doorway of the room. The camera peers over her naked left shoulder from behind, never showing her face, as she recounts the dream in which her murdered friend hands her baby to Martha. Martha holds it, and we see only Martha's hands gesturing in accord with the events of the dream. It's a beautiful and brilliant piece of scene composition.

Hillcoat is unflinching when it comes to violence, but he's equally forceful in showing tender moments between the Stanleys and the brothers, the chilling fear of Mikey, and the beauty of the land and the strength and flaws of the people. *The Proposition* features several outstanding performances: Huston is chilling as the articulate madman, wild man's hair framing his soft face. Pearce is magnificent as the little-spoken protagonist torn between loyalties, ethnicities, and ways of life, trying to find his moral compass; his character's development is essentially a long sojourn in a natural and ethical wilderness. Watson, who is adept at playing with the edge of sanity, is compelling as the frightened yet resourceful and brave wife. Hurt's two cameo scenes are like Shakespearean tour-de-forces. But the best performance of all comes from Winstone, who portrays the cunning contradictory impulses of a man desperately trying to find a way to bring order to his conquest by following unorthodox methods; he is both humane and absolutely amoral, and you see his sanity slipping as the forces he has unleashed spin out of his control. He is a stand-in for every underling who has to do the dirty work of colonialism, for every military strategist who finds he must throw out the rulebook to achieve success.

The Proposition has the clarity and audacity of a nightmare, the burning force of a living hell on earth, and yet it celebrates the elemental, essential beauty of the natural world with the same unsparing perspective it applies to the warring inhabitants vying to gain a measure of control over it. It is one of the most gripping and audacious westerns ever made, and one of the most fantastic films of the year, one that harkens back, in style and substance, to the best of the Australian New Waves films of the 1970s.

Michael Betzold

CREDITS

Charlie Burns: Guy Pearce
Captain Morris Stanley: Ray Winstone
Martha Stanley: Emily Watson
Arthur Burns: Danny Huston
Jellon Lamb: John Hurt
Eden Fletcher: David Wenham
Brian O'Leary: Noah Taylor
Jacko: David Gulpilil
Queenie: Leah Purcell
Two Bob: Tom Lewis
Mikey Burns: Richard Wilson
Origin: Austalia, Great Britain
Language: English
Released: 2005
Production: Chris Brown, Cat Villiers, Jackie O'Sullivan, Chiara Menage; U.K. Film Council, Surefire Films; released by Sony Pictures, Tartan Films
Directed by: John Hillcoat
Written by: Nick Cave
Cinematography by: Benoit Delhomme
Music by: Warren Ellis
Sound: Craig Walmsley
Editing: Jon Gregory
Art Direction: Bill Booth, Marita Mussett
Production Design: Chris Kennedy
MPAA rating: R
Running time: 104 minutes

REVIEWS

Chicago Sun-Times Online. May 19, 2006.
Entertainment Weekly Online. May 17, 2006.
Los Angeles Times Online. May 5, 2006.
New York Times Online. May 5, 2006.
Premiere Magazine Online. May 5, 2006.
Variety Online. September 16, 2005.

QUOTES

Samuel Stote: "What's a misanthrope?"
Arthur Burns: "A misanthrope is a bugger who hates every other bugger."
Samuel: "Are we misanthropes?"
Arthur: "Lord no! We're family."

TRIVIA

Screenwriter Nick Cave completed the script in three weeks.

PULSE

You are now infected.
—Movie tagline

Box Office: $20.2 million

In the modern world where technology like email, Blackberries, and mobile telephones are as ubiquitous as concrete, it was inevitable that moviemakers would turn these everyday friends into our worst nightmares. This was done by Japanese director Kiyoshi Kurosawa in his 2001 horror film *Kairo.* Of course, if the Japanese are going to make a horror film, it is also inevitable that an American director will come along and rip it off—perhaps successfully, but more often than not it just doesn't translate well. *Pulse,* this year's American remake of *Kairo,* falls solidly and firmly into the ranks of the latter.

Set against one of the dreariest college campuses ever captured on film, *Pulse* begins with computer whiz Josh (Jonathan Tucker) desperately searching the library for someone named Seigler. Josh is obviously terrified of something. He's nervous and easily spooked. And well he should be, for something finds him and then seems to suck the soul out of him. Meanwhile, Josh's girlfriend, Mattie (Kristen Bell) wonders aloud to her best friends Isabell (Christina Milian), Stone (Rick Gonzalez), and Tim (Samm Levine), as to why Josh has been avoiding her lately. So Mattie goes to Josh's apartment only to find that he acts like a walking ghost. While she's there, for no reason she can ascertain, he hangs himself in the bathroom.

A few days later, Mattie gets a package in the mail containing three rolls of red tape and a short, cryptic message indicating that it's the only thing that keeps them out. It's from Josh, but exactly who the "them" is the note refers to is a mystery. Later, while in a chat room, Mattie's friends suddenly get a message from Josh: "Help me." Thinking someone is playing around with Josh's computer, Stone goes to Josh's apartment only to face a similar soul sucking apparition.

Thinking Stone never got Josh's computer turned off, Mattie goes back to the apartment only to find his landlady has sold it to a man named Dexter (Ian Somerhalder). She tracks him down and the two begin to unravel the puzzle behind not only Josh's death, but also behind the area's suicide epidemic and the unusual occurrence of people just disappearing.

"Do you want to see a ghost?" is the computer message that kicks off the chaos. Seigler, it turns out, was working on a telecom project that found frequencies that no one knew existed. Because of this, another life form from another dimension has found its way into ours via our technology and all that sucking we've seen is their taking away one's will to live. The red tape is the only thing that blocks the spectrum on which they move and because of this everyone has been sealing their doors and covering their windows with tape. However, there's a better way to avoid the soul suckers and that's to find a dead zone, a place where all the PDAs and cell phones won't work and the Internet can't get in. Eventually, with everyone dying around them, that's what Dexter and Mattie are forced to do and with that we see a vision of civilization's future: tent cities in the middle of nowhere.

What makes Japanese horror films so watchable is not so much their plot as their atmosphere. They are subtle and creepy. Unfortunately, when they are remade in America the atmosphere is usually sacrificed in an attempt to make it as scary as possible. The result is that usually they are not atmospheric or scary. What is even more unfortunate is that in this particular remake, *Pulse* has attempted to create atmosphere by desaturating the colors in the film and making all the settings—apartments, classrooms, coffee shops, bathrooms and laundry rooms—the filthiest ever caught on film. One imagines the cast and crew having to shower every ten minutes to wash off the disgusting debris created by production designer Gary Matteson. This is the greyest, grimiest, dirtiest city ever filmed. The ugly, grainy and grey cinematography by director of photography Mark Plummer fails to provide a spooky atmosphere; it's merely distracting and just plain depressing. No one looks good in this movie and it is dismaying to see two of television's best looking actors—*Veronica Mars'* Kristen Bell and *Lost*'s Ian Somerhalder—lensed so unflatteringly. Instead of watching their emotional reaction to what's going on around them in their close-ups, all we can see arepores, bumps, and creases.

In the end director Jim Sonzero, who comes from a background in making commercials and is making his theatrical debut here, offers up an incredibly unattractive movie with a screamingly loud audio. It isn't very scary and it's not even very interesting. It's hard to care about these characters or to be terrified by the special effects or be cautioned by its apocalyptic vision of a future where the technology that's supposed to make us closer actually isolates us even more. In fact Brad Dourif's cameo as a scenery-chewing coffee shop prophet of doom is probably the highlight of the film. But those few minutes aren't worth the wait.

Beverley Bare Buehrer

CREDITS

Mattie: Kristen Bell
Dexter: Ian Somerhalder
Isabell: Christina Milian
Stone: Rick Gonzalez
Professor Cardiff: Zach Grenier
Dr. Waterson: Ron Rifkin
Josh: Jonathan Tucker
Tim: Samm Levine
Thin Bookish Guy: Brad Dourif (Cameo)
Origin: USA
Language: English
Released: 2006
Production: Anant Singh, Brian Cox, Michael Leahy, Joel Soisson; Dimension Films, Distant Horizon, Neo Art & Logic; released by Weinstein Co.
Directed by: Jim Sonzero
Written by: Wes Craven, Ray Wright
Cinematography by: Mark Plummer
Music by: Elia Cmiral
Sound: Larry Scharf, Tibi Borcoman
Editing: Bob Morri, Kirk Morri, Robert K. Lambert
Art Direction: Sorin Popescu, Jodi Ginnever
Costumes: Irene Bob
Production Design: Elmanno Di Febo-Orsini, Gary B. Matteson
MPAA rating: R
Running time: 90 minutes

REVIEWS

Boxoffice Online. August 11, 2006.
Entertainment Weekly Online. August 14, 2006.
Hollywood Reporter Online. August 14, 2006.
Los Angeles Times Online. August 11, 2006.
New York Times Online. August 12, 2006.
Variety Online. August 14, 2006.

THE PURSUIT OF HAPPYNESS

Box Office: $162.8 million

The Pursuit of Happyness was inspired by a true story, that of a determined man's arduous struggle to go from being broke to becoming a millionaire broker so he can support his young son. As plans got underway to turn a heart-tugging fifteen-minute profile on ABC's *20/20* into a feature-length drama, Chris Gardner had some initial reservations about being played by Will Smith, who had catapulted to multimillion-dollar superstardom through high-octane, special-effects-laden crowd pleasers like *Independence Day* (1996) and *Men in Black* (1997). "You think of Will," Gardner was quoted in *Entertainment Weekly*, "and you think of alien spacecraft, lots of violence, guns, fast cars." With his ebullient, boyish charm and hip-hop flavorings, could Smith play decidedly less hip and with less youthful, brash hop as a slightly graying, paternal, sorely-tested but ultimately triumphant magnet for woe? Smith admitted that well-known elements of both his personality and screen persona had to disappear in order for him to effectively disappear into character, the role calling on him to show even more depth and skill than he memorably exhibited in *Six Degrees of Separation* (1993) and *Ali* (2001).

Leading to its uplifting climax, the film makes hearts heavy with its chronicling of the seemingly endless hurdles to be cleared in Gardner's pursuit of happiness. While presidential campaign ads for Ronald Reagan declared with unwavering optimism that it was "morning in America," life for Gardner at the dawn of the 1980s was looking pretty dark. He had sunk his life savings into bulky but portable bone density scanners, which he doggedly lugs up and down the hilly streets of San Francisco in search of buyers. Unfortunately, Gardner seems infinitely more likely to wind up with a hernia than a fortune, as most doctors' offices find the machines expensive and nonessential. His car has been towed away. The tax bill is past due, as is the rent. Gardner's snappish, excruciatingly stressed-out working wife, Linda (Thandie Newton), exasperatedly harps on his inability to provide. An early close-up of the subdued, beleaguered, well-intentioned man clearly conveys the grim, painful vice in which he finds himself, completely at a loss for how to improve matters.

The one bright spot in Gardner's existence is his five-year-old son, Christopher (Jaden Christopher Syre Smith, Will's real-life son, in his feature film debut), to whom this distracted man is nonetheless warmly, attentively devoted. As his own father was absent from his life until he was an adult, Gardner has resolved to have and maintain a close, affectionate relationship with a son he clearly enjoys being around. It is his love for Christopher that keeps Gardner going.

One propitious day, Gardner trudges past the headquarters of stock brokerage titan Dean Witter Reynolds and, gazing admiringly at the employees' smiling contentment, well-tailored clothes, and fancy cars, suddenly thinks he may see a way of transforming his nightmare into the American Dream. The company has a posting for a broker trainee program, and the thirty-eight-year-old smart, personable high school graduate lobbies hard for this highly-selective, crucial opportunity. Showing an ability to think quickly on his feet, Gardner finagles a cab ride with the firm's Mr. Twistle (Brian Howe) and endeavors to win over his captive audience. Grappling with a Rubik's Cube, Twistle is particularly intrigued after this persistent man is able to solve it. Linda, however, remains much less impressed as her down-on-his-luck husband aims high, offering up snide, belittling comments instead of encouragement. One wishes she would at least leave him alone and soon she does, walking out on him but unfortunately doing so with Christopher in tow. Gardner will let her go, but he adamantly holds on to his son.

Over and over throughout *The Pursuit of Happyness*, Gardner is shown racing down streets, darting through traffic (one time even getting hit), and dashing onto multiple forms of public transportation, tearing around town trying to overcome the latest travail that is tearing him apart. For example, he must twice chase after people who have walked off with his machines, one of which he foolishly left in the temporary care of a stranger on the street while visiting Dean Witter Reynolds. On another occasion, Gardner is hauled off to the police station for unpaid parking tickets while painting his apartment on the eve of his interview at the brokerage firm, and thus is forced to run there upon his release in spattered, inappropriately-casual clothing. Nevertheless, once again showing himself to be as quick on his feet mentally as he is physically, Gardner uses humor and good-natured charm to snag a slot in the program. There is, however, one startling catch: only a single person will be hired at the end of a six-month internship which pays absolutely nothing. It is a risk he can ill-afford to take but must, and viewers' rooting for Gardner will undoubtedly now kick into high gear as he attempts to stand out in a highly-competitive crowd.

"Don't ever let anyone tell you you can't do something," Gardner tells his son. "You want something, you go get it—period." Based on what is presented here, it would seem that few are as qualified to impart an inspirational message about what can be accomplished through resolution and resiliency, to assert that one may be relentlessly beaten down by life and still not be beaten. It is tough to watch Gardner toiling to reel in clients at work at the same time he is continuously losing a place to call home. He and Christopher are kicked out of their apartment due to lack of funds and then a motel, finally having to struggle for a couple of cots in a stuffed-to-the-gills homeless shelter. Just when he is finally earning some money from the sale of his scanners, the government scoops up most of it for nonpayment of back taxes. Gardner's desperation is palpable when he almost roughs up a supposed friend in order to gain repayment for a mere but much-needed fourteen bucks. No one watching will be without sympathy and admiration for Gardner as he exhibits amazing perseverance, and many will find it hard, as Gardner himself does, to keep their emotions in check when he is finally rewarded with a job at Dean Witter Reynolds. In an exhilarating, highly affecting scene, he teeters between decorous self-control and surging, triumphant elation while walking down the street amongst a sea of people. As Gardner and his son walk down the street, the latter cracking up the former with knock-knock jokes, the audience is informed about his subsequent, multimillion-dollar success. It is important to note that the man the two walk past before the credits begin to roll is the real Chris Gardner.

What will unquestionably make viewers most sympathetic toward Gardner is his constant, striving to do his best for Christopher. They will notice such things as the way he first impresses upon the jabbering boy to stay safely put in a park playground before sprinting to retrieve one of his machines. There are the many times Gardner provides his son with reassurance, even when he himself is in tremendous need of it. The finest example of this is the superb, painfully-poignant scene in which he makes a game out of their having to take shelter for the night in a deserted subway station bathroom, pretending they are prehistoric men holing up in a cave to escape menacing dinosaurs. No one will be left unaffected by the sight of Gardner, tears streaming down his face, sitting on the floor with a sleeping Christopher protectively cradled in his arms and attempting to keep whoever is outside from getting in. The thoroughly realistic nature of the often enjoyable exchanges between father and son, as well as the believability of their endearing bond, are surely due at least in part to the talented actors' actual connection.

The Pursuit of Happyness (the misspelling taken from artwork outside Christopher's day care) is the first English-language film from Italian director Gabriele Muccino. It was written by Steve Conrad, most recently responsible for *The Weather Man* (2005), another character study of a man struggling to succeed in life. Changes were made in the conversion of fact to film, including the transformation of Gardner's infant into a five-year-old with whom he could interact. Also, the internship actually provided Gardner with a small stipend, surely deleted from the proceedings to further emphasize the riskiness of his pursuit. Made on a reported budget of $55 million, *The Pursuit of Happyness* earned well over twice that much. The film received many positive reviews, although some critics found the film veered to often toward manipulative sappiness. Smith received richly deserved Screen Actors Guild, Golden Globe, and Oscar® nominations. The gifted actor turned in an appealing, moving, wholly convincing performance of admirable restraint and subtlety. Gardner need not have been worried.

David L. Boxerbaum

CREDITS

Chris Gardner: Will Smith
Linda: Thandie Newton
Jay Twistle: Brian Howe
Martin Frohm: James Karen
Christopher: Jaden Christopher Syre Smith
Alan Frakesh: Dan Castellaneta
Walter Ribbon: Kurt Fuller
Origin: USA
Language: English
Released: 2006
Production: Todd Black, Jason Blumenthal, Steve Tisch, James Lassiter, Will Smith; Overbrook Entertainment, Escape Artists, Relativity, Columbia Pictures; released by Sony Pictures Entertainment
Directed by: Gabriele Muccino
Written by: Steve Conrad
Cinematography by: Phedon Papamichael
Music by: Andrea Guerra
Sound: Willie Burton
Editing: Hughes Winborne
Art Direction: David Klassen
Costumes: Sharen CQ Davis
Production Design: J. Michael Riva
MPAA rating: PG-13
Running time: 120 minutes

REVIEWS

Chicago Sun-Times Online. December 15, 2006.
Entertainment Weekly. December 15, 2006, p. 65.
Hollywood Reporter Online. December 8, 2006.
Los Angeles Times Online. December 15, 2006.
New York Times Online. December 15, 2006.
Premiere Magazine Online. December 14, 2006.
Rolling Stone Online. December 12, 2006.
San Francisco Chronicle. December 15, 2006, p. E1.
Variety Online. December 7, 2006.
Washington Post. December 15, 2006, p. C1.

QUOTES

Chris Gardner (to his son): "You got a dream, you gotta protect it. People can't do something themselves, they wanna tell you that you can't do it. You want something? Go get it. Period."

AWARDS

Nomination:

Oscars 2006: Actor (Smith)

Golden Globes 2007: Actor—Drama (Smith), Song ("A Father's Way")

Screen Actors Guild 2006: Actor (Smith)

Q

THE QUEEN

Tradition prepared her. Change will define her.
—Movie tagline

Box Office: $55.4 million

Because of its controversial subject matter—the state of the House of Windsor in time of crisis after the death of Princess Diana—*The Queen* would surely satisfy viewers hoping to get a glimpse into the reclusive monarchy at home. The tremendous popularity of Princess Diana and the disturbing circumstances surrounding her death would seem to assure a ready-made mass audience.

The story begins in 1997 with Tony Blair (Michael Sheen) becoming Prime Minister and negotiating the Queen's permission to form a new government just as disaster strikes and the "People's Princess" is killed in an auto accident in Paris. Thereafter, the Queen retreats to Balmoral Castle in Scotland, where she stays for a week, out of sight of her subjects. As Anthony Lane explained in the *New Yorker*, her decision to "pull up the drawbridge" was interpreted "by the public as evidence of a hard heart," as CNN television reported that the Royals were somehow remiss in not showing "enough remorse over Princess Diana's death," while commoners wept.

Before *The Queen* even opened in America, it had already won the best actress award at the Venice Film Festival. Remarkably, Helen Mirren has now played both Queen Elizabeth I (2005) and Queen Elizabeth II, the latter at a time when, as *Newsweek* noted, Her Majesty seemed entirely "out of touch with not just her people and her new prime minister, Blair, but with the entire planet." Mirren, was clearly trying to find the woman behind the throne, just as Forest Whitaker, in his portrayal of Idi Amin Dada, was looking for the man behind the monster. Interestingly enough, Peter Morgan penned both of these pictures.

For Mirren it was apparently a matter of self-control, self-discipline, and dignity, according to *Newsweek*. *USA Today* critic Claudia Puig noted that Mirren "inhabits the role of Queen Elizabeth so thoroughly that her transformation astounds." and a "lesser actress might have been able to pull off the ceremonial persona," but the genius of this film is that Mirren was able "to portray the queen as multidimensional and human," showing "steely determination along with vulnerability and confusion." Puig thought that the Motion Picture Academy should simply "hand her the Oscar® now."

Morgan claimed to have written most of the screenplay in about two weeks, as it came to him "in a fever," but, he told *USA Today*, he then spent "nine months fact-checking and editing" in the interest of accuracy. After Diana is killed in Paris in August of 1997, Queen Elizabeth apparently wanted a private funeral, since, in the words of Maria Puente in *USA Today*, "Showing one's feelings in public is definitely not in with her crowd." Prince Charles (Alex Jennings) is simply devastated. Prince Philip (James Cromwell) also wants to keep the affair private. Sensing a media frenzy, Blair advises otherwise, as he recognizes a crisis that could damage the monarchy. Reviewing the film for *The Spectator* in Britain, Diana's former private secretary claimed that this "might just be the best and most important film ever made about the Windsors," while *USA Today* reported that friends and retainers of the palace "have let it be known that the film is spot-on." Consultant Robert Lacey, who interviewed palace sources, approved of the film's pro-royalist spin. "People come away understanding the queen's perspective of herself as a grandmother, [and] as a human being," Lacey told *USA Today*: "they see the fallibility and the vulnerability, and that increases the affection."

New Yorker reviewer Anthony Lane approached the film with "grim trepidation," as he wondered, "How could Frears and his cast rise above the sins of the miniseries?" He was impressed with the "twin sides" of Mirren's appeal: "the warmth and the chill. How many actresses," Lane wondered, "since Dietrich and Bacall, have managed to make the forbidding seem so winning, and vice versa?" *Washington Post* reviewer Desson Thomson was impressed by the performance of Cromwell as an "extremely bombastic" Prince Philip, who coldly characterizes Diana's mourners as "a chorus line of soap stars and homosexuals" and by Sylvia Syms' "tipsy" Queen Mother. This sort of "royal razzing" is counterbalanced by Mirren's "finely calibrated performance [that] reveals a complex woman coping with a bewildering world," as Blair's "growing sympathy for his beleaguered monarch gradually becomes ours." Thomson perceptively remarks that when the Queen reads the "notes of contempt for the House of Windsor" included with the scattered flowers left as a tribute to Diana, her eyes suggest that she understands "what it truly means to reign but not to rule."

The Queen was eventually hailed as one of the year's best pictures by *Time*, *Newsweek*, *Rolling Stone*, the *New York Times*, the *Wall Street Journal*, the *Los Angeles Times*, and other newspapers. By the year's end Miramax was touting the film as not only "the best reviewed film of the year" but "the most honored film of the year."

That the film at times seems almost documentary is a tribute to the writer, director, and stellar cast. For Helen Mirren, it was, as John Lahr described it, a "command performance." There are certainly memorable images, as when the Queen notices a stag in the wild on her estate in Scotland, and senses a kinship and vulnerability. The Queen is able to show the veiled humanity of the monarch, hidden beneath opulent layers of regal dignity. Essaying Queen Elizabeth II, Mirren manages to give this most modern monarch a human dimension, and by doing so, she holds the film together.

James M. Welsh

CREDITS

Queen Elizabeth II: Helen Mirren
Tony Blair: Michael Sheen
Prince Philip: James Cromwell
Cherie Blair: Helen McCrory
Prince Charles: Alex Jennings
Queen Mother: Sylvia Sims
Origin: Great Britain, France, Italy
Language: English
Released: 2006
Production: Andy Harries, Tracey Seaward, Christine Langan; Pathe Productions, Granada; released by Miramax
Directed by: Stephen Frears
Written by: Peter Morgan
Cinematography by: Alfonso Beato
Music by: Alexandre Desplat
Sound: Peter Lindsay
Editing: Lucia Zucchetti
Art Direction: Peter Wenham
Costumes: Consolata Boyle
Production Design: Alan Macdonald
MPAA rating: PG-13
Running time: 101 minutes

REVIEWS

Boxoffice Online. September 29, 2006.
Entertainment Weekly. October 6, 2006, p. 48.
Hollywood Reporter Online. September 5, 2006.
Los Angeles Times Online. October 6, 2006.
New York Times Online. September 29, 2006.
Newsweek Online. October 2, 2006.
Rolling Stone Online. September 21, 2006.
Variety Online. September 2, 2006.
Washington Post. October 6, 2006, p. C5.

QUOTES

Tony Blair (on Diana's death and the royal family): "They screwed up her life, let's hope they don't screw up her death."

TRIVIA

Michael Sheen also played Tony Blair in the Stephen Frears/Peter Morgan TV movie *The Deal* (2003).

AWARDS

Oscars 2006: Actress (Mirren)
British Acad. 2006: Actress (Mirren), Film
Golden Globes 2007: Actress—Drama (Mirren), Screenplay
Screen Actors Guild 2006: Actress (Mirren)

Nomination:

Oscars 2006: Costume Des., Director (Frears), Film, Orig. Screenplay, Orig. Score
British Acad. 2006: Costume Des., Director (Frears), Film Editing, Makeup, Orig. Screenplay, Support. Actor (Sheen), Orig. Score

Directors Guild 2006: Director (Frears)
Golden Globes 2007: Director (Frears), Film—Drama
Writers Guild 2006: Orig. Screenplay

THE QUIET

Isn't it time everyone hears your secrets?
—Movie tagline

Distasteful, lurid, and finally nonsensical, *The Quiet* tries to be many things and fails at all of them. It is a thriller that does not thrill, a critique of suburbia that says nothing new on the subject, and a dark teen comedy whose only humor is purely unintentional. This movie is so insipid that it is a wonder it received the green light. The production notes speak glowingly of the film as the result of "the groundbreaking collaboration between Burnt Orange Productions and the University of Texas Film Institute," which allows students to work with professionals on independent features. But if *The Quiet* exemplifies the kind of work this collaboration is producing, then perhaps the partnership should be reconsidered.

The film's premise has promise. Withdrawn teenager Dot (Camilla Belle) has been left an orphan in the wake of her father's sudden death and is taken in by the Deer family, which includes parents Paul (Martin Donovan) and Olivia (Edie Falco), who was a friend of Dot's late mother, and daughter Nina (Elisha Cuthbert), the beautiful, blonde cheerleader. Dot is deaf and mute and sits alone in the school cafeteria, where Nina and her best friend, the obnoxious and bullying Michelle (Katy Mixon), make fun of her for her plain looks and inability to socialize with the other kids.

The dark secret at the heart of the screenplay, written by Abdi Nazemian and Micah Schraft, is the clandestine, incestuous relationship between Paul and Nina, who both loves and hates her father. Even with this risky subject matter, the film is curiously flat, never delving into the psyches of the predatory father or the victimized daughter. Indeed, for such a controversial story line, the film does nothing with the repercussions of such a bond, instead exploiting icky scenes of father-daughter intimacy.

Other events are fairly mundane. Nina and Michelle talk about sex, the parents bicker over how strict to be with the girls, and a classmate named Connor (Shawn Ashmore) takes an interest in Dot, who does not seem to realize or care that this attention makes her the envy of Michelle. When Dot and Connor eventually have sex, we have no idea what the experience means to this shy girl.

Connor and other characters feel free to share their innermost secrets with Dot, presumably because there is some perverse satisfaction in making very personal confessions to someone who cannot hear them. The situation changes, however, when Nina discovers, that Dot in fact can talk, and begins toying with her. Nina reveals how much she hates her father and says that she plans to kill him. The film looks like it is going to be a thriller, but it fails to generate any tension. At one juncture, for example, Nina seems about to get a gun from Michelle, but this plot point goes nowhere.

Making matters worse is the fact that the film has ambitions beyond a standard thriller, which means pretentious scenes wherein Dot plays Beethoven on the piano while musing in voice-over on the genius of his work even as he grew more deaf. There are also excruciating, trite passages in which she talks about how hard it is to face herself and shares inane nuggets of wisdom such as "Lies keep us safe from the truth." None of these overwrought voice-overs illuminate Dot—they just make an uninteresting character seem self-important.

The Quiet piles tawdry detail on tawdry detail, as when Nina, just inches from bashing in her father's head with a hot iron, suddenly changes her mind and pretends to be pregnant to extort $1,000 from him for an abortion. If such a scene were played as a parody of a teen soap opera, it still would not work. When Paul later discovers the truth and goes into a violent rage, Dot strangles him with a broken piano wire, an act that sends an already unbelievable movie into the realm of the ridiculous. Nina seems absolutely traumatized by her father's death, but very quickly puts aside these feelings and scurries off with Dot to the high school dance, somehow able to act as if nothing has happened, and then goes into the woods to bury the evidence of the killing. It seems that they have grown close and devised a plan together, which comes as a total surprise, since the relationship is so ill defined.

We do finally learn why Dot has pretended to be disabled—to be close to her deaf-mute father after her mother died, and to be invisible to the world. Her ruminations on being invisible are meant to be poignant and flesh out her troubled character, but she is still a cipher at the end. Nina's description of Dot as "a major enigma," is the film's only genuine insight about her. Adding to the sheer lunacy of *The Quiet*, Olivia, whose only distinctive trait throughout the film is her addiction to prescription drugs, assumes the guilt for the killing, leaving the girls together at the film's conclusion.

It is really hard to say what director Jamie Babbit was striving to accomplish in *The Quiet*, which was obviously inspired by *American Beauty* (1999), but, unlike that Oscar® winner, is marked by a lackluster plot, wildly inconsistent characters, lethargic pacing, and amateurish acting. Moreover, *The Quiet* cannot be taken seriously as a thriller because it does not have the genre's suspense or pacing and is so sloppily constructed that it never builds any dramatic momentum. It is also too somber and pretentious to be enjoyed as a sexy, trashy guilty pleasure. This is a thoroughly uninspired and unpleasant movie, easily one of the worst of the year.

Peter N. Chumo II

CREDITS

Dot: Camilla Belle
Nina: Elisha Cuthbert
Paul: Martin Donovan
Olivia: Edie Falco
Connor: Shawn Ashmore
Michelle: Katy Mixon
Origin: USA
Language: English
Released: 2005
Production: Carolyn Pfeiffer, Holly Wiersma, Andrea Sperling, Joel Michaely; Burnt Orange, Town Lake Films; released by Sony Pictures Classics
Directed by: Jamie Babbit
Written by: Abdi Nazemian, Micah Schraft
Cinematography by: M. David Mullen
Music by: Jeff Rona
Sound: Andrew Gohn
Editing: Joan Sobel
Costumes: Aimee Kandl
Production Design: John Frick
MPAA rating: R
Running time: 96 minutes

REVIEWS

Boxoffice Online. August 25, 2006.
Entertainment Weekly. September 1, 2006, p. 53.
Los Angeles Times Online. August 25, 2006.
New York Times Online. August 25, 2006.
Variety Online. September 13, 2005.

R

THE RETURN

The past never dies. It kills.
—Movie tagline

Box Office: $7.7 million

Asif Kapadia's *The Return* is a plodding thriller that builds up a set of eerie circumstances surrounding a murder from long ago, but ultimately does not lead anywhere very compelling. Believing that "If I keep moving forward, nothing bad can catch me," Joanna Mills (Sarah Michelle Gellar) is a go-getter of a sales rep for a trucking company and lives a rootless existence primarily, it seems, because she is haunted by some traumatic event from her childhood. As the film progresses, the past is filled out until, in a climactic revelation, her life is shown to be intertwined with the spirit of a dead woman. By the end, however, neither that woman's story nor Joanna's makes us care very much about either character or their supernatural connection.

Appearing primarily in flashbacks, playwright Sam Shepard is Ed, Joanna's widowed father, trying to care for his little girl, who has clearly been spooked by something that she cannot articulate and, as a result, grows into an adult prone to stabbing herself. As Joanna tries to bury the past by working a job that requires her to travel a lot, she has visions of a strange man stalking her, cannot escape hearing Patsy Cline's classic "Sweet Dreams (Of You)," and walks through the evidence of an auto accident that seems to be all in her head. She sees a picture of La Salle, Texas, in one of her sales catalogues and, because the photo contains a bar familiar from her visions, feels compelled to go there, even though La Salle is the place where, as a little girl, she first became violent and hurt herself.

La Salle looks like a ghost town, and the creepy woman who registers Joanna at the rundown, seemingly deserted hotel does not make the place more inviting. But Joanna finally meets a man named Terry Stahl (Peter O'Brien) when he protects her from an aggressive rival salesman, Kurt (Adam Scott), who just happens to show up in this remote town and gets violent with her. Kurt and Joanna probably have a history, but the movie never spells it out, and the confrontation feels like a contrived way to get Joanna and Terry together. Despite his apparent goodness, Terry holds an ambiguous place in his community as a man many believe killed his wife.

The film creates a desolate, washed-out atmosphere and provides a few shocks and scares along the way. Joanna looks at herself in the mirror, and her eye color seems to change; later, she sees the reflection of Annie (Erinn Allison), Terry's late wife, staring back at her. Joanna is chased by a mysterious pursuer, who may be a product of her mind, and slowly seems to realize that her life has somehow merged with Annie's. The clincher is Joanna's discovery of a mural on Terry's barn door matching pictures of a seahorse she drew as a child. After a while, the intermingling of Joanna's real life with ghostly visions becomes rather dull, when it should be building a sense of danger and suspense. Gellar, playing a role similar to her frightened heroine in *The Grudge* (2004) and this year's *The Grudge 2*, shows very little emotion as the troubled Joanna experiences one weird occurrence after another.

When Joanna finally happens upon Annie's killer, the scruffy Griff (J.C. MacKenzie), the film climaxes with a protracted chase and showdown intercut with Griff's murder of Annie long ago. Joanna finally kills him, but this is really Annie acting through Joanna's body. The solution to the puzzle proves rather underwhelming and not very well explained. When she was a little girl, Joanna was with her father in their station wagon when it was hit by Terry as he raced to get help for the dying Annie. Somehow this crash, which killed Annie, had a supernatural effect in which her spirit was reincarnated in Joanna, thus enabling Annie to return to Terry and avenge her own death. It is, finally, a rather flimsy and confusing conceit on which to hang the whole film, especially since Annie never becomes a real character to us, and the villainous Griff is nothing more than an anonymous bogeyman. The whole back story, including the motive for the murder, remains a mystery. Indeed, because so little is known about everyone involved, it is difficult to become emotionally invested in anyone's story. And the car accident as the device for supernatural transference feels very random and even awkward.

Perhaps the key to the film is Ed's musings to his daughter on why he never remarried after his wife's death—he had found his one true love and believes that one day he will find her again. It is a statement that is probably meant to apply to Terry and Annie's bond beyond the grave. But ultimately this is a poorly executed idea Screenwriter Adam Sussman does not bring any clarity or depth to these weighty supernatural and romantic notions so we are neither scared by the ghost story nor moved by the tale of lost love.

Peter N. Chumo II

CREDITS

Joanna Mills: Sarah Michelle Gellar
Terry Stahl: Peter O'Brien
Kurt: Adam Scott
Michelle: Kate Beahan
Ed Mills: Sam Shepard
Griff: J.C. MacKenzie
Annie: Erinn Allison
Origin: USA
Language: English
Released: 2006
Production: Aaron Ryder, Jeffrey Silver; Biscayne Pictures, Intrepid Pictures, Raygun Productions; released by Rogue Pictures
Directed by: Asif Kapadia
Written by: Adam Sussman
Cinematography by: Roman Osin
Music by: Dario Marianelli
Editing: Claire Simpson
Art Direction: Jeff Knipp
Costumes: John Dunn
Production Design: Therese DePrez
MPAA rating: PG-13
Running time: 85 minutes

REVIEWS

Boston Globe Online. November 10, 2006.
Entertainment Weekly. November 24, 2006, p. 84.
Los Angeles Times Online. November 13, 2006.
New York Times Online. November 11, 2006.
Variety Online. November 12, 2006.

QUOTES

Joanna: "Sometimes I think if I keep moving forward, nothing bad can catch me."

ROCKY BALBOA

It ain't over 'til it's over.
—Movie tagline

Box Office: $70.2 million

Sixteen years after the release of the last *Rocky* movie (*Rocky V* in 1990), which was largely a disappointment with critics and audiences, writer/director/star Sylvester Stallone returns to the popular boxing hero in an attempt to bring a more satisfying closure to the film franchise. *Rocky Balboa* strives to link itself back to the tone and thematic soul of the first *Rocky* (1976) rather than continue the storylines developed through the later installments of the series. The film evokes many moments of nostalgia as well as a sad reflection on the passage of time and the loss of loved ones.

In terms of simple story stripped of details and character development, there is very little originality in the basic plots of any of the *Rocky* films, and that continues to be the case with *Rocky Balboa.* In every movie, Rocky (Stallone) becomes an underdog who goes into training and pushes the limits to face an opponent he is not favored to beat. What keeps the best of the films from being carbon copies of the others is the character development, and in *Rocky Balboa* it centers mostly on Rocky's lonely sense of the passage of time and a feeling of having unfinished business that motivates him to prove he "has what it takes" in the boxing ring.

When the film begins, the audience learns that Rocky's beloved wife Adrian has been dead for several years, having succumbed to cancer. Rocky owns a restaurant called Adrian's, decorated with numerous pictures of his wife, where he entertains patrons with stories about his famous matches. On the anniversary of Adrian's death, Rocky visits her grave and embarks on a sad tour of key settings from the past—an ice rink where he and Adrian once skated...the building where his old trainer Mickey worked—only to find that they are in shambles or torn down. "The whole world's falling apart," says Paulie (Burt Young), Rocky's gruff brother-in-law. In fact, Paulie becomes frustrated with Rocky's preoccupation with the past and his regular trips down memory lane. "You're living backwards," Paulie complains. "I can't do this no more."

Even Rocky's son Rocky Jr. (Milo Ventimiglia) shies away from participating in his father's nostalgic ritual. Though Rocky wants a close relationship, his son has become distant and withdrawn, thanks to the perception that he lives in his father's shadow. Consequently, Rocky finds himself emotionally alone until he meets Marie (Geraldine Hughes) while visiting a bar he used to frequent. Discovering that he once met Marie years before when she was a smart-aleck teenager, Rocky soon forms a friendship with her and her teenaged son. Marie enables him to connect to his past but also find a bridge to the future. When Rocky asks her to come work as the hostess at Adrian's, she overcomes her doubts and agrees to do so when he insists he needs her help.

Meanwhile, the public eye returns to Rocky when the commentators on a TV sports show speculate about a theoretical match between the legendary Rocky Balboa and current heavyweight champion Mason "The Line" Dixon (Antonio Tarver), based on an imaginary scenario where each boxer was in his prime. A computer-simulated match picks Rocky as the winner, which leads others to declare that if Mason Dixon went up against Rocky today—when the former champion is much older, slower, and less in shape—Mason would be the obvious winner. When Rocky hears commentators joking about him, their dismissal of his potential stirs him to want to prove himself—to demonstrate that he can do more than stand around telling stories of the past. Surprising everyone except Marie, he applies for a license to fight professionally again. Initially he is turned down even though he passes the physical examination, but after an impassioned speech about freedom to chart one's own course in life, the board grants him a license. Soon thereafter, Rocky receives an invitation from Dixon's manager to participate in an exhibition match against the current champion, a scheme designed to bolster Dixon's waning popularity. Of course Rocky cannot resist the invitation, and he begins training for the fight while most of the "experts" predict he will not be able to last any longer than the first round. "You gotta get hit and keep on going," Rocky tells his son, relating his own experience to Jr.'s internal struggles. "Gotta believe in yourself."

When Rocky faces Mason Dixon in the ring, the public demonstrates its support for the legendary boxer despite the predictions of the announcers, showing they still remember him as a true champion and are intensely loyal to him. Although the match does not get off to a great start, Rocky soon proves that he is able to see it through to the end.

For audiences who enjoyed *Rocky* and any of its sequels, *Rocky Balboa* should be a satisfying film, one that brings closure to the series in a way that was not accomplished in *Rocky V*. It follows the typical *Rocky* formula but also explores character-oriented themes that are unique yet believable in the context of the films, and since these themes deal with the passage of time and the loss of an era, they are also metafictional, dealing with not only Rocky the character but also *Rocky* the film(s). Rocky does not have to actually win the match in order to prove himself; he needs merely to keep fighting until the end and demonstrate that he has the heart of a true champion. Some elements of the film could be more fully developed—Rocky Jr.'s personal struggle and journey over the course of the film is not explored with much depth, and Mason Dixon is given only one scene that attempts to paint a three-dimensional portrait of the character. The focus of the movie is on Rocky and Marie, and fortunately their relationship is portrayed well and is poignant enough to overshadow the weaknesses of other character portrayals. Assuming that *Rocky Balboa* really is the final film in the series, the movie serves as a more-than-adequate resolution to the story of Rocky's life as a boxing champion.

David Flanagin

CREDITS

Rocky Balboa: Sylvester Stallone

Paulie: Burt Young

Robert Jr.: Milo Ventimiglia

Duke: Tony Burton

Mason "The Line" Dixon: Antonio Tarver

Marie: Geraldine Hughes

L.C.: A.J. Benza

Steps: James Francis Kelly III

Origin: USA

Language: English

Released: 2006

Production: Charles Winkler, Robert Chartoff, David Winkler, Kevin King; Revolution Studios, Columbia Pictures; released by MGM

Directed by: Sylvester Stallone

Written by: Sylvester Stallone
Cinematography by: Clark Mathis
Music by: Bill Conti
Sound: Mark Ulano
Editing: Sean Albertson
Art Direction: Michael Atwell, Jesse Rosenthal
Costumes: Gretchen Patch
Production Design: Franco-Giacomo Carbone
MPAA rating: PG
Running time: 101 minutes

REVIEWS

Chicago Sun-Times Online. December 20, 2006.
Entertainment Weekly. December 22, 2006, p. 57.
Hollywood Reporter Online. December 15, 2006.
Los Angeles Times Online. December 20, 2006.
New York Times Online. December 20, 2006.
Rolling Stone Online. December 12, 2006.
San Francisco Chronicle. December 20, 2006, p. E1.
Variety Online. December 15, 2006.
Washington Post. December 20, 2006, p. C1.

QUOTES

Rocky: "I think I wanna fight. Y'know, nothing big. Just small things, like, local."

Paulie replies: "What? You haven't peaked yet?"

RUNNING SCARED

Ready. Aim. Run.
—Movie tagline

Every bullet leaves a trail.
—Movie tagline

It's Not How Far You Go For The Truth...It's How Fast You Get There.
—Movie tagline

Box Office: $6.8 million

There is a trend in contemporary adventure films toward creating more ridiculous and incredulous stories. However, the ridiculous should be balanced with the plausible. *Running Scared*, directed and written by Wayne Kramer, is 90 percent ridiculous.

Graphic violence is obviously the bait for the audience of *Running Scared*. However, the violence is not creatively executed, except in its exaggeration. Kramer has employed the most predictable suspects to maintain the bloodletting: dirty cops, drug dealers, pedophiles, pimps, Russian mobsters, Italian mobsters, and victimized children.

Small-time hood Joey (Paul Walker), a decent enough family man given his occupation, is charged with disposing of a gun used to kill some dirty cops at a drug drug deal gone wrong. He hides it in his basement, unaware that his son Nicky (Alex Neuberger) and a playmate, Oleg (Cameron Bright) saw his hiding place. Later that night, Oleg shoots his abusive, Russian mob affiliated father, Anzor (Karel Roden) with the same gun.

Oleg flees with the gun as Joe realizes that he has it, and that his bosses, as well as the surviving dirty cop (Chazz Palminteri) and the Russian mob will all be looking for them. From there, the film become a frenetic race against the clock, high speed chase thriller, as Joey traces the gun from Oleg through a dizzying array of underworld and fringe figures. His wife Teresa (Vera Farmiga) even joins the search, encountering and disposing of a particularly nasty husband and wife pedophile team (Bruce Altman and Elizabeth Mitchell). Where *Running Scared* lacks plausibility, it accounts for its absence with its abundance of spectacle and break-neck pacing. The effect is undeniable, but it doesn't create much empathy for the characters or their actions.

There is a point this film is trying to make about these characters that is lost in the pace and violence. While visually stunning, there is nothing human to grasp. There are actions and characters, but they all seem quite detached from each other. This overriding vision does not allow what is, for the most part a talented cast of actors, much of a chance for success. The dialogue is as difficult to tolerate as the plot. The actors may not have been directed to shout most of their lines, but such consistency scarcely seems accidental. Perhaps a little more attention to the cohesiveness of the human elements and a little less to attempting to shock and awe the audience could have created a less ridiculous film.

The lesson of the film seems to be that bad parents should be killed or beaten, and those who perform such acts will be rewarded with safety. Joey apparently beat his abusive father with a baseball bat, resulting in his current vegetative state. Oleg shoots his father because of his physical and emotional torment. Teresa murders the two pedophiles without any hesitation. When the spectrum is weighted so heavily towards the spectacularly violent, death becomes the only vehicle of retribution. With absolutely nothing subtle in *Running Scared's* 122 minute running time, this Kramer effort breaks all expectations created by the treatment of suspense in his film, *The Cooler* (2003).

Sporting a fantastic color palette, the film simply has neither a human touch nor accessible characters. There is something to be said about trying too hard, to do too many things all at once. The best part of the entire film was the end. The graphic storybook credit sequence is mythical and epic. Perhaps the pace and dense imagery of the prior 119 minutes should have been informed by the simpler structures and symbolism of those final pictures.

Nick Kennedy

CREDITS

Joey Gazelle: Paul Walker
Oleg Yugorsky: Cameron Bright
Teresa Gazelle: Vera Farmiga
Anzor Yugorsky: Karel Roden
Tommy "Tombs" Perello: Johnny Messner
Mila Yugorsky: Ivana Milicevic
Detective Rydell: Chazz Palminteri
Nicky: Alex Neuberger
Sal "Gummy Bear" Franzone: Michael Cudlitz
Dez: Bruce Altman
Adele: Elizabeth Mitchell
Perello: Arthur J. Nascarelli
Ivan Yugirsky: John Noble
Pimp Lester: David Warshofsky
Divina: Idalis DeLeon
Origin: USA
Language: English
Released: 2006
Production: Michael Pierce, Brett Ratner, Sammy Lee; Media 8 Entertainment, True Grit Production, VIP Medienfonds 1 & 2, MDP Filmproduktion; released by New Line Cinema
Directed by: Wayne Kramer
Written by: Wayne Kramer
Cinematography by: James Whitaker
Music by: Mark Isham
Sound: T.J. O'Mara
Music Supervisor: Brian Ross
Editing: Arthur Coburn
Costumes: Kristen M. Burke
Production Design: Toby Corbett
MPAA rating: R
Running time: 122 minutes

REVIEWS

Boxoffice Online. February 24, 2006.
Chicago Sun-Times Online. February 24, 2006.
Entertainment Weekly Online. February 22, 2006.
Los Angeles Times Online. February 24, 2006.
New York Times Online. February 24, 2006.
Premiere Magazine Online. February 24, 2006.
Variety Online. February 22, 2006.
Washington Post Online. February 24, 2006.

QUOTES

Tommy "Tombs" Perello: "You spill Perello blood, you're deep-six invested."

RUNNING WITH SCISSORS

He's looking forward to a memory he won't have to suppress.
—Movie tagline

Do not disturb them. They already are.
—Movie tagline

Box Office: $6.8 million

There is no doubt in the increasingly unhinged mind of aspiring poet Deirdre Burroughs (Annette Bening) that she is meant for greatness, but her essential, ferocious need for approbation is unfortunately as great as her need for medication. Her life marches on in a series of unsettling, deranged episodes while her fervent aspirations are left unattained. It is the same with *Running with Scissors*, a film that was billed as a comedy but is too dolorous and off-puttingly disturbing to be humorous and too outlandishly berserk to be relatable. The movie is based upon the supposedly truthful 2002 best-selling memoir by Deirdre's son, Augusten, which recounted the freakishly challenging 1970s adolescence he has since struggled to transcend. The memoir is a mixture of surrealistic loopiness and the spectacularly disturbing, related by an author who asserts that "humor is a kind of life raft" and "there's a lot of absurdity in life even in the darkest places." Like the book, the film *Running with Scissors* has endless absurdity and darkness, but even as a pitch-black comedy, there is painfully little light.

When viewers first meet Augusten, he is a sweet, sunny little boy (Jack Kaeding), comprising an adoring audience of one for his mother's poetry reading. Deirdre states that she is "meant" to be a famous and respected writer, and Augusten looks wholeheartedly convinced. He is even shown later pretending to be her, microphone in hand and bowing appreciatively. There is a clear bond (and similarity) between them, although one increasingly wonders whether Deirdre values him more as an uncritical fan than as a son.

Deirdre feels that a number of things are holding her back, none of which include her worsening mental illness or her lack of any significant talent. She sees herself as no mere housewife, and in the midst of the Women's Movement, she is determined not to have her voice squelched. She dreams of reciting at Carnegie Hall, but so far, when she makes an appearance to read her poetry, only one woman sits down to listen, and even she doesn't look especially thrilled. As such, she imperiously holds court in her living room amidst the other ladies in her neighborhood poetry group, scathingly dismissing the works of others while magazines like *The New Yorker* reject her own creations. As Deirdre crumbles the rejection letters in her hand, one senses she is crumbling too.

Less comforting, and viewed by Deirdre as a saboteur of her narcissistic dreams, is her college professor husband Norman (Alec Baldwin), who is alcoholic, disenchanted, and emotionally disconnected from his troubled family teetering on the bring of disaster. Their fights are both physically and verbally violent. Baldwin skillfully conveys the man's weariness and burdensome sense of defeat: he cannot bear his wife's combative volatility and forlornly assesses his only offspring as a mini-Deirdre. Norman does not see himself in his son, as he notes miserably, and Augusten agrees. Norman's watering, dejected eyes alone speak volumes: how in the world did it all come to this?

A teenaged Augusten (now played by Joseph Cross) expresses his desire that they "just be a normal family," and when the calm, sonorously-voiced Dr. Finch (Brian Cox) appears on the scene resembling St. Nicholas, one wonders if he might be there to deliver miraculous assistance. However, Finch, to borrow the title of Billy Bob Thornton's 2003 comedy, is one bad Santa. The mental health professional seems disturbingly abnormal and unprofessional almost from the start. When politely offered a little refreshment upon entering someone's home, few people request slices of bologna with a side order of horseradish. Finch also inquires with peculiar, intense interest about Deirdre's bowel movements. The doctor soon comes down hard on Norman when he understandably balks at Finch's request for daily, five-hour marriage counseling sessions, and is suspiciously laudatory towards Deirdre. When Deirdre and Augusten visit his office, Finch takes them on an abhorrent tour of "the adjacent room where I masturbate," devoid of *Playboys* but startlingly lined with framed photographs of such less than tempting world leaders as Queen Elizabeth and Golda Meir. Sure to make one's skin crawl further is the sight of Finch's daughter Hope (Gwyneth Paltrow) curled up on the lounge chair she knows her father uses for pleasuring himself, contentedly and revoltingly snuggling with his (quite possibly soiled) blanket. As the doctor is shown to freely dispense all sorts of pills, many viewers might be interested in taking something themselves to combat their nausea at this point. And, if they knew what was coming down the pike during the rest of *Running*'s running time, stocking up on drugs at this point might be a good idea.

Soon after Norman kisses his son's head and leaves the family, Deirdre drops Augusten off at Finch's house and follows the doctor to a highly unorthodox session of counseling and, one suspects, coupling. The teen, along with the audience, is startled by the doctor's residence from the start, a Pepto-Bismol-pink Victorian choked inside and out with countless knick-knacks, dirty dishes, and just plain rubbish. A fully decorated Christmas tree has continuously adorned the living room for over two years. The structure (inspired by the creepy work of Edward Gorey) should perhaps be condemned, and it quickly seems even more certain that most of its inhabitants should probably be committed. Agnes (Jill Clayburgh), Finch's bedraggled wraith of a wife, munches on dog food right out of the bag while staring blankly at the television. The aforementioned Hope receives God's guidance by opening the Bible, randomly pointing to a word, and ridiculously divining its meaning. (One night, for example, the Lord okays fish sticks for dinner.) There is a little tot nicknamed Poo (Gabriel Guedj), who constantly hides behind the Christmas tree, regularly announcing his regularity with a joyful, "I just pooped!" Finch's raccoon-eyed, rebellious adopted daughter Natalie (Evan Rachel Wood) initially gets acquainted with Augusten using electric shock equipment. Her heart (and collarbone) were recently broken by an affair gone terribly wrong with a pedophile patient of her father's, a relationship the good doctor sanctioned. Finally, and ominously, on the premises is Neil Bookman (a barely recognizable, mustachioed Joseph Fiennes), a thirty-seven-year-old schizophrenic homosexual pedophile patient adopted by Finch. It is a mad menagerie, led by this certifiable but (for the time being) certified doctor/patriarch who brings to mind the biblical phrase, "Physician, heal thyself," as he gathers his clan around the toilet bowl to read his feces like some people read tea leaves. The motley group makes the Addams Family resemble the wholesomeness and placidity of the Waltons.

Into this endlessly unsound environment, Deirdre abandons her horrified and hurt son, making Dr. Finch his legal guardian. Augusten tries to contact his father for help, but Norman simply hangs up before the collect call can be put through. The wrong member of the Burroughs family is now stuck in the madhouse, an asylum from which anyone would wish to seek asylum. Deirdre, now full of pills, feels poised for her ascent to literary greatness, but it seems obvious that Finch is simply hastening her descent into madness.

These troubled characters cannot be mistaken for mere kooky eccentrics, at whose antics one can warmly chuckle. The people around Augusten are actually (and often alarmingly) psychologically ill. Except in Deirdre's case, the accent here is on the exhibition of insanity rather than insight into how these people got that way.

In writing the script for his feature film directorial debut, Ryan Murphy, the creator of the FX Channel's lurid series *Nip/Tuck*, apparently wanted viewers to be able to sense the pained, pitiable humanity beneath the shockingly irrational and irresponsible behavior of the Finch family. Both Murphy and Burroughs insisted they were out to neither ridicule nor damn the damaged. However, people like Finch, Deirdre, and Neil are not only damaged but also damaging, and while incredibly adaptive Augusten and kindred spirit Natalie may be able to laugh in order to cope, it is clearly no laughing matter. Some viewers may be able to be amused by the amazing absurdity, but these moments are distinctly eclipsed by scene after scene that is depressing, increasingly distressing, and often distastefully disturbing. So, for example, when Augusten attempts suicide after Finch suggests it as a way to legitimately miss school, or when viewers see this naive young man engage in an ongoing sexual relationship with Neil, a man more than twice his age with a head full of reverberating voices, most watching will agree that the proceedings repel more than compel and will want to get Augusten—and themselves—away from it all.

It should be noted that the real-life Finches (sans the now-deceased doctor) filed a lawsuit in 2005 for defamation, invasion of privacy, and emotional distress, claiming that Burroughs' book is actually a work of fiction. It was settled in 2006, with no details made public. The film, made on a budget of approximately $12 million, was only able to gross about half of that during its limited release. Critics were much more impressed with the individual performances than the film as a whole. Although Bening drew early Oscar® buzz for her towering, pungent performance, she was also criticized as "histrionic." Cross is adequate, but his character mainly just reacts to the overwrought insanity around him and is thus overshadowed. The most memorable and affecting moments of the film actually come from perhaps its least showy performance, that of Clayburgh as the haggard kibble nibbler. As her Agnes watches the younger, more vibrant Deirdre mount the stairs on the way to more hands-on help from her husband, the threatened woman's insecurity is signaled by a touching, ineffectual little touch-up of her hair. Over time, Agnes becomes something of a mother figure to Augusten, gradually coming out of her shell enough to show some sincere thoughtfulness. Agnes courageously asserts herself by giving him money she has secretly stashed away—money her family desperately needs—so that he can make a liberating move to start anew in New York City. "You're the best son a mom could ever want," she adds tenderly and movingly. Despite all the dramatics that went before, this sweet, subdued moment of connection may be the most powerful, arresting moment in *Running with Scissors.*

David L. Boxerbaum

CREDITS

Augusten Burroughs: Joseph Cross
Deirdre Burroughs: Annette Bening
Dr. Finch: Brian Cox
Neil Bookman: Joseph Fiennes
Natalie Finch: Evan Rachel Wood
Norman Burroughs: Alec Baldwin
Agnes Finch: Jill Clayburgh
Hope Finch: Gwyneth Paltrow
Dorothy: Gabrielle Union
Fern Stewart: Kristin Chenoweth
Michael Shepherd: Patrick Wilson
Young Augusten: Jack Kaeding
Poo: Gabriel Guedj
Origin: USA
Language: English
Released: 2006
Production: Brad Grey, Ryan Murphy, Dede Gardner, Brad Pitt; Plan B Entertainment, TriStar Pictures; released by Sony Pictures
Directed by: Ryan Murphy
Written by: Ryan Murphy
Cinematography by: Christopher Baffa
Music by: James Levine
Sound: Marc Gilmartin
Music Supervisor: P.J. Bloom
Editing: Byron Smith
Art Direction: Lorin Flemming
Costumes: Lou Eyrich
Production Design: Richard Sherman
MPAA rating: R
Running time: 121 minutes

REVIEWS

Boxoffice Online. October 20, 2006.
Entertainment Weekly. October 27, 2006, p. 52.
Hollywood Reporter Online. October 16, 2006.
Los Angeles Times Online. October 20, 2006.
New York Times Online. October 20, 2006.
Premiere Magazine. November 2006, p. 42.
San Francisco Chronicle. October 20, 2006, p. E1.
Variety Online. October 13, 2006.
Village Voice Online. October 17, 2006.

QUOTES

Augusten: "I guess it doesn't matter when I begin. No one is gonna believe me anyway."

AWARDS

Nomination:

Golden Globes 2007: Actress—Mus./Comedy (Bening)

RUSSIAN DOLLS

(Les Poupees russes)

Cedric Klapisch's dizzy erotic comedy from France, *Russian Dolls*, blazons forth with an ambitious stylistic premise: in this digital age, the film storyteller need not remain content with a uniform filmic space but can visually fragment it so that it reflects our splintered cyberpersonalities. Had Klapisch been able to translate this vision into a set of equally refreshing plot elements, this sequel would have had the timely appeal of its predecessor, *L'Auberge Espagnole* (2002). As it stands, the film's own cyberpersonality takes the form of riffs from an all too conventional thirty-something coming-of-age sitcom narrative. As in Michel Gondry's *The Science of Sleep* (2006), Klapisch finds that the only way to rise above the frenetic confusion of contemporary desires and pressures is to resort to trusted, age-old values and sentiments.

Xavier (Romain Duris), a rakish freelance writer about to turn thirty, literally thinks through his laptop, which allows him to put down his experiences at the same time as he tries to make sense of them. The film, as if to keep up with him, occasionally transposes pieces of Xavier's memory and imagination onto an otherwise realistic scene, much like persistent unwanted pop-ups. What allows Klapisch to indulge in such free-form departures is the film's story line, most of which is told in flashback.

The story's present takes place at a wedding ceremony in St. Petersburg, which also functions as a reunion for its cast of multinational principals, most of whom were also featured in the previous film as denizens of a rambling apartment in Barcelona. Now, as all of them are waiting for a traffic light to change, Xavier's voiceover tells us that he feels his life is going to change forever as he eyes the beautiful, slinky Wendy (Kelly Reilly).

Before we get to know more, we are thrown into a flashback of Xavier's frantic life a year ago. In a washroom on a train between London and Paris, Xavier is "sorting" it all out as he's feeding his erotic experiences into a laptop. It is his way of deciding which of the desirable smart pretty women in his life mean the most to him. This shunts us to an even earlier flashback of Xavier trying to eke out a living as a freelance reporter in Paris. He is interviewing everyone from hot dog makers to tree cutters while also looking after a toddler who belongs to his longtime and deep attachment, the sharp-witted Martine (Audrey Tautou), while she is away attending a world conference on the environment. As fate hits him while he's down, he also has to move out of his apartment, a plight relieved by another old friend, the kindly Isabelle (Cecile De France), a sporty lesbian with short-cropped hair, who is now a financial reporter for CNN.

While choosing a present for Martine, Xavier gets to know the exotic Kassia (Aissa Maiga), an African store clerk from Senegal that Xavier easily lures into bed. There is a morning after scene suffused with genuine warmth between the two. Xavier later gives in to Martine when she calls to say that she's feeling unbearably lonely. Despite his pleading, she insists on sleeping with him. As she's about to leave the next morning, in walks Kassia, to whom Xavier introduces Martine as "just no one." This angers Martine to the point that she goes ballistic and insists that she will always be a part of his life as she storms out. Kassia then confronts Xavier with his lie, which results in his flying off the handle and denouncing all women. As Kassia leaves, he yells at her in rage, making it clear he doesn't want to see her again.

As if to compensate for this personal debacle, Xavier's professional life picks up. He is offered an assignment to write a TV movie for BBC 2 which, despite his faltering English, Xavier takes on, confident that he can draw upon the resources of another Barcelona friend, the congenial long-haired William (Kevin Bishop). Here the film introduces a digression which lacks the steam even of a subplot. As the two friends reunite, William narrates through an extended flashback how his work as a stagehand helped him find true love. To woo the beautiful Natacha (Evguenya Obraztsova), a Russian ballerina performing in London, William had to spend a year learning Russian before he could visit her in St. Petersburg. The only bearing this has on Xavier's story is to make him see what he's missing out on when it comes to the real thing.

Ironically, it is William's sister, Wendy, Xavier's collaborator, who eventually makes the deepest impact on him. While scripting their romantic soap, they also have to keep Wendy's hirsute brute of an ex-lover at bay. This brings out the violent side in Xavier as he chases him away, threatening to bludgeon him in the process. Good fortune, like ill luck, also seems to come in pairs for Xavier. Just as he's forming a congenial bond with Wendy, he gets an offer from his publisher to ghostwrite the memoirs of a top fashion model in Paris. His multitasking requires that Xavier flit between Paris and London on the express train, which is where we find him at the start of the second flashback.

Celia (Lucy Gordon), the fashion model, is clearly the most stylish thing to have ever happened to Xavier; so entranced is he by her personality, her figure and her walk (in reverse order). Celia for her part seems to find Xavier's openness disarming and, like Wendy, tries to incorporate Xavier into her lifestyle, an endeavor that doesn't quite succeed.

The conflict in Xavier leads to the film's most affecting scene when Wendy confesses to Xavier that she loves him for all his imperfections just as he's getting on the train to Celia. Xavier looks so knocked over by her frankness that he allows the train to pull him away from this moment of epiphany.

In the film's final sequence, Xavier's story returns to the present, the precise moment by the traffic light in St. Petersburg. Wendy, by now convinced that Xavier has dismissed her for Celia, slaps him as he approaches her. Klapisch uses William and Natasha's wedding as the culmination of all the forms of desire his film has explored. There is even a brief shot of Martine in Paris with her new lover. Wendy does forgive Xavier amidst the bonhomie of the wedding cruise. This leads him to eventually rush to her in London. On the train, he notes on his laptop that the women he has been drawn to have been like Russian dolls, and that he had to keep opening each before he could get to the innermost one.

Vivek Adarkar

CREDITS

Xavier: Romain Duris
Martine: Audrey Tautou
Isabelle: Cecile De France
Wendy: Kelly Reilly
William: Kevin Bishop
Celia: Lucy Gordon
Kassia: Aissa Maiga
Natacha: Evguenya Obraztsova
Origin: France, Great Britain
Language: English, French, Russian, Spanish
Released: 2005
Production: Bruno Levy; StudioCanal, France 2 Cinema, Ce Qui Me Meut, Lunar Films; released by Mars Distribution
Directed by: Cedric Klapisch
Written by: Cedric Klapisch
Cinematography by: Dominique Colin
Music by: Loik Dury, Laurent Levesque
Sound: Cyril Moisson, Stephane Brunclair, Dominique Dalmasso
Editing: Francine Sandberg
Costumes: Anne Schotte
Production Design: Marie Cheminal, Chris Edwards
MPAA rating: Unrated
Running time: 125 minutes

REVIEWS

Boxoffice Online. May 12, 2006.
Los Angeles Times Online. May 19, 2006.
New York Times Online. May 10, 2006.
Variety Online. June 15, 2005.
Village Voice Online. May 9, 2006.

QUOTES

Wendy: "I know most girls they get weak on their knees for what's beautiful, you know, that's all they see, that's all they want. But I'm not like that. I don't just see what's beautiful. I fall for the other stuff. I love what's not perfect. It's just how I am."

TRIVIA

The Kookai store where Kassia works is located at 155 Rue de Rennes.

RV

On A Family Vacation, No One Can Hear You Scream.
—Movie tagline

Box Office: $71.7 million

Bob Munro (Robin Williams) is a wimp and a liar. As will happen with wimps and liars, eventually they will have to stand up to their tormentors and admit the truth to those they have deceived. In a good story about wimps and liars there are interesting characters doing interesting things on their way to this conclusion. Unfortunately, *RV* is not a good movie. It is, however, a far-too-familiar movie.

Bob lies to his family. He was supposed to take his wife Jamie (Cheryl Hines), his daughter Cassie (Joanna "JoJo" Levesque), and his son Carl (Josh Hutcherson) on vacation to Hawaii, but his boss Todd (Will Arnett) demands that he make a presentation to a company in Boulder, Colorado during that same time period. Rescheduling the family vacation is impossible because of the camp his weightlifting, gangsta' wannabe son will be attending and college prep programs awaiting his permanently-disgusted-with-everything daughter. But Bob can't level with his family. Guess the filmmakers think it's funnier if he lies to them and suddenly changes their vacation plans without their input. And so the disgruntled Munros end up on vacation in one of the ugliest RVs ever to come off the assembly line. (Perhaps the only piece of interesting trivia about the film is that director Barry Sonnenfeld is pictured on the side of said RV as IRV beckoning the unwary to "rent me.")

Bob lies to his boss, too. Bob calls in to work claiming to be sick so he can begin the painfully slow trek to Boulder with his family in an RV not so affectionately called "The Rolling Turd." Todd thinks Bob is at home working on his presentation and will be flying in for the meeting, but a lot can happen between Pasadena and Boulder.

For example, before they've even left their own street, Bob discovers that he can't drive an RV very well. Not long afterward Bob finds out that the RV's parking brake is damaged requiring that the wheels be chocked each time he stops…or he won't stop. He also realizes that he hasn't a clue how to empty the RV's backed up sewage system. He learns that he can't cook a decent meal and that raccoons are hard to evict once they take up residence in the camper's oven. Bob discovers that in the western wilderness WiFi connections are hard to come by, preventing him from emailing his presentation to his boss, which is made even more difficult when a hitchhiking guitar player steals his laptop. And he notices that not only does his family have little in common with each other, but they also have even less in common with the other families who enjoy RV camping.

One of these families is the Gornickes: Dad Travis (Jeff Daniels), Mom Mary Jo (Kristen Chenoweth) and kids Earl (Hunter Parish), Moon (Chloe Sonnenfeld) and Billy (Alex Ferris). The Gornickes are terminally perky and good-natured and they live full-time in their RV. (Travis and Mary Jo are about the only interesting characters in *RV* and Daniels and Chenoweth look like the only ones not taking the movie too seriously and who allow themselves a bit of fun.) The kids are home schooled and smart, Mom earns $60,000 a year selling various beauty products in the trailer parks, and Dad knows all there is to know about camping, RVs, and the local terrain. They help Bob with his sewage problem, give them a dinner when Bob's epicurean attempts fail, and even find Bob's purloined computer and try to return it to him.

But Bob lies to the Gornickes, too. Uncomfortable with their folksy friendliness, Bob says they have to be on their way early the next morning and then spends the rest of the movie running into them, lying to them, and trying to avoid them. Even though, as anyone can guess, in the end the Gornickes will be the ones who save Bob's sorry soul.

In fact, there is nothing about the movie *RV* that one can't guess far in advance. Only someone who has led a fairly movie-deprived life would not recognize *National Lampoon's Vacation* (1983), but Robin Williams can't pull off the beleaguered dad as well as Chevy Chase did. *RV* is as much a retread as the tires that are fairly certain to be on "The Rolling Turd." This derivative road trip about a dysfunctional family and the disasters they encounter offers no surprises and virtually no laughs. Turning the emptying of a blocked sewage system into a spectator sport may amuse those in the campground, but watching the squirming Williams get covered in fecal matter just made this viewer squirm, too. And speaking of squirming, the saccharine ending followed by the entire cast singing "Route 66" in cowboy gear seems like just so much more groanable fecal matter.

Beverley Bare Buehrer

CREDITS

Bob Munro: Robin Williams
Travis Gornicke: Jeff Daniels
Jamie Munro: Cheryl Hines
Mary Jo Gornicke: Kristin Chenoweth
Cassie Munro: Joanna "JoJo" Levesque
Carl Munro: Josh Hutcherson
Moon Gornicke: Chloe Sonnenfeld
Billy Gornicke: Alex Ferris
Todd Mallory: Will Arnett
Howie: Brendan Fletcher
Garry Moiphine: Brian Markinson
Earl Gornicke: Hunter Parrish
Larry Moiphine: Rob LaBelle
Origin: USA
Language: English
Released: 2006
Production: Lucy Fisher, Douglas Wick; Columbia Pictures, Relativity, Red Wagon Films, Inc., Intermedia, IMF; released by Sony Pictures Entertainment
Directed by: Barry Sonnenfeld
Written by: Geoff Rodkey
Cinematography by: Fred Murphy
Music by: James Newton Howard
Sound: Peter Kurland
Editing: Kevin Tent
Art Direction: Kevin Humenny
Costumes: Mary Vogt
Production Design: Michael Bolton
MPAA rating: PG
Running time: 98 minutes

REVIEWS

Boxoffice Online. April 28, 2006.
Chicago Sun-Times Online. April 28, 2006.
Los Angeles Times Online. April 28, 2006.
New York Times Online. April 28, 2006.

Variety Online. April 27, 2006.
Washington Post. April 28, 2006, p. C5.

QUOTES

Jamie to husband Bob: "Try to remember we're not friendly."
Carl to dad Bob: "You have no idea what you're doing."
Bob replies: "Damn straight."

AWARDS

Nomination:

Golden Raspberries 2006: Worst Support. Actress (Chenoweth)

S

THE SANTA CLAUSE 3: THE ESCAPE CLAUSE

His time at the North Pole is about to go South.
—Movie tagline

'Twas the fight before Christmas.
—Movie tagline

Box Office: $84.5 million

As a general rule, when sequels start containing numbers higher than two, it is not smart to expect much in the way of quality. This is especially true when the original in the series was only middling to begin with. This rule is proven again with *The Santa Clause 3: The Escape Clause*. Since the first two installments made almost $300 million in theaters, it seems a subsequent *Santa Clause* movie was inevitable.

In the first film (1994), regular guy Scott Calvin (Tim Allen), stumbles into some magic and inadvertently inherits the job of becoming Santa Claus. In the second (2002), he finds a Mrs. Claus (Elizabeth Mitchell), which gives him the Clausian equivalent of tenure. In the third, he fends off in-laws and a would-be usurper.

This installment finds Mrs. Claus grumpy and pregnant. She is out of sorts because Santa is not paying enough attention to her and she misses her family. For reasons of security, she is not allowed to tell her family that her husband is Santa—though it seems fine for Santa's ex-wife and various other Santa-side relatives to know. Mrs. Claus tells them only that her husband is a toymaker and that they live in Canada.

Santa eventually realizes that the only way to appease his wife is to let her folks visit. He and the elves work on an elaborate plan to make the North Pole look like Canada. It is a mildly amusing conceit. Santa's in-laws (Alan Arkin and Ann-Margaret) are so busy looking for ways to criticize their son-in-law that they do not really question the whole Canada idea.

Santa has worse problems than disapproving in-laws. One of the other Legendary Creatures, Jack Frost (Martin Short), is jealous of Santa and wants to take over his job. He discovers that he can do just that, if only he can get Santa to wish for his old life back, but Santa must be holding a specific magic snow globe at the time he makes the wish. This is the escape clause of the title.

Appearances by old favorites Mother Nature (Aisha Tyler), Father Time (Peter Boyle), and Cupid (Kevin Pollak) enliven the proceedings. Also returning are main elf Curtis (Spencer Breslin), as well as Santa's extended family, his ex-wife (Wendy Crewson), her husband (Judge Reinhold), their daughter (Liliana Mumy), and Calvin's son (Eric Lloyd). The returnees probably added to the payroll budget, but they are not given all that much to do. Any zest in the film comes from the newcomers—Short, Ann-Margaret, and Arkin. Short brings the energy of someone who has not endured a third version of the same movie. He is an over-the-top performer, exactly the kind this role calls for. Arkin does a nice job of portraying the over-protective father. Ann-Margaret is particularly amazing, if only for the fact that she looks so surrealistically well-preserved.

More than one critic found their Grinch-like feelings aroused by the movie's Halloween release date, though for some, that was not enough to ruin the film. Elizabeth Weitzman of the *New York Daily News* wrote that "Allen and Short seem to be having so much fun that their enthusiasm is entirely contagious." Jeff Strickler of the *Minneapolis Star-Tribune* wrote that "the movie is more cute than funny. Smiles are plentiful, but outright laughs are more widely scattered." Peter Hartlaub of the *San Francisco Chronicle* wrote: "This plodding and unfunny sequel is (like) *Garfield: A Tail of Two Kitties* (2006)—appearing to exist mostly because the film before it made a lot of money." Keith Phipps of *The Onion A.V. Club* wrote: "Shot almost entirely on a single set possibly left standing from the last film, it features what looks like first-take performances and a script that's inane even by kiddie-movie standards." Ty Burr of the *Boston Globe* wrote that "*Santa Clause 3* is shallow, formulaic Yuletide good cheer that's nevertheless acceptable for small children and grown-ups who like to think like them." Of the film's G rating, Manola Dargis of the *New York Times* wrote: "It's squeaky clean, but you might die of boredom."

Jill Hamilton

CREDITS

Santa/Scott Calvin: Tim Allen
Mrs. Claus/Carol: Elizabeth Mitchell
Jack Frost: Martin Short
Curtis: Spencer Breslin
Neil Miller: Judge Reinhold
Laura Miller: Wendy Crewson
Charlie: Eric Lloyd
Lucy Miller: Liliana Mumy
Bud Newman: Alan Arkin
Sylvia Newman: Ann-Margret
Cupid: Kevin Pollak (Cameo)
Easter Bunny: Jay Thomas (Cameo)
Father Time: Peter Boyle (Cameo)
Mother Nature: Aisha Tyler (Cameo)
Origin: USA
Language: English
Released: 2006
Production: Brian Reilly, Robert Newmyer, Jeffrey Silver; Walt Disney Pictures, Outlaw Productions, Boxing Cat Films; released by Buena Vista
Directed by: Michael Lembeck
Written by: Edward Decter, John J. Strauss
Cinematography by: Robbie Greenberg
Music by: George S. Clinton
Sound: Marc Weingarten
Music Supervisor: Frankie Pine
Editing: David Finfer
Art Direction: Charlie Daboub, Gregory A. Berry
Costumes: Ingrid Ferrin
Production Design: Richard Holland
MPAA rating: G
Running time: 91 minutes

REVIEWS

Chicago Sun-Times Online. November 3, 2006.
Entertainment Weekly. November 17, 2006, p. 102.
Hollywood Reporter Online. November 3, 2006.
Los Angeles Times Online. November 3, 2006.
New York Times Online. November 3, 2006.
Variety Online. November 3, 2006.

QUOTES

Jack Frost: "You're not Santa anymore. You're just a guy who smells like a cookie."

AWARDS

Nomination:

Golden Raspberries 2006: Worst Actor (Allen), Worst Support. Actor (Short), Worst Sequel/Prequel

SAW III

Sometimes rules are meant to be broken.
—Movie tagline
To the victor goes the spoils.
—Movie tagline
Every game has its loopholes.
—Movie tagline
This time, he's pulling out all the stops.
—Movie tagline

Box Office: $80.2 million

Director Darren Lynn Bousman's sensation-filled gorefest, *Saw III,* proves inconclusively that the filmic subgenres of horror and porn have a lot more in common than one would have imagined. Both require a concentration within their form and content and both manage to achieve their commercial goals with a minimum of narrative. More importantly, both thrive on a repressed urge amongst their audiences to shut out the world. Bousman goes one step further: *Saw III* proves it is possible to keep the world as we know it at bay for the entire duration of a feature film and along with it, a rational chain of cause-and-effect with the result that as viewers are watching the film, they feel they are looking at a puppet show, only the blood and self-mortification are all too real.

The two main victims of Cramer (Tobin Bell), an ailing, aged torturer, are Lynn (Bahar Soomekh), a darkly attractive young surgeon, and her husband, Jeff (Angus MacFadyen), both recovering from the loss of a son in a traffic accident for which the errant driver was sentenced a mere six months. Lynn and Jeff are kidnapped (viewers are not shown how), and they find themselves in chains in an underground torture dungeon in an unspecified location.

What allows Bousman to get away with such filmic sleights-of-hand is that the film's narrative, or what passes for it, draws its lifeblood from the motif of Cramer's unquestionable power. Other recent forays in this direction have used such a motif to expose such potential traps as cut-rate global tourism, as in *Hostel* (2005), and fascist brutality, as in *Pan's Labyrinth* (2006). In *The Texas Chainsaw Massacre: The Beginning* (2006), the Massacre itself looked silly, and the Chainsaw was straight out of Home Depot. The scariest part of the film was how it portrayed Texas. *Saw III* adopts an opposing tactic: by sacrificing any hint of a geographical setting, it seems to draw its inspiration from the short stories of Edgar Allan Poe.

Had Bousman chosen to, this orgy of dismemberment could have been built around the two truly horrific ironies in American society today: a much too lenient system of justice and an uncaring, exploitative medical mafia. But the directorial impulse here clearly lies somewhere else. The fact that the film, for all its crudity, has succeeded at the box-office speaks volumes for a repressed urge amongst today's moviegoers to hit out viciously and, more important, blindly, at what oppresses them, as if there are just too many targets to isolate. And yet, the film does have one redeeming feature, one championed by Aristotle no less, and that is that after taking in all the cruelty the film has presented in all its revolting detail, a viewer will surely have gotten any latent urge to cause willful pain to others out of his or her system, at least for the time being. Thus, because of the film's unabated sensationalism and tastelessness, any critical take on the film would best serve its readers by writing around the film instead of about it, and to treat its form and content as symptoms rather than filmic motifs.

In keeping with today's hi-tech age, Cramer communicates with his victims through an avatar he has constructed for himself as Jigsaw, a grotesque harlequin mask with a computerized voice that his victims see before them on a television monitor and hear on voice recorders. Jigsaw embodies every personal computer nerd's worst nightmare: a cybergenerated stock figure who attains the power of life and death over the user.

In a pitch black room scattered with the remnants of bloody limbs attached to chains, Jeff is provided the wherewithal to undergo "a series of tests" at the end of which he will be able to confront the man responsible for his son's death. Lynn gets to meet Cramer himself who is bed-ridden with a tumor in his frontal lobe and needs Lynn to operate on him. "Death is a surprise party," Cramer says to her, "unless you're dead on the inside." The pressures on Lynn are explained to her by Amanda (Shawnee Smith), Cramer's villainously beautiful assistant, who puts on Lynn a metallic collar geared to explode if Cramer's monitored heartbeat falls to a fatal level. Lynn's surgery must keep Cramer alive until Jeff finishes his tests.

Jeff's first test involves Denica (Debra McCabe), a witness to the accident in question but who kept silent. Jeff is able to witness her torture as she's tied nude under a lethal shower. Despite her helpless apologies, Jeff sees her frozen to death. On her part, Lynn has to make do with the instruments of torture in order to "decompress" Cramer's brain. She drills through his skull and removes a part of the carapace, thereby revealing the inside of his head. Meanwhile Jeff is led to his second victim, Judge Halden (Barry Flatman), who has been chained at the bottom of a pit that slowly fills up with sewage. Halden convinces Jeff that it was the judicial system that was responsible for the light sentencing, which in turn leads to Jeff forgiving him and freeing him from torture, but not from a trigger mechanism that does away with the judge.

Instead of the elemental horror of Poe's "The Pit and the Pendulum," the film resorts to flashes and shocks that evoke nothing more than a montage from a preview of coming attractions. This is horror in the form of sound-bytes. Rigg (Lyriq Bent), the young black man driving the car that killed Jeff's son, is tied to a rack. Jeff can only watch as complex gears twist Rigg's arms and legs off until finally his head is made to rotate like a corkscrew.

The surgery complete, Cramer grants Lynn her freedom, but Amanda comes in the way, not wanting her to escape. Having finished his tests, Jeff enters Cramer's sanctum and shoots Amanda in the neck. Then Cramer, whose flashbacks have revealed how Amanda came to be his assistant, says to Amanda those two words abhorred by every video game enthusiast: "Game Over!" For Jeff, however, the final test is whether he can forgive Cramer. Jeff says he does as he fires at Cramer, but he finds there are no bullets in the gun, whereupon he proceeds to slash the archvillain's throat.

However, this is no resolution for what has proven to be so profitable a filmic franchise. A recorder informs Jeff that his daughter is being held prisoner in a chamber with a limited supply of air and that to save her he must play a game. Jeff's response is to emit a helpless primal wail after which the screen blacks out.

One leaves the film with the thought that while merchants of even softcore filmic porn are deprived of respectable theatrical venues via X ratings, Bousman and Company are allowed to reap their profits by capitalizing on the freedom to explicitly depict mutilations and other abominations with smug self-righteousness.

Vivek Adarkar

CREDITS

Cramer/Jigsaw: Tobin Bell
Amanda: Shawnee Smith
Jeff: Angus MacFadyen
Kerry: Dina Meyer
Lynn: Bahar Soomekh
Tim: Mpho Koaho
Denica: Debra McCabe
Judge Halden: Barry Flatman
Rigg: Lyriq Bent
Origin: USA
Language: English
Released: 2006
Production: Gregg Hoffman, Oren Koules, Mark Burg; Twisted Pictures; released by Lionsgate
Directed by: Darren Lynn Bousman
Written by: Leigh Whannell
Cinematography by: David Armstrong
Music by: Charlie Clouser
Sound: Richard Penn
Editing: Kevin Greutert
Art Direction: Anthony Ianni
Costumes: Alex Kavanagh
Production Design: David Hackl
MPAA rating: R
Running time: 107 minutes

REVIEWS

Hollywood Reporter Online. October 28, 2006.
Los Angeles Times Online. October 30, 2006.
New York Times Online. October 28, 2006.
Variety Online. October 27, 2006.

A SCANNER DARKLY

What Does A Scanner See?
—Movie tagline
Everything Is Not Going To Be OK.
—Movie tagline

Box Office: $5.5 million

Smack dab into a summer of sequels and blockbuster comic-book adaptations, something unique and sinister dropped into moviegoers' laps in mid-2006—Richard Linklater's latest experiment in fantasy, *A Scanner Darkly.* The emphasis should be on "darkly": Linklater's faithfully hallucinatory adaptation of Philip K. Dick's 1973 short story is one of the most harrowing depictions ever of the paranoid and powerless life of drug junkies. Its nightmarish quality is only slightly tempered by the fact that Linklater animates his story using the same amazing rotoscoping technique he pioneered for feature-length film with his marvelous philosophical saga *Waking Life* (2001). That is, he filmed his cast and then had a team of animators draw over the film with computer graphics, creating a realistic graphic-novel look that proves very useful for Dick's half-crazed storyline.

Dick, whose science fiction stories have inspired several successful films, including *Blade Runner* (1982) and *Minority Report* (2002), was a visionary genius whose personal life spiraled down through drug addiction into paranoid fantasies about aliens communicating with him. He wrote *A Scanner Darkly* during a drug rehabilitation stint, and it is both merciless in its depiction of the psychic ravages of drug addiction and sympathetic to its victims, among whom are many friends Dick named, as Linklater repeats in a sad end-credit dedication. The tale also weaves Dick's customary motifs of sinister corporate and government collusion in a future where individual liberties have been sacrificed for the sake of a wartime campaign—in this case, an all-out war against drugs.

That Linklater sees fit to place the story only seven years in the future—that is, forty years after Dick's original story—is testament to how close to that future our society has edged. The methods of police control in *A Scanner Darkly* don't seem all that far-fetched—even the "scramble suit" that the narc, Officer Fred, wears, a garment that keeps shifting his countenance and attire to make him unidentifiable, seems only a step beyond holographic techniques currently in use. The rotoscoping is ideal for the scramble suit, because its rapidly shifting images are only a short step removed from the rest of the film's animation.

The technique also comes in handy in the film's opening scene, in which the protagonist, Bob Arctor (Keanu Reeves), sweats his way through a hallucination that involves insects crawling all over him. Later, one of his friends turns into a giant beetle. Too bad there aren't a few more such scenes to liven up the film, but Linklater isn't into grandstanding with his technique—most of the time he merely uses it to render a hyperrealistic world, full of shifting and uncertain images filtered through the lens of the drug addict.

The animation is much improved from the rotoscoping in *Waking Life,* with beautifully drawn sequences that challenge the imagination at the same time they are grounded in reality. The effect of the technique is so compelling that the characters come alive even more than some live-action actors, and by the time the film is half over, everyone on screen looks more and more like real people, so easily does one accept this fluid, fanciful, but very realistic method of depicting them.

The story is compelling, too, but feels fleshed out in the first hour by superfluous, albeit highly entertaining exchanges. Both Woody Harrelson and Robert Downey Jr. have a great time with their roles as Bob's sidekicks in drug-addled misery, creating comic characters both hilarious and tragically dead-on. Harrelson's Ernie Luckman is an extension of the actor's often-used wild-man, goofball shtick, but in this film Harrelson has no restraints—since his actions are going to be animated anyway, he's able to let loose and make himself as outlandish as he wants to be. Downey's cartoonishness is something different, and so good you wish you could see it in live action: with his brush cut, oversized glasses, and nerdish outfits, Downey's James Barrish has a memorable look, and his overly intellectualized, verbose but rambling dialogue sounds just right—an addled prattling of almost-convincingly-articulated nonsense.

Unfortunately, in a key role that gets less dialogue and screen time, Winona Ryder's character is not one that stands out. Linklater had underwritten the role, perhaps, as Dick also did, to maximize the impact of revelations concerning her character later on. And Reeves, though sweaty and paranoid, doesn't have the range to pull off the complicated dual role to which he's assigned—a man who's being manipulated heavily, by unknown forces, into a split personality, both a narcotics officer and the drug kingpin he's supposedly trying to bring down.

Interestingly, all the actors in the cast have had their own highly publicized battles with substance abuse—making them ideal candidates for a film that knowingly plumbs the depraved depths of drug addiction. In Dick's world, and in the world Linklater re-creates, drugs make their victims pathetic and paranoid, and their behavior reprehensible. But there is a sinister conspiracy behind the widespread pushing of the drug, known as Substance D. It has rendered society into a battle zone between the addicted, those trying to catch them, those pushing the drug, and those trying to stay out of its grip.

Linklater is content, after introducing his characters, to let them wiggle on the hook of the confusing plot. The biggest mystery is what is happening to Agent Fred, who is obviously an addict but not so clearly the victim of a strange conspiracy whose dimensions are unfathomable. Before an exhilarating ending that provides hope for liberation, there are long stretches where the addicts seem to stew in their own paranoid juices. One extended sequence, which involves Barrish and Luckman breaking down on a car trip and then wondering who may have broken into their house—which Barrish has left unlocked in a strange effort to entrap intruders—is a tour de force of paranoia, deftly executed as a sort of comic opera. But too much of the remaining parts of the first hour-plus of *A Scanner Darkly* seem full of redundant and murky exposition.

It's too bad that, much as with *Waking Life,* marketers don't seem to know what to make of Linklater's hybrid film. Too many folks won't see it because they think it's a cartoon, but of course it's an adult feature, not an animated movie for families. Some viewers may find the technique distances them enough from the characters that they don't feel too dragged down into their hard-to-bear world. It might be the ideal method for telling a Phillip K. Dick story. The trouble with Dick's fantasies is that they strain a bit too hard to paint a shadowy authoritarian structure whose specific rules are inscrutable. They yield protagonists who are so manipulated they seem incapable of doing more than responding to unseen forces. This story is a little different in that the small window of hope that opens at the end comes from a surprise corner, from forces that use the protagonist, as Dick himself does, as a tool in the service of a larger war. Linklater and his animation team render this surreal world precisely as it might have unraveled in the brilliantly troubled mind of Dick himself—as a nightmarish vision that is slowly taking over what's known as the normal world.

Michael Betzold

CREDITS

Bob Arctor: Keanu Reeves

Donna Hawthorne: Winona Ryder

James Barris: Robert Downey Jr.

Ernie Luckman: Woody Harrelson

Charles Freck: Rory Cochrane

Arctor's Wife: Melody Chase

Connie: Lisa Marie Newmyer

Origin: USA

Language: English

Released: 2006

Production: Palmer West, Jonah Smith, Erwin Stoff, Anne Walker-McBay, Tommy Pallotta; Thousand Words, Section Eight; released by Warner Independent Pictures

Directed by: Richard Linklater

Written by: Richard Linklater
Cinematography by: Shane Kelly
Music by: Graham Reynolds
Sound: Ethan Andrus
Editing: Sandra Adair
Costumes: Kari Perkins
Production Design: Bruce Curtis
MPAA rating: R
Running time: 102 minutes

REVIEWS

Boxoffice Online. July 7, 2006.
Entertainment Weekly. July 14, 2006, p. 61.
Los Angeles Times Online. July 7, 2006.
New York Times Online. July 7, 2006.
Premiere Magazine Online. July 6, 2006.
San Francisco Chronicle. July 7, 2006, p. E1.
Variety Online. May 25, 2006.
Village Voice Online. July 5, 2006.
Washington Post. July 14, 2006, p. C1.

QUOTES

James Barris: "This is a world getting progressively worse. Can we not agree on that?"

SCARY MOVIE 4

The fourth and final chapter of the trilogy.
—Movie tagline

Bury the grudge. Burn the village. See the saw.
—Movie tagline

The funniest thing you ever sawed.
—Movie tagline

What Is With The Scary Movies?
—Movie tagline

Box Office: $90.7 million

It's fitting that director David Zucker has taken over the *Scary Movie* franchise. Started in 2000 by Keenan Ivory Wayans and his brothers Shawn and Marlon, the first two movies put a Wayans spin on the filmic form that Zucker and his brother Jerry pretty much invented with their classic *Airplane!* (1980). Here Zucker, and longtime collaborator Jim Abrahams, do what they do best: compress popular culture in a movie-length collection of visual gags, crude jokes and movie parodies. This rapid-fire joke technique is no longer the groundbreaking surprise it was when *Airplane!* debuted—it would be impossible to recapture the element of surprise of that film. But Zucker and Co. have faith in the comedy style they have developed. They pile on the jokes, keep them coming and hope that some of them hit. By sheer volume alone, invariably some do.

In this fourth installment, the movie parodies change, but Anna Faris faithfully returns as the dim Cindy Campbell. This time out, she gets a job in a seemingly haunted house that features a paralyzed elderly woman, Mrs. Norris (Cloris Leachman), and some sort of pale-faced spirit boy. She does not seem overly concerned about the creepy goings-on in the house and is more interested in the divorced dad, Tom Ryan (Craig Bierko), who lives next door. The plot, if that is the correct word, is not so much as unraveled as it is haphazardly tossed out. Abrahams, plus writers Craig Mazin and Pat Profit, string together chunks of *Brokeback Mountain* (2005), *Million Dollar Baby* (2004), *Saw* (2004), *The Village* (2004), *The Grudge* (2004), *War of the Worlds* (2005), and even Tom Cruise's notorious couch jumping moment on *Oprah,* in hopes that together a new, coherent plot will arise. It does not, but that is sort of beside the point.

Scary Movie 4 is populated with a strong cast. Leslie Nielsen makes his practically mandatory appearance in such a film as the President of the United States. As usual, his dignity lasts about two seconds, and soon he is standing naked in front of a United Nations meeting. Leachman hams it up as a paralyzed woman who is desperately trying to signal her dim caregiver, Cindy, that something is seriously amiss. And Faris is just the right actress to play Cindy. Whatever happens to her or her friends in these films, Cindy remains prettily wide-eyed and oblivious. Bierko plays the perfect soul mate to Cindy. His Tom Ryan is klutzy, unintelligent and perhaps even more oblivious than Cindy. And even though it is her fourth such film, Regina Hall brings a feisty energy to the one-note part of the sexually aggressive buddy, Brenda.

In the pop culture blender that is these types of films, guest stars pop up frequently, in odd roles or pairings. Dr. Phil and Shaquille O'Neal do a bit together and Anthony Anderson is a gay cowboy. Also cashing a paycheck are James Earl Jones, Molly Shannon, and Chingy. Something about this type of film seems to give permission to famous folks to leave their dignity at home. Mike Tyson cheerfully participates in an ear-biting segment and Charlie Sheen gamely plays along with a Viagra joke. Carmen Electra, Bill Pullman, and Chris Elliott band together in an extended *The Village* sequence.

Critics were pretty kind to the film. Liz Braun of the *Toronto Sun* wrote that "it's less offensive than earlier *Scary* outings. It's also less funny. But what the heck." Colin Covert of the *Minneapolis Star Tribune* wrote: "The six-year-old franchise shows its age, with some off-the-mark satire and prehistoric references (it reaches back to 1997 for a Mike Tyson ear-biting gag) but there are still enough solid jokes to outweigh the clunkers." Peter Hartlaub of the *San Francisco Chronicle* wrote: "Maybe 38 percent of the comedy hits its mark in this movie, and that's more than enough to satisfy." Wesley Morris of the *Boston Globe* wrote: "Part sketch-comedy cartoon, part *Cracked* magazine spoof, installment four is the most scornfully made yet." And for those viewers who wanted intellectual justification for their penchant for silly movies, Nathan Lee of the *New York Times* offered that "the fun of *Scary Movie 4* is that it isn't a movie at all. Organized on the principle of parody, not plot, driven by gags and cultural feedback, it's an exercise in lowbrow postmodernism, a movie-movie contraption more nuts than Charlie Kaufman's gnarliest fever dream. It's cleverly stupid."

Jill Hamilton

CREDITS

Cindy Campbell: Anna Faris
Brenda Meeks: Regina Hall
Tom Ryan: Craig Bierko
Mahalik: Anthony Anderson
Holly: Carmen Electra
Ezekiel: Chris Elliott
CJ: Kevin Hart
Mrs. Noris: Cloris Leachman
Oliver: Michael Madsen
President Baxter Harris: Leslie Nielsen
Henry Hale: Bill Pullman
George: Simon Rex
Tom: Charlie Sheen
Marilyn: Molly Shannon
Shaq: Shaquille O'Neal
Harper: Bryan Callen
Knifeman: Dave Attell
Rachel: Conchita Campbell
Oprah: Debra Wilson
Rasheed: Patrice O'Neal
Himself: Dr. Phil McGraw
Narrator: James Earl Jones (uncredited)
Himself: Chingy
Himself: Mike Tyrson (Cameo)
Origin: USA
Language: English
Released: 2006
Production: Robert K. Weiss, Craig Mazin; Dimension Films, Miramax, Brad Grey Pictures; released by Dimension Films
Directed by: David Zucker
Written by: Craig Mazin, Jim Abrahams, Pat Proft
Cinematography by: Thomas Ackerman
Music by: James L. Venable
Sound: Hamilton Sterling
Editing: Craig Herring, Tom Lewis
Art Direction: Willie Heslup
Costumes: Carol Ramsey
Production Design: Holger Gross
MPAA rating: PG-13
Running time: 83 minutes

REVIEWS

Boxoffice Online. April 14, 2006.
Detroit News. April 14, 2006, p. 1F.
Entertainment Weekly. April 21, 2006, p. 56.
Los Angeles Times Online. April 14, 2006.
New York Times Online. April 14, 2006.
San Francisco Chronicle. April 14, 2006, p. E5.
Variety Online. April 13, 2006.

SCHOOL FOR SCOUNDRELS

Nice guys graduate last.
—Movie tagline

Life's a game. Learn how to play.
—Movie tagline

Too nice? Too honest? Too 'you'? Help is on the way.
—Movie tagline

Anything you learn can and will be used against you.
—Movie tagline

Box Office: $17.8 million

For most of the running time in *School for Scoundrels*, an irritable Billy Bob Thornton sneers disgustedly, and an overwhelmed Jon Heder swoons precipitously. Struggling to make sub-par material work can do such things to an actor. A remake of a superior 1960 British production, *School for Scoundrels* is an inert blend of romantic comedy and endless, mean-spirited, and increasingly ridiculous male one-upmanship. In the 2006 remake, Billy Bob teaches a class meant to turn the ineffectual into the potently impressive. One only wishes that *School for Scoundrels* itself could have enrolled in that same seminar.

Heder, still best known as the star of *Napoleon Dynamite* (2004), continues to till familiarly feckless territory as Roger, a meek, male meter-maid. When first seen, he is sound asleep amongst stacks of self-help books, signaling his decidedly discontent lifestyle. In short order, one can see why. Diffident Roger scoots around the streets of New York City in a dorky little vehicle wearing even dorkier little shorts. After issuing a ticket to a pair of brawny, unsavory characters who are less than intimidated by his authority, a panic-stricken Roger must beat a hasty retreat (or, at least, as hasty as his pokey, diminutive contraption will permit). As he hyperventilates behind the wheel on the way to passing out, the tough-looking miscreants enthusiastically boot the sides of his cart, throwing derisive insults (and later bullets) his way. Once the shaken "little ticket man" regains consciousness, he apologizes if his anxiety-induced swoon had led the men to fear they had killed him and even agrees to their "request" that he cover their $80 ticket. Roger also gives up his badge, uniform, and regulation sneakers to compensate for their "emotional distress" and returns humiliated to the station in his underwear. His boss (Luis Guzman), who incompetently doubles as a counselor, is less than helpful.

As if Roger was not miserable enough, he is also belittled by his coworkers and rejected as an underwhelming Big Brother by three successive dissatisfied kids, leaving him hopelessly demoralized and sobbing down the street. It is no wonder that he lacks the confidence to ask out the cute Aussie sweetheart, Amanda (Jacinda Barrett), who lives in a neighboring apartment. After all, most women would much prefer finding a gallant Prince Charming on their threshold than simply a doormat.

Good news (of sorts) comes from sympathetic Big Brother coordinator Ian (David Cross), a former jellyfish himself who developed a spine thanks to an ultra-secret Adult Ed course one can apparently only learn of through the nebbish network of its former graduates. It is taught by brutally biting Dr. P (Thornton), who regularly refers to his students as "retards" and even less polite epithets, and is constantly accompanied by his massively intimidating assistant Lesher (Michael Clarke Duncan). Dr. P dispenses advice on how men can release their "inner lion" through emboldening but bad behavior. Examples of his advice include "Lie, lie and lie some more" to get a woman in bed, and "No compliments—ever!" Dr, P also retains the right to activate his students' beepers at any time, at which point, each man must not only assert himself but also "initiate a confrontation." This unsound advice paves the way for a series of ludicrously stupid scenes of an elderly hospital patient getting food shoved in his face, a street musician having her violin smashed to bits, a couple's car windshield getting bashed with a bat, and two ruffians on the subway being told to pipe down. (They do not respond well.) As for Roger, he grabs a magazine and the last cherry Danish from the office bully, getting an unpleasant, headfirst inspection of a toilet bowl as a result. Speaking of unhappy endings, more cringes than guffaws will be elicited when it is insinuated that Lesher rapes three of the students in the woods during a subsequently lame paintball scene. This sodomy comedy unfortunately and unpleasantly continues to resurface for the rest of *School for Scoundrels.*

With amazing rapidity and unbelievable ease, Roger soon becomes the boldest of the bunch. However, rising to become Dr. P's prize pupil could come with quite a high price, as Ian warns that the maniacal motivator has been known to resentfully (and rabidly) tear down what he has so successfully built up. It looks like that is where things may be headed when the married, not-so-good doctor throws down the gauntlet to his protege by suavely pursuing Amanda for himself, pretending to be a tender-hearted, widowed surgeon named Dennis. Throughout the scenes of nonsensical competition which follow, both Dr. P and the film itself endeavor to keep viewers guessing as to whether he is actually trying to help further embolden Roger or is merely helping himself to what Roger covets.

As a result, during a doubles tennis match in which the two men play opposite Amanda and her highly acerbic roommate, Becky (Sarah Silverman), Roger feigns innocence while repeatedly smashing Dr. P in the skull and crotch. Dr. P retaliates by getting his other students to break into Amanda's apartment and cover everything (including her poor dog) with bright red graffiti designed to make Roger look psychotically lovesick and jealous. Soon after, Roger has the doctor's car towed. Then Roger's boss, citing a fervid love letter that was actually penned by Dr. P, fires Roger for sexual harassment. This no-holds-barred tit for tat spirals increasingly out of control without giving the film any real sense of momentum. The over-the-top climax to all this inanity takes place at the airport where Dr. P is about to whisk away an unsuspecting Amanda to a non-existent medical convention in Florida. After Roger and the audience are jerked back and forth some more about Dr. P's true intentions, it all ends with both men writhing ridiculously on board an aircraft after getting zapped with a defibrillator. Few watching will get much of a charge out of any of this.

Except for some of Dr. P's humorously-cutting comments, the comedy in *School for Scoundrels* is as anemic as the story of Roger's ardor for Amanda. Few viewers will be drawn to Roger's faint flame, let alone be exultant when she finally realizes what is going on and happily deflowers him in Miami. While Heder succeeds in making the audience feel sorry for his character when he is at his most pathetic, Roger is simply too wan and wanting as the film's ostensible romantic hero. Barrett's Amanda is endlessly sweet, but bland. Their one date scene together is a sparkless yawn which includes Roger trying to impress animal-loving Amanda by liberating a restaurant's lobsters and tossing them into the river. How lucky they are, not only to be free but also absent for the rest of the boring sequence. Of even less interest are the romantic "achievements" of fellow students Eli (Todd Louiso) and Diego (Horatio Sanz), noted in the film's denouement. While the characters are now doing their equivalent of roaring, the film itself ends with a weak whimper.

Made on a budget estimated at $20 million, *School for Scoundrels* grossed over $17 million at the domestic box office. Critical reaction was not positive. The film was directed and co-written by Todd Phillips (along with continued collaborator Scot Armstrong), who provided more fun in the past with *Old School* (2003). Overall, their latest effort fails to make the grade.

David L. Boxerbaum

CREDITS

Dr. P: Billy Bob Thornton
Roger: Jon Heder
Amanda: Jacinda Barrett
Lesher: Michael Clarke Duncan
Lonnie: Ben Stiller
Sergeant Moorehead: Luis Guzman
Diego: Horatio Sanz
Becky: Sarah Silverman
Ian: David Cross
Eli: Todd Louiso
Origin: USA
Language: English
Released: 2006
Production: Todd Phillips, Daniel Goldberg, J. Geyer Kosinski; Dimension Films, Picked Last, Media Talent Group; released by MGM
Directed by: Todd Phillips
Written by: Todd Phillips, Scot Armstrong
Cinematography by: Jonathan Brown
Music by: Christophe Beck
Sound: Kim Harris Ornitz
Editing: Leslie Jones, Daniel Schalk
Art Direction: Scott A. Meehan
Costumes: Louise Mingenbach
Production Design: Nelson Coates
MPAA rating: PG-13
Running time: 101 minutes

REVIEWS

Boxoffice Online. September 29, 2006.
Chicago Sun-Times Online. September 29, 2006.
Entertainment Weekly Online. September 27, 2006.
Hollywood Reporter Online. September 26, 2006.
Los Angeles Times Online. September 29, 2006.
New York Times Online. September 29, 2006.
Rolling Stone Online. September 21, 2006.
San Francisco Chronicle. September 29, 2006, p. E4.
Variety Online. September 24, 2006.
Washington Post. September 29, 2006, p. C5.

QUOTES

Dr. P (to his students): "You can't help yourself because your self sucks!"

THE SCIENCE OF SLEEP

(La Science des reves)

Close your eyes. Open your heart.
—Movie tagline

In dreams emotions are overwhelming.
—Movie tagline

Box Office: $4.6 million

Michel Gondry's trippy romantic comedy from France, *The Science of Sleep*, revolves around youthful but misguided attempts to find art, sex, and romance in today's Paris. But on a more profound level, the film's grandiose title masks a reflection on the seismic shift taking place in human culture globally. We ourselves need to create the art we need, the film seems to say, no matter how crude our attempts to externalize our visions. Like no other film before it, Gondry's film reflects this paradigmatic shift, crudity and all. If his effort goes overboard in his tribute to homemade art, it is because he extends the idea of home as a source for a new kind of artistic form into the realm of artistic content as well, with the result that the lackluster domesticity (read the domination of the mother) and the tired view of sex he portrays rob his film of the refreshing originality it might have imparted.

The handsome young Stephane (Gael Garcia Bernal), the film's protagonist, is a talented graphic artist, but a dork when it comes to romance. His mother, the congenial Christine (Miou-Miou), has invited him to return to Paris from Mexico, with the lure of a job suited to his talents. As he settles into the cramped bedroom of his childhood, in a building owned by his mother, he finds his mechanical robotic toys are still functioning. Stephane looks forward to working as a designer in an outfit that produces calendars. What Stephane is not prepared for is that the operation consists of only three employees: the sex-obsessed middle-aged Guy (Alain

Chabat), who becomes his buddy of sorts, largely owing to the fact that he shares with Stephane the dilemma that, despite his good looks, he has not been able to find romance; the neurasthenic asexual Serge (Sacha Bourdo); and the repressed nymphomaniac Martine (Aurelia Petit). Stephane soon feels betrayed by the fact that his duties consist of nothing more than cut-and-paste jobs, but Guy gets him to show his portfolio to their eccentric boss, Pouchet (Pierre Vaneck). Stephane has designed a calendar conforming to his vision of what he calls "Disasterology," illustrating the worst human disaster that occurred in each month, from Flight 800 to the Mexico City Earthquake. Needless to say, Pouchet has nothing to offer in the way of an outlet for Stephane's imagination.

This rejection hits us as hard as it does Stephane, since the film opens with Stephane performing and televising from the studio of his dreams. Here, he is his own back-up band, his own cameraman behind a mock TV camera, and the host of his own educational cooking program. The recipe he is sharing with an unseen audience is one for dreams. Into a large saucepan, he mixes up the ingredients: random thoughts, reminiscences, memories of the past, loves, friendships, as well as things seen during the day. This studio functions as Stephane's child-like refuge throughout the film from a world he does not understand, but he is not always in control of the proceedings. A monitor on the wall behind him shows a day-glow reality, a vortex into which Stephane disappears the first time we see it. A voiceover recounts his past experience of attending a Duke Ellington concert with his Dad, but then the performer turns out to be Duck Ellington, and Stephane tells his father on the soundtrack, "But you're dead, lost to cancer."

This opening sums up what is at the deepest level in Stephane's unconscious: the unresolved issue of having lost his father whom he loved, and his inability to accept the erudite Gerard (Alain de Moyencourt), his mother's current lover. To this conflict is added his out-of-place feelings at work. A comment from Guy about the stubble on his face leads to his dreaming of a menacing electric shaver that takes the form of a spider that attacks Pouchet. Instead of shaving him, the shaver makes Pouchet grow a long beard, after which Pouchet jumps out the window and takes his place on the street, pushing a cart like a tramp. As a counterpoint, Stephane flies like Superman over a cardboard world, an escape within his escape, the correlative of a distant memory of inventing toys with his father.

Stephane's control over this jumble of repressed desires is tested when he comes to know his neighbor across the hall, the attractive but spectacled and circumspect Brit, Stephanie (Charlotte Gainsbourg), who has just moved in. Initially, Stephane is drawn to her blonde friend, the less reserved and pretty Zoe (Emma de Caunes), someone who makes him feel at home by telling him about herself and Stephanie as having glamorous jobs as concert managers (which the gullible Stephane believes). In fact, they both work as clerks in a clinical laboratory. Zoe soon feels that her new friend and Stephanie are meant for each other. She says to him, "Stephane...Stephanie," then adds, "She doesn't have a boyfriend." Stephane finds this embarrassing, so much so that he does not even tell them that he lives across the hall. He does, however, try to explain their being brought together through his theory of human behavior, a theory he calls "Synchronized Parallel Randomness." He illustrates this with the example of two men brought face to face who both keep stepping aside so that the other can proceed; their thinking is so similar that they keep stepping aside at the same time, the path of one being blocked by the other, the result being that neither can move ahead.

What might appear to be a dry philosophical conundrum takes on a romantic tinge when Stephane finds that Stephanie is also a craftsperson like him. He shows her and Zoe the 3-D glasses he has invented, which enables one to see life in 3-D. "But life is already in 3-D!" Stephanie retorts. She then sees what Stephane means when she looks through them, and a painting appears to take on a holographic depth. As for Stephanie, her toys are far less flamboyant—an embroidered pony, a little white boat made out of fabric—but they impress Stephane nevertheless. When Stephanie says she wants to prepare a forest in which to place the boat, Stephane suggests the forest be inside the boat. Stephanie looks puzzled at first, but then acknowledges Stephane's outlandish idea with a smile.

From this point on, Stephane and Stephanie become the two central figures in the philosophical conundrum. This results in the film's narrative stalling and its dramatic quotient plummeting, as it revolves around the inability of its two leads to move ahead in their relationship. Stephane has been shown to have normal sexual longings when he dreams of having his way with Martine, laying her across the photocopy machine, while his painted vista of the Mexico City Earthquake undulates in the background. Similarly, we cannot see why someone like Stephanie would want to keep Stephane at bay, shirking from any kind of physical intimacy whenever the occasion arises, such as when Stephane demonstrates his time machine, which allows him to kiss her in the future, resulting in her slapping him in the present. When he proposes marriage, her answer is that she does not want a boyfriend. No doubt Gondry as writer/director needs this distance between his romantic couple to drive home his lyrical thrust at the end of the film, but it reduces his formally innovative enterprise to the level of a simple date movie.

Guy's continuing advice to Stephane on sex—from how to get Martine to perform fellatio on him to French-kissing Stephanie—doesn't help Stephane or the film. It does, however, inspire Stephane to make out with a night-bird on the club scene while Guy tries his luck with Zoe. Another subplot has to do with Stephane and Stephanie making an animated film using the boat, but it never gets off the ground. Yet another has to do with Stephane interviewing Christine and Gerard in his dream studio when he imagines himself a celebrity, and Christine tells the camera that "since he was six, he inverted dream and reality." This leads Stephane to devise a contraption whereby he can control the movement of his eyes while asleep, and thereby control his dreams.

This ultimately works because he dreams of Stephanie. He also dreams of himself as a successful and famous graphic designer with a museum named after him. However, the Stephanie that Stephane dreams about advises him to be more persistent, thereby reducing Stephane to a schizoid state. In a dream, he is with Stephanie on a ski lift, but their intimacy is ruined by Guy, Serge, and Martine in the car behind him shouting advice, with Guy telling him to grab the moment and Martine telling him not to rush. Stephane kisses the face of his beloved, but then in the snow, the earth opens up under his feet, revealing its red core.

The dream, however, seems to give Stephane the courage to break into Stephanie's apartment by climbing in a window, if, for no other purpose, than to fix her damaged pony. When Stephanie returns to find him there, she throws him out, but later relents when her pony starts to gallop once again. These ups and downs, spanning the worlds of Stephane's imagination and reality, prove too much for him, and he collapses in tears outside Stephanie's door.

As Stephane gets ready to return to Mexico, he pays Stephanie one last visit. With nothing to lose, he resorts to explicit sex talk, which she does not encourage, claiming that he is distorting reality. He then climbs up onto the bunk bed she has built and, like a child, refuses to come down. "I'll call your mother!" she screams up at him. In desperation, he asks her to feel his hair. She refuses. At that moment, he seems to have an epiphany of sorts as he sees the white boat with trees inside it: Stephanie has brought his suggestion to life. This piece of craftwork fashioned by her hands seems to say far more to him than any words or gesture from her. As he falls asleep, Stephanie gently feels his hair.

In his dream world, he and Stephanie ride the pony he fixed over rolling pastures, then onto the white boat which sets sail on a cellophane sea, below clouds of cotton wool. For those of us who can create art from our dreams, the film seems to say, true happiness can only be found in an artificial world and not the one we take to be real.

Vivek Adarkar

CREDITS

Stephane Miroux: Gael Garcia Bernal
Stephanie: Charlotte Gainsbourg
Guy: Alain Chabat
Christine Miroux: Miou-Miou
Monsieur Pouchet: Pierre Vaneck
Zoe: Emma de Caunes
Serge: Sacha Bourdo
Martine: Aurelia Petit
Gerard: Alain de Moyencourt
Origin: France, Italy
Language: English, French
Released: 2006
Production: Georges Bermann, Michel Gondry, Frederic Junqua; Partizan Films, France 3 Cinema; released by Warner Independent
Directed by: Michel Gondry
Written by: Michel Gondry
Cinematography by: Jean-Louis Bompoint
Music by: Jean-Michel Bernard
Sound: Guillaume Sciama
Editing: Juliette Welfing
Costumes: Florence Fontaine
MPAA rating: R
Running time: 105 minutes

REVIEWS

Boxoffice Online. September 15, 2006.
Entertainment Weekly. September 29, 2006, p. 55.
Los Angeles Times Online. September 22, 2006.
New York Times Online. September 22, 2006.
Premiere Magazine Online. September 8, 2006.
Rolling Stone Online. September 7, 2006.
San Francisco Chronicle. September 22, 2006, p. E5.
Variety Online. January 23, 2006.
Washington Post. September 22, 2006, p. C5.

QUOTES

Stephane: "It's a dream. We don't have to work in dreams."

SCOOP

The Perfect Man. The Perfect Story. The Perfect Murder.
—Movie tagline

Box Office: $10.5 million

Match Point (2005) is a dark melodrama with deeper psychological shadings than anything writer/director

Woody Allen has created since *Hannah and Her Sisters* (1986). Not only the London setting but the characters and dialogue have an unexpected polish missing from Allen's recent films. *Scoop*, in contrast, represents a return to Allen's past. If *Anything Else* (2003) is a reworking of *Annie Hall* (1977), in a decidedly minor key, *Scoop* revisits *Manhattan Murder Mystery* (1993), with a side trip to the mystery spoof *The Curse of the Jade Scorpion* (2001).

In *Manhattan Murder Mystery*, the character played by Allen refuses to accept the assertions of his wife, (Diane Keaton) that one of their neighbors has murdered his spouse. A similar plot unfolds in *Scoop*. Journalist Joe Strombel (Ian McShane) has died of a coronary, but on the way to the other side, he learns the possible identity of the Tarot Killer, a serial murderer currently preying on London prostitutes. A determined reporter to the end, Joe manages to animate his spirit to American journalism student Sondra Pransky (Scarlett Johansson) to tell her what he has discovered. This meeting, which recalls Allen's use of the ghost of Humphrey Bogart in *Play It Again, Sam* (1972), occurs while Sondra is a volunteer in a vanishing trick performed by magician Sid Waterman (Woody Allen), also known as Splendini. Sondra enlists Sid's help to find evidence against the aristocratic playboy, Peter Lyman (Hugh Jackman), whom Joe believes to be the Tarot Killer, by posing as father and daughter. Peter and Sondra immediately find themselves falling for each other despite her suspicions, while Sid remains skeptical of Lyman's guilt, even after meeting Joe. The pair nevertheless take their circumstantial evidence to journalist Mr. Malcolm (Charles Dance), who says that Sondra does not yet have a story. Again as with *Manhattan Murder Mystery*, everything is not as it seems.

Allen invokes a Hitchcockian element by having Sondra and Sid invade the locked room where Peter keeps his collection of antique musical instruments, which results in a series of scenes recalling Cary Grant, Ingrid Bergman, and Claude Rains' wine cellar encounter in *Notorious* (1946). While *Scoop* doesn't have as many direct references as the heavily allusive *Match Point,* one of the most interesting is taken from Theodore Dreiser's *An American Tragedy* (1925) and George Stevens' adaptation of *A Place in the Sun* (1951), both of which are also major sources for *Match Point.* In addition to the previously mentioned echoes of his films, Allen also borrows the image of Death from *Love and Death* (1975), whose ending is similar to that of *Scoop*.

As usual with Allen, the performances are solid. McShane is agreeably manic as the reporter who cannot rest peacefully until the mystery is resolved. Jackman's pleasant likeability is perfect for a character Sondra hopes is not a murderer. Going from the sultry femme fatale of *Match Point* to a more naive seductress, Johansson is charming and even displays some comedic skills reminiscent of Keaton's. The always generous Allen even gives her some punchlines to deliver. The film's weakest link is initially Allen himself. Splendini's stage patter is meant to be bad, but his introductory scene goes on so long that Allen almost becomes embarrassing. When Sid meets Sondra, he keeps his eyes focused on the floor for no obvious reason. Yet after this inauspicious beginning, Allen the actor settles down and slowly assumes his familiar neurotic persona.

The mystery element of *Scoop* is well-handled, keeping the audience guessing about the killer's identity as Peter seems such an unlikely murderer, and the film's unexpected twist is satisfying. The slapstick, which occasionally resembles something out of a Bowery Boys comedy, is also effective.

After taking a step forward with *Match Point*, Allen regresses with *Scoop*. This murder-mystery comedy is much more accomplished and entertaining than its reviews would indicate, but it represents a return to material Allen can seemingly produce on automatic pilot.

Michael Adams

CREDITS

Sid Waterman: Woody Allen
Sondra Pransky: Scarlett Johansson
Peter Lyman: Hugh Jackman
Joe Strombel: Ian McShane
Mr. Malcolm: Charles Dance
Vivian: Romola Garai
Jane Cook: Fenella Woolger
Lord Lyman: Julian Glover
Jan: Victoria Hamilton
Detective: Anthony Head
Origin: USA
Language: English
Released: 2006
Production: Letty Aronson, Gareth Wiley; Ingenious Film Partners; released by Focus Features
Directed by: Woody Allen
Written by: Woody Allen
Cinematography by: Remi Adefarasin
Sound: Peter Glossop
Editing: Alisa Lepselter
Art Direction: Nick Palmer
Costumes: Jill Taylor
Production Design: Maria Djurkovic
MPAA rating: PG-13
Running time: 96 minutes

REVIEWS

Boxoffice Online. July 28, 2006.
Chicago Sun-Times Online. July 28, 2006.

Entertainment Weekly. August 4, 2006, p. 48.
Los Angeles Times Online. July 28, 2006.
New York Times Online. July 28, 2006.
San Francisco Chronicle. July 28, 2006, p. E7.
Variety Online. July 16, 2006.
Washington Post. July 28, 2006, p. C6.

QUOTES

Sid: "I was born into the Hebrew persuasion, but when I got older I converted to narcissism."

THE SECOND CHANCE

Same faith. Same city. Different worlds.
—Movie tagline

Independent religious films are generally stereotyped as lower-quality movies suffering from low production values, weak writing, either simplistic or outlandish (and preachy) plots, frequently unrealistic characterizations, and/or sanitized representations of reality. Unfortunately (for faith communities, at least), those stereotypes have been justified more often than not. *The Second Chance* is an attempt to break away from the typical "Christian movie" mold and tell a good story—a realistic and frank one—with high production values. Co-written and directed by a former contemporary Christian music recording artist and starring another well-known Christian recording artist, the film manages to break significant ground for its genre, though it still may not resonate much with non-church-going audiences. Director Steve Taylor occasionally courted controversy in Christian circles when he recorded music in the 1980s and 1990s, choosing to be upfront and frank about personal and social issues and often encouraging "the church" to take an honest look at itself, and this is generally what he has done in *The Second Chance*. The movie does not attempt to "preach" to or at the audience; it strives not to be a "Christian movie" per se but a story about real people who happen to be Christians. Issues of faith are not the focus of the movie; they are simply part of the world of the characters because their faith—or sometimes lack of it—is something the characters have in common. Yet, since the setting of the film involves two churches and the relationships between them, overall *The Second Chance* seems more directed to audiences of the faithful. Due to its grittier elements, however, it is not likely to be screened in many churches on a Sunday morning.

Real-life recording artist Michael W. Smith plays Ethan Jenkins, music minister at an affluent suburban mega-church called The Rock, where his father Jeremiah (J. Don Ferguson) is the pastor. The church helps support the mostly African American church Second Chance, a congregation planted in a now-poor area of town by Jeremiah many years before. When Ethan invites the pastor of Second Chance, Jake Sanders (Jeff Obafemi Carr), to speak before the congregation at The Rock one Sunday, the huge audience is shocked by Jake's attitude. Perturbed that the charismatic audience seems to be congratulating itself on raising a large sum of money to give the Second Chance congregation, Jake talks about their sheltered vision and the true nature of ministry. "Keep your damn money!" he says angrily. This awkward situation is the tip of the iceberg for the elders at The Rock, who have been annoyed with some of Ethan's tendencies, so they assign him to work with Jake at Second Chance.

Both Ethan and Jake must confront prejudices and preconceptions as they are forced to work together. Ethan arguably learns the most, witnessing the street-wise Jake minister in a real way to those who need help—drug addicts, gang members, poor single mothers—and realizes that truly ministering to people involves a lot more than preaching to them or getting them excited on Sunday. Gradually Ethan realizes that this is the kind of ministry that he wants to be involved in, where the focus is not on leading others—not on himself or his own needs—but on serving others. Jake, too, learns from Ethan, realizing that his anger often prevents him from seeing clearly and discovering that he harbors a few prejudices of his own against people with backgrounds like Ethan's. Ultimately, even Ethan's father comes to a significant epiphany, discovering that he has lost sight of the original vision he had many years before when he planted Second Chance.

Many of the basic themes in *The Second Chance*—bridging the divide between ethnic and racial groups or between the wealthy and the poor—are significant and do not limit themselves to religious audiences. Yet the film also conveys a clear message directed to a more specific audience of the faithful—that the truest ministry of churches is meaningful service to those in need, to those who are hurting and struggling—and urges churches to reach across racial and social barriers to work together. Both Smith and Carr play their roles convincingly, revealing the complexity and earnestness of the characters. Stylistically, the film maintains a dynamic, fast pace throughout, punctuated with interesting movements, camera angles, and a hip music score that is engaging and mood-appropriate.

The Second Chance has its limitations—because of its grittier elements, it is not likely to be widely embraced within Christian communities. However, it is also unlikely to engender much interest outside of church-going viewers simply because of the setting and the role played by Christian faith. Yet it is a well-made, interesting film that tells an important story and shares an insightful and useful message. Even apart from the church setting, the message that throwing money at a cause is not as effective as getting personally involved is one that can be taken to heart.

David Flanagin

CREDITS

Ethan Jenkins: Michael W. Smith
Jeremiah Jenkins: J. Don Ferguson
Amanda Sanders: Lisa Arrindell Anderson
Parker Richards: David Alford
Jake Sanders: Jeff Obafemi Carr
Sonny: Henry Haggard
Valerie: Kenda Benward
Tony: Jonathan Thomas
Julius: Calvin Hobson
Mayor: Bobby Daniels
Miss Burdoe: Shirley Cody
Claudia Jenkins: Peggy Walton Walker
Trina: Vilia Steele
Origin: USA
Language: English
Released: 2006
Production: Clarke Gallivan, Coke Sams, Steve Taylor; Triumph Films, Cedar Partners, Ruckus Films; released by Sony Pictures Entertainment
Directed by: Steve Taylor
Written by: Steve Taylor, Henry O. Arnold, Ben Pearson
Cinematography by: Ben Pearson
Music by: Michael W. Smith
Sound: Nick Palladino
Editing: Matthew Sterling
Art Direction: Sheila B
Costumes: Alonzo V. Wilson
Production Design: Ruby Guidara
MPAA rating: PG-13
Running time: 102 minutes

REVIEWS

Los Angeles Times Online. February 17, 2006.
New York Times Online. February 17, 2006.
Variety Online. February 18, 2006.

SEE NO EVIL

Eight Teens, One Weekend, One Serial Killer.
—Movie tagline

This Summer, someone is raising Kane.
—Movie tagline

This Summer, Evil Gets Raw.
—Movie tagline

Box Office: $15 million

On paper, *See No Evil* doesn't exactly sound like masterpiece material. The movie was produced by wrestling kingpin Vince McMahon and penned by *WWF Smackdown!* writer Dan Madigan. The villain, Jacob Goodnight, is played by Glen Jacobs, who is better known as wrestler Kane. And Gregory Dark, whose resume is populated with adult films, directs the film.

Considering its pedigree, *See No Evil* is better than it could have been. Credit for that should go to director of photography Ben Nott, who at least gave the movie an artistically creepy look. The action takes place in the old, run-down downtown Blackwell Hotel. Although the once grand lodgings has had mainly rodent guests since its heyday in the 1920s, the way that Nott lovingly films the old hotel makes it by far the most memorable character in the film.

Less interesting is the group of juvenile delinquents that are sent to the hotel for a three-day tour of duty. If they help clean up the place, they will get a month shaved off their sentences. For some reason, the powers-that-be at the detention center has decided that the cleanup crew will be coed. (They also seem to have chosen the crew on the basis of bodily attractiveness.) The female inmates include a Paris Hilton-like rich blonde, Zoe (Rachael Taylor), animal rights activist Melissa (Penny McNamee) and abuse victim, Christine (Christina Vidal). The male inmates include a computer geek, Richie (Craig Horner) and a lock picker, Tyson (Michael J. Pagan). Former prostitute, Kira (Samantha Noble), is horrified to see that she will be working with her abusive ex-boyfriend, Michael (Luke Pegler).

The crew is led by Officer Williams (Steven Vidler) who is trying to escape a dark past. Four years previously as a rookie cop, he and his partner encountered a psycho killer (Jacob) who liked to gouge out eyes. The partner was killed, Williams lost a hand, and the killer got away.

None too surprisingly, Jacob has set up house in this same hotel and the killer doesn't seem to have changed much. He still enjoys killing and gouging out eyeballs with his thick, yellow fingernails. There are plenty of shots of him performing this act, after which he plops the eyeballs into murky jars filled with some sort of fluid.

The movie gets down to the business of killing teens quickly. The action generally goes thusly: a teen or two goes up in the old art deco elevator and gets off at a cobweb-covered upper floor. Once there, they encounter the killer and Jacob either kills them right away, or for variety, chases them about a bit before killing them. Either way, the death and all its accompanying gruesomeness is plainly visible to all audience members who are not covering their eyes.

Of course, a film whose sole purpose is to show attractive teens gruesomely picked off one by one is not going to be a shining example of humanitarianism, but there is a certain unsettling mean-spiritedness that permeates the film. When Melissa, the animal rights activist, is killed, she is eaten by a pack of hungry, wild dogs. And when Zoe, the rich society girl, meets her end, it is by being gagged with her ever-present cell phone. Both of these deaths are played for laughs.

In the end, though, the fatal flaw of *See No Evil* is that poor, hulking Kane is a terrible actor. The hulking, bald mountain of a man looks menacing enough but he simply isn't able to deliver an adequate level of scariness. This is bad, since it is his sole acting duty in the film. When Kane is filmed in shadows, he is very frightening. But when the director lets him come out into the scene, he loses all mystery and just looks like he is performing wrestling moves, albeit with an old rusty hook.

Critics did not like this film one bit. Peter Hartlaub of the *San Francisco Chronicle* wrote: "*See No Evil* is a horror movie that doesn't just show a woman with her eyeballs ripped out, it has a camera zoom into one of the sockets. If you're the type of person who loves seeing people get their eyes gouged in graphic fashion, then run—don't walk—to this film. Seriously, this is your *Citizen Kane*." Lisa Rose of the *Newark Star-Ledger* called the movie a "dumb splatter film" and wrote, "With its raw brutality, decayed urban setting and less-than-innocent victims, *See No Evil* is a poor man's *Saw*." Robert Abele of the *Los Angeles Times* called it "hyper-directed dreck," while Ty Burr of *The Boston Globe* was kinder, labeling it "proficient junk."

Jill Hamilton

CREDITS

Tyson: Michael J. Pagan
Christine: Christina Vidal
Williams: Steven Vidler
Melissa: Penny McNamee
Jacob Goodnight: Glen "Kane" Jacobs
Kira: Samantha Noble
Michael: Luke Pegler
Zoe: Rachael Taylor
Richie: Craig Horner
Origin: USA
Language: English
Released: 2006
Production: Joel Simon, Vince McMahon; WWE Films; released by Lionsgate Films
Directed by: Gregory Dark
Written by: Dan Madigan
Cinematography by: Ben Nott
Music by: Tyler Bates
Sound: Guntis Sics
Editing: Scott Richter
Art Direction: Adam Head
Costumes: Phil Eagles
Production Design: Michael Rumpf
MPAA rating: R
Running time: 84 minutes

REVIEWS

Boxoffice Online. May 19, 2006.
Entertainment Weekly Online. May 24, 2006.
Los Angeles Times Online. May 22, 2006.
New York Times Online. May 20, 2006.
Variety Online. May 19, 2006.

TRIVIA

The tagline "This Summer, Evil Gets Raw" refers to the WWE wrestling show Glen Jacobs/Kane (Jacob Goodnight) appears on, *Raw Is War.*

THE SENTINEL

In 141 years, there's never been a traitor in the Secret Service...until now.
—Movie tagline

Box Office: $36.2 million

The Presidential assassination thriller *The Sentinel* is a mostly competent popcorn entertainment. Not only is it a perfect film to eat popcorn by but also it is not filling and has no aftereffects. *The Sentinel* recalls many similar films that stick more to the ribs and the memory.

Pete Garrison (Michael Douglas) is a veteran Secret Service agent who was wounded during the 1981 attempt on the life of Ronald Reagan. How someone this old—Douglas is sixty-one—is still on the job is one of several plot points the film glosses over. While the film's reviewers were annoyed by such flaws, Clark Johnson's energetic direction makes matters swirl so fast that it is difficult to concentrate on the many lapses in continuity and logic.

Garrison is told by a colleague, Charlie Merriweather (played by the director), that he has something important to tell his friend. *The Sentinel* is the kind of film in which delaying such information can be fatal. After Merriweather's murder, a former source (Raynor Scheine) tells Garrison of a plot to kill the President (David Rasche) involving a mole within the Secret Service. Garrison's actions are complicated by his affair with First Lady Sarah Ballentine (Kim Basinger) and by the suspicions of his former protege David Breckinridge (Kiefer Sutherland). Breckinridge's belief that Garrison was having an affair with his wife (Kristin Lehman) led to the breakup of his marriage. While Breckinridge strives to prove that Garrison is the mole, his new partner, Jill Marin (Eva Longoria), also trained by Garrison, has her doubts.

Garrison's situation is compromised further when surveillance photographs of him and Sarah arrive and he is tricked into walking into an FBI stakeout. Convinced that Garrison is the mole, Breckinridge arrests him, only for the older agent to escape. (The Secret Service is shown to be lax and uses questionable judgment several times.) On his own, Garrison must survive by his wits while proving his innocence.

Best known as Detective Meldrick Lewis on *Homicide: Life on the Street* (1993-1999), Johnson directed episodes of that series, other episodic television, and the Martin Luther King, Jr., television drama *Boycott* (2001) before making his first feature film, *S.W.A.T.* (2003). *The Sentinel* has lots of style, with quick cuts and a frenetically moving camera. Johnson seems to want to keep the action nonstop not only to heighten the excitement but to keep his viewers from thinking too much about the proceedings. Johnson handles a shootout in a mall in Allendale, Virginia, quite well, but with the final showdown in a stairwell in Toronto, it is not always easy to know what is going on.

The film's look varies from scene to scene with cinematographer Gabriel Beristain altering the lighting to reflect Garrison's psychological state. When the protagonist is on the run, Beristain, whose credits include *The Spanish Prisoner* (1997), gives the exterior shots a reddish tint to underscore Garrison's tension.

Adapting the 2003 novel by former Secret Service agent Gerald Petievich, screenwriter George Nolfi, who wrote *Ocean's Twelve* (2004), may have inherited some oversights but does little to resolve them. The motives of the sinister group out to kill the president are a bit muddy, as are those of the mole, whose identity is more obvious than it should be. *The Sentinel* is also vague about the subdued marital tensions in the White House and why Breckinridge thinks Garrison has cuckolded him. This latter plot device serves only as an excuse for Breckinridge's hostility.

Several reviewers compared *The Sentinel* unfavorably to *In the Line of Fire* (1993). The two are similar in having older agents trying to prove themselves, with Clint Eastwood even older at the time than Douglas is in *The Sentinel.* Both films attempt to be character studies, with *In the Line of Fire* offering considerably more depth. Beyond Garrison's obviously ill-fated love for Sarah, he remains rather sketchy.

Douglas tries to fill in the gaps by making Garrison alternately cocky and uncertain. Until he softens a bit toward the end, Sutherland's Breckinridge is essentially a no-nonsense pursuer. Longoria and Basinger are fine in underwritten roles. Basinger is especially effective in her one love scene with Douglas. With his rugged, Reaganesque appearance, Rasche looks presidential. The always-reliable Martin Donovan manages to find a few shadings of character as a senior Secret Service agent.

Some reviewers complained that *The Sentinel* resembles something made for television because it is plot-driven with no nuances. Ballentine is a generic president belonging to no party and espousing no philosophy. The bad guys want him dead simply because he is the president. *The Sentinel* has superficial similarities to other thrillers, including *The Manchurian Candidate* (1962) and *Three Days of the Condor* (1975), but those films explored Cold War tensions, looking at such issues as whether the American government can be trusted. In *Seven Days in May* (1964), only army officer Kirk Douglas stands in the way of a right-wing conspiracy to overthrow the presidency. *The Sentinel* is fun to watch, despite its flaws, but by completely ignoring any political, social, or psychological concerns, it is not about anything. It is just a popcorn film that evaporates from memory minutes after it is over.

Michael Adams

CREDITS

Pete Garrison: Michael Douglas
David Breckinridge: Kiefer Sutherland
William Montrose: Martin Donovan
The Handler: Ritchie Coster
Jill Marin: Eva Longoria
Sarah Ballentine: Kim Basinger
National Security Advisor: Blair Brown
President Ballentine: David Rasche
Cindy Breckinridge: Kristin Lehman
Walter Xavier: Raynor Scheine
Director Overbrook: Chuck Shamata
Deputy Director Cortes: Paul Calderon
Charlie Merriweather: Clark Johnson
Origin: USA
Language: English
Released: 2006

Production: Michael Douglas, Arnon Milchan, Marcy Drogin; Regency Enterprises, Further Films, New Regency; released by 20th Century Fox
Directed by: Clark Johnson
Written by: George Nolfi
Cinematography by: Gabriel Beristain
Music by: Christophe Beck
Sound: John J. Thomson
Music Supervisor: Evyen Klean
Editing: Cindy Mollo
Art Direction: Rocco Matteo
Costumes: Ellen Mirojnick
Production Design: Andrew McAlpine
MPAA rating: PG-13
Running time: 105 minutes

REVIEWS

Boxoffice Online. April 21, 2006.
Chicago Sun-Times Online. April 21, 2006.
Detroit News. April 21, 2006, p. 3F.
Entertainment Weekly. April 28, 2006, p. 116.
Los Angeles Times Online. April 21, 2006.
New York Times Online. April 21, 2006.
San Francisco Chronicle. April 21, 2006, p. E5.
USA Today Online. April 20, 2006.
Variety Online. April 20, 2006.
Washington Post. April 21, 2006, p. C5.

TRIVIA

Director Clark Johnson cameos as the first Secret Service agent who's killed.

SHADOWBOXER

Feeling protected is very seductive.
—Movie tagline

This edgy, innovative, and unpredictable assassin movie serves up almost unwatchable, disturbing violence interspersed with surprising interludes of intelligence, compassion, and tenderness, even if *Entertainment Weekly* reviewer Owen Gliebermann dismissed it as pornographic and graded it a failure. On the other hand, *Variety* had a different take on what the film was and why it could be considered significant.

The plot begins with Rose (Helen Mirren), a maternal killer who, in a moment of weakness, spares the life of Vickie (Vanessa Ferlito), the pregnant moll of a ruthless and sadistic crimelord named Clayton (Stephen Dorff). Clayton wanted Vickie killed because he believed she had become pregnant by another man, one of his associates who Clayton is seen sodomizing with a pool cue stick at the start of the film on top of a pool table, witnessed by assorted gunsels. Clayton puts out a contract through a handicapped man confined to a motorized wheelchair (Tom Pasch plays this villain, made all the more scary because he seems to be perfectly harmless and mild-mannered). Rose and her partner, Mikey (Cuba Gooding Jr.), set forth to execute the contract, invading Clayton's house while the crimelord is conveniently out of town. Mikey kills the gunsels, catching them off guard in a card game. Meanwhile, Rose goes for Vickie, but is taken somewhat aback when she notices Vickie is pregnant. Then, as Vickie stands by her bed, paralyzed with fear, Vickie's water breaks and she goes into labor. Rose sees this as a signal from God, believing she was placed in that bedroom because she was fated to save Vickie and the child. She delivers the baby, then takes mother and child to Dr. Don (Joseph Gordon-Levitt, looking rather too young to be a working doctor). At the hospital they are treated by Dr. Don and his obstetric nurse, Precious (Mo'Nique), who turns out later to be a vindictive junkie whose jealousy causes complications. There are few admirable characters in this plot, ingeniously scripted by William Lipz, but they are somehow mostly believable.

However, Rose has problems of her own. Diagnosed with cancer, her days are numbered. She medicates, she smokes, and she kills. The script fails to provide a coherent backstory to explain her profession. She is apparently British and came to America as a medical student. She fell in with a mobster hitman, from whom she apparently learned her trade. The hitman abused, then killed, his wife. After the funeral, he finds his son, Mikey, playing with his silenced revolver. Enraged, the father starts beating Mikey, who is spared when Rose coolly fires a bullet into the brute. Consistently in the film the killings are casual and generally without conscience. Rose thereafter becomes Mikey's surrogate mother. They work together as hired killers and watch each other's back.

Rose is worried about who will take care of Mikey after she is gone, but is clever enough to imagine a solution to this dilemma. The two assassins take Vickie and her newborn son under their care and protection. They find a house in the suburbs of an undisclosed city and set up housekeeping as a "family." All is well until nurse Precious discovers Dr. Don fondling and fiddling with an attractive female patient and informs Clayton that Vickie is still alive as is Clayton's (perhaps) illegitimate son. Enraged, Clayton tracks them down, breaks into the house, and takes them prisoner, though by the time this happens, Rose has long since died and the son appears to be about seven or eight years old.

Clayton makes a mistake of attempting to torture Mikey before killing him. He amputates a finger by using pinking shears. Mikey, a trained killer, retaliates and disables Clayton's latest set of gunsels and then goes for Clayton. Clayton gets the upper hand and appears ready to deliver the coup de grace, but then the unexpected happens. Vickie's son, who was fascinated by firearms just as young Mikey was before him, picks up a loose pistol and, gripping it with both hands, shoots Clayton in the back. "You know, there may be more of them?" Mikey remarks to the boy. "Then, we'll kill 'em," the boy responds, providing a chilling conclusion to an ugly story.

As noted above, reviewer Owen Gleibermann in *Entertainment Weekly* was outraged by the picture. He hated the characters and their relationships. Gleibermann strongly objected to the "May-December interracial quasi-incest" on display in this "brutally incoherent" movie (though the charge of incest is highly debatable). Since the film was carefully placed in limited release in urban markets and arthouses, producer and first-time director Lee Daniels surely knew it was not likely to succeed in the summer mass market, competing against high-budget mainstreamed vehicles like *Miami Vice* (2006), which opened the week after *Shadowboxer* was released.

In Robert Koehler's *Variety* review, by contrast, the film was described as "strange and exotic." Koehler was very impressed by the way *Shadowboxer* "admirably jostles and upends the fatigued killer-for-hire genre." Koehler claimed that the picture is "centrally concerned with how a parent's lifestyle can be passed down to a child." This is clearly seen when what happened to Mikey as a boy is passed on to Vickie's son, who regards Mikey as his true father. *Baltimore Sun* critic Michael Sragow was not so impressed, however. For him the final shoot-out, "starring Vickie's grade-school kid, proves that 'the circle of violence' is as useless and cliched a concept in garish gangster dramas as it is in editorials about the Middle East."

Journalistic reviews were mixed, but predominantly negative. *The Washington City Paper* considered the film "unintentionally hilarious," for example. Noting graphic and thematic resemblances to the work of John Woo and Quentin Tarantino, *Washington Post* reviewer Desson Thomson found echoes in the Lipz script of "better movies about hired killers" and lamented that the "authoritatively cool" Cuba Gooding Jr. might have chosen a better project "to show his previously untapped abilities."

In his *New York Times* review, Stephen Holden wrote that the "extravagance" of this "gaudy" thriller "leaves you with your mouth hanging open—partly in admiration of its audacity and partly in disbelief at its preposterousness." The interracial sex scenes involving Gooding and Mirren that so offended the *Entertainment Weekly* reviewer constitute little more than an absurd, merely vulgar spectacle that is both distasteful and geriatrically insulting. But there is more to this "gaudy thriller" than the fact that it appears to be a thriller for those willing to look beyond the "gaudy" surfaces. Daniels is constantly risking absurdity in this film, but deserves more than a little credit for taking chances.

Shadowboxer has all the earmarks of a cult movie, a layered plot with frequent flashbacks (even flashbacks within flashbacks), psychotic characters, and explosive and unexpected violence. It is more intelligent than most recent Hollywood products, but because it rather too eagerly courts taboos and risks ridicule, it could still go very quickly into video markets. *Variety* was cautious in its prediction: "pic faces a possible B.O. mission impossible." The nearest competition was surely the new *Miami Vice*, made on a far larger budget and featuring far more recognizable star talent. Cuba Gooding Jr. is a still developing talent, but not likely to compete too strongly against Jamie Foxx.

In his hostile *Baltimore Sun* review, Michael Sragow criticized Helen Mirren for playing the "ailing hitwoman with her usual craft, conviction and daring," but "without a lick of her usual sense." Mirren is far more recognizable in Britain than in America, where she has not worked steadily in feature films. Mirren is probably best known for starring as the lead detective in the *Prime Suspect* television series imported by PBS, but also, perhaps, for playing the unfaithful wife for Peter Greenaway in *The Cook, the Thief, His Wife, and Her Lover*, a nasty piece of work released in 1990, or for her performance as Queen Elizabeth II in 2006's *The Queen.* She is no stranger to oddly motivated roles in plots that may seem borderline incoherent. Rose is conflicted. Mikey is also conflicted. The film's metaphorical title, *Shadowboxer,* suggests an inner struggle, visualized frequently in the film as Cuba Gooding Jr. works out with punching bags, releasing his frustrations. Too bad there is no comparable release for the viewer.

James M. Welsh

CREDITS

Mikey: Cuba Gooding Jr.
Rose: Helen Mirren
Vickie: Vanessa Ferlito
Neisha: Macy Gray
Dr. Don: Joseph Gordon-Levitt
Precious: Mo'Nique

Clayton: Stephen Dorff
Origin: USA
Language: English
Released: 2006
Production: Lee Daniels, Damon Dash, Brook Linfest, Lisa Cortes, David Robinson; released by Teton Films
Directed by: Lee Daniels
Written by: William Lipz
Cinematography by: M. David Mullen
Music by: Mario Grigorov
Sound: Thomas J. Varga
Music Supervisor: A. J. Azzarto
Editing: William Chang Suk-ping, Brian A. Kates
Art Direction: Tim Galvin
Costumes: Teresa Binder-Westby
Production Design: Steve Saklad
MPAA rating: R
Running time: 93 minutes

REVIEWS

Boxoffice Online. July 21, 2006.
Chicago Sun-Times Online. July 28, 2006.
Hollywood Reporter Online. September 27, 2005.
Los Angeles Times Online. July 21, 2006.
New York Times Online. July 21, 2006.
San Francisco Chronicle. July 28, 2006, p. E6.
Variety Online. July 18, 2006.
Village Voice Online. July 18, 2006.
Washington Post Online. July 21, 2006.

THE SHAGGY DOG

Raise The Woof.
—Movie tagline

Box Office: $61.1 million

The Shaggy Dog is a Disney remake of a semi-classic Disney film. The original (1959) starred Fred MacMurray as the father of a boy named Wilby (Tommy Kirk), who comes into possession of a magic ring that periodically turns him into a sheepdog. That movie was successful and led to a follow-up in 1976 called *The Shaggy D.A.*, starring Dean Jones as an adult Wilby. Walt Disney, like every other studio, has made a recent practice of attempting to capitalize on past successes by resurrecting old films and television series, a trend that arguably has not resulted in very many "new" versions as good as the old ones. Such is the case with Disney's latest *Shaggy Dog*, starring Tim Allen. Even though the film has some amusing moments, overall it comes across as formulaic, generally uninspired, and trite. A movie about a man who turns into a dog has been done before, but the premise still holds potential that it could be developed into a successful comic film. Unfortunately that is not what happened with Tim Allen's *Shaggy Dog*.

Allen plays Dave Douglas, a Deputy District Attorney caught up in his job and disconnected from his family because he aspires to be promoted to District Attorney. Dave is presently involved in a case prosecuting a high school social studies teacher named Justin Forrester (Joshua Leonard), who has been accused of setting a fire at Grant & Strictland research labs. Dave's daughter Carly (Zena Grey) is one of Forrester's students, and she insists her teacher could not have been the arsonist even though he is passionate about his cause. Forrester is an animal rights activist who claims that Grant & Strictland is guilty of illegal animal experimentation. In fact, the company is indeed using a very special animal in its experiments—a three hundred year-old sheepdog from Tibet. The dog escapes from the laboratory and is lucky to be found by Carly, who takes him home.

Dave does not like the dog and the feeling seems to be mutual, because it bites him. Predictably, the wound does something to Dave, altering his DNA, and he soon finds himself turning into a sheepdog. Mishap after mishap and plenty of occasions for slapstick humor follow as Dave turns into a canine during the day and returns to his human form at night. However, as an animal, he has the opportunity to learn things he was previously unaware of. He realizes that his relationship with his wife Rebecca (Kristin Davis) is not what it should be (and his apparent disappearances during the day make things worse); he also learns that his son Josh (Spencer Breslin) actually hates football and only plays because he thinks his father expects him to. In addition, he discovers that scientists at Grant & Strictland, led by Dr. Kozak (Robert Downey Jr.), have been using the 300-year-old dog to try to develop a life-extending drug, but their experiments have resulted in bizarre animal mutations.

The experience forces Dave to examine himself and his priorities. When he misses his wedding anniversary, Dave says, "I'm not a bad dog but I'm a terrible man." Eventually he communicates to his children that he has been transforming into a dog, and in the end, after a confrontation with Kozak that leaves the villain turning into a canine himself, everything is happily resolved and Dave turns his priorities around.

There have been numerous movies about a father who realizes he is a workaholic and needs to devote more time to knowing and supporting his family. That is the basic plot of *The Shaggy Dog*, and unfortunately the movie does not offer anything new or meaningful to the theme. Dave's transformation into a dog simply functions as a device for him to learn who he really is and how others see him—that and an excuse for Tim Allen to engage in a lot of physical comedy. If *The Shaggy Dog* had put a new spin on the original movie or explored a storyline that was truly unique or at least more creative, it might have been a memorable, worthwhile comedy. As it is, the movie lacks anything to set it apart from countless films that have come before.

David Flanagin

CREDITS

Dave Douglas: Tim Allen
Dr. Kozak: Robert Downey Jr.
Rebecca Douglas: Kristen Davis
Josh Douglas: Spencer Breslin
Justin Forrester: Joshua Leonard
Ken Hollister: Danny Glover
Judge Claire Whittaker: Jane Curtin
Carly Douglas: Zena Grey
Lance Strictland: Philip Baker Hall
Baxter: Craig Kilborn
Justin Forrester's Attorney: Annabelle Gurwitch
Dr. Gwen Lichtman: Bess Wohl
Trey: Shawn Pyfrom
Ms. Foster Teacher: Laura Kightlinger
Larry: Jarrad Paul
Origin: USA
Language: English
Released: 2006
Production: David Hoberman, Tim Allen; Walt Disney Pictures, Mandeville Films, Boxing Cat Films; released by Buena Vista
Directed by: Brian Robbins
Written by: Cormac Wibberley, Marianne S. Wibberley, Geoff Rodkey, Jack Amiel, Michael Begler
Cinematography by: Gabriel Beristain
Music by: Alan Menken
Sound: Jose Antonio Garcia
Editing: Ned Bastille
Art Direction: Daniel T. Dorrance
Costumes: Molly Maginnis
Production Design: Leslie McDonald
MPAA rating: PG
Running time: 98 minutes

REVIEWS

Boxoffice Online. March 10, 2006.
Chicago Sun-Times Online. March 10, 2006.
Entertainment Weekly Online. March 8, 2006.
Los Angeles Times Online. March 10, 2006.
New York Times Online. March 10, 2006.
Variety Online. March 5, 2006.

AWARDS

Nomination:

Golden Raspberries 2006: Worst Actor (Allen), Worst Remake

SHERRYBABY

No one makes it alone.
—Movie tagline

In *SherryBaby*, Maggie Gyllenhaal has finally shown, beyond a shadow of a doubt, why critics have been so rapturous about her rising fame in Hollywood. Gyllenhaal's no-holds-barred performance as a drug addict trying to get her life back in order makes this otherwise modest sophomore feature of writer-director Laurie Collyer well worth seeing.

Up until this 2006 effort, Gyllenhaal could have been accused by some to be coasting on nepotism (her father, Stephen Gyllenhaal, directed the first six movies she appeared in, and her younger brother, Jake Gyllenhaal, was a Hollywood up-and-comer before she became well known herself). But many have admired Maggie Gyllenhaal's quirky screen persona and "daring" choices of roles since her screen debut, including her titular part in the offensive and overrated *Secretary* (2002). However, her true abilities as an actor have only begun to materialize.

Moving without being overly melodramatic, *SherryBaby* tells the story of a narcotics-addicted former convict struggling to reconnect with the daughter she abandoned years earlier. Gyllenhaal plays Sherry Swanson with aching fervor and is capably supported by a strong ensemble cast. Collyer's story starts with Sherry having just been released from prison. As part of her conditional release, Sherry has to meet with a tough-talking parole officer, Hernandez, played by Giancarlo Esposito. After their initial meeting, Sherry presses the resistant Hernandez about arranging a meeting between Sherry and her young daughter, Alexis (Ryan Simpkins), who is in the care of Bobby (Brad Henke), her laid-back brother, and Lynette (Bridget Barkan), her resentful sister-in-law. Rebuffing the strong advice of her parole officer, Sherry meets with her daughter anyway and further jeopardizes her release by moving out of her state-mandated halfway house and moving into Bobby's more comfortable digs to be closer to her daughter.

After a clumsy reunion with Alexis, Sherry encounters a series of roadblocks to her rehabilitation, which come to the surface in arguments with her family over her inability to find a decent job and how involved the family is willing to let Sherry become in Alexis' life. These emotional hurdles take their toll on Sherry, resulting in her retreating into her former, unhealthy habits including drinking and indulging in casual sex. During a family gathering with her father, Bobby Sr. (Sam Bottoms), Sherry has a revelation about early sexual abuse she'd suffered during her childhood and recognizes the parallels between her self-destructive behavior and her antisocial tendencies. Unwilling to fully face the truth, Sherry starts taking drugs again. As a result of her substance abuse, Sherry's parole violations come to the attention of Hernandez, who, unexpectedly, shows Sherry an unusual degree of compassion. With yet another second chance, Sherry enrolls in rehabilitation for her substance abuse, fully aware that the treatment, while necessary to save her life, will ultimately keep her away from Alexis for even longer.

It is a credit to Laurie Collyer's ability as a filmmaker that she is able to make Sherry such an engaging character, particularly since the "troubled addict ventures down the long, hard road to recovery" has become such an overly familiar, almost trite, plot device. But, as she demonstrated in her debut feature, the 1999 documentary *Nuyorican Dream*, about a Puerto Rican family living in poverty, Collyer manages to avoid most of the obvious cliches in *SherryBaby* and, thankfully, never exploits the more sensational aspects of her troubled title character. (The implied incest between Sherry and her father is handled with a much appreciated sense of restraint and delicacy.)

However, since this is Collyer's first fictional work, there were bound to be a few narrative missteps. The character of Lynette (Bridget Barkan) is particularly troubling as she vacillates throughout the film, supporting Sherry in one scene while she glares at her in another. Collyer fails to make Lynette's character shifts ring true and, as such, her inconsistency stands out against the rest of the film. A few critics took issue with Collyer's storyline itself: Ella Taylor in the September 5 *Village Voice* wrote: "…we know exactly where the transparent action is going from word one, and the movie never shakes free of a twelve-step psychology that carries its subject doggedly from good intentions through relapse, more relapse, to the big secret that explains why this confused young woman is as she is, and to the inevitable glimmer of hope."

But other reviewers overlooked these apparent narrative problems, such as A.O. Scott, who stated in his September 8, 2006 *New York Times* review: "What screenwriters call the arc of the story is visible from the outset, and some of the scenes in *SherryBaby* have a familiar look and feel. But what distinguishes the film from its many peers is the quality of Ms. Collyer's writing—which rarely reaches for obvious, melodramatic beats—and the precision of Ms. Gyllenhaal's performance. She treats the character neither as a case study nor as an opportunity to show off her range, but rather as a completely ordinary and therefore arrestingly complicated person."

This respect for her character is, perhaps, the strongest aspect of *SherryBaby*, and Collyer's even-handed directorial approach seems perfectly suited to tell Sherry's story. Collyer brings an intimacy to her characterizations that is reminiscent of the films of John Cassavettes or Alison Anders, knowing how to underscore dramatic moments without resorting to flashy cinematic excess. This reserved touch makes the few moments of stylization seem that much more effective, particularly in the lyrical montage of Sherry's return to her past addictions, luminously scored by Jack Livesy and Susan Jacobs.

And, to the great credit of the film's casting director, Collyer's character-driven narrative is backed up by a truly impressive ensemble who seem committed to making their roles appear real and three-dimensional. The entire cast is natural and believable: Gyllenhaal (whose bravery in the complex lead fails to come across like a stunt), Ryan Simpkins, Danny Trejo, Barkan, Henke, Esposito, and Sam Bottoms all deliver exceptionally strong performances.

It is a tribute to *SherryBaby* to say that Collyer brings such a sense of the real to her subject that the film is almost hard to watch—as viewers, we're allowed an unusually intimate entrance into the life of this troubled young woman. But despite the harshness of Sherry's journey, the experience is rewarding for her as a character and for audiences as well.

Eric Monder

CREDITS

Sherry Swanson: Maggie Gyllenhaal
Bobby: Brad Henke
Dean: Danny Trejo
Officer Hernandez: Giancarlo Esposito
Lynette: Bridget Barkan
Alexis: Ryan Simpkins
Bobby Sr.: Sam Bottoms
Origin: USA
Language: English
Released: 2006
Production: Lemore Syvan, Marc Turtletaub; Big Beach, Elevation Filmworks; released by IFC Films
Directed by: Laurie Collyer
Written by: Laurie Collyer

Cinematography by: Russell Fine
Music by: Jack Livesey, Susan Jacobs
Sound: Ira Spiegel
Editing: Curtiss Clayton, Joe Landauer
Costumes: Jill Newell
Production Design: Stephen Beatrice
MPAA rating: Unrated
Running time: 95 minutes

REVIEWS

Boxoffice Online. September 8, 2006.
Chicago Sun-Times Online. September 15, 2006.
Entertainment Weekly. September 15, 2006, p. 53.
Los Angeles Times Online. September 8, 2006.
New York Times Online. September 8, 2006.
Variety Online. January 22, 2006.

AWARDS

Nomination:
Golden Globes 2007: Actress—Drama (Gyllenhaal)

SHE'S THE MAN

Everybody has a secret...Duke wants Olivia who likes Sebastian who is really Viola whose brother is dating Monique so she hates Olivia who's with Duke to make Sebastian jealous who is really Viola who's crushing on Duke who thinks she's a guy...
—Movie tagline

Box Office: $33.7 million

Following in the footsteps of the teen hits, *10 Things I Hate About You* (1999), based on William Shakespeare's *Taming of the Shrew,* and *O* (2001), an update of *Othello,* comes the romantic comedy *She's the Man,* inspired by Shakespeare's gender-bender *Twelfth Night.* With its upbeat "girl power" message, buoyant pop soundtrack, and an eclectic cast that includes comedy veterans Julie Hagerty and David Cross, *She's the Man* takes a proven premise, combines it with proven writers (Karen McCullah Lutz and Kirsten Smith also penned the aforementioned *10 Things I Hate About You*), and makes it work for modern day audiences. While star Amanda Bynes dressed as a man proves less than convincing, it is nonetheless as much campy fun as the rest of this over-the-top romantic comedy.

Viola Hastings (Amanda Bynes) is an accomplished soccer player on the girls team at Cornwall Prep who gets a taste of typical teen angst when the program is cut and the boys team coach ridicules the notion of allowing girls on their team. Spunky Viola dumps her handsome jock boyfriend Justin (Robert Hoffman) when he echoes the chauvinist coach's sentiments. Naturally, things aren't going any better at home with her pushy mother Daphne (Julie Hagerty) insisting her tomboy daughter attend debutante training.

Although Viola's Elizabethan-era counterpart thought her brother was in Elysium, this Viola's twin Sebastian (James Kirk) is merely sneaking off to London to a gig with his band for a few weeks, ditching both his uber-bitch girlfriend Monique (Alex Breckinridge) and classes at Illyria Prep where he is a new transfer student (having been booted from Cornwall). This gives Viola the brilliant idea of assuming his identity in order to attend Illyria and join their soccer team—Cornwall's rival—to prove she's as good as any boy.

With Joan Jett singing "Love is All Around," the theme song from *The Mary Tyler Moore Show,* in the background, Viola teaches herself to walk, talk, and act like a dude while her friend, Paul (Jonathan Sadowski), performs an extreme makeover to make her look like one too. Sounding like a hybrid of David Spade and Eminem, Viola/Sebastian makes a bad first impression on her hunky new roommate, Illyria's star soccer player Duke Orsino (Channing Tatum), along with buddies Andrew (Clifton McCabe Murray) and Toby (Brandon Jay McLaren). Worse yet, tough-as-nails soccer coach Dinklage (Vinny Jones) banishes her to the second string.

Desperate to up her stock at Illyria, Viola again calls on the wily Paul who orchestrates a scene where, one by one, a bevy of beautiful girls confront Viola/Sebastian accusing him of breaking her heart in front of Duke and the other guys. Figuring there must be something to it, Duke bargains with Viola/Sebastian to help him get a date with his crush Olivia (Laura Ramsey) in exchange for private soccer lessons. As in Shakespeare's comedy, Viola falls for Duke causing the lovestruck teen to more frequently break "character" in his presence. Despite a few close calls, Viola/Sebastian avoids being found out and apparently, plays the part so well that Olivia develops a crush on the sensitive "boy" Viola, spurning Duke. Other humorous pitfalls Viola faces include getting around the thankfully oblivious Principal Gold, who unfortunately takes a special interest in transfer students, and avoiding Sebastian's hilariously psychotic girlfriend Monique who has no idea the real Sebastian is in London.

The Junior League Carnival affords a chance meeting between Viola and Duke as her mother has recruited her to work the kissing booth. After frantically running around the carnival changing from Viola to Sebastian and back again, Viola ends up in the booth just as Olivia is relieved of her duties and Duke is next in line. They share a meaningful kiss and soon Duke is pondering dating Viola now, which "Sebastian" is only too happy to arrange for him. Viola's plans are thwarted, however, as Olivia sees her chance to make "Sebastian" jealous by dating Duke. Viola ends up on a double date with Duke and Olivia, her date being the overly enthusiastic class geek Eunice (a brilliant Emily Perkins).

Fans of the play will be happy to see Malvolio finally turn up: he's the pet tarantula of Malcolm, who has an unrequited crush on Olivia. He turns the beast loose in Duke's room where Duke and Viola/Sebastian both jump up on the bed screaming like girls. Duke is appropriately weirded out by the strange behavior of his roommate and decides he wants nothing to do with him or his sister. Sebastian finally returns to Illyria from London where he is pleased but confused to be greeted with kisses by a strange but attractive girl—Olivia. He is not so pleased, however, when he is thrown into the much anticipated soccer game against Cornwall the next day, being mistaken for his sister. Not long into the game, Principal Gold, acting on information given to him by Malcolm, interrupts with the news that Sebastian is, in fact, not a boy. Sebastian, being, in fact, Sebastian proves this wrong in a very public manner as he pulls down his shorts. Viola, watching from under the bleachers, then switches clothes with her brother and steps in to play in his stead. Viola proves more than capable but is distracted by Duke's continued rebukes throughout the game—refusing to pass to her when she's clearly open. To make things plain to Duke, she, then, too publicly reveals that she is actually a girl. Despite the opposing team's objections, Coach Dinklage lets her finish the game, most triumphantly, as a girl. As in Shakespeare's comedy, all's well that end's well: Illyria wins the game and everyone winds up with the right person.

Hilary White

CREDITS

Viola: Amanda Bynes
Duke: Channing Tatum
Olivia: Laura Ramsey
Coach Dinklage: Vinnie Jones
Justin: Robert Hoffman
Daphne: Julie Hagerty
Principal Gold: David Cross
Monique: Alex Breckinridge
Paul: Jonathan Sadowski
Eunice: Emily Perkins
Sebastian: James Kirk
Andrew: Clifton McCabe Murray
Toby: Brandon Jay McLaren
Origin: USA
Language: English
Released: 2006
Production: Lauren Shuler-Donner, Ewan Leslie; DreamWorks Pictures, Lakeshore Entertainment, Donners' Company; released by DreamWorks
Directed by: Andy Fickman
Written by: Karen McCullah Lutz, Kirsten Smith, Ewan Leslie
Cinematography by: Greg Gardiner
Music by: Nathan Wang
Sound: Rob Young
Music Supervisor: Jennifer Hawks
Editing: Michael Jablow
Art Direction: John R. Jensen, John Burke
Costumes: Katia Stano
Production Design: David J. Bomba
MPAA rating: PG-13
Running time: 105 minutes

REVIEWS

Boxoffice Online. March 18, 2006.
Chicago Sun-Times Online. March 17, 2006.
Los Angeles Times Online. March 17, 2006.
New York Times Online. March 17, 2006.
San Francisco Chronicle Online. March 17, 2006.
Variety Online. March 9, 2006.
Washington Post. March 17, 2006, p. WE30.

SILENT HILL

Enjoy your stay. We've been expecting you.
—Movie tagline

Box Office: $46.9 million

The usual objective one has when playing a video game is to progress through varying layers of obstacles and difficulties until one achieves a final goal. The usual objective of watching a film is to follow interesting characters as they travel through a coherent storyline to a satisfying conclusion. Problems arise, however, when filmmakers try to turn successful video games into movies. Which objective will they pursue? If they do the first, filmgoers will be unsatisfied. If they do the second, the loyal gamers will be unhappy. *Silent Hill,* which is not the first movie to be based on a video game, unfortunately suffers from this dilemma. In an attempt to not alienate gamers, the movie sacrifices an intelligible plot on the altar of demons, monsters, and evil ghosts.

"Silent Hill" is the name yelled by young Sharon (Jodelle Ferland) as she sleepwalks in the dead of night only to be rescued by her parents Rose (Radha Mitchell) and Christopher DaSilva (Sean Bean) as she teeters precariously over a watery abyss. With a little research, Rose discovers that Silent Hill is a ghost town in West Virginia (Sharon was apparently adopted from an orphanage in West Virginia). Rose loads her daughter up in the family car and heads for Silent Hill—in the dark of night—and never bothers to tell her husband. When he discovers what she's done, he cancels her credit cards and takes off after her.

Meanwhile, at a roadside gas and food stop, Rose attracts the attention of an overly-butch, suspicious-looking female motorcycle cop, Cybil (Laurie Holden). Cybil, evidently, was traumatized a few years back in an incident involving a kidnapped little boy. Fearing Sharon might be kidnapped, she follows Rose. Inexplicably, after stopping for Cybil's police lights, Rose suddenly takes off and crashes through the gates leading into the unsafe ghost town of Silent Hill. The reason the town has been abandoned and gated off from outsiders is that fires in the coalmines below the city are still burning and the town is awash in toxic fumes. Just the kind of place one wants to go to in the middle of the night with one's young daughter in the car.

Rose crashes during the chase, blacks out and wakes up to find herself in an uninhabited town where it rains ash and her daughter is missing. Rose desperately begins searching the abandoned town for Sharon, following what she believes to be a little girl and eventually finds herself in some kind of underground fence maze when an air raid siren goes off. Suddenly everything goes black and Rose finds herself surrounded by glowing, twisted, charred, and misshapen bodies that can spit out burning sludge.

These visually dark and menacing periods in Silent Hill alternate in time with foggy, washed-out, relatively safe periods in the abandoned town. But at the same time, these two periods are overlaid with another version (or possibly another dimension) of Silent Hill in which Rose's husband and Officer Gucci (Kim Coates) look for them. This Silent Hill is filmed in a golden twilight and is devoid of all ghosts, demons, or people of any kind.

Eventually Rose is joined by Officer Cybil, who crashed her motorcycle during the earlier chase and also blacked out, and the two fight various strange and unexplained monsters (including a contortionist trussed up in barbed wire, a big man with a metal pyramid on his head, people-eating cockroaches, and zombie nurses) during the dark periods and try to find Sharon and learn the truth about the town during the foggy periods. The truth, by the way, involves a cult of witch hunters headed by Cristabella (Alice Krige) and has nothing to do with coal mine fires.

If one expects the story to finally reveal who all the monsters are or even why Sharon has to come back to the town, one will be disappointed. As mentioned, coherence is not a priority for this movie. Most of it is simply disturbing and bizarre. It is easy to see the video game origins of *Silent Hill,* from the various levels of menace to the picking up of items (keys, lamps, maps, etc) that might be useful to defeat whatever obstacles one encounters. The final goal is obvious—rescuing Sharon—but explaining it all in a logical and consistent manner is not. If there is an upside to *Silent Hill,* it is the cinematography. Dan Laustsen has done an excellent job of creating an eerie and nightmarish world. However, his work is almost wasted in service of atmospheric nonsense that should have been a half hour shorter and a lot less cryptic.

Beverley Bare Buehrer

CREDITS

Rose Da Silva: Radha Mitchell
Christopher Da Silva: Sean Bean
Cybil Bennett: Laurie Holden
Dahila Gillespie: Deborah Kara Unger
Sharon/Alessa: Jodelle Ferland
Christabella: Alice Krige
Officer Thomas Gucci: Kim Coates
Anna: Tanya Allen
Origin: Canada, France
Language: English
Released: 2006
Production: Victor Hadida, Don Carmody; TriStar Pictures, Samuel Hadida, Davis Films, Silent Hill DCP, Konami; released by Sony Pictures Entertainment
Directed by: Christophe Gans
Written by: Roger Roberts Avary
Cinematography by: Dan Laustsen
Music by: Jeff Danna
Sound: Nicolas Becker
Editing: Sebastien Prangere
Art Direction: Elinor Rose Galbraith, James McAteer
Costumes: Wendy Partridge
Production Design: Carol Spier
MPAA rating: R
Running time: 127 minutes

REVIEWS

Boxoffice Online. April 21, 2006.
Chicago Sun-Times Online. April 21, 2006.

Hollywood Reporter Online. April 21, 2006.
Los Angeles Times Online. April 24, 2006.
New York Times Online. April 22, 2006.
Variety Online. April 21, 2006.

QUOTES

Christabella (to Rose): "To find your daughter, you must face the darkness of Hell."

16 BLOCKS

For a New York cop and his witness, the distance between life and death just got very short.
—Movie tagline

1 Witness…118 Minutes…
—Movie tagline

Box Office: $36.8 million

In director Richard Donner's latest suspense thriller, *16 Blocks*, written by Richard Wenk, Bruce Willis plays a burnt-out, over-the-hill police detective named Jack Mosley, a world-weary boozehound, who gets roped into a last-minute assignment on overtime. The assignment is as simple as the movie's plot: he has todeliver small-time crook Eddie Bunker (Mos Def) from here to there, from the stationhouse to the grand jury, sixteen blocks across Lower Manhattan (with Toronto convincingly passing for New York). But this assignment is not as easy as it sounds. It turns out that Eddie's testimony will uncover some horrendously deep corruption and brutality in the New York Police Department, implicating Jack's former partner, Frank Nugent (played with cold-hearted and scary efficiency by David Morse), who is coordinating a hit team to insure that Eddie never gets to the grand jury. The kicker, we learn as the plot deepens, is that this ring of corruption also encircles Jack Mosley. But, miraculously, Jack sees his assignment as a chance to redeem himself. Frank begs him to back off, to walk away, but Jack refuses, resulting in a chase across Manhattan, south of Canal Street, involving cars, busses, and subway trains, easily transporting us into the familiar movie-chase terrain familiarized by many of Donner's earlier works, most famously, perhaps, the *Lethal Weapon* series (1987-1998).

But Bruce Willis is not simply doing a Mel Gibson imitation in *16 Blocks*. In fact, he is not clowning around at all, though at times he seems almost as suicidal as Gibson's character in the first *Lethal Weapon* (1987). Instead, Willis more nearly resembles the shell-shocked Vietnam vet he played for Norman Jewison in the film adaptation of Bobbi Ann Mason's novel, *In Country* (1989). In that film, Willis, in the words of one critic, did a "terrific job of looking seedy, fortyish, stoic, and solid." In *16 Blocks,* at the age of fifty-one, the actor looks even more astonishingly seedy and stoic. He truly resembles the alcoholic he plays, who cannot move his prisoner more than a few blocks without stopping for a drink. It is the sort of role an actor better known for his dramatic work might be expected to play, but Willis is more than up to the challenge.

Despite Willis's unusually strong lead performance, *16 Blocks* does not escape entirely from the *Lethal Weapon* formula. It is not exactly a buddy movie, but at times plays that way, with Bruce Willis in the "serious" Danny Glover role and Mos Def standing in for Glover's manic motor-mouthed sidekick. It turns out that Eddie is not much of a hardened criminal, just a "kid," as the cops, good and bad, refer to him, with ambition and aspirations. Eddie wants to own his own business, a bakery, and specialize in designing birthday cakes, hoping to move to Seattle in order to realize his dreams. He speaks endlessly about his plans, as if to keep his mind off the more immediate threats. Mos Def plays this optimistic and innocent role brilliantly against the more cynical Willis, giving what would otherwise be a fairly silly movie a pace and a heart. If ever a movie was saved by its performances, *16 Blocks* is at the top of the list. However, her *USA Today* review, Claudia Puig was less considerate of the elder star, commenting that: "Willis's performance mystifies, while Mos Def's mesmerizes." Alternately, *Variety* reviewer Robert Koehler objected to what he construed to be minority stereotyping, since, in his opinion, Eddie's constant babbling was "dangerously close to the stereotype of the dim, shuffling black man out of Hollywood's sorry past."

Once the sixteen-block journey is set into motion, the plot bounces along from one improbable dilemma to another. *Washington Post* reviewer Stephen Hunter reasonably complained that the movie "is too full of nonsense." The story puts Jack and Eddie into numerous impossible situations with no way out, then conjures up lame means of escape. At one point, for example, they are trapped in an apartment, with several experienced detectives about to catch up with them yet they still escape somehow. (Shrewd Jack telephones in the wrong apartment number to headquarters, drawing the assassins to one floor, while he and Eddie escape from another.) Later, they are trapped on a city bus, and it looks as though Jack has reached the end of the line. The tires of the bus have been shot off the rims, and their hostages have been released, including Eddie, disguised as a businessman, who is somehow able to calmly walk past the army of cops that has been trying to assassinate him all morning. So what does he do? Fly to Seattle? No. He comes back, to save Jack, and after a crunching chase, they both escape in an ambulance, with Jack's sister, Diane (Jenna Stern), an emergency room nurse, conveniently on board to stitch up the wounded Eddie.

In the end, Jack lets Eddie go rather than sending him to his certain death at the court house, where he knows the police assassins will be waiting. Jack decides to testify himself, since he was one of the dirty cops Eddie's testimony would have inadvertently put away. In a tense stand-off, Jack announces his intentions to selflessly sacrifice himself for truth and justice, and a cop assassin is barely stopped by a SWAT sniper just as he is about to shoot Jack. Eddie escapes to Seattle to fulfill his dreams of entrepreneurship, while Jack lives on to cooperate with the grand jury and serve out his time, paying his debt to society. Jack the cynic does not like birthdays, but at the end of the film, after Jack's release from prison, Eddie sends him a birthday cake.

Regarding the film's direction, *The Washington Post's* Stephen Hunter gleefully dismissed Donner as "a clever hack, but at least a craftsman of some merit." Manohla Dargis of the *New York Times* was far more generous, calling Donner an "action auteur," while *Variety* noted that the movie was "closer to a compact film noir" than the slick entertainments the director is famous for. The fault for the logical absurdities of the screenplay would be more fairly credited to Richard Wenk than to Donner, who was almost able to cover the plot flaws by keeping the frantic plot in motion and the characters on the run.

The screenplay also drew criticism for trying to be too clever for its own good. *The New York Times* noted, for example, the screenwriter's "fondness for naming his characters after famous crime writers—Bunker for Edward Bunker, Mosley for Walter Mosley," a tendency that also extends to the David Morse character, "called Frank Nugent, after the great Hollywood screenwriter." While this may thrill movie geeks and fans of crime fiction, average moviegoers will most likely remain clueless.

Claudia Puig further complained that this "familiar story of police corruption" had been "around the block a time or two," and Stephen Hunter pointed out the similarities between *16 Blocks* and Clint Eastwood's "utterly brainless 1977 loser *The Gauntlet*, which featured bad cops also subverting the system from within, forcing Eastwood and a witness (Sondra Locke) to ride a bus through town while every lawman in Phoenix county fired away at them." Manohla Dargis of the *New York Times* also remembered Donner's "debt" to *The Gauntlet*.

But by simply looking past the car chases in *16 Blocks*, viewers will find a movie about hope, ambition, and second chances. This is, ultimately, an upbeat actor's movie, marking an impressive performance by Mos Def and a courageous and solid turn by Bruce Willis, who had the courage to both look and act his age and embrace a mature role with dignity. As Baltimore critic Chris Kaltenbach wrote, "Long one of Hollywood's most under-rated actors, Willis may finally get the recognition for versatility he deserves through this film." One hopes so, for Richard Donner's film is not just an actor's film in an action setting, not unlike the *Lethal Weapon* franchise, but is also a well-performed allegory about police corruption and redemption. The movie offers an affirming message about second chances, while, in turn, offering a few nice chances to Mos Def and an over-the-hill action hero who apparently still has something to contribute to the genre.

James M. Welsh

CREDITS

Jack Mosley: Bruce Willis
Eddie Bunker: Mos Def
Frank Nugent: David Morse
Jimmy Mulvey: Cylk Cozart
Capt. Gruber: Casey Sander
Robert Torres: David Zayas
Diane Mosley: Jenna Stern
Jerry Shue: Robert Racki
Origin: USA
Language: English
Released: 2006
Production: Jim Van Wyck, John Thompson, Arnold Rifkin, Avi Lerner, Charlotte Street; Cheyenne Enterprises, Alcon Entertainment, Randall Emmett; released by Warner Bros.
Directed by: Richard Donner
Written by: Richard Wenk
Cinematography by: Glen MacPherson
Music by: Klaus Badelt
Sound: Greg Chapman
Music Supervisor: Ashley Miller
Editing: Steve Mirkovich
Art Direction: Brandt Gordon
Costumes: Vicki Graef
Production Design: Art Greywal
MPAA rating: PG-13
Running time: 105 minutes

REVIEWS

Boxoffice Online. March 3, 2006.
Chicago Sun-Times Online. March 3, 2006.
Entertainment Weekly Online. March 1, 2006.
Los Angeles Times Online. March 3, 2006.
New York Times Online. March 3, 2006.
Variety Online. February 25, 2006.
Washington Post Online. March 3, 2006.

QUOTES

Frank Nugent (reloading weapon): "You know, when I woke up this morning, I didn't expect to be trading nine millies with my friend."

SLITHER

What Ever You Do…Don't Scream.
—Movie tagline

Box Office: $7.8 million

Writer/director James Gunn comes to movie making via Lloyd Kaufman's Troma Enterprises. If you're not familiar with Troma, then you've never seen or heard of *The Toxic Avenger* (1985) or Gunn's own *Tromeo and Juliet* (1996). Troma's trademark is schlocky, campy horror films. From Troma, Gunn went on to write the remake of *Dawn of the Dead* (2004) and the two live-action Scooby Doo flicks. It's easy to see Troma's influence on his directorial debut, *Slither*, and maybe a bit of Scooby, too.

Slither is the story of the little town of Wheelsey and what happens to it when a meteor lands there just as deer season is about to open. The town's sheriff, Bill Pardy (Nathan Fillion), is snoozing in his squad car late one night while his deputy uses the radar gun on whip-poorwills (27 m.p.h.). Suddenly, there is a bright crash seen through the squad car's rear window. They, however, notice nothing. It turns out the meteor is only about the size of a baseball, but it does pulse and glow as movie meteors are inclined to do. And then it breaks open and out slithers what can only be described as a slug.

The next day we are introduced to several more of the sleepy little speed trap's inhabitants. There's Jack MacReady (Gregg Henry), Wheelsey's foul-mouthed mayor; Starla Grant (Elizabeth Banks), the town's high school biology teacher; and the redundantly named Grant Grant (Michael Rooker), the richest man in Wheelsey and Starla's husband. Starla grew up in poverty and although she wanted to run off to Hollywood and become a movie star, she ended up married to Grant. For Stella it is a loveless marriage while Starla is the love of Grant's life. Obviously, this is the source of much confusion and frustration for Grant.

One night the lovelorn Grant goes off and gets drunk, picks up Brenda (Brenda James) in a bar, and wanders off into the woods for a little whoopee. Instead, Grant stumbles upon the meteor, follows an oozy trail, finds the slug, and naturally, just has to give it a poke. The result is a needle-like appendage being shot from the slug into Grant's abdomen resulting in an alien taking up residence inside of him. The richest man in town now craves meat, lots of meat, lots of raw meat and it's not long before the town is flooded with fliers for lost pets.

Grant then goes back to take care of some unfinished business with Brenda. But the alien Grant's idea of showing Brenda a good time consists of similarly needling her in the gut and getting her pregnant with alien babies. Of course, Brenda can't be left where her husband might find her so she is taken to an old barn and chained there to wait for the not-so-blessed event.

Back at the Grant home, Starla begins to notice that Grant isn't acting normal. He's also not looking so good. When she breaks into the newly locked basement and finds it filled with dead animals, she knows that there's a problem. Starla and Sheriff Pardy then go out to find Grant who has turned into a giant Jabba the Hutt, squid-type thing. The hunt leads them to the now hugely rotund Brenda who suddenly explodes, sending thousands of little slugletts off into the woods and into the mouths of all the deputies in the area. Of course the deputies aren't dead and it isn't long before they're walking around like alien zombies, stalking the uninfected as food.

There's nothing new or innovative in this story, in fact, one can pick out specific plot points "borrowed" from other movies, probably deliberately. But that's part of the film's homage nature. It purposely incorporates images and ideas from other films and then gleefully makes fun of them. It is unashamedly imitative and campy and retro in its look and feel.

Since the plot is thin and well-known, *Slither* has to depend on its actors to carry it and they do an admirable job. Michael Rooker's Grant is sleazy and basically unlovable but we do feel sorry for him. Gregg Henry's profanity-inclined mayor chews scenery but it is fun to imagine how he ever got elected. Elizabeth Banks' Starla is sufficiently sweet as a love interest not only for her husband but also for the lovelorn sheriff. But Nathan Fillion's sheriff is the character that truly gives the film its tone and humor. His deputies are more like the F Troop than a SWAT team. As played by Fillion, Pardy's not some super heroic alien fighter but a regular guy who can just barely figure out what's going on. In fact, when he's attacked by an alien-infected deer and has to be saved by a teenager, he makes a point of telling her that when she recounts the story in the future, he will have to be the hero. Fillion makes Pardy almost a detached observer of the action in the film, as if he's simply there to make wry comments on the absurdity of it all while actually saving the day…barely. While not always successful in its comedy (very broad) or its horror (very gross), *Slither* is an entertaining hybrid that's good for whiling away an hour and a half.

Beverley Bare Buehrer

CREDITS

Bill Pardy: Nathan Fillion
Starla Grant: Elizabeth Banks
Jack MacReady: Gregg Henry
Grant Grant: Michael Rooker
Brenda Gutierrez: Brenda James
Wally: Don Thompson
Kylie Strutemyer: Tania Saulnier
Shelby: Jenna Fischer
Origin: USA, Canada
Language: English
Released: 2006
Production: Paul Brooks, Eric Newman; Universal Pictures, Gold Circle Films, Strike Entertainment; released by Universal
Directed by: James Gunn
Written by: James Gunn
Cinematography by: Gregory Middleton
Music by: Tyler Bates
Sound: William Skinner
Editing: John Axelrad
Art Direction: Michael Norman Wong
Costumes: Patricia Louise Hargreaves
Production Design: Andrew Neskoromny
MPAA rating: R
Running time: 95 minutes

REVIEWS

Chicago Sun-Times Online. March 31, 2006.
Entertainment Weekly Online. March 31, 2006.
Los Angeles Times Online. March 31, 2006.
New York Times Online. March 31, 2006.
San Francisco Chronicle Online. March 31, 2006.
USA Today Online. March 31, 2006.
Variety Online. March 19, 2006.
Village Voice Online. March 28, 2006.
Washington Post Online. March 31, 2006.

SNAKES ON A PLANE

Sit back. Relax. Enjoy the fright.
—Movie tagline

Box Office: $34 million

Can a cult-film phenomenon be created even before the movie hits theaters? Such a question may seem odd since the very notion of a cult film revolves around it finding a loyal and impassioned following. But in the age of the Internet, word of mouth on a movie can begin even while it is still in production. Such was the case with David R. Ellis's *Snakes on a Plane*, a comic thriller that Internet geeks were chatting up months before its release and whose title baldly tells us what to expect. Reports surfaced that Ellis shot extra scenes beefing up the violence and language to satisfy the wishes of bloggers and to garner the movie an R rating. But if, ultimately, the tepid box office results were a letdown in light of all the prerelease hype, then perhaps the lesson is that Internet buzz does not automatically translate into blockbuster status.

The real success of *Snakes on a Plane* may not be in its nontraditional marketing but in its simple, silly, and fun concept and the entertaining way it is executed. The eyewitness to a gangland murder, a surfer named Sean (Nathan Phillips), has to be transported from Honolulu to Los Angeles to testify against ruthless crime lord Eddie Kim (Byron Lawson). Sean is in the custody of FBI agent Neville Flynn (Samuel L. Jackson), who has commandeered the entire first class section of an airplane to protect Sean, leaving everyone else to fly coach. But the bad guys have concocted a nefarious and far-fetched plot to kill the witness. They have stashed poisonous snakes in the cargo hold and sprayed the passengers' leis with pheromones guaranteed to arouse the slithery creatures. Once the plane is in the air and securely away from shore, a timer is set to release the snakes.

The plane is filled with a variety of characters who occasionally butt heads but ultimately have to work together to survive. Claire (Julianna Margulies), who emerges as a leader in the battle, is a flight attendant on her last mission before starting law school. Another flight attendant, the attractive Tiffany (Sunny Mabrey), flirts with Sean. Mercedes (Rachel Blanchard) is a pretty, rich, blonde passenger carrying a pampered Chihuahua in her handbag. Accompanied by his comic bodyguards, narcissistic rap star Three G's (Flex Alexander) is constantly worried about germs and frets over people touching him. Two little brothers taking their first flight alone, a young mother with her baby, and a disgruntled British businessman round out the major players.

Since the characters are essentially stereotypes, their main function is to be terrorized by the snakes and run around in a panic, the screenplay, credited to John Heffernan and Sebastian Gutierrez from a story by Heffernan and David Dalessandro, comes up with some suitably gross and inventive ways for the snakes to kill their victims. One couple is attacked while having sex in the rest room. Another man is bit in the genitals, and an unsuspecting woman finds a snake in her airsickness bag. The snooty businessman is eventually wrapped by a python and then devoured head first. Yet, because such violence is so over-the-top, the film, while providing some jolts, is rarely downright scary. But thrilling it is, even if the overall plot is rather predictable.

Given the limited concept, it is surprising that the story does not grow tiresome. But the passengers' quirky personalities keep us amused, and Ellis makes the most of the various parts of the aircraft, keeping the survivors on the run and on their toes to outwit their reptilian foes. The screenplay generates some suspense on the ground when the FBI agent in charge, Hank Harris (Bobby Cannavale), has to race against time with a snake expert to secure antivenom for the passengers who are still alive but have been bitten. And while the role of the tough-talking, no-nonsense FBI agent Flynn is hardly a stretch for Jackson—indeed, it is a quintessential role for him—without his charisma and authority grounding the story, the whole enterprise would probably collapse. Flynn is a force to be reckoned with in the most ridiculous of situations, whether he is leading the passengers on a run for safety to the front of the plane or uttering the movie's signature line: "I have had it with these motherf**kin' snakes on this motherf**kin' plane!" which, incidentally, had its genesis on the Internet.

There are also some very humorous touches amidst the tension, including seeing the action from the snakes' point of view via a green-tinted screen, as if they were wearing night-vision goggles. The big finale is a great mix of the comic and the thrilling. With both pilots dead, it is left to Troy (Kenan Thompson), a bodyguard to Three G's and the only passenger with flight experience, to bring the plane in for a safe landing. But soon we learn that his only "experience" is behind the controls of a video game. Nonetheless, true to the film's spirit of cheerful fun amongst utter chaos, he succeeds against the odds while the surviving passengers cling to whatever they can for dear life.

If *Snakes on a Plane* is an entertaining thrill ride with an original premise, it is, nonetheless, hard to overlook the fact that, in its broad outlines, the screenplay is a formulaic disaster movie, complete with a diverse ensemble sometimes fighting each other but ultimately overcoming their differences and bonding together to survive a deadly threat. Yet the movie carries viewers along through its sheer energy and bursts of comic mayhem, and one can surmise that seeing it with a huge, enthusiastic audience could only make the experience livelier. While it is a great B-movie adventure for late summer, it is, however, hardly the next cult classic that so many people were expecting (or maybe just hoping for). Perhaps the lesson from all the hype is simply that such phenomena cannot be predicted or built online—they can only happen when enough people discover and embrace a movie for themselves.

Peter N. Chumo II

CREDITS

Neville Flynn: Samuel L. Jackson
Claire Miller: Julianna Margulies
Troy: Kenan Thompson
Sean Jones: Nathan Phillips
Three G's: Flex Alexander
Hank Harris: Bobby Cannavale
Rick: David Koechner
Tiffany: Sunny Mabrey
Dr. Steven Price: Todd Louiso
Eddie Kim: Byron Lawson
Mercedes: Rachel Blanchard
Origin: USA
Language: English
Released: 2006
Production: Gary Levinsohn, Don Granger, Craig Berenson; Mutual Film Corporation; released by New Line Cinema
Directed by: David R. Ellis
Written by: Sebastian Gutierrez, John Heffernan
Cinematography by: Adam Greenberg
Music by: Trevor Rabin
Sound: Michael McGee
Editing: Howard E. Smith
Art Direction: John Alvarez
Costumes: Karen Matthews
Production Design: Jaymes Hinkle
MPAA rating: R
Running time: 105 minutes

REVIEWS

Chicago Sun-Times Online. August 18, 2006.
Time Magazine Online. August 18, 2006.
Village Voice Online. August 18, 2006.

QUOTES

Neville Flynn: "I have had it with these motherf**kin' snakes on this motherf**kin' plane."

SOMERSAULT

Love can turn you upside down.
—Movie tagline

Somersault is a slow-moving, impressionistic study of a young woman's quest for acceptance and meaning in life. It is a small, closely observed film that demands patience. The plot is slight and slow, more of a character study than anything else. The trouble is, the characters are also rather thinly drawn.

The movie, which is set in an unidentified part of Australia, begins with Heidi (Abbie Cornish) making a pass at her mother's boyfriend. He is lounging on a bed half-naked, and she asks if she can touch a tattoo of a snake on his chest. Soon, she is kissing him. Her mother appears in the doorway, and flies into a rage. Heidi, whose age is not clear but who presumably is in her later teens, decides to leave home. She takes a bus to a ski-resort area where she thought she had a friend. When she gets there she finds out she is utterly alone.

She quickly finds a club where boys are eager to offer her drinks and a chance to dance. She goes back to a cabin with one of them and has sex, but the next morning the boys leave. Heidi quickly hooks up with Joe (Sam Worthington), a hunk of few words and a rather puzzling indifference to her charms. After a bit of very obvious wooing, Heidi captures his attention—at least sexually. She spends most of the rest of the movie trying to secure him as a boyfriend while he occupies himself with work, family, and a brief exploration into the possibility that he is bisexual.

Meanwhile, Heidi secures a room to rent at a hotel where she is befriended by a proprietress whose husband is in prison and who functions as a substitute mother figure. She also gets a job at a gas station convenience store, but only because she seduces the owner.

This is writer/director Cate Strickland's first feature film after a series of shorts that were acclaimed in her native land, and perhaps this should really have been a short-film subject. The film is long on rather stereotypical "indie" aesthetics—including an overuse of slow motion, puzzling abrupt cutaways, and throwaway moments that are supposed to signal character moods, such as one in which Heidi puts on rose-colored goggles and sees the world in a new light.

Strickland seems to be constantly fumbling to invest meaning in a story that is also striving for everyday realism. The missing element is character delineation and complexity, something that might help the audiences care about Heidi and her plight. Instead, there is no backstory to explain why Heidi kissed her mother's boyfriend, whether she is just impulsive or curious or whether she has a need for affection or danger. There is absolutely no information about Heidi's relationship with her mother; in fact, her mother barely registers as a character in her few scenes.

Strickland instead presents a character study of a young woman of indeterminate age, background, and personality, as if to suggest that Heidi may be a stand-in for all adolescent girls. She doesn't make her into either a romantic or sympathetic protagonist, which is fine if realism is the goal, but without context her actions make no sense. The film suggests that Heidi is merely hungry—for food, shelter, and affection—the basic needs, and she is willing to prostitute herself to get those needs met. Yet she is not cruel or mean, merely weak.

Cornish, who is on screen for practically the entire film, does a marvelous job of investing subtle spirit and complexity into what is essentially a blank main character. Her face is both girlish and womanly, perfect for a movie that suggests, at times rather clumsily, a female with feet in both the world of childhood and adulthood. When Cornish plays flirtatious, it is usually subtle; when she is nude in sex scenes, she suggests a combination of shattering innocence and womanly ardor.

Worthington also tries hard, but his character is even more inscrutable. Strickland doesn't believe in dialogue that sheds much light on the inner workings of her characters. Neither Heidi nor Joe has a lot to say; they speak mostly in clipped mumbles.

In the service of realism, the lack of dialogue rings true to life. And the fact that its characters stumble through mundane days where not much happens, *Somersault* could also make claims to being uncontrived. Except that the story *is* highly contrived: the kiss, the couplings, all the coming-of-age motifs, it's all been done before. It is the story of the prodigal child, and you know where she will end up, despite hints at tragedy, because this is clearly a gentle, sweet-hearted film at bottom.

It's fine to make a minimalist kind of film, but it's hard to make an effective character study when your characters don't carry much weight. Their actions must carry meaning if their words don't. Artsy aesthetics don't confer either substance or authenticity on their own.

For much of the film, scenes pile on one by one without much clarity. The awkward scene in which he exhibits confusion about his sexual preference seems much too easy and convenient a red herring, especially since it goes nowhere.

Everything in *Somersault* is indefinite and inconclusive, as if Strickland were afraid to commit to anything, much like her adolescent characters. It might be a film that teenage girls would identify with, because it delineates a world of confusion and impermanence. Cornish adeptly portrays a young woman unsure of her status in the world, struggling with some basic ethical choices—what will she do to survive? Steal? Prostitute her body? Strickland presents these dilemmas rather delicately and doesn't carry them through to their logical conclusions, and her techniques keep the audience at a distance.

Viewers looking for action, plot, dialogue, or character development will be disappointed by *Somersault.* For those wanting artistry, Strickland makes an effort at quiet, trenchant observation—but too many of her techniques are cliched. There are moments of quiet contemplative beauty and anguish, but they are fragile and fleeting, and it is a lack of emotional connection to Heidi and her plight that keep these moments from being compelling. *Somersault* would have been a nice short film, but it lacks the story, weight, dramatic tension, and depth of character to be plausible as a feature.

Michael Betzold

CREDITS

Joe: Sam Worthington
Irene: Lynette Curran
Diane: Leah Purcell
Stuart: Nathaniel Dean
Heidi: Abbie Cornish
Richard: Erik Thomson
Bianca: Hollie Andrew
Nicole: Olivia Pigeot
Karl: Blake Pittman
Origin: Australia
Language: English
Released: 2004
Production: Anthony Anderson; Film Finance Corp, New South Wales Film & Television Office, Red Carpet Prods., Showtime Australia; released by Magnolia Pictures
Directed by: Cate Shortland
Written by: Cate Shortland
Cinematography by: Robert Humpherys
Sound: Sam Petty
Editing: Scott Gray
Art Direction: Janie Parker
Costumes: Emily Seresin
Production Design: Melinda Doring
MPAA rating: Unrated
Running time: 106 minutes

REVIEWS

Boxoffice Online. April 14, 2006.
London Times Online. March 3, 2005.
Los Angeles Times Online. April 21, 2006.
New York Times Online. April 21, 2006.
Variety Online. May 18, 2004.
Village Voice Online. April 18, 2006.

SOMETHING NEW

She had it all under control. Except her heart.
—Movie tagline

A romantic comedy with a whole lot of drama.
—Movie tagline

Box Office: $11.4 million

The interracial romantic comedy *Something New* isn't really new at all. Released the week before Valentine's Day 2006, it's a date movie that's sweet and affecting and well cast, as well as talky and predictable. It's also the first screen effort for sitcom writer and producer Kriss Turner, who's worked on such shows as *Living Single, Whoopi,* and *Everybody Hates Chris,* and music video director Sanaa Hamri. The movie stars beautiful Sanaa Lathan and Aussie-born hunk Simon Baker and, thankfully, the two have a lot of sensual chemistry. You want to see their characters find love because they seem right for each other—no matter what bumps present themselves along the way.

And bumps there are. First we are introduced to Kenya McQueen (Lathan), whose wedding dream is interrupted by her chiming alarm clock. She wakes up alone on Valentine's Day and looks out on the dismal weed-filled backyard of her new home. Kenya is a disciplined, early thirty-something senior accountant at a big (apparently mostly white male) Los Angeles firm where she learns she's up for a partnership. She's greeted by perky co-worker Leah (Katharine Towne), who wants to set Kenya up on a blind date since she has no social life, that is, except with her equally successful girlfriends: Cheryl (Wendy Raquel Robinson) is a judge, Suzzette (Golden Brooks) is a pediatrician, and Nedra (Taraji P. Henson) is a banker. All are unmarried and lament the fact that, according to an article, 42.4 percent of all African American women haven't married, and the statistics are worse for educated professional women like themselves. Kenya, however, doesn't believe that a "single, black professional woman [is] destined to be unhappy and alone." But her girlfriends are quick to mock the list of traits she expects in her IBM (Ideal Black Man).

Upset after she hears an old boyfriend is getting married, Kenya agrees to let Leah set her up and meets her blind date at Starbucks. But she's shaken when the date turns out to be with Brian Kelly (Baker), a blond, blue-eyed, white man. She's obviously uncomfortable and quickly breaks off the meeting only to see Brian again at Leah's engagement party. She admires the landscaping he did at the home of Leah's parents, and Brian agrees to check out her own pitiful yard. He arrives in a beat-up work truck with a friendly golden retriever that makes Kenya nervous (she doesn't "do" dogs). Brian likes to "take hard earth and make things bloom" and begins to work on Kenya's garden and Kenya herself. He's smitten from the start; she's skittish and circumspect, especially after seeing the reaction of her obnoxious, womanizing younger brother Nelson (Donald Faison), who refers to Brian as "the help."

Kenya is the product of a socially prominent, well-to-do family: Nelson is a newly-minted lawyer, their father Edmond (Earl Billings) is a neurosurgeon, and their status-minded mother Joyce (Alfre Woodard) is, well, free with her opinions. When Brian works late, Kenya invites him in for takeout, and he inquires why her house is so beige and impersonal (her mother "thinks bright colors are for children and whores."). He then bluntly asks her, "So, I take it you don't do white guys?" She replies: "I just happen to prefer black men. It's not a prejudice, it's a preference." Brian is skeptical but persistent. He insists that workaholic Kenya go hiking with him; they get caught in a rain shower, and—cue the music—have their first kiss in the rain. Brian spends the night but, the next morning, mistakenly questions why she wears a hair weave instead of her natural hair. Outraged, Kenya dismisses him and complains to her girlfriends about his obtuseness. They tell her if the sex was great (and it was), she should just enjoy herself. Kenya decides to get the hair weave removed and begins to add some color to her power-suited wardrobe.

The romance is kept on the QT, and Brian is the one who's uncomfortable when they join Cheryl and her boyfriend Walter (Mike Epps) at a black club where Kenya tries to downplay their connection. Cheryl tells Kenya to relax. Kenya is also having trouble with a nervous white male client and complains to Brian about having to pay the "black tax," meaning she has to work twice as hard to be considered equal. Brian really doesn't understand. He's also the outsider at her housewarming party since Kenya is reluctant to make their romance clear when he meets her parents. To make the situation more awkward, Nelson has invited his mentor, suave tax attorney Mark Harper (Blair Underwood), in hopes Kenya will be attracted to him. Kenya, who was a debutante as a girl, is also reluctant to bring Brian along as her date to an annual African American cotillion.

The couple's insecurities come to a boil when (both having had a rough day at work) they get into a harsh argument about race. Kenya complains that she doesn't get to take the night off from being black and the only time "you guys know you're white is when you're in a roomful of black people." He replies that he's "never going to be on the right side of the war going on inside your head because I'm not black." They break up, and Kenya accepts a date with Mark. After two weeks apart, Brian tries to make amends: "I want to be there for you, Kenya.... I may not always relate but I can promise I'll empathize." Brian says he loves her; Kenya tells him she's seeing someone else. She takes Mark to Leah's wedding but is furious when Brian also turns up with a date and then gets into an argument with her exasperated girlfriends. Kenya soon decides that Mark isn't her IBM and talks with Cheryl and Walter about her dilemma. Walter offers the advice that "at the end of the day it's not about skin color or race, it's about the love connection, the vibe that's between a man and a woman."

Kenya thinks that after disagreeing with her client that she's lost her partnership but eventually gets her promotion. But when she goes to the cotillion with her family, Kenya drinks too much and winds up crying in the bathroom. Her father comes in for a heart-to-heart and admits he likes Brian: "Anyway, the boy's just white. He ain't a Martian." Kenya leaves the cotillion to find Brian and finally admits: "You're the one I want, Brian. I love you." She brings Brian back to the cotillion to publicly declare their coupledom, and as the two dance together, the scene shifts to them happily dancing at their backyard wedding.

Something New is about the process of falling in love. Kenya, who had a sheltered, privileged childhood, wants to be open and adventurous but needs someone to help her take that first step. Brian, a college-educated former ad exec, decided to leave the suit-and-tie world behind and can't understand why it isn't so easy for Kenya to go beyond her comfort zone. Kenya is unhappy being judged by others for dating outside her race; Brian is disconcerted at being the odd-man-out with her friends and family. You want the adorable twosome to have a happy ending because they make each other better people—despite the racial difference, despite the discomfort of others. It may be a fairy tale but here's to living happily-ever-after.

Christine Tomassini

CREDITS

Kenya McQueen: Sanaa Lathan
Brian Kelly: Simon Baker
Walter: Mike Epps
Nelson McQueen: Donald Faison
Mark Harper: Blair Underwood
Cheryl: Wendy Raquel Robinson
Suzzette: Golden Brooks
Nedra: Taraji P. Henson
Edmond McQueen: Earl Billings
Leah: Katharine Towne
Joyce: Alfre Woodard
Origin: USA
Language: English
Released: 2006
Production: Stephanie Allain; released by Focus Features
Directed by: Sanaa Hamri

Written by: Kristopher Turner
Cinematography by: Shane Hurlbut
Music by: Wendy Melvoin, Lisa Coleman, Paul Anthony Stewart
Sound: Susumu Tokunow
Music Supervisor: Spring Aspers
Editing: Melissa Kent
Costumes: Hope Hanafin
Production Design: Mayne Berke
MPAA rating: PG-13
Running time: 100 minutes

REVIEWS

Boxoffice Online. February 3, 2006.
Chicago Sun-Times Online. February 3, 2006.
Entertainment Weekly Online. February 1, 2006.
Los Angeles Times Online. February 3, 2006.
New York Times Online. February 3, 2006.
Variety Online. January 22, 2006.
Washington Post Online. February 3, 2006.

QUOTES

Nelson McQueen: "Mommie, Kenya's dating white boys now."

STAY ALIVE

You Die in the Game—You Die for Real.
—Movie tagline

Play It To Death.
—Movie tagline

The only thing you'll lose in this game is YOUR LIFE.
—Movie tagline

Box Office: $23 million

The makers of *Stay Alive* showed some savvy with their film in one respect: predicting how it would be received by critics. The film was not prescreened for critics for fear of bad reviews and, indeed, reviews for the film were scathing.

The premise the film was not completely awful. The beta version of an underground game called Stay Alive falls into the hands of a couple of Hutch's (Jon Foster) friends. The next morning, the friends are dead. Hutch's irreverent buddy, Phineus (Jimmi Simpson), suggests paying tribute to the fallen by playing the game. The two, plus Phineus' goth sister, October (Sophia Bush), nerdy Swink (Frankie Muniz) and intriguing new girl Abigail (Samaire Armstrong) start up the game. Hutch's boss, Miller (Adam Goldberg), links into their game from his office.

When the game comes on, the players are asked to recite a creepy incantation. Somehow this raises the spirit of seventeenth century spirit Elizabeth Bathory. According to legend, Bathory's habits included killing people on her plantation with a pair of large scissors. When scissors were not convenient, she also enjoyed running over victims with her horse-drawn carriage.

Hutch and his fellow players recite the chant, marveling over the game's apparent voice-recognition capabilities. What they should be more concerned with are the game's raising-the-dead capabilities.

Goldberg is the first to see the words "game over" and the kids are horrified when he is found dead the next morning, killed in the same manner in which he died in the game. The teens do not quite make the connection between the game and the rash of odd deaths until Phineus is killed by a horse-drawn carriage, when they start to figure it out. They tackle the problem as teens in horror films are wont to do—they separate and explore a creepy mansion.

Their vaguely-defined plan has something to do with capturing Bathory, putting some nails in her, then boiling her blood. Swink is in charge of protecting the players by playing the game while Hutch and Abigail enter Bathory's real life New Orleans mansion, in order to apply the nails and boiling treatment. This sequence could have been pretty suspenseful, but the movie does not follow the few rules of logic that it has set. Players are supposed to die in real life when they die in the game, but some die even though they are still alive in the game. Poor Bathory probably became frustrated that, although she was able to come alive centuries after her death, her killing opportunities were limited by the video game skills of a bunch of slacker teens.

The most interesting characters are killed off first and soon the audience is stuck with Hutch and Abigail and their tepid romance. Foster's Hutch is not without his charms, but he lacks the charisma of a leading man

Blame must lie with director/writer William Brent Bell and co-writer Matthew Peterman. They waste an interesting premise and a cast of good young actors.

Stay Alive was not exactly a critical favorite. Roger Moore of the *Orlando Sentinel* wrote: "Not frightening or affecting or even titillating." Neil Genzlinger of the *New York Times* wrote that "the star of *Stay Alive* is a cutting-edge video game, but the film still has hackneyed horror at its heart. And worse, it's not even the stylishly, wittily executed hackneyed horror of the *Scream* movies." Neva Chonin of the *San Francisco Chronicle* wrote: "*Stay Alive* is so devoid of tension, much less error, that it works better as unintentional comedy than horror." Finally, Gregory Kirschling of *Entertainment Weekly* gave the film a D- grade, writing, "Videogames are no longer brainless, so why are videogame movies so slow to evolve?"

Jill Hamilton

CREDITS

Hutch: Jon Foster
Abigail: Samaire Armstrong
Swink: Frankie Muniz
Phineus: Jimmi Simpson
Detective Thibodeaux: Wendell Pierce
October: Sophia Bush
Miller Banks: Adam Goldberg
Origin: USA
Language: English
Released: 2006
Production: McG, Peter Schlessel, James Stern, Matthew Peterman; Hollywood Pictures, Spyglass Entertainment, Endgame Entertainment, Wonderland Sound and Vision, Stay Alive; released by Buena Vista
Directed by: William Brent Bell
Written by: William Brent Bell, Matthew Peterman
Cinematography by: Alejandro Martinez
Music by: John (Gianni) Frizzell
Sound: Whit Norris
Editing: Harvey Rosenstock
Art Direction: Alan Hook
Costumes: Caroline Eselin
Production Design: Bruton Jones
MPAA rating: PG-13
Running time: 85 minutes

REVIEWS

Los Angeles Times Online. March 27, 2006.
New York Times Online. March 25, 2006.
San Francisco Chronicle Online. March 27, 2006.
Variety Online. March 24, 2006.

STEP UP

Every second chance begins with a first step.
—Movie tagline

Box Office: $65.3 million

Step Up follows an age-old Hollywood formula. Boy meets girl, they dance, and they fall in love. It also adds the familiar element of the big city *Fame*-style art school that is popping with good-looking creative young people. (Director of photography Michael Seresin also shot *Fame* [1980].) There is the more recent de rigueur element of combining classical dance and hip-hop moves to create a new exciting dance form. Indeed the whole movie is practically a remake of *Save the Last Dance* (2001). But plagiarism lawsuits will probably not be filed since writer Duane Adler was behind both scripts.

Besides, this basic style of film has been around since Rogers and Astaire. There is a reason for that—it is entertaining to watch the courtship dance portrayed literally as a dance. Channing Tatum plays Tyler Gage, a white foster kid who hangs out with black kids. He spends his days with Mac (Damaine Radcliff) and Mac's little brother, Skinny (De'Shawn Washington) playing basketball, stealing cars, and practicing his dance moves. After getting caught vandalizing an art school, Tyler is sentenced to two-hundred hours of community service at the school. He is to be the janitor but soon catches the eye of comely rich girl Nora Clark (Jenna Dewan). Nora is working on her senior dance routine that will determine whether she has a future in dance. Her prim mother (Deidre Lovejoy) has decreed that if Nora fails, she will be sentenced to a college stint at Cornell or Brown.

Nora's dance partner sprains his ankle and she needs to find a new partner. Somehow, all of the dancers at her school are not good enough and she enlists Tyler. Tyler, who previously communicated primarily through grunts and shrugs, learns to do plies, falls in love, and finds a dream to follow. The good thing about Tatum is that he is a very capable dancer. He brings a strong masculine presence to the dance floor. However, he also appears to have the personality of a block of wood. He seems almost pre-verbal and has an array of facial expressions that range from A to B in his acting repertoire. Luckily, Nora does not come across as terribly bright either, so it seems fine enough that she has cast her lot with this dullish guy wearing oversized clothing.

In between the dance sequences, there are other half-hearted plot strands. Mac resents Tyler for neglecting their friendship. Nora resents her mother for not supporting her dream. Skinny resents his brother for treating him like a kid. Tyler tries to impress tough school director (Rachel Griffiths) that he is worthy of coming to the school. Nora and Tyler fight and break up a few times, but there is never much of a worry that they are one big dance number away from patching everything up.

Since first time director Anne Fletcher has a background in choreography, the strongest moments in the film are the dance numbers. In one scene, Nora takes Tyler to a local dance club and the evening turns into a girls-against-boys dance-off. It is a high-energy romp, filled with good moves and great music. It is also a chance to highlight the musical talents of supporting characters Miles (musician Mario) and Lucy (Drew Sidora). It is too bad that Miles and Lucy are relegated to best friend roles. In a movie so infused with hip-hop energy, it seems odd that the two main characters would be among the few white students at the school.

Critics had seen it all before and they varied on how acceptable that was to them. Jeannette Catsoulis of the *New York Times* wrote: "Though most of the cast appears to be on its ninth repeat of 12th grade, *Step Up* is a likable product that's refreshingly free of vulgarity." Ruthe Stein of the *San Francisco Chronicle* wrote: "A lot of movies are derivative. What makes *Step Up* particularly dispiriting is that it has nothing fresh to add." Ty Burr of the *Boston Globe* knew the script was rehashed, but liked the movie anyway: "*Step Up* has appeal beyond its crummy obvious screenplay because joy in physical movement courses through every frame."

Jill Hamilton

CREDITS

Tyler Gage: Channing Tatum
Director Gordon: Rachel Griffiths
Mac Carter: Damaine Radcliff
Nora Clark: Jenna Dewan
Omar: Heavy D
Skinny Carter: De'Shawn Washington
Brett Dolan: Josh Henderson
Katherine Clark: Deidre Lovejoy
Origin: USA
Language: English
Released: 2006
Production: Patrick Waschsberger, Adam Shankman, Erik Feig, Jennifer Gibgot; Summit Entertainment, Touchstone Pictures, Offspring Entertainment; released by Buena Vista
Directed by: Anne Fletcher
Written by: Duane Adler, Melissa Rosenberg
Cinematography by: Michael Seresin
Music by: Aaron Zigman
Sound: John McCormick
Music Supervisor: Buck Damon
Editing: Nancy Richardson
Art Direction: Laura Ballinger Gardner
Costumes: Alix Hester
Production Design: Shepherd Frankel
MPAA rating: PG-13
Running time: 98 minutes

REVIEWS

Boston Globe Online. August 11, 2006.
Entertainment Weekly Online. August 9, 2006.
USA Today Online. August 11, 2006.

STICK IT

Defy and conquer.
—Movie tagline

Box Office: $26.9 million

Stick It was written and directed by Jessica Bendinger, who also wrote the fresh and exuberant cheerleading comedy *Bring It On,* one of 2000's most pleasant surprises. Set in the world of elite female gymnastics, *Stick It* tries to present a similarly feisty and quirky take on girls' competitive sports. Unfortunately, while the film has some fun moments and a few memorable lines, a weak screenplay—in which triteness too often takes the place of invention and MTV-style montages and fast-motion camera tricks become a substitute for a solid storyline—finally undoes it.

Pretty in a tomboyish, athletic way, Missy Peregrym stars as Haley Graham, a rebellious teenager from a broken home who is sentenced to the Vickerman Gymnastics Academy (VGA) after she busts through a glass window while doing some daring dirt-bike stunts in an empty swimming pool. While Haley's father essentially strikes a deal to get her into the VGA, Haley hates the prospect of going there. She has a notorious reputation as the girl who walked out in the middle of the World Gymnastics Championships two years ago, thus losing the gold medal for the United States. It is not surprising, then, that her fellow gymnasts do not welcome her with open arms. Haley is, of course, a rebel who needs a good coach to motivate her for a return to competition, and Burt "Vick" Vickerman (Jeff Bridges) is just the man for the job. He is a seasoned, inspiring coach, but also has the unrealistic expectation that he will turn every little girl into an Olympian.

The main problem with *Stick It* is that, in the broad strokes, the story is very perfunctory and hits all of the expected beats of the genre—from the maverick athlete forced to learn discipline to the firm but loving coach lecturing her not to waste her talent. Indeed, too many of the conflicts feel uninspired and derivative of other teen films. For example, in the middle of a tense meet, Haley has to deal not only with her rival, Joanne Charis (Vanessa Lengies), convincing their teammates that Haley is trying to sabotage them but also with her mother revealing that Vick took her on only because her father is paying him an enormous fee. A distraught Haley is about to walk away from the competition when Vick tries to persuade her not to let history repeat itself. She then discloses the dark secret of why she choked at Worlds—she discovered that her coach and her mother were having an affair. After such build-up, it is a contrived and rather unimaginative revelation designed to wring our emotions for poor Haley.

Helped by the fact that she actually has male friends (an anomaly, it seems, in the world of female gymnastics), the loathing and suspicion the other girls direct toward Haley slowly turns to admiration and respect. Haley's social transformation may be too easy, but this is, after all, a fairly good-natured story that, for the most part, is content to skim over serious tensions in favor of female bonding.

Vick's redemption also comes pretty easily. Not only does he write a letter to the judge on Haley's behalf, but he also pays for the damage she did at the beginning, thus atoning for the fact that he is making four times off Haley what he makes off the other girls. In his big scene demonstrating what a changed man he has become, Vick even levels with the mothers about their daughters' Olympic chances. His arc, like so much of the film, is pretty obvious, but Bridges, ever the consummate actor, brings as much shading as he possibly can to the familiar role.

Despite the script's predictability, there are, nonetheless, some fun touches along the way, hints of Bendinger's unique spirit that the film could have used more of. One of the practice sessions is filmed from above, turning the group of gymnasts into geometric shapes resembling a Busby Berkeley dance number. Haley's voice-overs have some wit, and the fast and snappy banter, especially among the girls, involves some sharp wordplay and clever one-liners ("Who died and made you Nadia?"), even if the cliques and rivalries echo better films like *Mean Girls* (2004).

And while most of the other gymnasts barely register as individuals, Joanne is actually a very funny character. Jealous of Haley, Joanne is initially an antagonist, but soon proves she can be cute and even endearing as she mangles the English language to great comic effect. Joanne also grows when a boy asks her to the prom and, realizing for the first time that there is more to life than gymnastics, she becomes giddy with excitement. Her mother wants her only to focus on the sport, and when Joanne stands up for herself and declares that she is going to the prom anyway, as predictable as the moment may be, it is nonetheless refreshing to see the change in what seemed to be a stock comic villain.

But if much of the film too often feels formulaic, that cannot be said of its conclusion, which is unbelievable and seems like it comes from another movie. At the final competition, the National Gymnastics Championships, the very subjective, unfair scoring of the judges all of a sudden becomes the central issue. A teammate named Mina Hoyt (Maddy Curley) does a perfect vault and is given a 9.5 out of 10, allegedly because her bra strap was showing but really because the judges hate Vick.

The girls, led by Haley, protest by intentionally "scratching" or not completing their routines so that the gymnast they deem most deserving can win each event. While Haley's big rival, Tricia Skilken (Tarah Paige), at first does not go along with the scheme (and thus becomes the villain simply because she wants to compete), everyone else does. This is completely implausible since girls who put so much time and dedication into this sport are not going to launch a spontaneous rebellion and throw away their chances at winning a medal. It is a very odd sports movie, indeed, in which fixing the results is seen as an act of empowerment and the desire to compete makes someone bad. Of course, even Tricia must come around to the group's point of view so that Haley can "win" the floor event, in which she is favored.

Bendinger's directorial debut is not without a certain charm, but ultimately lacks a coherent script and the extra spark that made *Bring It On* such an unexpected delight. For all of its spunky attitude and appealing young actresses, *Stick It* too often feels like a retread that relies on sports cliches we have seen before and an ending that rings completely hollow. No one should expect something profound from a teen gymnastics comedy, but a unique point of view on the sport and a few more original characters would have gone a long way to giving the movie the energy it needs.

Peter N. Chumo II

CREDITS

Haley Graham: Missy Peregrym
Burt Vickerman: Jeff Bridges
Joanne Charis: Vanessa Lengies
Poot: John Patrick Amedori
Wei Wei Yong: Nikki SooHoo
Mina Hoyt: Maddy Curley
Frank: Kellan Lutz
Dorrie: Svetlana Efremova
Ivan: Mio Dzakula
Brice Graham: Jon Gries
Alice: Gia Carides
Judge Westreich: Polly Holliday
Mrs. Charis: Julie Warner
Chris DeFrank: John Kapelos
Himself: Bart Conner (Cameo)
Tricia Skilken: Tarah Paige
Origin: USA
Language: English
Released: 2006
Production: Gail Lyon; Touchstone Pictures, Spyglass Entertainment, Barber/Birnbaum, Jessica Bendinger/Gail Lyon; released by Buena Vista

Directed by: Jessica Bendinger
Written by: Jessica Bendinger
Cinematography by: Daryn Okada
Music by: Mike Simpson
Sound: Douglas Axtell
Music Supervisor: Spring Aspers
Editing: Troy Takaki
Art Direction: Chris Cornwell
Costumes: Carol Ramsey
Production Design: Bruce Curtis
MPAA rating: PG-13
Running time: 105 minutes

REVIEWS

Chicago Sun-Times Online. April 28, 2006.
Los Angeles Times Online. April 28, 2006.
New York Times Online. April 28, 2006.
San Francisco Chronicle. April 28, 2006, p. E5.
Variety Online. April 27, 2006.

QUOTES

Burt (to Haley): "Just don't get blood on the equipment."

STRANGER THAN FICTION

Harold Crick isn't ready to go. Period.
—Movie tagline

Box Office: $40.4 million

Earlier this year in *Talladega Nights: The Ballad of Ricky Bobby*, Will Ferrell entertained audiences by running around wildly in his jockey shorts while shrieking hysterically. It was typical Ferrell, unlike *Stranger Than Fiction*, which calls on the comedian to calm down and underplay instead of strip down to his underwear. Following in the footsteps of other comedic talents who have tried their hand at something a little more serious, Ferrell acquits himself nicely as a man who is shaken to realize he is actually a character in someone's nearly-completed novel, and that his life may very well be finished when the book is. Only when this exceedingly sober, solitary figure accepts that his time is short does he pursue the things for which he has longed, breaking loose from his profoundly regimented existence to finally and rather poignantly experience what life has to offer. "I can't die right now. It's bad timing," the man laments, and now that he actually has a life to lose, he aims to save it by somehow contacting his creator and appealing for a happier ending.

When viewers first encounter Ferrell's Harold Crick, he is beginning his morning as he has begun all of his mornings. He meticulously brushes his teeth, carefully counting every upstroke and downstroke. He takes the same number of steps (keeping track as he goes) to catch the same bus to work. Harold is employed at the Internal Revenue Service, where his job is as dull and repetitive as the rest of his existence. He painstakingly times his breaks during the day, relying on a remarkable wristwatch that seems to take as much interest in him as he in it. Harold walks home alone, eats alone, and crawls into bed at exactly the same time every night—alone. All in all, a pretty lifeless life. It is mentioned that he ties his tie in a single knot instead of a double to save time. For what, one wonders?

All this information about Harold is provided to the audience through the omniscient narration of an articulate, unseen, female Brit, who then gives Harold a shock when he starts to be able to hear her, just like a member of the audience. He does not know what to make of this detailed audible chronicling of his daily endeavors, which no one else seems able to hear. Especially for a man unaccustomed to having women follow him around, viewers can certainly appreciate how Harold might be thrown upon by being stalked by a disembodied voice. (He was once engaged, but his fiance threw him over for the heart-pounding excitement of an actuary.)

Despite endeavoring to maintain his carefully controlled exterior, Harold is soon so preoccupied with this mystifying development that he cannot concentrate at work. When he goes to audit spirited, tattooed baker Ana Pascal (Maggie Gyllenhaal), it is hard to know what unnerves him more, her tempting form or the voice's knowledge (and racy description) of his temptation. Anarchic Ana's pugnacious recalcitrance, her cries of "miscreant taxman!" and the booing from her customers do nothing to lighten poor Harold's load.

Human Resources counselor Dr. Cayly (Oscar®-winner Tom Hulce, onscreen for the first time in thirteen years) suggests that Harold take a long-overdue vacation. Psychiatrist Dr. Mittag-Leffler (the always welcome Linda Hunt) gravely suggests he might be schizophrenic and in need of medication. "The voice isn't telling me to do anything," Harold counters, "it is telling me what I've already done...accurately, and with a better vocabulary." Mittag-Leffler alternately suggests that he seek out an expert in literature, which leads Harold to English Professor Jules Hilbert (Dustin Hoffman), who becomes intrigued with his predicament. Harold feels as if he is a character in his own life story, and so the professor quite humorously endeavors to methodically pinpoint what kind of character and in what kind of story. After all, things end quite happily for protagonists in comedies, but much less so in tragedies.

Unfortunately for Harold, the all-knowing, erudite utterances have recently included a startling reference to his "imminent death," which leads to some hilarious screaming at the heavens for explanations that do not come. That is partly because acclaimed, reclusive author Karen "Kay" Eiffel (the marvelously skilled, delightful Emma Thompson), who gave Harold life, is across town suffering from an agonizing case of writer's block and cannot decide how she wants to take that life away from him. She is a twitchy, petulant mess, with the peculiar and rather nauseating habit of carefully extinguishing the cigarettes she chain smokes into slobber-soaked tissues.

Kay is repeatedly shown imaging all sorts of perfectly lethal ways one could die—falling from a great height, careening off the side of a bridge—but none seem to fit quite happily enough into her tragedy to be titled "Death and Taxes." Since the author is having such a tough time finishing-off both Harold and her book, Kay's publisher decides it is high time to send in no-nonsense, let's-cut-to-the-chase assistant Penny Escher (Queen Latifah) to carry this basket case across the finish line. Penny is soon keeping a watchful, wary eye on her resistant charge, especially when Kay soggily sits in the midst of a deluge contemplating pneumonia or politely inquires of a hospital's nurse where they keep all the "dead for sure people." Thompson's Kay is hilariously unhinged.

Gradually, events convince Hilbert that Harold does not control his ultimate fate, and so the professor simply (but sagely) points out that there is nothing for the man to do but live—really live—before he dies, to make his life "the one you've always wanted." It is an interesting thing for all to ponder: if we knew death was coming soon, what specifically would truly getting down to living entail? Furthermore, since we know full well that death, whether "imminent" or not, is nonetheless inevitable, is there really ever any time to waste in living life well and to the fullest? For one's enjoyment of this film, it is best not to ruminate too much about (among other things) how Harold can make up his mind to do anything that has not first been made up in the mind of Kay Eiffel. Regardless, the character asserts his free will, screwing up his courage and adopting the philosophy of a coworker (Tony Hale), who still retains a childhood yearning to go to space camp, that it is never too late to go after what your heart desires. Harold always wanted to play the guitar, so he goes out and buys just the right one. He is seen wearing a brightly colored sweater instead of his usual drab tie and suit. He stops all his tedious tallying of brushstrokes and steps, and his rigid attention to time. When this happens, the on-screen graphics that have continually popped up to visually represent the workings of Harold's mind disappear for good. He no longer eats alone. He smiles. In short, as Kay puts it with an accent on the third word, "Harold Crick lived his life."

Most significant of all, though, Harold pursues his interest in Ana, wooing the baker by giving her a bunch of flours. (Earlier, the two had a brief, lovely interlude, during which she introduced him to the simple but considerable pleasures of freshly baked cookies.) She senses a sweet sincerity about him, finally drops all attitude, and invites him up to her place where they laugh and eat. Colored lights throw hues upon the proceedings, emphasizing that Harold's existence is no longer colorless. He plays the guitar and expresses himself through song. Ana rewards him with a passionate kiss, which leads the two burgeoning lovers to bed. Harold has never felt such blissful contentment and excitedly reports to Hilbert that his story is not headed toward a tragic end, after all.

The most touching part of *Stranger Than Fiction* comes when, at his height of happiness, Harold recognizes Kay's voice on a tape playing in Hilbert's office and is shaken to learn that his creator only writes tragedies in which the protagonists are eliminated with the cruelest of timing. Thus, since he does not want to die, Harold must go to meet his maker. Suspense builds for Harold, Kay, and the audience when, after contacting the flabbergasted writer by phone, he arrives at her apartment to plead for his life. Kay gives him her manuscript and the outline for the—his—ending to read, but he cannot bring himself to do so and hands it to Hilbert. The bottom falls out of Harold's world when Hilbert gently informs him that the work is an absolute masterpiece that unfortunately would be ruined if it ended in any other way but with his death. In a potent, truly affecting moment, Harold, after having read the manuscript himself, returns it to Kay and, movingly accepting his fate, asserts that she must not change a single word. On a morning soon after, just as Kay is halfway through typing the word "dead," Harold courageously grabs a boy out from the path of an oncoming bus and is hit himself.

It is a heroic and unquestionably tragic end, except there is a twist to Harold's fate. Some will find it false and too sentimental, while others will happily embrace it as both intriguing and satisfying. After brooding about whether any of the other poor characters she had killed off might also have actually existed, Kay could not in good conscience do away with the one she knew for sure was real. Even though her rewritten work is, in Hilbert's opinion, perfectly adequate but no longer perfection, Kay says she can live with not killing Harold. Anyway, she says, as Harold is seen recuperating in the hospital with Ana at his side, is her character not even more exceptional now since, possessing the certain knowledge that he would lose his life in saving the boy's, the man still headed to the bus stop that morning?

Made on a budget of approximately $38 million, *Stranger Than Fiction*'s box office take passed the $40 million mark. Critical reaction was predominantly positive, and it began earning nominations and awards. The film was compared to *The Truman Show* (1998) and the screenplays of Charlie Kaufman, although some critics called it "Kaufman-lite." Still, *Stranger Than Fiction* is a smart, clever, thought-provoking, pleasure of a fable. There's certainly nothing lowbrow about this Ferrell film, which is sure to raise some eyebrows in Hollywood about his range.

David L. Boxerbaum

CREDITS

Harold Crick: Will Ferrell
Ana Pascal: Maggie Gyllenhaal
Professor Jules Hilbert: Dustin Hoffman
Kay Eiffel: Emma Thompson
Penny Escher: Queen Latifah
Dave: Tony Hale
Dr. Cayly: Tom Hulce
Dr. Mittag-Leffler: Linda Hunt
Origin: USA
Language: English
Released: 2006
Production: Lindsay Doran; Three Strange Angels, Columbia Pictures, Mandate Pictures; released by Sony Pictures
Directed by: Marc Foster
Written by: Zach Helm
Cinematography by: Roberto Schaefer
Music by: Brian Reitzell, Britt Daniel
Sound: David Obermeyer
Editing: Matt Chesse
Art Direction: Craig Jackson
Costumes: Frank Fleming
Production Design: Kevin Thompson
MPAA rating: PG-13
Running time: 113 minutes

REVIEWS

Boxoffice Online. November 10, 2006.
Chicago Sun-Times Online. November 10, 2006.
Entertainment Weekly. November 17, 2006, p. 99.
Hollywood Reporter Online. September 11, 2006.
Los Angeles Times Online. November 10, 2006.
New York Times Online. November 10, 2006.
San Francisco Chronicle. November 10, 2006, p. E5.
Variety Online. September 12, 2006.
Washington Post. November 10, 2006, p. C1.

QUOTES

Dr. Mittag-Leffler: "You have a voice speaking to you?"
Harold: "About me—accurately—and with a better vocabulary."

AWARDS

Nomination:

Golden Globes 2007: Actor—Mus./Comedy (Ferrell)
Writers Guild 2006: Orig. Screenplay

STRANGERS WITH CANDY

Going to high school for the first time is always scary...Especially the second time around.
—Movie tagline

Box Office: $2 million

Out of Comedy Central's cancelled cult hit of the same name comes its cinematic prequel, *Strangers with Candy,* the maiden theatrical effort of David Letterman's Worldwide Pants production company. Fans of the show and Stephen Colbert enthusiasts will doubtless find endless amusement in the antics of forty-seven-year-old high school freshman, former "boozer, user, and loser" Jerri Blank, played by co-writer Amy Sedaris, and the talented cast that includes co-writer Colbert, Dan Hedaya, Matthew Broderick and creative cameos by Philip Seymour Hoffman, Alison Janney, and Sarah Jessica Parker. Castmate, co-writer, and first time director Paul Dinello smoothly and capably orchestrates the transition of the show to the big screen.

Jerri, with her bulging midsection and comically misshapen mug, was conceived as the unlikely heroine of an after school special-type sitcom. A former prostitute and junkie newly released from prison, Jerri goes back to high school in order to get a fresh start on life. There, she learns lessons that she either misinterprets or misses altogether. Here, Jerri goes back to try to help her father Guy Blank (Dan Hedaya) wake from his twenty-five-year coma by proving herself a worthy daughter, much to the chagrin of her evil stepmother (Deborah Rush) and dim-witted teenage stepbrother Derrick (Joseph Cross), a proud member of the junior varsity squat-thrust team.

Just as Sedaris has a gleeful lack of shame in her portrayal of the gargoylesque Jerri, the character is also not shy about graphically divulging her past. This is evident when Jerri introduces herself to her classmates: "Hello, I'm Jerri Blank and...and I'm an alcoholic. I'm also addicted to amphetamines as well as main line narcotics. Some people say I have a sex addiction, but I think all those years of prostitution was just a means to feed my ravenous hunger for heroin. It's kinda like the chicken or the nugget. The point is, I'm addicted to gambling. Thank you. Oh, and my daddy's in a coma."

While Principal Blackman (the hysterically funny Greg Hollimon) cannot stop the less-than-academic Jerri from attending Flatpoint High, neither is he particularly thrilled as he needs to somehow prove that his low-test score students have improved. He explains to Jerri: "Why would I doctor the books to improve the overall test scores of the student body just so I could collect bonus funds from the state which I willfully misappropriated in order to pay off large gambling debts? It just doesn't add up." Because of Blackman's transgressions, he's now "got the school board breathing down my neck like a drunken jock at a roofie party." His answer? To have his students win the school science fair, which Jerri has also signed up for in order to help save her daddy.

Science teacher Mr. Noblet (Colbert) wants to win the science fair as well, if only to annoy the ringer that Blackman has brought in to ensure a win, Noblet's nemesis Roger Beekman (Matthew Broderick). Noblet is a married, born-again Creationist who has recently, and unfeelingly, ended his affair with the school's good-natured naif, art teacher Mr. Jellineck (Dinello) and who is prone to spouting to his class, "Eyes to the back of the room!" when he has a weepy moment. Beekman's hand-picked dream team of popular kids is challenged when Noblet creates his own science fair team but Noblet is unsuccessful in his attempts to eject the well-meaning but incompetent Jerri by sending her to the school's self-involved grief counselor (Sarah Jessica Parker).

Jerri is somewhat successful as a sophomore, winning a small circle of nerdy but true-blue friends, the redheaded Tammi (Maria Thayer) and Megawatti (Carlo Alban). Jerri's still used to jailhouse life, though, and the long-suffering Tammi puts up with Jerri's constant romantic advances while Megawatti secretly pines for Jerri. Jerri's more interested in the blond, buff jock Brason (Chris Pratt) and finds the opportunity she's looking for when he's sent to "seduce" her in order to get her team's science fair plans for Beekman's team. Brason easily gets the plans but Jerri feels bad and, at the last minute, comes up with a clever idea for a homemade battery taken from her prison days. Jellineck, unceremoniously ousted as the evil Beekman's aide, decides to help out his former lover's team in the showmanship area. The science fair showdown is hilarious its in excess, with both teams staging musical numbers in elaborate costume to highlight their inventions. A fitting ending, Noblet and Jerri's team wins, and then loses when it catches fire, while Jerri's dad remains comatose and she learns little to nothing in the process.

The gifted Sedaris owns the film, breezing through each tasteless and crass scenario as fearlessly funny as ever. The original TV cast, including Dinello, Colbert, and Holliman are just as polished and witty in the film. Broderick is capable as Beekman. Among the cameos, Janney, as the bitter, school board member and tossed aside fling of Blackman, and Hoffman, her toadying, adoring peer, are standouts. While some critics noted the film's sometimes controversial humor, Dennis Harvey observed in his *Variety* review that "the incessantly voiced racist and homophobic remarks are so pointedly ludicrous that they parody prejudice itself."

Hilary White

CREDITS

Jerri Blank: Amy Sedaris
Geoffrey Jellineck: Paul Dinello
Chuck Noblet: Stephen Colbert
Sara Blank: Deborah Rush
Principal Blackman: Greg Hollimon
Guy Blank: Dan Hedaya
Alice: Allison Janney
Henry: Philip Seymour Hoffman
Coach Divers: Kristen Johnston
Carlo Honklin, Drivers Ed Teacher: Justin Theroux
Roger Beekman: Matthew Broderick
Grief Counselor Peggy Callas: Sarah Jessica Parker
Dr. Putney: Ian Holm
Megawatti Sacranaputri: Carlo Alban
Tammi Littlenut: Maria Thayer
Monica: Elisabeth Harnois
Brason: Chris Pratt
Derrick Blank: Joseph Cross
Stew: David Pasquesi
Rolanda: Alicia Ashley
Stanley: Ryan Donowho
Origin: USA
Language: English
Released: 2006
Production: Mark Roberts, Lorena David, Valerie Schaer Nathanson; Comedy Central, Worldwide Pants; released by Warner Independent Pictures, ThinkFilm
Directed by: Paul Dinello
Written by: Amy Sedaris, Paul Dinello, Stephen Colbert
Cinematography by: Oliver Bokelberg
Sound: Sandy Berman
Editing: Michael R. Miller
Art Direction: Mylene Santos

Costumes: Victoria Ferrell
Production Design: Teresa Mastropierro
MPAA rating: R
Running time: 97 minutes

REVIEWS

Boxoffice Online. June 28, 2006.
Entertainment Weekly Online. June 21, 2006.
Los Angeles Times Online. July 7, 2006.
New York Times Online. June 28, 2006.
Premiere Magazine Online. June 27, 2006.
Variety Online. March 1, 2005.
Washington Post. July 7, 2006, p. C1.

TRIVIA

The band whose logo appears on apparel worn by characters in the movie, Snowball 37, is an actual touring band made up of three members of the Fagan family, who appear as students in the movie and all but one episode of the TV series.

SUPERMAN RETURNS

Box Office: $200 million

After a nineteen-year sabbatical, the Last Son of Krypton soars to the silver screen again. In the making for over ten years, a new Superman film had been tossed around among several potential directors. Initially given to Kevin Smith, director/producer of the indie hit, *Clerks* (1994), the project tanked and was passed on to Tim Burton (director of both *Batman* [1989] and *Batman Returns* [1992]). Burton cast Nicolas Cage to play the character. When Burton's film never materialized, the title was handed off to McG and later Brett Ratner before finally coming to rest with Bryan Singer.

Singer, who directed the first two installments of the "X-Men" franchise, has an enduring respect and affection for the first two Richard Donner Superman films and did not complicate the simple formula that has historically spelled success for the Man of Tomorrow. Prior to Singer's commission, Superman was being rethought. One script had him stripped of his ability to fly; consigned to wearing a black suit, deprived him of his birth name, and had him fighting a gigantic spider in its climax. Singer felt it necessary to focus on Donner's take on the character: a noble, good-hearted alien who at his core is a lonely orphan striving to fit in. The result is *Superman Returns,* both an homage to *Superman: The Movie* (1978) and *Superman II* (1980) as well as being a loosely based sequel to them.

Contrary to his current image, Superman, created by Jerry Siegel and Joe Schuster, was initially envisioned as a bald mad scientist obsessed with world domination via the power of mental telepathy (similar in the former aspect to his future nemesis, Lex Luthor). In January 1933, their story "Reign of the Super-Man" was published in their own fanzine where Siegel wrote the stories and Schuster illustrated them. This idea was scrapped and Superman was recreated as a heroic figure who protected the world from evildoers by means of Herculean strength, great speed and stamina, and near invulnerability. It is speculated that the conception of Superman's name stemmed from Friedrich Nietzsche's Ubermensch which can translate to "Overman," or "Superman." From this tinkering came the secret identity (much like Zorro, or the Shadow). But in the Superman mythos, however, it is his civilian persona that bears the disguise, wearing a fedora and glasses. Although his iconic costume has endured minor alterations, it is primarily the same with his red cape and tight blue and red body suit with the diamond shaped emblem on his chest bearing the famous "S."

The character was sold to Detective Comics, Inc. (today's DC Comics) and his own book was launched in June 1938 with the publishing of *Action Comics* No. 1. An immediate hit that flew off newsstands in a blur of primary colors, Superman became the template for a legion of costumed superheroes covering three ages of comic book history spanning close to seven decades. Among them were imitations such as Fawcett Comics' Captain Marvel (whose powers so closely mirror Superman's that a copyright infringement suit from DC Comics put Captain Marvel in publication limbo for decades) or Timely's Captain America who could easily abide with the Superman mantra of fighting for "Truth, Justice, and the American Way" (the latter part of the phrase was deleted from *Superman Returns* perhaps due to the geo-political climate that has fostered a bit of anti-American sentiment). In less than a year, Superman had a daily comic strip appearing in newspapers nationwide and had a second comic title, "Superman." In short order, Superman transcended from the page of illustrated pulp into radio serials and film. From radio came the memorable phrases which have remained in the titan's tradition such as, "Up, up and away!", "This looks like a job for Superman!", and the most often heard in radio, TV, film and comics alike, "Look...up in the sky...it's a bird...it's a plane...it's...Superman!"

By casting Brandon Routh as the title character, Singer, like Donner, ditched the idea of casting an established Hollywood hunk in favor of an unknown actor. The reasoning behind this being both directors wanted to avoid Superman being "upstaged" by a movie star. Singer commented in the *San Diego Union-Tribune,* "What mattered was never his looking somewhat like Chris Reeve. But he must step out of our collective memory, as Superman." That being said, Routh resembles a baby-faced, slimmed down Christopher Reeve and looks more like a Superboy than a Superman. When Routh delivers his lines, it is as though this Midwestern boy from Des Moines, Iowa is channeling the deceased actor. Although generally convincing as the Man of Steel and given an overall thumbs up by most critics, it is difficult not to compare him to his cinematic predecessor. Consequently, not all critics were accepting of the newcomer. Roger Ebert, who has generally given praise for the avalanche of superhero films released in recent years, had a problem with the casting: "Routh lacks charisma as Superman, and I suppose as Clark Kent, he isn't supposed to have any."

Keeping in step with this veneration, Singer also resurrected Marlon Brando, who played Superman's Kryptonian father, Jor-El. Singer inserts many of Brando's lines (from both used and unused footage) as the scientist who became a pariah on Krypton when he accurately foretold of the planet's doom. Brando is posthumously reunited with former costar Eva Marie Saint, with whom he starred with in Elia Kazan's *On the Waterfront* (1954) and for which both actors received Oscars® (Brando for Best Actor and Saint for Best Supporting Actress). Saint plays Clark's adoptive mother, Martha Kent. Also due honorable mention among the credits is the casting of Noel Neill and Jack Larson who played Lois Lane and Jimmy Olson respectively on the 1950s TV hit, *The Adventures of Superman*. In *Superman Returns*, Larson plays a bartender who serves Clark and the new Jimmy, Sam Huntington. Neill is briefly seen as the elderly dying heiress, Gertrude Vanderworth, charmed and courted by that devious, brilliant megalomaniacal sociopath, Lex Luthor, who inherits considerable wealth upon Gertrude's passing.

At the beginning of *Superman Returns*, it is learned that Superman has been on a five-year hiatus due to astronomers reporting a sighting of what they theorize to be remnants of the planet Krypton. Kal-El departs to investigate with a hope of finding survivors from his native world. Throughout this summary, Singer reintegrates John Williams' classic Superman score, which has become as indelible a signature for him as the James Bond Theme is for Agent 007. During his long absence, the world has moved on as evidenced by an editorial piece by Lois Lane entitled, "Why the World Doesn't Need a Superman." Kal-El returns to Earth the same way he did as a toddler, entering the atmosphere like a burning meteor in a crystal spiked space pod and crash landing on the Kent's farmland, burrowing a trench stretching a length close to that of a football field. Unlike Christopher Nolan's *Batman Begins* (2005), *Superman Returns* is not glutted with exposition by retelling the character's origin, but is more faithful to continuity. As he recovers, Clark overlooks the expanse of the Kent farm and gets caught in a reverie, reflecting back upon his adolescence when his powers began to manifest themselves and he sped through acres of corn with blinding acceleration. It is during one of his many bounds through the air that he learns he can levitate; a foretoken of perhaps Superman's most defining attribute, the ability to fly. In this scene, Singer's attention to minutia may be seen on the Kent's fireplace mantel among an array of family portraits. One of the photographs is of Glenn Ford who played Clark's stepfather in *Superman: The Movie.*

Clark returns to his old job at The Daily Planet located in Metropolis. Donner's Metropolis was indistinguishable from New York City, complete with the Statue of Liberty. Singer's is almost anachronistic, with antiquated buildings and cars blending in with cellular camera phones and a Boeing 777 piggy-backing a futuristic looking space shuttle. It is here that Superman responds on cue to an emergency and makes his entrance in the nick of time to save the astronauts on the shuttle (by severing its moorings with his smoldering CGI-vision) and all aboard the 777 including, of course, Lois Lane. Lois seems to be a favorite focus for fate, who, acting like a formidable villain in Superman's gallery of nefarious rogues, has repeatedly predestined this feisty reporter to die despite Superman's reliable interventions. In line with the All-American component surrounding his story telling, Superman gently sets down the 777's fuselage on a baseball diamond where a baseball game is in progress. It is his reintroduction to the world, which welcomes him back with euphoric applause. Here, Routh exudes the boy scout-in-blue-tights mannerisms in such a sincere delivery, it is hard to determine if he is acting as he boards the aircraft and dutifully asks everyone if they are all right.

What Routh lacks is a certain duplicity involved in playing two distinct alter egos. Although bumbling and awkward as Kent—complete with comedic moments, like flashing Lois a geeky smile in an overcrowded elevator and looking like a self-conscious outsider—the polarity is one rung up from George Reeves' performance in *The Adventures of Superman.* In that TV show, primarily targeted for young boys, Reeves made no distinction whatsoever between the personas of Superman and Clark. He was always one-dimensional; charming and confident, but never alternating in personality whether in red boots or spectacles. Christopher Reeve played both characters best. As Superman, he was articulate; speaking from his gut while walking upright and looking straight ahead. He was composed; with his chin up and chest out. As Clark he raised his voice an octave, stuttering about with nasal uncertainty, looking too big as he stooped his shoulders in a slouch, looking down at the ground through those ridiculously large 1970s style goggles he wore as he lumbered after Margot Kidder like a newly castrated bull in a china shop. The act was the disguise, not the glasses. No way could this guy be Superman.

Similarly, Kate Bosworth's Lois Lane just doesn't hit the mark as the obstinate Pulitzer Prize-winning journalist. Cute and emoting, Bosworth shares the best chemistry with Tristan Lake Leabu, who plays her five-year-old son, Jason White. During Superman's absence, Lois shacked up with her editor's flyboy nephew, Richard White. However, a later action scene shows the young, asthmatic Jason launching a grand piano against a monstrous thug bent on killing his mom and crushing him to death and proves the kid's a hybrid (never mind his immunity to kryptonite as tested by the paranoid Luthor). Perhaps the blossoming supertot's existence can be better explained by the intimate scene in *Superman II* after Kal-El gave up his powers to live as a human with Lois.

As Lex Luthor, Kevin Spacey is reunited with Singer who directed him in *The Usual Suspects* (1995). Spacey's Luthor is darker and edgier than Gene Hackman's. In Spacey's portrayal of the character, you see the genius criminal spiraling down and becoming more embittered and consumed with an appetite for vengeance against his Kryptonian foe whom he blames for his time in prison. This blood lust almost parallels Luthor's obsession with owning continental sized portions of real estate. When telling his Bonnie-in-crime, Kitty Kowalski (zanily played by Parker Posey) of his intent to steal and manipulate Kryptonian crystals (for which most of this superior alien technology is based), he uses the story of Prometheus as an analogy. "Sounds great, Lex. But you're not a god," Kowalski tells him. "God?" he replies. "Gods are selfish beings who fly around in little red capes and don't share their power with mankind."

Among observations about the film is that it harbors a theological theme. This is a well-deserved insight. When Superman literally slow dances with Lois to the clouds above Metropolis, he explains to her, "You wrote that the world doesn't need a savior, but every day I hear people crying for one." There is also Brando's proclamation that could serve as a paraphrase for John 3:16, "For this reason above all, their capacity for good, I have sent them you, my only son." During the movie's climax (most of the plot could be described as a distorted reflection of Donner's first installment) Superman is betrayed by Kowalski in that she was in league with Luthor but was saved by Superman from certain death by being trapped in a runaway car complete with severed brakes. He is weakened by Kryptonite and receives severe kicks to the ribs by Lex (Lucifer) and beaten by his thugs (Roman centurions) before being shanked in the back by a kryptonite knife. When Superman is rescued by Lois, Richard, and Jason, he excises the crystalline baby continent and sends it off into space before falling back to earth in a Christ like crucifixion pose. He flat-lines, but quickly regains a pulse.

Superman has survived Kryptonite, magic, camp, Dr. Fredric Wertham's anti-comic book campaign (which echoed McCarthyism as outlined in his book, *Seduction of the Innocent*), and the rampant superhero angst that has plagued so many of his colleagues. Despite these challenges, Superman remains the champion of hope that has been seen on both the tiny screen and the silver screen and will no doubt continue to do so in some capacity for an additional seventy years.

David Metz Roberts

CREDITS

Superman/Clark Kent: Brandon Routh

Lois Lane: Kate Bosworth

Lex Luthor: Kevin Spacey

Richard White: James Marsden

Martha Kent: Eva Marie Saint

Kitty Kowalski: Parker Posey

Perry White: Frank Langella

Jimmy Olsen: Sam Huntington

Stanford: Kal Penn

Gertrude Vanderworth: Noel Neill

Bo the Bartender: Jack Larson

Jor-El: Marlon Brando

Jason White: Tristan Lake Leabu

Brutus: David Fabrizio

Origin: USA

Language: English

Released: 2006

Production: Jon Peters, Bryan Singer, Gilbert Adler; Legendary Pictures, Bad Hat Production; released by Warner Bros.

Directed by: Bryan Singer

Written by: Bryan Singer, Michael Dougherty, Daniel P. "Dan" Harris

Cinematography by: Newton Thomas (Tom) Sigel

Music by: John Ottman

Sound: Sally Brincat

Editing: John Ottman, Elliot Graham

Art Direction: Lawrence A. Hubbs, Damien Drew, Catherine Perez-Mansill, John Pryce-Jones, Charlie Revai

Production Design: Guy Hendrix Dyas

MPAA rating: PG-13
Running time: 140 minutes

REVIEWS

Boxoffice Online. June 28, 2006.
Chicago Sun-Times Online. June 27, 2006.
Entertainment Weekly Online. June 21, 2006.
Los Angeles Times Online. June 27, 2006.
New York Times Online. June 27, 2006.
Premiere Magazine Online. June 26, 2006.
Variety Online. June 18, 2006.
Washington Post. June 28, 2006, p. C1.

QUOTES

Jor-El: "You will travel far, my little Kal-El, but we will never leave you—even in the face of our deaths. You will make my strength your own. You will see my life through your eyes, as your life will be seen through mine. The son becomes the father. And the father, the son."

TRIVIA

Originally set to direct, Brett Ratner left the project primarily because he and Warner Bros. executives could not agree on whom to cast as Superman. Among those considered for the role were actors Josh Hartnett, Paul Walker, Matthew Bomer, Brendan Fraser, Ashton Kutcher, David Boreanaz, Ian Somerhalder, Henry Cavill, and Jerry O'Connell.

AWARDS

Nomination:
Oscars 2006: Visual FX
British Acad. 2006: Visual FX
Golden Raspberries 2006: Worst Support. Actress (Bosworth)

T

TAKE THE LEAD

Never Follow.
—Movie tagline

Nobody gave them a chance until one man gave them a dream.
—Movie tagline

Box Office: $34.7 million

Take the Lead is loosely based on the life of Pierre Dulaine, a New York ballroom dance teacher who helped inspired the ballroom dance movement captured in the film *Mad Hot Ballroom* (2005). In *Take the Lead*, which marks the feature debut of music video director Liz Freidlander, Dulaine is played by Antonio Banderas. Dulaine runs an upscale dance studio where he teaches well-heeled young people how to fox-trot and waltz for the various cotillions they will be attending.

Dulaine is directed to his true life's purpose after he witnesses a young man, Rock (Rob Brown), smashing in the window of a car. Dulaine finds an i.d. that indicates that the car belongs to Augustine James (Alfre Woodard), the principal of a rough urban school. The next day he shows up at the hard-nosed principal's school. He offers to teach her students ballroom dancing. James, who thinks that Dulaine's courtly manners and love of dance will make him an easy target for her tough students, offers him her detention kids. She bets him five dollars that he will not make it through a single day.

The plot unfolds in predictable fashion. At first the kids resist Dulaine's methods, and especially his square Gershwin music, but they are gradually won over. Many of these kids have nothing going for them and, at the very least, Dulaine pays attention to them. Dulaine's way of living, with his impeccable manners and old-style suaveness is appealing to the kids. So is the way that he is willing to work within their culture. He takes their love of modern dance music and moves and lets them do "smash ups" of new music with old standards.

Each of the students has a bit of a story. There is a skinny white kid who harbors a secret crush on his large partner. There is a love triangle between two guys and a girl that climaxes in a dramatic tango. The story line with the most airtime is with Rock and LaRhette (YaYa DaCosta). Rock is practically raising himself since his parents, overcome with grief over the death of his older brother, have become addicts. Over at LaRhette's house, things are not much better. She watches over her younger brother while her mother works as a prostitute. LaRhette's brother was also killed with Rock's, and consequently the two hate each other. But, through Dulaine's gentle coaching and the power of dance, the two learn to come together and blossom.

Dulaine is not surprised. As he says in a speech to a PTA meeting filled with parents concerned about his unorthodox methods, Dulaine believes that he is not merely teaching the kids ballroom dance, but rather a way of behaving in the world. By teaching the men to hold their partners with respect, he reasons, he is teaching them to respect women in general. By giving them something to excel in, they learn to believe in themselves. In the end, even Principal James is swooning over the charming dance instructor.

In much the same way that Dulaine wins over the principal, Banderas wins over the audience. The material of the film is not great, and it is certainly not original, or even particularly well-filmed, but Banderas pulls it off using considerable charm. Banderas inhabits a world that is more cultured and graceful that the regular world, and he makes that world mighty attractive.

Critics split on the merits of *Take the Lead*, often influenced by just how charming they found Banderas to be, a division that often followed gender lines. Wesley Morris of the *Boston Globe* called the film a "pandering dramedy" and wrote that "the movie partners all the cliches of the inner-city school drama with the cliches of the dance instructional, and the two keep stomping on each other's toes." Stephen Holden of the *New York Times* wrote that "despite its nifty concept and fiery leading man, [the film] feels sloppy and rushed." Carrie Rickey of the *Philadelphia Inquirer* wrote: "Antonio Banderas has boudoir eyes, flamenco hips, and the attitude that anyone can make it if he knows how to shake it. In *Take the Lead* this combination is so potent that it should be a controlled substance." Stephanie Zacharek of *Salon* wrote that "while we may be able to pretty much guess everything that's going to happen in *Take the Lead*, its considerable charm lies in the way it fulfills, rather than bucks, our expectations."

Jill Hamilton

CREDITS

Pierre Dulaine: Antonio Banderas
Augustine James: Alfre Woodard
Sasha: Jenna Dewan
Ramos: Dante Basco
Rock: Rob Brown
LaRhette: Yaya DaCosta
Caitlin: Lauren Collins
Joe Temple: John Ortiz
Monster: Brandon D. Andrews
Origin: USA
Language: English
Released: 2006
Production: Diane Nabatoff, Michelle Grace, Christopher Godsick; Tiara Blu Films; released by New Line Cinema
Directed by: Liz Friedlander
Written by: Dianne Houston
Cinematography by: Alex Nepomniaschy
Music by: Aaron Zigman
Sound: John Ross
Editing: Robert Ivison
Art Direction: Nigel Churcher
Costumes: Melissa Toth
Production Design: Paul Denham Austerberry
MPAA rating: PG-13
Running time: 117 minutes

REVIEWS

Boxoffice Online. April 7, 2006.
Chicago Sun-Times Online. April 7, 2006.
Entertainment Weekly. April 14, 2006, p. 61.
Los Angeles Times Online. April 7, 2006.
New York Times Online. April 7, 2006.
People. April 17, 2006, p. 37.
San Francisco Chronicle Online. April 7, 2006.
USA Today Online. April 6, 2006.
Variety Online. April 2, 2006.
Village Voice Online. April 4, 2006.
Washington Post. April 7, 2006, p. C5.

QUOTES

Pierre: "What I teach has value."
Ramos: "Not where I live."

TRIVIA

The 2005 documentary *Mad Hot Ballroom* followed actual elementary students of Pierre Dulaine's program.

TALLADEGA NIGHTS: THE BALLAD OF RICKY BOBBY

The story of a man who could only count to #1.
—Movie tagline

Box Office: $148.2 million

Put Will Ferrell in a comedy about an oblivious NASCAR driver with two first names and "ballad" in the title and you already know you're halfway to a good time; add writer/director Adam McKay, a fellow *Saturday Night Live* alum who also teamed with Ferrell on *Anchorman: The Legend of Ron Burgundy* (2004), along with a talented supporting cast and you end up with an inspired sports comedy that is nearly as entertaining as the pair's previous effort. The film is littered with shameless but somehow weirdly appropriate product placement from the likes of Wonder Bread and Old Spice along with irresistible catchphrases like, "Shake 'n' Bake!" While mocking the sport and its macho Southern practitioners, the film is also an earnest comic homage to racers and fans alike.

Ricky Bobby, born in the back seat of a Chevelle, is a man with driving in his blood. His meteoric rise to fame, quickly chronicled in the opening montage, began while working in the pit crew of the Dennit racing team alongside his best buddy Cal (John C. Reilly) and pit chief Lucius (Michael Clarke Duncan). Fate intervenes when Ricky volunteers as the replacement for one of the drivers and somehow wins the race. The newly crowned king of the NASCAR circuit, Ricky is driven to enormous success by the words of his no-good, absentee father Reese (Gary Cole), a semi-professional stock car racer: "If you ain't first, you're last." Helping to make sure Ricky always finishes first is teammate Cal, who seems satisfied with his perennial second-place status. With trophy wife Carley (Leslie Bibb) and spoiled sons Walker (Houston Tumlin) and Texas Ranger (Grayson Russell) at home, Ricky's arrogance grows as his success goes virtually unchallenged.

Ricky, who refuses to let the humble Cal win even one race, is due for a comeuppance which he finds in the form of gay French Formula One driver Jean Girard, played by *Borat*'s Sacha Baron Cohen. The antithesis of all things American and NASCAR, Bobby's new nemesis Girard is sponsored by Perrier, reads Camus, drinks macchiatos, and likes jazz, but is also a gifted racer hell-bent on defeating the pompous win-aholic Bobby. Cohen makes the character his own as much as Ferrell does his, with his faux French accent sounding as authentic as his Kazakh and equally hilarious, pronouncing Ricky's last name more like "Booby." Ferrell shares his screen time with Cohen with aplomb, with the two comic favorites facing off for a zesty on-screen kiss.

Ferrell and Cohen have much in common. Both are fearless character actors prone to displaying an un-toned, hirsute physique for the sake of a laugh. Although Ferrell and McKay's *Talladega Nights* has not generated the same award-generating buzz as Cohen's *Borat,* it is nevertheless similar in that it is also a social commentary wrapped in a comedy, without the accompanying malice of the latter. In one of the film's highlights, the over-privileged Bobby family gathers for a dinner that begins with Ricky leading his family in a wacky version of grace that thanks the "baby Jesus" for the "bountiful harvest of Dominos, KFC, and the always delicious Taco Bell...and of course my red hot smokin' wife Carley, who is a stone cold fox," while the precocious and offensive Walker and "TR" are encouraged to mercilessly abuse their grandfather and ends with a turned-on Carley and Ricky in a spur-of-the-moment make-out session. Another memorable dinner scene begins with a Grace sponsored by Powerade, while Cal and the Bobbys discuss their favorite incarnations of Jesus—Ricky's, naturally, being the baby Jesus while Cal's more creative embodiments include Jesus as "a mischievous badger" or singing lead for Lynyrd Skynyrd.

The signature scantily-clad Ferrell scene comes when a nasty crash has a delusional Ricky stripping down to his skivvies and running wildly around the track, believing he is on fire. Ricky winds up in the hospital, convinced he can't walk, which leads to one of the films funniest bits as Cal and Lucius, in order to show Ricky that he does have use of his legs, first stab Ricky in the leg with one knife then try to remove that knife by plunging in a second. Although Ricky does indeed have use of his legs, the crash causes him to lose all confidence and he stops racing altogether.

A surreal plot twist then has Carley leave Ricky for Cal, who's now taking Ricky's place as the number one racer. While it is believable that the gold-digging Carley would leave her husband for a more successful racer, it is less so that the faithful, soft-spoken Cal would run off with Ricky's wife, move into Ricky's house, and even invite his former best pal to their wedding. Ricky, now strangely broke, takes the kids and moves in with his mom Lucy (Jane Lynch), who disciplines the boys for the first time in their rotten young lives. Meanwhile, Reese returns long enough to help Ricky regain his confidence, which he does in rather unorthodox ways, including having Ricky drive blindfolded and with a wild cougar in the car.

Predictably, the newly humbled Ricky returns to the top of the racing heap with a new woman by his side—his buttoned-down, bespectacled former assistant Susan played by Oscar®-nominee Amy Adams (*Junebug* [2005]) who transforms into a sexy vixen as she delivers a wonderful motivational speech ("Ricky Bobby is not a thinker! Ricky Bobby is a driver!") that inspires Ricky in more ways than just racing. Cal dumps Carley and he and Ricky are once again bumping knuckles to their beloved "Shake 'n' Bake!"

Talladega Nights is good Southern-fried fun that NASCAR fans should also appreciate for extremely well-shot racing scenes that included staging several crashes for the sake of authenticity. Real NASCAR stars may be seen in cameos, including Dale Earnhardt Jr.

Hilary White

CREDITS

Ricky Bobby: Will Ferrell
Cal Naughton Jr.: John C. Reilly
Jean Girard: Sacha Baron Cohen
Lucius Washington: Michael Clarke Duncan
Carley Bibb: Leslie Bibb
Susan: Amy Adams
Reese Bobby: Gary Cole
Mrs. Dennit: Molly Shannon
Lucy Bobby: Jane Lynch
Gregory: Andy Richter
Walker: Houston Tumlin
Texas Ranger: Grayson Russell
Origin: USA
Language: English
Released: 2006
Production: Jimmy Miller, Judd Apatow; Relativity, Mosaic Media Group, Columbia Pictures; released by Sony Pictures

Directed by: Adam McKay
Written by: Will Ferrell, Adam McKay
Cinematography by: Oliver Wood
Music by: Alex Wurman
Sound: Mark Ulano
Music Supervisor: Hal Willner
Editing: Brent White
Art Direction: Virginia Randolph-Weaver
Costumes: Susan Matheson
Production Design: Clayton Hartley
MPAA rating: PG-13
Running time: 108 minutes

REVIEWS

Rolling Stone Online. August 3, 2006.
Salon.com. August 4, 2006.
Washington Post Online. August 4, 2006.

TENACIOUS D IN THE PICK OF DESTINY

The greatest motion picture of all time.
—Movie tagline

Box Office: $8.3 million

Jack Black has made a career out of mocking rock and roll pretentiousness, and the surprising thing is that his shtick is still so funny. In his latest film, the awkwardly titled *Tenacious D in the Pick of Destiny,* he skewers his own mock band's fanciful claims to greatness. The key to his success is that he does not just write satirical songs, he incessantly dismembers the cocky attitude of male rockers.

Black has done this routine so many times that he has basically become his own parody. A few years back he started the group Tenacious D with Kyle Gass, and the band became a cult favorite, churning out songs that made absurd claims to greatness while imitating heavy metal icons and their classic guitar riffs. Tenacious D's songs are not only hilarious, they are well executed. Making fun of rock's excesses, Black and his mate are clever and lewd, but it is all done in tongue-in-cheek lighthearted fun, so even when real bands and their fans are being mocked, they are not put off.

Black imported this persona wholesale into his breakthrough role in Richard Linklater's *School of Rock* (2003), in which he played a substitute teacher at a private school who instructs his privileged, precocious students in the intricacies of rock history and showmanship. It helps that Black himself—short and Hobbit-like, with eyebrows that are devilishly upturned and facial expressions of wide-eyed, open-mouthed inanity—looks nothing like a typical rock star. So when he overenthusiastically vows to rock the world like it has never been rocked before, he is automatically absurd. His comic style is simply to heighten the absurdity, to keep shouting rock-and-roll cliches and putting them to over-the-top music until he wears down all resistance.

In *Pick of Destiny,* Black teams up with bandmate Gass to ostensibly tell the story of Tenacious D's genesis. It is a real gamble. Not only have audiences seen Black's act a number of times, but Gass looks even less like a rock star than Black does. Balding, middle-aged, and paunchy, Gass does not radiate much energy, especially next to Black's hyperkinetic persona. He also lacks his partner's acting chops. It turns out, however, that Gass is a suitable straight man for Black, and it actually helps that "J.B.," as Black calls his character in the film, has someone a little more down-to-earth to bounce off. (It is not entirely clear whether Black the actor is playing Black the Tenacious D front man, or whether J.B. is an entirely new character—and it matters not at all.) Gass does a passable job of playing forlorn, dopey, put-upon, and distracted, and Black does not need much else.

In fact, there is not much else in *Tenacious D in the Pick of Destiny* except the wicked imagination of Black and his cohorts (Gass and director and co-writer Liam Lynch) riffing on the familiar story of a band's origins. The songs are terrific in this quasi-musical that veers audaciously between mockery and mayhem. The opening scene puts a new kick into generational conflict, as a young Black brings down the house of his conservative, God-fearing parents with a profanity-laced anthem to his own ambitions for stardom (the boy's father is played by the rocker Meat Loaf). Notably, the rest of the film clearly positions rock as divine, and its players as gods—and this is the core of Black's satire: his posing has cosmic pretensions even though its subject matter is usually quite mundane. What Black slices and dices most deliciously is male-dominated heavy metal's preoccupation with juvenile virility, sexual conquest, and obsession with grand meaning.

It is pleasing how the film uses a set of heraldic-themed tarot cards to announce various scenes, positioning the story as a quest to achieve the holy grail of rock stardom. It works, too, as a reminder that many hard-rock bands draw heavily on such medieval themes to churn out pretentious songs that position themselves as princes and knights winning the hearts of maidens and wenches. The movie is in fact a satire of the very idea of achieving heroism through celebrity, and it succeeds because Black makes himself the object of his own ridiculousness. It is not vicious rather, it is vivacious.

In this case, the "grail" is a special sort of guitar pick (thus, "the pick of destiny") supposedly used only by rock giants and fancifully descended from the tooth of Satan—who, in heavy-metal mythology, is the wellspring of rock inspiration. "J.B." and "K.G." learn of the pick from a guitar-store employee (Ben Stiller). They must "rescue" it from a castle of sorts—a "Rock and Roll History Museum" that's somehow located between Los Angeles and Sacramento. They run into a competitor for the grail, a menacing villain played with obvious fun by Tim Robbins, and Gass is temporarily waylaid by a trio of seductive sorority girls.

The telling of this tall tale is rife with diversions that have to do with drugs (always dope, nothing harder) and sex (mainly puerile)—merely because they are part of the famous trio that includes rock. Prepare yourself for adolescent jokes that are sometimes done so well that you cannot keep from laughing, as when Black uses his manly powers to reach an important button that deactivates lasers guarding the pick. What is even funnier than these scenes are the songs that make reference to the events themselves. The whole film is a sort of minor rock opera that includes scenes as fanciful as a hallucinogenic-mushroom-induced encounter with the pastel world of the Sasquatch.

At its best, *The Pick of Destiny* has the no-holds-barred mayhem of a Marx Brothers comedy, though its high points are intermittent. The filmmakers have the wisdom to keep the whole thing short at ninety-three minutes. By all rights, Black's act should wear thin long before that, but his energy and craziness transcend the often-trivial material. Rock pretentiousness is low-hanging fruit—an easy target—but Black makes it a savory meal of mischief. Black is a comic genius in this role he's created for himself, but what's unclear is whether he can succeed when he steps outside of it (his other 2006 star vehicle, *Nacho Libre,* garnered universally bad reviews, and he seemed out of place in the frothy romantic comedy *The Holiday*). It is time for him to conquer new frontiers, but you cannot help admiring how amusingly he's decimated the sacred cows of rock. Against all odds, the supremely silly *Tenacious D in the Pick of Destiny* rocks the house.

Michael Betzold

CREDITS

JB: Jack Black
KG: Kyle Gass
Lil' JB: Troy Gentile
Lee: Jason Reed
Guitar Store Guy: Ben Stiller
The Stranger: Tim Robbins
JB's Father: Meat Loaf Aday
Origin: USA
Language: English
Released: 2006
Production: Stuart Cornfeld, Jack Black, Kyle Gass; Red Hour; released by New Line Cinema
Directed by: Liam Lynch
Written by: Jack Black, Kyle Gass, Liam Lynch
Cinematography by: Robert Brinkmann
Music by: Tenacious D
Sound: Pud Cusack
Editing: David Rennie
Art Direction: Maria Baker
Costumes: Dayna Pink
Production Design: Martin Whist
MPAA rating: R
Running time: 93 minutes

REVIEWS

Chicago Sun-Times Online. November 22, 2006.
Hollywood Reporter Online. October 30, 2006.
Los Angeles Times Online. November 22, 2006.
New York Times Online. November 22, 2006.
San Francisco Chronicle. November 22, 2006, p. E4.
Variety Online. November 2, 2006.
Washington Post. November 22, 2006, p. C4.

QUOTES

JB: "We're going to pay the rent with our rock."

THE TEXAS CHAINSAW MASSACRE: THE BEGINNING

Witness the Birth of Fear.
—Movie tagline

Every Legend Has a Beginning.
—Movie tagline

Box Office: $39.5 million

The latest addition to the *The Texas Chainsaw Massacre* franchise is *The Texas Chainsaw Massacre: The Beginning,* which serves up the backstory of Tommy Hewitt and his clan's seemingly endless appetite for bloody mayhem, torture, and cannibalism. *The Texas Chainsaw Massacre: The Beginning* is the sixth film to shoulder the weight and lofty expectations of Tobe Hooper's original, *The Texas Chain Saw Massacre* (1974), the film that thrust the slasher subgenre into mainstream consciousness. *The Beginning* is not a prequel to the 1974 film, but the backstory and subsequent rehashing of *The Texas Chainsaw Massacre* (2003) starring Jessica Biel.

A prequel to *The Texas Chainsaw Massacre* should have been an exciting, enlightening, and much-anticipated addition to the franchise. This installment, however, falls well short of the mark by giving viewers forty minutes of *The Beginning* and using the remaining fifty minutes to regurgitate whole scenes from the earlier films.

The story opens in a backwoods Texas slaughterhouse as grim and grimy as anything depicted in Upton Sinclair's *The Jungle*. The year is 1939 and Tommy Hewitt (a.k.a Leatherface) claws his way out of his dead mother's womb and into the hearts, minds, and nightmares of filmgoers everywhere. The baby is left for dead and is discovered by a local woman while scrounging through the trash. She takes the infant home for Charlie Hewitt, Jr. (R. Lee Ermey) to raise along with the rest of their cannibalistic clan.

Flash forward thirty years and the massive, disfigured young Tommy (Andrew Bryniarski) is working on the same killing floor where he clawed his way to life. Unfortunately for Tommy and everyone else in the small town, the slaughterhouse is closing. Rather than leave, Tommy instead savagely smashes in the skull of his boss. During the rampage, he discovers a more effective and brutal implement for killing and destruction: a chainsaw. Leaving the slaughterhouse still carrying his blood-drenched, newfound toy, Tommy bumps into his uncle Charlie and Sheriff Hoyt (Lew Temple). As the sheriff leaves the squad car to confront Tommy, Charlie plucks the shotgun from the car dashboard and shoots the sheriff in the back noting that he has, in fact, gotten rid of the town's entire police force with one shot. Dragging the body home, Charlie serves up sauteed sheriff to his clan and like a backwoods Scarlett O'Hara, proclaims, "We ain't never gonna starve again." Donning the dead man's uniform, it's clear there's a (sadistic) new sheriff in town.

Going forward, the film tracks familiar ground as two Vietnam-bound brothers Eric (Matt Bomer) and Dean (Taylor Handley) and their girlfriends Chrissie (Jordana Brewster) and Bailey (Diora Baird) traverse rural Texas in search of a little tranquility before the boys ship out. The foursome's trip is rudely interrupted when they crash into a cow on a lonely stretch of road. The impact throws Chrissie into the weeds on the side of the road and before the quartet can regroup, "Sheriff Hoyt" appears and brings Eric, Dean, and Bailey home to meet the family. We've been down this road before and the gore that follows is a veritable cornucopia of contemporary cinematic cliches with tight, hand-held shots filled with crimson rivers of blood, piles of human remains, ear-splitting screams, the smash of bones, and a even a tongue extraction for good measure.

Director Jonathan Liebesman serves up a repulsive mix that had more than one reviewer likening *The Beginning* to a snuff film. *The Beginning* lacks the suspense and cat-and-mouse quality that made the 1974 version the standard bearer of the genre. Moviegoers looking for the nightmare-worthy dinner scene from the original will find an updated and amped-up version that was not one of the seventeen scenes left on the cutting room floor in order for the movie to secure and R rating. Liebesman and cinematographer Lukas Ettlin, who also collaborated on the straight-to-video film *Rings* (2005), do create surprisingly well-crafted visuals that belie the film's subject matter. An early Leatherface montage depicting his troubled youth is a brief but fine example.

As prequels go, *The Beginning* is surprisingly short on actual backstory. The story does show in graphic detail the origin of Thomas Hewitt's "Leatherface" mask that was inspired by the real-life cannibal Ed Gein. Aside from this and his horrid birth, the movie covers very little new ground and lacks the suspense and social commentary of the original. As Chris Cabin from *Filmcritic.com* writes, the film " commits the crime of being totally and utterly tiresome."

Michael White

CREDITS

Chrissie: Jordana Brewster
Sheriff Winston Hoyt: Lew Temple
Charlie Hewitt Jr./Sheriff Hoyt: R. Lee Ermey
Leatherface: Andrew Bryniarski
Bailey: Diora Baird
Dean: Taylor Handley
Eric: Matt Bomer
Holden: Lee Tergesen
Origin: USA
Language: English
Released: 2006
Production: Andrew Form, Brad Fuller, Tobe Hooper, Kim Henkel; Platinum Dunes, Next Entertainment; released by New Line Cinema
Directed by: Jonathan Liebesman
Written by: Sheldon Turner
Cinematography by: Lukas Ettlin
Music by: Steve Jablonsky
Sound: Stacy Brownrigg
Editing: Jonathan Chibnall
Art Direction: John Frick
Costumes: Mari-An Ceo
Production Design: Marco Rubeo

MPAA rating: R
Running time: 84 minutes

REVIEWS

Entertainment Weekly. October 13, 2006, p. 111.
Hollywood Reporter Online. September 25, 2006.
New York Times Online. October 6, 2006.
Variety Online. October 5, 2006.

QUOTES

Hoyt (about eating human flesh): "Meat's meat, bone is bone."

AWARDS

Nomination:

Golden Raspberries 2006: Worst Sequel/Prequel

THANK YOU FOR SMOKING

Nick Naylor doesn't hide the truth...he filters it.
—Movie tagline

Box Office: $24.7 million

Jason Reitman's slick satire centers on shrewd spin-doctor Nick Naylor (Aaron Eckhart), a powerful, seemingly soulless Washington tobacco lobbyist who is ultimately humanized during his journey throughout the film. Directing his first feature, Reitman (son of filmmaker Ivan Reitman) gets it right with a smart script he adapted from the novel by Christopher Buckley, sophisticated visuals, and an impressive cast led by Eckhart who embodies Naylor with just the right amount of cynicism and greed while effortlessly adding genuine earnestness and vulnerability. The film's appealing brand of subtle, dark comedy, brisk pacing, and an absolute unwillingness to indulge in cheap sentimentality keeps this engagingly funny film on track right up to the end.

Thank You for Smoking starts appropriately enough with Tex Williams crooning "Smoke Smoke Smoke That Cigarette!" while the savvy script introduces the good-looking, smooth talking Nick, Vice President of the Academy of Tobacco Studies and the self-proclaimed "Colonel Sanders of nicotine," who amusingly narrates in voiceover. Representing Big Tobacco on a talk show outlining the dangers of smoking hosted by Joan Lunden (playing herself), Nick is the reviled pariah among the guests, who include representatives from the Lung Cancer Association and a teenage cancer victim ravaged from smoking. As his job is being "paid to talk," Nick, a naturally consummate debater, manages to convince both Lunden and the studio audience that tobacco cares and by the show's end, even "Cancer Boy" is shaking his hand. He has learned from the best: Nick describes the workings of his company, which employs a doctor ("they found him in Germany") who after much research, can find no conclusive link between nicotine and lung cancer ("The man's a genius. He could disprove gravity.") as well as a team of lawyers known as "sharks" who, he explains, function "just like a John Grisham novel but without all the espionage."

If the script has any obvious flaws, it is perhaps in the opening as Nick's glowing descriptions of himself border on the gratingly narcissistic: "You know that guy who could pick up any girl? I'm him. On crack....I have a Bachelor's degree in kicking ass and taking names." B.R. (J.K. Simmons), Nick's even more soulless boss, earned those initials during his tour in Vietnam and those who know what it means, Nick explains, are all dead. Nick is divorced and reviled by both his ex-wife and her boyfriend who would like to limit his contact with his only son Joey (Cameron Bright). His only friends are the members of a secret group called the "M.O.D. Squad" ("Merchants of Death"): Polly Bailey (Maria Bello), an alcohol industry lobbyist, and Bobby Jay Bliss (David Koechner), the face of firearms in Washington. They meet at the dimly lit Bert's to commiserate and argue over whose industry kills more of it's consumers, with Nick trumping his comrades with 1,200 deaths per day. Bello is refreshing in a darkly comic turn as a bitter alcohol-pusher who began her drinking career at fourteen and earned her the tolerance of "an Irish dockworker" while Koechner, becoming a ubiquitous face in big-screen comedies, turns in another adept performance as a chauvinist gun-toter. These scenes, among the funniest, are made especially entertaining by their rampant political incorrectness and Reitman took care not to disappoint fans of the book who especially enjoyed the M.O.D. Squad.

Whether he's selling a classroom of elementary school children on the idea of their right to challenge authority and try smoking for themselves when they get older or chatting with fellow airplane passengers hoping it will result in at least one person becoming a smoker, Nick enjoys what he does. He enjoys his job because he's good at it, not to mention it more than amply "pays the mortgage," a phrase that turns up throughout the film. Talking is what Nick has to offer to the world and he explains the power of such a gift to his son during one of his weekend visits. When Joey asks his dad for help on his homework assignment, a paper arguing why the American government is the best government in the world, Nick explains that it doesn't matter what he writes about as long as he argues it correctly. Then he can never be wrong.

With nicotine sales plummeting due to health concerns and annoying politicians like Vermont Senator Ortolan K. Finistirre (William H. Macy) lobbying for stricter warning labels on cigarette packages, B.R. demands his staff come up with effective counter tactics. While watching an old John Wayne movie, Nick has the brilliant idea of bringing smoking back to the movies and not just among R.A.V.s ("Russians, Arabs, and villains") and is summoned to Winston-Salem to meet with the Captain (Robert Duvall), Big Tobacco's head honcho. Nick's spiritual father, the Captain is a grizzled nicotine veteran who invented the cigarette filter after *Reader's Digest* slammed the industry in the 1950s and who drinks mint juleps that Fidel Castro taught him the secret of making. He loves Nick like the son he never had and sends him back in style on his private jet, the hilariously named "Tobacco One."

B.R. sets up a meeting for Nick in Hollywood with powerful super-agent Jeff Megall (Rob Lowe) from E.G.O. (Entertainment Global Offices; the film is rife with amusing acronyms) and Joey, using the verbal techniques his father taught him, finagles his mother Jill (Kim Dickens) into letting him go along to see his dad in action. They are ushered into the office by Megall's fast-talking assistant Jack (Adam Brody). In hands-down the funniest supporting role of the film, Brody's Jack acts as a sort of a coked-up tour guide during the long walk to Jeff's office. He points out the $12,000 Koi fish that was a gift from Oprah, discusses a sculpture gifted by Matthew McConnaghay (before Jeff represented him he was a "face" and now, he's a "name"), casually offers Joey a Red Bull, and manages to crack up a passing coworker with this most outrageous "inside joke": "I'm going to impale your mom on a spike and feed her dead body to my dog with syphilis."

Lowe's eccentric agent wastes no time in getting Nick's idea implemented and soon he's making the deal. A futuristic movie starring Brad Pitt and Catherine Zeta-Jones entitled *Message from Sector Six,* will be the vehicle that will have Americans lighting up in droves once they get a load of the sexy stars puffing away post-coital, all for a mere $25 million. Nick agrees with the caveat that for that kind of money, Brad would be expected to blow smoke rings. Jeff takes the idea one step further with the innovative suggestion to market a cigarette specifically designed as a movie tie-in called Sector Six.

The Captain also sends Nick on a mission to take care of another thorn in Big Tobacco's side: a disgruntled and now cancer-ridden former Marlboro Man, Lorne Lutch (Sam Elliott), who is complaining loudly to the media. Nick is instructed to offer him a briefcase full of money with no strings attached other than their hope that he will feel enough "gratitude" that he will keep quiet. With Lorne outraged that they think he can be "bought," Nick takes a clever tack—suggesting he summon the media to witness this tobacco "bribe" and then declare he will donate the whole thing to charity. Lutch does what Nick knows he will: takes the money and stops talking.

With these successes under his belt, Nick wings back to Washington and into the arms of his new lover, Heather Holloway (Katie Holmes), a perky young reporter he previously became involved with as she interviewed him for a story in the *Washington Probe* newspaper. Still flying high, Nick appears on the Dennis Miller show where the first sign of trouble creeps into his life in the form of a live, on-air death threat. The caller claims that Nick will be dead within the week for all the wrongs he has committed through his work. It also makes for a particularly lively M.O.D. Squad discussion as they bicker about who is a bigger target for a terrorist. "I'm surprised I didn't get shot on my way to work today," brags Polly.

Cross-cut scenes show a classmate of Joey's reading her aforementioned "America" essay to the class at St. Euthanasius as Nick is grabbed off the street and thrown into a van. As one little girl makes her point that the American government is the best because we are free to do whatever we want, the kidnappers paste dozens of nicotine patches all over his body, berating him for doing his job: defending America's right to choose. He is found naked and unconscious in the lap of the Lincoln Memorial. Ironically, the kidnappers attempts to kill Nick have backfired. Now hospitalized, the doctor tells Nick that no nonsmoker could have survived such an attack and that smoking actually saved his life while his boss praises him for now garnering the sympathy of the American public.

A greater threat to Nick than the kidnappers, apparently, is Holloway's scandalous article. She includes everything he told her that he assumed would be "off the record" during their bedroom romps which included potentially damaging conversations held by the M.O.D. Squad, bribing the Marlboro Man, and negatively affecting his son's morals. All the good will his kidnapping created is destroyed by the article, his boss notes just before firing him. His seemingly endless well of confidence run dry, Nick retreats to his apartment where his son, who still believes in his dad and what he does, inspires his comeback in the film's final act.

He testifies, as scheduled, at a hearing led by Senator Finistirre on making cigarette makers carry a skull and crossbones symbol on every pack. With his proud son watching, he makes a rousing argument against the measure that the press eats up. B.R. swoops back in to offer him his job back which he promptly refuses, preferring to use his God-given gift of gab in another politically incorrect arena and is later seen showing cell phone makers how to refute the claims of a link to their product and brain cancer. But Finistirre is not to be deterred either and is seen in the final frames pitching his new idea: retouching classic films to take the smoking out, showing a clip of Bette Davis holding a candy cane.

That Eckhart manages to make this "Merchant of Death" likeable is a feat but he is given ample support by costar Bright who plays Joey as an intelligent sidekick, bewildered by the fact that the world would hate his dad just for doing his job. It is their relationship that gives the film a seriousness that balances the sometimes outrageous humor, aspiring to the excellence of such satires as *The Player* (1992) or *Wag the Dog* (1997).

Ironically, no one actually smokes in the film although some of the characters, particularly Eckhart's, are supposed to have the habit (he reaches for one at one point to find his pack empty). It is a pointed statement the film itself references: that in Hollywood films no one smokes anymore. Particularly not the leading man.

Hilary White

CREDITS

Nick Naylor: Aaron Eckhart
Polly Bailey: Maria Bello
Joey Naylor: Cameron Bright
Jack: Adam Brody
Lorne Lutch: Sam Elliott
Bobby Jay Bliss: David Koechner
Heather Holloway: Katie Holmes
Jeff Megall: Rob Lowe
Senator Ortolan K. Finistirre: William H. Macy
B.R.: J.K. Simmons
The Captain: Robert Duvall
Jill Naylor: Kim Dickens
Pearl: Connie Ray
Ron Goode: Todd Louiso
Origin: USA
Language: English
Released: 2006
Production: David O. Sacks; ContentFilm, Room 9 Entertainment; released by Fox Searchlight
Directed by: Jason Reitman
Written by: Jason Reitman
Cinematography by: James Whitaker
Music by: Rolfe Kent
Sound: Steve Morrow
Editing: Dana E. Glauberman
Costumes: Danny Glicker
Production Design: Steven A. Saklad
MPAA rating: R
Running time: 92 minutes

REVIEWS

Boxoffice Online. March 17, 2006.
Chicago Sun-Times Online. March 24, 2006.
Los Angeles Times Online. March 17, 2006.
New York Times Online. March 17, 2006.
San Francisco Chronicle Online. March 24, 2006.
Variety Online. September 12, 2005.
Village Voice Online. March 14, 2006.
Washington Post. March 17, 2006, p. C1.

QUOTES

Nick: "The message Hollywood needs to send out is 'Smoking Is Cool!'"

AWARDS

Ind. Spirit 2007: Screenplay
Nomination:
Golden Globes 2007: Actor—Mus./Comedy (Eckhart), Film—Mus./Comedy
Ind. Spirit 2007: Actor (Eckhart)
Writers Guild 2006: Adapt. Screenplay

THE THREE BURIALS OF MELQUIADES ESTRADA

For justice. For loyalty. For friendship.
—Movie tagline

Box Office: $5 million

Tommy Lee Jones's directorial debut is a critically-acclaimed Tex-Mex drama that won the Best Actor and Best Screenplay award at the Cannes Film Festival. The screenplay was written by Mexico's Guillermo Arriaga, who also penned *21 Grams* (2003) and 2006's much-lauded *Babel.* Critics favorably compared the film's style to the works of Sam Peckinpah, with *Chicago Sun-Times*' Roger Ebert calling it, "the kind of story that John Huston or Sam Peckinpah might have wanted to film. It begins with a bedrock of loyalty and honor between men, and mixes it with a little madness." *Three Burials* also reminded Ebert of Pekinpah's seminal cult classic *Bring Me the Head of Alfredo Garcia.*

With a narrative that jumps from present to past and back again, Jones helps clarify the timeline with intermittent titles that appear on screen. A hard-scrabble border town in Cibolo County, Texas, is home to the cast of characters, which includes grizzled ranch foreman Pete Perkins (Tommy Lee Jones). Pete hires Melquiades Estrada (Julio Cesar Cedillo), a young illegal Mexican migrant worker, and the two form a strong bond of friendship. Melquiades falls victim to a shooting accident involving the rookie border patrol agent Mike Norton (Barry Pepper), who tries to cover up the mess by hastily burying the body. Mike loses the audience's sympathy early after he is shown cruelly roughing up a Mexican woman trying to illegally enter the country earlier in the film. When Pete goes to the police, however, it is clear the local Sheriff Belmont (a well-used Dwight Yoakum) cares little for embarking on a proper investigation. Meanwhile, the troubled brute Norton broods at home with his beautiful wife Lou Ann (January Jones), a young girl having trouble adjusting to her depressing, new married life in the desolate Texas town. She finds a friend in Rachel (Melissa Leo), a married waitress who finds pleasant distraction in her affairs with both the sheriff and Pete.

With the police apparently not caring that one more illegal immigrant is dead, Pete takes the matter into his own hands. Seemingly mad with grief, Pete bursts into Mike's mobile home, binds Lou Ann (shown in flashback as carrying on an affair with the kindly Melquiades), and kidnaps Mike.

The rest of the film involves the journey of the three men: Pete, Mike and the corpse of Melquiades, who all travel on horseback to Mexico where Pete plans to bury Melquiades in his hometown, near his wife and family, as he promised his friend he would some time back. Along the way, Pete tries to not only wrangle a confession from Mike, but also make him keenly aware of what he's done and the consequences it will bring.

During the excruciating trek, much of the film's black comedy arises out of the cowboy's devoted care of his friend's decomposing body, which he tries to preserve by filling it with anti-freeze at one point. There is also irony, as Mike is bitten a poisonous snake and healed by the same Mexican woman whom he beat so brutally in an earlier scene.

When they arrive at their destination, Mike certainly much altered along the way, it becomes apparent that Melquiades had invented the fact that he had a wife and children and, no one in the town will claim him. Pete conducts a fitting burial in an appropriate place in honor of his old friend, finally freeing the cut-and-bruised Mike, who is nonetheless emotionally healthier.

Jones' direction is as flawless as his performance and his uniformly strong cast. As *Variety*'s Todd McCarthy noted, "Arriaga's script is so deeply conceived that, even though the characters do many profoundly misguided things, the viewer understands these people well enough to accept them; there's no melodramatic good-and-evil here, but a range of human pros and cons hopelessly intertwined."

Hilary White

CREDITS

Pete Perkins: Tommy Lee Jones
Mike Norton: Barry Pepper
Sheriff Belmont: Dwight Yoakam
Lou Ann Norton: January Jones
Rachel: Melissa Leo
Old Man With Radio: Levon Helm
Mariana: Vanessa Bauche
Melquiades Estrada: Julio Cesar Cedillo
Captain Gomez: Mel Rodriguez
Rosa: Cecilia Suarez
Lucio: Ignacio Guadalupe
Origin: USA, France
Language: English, Spanish
Released: 2005
Production: Michael Fitzgerald, Luc Besson, Pierre Ange Le Pogam, Tommy Lee Jones; Europacorp, Javelina Film Co.
Directed by: Tommy Lee Jones
Written by: Guillermo Arriaga
Cinematography by: Chris Menges
Music by: Marco Beltrami
Sound: Marc Weingarten
Editing: Roberto Silvi
Art Direction: Jeff Knipp
Costumes: Kathleen Kiatta
Production Design: Meredith Boswell
MPAA rating: R
Running time: 120 minutes

REVIEWS

Boxoffice Online. December 14, 2005.
Entertainment Weekly Online. December 14, 2005.
Los Angeles Times Online. December 14, 2005.
New York Times Online. December 14, 2005.
Premiere Magazine Online. December 16, 2005.
Variety Online. May 23, 2005.

TIDELAND

The squirrels made it seem less lonely.
—Movie tagline

Filmmaker Terry Gilliam first earned his stripes on the hugely successful satiric *Monty Python* television series and later collaboratedwith Terry Jones on the troupe's big-screen features *Monty Python and the Holy Grail* (1974) and *Monty Python's Life of Brian* (1979). This hugely talented artist and designer broke into the movies with a vengeance in his post-Python career with the success of *Time Bandits* (1981) and the critical acclaim for his vastly creative *Brazil* (1985). But, in the last decade or so, his career has floundered with several highly inventive but largely incoherent films, including *Fear and Loathing in Las Vegas* (1998) and, more recently, *The Brothers Grimm* (2005). Gilliam has also had his fair share of troubled or uncompleted productions, such as his failed "The Man Who Killed Don Quixote." Like Orson Welles before him, Gilliam has apparently become modern cinema's patron saint of hopeless bravado, desperate gambles, and lost causes.

Some have wondered lately if Gilliam's bizarre imagination has spun out of control, revealing a decidedly nasty and gruesome edge. His newest film, *Tideland*, adapted by Gilliam and Tony Grisoni from the cult novel by Mitch Cullin, is just such a film. It shakes out a fantastic cocktail of allusions to books and films and paintings, such as *Alice in Wonderland*, *Texas Chainsaw Massacre*, Alfred Hitchcock's *Psycho*, Andrew Wyeth's painting "Christina's World," and Gilliam's own drug-addled *Fear and Loathing in Las Vegas*. Gilliam has described the film himself as "*Alice in Wonderland* meets *Psycho*."

On balance, Alice's adventures down the rabbit hole were less gruesome, frightening, and downright nasty than those encountered by the heroine of *Tideland*, a ten-year-old girl named Jeliza-Rose (Jodelle Ferland in a remarkable performance). Her descent into hell begins with the death of her drugged-out mother, the preposterously named Queen Gunhilda (Jennifer Tilly). After covering her corpse with a rug, books, and other articles, she and her equally snockered father, rock guitarist Noah (Jeff Bridges), quit the scene and take a bus to Grandma's house amidst the grassy wastes of Tideland (shot in Saskatchewan, Canada). But Grandma is only a desiccated corpse in a wind-blown shack. So, what's a father and daughter to do but set up housekeeping of their own? Jeliza-Rose prepares Dad's heroin injection and leaves him to sleep off what he calls his "vacation." That's where Dad remains, for most of the rest of the picture, which is to say his remains sit in the chair, slowing decaying, as Jeliza-Rose scampers about in more adventures. And those adventures are just beginning.

These include a frightening encounter with Dell (Janet McTeer), a gaunt woman who abruptly shows up clad in a black bee-keeper's outfit; a mentally-disabled boy named Dickens (Brendan Fletcher), who wanders the grasses wearing a scuba-diver's face mask and flippers; the frightening appearances of the "monster shark," which is actually a passenger train that comes roaring by on occasion; and the disappearance of her beloved doll's head, "Mystique," down a rabbit hole. (Jeliza-Rose even goes down the rabbit hole at one point, or is it only a dream?) Dell turns out to be Dad's sister, who lives downstairs with Dickens and sleeps upstairs with the rotted corpse of Grandma. One day, the whole gang gathers around the likewise rotting form of Dad, now wearing a golden wig placed on his head by Jeliza-Rose, for some housecleaning. Dell lays out Dad's corpse, disembowels it, stuffs it with Jeliza-Rose's dolls, and places it at the head of the dinner table in a cozy domestic scene (shades of *Texas Chainsaw Massacre*). Later, while a sewed-up Dad lies browning and crackling on the bed, Jeliza-Rose strikes up a peculiar romance with Dickens. He tells her his big "secret," that he is preparing for the End of the World with a hidden stash of dynamite sticks. Jeliza-Rose regards her developing relationship with Dickens as a marriage and sees herself as the mother whose grumbling stomach surely betokens an impending baby. They exchange a few kisses, which obviously agitates the addled Dickens. When Dell discovers them in bed, she goes crazy. Incest and child molestation are apparently no strangers to this household.

There is a big fight, and Jeliza-Rose flees back to her house. That night, a great disturbance shakes the windows. Clambering down the meadow, the little girl discovers that the Monster Shark has been blown up by Dickens' dynamite sticks. The End of the World, indeed! More confused than ever, the girl crouches by the tracks while the survivors of the train-wreck stagger around her. A woman comes to Jeliza-Rose and comforts her. Tender words imply the child has found a mother at last.

Tideland is gruesome, funny, frequently tasteless, and profoundly disturbing all at the same time. There are scenes that are tasteless in the extreme (although one doubts if Gilliam cares much), such as the death scene of Queen Gunhilda, as she lies choking and gasping, splayed out on her bed; the bus ride as an obscenely farting father and daughter travel to the grassy country; and the weirdly pathetic sex scene between Dell and the village delivery boy. In short, this picture is not for the squeamish, particularly due to the not-so-subtle implications of family incest (apparently, Dad and Dell, brother and sister, had been lovers); child abuse (the parody of romantic love between the cosmetic-smeared Jeliza-Rose and the puppet-like contortions of Dickens could make viewers writhe in discomfort, especially when he climbs atop her in the bed); and the grisly fate that awaits the corpse of poor Dad, whose face, as the picture transpires, suffers the indignity of Jeliza-Rose's blond fright-wig, smeared lipstick, and Dell's clumsy taxidermy. What in the world is Jeff Bridges doing in this picture? Surely it was not for the money, since Terry Gilliam's budgets have shrunk radically since his *Brazil* days.

But most disturbing of all is the performance by little Jodelle Ferland as Jeliza-Rose. She greets each new horror, grotesque behavior, and crazy apparition with unflappable aplomb. She confides in her only companions, the finger puppets waggling on her fingers and, strangely enough, they talk back. She hugs the desiccated form of Dad with motherly tenderness. She sits down to the gruesome dinner table and eats with relish. She delights in her visits with Dickens in his "Submarine," an overturned, rotting automobile. And the screams she emits while crouching in the upside-down car while the train roars by outside are not of fright but of some kind of manic ecstasy. A scene that particularly sticks in the mind is her horrible parody of her mother's death, shot from a high angle as the capering, gesticulating child, dressed before the mirror in her mother's furs and gowns, takes shrill delight in her feigned death-throes. One fears that there might be something equally perverse in Gilliam's direction of this child, of placing her amidst this chamber of grotesques, of what he must have advised her in the direction, and what the child might have made of all this.

New York Times reviewer A.O. Scott found the acting luridly exaggerated: "The aesthetic is at once grotesque and dreamy, but not coherently so, since no distinction is made between the filmmaker's perception and his heroine's." Scott also found the first two-thirds of the film merely "tiresome," and the ending "creepy, and not in a good way." In short, the reviews were decidedly mixed, but most were negative, with Philip French of *The Guardian* calling the film "deeply disappointing" to "borderline unwatchable." Many reviewers were simply outright puzzled: Jessica Winter of *Time Out*, for example, found Gilliam's "brash disregard for conventional narrative rhythms and structures" simply "bewildering."

And yet, there are moments and images of a strangely memorable beauty in *Tideland*, such as the lyric, Arnold Bax-like music score by Michyel and Jeff Danna. Similarly affecting were Gilliam's trademark sharply contrasting light and dark palette (photography by Nicola Pecorini); the collapse of Dell's mansion down into the grassy depths, like a ship drowning in the ocean (apparently a dream image); the blowing interiors of the mansion; the monstrous train which explodes the stillness; the rabbit-hole sequence as the girl drifts down and down (lensed in a reverse angle as she falls away from the circle of light of the tunnel entrance); and, finally, the conversation between Dickens and Jeliza-Rose about the End of the World, while enormous earth-moving machinery gobbles up the valley below.

When all is said and done, one cannot help but admire the bravery, even the bravado of this crazy, disjointed nightmare of a picture. It is decidedly not a commercial film, much less a pleasant entertainment. It might even be something of a testament, a culmination of all the quirks, frenzies, comic idiocies, and horrors that populate the mind of Terry Gilliam. The movie was sufficiently confused that it appeared on the Ten Worst lists of some critics and the Ten Best lists of others. In other words, not a good pick for mainstream audiences.

John C. Tibbetts and James M. Welsh

CREDITS

Jeliza-Rose: Jodelle Ferland
Dell: Janet McTeer
Dickens: Brendan Fletcher
Noah: Jeff Bridges
Queen Gunhilda: Jennifer Tilly
Origin: Canada, Great Britain
Language: English
Released: 2005
Production: Jeremy Thomas, Gabriella Martinelli; Recorded Pictures Company, Capri Films; released by ThinkFilm
Directed by: Terry Gilliam
Written by: Terry Gilliam, Tony Grisoni
Cinematography by: Nicola Pecorini
Music by: Mychael Danna, Jeff Danna
Sound: David Lee
Editing: Lesley Walker
Art Direction: Anastasia Masaro
Costumes: Mario Davignon
Production Design: Jasna Stefanovic
MPAA rating: R
Running time: 122 minutes

REVIEWS

Los Angeles Times Online. October 20, 2006.
New York Times Online. October 13, 2006.
San Francisco Chronicle. October 27, 2006, p. E5.
Variety Online. September 12, 2005.
Village Voice Online. October 10, 2006.

TIME TO LEAVE

(Les Temps qui reste)

Writer/director Francois Ozon's 2005 film *Time to Leave* (*Les Temps qui reste*) follows 2000's *Under the Sand* (*Sous le sable*) in what the director has described as the second of a trilogy on confronting death. In this installment it is thirty-one-year-old Romain (Melvil Poupard) who is unwillingly confronting his own mortality. A handsome, arrogant, successful fashion photographer in Paris, Romain collapses at a shoot and then learns from his doctor that he has terminal cancer. His doctor urges chemotherapy, admitting that even with treatment, Romain has less than a five percent chance of surviving. Without the treatment, he has maybe three months. Romain decides against the chemo and finally reacts to the news by breaking down crying on a park bench.

At first he intends to tell his family about his diagnosis when they have dinner together; Romain seems calm enough while playing with his sister Sophie's (Louise-Anne Hippeau) baby son,but he reacts to his mother's normal solicitousness with impatience, and cruelly lashes out at Sophie for her supposed inadequacies. Claiming he's drunk, Romain asks his father (Daniel Duval) to drive him home and the two share a conversation about his parents' long-but-rocky marriage. It seems as if he may confide in his father, but the moment passes. Seemingly determined to drive everyone out of his life, Romain also throws his younger boyfriend Sasha (Christian Sengewald) out of the apartment, saying he doesn't feel anything anymore. Sasha doesn't seem too surprised, as their affair has been cooling off.

While driving to visit his widowed, paternal grandmother in the country, Romain stops off at a cafe where middle-aged waitress Jany (Valeria Bruni-Tedeschi) notices him watching the children on the playground. They converse for a few minutes and she finds out that Romain is single and childless. Later, while Romain and his grandmother Laura (Jeanne Moreau) prepare dinner, she asks why he hasn't told his family. He tells her that "I don't think anyone wants to hear it." and "I think I like it that nobody knows." When asked why he told her, Romain replies "Because you're like me, you'll be dying soon." Laura accepts his reasons with a complicit smile and a shrug and offers comfort when Romain breaks down and tells her: "I don't know what to do. I don't know what's right. I'm following my instincts." He walks in the woods and sees his old treehouse, remembering when he and Sophie were once so close. Romain also frequently envisions his childhood self (Ugo Soussan Trabelsi) as he revisits his past.

While driving back to Paris, Romain stops at another cafe and Jany walks in; her husband, Bruno (Walter Pagano) works there. She covertly watches Romain as she and Bruno talk and then sits down at Romain's table. Timidly, she reveals that she and her husband want children but he is sterile. They both think Romain is handsome and she politely asks if he will sleep with her. Rather than explaining that he is ill—or even gay—he replies that he doesn't like children. Romain continues to cut himself off, pretending he is on vacation, not answering the phone, and rarely leaving his apartment as his health deteriorates. He reads a letter Sophie sends him; she doesn't understand why he has been hostile to her and wants to reconcile. Romain phones her to apologize while watching Sophie play with her two sons in the park. Perhaps as a result of this tender moment, Romain changes his mind, and agrees to father Jany's child, but only if Bruno will join them in bed. This entire situation is more than a little ludicrous and the actors don't quite pull it off.

Romain becomes decidedly more frail, and his last act is to make a will, witnessed by the pregnant Jany and Bruno, leaving his property to his unborn child. He then takes a train to the seaside, where he went as a child. This last section is without dialogue; only Valentin Silvestrov's score accompanies Romain as he walks the promenade, takes a swim, and then stretches out on a towel in the sand like so many others around him. As the sun sets, the other beachgoers leave while he remains, smiling as the darkness approaches.

The literal translation of the French title, *The Time That's Left*, might have been more suitable. It is Romain's "time to leave" because he has terminal cancer but it is how he deals with the "time that's left" that makes up Ozon's frequently wordless portrait. There are numerous dialogue-free scenes of Romain walking, drinking, taking photos, and staring into space. Romain tells Jany that he is "not a nice man," but his cruelty to those around him seems more to be his aversion to being an object of their pity. Only with his strong-willed grandmother can Romain tell the truth; she has her own regrets about the choices she made in life. These too-few scenes between the iconic Moreau and Poupard are tender and heartbreaking and to be treasured. Poupard must be commended, as his somewhat enigmatic and unlikable character deteriorates into a pale, stick figure who communicates both anguish and final acceptance with his eyes rather than in speech.

Christine Tomassini

CREDITS

Romain: Melvil Poupaud
Laura: Jeanne Moreau
Jany: Valeria Bruni-Tedeschi
Father: Daniel Duval
Mother: Marie Riviere
Sasha: Christian Sengewald
Sophie: Louise-Anne Hippeau

Bruno: Walter Pagano
Young Romain: Ugo Soussan Trabelsi
Origin: France
Language: French
Released: 2005
Production: Olivier Delbosc, Marc Missonnier; Fidelite Productions, France 2 Cinema, Canal Plus
Directed by: Francois Ozon
Written by: Francois Ozon
Cinematography by: Jeanne Lapoirie
Sound: Brigitte Taillandier, Aymeric Devoldere
Editing: Monica Coleman
Costumes: Pascaline Chavanne
Production Design: Katia Wyszkop
MPAA rating: Unrated
Running time: 85 minutes

REVIEWS

Hollywood Reporter Online. May 17, 2005.
Los Angeles Times Online. July 21, 2006.
New York Times Online. July 14, 2006.
The Observer Online. May 14, 2006.
San Francisco Chronicle. July 28, 2006, p. E7.
Variety Online. May 16, 2005.
Village Voice Online. July 11, 2006.

QUOTES

Romain (explaining why he's only telling his grandmother he's dying): "Because you're like me. You'll be dying soon."

TRISTAN & ISOLDE

Before Romeo & Juliet, there was...
—Movie tagline

Box Office: $14.7 million

Tristan's dying words, "Life is greater than death. Love is greater than both," neatly encapsulates the legend chronicled in Kevin Reynolds's epic *Tristan & Isolde,* which Roger Ebert dubbed, "a lean and effective action romance." The story of the tragic love between the Cornish knight and his Irish princess has timeless appeal, first surfacing in the twelfth century. Since then, there have been more variations on the tale in more countries than there are different spellings of Isolde's name (Iseult, Isolde, Yseut), including the famous Wagner opera. Granted, there are a plethora of anachronisms in Reynolds's version of the legend, chief among them technically incorrect references to the English and the Celts (not actually used at the time) and a prominently featured Elizabethan-era John Donne poem, "The Good-Morrow." But Donne's words are beautiful and fitting, and although *Tristan & Isolde* is not a wholly historically accurate romance (the original story contained a love potion, after all), it is nonetheless a well-made and compelling one.

The time is The Dark Ages, circa 600 A.D. The fall of the Roman Empire has left the fate of Britain in the hands of chaotic tribes fighting amongst themselves for power while a united Ireland dominates them all from across the sea, led by King Donnchadh (a wonderful but sometimes unintelligible David O'Hara). This is, clearly, a very different dynamic between the two countries than audiences are used to seeing. As Keith Phipps wryly notes in his review in *The Onion,* "Oh, when will the Irish stop oppressing the British?" Benefiting greatly from the inter-tribal warfare, Donnchadh is sends his soldiers over to England to stir up trouble whenever there is the threat of an alliance.

James Franco (*Spider-Man*'s Harry Osborn), speaking with a passable British accent, is the heroic Tristan. He was raised by the benevolent Lord Marke (a regal Rufus Sewell), a fellow proponent of an allied Britain and friend of Tristan's father, who, along with Tristan's mother, died during an Irish siege in front of their young son. Marke more than shows his courtly character when, attempting to save the young Tristan (played by Thomas Sangster) in the fight that claimed the boy's parents, he is struck by one of the Irish and loses a hand. Along with Marke's natural son, Melot (Henry Cavill), Tristan is being groomed to become a warrior at an early age due to the country's constant warmongering. After witnessing the bloody skirmish that caused his parents' death and surrogate father's dismembering, Tristan is understandably reluctant to fight. However, after some schoolyard taunts brand him a coward, Tristan quickly overtakes the supervised bands of brawling children armed with their little wooden swords.

Lord Marke is the leader of one of the British tribes, and the favored Tristan grows up to become his fiercest soldier, much to the neglected Melot's chagrin. Tristan is sent to lead an attack on Donnchadh's men, who are kidnapping and enslaving the British. After a fierce battle, Tristan and his men are victorious, but not before Tristan tangles with a particularly strapping Irish soldier who, before his death, cuts Tristan with his poisoned sword. Thinking him dead, the men send Tristan's body out for the traditional "burial" at sea, which consists of setting him afloat atop a raft of logs.

Still clinging to life, Tristan's body reaches the Irish shore where he is luckily found by the equally comely Isolde (Sophia Myles), King Donnchadh's only daughter. Thankfully, she is practiced in the art of healing herbs and, correctly guessing his poison, covertly nurses the handsome stranger back to health with the help of her disapproving maid, played by Irish actress Bronagh Gallagher (*Pulp Fiction, Mary Reilly*). When he regains consciousness, she lies to Tristan, giving him a fake name and saying she's a commoner while sneaking away from the castle each day to aid him in a small shack by the sea. Despite the fact that Tristan is her sworn enemy and Isolde has been promised to her father's best soldier, Morholt (Graham Mullins), they proceed to fall in love anyway. When Tristan is well enough, Isolde prompts him to return to Britain.

While Isolde is thrilled, scheming Donnchadh is enraged when he hears from the few remaining soldiers returning from Britain that Tristan of Cornwall has slain his best soldier and Isolde's intended in battle (the soldier with the poison sword, in fact). In order to kill two birds with one stone, Donnchadh cooks up a tournament to set the English against one another to win a title, land, and his daughter's hand in marriage. Marke sees through the ruse, knowing it is just another of the Irish's king's ploys to keep them from uniting but all the other factions agree to participate and Tristan volunteers to be Marke's champion.

With a veiled Isolde looking on, Tristan wins the contest, and it is heartbreaking as she excitedly lifts her veil and proclaims, "I'm yours!" Tristan is shocked, realizing that Isolde is his beloved while King Donnchadh corrects her: "No, Tristan has won you on behalf of Lorde Marke." It is all downhill for the lovers from this point on.

Isolde begs him to run off with her, but Tristan, always the dutiful soldier, delivers his true love to his loving Lord, believing it is the only way to save his country. He pines for her, watching and wincing from a distance as she actually begins to look happy with Marke. And why not? Marke is handsome, kind, and more charismatic than the mopey, ineffective person Tristan suddenly devolves into—in any other film she would have fallen for him. Reynolds errs here with his dubious direction of making Tristan out as a total wimp and his casting of the too-young-and-good-looking Sewell.

Tristan perks up a bit when, egged on by the eager Isolde, they begin to meet regularly for secret trysts. An enemy camp susses out what is going on between them and uses the information to bring down Marke and his beloved protege. Marke and his men are out riding when they spy the lovers, and Marke is forced to imprison them both. Tristan gives no excuses, while the more practical Isolde tells Marke of their dilemma: they fell in love long before and without Tristan knowing who she even was. Marke sets them free to go off together. Meanwhile, Melot has finally had it when Marke chooses Tristan as his second over his own son and aids the encroaching enemy seeking to breach Marke's castle with his knowledge of a secret underground passage. Of course, the dutiful and loyal Tristan does not leave with Isolde, but instead remains to fight to the death alongside Marke one last time.

Franco and Myles make a lovely couple and, while Franco is suitably dashing and energetic in his battle scenes, Myles's spark and verve makes her consistently outshine her costar. Sewell and O'Hara give standout performances while Cavill is strong and sympathetic in a smaller role as the neglected son. All are given credible action and dialogue courtesy of screenwriter Dean Gregoris, whose eclectic background includes penning 2004's *Manchurian Candidate,* John Woo's *Paycheck* (2003), and *Lara Croft Tomb Raider: The Cradle of Life* (2003).

Tony Scott (*Top Gun*) produced *Tristan & Isolde*, along with his brother Ridley Scott, who originally sought to make the film himself, but ultimately directed the Academy Award®-winning *Gladiator* (2000) instead. They made a capable choice in Reynolds, director of *Robin Hood: Prince of Thieves* (1991), *Rapa Nui* (1994), *Waterworld* (1995), and *The Count of Monte Cristo* (2002), who is certainly no stranger to period, costume dramas with plenty of action. *Tristan & Isolde* is no exception, and the battle scenes are legitimately exciting. *The Onion*'s Phipps makes another good point, however, when he complains that "Britain and Ireland appear to be home to about three dozen people, and the action scenes all involve the same five characters fighting in close-up." Budget issues aside, those three dozen people, guided by stunt coordinator Nick Powell (*Braveheart*), certainly do a nice job of making the combat realistic and entertaining. As an added bonus, the beautiful, rugged coastlines and windswept exteriors of Ireland and the Czech Republic are expertly captured by cinematographer Arthur Reinhart.

Hilary White

CREDITS

Tristan: James Franco
Isolde: Sophia Myles
Lord Marke: Rufus Sewell
King Donnchadh: David Patrick O'Hara
Wictred: Mark Strong
Melot: Henry Cavill
Bragnae: Bronagh Gallagher
Bodkin: Ronan Vibert
Edyth: Lucy Russell
Young Tristan: Thomas Sangster
Leon: JB Blanc

Morholt: Graham Mulins
Origin: Great Britain, Germany, USA
Language: English
Released: 2006
Production: Lisa Ellzey, Moshe Diamant, Elie Samaha, Giannina Facio; Scott Free, ApolloProMedia, QI Quality Intl., MFF, Stillking; released by 20th Century Fox
Directed by: Kevin Reynolds
Written by: Dean Georgaris
Cinematography by: Arthur Reinhart
Music by: Anne Dudley
Sound: Reinhard Stergar
Editing: Peter Boyle
Art Direction: Johnny Byrne
Costumes: Maurizio Millenotti
Production Design: Mark Geraghty
MPAA rating: PG-13
Running time: 125 minutes

REVIEWS

Boxoffice Online. January 13, 2006.
Chicago Sun-Times Online. January 13, 2006.
Entertainment Weekly Online. January 18, 2006.
Los Angeles Times Online. January 13, 2006.
New York Times Online. January 13, 2006.
Premiere Magazine Online. January 13, 2006.
Variety Online. January 12, 2006.
Washington Post Online. January 13, 2006.

QUOTES

Isolde: "Know that I love you, Tristan. Wherever you go, whatever you see, I'll be there with you."

Tristan: "You were right. Life is greater than death. And love is greater than either."

TRIVIA

Ridley Scott was originally going to direct this film in the late 1970s immediately after his debut film, *The Duellists* (1977). However, he put the film aside to direct *Alien* (1979).

TRISTRAM SHANDY: A COCK AND BULL STORY

Because everyone loves an accurate period piece.
—Movie tagline

He's About To Play The Role Of His Life.
—Movie tagline

Box Office: $1.2 million

Michael Winterbottom is a maverick, offbeat British director who likes to explore the limits of cinematic storytelling (among his numerous films are *24 Hour Party People* [2002] and *Code 46* [2003]). In *Tristram Shandy: A Cock and Bull Story*, he's certainly met his match in the famously eccentric eighteenth-century novel by Laurence Sterne—*The Life and Opinions of Tristram Shandy, Gentleman*—long a favorite of advanced English literature classes but widely considered unfilmable. Winterbottom is determined to prove that judgment right, by making his "adaptation" into something like what was depicted in Spike Jonze's more accessible *Adaptation* (2002)—an exercise in the improbabilities of cinema.

Sterne's novel is a fascinating, comic, and often annoying excursion into mock biography, full of asides, interruptions, and literary cul de sacs. As such, it is, as the lead actor in this movie Steve Coogan calls it, "a postmodern classic written before there was anything modern to be post- about." The most postmodern thing about Sterne's work is that it is self-referential. The lead character, Tristram Shandy, is trying to write his life story but keeps getting interrupted by life itself and by his own curious thoughts.

In the spirit of this novel, Winterbottom presents us with a movie about a movie being made about the character Tristram Shandy. First, we are introduced to the two main actors in the movie—Coogan and Rob Brydon—who squabble constantly throughout the production about who has the bigger role, the best teeth, and the better agent. It is clear from the start, then, that this is a movie about the ego involved in playing a role. At the center of this exercise, which is by turns wickedly satiric, pedantic, and excruciatingly dull, is Coogan, who parlayed a radio character into a comic career in the United Kingdom and also starred in Winterbottom's *24 Hour Party People*. Coogan is funny, but his status as a celebrity is questionable for American audiences; Winterbottom plays off Coogan's character and notoriety in dozens of ways, many of which are inscrutable to those who are not Coogan fans.

At the outset, Coogan tells us he is playing Shandy, but in an early sequence in which Tristram, while a boy, suffers an unfortunate incident involving urination, a nurse, and a broken window sash, Coogan appears to tell us that various child actors are also playing his character, and not well. Coogan also plays Tristram's father, Walter, an odd duck who is forever cataloguing experiences rather than enjoying them. He has ordered his wife to have their child at home, but wants a besotted local doctor to deliver the baby rather than a midwife. The doctor arrives bearing "the latest invention"—a pair of crude forceps.

At some of its better moments, Winterbottom's film toys with a sort of Marx Brothers anarchy—indeed, Groucho Marx is quoted not once, but twice in the film—and the doctor's demonstration of the forceps' power, first on Tristram's Uncle Toby's hand, and then on a cantaloupe, approaches a deadpan filmic Marxism. While Tristram's mother is screaming in the agony of a difficult childbirth, the men are debating finer points of language, logic, and science in the drawing room, but they are all buffoons. The doctor looks nervous and uncertain, and Toby (Brydon) is obsessed with recreating the Battle of Flanders, in which he apparently suffered a most undignified injury from a bomb blast. Twice in the film, when Toby's character is asked where exactly he was wounded, he leads his questioner by the hand, across his miniature battlefield, and replies, "Right here, in this ditch."

After circling in time around the moment of Tristram's birth, Winterbottom's camera pulls back to reveal the film crew making the movie, and the film changes entirely, into something like a less complex and less densely plotted version of David Mamet's *State and Main* (2000). Less funny, too, unfortunately. Whereas the first half-hour of the film focuses on the character Tristram Shandy's inability to come to terms with the circumstances of his own birth—and his attempts to explain the peculiarities of that event as the narrator of the filmic story—the rest of *Tristram Shandy: A Cock and Bull Story* follows Coogan's difficulties in coming to term with his life as a movie star marooned on the set of *Tristram Shandy.*

Coogan's dilemmas beset him for the rest of the evening, as the day's shooting ends with the birth of Tristram still not completed. Coogan, trying to control what is happening to the still-in-progress movie involving his character, is continuously frustrated by demands and circumstances. (It's eventually explained that this is exactly the theme of Sterne's novel: that Tristram, attempting to write his own life story, is constantly interrupted; and that Walter Shandy's efforts to exhaustively chronicle his son's birth, and thus control his progeny's place in the world, is also doomed.) Coogan's girlfriend Jenny (Kelly Macdonald) has flown over from the United States with their infant son in order to spend one night with Coogan. But other predicaments plague Coogan, one of which is his flirtatious relationship with a production assistant named Jennie (Naomie Harris). While he is conflicted emotionally about which woman to bed, Coogan also has to meet with his agent and his agent's assistant, and do an interview with a magazine writer who has been ordered to write a story about Coogan's dalliances with a stripper—but instead might be persuaded to write a fluff piece about how being a father has changed Coogan.

While all this is swirling about him Coogan engages in a comic battle to keep his much-cherished spot as the "leading man" in the farce that *Tristram Shandy* has become. He is fitted into a harness and placed upside down into a giant synthetic womb that's been created for a potential birth scene; he is concerned about whether his shoes make him look sufficiently tall compared to Brydon; and, as the evening wears on, he eventually passes along an idea broached by Jennie that the movie be changed to include a long romantic sequence featuring the Widow Wadman, not realizing it means he has given his co-star a larger role and a chance to play opposite his dream actress, Gillian Anderson, who is recruited to play the part. Meanwhile, a group of battle re-enactors has camped out around the castle where the film crew is headquartered, and there is a debate about whether there should be a battle scene, and if so, how authentic it should be.

All of this creates a film that is a bit reminiscent of Robert Altman—a satirical look inside the set of a movie, where decisions are made on what seem to be whimsy. The protagonist's dilemmas seem to center around his sexual equipment and performance. What results is a movie that is alternately hilarious, ridiculous, and boring. It is a bit obvious too: Jennie, a movie buff, explains the theme in a plot summary of a film about two knights who beat each other up without effect: it's a lot like postmodern life, she says, where everyone is armored with so many characters that people's interactions seem to have no effect.

Winterbottom occasionally gets the interplay between his multiple stories about Coogan's personal and professional life, and his character's story about his own birth, stunningly right. When Coogan argues that it would make Shandy's father more human and sympathetic if he were (contrary to historical verisimilitude) present in the room at his son's birth, we see Coogan retreat to pick up and comfort his own crying baby, and Coogan instantly becomes more sympathetic, and turns out to do the right thing by his fatherhood. It is a wry piece of filmmaking, but Winterbottom too often settles for less than maximum impact. Played as outright farce, *Tristram Shandy* could have been a cult classic, clever and cutting, but the director seems not to care so much about comic impact as he does about proving his story unfilmable. Movie industry insiders may enjoy this effort, while fans of Sterne may be simultaneously enthused and/or outraged—the movie has chosen to essentially riff on the story rather than tell it, and that's probably a wise choice. Mainstream audiences, especially those who are unfamiliar with Coogan or Sterne, will likely find this unwatchable.

In a film about how we distance ourselves from the roles we play in life, Winterbottom's choice is to distance the movie from the audience so much that we stay uninvolved and view this as more of an academic exercise than a filmic experience. Oddly delightful at times, *Tristram Shandy* is mostly just odd, and Winterbottom displays far too much confidence in Coogan's talents as a skit artist to make Coogan believable when his protagonist turns sentimental. If Winterbottom had made this more of a romp, and had put even more obstacles in his lead actor's way, it would have worked better as entertainment; instead, it falls short of its promise.

Michael Betzold

CREDITS

Tristram Shandy, Walter Shandy, "Steve Coogan": Steve Coogan
Toby Shandy, "Rob Brydon": Rob Brydon
Elizabeth Shandy, "Keeley Hawes": Keeley Hawes
Susannah, "Shirley Henderson": Shirley Henderson
Dr. Slop, "Dylan Moran": Dylan Moran
Mark: Jeremy Northam
Jennie: Naomie Harris
Jenny: Kelly Macdonald
Debbie: Elizabeth Berrington
Ingoldsby: Mark Williams
Simon: James Fleet
Joe: Ian Hart
Gary: Kieran O'Brien
Patrick Curator, Parson Yorick: Stephen Fry
Widow Wadman, "Gillian Anderson": Gillian Anderson
Parson: David Walliams
TV Interviewer: Anthony H. Wilson
Origin: Great Britain
Language: English
Released: 2005
Production: Andrew Eaton; BBC Films, Revolution Films, Scion Films, EM Media, Baby Cow Productions; released by Picturehouse
Directed by: Michael Winterbottom
Written by: Martin Hardy
Cinematography by: Marcel Zyskind
Music by: Michael Nyman, Erik Nordgren, Nino Rota
Sound: Stuart Wilson
Editing: Peter Christelis
Art Direction: Emma MacDevitt
Costumes: Charlotte Walter
Production Design: John Paul Kelly
MPAA rating: R
Running time: 91 minutes

REVIEWS

Boxoffice Online. January 27, 2006.
Chicago Sun-Times Online. February 17, 2006.
Entertainment Weekly Online. January 25, 2006.
Los Angeles Times Online. February 10, 2006.
New York Times Online. January 27, 2006.
Variety Online. September 18, 2005.
Washington Post Online. February 17, 2006, p. C01.

QUOTES

Steve Coogan: "*Tristram Shandy,* it was actually number eight in the top one hundred books of all time."
Tony Wilson: "That was a chronological list."

TRIVIA

The screenplay was credited to one Martin Hardy, which is actually a pseudonym for the real screenwriter Frank Cottrell Boyce.

TRUST THE MAN

Love is a four-letter word.
—Movie tagline

Box Office: $1.5 million

Trust the Man is writer/director Bart Freundlich's take on that favorite Woody Allen genre, the upscale New York romantic comedy. Unfortunately, as most critics noted, the comparison to Allen ends there, although Freundlich's talkfest is certainly populated with a lot of restless, unfulfilled artist-types looking for a purpose in life and extra-curricular sex. While his family dramedy *The Myth of Fingerprints* (1997) managed to cause a stir at Sundance, it didn't translate into box office, with his latest effort following suit, recouping a mere $1.5 million of its $10 million budget.

The metaphorical opening scene sets the stage. "I'm trying to poop, but I can't." says little David (Liam Broggy). It turns out he's no different than the rest of the ineffectual men in this film, including his father Tom (David Duchovny), a discontented, sex-addicted stay-at-home dad, and Tobey (Billy Crudup), a sportswriter who doesn't do much of anything. Tom's wife is Rebecca (Freundlich's real-life wife Julianne Moore), a successful film actress making her stage debut at Lincoln Center, while Tobey's girlfriend of seven years, Elaine (Maggie Gyllenhaal), is an aspiring children's book author who wants to have children before it's too late. Rebecca and Tobey are brother and sister, and the couples are best friends. The inherent drama in the situation is painfully clear and all but ignored by the director, who prefers glib dialogue and trite situations to tell his story.

It doesn't help that Freundlich enlists Garry Shandling as Tom and Rebecca's marriage counselor Dr. Beekman, whom they visit once a year, thus making the whole situation as patently cute as the rest of the script.

While the apparently frigid Rebecca urbanely recounts Tom's "sex mania," wanting it twice a day, and blithely references his porn collection, Tom goes out and gets some on the side with a divorced hottie from David's preschool. Meanwhile, Rebecca is chased by her young costar, Jasper (Justin Bartha), who just wants to brag about sleeping with a world-famous actress.

In a perpetual state of arrested development, Tobey spends his days obsessing about his car, primo parking spot, and engaged ex-girlfriend Faith (Eva Mendes), while avoinding committing to starting a family with Elaine. Not surprisingly, Tobey is also in therapy and is so neurotic, he actually stalks his therapist (Bob Balaban).

While Tobey is charming and funny—presumably the reason Elaine has put up with him for so long—a finally fed-up Elaine decides to find a more suitable partner, beginning with a European caricature with a groan-inducing accent that resembles, as *The Onion*'s Scott Tobias noted, "a character on *Sprockets.*" Tobey counters by carrying on an affair with the now-married Faith. Freundlich even employs Ellen Barkin as lesbian children's book publisher Norah who is turned on by Elaine's sexy author photo in yet another fluffy bit of sexy fun. Elaine also finds comfort in the arms of refreshingly honest coffeehouse musician Dante (James Le Gros).

The hokey final scene has Freundlich inexplicably reuniting the hapless couples in the most public manner possible at Lincoln Center, and forcing his equally hapless actors into the Lincoln Center equivalent of screwball comedy.

Crudup fares better than the rest of his castmates, as his more likeably loathsome character delivers most of the script's best lines. The usually dramatic actor shows a wonderful and as-yet-underutilized talent for comedy. Duchovny and Moore are thoroughly believable as the bickering couple, but have little meat to sink their acting chops into, while Gyllenhaal gamely tries to rise above the middling material. Freundlich's New York is charmingly glossy, to the point of being precious. In fact, as *The Onion*'s Tobias also noted, Freundlich seems to have cornered the market on taking a low-budget indie and somehow making it look and feel just as vapid and soulless as most big-budget Hollywood romantic comedies.

The *Los Angeles Times*' Carina Chocano called the film "bizarrely off-key" with *Variety*'s John Anderson wryly noting that "the closing scenes of *Trust the Man* are so contrived and madcap, the viewer fully expects someone to start throwing pies. That they don't is a disappointment, all things considered."

Hilary White

CREDITS

Rebecca: Julianne Moore
Tom: David Duchovny
Tobey: Billy Crudup
Elaine: Maggie Gyllenhaal
Dr. Beekman: Garry Shandling
Faith: Eva Mendes
Norah: Ellen Barkin
Dante: James LeGros
David: Liam Broggy
Pamela: Dagmara Dominczyk
Jasper: Justin Bartha
Origin: USA
Language: English
Released: 2006
Production: Tim Perell, Sidney Kimmel, Bart Freundlich; Fox Searchlight Pictures, Process Prods.; released by 20th Century Fox
Directed by: Bart Freundlich
Written by: Bart Freundlich
Cinematography by: Tim Orr
Music by: Clint Mansell
Sound: William Sarokin
Music Supervisor: Daniel Wise
Editing: James Gilroy
Art Direction: John Mymarkay
Costumes: Michael Clancy
Production Design: Kevin Thompson
MPAA rating: R
Running time: 103 minutes

REVIEWS

Boxoffice Online. August 18, 2006.
Chicago Sun-Times Online. August 18, 2006.
Entertainment Weekly Online. August 25, 2006.
Los Angeles Times Online. August 18, 2006.
New York Times Online. August 18, 2006.
San Francisco Chronicle. August 18, 2006, p. E5.
Variety Online. August 14, 2006.
Village Voice Online. August 15, 2006.
Washington Post. August 18, 2006, p. C5.

TRIVIA

The children of Tom and Rebecca are played by the real-life offspring of Julianne Moore and Bart Freundlich.

TSOTSI

Hope Set Him Free.
—Movie tagline

In this world...redemption just comes once.
—Movie tagline

Box Office: $2.9 million

The global intertextuality of cinematic social realism in our time once again asserts itself in Gavin Hood's Oscar®-winning gritty fable from South Africa, *Tsotsi.* Set in the shanty towns that accompany urban development and comprise the underbelly of progress, Hood's debut feature takes a Christian belief and recontextualizes it to create a hero for our times. Here, it is not sinning that can lead to sainthood as much as a sense of revolt. In so doing, *Tsotsi* evokes its compatriots in similar memorable struggles, from Hector Babenco's *Pixote* (1980) to Mira Nair's *Salaam, Bombay!* (1988) to Fernando Meirelles's *City of God* (2002).

In relation to his cinematic brethren, however, Tsotsi (Presley Chweneyagae), as the leader of a violent youth gang, emerges as wiser and more mature. As a result that Hood's effort is nowhere as sensational as its antecedents, but stands to rival them in the way it juxtaposes beauty and squalor, a cinematic tradition that stretches all the way back to Marcel Camus's *Black Orpheus* (1958), set in the shanties above Rio. All Hood's film lacks, it would seem, is an overt political dimension related to post-apartheid South Africa built into its plot. Instead, the film locates Tsotsi's plight as an internal conflict, which in turn allows its narrative, based on a novel by Nobel Prize-winning author Athol Fugard, to keep on the safe side of a universal parable.

The film opens by juxtaposing two male preoccupations the world over: power and gambling. The dice, wielded by unseen members of Tsotsi's gang, are shown in slow motion as the main title fill the screen. It is only when the camera pulls back that we see Aap (Kenneth Nkosi), also known as Fatso, the spectacled Boston (Mothusi Magano), and the malevolent Butcher (Zenzo Ngqobe), their eyes fixed on the dice while Tsotsi stands watch outside. The exterior of shanties shot at twilight bestows an ethereality upon the dirt and despair as Tsotsi strides with his gang, raising his middle finger to the rest of the world.

We soon see that the gang's command over the alleyways of the shanty town also extends into a sense of power they feel in the big city. Tsotsi and his gang follow a fat businessman onto a crowded train, then surround him. The victim smiles smugly, until Butcher takes out an ice pick and silently stabs the man to death while Tsotsi takes his money. When the carriage empties, the man is shown lying on the floor.

This crime serves to put Tsotsi into relief against the others of his gang. He begins to come into his own before our eyes. That night, at the gang hangout, Boston, who cannot handle the guilt of what Tsotsi has done, stabs himself in the arm in atonement. Envious of Tsotsi's cool, Boston questions him about his real name, since "Tsotsi" is the South African appellative for thug. Tsotsi remains silent, presumably not wanting to reveal the names of his parents. But Boston will not let the matter rest. He calls Tsotsi someone without a mother or father, in effect "a dog." Tsotsi erupts in rage, knocks Boston down, and pummels him with blows. He then runs off, across a dark field, the incessant beat of the African music on the soundtrack affirming his ethnic identity.

We come to know of Tsotsi's past when his run is intercut with that of a much younger Tsotsi, thereby giving the impression that he has been running all his life. A later flashback will make this clear. Now, as Tsotsi shivers in the pouring rain, we see Little Tsotsi shivering inside an abandoned steel drainpipe, along with other homeless children. He may look as helpless as them, except the audience knows that he is headed for bigger things.

In the film's present, as a car stops outside an elite bungalow, Tsotsi ends up shooting the lone female driver in the legs. Pumla (Nambitha Mpumlwana), a housewife, collapses in the middle of the road as Tsotsi drives off in her car. It is only when he hears a baby crying in the back seat that he careens to a stop, not knowing his life will change irrevocably. Unable to abandon the baby along with the car, Tsotsi packs the baby's food and a blanket into a shopping bag and starts off downhill. Curiously, the baby falls silent, as if accepting Tsotsi as a parent.

The film now sets out to contrast this new phase in Tsotsi's life—his kindness and sense of responsibility towards the baby—with his life as a gang member. In the process, it loses the raw energy and dramatic steam hitherto generated in favor of the social comedy arising from Tsotsi having to play mother.

At the opposite end of the power spectrum, the film introduces us to Police Captain Smit (Ian Roberts), a white holdover from the colonialist regime, cursing beside the car Tsotsi abandoned, as he looks out over the shanties. It is clear who has the upper hand in this equation, since according to Smit, it is impossible to track anyone down in that pit of squalor.

To reinforce this irony, the film cuts to the interior of Tsotsi's hut. We find a small TV and even an amplifier, powered by a car battery, no doubt typical of Third World poverty. Tsotsi looks repelled as he changes the baby's diapers. When Butcher and Aap come calling, they too are assaulted by the stink of the baby's excrement, though Tsotsi doesn't tell them it is from inside his hut. Nothing could contrast more with Tsotsi's world than that of the elite Pumla, recovering in her hospital bed, as Smit and his men explain to her: "There are a million people in those shanties!" John (Rapulana

Seiphemo), the baby's father, wants the baby found, come what may.

Weakening its already depleted dramatic thrust, the film now broadens its focus, no doubt to accommodate more social realism. Three subplots emerge, none able to rival the main story in dramatic intensity.

The first concerns the defiant lame Beggar (Jerry Mofokeng). Tsotsi stumbles over his wheelchair at the train station, whereupon the Beggar spits at his feet. Tsotsi in turn follows him to an underpass. In the background, we glimpse a wall splattered with graffiti, indicative of independent South Africa taking to the futility of western-style street protest. Tsotsi at first believes the Beggar is feigning his disability and so, shows him a gun to force him to stand up. When he learns that the Beggar lost the use of his feet while working in the mines, Tsotsi is forgiving. This foreshadows the compassion in Tsotsi and, more importantly, situates it within a socio-economic context. During his phase of atonement, Tsotsi will return to hunt the Beggar down and even kneel before him.

The second subplot concerns Miriam (Terry Pheto), an attractive single mother living by herself in the shanties, who makes a living from making glass ornaments. Tsotsi uses her as a midwife, and is nearly tempted to leave the baby with her, securing visiting rights for himself, but then changes his mind at the last minute.

The third subplot focuses on gang rivalry as Fela (Zola), a gang leader tries to get Tsotsi's gang to work for him. Tsotsi refuses, while the quick-tempered Butcher chases Fela away with an ice pick. Tsotsi eventually sets Aap free to join Fela.

Excitement returns as the film's narrative gets back onto its main track when Tsotsi and his gang stalk Pumla's house to get money for Boston to complete his education. When John drives up, Tsotsi puts a gun to his head and gets him to turn off the electronic alarm. This allows the gang to enter the house and tie John to a chair. Aap then disconnects the phone. As Tsotsi looks at the baby's nursery, it seems to evoke for him the life of love and comfort he never had. An earlier flashback has shown Little Tsotsi running from the rage of a drunken father. Now, as if to remind him of where he stands in relation to this elite domesticity, the scene around him explodes into sudden violence. Tsotsi himself contributes to it, as if it were a conditioned reflex ingrained in him. Butcher finds a handgun in a drawer. As Tsotsi is filling up the baby's bottle from a can of milk, John sets off the alarm in his key chain. Butcher is about to shoot John when Tsotsi shoots Butcher dead, then makes a getaway with Aap in John's car, which he later sells to Fela's chop shop. The police arrive at the house too late.

When Tsotsi learns from Miriam, who has found out from the newspapers, that Pumla has lost both her legs, Tsotsi is grief-stricken by the guilt. His life now becomes driven by an inner urge to atone. This brings him closer to the wounded Boston, to whom he offers refuge and a gun. Racked by an inner conflict as to whether or not to keep the baby, Tsotsi follows Miriam's advice and decides to return the baby to its mother, in exchange for which Miriam tacitly agrees to allow him to see her.

We then see Tsotsi, alone, outside the gate of the house, speaking to John on the intercom to tell him he is leaving the baby there in a duffel bag. This time, however, he is spotted by a police deputy. As the sirens close in, Tsotsi is trapped, but Pumla's wails to save her baby result in a standoff. When John pleads with the police, Smit orders them to lower their weapons. Speechless and in tears, Tsotsi hands the baby over to its father, then dutifully obeys the command to raise his hands over his head.

Lit from behind, the young rebel, from a newly emergent Africa, looks almost Christ-like, his virtuous qualities having redeemed his brutal sins. Or so the film would no doubt have us believe, itself having veered from becoming a film noir of post-colonialist despair into a sentimental, but hopeful, plea for the human heart to rise above the rage borne out of social injustice.

Vivek Adarkar

CREDITS

Aap: Kenneth Nkosi
Butcher: Zenzo Ngqobe
Tsotsi: Presley Chweneyagae
Miriam: Terry Pheto
Boston: Mothusi Magano
Tsotsi's father: Israel Makoe
Sgt. Zuma: Percy Matsemela
Young Tsotsi: Benny Moshe
Pumla C.: Nambitha Mpumlwana
John: Rapulana Seiphemo
Captain Smit: Ian Roberts
Beggar: Jerry Mofokeng
Origin: Great Britain, South Africa
Language: Afrikaans
Released: 2005
Production: Peter Fudakowski; U.K. Film and TV Productin Co., Industrial Development Corp., National Film and Video Foundation, Moviworld
Directed by: Gavin Hood
Written by: Gavin Hood

Cinematography by: Lance Gewer
Music by: Mark Kilian, Paul Hepker
Sound: Shaun Murdoch
Editing: Megan Gill
Art Direction: Mark Walker
Costumes: Nadia Kruger, Pierre Vienings
Production Design: Emelia Weavind
MPAA rating: R
Running time: 94 minutes

REVIEWS

Boxoffice Online. February 24, 2006.
Chicago Sun-Times Online. March 10, 2006.
Entertainment Weekly Online. February 22, 2006.
Los Angeles Times Online. February 24, 2006.
New York Times Online. February 24, 2006.
Premiere Magazine Online. February 24, 2006.
Variety Online. August 23, 2005.
Washington Post Online. March 10, 2006.

TRIVIA

"Tsotsi" loosely translates to "thug" in the urban slang of Johannesburg.

AWARDS

Oscars 2005: Foreign Film

Nomination:

British Acad. 2005: Foreign Film
Golden Globes 2006: Foreign Film

TURISTAS

Go Home.
—Movie tagline

Box Office: $7 million

John Stockwell's cinematically highbrow slasher film, *Turistas*, violates a cardinal principle of the subgenre it wishes to cash in on: it justifies its generic staples by appealing to the viewer's intelligence, thereby trying to appear convincing, for the most part. This proves a big mistake, in the context of the recent successes of senseless mutilation scarefests, such as *Saw III* (2006).

Of course the film that *Turistas* seeks to emulate is Eli Roth's *Hostel* (2005), whose horror grew out of the traps awaiting cut-rate American tourists in the remote reaches of Eastern Europe. On the face of it, one can speculate that if Stockwell had merely combined Roth's recipe with his own gritty on-location work in the jungles of Brazil, he might have ended up with a horrific version of Robert Zemeckis's *Romancing the Stone* (1984). Instead, Stockwell gravitates to the mutilation table after such a lengthy build-up that the little demonic surgery he does show appears absurdly out of place. Thus, in view of the kind of indulgence this subgenre has profited from, Stockwell's film falls between two stools, or to be more precise, between two scalpels, which could explain the film's miserable box office performance.

To make up for the menace it tries to generate in its first half, the film opens with a scene of one of its female leads on an operating table pleading for her life. This scene shamelessly functions as a kind of teaser trailer for the film itself, assuring the viewer that good things are worth waiting for. Not that the wait here isn't entertaining. The film's fresh crop of young faces, though playing stereotypes, in the midst of a forbiddingly savage terrain hold out the promise of an exotic horror film, if nothing else. There's the sinewy Alex (Josh Duhamel), who is traveling with his darkly attractive sister, Bea (Olivia Wilde) and her blond girlfriend, Amy (Beau Garrett). There's the sardonic Brit, Finn (Desmond Askew) and his buddy, Liam (Max Brown). And as if from a world apart, there's the beautiful Australian Pru (Melissa George), an exogamous world traveler with blond dreadlocks, fresh from a jaunt in Cambodia. There are others, but these six form the group we become most concerned about, largely because they remain a likeable lot.

The first blow to their plans comes when their bus veers off a hill road, giving everyone a chance to scramble out before it rolls down a precipice and breaks apart. When Bea starts taking snapshots of the natives, they become violently paranoid. This is because their kids are being abducted and scavenged for body parts, which are then sold to Americans. Unable to wait in the sun for the next bus, which is ten hours away, our group, proceeding on hearsay, decides to follow a path through the jungle and discover a beach complete with a cafe.

The film shows them enjoying the ideal tropical life, dancing suggestively with the dark-skinned Romeos and sirens to hot rhythms at night. Finn even manages to get it on inside a shack with a lovely local who reveals herself to be a hooker. The second blow comes when they wake up at dawn the next day to find that they were drugged and all their passports, money, and valuables have been stolen. At this point, Kiko (Agles Steib), a lovable long-haired native beachcomber, who leads them to the nearest town. On the way, he shows them scenic lagoons and idyllic waterfalls. For a horror film, nature seems to be bending over backwards to provide the four with touristy memories. In the town, however, urchins start throwing stones at them until

Kiko presses on them the need to get away from a place that has no police station.

For a while the six get lost in the jungle after trekking for ten hours, or so it feels like to Finn. Kiko however comes through and leads them to a house in the middle of nowhere. This is the retreat of the evil Dr. Zamora (Miguel Lunardi) who is away with his men hunting for the group. Alex explores the estate to find all manner of surgical implements, a sheaf of passports belonging to western tourists, and most important, a gun. Pru on her part uncovers a stash of medicines, which she uses to treat Kiko, who was earlier wounded in a jump from a high rock. Bea finds cans of food with which she feeds the animals kept in cages. That night the group enjoys a civilized dinner around a dinner table.

It is when the others are asleep and Alex is looking at images on a bank of TV sets that Zamora and his men return in his helicopter. A female assistant tells Alex and the group to run. But it's too late, as anyone would have imagined. Pru is grabbed, Alex is attacked and both are bound. Amy finds herself under the bright lamp of an operating table, which is how the film opened.

Zamora's surgical skills now hold sway as he cuts open Amy, while pointing out how one has to wait seven years for a healthy kidney in the States. So, when rich gringos need one, Zamora's operation is ready to oblige. But with American tourists, Zamora feels infused with a historical purpose: "You've taken our land, our gold...I have had enough! It has been your greed and our weakness. Now I want to even the scales, so you can give back. Your livers and kidneys are going to a hospital in Rio." It is an intelligent observation that the film merely touches upon, instead of exploiting this ideological edge over its generic rivals.

As if having delivered the goods, the film now rushes headlong towards the predictable escape of the survivors, much as a classical western would towards the climactic gunfight. Pru fights off her attacker with her feet as Alex hacks him from behind. Alex is able to save Finn but not Amy. The group sets off the way they came, through the jungle and into the grotto. Zamora pursues them, instructing his men that the group has to be taken alive. Seeing no value in Kiko's organs, however, he is shot dead. The climax takes place in an underwater cavern as Alex bludgeons Zamora, who then instructs his man to shoot Alex. At this point Pru intervenes by using her knowledge of Portugese. After her pleading, the man shoots Zamora instead. In the final scene, as Alex and a saddened Bea are waiting to get onto a copter, they overhear a couple behind them debating whether to take the bus or the plane. Quips Alex: "Take the plane."

Vivek Adarkar

CREDITS

Alex: Josh Duhamel
Pru: Melissa George
Bea: Olivia Wilde
Finn: Desmond Askew
Amy: Beau Garrett
Liam: Max Brown
Kiko: Agles Steib
Dr. Zamora: Miguel Lunardi
Origin: USA
Language: English
Released: 2006
Production: Scott Steindorff, Marc Butan, Bo Zenga, John Stockwell; 2929 Productions, Stone Village, Boz Productions; released by Fox Atomic
Directed by: John Stockwell
Written by: Michael Arlen Ross
Cinematography by: Enrique Chediak
Music by: Paul Haslinger
Sound: Jonathan Miller
Music Supervisor: David Falzone
Editing: Jeff McEvoy
Art Direction: Cecia Richters
Production Design: Marlise Storchi
MPAA rating: R
Running time: 89 minutes

REVIEWS

Boxoffice Online. December 1, 2006.
Entertainment Weekly. December 8, 2006, p. 58.
Hollywood Reporter Online. December 1, 2006.
Los Angeles Times Online. December 1, 2006.
New York Times Online. December 1, 2006.
San Francisco Chronicle. December 1, 2006, p. E5.
Variety Online. November 30, 2006.
Washington Post. December 1, 2006, p. C5.

U

ULTRAVIOLET

The Blood War Is On.
—Movie tagline

Box Office: $18.5 million

Ultraviolet begins with the main character warning that she was "born into a world you may not understand." While this foretells a mystifying film, there is in fact very little that requires explanation as this has been seen several times before and to greater affect. Writer/director Kurt Wimmer is perhaps better known for his screenwriting credits (*The Recruit* [2003] and *The Thomas Crown Affair* [1999]) than for his directing (which includes the 2002 science-fiction adventure *Equilibrium*). In *Ultraviolet* he blends the worlds of anime and video games and produces a very unsatisfying homage to and rip-off of films like *The Matrix* (1999), *Underworld* (2003), *The Fifth Element* (1997), and *Resident Evil* (2002).

In the mid-twenty-first century, a botched genetic experiment designed to create a super-soldier spawns a virus that turns a sizable portion of the planet's population into beings called "hemophages." These "infected" humans are blessed with heightened speed and reflexes but suffer from light sensitivity and a physiological need for blood plasma, as well as a shortened lifespan. To add to their woes, a tyrannically fascist government is systematically eradicating the vampire-like hemophages for fear of their growing numbers. Violet (Milla Jovovich) is an especially violent and dangerous hemophage with a limited chameleon-like ability to alter her appearance at will (in the form of clothes, hair, etc.). She can also handle guns and swords quite deftly and is a formidable fighter, using an amalgam of several martial arts styles. While working for the hemophage resistance, she is charged with stealing the government's new anti-hemophage weapon. Unfortunately, Violet learns that this "weapon" is actually a genetically engineered ten-year-old boy named Six (Cameron Bright) and her dormant maternal instincts take over. She now must not only protect the boy from the government who created him but also from her own kind, who would simply execute him as an enemy.

Jovovich does a competent job as Violet, though it seems that these video-game heroine/vixen roles aren't too emotionally taxing for her anymore. Other characters, such as the naive, confused, lost boy Six; the over-the-top villain and architect of the war against the hemophages, Daxus (Nick Chinlund); and the platonic sidekick who apparently wants more from his relationship with Violet, Garth (William Fichtner), never develop beyond their stock behavior (although Daxus's real motivation is suddenly revealed at the end of the film during an incongruous sword fight with Violet wherein all the lights are extinguished and the swords are inexplicably lit on fire).

Violet's voiceover narration propels the film's plot, which exists solely to get her from fight scene to fight scene, from outfit to outfit, and from hair color to hair color. There is little emphasis on story or characterization other than the recycled situations and stock characters lifted from other films. This shouldn't necessarily mean that a film is destined to fail. In fact, *Resident Evil* (2002) proved that it was possible to have a predictable plot and cookie-cutter characters yet still produce quality pulp-entertainment. That film was successful because the filmmakers embraced the idiom they were working in and shied away from trying to create the next *Matrix*. *Ultraviolet* aspires to be much better than it is and suffers for it. It follows a typical boilerplate for comic book action films. There is nothing extraordinary about the film; it is derivative of others in the genre. It could possibly have been a slicker genre picture had the characters been more developed or had the story been less formulaic, or even if it were less "serious" and a bit more fun. But, as Jeannette Catsoulis noted in the *New York Times*, "none of this really matters, as Mr. Wimmer is more concerned with fetishizing his heroine and patronizing his audience."

Despite its shortcomings, *Ultraviolet* does feature a few striking fight sequences. Stunt coordinator Mike Smith trained extensively with Jovovich to prepare her for these impressively choreographed scenes. Their work is rather exciting when the movie begins, but, as Peter Hartlaub points out in the *San Francisco Chronicle*, "after a few fun scenes in the first fifteen minutes, the action becomes unoriginal. It seems like half the battles consist of five to fifty henchmen surrounding Violet, who dispatches them instantly with one swing of her sword or a few bursts of gunfire." Despite the mounting tedium, the film's pacing remains rather brisk. This thankfully allows for the bridges between action sequences to pass quickly.

While director of photography Arthur Wong Ngok Tai does manage to give production designer Choo Sung Pong's landscape an acceptable futuristic look, the film is unemotional and rather dull. As Robert Koehler writes in *Variety*, the film is "hermetically sealed in a synthetic wrapping that's so total—Sony's top-flight high-def cameras, visibly low-budget CG work, exceptionally hackneyed and imitative action and dialogue—that it arrives a nearly lifeless film."

According to writer/director Wimmer, *Ultraviolet* was inspired by the John Cassavetes film *Gloria* (1980) and then adapted to the world of comic book adventures. (The plot of the Cassavetes film follows a woman who takes it upon herself to protect a child from the mafia.) While that film was an adept character study, *Ultraviolet* is ultimately just another entry in the endless parade of uninspired, unoriginal, and unenjoyable comic-book films. The studio reportedly removed thirty minutes from Wimmer's original cut of the film, which purportedly emphasized character over action, but it is hard to imagine that the additional footage could have made any real difference.

Michael J. Tyrkus

CREDITS

Violet: Milla Jovovich
Six: Cameron Bright
Daxus: Nicholas Chinlund
Garth: William Fichtner
Nerva: Sebastien Andrieu
Origin: USA
Language: English
Released: 2006
Production: John Baldecchi; Screen Gems; released by Sony Pictures Entertainment
Directed by: Kurt Wimmer
Written by: Kurt Wimmer
Cinematography by: Arthur Wong Ngok Tai
Music by: Klaus Badelt
Sound: Bob Clayton
Editing: William Yeh
Art Direction: Joel Chong
Costumes: Joseph Porro
Production Design: Choo Sung-pong
MPAA rating: PG-13
Running time: 89 minutes

REVIEWS

Boxoffice Online. March 3, 2006.
Entertainment Weekly. March 8, 2006.
Los Angeles Times Online. March 6, 2006.
Premiere Magazine Online. March 3, 2006.
Variety. March 3, 2006.
Hollywood Reporter. March 6, 2006.
New York Times. March 4, 2006.
San Francisco Chronicle. March 6, 2006.

QUOTES

Violet: "Hi. My name is Violet. And I was born in a world you may not understand."

TRIVIA

Milla Jovovich's character uses a more authentic variant of "Gun Kata," a blend of gunfighting and martial arts developed by director Kurt Wimmer.

UNACCOMPANIED MINORS

Silent night... yeah, right.
—Movie tagline

Six kids, snowbound in an airport on Christmas Eve, without supervision. Someone please call security.
—Movie tagline

Box Office: $16.6 million

The target audience for Paul Feig's kid-friendly *Unaccompanied Minors* is most likely unaware of its origins. It was inspired by a segment by Susan Burton for an episode of Chicago Public Radio's *This American Life* called "Babysitting," which aired in 2001. This short piece, however, which is a bittersweet reflection on children of divorce being stranded in the airport the day after Christmas, bears little resemblance to the movie, which is not much more than a hodgepodge of stale slapstick, tiresome chases, and seemingly endless scenes of kids running amok.

The true inspiration for this movie seems to be two popular movies penned by John Hughes, *The Breakfast Club* (1985) and *Home Alone* (1990). But, whereas those popular entertainments have solid screenplays and likeable characters, the script for *Unaccompanied Minors* includes stock characters, very little plot, and silly montages to cover for the lack of a compelling story. Credited to Jacob Meszaros and Mya Stark, the screenplay focuses on several children thrown together during a blizzard at a Midwestern airport on Christmas Eve. Spencer Davenport (Dyllan Christopher) is flying with his sister, Katie (Dominique Saldana), to see their father for Christmas. (The whole notion of being an "unaccompanied minor" because of divorce and shuttling back and forth between parents is the theme of the radio program and is touched on briefly in the film via the Davenport siblings.) But when Spencer busts out of the holding area, he is separated from Katie and finds himself with some other semi-delinquents, each representing a different social group and unique set of personality quirks: Grace Conrad (Gina Mantegna), the pretty, rich, and snobby girl Spencer is immediately smitten with; Charlie Goldfinch (Tyler James Williams), a natural entertainer who spontaneously sings karaoke and just happens to be both black and Jewish; Timothy Wellington (Brett Kelly), better known as "Beef," a lonely, heavy boy who clings to his Aquaman action figure as if it were a security blanket; and Donna Malone (Quinn Shephard), a poor girl who so hates to be touched that she reflexively punches anyone who does so. Their adversary is Oliver Porter (Lewis Black), the disgruntled authority figure who hates Christmas (we eventually learn that he is bitter because his wife left him five Christmases ago) and is angrier this year because the blizzard prevented him from taking his Hawaiian vacation. His assistant is Zach Van Bourke (Wilmer Valderrama), who has a soft spot for the kids and clearly does not like being a disciplinarian.

The only engine driving the kids' antics is their quest to get to the nearby lodge (where the well-behaved unaccompanied minors get to stay) so that Spencer can deliver Katie's Christmas present and thus ensure that her faith in Santa will not be shattered. Meanwhile, Katie is virtually a prisoner of a bully named Mary Lynn (Michelle Sandler), a bratty girl who makes up Katie like a hideous human doll. The other subplots do not add up to much. Spencer and Katie's dad, Sam (Rob Corddry), makes the long drive to retrieve them but runs into so many obstacles because he is an environmental nut whose car, powered by biodiesel fuel, is not up to the task. Their mother, Val (Paget Brewster), bides her time with her wacky sister, Judy (an uncredited Teri Garr), a Christmas fanatic whose house and lawn are ridiculously overdecorated.

The half-baked screenplay has the kids run wild through the various parts of the airport while the perpetually irritated Oliver obsesses over catching them. Beef separates from the group to go on a quest for a Christmas tree, but the others goof off, elude the authorities, and gradually set their differences aside to work together. Unfortunately, the comic routines, such as Charlie hiding in a piece of luggage and being buffeted every which way along a conveyor belt, are not especially funny. In the unclaimed luggage area, the kids have a blast scavenging through bags, playing with what they find, and dancing with each other. The once snooty Grace shows that she really has a heart and starts to fall for Spencer, and tomboyish Donna bonds with Charlie. But the characters do not develop any genuine connections other than their battle with a common enemy, and the eventual couplings at the end feel forced, a shadow of the poignant moments that conclude *The Breakfast Club*.

Indeed, as relentless slapstick and action get in the way of the relationships, *Unaccompanied Minors* proves that John Hughes's talent for getting to the heart of adolescent and preadolescent characters is not easily duplicated. The kids triumphantly use a canoe to slide down a snow-covered hill to get the gift to Katie. Afterwards, they are caught by Oliver, who locks them up, but they stage yet another escape and blunder into the airport's decorations room.

Despite the redundancy of the plot, the movie works its way to a sweet, warmhearted ending that actually would be enjoyable if it were earned and the character changes were credible. Beef brings in a huge tree—presumably he has traded Aquaman in a nonsensical deal that is probably meant to suggest that he has matured—and the kids proceed to adorn the airport with all the holiday decorations that Oliver left in storage. So transformative is the kids' magic, moreover, that Oliver himself has a change of heart and, in a completely unbelievable finale, dons a Santa suit and distributes gifts to the stranded passengers.

While *Unaccompanied Minors* fails with its script, the young actors are fairly likable and do the best they can with the obvious material and the stereotypical characters they are playing. But Black's villainous foil wears out his welcome, and Valderrama seems like he is caught in the middle just looking flummoxed. As silly as her character is, it might have been fun to see more of Garr's crazy Christmas lady.

There is a thoughtful idea behind *Unaccompanied Minors*—the effect of divorce on children's Christmas celebrations—but very little imagination behind the execution, leaving not only the characters stranded at the airport but the actors as well with very little to do that is comical or moving. The movie has been derisively called "*Home Alone* in an airport," but it should be remembered that that film does not work on slapstick alone; it charms audiences with the emotion behind not only the fear and wonder of being left alone but also the small miracle of connecting with another human being. The absurdity is grounded in something real, which *Unaccompanied Minors* does not try to summon until the end, by which time it is too late.

Peter N. Chumo II

CREDITS

Timothy "Beef" Wellington: Brett Kelly
Oliver Porter: Lewis Black
Zach Van Bourke: Wilmer Valderrama
Valerie: Paget Brewster
Charlie: Tyler James Williams
Spencer: Dyllan Christopher
Grace: Gina Mantegna
Donna: Quinn Shephard
Katie: Dominique Saldana
Cindi: Jessica Walter
Ernie: David Koechner
Sam: Rob Corddry
Judy: Teri Garr
Mary Lynn: Michelle Sandler
Origin: USA
Language: English
Released: 2006
Production: Lauren Shuler Donner, Michael Aguilar; Village Roadshow Pictures; released by Warner Bros.
Directed by: Paul Feig
Written by: Jacob Meszaros, Mya Stark
Cinematography by: Christopher Baffa
Music by: Michael Andrews
Sound: Christopher Aud
Music Supervisor: Jennifer Hawks
Editing: George Folsey Jr., Brad E. White
Art Direction: Erin Cochran
Costumes: Lisa Tomczeszyn
Production Design: Aaron Osborne
MPAA rating: PG
Running time: 87 minutes

REVIEWS

Chicago Sun-Times Online. December 8, 2006.
Entertainment Weekly. December 15, 2006, p. 70.
Hollywood Reporter Online. December 3, 2006.
Los Angeles Times Online. December 8, 2006.
New York Times Online. December 8, 2006.
San Francisco Chronicle. December 8, 2006, p. E5.
Variety Online. December 3, 2006.
Washington Post Online. December 7, 2006.

UNDERWORLD: EVOLUTION

Box Office: $62.3 million

Underworld: Evolution is the sequel to 2003's Goth action-horror *Underworld,* with director Len Wiseman and screenwriter Danny McBride returning as well as stars Kate Beckinsale and Scott Speedman. With the success of the first film, Wiseman got approximately double the budget to play with (estimated at some $50 million), which meant production/creature designer Patrick Tatopoulos was able to improve the prosthetics and mechanics for his creations and the film contains hundreds of visual effects and miniatures as well as green screen and wire work and whatever else was needed to keep the action moving. While the first *Underworld,* which was filmed in Budapest, Hungary, has an Old World, decaying city look, the sequel takes to the countryside and mountains of a nameless Eastern European locale (though it was shot in Vancouver, British Columbia). The dark, subterranean world of the original, with its blue/grey/brown palette, remains, though cinematographer Simon Duggan took over the camera from Tony Pierce-Roberts. Also remaining are the gore, violence, and Beckinsale's tight latex/vinyl/leather catsuit.

Another thing that hasn't changed in the sequel is the convoluted plot. It's best to have recently seen *Underworld* before tackling *Underworld: Evolution* but Wiseman thoughtfully provides lots of exposition in the form of a title crawl and prologue to help newcomers catch up. The crawl informs that a "blood feud raged between a ruling class of vampires and a rebellious legion of werewolves." The immortal Alexander Corvinus sired twin sons: Marcus (Tony Curran), who was bitten by a bat and leads the vampires, and William (Brian Steele), who was bitten by a wolf and leads the lycans. Only these prototype werewolves cannot resume their human form and are incredibly and indiscriminately vicious. The prologue then finds us in 1202 A.D. in the midst of a village slaughter caused by William. He is being hunted by Marcus and vampire lord Viktor (Bill Nighy). According to legend, if either Marcus or William is killed, anyone from their bloodlines would also die. So when William is captured, Viktor breaks his promise to Marcus and insists on imprisoning William far away from his brother.

Then we return to the present, picking up immediately after the first film ended. Vampire Selene (Beckinsale) and lycan hybrid Michael (Speedman) are hiding out in an underground vampire safe house (that is unfortunately connected to an overall security network). Since Selene killed Viktor in the first film, she's persona non grata amongst the rest of the vampires. However, she wants to return to the vampire mansion to prevent Kraven (Shane Broly), who escaped death in *Underworld*, from killing Marcus who is supposed to be in vampire hibernation. However, Marcus has revived and drains Kraven's blood, thus learning what has been happening while he's been asleep. He also knows about Michael and, thanks to camera security, where he is hiding.

Also hooked up to visuals is a mystery man, eventually revealed to be Alexander Corvinus, played with distinguished gravitas by Sir Derek Jacobi, who has had his men gather the bodies of vampire elders Viktor and Amelia as well as lycan Lucian and fly them to his cargo ship. He removes a medallion from inside Viktor's body; a similar medallion (once worn by Lucian) is now in Michael's possession.

Selene urges Michael to learn to feed on blood, saying that human food is probably lethal to him now. Michael can't bring himself to drink blood and leaves the safe house for the questionable comforts of an isolated tavern that is a stopover for Russian-speaking soldiers. When the human food he consumes makes him violently ill, Michael begins to change into his hybrid beast form just as a news report broadcasts that he is a wanted man. The soldiers try to capture Michael, wounding him badly as he escapes. Selene hears shots and rescues Michael though it's almost sunrise. Michael feeds from Selene to stem his blood loss as Marcus appears. He wants to know why Viktor kept Selene alive after slaughtering her family. Selene and Michael escape in a stolen truck after battling Marcus and hide out in an abandoned factory as the sun rises.

They get to take a breather and have a moment, allowing Selene to lose the catsuit for a golden-lit sex scene. Pheromones must be drawing them together since Selene generally acts more like a big sister who must protect a vulnerable little brother than a lover. Selene suddenly remembers Lucian's medallion from her childhood and tells Michael that they need to get to Tanis, the official historian of the covens, who was exiled by Viktor. Tanis (Steven Mackintosh) is a nervous weasel who allied himself with Lucian and the werewolves for protection. He tells her that Marcus made Viktor, a local ruler, into a vampire in exchange for his army helping to defeat the rampaging lycans. It was Selene's father who built William's prison and the memory of its location is hidden in her blood. Lucian's medallion, which was originally worn by Viktor's daughter (who was Lucian's lover), is one of two keys; Viktor had the other. Tanis sends Selene and Michael to Corvinus for further information.

Marcus finds out what Tanis knows before killing him and then goes after Selene and Michael again. In the meantime, Alexander tells the duo that he could never kill his sons, no matter the destruction they caused. Marcus arrives to wreck havoc and fights Michael, taking the medallion and leaving the lycan for dead. Selene is attacked and bitten and Marcus learns the location of William's prison. She tries to revive Michael with her blood but this doesn't seem to work. Marcus goes after his father in order to get Viktor's medallion. Marcus wants to establish a new—and superior—race while Alexander proclaims: "We are oddities of nature, you and I. Nothing more. This is a world for humanity." Marcus stabs Alexander and takes the medallion. When Selene finds him dying, Alexander insists she feed from him, which will offer her additional strength and further blur the bloodlines, making her "the future." Selene takes Alexander's remaining men and his helicopter to go after Marcus. Since she can't bear to leave Michael behind, she also takes his body with her.

Marcus finds William's fortress prison and releases him (that's agile creature performer Brian Steele inside the elaborate werewolf suit). Selene and her men follow and she manages to temporarily trap Marcus before going after William. Michael finally revives and comes to Selene's aid. Marcus gets free and brings down the hovering helicopter, which crashes into the cavern, rotors spinning. Lycans William and Michael battle while vampires Marcus and Selene go at it. Michael rips William's head off while Selene stabs Marcus with one of his own talons and then pushes him into the helicopter's whirling blades. Dawn filters into the cavern and Selene discovers she can now withstand sunlight, thanks to Alexander's blood. She and Michael are together while Selene announces (in voiceover) that more chaos will follow "but for now, for the first time…I look into the light with new hope."

It's been written that Wiseman conceived of his story as a trilogy and he certainly left room for another sequel with this ending. Whether *Underworld: Evolution* made enough money to satisfy Sony Pictures is anyone's guess, but it's probable that if fans were as vocal about the sequel as the original, Wiseman could be checking his notes to see what else he can do. Maybe next time he can make the story's obsession with bloodlines and genetic purity a viable part of the plot while continuing to ramp up the action. Maybe he can even make the imperious Selene and the studly Michael a believable sexual couple The films so far have been too bloody to allow for romance. And surely he can find additional well-regarded British actors to go slumming—even thespians are allowed to have some fun.

Christine Tomassini

CREDITS

Selene: Kate Beckinsale
Michael Corvin: Scott Speedman
Marcus Corvinus: Tony Curran
Kraven: Shane Brolly
Alexander Corvinus: Derek Jacobi
Viktor: Bill Nighy
Andreas Tanis: Steven Mackintosh
William Corvinus: Brian Steele
Samuel: John Mann
Lucian: Michael Sheen
Erika: Sophia Myles
Pierce: Richard Cetrone
Origin: USA
Language: English
Released: 2005
Production: David Coatsworth, Tom Rosenberg, Richard Wright; Lakeshore Entertainment; released by Screen Gems
Directed by: Len Wiseman
Written by: Len Wiseman, Danny McBride
Cinematography by: Simon Duggan
Music by: Marco Beltrami
Editing: Nicolas De Toth
Art Direction: Chris August
Costumes: Wendy Partridge
Production Design: Patrick Tatopoulos
MPAA rating: R
Running time: 106 minutes

REVIEWS

Entertainment Weekly Online. January 25, 2006.
Philadelphia Inquirer Online. January 21, 2006.
Variety Online. January 21, 2006.

UNITED 93

September 11, 2001. Four planes were hijacked. Three of them reached their target. This is the story of the fourth.
—Movie tagline

Box Office: $31.5 million

Written and directed by Paul Greengrass, this critically acclaimed docudrama details the events aboard United Airlines Flight 93 on the morning of September 11, 2001. The goal of the film was to be as accurate as possible, but imagination had to be infused to fill in gaps of uncertainty. The last minutes aboard this plane have rendered its occupants as heroes due to their decision and actions. According to Greengrass, the film benefited from the cooperation of all the families of the passengers aboard.

Flight 93 was a Boeing 757 that was hijacked by terrorists in tandem with a coordinated effort planned by al-Qaeda radicals. Three other commuter airliners were also hijacked resulting in successive attacks to both towers of the World Trade Center and the Pentagon. It is believed that Flight 93 was heading for the Capitol in Washington DC. Of the four planes commandeered, it was the only one that did not hit its intended target but was forced down into a field close to Shanksville, Pennsylvania.

The film begins with the terrorists praying in their hotel room on the early morning of September 11, 2001. The flight crew was concurrently gathering at the airport and began their scheduled, rote tasks in preparation for takeoff. Several passengers are seen boarding, and air traffic control employees are seen changing shifts and continuing the unending monitoring of the national skies.

After an uneventful, commonplace delay, United Airlines Flight 93 takes off from Newark Airport. Shortly thereafter, the first of the two planes crashes into the World Trade Center and chaos ensues as air traffic control crews frantically try to decipher what is transpiring. The Air Force is notified that something may be out of its proper course and they are placed on alert.

Aboard Flight 93, the hijackers have killed both pilots and taken over the cockpit. Two other terrorists inform the passengers that they have explosives bound to their torsos and keep them at bay with this threat as well as with box cutters. As further disincentive, one of the passengers is stabbed and bleeds to death. The Air Force's response is sluggish and they do not have enough planes to scramble to a hijacked airliner crisis. Ben Sliney, who plays himself, decides to shut down all airspace in the United States and incoming international flights are diverted away from the country. The passengers become aware of the national crisis via cell phones and the on-board Airfone service. Upon hearing of the WTC and Pentagon disasters, the people realize their fate and take a hasty vote in favor of taking back the plane. Passengers are seen making their phoned last goodbyes to loved ones and inform them of their plan to fight back.

Weapons are fashioned from anything: soda cans, bottles, fire extinguishers, silverware. After one of the passengers informs them that he is a pilot but hasn't flown anything the size or sophistication of a Boeing 757, the group decides that he is their only hope in landing the plane. They lunge forward using a beverage and meal cart as well as pillows to guard against the weapons of the terrorists. The cockpit is broken breached, the terrorist piloting the plane spins into an upside down nosedive. The film does not show the plane crash into the Pennsylvania field but shows the ground rushing up towards the cockpit window.

Of the movie's cast, eleven played themselves. The narrative was pieced together from accounts of all parties involved: families, friends, military and air control personnel. Originally titled *Flight 93*, the title was changed to to distinguish the film from A&E's *Flight 93* and "Dedicated to the memory of all those who lost their lives on September 11, 2001."

David Metz Roberts

CREDITS

Todd Beamer: David Alan Basche
William Joseph Cashman: Richard Bekins
Jane Folger: Susan Blommaert
Thomas E. Burnett Jr.: Christian Clemenson
Joseph DeLuca: Ray Charleson
Colonel Robert Marr: Gregg Henry
Deborah Welsh: Polly Adams
Colleen Fraser: Denny Dillon
Ziad Jarrah: Khalid Abdalla
Saeed Al Ghamdi: Lewis Alsamari
Himself: Ben Sliney
Himself: Maj. James Fox
Sandra Bradshaw: Trish Gates
Mark Bingham: Cheyenne Jackson
Origin: USA
Language: English
Released: 2006
Production: Tim Bevan, Eric Fellner, Lloyd Levin, Peter Greengrass; Studio Canal Plus, Sidney Kimmel, Working Title Productions; released by Universal
Directed by: Paul Greengrass
Written by: Paul Greengrass
Cinematography by: Barry Ackroyd
Music by: John Powell
Sound: Chris Munro
Editing: Clare Douglas, Christopher Rouse, Richard Pearson
Art Direction: Alan Gilmore
Costumes: Dinah Collin
Production Design: Dominic Watkins
MPAA rating: R
Running time: 111 minutes

REVIEWS

Chicago Sun-Times Online. April 28, 2006.
Entertainment Weekly. April 28, 2006, p. 113.
Hollywood Reporter Online. April 20, 2006.
Los Angeles Times Online. April 28, 2006.
New York Times Online. April 28, 2006.
San Francisco Chronicle. April 28, 2006, p. E1.
Variety Online. April 19, 2006.
Village Voice Online. April 18, 2006.
Washington Post. April 28, 2006, p. C1.

QUOTES

Todd Beamer: "Let's roll."

AWARDS

British Acad. 2006: Director (Greengrass), Film Editing
Nomination:
Oscars 2006: Director (Greengrass), Film Editing
British Acad. 2006: Cinematog., Orig. Screenplay, Sound
Writers Guild 2006: Orig. Screenplay

UNKNOWN WHITE MALE

If you lost your past, would you want it back?
—Movie tagline

Unknown White Male may go down in history as the most problematic documentary of 2006. Blessed with perhaps the most intriguing premise for a documentary since *Fahrenheit 9/11* (2004), the film spends a good portion of its time working against itself, thwarting possible audience interest by emphasizing questions and then not fully exploring those questions. *Unknown White Male* traces the journey of Doug Bruce, a man who wakes up on a New York subway the morning of July 3, 2003, with no idea of who he is. Neither a clinical, scientific analysis in the tradition of the long-running television show *Nova* nor a very personal (or complete) narrative, this guerrilla-style, yet somehow very consciously produced film leaves the viewer wondering if the eighty-eight minutes spent in Doug's world is really worth it.

Unknown White Male is roughly comprised of three sections that explore Doug's condition at various stages: the first section traces Doug's path on July 3, 2003, as he regains consciousness on a subway in Coney Island, unaware of who he is; the second section focuses on Doug's attempts to settle into a life he has no memory of, with an emphasis on relating to people from his life before the amnesia, like his family and friends; and the third section briefly explores the possibility that Doug may never get his memory back.

The film opens with a montage of black-and-white images, the announcement of the situation, and the questions, "How much is our personality, our identity, determined by the experiences we have? And how much is already there—pure us?" *Unknown White Male* then shifts to footage of Doug on the subway recounting his initial experience of coming to on the subway, not knowing who he is. Professor Daniel Schacter, Chair of Psychology at Harvard, appears onscreen and talks generally about what Doug seems to have experienced, something called a "fugue state"—a functional state of action in which the subject is unaware that he has no memory and that ends when the subject becomes aware of the lack of memory. Doug recalls attempting to remember who he was and where he was going. He had only a backpack with him with nothing in it to really give him a clue as to his identity. Not knowing what else to do, he turns himself in to the police. They search the backpack and come up with a phone number. Yet when they call the number, the woman who answers has no idea whom Doug is. All the police have to go on is this phone number and the fact that Doug has an English dialect. It seems that Doug has suffered from retrograde amnesia and has lost his episodic memory, which is made up of personal individual experiences. Doug is eventually hospitalized in a psychiatric ward. When asked to sign some paperwork, he is stunned to find that he has a distinct signature. With only his signature and the phone number as clues to who he is, Doug keeps calling the number found in his backpack and, eventually, the woman on the other end, the mother of a friend, finally figures out who Doug is. She and the friend retrieve him from the hospital, and Doug begins the process of finding out who he was prior to the memory loss.

The second section of *Unknown White Male* documents Doug's various encounters with portions of his old life, and his reactions to them as a person with amnesia. The first, and in many ways most poignant encounter, is with his family in Spain. Doug himself films the entire experience. They do not know how to react to one another. Doug's father and sister each confess to being frightened to meet Doug for the first time. They note the differences in him: how he was very gregarious prior to the amnesia and how he seems to be more reflective and emotional since the memory loss. Doug discovers that his mother has died, but, of course, cannot remember it, which saddens him. He goes through some of his possessions in Paris, where he once lived apparently, and talks about how this differs from simply hearing about his past from other people. He calls the place where his things are stored, a room of "complete truth, unfiltered experiences." Doug then returns to New York and begins attempting to live life without a past. He reports everything being new to him, especially food. Doug is shown meeting with old acquaintances in the United Kingdom, relearning photography (something he had begun to pursue prior to his amnesia), and falling in love. Nearly everyone expresses the sentiment that Doug is more open than before, and that his circumstances give him the unique ability to see everything with the eyes of a newborn, yet to appreciate his experiences with the mind of an adult. The upshot of all of these encounters, though, is to make the audience feel as though it has as little investment in Doug's life as he does.

The third and final portion of *Unknown White Male* addresses Doug's life as a possible permanent amnesiac. Fourteen months after the memory loss, Doug's friends and family report that he is really "finding himself." Many of Doug's friends, including Rupert Murray, the director of *Unknown White Male*, have come to accept Doug as he is and do not particularly want Doug to recover his memory unless he desires it. Doug does express some newfound interest in pursuing certain parts of his past. He wishes he could remember his mother, for instance. Doug also, however, expresses some interest in what will happen if his memory ever does return. At the end of *Unknown White Male*, both Doug and the audience are left to ponder what may happen should Doug's memory come back and he is forced to face the moment when who he was and who he is collide.

While the facts that underlie *Unknown White Male* certainly raise some interesting questions, Doug's and, more disappointingly, the director's seemingly complete lack of interest in tenaciously pursuing answers to these questions ultimately makes *Unknown White Male* a lost opportunity. Perhaps Doug is more interested in going forward with his life than doggedly pursuing his past, but it is precisely the journey to regain his memory for which the audience longs. Perhaps the fact that the director was and is a friend of his subject is part of the problem for, even taking into account Doug's lack of desire to remember who he was or to discover why or how he lost his memory in the first place, it should be the job of the filmmaker to pursue relentlessly the questions he himself poses. For better or worse, Murray stays with his subject, never pushing Doug or prodding him with the difficult questions he leaves to the audience, never seeking for answers in case studies that might shed light on Doug's condition nor attempting to get Doug to submit to on-screen interviews with experts in the field of neurology. Unfortunately, Murray seems content, like Doug, to accept the very general diagnosis of "retrograde amnesia," to embrace the new and past-less Doug, and to allow *Unknown White Male* never fully to become the compelling documentary it might have been.

John Boaz

CREDITS

Origin: USA

Language: English

Released: 2005

Production: Beadie Finzi; Film Four, Spectre Broadcast; released by Wellspring

Directed by: Rupert Murray

Cinematography by: Orlando Stuart

Music by: Mukul

Editing: Rupert Murray

MPAA rating: PG-13

Running time: 88 minutes

REVIEWS

Boxoffice Online. February 24, 2006.
Chicago Sun-Times Online. March 10, 2006.
Entertainment Weekly Online. February 22, 2006.
Los Angeles Times Online. February 24, 2006.
New York Times Online. February 24, 2006.
Variety Online. February 1, 2005.

THE U.S. VS. JOHN LENNON

Musician. Humanitarian. National Threat.
—Movie tagline

Box Office: $1.1 million

In watching the documentary, *The U.S. vs. John Lennon,* audiences unfamiliar with the former Beatle's anti-war activism will get a thorough education in how Lennon used his creativity and celebrity to move from being a global entertainer to an enemy of the Richard Nixon administration and J. Edgar Hoover's FBI. David Leaf and John Scheinfeld have written and directed a powerful film that serves both as a history lesson and a timely warning about the abuse of power. It is an intriguing movie, one that will resonate with anyone who lived through the 1960s and 1970s or is curious about that era's history, particularly the protest movement against the Vietnam War. The film does raise some questions it neglects to answer, and it ignores some inconvenient truths.

There is no doubt right from the start whose side the filmmakers are on. Lennon is not presented as a saint, exactly, but he's certainly almost immune from critical assessment. Among the dozens of people interviewed the only one who seems to scoffingly question Lennon's motives is the notorious Watergate operative and ex-felon G. Gordon Liddy, and his few comments serve mainly to praise Lennon with faint damnation, considering the source.

What's utterly captivating about this portrayal of Lennon, however, is the extent to which it catches the very public protester's sense of humor and his positive, cheerful attitude toward life, even as he's angrily railing against Vietnam. In scenes with Yoko Ono and, late in the film, their son Sean, Lennon seems genuine, unaffected, and content. It helps that Leaf and Scheinfeld had the complete cooperation of Ono, who provides many of the movie's most memorable commentaries, especially as she talks about one night, during the "bed-in" in Montreal, when the couple saw a full moon out their hotel window and snuggled together in complete harmony with their place in the world. It's clear that Lennon's simple pronouncements on peace and love were both heartfelt and genuine and reflected in the way he lived his life.

What doesn't emerge as clearly is how Lennon was transformed into a peace activist, though the movie certainly strives to tell the story. It notes his working-class background, his being abandoned by both his parents, and his troubles at school. But, all the Beatles were working-class in origin, and the complexity of John's personality is left somewhat obscured. Since this is an authorized Yoko Ono version of one aspect of his life—her participation obviously comes with a certain amount of control—we have pieces of John's life completely omitted, including his first marriage and his son Julian by that marriage, his artistic and political squabbles with Paul McCartney, his heroin addiction, and the rough parts of his relationship with Ono, including a fifteen-month separation.

These personal details are relevant because *The U.S. vs. John Lennon* portrays the political battle, which centered eventually on the government's efforts to deport Lennon, through the prism of Lennon's strong personal beliefs. His position as one of the most influential leaders of counter-culture thinking is made obvious and driven home by the connections some may have forgotten about—his authorship of the antiwar anthem "Give Peace A Chance," his rejection of violence in the seminal Beatles song "Revolution," and his much-played anti-war Christmas song, "Happy Xmas (War Is Over)." Unfortunately, the film gives short shrift to his most impactful composition, "Imagine."

Snippets of these and many other Lennon songs, interspersed with images from Vietnam and from anti-war protests, and with interviews with a motley cast of observers from Walter Cronkite and Geraldo Rivera to Gore Vidal and Angela Davis, provide viewers with a thorough and trenchant tour through 1960s counterculture. Though this is a subject often tackled, it's rarely been done so forcefully, and anyone who doesn't understand why music such as Lennon's was a crucial component of the era's political protest should pay close attention. Rather than proceeding strictly chronologically, the film moves its story along both logically and emotionally, circling around the turmoil of the times with an eagle's-eye view.

What might be arguable is the film's view that Lennon was at the center of the politics of the anti-war movement; some would say his involvement was more at the periphery. The movie devotes considerable time to Lennon and Ono's "bed-ins" on their honeymoon in Amsterdam, and later in Montreal, where the couple stayed in hotel beds to protest the war and also to capitalize upon media attention. Certainly they were among the first celebrities to play the media in this self-referential fashion, and they get full credit for the originality of their idea. At the same time the film doesn't shrink from portraying the media's questioning of this tactic, and there's priceless footage of a *New York Times* reporter berating Lennon for trivializing his fame, scolding him as being naive and his actions as being unworthy of his artistic stature. Also remarkable is the scene showing the recording of "Give Peace A Chance" in their Montreal hotel room, an event that included Tom Smothers (who is interviewed) accompanying John on guitar and a shirtless Timothy Leary (unmentioned in the film) sitting on the floor.

This and the couple's placing of "War Is Over" posters in a dozen cities around the world, as well as Lennon's appearance at an Ann Arbor, Michigan, benefit concert in April 1971 to push for freeing political activist John Sinclair (a success), are given plenty of attention. These activities, but more importantly Lennon's anti-war and political songs, were indeed influential, but they constitute the sum of Lennon and Ono's major anti-war activity. He is also shown speaking at a rally, and in several TV interviews giving his views quite strongly, but on balance the documentary seems to pump up Lennon's importance in the anti-war movement.

There's no doubt, however, that the FBI surveillance of Lennon was a chilling testament to the mentality of the era—and, some would say, has resonance during a similar era these days. Lennon talks about his phone being tapped and his being followed. Surprisingly, however, the film glosses over exactly what was in the FBI files. Instead of dissecting the most important details of the dispute that is the title of the film, Leaf and Scheinfeld seem to back away, as if what exactly the government was doing and saying about John and Yoko wasn't as important as the fact that the Nixon administration considered him an enemy of the state.

The lack of information leads to a puzzle: It's revealed that, following the success of the Sinclair concert, radical anti-war activist-showmen Jerry Rubin and Abbie Hoffman were planning with Lennon a nationwide concert tour that would follow the Nixon presidential campaign of 1972 and culminate in a massive rally and concert outside the Republican convention in Miami. The film makes clear that the government's discovery of these plans prompted the crackdown by the INS that resulted in deportation proceedings against Lennon and Ono. But, given how ardently Lennon is portrayed as an anti-war activist, the motivation for the couple's refusal to follow through on these incendiary plans is left unclear. Some viewers may be left wondering: if John and Yoko were so opposed to the war why didn't they escalate their protests and go ahead with the plans for the political concert tour? Ono's explanation is chilling: she says they had the strong feeling that if they went to Miami their lives would be in danger.

The film moves on to a rather dull exposition of the deportation case; Lennon eventually won after their lawyer dragged on the proceedings for years with procedural delays. But the viewer wants to know: What in the FBI files can back up Yoko's assertion that they were assassination targets? The documentary is silent on this issue and on the general subject of death threats. This omission is more glaring when the film ends with Lennon's assassination, years later, in December 1980, long after the war was over when the tensions between the government and activists had cooled, and Lennon had spent five years raising his son and taking a hiatus from both music and public life.

To explore the possible connections between Mark David Chapman (Lennon's assassin) and previous plots, if indeed there were any, against Lennon, would have required another movie, but it's not satisfying that the film leaves a general, unsupported inference that Lennon was killed for his beliefs, rather than by a deranged gunman. It's not for lack of material. Several books have been published since Lennon's FBI files were released in the mid-1990s, and the film slides by some of the personal complications and details that clouded the issue, including Yoko's custody battle with her ex-husband over their daughter—a major reason she and Lennon decided to stay in New York. To include these details might have made the picture more complicated, but it's a pity that Leaf and Scheinfeld didn't trust the power of their story and protagonist to survive a more nuanced, balanced treatment.

In the end, *The U.S. vs. John Lennon* plays it safe by keeping viewers at a distance from some of the messier facts of the case, in order to make its depiction of Lennon a cleaner portrait of good (sincere artist and anti-war protestor) against evil (a paranoid, immoral government). But, as the film makes clear, the power and vision and sincerity of Lennon's actions, the courage of his stance, the originality of his ideas, his unfailing sense of humor, and his very post-modern appreciation of the possibilities afforded by his celebrity status were so effective and influential that being honest about the mitigating circumstances of his personal life would not detract from the message. To gloss over drug use, marital squabbles, child custody battles, and political disputes was unnecessary. Lennon's image would have survived, and in fact would have been more powerful and human, if his halo were more accurately portrayed as slightly askew. In the end, the film is both too worshipful and not ambitious enough. It needlessly treats its subject with kid gloves. While it succeeds in capturing Lennon's power in those turbulent times, it leaves too many questions unanswered.

Michael Betzold

CREDITS

Origin: USA
Language: English
Released: 2006
Production: David Leaf, John Scheinfeld; Authorized Pictures; released by Lionsgate
Directed by: David Leaf, John Scheinfeld
Written by: David Leaf, John Scheinfeld
Cinematography by: James Mathers
Sound: Tom Bergin, Christopher Knell
Editing: Peter S. Lynch II
MPAA rating: PG-13
Running time: 99 minutes

REVIEWS

Boxoffice Online. September 15, 2006.
Chicago Sun-Times Online. September 29, 2006.
Entertainment Weekly. September 22, 2006, p. 76.
Hollywood Reporter Online. September 1, 2006.
Los Angeles Times Online. September 15, 2006.
New York Times Online. September 15, 2006.
San Francisco Chronicle. September 29, 2006, p. E4.
Variety Online. August 31, 2006.
Village Voice Online. September 5, 2006.

QUOTES

G. Gordon Liddy (on Lennon): "He was a high-profile figure so his activities were monitored."

V

V FOR VENDETTA

Freedom! Forever!
—Movie tagline

Remember, remember the 5th of November.
—Movie tagline

People should not be afraid of their governments. Governments should be afraid of their people.
—Movie tagline

Box Office: $70.5 million

"Remember, remember the fifth of November," goes the sing-song chant of English children as they go door-to-door on that same date every year collecting "pennies for the Guy" which they will then use to buy fireworks to set off during the annual nighttime bonfire. The holiday is Guy Fawkes' Day. Fawkes was a Catholic fanatic dismayed by the Protestant rule of King James I. As a result he joined with several other Catholic conspirators and planted thirty-six barrels of gunpowder in the cellars of Parliament with the intent of blowing up the king and his government on November 5, 1605. The plot was discovered, however, and Fawkes was arrested, tortured and executed. Now it is left to children to celebrate the foiling of the Gunpowder Plot. Children and the movie *V for Vendetta.*

In the year 2020, England is ruled by Chancellor Adam Sutler (John Hurt) and his Nazi-like Norsefire Party. It is a dreary dystopia that allows for no dissent, no questioning, no freedom and no ideas not approved by the party. To enforce this oppressive rule, Sutler's Secret Police, headed by Creedy (Tim Piggot-Smith) uses thugs called Fingermen who more often than not use their jobs to create sadistic mayhem among the populace.

For example, one night, young Evey Hammond (Natalie Portman), a gopher at the British Television Network, is on her way to a secret rendezvous with on-air personality Gordon Deitrich (Stephen Fry). She is stopped in the street for curfew violation by several Fingermen, who are about to take the law and Evey into their own hands. Before they can have their fun, Evey is saved by a mysterious man dressed in a black cape, hat and boots, wearing a black Prince Valiant wig and an eerily smiling, unmoving mask depicting Guy Fawkes. His name is V (Hugo Weaving), and after rescuing Evey he takes her up to a nearby roof to watch something extraordinary. As Tchaikovsky's "1812 Overture" blares over what is supposed to be a tightly controlled public address system, fireworks go off and the symbol of British law, the Old Bailey, explodes.

Not long afterward, V reappears in Evey's life after he invades the BTN with a cartload of Guy Fawkes masks and explosives strapped to his chest. He takes control of the transmission, tells the viewers that there is something terribly wrong in England and challenges them to meet him in one year outside Parliament...on Guy Fawkes Day.

During the ensuing year several events intertwine. Because Evey has been seen twice with V she is mistakenly identified as his co-conspirator and police begin to look for her. This is the job of Chief Inspector Finch (Stephen Rea) and his sidekick Dominic (Rupert Graves). But as Finch delves deeper into V and Evey's backgrounds, he makes some startling discoveries about the government he works for.

Since Evey is now hunted by the police, V gives her sanctuary in his home, the Shadow Gallery, where she discovers a trove of priceless art, books, movies, and music, which have been declared dangerous and therefore forbidden by Sutler's government. Once outside the Shadow Gallery, she is arrested and tortured, but comforted by brave notes she finds from a previous prisoner, Valerie (Natasha Wightman), who was imprisoned for being a lesbian. Given an ultimatum to reveal V's whereabouts or die, Evey chooses death and is inexplicably released. V confesses he arranged the whole thing to teach her to live without fear. Evey had been haunted by the childhood memory of her parents, both political protesters, being taken away by the government to Belmarsh, where they died. Thanks to V, Evey finds she now has all the strength and integrity she needs, vowing to meet up with V again before the fifth of November.

During this time, V is also busy exacting his own personal revenge on all those connected with a secretive government detention center called Larkhill. V himself had once been imprisoned there, enduring mental and physical torture. During his time at Larkhill, he also learned how far a government would go to terrify its people into obedience. While all this is going on, the people start to question their government and the kind of lives they are forced to live because of it.

V for Vendetta began as a graphic novel co-created by Alan Moore (who has basically disowned the film) and David Lloyd. Begun in 1981 and finished in 1988, it appeared on the scene just as conservative British Prime Minister Margaret Thatcher was starting her third term. It envisioned an Orwellian England of the not-too-distant future in which a repressive government keeps its people in line by keeping them in a constant state of fear. It is a government that manipulates its people through an endless series of crises into an unquestioning acceptance of their totalitarian rule, surrendering their freedom as the price for safety. At the time of original publication, the graphic novel was seen as a broadside against Thatcher's more conservative policies, but when translated for the screen in 2006 by the Wahcowski brothers, some say *V for Vendetta* now seems more aimed at the Geroge W. Bush administration.

Initially set for release in November 2005, to coincide with Guy Fawkes' Day, the date was changed to March 2006 as a result of the terrorist bombings in London in July, and the ambiguous nature of terrorist activities in the movie. This fact alone indicates both a weakness and a strength of the movie. By forcing the audience to admire V's activities, the film makes us complicit in its moral ambiguity.

Some have decried *V* as a movie that glorifies terrorism, but others will find that the intelligent script actually makes one think about the nature of terrorism. Those who see the world in black and white will not be happy with the infinite shades of grey. Actually, part of the movie's appeal is that it is so ambiguous, and that makes it intriguing. It forces recognition that religion and governments can win and maintain power through terror and manipulation. It also invites contemplation on the function and consequences of extremist thinking of any stripe.

There is no doubt that some people will find *V for Vendetta* an uncomfortable film. It offers no easy answers, but it bravely asks some questions that everyone should face...even if they don't want to. As V says, "an idea can change the world. We die defending them and kill in the name of them." Is it asking too much that we actually think about them?

While this intelligent story has an appeal all its own for thinking moviegoers, the way in which it is told is also quite appealing. It is amazing that Hugo Weaving can breathe such life into a character using just his physical actions and his expressive voice. Always hidden behind a mask, he can never use his face to convey emotion, and yet we know exactly what V is feeling. Weaving makes V a charismatic character who is both victim and villain. He is also tormented and tormentor, cunning and vindictive, agile and tender, smart and verging on insanity. In other words, he is complex and mysterious, and we have no trouble believing that this man truly is capable of exciting the masses while successfully challenging and infuriating those in power.

The rest of the cast is equally good. John Hurt positively foams at the mouth as the repressive Chancellor. Stephen Rea provides his typical low-key but edgy presence, Stephen Fry is amusing as a TV personality turned gadfly, and Natalie Portman glows as the everywoman thrown into a situation beyond her control.

V for Vendetta is a fascinating, thinking person's action film. It is well-acted, solidly told, fast-paced, and visually stylish.

Beverley Bare Buehrer

CREDITS

V: Hugo Weaving
Evey: Natalie Portman
Finch: Stephen Rea
Deitrich: Stephen Fry
Adam Sutler: John Hurt
Creedy: Tim Pigott-Smith

Dominic: Rupert Graves
Lewis Prothero: Roger Allam
Dascomb: Ben Miles
Delia Surridge: Sinead Cusack
Etheridge: Eddie Marsan
Valerie: Natasha Wightman
Origin: USA
Language: English
Released: 2006
Production: Joel Silver, Grant Hill, Andy Wachowski, Larry Wachowski; Silver Pictures, Anarchos Prods.; released by Warner Bros.
Directed by: James McTeigue
Written by: Andy Wachowski, Larry Wachowski
Cinematography by: Adrian Biddle
Music by: Dario Marianelli
Sound: Tom Sayers
Editing: Martin Walsh
Art Direction: Sarah Horton, Sebastian Krawinkel, Steve Bream
Costumes: Sammy Sheldon
Production Design: Owen Paterson
MPAA rating: R
Running time: 132 minutes

REVIEWS

Boxoffice Online. March 17, 2006.
Chicago Sun-Times Online. March 16, 2006.
Los Angeles Times Online. March 17, 2006.
New York Times Online. March 17, 2006.
Rolling Stone Online. March 7, 2006.
San Francisco Chronicle Online. March 16, 2006.
USA Today Online. March 17, 2006.
Variety Online. February 13, 2006.
Village Voice Online. March 14, 2006.

QUOTES

V: "Behind this mask is a man and behind this man is an idea. And ideas are bulletproof."

VENUS

Box Office: $3.1 million

If Peter O'Toole had never found fame and fortune as an international star of the silver screen but had continued acting anyway with a modest measure of success, it is possible that his fate would have been similar to that of Maurice Russell, his character in Roger Michell's *Venus.* Penned by Hanif Kureishi, the film is a bittersweet meditation on facing old age and impending death while also trying to cling to some last vestige of vitality. It is at turns sad and wistful but also fairly slight dramatically. There is little doubt that, if O'Toole were not providing his own dramatic heft and charisma, as well as the gravitas of his persona, the film itself could have crumbled under its thin framework.

Maurice is a journeyman actor who has had his heyday and his share of fame. His command of Shakespeare suggests that he has played the great roles, but, nearing the end of his life, he is relegated to playing the dying father confined to a hospital bed, where he simply lies motionless. He must slap himself to start his day, which he generally spends in the company of two buddies, Ian (Leslie Phillips) and Donald (Richard Griffiths). When Ian's grandniece, Jessie (Jodie Whittaker), moves in with him, Maurice's life gets shaken up. She has left the country to come to London to try her hand at modeling, but very soon Ian is at a loss as to how to control this wild, young woman. Little more than a spoiled child, she is rude and a tad vulgar, drinking Ian's liquor and lounging around the house. Maurice, however, takes an instant interest in Jessie, who obviously sparks his lust and curiosity. He gets her a job modeling for an art class and then makes a mess of the studio when he crashes into the room trying to sneak a peek at her. A broad piece of slapstick, it is one of the movie's funniest scenes.

Between monitoring his mounting prostate problems and pursuing Jessie, Maurice occupies his days as best he can, but Jessie can be such a coarse, selfish girl that, at times, we just feel sorry for the hapless Maurice as he makes a fool of himself to win her affection, if not her love, and being treated badly in return. He exposes her to some culture via a trip to the theater and a visit to a museum, where he shows her a painting of the goddess Venus. He henceforth playfully calls her by that name, all the while yearning for the chance to touch her hand or kiss her neck. Because he is, as he puts it, "a little bit" famous, she is intrigued by him. At times, their exchanges border on the lascivious, but the screenplay is unafraid to go to raw, somewhat uncomfortable areas with an old man whose appetites have been rejuvenated. At other times, the relationship is quite poignant, as when Jessie shares her own embarrassing story of love gone bad and the abortion her mother forced her to have and Maurice responds with a recitation of Shakespeare's sonnet "Shall I compare thee to a summer's day?"

Every now and then, Maurice drops in to visit Valerie (Vanessa Redgrave), the wife he deserted long ago with three small children. Their scenes are tender, and the actors effortlessly communicate a lifetime's worth of struggles and Maurice's little attempts to make amends for his failures.

There are really two movies somewhat uncomfortably coexisting in *Venus*. The first is a geriatric *Lolita*, and the other is a swan song for the legend of O'Toole, a tribute not only to him, but to the acting life as well. We are treated to a scene of Maurice filming a small role in a costume drama and another of Maurice and Ian dancing in St. Paul's in Covent Garden, which houses the remains of such famed thespians as Boris Karloff and Robert Shaw. In another digression, Maurice journeys to an outdoor theater and begins Hamlet's "To be or not to be" soliloquy. These scenes really have little to do with the main plot but feel like a tribute to the passing of a generation of British actors, of which O'Toole/Maurice is a representative or perhaps the last survivor.

The central plot, nonetheless, revolves around Maurice gradually breaking down Jessie's resistance to being touched and allowing him little gestures of intimacy. While it seems that his prostate surgery has made him impotent, he still enjoys small pleasures, "a theoretical interest," as he puts it, in the opposite sex. The big turn in their relationship comes when Maurice has an altercation with her lowlife boyfriend and Jessie ends up knocking Maurice down. Confined to a bed, Maurice is in worse shape then ever but asks for Jessie to look after him, which she does. This once snotty girl has had a change of heart, and she stays with him, ultimately taking a trip with him to the coastal area where he grew up. In a beautiful instance of life having come full circle, an increasingly enfeebled Maurice has Jessie take off his shoe so that he can dip his foot in the water one last time before he quietly dies. Maurice has somehow brought out the goodness in Jessie, a shift that Whittaker, in her film debut, makes credible. Her character may not be as well defined as Maurice, but Whittaker holds her own opposite the legendary O'Toole.

Ultimately this modest character study, with all of its rough edges and digressions, works as well as it does because of O'Toole, who brings his rakish charm and dry wit to a part that, in other hands, could have devolved into the stereotypical dirty old man. He lets us see the neediness of a fellow who may be a scoundrel but knows that the end is near and soldiers on, basking in the one beautiful thing in his life that can bring him joy. If this role ends up being O'Toole's last, it would be a testament to his boldness in taking on a character who is sometimes less than admirable while gently playing with his own screen image, presenting an alternate reality in which stardom never happened and the punishing vicissitudes of old age are a daily battle. For more than any other film in recent memory, *Venus* unsentimentally lays bare the harsh existence of coping with a deteriorating body and living in the shadows of past glory while finding some bit of solace and beauty to carry one through.

Peter N. Chumo II

CREDITS

Maurice: Peter O'Toole
Ian: Leslie Phillips
Donald: Richard Griffiths
Jessie: Jodie Whittaker
Valerie: Vanessa Redgrave
Origin: Great Britain
Language: English
Released: 2006
Production: Kevin Loader; FilmFour, U.K. Film Council, Free Range Films; released by Miramax Films
Directed by: Roger Michell
Written by: Hanif Kureishi
Cinematography by: Haris Zambarloukos
Music by: David Arnold, Corinne Bailey Rae
Sound: Danny Hambrook
Editing: Nicolas Gaster
Art Direction: Emma MacDevitt
Costumes: Natalie Ward
Production Design: John Paul Kelly
MPAA rating: R
Running time: 94 minutes

REVIEWS

Boxoffice Online. December 20, 2006.
Los Angeles Times Online. December 20, 2006.
New York Times Online. December 21, 2006.
Newsweek Online. December 18, 2006.
Rolling Stone Online. November 21, 2006.
Variety Online. September 7, 2006.
Village Voice Online. December 19, 2006.

QUOTES

Maurice (to Jessie, showing her a classical painting): "There, you see, Venus is a goddess. She creates love and desire in us mortals, leading often to foolishness and despair."

TRIVIA

The third collaboration between writer Hanif Kureishi and director Roger Michell after *The Buddha of Suburbia* and *The Mother.*

AWARDS

Nomination:

Oscars 2006: Actor (O'Toole)
British Acad. 2006: Actor (O'Toole), Support. Actor (Phillips)

Golden Globes 2007: Actor—Drama (O'Toole)
Screen Actors Guild 2006: Actor (O'Toole)

VOLVER
(To Return)

Box Office: $12.5 million

Acclaimed Spanish director Pedro Almodovar plumbs his customary themes of mothers, daughters, sisters, abusive men, and separation and reconciliation in the quietly effective feature *Volver.* Almodovar's sixteenth feature film won widespread critical acclaim, starting with accolades at the Cannes Film Festival and continuing with mentions on many American critics' best-of-2006 lists. It is hard to see what all the fuss is about, though. *Volver* may be Almodovar's most accessible film, but it is also one of his least interesting. Compared to his other works that are full of blasphemy, bizarre sex, violence, and inventive magical realism, *Volver* is both visually and thematically tame and tepid.

Perhaps it's this very turn away from excessthat has aroused such widespread praise. *Volver* is not a difficult film to follow; it doesn't take on church or state, staying completely away from Almodovar's penchant for anti-Catholic and anti-government rhetoric and themes; it's not drenched in sexual perversions; and its characters are all sympathetic, except for one husband who is quickly disposed of and another man who is talked about, but never appears—they are both brutes, as almost all men are in Almodovar films). Though the film is lushly observant, it avoids challenging and unconventional techniques. Even the apparent mysticism that unfolds turns out to be, when all is said and done, a huge red herring.

None of the women in the film are crazy or overly flamboyant, unlike the females in many of Almodovar's other movies. Drug use is confined to one character smoking pot, an act that her friends seem to disapprove of. When the revelations come at the end of the film, they underline *Volver's* more universal appeal: this could be the story of any family of women and their friends, and this is what makes *Volver* so easy to praise. A man making a thoughtful movie about men's inhumanity to women gets plenty of appreciation just for his stance.

It helps, also, that Penelope Cruz—an actress so beautiful, graceful, and likeable that she is difficult to resist—is in the lead role. Her character, Raimunda, is hard-working and resourceful, courageous and forgiving, determined and spirited, and is in fact, a saint. She works several jobs, is a dutiful and understanding mother, and tolerates the indolence of her husband. The other women in the film are, though not completely without flaws, all worthy of praise too. Raimunda's daughter, Paula (Yohana Cobo), is brave and principled, though otherwise a typical young teenager. Raimunda's sister, Sole (Loa Duenas), makes a living through her own resources, running a hair salon out of her home, where she lives alone after being abandoned by her husband. The sisters live in Madrid; their parents both died a few years earlier in a fire. Their Aunt Paula, who raised Raimunda, is dying back in the village of their origin, in a fictional region of Spain that is supposedly beset by an east wind that makes people crazy (this seems a rather clumsy and threadbare artifice). Her neighbor and longtime friend of the family, Agustina (Blanco Portillo), is taking care of Paula. Agustina is also something of a saint: kind and generous, thoughtful and principled, but troubled by the disappearance of her own mother.

Almodovar's method for moving the plot along is to have people die or be in the process of dying. Raimunda's husband dies first, killed with a kitchen knife after he makes advances on Paula. When Raimunda cleans up the mess, there is a fine obsessiveness in the way Almodovar's camera clings to the mop with which she wipes up his blood. Raimunda dumps the body in a freezer of the restaurant next door to the their apartment complex; the restaurant's owner is going on a trip to Barcelona and leaves the place, which he wants to sell, in Raimunda's care. She reopens it by catering lunch for several days to a film crew shooting nearby. Almodovar expends quite a bit of *Volver* delving into the details of Raimunda's resourcefulness and determination in getting the meals cooked; it illustrates her strength of character but doesn't otherwise advance the plot and seems like a diversion.

The mystical red herring appears when the two sisters' mother, Irene (Carmen Maura), who was rumored to be a ghostly presence around Paula's house in the village, reappears in a comical fashion, hiding out in the trunk of Sole's car and revealing herself after Sole has come back to Madrid after Paula's funeral. Sole rather quickly overcomes her skepticism at things supernatural and accepts her mother as a houseguest. They disguise her as a Russian immigrant whom Sole has taken in to help with her hair salon treatments. When Raimunda visits, Irene hides under the bed.

All this is rather playfully done, and Maura makes Irene into another sympathetic woman, kind and witty if fearful of encountering Raimunda, who rejected her as a child. Lots of time goes by with Irene hiding from Raimunda; this artifice gets a little tedious, especially since audiences don't know why she is not revealing herself to both her daughters. Finally, the important revelations are set in motion by the news that Agustina is dying, and by her questions about her mother's interlocking history with her friends' family.

Some of this material could have been played as black comedy, but Almodovar shies away from something that intense. The tone is not one of farce, but of light melodrama. It's a winning formula to make a film out of how strong, brave women have been victimized by the acts of men unseen, but the idea doesn't provide much ongoing tension. The women aren't at war with one another or even with themselves; they are doing their best to make a life, but they are not deluding themselves either. Secrets aren't hidden for nefarious motives; everybody is well-meaning. Even death doesn't seem to muddle the little triumphs of everyday life.

It is difficult not to enjoy a film, so full of sympathetic characters. The entire cast gives strong performances, no doubt happy to be playing wonderful roles for Almodovar. But the famously acerbic director seems to have lost his edge: *Volver* is a bit like Ingmar Bergman making a happy domestic movie. *Volver* is a rich enough tapestry of a family history, though the history seems a bit contrived and its universality too forced. It is richly detailed, bright, and respectful, almost adoring of its female characters. Even the local prostitute seems like a good person. They're all women anyone would love to have as family members, friends or neighbors. But none of them seems all that tortured even by the most difficult events and confessions: Cruz, in particular, plays her pivotal character with an unflappable sunniness. Perhaps Almodovar has simply run out of venom and perversity. If so, the result will be movies like this that get lots of acclaim but don't have nearly as much bite or substance as his earlier work.

Michael Betzold

CREDITS

Raimunda: Penelope Cruz
Sole: Lola Duenas
Abuela Irene: Carmen Maura
Tia Paula: Chus Lampreave
Agustina: Blanca Portillo
Paula: Yohana Cobo
Regina: Maria Isabel Diaz
Paco: Antonio de la Torre
Emilio: Carlos Blanco
Auxiliar: Leonardo Rivera
Origin: Spain
Language: Spanish
Released: 2006
Production: Esther Garcia; El Deseo; released by Sony Pictures Classics
Directed by: Pedro Almodovar
Written by: Pedro Almodovar
Cinematography by: Jose Luis Alcaine
Music by: Alberto Iglesias
Sound: Miguel Rejas
Editing: Jose Salcedo
Art Direction: Salvador Parra
MPAA rating: R
Running time: 111 minutes

REVIEWS

Boxoffice Online. November 3, 2006.
Entertainment Weekly. November 10, 2006, p. 56.
Hollywood Reporter Online. May 20, 2006.
Los Angeles Times Online. November 3, 2006.
New York Times Online. November 3, 2006.
Variety Online. March 26, 2006.
Village Voice Online. October 31, 2006.

AWARDS

Nomination:
Oscars 2006: Actress (Cruz)
British Acad. 2006: Actress (Cruz), Foreign Film
Golden Globes 2007: Actress—Drama (Cruz), Foreign Film
Screen Actors Guild 2006: Actress (Cruz)

W

WAH-WAH

Every family has its own language.
—Movie tagline

Actor Richard E. Grant makes his directorial/screenwriting debut with this well-received, semi-autobiographical independent drama that chronicles one young man's coming of age in late 1960s Swaziland on the eve of its independence. Grant's long and varied career, along with a childhood spent in Swaziland, has doubtless aided in creating memorable characters and a lushly filmed, detailed portrait of life among the British colonists in the Southeast African country.

Nearly twelve years old, Ralph Compton (Zachary Fox), presumably asleep in the back seat of the family car, wakes to catch his mother Lauren (Miranda Richardson) in flagrante delicto with his father's best friend, John Traherne (Ian Roberts), in the front seat. His father Harry (Gabriel Byrne), the well-liked and respectable minister of education confronts the man at a social gathering. It is clear the marriage has been in trouble for some time, but it is a shock to Harry when Lauren runs off with her lover back to Britain, vowing never to return, leaving a crushed Ralph behind. While everyone in their circle seems to drink and have affairs, it is still frowned upon to desert one's family.

Harry sends his son off to boarding school to avoid the shame and embarrassment he would surely feel in their tight-knit community. Fourteen-year-old Ralph (Nicholas Hoult) returns to find things much changed at home. While it seemed that his father might conveniently couple with Gwen Traherne (Julie Walters), the likeable wife John abandoned, his father has instead impulsively married Ruby (Emily Watson), a former airline hostess. Ralph is determined not to like her, but quickly falls for her independence and easygoing charm, refreshing in the sea of snobbish, elitist expatriats. Harry's circle is not an easy one to break into and, led by the uber-snooty Lady Riva Hardrick (a wonderfully hateful Celia Imrie), they shun the American intruder. The film's title refers to what the stuffy Brits sounds like to Ruby, the film's sole American character; their quirky "hubbly-jubblys" and "toodle-pips" merely sounding like "wah-wah" to her. Despite his new wife and son happily coming together, Harry is tortured by the fact that his beloved Lauren has left, and slips into alcoholism. When drunk, Harry becomes an abusive monster.

Princess Margaret's visit to mark Swaziland's independence ceremonies is much anticipated among the colonists and they plan to perform a production of *Camelot.* Ralph auditions and wins a spot in the cast. The rehearsal scenes are some of the film's funniest, with everyone behaving much as one would expect, the amateur actors exhibiting their diva-like antics and the put-upon director escaping to the bar whenever possible. Similarly, Harry is deeper in the bottle than ever himself, to the point of finally alienating the ever-faithful and understanding Ruby, who leaves out of desperation.

It seems Ralph may have his dream family back intact after all when a seemingly contrite Lauren unexpectedly returns. For a brief shining moment, Harry and Lauren blissfully reunite in what almost appears to be a dream sequence. They slow dance in the living room as a smiling Ralph looks on. Of course, the bliss doesn't last. Harry learns that Lauren has only returned due to John's transfer to South America, apparently not wanting to relocate there herself. Tired of being her fail-safe, Harry shuts the door on her, literally and figuratively, for good.

The film errs a bit in its simplistic treatment of Harry's alcoholism. Ralph intervenes, consulting a doctor about his father's drinking. Harry agrees to meet with the doctor, who gives him pills that work like Antabuse. Harry immediately, and seemingly without any trouble, stops drinking cold turkey. Ruby returns, the play goes reasonably well—despite Princess Margaret leaving before the end—and Ralph is part of a happy family once again. However, and in a final twist, Harry is hospitalized with a brain tumor and dies. Ralph bonds with his friends atop a picturesque hilltop as the sun sets on a dramatic South African landscape.

Grant's personal touches are clearly evident, such as when Ralph, becoming enamored with all things dramatic, and clearly influenced by Ruby's independence, is shown sneaking out to see Kubrick's seminal *A Clockwork Orange* (1971) at a local cinema and afterwards, painting his face to resemble the film's malignant main character.

Grant did exceedingly well casting the film, and elicits memorable performances from the talented cast, with Byrne a standout. Although Grant eschews a completely realistic tone, his reality is a tad heightened, Byrne's depth brings a needed gravitas, nicely balancing the flightier performances of Richardson and Imrie. Watson finds a multitude of levels within what could have been a stereotypical "kooky American" character. Wisely focusing on character over political statement, Grant steers clear of an overtly biased portrait of the country and its people. Derek Elley notes in his *Variety* review, "though the pic is set in a similar milieu as *White Mischief* (1988), with colonials leading a charmed life of boozing and fornication, there's an appealing lack of bitterness to Grant's take on a later period."

Hilary White

CREDITS

Harry Compton: Gabriel Byrne
Lauren Compton: Miranda Richardson
Ruby Compton: Emily Watson
John Traherne: Ian Roberts
Gwen Traherne: Julie Walters
Ralph Compton: Nicholas Hoult
Lady Riva Hardwick: Celia Imrie
Charles Bingham: Julian Wadham
June Broughton: Fenella Woolger
Vernon: Sid Mitchell
Young Ralph: Zachary Fox
Origin: Great Britain, France
Language: English
Released: 2005
Production: Marie-Castille Mention-Schaar, Pierre Kubel, Jeff Abberley; Scion Films, Loma Nasha Productions, Wah Films Prods.
Directed by: Richard E. Grant
Written by: Richard E. Grant
Cinematography by: Pierre Aim
Music by: Patrick Doyle
Sound: Dominique Levert
Editing: Isabelle Dedieu
Costumes: Sheena Napier
Production Design: Gary Williamson
MPAA rating: R
Running time: 97 minutes

REVIEWS

Boxoffice Online. May 12, 2006.
Entertainment Weekly Online. May 10, 2006.
Los Angeles Times Online. May 12, 2006.
New York Times Online. May 12, 2006.
Variety Online. August 22, 2005.
Washington Post. May 12, 2006, p. WE33.

TRIVIA

The teacher in the school scene was Richard E. Grant's real-life history teacher, who taught him in the very classroom where the scene takes place.

WAIST DEEP

His son. His life. His freedom. He's taking them all back.
—Movie tagline

Bonnie And Clyde—On The Flip Side.
—Movie tagline

Box Office: $21.3 million

Movie ads frequently feature the phrase, "From the director of." *Waist Deep* did not, probably because the phrase would have been followed by "*Glitter.*" Even without Mariah Carey, director and writer Vondie Curtis Hall has created a movie that will not be found on any critics' top ten lists.

Waist Deep, a movie whose title has no particular meaning with regards to the film, concerns a day and night in the life of O2 (Tyrese Gibson). O2, so named because he can disappear like oxygen, is a former convict with two strikes on his record. He tries to live on the right side of the law by taking a job as a security officer and looking after his surrealistically cute son, Junior (H. Hunter Hall, the director's son). O2 is not very successful in these endeavors, as he ends up losing his son and having a mid-street shoot-out within minutes of the film's start.

The tomfoolery starts when O2's irresponsible cousin Lucky (Larenz Tate) fails to pick Junior up from school. O2 is forced to leave work and, for some unknown reason, also takes his job-issued gun with him. It is never explained why someone would provide a gun for an ex-con security guard. After Junior is finally picked up, the car with Junior in the back seat is stolen. O2 chases the car thieves on foot for awhile then shoots some people, but still does not get his son. He enlists the help of a comely prostitute, Coco (Meagan Good), to help him find his boy. It seems that Junior's kidnapping was orchestrated by the local gang kingpin, Big Meat (hip-hop star The Game). Big Meat wants $100,000 for the boy's safe return. The audience can be quite sure that Meat means business because there is a graphic scene in which he cuts off the hand of someone who has betrayed him then uses the severed hand to slap the poor fellow on the face. The extreme violence of this scene is, however, out of the step with the rest of the film.

O2 decides the best way to raise the ransom money is through a combination of house break-ins and bank robberies. He and Coco drive around a posh section of Los Angeles until they spot a wealthy couple leaving their house. The two break into the sleek, modern home, find some cash and safe deposit box keys, and then attend to the next important matter of business—having sex. This taken care of, while poor Junior languishes under Meat's care, Coco and O2 set out to rob some local banks.

The bank robberies are the most enjoyable scenes in the film, with the possible exception of admiring the sheer perfection of Gibson and Good's physiques. The sequences in which O2 and Coco perform their clever scams to weasel their way into the various banks' safes are fun to watch. A character in the movie likens the duo to a modern-day Bonnie and Clyde and it would have been nice if the movie could have stuck with that idea throughout. Instead, it is more of a mishmash. There are some car chases, shoot-out, scams and other common action film elements, but it is all done halfheartedly. It is as if no one in the movie particularly enjoyed such elements, but put them in because that is how it is usually done.

Critics were not horribly impressed with the film. David Hiltbrand of the *Philadelphia Inquirer* gave it one out of four stars and wrote that the film "is tissue thin, a music video's worth of plot stretched over a feature-length frame." Randy Cordova of the *Arizona Republic* gave the film a "bomb" rating and called it "a mean and depressing B movie in which there's no one to root for or even care about." Jessica Reaves of the *Chicago Tribune* was kinder, calling it "a truly schizophrenic, although not unlikable, movie." Wesley Morris of the *Boston Globe* wrote: "Had *Waist Deep* been 101 minutes of holdups, it could have been something. Instead, the movie is full of plodding chases and bad acting from the supporting cast." Finally, A. O. Scott of the *New York Times* wrote that the film "is unapologetically a B movie, its narrative premise whittled down to a mean little nub and placed carefully on the borderline between the wildly implausible and the completely absurd."

Jill Hamilton

CREDITS

O2: Tyrese Gibson
Coco: Meagan Good
Lucky: Larenz Tate
Fencing House Lady: Kimora Lee Simmons
Junior: H. Hunter Hall
Big Meat: The Game
Origin: USA
Language: English
Released: 2006
Production: Preston Holmes; Rogue Pictures, Radar Pictures, Intrepid Pictures, RSVP Productions; released by Rogue Pictures
Directed by: Vondie Curtis-Hall
Written by: Vondie Curtis-Hall, Darin Scott
Cinematography by: Shane Hurlbut
Music by: Terence Blanchard
Sound: David Parker
Editing: Terilyn Shropshire
Art Direction: Yoojung Han
Costumes: Marie France
Production Design: Warren Alan Young
MPAA rating: R
Running time: 97 minutes

REVIEWS

Boxoffice Online. June 23, 2006.
Entertainment Weekly Online. July 5, 2006.
Los Angeles Times Online. June 23, 2006.
New York Times Online. June 23, 2006.
Premiere Magazine Online. June 22, 2006.
Variety Online. June 21, 2006.
Washington Post. June 23, 2006, p. C5.

THE WAR TAPES

Deborah Scranton's award-winning documentary (Best Documentary, 2006 Tribeca Film Festival), *The War*

Tapes, condenses video footage about and behind today's headlines to provide not only a fresh view of the nature of contemporary military warfare but also of the immediacy of video as an extension of the film medium. Primarily shot by three National Guardsmen—the handsome twenty-four-year-old carpenter, Sergeant Stephen Pink; the thirty-four-year-old rotund forklift driver, Specialist Michael Moriarty; and the twenty-four-year-old Lebanese-born college student, Sergeant Zack Bazzi—the film provides a self-effacing, grittily factual view of the Iraqi conflict.

None of the three have a distinguishable video style. The footage is simplistic in nature, almost like a home movie. What Scranton is counting on to lift her film out of the monotony that quickly sets in are the disturbing visuals of roadside battles and of the helpless civilians trapped in a war zone. But even here there is little to shock anyone used to widely-reported news features on the subject. Where Scranton's film scores big is in its homespun crudity, which forces the viewer to contemplate the conflict, and beyond. Those who have risked their lives within it expound upon this idea. It is their informality that proves unique; they speak much as they would amongst their friends at a bar.

By making the audience value filmic crudity, *The War Tapes* harkens back to the inception of film, leaving the viewer to wonder how the medium would have developed had it been used in a personalized manner, like the motor car, instead of as the collective cash cow it has turned out to be. The French thinker Paul Virilio argues in his book *War and Cinema* that conventional films, whether fact or fiction, train whole societies for war through the one basic process of having everyone in a hall look at a projected image from one perspective. With Scranton's film, it is as if that very audience, whose experience of the movies is confined to a passive weekend jaunt, is brought alive by the soldiers' video cameras. Every second of footage they shoot thus becomes an assertion, and a life-affirming one at that, of their will to survive. Thus, it is through these flashes, fortuitous and accidental, that the film can best be described.

The film opens with a seemingly routine operation to locate insurgents in the abandoned civilian dwellings of Fallujah on November 29, 2004. The terrain appears scorchingly hot. Titles superimposed indicate that there are 160,000 American ground troops in Iraq, out of which 64,000 are National Guardsmen (NG). As opposed to those on active duty, these are Citizen Soldiers, many of whom hold decent jobs and occupations to which they plan on returning to after their tour of duty.

A long shot of the operation is shattered by an explosion, which causes the camera to lose its balance and zigzag to the ground. We quickly return to the NGs and hear the instructions they bark to each other. Following a command, we see an NG holding his weapon up as he nears the darkness inside a cottage, but he does so awkwardly, making his fear apparent. The word goes out that "Sergeant Smith is down!" We then see the action of the operation through the front windshield of a Humvee. Again, as we watch, we can feel the vehicle tipping over in the midst of a barrage of ammo.

Switching from the interpersonal to the intrapersonal, the film cuts to a letter being written by one of the NGs as his voiceover recounts: "I want to kill…I have a reoccurring epiphany. This is happening and it will have a lasting impact on me for the rest of my life." The close-up of a face that we will come to know as Sgt. Pink fades out.

This opening proves a condensation of the ideas the film will explore in its mode of factual exposition: raw combat footage, the NGs as soldiers, the NGs as men with home lives, and the NGs revealing their true feelings about the war. Each of these subjects packs a wallop, but with varying degrees of originality. Ironically, it is the non-combat footage that remains etched in the viewer's memory the longest.

Something that doesn't get emphasized in news reports is that the ground action of the American military abroad, from Vietnam onwards, has always involved pleasures and pastimes the troops have been deprived of at home. To this end, Pink's camera shows us a scorpion fight organized as a betting operation by the soldiers. This becomes an extended sequence of a single fight turning into a tournament with the battlers growing in size and excited voiceovers underscoring the cruelty of the proceedings.

With its informal footage, we see scenes of the kind we could never imagine. Moriarty's camera reveals a harrowing moment, on a pitch-black night, as he and his Humvee, providing escort to a convoy of fuel tankers, swerve to avoid a collision with an errant truck, they suddenly find themselves overrunning a young girl who had darted in their path. Through Thermal Imaging videography, we see the convoy running over her body. When the men with Moriarty are able to drag what is left of her off the road, they find that she was carrying cookies. Men hardened by war are heard saying on the soundtrack, "Don't look at that!" A close-up of the Squad Leader looking shaken is accompanied by his voiceover: "I'll remember that for the rest of my life. The Iraqi people are who we're here to help and we just killed them."

But it is only in the film's closing segments, that it points to the ideological implications of the conflict that are left out of even newspaper coverage. From what the NGs say, after they have returned home, it becomes clear that what we've been watching has not been part of a war at all, despite the film's title, it has only been a military action which, like any defense initiative, has only benefited certain defense industries. Ironically, what *The War Tapes* points out is that in a time of global capitalism, war could well have become obsolete. Instead, what we have are military maneuvers, taking their small but steady toll in human lives, too profitable to end quickly.

Vivek Adarkar

CREDITS

Origin: USA
Language: Arabic, English
Released: 2006
Production: Steve James, Robert May; SenArt Films; released by SenArt Films
Directed by: Dan Wallin
Cinematography by: P.H. O'Brien, Peter Ciardelli
Music by: Norman Arnold
Sound: Tom Efinger
Music Supervisor: Tracy McNight
Editing: Steve James, Leslie Simmer
MPAA rating: Unrated
Running time: 97 minutes

REVIEWS

Entertainment Weekly Online. May 31, 2006.
LA Weekly Online. May 30, 2006.
Village Voice Online. May 30, 2006.

WASSUP ROCKERS

"There's no place like home" is the lesson that a group of Latino skateboarders from the ghetto in South Central L.A. learn after spending an adventure-filled day in Beverly Hills. While the African Americans in their neighborhood pick fights with them for wearing tight clothes and listening to punk rock music, they sure are better than the creeps they encounter while in the glamorous suburb, where every white person they meet is a campy stereotype. One could argue that this quasi-documentary is writer/director Larry Clark's (*Kids* [1995], *Bully* [2001] and the similarly-themed *Ken Park* [2002]) attempt to turn the tables on the racist films of yore, which depict minorities in much the same way as the whites here, but his skate punk antiheroes do not give the viewer much to care about or identify with to support such an experiment. While some critics praised the film—Roger Ebert, among them, compares the film to *Ferris Bueller's Day Off* (1986)—most did not, with Richard Roeper summarizing, "the music sucks, the acting is weak, and the skating isn't very good."

Many critics also noted Clark's penchant for rather ogling shots of teens, with Roeper not surprised that the film opens with "shirtless, teenage boys. One of Clarks rather disturbing obsessions." The boys include Kico (Francisco Pedrasa), Milton a.k.a. Spermball (Milton Velasquez), Porky (Yunior Usualdo Panameno), Eddie (Eddie Velasquez), Louie (Luis Rojas-Salgado) and Carlos (Carlos Velasco). Many of the boys live together in a ratty house with no parental supervision, for the most part. Chief among them is Jonathan (Jonathan Velasquez), the film's teenage Romeo whose mere presence causes women of all ages, and at least one man, to immediately want to bed him. Extremely inarticulate, the framework for the way Jonathan tells stories is uniformly the same: "And then...And then...So Then...And then...And then...But then...And then..." ad infinitum. The tedious story goes on, the camera transfixed, the audience bored beyond belief. Indeed, many scenes are incredibly tedious, as when the boys decide to head to a park to go skateboarding in Beverly Hills. Take after take shows the boys wiping out on the cement stairs, and the whole film devolves into a sports documentary.

But just when you think Clark is creating a skateboarding instructional film, he introduces the boys first taste of white culture. Two pretty girls, Jade and Nikki (Laura Cellner and Jessica Steinbaum) that have been admiring them from afar, approach them. The blonde immediately makes out with Jonathan and brazenly grabs his behind before inviting the gang to her house...anytime. Three obnoxiously preppie-looking boys stroll past to claim the girls, and it is clear she is just using Jonathan and his friends to make them jealous. A bumbling and incompetent cardboard cop (the first of the two scenes that portray the Beverly Hills police as immoral and incompetent) cruises up to hassle the carefree youths, mistaking them for Mexicans, and impotently tries to wrangle information out of them. The boys laugh at him and take off, though he manages to take one down in handcuffs.

They head to the girls' house where Jonathan naturally has the blonde in one room, while buddy Kico has the brunette in another. Kico's conversation with her, seemingly intended as naturalistic teen-speak, comes off as heavy-handed compared to the girl's rapid-fire, incisive questioning, suggesting she is just a place card for the middle-aged director. When asked if the other skateboarders are his "best friends" "No," Kico says simply, "We're all the same." He repeats this over and over, hammering home Clark's point about the healthy attitudes held by the "innocent" boys that he holds up as martyrs.

The three white boys show up on cue for a brawl and, as they are outnumbered, resort to calling the police. From this point on, the boys are on the run. They scale the impressively huge gates and walls separating the rich, evil white people and scurry through their grounds to the next wall. One of them, a dead ringer for Clint Eastwood, portrays a filmmaker who shoots and kills one of the boys scaling the wall to the next yard. When the police arrive, one remarks that he is a big fan of the filmmaker and assures him that things will be handled quickly and quietly.

Things get continually more unlikely at the next mansion. After scaling the wall, they unwittingly crash a hipster party, where they seamlessly mingle with the artsy types who find them charming. Especially Jonathan, who gets personally ushered upstairs by the party's homosexual host who, naturally, has designs on the boy. After he accidentally tumbles down a dangerous looking flight of stairs, the boys continue lamming it, finding help at the mansion next door.. The maids, smoking outside, spy the boys and have heard they are wanted by police so they arrange for the gardener's truck to take them to safety. Not before the drunken mistress of the manse (Janice Dickinson) spies cute Kico and takes him upstairs to give him a bubble bath. After he leaves, she (supposedly hilariously) accidentally electrocutes herself in the tub—one more rich, evil white person getting their comeuppance. The boys finally make it home to the welcoming taunts of the gun-toting African Americans who sneer, "Wassup Rockers!"

One reviewer noted that the film has a certain "grungy charm", and Clark's nonprofessional cast of Salvadorian and Guatemalan skaters are certainly natural, convincing, and sometimes appealing in their roles. A true documentarian's approach with a congruent style would have made for an interesting film on this previously untapped L.A. subculture. Instead, Frank Scheck of the *Hollywood Reporter* sees Clark's film, "approaching a level of camp commensurate with John Waters." While Elizabeth Weitzman from the *New York Daily News* notes that when it comes to the kids, "there are too many adults they can't trust, and it's hard to shake the feeling that their director is also one of them."

While *Kids* was infinitely more nihilistic, the unarguably more good-natured *Wassup* is also not any the better for it.

Hilary White

CREDITS

Carlos: Carlos Velasco
Jonathan: Jonathan Velasquez
Kico: Francisco Pedrasa
Milton/Spermball: Milton Velasquez
Porky: Yunior Usualdo Panameno
Eddie: Eddie Velasquez
Louie: Luis Rojas-Salgado
Iris: Iris Zelaya
Ashley Maldonado: Rosalia
Jade: Laura Cellner
Nikki: Jessica Steinbaum
Beverly Hills Actress: Janice Dickinson
Origin: USA
Language: English
Released: 2006
Production: Larry Clark, Kevin Turen, Henry Winterstern; Glass Key; released by First Look Pictures
Directed by: Larry Clark
Written by: Larry Clark
Cinematography by: Steve Gainer
Music by: Harry Cody
Sound: Steve Weiss
Editing: Alex Blatt
Costumes: Maryam Malakpour
Production Design: John Demeo
MPAA rating: R
Running time: 99 minutes

REVIEWS

Boxoffice. April, 2006, p. 152.
Chicago Sun-Times Online. June 30, 2006.
Entertainment Weekly Online. July 5, 2006.
Los Angeles Times Online. June 30, 2006.
New York Times Online. June 23, 2006.
Variety Online. January 20, 2006.
Village Voice Online. September 20, 2005.

WATER

For five years, extremist groups waged a campaign of death threats, arson and riots to stop the production of "Water." But the filmmakers were not to be silenced.
—Movie tagline

Box Office: $5.5 million

Asian Indian expatriate Deepa Mehta's exotic period piece about female bonding, *Water* (2005), espouses social protest against the forces of patriarchal Hindu dogma. The initial attempt to film on location in Benaras, Hinduism's holiest city, could be a film on its own. Threatened by zealous mobs who burnt an effigy of her, Mehta had to flee to her home in Canada, where she worked instead on *Bollywood Hollywood* (2002).

When Mehta attempted to film *Water* again, she chose Sri Lanka, whose landscape appears suffused with the same historical past as India. The scenery also propels her narrative, casting her vast array of characters as pawns who are seemingly helpless against the weight of Brahman rule. While the situations and narrative events appear shocking in terms of the socio-religious dimension to which they allude—especially since it still provides a bedrock of faith in today's economically progressive India—as plot motifs, they remain insipid.

Mehta, as writer-director, grounds her film in the opening titles by quoting from "The Laws of Manu," the seminal prescriptive text that guides the behavior of conventional Hindus: a virtuous wife who remains true to her husband even after his death enters heaven, whereas a woman who is unfaithful will be "reborn in the womb of a jackal." The inner turmoil caused by such an edict is played out against the backdrop of a rundown home for widows in Benaras of 1938. The recalcitrant Chuyia (Sarala), a child bride whose shaven head indicates that she is a widow, is brought to the home by her father against her will. The domineering Head Mother (Meera Biswas) offers her solace, but Chuyia quickly rejects it, wanting instead to be with her own mother.

As Chuyia, whose name ironically translates as "mouse," conforms to the daily rituals of the widows' home, she strikes a special rapport with the angelic Kalyani (Lisa Ray). One day as Chuyia is chasing Kalyani's pup through the narrow alleyways, her path crosses that of Narayan (John Abraham), a young, handsome scholar. When Chuyia introduces him to Kalyani, a flash of mutual attraction can be detected, yet must be remain suppressed. Narayan quickly returns to his elite abode where he lives with his parents, his father Dwarkanath (Gerson Da Cunha) being a prosperous merchant.

The character of Narayan allows Mehta to broaden her canvas to include the historical socio-political changes taking place in an India striving to cast off the yoke of British rule. This ferment is driven by the charismatic figure of M. K. Gandhi, later known as "Mahatma," whom is not seen at this point, but whose views are debated. Gulabi (Raghuvir Yadav), the eunuch who serves as a link between the Head Mother and the outside world, has his own opinion on this thinker, who has come from Africa and claims to have forsworn sex. The Head Mother remains cynical, herself a hypocrite reaping the best of both worlds: while championing the tradition that keeps widows in servility, she has her head massaged through the bars of her window by Gulabi and smokes cannabis nectar as an invocation to the Hindu Lord Shiva. Ideological barriers encountered by Gandhi also become evident in the behavior of Rabindra (Vinay Pathak), Narayan's pro-British friend, who slugs Scotch whiskey and sees no use in political freedom for his country. Narayan, on the other hand, places his trust in Gandhi's ideal of "passive resistance" to alien oppression.

Mehta's narrative at this point loses its initial steam, and it never quite recovers until the last scene. Shifting its focus from Chuyia's story to that of Kalyani, the film sinks under the weight of age-old platitudes, which are spouted first by Narayan as his way of courting Kalyani and then by the Pandit (Kulbhushan Kharbanda), a rotund compassionate sage, whom Chuyia is taken to see by Shakuntala (Seema Biswas), the widow who looks after the day-to-day affairs of the home.

Narayan is depicted as a Krishna figure, playing his flute by the river under the light of the full moon. Even so, he is unwilling to touch Kalyani in what must be one of the more unusual love scenes. He is prepared, however, to defy his parents' wishes and marry her. For her part, Kalyani yearns to escape from the home and start a new life with him. When the Head Mother becomes aware of the situation, she locks Kalyani in her room, where she remains until Shakuntala frees her.

A plot twist ensues when Narayan discovers that Kalyani has been serving his father as a devadasi, or temple prostitute. This explains his father's advice to keep her as a mistress. Narayan renounces this Brahman privilege and decides instead to leave home. But his actions are too late: Kalyani lays her bangles and folded white robe on the steps beside the holy Ganges River and drowns herself.

Later, as a means of acquiring funds for the home, the Head Mother orders Gulabi to initiate Chuyia into the life of a devadasi. Shakuntala, however, intercedes in a timely manner and carries the sleeping Chuyia to the train station, where Gandhi (Mohan Jhangiani), bathed in beatific sunlight, is holding a prayer meeting on the platform. After a silent meditation, Gandhi states: "For a long time I believed that God is Truth. But today I know that Truth is God."

In the swarming melee of Gandhi's stopover, Shakuntala seizes the opportunity to hand Chuyia to Narayan, who has decided to leave with Gandhi's entourage. As the train departs, the sadness on Shakuntala's face is tinged by a sense of bitter triumph. An end title imparts that according to the 2001 census, there are thirty-four million Asian Indian widows living in accordance with "The Laws of Manu."

Vivek Adarkar

CREDITS

Shakuntala: Seema Biswas
Kalyani: Lisa Ray

Gulabi: Raghuvir Yadav
Pandit/Sadananda: Kulbashan Kharbanda
Narayan: John Abraham
Chuyia: Sarala
Madhumati: Manorama
Patiraji, aka "Auntie": Vidula Javalgekar
Gyanvati/Head Mother: Meera Biswas
Dwarkanath: Gerson Da Cunha
Gandhi: Mohan Jhangiani
Rabindra: Vinay Pathak
Origin: Canada
Language: Hindi
Released: 2005
Production: David Hamilton; released by Mongrel Media, Fox Searchlight
Directed by: Deepa Mehta
Cinematography by: Giles Nuttgens
Music by: Mychael Danna, A.R. Rahman
Editing: Colin Monie
MPAA rating: PG-13
Running time: 117 minutes

REVIEWS

Boxoffice Online. April 28, 2006.
Hollywood Reporter Online. September 9, 2005.
Los Angeles Times Online. April 28, 2006.
New York Times Online. April 28, 2006.
San Francisco Chronicle. April 28, 2006, p. E4.
Variety Online. September 8, 2005.
Village Voice Online. April 25, 2006.

TRIVIA

The director originally began filming in Benares, India, in 2000, but the production was shut down and sets destroyed by Hindu fundamentalists. Mehta eventually re-created her film in Sri Lanka.

WE ARE MARSHALL

From the Ashes We Rose.
—Movie tagline

Box Office: $43.5 million

We Are Marshall is at once a moving, sad, and inspiring film based on a true story of hope arising from tragedy. Set in West Virginia in 1970 and 1971, the story explores the aftermath of a terrible accident when a plane carrying Marshall University's football team, coaching staff, and prominent local citizens goes down in a horrific crash just short of home. All on board are killed, and suddenly the university town finds itself struggling with a kind of shared grief and bewilderment that no one could have ever anticipated. The question that then begins to trouble many citizens, students, and administration officials is whether the football program should be continued. Some feel that putting together another team—which would take time and resources the university does not really have—would in some way dishonor those who were killed.

Football player Nate Ruffin (Anthony Mackie), one of a few players who escaped the tragedy because he was not on the plane, does not agree with the idea that continuing the program would be a dishonor to his late teammates. In fact, he believes the opposite, that Marshall should assemble another team for the very purpose of honoring the memory of those who lost their lives—to give players like himself an opportunity to continue their legacy and do something special "for our team." The board of trustees, influenced largely by board member Paul Griffen (Ian McShane), who lost his son in the crash, intends to suspend the program, but Nate organizes a rally of supporters who show their loyalty to the team by gathering in an enormous crowd outside the administration building and chanting "We...are...Marshall!"—the school's spirit cry. University President Donald Dedmon (David Strathairn), who is inclined to agree with the need to continue the football program, nevertheless is unsure of how to proceed. "You can start with a coach, sir," Nate tells him. Thus Dedmon begins searching for coaching candidates, but he rapidly discovers that no alumni are interested because of the tragic nature of the situation. Finally he receives a call from Jack Lengyel (Matthew McConaughey), a coach from a small college in Wooster. When Dedmon interviews Jack and asks him why he is interested in this job given the unusual circumstances, Jack—in his simple, straightforward way—explains that when he heard about the horrible accident and realized what the college town must be going through, he decided to call about the position because "I thought maybe I could help."

When Jack arrives at Marshall to build a new team for the 1971 season, he visits Red Dawson (Matthew Fox), who was the only member of the coaching staff not on the plane that fateful day. Red had already turned down an offer from Dedmon to take the position of Head Coach, burdened with feelings of guilt and unwilling to take on the responsibility of telling parents he would watch out for their children when he no longer believed he could do so. Nevertheless, Jack asks Red to come back as his assistant—an offer Red initially turns down but then accepts, telling Jack he will give him one year.

Jack and Red manage to assemble a coaching staff without much trouble, but finding players is another matter. After weeks of frustration, Jack approaches President Dedmon with a seemingly futile idea; if Dedmon can convince the NCAA to allow an exception to its rules and permit Marshall to play freshmen, Jack believes they will be able to recruit some good players who are enticed by the idea of taking the field three years earlier than would be possible anywhere else. Dedmon ultimately succeeds in this unprecedented request, though only after going to the NCAA in person, and immediately Jack and Red set out to find athletes with potential. In some of the movie's lighter scenes, the two coaches end up recruiting several players who are skilled athletes in other sports, betting that their talent will translate into success on the football field.

During the off-season, Jack and Red put all their energy into training this rookie team, captained by Nate. Unfortunately, when they take to the field for their first game, they suffer a humiliating defeat, and right away people begin to wonder if it was a bad idea to keep the program going. Nate, for one, is devastated and feels as if he has let his late teammates down. "That was my team. They left it in my hands," he weeps, but Coach Jack tries to correct him. "No. No!" he tells Nate, insisting that his teammates did *not* leave the team for him to bring back to glory. But Nate is not the only one to question himself. Red also questions what they have done, believing they have made a mockery of the team. Once again, Jack imparts some useful wisdom: "Right now, winning or losing doesn't matter. Not even *how* we play. What matters is that we *do* play."

Events take a more hopeful turn when they play their first home game. After Jack makes an impassioned, inspiring speech to the team at the cemetery where several of the former players are buried, the players focus on trying to be a true team, working together to honor not only their predecessors and former teammates but also the school and the community. In an exciting, hard-fought game, Marshall emerges victorious. The narrator soon explains that the team managed to win one more game that season and struggled throughout the 1970s to eventually become a championship team—a goal they finally reached in the 1980s.

Certainly there has been no shortage of sports movies telling stories of underdog teams beating the odds to emerge as victors, and many of these movies have been quality films, compelling and inspiring in the dramatic struggles they portray. *We Are Marshall* is not a typical sports, however, and that is partially what makes it stand out as unique and powerful. Though the specific subject matter of the plot deals with a football team, the larger issue explored is the human pain—the personal and communal struggle with grief—that comes after a tragedy that affects many. The story asks pertinent questions about how to respond to that kind of pain and how to move forward. Less a story about football than a story about "bouncing back" after a tremendous loss greater than a mere loss of a game, *We Are Marshall* explores the various responses of those who are most touched by such a tragedy. Thanks largely (but not exclusively) to the ever-positive and determined character of Jack, these individuals eventually discover that they must let go of their feelings of guilt; the best way to honor those they have lost is to strive forward with dignity and hope. It explores themes of sorrow, loss, and redemption, conveying a sense of victory that arises not merely from winning games and proving one's self but from persevering alongside others in the midst of pain and seeing hope where circumstances make it difficult to see.

David Flanagin

CREDITS

Jack Lengyel: Matthew McConaughey
Red Dawson: Matthew Fox
Nate Ruffin: Anthony Mackie
President Dedmon: David Strathairn
Paul Griffen: Ian McShane
Annie Cantrell: Kate Mara
Carol Dawson: January Jones
Sandy Lengyel: Kimberly Williams-Paisley
Origin: USA
Language: English
Released: 2006
Production: Basil Iwanyk, McG; Wonderland Sound and Vision, Thunder Road Productions, Legendary Pictures; released by Warner Bros.
Directed by: McG
Written by: Jamie Linden
Cinematography by: Shane Hurlbut
Music by: Christophe Beck
Sound: Mary H. Ellis
Editing: Priscilla Nedd Friendly, Gregg London
Art Direction: Jonah Markowitz
Costumes: Danny Glicker
Production Design: Tom Meyer
MPAA rating: PG
Running time: 131 minutes

REVIEWS

Boxoffice Online. December 22, 2006.
Entertainment Weekly. December 22, 2006, p. 57.
Hollywood Reporter Online. December 14, 2006.
Los Angeles Times Online. December 22, 2006.

New York Times Online. December 22, 2006.
San Francisco Chronicle. December 22, 2006, p. E6.
Variety Online. December 15, 2006.
Washington Post Online. December 22, 2006.

WHEN A STRANGER CALLS

Whatever You Do, Don't Answer The Phone.
—Movie tagline

Box Office: $47.8 million

When a Stranger Calls was a film that was not screened in advance for critics—the usual sign that the studio does not expect the film to get good reviews. In this case, they were quite right. When critics finally got to see *When a Stranger Calls*, they gave it scathing reviews. But it was too late to warn the public. Most newspaper reviews of the movie did not appear until the week following the film's debut. The movie was number one for that weekend. Maybe the poor reviews would not have changed anything, but perhaps a few people could have found a better way to spend eighty-three minutes of their lives.

The movie is billed as a remake of a 1978 stalker film starring Carol Kane. But it is really not a remake. The first film began with a stalker calling a babysitter and harassing her. This is the most memorable aspect of the film and was memorably spoofed in *Scream* (1996). The majority of the rest of the film involved Charles Durning's efforts to capture the killer. The new version just takes the babysitter and killer part and forces it into the shape of a full-length movie. First-time screenwriter Jake Wade Wall, who reportedly attended Yale and NYU, seems at a loss to figure out the alchemy involved in turning a twenty-minute concept into a full-length movie. He gets no help from director Simon West who had already quite definitively demonstrated his ineptitude in *Lara Croft: Tomb Raider* (2001). With no one having a clue about how to build suspense, there are plenty of scenes that go nowhere. In one scene, Jill (Camilla Belle), wanders down dark hallways, turns corners slowly, and creeps through doorways. Finally the creepy sound she hears turns out to be...an ice maker. It is difficult to imagine this spawning nightmares for anyone.

Jill got into her predicament by getting grounded. After spending over eight hundred cell phone minutes listening to her boyfriend apologize for kissing her best friend, Tiffany (Katie Cassidy), Jill went over her monthly allotment. To pay her parents back, Jill takes a job babysitting at a remote, architecturally stunning house. The house has huge two-story picture windows that overlook a pond and an atrium filled with yellow canaries. In some sense, the filmmakers should be given credit for making such a showplace seem even slightly menacing.

The children are asleep and Jill has been given orders not to wake them. Instead of raiding the refrigerator and watching TV, as any other babysitter would do, Jill chooses to sit in the darkened living room reading a schoolbook. Then she starts getting prank phone calls. Mostly, the caller breathes menacingly into the phone. Later he says creepily, "Have you checked the children?" (In the first movie, said children were dead. In this version, they are merely sleeping.)

The killer does not seem to be a man of action because instead of simply killing Jill, he keeps calling her. After Jill calls the police in a panic, they trace the call and report the bad news that the calls are coming from inside the house. This would be a whole lot scarier if this information was not readily apparent in every ad and preview for the film. Not that such an obvious hack job should be airtight, but the film has a few too many incongruities and the slow pace gives moviegoers plenty of time to ruminate on them. The house's lights, for instance, are supposed to go on whenever someone enters a room. But they do not. When Jill is sneaking around dark hallways, they stay off. But when the killer is creeping around upstairs, they go on—sometimes. Also, the killer is tremendously crafty in figuring out how Jill will react to certain situations and takes great care in setting gory scenes for her to discover. But when he finally tries to catch her, he becomes hopelessly inept and they end up spending the last several minutes of the film in hand-to-hand combat.

Lisa Rose of the *Newark Star-Ledger* wrote: "The quiet scenes don't build tension. They bore you silly. All the action is wedged into the last fifteen minutes and the showdown is a yawn rather than a scream." Matt Pais of the *Chicago Tribune* wrote that the film "offers a new record for red herrings, the most manipulative score imaginable and no payoff whatsoever." Lou Lumenick of the *New York Post* called the film "ineptly directed," but added that it "has unusually nice cinematography and sets for the genre." Finally, Wesley Morris of the *Boston Globe* wrote: "Even by the lowest standards, this is a frightless, cynically made movie...Audiences are bound to exit *Stranger* booing, knowing full well the movie belongs on their do-not-call list."

Jill Hamilton

CREDITS

Jill Johnson: Camilla Belle
Stranger: Tommy Flanagan
Scarlet: Tessa Thompson
Bobby: Brian Geraghty

Mr. Johnson: Clark Gregg
Dr. Mandrakis: Derek De Lint
Officer Burroughs: David Denman
Allison Mandrakis: Madeleine Carroll
Mrs. Mandrakis: Kate Jennings Grant
Will Mandrakis: Arthur Young
Detective Hines: Steve Eastin
Voice of the Stranger: Lance Henriksen (Voice)
Tiffany: Katie Cassidy
Origin: USA
Language: English
Released: 2006
Production: John Davis, Wyck Godfrey, Ken Lemberger; Screen Gems, Davis Entertainment Company; released by Sony Pictures Entertainment
Directed by: Simon West
Written by: Jake Wade Wall
Cinematography by: Peter Menzies Jr.
Music by: James Dooley
Sound: Glenn Berkovitz
Editing: Jeff Betancourt
Art Direction: Gerry Sullivan
Costumes: Marie-Sylvie Deveau
Production Design: Jon Gary Steele
MPAA rating: PG-13
Running time: 100 minutes

REVIEWS

Entertainment Weekly Online. February 8, 2006.
Los Angeles Times Online. February 6, 2006.
Premiere Magazine Online. February 3, 2006.
Variety Online. February 3, 2006.
Washington Post Online. February 4, 2006.

QUOTES

Jill Johnson: "You really scared me, if that's what you wanted. Is that what you wanted!?"
Stranger: "No."
Jill Johnson: "What do you want?"
Stranger: "Your blood all over me."

TRIVIA

Based on an urban legend, "The Babysitter and The Man Upstairs."

WHO KILLED THE ELECTRIC CAR?

In 1996, electric cars began to appear on roads all over California. They were quiet and fast, produced no exhaust and ran without gasoline. Ten years later, these cars were destroyed.
—Movie tagline

Box Office: $1.6 million

While Davis Guggenheim's *An Inconvenient Truth* (2006) tackles the larger issues related to global warming, Chris Paine's *Who Killed the Electric Car?* (2006) looks at one cause, the internal-combustion engine, and one failed attempt to address the problem, the electric car. Mixing interviews with automobile and oil company executives, engineers, scientists, politicians, bureaucrats, and owners of electric cars with news footage and scenes of protests, Paine tries to examine all sides of the complicated issue within ninety minutes.

Much of *Who Killed the Electric Car?* centers around the actions of the California Air Resources Board (CARB), which adopted a zero-emission mandate in 1990 to try to fight the state's overwhelming smog problem. As a result, electric cars with rechargeable batteries were marketed in California by General Motors, Ford, Toyota, Honda, and other manufacturers, and charging stations were erected throughout the state. Then the automakers suddenly turned against their own products. The person in charge of marketing GM's EV1 recalls being told by another marketing executive that he was the enemy.

Paine's major scapegoat is Dr. Alan C. Lloyd, chairman of CARB, who essentially leads the fight to rescind his board's mandate before joining the California Fuel Cell Partnership. The George W. Bush administration's solution to the emissions dilemma is cars that run on hydrogen fuel cells, a solution Paine and his experts paint as too impractical. Hydrogen is depicted as nothing more than a public-relations smokescreen. The film's most amusing moment comes with President Bush's appearance at a hydrogen fueling station. Presidential advisor Karl Rove is seen in the background talking on his mobile phone, his body language making clear that hydrogen is merely an excuse for a photo opportunity and a serious concern.

The centerpiece of *Who Killed the Electric Car?* is GM's efforts to round up and destroy all of California's EV1s. Apparently, though Paine does not make this clear, all the GM electric cars were leased, giving the company the right to take them away when the leases expired. Actor-director Peter Horton, possessor of the last EV1 in the state, is shown watching his beloved vehicle being taken away. Although GM had claimed that the vehicles would be preserved, Paine shows them being compacted in the Arizona desert.

In perhaps an effort at bipartisanship, Mel Gibson, known for his conservative politics, is interviewed about his passion for his EV1. It is hard to imagine GM's taking away the superstar's car, but apparently this happened.

The star of *Who Killed the Electric Car?* is Chelsea Sexton, a former EV1 salesperson heartbroken by GM's treachery. She, along with the former electric-car owners turned protestors, puts a human face on the controversy. Inventor Stanford R. Ovshinsky, whose Ovonic battery ran the EV1s, makes a charming spokesman for why electric cars remain a good idea.

Martin Sheen, well known for his support of liberal causes, narrates the film with a surprisingly impartial tone, never stooping to overly dramatize the issues. Paine's argument is generally logical and well balanced, always anticipating what opponents might say and counterbalancing their views. There are occasional flaws, as when Paine cites the enormous recent profits of the oil companies without citing a source.

Paine makes the demise of the EV1 and the other electric cars so painfully personal that some viewers might be more depressed than stirred to action. For much of the film, fighting the corporations, the politicians, and the bureaucrats seems pointless. Yet *Who Killed the Electric Car?* ends by painting a rosy picture of the future, with gas-electric hybrids like the Toyota Prius seen as a viable solution. Paine might have spent more time exploring this option at the expense of the tears shed over the EV1.

Michael Adams

CREDITS

Origin: USA

Language: English

Released: 2006

Production: Jessie Deeter; Plinyminor, Papercut Films, Electric Entertainment; released by Sony Pictures Classics

Directed by: Charles Paine

Written by: Charles Paine

Cinematography by: Thaddeus Wadleigh

Music by: Michael Brook

Sound: Alex Lamm, Jayme Roy, James Ridgely, Bill Stefanacci

Music Supervisor: Peter Afterman, Margaret Yen

Editing: Michael Kovalenko, Chris A. Peterson

MPAA rating: PG

Running time: 92 minutes

REVIEWS

Boxoffice Online. June 30, 2006.

Entertainment Weekly Online. July 5, 2006.

Los Angeles Times Online. June 28, 2006.

New York Times Online. June 28, 2006.

Premiere Magazine Online. June 29, 2006.

Variety Online. May 8, 2006.

WHY WE FIGHT

It is nowhere written that the American empire goes on forever.
—Movie tagline

Box Office: $1.4 million

Among the values outlined in U.S. President George Washington's farewell address to the fledgling nation in 1797 were the need for national unity, freedom of foreign interests, loyalty to the Constitution, and service to the common good. A similar message is delivered at the beginning of the Eugene Jarecki's documentary *Why We Fight* (2005).

A documentarian who won the Grand Jury Prize at the Sundance Film Festival for his film *The Trials of Henry Kissinger,* Jarecki opens his newest film with the televised farewell address of Dwight D. Eisenhower, in which the outgoing commander-in-chief delivered a foreboding warning against the nation's development of a "vast military-industrial complex." According to Eisenhower, outgoing doing so would place the United States in a perpetual state of war. Jarecki provides compelling evidence that Eisenhower's prophecy was not only an insightful forecast, but that war has become a profitable venture for the United States. Examples include U.S. Vice President Dick Cheney supporting legislation that guarantees contracts to companies like Halliburton and the Carlyle Group to rebuild the infrastructure of war-torn Iraq.

Ironically adopting the title of the World War II propaganda film series created by Frank Capra, *Why We Fight* features Jarecki interviewing a diverse crowd, including the common civilian, the political leader, and both active and retired military personnel, all of whom he queries, "Why do we fight?" The most common answer is for freedom, but global power, democracy, and oil also are expressed.

The film chronicles the rise of U.S. military hegemony from an emerging superpower engaged with its primary communist nemesis, the former Soviet Union, to the leading force against the war on terrorism. The movie intersperses chapters from the lives of three U.S. citizens, and these provide the film with a humanist viewpoint. Among them is the story of a young New York man, William Solomon, who, upon the death of his mother, realizes that he cannot afford to elevate his station on the socio-economic ladder and adequately provide for himself. A visit to the neighborhood military recruitment office gives him the assurance of a brighter future—if he joins the service. Portrayed as somewhat of an orphan in the world, Solomon makes the decision to leave behind his childhood residence. He is last seen being driven by his recruiter to basic training. The DVD version of this film reveals that Solomon spent eighteen months in Iraq as a helicopter mechanic.

Another story focuses on retired Lt. Col. Karen Kwiatkowski, who served as a military expert at the Pentagon. She soon became disillusioned with U.S. government executive decisions that were based on the political and economic interests of private-sector think tanks and defense contractors. In the film, Kwiatkowski is outspoken in her belief that the U.S. heads of state are primarily concerned with rewarding large defense contractors in order to maintain their positions of power.

Perhaps the most poignant story is that of retired New York City police officer and Vietnam War veteran Wilton Sekzer. While riding on a metropolitan bus on the morning of September 11, 2001, he saw the first tower of the World Trade Center being hit by a high-jacked airliner. His son, who worked in one of the towers, was among those that tragically perished. Heartbroken, Sekzer abides with the national sentiment to respond with force and initially places his trust in U.S. government decisions, including the unilateral invasion of Iraq. To demonstrate his convictions, he petitions the U.S. military to inscript his son's name on a bomb. Scrolling through the lengthy threads of email, Sekzer learns that his request is granted. However, he later expresses a sense of betrayal and anger when U.S. President George W. Bush admits that there was no connection between the deposed regime of former Iraqi dictator Saddam Hussein and the attack on the World Trade Center.

Jarecki crafts a film with snippets of archived footage and sound bites, as well as with interviews of both contemporary conservative and liberal pundits. Perhaps the most memorable quote is given by Gore Vidal, who describes the U.S as the "United States of Amnesia." Through this multi-layered lens, *Why We Fight* hopes to avoid excessive spin and focuses instead, with objective acuity, on the national rationale for this ongoing state of warfare. Although clearly a voice of dissent, Jarecki avoids two pitfalls demonstrated in documentarian Michael Moore's *Fahrenheit 9/11* (2004): he shuns iconoclastic smarminess by not appearing in his film and also steers clear of excessive castigation of the second Bush administration, choosing instead to focus on the rapid ascent of the United States' "military-industrial complex."

Film critic Roger Ebert of the *Chicago Sun-Times* provides an insightful observation about documentaries like *Why We Fight*. While agreeing with its politics, Ebert finds its content somewhat redundant and ineffective. He offers this description: "Few people are likely to see this film unless they already agree with its conclusions, and few of those will learn anything new from it." Comparing Jarecki's film to Moore's, Ebert reinforces his point by stating: "When one of its distributors said Michael Moore's *Fahrenheit 9/11* would defeat George Bush in 2004, he miscalculated, because there was little overlap between those planning to vote for Bush and those planning to see the movie."

David Metz Roberts

CREDITS

Origin: USA
Language: English
Released: 2005
Production: Eugene Jarecki, Susanna Shipman; Charlotte Street; released by Sony Pictures Classics
Directed by: Eugene Jarecki
Written by: Eugene Jarecki
Cinematography by: Chris Li, Etienne Sauret, May-Ying Welch, Sam Cullman
Music by: Robert Miller
Sound: Peter Miller, Brian Buckley, Paul Rusnak
Music Supervisor: Sue Jacobs
Editing: Nancy Kennedy
MPAA rating: PG-13
Running time: 98 minutes

REVIEWS

Boxoffice Online. January 20, 2006.
Chicago Sun-Times Online. February 17, 2006.
Entertainment Weekly Online. January 18, 2006.
Los Angeles Times Online. January 20, 2006.
New York Times Online. January 20, 2006.
Variety Online. January 24, 2005.
Washington Post Online. February 10, 2006, p. C05.

QUOTES

Sen. John McCain: "When does the United States go from a force for good, to a force of imperialism?"

THE WICKER MAN

Some sacrifices must be made.
—Movie tagline

Box Office: $23.6 million

The Wicker Man is unlikely to satisfy either the fans of the British cult horror picture on which it is based or the fans of writer/director Neil LaBute. After all, the original film had been called "the *Citizen Kane* of horror movies." The remake, with its setting changed from the magical coast of Scotland to the Pacific Northwest, offers an impressive example of a plot gone wrong that doesn't make sense and doesn't seem to be the least bit bothered about it.

Highway patrolman Edward Malus (Nicolas Cage) gets an urgent letter from an old girl friend named Willow (Kate Beahan), who disappeared some years before and now desperately needs Edward's help in order to find her daughter Rowan, who seems to have gone missing from the cult community on the secluded island where Willow now lives. Edward, now employed as a California police detective, decides to take off for this remote island off the coast of Washington, improbable though that decision may seem. Guilt involving a roadside accident he witnessed seems to be his main motive; that memory must really bother him, since it comes to him only in disturbing monochrome flashbacks. A little girl was trapped in a car that burst into flames before Edward, then a highway patrol cop, could rescue her. For whatever reason, then, and by whatever flawed logic (it later turns out that the missing girl was Edward's daughter), Edward seeks out Summers Isle, an island so remote he can only reach it by biplane and by bribing the pilot who brings provisions to the island. That pilot later ends up inexplicably dead, the radio on his airplane smashed.

A smarter protagonist might have worried more about how he might get off of this peculiar and apparently demented island. But Edward is more bossy, assertive, and obnoxious than smart and believes in his authority as a policeman from California, though he is seriously out of his jurisdiction. He does not help his case by being noisy and obnoxious and by constantly reminding the unimpressed natives that he is a police officer from California. He believes the little girl he seeks is the designated ritual victim to the God of the Harvest, a burnt offering to be served up in a huge human effigy made of wicker, a very odd and dominant construction that the policeman seems not to encounter until the very and of the film. Yes, there will be a human sacrifice. No, it will not be pleasant. The viewer will not understand Edward's role in this ritual until the very end of the movie. Problem is, the story as retold is more laughable than scary.

Watching this updated remake, it is difficult to understand why the original became a cult hit. The first film was made in 1972, released in 1973, directed by Robin Hardy and starred Edward Woodward (later to become famous as the star of an American television series, *The Equalizer*), as the police officer, Sergeant Howie, Britt Ekland as Willow, and Christopher Lee as Lord Summersisle. The original enjoyed a limited release in Britain but was not, initially, released in the United States. The fantasy fanzine *Cinefantastique* (Vol. 6, No. 3, 1977) published an essay by David Bartholomew that established the film's cult standing.

The original, of course, was set on an island off the coast of Scotland, lending a touch of Celtic mysticism and Druid paganism not present in the new version. The switch to a matriarchal beekeeping commune also complicates credibility. Men in the remake are mute drones and little more. The women call the shots, and most of them are incredibly smug. Instead of Lee as a magisterial Scots "laird," Ellen Burstyn plays the parallel role of Sister Summersisle with quiet, understated dignity and restraint, a pleasant counter-balance to Cage's constant anger, frustration, and frenzy. All Cage can do is to shout and bluster and wave his weapon menacingly. In extreme situations, he punches women in the face. One understands his anger and frustration, since most of the women are far more articulate than the script allows him to be. Cage's acting is so irrational and irritating that one almost feels a sense of profound satisfaction when he finally has to face the Wicker Man.

The writer who originally concocted this metaphysical morass was Anthony Shaffer, the twin brother of playwright Peter Shaffer (who was best known for the equally "primitive" and puzzling drama *Equus* [1977] and his later moral allegory involving Mozart and Hapsburg court composer Antonio Salieri *Amadeus* [1984]). Anthony Shaffer is probably best known for his play *Sleuth*, which was adapted to film in 1972, the same year he adapted *Frenzy* for Alfred Hitchcock, at about the same time he would have been working on *The Wicker Man*. Neil LaBute gets writing credit for the remake, Shaffer having died in 2001, though LaBute's credits mention a novel entitled *The Ritual* as the ultimate source, while *The Films of Christopher Lee* (Scarecrow Press, 1983, Robert W. Pohle, Jr., and Douglas C. Hart) mentions only a "novelization" of the screenplay, attributed to Shaffer and director Robin Hardy.

Casting surprises include Cage as Edward Malus and Burstyn as Chief Priestess Sister Summersisle. Probably the cult standing of the 1973 film, along with the reputation of playwright and director LaBute helped to make the actors agreeable to roles that were so foolish and embarrassing in a plot that was lamentably incoherent. Even the most simple and basic communications are made to seem awkward and artificial. Such problems are surprising, considering that LaBute began as a playwright and has now written seventeen plays and a collection of short stories. Born in Detroit in 1963 educated at Brigham Young University, LaBute adapted his play *In the Company of Men* to the screen in 1997 and went on to direct several films, including *Nurse Betty* (2000) and *The Shape of Things* (2003). LaBute told Ellen McCarthy of the *Washington Post* that he agreed to remake *The Wicker Man* because he "liked the film...[and]...didn't feel compelled to copy it or say, 'Well, I think I can do better.'" Instead, he "wanted to be able to say, 'This is a movie that interests me.'"

LaBute's remake opened on a rainy Labor Day weekend in the wake of Hurricane Ernesto in the Mid-Atlantic and Northeast. The film grossed just under $12 million that weekend and was not available to media reviewers in pre-release screenings. *Entertainment Weekly* came back with a proper review a week later. Reviewer Owen Gleiberman wrote favorably of the original's "bizarre Scottish commune", concluding that the film, "kitschy as much of it is, does exert an eerie power." He approved of LaBute's "big innovation" of turning Christopher Lee into Ellen Burstyn and the pagan commune into a "honey-harvesting" matriarchy. His review generously claimed that the remake had "just enough enigma and weirdness" to justify a B-minus.

Other reviewers were less kind. "A movie like this can survive an absurd premise but not incompetent execution," A.O. Scott wrote in his *New York Times* review, adding that "LaBute, never much of an artist with the camera, proves almost comically inept as a horror-movie technician." Scott concluded that the film was "neither haunting nor amusing: just boring." *Washington Post* reviewer Stephen Hunter called the film "dreadfully funny." The "fundamental problem," according to Hunter, was that "the mechanics of the thriller are utterly alien to poor LaBute." Moreover, Hunter concluded, that the film is "quite unpleasant, when it isn't completely goofy."

James M. Welsh

CREDITS

Edward Malus: Nicolas Cage
Sister Summersisle: Ellen Burstyn
Sister Willow: Kate Beahan
Dr. Moss: Frances Conroy
Sister Rose/Sister Thorn: Molly Parker
Sister Honey: Leelee Sobieski
Sister Beech: Diane Delano
Origin: USA
Language: English
Released: 2006
Production: Nicolas Cage, Norm Golightly, Avi Lerner, Randall Emmett; Alcon Entertainment, Millennium Films; released by Warner Bros.
Directed by: Neil LaBute
Written by: Neil LaBute
Cinematography by: Paul Sarossy
Music by: Angelo Badalamenti
Sound: Darren Brisker
Editing: Joel Plotch
Costumes: Lynette Meyer
Production Design: Phillip Barker
MPAA rating: PG-13
Running time: 97 minutes

REVIEWS

Entertainment Weekly. September 15, 2006, p. 54.
Hollywood Reporter Online. September 5, 2006.
Los Angeles Times Online. September 4, 2006.
New York Times Online. September 2, 2006.
San Francisco Chronicle. September 1, 2006, p. E2.
Variety Online. September 1, 2006.

AWARDS

Nomination:

Golden Raspberries 2006: Worst Picture, Worst Actor (Cage), Worst Screenplay, Worst Remake

THE WILD

A whole new breed of tourist.
—Movie tagline

The Circle of Life meets The Big Apple.
—Movie tagline

Box Office: $37.3 million

Computer-generated animation has given writers and animators an unprecedented opportunity. Using the technology, they can create stories set in lands limited only by their imaginations, and it is all rendered crisply, clearly, and relatively inexpensively. With unlimited creative tools at their command, the storytellers have somehow all come upon the same idea—make kiddie movies featuring wacky talking animals.

Walt Disney Studio's *The Wild* suffered from the recent proliferation of such films. It was pretty much lost between such similarly-themed fare as *Barnyard, Over the Hedge,* and *Ice Age 2: The Meltdown*, all released in the same year. But the film that overshadowed *The Wild* the most was *Madagascar* (2005). Not only did the two films share the usual crew of sassy animals but both involved zoo animals escaping to the wild and trying to apply their city ways to jungle life. By the time *The Wild* finally rolled into theaters (though it was actually in development before *Madagascar*), it was probably a rare parent who was looking forward to sitting through this particular story again.

The Wild also has a familiar feel with its father-son relationship. As in *The Lion King* (1994), it has a young lion, Ryan (voice of Greg Cipes), who must emerge from the shadow of his more powerful father, Samson (voice of Kiefer Sutherland), to prove that he is also a strong leader. The twist is that, while Simba's father was genuinely a strong leader, Ryan's father Samson is a fraud. In their big city zoo home, Samson is the main attraction. He is billed as a ferocious predator taken straight from the wild. Samson enjoys his role and celebrity. He is not anxious to reveal to anyone, especially his young cub, that he is actually not from the wild, but rather from a small-time circus. Samson likes to regale Ryan with (fictitious) tales of his exploits. It all just serves to make Ryan feel even more inferior. The poor cub has not even found his roar yet, which is a point of embarrassment for him. Fed up with not measuring up, Ryan hops on a container ship bound for Africa.

Samson gathers his pals and they set off to find the cub. Along on the journey are the none-too-bright snake, Larry (voice of Richard Kind) and a hyper little squirrel, Benny (voice of Jim Belushi), who is in love with a comedic giraffe, Bridget (voice of Janeane Garofalo). The main bit of originality comes from the character of Nigel (voice of Eddie Izzard), a Aussie koala. Izzard improvised most of the dialogue and he comes up with some unexpected comments. "Does anyone have any eucalyptus wipes?" he asks daintily after soiling himself. It is also a nice touch that he sports a hideous set of crooked teeth.

Once ensconced in the wild, the animals find themselves pitted against a herd of wildebeests, led by Kazar (voice of William Shatner). Kazar intends to change the animal hierarchy and put wildebeests above lions. He plans to do this is by eating a lion—Samson. There is also a none-too-original side story about the wildebeests seeing Nigel and worshipping him as a god. Attentive moviegoers will remember that the sloth in *Ice Age 2* was also treated as a god, as were many other jungle visitors in previous films.

The film was directed by Steve "Spaz" Williams, who has honed his visual sense with his work on *The Abyss* (1989) and *The Mask* (1994). The animation is very detailed and precise. For example, Samson's mane reportedly contains six million hairs. Roger Ebert of the *Chicago Sun-Times* found the look disturbing. "The cartoon illusion is lost," he wrote, "and we venture toward the Uncanny Valley—that shadowy area known to robot designers and animators, in which artificial creatures so closely resemble humans that they make us feel kinda creepy." Other critics generally liked the look of the film, but found the rest to be a narrative rehash. Michael Wilmington of the *Chicago Tribune* wrote that the film "has a good director, snazzy visuals and some really funny animals, and that's at least half the battle." Desson Thomson of the *Washington Post* thought that the film seemed "like a sampling of other, better Disney films." Peter Hartlaub of the *San Francisco Chronicle* wrote: "*The Wild* is a decent-looking and harmless computer animated film that is notable mostly because it doesn't appear to contain a single original idea." Finally, Ty Burr of the *Boston Globe* wrote: "How's the movie? Technologically incredible, aesthetically pretty hideous, and narratively lumpy."

Jill Hamilton

CREDITS

Samson: Kiefer Sutherland (Voice)
Benny: Jim Belushi (Voice)
Nigel: Eddie Izzard (Voice)
Bridget: Janeane Garofalo (Voice)
Ryan: Greg Cipes (Voice)
Larry: Richard Kind (Voice)
Kazar: William Shatner (Voice)
Fergus Flamingo: Colin Hay (Voice)
Penguin MC: Don Cherry (Voice)
Carmine: Lenny Venito (Voice)
Blag: Patrick Warburton (Voice)
Samson's Father: Kevin M. Richardson (Voice)
Origin: USA
Language: English
Released: 2006
Production: Clint Goldman, Beau Flynn; Walt Disney Pictures, Hoytyboy Pictures, Sir Zip Studios/Contrafilm; released by Buena Vista
Directed by: Steve "Spaz" Williams
Written by: Edward Decter, John J. Strauss, Mark Gibson, Philip Halprin
Music by: Alan Silvestri
Sound: Andy Newell
Editing: V. Scott Balcerek, Steven L. Wagner
Production Design: Chris Farmer
MPAA rating: G
Running time: 85 minutes

REVIEWS

Chicago Tribune Online. April 14, 2006.
New York Times Online. April 14, 2006.
San Francisco Chronicle. April 14, 2006, p. E5.
USA Today Online. April 13, 2006.
Variety Online. April 12, 2006.
Washington Post. April 14, 2006, p. C1.

QUOTES

Samson (about a sewer system): "Appears to be a human bathing area."
Nigel (replies): "You mean humans don't lick themselves clean? Disgusting!"

WINTER PASSING

Sometimes you go looking for something you want...and find what you need.
—Movie tagline

Adam Rapp's bleak but sentimental little film, *Winter Passing,* is an odd piece of work. For one thing, the splendid Ed Harris manages to make almost no impact in the juicy role of a dissipated aging writer. Even stranger is the presence of Will Ferrell who, in between making blockbuster comedy hits took a small deadpan part in this low-budget character study. He struggles to rein in his anarchic comic wildness.

The equally unlikely protagonist is played by Zooey Deschanel as if she were on emotion-suppressing medication. Yes, she's supposed to be a depressed and depressing character, and she's emblematic of a generational style in which expressiveness is considered bad form. Even so, Deschanel seems to be straining to make as little impact on screen as possible. Her face shrouded in dark bangs, her small body hunched and shrinking away from human contact, her speech always delivered in a soft, mumbling monotone, Deschanel almost disappears from the center of a film that seems to strive for a muted impact.

First-time writer/director Rapp might be mistaking subtlety for substance. The film is quiet, though often observant, and the story is thin and slow. Deschanel plays Reese Holden, a twenty-something Manhattan waif who works as a bartender, acts occasionally in small productions off-off-Broadway, and consumes both alcohol and cocaine, though neither drug seems to have much effect on her somnolent personality. Rapp signals that *Winter Passing* will be lackadaisical in its approach right from the start, in a scene in which Reese, auditioning for an unknown part, is asked to sing, and croons "My Bonnie Lies Over the Ocean" in utterly unremarkable fashion; the pointlessness of her starving-artist existence is the only point.

Reese seems half alive at best, barely responsive to suitors and friends, and we start to find out why when a literary agent (Amy Madigan) finds her and offers her $100,000 in exchange for a box of letters between her parents. Her mother is dead, and her father Don (Ed Harris), a former best-selling author turned recluse, hasn't written anything of note in many years. But both remain famous enough writers to excite literary interest in this correspondence, which has been left to Reese by an uncle. The agent informs her of this fact, though why the uncle hadn't contacted Reese directly is unclear.

After cruelly disposing of a cat that has been diagnosed with leukemia by zipping her into a sports bag and dumping her into the Hudson River, Reese travels by bus to northern Michigan, to her parents' woodland estate. She is greeted by Corbit (Ferrell), a caretaker of sorts, who keeps intruders away. Helping out with the cooking and housework is Shelley (Amelia Warner), a former student of Don's. Reese's father has not only retired from teaching—as well as writing—he has taken to living in the garage.

His face framed by long, stringy white hair, Harris plays Holden as a stumbling, barely-there old alcoholic, who struggles to hold his fork while feeding himself. It is unclear whether his feebleness is a result of drink, senility, fading interest in life, or a combination of all three. Apart from one small confrontation with his daughter, however, Holden isn't a character with much of a discernible personality. Whatever impact he used to have—and judging by the adulation of his acolytes, it must have been mighty—has left few traces behind. Harris misses an opportunity to make Holden into a memorable curmudgeon, a prodigious thinker, or a radical artist. It's implied that he once was all three, as well as a prolific writer, but we learn that from others' dialogue, not his.

Sadly lacking, too, is much of a backstory for his two new housemates. We don't know why they're present or what they see in the old literary lion. It's left for Ferrell to fill the idle time that ticks away in this movie with an understated comic characterization, not really his forte. He's a shy, born-again Christian rocker who was once a member of a group called Punching Pilate (the best joke in a film short on humor). Since no one else in the film is funny—or even memorably quirky—Ferrell seems to be stumbling on set from another movie, but he is held mostly in check by a director who seems unsure of how to handle his material other than to consistently downplay it.

What is left is a collection of small moments: Reese and Shelley fighting over which one is the patriarch's favorite, Reese finding and reading the letters and demanding details of her mother's suicide, Ferrell singing a Beatles song in a falsetto at the open mike night at the local bar in town. Given the setup, it will come as no surprise to most viewers that the return of the prodigal daughter and the halting attempts at reawakening human connections with her father will have a redemptive effect at the end. One sure bet about films like *Winter Passing,* which take such pains to portray characters as cynical and damaged, is that they will end up awash in sentimentality, though it will be packaged in a muted shroud of shrugging anomie. Writer's block will be conquered, estranged relatives will reconnect, and even an anti-romantic girl will find love.

Rapp has the bones of a story but his characters are narratively malnourished, not to say anorexic. It is not enough to be small and artsy, in order to succeed as an independent sleeper you need rich characters. The lack of this key ingredient makes Rapp's slacker filmmaking style even less impactful.

Michael Betzold

CREDITS

Reese Holden: Zooey Deschanel
Don Holden: Ed Harris
Corbit: Will Ferrell
Shelly: Amelia Warner
Lori Lansky: Amy Madigan
Ray: Dallas Roberts
Deirdre: Deirdre O'Connell
Rob: Robert Beitzel
Origin: USA
Language: English
Released: 2005
Production: Jennifer Dana, David Koplan; Focus Features, Stratus Film Co., Laura Bickford, Mint Pictures; released by Yari Film Group
Directed by: Adam Rapp
Written by: Adam Rapp
Cinematography by: Terry Stacey
Music by: John Kimbrough, John Kimbrough
Sound: Noah Vivekanand Timan
Editing: Meg Reticker
Art Direction: Lucio Seixas
Costumes: Victoria Farrell
Production Design: David Korins
MPAA rating: R
Running time: 98 minutes

REVIEWS

Boxoffice Online. February 17, 2006.
Chicago Sun-Times Online. March 10, 2006.
Entertainment Weekly Online. February 22, 2006.
Los Angeles Times Online. February 17, 2006.
New York Times Online. February 17, 2006.
Premiere Magazine Online. February 17, 2006.
Variety Online. September 16, 2005.
Washington Post Online. March 10, 2006, p. WE32.

TRIVIA

The kitten playing Spike was rescued from an animal shelter and adopted by the producer's brother.

WORDPLAY

Discover a world that thinks inside the box.
—Movie tagline

Box Office: $3.1 million

Legendary *New York Times* crossword puzzle editor and NPR personality Will Shortz is the focus of Patrick Creadon's documentary *Wordplay*—an intellectual feel-good film that takes a fascinating look at crossword puzzle creators, competitors, and famous fans. Creadon takes a difficult topic to bring to life onscreen and makes it visually innovative and actually exciting to watch, showing high-profile puzzlers from all walks of life, from athletes to musicians and politicians.

The profile of Shortz, who has edited the *New York Times* crossword since 1994, reveals his lifelong obsession with crossword puzzles. He created his first puzzle as a youth and then went on to receive a degree in the self-created major of "enigmatology" from Indiana University, admitting he consigned himself to a life of poverty and puzzles. Also inhabiting this tight-knit world of professional puzzlers is crossword puzzle creator Merl Reagle, who provides engrossing, step-by-step instructions on puzzle creation with one he creates on the spot for the film, called "Word Play."

Celebrity puzzlers feature prominently in the film and Creadon frequently cuts between former president Bill Clinton, *The Daily Show* host Jon Stewart, documentarian Ken Burns, folk musicians the Indigo Girls, and Yankees pitcher Mike Mussina who share fascinating stories about their experience with the *New York Times* puzzle, which they all acknowledge as the preeminent crossword. Stewart notes, "I am a *Times* puzzle fan. I will solve the *USA Today*, but I don't feel good about myself." Reflecting the solitary nature of crossword solving, all these high-profile people are shown by themselves with only the folded section of the paper in front of them. A highlight is a clever montage showing all the celebrities solving the same crossword simultaneously. Although sometimes allowing the viewer to see the puzzle being solved by hand, more frequently Creadon, along with titling and graphics designer Brian Oakes, shows a close-up of the clues in large letters on the upper portion of the screen while the squares are being filled in below.

Even more interesting than the celebrities are the slavish devotees of the *New York Times* crossword puzzle. Creadon introduces some of the best puzzlers in the country when they gather at the 28th annual American Crossword Puzzle Tournament, an event founded and hosted by Shortz and held each year at the Marriott in Stamford, Connecticut. With so many of the same people returning each year, it is akin to a family reunion complete with talent contest, crossword-related songs being sung, and contestants and judges wearing colorful, crossword-themed garb.

The tournament takes place one weekend in March where the contestants must complete six puzzles on

Saturday and are graded on speed and accuracy. The standings are posted the next morning followed by puzzle number seven which decides the top three finalists. The finalists then take the stage to solve one last puzzle in front of an audience with live commentary from the judges (contestants wear large earphones to block any sound). Some tension is created as one of the top three contestants after the first round is eliminated for an error and fourth place contestant, perpetual runner-up Al Sanders, makes it into the top three, along with Trip Payne, a professional crossword constructor from Florida, and Rensselaer Polytechnic Institute student Tyler Hinman. The showdown of the top three provides a dramatic ending to Creadon's film, with underdog Sanders finishing far ahead of the other two contestants only to realize too late that he forgot to fill in two of the squares. Throwing off the headphones, Sanders is red in face as he utters an unprintable but understandable expletive. Old pro Trip is shown up by newcomer Tyler, who, at twenty-years-old, becomes the tournament's youngest winner ever (and, although not noted in the documentary, repeated his win in 2006).

One of the film's more sympathetic characters is Ellen Ripstein, a puzzle editor from New York. Ripstein, dubbed the Susan Lucci of the tournament, regularly finished in the top three for eighteen years, but had never won the tournament until 2001. Like most of the other puzzlers featured, she is an eccentric intellectual who exhibits a playful side during the talent competition when she shows off her baton-twirling skills.

Produced by Creadon and fellow screenwriter Christine O'Malley, *Wordplay* is certainly worthy of its Grand Jury nomination at the 2006 Sundance Film Festival. Doug Blush's fast-paced editing keeps the film moving briskly along while Peter Golub and Vic Fleming's original music is complemented by songs such as Cake's apt "Shadow Stabbing" which plays during the opening credits.

Hilary White

CREDITS

Origin: USA

Language: English

Released: 2006

Production: Patrick Creadon, Christine O'Malley; Grinder Films; released by IFC Films

Directed by: Patrick Creadon

Written by: Patrick Creadon, Christine O'Malley

Cinematography by: Patrick Creadon

Music by: Peter Golub

Music Supervisor: Tracy McNight

Editing: Doug Blush

MPAA rating: Unrated

Running time: 90 minutes

REVIEWS

Boxoffice Online. June 16, 2006.

Chicago Sun-Times Online. June 23, 2006.

Entertainment Weekly Online. June 14, 2006.

Los Angeles Times Online. June 23, 2006.

New York Times Online. June 16, 2006.

Premiere Magazine Online. June 16, 2006.

Variety Online. January 23, 2006.

Washington Post. June 23, 2006, p. C5.

QUOTES

Jon Stewart: "I am a *Times* puzzle fan. I will solve the *USA Today,* but I don't feel good about myself."

WORLD TRADE CENTER

A true story of courage and survival.
—Movie tagline

Box Office: $70.2 million

The year 2006 marked five years since the events of September 11 and on this anniversary, filmmakers felt that enough time had passed and wounds had sufficiently healed to address the event that scarred the American national consciousness. Earlier in the year, Paul Greengrass' *United 93* opened to almost universal critical acclaim but not box office success. *World Trade Center* is controversial auteur Oliver Stone's effort to address those dark days.

While Greengrass' film concerned the heroic events aboard the hijacked plane that missed the terrorists' target, crashing in a Pennsylvania field because of the actions of the passengers, Stone chose to focus on one small event that happened when two hijacked planes crashed into the World Trade Center towers in New York City. Instead of telling the broader story of that day, Stone distills it down to the story of two rescuers trapped beneath the rubble of the fallen towers. Their stories become symbolic of the larger and more overwhelming event.

To Stone's credit, this sincere acknowledgment of the men and women who risked their lives to help others that day does not contain any of the elements usually found in his films. For an event that became politically galvanizing, the filmic recounting is amazingly devoid of partisanship. There are no veiled hints of conspiracy theories or political agendas evident in the story, although many right-wing media commentators have flag-wavingly adopted the film as if it were made by one of their own. The liberal Stone, however, presents this true-life story in an extremely straightforward and respectful way.

World Trade Center opens with dawn on an average September day in New York as millions of people made their way to work. The focal points are two men and their families. Sergeant John McLoughlin (Nicholas Cage) is a twenty-one-year vet of the NYPD and a veteran of the World Trade Center bombing in 1993 who now works for the Port Authority. Will Jimeno (Michael Pena) is a Columbian immigrant who recently graduated from the police academy. He is now an eager rookie at the Port Authority and is more than a little anxious about doing well.

Not long after the men report for work that morning the first plane hits the first World Trade Center tower and all forcers are marshaled to get the situation under control. John and his crew are sent to help with the evacuation. On the way, they begin to get confusing information. The Pentagon has been hit by a missile, the other tower has been attacked…no it hasn't…yes it has. They're right there and they probably have less information than someone at home watching the events unfold on CNN. However, John and his crew do what they must and rush into a building that everyone else is fleeing. While gathering their equipment in the concourse between the two towers, the unthinkable happens. The first tower falls. John and Will are alive but trapped in debris. Better off is Officer Dominick Pezzulo (Jay Hernandez) who manages to free himself but is killed when the second tower falls, dumping additional debris on John and Will. The two men now must talk to and encourage each other to keep alive.

As John and Will lay immobile in the rubble, we also witness the paralysis that envelopes their families as they wait for news and tend to their families. Donna McLoughlin (Maria Bello) and Allison Jimeno (Maggie Gyllenhaal) alternate between concern, hope, fear, despair, and anger. They feel the need to do something, but they are as helpless as their husbands.

The one person who doesn't seem powerless is an accountant and ex-Marine who feels called by God to go to the accident site and help. Master Sergeant Dane Karnes (Michael Shannon) gets himself a buzz cut, dons his old uniform, and walks right onto the site to begin his own search and rescue operation. It will be he who finally finds John and Will and leads others to free them after thirteen hours (for Will) and twenty-two hours (for John) of pain, agony, and thirst.

This is a small story set against a huge event. It is representative of all the men and women who went to help that day, many of whom sacrificed their own lives. It is also a story of the human spirit, of how we band together in times of emergency, of how the worst of times can bring out the best in people. It is a very personal and human story told in a very respectful manner.

Just as Stone's filmmaking here is relatively reserved, so too are the performances. Cage and Pena spend almost the entire film acting using only their voices and grit-covered faces. The impotence their families feel when confronted by the situation keeps the wives actions tightly bound, as well. In light of the incredible emotions of that day, these constrained people reflect a national emotion. These people are heroes but they're also human and Stone ably portrays both identities. He shows us the faces of the Port Authority police as they look out the window of their bus as they approach the towers. These men look scared and worried, but they will do their job. Cage and Pena take the heroic and make it human, they take the very human and make it heroic.

World Trade Center is not only well acted and well told, it is also well made. From David Brenner's and Julie Monroe's balanced editing blending the separate yet intertwined stories to Craig Armstrong's solemnly appropriate music, there's not a wrong note in the film. Special mention has to go to Jan Roelf's incredibly authentic recreation of the Twin Towers and Seamus McGarvey's clear-cut camerawork, which, when coupled with the sound effects, actually put one at ground zero as the towers fell. Add these elements together and Stone has given audiences a caring and psychologically compelling re-creation of a day that still resonates in the collective American consciousness.

Beverley Bare Buehrer

CREDITS

John McLoughlin: Nicolas Cage

Will Jimeno: Michael Pena

Donna McLoughlin: Maria Bello

Allison Jimeno: Maggie Gyllenhaal

Dominick Pezzulo: Jay Hernandez

Scott Strauss: Stephen Dorff

Dave Karnes: Michael Shannon

Origin: USA

Language: English

Released: 2006

Production: Michael Shamberg, Stacey Sher, Moritz Borman, Debra Hill; released by Paramount Pictures

Directed by: Oliver Stone

Written by: Andrea Berloff

Cinematography by: Seamus McGarvey
Music by: Craig Armstrong
Sound: John Pritchett
Music Supervisor: Budd Carr
Editing: David Brenner, Julie Monroe
Art Direction: Richard Johnson
Costumes: Michael Dennison
Production Design: Jan Roelfs
MPAA rating: PG-13
Running time: 129 minutes

REVIEWS

Los Angeles Times Online. August 9, 2006.
Newsday Online. August 4, 2006.
Time Magazine Online. July 31, 2006.

THE WORLD'S FASTEST INDIAN

Based on one hell of a true story.
—Movie tagline

Box Office: $5.1 million

"I've had a good career playing psychopaths or uptight people," notes Anthony Hopkins, "and I'm fed up with those. I don't want to play any more of them." In *The World's Fastest Indian,* he is light years away from the unsettling Hannibal the Cannibal, as well as those stiff, remote Merchant-Ivory characters who tried to keep everything rigidly and oh-so-properly repressed. This film tells the true story of colorful New Zealand codger Burt Munro, who dreamt of testing out his prized, lovingly-modified 1920 Indian twin motorcycle on Utah's famous Bonneville Flats to see how fast it would take him. When the senior cyclist showed up there with his beloved "old girl" in 1967, they must have seemed like a matched pair of out-dated curiosities. The other bikers, proud of their newer equipment and with less years but more financial backing behind them, must have dismissed him as an unrealistic old coot, as crusty, salty, and dried up as the flats themselves. However, no one could put the brakes on Burt. Spunkily, unswervingly determined to reach his goal "before I fall off the perch," he flabbergasted all by setting a new land speed record of 201.851 mph, which still stands today. While Burt may have been thought by some to be nuts for venturing thousands of miles on such an improbable quest, he is a richly rewarding character of sound mind (if somewhat eccentric) for Hopkins to portray. There is also no repression here as his Burt is a warm, vibrant, admirably plucky, amiable old teddy bear, with a delightful, cheerful chortle and a piquant dash of vinegar when needed. It is an engaging, charming performance, convincing and memorable, and one which Hopkins rightly rated as among his best. How unfortunate that the film, made on a budget of approximately $20 million, grossed just over $5 million in limited release despite quite positive reviews.

The World's Fastest Indian was written and directed by Roger Donaldson, who grew up in New Zealand with an interest in motorcycles and was understandably drawn to learn more about Munro. Donaldson eventually got to know him, and made a documentary entitled *Burt Munro: Offerings to the God of Speed* (1971), a phrase Burt had scrawled in his garage above the shelves of parts he hoped would accelerate his cycle. Donaldson felt that his first film did not do justice to its subject, and wrote the first script for *Indian* in 1979, the year after Burt's death. It is clear here how much respect and affection he has for Burt, and those watching will quickly feel the same upon meeting this uncommonly common man.

Donaldson effectively makes clear that Burt's single-minded, devoted improvement of the Indian is beyond idle tinkering. The bike is the driving force in his life. He stubbornly aims to get to the hallowed proving grounds of Bonneville to break the 200 mph mark. The idea of getting the chance to do so clearly consumes and thrills him. However, the place is so far away and his goal seems a tad far-fetched. After all, elderly Burt strains to hear and to urinate, and he is also whisked off in an ambulance with chest pains to learn that both his arteries and his chances for success have now exceedingly narrowed. The Indian seems somewhat dotty too, with no effective braking mechanism and makeshift parts that include a kitchen door hinge and the cork from a brandy bottle. "I think your motorcycling days are over," a doctor tells Burt, to which he chuckles, "Like hell they are." There is unquestionably still a lot of life left in the man, something jauntily, inspiringly indomitable. In addition, when Burt obliviously revs up the Indian at night and his sleepy neighbors threaten to call the police, his venerable vehicle sounds remarkably chipper as well.

Despite Burt's nocturnal inconsiderateness, his unwise, incendiary solution for an overgrown lawn, and his penchant for publicly peeing on his lemon tree to make it grow, it seems that even his periodically puzzled and/or exasperated neighbors cannot help but wish him well. For those watching the film, these quirks merely add entertaining colorfulness rather than diminishing the work's sympathetic portrait. In short order, Hopkins successfully imbues Burt with a highly agreeable, endearing appeal, and both his portrayal and the screenplay engender fondness, admiration, and respect for this resourceful, resolute, resilient man whom viewers wish to succeed. They will fully understand the warmth shown toward Burt by Tom (Aaron Murphy), the companionable redheaded boy next door (their scenes together are sweetly affecting), his lady friend (Annie Whittle), and the assorted locals who wish him well on his quest and offer what they can in the way of financial assistance. Even some initially antagonistic cycle-riding punks who once Burt challenged to a race now admire his grit and honor him with an escort to his port of departure.

There are a number of humorous examples of culture shock once Burt arrives in Los Angeles. He is awed by the bright lights of Hollywood, and ponders the considerable sum it must take to keep them lit. He has never seen so many cars and such traffic congestion. When Burt learns of his cab fare, the astonished man clarifies that he merely wanted to ride in the vehicle and not purchase it. He is taken advantage of by a street vendor and is offered the services of a streetwalker. Once at his hotel, he is welcomed to "Hollyweird" by Tina (Chris Williams), who, unbeknownst to Burt, is actually a man. The transvestite is extremely kind and helpful, and Burt barely bats an eye when Tina comes clean to him about her gender. "You're still a sweetheart," he says congenially, with undiminished affection.

Despite the fact that ten tons of fertilizer fell on the Indian's crate during passage, the remarkably unscathed bike, like its owner, seems smiled upon by fate. Burt is also warmly received by the many people he meets as he endeavors to make it to Bonneville despite both mechanical and medical challenges. He takes nitroglycerin tablets for his increasingly troublesome heart, and the crushed dog testicles benevolently bestowed upon him by a Native American allow Burt to relieve himself despite continued prostate problems. A widow (Diane Ladd) invites him into both her house and her bed. Conversations he has with her about her late husband, another talk with a young soldier temporarily back from the Agent Orange-blanketed jungles of Vietnam, as well as Burt's dreams about the tree-felling accident that killed his twin brother years before, all warn of the fragile and finite nature of life. No one knows what lies around the corner, the film is pointing out, and so, especially for anyone like Burt with a hankering to do something, there is great meaning and wisdom in the phrase "carpe diem."

Perhaps the most powerful and moving scene in *The World's Fastest Indian* is when Burt finally sees Bonneville's arrestingly beautiful, wide-open landscape. Tears well up in his eyes as he stares in reverent disbelief upon reaching the promised land of his dreams. J. Peter Robinson's music also wells up, suitably reflecting the scene's soaring emotions. Hopkins so masterfully conveys just how much the overwhelmed man is feeling inside at that moment that viewers will undoubtedly be touched and rejoice both with and for him.

The hearts of those watching will subsequently sink when Burt is told that registration for the competition closed the month before and that his uniquely-outfitted Indian would probably not pass the technical inspection. Feeling sorry for the old guy who came all this way to fulfill a lifelong dream, fellow motorcycle enthusiast Jim Enz (Christopher Lawford) lobbies on behalf of "the most determined man I've ever seen in my life" to break the rules just this once. Although the film's title reveals the outcome, the run during which Burt breaks the world's record is gripping and wholly satisfying.

David L. Boxerbaum

CREDITS

Burt Munro: Anthony Hopkins
Ada: Diane Ladd
Tom: Aaron Murphy
Fernando: Paul Rodriguez
Tina: Chris Williams
Jim Enz: Christopher Lawford
Fran: Annie Whittle
Origin: USA, New Zealand
Language: English
Released: 2005
Production: Hannam Donaldson; New Zealand Film Commission, OLC/Rights Entertainment, Tanlay, New Zealand Film Production Fund, 3 Dogs and A Pony; released by Magnolia Pictures
Directed by: Roger Donaldson
Written by: Roger Donaldson
Cinematography by: David Gribble
Music by: J. Peter Robinson
Sound: Douglas Cameron
Editing: John Gilbert
Costumes: Jane Holland, Nancy Cavallaro
Production Design: Robert Gillies, J. Dennis Washington
MPAA rating: PG-13
Running time: 127 minutes

REVIEWS

Boxoffice Online. December 7, 2005.
Entertainment Weekly Online. December 7, 2005.
Variety Online. September 11, 2005.

X–Z

X-MEN: THE LAST STAND

Take a stand.
—Movie tagline

Box Office: $234.3 million

The third installment of the film franchise based on Marvel Comics' *X-Men* series, *X-Men: The Last Stand* is plainly constructed as a pseudo-conclusion to a trilogy that began with *X-Men* (2000); as such, it cannot be viewed easily as a stand-alone film. The first two movies developed three primary plot threads that continue to some extent in the third film. The first thread is the tension between the growing community of mutants and "normal" humans. The second plot follows the conflict between the X-Men organization led by Professor Charles Xavier (Patrick Stewart), intent on forging a peaceful coexistence with non-mutants, and a group of angst-ridden mutants led by Magneto (Ian McKellen), who believe coexistence is not possible and fight for mutant dominance of the human world. A third storyline involves a love triangle between tough, wise-cracking mutant Wolverine (Hugh Jackman), beautiful psychic Jean Grey (Famke Janssen), and Jean's boyfriend, Scott Summers (James Marsden), also known as Cyclops. The second movie (*X2* [2003]) ended with Jean sacrificing herself to save her friends but it also set up a potential for her to return in a form familiar to readers of the comic. This return forms the basis for one of the plot developments and conflicts in *X-Men: The Last Stand*.

Two major developments drive the storyline of *The Last Stand*. Wealthy businessman Warren Worthington II (Michael Murphy) has funded research to find a way to "cure" mutants, motivated by his distress at learning that his own son (Ben Foster) has developed a mutation in which his body sprouts huge wings. Worthington's researchers succeed in their quest when they find a young boy, Jimmy (Cameron Bright), whose unique mutation enables him to temporarily reverse the effects of mutation in others. When Worthington announces the existence and availability of a serum capable of making mutants "normal," controversy erupts. Some mutants can understand the appeal of the drug. Dr. Hank McCoy (Kelsey Grammer), nicknamed Beast, who is a former member of the X-Men and current Secretary of Mutant Affairs, discusses the situation with Xavier and concedes that he can understand why a mutant might want to be free from the persecution and isolation that has troubled the mutant community. At the same time, he and Xavier worry about what might happen if public opinion turned against the mutants as it has in the past. Elsewhere, the powerful Magneto uses the controversy as a catalyst for raising a mutant army determined to overthrow non-mutants once and for all, insisting that the "cure" will become public policy and that all mutants will ultimately be forced to undergo treatment. When Magneto's army begins to make trouble, at least some of his warnings seem to be justified, because the government authorizes turning the drug into a weapon.

Meanwhile, as set up in the second film, Jean Grey makes a surprising return but has been partially transformed, gaining increasing power and struggling with a dark side of her psyche that cannot control her emotions. When Scott seeks her out and discovers she is alive, she gives in to her darker impulses and apparently destroys him (a tragedy that is not witnessed by any of the other X-Men). Soon she ends up back at Xavier's mansion, where Xavier explains to Wolverine that Jean's psychic powers make her one of the most powerful mutants alive, but when her mutation developed, she became torn between two dueling personalities—that of Jean and that of Phoenix, the more powerful of the two but also the one without control of dangerous emotions. For years, Xavier has been using his psychic powers to suppress Phoenix and keep Jean stable, but now he finds that he is losing the ability to do so.

When Magneto learns of Phoenix's existence, he sets out to recruit her for his cause. An ensuing showdown between Jean, Xavier, and Magneto in which the Professor attempts to reach out to Jean and help her regain control leads to tragedy when Xavier is pulled apart at the molecular level. Wolverine witnesses the Professor's destruction and is devastated, as are Storm (Halle Berry) and the other X-Men, who consider closing Xavier's School for Gifted Youngsters. However, realizing that a war is about to begin in which everyone could be destroyed, Wolverine, Storm, and Beast set out to stop Magneto.

The final showdown takes place on Alcatraz Island, where Worthington has set up his research facility. Magneto's army assaults the island to get to little Jimmy, but the X-Men arrive to intervene. Though she has accompanied Magneto, Jean/Phoenix does not get involved in the fighting until she is threatened herself, at which point she begins tearing the island apart, starting with the army attempting to protect the facility. In the end, Beast brings down Magneto with one of the anti-mutant shots, causing Magneto to lose his powers, and it is Wolverine who finds a way to stop Jean/Phoenix. When he approaches her to say that he loves her and would die for her, she lowers her defenses and, briefly becoming Jean again, asks him to save her. Wolverine does just that...by stabbing her and putting her misery to an end.

X-Men: The Last Stand is action packed and visually exciting, with convincing and generally amazing effects work. The story, however, misses much of its potential. While some of the character development is interesting and unexpected, many of the plot turns seem unnecessary or at least unnecessarily final. Scott, for example, has only a very small role and is dispensed with rather suddenly, doing little justice to the character. Other characters suffer similar fates; though they may not be killed off, their roles are significantly reduced to the point that they seem underdeveloped and unessential to the story. The loss of some endearing characters such as Xavier does serve to develop the growth of others—particularly Wolverine and to a lesser extent Storm and Beast. In fact, one of the main weaknesses of the film is that it focuses on Wolverine and Storm. The former has always been one of the most important characters in the X-Men films, but Storm is simply not as interesting a character. Also, Jean's struggle with her dual identity should be a major element of the story, yet by the end it seems as if she, too, has not been given the attention that her character deserves. More often than that, she simply stands on the sidelines watching events transpire around her.

Generally, while the movie works as an action film and succeeds to some extent in charting interesting emotional journeys for some of the characters, it also feels rushed and underdeveloped. Indeed, production of the film was in fact accelerated, as the studio wanted it ready to be released in the summer of 2006, so it is quite possible that the studio's mandate hurt the story. Bryan Singer, the director of the first two films, left the franchise to make *Superman Returns* (2006) when Twentieth Century Fox insisted on having the new X-Men film in theaters in 2006. Even though *X-Men: The Last Stand* performed well at the box office, surprising analysts with what turned out to be the number three opening day gross of all time and in fact going on to ultimately out-gross its two predecessors, the movie was also widely regarded as the worst of the three films, owing significantly to its treatment and underdevelopment of characters.

David Flanagin

CREDITS

Professor Charles Xavier: Patrick Stewart
Eric Lensherr/Magneto: Ian McKellen
Logan/Wolverine: Hugh Jackman
Jean Grey/Phoenix: Famke Janssen
Ororo Munroe/Storm: Halle Berry
Marie/Rogue: Anna Paquin
Raven Darkholme/Mystique: Rebecca Romijn
Dr. Hank McCoy/Beast: Kelsey Grammer
Warren Worthington III/Angel: Ben Foster
Scott Summers/Cyclops: James Marsden
Bobby Drake/Iceman: Shawn Ashmore
Peter Rasputin/Colossus: Daniel Cudmore
Kitty Pryde: Ellen Page
John Allerdyce/Pyro: Aaron Stanford
Cain Marko/Juggernaut: Vinnie Jones
Callisto: Dania Ramirez
Dr. Moira MacTaggart: Olivia Williams
Dr. Kavita Rao: Shohreh Aghdashloo
Jimmy/Leech: Cameron Bright
Warren Worthington II: Michael Murphy

Bolivar Trask: Bill Duke
Jamie Madrox/Multiple Man: Eric Dane
Young Jean Grey: Haley Ramm
Quill: Ken Leung
FBI Interrogator: Anthony Heald
Origin: USA
Language: English
Released: 2006
Directed by: Brett Ratner
Written by: Zak Penn, Simon Kinberg
Cinematography by: Dante Spinotti
Music by: John Powell
Sound: Karen Schell
Editing: Mark Goldblatt, Mark Helfrich, Julia Wong
Art Direction: Helen Jarvis, Sandra Tanaka, Chad S. Frey, Justin Scoppa Jr.
Costumes: Judianna Makovsky, Lisa Tomczeszyn
Production Design: Ed Verreaux
MPAA rating: PG-13
Running time: 104 minutes

REVIEWS

Boxoffice Online. May 26, 2006.
New York Times Online. May 26, 2006.
Time Magazine Online. May 22, 2006.
Variety Online. May 22, 2006.

YOU, ME AND DUPREE

Two's company. Dupree's a crowd.
—Movie tagline

Box Office: $75.6 million

Hopefully, an off-kilter, highly problematic Peter Pan of a houseguest will never land on one's living room couch, but that is what happens in the middling comedy *You, Me and Dupree.* The Dupree of the title (Owen Wilson) crosses the threshold with his treasured mounted moose head, its glass-eyed countenance managing to appear more perceptive than the affable but heedless slacker lugging it. Dupree has acquired a highly inconvenient invitation from a newly married couple whose plans for wedded bliss did not include him. Still, upon learning that Dupree has lost his job, his home, and only has a bicycle on which to get around, long-time buddy Carl (Matt Dillon) convinces his sweet but understandably reluctant wife Molly (Kate Hudson) to temporarily take in this unwieldy third wheel. Viewers fully expect what the goodhearted newlyweds surely must also know will transpire, and the couple does, indeed, repeatedly and somewhat amusingly pay for their charity. However, as the film progresses, it may lose many viewers with its significant and hard-to-swallow shifts in tone and characterization.

An obvious effort is made to emphasize Carl and Molly's initial closeness and contentment. In the film's opening scenes, the two are shown on the eve of their wedding relaxing on a Hawaiian beach under bright blue skies. Blond and beguiling Molly is utterly charming, and as radiant as their surroundings. The line "Remember, when this is all over, it's just you and me!" signals the arrival of best man Dupree, setting the stage for him to start making his own waves in a quirky, cheerfully-oblivious fashion.

Once cozily ensconced in their new home, the couple's new life is also idealized and their harmoniousness underscored. They decide to share the writing of "thank you" notes and the recording of their answering machine message, laughing and giggling all the while. Carl has a great job designing a new and potentially lucrative real estate development for his business titan of a boss, and new father-in-law, Mr. Thompson (Michael Douglas, with clear echoes of his Gordon Gekko from 1987's *Wall Street*). Molly works with young children as a schoolteacher, which might to some extent prepare her for her husband's handful of a pal. Dupree is indeed childlike, and, upon moving in, is a big hit with the neighborhood kids with whom he spends much time playing.

It is clear from the beginning that Dupree means no harm, and seems grateful for what Carl and Molly are doing for him. He is caring—just much too carefree and not at all careful. The assurance is given that Dupree will soon "land on his feet," but until he does he will clearly be stepping on some toes while being more than a little underfoot. He makes a point of promising the newlyweds that they can go upstairs and "explore each other" without any fear that he will listen. When the two come down for breakfast, their appetites are suppressed upon seeing more of their still-snoozing houseguest than they ever cared to. Dupree then gets an out-of-practice Carl to get on a skateboard despite Molly's protestations, and, of course, the wipeout is not pretty. After Carl has a particularly hard day at work, Dupree's prescription is to chill out by inviting a slew of guys over to imbibe, scarf down food, and watch football. When Molly arrives home, the house is a mess, her grandmother's expensive silver platter has been used to serve nachos, and there are strippers at the door. The film often ventures into gross-out, lowbrow humor, such as when Dupree interrupts the lovers in bed with a mad, diarrhea-induced dash to use their "crapper." (In a previous scene, he had desperately called in the middle of Carl's meeting with Thompson concerning the whereabouts of a plunger for an overflowing toilet.) After a joke about the probable necessity for using matches when he is finished, viewers not only have to watch Molly nearly vomit and swoon from her guest's gas but also Dupree's description of the intake which set his disgusting output in motion.

Unfortunately, Carl feels responsible for his friend, as if he had somehow ditched Dupree by getting married, and is still reluctant to send him packing. His frustrated wife meaningfully suggests that her husband start "prioritizing his responsibilities." Perhaps in the hope that Dupree will find love and leave, Molly sets him up with a coworker. No one seems able to see that no good can come of this. His candle-lit tryst with the surprisingly wanton Mormon librarian ends with the accidental incineration of Carl and Molly's home. Molly has had enough. "Tonight!" she orders, and Carl cannot help but agree. Dupree thanks them kindly but ludicrously for a "lovely stay," and leaves bearing "no hard feelings."

Once Dupree peddles away on his bike (his departure nearly aborted when he collides with a car), *You, Me and Dupree* shifts gears. Character's feelings and personalities make 180-degree turns as the film itself suddenly goes in a completely new direction. When the couple later spots Dupree sitting forlornly on a bus stop bench in the rain, it is Carl who suggests they leave him there and Molly who, is adamant in her insistence that they retrieve him. As she barks commands at Carl, it steps up the film's emasculation and demoralization of her husband, which was already begun by Molly's creepily possessive father. Thompson has begun undercutting his new son-in-law's work, requested Carl, not Molly, adopt a hyphenated surname, and even suggested he get a vasectomy. (After Carl endures one eye-opening conversation with Thompson and is left standing at the desolate site of the proposed development, the location's ominous resemblance to that of the famous crop-dusting scene in Hitchcock's classic *North by Northwest* [1959] makes him seem even more under attack.) Under such pressure, Carl slicks his hair back, becomes distant, surly, and insanely jealous of Dupree, to whom Molly has increasingly looked to for emotional support. Indeed, she is now his prime defender, as well as densely sticking up for her dear old dad who is making Carl suffer so.

As for the slacker goof, he has suddenly begun cooking, cleaning, and mending what he had previously destroyed. Dupree has also gone on a sudden fitness craze, and come to idolize indomitable bicyclist Lance Armstrong (who makes a dream sequence cameo). He is now insightful and considerate. Dupree is then revealed to be a sucker for romantic Audrey Hepburn films and a writer of gooey poetry. He is suddenly presented as possessing heretofore hidden depth, an unlikely shaggy sage. It is Dupree as teacher and healer. The careerless man gives a rambling inspirational talk to Molly's class on career day. Dupree swings into action to make Carl see the light, get his bearings, and rediscover his "Carlness."

As the film zigzags in and out of a more slapstick sort of humor, there is a lame scene (which goes on too long) in which a hulking security guard races after decoy Dupree while Carl sneaks up to Thompson's office to get some things straight. Now Thompson's personality abruptly changes. He apologizes for being "a little rough" and "excessive."

Now that Dupree has made it all better, Molly and Carl quickly, easily, and sappily meld back into one. "My work is done here," Dupree declares triumphantly, and marches out into the world to help others find their inner "ness" and live better lives. In the final scene, an adoring throng applauds him and snaps up copies of the inspirational self-help book he has written.

Made on an estimated budget of $54 million, *You, Me and Dupree* succeeded in grossing just under $74 million. It seems wholly appropriate that brothers Anthony and Joe Russo, previously associated with the award-winning television series *Arrested Development*, were chosen to tell Dupree's story. However, far fewer people sang the praises of their film, with its unspectacular, multi-tonal screenplay by first-timer Mike LeSieur which failed to pinpoint a single "ness." The material which produces real laughs is as skimpy as some of Hudson's fetching outfits, and what modest entertainment value there is here quickly depreciates after viewing.

David L. Boxerbaum

CREDITS

Randy Dupree: Owen Wilson

Carl Peterson: Matt Dillon

Molly Peterson: Kate Hudson

Mr. Thompson: Michael Douglas

Annie: Amanda Detmer

Neil: Seth Rogen

Origin: USA

Language: English

Released: 2006

Production: Scott Stuber, Mary Parent, Owen Wilson; Stuber-Parent, Avis-Davis Production; released by Universal

Directed by: Anthony Russo, Joe Russo, Peter Ellis

Written by: Michael LeSieur

Cinematography by: Charles Minsky

Music by: Rolfe Kent

Sound: Petur Hliddal

Editing: Debra Neil-Fisher

Art Direction: Paul Sonski

Costumes: Karen Patch

Production Design: Barry Robison
MPAA rating: PG-13
Running time: 108 minutes

REVIEWS

Boxoffice Online. July 14, 2006.
Chicago Sun-Times Online. July 14, 2006.
Entertainment Weekly. July 21, 2006, p. 47.
Los Angeles Times Online. July 14, 2006.
New York Times Online. July 14, 2006.
Premiere Magazine Online. July 12, 2006.
San Francisco Chronicle. July 14, 2006, p. E1.
Variety Online. July 7, 2006.
Washington Post. July 14, 2006, p. C5.

ZOOM

They're going to save the world...as long as they're home for dinner.
—Movie tagline

Box Office: $11.9 million

Despite a cast including Tim Allen, Courteney Cox, and Chevy Chase, plus a Disney pedigree, *Zoom* was rushed into theaters with little fanfare (or pre-screenings for critics). It left just as quickly. It was probably a matter of Disney trying to cut their losses. Not surprisingly, neither audiences nor critics ended up being very fond of the film.

The main gripe that the critics seemed to have with the film was that they had seen it all before. Recent films like *The Incredibles* (2004), *Sky High* (2005), the *Spy Kids* films (2001-2003), and the first two *X-Men* films (2000 and 2003) had covered the same territory, and covered it better. The rehashed plot concerns Jack Shepard (Allen), a middle-aged man formerly called Captain Zoom. Zoom, known for his super-speed, was part of the high-powered Zenith Team, a group of government-employed superheroes. On the team's last mission, Zoom's brother Connor, known by the superhero name of Concussion (Kevin Zegers), was given too many gamma rays, or something like that, and turned evil.

Years later, government officials, led by General Larraby (Rip Torn), have recruited Zoom to whip a team of budding child superheroes into shape. What they fail to tell Zoom is that he is training them in preparation for Concussion's return. Zoom, who has become disillusioned with his government bosses and the way they treated superheroes, is disinclined to help the children. But the young prodigies eventually melt the bitter man's heart. There is Dylan (Michael Cassidy), the good-looking teen who can become invisible. He has a crush on Summer (Kate Mara), who practices telekinesis and levitation. Also on the team is a chubby kid, Tucker (Spencer Breslin), who can expand his body parts at will, and cute little Cindy (Ryan Newman), who has super strength and wants to be called Princess.

There is a strong supporting cast with Cox and Chase, but instead of helping matters, they somehow make it worse. It is particularly embarrassing for older audience members to see these notable comedic actors flailing about in such dreck. Cox plays Marsha, a scientist on the government team, who has collected Captain Zoom comics since she was a child. Cox does a nice job conveying her character's disillusionment at seeing her favorite superhero act all-too human, but other than that, writers Adam Rifkin and David Berenbaum did not give her much else in the way of personality—unless you consider being klutzy a personality trait. Faring worst of all is Chase who plays bumbling scientist Dr. Grant. Chase looks strangely over-made up and almost waxen. Chase seems lost and shows no hint of his former comedic skill. It is difficult to tell if it is his fault or the way the part was written. The low point of his performance comes after he is struck by lightning and, inexplicably, starts speaking in a parodied Chinese accent. Such ethnic humor might have worked in the 1940s, but in 2006, it is shockingly inappropriate.

As noted earlier, critics brought out the low grades for the film. Stephen Williams of *Newsday* wrote: "Although it's got a flying saucer that can do a Wendy's drive-though and a robot eerily like R2-D2, the film lacks pace and rhythm. There's really just fifteen minutes of content puffed into ninety." Stephen Whitty of the *Newark Star-Ledger* wrote: "Why does this eighty-three-minute movie feel like two hours?" Peter Hautlaub of the *San Francisco Chronicle* wrote that "*Zoom* is a C-list production in every possible way, from the actors and the special effects to the music and the script." Finally, Ty Burr of the *Boston Globe* wrote: "Shabbily filmed and resolutely unfunny, *Zoom* reflexively falls back on poop gags when the inspiration flags, which is most of the time."

Jill Hamilton

CREDITS

Jack Shepard/Captain Zoom: Tim Allen
Marsha Holloway: Courteney Cox
Tucker Williams/Mega-Boy: Spencer Breslin
Dr. Grant: Chevy Chase
Summer Jones/Wonder: Kate Mara
General Larraby: Rip Torn

Connor Shepard/Concussion: Kevin Zegers
Cindy Collins/Princess: Ryan Newman
Dylan West/Houdini: Michael Cassidy
Dylan's Teacher: Thomas F. Wilson
Dick: Willie Garson
Origin: USA
Language: English
Released: 2006
Production: Suzanne Todd, Jennifer Todd, Todd Garner; Team Todd, Boxing Cat Films, Revolution Studios, Columbia Pictures; released by Sony Pictures
Directed by: Peter Hewitt
Written by: Adam Rifkin, David Berenbaum
Cinematography by: David Tattersall
Music by: Christophe Beck
Sound: Robert F. Scherer
Music Supervisor: John Houlihan
Editing: Lawrence Jordan
Art Direction: Joshu de Cartier
Costumes: Ha Nguyen
Production Design: Barry Chusid
MPAA rating: PG
Running time: 88 minutes

AWARDS

Nomination:

Golden Raspberries 2006: Worst Actor (Allen)

List of Awards

Academy Awards

Film: *The Departed*
Animated Film: *Happy Feet*
Director: Martin Scorsese (*The Departed*)
Actor: Forest Whitaker (*The Last King of Scotland*)
Actress: Helen Mirren (*The Queen*)
Supporting Actor: Alan Arkin (*Little Miss Sunshine*)
Supporting Actress: Jennifer Hudson (*Dreamgirls*)
Original Screenplay: Michael Arndt (*Little Miss Sunshine*)
Adapted Screenplay: William Monahan (*The Departed*)
Cinematography: Guilermo Navarro (*Pan's Labyrinth*)
Editing: Thelma Schoonmaker (*The Departed*)
Art Direction: Eugenio Caballero, Pilar Revuelta (*Pan's Labyrinth*)
Visual Effects: John Knoll, Hal T. Hickel, Charles Gibson, Allen Hall (*Pirates of the Caribean: Dead Man's Chest*)
Sound: Michael Minkler, Bob Beemer, Willie D. Burton (*Dreamgirls*)
Makeup: David Marti, Montse Ribe (*Pan's Labyrinth*)
Costume Design: Milena Canonera (*Marie Antoinette*)
Original Score: Gustavo Santaolalla (*Babel*)
Original Song: "I Need to Wake Up" (Melissa Etheridge, *An Inconvenient Truth*)
Foreign Language Film: *The Lives of Others*
Documentary, Feature: *An Inconvenient Truth*

Directors Guild of America Award

Director: Martin Scorsese (*The Departed*)

Writers Guild of America Awards

Original Screenplay: Michael Arndt (*Little Miss Sunshine*)
Adapted Screenplay: William Monahan (*The Departed*)

Golden Globes

Film, Drama: *Babel*
Film, Musical or Comedy: *Dreamgirls*
Director: Martin Scorsese (*The Departed*)
Actor, Drama: Forest Whitaker (*The Last King of Scotland*)
Actor, Musical or Comedy: Sacha Baron Cohen (*Borat: Cultural Learnings of America for Make Benefit Glorious Nation of Kazakhstan*)
Actress, Drama: Helen Mirren (*The Queen*)
Actress, Musical or Comedy: Meryl Streep (*The Devil Wears Prada*)
Supporting Actor: Eddie Murphy (*Dreamgirls*)
Supporting Actress: Jennifer Hudson (*Dreamgirls*)
Screenplay: Peter Morgan (*The Queen*)
Score: Alexandre Desplat (*The Painted Veil*)
Song: "The Song of the Heart" (Prince, *Happy Feet*)
Foreign Language Film: *Letters from Iwo Jima*

Independent Spirit Awards

Film: *Little Miss Sunshine*
First Film: *Sweet Land*
Director: Jonathan Dayton, Valerie Faris (*Little Miss Sunshine*)
Actor: Ryan Gosling (*Half Nelson*)
Actress: Shareeka Epps (*Half Nelson*)
Supporting Actor: Alan Arkin (*Little Miss Sunshine*)
Supporting Actress: Frances McDormand (*Friends with Money*)
Screenplay: Jason Reitman (*Thank You For Smoking*)
First Screenplay: Michael Arndt (*Little Miss Sunshine*)
Cinematography: Guillermo Navarro (*Pan's Labyrinth*)
Foreign Language Film: *The Lives of Others*
Documentary: *The Road to Guantanamo*

Los Angeles Film Critics Awards

Film: *Letters from Iwo Jima*
Director: Paul Greengrass (*United 93*)
Actor: Forest Whitaker (*The Last King of Scoland*) and Sacha Baron Cohen (*Borat: Cultural Learnings of America for Make Benefit Glorious Nation of Kazakhstan*)
Actress: Helen Mirren (*The Queen*)
Supporting Actor: Michael Sheen (*The Queen*)
Supporting Actress: Luminita Gheorghiu (*The Death of Mr. Lazarescu*)
Screenplay: Peter Morgan (*The Queen*)
Cinematography: Emmanuel Lubezki (*Children of Men*)
Score: Alexandre Desplat (*The Painted Veil* and *The Queen*)
Animated Film: *Happy Feet*
Foreign Language Film: *The Lives of Others*
Documentary: *An Inconvenient Truth*

National Board of Review Awards

Film: *Letters from Iwo Jima*
Director: Martin Scorsese (*The Departed*)
Actor: Forest Whitaker (*The Last King of Scotland*)
Actress: Helen Mirren (*The Queen*)
Supporting Actor: Djimon Hounsou (*Blood Diamond*)
Supporting Actress: Catherine O'Hara (*For Your Consideration*)
Foreign Language Film: *Volver*
Documentary: *An Inconvenient Truth*

National Society of Film Critics Awards

Film: *Pan's Labyrinth*
Director: Paul Greengrass (*United 93*)
Actor: Forest Whitaker (*The Last King of Scotland*)
Actress: Helen Mirren (*The Queen*)
Supporting Actor: Mark Wahlberg (*The Departed*)
Supporting Actress: Meryl Streep (*The Devil Wears Prada* and *A Prairie Home Companion*)
Cinematography: Emmanuel Lubezki (*Children of Men*)

New York Film Critics Awards

Film: *United 93*
Director: Martin Scorsese (*The Departed*)
Actor: Forest Whitaker (*The Last King of Scotland*)
Actress: Helen Mirren (*The Queen*)
Supporting Actor: Jackie Earle Haley (*Little Children*)
Supporting Actress: Jennifer Hudson (*Dreamgirls*)
Screenplay: Peter Morgan (*The Queen*)
Cinematography: Guillermo Navarro (*Pan's Labyrinth*)
Foreign Language Film: *Army of Shadows*
Documentary: *Deliver Us from Evil*
Animated Film: *Happy Feet*

Screen Actors Guild Awards

Actor: Forest Whitaker (*The Last King of Scotland*)
Actress: Helen Mirren (*The Queen*)
Supporting Actor: Eddie Murphy (*Dreamgirls*)
Supporting Actress: Jennifer Hudson (*Dreamgirls*)
Ensemble Cast: *Little Miss Sunshine*

Obituaries

Edward Albert (February 20, 1951–September 22, 2006). Born in Los Angeles, the actor was the son of actors Margo and Eddie Albert. Albert made his film debut at thirteen in 1965's *The Fool Killer*; he was studying psychology at UCLA when he co-starred in *Butterflies Are Free* (1972) for which he received a Golden Globe award as most promising male newcomer. Albert appeared in numerous movie and television productions as well as on stage. Like his father (who died in 2005), Edward Albert was also a dedicated environmentalist. Screen appearances include *Forty Carats* (1973), *The Greek Tycoon* (1978), *The Ice Runner* (1993), *Guarding Tess* (1994), and *Extreme Honor* (2001).

Elizabeth Allen (January 25, 1929–September 19, 2006). Born Elizabeth Ellen Gillease in Jersey City, New Jersey, the actress was a model before getting a job introducing the skits on *The Jackie Gleason Show* in the early 1950s. Allen first appeared on Broadway in 1957's *Romanoff and Juliet* and she received Tony nominations for *The Gay Life* (1961) and *Do I Hear a Waltz?* (1965). Among her film appearances were *From the Terrace* (1960), *Donovan's Reef* (1963), *Cheyenne Autumn* (1966), and *The Star Spangled Girl* (1971). Allen retired in 1983.

Jay Presson Allen (March 3, 1922–May 1, 2006). Born Jacqueline Presson in Fort Worth, Texas, the writer moved to New York in the early 1940s and began writing television scripts. She changed her name after marrying producer Lewis M. Allen in 1955. Allen's unproduced first play, *The First Wife*, was filmed as *Wives and Lovers* in 1963. She became well known for her adaptations, beginning with *The Prime of Miss Jean Brodie*, which Allen adapted for the stage in 1966 and for the screen in 1969. Among Allen's other works were *Marnie* (1964), *Cabaret* (1972, for which Allen received an Oscar® nomination), *Travels with My Aunt* (1972), *Forty Carats* (1973), *Funny Lady* (1975), *Just Tell Me What You Want* (1980), *Prince of the City* (1981), and *Deathtrap* (1982).

June Allyson (October 7, 1917–July 8, 2006). Born Ella Geisman in the Bronx, New York, the actress with the blonde pageboy and perky manner was raised by her mother after her alcoholic father left the family. Inspired by the dancing of Ginger Rogers, she won a Broadway chorus job in 1938 and changed her name: June, after the month, and Allyson, from a family friend. In 1941, Allyson was appearing in the musical *Best Foot Forward* and when MGM (Metro-Goldwyn-Mayer) bought the movie rights, they offered her a contract. She worked for the studio for eleven years and twenty-five films. In 1945, Allyson married fellow star Dick Powell; he died in 1963. When her film career slowed in the late 1950s, Allyson turned to television and stage work; her autobiography (which revealed her own alcoholism) was published in 1982. Among her films were *Meet the People* (1944), *Two Girls and a Sailor* (1944), *Her Highness and the Bellboy* (1945), *The Sailor Takes a Wife* (1946), *High Barbaree* (1947), *The Bride Goes Wild* (1948), *Little Women* (1949), *The Stratton Story* (1949), *The Reformer and the Redhead* (1950), *Right Cross* (1950), *Too Young to Kiss* (1951), *Remains to Be Seen* (1953), *Executive Suite* (1954), *The Glenn Miller Story* (1954), *The McConnell Story* (1955), *Strategic Air Command* (1955), *My Man Godfrey* (1957), *A Stranger in My Arms* (1959), and *They Only Kill Their Masters* (1972).

Robert Altman (February 20, 1925–November 20, 2006). Born in Kansas City, Missouri, the director enlisted in the Army in 1943 and was a B-24 co-pilot. After his discharge, Altman tried acting and writing in Hollywood but moved back to Kansas City and began making industrial films. He made his first low-budget feature, *The Delinquents*, there in 1957. Altman then began to work in television as a writer, director, and producer before his next features: *Countdown* (1968) and *That Cold Day in the Park* (1969). In 1970, he directed the unexpected hit *M*A*S*H*, which featured Altman's trademark ensemble acting and overlapping dialogue, and received the first of his Oscar® nominations as best director. Altman also received a nomination for 1975's *Nashville*, but did not see critical success again until 1992's *The Player* (another nomination). Altman also received best director nominations for *Short Cuts* (1993) and *Gosford Park* (2001), and finally received an honorary lifetime achievement Oscar® in 2006. It was at the Academy Awards® ceremony that the director revealed that he'd had a heart transplant in the mid-1990s. His last film was 2006's *A Prairie Home Companion*. Among his other features were *McCabe & Mrs. Miller* (1971), *The Long Goodbye* (1973), *California Split* (1974), *Thieves Like Us* (1974), *Buffalo Bill & the Indians* (1976), *Quintet* (1979), *Popeye* (1980), *Streamers* (1983), *Fool for Love* (1985), *Vincent & Theo* (1990), *Ready to Wear* (1994), *Kansas City* (1995), *Dr. T & the Women* (2000), and *The Company* (2003). Altman also received an Emmy for HBO's *Tanner '88* (1988) and returned to the character in 2004's *Tanner on Tanner*.

Sir Malcolm Arnold (October 21, 1921–September 23, 2006). The prolific composer was born in Northampton, England, and was privately educated before studying at the Royal College of Music. He became a trumpet player with the London Philharmonic Orchestra, which recorded an Arnold overture in 1946, but his life was blighted by a diagnosis of schizophrenia in his twenties as well as mental breakdowns and alcoholism. Arnold composed numerous film scores and won an Oscar® for *The Bridge on the River Kwai* (1957). Among his other soundtracks were *The Belles of St. Trinian's* (1954), *Hobson's Choice* (1954), *I Am a Camera* (1955), *The Inn of the Sixth Happiness* (1958), *Suddenly, Last Summer* (1959), *Whistle Down the Wind* (1961), *The Chalk Garden* (1964), *Battle of Britain* (1969), and *David Copperfield* (1970).

Joseph Barbera (March 24, 1911–December 18, 2006). Born in New York, the animation pioneer partnered with William Hanna to form Hanna-Barbera Productions and made over one hundred cartoon series in a collaboration that lasted decades. Barbera began his career with Van Beuren Studios in 1932, moved to Terrytown Studios, and then to MGM (Metro-Goldwyn-Mayer) in 1937. He and Hanna began a series with a cat named Jasper and mouse called Jinx; the 1940 short, *Puss Gets the Boot*, received an Oscar® nomination. In 1941's *The Midnight Snack*, the cat was renamed Tom and the mouse Jerry; the duo won Hanna-Barbera seven Oscars® between 1943 and 1952 (as well as thirteen nominations) and were featured opposite Gene Kelly in *Anchors Aweigh* (1945) and Esther Williams in *Dangerous When Wet* (1953). When MGM closed their animation studio in 1957, Hanna-Barbera turned to television production, including *The Huckleberry Hound Show, Yogi Bear, The Flintstones, The Jetsons*, and *The Adventures of Jonny Quest*; they sold their production company in 1967. Barbera remained active in the industry and was the writer, director, and storyboard artist of the 2005 short, *The Karateguard*. Barbera's 1994 autobiography was entitled *My Life in 'Toons: From Flatbush to Bedrock in Under a Century.*

Frances Bergen (September 14, 1922–October 2, 2006). The wife of ventriloquist Edgar Bergen and mother of actress Candice Bergen was born Frances Westerman in Birmingham, Alabama, and moved to Los Angeles at the age of ten. The model was in the audience at Bergen's radio show when he spotted her and they married in 1945. Bergen appeared in small roles in several films in the 1950s, co-starred in the 1958 television series *Yancy Derringer* (1958), and sang in nightclubs (though she limited her career because of her marriage). Bergen resumed acting after her husband's death in 1978. Among her films were *Titanic* (1953), *American Gigolo* (1980), *Rich and Famous* (1981), *The Sting II* (1983), and *Eating* (1990).

Ted Berkman (January 9, 1914–May 12, 2006). Born Edward Oscar Berkman in Brooklyn, New York, the writer graduated from Cornell University in 1933 and began working at *The New York Mirror* and later as a radio correspondent for ABC. His screen credits include *Bedtime for Bonzo* (1951), *Fear Strikes Out* (1957), *Short Cut to Hell* (1957), *Edge of Fury* (1958), *Girl of the Night* (1960), and *Cast a Giant Shadow* (1966).

Frank Beyer (May 26, 1932–October 1, 2006). Born in Nobitz, Germany, the East German director's career was both aided and censored by the state film monopoly, DEFA, which eventually banned both Beyer and his controversial 1965 film, *Traces of Stones*. Beyer studied in Prague and made his first feature, *Two Mothers*, in 1957. His 1975 drama, *Jacob the Liar*, was the only East German production to be nominated for a best foreign film Academy Award®. Other works include *Five Cartridges* (1960), *Carbide and Sorrel* (1963), *Naked Among Wolves* (1963), *The Turning Point* (1983), and *Nikolaikirche* (1995). Beyer published his autobiography, *When the Wind Changes*, in 1990.

Fabian Bielinsky (February 3, 1959–June 28, 2006). Born in Buenos Aires, Argentina, the director died of a heart attack. He studied at the National Cinematographic Institute and, after graduating in 1983, he worked as an assistant director and made hundreds of commercials before releasing his first feature, *Nine Queens*, in 2000. Bielinsky's second feature was 2005's *The Aura*.

Peter Boyle (October 18, 1935–December 12, 2006). The actor was born in Philadelphia, Pennsylvania, and joined the Christian Brothers after graduating from La Salle College. Boyle left the monastery after three years and eventually went to New York to study acting with Uta Hagen. He played the title character in *Joe* (1970) and was generally typecast as an angry everyman before his comedic portrayal of the monster in Mel Brooks' *Young Frankenstein* (1974). Other film appearances include *The Candidate* (1972), *Taxi Driver* (1976), *F.I.S.T.* (1978), *Where the Buffalo Roam* (1980), *Yellowbeard* (1983), *The Dream Team* (1989), *Malcolm X* (1992), *While You Were Sleeping* (1995), *Monster's Ball* (2001), and *Scooby-Doo 2: Monsters Unleashed* (2004). Boyle also played patriarch Frank Barone on the TV comedy *Everybody Loves Raymond* from 1996 to 2005, receiving five Emmy nominations.

Richard Bright (June 11, 1937–February 18, 2006). The character actor was born in Brooklyn, New York, and made his film debut in *Odds Against Tomorrow* (1959). Bright played mob enforcer Al Neri in all three *Godfather* pictures and had a number of theater and television credits as well. Other films include *Panic in Needle Park* (1971), *The Getaway* (1972), *Looking for Mr. Goodbar* (1977), *Once Upon a Time in America* (1984), *The Ref* (1993), and *Beautiful Girls* (1996).

Phil Brown (April 30, 1916–February 9, 2006). Born in Cambridge, Massachusetts, the actor was best known for playing Owen Lars, uncle to Luke Skywalker, in 1977's *Star Wars*. Brown was accepted into the Group Theatre in 1938 and after the company folded in 1941, he moved to Hollywood and founded the Actor's Laboratory where he directed a number of plays. He also directed the 1949 feature *The Harlem Globetrotters*. But Brown was blacklisted in the early 1950s and moved his family to London where he found work on stage and in films. Other credits include *Tropic of Cancer* (1970) and *Twilight's Last Gleaming* (1977).

Henry Bumstead (March 17, 1915–May 24, 2006). Lloyd Henry Bumstead was born in Ontario, California, and worked summers for RKO Radio Pictures before taking a job with Paramount in 1937. Bumstead worked as a production designer or art director on more than one hundred films, winning Oscars® for *To Kill a Mockingbird* (1962) and *The Sting* (1973). He worked with Clint Eastwood on thirteen films, including the 2006 releases *Flags of Our Fathers* and *Letters from Iwo Jima*. Bumstead's first credit was 1948's *Saigon*; other films include *The Man Who Knew Too Much* (1956), *Vertigo* (1958), *Topaz* (1959), *Joe Kidd* (1972), *High Plains Drifter* (1973), *Family Plot* (1976), *Slap Shot* (1977), *The World According to Garp* (1982), *Cape Fear* (1991), *Unforgiven* (1992), *Midnight in the Garden of Good and Evil* (1997), *Blood Work* (2002), *Mystic River* (2003), and *Million Dollar Baby* (2004).

Red Buttons (February 5, 1919–July 13, 2006). Born Aaron Chwatt in New York, the comedian earned his professional name because of his red hair and the brass buttons on his bellboy uniform, which he wore while working at a Bronx tavern. He worked the so-called Borscht Circuit in the Catskills before moving into burlesque and Broadway. Inducted into the Army in 1943, Buttons joined the cast of the Army Air Force play, *Winged Victory*, eventually re-creating his role in the 1944 film version. He continued to work on Broadway after his discharge and did a weekly comedy-variety show for CBS, beginning in 1952. Buttons won a best supporting actor Oscar® for 1957's *Sayonara*. He also appeared in such films as *Hatari!* (1962), *The Longest Day* (1962), *They Shoot Horses, Don't They?* (1969), *The Poseidon Adventure* (1972), *Pete's Dragon* (1977), *18 Again!* (1988), and *It Could Happen to You* (1994). Buttons continued his nightclub and television work and had recurring roles on *Knot's Landing*, *Roseanne*, and *Street Time*.

Oleg Cassini (April 11, 1913– March 17, 2006). The fashion designer was born in Paris, France (some sources say Russia) to Russian diplomat Alexander Loiewski and Italian countess Marguerite Cassini. The family eventually settled in Florence, Italy, where Oleg learned the dress business from his mother. He came to New York in 1936 and moved to Hollywood in 1940, working in the costume departments of Paramount Studios and 20th Century Fox, where he designed for such stars as Veronica Lake, Marilyn Monroe, Grace Kelly, and Gene Tierney, whom Cassini married in 1941 (they divorced in 1952). Cassini later returned to New York to open his own fashion house and became the official designer to first lady Jacqueline Kennedy. Cassini's autobiography, *In My Own Fashion*, was published in 1987.

Betty Comden (May 3, 1917–November 23, 2006). Born Elizabeth Cohen in Brooklyn, New York, the lyricist had a professional partnership with Adolph Green that lasted more than sixty years (until his 2002 death). After graduating from New York University in 1938, Comden joined the Washington Street Players, where she first met Green. Along with Judy Holliday, Alvin Hammer, and John Frank, they formed a cabaret act called the Revuers, who were given a part in the 1944 film *Greenwich Village*. The first Comden-Green collaboration was the 1944 Broadway musical, *On the Town* (filmed in 1949). The duo then did the films *Good News* (1947) and *The Barkleys of Broadway* (1949). Their 1956 musical, *Bells Are Ringing*, which starred Holliday, was filmed in 1960. Among their other film credits were *Take Me Out to the Ball Game* (1949), *Singin' in the Rain* (1952), *The Band Wagon* (1953, Oscar®-nominated screenplay), *It's Always Fair Weather* (1955, Oscar®-nominated screenplay), and *Auntie Mame* (1958). The Comden-Green duo also won seven Tony Awards. Comden published her memoirs, *Off Stage*, in 1995.

John Conte (September 15, 1915–September 4, 2006). The actor was born in Palmer, Massachusetts, but moved to Los Angeles as a teenager. He got his start on radio, including a part on the *Burns and Allen* show. Conte appeared on stage beginning in the late 1940s and had numerous guest roles on television from the early 1950s on. Films include *Lost in a Harem* (1943), *The Man with the Golden Arm* (1955), *Trauma* (1962), and *The Carpetbaggers* (1964). Conte quit acting after founding the NBC affiliate, KMIR-TV, in 1968.

Pat Corley (June 1, 1930–September 11, 2006). The character actor was born in Dallas, Texas, and began his career in summer stock in California. He had recurring roles on such television shows as *The Bay City Blues* and *Hill Street Blues* before joining the CBS sitcom *Murphy Brown*, where he played Phil the bartender from 1988–96. Films include *Coming Home* (1978), *Nightwing* (1979), *True Confessions* (1981), *Night Shift* (1982), *Against All Odds* (1984), *Silent Witness* (1985), and *Mr. Destiny* (1990).

Tamara Dobson (May 14, 1947–October 2, 2006). Born in Baltimore, Maryland, the six foot, two inch tall actress began modeling in her hometown before moving to New York where she enrolled in acting classes. Dobson made her screen debut in 1972's *Fuzz*. In 1973, she starred as the first blaxploitation heroine in *Cleopatra Jones*, reprising her role in 1975's *Cleopatra Jones and the Casino of Gold*. Other films include *Come Back, Charleston Blue* (1972), *Norman, Is That You?* (1976), *Murder at the World Series* (1977), *Chained Heat* (1983), and *Amazons* (1984).

Robert Donner (April 27, 1931–June 8, 2006). Born in New York, the character actor appeared in more than one hundred films and television shows, often cast as an eccentric. He moved to California after serving in the Navy and studied acting, beginning his film career with uncredited roles in *Rio Bravo* (1959) and *The Man Who Shot Liberty Valance* (1962). Other films include *Cool Hand Luke* (1967), *Vanishing Point* (1971), *High Plains Drifter* (1973), *The Man Who Loved Cat Dancing* (1973), *Under the Rainbow* (1981), and *Hoot* (2006). Donner also had recurring TV roles on *The Waltons* (as Yancy Tucker) and *Mork & Mindy* (as Exidor).

Richard Fleischer (December 8, 1916–March 25, 2006). Born in Brooklyn, New York, the director was the son of animation pioneer Max Fleischer. He studied psychology before transferring to Yale University's School of Drama. Fleischer was hired as a writer of newsreels at RKO Radio Pictures and began directing shorts; after serving in World War II, he became a contract director for the B-picture unit at the studio. His work caught the eye of Walt Disney, who offered Fleischer the job of directing the big-budget, A-list 1954 movie, *20,000 Leagues Under the Sea*. Directorial credits include *Follow Me Quietly* (1949), *Trapped* (1949), *The Happy Time* (1952), *The Narrow Margin* (1952), *The Vikings* (1958), *Compulsion* (1959), *Barabbas* (1962), *Fantastic Voyage* (1966), *Doctor Doolittle* (1967), *The Boston Strangler* (1968), *Che!* (1969), *Tora! Tora! Tora!* (1970), *10 Rillington Place* (1971), *The New Centurions* (1972), *Soylent Green* (1973), *Mr. Majestyk* (1974), *Mandingo* (1975), *The Jazz Singer* (1980), *Conan the Destroyer* (1984), *Red Sonja* (1985), and *Million Dollar Mystery* (1987). His only Oscar® came as the producer of the 1947 documentary *Design for Death*. Fleischer's memoir, *Just Tell Me When to Cry*, was published in 1993.

Glenn Ford (May 1, 1916–August 30, 2006). Born Gwyllyn Samuel Newton Ford in Sainte-Christine, Quebec, the actor took his professional name from the site of the family paper mill, Glenford. The family moved to California when Ford was seven and he toured with a number of theater groups after high school. Ford made his film debut in the low-budget *Heaven with a Barbed Wire Fence* (1939) and became a contract player at Columbia Pictures later that same year. After serving in World War II, Ford returned to the studio and starred in *Gilda, A Stolen Life*, and *Gallant Journey* (all 1946). Other screen credits include *Men Without Souls* (1940), *My Son Is Guilty* (1940), *The Desperadoes* (1941), *Destroyer* (1941), *The Big Heat* (1953), *The Man from the Alamo* (1953), *Human Desire* (1954), *Blackboard Jungle* (1955), *Teahouse of the August Moon* (1956), *Don't Go Near the Water* (1957), *3:10 to Yuma* (1957), *Imitation General* (1958), *Cimarron* (1960), *Pocketful of Miracles* (1961), *The Courtship of Eddie's Father* (1963), *The Rounders* (1965), *Heaven with a Gun* (1969), *Midway* (1976), and *Superman* (1978). He also starred on television in *Cade's County* and *The Family Holvak*. Among Ford's four wives was actress-dancer Eleanor Powell, from 1943–59.

Anthony "Tony" Franciosa (October 25, 1928–January 19, 2006). Born Anthony Papaleo in New York, the actor adopted his mother's maiden name professionally. He studied at the Actor's Studio and made his Broadway debut in 1953. Franciosa received a Tony nomination for 1956's *A Hatful of Rain* and played the same role in the 1957 film version, for which he received an Oscar® nomination. Other films include *A Face in the Crowd* (1957), *The Long, Hot Summer* (1958), *Career* (1959), *The Naked Maja* (1959), *Period of Adjustment* (1962), *Rio Conchos* (1964), *Assault on a Queen* (1966), *Across 110th Street* (1972), *The Drowning Pool* (1975), and *City Hall* (1995). Franciosa also appeared on television in the series *Valentine's Day, The Name of the Game, Search, Matt Helm*, and *Finder of Lost Loves*. Franciosa was married to actress Shelley Winters (1920–2006) from 1957–60.

Arthur Franz (February 29, 1920–June 17, 2006). Born in Perth Amboy, New Jersey, Franz was a prolific character actor in film and television whose first screen credit was 1948's *Jungle Patrol*. His only starring role was in *The Sniper* (1952). Other credits include *Sands of Iwo Jima* (1949), *Abbott and Costello Meet the Invisible Man* (1951), *Invaders from Mars* (1953), *The Caine Mutiny* (1954), *Hellcats of the Navy* (1957), *Missiles of October* (1974), and *That Championship Season* (1982).

Paul Gleason (May 4, 1939–May 27, 2006). The actor was born in Jersey City, New Jersey, and grew up in Miami. Gleason studied with Lee Strasberg at the Actor's Studio in the early 1960s and appeared in more than sixty films. Credits include *Trading Places* (1983), *The Breakfast Club* (1985), *Die Hard* (1988), *The Giving Tree* (2000), *Not Another Teen Movie* (2001), *National Lampoon's Van Wilder* (2002), and *The Passing* (2005).

James Glennon (August 29, 1942–October 19, 2006). The cinematographer was born in Los Angeles, the son of cinematographer Bert Glennon. He earned a bachelor's in filmmaking at UCLA and started in the mailroom at Warner Bros. before working in the camera department on such TV series as *Gilligan's Island* and *Batman*. Glennon's first film credit was 1977's *Jaws of Death*. Credits include *El Norte* (1983), *Smooth Talk* (1985), *Flight of the Navigator* (1986), *Citizen Ruth* (1996), *Election* (1999), *About Schmidt* (2002), and *The United States of Leland* (2003). Glennon also worked on numerous television shows, winning a 2004 Emmy for *Deadwood*.

Pedro Gonzalez Gonzalez (May 24, 1925–February 6, 2006). Born in Aguilares, Texas, the comedic actor began entertaining with his family at the age of seven. He appeared as a contestant on the Groucho Marx quiz show, *You Bet Your Life*, which brought him to the attention of John Wayne, who signed Gonzalez Gonzalez to a contract with his production company. Screen credits include *The High and the Mighty* (1954), *Rio Bravo* (1959), *McLintock!* (1963), *Hellfighters* (1968), *The Love Bug* (1969), *Chisum* (1970), and *Support Your Local Gunfighter* (1971).

Gary Graver (July 20, 1938–November 16, 2006). The cinematographer was born in Portland, Oregon, and began working as a cameraman with the Navy Combat Camera Group in the early 1960s. Graver shot a number of low-budget and independent films, including *Satan's Sadists* (1969), *Dracula vs. Frankenstein* (1971), *Invasion of the Bee Girls* (1973), *The Student Body* (1976), *Grand Theft Auto* (1977), *Moonshine County Express* (1977), *Death Sport* (1978), *The Toolbox Murders* (1978), *Sorceress* (1995), *Vice Girls* (2000), *Usher* (2002), and *Quigley* (2003). Graver met Orson Welles in 1970 and worked with the director until his 1985 death on such projects as *F for Fake* (1975), *Filming Othello* (1978), and his uncompleted final film, *The Other Side of the Wind*. Graver's own directorial efforts include *The Great Dream* (1963), *Texas Lightning* (1981), *Party Camp* (1987), *Evil Spirits* (1991), *The Escort* (1997), and numerous erotic films under the pseudonym Robert McCallum.

Gary Gray (December 18, 1936–April 4, 2006). The child actor was born in Los Angeles, the son of Hollywood business manager Bill Gray, who was encouraged by his clients to get Gary into films. Gray made his uncredited debut at three in 1941's *A Woman's Face*. His role in 1950's *The Next Voice You Hear* led to an MGM (Metro-Goldwyn-Mayer) contract. Among his other films were *Rachel and the Stranger* (1948), *Return of the Bad Men* (1948), *The Girl from Jones Beach* (1949), *The Great Lover* (1949), *Leave It to Henry* (1949), *Father Makes Good* (1950), *Pal, Canine Detective* (1950), *The Painted Hills* (1951), *Rodeo* (1952), *Teenage Rebel* (1956), *The Party Crashers* (1958), and *Terror at Black Falls* (1962). Gray retired in the early 1960s.

Valmond "Val" Guest (December 11, 1911–May 10, 2006). The producer, director, and screenwriter was born in London, England. Guest was working as a songwriter when he met director Lupino Lane, who offered him a job writing and acting in *The Maid of the Mountains* (1932); other early scripts were *No Monkey Business* (1935), *Public Nuisance No 1* (1936), *Good Morning, Boys* (1937), *Oh, Mr. Porter* (1937), and *Ask a Policeman* (1938). Guest made his directorial debut with 1943's *Miss London Ltd.* Guest directed some fifty films, including *Murder at the Windmill* (1949), *Miss Pilgrim's Progress* (1950), *Mr. Drake's Duck* (1950), *Penny Princess* (1952), *The Runaway Bus* (1953), *Family Affair* (1954), *The Quatermass Xperiment* (1955), *The Abominable Snowman* (1957), *Camp on Blood Island* (1957), *Express Bongo* (1959), *Life Is a Circus* (1959), *Hell Is a City* (1960), *The Day the Earth Caught Fire* (1961), *Casino Royale* (1967), and *Killer Force* (1975). His autobiography, *So You Want to Be in Pictures*, was published in 2001.

Lois Hall (August 22, 1926–December 21, 2006). Born in Grand Rapids, Minnesota, the actress moved with her family to California after World War II and she attended the drama school at the Pasadena Playhouse. Hall's screen debut came with an uncredited bit in 1948's *Every Girl Should Be Married*. She appeared in the movie serials *The Adventures of Sir Galahad* (1949) and *Pirates of the High Seas* (1950) and was frequently cast in westerns for Republic Pictures. Hall semi-retired after her marriage but made occasional film appearances and guest-starred on television. Credits include *Horsemen of the Sierras* (1949), *Roaring Westward* (1949), *Cherokee Uprising* (1950), *Frontier Outpost* (1950), *Texas Dynamo* (1950), *Blazing Bullets* (1951), *Colorado Ambush* (1951), *Night Raiders* (1952), *Texas City* (1952), *Dead Again* (1991), *Gone in Sixty Seconds* (2000), *Bad Boy* (2002), and *Flightplan* (2005).

Miklos "Mickey" Hargitay (January 6, 1926–September 14, 2006). Born in Budapest, Hungary, the bodybuilder-turned-actor came to the United States in 1947. He turned his 1955 Mr. Universe title into a show business career, performing in Mae West's nightclub act, which actress Jayne Mansfield came to see in 1956. Hargitay and Mansfield married in 1958 and appeared together in the movies *Will Success Spoil Rock Hunter?* (1957), *The Loves of Hercules* (1960), *Promises! Promises!* (1963), and *Primitive Love* (1964); the couple divorced in 1964. Hargitay's other screen credits include *The Bloody Pit of Horror* (1965), *Three Graves for a Winchester* (1966), *Wanted Ringo* (1970), and *Lady Frankenstein* (1972). Hargitay later became a contractor and real estate investor.

Arthur Hill (August 1, 1922–October 22, 2006). The actor was born in Melfort, Saskatchewan, and worked his way through the University of British Columbia by performing in radio theater for the Canadian Broadcasting Company. Hill appeared on stage in London and New York, winning a Tony Award for the original Broadway production of *Who's Afraid of Virginia Woolf?* in 1963. He moved to Los Angeles in 1968 and starred in the television series *Owen Marshall: Counselor at Law* from 1971 to 1974. Hill's screen credits include *The Young Doctors* (1961), *In the Cool of the Day* (1963), *The Ugly American* (1963), *Harper* (1966), *Petulia* (1968), *The Andromeda Strain* (1971), *Futureworld* (1976), *A Bridge Too Far* (1977), *The Champ* (1979), *Making Love* (1982), *The Guardian* (1984), and *Tales of the Unexpected* (1991).

George Hively (April 28, 1933–February 7, 2006). Born in Los Angeles, the film editor followed in the career footsteps of his father (also George). Hively began his career working on the *Perry Mason* television series from 1957 to 1966. Films include *Deadhead Miles* (1972), *The Little Prince* (1974), *Lucky Lady* (1975), *The Savage Bees* (1976), *Movie Movie* (1978), *Bill* (1981), *Friday the 13th, Part III* (1982), *Blame It on Rio* (1984), and *Blind Justice* (1986). Hively worked for the last fourteen years as staff editor at Sony Pictures.

Barnard Hughes (July 16, 1915–July 11, 2006). Born in Bedford Hills, New York, the actor began his professional career in 1934 with the Shakespeare Fellowship Repertory Company and went on to play more than four hundred roles on stage and in film and television. Hughes won the best actor Tony Award for *Da* in 1978, reprising his role for the 1988 film version. He had recurring roles on such TV series as *Blossom, The Bob Newhart Show, The Cavanaughs, Doc*, and *Mr. Merlin*. Screen credits include *Midnight Cowboy* (1969), *Cold Turkey* (1971), *The Hospital* (1971), *Oh, God!* (1977), *First Monday in October* (1981), *Tron* (1982), *Doc Hollywood* (1991), *Sister Act 2* (1993), *The Fantasticks* (1995), and *The Cradle Will Rock* (1999). Hughes' last performance came on Broadway in 2000 in *Waiting in the Wings*.

Akira Ifukube (May 31, 1914–January 8, 2006). Born in Kushiro, Hokkaido, the composer was self-taught and wrote more than three hundred film compositions. Ifukube worked as a forestry official until 1946 when he became a music instructor. His best known work is the main theme for *Godzilla* (1954), which reappeared in many of the later movies. Other credits include *Children of Hiroshima* (1952), *The Harp of Burma* (1956), and the *Daimajin* series (1966). He was named a Person of Cultural Merit in Japan in 2003.

Shohei Imamura (September 15, 1926–May 30, 2006). Born in Tokyo, Japan, the director joined the Shochiku film company in 1951, later moving to the rival Nikkatsu studio. His directorial debut came with 1958's *Stolen Desire*. Imamura won the Palme d'Or at the Cannes Film Festival twice: for *The Ballad of Narayama* (1983) and *The Eel* (1997). Other credits include *Endless Desire* (1958), *Nishi Ginza Station* (1958), *Stolen Desire* (1958), *The Second Brother* (1959), *Pigs and Battleships* (1961), *The Insect Woman* (1963), *Unholy Desire* (1964), *The Pornographers* (1966), *The Profound Desire of the Gods* (1968), *Vengeance Is Mine* (1979), *Why Not?* (1981), *Black Rain* (1989), *Dr. Akagi* (1998), and *Warm Water Under a Red*

Bridge (2001). His last work was a short film included in the anthology *11'09"01* about the events of September 11, 2001. Imamura was also the founder of the Japan Academy of Moving Images, a film school.

Claude Jade (October 8, 1948–December 1, 2006). Born Claude Jorre in Dijon, France, the actress was appearing on stage when director Francois Truffaut cast her in the third of his Antoine Doinel films, *Stolen Kisses* (1968). This was followed by *Bed and Board* (1970) and *Love on the Run* (1978). Jade also appeared in such films as *My Uncle Benjamin* (1969), *Topaz* (1969), *Lenin in Paris* (1980), *Tegeran-43* (1981), and *Bon Soir* (1992), while continuing her career on stage and in television. Jade published her autobiography, *Flying Kisses*, in 2004.

Lois January (October 5, 1912–August 7, 2006). The actress was born Laura Lois January in McAllen, Texas. After her family moved to Los Angeles, January graduated from the Marborough School for Girls and toured with the Denishawn dancers. She was discovered by a Universal talent scout while performing at the Pasadena Community Playhouse and made twelve studio westerns from 1935–37. January also appeared as the manicurist who sings to Dorothy in 1939's *The Wizard of Oz* although the footage didn't survive the final cut. January's films include *Arizona Bad Man* (1935), *Bulldog Courage* (1935), *Border Caballero* (1936), *Cocaine Fiends* (1936), *Rogue of the Range* (1936), *Bar-Z Bad Men* (1937), *Courage of the West* (1937), *Lightning Bill Crandall* (1937), *Moonlight on the Range* (1937), *The Roamin' Cowboy* (1937), *The Red Rope* (1937), and *The Trusted Outlaw* (1937). She later guest-starred on a number of television shows until retiring in 1987.

Robert Earl Jones (February 3, 1910–September 7, 2006). The actor (and father of actor James Earl Jones) was born in Senatobia, Mississippi, and worked as a sharecropper before moving first to Memphis for a railroad job and later to Chicago where he worked as a boxer and sparring partner of Joe Louis. Eventually moving to New York, Jones' first acting role was in a one-act play by Langston Hughes. He appeared in two movies by black filmmaker Oscar Micheaux, *Lying Lips* (1939) and *The Notorious Elinor Lee* (1940), and made his stage debut in 1945 in *The Hasty Heart*. The actor's career was interrupted when he was blacklisted in the 1950s. Screen credits include *The Sting* (1973), *Cockfighter* (1974), *Trading Places* (1983), *The Cotton Club* (1984), *Witness* (1985), and *Rain Without Thunder* (1993).

Andreas Katsulas (May 18, 1946–February 13, 2006). Born in St. Louis, Missouri, the sinister-looking character actor often played villains on film and television. Katsulas majored in theater at St. Louis University and had a master's degree in theater from Indiana University. He moved to Los Angeles in 1986 and appeared on such science fiction shows as *Alien Nation* and *Star Trek: The Next Generation* before his continuing role as Ambassador G'Kar on *Babylon 5*. Screen credits include *Someone to Watch Over Me* (1987), *Sunset* (1988), *Next of Kin* (1989), *The Fugitive* (1993), *Hot Shots! Part Deux* (1993), and *Executive Decision* (1996).

Bruno Kirby (April 28, 1949–August 14, 2006). Born Bruno Giovanni Quidaciolu in New York, Kirby was the son of actor Bruce Kirby. The character actor died from complications related to leukemia. He moved to Los Angeles in the late 1960s, appearing in a number of television series over the years, including *Room 222, Kojak, Fame, Mad About You, Frasier*, and *Entourage*. Screen credits include *Young Graduates* (1971), *The Harrad Experiment* (1973), *The Godfather, Part II* (1974), *This Is Spinal Tap* (1984), *Good Morning, Vietnam* (1987), *Tin Men* (1987), *When Harry Met Sally* (1989), *The Freshman* (1990), *City Slickers* (1991), *The Basketball Diaries* (1995), *Donnie Brasco* (1996), *Sleepers* (1996), and *American Tragedy* (2000).

Phyllis Kirk (September 18, 1929–October 19, 2006). Born Phyllis Kirkegaard in Plainfield, New Jersey, the actress was best known as the damsel in distress opposite Vincent Price in 1953's 3-D horror film, *House of Wax*. Kirk shortened her last name when she moved to New York to study acting. She made her movie debut in *Our Very Own* (1950); other credits include *A Life of Her Own* (1950), *Two Weeks with Love* (1950), *River Beat* (1954), *Back from Eternity* (1956), *Johnny Concho* (1956), and *The Sad Sack* (1957). Kirk also starred opposite Peter Lawford in *The Thin Man* television series from 1957 to 1959. Kirk was heavily involved in social causes and later launched a public relations career in the 1970s.

Don Knotts (July 21, 1924–February 24, 2006). The skinny, frequently nervous-appearing comedic actor with the high-pitched voice was born Jesse Donald Knotts in Morgantown, West Virginia, and started performing a ventriloquism act in his teens. After serving in World War II and graduating from West Virginia University, Knotts moved to New York and appeared on the soap opera *Search for Tomorrow* from 1953–55 and *The Steve Allen Show* from 1956–60. Knotts appeared on Broadway in 1955's *No Time for Sergeants* opposite Andy Griffith and both men reprised their roles for the 1958 film version. The actors kept in touch and, in 1960, Knotts was cast as deputy Barney Fife in *The Andy Griffith Show*, a role for which he won five Emmys. Knotts later played Ralph Furley in *Three's Company* from 1979–84. Screen credits include *The Incredible Mr. Limpet* (1964), *The Ghost and Mr. Chicken* (1966), *The Reluctant Astronaut* (1967), *The Shakiest Gun in the West* (1968), *The Apple Dumpling Gang* (1975), *Gus* (1976), *No Deposit, No Return* (1976), *Herbie Goes to Monte Carlo* (1977), *The Apple Dumpling Gang Rides Again* (1979), *Cats Don't Dance* (1997), *Pleasantville* (1998), and *Chicken Little* (2005). Knotts published his memoirs, *Barney Fife and Other Characters I Have Known*, in 2000.

Robert "Buzz" Knudson (September 29, 1925–January 21, 2006). Born in Los Angeles, Knudson was an Oscar®-winning sound re-recording mixer. His father got him into the sound union after World War II but Knudson pitched minor-league baseball instead. He went to work for RCA in 1952 and then joined Todd-AO in 1960 as a recording engineer. Knudson was president of the company from 1982 to 1990 and served as a consultant until his 2003 retirement. Knudson amassed some ninety credits; he won Oscars® for *Cabaret* (1972), *The Exorcist* (1973), and *E.T. the Extra-Terrestrial* (1982), and was nominated for *A Star Is Born* (1976), *Close Encounters of the Third Kind* (1977), *Sorcerer* (1977), *Hooper* (1978), *1941* (1979), *Empire of the Sun* (1987), and *Who Framed Roger Rabbit?* (1988).

Kurt Kreuger (July 23, 1916–July 12, 2006). Born in Michenberg, Germany, the actor was raised in Switzerland. Kreuger dropped out of Columbia University to study acting and received a contract with 20th Century Fox where he was soon typecast as a Nazi or German officer in numerous World War II movies. He primarily appeared on television in the 1950s and 1960s before starting a career in real estate. Screen credits include *Mademoiselle Fifi* (1944), *None Shall Escape* (1944), *Escape in the Desert* (1945), *Hotel Berlin* (1945), *Paris Underground* (1945), *The Spider* (1945), *Sentimental Journey* (1946), *The Dark Corner* (1946), *Unfaithfully Yours* (1948), *The Enemy Below* (1957), *Legion of the Doomed* (1958), and *The St. Valentine's Day Massacre* (1967).

Otto Lang (January 21, 1908–January 30, 2006). Born in Tesanta, Austria-Hungary, the producer/director's career had an unusual beginning. A ski instructor, Lang emigrated to the United States in 1935 and opened the first ski school in Mt. Rainier, Washington, where his skills were featured in the 1936 short, *Ski Flight*. Lang doubled for Sonja Henie in a ski sequence in 1937's *Thin Ice*, which was filmed at the Paradise Lodge. After moving to Sun Valley, Lang worked on Henie's 1941 film *Sun Valley Serenade*, which was produced by Daryl F. Zanuck, whom he taught to ski. Zanuck helped Lang launch his filmmaking career by directing military training films for the Mountain Troops. As a documentary producer/director, Lang received Academy Award® nominations for the 1950s shorts *Jet Carrier, The First Piano Quartette,* and *Vesuvius Express*. Producer film credits include *Call Northside 777* (1948) and *5 Fingers* (1952). Lang's memoir, *A Bird of Passage: The Story of My Life from the Alps of Austria to Hollywood, USA*, was published in 1994.

Al Lewis (April 30, 1923–February 3, 2006). Born Albert Meister in Wolcott, New York, the character actor grew up in Brooklyn, becoming a vaudeville and circus performer. Lewis' big break came on television, first with Fred Gwynne in *Car 54, Where Are You?* (1961–63) and then as Grandpa the vampire, again opposite Gwynne, in *The Munsters* (1964–66). Lewis never complained about typecasting and made numerous appearances in character as well as opening a restaurant called Grandpa's. Films include *Pretty Boy Floyd* (1960), *Munster, Go Home* (1966), *They Shoot Horses, Don't They?* (1969), *The Boatniks* (1970), *Used Cars* (1980), *Married to the Mob* (1988), *Car 54, Where Are You?* (1994), *South Beach Academy* (1996), and *Night Terror* (2002).

Stu Linder (November 8, 1931–January 12, 2006). The film editor was born Stewart Bridgewater Linder in Geneva, Illinois, but grew up in Hermosa Beach, California. He was a pioneer of surf and beach culture, designing the first surfboard logos for commercial boards in the 1950s. Linder began at Paramount as an apprentice after World War II. He edited numerous movies for director Barry Levinson, beginning with 1982's *Diner*, and received an Oscar® nomination for *Rain Man* (1988). Among Linder's other Levinson films were *The Natural* (1984), *Good Morning, Vietnam* (1987), *Tin Men* (1987), *Avalon* (1990), *Bugsy* (1991), *Disclosure* (1994), *Sleepers* (1996), *Wag the Dog* (1997), *Bandits* (2001), and *Man of the Year* (2006). Linder shared an Oscar® win for the 1966 John Frankenheimer film *Grand Prix*.

Moss Mabry (1918–January 25, 2006). Born in Marianna, Florida, the costume designer earned a degree in mechanical engineering before attending the Chouinard Art Institute in California and eventually signing a contract with Warner Bros. He worked on more than eighty films between 1953 and 1988, including designing the red jacket worn by James Dean in 1955's *Rebel Without a Cause*. Mabry received Oscar® nominations for *Giant* (1956), *What a Way to Go!* (1964), *Morituri* (1965), and *The Way We Were* (1973). Among his other films were *The Bad Seed* (1956), *The Manchurian Candidate* (1962), *Mutiny on the Bounty* (1962), *Bob & Carol & Ted & Alice* (1969), *Butterflies Are Free* (1972), *King Kong* (1976), *The Shootist* (1976), *The Toy* (1982), and *Yellow Pages* (1988).

Mako (December 10, 1933–July 21, 2006). The actor was born Makoto Iwamatsu in Kobe, Japan; he joined his parents, who were studying in New York, when he was fifteen. Mako moved to California after serving two years in the Army and studied at the Pasadena Playhouse. In 1965, he co-founded the East West Players, the first Asian American theater company. Mako earned an Academy Award® nomination for an early film role, 1966's *The Sand Pebbles*. Other films include *Conan the Barbarian* (1982), *Conan the Destroyer* (1984), *Pacific Heights* (1990), *Rising Sun* (1993), *Seven Years in Tibet* (1997), *Pearl Harbor* (2001), *Bulletproof Monk* (2003), and *Memoirs of a Geisha* (2005).

Marian Marsh (October 13, 1913–November 9, 2006). The actress was born Violet Ethelred Krauth in Trinidad, West Indies, but her family later moved to Boston. Marsh followed her older sister, who acted under the names Jean Morgan and Jean Fenwick, to Hollywood. Marsh began her own career under the name Marian Morgan, including a bit in 1930's *Hell's Angels*. John Barrymore picked the teenager for the role of Trilby in 1931's *Svengali* because she resembled his wife Delores; Marsh appeared opposite Barrymore again in *The Mad Genius* (also 1931). Screen credits include *Five Star Final* (1931), *A Girl of the Limberlost* (1934), *The Black Room* (1935), *Crime and Punishment* (1935), *In Spite of Danger* (1935), *Unknown Woman* (1935), *Counterfeit* (1936), *Lady of Secrets* (1936), *The Man Who Lived Twice* (1936), *The Great Gambini* (1937), *Saturday's Heroes* (1937), *Youth on Parole* (1937), and *When's Your Birthday?* (1937). Her last film was 1942's *House of Errors*.

Osa Massen (January 13, 1916–January 2, 2006). Born in Copenhagen, Denmark, the actress was frequently cast as a femme fatale. Massen trained as a photographer but was persuaded by Danish director Alice O'Fredericks to take a role in 1935's *Kidnapped*. Massen's first Hollywood film was *Honeymoon in Bali* (1939). Screen credits include *Accent on Love* (1941), *Devil Pays Off* (1941), *A Woman's Face* (1941), *You'll Never Get Rich* (1941), *Background to Danger* (1943), *Jack London* (1943), *Cry of the Werewolf* (1944), *Tokyo Rose* (1946), *Million Dollar Weekend* (1948), and *Rocketship X-M* (1950).

Darren McGavin (May 7, 1922–February 25, 2006). Born in Spokane, Washington, the actor was living in Los Angeles and painting sets at Columbia Pictures when he landed a role in 1945's *A Song to Remember*. McGavin went on to a steady career in both film and television, appearing in five series, including cult favorite *Kolchak: The Night Stalker.* Screen credits include *The Man with the Golden Arm* (1955), *Summertime* (1955), *The Delicate Delinquent* (1957), *No Deposit, No Return* (1976), *A Christmas Story* (1983), *The Natural* (1984), and *Billy Madison* (1994).

Richard Morgan (August 12, 1958–December 23, 2006). Born in Hobart, Australia, the actor died from motor neuron disease. Morgan found his greatest success in Australian television, beginning at eighteen with his role as Terry Sullivan in *The Sullivans* (1976). Film credits include *Break of Day* (1976), *The Devil's Playground* (1976), *Phar Lap* (1983), *Innocent Prey* (1984), *Silver City* (1984), *Outback Vampires* (1987), and *Farewell to the King* (1989). Morgan quit acting from 1990 to 2000 for a business career but later returned to various television roles.

Jan Murray (October 4, 1916–July 2, 2006). The comedian was born Murray Janofsky in the Bronx, New York, and first made his reputation working at resorts in the Catskills, changing his name at the request of an agent to something easy to remember. Murray hosted a number of TV game shows in the 1950s, including *Go Lucky, Sing It Again, Meet Your Match, Dollar a Second,* and *Treasure Hunt.* Murray moved to Los Angeles in 1965 to find acting work; credits include *Who Killed Teddy Bear?* (1965), *The Busy Body* (1967), *A Man Called Dagger* (1967), *Thunder Alley* (1967), *The Angry Breed* (1968), and *Which Way to the Front?* (1970). Murray stopped performing at eighty-three, citing his worsening asthma, which threw off his comedic timing.

Fayard Nicholas (October 20, 1914–January 24, 2006). Born in Mobile, Alabama, Fayard was the elder of the tap-dancing Nicholas Brothers (Harold died in 2000). Their parents were musicians who played in vaudeville orchestras and Fayard learned to dance by watching the routines, which he then taught to the younger Harold; they started in vaudeville in 1928. They debuted at the Cotton Club in 1932 and also appeared in a short, *Pie, Pie Blackbird.* The dance team was seen in *Kid Millions* (1934), *The Big Broadcast of 1936* (1935), *Down Argentine Way* (1940), *Sun Valley Serenade* (1941), *Orchestra Wives* (1942), *Stormy Weather* (1943), and *The Pirate* (1948). The brothers began to perform separately after touring in the 1950s and Fayard had a dramatic role in *The Liberation of L.B. Jones* (1970). He also won a 1989 Tony award for his choreography of the Broadway revue *Black and Blue.* The Nicholas Brothers were the subject of the 1992 documentary, *The Nicholas Brothers: We Sing and We Dance.*

Leon Niemczyk (December 15, 1923–November 29, 2006). Born in Warsaw, Poland, the actor co-starred in hundreds of Polish films and television series. He starred in Roman Polanski's first feature film, *Knife in the Water* (1962), and his last role was in the David Lynch film *Inland Empire* (2006). An attempt to flee communist-led Poland landed Niemczyk in prison and he believed his criticism of the party cost him leading roles. However, he had a successful career as a character actor.

Philippe Noiret (October 1, 1933–November 23, 2006). Born in Lille, France, the actor made some 125 movies over a fifty-year career. Noiret began his career in 1953, touring with the Theatre Nationale Populaire. His film debut was in *La Pointe Courte* (1955) and he won Cesar awards for *The Old Gun* (1972) and *Life and Nothing But* (1990). Other credits include *Zazie in the Metro* (1960), *Night of the Generals* (1967), *The Assassination Bureau* (1969), *Murphy's War* (1971), *Le Grand Bouffe* (1973), *The Clockmaker* (1974), *The Judge and the Assassin* (1975), *Coupe de Torchon* (1981), *My New Partner* (1984), *Cinema Paradiso* (1988), *Il Postino* (1994), *On Guard!* (2003), and *Three Friends* (2006).

Carrie Nye (October 14, 1936–July 14, 2006). Born Carolyn Nye McGeoy in Greenwood, Mississippi, the husky-voiced actress was best known for her stage work, especially with the Williamstown Theatre Festival. She went to Yale Drama School where she met Dick Cavett, whom Nye married in 1964. Nye made her Broadway debut in 1960's *A Second String* and was nominated for a 1965 Tony award for *Half a Sixpence.* Among her screen credits were *The Group* (1966), *Divorce His/Divorce Hers* (1973), *The Scarlett O'Hara War* (1980), *Creepshow* (1982), and *Hello Again* (1987). Nye's last acting role was as Carolyn Carruthers on the daytime soap opera *The Guiding Light* in 2003.

Sven Nykvist (December 3, 1922–September 20, 2006). The award-winning cinematographer was born in Moheda, Sweden. He began his career as a camera assistant in 1941 and debuted as a cinematographer in 1945. Nykvist worked with director Ingmar Bergman on twenty-two films and won Oscars® for *Cries and Whispers* (1973) and *Fanny and Alexander* (1982). Other credits include *Sawdust and Tinsel* (1953), *The Virgin Spring* (1960), *Through a Glass Darkly* (1961), *The Winter Light* (1962), *Persona* (1966), *Hour of the Wolf* (1968), *The Passion of Anna* (1970), *Scenes from a Marriage* (1973), *The Tenant* (1976), *Pretty Baby* (1978), *From the Life of the Marionettes* (1980), *Star 80* (1983), *Agnes of God* (1985), *Crimes and Misdemeanors* (1989), *Chaplin* (1992), *Sleepless in Seattle* (1993), *What's Eating Gilbert Grape?* (1993), *Something to Talk About* (1995), *Celebrity* (1998), and *Curtain Call* (1999). Nykvist also received an Oscar® nomination for cinematography for *The Unbearable Lightness of Being* (1988) and a best foreign film Oscar® nomination for his feature directorial film, 1991's *The Ox.* Nykvist retired in 1999.

Gerard Oury (April 29, 1919–July 20, 2006). Born in Paris, France, the director was best known for his comedies. Oury began his career as an actor; he fled the Nazi occupation but returned to France after World War II and directed his first film in 1959. Films include *The Sucker* (1964), *La Grande Vadrouille* (1966), *The Brain* (1968), *La Folie des Grandeurs* (1971), *Les Aventures de Rabbi Jacob* (1973), *L'As des As* (1982), and *La Schpountz* (1999).

Jack Palance (February 18, 1919–November 10, 2006). The gravel-voiced actor was born Volodymir Ivanovich Palaniuk in Lattimer Mines, Pennsylvania. Palance became a professional boxer under the name Jack Brazzo in the late 1930s and, after serving in World War II, he studied journalism at Stanford University but switched to the drama department. Palance (he changed his name when he became an actor) headed to New York where he first appeared on Broadway in 1947's *The Big Two.* He made his screen debut under the name Walter Palance in 1950's *Panic in the Streets.* Palance received best supporting actor Oscar® nominations for *Sudden Fear* (1952) and *Shane* (1953) and won for *City Slickers* (1991). Screen credits include *Arrowhead* (1953),

The Silver Chalice (1954), *The Big Knife* (1955), *I Died a Thousand Times* (1955), *Attack!* (1956), *Barabbas* (1962), *The Professionals* (1966), *Dr. Jekyll and Mr. Hyde* (1968), *Monte Walsh* (1970), *Dracula* (1973), *Oklahoma Crude* (1973), *Bagdad Cafe* (1988), *Young Guns* (1988), *Batman* (1989), *City Slickers II: The Legend of Curly's Gold* (1994), and *Prancer Returns* (2001). Palance also won an Emmy for 1956's *Requiem for a Heavyweight* and had regular roles on the television series *The Greatest Show on Earth, Bronk*, and *Ripley's Believe It or Not.*

Gordon Parks (November 30, 1912–March 7, 2006). The author, photojournalist, composer, and filmmaker was born the youngest of fifteen children in Fort Scott, Kansas. Parks worked a series of menial jobs and was working as a railroad car waiter in 1937 when he was inspired to try his hand at photography, eventually landing fashion shoots and society portraits. In 1942, Parks received a fellowship and moved to Washington DC, where he was a trainee at the photography unit of the Farm Security Administration and then at the Office of War Information, as well as freelancing for magazines. He became the first African American photojournalist for *Life* magazine from 1948–72. He was also the first African American to write and direct a Hollywood feature film with 1969's *The Learning Tree*, which was based on his own 1963 novel. This was followed by *Shaft* (1971), *Shaft's Big Score* (1972), *The Super Cops* (1974), *Leadbelly* (1976), and *Solomon Northup's Odyssey* (1984). Parks wrote several memoirs, including *A Choice of Weapons* (1966), *To Smile in Autumn* (1979), *Voices in the Mirror* (1990), and *A Hungry Heart* (2005).

Christopher Penn (October 10, 1965–January 24, 2006). Born in Los Angeles, the actor came from a show business family: father Leo was a director, mother Eileen Ryan and brother Sean are actors, and brother Michael Penn is a musician. Penn's death was apparently related to an enlarged heart and heart disease. He began his career as a child actor in the 1970s. Credits include *Rumble Fish* (1983), *Footloose* (1984), *Pale Rider* (1985), *At Close Range* (1986), *Mobsters* (1991), *Reservoir Dogs* (1992), *Short Cuts* (1993), *True Romance* (1993), *Mulholland Falls* (1995), *One Tough Cop* (1998), *American Pie 2* (2001), *Corky Romano* (2001), *Murder by Numbers* (2002), *After the Sunset* (2004), *Starsky and Hutch* (2004), and *The Darwin Awards* (2006).

Basil Poledouris (August 21, 1945–November 8, 2006). The composer was born in Kansas City, Missouri, and studied film and music at the University of Southern California. He began by scoring educational films and went on to film and television work, receiving an Emmy for the 1989 miniseries *Lonesome Dove*. Credits include *Big Wednesday* (1978), *The Blue Lagoon* (1980), *Conan the Barbarian* (1982), *Conan the Destroyer* (1984), *Red Dawn* (1984), *Flesh and Blood* (1985), *Robocop* (1987), *Farewell to the King* (1989), *The Hunt for Red October* (1990), *Flight of the Intruder* (1991), *Free Willy* (1993), *Serial Mom* (1994), *Free Willy 2* (1995), *It's My Party* (1995), *Starship Troopers* (1997), *For Love of the Game* (1999), and *Cecil B. Demented* (2000).

Gillo Pontecorvo (November 19, 1919–October 12, 2006). The director was born in Pisa, Italy, to a Jewish family. Pontecorvo moved to France in 1939 to escape the Fascist regime but eventually returned to Italy as part of the Milan resistance. He worked as a journalist and started directing documentaries; his first feature film was 1957's *The Wide Blue Road*. Pontecorvo received an Oscar® nomination for *The Battle of Algiers* (1966). Other credits include *Kapo* (1959), *Burn* (1969), and *Operation Ogre* (1979).

Gretchen Rau (July 6, 1939–March 29, 2006). Born in New Orleans, Louisiana, the set decorator moved to New York in 1966 and worked as a property master for a commercial production house before moving into feature films. Rau received an Oscar® nomination for *The Last Samurai* (2003) and won for *Memoirs of a Geisha* (2005). Other credits include *Once Upon a Time in America* (1984), *Crocodile Dundee* (1986), *Mississippi Burning* (1988), *A River Runs Through It* (1992), *Six Degrees of Separation* (1993), *What's Eating Gilbert Grape?* (1993), *Nobody's Fool* (1994), *The Crucible* (1996), *City of Angels* (1998), *The Horse Whisperer* (1998), *The Shipping News* (2001), *The Life Aquatic with Steve Zissou* (2004), and *The Good Shepherd* (2006).

Dana Reeve (March 17, 1961–March 6, 2006). Born Dana Morosini in Teaneck, New Jersey, the actress and head of the Christopher Reeve Foundation died of lung cancer. Reeve was working in cabaret when she met her husband in 1987; they married in 1992 (Christopher Reeve died in 2004). Although she did commercials, television, and stage work, after Christopher Reeve's paralyzing accident in 1995, she limited her career. Reeve's last role was as the voice of Emily Irving in the 2006 animated feature *Everyone's Hero.*

Kasey Rogers (December 15, 1925–July 6, 2006). Born Imogene Rogers in Morehouse, Missouri, the actress earned her nickname, "Casey," for her childhood baseball prowess. She was working as a contract player at Paramount under the screen name Laura Elliot, but was loaned to Warner Bros. for her best known role in 1951's *Strangers on a Train.* Others credits include *Special Agent* (1949), *Silver City* (1951), *Two Lost Worlds* (1951), and *Denver and Rio Grande* (1952). Rogers also had recurring roles on the television series *Peyton Place* and *Bewitched.* In the 1970s, Rogers took up motocross racing and promotion and established the PowderPuff's Unlimited Riders and Racers association.

Leonard Schrader (November 30, 1943–November 2, 2006). Born in Grand Rapids, Michigan, the screenwriter grew up in a family of strict Dutch Calvinists who forbade moviewatching and Schrader didn't see his first film until he went to college. Schrader graduated from Calvin College and received a master's degree from the University of Iowa Writers' Workshop. He based his first screenplay, *The Yakuza* (1975), co-written with his brother Paul Schrader, on the knowledge he acquired while teaching American literature in Japan. Schrader was nominated for an adapted screenplay Oscar® for the film *Kiss of the Spider Woman* (1985). His only directorial effort was 1991's *Naked Tango*, which he also scripted. Additional credits include *Blue Collar* (1978), *Old Boyfriends* (1979), and *Mishima* (1985). Schrader was also the filmmaker-in-residence at the American Film Institute where he taught graduate screenwriting.

Moira Shearer (January 17, 1926–January 31, 2006). The ballerina and actress was born in Dunfermline, Scotland. She joined the Sadler's Wells School in 1940 and the ballet company itself in 1942. The flame-haired dancer starred in

The Red Shoes in 1948, but later complained the successful dance melodrama ruined her ballet career. Other films include *The Tales of Hoffmann* (1950), *The Story of Three Loves* (1952), *The Man Who Loved Redheads* (1954), *Peeping Tom* (1960), and *Black Tights* (1961). Shearer quit dancing in 1954 to concentrate on acting and worked primarily in the theatre; she also lectured on ballet history and wrote book reviews.

Adrienne Shelly (June 16, 1966–November 1, 2006). The actress/writer/director, born Adrienne Levine in Queens, New York, was the victim of a homicide. Shelly starred in director Hal Harley's films *The Unbelievable Truth* (1989) and *Trust* (1990). Other acting credits include *Sleep with Me* (1994), *Teresa's Tattoo* (1994), *Wrestling with Alligators* (1998), *Revolution No. 9* (2002), and *Factotum* (2006). She wrote and directed the features *Sudden Manhattan* (1997), *I'll Take You There* (1999), and *Waitress* (2006).

Vincent Sherman (July 16, 1906–June 18, 2006). Born Abraham Orovitz in Vienna, Georgia, the director was working as a newspaper police reporter when he and a former classmate wrote a play and decided to try their luck in New York. A talent agency suggested his name change when Sherman began looking for acting work. A role in the 1932 play *Counsellor-at-Law* led Sherman to re-create the part for the 1933 film version. In 1937, he became a writer for Warner Bros. B-picture unit, including *Crime School* (1938) and *King of the Underworld* (1939). Sherman also became a contract director at Warner Bros. with 1939's *The Return of Dr. X.* Credits include *All Through the Night* (1942), *The Hard Way* (1942), *Old Acquaintance* (1943), *Mr. Skeffington* (1944), *The New Adventures of Don Juan* (1948), *The Hasty Heart* (1949), *The Damned Don't Cry* (1950), *Harriet Craig* (1950), *Goodbye, My Fancy* (1951), *An Affair in Trinidad* (1952), *Lone Star* (1952), *The Young Philadelphians* (1959), *Ice Palace* (1960), *The Second Time Around* (1961), and *Cervantes* (1967). Sherman was dropped by Warner Bros. in the early 1950s because of the Communist blacklist and later turned to television directing, including the TV movies *The Last Hurrah* (1977), *Women at West Point* (1979), *Bogie: The Last Hero* (1980), and *The Love Goddess* (1983). His 1996 autobiography was entitled *Studio Affairs: My Life as a Film Director.*

Sig Shore (May 13, 1919–August 17, 2006). Born in the Bronx, New York, the independent producer worked in advertising and imported foreign films. His first producer credit was for 1972's *Superfly*. Shore directed and produced the features *That's the Way of the World* (1975), *The Act* (1984), and *Return of Superfly* (1990). He also produced *Superfly T.N.T.* (1973), wrote and directed *Sudden Death* (1985), and directed *The Survivalist* (1987).

Vilgot Sjoman (December 2, 1924–April 9, 2006). The director, born in Stockholm, Sweden, was a protege of Ingmar Bergman, whom Sjoman met in the 1940s. The director often worked with controversial and/or sexually explicit material. Credits include *The Mistress* (1962), *491* (1964), *My Sister, My Love* (1966), *I Am Curious (Yellow)* (1967), *I Am Curious (Blue)* (1968), and *Alfred Nobel* (1995).

Mickey Spillane (March 9, 1918–July 17, 2006). The creator of hard-boiled PI Mike Hammer was born Frank Morrison Spillane in Brooklyn, New York. His father called him Mickey after his baptismal saint's name, Michael. Spillane began writing and selling stories right out of high school, eventually working at comic book company Funnies Inc. where he developed a detective called Mike Danger. Hammer first appeared in the 1947 novel, *I, the Jury*, which was filmed in 1953 and 1982. Other filmed Hammer novels were *Kiss Me Deadly* (1955), *My Gun Is Quick* (1957), and *The Girl Hunters* (1963), which starred Spillane as Hammer. From 1973 to 1989, Spillane spoofed his image and his character in a number of Miller Lite beer commercials. The character was also featured in a radio show, a cartoon strip, three TV series, and several made-for-TV movies. Spillane also played himself in 1954's *Ring of Fear* and had roles in the horror films *Mommy* (1995) and *Mommy 2* (1996).

Richard Stahl (January 4, 1932–June 18, 2006). The character actor was born in Detroit, Michigan, and began his career doing magic tricks. Stahl was a graduate of New York's American Academy of Dramatic Arts. Screen credits include *Five Easy Pieces* (1970), *The Student Nurses* (1970), *Beware! The Blob* (1972), *High Anxiety* (1977), *9 to 5* (1980), *Private School* (1983), and *Ghosts of Mississippi* (1996).

Maureen Stapleton (June 21, 1925–March 13, 2006). Born in Troy, New York, the actress came to New York City after her high school graduation to study acting, including at the Actor's Studio. Stapleton made her Broadway debut in 1946 and won Tony awards for 1951's *The Rose Tattoo* and 1971's *The Gingerbread Lady.* She won a best supporting actress Oscar® for 1981's *Reds* and was nominated for *Lonelyhearts* (1958), *Airport* (1970), and *Interiors* (1978). Other screen credits include *The Fugitive Kind* (1960), *Bye Bye Birdie* (1963), *Plaza Suite* (1971), *Johnny Dangerously* (1984), *Cocoon* (1985), *The Money Pit* (1986), *Cocoon: The Return* (1988), and *Addicted to Love* (1996). Stapleton also won a 1967 Emmy for *Among the Paths to Eden* and was nominated for *Queen of the Stardust Ballroom* (1975), *The Gathering* (1977), *Miss Rose White* (1992), and *Road to Avonlea* (1996). Her 1995 autobiography was entitled *A Hell of a Life.*

Joseph Stefano (May 5, 1922–August 25, 2006). Born in Philadelphia, Pennsylvania, the writer began his career touring as a singer and dancer in operettas and wrote songs for nightclub acts. He was hired as a writer in the 1950s for the *Ted Mack Family Hour* and his first screenplay was 1958's *The Black Orchid.* He became a scriptwriter for 20th Century Fox in 1960 and wrote the adapted screenplay for *Psycho* (1960) as well as *The Naked Edge* (1961), *Eye of the Cat* (1969), *Futz* (1969), *Home for the Holidays* (1972), *Snowbeast* (1977), *The Kindred* (1987), *Psycho IV: The Beginning* (1990), and *Two Bits* (1995). Stefano also produced *The Outer Limits*, which ran from 1963 to 1965, and wrote many of the episodes.

Robert Sterling (November 12, 1917–May 30, 2006). The actor was born William Sterling Hart in New Castle, Pennsylvania, and changed his name when he signed with Columbia Pictures in 1939 to avoid confusion with silent western star William S. Hart. Sterling moved to MGM (Metro-Goldwyn-Mayer) in 1941 where he appeared in *The Getaway* (1941), *I'll Wait for You* (1941), *The Penalty*

(1941), *Ringside Maisie* (1941), *Two-Faced Woman* (1941), *Johnny Eager* (1942), *Somewhere I'll Find You* (1942), *This Time for Keeps* (1942), *Roughshod* (1949), *Bunco Squad* (1950), *The Sundowners* (1950), *Show Boat* (1951), *Return to Peyton Place* (1961), *Voyage to the Bottom of the Sea* (1961), and *A Global Affair* (1964). Sterling and wife Anne Jeffreys co-starred as the ghostly George and Marion Kirby in the TV sitcom *Topper* from 1953 to 1956. Sterling continued to make occasional guest appearances on television but essentially turned from acting to a business career.

Frankie Thomas (April 9, 1921–May 11, 2006). Born in New York, the actor began as a child performer on stage in the 1930s. He appeared in the drama *Wednesday's Child* and came to Hollywood for the 1934 film version. Thomas also appeared in *A Dog of Flanders* (1935), *Tim Tyler's Luck* (1937), *Boys Town* (1938), *Nancy Drew, Detective* (1938), *Nancy Drew, Reporter* (1939), *Nancy Drew, Troubleshooter* (1939), *Nancy Drew and the Hidden Staircase* (1939), *Flying Cadets* (1941), and *The Major and the Minor* (1942). After serving in the Coast Guard in World War II, Thomas moved back to New York for stage and television work. He was cast as the lead in *Tom Corbett, Space Cadet*, which ran from 1950 to 1955. Thomas retired when the show ended and became an author. At his request, Thomas was buried in his Tom Corbett costume.

Alida Valli (May 31, 1921–April 22, 2006). Born Alida von Altenburger in Pula, which was then part of Italy and is now Croatia, the actress studied at the Centro Sperimentale in Rome and made her screen debut in 1936's *The Two Sergeants*. Valli changed her name and made five films in 1937, including *It Was I* and *The Last Enemy*. Other credits include *Manon Lescaut* (1940), *Old-Fashioned World* (1941), *Schoolgirl Diary* (1941), *We the Living* (1942), *Laugh Pagliacci* (1943), *Life Begins Anew* (1945), and *Eugenie Grandet* (1947). Valli was offered a Hollywood contract by David Selznick and made *The Paradine Case* (1947), *Miracle of the Bells* (1948), and *The Third Man* (1949). She returned to Italy and was featured in such films as *Senso* (1954), *Il Grido* (1957), *The Wide Blue Road* (1957), *The Castilian* (1963), *Oedipus Rex* (1967), *The Spider's Strategem* (1970), *1900* (1976), *La Luna* (1979), and *Semana Santa* (2002). Valli also appeared on stage and television.

Shirley Walker (April 10, 1945–November 30, 2006). Born in Napa, California, the composer attended San Francisco State on a piano scholarship. Walker composed music for industrial films and wrote jingles before she began her film career playing synthesizers on *Apocalypse Now* (1979). Film scores include *The End of August* (1982), *Ghoulies* (1985), *Chicago Joe and the Showgirl* (1990), *Memoirs of an Invisible Man* (1992), *Batman: Mask of the Phantasm* (1993), *Escape from L.A.* (1996), *Turbulence* (1997), *Final Destination* (2000), *Final Destination 2* (2003), *Willard* (2003), *Final Destination 3* (2006), and *Black Christmas* (2006). Walker also worked heavily in television and scored a number of series and made-for-TV movies; she was hired by Warner Bros. in 1990 as supervising composer on a number of animated series and won Emmys for *The Adventures of Batman & Robin* and *Batman Beyond*.

Jack Warden (September 18, 1920–July 19, 2006). The gruff-voiced actor was born John H. Lebzelter in Newark, New Jersey, and pursued his career in New York after serving in World War II, taking his father's middle name as his stage name. Warden joined the Alley Theatre in Dallas in 1946 and debuted on television in 1950 before his breakthrough film role as Juror No. 7 in 1957's *Twelve Angry Men*. Warden was nominated for best supporting actor Oscars® for *Shampoo* (1975) and *Heaven Can Wait* (1978). He won an Emmy for the 1971 TV movie, *Brian's Song*. Films include *From Here to Eternity* (1953), *The Man Who Loved Cat Dancing* (1973), *The Apprenticeship of Duddy Kravitz* (1974), *All the President's Men* (1976), *And Justice for All* (1979), *Being There* (1979), *Used Cars* (1980), *So Fine* (1981), *The Verdict* (1982), *Bullets Over Broadway* (1994), *Mighty Aphrodite* (1995), *Bulworth* (1998), and *The Replacements* (2000).

Dennis Weaver (June 4, 1924–February 24, 2006). Born in Joplin, Missouri, the lanky actor studied at the Actor's Studio after serving in World War II. Weaver made his screen debut in *The Raiders* (1952) but was better known for his television roles. He played deputy Chester Goode on *Gunsmoke* from 1955 to 1964, as well as starring in *Kentucky Jones* (1964), *Gentle Ben* (1967–69), *McCloud* (1970–77), *Stone* (1980), *Emerald Point N.A.S.* (1983), *Buck James* (1987), and the cable series *Wildfire* (2005). Weaver was also featured in such miniseries as *Centennial* (1978) and *Lonesome Dove* (1994). Other credits include *The Nebraskan* (1953), *Touch of Evil* (1958), *The Gallant Hours* (1960), *Gentle Giant* (1967), *Duel* (1971), *The Virginian* (1999), *High Noon* (2000), and as the voice of Abner in *Home on the Range* (2004). Weaver's autobiography, *All the World's a Stage*, was published in 2001.

Nicholas Webster (July 24, 1912–August 12, 2006). Born in Spokane, Washington, the director started as a film cutter at MGM (Metro-Goldwyn-Mayer) and worked as an Army cinematographer during World War II and a documentary and commercial director after the war. Webster didn't begin directing in Hollywood until the early 1960s. Credits include *Dead to the World* (1961), *Gone Are the Days!* (1963), *Santa Claus Conquers the Martians* (1964), *Mission Mars* (1968), and *No Longer Alone* (1978). Webster also filmed a number of documentaries for television and directed numerous TV series. His 1997 autobiography was called *How to Sleep on a Camel: Adventures of a Documentary Film Director*.

Johnny Weissmuller Jr. (September 23, 1940–July 27, 2006). Born in San Francisco, the actor swam competitively in college, served in the Navy, and worked as a longshoreman. Among his film roles were *Andy Hardy Comes Home* (1958), *THX 1138* (1971), and *American Graffiti* (1973), and he appeared on television beginning in the 1960s. Weissmuller Jr. also published the 2002 memoir, *Tarzan, My Father*.

Jack Wild (September 30, 1952–March 1, 2006). Born in Royton, England, the actor was nominated for a best supporting actor Oscar® at sixteen for his role as the Artful Dodger in the 1968 musical *Oliver!* He then starred on television in 1969's *H.R. Pufnstuf* and in the 1970 movie version. Wild was a teen idol in Great Britain and also made *Melody* (1971), *The Pied Piper* (1972), and *The 14* (1973), but his career was essentially over by the age of twenty-one. Wild's last screen role was in 1991's *Robin Hood: Prince of*

Thieves. He was diagnosed with oral cancer in 2000 and was left unable to speak after surgery.

Shelley Winters (August 18, 1920–January 14, 2006). Born Shirley Schrift in St. Louis, Missouri, the actress grew up in Brooklyn and took acting lessons at the New Theater School. She allegedly took her stage name from poet Percy Bysshe Shelley and her mother, Rose Winter. Winters signed a contract with Columbia Pictures and was first molded into bombshell roles before evolving into a character actress. She had a one-line part in 1943's *What a Woman!* and also had small roles in *Knickerbocker Holiday* (1944) and *A Thousand and One Nights* (1945). Columbia dropped her but Winters then signed with Universal Studios and her breakthrough role came with 1947's *A Double Life*. Winters earned a best actress Oscar® nomination for 1951's *A Place in the Sun*; she won best supporting actress Oscars® for *The Diary of Anne Frank* (1959) and *A Patch of Blue* (1965) and was nominated for *The Poseidon Adventure* (1972). Other credits include *Larceny* (1948), *The Great Gatsby* (1949), *Frenchie* (1950), *Winchester 73* (1950), *Meet Danny Wilson* (1952), *The Night of the Hunter* (1955), *The Young Savages* (1961), *The Chapman Report* (1962), *Lolita* (1962), *Alfie* (1966), *Harper* (1966), *Bloody Mama* (1970), *Who Slew Auntie Roo?* (1971), *Blume in Love* (1973), *Next Stop, Greenwich Village* (1976), *S.O.B.* (1981), *Heavy* (1994), and *Portrait of a Lady* (1996). Winters also wrote two autobiographies: *Shelley, Also Known as Shirley* (1980) and *Shelly II: In the Middle of My Century* (1989).

Jane Wyatt (August 12, 1910–October 20, 2006). The actress was born in Campgaw, New Jersey, and took drama courses at Barnard College before apprenticing at the Berkshire Playhouse. She first appeared on stage in 1931 and signed a short contract with Universal in 1934, appearing in *One More River* and *Great Expectations*. Wyatt alternated between film and stage work during the 1930s and 1940s; screen credits include *Lost Horizon* (1937), *The Kansan* (1943), *None But the Lonely Heart* (1944), *Boomerang* (1947), *Gentleman's Agreement* (1947), *Pitfall* (1948), *Canadian Pacific* (1949), *Task Force* (1949), and *My Blue Heaven* (1950). Wyatt was a three-time Emmy winner for her role as understanding wife and mother Margaret Anderson in the TV series *Father Knows Best* (1954–60). She later appeared as Spock's human mother, Amanda, in the *Star Trek* TV series and reprised her role in 1986's *Star Trek IV: The Voyage Home*.

Selected Film Books of 2006

Anderson, John and Laura Kim. *I Wake Up Screening: What to Do Once You've Made That Movie.* Watson-Guptill, 2006. Offers advice for emerging filmmakers from more than 60 industry insiders.

Angell, Callie. *Andy Warhol Screen Tests: The Films of Andy Warhol: Catalogue Raisonne.* Abrams, 2006. The first of a two-volume catalogue of Andy Warhol's Factory studio work, beginning with his silent shorts in 1963. Includes 780 photographs.

Avni, Sheerly. *Cinema by the Bay.* George Lucas Books, 2006. Film history of San Francisco; includes profiles of directors and studios located in Northern California.

Badley, Linda, R. Barton Palmer, and Steven Jay Schneider, editors. *Traditions in World Cinema.* Rutgers University Press, 2006. Essays discussing film movements from German expressionism and Italian neorealism to Japanese horror, Chinese melodrama, and African, Middle Eastern, and South American film.

Barbeau, Adrienne. *There Are Worse Things I Could Do.* Carroll & Graf, 2006. The actress discusses her forty-year career in movies, television, and stage.

Bast, William. *Surviving James Dean.* Barricade, 2006. The TV writer and journalist met Dean in 1950 and details their friendship, focusing on Dean's sexuality and the long-term impact Dean had on the author's life.

Beauchamp, Cari, editor. *Adventures of a Hollywood Secretary: Her Private Letters from Inside the Studios of the 1920s.* University of California Press, 2006. Collection of missives from Valeria Belletti, who worked as a secretary for Samuel Goldwyn and Cecil B. DeMille from 1925 to 1929.

Bengtson, John. *Silent Traces: Discovering Early Hollywood Through the Films of Charlie Chaplin.* Santa Monica Press, 2006. Bengtson combines images from Chaplin's films with archival photos, maps, and current comparisons to showcase the evolving California landscape.

Berry, Jo. *The Parents' Guide to Kids' Movies: Over 500 Children's and Family Films Reviewed.* Orion, 2006. Covers films marketed to youngsters from preschool to preteens for language, violence, and adult situations.

Bordwell, David. *The Way Hollywood Tells It: Story and Style in Modern Movies.* University of California Press, 2006. Examines visual storytelling styles in both mainstream and independent films made since 1960.

Brode, Douglas. *Elvis Cinema and Popular Culture.* McFarland, 2006. Provides a film-by-film study of Elvis Presley's thirty-one movies as a reflection of American society.

Bruzzi, Stella. *Bringing Up Daddy: Fatherhood and Masculinity in Postwar Hollywood.* British Film Institute, 2006. Decade-by-decade examination of the Hollywood dad from World War II to the present.

Burstyn, Ellen. *Lessons in Becoming Myself.* Riverhead, 2006. The actress details her tumultuous childhood, her career on stage and screen, and her personal struggles and triumphs.

Cahir, Linda Costanzo. *Literature into Film: Theory and Practical Approaches.* McFarland, 2006. Comprehensive guide to literature-based films that provides a relationship between the movies and the original texts.

Callow, Simon. *Orson Welles, Volume 2: Hello Americans.* Viking, 2006. Covers Welles' career from 1941 to 1947, from the premiere of *Citizen Kane* to his self-imposed exile in Europe.

Capua, Michelangelo. *Yul Brynner: A Biography.* McFarland, 2006. Biography covers the actor's early years in Russia, France, and China through his success in *The King and I.*

Carlyle, John. *Under the Rainbow: A Memoir of Judy Garland, Rock Hudson, and the End of Old Hollywood.* Carroll & Graf, 2006. Former actor Carlyle discusses his own life and his friendship with Garland in the 1960s.

Chandler, Charlotte. *The Girl Who Walked Home Alone: Bette Davis, a Personal Biography.* Simon & Schuster, 2006. Chandler presents interviews she did with Davis and minimal synopses of her movies.

Charyn, Jerome. *Raised by Wolves: The Turbulent Art and Times of Quentin Tarantino.* Thunder's Mouth, 2006. Analysis of the director and his films.

Chung, Hye Seung. *Hollywood Asian: Philip Ahn and the Politics of Cross-Ethnic Performance.* Temple University Press, 2006. Investigates the career of the Korean-American actor, who made more than two hundred screen appearances.

Cocks, Geoffrey, James Diedrick, and Glenn Perusek, editors. *Depth of Field: Stanley Kubrick, Film, and the Uses of History.* University of Wisconsin Press, 2006. Screenwriters and scholars analyze Kubrick's thirteen films from numerous perspectives.

Conard, Mark T., editor. *The Philosophy of Neo-Noir.* University Press of Kentucky, 2006. Contributors analyze recent films that utilize noir conventions of alienation, pessimism, moral ambivalence, and disorientation.

Cowie, Peter. *Louise Brooks: Lulu Forever.* Rizzoli, 2006. The silent screen actress is celebrated in film stills, private photos, letters, and interviews that explore her status as a cult icon.

Cropper, Simon. *Time Out 1000 Films to Change Your Life.* Time Out, 2006. Actors, directors, cinematographers, animators, and others write about their favorite films.

Crosse, Jesse. *The Greatest Movie Car Chases of All Time.* MBI Publishing Company, 2006. Close-up look at the ten most amazing car chases ever filmed.

D'Lugo, Marvin. *Pedro Almodovar.* University of Illinois Press, 2006. Chronological examination of the Spanish director's career from his Super 8 shorts to his award-winning feature films.

Davis, Ronald L. *Zachary Scott: Hollywood's Sophisticated Cad.* University Press of Mississippi, 2006. Biography of the actor who was typecast as a debonair villain in American films, especially in the 1940s.

De la Mora, Sergio. *Cinemachismo: Masculinities and Sexuality in Mexican Film.* University of Texas Press, 2006. Analysis of how Mexican cinema has represented machismo in relationship to national identity from 1950 to 2004.

De Vito, John and Frank Tropea. *The Immortal Marilyn: The Depiction of an Icon.* Scarecrow Press, 2006. Decade-by-decade review of how Marilyn Monroe has been depicted from the 1950s to the present day.

Dick, Bernard F. *Forever Mame: The Life of Rosalind Russell.* University Press of Mississippi, 2006. Relies primarily on Russell's own memoir and film archives as well as interviews to recount the actress's life.

Dixon, Wheeler Winston. *Visions of Paradise: Images of Eden in the Cinema.* Rutgers University Press, 2006. Explores images of heaven, earthly paradises, and utopias in European and Hollywood films.

Dobson, Terence. *The Film Work of Norman McLaren.* Indiana University Press, 2006. Looks at the achievements of the animation pioneer and the technical processes used in his films.

Dubas, Rita. *Shirley Temple: A Pictorial History of the World's Greatest Child Star.* Applause Books, 2006. Provides a concise history of Temple's career, as well as an extensive look at the collectibles that bear her image.

Ebert, Roger. *Awake in the Dark: The Best of Roger Ebert.* University of Chicago Press, 2006. The *Chicago Sun-Times* film critic offers his reviews of the best films over his thirty-eight-year career, as well as interviews and companion pieces.

Eliot, Marc. *Jimmy Stewart: A Biography.* Harmony, 2006. Extensive biography of cinema's everyman.

Erwin, Ellen and Jessica Z. Diamond. *The Audrey Hepburn Treasures.* Atria, 2006. Heavily illustrated biography that uses the actress's own words and copies of personal mementos to provide a narrative of her life and work.

Eszterhas, Joe. *The Devil's Guide to Hollywood: The Screenwriter as God.* St. Martin's, 2006. The screenwriter of some fifteen films offers reminiscences and Hollywood trivia, as well as some basic advice for would-be writers.

Everett, Rupert. *Red Carpets and Other Banana Skins.* Little, Brown, 2006. Autobiography of the openly gay British actor that covers his personal and professional lives.

Falk, Peter. *Just One More Thing: Stories from My Life.* Carroll & Graf, 2006. The actor discusses his personal and professional lives, including his work with John Cassavetes and his popular television role as Lt. Columbo.

Feldman, Edward S., with Tom Barton. *Tell Me How You Love the Picture: A Hollywood Life.* St. Martin's, 2006. The film producer looks back on his career, beginning as a publicist in the 1950s through his studio days.

Fine, Marshall. *Accidental Genius.* Miramax, 2006. Biography of independent actor/director John Cassavetes.

Frayling, Christopher. *Ken Adam: The Art of Production Design.* Faber & Faber, 2006. Question-and-answer text between Adam and Frayling covers Adam's career in the post-World War II British film industry, including the James Bond films and his work with Stanley Kubrick.

Freedland, Michael. *Dean Martin: King of the Road.* Robson, 2006. Biography of the singer/actor includes his partnership with Jerry Lewis, his Rat Pack years, and his television work.

Fridlund, Bert. *The Spaghetti Western: A Thematic Analysis.* McFarland, 2006. Examines the Italian western and the construction of its stories.

Friedman, Lester D. *Citizen Spielberg.* University of Illinois Press, 2006. Analysis of the director's work in various genres, from science fiction to adventure to war films.

Gabler, Neal. *Walt Disney: The Triumph of the American Imagination.* Knopf, 2006. Biography of the entertainment mogul that is especially interested in the early years of the Disney studio.

Galloway, Patrick. *Asia Shock: Horror and Dark Cinema from Japan, Korea, Hong Kong, and Thailand.* Stone Bridge Press, 2006. Surveys suspense, exploitation, supernatural, and other aspects of Asian Extreme cinema.

Gaspard, John. *Fast, Cheap, and Under Control: Lessons from the Greatest Low-Budget Movies of All Time.* Michael Wiese Productions, 2006. An independent filmmaker himself, Gaspard offers useful advice on making low-budget movies.

Getz, Leonard. *From Broadway to the Bowery: A History and Filmography of the Dead End Kids, Little Tough Guys, East Side Kids and Bowery Boys Films, with Cast Biographies.* McFarland, 2006. Chronicles the origin of the various street kid film incarnations, casts, and studios.

Grahame-Smith, Seth. *The Big Book of Porn: A Penetrating Look at the World of Dirty Movies.* Quirk, 2006. A chronology of the porn industry and its stars.

Gresh, Lois H. and Robert Weinberg. *The Science of James Bond: From Bullets to Bowler Hats to Boat Jumps, the Real Technology Behind 007's Fabulous Films.* Wiley, 2006. Examines the gadgets and weapons that fill the James Bond movies.

Harness, Kyp. *The Art of Laurel and Hardy: Graceful Calamity in the Films.* McFarland, 2006. Explores the comedy and up-and-down careers of the duo.

Harry, Lou and Eric Furman. *In the Can: The Greatest Career Missteps, Sophomore Slumps, What-Were-They-Thinking Decisions and Fire Your Agent Moves in the History of the Movies.* Emmis Books, 2006. Cinematic flops that both critics and moviegoers agree on, as well as TV stars who couldn't transition to film, and other embarrassing choices made by performers and directors alike.

Higgins, Steven. *Still Moving: The Film and Media Collections of the Museum of Modern Art.* Museum of Modern Art, 2006. Catalogue offers some five hundred images from MoMA's collection, which was founded in 1935.

Hirshenson, Janet, and Jane Jenkins, with Rachel Kranz. *A Star Is Found: Our Adventures Casting Some of Hollywood's Biggest Movies.* Harcourt, 2006. Hirshenson and Jenkins, casting partners since 1981 and the owners of the Casting Company, offer practical advice to actors about auditions, as well as anecdotes about the films they've worked on.

Horowitz, Josh. *The Mind of the Modern Moviemaker: 20 Conversations with the New Generation of Filmmakers.* Plume, 2006. Horowitz asked such diverse directors as Kerry Conran, Karyn Kusama, Michel Gondry, Neil LaBute, and others about their aspirations, influences, and approaches to filmmaking.

Humphries, Reynold. *The Hollywood Horror Film, 1931–1941: Madness in a Social Landscape.* Scarecrow Press, 2006. Analyzes representative films of the decade through audience reaction as well as societal implications.

Indick, William. *Psycho Thrillers: Cinematic Explorations of the Mysteries of the Mind.* McFarland, 2006. Analysis of the genre, including character traits and themes.

Jackson, Kathy Merlock, editor. *Walt Disney: Conversations.* University Press of Mississippi, 2006. Jackson examines interviews and speeches delivered by Disney between 1929 and 1966.

Jaikumar, Priya. *Cinema at the End of Empire: A Politics of Transition in Britain and India.* Duke University Press, 2006. Examines British and Indian films of the 1930s and 1940s in relation to the end of colonialism.

Joslin, Lyndon W. *Count Dracula Goes to the Movies: Stoker's Novel Adapted, 1922–2003.* McFarland, 2006. This updated edition of Joslin's 1999 guide includes additional titles, the Dracula series films from Universal and Hammer studios, and films clearly influenced by Stoker's creation.

Kamir, Orit. *Framed: Women in Law and Film.* Duke University Press, 2006. Examines films from 1928–2001 in Europe, Japan, and the United States that relate to women committing crimes against men and how society deals with their legal rights.

Kamp, David, with Lawrence Levi. *The Film Snob's Dictionary: An Essential Lexicon of Filmological Knowledge.* Broadway Books, 2006. An A-Z reference guide to film geek speak.

Kazanjian, Howard and Chris Enss. *The Young Duke.* Globe Pequot Press, 2006. Looks at John Wayne's early life and his first Hollywood roles.

Keesey, Douglas. *The Films of Peter Greenaway: Sex, Death and Provocation.* McFarland, 2006. Examines nine of Greenaway's feature films.

Kimmel, Daniel M. *The Dream Team: The Rise and Fall of DreamWorks and the Lessons of Hollywood.* Ivan R. Dee, 2006. Story of the studio started in 1994 by Steven Spielberg, Jeffrey Katzenberg, and David Geffen to its demise in 2005.

Kipen, David. *The Schreiber Theory: A Radical Rewrite of American Film History.* Melville House Publishing, 2006. Posits the theory that screenwriters should be given as much, if not more, consideration as directors in shaping a film.

Klein, Shelley. *Frankly, My Dear: Quips and Quotes from Hollywood.* Barron's, 2006. Collection of witty and acerbic quotes on the film industry.

Klinger, Barbara. *Beyond the Multiplex: Cinema, New Technologies, and the Home.* University of California Press, 2006. A study of how contemporary technologies and media, including home theater, DVD, and the Internet, change and affect the viewing experience.

Koven, Mikel J. *La Dolce Morte: Vernacular Cinema and the Italian Giallo Film.* Scarecrow Press, 2006. Explores the history and evolution of this subgenre of the Italian horror film and how it fits within the context of the country's filmmaking.

Krampner, Jon. *Female Brando: The Legend of Kim Stanley.* Watson-Guptill, 2006. Biography of the actress whose alcoholism derailed her film and stage career.

Leguizamo, John. *Pimps, Hos, Playa Hatas, and All the Rest of My Hollywood Friends.* Ecco, 2006. Autobiography of the comic and actor.

Lemmon, Chris. *A Twist of Lemmon: A Tribute to My Father, Jack Lemmon.* Algonquin, 2006. Since his parents divorced when he was three, Lemmon's memoir focuses on activities he shared with his father, as well as time spent with such family friends as Walter Matthau.

Lenburg, Jeff. *Who's Who in Animated Cartoons: An International Guide to Film and Television's Award-Winning and Legendary Animators.* Applause Books, 2006. Offers biographical information on some three hundred animators.

Leonard, Richard. *Movies That Matter: Reading Film Through the Lens of Faith.* Loyola, 2006. The Jesuit film critic and writer examines fifty films for their theological themes.

Littger, Stephan. *The Director's Cut: Picturing Hollywood in the 21st Century.* Continuum, 2006. Interviews with twenty-one Hollywood directors.

Lopate, Phillip, editor. *American Movie Critics: An Anthology from the Silents Until Now.* Library of America, 2006. Traces the evolution of the medium and those who wrote about it, from professional critics to such writers as James Baldwin, Susan Sontag, and Brendan Gill.

Lott, M. Ray. *Police on Screen: Hollywood Cops, Detectives, Marshals and Rangers.* McFarland, 2006. Provides a critical and historical analysis of law enforcement in American film.

Louvish, Simon. *Mae West: It Ain't No Sin.* St. Martin's/Dunne, 2006. Louvish had access to the archive of West memorabilia, which enhances his biography of the writer and performer.

Mann, William J. *Kate: The Woman Who Was Hepburn.* Holt, 2006. Biography of the actress that details her complex and rocky relationships, both professional and personal.

Maren, Jerry. *Short and Sweet: The Life of the Lollipop Munchkin.* Cumberland House Publishing, 2006. Maren, who stands a little over three feet tall, offers anecdotes about his sixty years in show business.

Marubbio, M. Elise. *Killing the Indian Maiden: Images of Native American Women in Film.* University Press of Kentucky, 2006. A study of thirty-four Hollywood films that explore the sacrificial role of female Native American characters.

McBride, Joseph. *What Ever Happened to Orson Welles?: A Portrait of an Independent Career.* University Press of Kentucky, 2006. Film critic McBride examines Welles' work during the 1970s and 1980s.

McClean, Shilo T. *Digital Storytelling: The Narrative Power of Visual Effects in Film.* MIT Press, 2006. Shows how computer-generated effects can add to a film's narrative rather than overwhelm the story.

McGivern, Carolyn. *The Lost Films of John Wayne.* Cumberland House, 2006. Looks at the 1950s aerial films *Island in the Sky* and *The High and the Mighty,* which were unavailable until 2005.

McLaughlin, Robert L. and Sally E. Parry. *We'll Always Have the Movies: American Cinema During World War II.* University Press of Kentucky, 2006. Analysis of more than six hundred films made between 1937 and 1946 in regards to their cultural and historical importance.

Mottram, James. *The Sundance Kids: How the Mavericks Took Back Hollywood.* Faber & Faber, 2006. Analysis of directors who were first discovered at the Sundance Film Festival, including Sofia Coppola, Wes Anderson, David Fincher, and Bryan Singer.

Muir, John Kenneth. *Mercy in Her Eyes: The Films of Mira Nair.* Applause Books, 2006. Examines the films of the Indian-born director.

Mustazza, Leonard. *The Literary Filmography: 6,200 Adaptations of Books, Short Stories and Other Nondramatic Works.* McFarland, 2006. A guide to English-language works that have been adapted as theatrical and television films.

Nickens, Daryl G., editor. *Doing It for Money: The Agony and Ecstasy of Writing and Surviving in Hollywood.* Tallfellow Press, 2006. Essays from forty-eight movie and television writers on writing, pitching, selling, and rewriting.

Nixon, Marni and Stephen Cole. *I Could Have Sung All Night: My Story.* Watson-Guptill, 2006. Autobiography of the singer who dubbed many of Hollywood's leading ladies, including Natalie Wood, Audrey Hepburn, and Deborah Kerr.

Nogami, Teruyo. *Waiting on the Weather: Making Movies with Akira Kurosawa.* Stone Bridge Press, 2006. Hired in 1950 as a script assistant, Nogami offers a candid account of her long professional involvement with the acclaimed Japanese director, which lasted until his death.

Nourmand, Tony and Graham Marsh, editors. *Exploitation Poster Art.* Aurum, 2006. Poster anthology and mini-history of exploitation films from the 1910s to the mid-1970s.

Paffenroth, Kim. *Gospel of the Living Dead: George A. Romero's Visions of Hell on Earth.* Baylor University Press, 2006. Detailed narrative analysis of the director's zombie films and their religious meanings.

Phillips, Alastair and Ginette Vincendeau, editors. *Journeys of Desire: European Actors in Hollywood: A Critical Companion.* British Film Institute, 2006. Guide to more than nine hundred European performers, from stars to character actors, who worked in American films.

Phillips, Gene D. *Beyond the Epic: The Life and Films of David Lean.* University Press of Kentucky, 2006. Examines the screenplays and production histories of the director's sixteen films.

Quirk, Lawrence J. and William Schoell. *The Sundance Kid: An Unauthorized Biography of Robert Redford.* Taylor Trade Publishing, 2006. Biography of the actor that covers not only his career but also his work on environmental and conservation causes.

Rasmussen, Randy. *Orson Welles: Six Films Analyzed, Scene by Scene.* McFarland, 2006. Critical study of six major Welles films.

Raw, Laurence. *Adapting Henry James to the Screen: Gender, Fiction and Film.* Scarecrow Press, 2006. Discusses how film adaptations of James' work examine the theme of gender relations and how changing priorities affect these films.

Rich, John. *Warm Up the Snake: A Hollywood Memoir.* University of Michigan Press, 2006. The radio, television, and film director and producer tells all about his decades-long career.

Robinson, Chris. *Unsung Heroes of Animation.* Indiana University Press, 2006. Focuses on the work of independent contemporary animators of the late 20th and early 21st centuries.

Ruoff, Jeffrey. *Virtual Voyages: Cinema and Travel.* Duke University Press, 2006. Examines the pivotal role of travelogues in cinematic history and the role of travel imagery in film.

Ryan, Jim. *The Rodeo and Hollywood: Rodeo Cowboys on Screen and Western Actors in the Arena.* McFarland, 2006. Provides career profiles of rodeo stars who appeared in films, as well as entertainers who made rodeo appearances from the 1930s to the 1970s.

Ryder, Rob. *Hollywood Jock: 365 Days, Four Screenplays, Three TV Pitches, Two Kids, and One Wife Who's Ready to Pull the Plug.* Harper, 2006. A year in the life of the Hollywood freelancer.

Saltzman, Devyani. *Shooting Water: A Memoir of Second Chances, Family, and Filmmaking.* Newmarket, 2006. The daughter of filmmaker Deepa Mehta looks back on her childhood, estrangement from her mother, and their eventual work together.

Sanders, James, editor. *Scenes from the City: Filmmaking in New York 1966–2006.* Rizzoli, 2006. Includes over 200 stills that cover the changing face of New York in film from *Breakfast at Tiffany's* to the work of Woody Allen, Martin Scorsese, and Spike Lee.

Schatz, Howard. *In Character: Actors Acting.* Bulfinch, 2006. The photographer snapped close-ups of dozens of actors, directing their reactions to specific scenarios, to capture even the most subtle change of expression.

Schickel, Richard, editor. *The Essential Chaplin: Perspectives on the Life and Art of the Great Comedian.* Ivan R. Dee, 2006. Collection of thirty essays on Chaplin's life and work.

Schwarz, Ted. *Hollywood Confidential: How the Studios Beat the Mob at Their Own Game.* Taylor Trade Publishing, 2006. In-depth look at the mob influence in Hollywood from the 1920s to the 1980s.

Scott, Ian. *In Capra's Shadow: The Life and Career of Screenwriter Robert Riskin.* University Press of Kentucky, 2006. Analysis of the screenwriter's life and work and how his style contributed to the films of director Frank Capra.

Server, Lee. *Ava Gardner: "Love Is Nothing."* St. Martin's, 2006. Biography of the beautiful MGM (Metro-Goldwyn-Mayer) star whose off-screen life was marred by alcohol and tempestuous romances.

Shearer, Stephen Michael. *Patricia Neal: An Unquiet Life.* University Press of Kentucky, 2006. Biography and cinematic study of the actress's career and her comeback after a massive stroke suffered in 1965.

Silet, Charles L.P., editor. *The Films of Woody Allen: Critical Essays.* Scarecrow Press, 2006. Contains twenty-four essays addressing Allen's work from a variety of cultural and theoretical perspectives.

Singer, Barnett. *Brigitte Bardot: A Biography.* McFarland, 2006. Chapters cover the French actress's childhood, career, personal life, and her involvement in animal welfare activism.

Smyth, J.E. *Reconstructing American Historical Cinema: From Cimarron to Citizen Kane.* University Press of Kentucky, 2006. Explores Hollywood's interpretations of national history from frontier epics to gangster biopics.

Spoto, Donald. *Enchantment: The Life of Audrey Hepburn.* Harmony, 2006. Celebrity biography of the actress that covers her childhood, film career, and her later work with the United Nations Children's Fund (UNICEF).

Stalter, Katharine. *The Indie Filmmakers: The Directors.* Zoom Lens Media, 2006. Interviews with fourteen independent filmmakers, including Justin Lin, Matthew Bright, Michele Maher, and C. Jay Cox.

Stevens, George Jr., editor. *Conversations with the Great Moviemakers of Hollywood's Golden Age at the American Film Institute.* Knopf, 2006. Interviews gathered from AFI seminars, including Harold Lloyd, Alfred Hitchcock, Billy Wilder, James Wong Howe, Hal Wallis, Ingmar Bergman, and many more.

Stoehr, Kevin L. *Nihilism in Film and Television: A Critical Overview from Citizen Kane to The Sopranos.* McFarland, 2006. Explores German philosopher Friedrich Nietzsche's idea that nothing matters through its inclusion in popular culture.

Stubbs, John C. *Federico Fellini as Auteur: Seven Aspects of His Films.* Southern Illinois University Press, 2006. Discussion of the director's films, organized by categories. Includes elements of his style, comic strategies, and adaptations of Fellini's work.

Taraborrelli, J. Randy. *Elizabeth.* Warner, 2006. As in Elizabeth Taylor in this sympathetic biography that also focuses on the actress's extensive AIDS activism.

Toplin, Robert Brent. *Michael Moore's Fahrenheit 9/11: How One Film Divided a Nation.* University Press of Kansas, 2006. An appraisal of the 2004 documentary and the controversy surrounding it.

Torregrossa, Richard. *Cary Grant: A Celebration of Style.* Bulfinch, 2006. Grant was not only an actor but a fashion icon and his sense of style is discussed by film and fashion personalities.

Tremper, Ellen. *I'm No Angel: The Blonde in Fiction and Film.* University of Virginia Press, 2006. The role of the blonde in modern fiction and film, including Harlow, Dietrich, and Monroe.

Turan, Kenneth. *Now in Theaters Everywhere: A Celebration of a Certain Kind of Blockbuster.* Public Affairs, 2006. The *Los Angeles Times* film critic offers a collection of reviews focusing on popular and/or critically admired films that deserve a viewer's attention.

Tzioumakis, Yannis. *American Independent Cinema.* Rutgers University Press, 2006. A chronological look at key films, filmmakers, and companies from the early 20th century to the present.

Vachon, Christine, with Austin Bunn. *A Killer Life: How an Independent Film Producer Survives Deals and Disasters in Hollywood and Beyond.* Simon & Schuster, 2006. Vachon, the head of Killer Films, details the difficult world of independent production.

Vitali, Valentina and Paul Willemen, editors. *Theorising National Cinema.* British Film Institute, 2006. Essays on the relationship between cinema and national identity.

Williams, Randy. *Sports Cinema—100 Movies: The Best of Hollywood's Athletic Heroes, Losers, Myths, and Misfits of the Silver Screen.* Limelight Editions, 2006. Guide centers on sports-oriented stories, characters, events, or backdrops from 1932 to the present.

Winter, Jessica. *The Rough Guide to American Independent Film.* Rough Guides, 2006. A history of indie cinema, beginning with the 1960s and continuing to the present.

Yankee, Luke. *Just Outside the Spotlight: Growing Up with Eileen Heckart.* Watson-Guptill, 2006. The son of the legendary character actress provides a memoir of his mother's fifty-year career.

Youngblood, Denise J. *Russian War Films: On the Cinema Front, 1914–2005.* University Press of Kansas, 2006. Explores more than 160 fictional narratives, from World War I to Chechnya, which reflect Soviet views of war.

Director Index

J.J. Abrams (1966-)
Mission: Impossible III *264*

Alejandro Agresti (1961-)
The Lake House *225*

Alexandre Aja
The Hills Have Eyes *178*

Elizabeth Allen (1934-)
Aquamarine *14*

Woody Allen (1935-)
Scoop *349*

Roger Allers
Open Season *294*

Pedro Almodovar (1951-)
Volver *423*

Robert Altman (1925-2006)
A Prairie Home Companion *311*

Darren Aronofsky (1969-)
The Fountain *144*

Doug Atchison
Akeelah and the Bee *2*

Jamie Babbit
The Quiet *325*

Kevin Bacon (1958-)
Loverboy *247*

Bryan Barber
Idlewild *194*

Mike Barker (1966-)
A Good Woman *163*

Timur Bekmambetov
Night Watch *283*

William Brent Bell
Stay Alive *371*

Jessica Bendinger
Stick It *373*

Fabian Bielinsky
The Aura *22*

Tony Bill (1940-)
Flyboys *140*

Uwe Boll
BloodRayne *44*

John Bonito
The Marine *259*

Darren Lynn Bousman
Saw III *340*

David Bowers
Flushed Away *139*

Colin Brady
Everyone's Hero *122*

Albert Brooks (1947-)
Looking for Comedy in the Muslim World *244*

Gregory Brown (1954-)
See No Evil *352*

Neil Burger
The Illusionist *196*

Edward Burns (1968-)
The Groomsmen *167*

Steve Buscemi (1957-)
Lonesome Jim *242*

Martin Campbell
Casino Royale *65*

Danny Cannon
Goal! The Dream Begins *157*

Christian Carion
Joyeux Noel *211*

Michael Caton-Jones (1958-)
Basic Instinct 2 *31*

Nuri Bilge Ceylan
Climates *80*

Claude Chabrol (1930-)
The Bridesmaid *55*

Jay Chandrasekhar
Beerfest *32*

Larry Charles
Borat: Cultural Learnings of America for Make Benefit Glorious Nation of Kazakhstan *48*

Patrice Chereau (1944-)
Gabrielle *151*

Larry Clark (1943-)
Wassup Rockers *429*

Laurie Collyer
Sherrybaby *358*

Cristina Comencini
Don't Tell *108*

Bill Condon (1955-)
Dreamgirls *111*

Greg Coolidge
Employee of the Month *118*

Martha Coolidge (1946-)
Material Girls *261*

Trent Cooper
Larry the Cable Guy: Health Inspector *227*

Sofia Coppola (1971-)
Marie Antoinette *257*

Frank Coraci (1965-)
Click *78*

Ericson Core
Invincible *204*

Allen Coulter
Hollywoodland *183*

Patrick Creadon
Wordplay *442*

Alfonso Cuaron (1961-)
Children of Men *74*

Jill Culton
Open Season *294*

Vondie Curtis-Hall (1956-)
Waist Deep *426*

Lee Daniels
Shadowboxer *355*

Jean-Pierre Dardenne (1951-)
The Child *73*

Luc Dardenne (1954-)
The Child *73*

Gregory Dark
See Gregory Brown

Andrew Davis (1946-)
The Guardian *170*

John A. Davis
The Ant Bully *11*

Jonathan Dayton
Little Miss Sunshine *240*

Robert De Niro (1943-)
The Good Shepherd *161*

Brian De Palma (1941-)
The Black Dahlia *39*

Guillermo del Toro (1964-)
Pan's Labyrinth *299*

Jonathan Demme (1944-)
Neil Young: Heart of Gold *278*

Tom Dey
Failure to Launch *127*

Paul Dinello
Strangers with Candy *377*

Bob Dolman
How to Eat Fried Worms *189*

Roger Donaldson (1945-)
The World's Fastest Indian *445*

Richard Donner (1939-)
16 Blocks *363*

Dennis Dugan (1946-)
The Benchwarmers *34*

Laurence Dunmore
The Libertine *236*

Clint Eastwood (1930-)
Flags of Our Fathers *135*
Letters from Iwo Jima *234*

Cory Edwards
Hoodwinked *185*

Fernando Eimbcke
Duck Season *113*

David R. Ellis
Snakes on a Plane *366*

Peter Ellis
You, Me and Dupree *449*

Emilio Estevez (1962-)
Bobby *45*

Richard Eyre (1943-)
Notes on a Scandal *284*

Stefan Fangmeier
Eragon *121*

Valerie Faris
Little Miss Sunshine *240*

Paul Feig
Unaccompanied Minors *408*

Sam Fell
Flushed Away *139*

Jeff Feuerzeig
The Devil and Daniel Johnston *102*

Andy Fickman
She's the Man *360*

Todd Field (1964-)
Little Children *237*

Anne Fletcher
Step Up *372*

Marc Foster
Stranger Than Fiction *375*

David Frankel (1960-)
The Devil Wears Prada *104*

Stephen Frears (1941-)
The Queen *323*

Bart Freundlich (1970-)
Trust the Man *400*

Liz Friedlander
Take the Lead *383*

Christophe Gans (1960-)
Silent Hill *361*

Andy Garcia (1956-)
The Lost City *245*

James Gartner
Glory Road *156*

Mel Gibson (1956-)
Apocalypto *12*

Terry Gilliam (1940-)
Tideland *392*

Tony Goldwyn (1960-)
The Last Kiss *232*

Michel Gondry
Dave Chappelle's Block Party *92*
The Science of Sleep *347*

Nicholaus Goossen
Grandma's Boy *166*

Richard E. Grant (1957-)
Wah-Wah *425*

Paul Greengrass
United 93 *412*

Christopher Guest
For Your Consideration *142*

Davis Guggenheim
An Inconvenient Truth *199*

James Gunn
Slither *365*

Sturla Gunnarsson
Beowulf & Grendel *35*

Bent Hamer
Factotum *125*

Sanaa Hamri
Something New *369*

Michael Haneke (1942-)
Cache *61*

Jim Hanon
End of the Spear *119*

Catherine Hardwicke
The Nativity Story *276*

Renny Harlin (1959-)
The Covenant *81*

Mary Harron
The Notorious Bettie Page *286*

Jared Hess
Nacho Libre *273*

Peter Hewitt
Zoom *451*

Tim Hill
Garfield: A Tail of Two Kitties *154*

John Hillcoat
The Proposition *316*

Michael Hoffman
Game 6 *152*

Nicole Holofcener (1960-)
Friends with Money *148*

Gavin Hood
Tsotsi *401*

Ron Howard (1954-)
The Da Vinci Code *88*

Nicholas Hytner
The History Boys *179*

Alejandro Gonzalez Inarritu
Babel *27*

Dan Ireland
Mrs. Palfrey at the Claremont *266*

David Jacobson
Down in the Valley *109*

Eugene Jarecki
Why We Fight *436*

Julian Jarrold
Kinky Boots *220*

Clark Johnson (1954-)
The Sentinel *353*

Niall Johnson
Keeping Mum *215*

Rian Johnson
Brick *53*

Tim Johnson
Over the Hedge *295*

Kirk Jones
Nanny McPhee *275*

Tommy Lee Jones (1946-)
The Three Burials of Melquiades Estrada *391*

Mike Judge (1962-)
Idiocracy *192*

Chen Kaige (1952-)
The Promise *315*

Asif Kapadia
The Return *327*

Gil Kenan
Monster House *268*

Karey Kirkpatrick
Over the Hedge *295*

Cedric Klapisch (1961-)
Russian Dolls *334*

Wayne Kramer
Running Scared *330*

Neil LaBute (1963-)
The Wicker Man *437*

John Lasseter (1957-)
Cars *63*

David Leaf
The U.S. vs. John Lennon *415*

Spike Lee (1957-)
Inside Man *202*

Michael Lembeck (1948-)
The Santa Clause 3: The Escape Clause *339*

Barry Levinson (1942-)
Man of the Year *252*

Shawn Levy
Night at the Museum *280*
The Pink Panther *304*

Jonathan Liebesman
The Texas Chainsaw Massacre: The Beginning *387*

Nnegest Likke
Phat Girlz *301*

Justin Lin
Annapolis *10*
The Fast and the Furious: Tokyo Drift *128*

Richard Linklater (1961-)
A Scanner Darkly *342*

Richard Loncraine (1946-)
Firewall *133*

Sidney Lumet (1924-)
Find Me Guilty *131*

David Lynch (1946-)
Inland Empire *201*

Liam Lynch
Tenacious D in the Pick of Destiny *386*

Kevin MacDonald
The Last King of Scotland *231*

Michael Mann (1943-)
Miami Vice *262*

James Marsh (1963-)
The King *218*

Frank Marshall (1954-)
Eight Below *117*

Neil Marshall
The Descent *101*

Scott Marshall
Keeping Up with the Steins *216*

Michael Mayer
Flicka *138*

McG
We Are Marshall *432*

Douglas McGrath (1958-)
Infamous *200*

Paul McGuigan
Lucky Number Slevin *249*

Adam McKay
Talladega Nights: The Ballad of Ricky Bobby *384*

James McTeigue
V for Vendetta *419*

Deepa Mehta (1950-)
Water *430*

Jean-Pierre Melville (1917-73)
Army of Shadows *16*

Nancy Meyers (1949-)
The Holiday *181*

Roger Michell (1957-)
Venus *421*

George Miller (1943-)
Happy Feet *173*

John Moore
The Omen *292*

Glen Morgan
Black Christmas *38*

Gabriele Muccino
The Pursuit of Happyness *319*

Ryan Murphy
Running with Scissors *331*

Rupert Murray
Unknown White Male *413*

Mark Neveldine
Crank *83*

Christopher Nolan (1970-)
The Prestige *313*

Phillip Noyce (1950-)
Catch a Fire *67*

Matthew O'Callaghan
Curious George *85*

Steve Oedekerk (1961-)
Barnyard *30*

Francois Ozon (1967-)
Time to Leave *394*

Charles Paine
Who Killed the Electric Car? *435*

Ol Parker
Imagine Me & You *197*

Tyler Perry
Madea's Family Reunion *251*

Wolfgang Petersen (1941-)
Poseidon *308*

Donald Petrie
Just My Luck *213*

Todd Phillips
School for Scoundrels *345*

Steve Pink (1966-)
Accepted *1*

Cristi Puiu
The Death of Mr. Lazarescu *94*

Stephen Quay (1947-)
The Piano Tuner of Earthquakes *303*

Timothy Quay (1947-)
The Piano Tuner of Earthquakes *303*

Adam Rapp
Winter Passing *441*

Brett Ratner (1970-)
X-Men: The Last Stand *447*

Peyton Reed
The Break-Up *51*

Christopher Reeve (1952-2004)
Everyone's Hero *122*

Kelly Reichardt
Old Joy *291*

Ivan Reitman (1946-)
My Super Ex-Girlfriend *270*

Jason Reitman
Thank You for Smoking *389*

Kevin Reynolds (1950-)
Tristan & Isolde *396*

Brian Robbins (1964-)
The Shaggy Dog *357*

Chris Robinson
ATL *21*

Eli Roth
Hostel *188*

Joe Roth (1948-)
Freedomland *146*

Anthony Russo
You, Me and Dupree *449*

Joe Russo
You, Me and Dupree *449*

Daniel St. Pierre
Everyone's Hero *122*

Carlos Saldanha
Ice Age: The Meltdown *191*

John Scheinfeld
The U.S. vs. John Lennon *415*

Martin Scorsese (1942-)
The Departed *99*

Ridley Scott (1939-)
A Good Year *164*

Tony Scott (1944-)
Deja Vu *97*

Susan Seidelman (1952-)
The Boynton Beach Club *49*

Aaron Seltzer
Date Movie *91*

Ward Serrill
The Heart of the Game *177*

Richard Shepard
The Matador *260*

Takashi Shimizu
The Grudge 2 *169*

Cate Shortland
Somersault *367*

Will Shriner
Hoot *186*

M. Night Shyamalan (1970-)
Lady in the Water *223*

Bryan Singer (1966-)
Superman Returns *379*

David Slade
Hard Candy *175*

Kevin Smith (1970-)
Clerks II *76*

Steven Soderbergh (1963-)
Bubble *57*
The Good German *159*

Courtney Solomon (1971-)
An American Haunting *8*

Barry Sonnenfeld (1953-)
RV *335*

Jim Sonzero
Pulse *318*

Sylvester Stallone (1946-)
Rocky Balboa *328*

Patrick Stettner
The Night Listener *282*

John Stockwell (1961-)
Turistas *404*

Oliver Stone (1946-)
World Trade Center *443*

Charles Sturridge (1951-)
Lassie *228*

Zhang Tan
The Promise *315*

Brian Taylor
Crank *83*

S. Lee Taylor
See Steve Taylor

Steve Taylor
The Second Chance *351*

Andre Techine (1943-)
Changing Times *69*

Betty Thomas (1949-)
John Tucker Must Die *209*

Robert Towne (1936-)
Ask the Dust *19*

Jeff Tremaine
Jackass Number Two *207*

Zak Tucker
Poster Boy *309*

Gore Verbinski
Pirates of the Caribbean: Dead Man's Chest *306*

Lars von Trier (1956-)
Manderlay *254*

Dan Wallin
The War Tapes *427*

Wayne Wang (1949-)
Last Holiday *229*

Keenen Ivory Wayans (1958-)
Little Man *239*

Paul Weitz (1966-)
American Dreamz *6*

Wim Wenders (1945-)
Don't Come Knocking *106*

Simon West (1961-)
When a Stranger Calls *434*

John Whitesell
Big Momma's House 2 *37*
Deck the Halls *96*

Steve "Spaz" Williams
The Wild *439*

Kurt Wimmer
Ultraviolet *407*

Gary Winick
Charlotte's Web *71*

Michael Winterbottom (1961-)
Tristram Shandy: A Cock and Bull Story *398*

Len Wiseman
Underworld: Evolution *410*

James Wong
Final Destination 3 *130*

Adam "MCA" Yauch (1964-)
Awesome! I F***in' Shot That! *23*

Zhang Yimou (1951-)
Curse of the Golden Flower *86*

Ronny Yu
Jet Li's Fearless *208*

Steven Zaillian (1951-)
All the King's Men *4*

David Zucker (1947-)
Scary Movie 4 *344*

Edward Zwick (1952-)
Blood Diamond *41*

Terry Zwigoff (1948-)
Art School Confidential *18*

Screenwriter Index

Jim Abrahams (1944-)
Scary Movie 4 *344*

J.J. Abrams (1966-)
Mission: Impossible III *264*

Milo Addica
The King *218*

Duane Adler
Step Up *372*

Woody Allen (1935-)
Scoop *349*

Pedro Almodovar (1951-)
Volver *423*

Jack Amiel
The Shaggy Dog *357*

Terry Anderson (1959-)
The Night Listener *282*

Scot Armstrong
School for Scoundrels *345*

Michael Arndt
Little Miss Sunshine *240*

Henry O. Arnold
The Second Chance *351*

Darren Aronofsky (1969-)
The Fountain *144*

Guillermo Arriaga
Babel *27*
The Three Burials of Melquiades Estrada *391*

Tom J. Astle
Failure to Launch *127*

Doug Atchison
Akeelah and the Bee *2*

Paul Attanasio
The Good German *159*

David Auburn
The Lake House *225*

Roger Roberts Avary (1967-)
Silent Hill *361*

Bryan Barber
Idlewild *194*

Leora Barish
Basic Instinct 2 *31*

Peter Baynham
Borat: Cultural Learnings of America for Make Benefit Glorious Nation of Kazakhstan *48*

Henry Bean
Basic Instinct 2 *31*

Michael Begler
The Shaggy Dog *357*

Timur Bekmambetov
Night Watch *283*

William Brent Bell
Stay Alive *371*

Steve Bencich
Open Season *294*

Jessica Bendinger
Aquamarine *14*
Stick It *373*

Alan Bennett (1934-)
The History Boys *179*

David Berenbaum
Zoom *451*

Andrea Berloff
World Trade Center *443*

Paul Bernbaum
Hollywoodland *183*

Jon Bernstein
Larry the Cable Guy: Health Inspector *227*

Andrew Rai Berzins
Beowulf & Grendel *35*

Fabian Bielinsky
The Aura *22*

Wang Bin
Jet Li's Fearless *208*

Jack Black (1969-)
Tenacious D in the Pick of Destiny *386*

Len Blum
Over the Hedge *295*
The Pink Panther *304*

Pascal Bonitzer
Changing Times *69*

Ron L. Brinkerhoff
The Guardian *170*

Jeremy Brock
The Last King of Scotland *231*

Albert Brooks (1947-)
Looking for Comedy in the Muslim World *244*

William Broyles, Jr. (1944-)
Flags of Our Fathers *135*

Peter Buchman
Eragon *121*

Neil Burger
The Illusionist *196*

Edward Burns (1968-)
The Groomsmen *167*

Adrian Butchart
Goal! The Dream Begins *157*

Dan Calame
Employee of the Month *118*

Giulia Calenda
Don't Tell *108*

Lorne Cameron
Over the Hedge *295*

J.S. Cardone
The Covenant *81*

Christian Carion
Joyeux Noel *211*

Nick Cave
The Proposition *316*

Nuri Bilge Ceylan
Climates *80*

Claude Chabrol (1930-)
The Bridesmaid *55*

Jay Chandrasekhar
Beerfest *32*

Patrice Chereau (1944-)
Gabrielle *151*

Tina Gordon Chism
ATL *21*

Chris Chow
Jet Li's Fearless *208*

Larry Clark (1943-)
Wassup Rockers *429*

Dick Clement (1937-)
Flushed Away *139*
Goal! The Dream Begins *157*

Chris Cleveland
Glory Road *156*

Sean Cliver
Jackass Number Two *207*

Daniel Clowes
Art School Confidential *18*

Etan Cohen
Idiocracy *192*

Joel Cohen
Garfield: A Tail of Two Kitties *154*

Sacha Baron Cohen (1971-)
Borat: Cultural Learnings of America for Make Benefit Glorious Nation of Kazakhstan *48*

Stephen Colbert
Strangers with Candy *377*

Warren Coleman
Happy Feet *173*

Bill Collage
Accepted *1*

Dave Collard
Annapolis *10*

John Collee
Happy Feet *173*

Laurie Collyer
Sherrybaby *358*

Cristina Comencini
Don't Tell *108*

Bill Condon (1955-)
Dreamgirls *111*

Steve Conrad
The Pursuit of Happyness *319*

Chris Conroy
Employee of the Month *118*

Greg Coolidge
Employee of the Month *118*

Adam Cooper
Accepted *1*

Sofia Coppola (1971-)
Marie Antoinette *257*

Matt Corman
Deck the Halls *96*

Allen Covert
The Benchwarmers *34*
Grandma's Boy *166*

Wes Craven (1939-)
Pulse *318*

Patrick Creadon
Wordplay *442*

Alfonso Cuaron (1961-)
Children of Men *74*

Vondie Curtis-Hall (1956-)
Waist Deep *426*

Jean-Pierre Dardenne (1951-)
The Child *73*

Luc Dardenne (1954-)
The Child *73*

William Davies
Flushed Away *139*

John A. Davis
The Ant Bully *11*

Geoff Deane
Kinky Boots *220*

Edward Decter (1959-)
The Santa Clause 3: The Escape Clause *339*
The Wild *439*

Guillermo del Toro (1964-)
Pan's Labyrinth *299*

Don DeLillo
Game 6 *152*

Dave Digilio
Eight Below *117*

Paul Dinello
Strangers with Candy *377*

Bob Dolman
How to Eat Fried Worms *189*

Roger Donaldson (1945-)
The World's Fastest Indian *445*

Michael Dougherty
Superman Returns *379*

Cory Edwards
Hoodwinked *185*

Todd Edwards
Hoodwinked *185*

Fernando Eimbcke
Duck Season *113*

Ted Elliott
Pirates of the Caribbean: Dead Man's Chest *306*

Matt Ember
Failure to Launch *127*

Emilio Estevez (1962-)
Bobby *45*

Blake T. Evans
Flyboys *140*

Bill Ewing
End of the Spear *119*

Li Feng
Jet Li's Fearless *208*

Will Ferrell (1968-)
Talladega Nights: The Ballad of Ricky Bobby *384*

Jeff Feuerzeig
The Devil and Daniel Johnston *102*

Todd Field (1964-)
Little Children *237*

Tim Firth
Kinky Boots *220*

Antwone Fisher
ATL *21*

Dan Fogelman
Cars *63*

Joe Forte
Firewall *133*

Bart Freundlich (1970-)
Trust the Man *400*

Jason Friedberg
Date Movie *91*

Josh Friedman
The Black Dahlia *39*

Michell Gallagher
The Marine *259*

Brad Gann
Invincible *204*

Robert Ben Garant
Night at the Museum *280*

Jeremy Garelick
The Break-Up *51*

Kyle Gass
Tenacious D in the Pick of Destiny *386*

Peter Gaulke
Ice Age: The Meltdown *191*

Bart Gavigan
End of the Spear *119*

Dean Georgaris
Tristan & Isolde *396*

Russell Gewirtz
Inside Man *202*

Mark Gibson
The Wild *439*

Mel Gibson (1956-)
Apocalypto *12*

Terry Gilliam (1940-)
Tideland *392*

Bettina Gilois
Glory Road *156*

Shelly Gitlow
The Boynton Beach Club *49*

Akiva Goldsman (1963-)
The Da Vinci Code *88*

Michel Gondry
The Science of Sleep *347*

Richard E. Grant (1957-)
Wah-Wah *425*

Susannah Grant (1963-)
Charlotte's Web *71*

Paul Greengrass
United 93 *412*

James Greer
Larry the Cable Guy: Health Inspector *227*

Tony Grisoni
Tideland *392*

Christopher Guest
For Your Consideration *142*

James Gunn
Slither *365*

Sebastian Gutierrez
Snakes on a Plane *366*

Laurent Guyot
Changing Times *69*

Paul Haggis
Casino Royale *65*
Flags of Our Fathers *135*
The Last Kiss *232*

Philip Halprin
The Wild *439*

Bent Hamer
Factotum *125*

Jeff Hand
Everyone's Hero *122*

Michael Haneke (1942-)
Cache *61*

Jim Hanon
End of the Spear *119*

Martin Hardy
Tristram Shandy: A Cock and Bull Story *398*

Dan Harmon
Monster House *268*

Laura Elena Harring (1964-)
The King *218*

Amy Harris
Just My Luck *213*

Daniel P. "Dan" Harris (1979-)
Superman Returns *379*

Mary Harron
The Notorious Bettie Page *286*

Jim Hecht
Ice Age: The Meltdown *191*

John Heffernan
Snakes on a Plane *366*

Kevin Heffernan
Beerfest *32*

Zach Helm
Stranger Than Fiction *375*

Jared Hess
Nacho Libre *273*

Jerusha Hess
Nacho Libre *273*

Howard Himelstein
A Good Woman *163*

Anthony Hines
Borat: Cultural Learnings of America for Make Benefit Glorious Nation of Kazakhstan *48*

Nicole Holofcener (1960-)
Friends with Money *148*

Gavin Hood
Tsotsi *401*

David Hoselton
Over the Hedge *295*

Coleman Hough
Bubble *57*

Dianne Houston
Take the Lead *383*

G. Cabrera Infante
The Lost City *245*

David Jacobson
Down in the Valley *109*

Eugene Jarecki
Why We Fight *436*

Stephen Jeffreys
The Libertine *236*

Niall Johnson
Keeping Mum *215*

Rian Johnson
Brick *53*

Mike Judge (1962-)
Idiocracy *192*

Chen Kaige (1952-)
The Promise *315*

Ken Kaufman
Curious George *85*

Joe Keenan
Flushed Away *139*

Garrison Keillor
A Prairie Home Companion *311*

Simon Kinberg
X-Men: The Last Stand *447*

I. Marlene King
Just My Luck *213*

Karey Kirkpatrick
Charlotte's Web *71*
Over the Hedge *295*

Cedric Klapisch (1961-)
Russian Dolls *334*

Marc Klein
A Good Year *164*

Jorgen Klubien
Cars *63*

Larry Konner
Flicka *138*

Steve Koren
Click *78*

Wayne Kramer
Running Scared *330*

Hanif Kureishi (1954-)
Venus *421*

Robert Kurtz
Everyone's Hero *122*

Alex Kurtzman
Mission: Impossible III *264*

Ian La Frenais (1937-)
Flushed Away *139*
Goal! The Dream Begins *157*

Neil LaBute (1963-)
The Wicker Man *437*

Preston Lacy
Jackass Number Two *207*

Ian LaFrenais
See Ian La Frenais

John Lasseter (1957-)
Cars *63*

Jay Lavender
The Break-Up *51*

David Leaf
The U.S. vs. John Lennon *415*

Charles Leavitt
Blood Diamond *41*

Peter Leccia
The Bridesmaid *55*

Tony Leech
Hoodwinked *185*

Steve Lemme (1973-)
Beerfest *32*

Thomas Lennon (1969-)
Night at the Museum *280*

Michael LeSieur
You, Me and Dupree *449*

Ewan Leslie
She's the Man *360*

Gregory Levasseur
The Hills Have Eyes *178*

Barry Levinson (1942-)
Man of the Year *252*

Eugene Levy (1946-)
For Your Consideration *142*

Nnegest Likke
Phat Girlz *301*

Jamie Linden
We Are Marshall *432*

Richard Linklater (1961-)
A Scanner Darkly *342*

William Lipz
Shadowboxer *355*

Chris Lloyd
Flushed Away *139*

Phil Lorin
Cars *63*

Jeff Lowell
John Tucker Must Die *209*

Sergei Lukyanenko
Night Watch *283*

Sidney Lumet (1924-)
Find Me Guilty *131*

Karen McCullah Lutz
She's the Man *360*

David Lynch (1946-)
Inland Empire *201*

Liam Lynch
Tenacious D in the Pick of Destiny *386*

Dan Madigan
See No Evil *352*

T.J. Mancini
Find Me Guilty *131*

Michael Mann (1943-)
Miami Vice *262*

Patrick Marber (1964-)
Notes on a Scandal *284*

Francesca Marciano
Don't Tell *108*

Paula Markovitch
Duck Season *113*

James Marsh (1963-)
The King *218*

Neil Marshall
The Descent *101*

Bill Marsilii
Deja Vu *97*

Steve Martin (1945-)
The Pink Panther *304*

Nat Maudlin
Open Season *294*

Armistead Maupin
The Night Listener *282*

Dan Mazer
Borat: Cultural Learnings of America for Make Benefit Glorious Nation of Kazakhstan *48*

Craig Mazin
Scary Movie 4 *344*

Danny McBride
Underworld: Evolution *410*

Robert J. McCrea
Find Me Guilty *131*

Alan B. McElroy
The Marine *259*

Douglas McGrath (1958-)
Infamous *200*

Adam McKay
Talladega Nights: The Ballad of Ricky Bobby *384*

Aline Brosh McKenna
The Devil Wears Prada *104*

Jean-Pierre Melville (1917-73)
Army of Shadows *16*

Maurizio Merli
Open Season *294*

Jacob Meszaros
Unaccompanied Minors *408*

Nancy Meyers (1949-)
The Holiday *181*

George Miller (1943-)
Happy Feet *173*

Brent Monahan
An American Haunting *8*

William Monahan
The Departed *99*

Chris Morgan
The Fast and the Furious: Tokyo Drift *128*

Glen Morgan
Black Christmas *38*
Final Destination 3 *130*

Peter Morgan
The Last King of Scotland *231*
The Queen *323*

Judy Morris (1947-)
Happy Feet *173*

Ryan Murphy
Running with Scissors *331*

Kiel Murray
Cars *63*

Wu Nan
Curse of the Golden Flower *86*

Abdi Nazemian
The Quiet *325*

Brian Nelson
Hard Candy *175*

Mark Neveldine
Crank *83*

Christopher Nolan (1970-)
The Prestige *313*

Jonathan Nolan
The Prestige *313*

George Nolfi
The Sentinel *353*

Steve Oedekerk (1961-)
Barnyard *30*

Mark O'Keefe
Click *78*

Christine O'Malley
Wordplay *442*

Roberto Orci
Mission: Impossible III *264*

Chris Ord
Deck the Halls *96*

Jessica O'Toole
Material Girls *261*

Francois Ozon (1967-)
Time to Leave *394*

Charles Paine
Who Killed the Electric Car? *435*

Ol Parker
Imagine Me & You *197*

Don Payne
My Super Ex-Girlfriend *270*

Ben Pearson
The Second Chance *351*

Zak Penn (1968-)
X-Men: The Last Stand *447*

Mark Perez
Accepted *1*

Tom Perrotta
Little Children *237*

Tyler Perry
Madea's Family Reunion *251*

Matthew Peterman
Stay Alive *371*

Pamela Pettler
Monster House *268*

Todd Phillips
School for Scoundrels *345*

Jeffrey Price
Last Holiday *229*

Richard Price (1949-)
Freedomland *146*

Pat Proft
Scary Movie 4 *344*

Mark Protosevich
Poseidon *308*

Cristi Puiu
The Death of Mr. Lazarescu *94*

Neal Purvis
Casino Royale *65*

John Quaintance
Aquamarine *14*
Material Girls *261*

Stephen Quay (1947-)
The Piano Tuner of Earthquakes *303*

Timothy Quay (1947-)
The Piano Tuner of Earthquakes *303*

Razvan Radulescu
The Death of Mr. Lazarescu *94*

Joe Ranft
Cars *63*

Adam Rapp
Winter Passing *441*

Amy Rardin
Material Girls *261*

Jonathan Raymond
Old Joy *291*

Kelly Reichardt
Old Joy *291*

Jason Reitman
Thank You for Smoking *389*

Don Rhymer
Big Momma's House 2 *37*
Deck the Halls *96*

Mike Rich
The Nativity Story *276*

Adam Rifkin (1966-)
Zoom *451*

Matt Robinson
Nanny McPhee *275*

Geoff Rodkey
RV *335*
The Shaggy Dog *357*

Melissa Rosenberg
Step Up *372*

Lecia Rosenthal
Poster Boy *309*

Mark Rosenthal
Flicka *138*

Michael Arlen Ross
Turistas *404*

Terry Rossio
Deja Vu *97*
Pirates of the Caribbean: Dead Man's Chest *306*

Eli Roth
Hostel *188*

Eric Roth
The Good Shepherd *161*

Richard Russo
Keeping Mum *215*

Ruth Sacks
Mrs. Palfrey at the Claremont *266*

Farhad Safinia
Apocalypto *12*

John Scheinfeld
The U.S. vs. John Lennon *415*

Rob Schrab
Monster House *268*

Micah Schraft
The Quiet *325*

Darin Scott
Waist Deep *426*

Peter S. Seaman
Last Holiday *229*

Phil Sears
Flyboys *140*

Amy Sedaris (1961-)
Strangers with Candy *377*

Susan Seidelman (1952-)
The Boynton Beach Club *49*

Aaron Seltzer
Date Movie *91*

David Seltzer (1940-)
The Omen *292*

Ward Serrill
The Heart of the Game *177*

Timothy J. Sexton
Children of Men *74*

Hannah Shakespeare
Loverboy *247*

Richard Shepard
The Matador *260*

Sam Shepard (1943-)
Don't Come Knocking *106*

Ryan Shiraki
Poster Boy *309*

Cate Shortland
Somersault *367*

Will Shriner
Hoot *186*

M. Night Shyamalan (1970-)
Lady in the Water *223*

Bryan Singer (1966-)
Superman Returns *379*

Shawn Slovo
Catch a Fire *67*

Jason Smilovic
Lucky Number Slevin *249*

Kevin Smith (1970-)
Clerks II *76*

Kirsten Smith
She's the Man *360*

Alec Sokolow
Garfield: A Tail of Two Kitties *154*

Courtney Solomon (1971-)
An American Haunting *8*

Paul Soter (1972-)
Beerfest *32*

Sylvester Stallone (1946-)
Rocky Balboa *328*

Jim Stark
Factotum *125*

Mya Stark
Unaccompanied Minors *408*

Patrick Stettner
The Night Listener *282*

Erik Stolhanske
Beerfest *32*

John J. Strauss
The Santa Clause 3: The Escape Clause *339*
The Wild *439*

James C. Strouse
Lonesome Jim *242*

Charles Sturridge (1951-)
Lassie *228*

Stephen Susco
The Grudge 2 *169*

Adam Sussman
The Return *327*

Gerry Swallow
Ice Age: The Meltdown *191*

Nick Swardson
The Benchwarmers *34*
Grandma's Boy *166*

Brian Taylor
Crank *83*

S. Lee Taylor
See Steve Taylor

Steve Taylor
The Second Chance *351*

Andre Techine (1943-)
Changing Times *69*

Emma Thompson (1959-)
Nanny McPhee *275*

Christine To
Jet Li's Fearless *208*

Robert Towne (1936-)
Ask the Dust *19*

Anne-Louise Trividic
Gabrielle *151*

Guinevere Turner (1968-)
BloodRayne *44*
The Notorious Bettie Page *286*

Kristopher Turner
Something New *369*

Sheldon Turner
The Texas Chainsaw Massacre: The Beginning *387*

Lars von Trier (1956-)
Manderlay *254*

Andy Wachowski (1967-)
V for Vendetta *419*

Larry Wachowski (1965-)
V for Vendetta *419*

Robert Wade
Casino Royale *65*

Jake Wade Wall
When a Stranger Calls *434*

David S. Ward (1947-)
Flyboys *140*

Keenen Ivory Wayans (1958-)
Little Man *239*

Marlon Wayans (1972-)
Little Man *239*

Shawn Wayans (1971-)
Little Man *239*

Paul Weitz (1966-)
American Dreamz *6*

Wim Wenders (1945-)
Don't Come Knocking *106*

Richard Wenk
16 Blocks *363*

Barry Wernick
Grandma's Boy *166*

Leigh Whannell (1977-)
Saw III *340*

Mike White (1970-)
Nacho Libre *273*

Cormac Wibberley
The Shaggy Dog *357*

Marianne S. Wibberley
The Shaggy Dog *357*

Kurt Wimmer
Ultraviolet *407*

Len Wiseman
Underworld: Evolution *410*

James Wong
Final Destination 3 *130*

Ray Wright
Pulse *318*

Iris Yamashita
Letters from Iwo Jima *234*

Zhang Yimou (1951-)
Curse of the Golden Flower *86*

Steven Zaillian (1951-)
All the King's Men *4*

Mark Zakarin
Keeping Up with the Steins *216*

Bian Zhihong
Curse of the Golden Flower *86*

Cinematographer Index

Phil Abraham
Annapolis *10*

Thomas Ackerman
The Benchwarmers *34*
Looking for Comedy in the Muslim World *244*
Scary Movie 4 *344*

Barry Ackroyd
United 93 *412*

Lance Acord
Marie Antoinette *257*

Remi Adefarasin
Scoop *349*

Pierre Aim
Wah-Wah *425*

Jose Luis Alcaine (1938-)
Volver *423*

Maxime Alexandre
The Hills Have Eyes *178*

Jamie Anderson
Art School Confidential *18*

Peter Andrews
See Steven Soderbergh

David Armstrong
Saw III *340*

Howard Atherton
Lassie *228*

Christopher Baffa
Running with Scissors *331*
Unaccompanied Minors *408*

Florian Ballhaus
The Devil Wears Prada *104*

Michael Ballhaus (1935-)
The Departed *99*

Lance Bangs
Jackass Number Two *207*

Michael Barrett
Bobby *45*
Goal! The Dream Begins *157*

Alfonso Beato
The Queen *323*

Dion Beebe
Miami Vice *262*

Christian Berger
Cache *61*

Gabriel Beristain
The Sentinel *353*
The Shaggy Dog *357*

Steven Bernstein
Little Man *239*

Adam Biddle
Crank *83*

Adrian Biddle (1952-2005)
An American Haunting *8*
V for Vendetta *419*

Oliver Bokelberg
Strangers with Candy *377*

Alexis Boling
Awesome! I F***in' Shot That! *23*

Jean-Louis Bompoint
The Science of Sleep *347*

Henry Braham
Flyboys *140*
Nanny McPhee *275*

Brian J. Breheny
Aquamarine *14*

Robert Brinkmann (1962-)
Tenacious D in the Pick of Destiny *386*

Jonathan Brown
The Pink Panther *304*
School for Scoundrels *345*

Eigil Bryld
The King *218*
Kinky Boots *220*

Don Burgess
Eight Below *117*
My Super Ex-Girlfriend *270*

Antonio Calvache
Little Children *237*

Paul Cameron
Deja Vu *97*

Jan Carlee
Everyone's Hero *122*

Milan Chadima
Hostel *188*

Michael Chapman (1935-)
Hoot *186*

Enrique Chediak
Down in the Valley *109*
Turistas *404*

Fabio Cianchetti
Don't Tell *108*

Peter Ciardelli
The War Tapes *427*

Dominique Colin
Russian Dolls *334*

Peter Lyons Collister (1956-)
Garfield: A Tail of Two Kitties *154*

Ericson Core
Invincible *204*

Patrick Creadon
Wordplay *442*

Sam Cullman
Why We Fight *436*

Dean Cundey
The Holiday *181*

Benjamin Davis
Imagine Me & You *197*

Elliot Davis
The Nativity Story *276*

Bruno Delbonnel
Infamous *200*

Benoit Delhomme
The Proposition *316*

Frank DeMarco
Beerfest *32*

John Ndiaga Demps
Phat Girlz *301*

Caleb Deschanel (1941-)
Ask the Dust *19*

Christopher Doyle (1952-)
Lady in the Water *223*

Robert A. Driskell, Jr.
End of the Spear *119*

Simon Duggan
Underworld: Evolution *410*

David M. Dunlap
Game 6 *152*

Andrew Dunn
The History Boys *179*

Pawel Edelman
All the King's Men *4*

Eric Alan Edwards
The Break-Up *51*

David Eggby
The Marine *259*

Robert Elswit
American Dreamz *6*

Dimitry Elyashkavich
Jackass Number Two *207*

Lukas Ettlin
The Texas Chainsaw Massacre: The Beginning *387*

Russell Fine
Sherrybaby *358*

Gavin Finney
Keeping Mum *215*

George Folsey, Jr.
The Pink Panther *304*

Ron Fortunato
Catch a Fire *67*
Find Me Guilty *131*

Jonathan Freeman
Hollywoodland *183*

Steve Gainer
Wassup Rockers *429*

Greg Gardiner
She's the Man *360*

Eric Gautier
Gabrielle *151*

Luke Geissbuhler
Borat: Cultural Learnings of America for Make Benefit Glorious Nation of Kazakhstan *48*

Lance Gewer
Tsotsi *401*

Pierre Gill
The Covenant *81*

Adam Greenberg
Snakes on a Plane *366*

Robbie Greenberg
The Santa Clause 3: The Escape Clause *339*

David Gribble
The World's Fastest Indian *445*

Xavier Perez Grobet
Monster House *268*
Nacho Libre *273*

Davis Guggenheim
An Inconvenient Truth *199*

Anthony Hardwick
Borat: Cultural Learnings of America for Make Benefit Glorious Nation of Kazakhstan *48*

Wolfgang Held
Poster Boy *309*

Julien Hirsch
Changing Times *69*

Harry Hitner
Ice Age: The Meltdown *191*

Robert Humpherys
Somersault *367*

W. Mott Hupfel, III
The Notorious Bettie Page *286*

Shane Hurlbut
Something New *369*
Waist Deep *426*
We Are Marshall *432*

Mark Irwin
Big Momma's House 2 *37*
Deck the Halls *96*
Grandma's Boy *166*

Johnny E. Jensen
Material Girls *261*

Hugh Johnson
Eragon *121*

Emmanuel (Manu) Kadosh
The Lost City *245*

Jean-Claude Kalache
Cars *63*

Shane Kelly
A Scanner Darkly *342*

Jan Kiesser
Beowulf & Grendel *35*

Jeffrey L. Kimball
Glory Road *156*

Alar Kivilo
The Lake House *225*

David Klein
Clerks II *76*

Nicholas D. Knowland
The Piano Tuner of Earthquakes *303*

Rick Kosick
Jackass Number Two *207*

Ellen Kuras
Dave Chappelle's Block Party *92*
Neil Young: Heart of Gold *278*

Toyomichi Kurita
Madea's Family Reunion *251*

Edward Lachman (1948-)
A Prairie Home Companion *311*

Jeanne Lapoirie
Time to Leave *394*

Dan Laustsen
Silent Hill *361*

Philippe Le Sourd
A Good Year *164*

Dean Lent
Phat Girlz *301*

Matthew F. Leonetti (1941-)
Accepted *1*

Pierre Lhomme
Army of Shadows *16*

Chris Li
Why We Fight *436*

Matthew Libatique (1969-)
The Fountain *144*
Inside Man *202*

Emmanuel Lubezki
Children of Men *74*

Franz Lustig
Don't Come Knocking *106*

Glen MacPherson
16 Blocks *363*

Anthony Dod Mantle (1955-)
The Last King of Scotland *231*
Manderlay *254*

Alain Marcoen
The Child *73*

Kim Marks
Larry the Cable Guy: Health Inspector *227*

Alejandro Martinez
Stay Alive *371*

James Mathers
The U.S. vs. John Lennon *415*

Clark Mathis
Rocky Balboa *328*

Shawn Maurer
Date Movie *91*

Sam McCurdy
The Descent *101*

Seamus McGarvey
Charlotte's Web *71*
World Trade Center *443*

Robert McLachlan
Black Christmas *38*
Final Destination 3 *130*

Phil Meheux
Casino Royale *65*

Alexander Melman
The Libertine *236*

Chris Menges (1940-)
Notes on a Scandal *284*
The Three Burials of Melquiades Estrada *391*

Peter Menzies, Jr.
When a Stranger Calls *434*

Anastas Michos
Freedomland *146*

Gregory Middleton
Slither *365*

Dan Mindel
Mission: Impossible III *264*

Charles Minsky
Keeping Up with the Steins *216*
You, Me and Dupree *449*

Eric Moynier
The Boynton Beach Club *49*

M. David Mullen (1962-)
Akeelah and the Bee *2*
The Quiet *325*
Shadowboxer *355*

J. Michael Muro
Flicka *138*

Fred Murphy
RV *335*

Oleg Mutu
The Death of Mr. Lazarescu *94*

Guillermo Navarro
Night at the Museum *280*
Pan's Labyrinth *299*

Alex Nepomniaschy
Take the Lead *383*

Mathias Neumann
BloodRayne *44*

Ben Nott
See No Evil *352*

Giles Nuttgens
Water *430*

P.H. O'Brien
The War Tapes *427*

Daryn Okada (1960-)
Stick It *373*

Tim Orr
Trust the Man *400*

Roman Osin
The Return *327*

Gyula Pados
Basic Instinct 2 *31*

Phedon Papamichael
The Pursuit of Happyness *319*

Phil Parmet
Lonesome Jim *242*

Peter Pau
The Promise *315*

Ben Pearson
The Second Chance *351*

Nicola Pecorini
Tideland *392*

Wally Pfister
The Prestige *313*

Garry Phillips
Catch a Fire *67*

Mark Plummer
Pulse *318*

Marco Pontecorvo
Firewall *133*

Hang-Seng Poon
Jet Li's Fearless *208*

Dick Pope
The Illusionist *196*
Man of the Year *252*

Rodrigo Prieto
Babel *27*

Fortunato Procopio
The Devil and Daniel Johnston *102*

Pascal Rabaud
Idlewild *194*

Arthur Reinhart
Tristan & Isolde *396*

William Rexer
The Groomsmen *167*

Robert Richardson (1955-)
The Good Shepherd *161*

Bob Richman
An Inconvenient Truth *199*

Anthony B. Richmond (1942-)
Employee of the Month *118*
John Tucker Must Die *209*

Lisa Rinzler
The Night Listener *282*

Claudio Rocha
Mrs. Palfrey at the Claremont *266*

Julie Rogers
Curious George *85*

John Christian Rosenlund
Factotum *125*

Richard Rutkowski
How to Eat Fried Worms *189*

Odd Geir Saether
Inland Empire *201*

Stephen St. John
The Guardian *170*

Paul Sarossy (1963-)
The Wicker Man *437*

Etienne Sauret
Why We Fight *436*

Roberto Schaefer
For Your Consideration *142*
Stranger Than Fiction *375*

Tobias Schliessler
Dreamgirls *111*

Nancy Schreiber
Loverboy *247*

John Seale (1943-)
Poseidon *308*

Jonathan Sela
The Omen *292*

Dean Semler (1943-)
Apocalypto *12*
Click *78*
Just My Luck *213*

Ben Seresin
A Good Woman *163*

Michael Seresin
Step Up *372*

Eduardo Serra
Blood Diamond *41*
The Bridesmaid *55*

Ward Serrill
The Heart of the Game *177*

Newton Thomas (Tom) Sigel (1961-)
Superman Returns *379*

Peter Sillen
Old Joy *291*

Geoffrey Simpson
Last Holiday *229*

Steven Soderbergh (1963-)
Bubble *57*
The Good German *159*

Peter Sova
Lucky Number Slevin *249*

Dante Spinotti (1943-)
X-Men: The Last Stand *447*

Terry Stacey
Friends with Money *148*
Winter Passing *441*

Tom Stern
Flags of Our Fathers *135*
The Last Kiss *232*
Letters from Iwo Jima *234*

Orlando Stuart
Unknown White Male *413*

Tim Suhrstedt
Idiocracy *192*
Little Miss Sunshine *240*

David Tattersall
The Matador *260*
Zoom *451*

Gokhan Tiryaki
Climates *80*

John Toon
Glory Road *156*

Salvatore Totino
The Da Vinci Code *88*

Sergei Trofimov
Night Watch *283*

Walther Vanden Ende
Joyeux Noel *211*

Checco Varese
The Aura *22*

Thaddeus Wadleigh
Who Killed the Electric Car? *435*

Andy Wang
Everyone's Hero *122*

May-Ying Welch
Why We Fight *436*

James Whitaker
Running Scared *330*
Thank You for Smoking *389*

Jo Willems
Hard Candy *175*

Stephen Windon
The Fast and the Furious: Tokyo Drift *128*

Darius Wolski
Pirates of the Caribbean: Dead Man's Chest *306*

Arthur Wong Ngok Tai
Ultraviolet *407*

Oliver Wood
Talladega Nights: The Ballad of Ricky Bobby *384*

Katsumi Yanagijima
The Grudge 2 *169*

Steve Yedlin
Brick *53*

Alexis Zabe
Duck Season *113*

Haris Zambarloukos
Venus *421*

Xiaoding Zhao
Curse of the Golden Flower *86*

Vilmos Zsigmond (1930-)
The Black Dahlia *39*

Marcel Zyskind
Tristram Shandy: A Cock and Bull Story *398*

Editor Index

Sandra Adair
A Scanner Darkly *342*

Sean Albertson
Rocky Balboa *328*

Craig Alpert
Borat: Cultural Learnings of America for Make Benefit Glorious Nation of Kazakhstan *48*
Bubble *57*

Tariq Anwar
The Good Shepherd *161*

Pamela Scott Arnold
Poster Boy *309*

Zack Arnold
Phat Girlz *301*

John Axelrad
Slither *365*

Stuart Baird
Casino Royale *65*

V. Scott Balcerek
The Wild *439*

Roger Barton
Eragon *121*

Ned Bastille
The Shaggy Dog *357*

Baxter
The Hills Have Eyes *178*

Alan Edward Bell
Hoot *186*

Brian Berdan
Crank *83*

Michael Berenbaum
Hollywoodland *183*

Mary Ann Bernard
See Steven Soderbergh

Jeff Betancourt
The Grudge 2 *169*
When a Stranger Calls *434*

Jill Bilcock
Catch a Fire *67*
The Libertine *236*

David Blackburn
ATL *21*

Alex Blatt
Wassup Rockers *429*

John Bloom
Notes on a Scandal *284*

Christopher Blunden
Flyboys *140*

Doug Blush
Wordplay *442*

Francoise Bonnot
Army of Shadows *16*

Peter Boyle
Tristan & Isolde *396*

Marianne Brandon
Mission: Impossible III *264*

David Brenner
World Trade Center *443*

Alejandro Brodersohn
The Lake House *225*

Barry Alexander Brown
Inside Man *202*

John Bryant
Everyone's Hero *122*

Jeff Buchanan
Dave Chappelle's Block Party *92*

Dana Bunescu
The Death of Mr. Lazarescu *94*

Anita Brant Burgoyne
Looking for Comedy in the Muslim World *244*

John Carr
Over the Hedge *295*

John Carter
Madea's Family Reunion *251*

Seth Casriel
Jackass Number Two *207*

Jay Cassidy
An Inconvenient Truth *199*

Nuri Bilge Ceylan
Climates *80*

Matt Chesse
Stranger Than Fiction *375*

Richard Chew
Bobby *45*

Jonathan Chibnall
The Texas Chainsaw Massacre: The Beginning *387*

Peter Christelis
Tristram Shandy: A Cock and Bull Story *398*

Lisa Zeno Chrugin
The Last Kiss *232*

Christopher Cibelli
The Lost City *245*

Curtiss Clayton
Sherrybaby *358*

Arthur Coburn
Running Scared *330*

Steven Cohen
Material Girls *261*

Monica Coleman
Time to Leave *394*

Richard Comeau
An American Haunting *8*

Tricia Cooke
The Notorious Bettie Page *286*

Tom Costain
Grandma's Boy *166*

Peter Coulson
Lassie *228*

Joel Cox
Flags of Our Fathers *135*
Letters from Iwo Jima *234*

Jacob Craycroft
A Prairie Home Companion *311*

Douglas Crise
Babel *27*

Alfonso Cuaron (1961-)
Children of Men *74*

Blair Daily
Man of the Year *252*

Nicolas De Toth
The Covenant *81*
Underworld: Evolution *410*

Isabelle Dedieu
Wah-Wah *425*

Keiko Deguchi
The Boynton Beach Club *49*

Nicolas DeToth
See Nicolas De Toth

Chris Dickens
Goal! The Dream Begins *157*

Dody Dorn (1955-)
A Good Year *164*

Clare Douglas
United 93 *412*

Marie-Helene Dozo
The Child *73*

Antonia Van Drimmelen
Notes on a Scandal *284*

Peter S. Elliott
Garfield: A Tail of Two Kitties *154*

Ayhan Ergursel
Climates *80*

Monique Fardoulis
The Bridesmaid *55*

Glenn Farr
Akeelah and the Bee *2*

Neil Farrell
A Good Woman *163*

Greg Featherman
Larry the Cable Guy: Health Inspector *227*

David Finfer
The Santa Clause 3: The Escape Clause *339*

Eric Firth
The Heart of the Game *177*

Sarah Flack
Dave Chappelle's Block Party *92*
Marie Antoinette *257*

George Folsey, Jr.
Hostel *188*
Unaccompanied Minors *408*

Rob Frazen
Friends with Money *148*

Matthew Friedman
John Tucker Must Die *209*

Priscilla Nedd Friendly
Big Momma's House 2 *37*
We Are Marshall *432*

Nigel Galt
Mrs. Palfrey at the Claremont *266*

Nicolas Gaster
Venus *421*

Christian Gazal
Happy Feet *173*

Francois Gedigier
Gabrielle *151*

Pal Gengenbach
Factotum *125*

Naomi Geraghty
The Illusionist *196*

John Gilbert
The World's Fastest Indian *445*

Megan Gill
Tsotsi *401*

James Gilroy
Trust the Man *400*

Martine Giordano
Changing Times *69*

Dana E. Glauberman
Thank You for Smoking *389*

Jinx Godfrey
The King *218*

Mark Goldblatt
X-Men: The Last Stand *447*

William Goldenberg
Miami Vice *262*

Anne Goursaud
Idlewild *194*

Jeff Gourson
Click *78*

Elliot Graham
Superman Returns *379*

Scott Gray
Somersault *367*

Adam Green
Lassie *228*

Jerry Greenberg
Invincible *204*

Jon Gregory
The Proposition *316*

Kevin Greutert
Saw III *340*

Janice Hampton
How to Eat Fried Worms *189*

Dan Hanley
The Da Vinci Code *88*

Miles Hanon
End of the Spear *119*

Jon Harris
The Descent *101*

Lee Haxall
Beerfest *32*

Mark Helfrich
X-Men: The Last Stand *447*

Jason Hellmann
Deja Vu *97*

Craig Herring
Scary Movie 4 *344*

Emma E. Hickox
Kinky Boots *220*

Mike Hill
The Da Vinci Code *88*

Scott Hill
Accepted *1*

Paul Hirsch
Date Movie *91*
Deck the Halls *96*

Michael Hofacre
Down in the Valley *109*

Robert Hoffman
Art School Confidential *18*

Peter Honess
Poseidon *308*

Tyler Hubby
The Devil and Daniel Johnston *102*

Michael Hudecek
Cache *61*

Andrew Hulme
Lucky Number Slevin *249*

Joe Hutshing
The Holiday *181*

Robert Ivison
Take the Lead *383*

Michael Jablow
She's the Man *360*

Mike Jackson
Little Man *239*

Steve James
The War Tapes *427*

Art Jones
Hard Candy *175*

Leslie Jones
School for Scoundrels *345*

Lawrence Jordan
Zoom *451*

Sheldon Kahn
My Super Ex-Girlfriend *270*

Brian A. Kates
Shadowboxer *355*

Virginia Katz
Dreamgirls *111*
Jet Li's Fearless *208*
Mrs. Palfrey at the Claremont *266*

Andrew Keir (1926-97)
The Night Listener *282*

Andy Keir
Neil Young: Heart of Gold *278*

Nancy Kennedy
Why We Fight *436*

Melissa Kent
Something New *369*

Myron Kerstein
American Dreamz *6*

Istvan Kiraly
Basic Instinct 2 *31*

Jamie Kirkpatrick
The Groomsmen *167*

Dmitri Kiselev
Night Watch *283*

Lynzee Klingman
Down in the Valley *109*
The Lake House *225*

Michael Kovalenko
Who Killed the Electric Car? *435*

Carole Kravetz-Akyanian
The Matador *260*

Justin Krish
Nanny McPhee *275*

Robert K. Lambert
Ask the Dust *19*
The Nativity Story *276*
Pulse *318*

Joe Landauer
Sherrybaby *358*

Simon Laurie
The Piano Tuner of Earthquakes *303*

Richard Learoyd
Jet Li's Fearless *208*

Dan Lebental
The Break-Up *51*

Chris Lebenzon
Deja Vu *97*

Tony Leech
Hoodwinked *185*

Robert Leighton
For Your Consideration *142*

Alisa Lepselter
Scoop *349*

Stuart Levy
The Nativity Story *276*

Tom Lewis
Employee of the Month *118*
Scary Movie 4 *344*

Susan Littenberg
Charlotte's Web *71*

Mark Livolsi
The Devil Wears Prada *104*

Gregg London
We Are Marshall *432*

Cheng Long
Curse of the Golden Flower *86*

David Lynch (1946-)
Inland Empire *201*

Peter S. Lynch, II
The U.S. vs. John Lennon *415*

Alex Mackie
Imagine Me & You *197*

Andrew Marcus
Flicka *138*

Mary Jo Markey
Mission: Impossible III *264*

Pamela Martin
Little Miss Sunshine *240*

Kelly Matsumoto
The Fast and the Furious: Tokyo Drift *128*

Jeff McEvoy
Turistas *404*

Michael R. Miller
Strangers with Candy *377*

Steve Mirkovich
16 Blocks *363*

Stephen Mirrione
Babel *27*

Cindy Mollo
The Sentinel *353*

Colin Monie
Water *430*

Julie Monroe
World Trade Center *443*

Nick Moore
Freedomland *146*
Little Man *239*
Nanny McPhee *275*

Jane Moran
Aquamarine *14*

Bob Morri
Pulse *318*

Kirk Morri
Pulse *318*

Rupert Murray
Unknown White Male *413*

Nadine Muse
Cache *61*

Debra Neil-Fisher
Just My Luck *213*
You, Me and Dupree *449*

Tom Nordberg
The Guardian *170*

John Ottman (1964-)
Superman Returns *379*

Jim Page
Firewall *133*

Bill Pankow
The Black Dahlia *39*

Fernando Pardo
The Aura *22*

Richard Pearson
United 93 *412*

Alejandro Carrillo Penovi
The Aura *22*

Chris A. Peterson
Who Killed the Electric Car? *435*

Sabrina Pilsco
Charlotte's Web *71*

Joel Plotch
The Wicker Man *437*

Sebastien Prangere
Silent Hill *361*

Jon Michael Price
The Ant Bully *11*

Peck Prior
The Benchwarmers *34*

Matthew Probst
Jackass Number Two *207*

Peter Przygodda
Don't Come Knocking *106*

Dallas S. Puett
The Marine *259*

Jay Rabinowitz
The Fountain *144*

Gary D. Raoch
Letters from Iwo Jima *234*

Fred Raskin
Annapolis *10*
The Fast and the Furious: Tokyo Drift *128*

David Ray
Loverboy *247*

Kimberly A. Ray
Employee of the Month *118*

Kelly Reichardt
Old Joy *291*

David Rennie
Idiocracy *192*
Tenacious D in the Pick of Destiny *386*

Meg Reticker
Winter Passing *441*

David Richardson
BloodRayne *44*

Nancy Richardson
Step Up *372*

Scott Richter
See No Evil *352*

Stephen E. Rivkin
Pirates of the Caribbean: Dead Man's Chest *306*

Alex Rodriguez
Children of Men *74*

Maria Rodriguez
Duck Season *113*

Ron Rosen
Flyboys *140*

David Rosenbloom
The Break-Up *51*

Steven Rosenblum
Blood Diamond *41*
Failure to Launch *127*

Harvey Rosenstock
Stay Alive *371*

Christopher Rouse
Eight Below *117*
United 93 *412*

Paul Rubell
Miami Vice *262*

Jose Salcedo
Volver *423*

Robin Sales
Keeping Mum *215*

Francine Sandberg
Russian Dolls *334*

Daniel Schalk
School for Scoundrels *345*

Thelma Schoonmaker
The Departed *99*

Ken Schretzmann
Cars *63*

Adam Scott
Monster House *268*

John Scott
Basic Instinct 2 *31*

Andrea Sedlackova
Joyeux Noel *211*

Terilyn Shropshire
Waist Deep *426*

Roberto Silvi
The Three Burials of Melquiades Estrada *391*

Leslie Simmer
The War Tapes *427*

Scott Simmons
Jackass Number Two *207*

Claire Simpson
The Return *327*

Margaret Sixel
Happy Feet *173*

Deidre Slevin
Last Holiday *229*

Byron Smith
Running with Scissors *331*

Howard E. Smith
Snakes on a Plane *366*

Kevin Smith (1970-)
Clerks II *76*

Lee Smith
The Prestige *313*

Joan Sobel
The Quiet *325*

Steven Soderbergh (1963-)
Bubble *57*
The Good German *159*

Sandy Solowitz
The Benchwarmers *34*

Molly Marlene Stensgard
Manderlay *254*

Matthew Sterling
The Second Chance *351*

William Chang Suk-ping
Shadowboxer *355*

Tom Swartwout
Find Me Guilty *131*

Dan Swietlik
An Inconvenient Truth *199*

Troy Takaki
Stick It *373*

Kevin Tent
RV *335*

Tara Timpone
Keeping Up with the Steins *216*

Camilla Toniolo
Game 6 *152*
Infamous *200*

Leo Trombetta
Little Children *237*

Plummy Tucker
Lonesome Jim *242*

Barbara Tulliver
Lady in the Water *223*

Neal Usatin
Awesome! I F***in' Shot That! *23*

John Venzon
Flushed Away *139*

Bernat Vilaplana
Pan's Labyrinth *299*

Dennis Virkler
The Guardian *170*

Steven L. Wagner
The Wild *439*

Wayne Wahrman
All the King's Men *4*

Lesley Walker
Tideland *392*

Martin Walsh
V for Vendetta *419*

Jeff Warren
Beowulf & Grendel *35*

Billy Weber
Nacho Libre *273*

Steven Weisberg
Man of the Year *252*

Oli Weiss
Don't Come Knocking *106*

Juliette Welfing
The Science of Sleep *347*

Brad E. White
The Pink Panther *304*
Unaccompanied Minors *408*

Brent White
Talladega Nights: The Ballad of Ricky Bobby *384*

Chris Willingham
Black Christmas *38*
Final Destination 3 *130*

John D. Wilson
The History Boys *179*

Hughes Winborne
The Pursuit of Happyness *319*

Julia Wong
X-Men: The Last Stand *447*

Craig Wood
Pirates of the Caribbean: Dead Man's Chest *306*

John Wright
Apocalypto *12*
Glory Road *156*

Justine Wright
The Last King of Scotland *231*

William Yeh
Ultraviolet *407*

Cecilia Zanuso
Don't Tell *108*

Pamela Ziegenhagen-Shefland
Open Season *294*

Don Zimmerman
Night at the Museum *280*
The Omen *292*

Lucia Zucchetti
The Queen *323*

Art Director Index

Kevin R. Adams
Everyone's Hero *122*

Gilles Aird
The Last Kiss *232*

Mercedes Alfonsin
The Aura *22*

John Alvarez
Snakes on a Plane *366*

Miguel Alvarez
Poster Boy *309*

Thomas Ambrose
The Notorious Bettie Page *286*

Kate Aronsson Brown
Game 6 *152*

Michael Atwell
Down in the Valley *109*
Rocky Balboa *328*

Alan Au
Click *78*
Grandma's Boy *166*

Chris August
Underworld: Evolution *410*

David Baca
Beerfest *32*

Maria Baker
Tenacious D in the Pick of Destiny *386*

Laura Ballinger Gardner
Infamous *200*
Step Up *372*

Patrick Banister
Hollywoodland *183*

Maria Teresa Barbasso
The Nativity Story *276*

Christina Barbu
The Death of Mr. Lazarescu *94*

Guy Barnes
Employee of the Month *118*

Pier Luigi Basile
A Good Woman *163*

Gary Baugh
All the King's Men *4*

David Baxa
Hostel *188*

Charley Beal
Invincible *204*

Emily Beck
Find Me Guilty *131*

Gregory A. Berry
The Santa Clause 3: The Escape Clause *339*

Zhao Bin
Curse of the Golden Flower *86*

J.P. Blackmon
Jackass Number Two *207*

Roberto Bonelli
Apocalypto *12*

Bill Booth
Aquamarine *14*
The Proposition *316*

Peter Borck
Art School Confidential *18*
Flicka *138*

Dennis Bradford
Just My Luck *213*

Ze Branco
Changing Times *69*

Steve Bream
V for Vendetta *419*

William Budge
Don't Come Knocking *106*

John Burke
She's the Man *360*

Johnny Byrne
Tristan & Isolde *396*

Andrew Max Cahn
The Guardian *170*

Thomas Cardone
Ice Age: The Meltdown *191*

Terri Cariiker-Thayer
The Departed *99*

Stephen Carter
Friends with Money *148*

Sue Chan
American Dreamz *6*

Joel Chong
Ultraviolet *407*

Nigel Churcher
Take the Lead *383*

Erin Cochran
Unaccompanied Minors *408*

Sylvia Conde
The Lost City *245*

Chris Consani
The Ant Bully *11*

Kevin Constant
Failure to Launch *127*
Glory Road *156*

Colman Corish
Lassie *228*

Chris Cornwell
Crank *83*
Stick It *373*

Christian Corvin
BloodRayne *44*

Robert Cowper
A Good Year *164*

Bruce Crone
Pirates of the Caribbean: Dead Man's Chest *306*

Charlie Daboub
The Santa Clause 3: The Escape Clause *339*

Joshu de Cartier
Man of the Year *252*
Zoom *451*

David Saenz de Maturana
Borat: Cultural Learnings of America for Make Benefit Glorious Nation of Kazakhstan *48*

Stefan Dechant
Lady in the Water *223*

Marcel Del Rio
The Matador *260*

Gary Diamond
Idlewild *194*

Daniel T. Dorrance
Mission: Impossible III *264*
The Shaggy Dog *357*

Damien Drew
Superman Returns *379*

Philip Elton
Kinky Boots *220*

Freddy Evard
A Good Year *164*

Marc Fisichella
Clerks II *76*

Lorin Flemming
Running with Scissors *331*

James Foster
Basic Instinct 2 *31*

Luke Freeborn
Poseidon *308*

Gary Freeman
Children of Men *74*

Chad S. Frey
X-Men: The Last Stand *447*

John Frick
How to Eat Fried Worms *189*
The Texas Chainsaw Massacre: The Beginning *387*

Daran Fulham
Blood Diamond *41*

Elinor Rose Galbraith
Silent Hill *361*

Tim Galvin
Shadowboxer *355*

Alan Gilmore
United 93 *412*

Jodi Ginnever
Pulse *318*

Brandt Gordon
16 Blocks *363*

Austin Gorg
The Guardian *170*

Adrian Gorton
Flags of Our Fathers *135*

Peter Grant
Manderlay *254*

Matthew Gray
Flyboys *140*

Isabelle Guay
The Fountain *144*

Robert Guerra
The Good Shepherd *161*

Yoojung Han
Waist Deep *426*

Tom Hannam
Ask the Dust *19*

Andy Harkness
Open Season *294*

William Hawkins
Pirates of the Caribbean: Dead Man's Chest *306*

Adam Head
See No Evil *352*

Dan Hermansen
Deck the Halls *96*

Willie Heslup
Scary Movie 4 *344*

Alan Hook
Stay Alive *371*

Sarah Horton
V for Vendetta *419*

Lawrence A. Hubbs
Superman Returns *379*

Denise Hudson
Accepted *1*

Kevin Humenny
RV *335*

Anthony Ianni
Saw III *340*

Paul Inglis
Basic Instinct 2 *31*

Craig Jackson
Stranger Than Fiction *375*

Helen Jarvis
Firewall *133*
Night at the Museum *280*
X-Men: The Last Stand *447*

John R. Jensen
She's the Man *360*

Bo Johnson
John Tucker Must Die *209*

Richard Johnson
Last Holiday *229*
World Trade Center *443*

John J. Kasarda
Little Children *237*

Kevin Kavanaugh
The Lake House *225*
The Prestige *313*

Akio Kikuchi
The Grudge 2 *169*

David Klassen
The Pursuit of Happyness *319*

Jeff Knipp
The Return *327*
The Three Burials of Melquiades Estrada *391*

Jason Knox-Johnston
The Descent *101*

Katerina Kopicova
The Omen *292*

Tomoko Kotakemori
The Grudge 2 *169*

Stefan Kovacik
The Illusionist *196*

Sebastian Krawinkel
V for Vendetta *419*

Martin Kurel
The Omen *292*

Michele Laliberte
The Fountain *144*

Simon Lamont
Casino Royale *65*
Keeping Mum *215*

Jeff LeGore
End of the Spear *119*

Gregory Levasseur
The Hills Have Eyes *178*

Nicole Lobart
Don't Come Knocking *106*

Daniel A. Lomino
Date Movie *91*

Nicholas Lundy
The Departed *99*

Emma MacDevitt
Tristram Shandy: A Cock and Bull Story *398*
Venus *421*

Kenneth Mak
Jet Li's Fearless *208*

Louis M. Mann
Garfield: A Tail of Two Kitties *154*

Gwen Margetson
Little Man *239*

Tamara Marini
The Hills Have Eyes *178*

Jonah Markowitz
We Are Marshall *432*

Naaman Marshall
Apocalypto *12*

Anastasia Masaro
Tideland *392*

Giles Masters
The Da Vinci Code *88*

Rocco Matteo
The Sentinel *353*

James McAteer
Silent Hill *361*

Jonathan McKinstry
Eragon *121*

Scott A. Meehan
School for Scoundrels *345*

Doug Meerdink
The Good German *159*

Carlos Menendez
The Lost City *245*
Miami Vice *262*

Malcolm Middleton
Children of Men *74*

Hannah Moseley
Notes on a Scandal *284*

Jeff Mossa
Click *78*
Grandma's Boy *166*

Alan E. Muraoka
Little Miss Sunshine *240*

Desma Murphy
Poseidon *308*

Marita Mussett
The Proposition *316*

John Mymarkay
Trust the Man *400*

Norman Newberry
Monster House *268*

Felicity Nove
Hard Candy *175*

Tom Nursey
Charlotte's Web *71*

Irene O'Brien
Lassie *228*

Nick Palmer
Scoop *349*

Greg Papalia
Monster House *268*

Janie Parker
Somersault *367*

Salvador Parra
Volver *423*

Catherine Perez-Mansill
Superman Returns *379*

Pierre Perrault
The Covenant *81*
Lucky Number Slevin *249*

Ian Phillips
Material Girls *261*

Scott Plauche
Deja Vu *97*

Sorin Popescu
Pulse *318*

Daryl Porter
The Marine *259*

John Pryce-Jones
Superman Returns *379*

Colombe Raby
Lucky Number Slevin *249*

Eva Radke
The Night Listener *282*

Olivier Radot
Gabrielle *151*

Virginia Randolph-Weaver
Talladega Nights: The Ballad of Ricky Bobby *384*

Anthony Reading
The Da Vinci Code *88*

Tom Reta
The Fast and the Furious: Tokyo Drift *128*

Charlie Revai
Superman Returns *379*

Cecia Richters
Turistas *404*

Hania Robledo
Nacho Libre *273*

Peter Rogness
The Pink Panther *304*

Patrick Rolfe
The Libertine *236*

Jesse Rosenthal
Rocky Balboa *328*

G. Victoria Ruskin
Friends with Money *148*

David Sandefur
The Break-Up *51*

Mylene Santos
Strangers with Candy *377*

Christian Schellewald
Over the Hedge *295*

Jeffrey Schoen
A Prairie Home Companion *311*

Justin Scoppa, Jr.
X-Men: The Last Stand *447*

Anne Seibel
Marie Antoinette *257*

Lucio Seixas
Winter Passing *441*

Paul Shardlow
Over the Hedge *295*

Sheila B
The Second Chance *351*

Jonathan Short
ATL *21*

Chris Shriver
Inside Man *202*
Loverboy *247*

Jean-Michel Simonet
Joyeux Noel *211*

William Ladd Skinner
Idiocracy *192*
Pirates of the Caribbean: Dead Man's Chest *306*

Paul Sonski
You, Me and Dupree *449*

Fabrice Spelta
Mrs. Palfrey at the Claremont *266*

Jeremy Stanbridge
Eight Below *117*

Craig Stearns
Big Momma's House 2 *37*

Joannah Stutchbury
The Last King of Scotland *231*

Gerry Sullivan
When a Stranger Calls *434*

Vlasta Svobodova
The Illusionist *196*

Pat Tagliaferro
For Your Consideration *142*

Sandra Tanaka
X-Men: The Last Stand *447*

Christopher Tandon
Annapolis *10*
The Black Dahlia *39*

Antonio Tarolla
The Nativity Story *276*

Jack G. Taylor, Jr.
Flags of Our Fathers *135*

Thomas T. Taylor
Goal! The Dream Begins *157*

James E. Tocci
Big Momma's House 2 *37*

Einar Unnsteinsson
Beowulf & Grendel *35*

Eric Veenstra
The Piano Tuner of Earthquakes *303*

Vieru Vlad
BloodRayne *44*

Thomas Voth
Dreamgirls *111*
The Lake House *225*

Delarey Wagener
Catch a Fire *67*

Mark Walker
Tsotsi *401*

Peggy Wang
Phat Girlz *301*

Tom Warren
The Devil Wears Prada *104*

Dan Webster
The Holiday *181*

Peter Wenham
The Queen *323*

Andrew White
Larry the Cable Guy: Health Inspector *227*

Simon Whiteley
Happy Feet *173*

Christina Wilson
Inland Empire *201*
Lady in the Water *223*

Tony Wohlgemuth
Final Destination 3 *130*

Michael Norman Wong
Slither *365*

Patricia Woodbridge
Freedomland *146*
My Super Ex-Girlfriend *270*

Music Index

Michael Andrews
Unaccompanied Minors *408*

Craig Armstrong
World Trade Center *443*

David Arnold (1962-)
Casino Royale *65*
Venus *421*

Norman Arnold
The War Tapes *427*

Kristin Asbjornsen
Factotum *125*

Michael Bacon
Loverboy *247*

Angelo Badalamenti (1937-)
The Wicker Man *437*

Klaus Badelt
Poseidon *308*
The Promise *315*
16 Blocks *363*
Ultraviolet *407*

Nathan Barr
Beerfest *32*
Hostel *188*

Stephen Barton
Mrs. Palfrey at the Claremont *266*

Tyler Bates
See No Evil *352*
Slither *365*

Christophe Beck
Garfield: A Tail of Two Kitties *154*
The Pink Panther *304*
School for Scoundrels *345*
The Sentinel *353*
We Are Marshall *432*
Zoom *451*

Marco Beltrami
The Omen *292*
The Three Burials of Melquiades Estrada *391*
Underworld: Evolution *410*

Jean-Michel Bernard
The Science of Sleep *347*

Terence Blanchard (1962-)
Inside Man *202*
Waist Deep *426*

Jon Brion
The Break-Up *51*

Michael Brook
An Inconvenient Truth *199*
Who Killed the Electric Car? *435*

T-Bone Burnett (1948-)
Don't Come Knocking *106*

Teddy Castellucci
Just My Luck *213*
Little Man *239*
My Super Ex-Girlfriend *270*

Matthieu Chabrol
The Bridesmaid *55*

George S. Clinton (1947-)
Big Momma's House 2 *37*
Deck the Halls *96*
The Santa Clause 3: The Escape Clause *339*

Charlie Clouser
Saw III *340*

Elia Cmiral
Pulse *318*

Harry Cody
Wassup Rockers *429*

Erran Baron Cohen
Borat: Cultural Learnings of America for Make Benefit Glorious Nation of Kazakhstan *48*

Lisa Coleman
Something New *369*

Bill Conti (1942-)
Rocky Balboa *328*

Britt Daniel
Stranger Than Fiction *375*

Jeff Danna (1964-)
Silent Hill *361*
Tideland *392*

Mychael Danna (1958-)
Little Miss Sunshine *240*
The Nativity Story *276*
Tideland *392*
Water *430*

Caine Davidson
An American Haunting *8*

Don Davis
The Marine *259*

Eric De Marsen
Army of Shadows *16*

John Debney (1957-)
The Ant Bully *11*
Barnyard *30*
Everyone's Hero *122*
Idlewild *194*
Keeping Up with the Steins *216*

Alexandre Desplat
Firewall *133*
The Queen *323*

Ramin Djawadi
Ask the Dust *19*
Open Season *294*

James Dooley
When a Stranger Calls *434*

Patrick Doyle (1953-)
Eragon *121*
Nanny McPhee *275*
Wah-Wah *425*

Anne Dudley (1956-)
Tristan & Isolde *396*

Loik Dury
Russian Dolls *334*

Clint Eastwood (1930-)
Flags of Our Fathers *135*

Kyle Eastwood (1968-)
Letters from Iwo Jima *234*

Todd Edwards
Hoodwinked *185*

Danny Elfman (1953-)
Charlotte's Web *71*
Nacho Libre *273*

Warren Ellis
The Proposition *316*

Stephen Endelman
Phat Girlz *301*

Harry Esscott
Hard Candy *175*

George Fenton
The History Boys *179*
Last Holiday *229*

Bruce Fowler
The Good Shepherd *161*

John (Gianni) Frizzell (1966-)
Stay Alive *371*

Andy Garcia (1956-)
The Lost City *245*

Mark Garcia
Poster Boy *309*

Juliette Garrigues
Changing Times *69*

Michael Giacchino
Looking for Comedy in the Muslim World *244*
Mission: Impossible III *264*

Richard Gibbs
John Tucker Must Die *209*

Philip Glass (1937-)
The Illusionist *196*
Notes on a Scandal *284*

Richard Glasser
Find Me Guilty *131*

Lucio Godoy
The Aura *22*

Peter Golub
Wordplay *442*

Robert Gray
The Groomsmen *167*

Harry Gregson-Williams
Deja Vu *97*
Flushed Away *139*

Rupert Gregson-Williams
Click *78*
Over the Hedge *295*

Mario Grigorov
Shadowboxer *355*

Andrea Guerra
The Pursuit of Happyness *319*

Paul Haslinger
Crank *83*
Turistas *404*

Alex Heffes
Imagine Me & You *197*
The Last King of Scotland *231*

Paul Hepker
Tsotsi *401*

Hilmar Orn Hilmarsson (1958-)
Beowulf & Grendel *35*

Dickon Hinchliffe
Keeping Mum *215*

David Hirschfelder (1960-)
Aquamarine *14*

James Horner (1953-)
All the King's Men *4*
Apocalypto *12*

Adam Horovitz (1966-)
Awesome! I F***in' Shot That! *23*

James Newton Howard (1951-)
Blood Diamond *41*
Freedomland *146*
Lady in the Water *223*
RV *335*

Alberto Iglesias
Volver *423*

Mark Isham (1951-)
The Black Dahlia *39*
Bobby *45*
Eight Below *117*
Invincible *204*
Running Scared *330*

Steve Jablonsky
The Texas Chainsaw Massacre: The Beginning *387*

Nathan Johnson
Brick *53*

Adrian Johnston
Kinky Boots *220*
Lassie *228*

Daniel Johnston
The Devil and Daniel Johnston *102*

Rickie Lee Jones
Friends with Money *148*

David Julyan
The Descent *101*
The Prestige *313*

Rolfe Kent (1963-)
Failure to Launch *127*
The Matador *260*
Thank You for Smoking *389*
You, Me and Dupree *449*

Mark Kilian
Tsotsi *401*

John Kimbrough
Winter Passing *441*

David Kitay
Art School Confidential *18*
Date Movie *91*

Henry Krieger
Dreamgirls *111*

Laurent Levesque
Russian Dolls *334*

James Levine
Running with Scissors *331*

Max Lichtenstein
The King *218*

Mei Linmao
Jet Li's Fearless *208*

Jack Livesey (1901-61)
Sherrybaby *358*

Henning Lohner
BloodRayne *44*

Henry Mancini (1924-94)
The Pink Panther *304*

Clint Mansell
The Fountain *144*
Trust the Man *400*

Dario Marianelli
The Return *327*
V for Vendetta *419*

Phil Marshall
Hoot *186*

Mac McAnally
Hoot *186*

Wendy Melvoin (1964-)
Something New *369*

Alan Menken (1949-)
The Shaggy Dog *357*

Mike D (1965-)
Awesome! I F***in' Shot That! *23*

Philip Miller
Catch a Fire *67*

Robert Miller
Why We Fight *436*

Mukstar Mirzakeev
Night Watch *283*

Richard G. Mitchell
A Good Woman *163*

Bob Mothersbaugh
How to Eat Fried Worms *189*

Mark Mothersbaugh (1950-)
How to Eat Fried Worms *189*

Mukul
Unknown White Male *413*

John Murphy
Basic Instinct 2 *31*
Miami Vice *262*

Jennie Muskett
Material Girls *261*

Peter Nashel
The Night Listener *282*

Javier Navarrete
Pan's Labyrinth *299*

Randy Newman (1943-)
Cars *63*

Thomas Newman (1955-)
The Good German *159*
Little Children *237*

Erik Nordgren
Tristram Shandy: A Cock and Bull Story *398*

Michael Nyman
The Libertine *236*
Tristram Shandy: A Cock and Bull Story *398*

Molly Nyman
Hard Candy *175*

John Ottman (1964-)
Superman Returns *379*

Ronald Owen
End of the Spear *119*

Andreea Paduraru
The Death of Mr. Lazarescu *94*

Michael Penn
The Last Kiss *232*

Heitor Pereira
Ask the Dust *19*
Curious George *85*

Tyler Perry
Madea's Family Reunion *251*

Steven R. Phillips
Larry the Cable Guy: Health Inspector *227*

Franco Piersanti
Don't Tell *108*

Douglas Pipes
Monster House *268*

Robert Pollard
Bubble *57*

Rachel Portman (1960-)
Infamous *200*
The Lake House *225*

Randall Poster
The Pink Panther *304*

Yuri Potyeyenko
Night Watch *283*

John Powell
Happy Feet *173*
Ice Age: The Meltdown *191*
United 93 *412*
X-Men: The Last Stand *447*

Trevor Rabin (1954-)
Flyboys *140*
Glory Road *156*
The Guardian *170*
Snakes on a Plane *366*

Corinne Bailey Rae
Venus *421*

A.R. Rahman
Water *430*

J. Ralph
Lucky Number Slevin *249*

Brian Reitzell
Stranger Than Fiction *375*

Graeme Revell (1955-)
Goal! The Dream Begins *157*
Man of the Year *252*

Graham Reynolds
A Scanner Darkly *342*

Craig Richey
Friends with Money *148*

J. Peter Robinson
The World's Fastest Indian *445*

Philippe Rombi
Joyeux Noel *211*

Jeff Rona (1957-)
The Quiet *325*

Elvin D. Ross
Madea's Family Reunion *251*

Alejandro Rosso
Duck Season *113*

Nino Rota (1911-79)
Tristram Shandy: A Cock and Bull Story *398*

Gustavo Santaolalla
Babel *27*

David Schommer
Accepted *1*

Theodore Shapiro
The Devil Wears Prada *104*
Idiocracy *192*

Howard Shore (1946-)
The Departed *99*

Alan Silvestri (1950-)
Night at the Museum *280*
The Wild *439*

Mike Simpson
Stick It *373*

Christopher Slaski
The Piano Tuner of Earthquakes *303*

Michael W. Smith
The Second Chance *351*

Michael Stevens
Letters from Iwo Jima *234*

Paul Anthony Stewart
Something New *369*

Marc Streitenfeld
A Good Year *164*

Mark Suozzo
The Notorious Bettie Page *286*

John Swihart
Employee of the Month *118*

Tenacious D
Tenacious D in the Pick of Destiny *386*

Yo La Tengo
Game 6 *152*

Tim P.
Larry the Cable Guy: Health Inspector *227*

Tomandandy
The Covenant *81*
The Hills Have Eyes *178*

Stephen Trask
American Dreamz *6*

Brian Tyler
Annapolis *10*
The Fast and the Furious: Tokyo Drift *128*

Shingeru Umebayashi
Curse of the Golden Flower *86*

Michael Utley
Hoot *186*

Fabio Vacchi
Gabrielle *151*

C.J. Vanston
For Your Consideration *142*

James L. Venable
Clerks II *76*
Scary Movie 4 *344*

Valera Viktorov
Night Watch *283*

Waddy Wachtel
The Benchwarmers *34*
Grandma's Boy *166*

Shirley Walker
Black Christmas *38*
Final Destination 3 *130*

P.T. Walkley
The Groomsmen *167*

Nathan Wang
She's the Man *360*

Paul Westerberg
Open Season *294*

Alex Wurman (1966-)
Talladega Nights: The Ballad of Ricky Bobby *384*

Adam "MCA" Yauch (1964-)
Awesome! I F***in' Shot That! *23*

Christopher Young (1954-)
The Grudge 2 *169*

Neil Young (1945-)
Neil Young: Heart of Gold *278*

Marcelo Zarvos
The Boynton Beach Club *49*
The Good Shepherd *161*
Hollywoodland *183*

Aaron Zigman
Akeelah and the Bee *2*
ATL *21*
Flicka *138*
Step Up *372*
Take the Lead *383*

Hans Zimmer (1957-)
The Da Vinci Code *88*
The Holiday *181*
Pirates of the Caribbean: Dead Man's Chest *306*

Performer Index

Hiam Abbass
The Nativity Story *276*

Khalid Abdalla
United 93 *412*

Ian Abercrombie (1933-)
Garfield: A Tail of Two Kitties *154*
Inland Empire *201*

Michael Abiteboul
Manderlay *254*

Simon Abkarian
Casino Royale *65*

John Abraham
Water *430*

Kirk Acevedo
Invincible *204*

Amy Adams
Talladega Nights: The Ballad of Ricky Bobby *384*

Jane Adams (1921-)
Last Holiday *229*

Joey Lauren Adams (1971-)
The Break-Up *51*

Polly Adams
United 93 *412*

Meat Loaf Aday (1948-)
BloodRayne *44*
Tenacious D in the Pick of Destiny *386*

Jerry Adler (1929-)
Find Me Guilty *131*

Sean Michael Afable (1988-)
Akeelah and the Bee *2*

Ben Affleck (1972-)
Clerks II *76*
Hollywoodland *183*

Casey Affleck (1975-)
The Last Kiss *232*
Lonesome Jim *242*

Walid Afkir
Cache *61*

Shohreh Aghdashloo
American Dreamz *6*
The Lake House *225*
The Nativity Story *276*
X-Men: The Last Stand *447*

Waris Ahluwalia
Inside Man *202*

Danny Aiello (1933-)
Lucky Number Slevin *249*

Carrie Aizley
For Your Consideration *142*

Lucy Akhurst
Don't Tell *108*

Carlo Alban
Strangers with Candy *377*

Shari Albert
The Groomsmen *167*

Tom Aldredge (1928-)
Game 6 *152*

Kelly Aldridge
Deck the Halls *96*

Sabrina Aldridge
Deck the Halls *96*

Erika Alexander
Deja Vu *97*

Flex Alexander
Snakes on a Plane *366*

Sasha Alexander
Mission: Impossible III *264*

David Alford
The Second Chance *351*

Roger Allam
V for Vendetta *419*

Chad Allen (1974-)
End of the Spear *119*

Karen Allen (1951-)
Poster Boy *309*

Tanya Allen
Silent Hill *361*

Tim Allen (1953-)
The Santa Clause 3: The Escape Clause *339*
The Shaggy Dog *357*
Zoom *451*

Woody Allen (1935-)
Scoop *349*

Erinn Allison
The Return *327*

Maria Conchita Alonso (1957-)
Material Girls *261*

Lewis Alsamari
United 93 *412*

Bruce Altman
Running Scared *330*

John Patrick Amedori (1987-)
Stick It *373*

Doru Ana
The Death of Mr. Lazarescu *94*

Anthony Anderson (1970-)
The Departed *99*
Hoodwinked *(V)* *185*
Scary Movie 4 *344*

Gillian Anderson (1968-)
The Last King of Scotland *231*
Tristram Shandy: A Cock and Bull Story *398*

Jeff Anderson
Clerks II *76*

Kevin Anderson (1960-)
Charlotte's Web *71*

Pamela Anderson (1967-)
Borat: Cultural Learnings of America for Make Benefit Glorious Nation of Kazakhstan *48*

Sam Anderson
The History Boys *179*

Andre 3000
See Andre Benjamin

Hollie Andrew
Somersault *367*

Brandon D. Andrews
Take the Lead *383*

Sebastien Andrieu
Ultraviolet *407*

Maya Angelou (1928-)
Madea's Family Reunion *251*

Alex Angulo
Pan's Labyrinth *299*

Christien Anholt (1971-)
Flyboys *140*

Jennifer Aniston (1969-)
The Break-Up *51*
Friends with Money *148*

Ann-Margret (1941-)
The Break-Up *51*
The Santa Clause 3: The Escape Clause *339*

Francesca Annis (1944-)
The Libertine *236*

John Archie
Hoot *186*

Lee Arenberg (1962-)
Pirates of the Caribbean: Dead Man's Chest *306*

Asia Argento (1975-)
Marie Antoinette *257*

Moises Arias
Nacho Libre *273*

Alan Arkin (1934-)
Firewall *133*
Little Miss Sunshine *240*
The Santa Clause 3: The Escape Clause *339*

Alun Armstrong (1946-)
Eragon *121*

Curtis Armstrong (1953-)
Akeelah and the Bee *2*

Samaire Armstrong
Just My Luck *213*
Stay Alive *371*

Will Arnett
Ice Age: The Meltdown *(V)* *191*
RV *335*

Enrique Arreola
Duck Season *113*

Lisa Arrindell Anderson
Madea's Family Reunion *251*
The Second Chance *351*

Arif Asci
Climates *80*

Ashanti
John Tucker Must Die *209*

Clare-Hope Ashitey
Children of Men *74*

Heather Ashleigh
Down in the Valley *109*

Alicia Ashley
Strangers with Candy *377*

Dustin Ashley
Bubble *57*

Shawn Ashmore (1979-)
The Quiet *325*
X-Men: The Last Stand *447*

Desmond Askew
The Hills Have Eyes *178*
Turistas *404*

Sean Astin (1971-)
Click *78*

Eileen Atkins (1934-)
Ask the Dust *19*

Rowan Atkinson (1955-)
Keeping Mum *215*

Dave Attell
Scary Movie 4 *344*

Jake T. Austin (1994-)
The Ant Bully *(V)* *11*
Everyone's Hero *(V)* *122*

Daniel Auteuil (1950-)
Cache *61*

Aviva
Down in the Valley *109*

Alejandro Awada
The Aura *22*

Rochelle Aytes
Madea's Family Reunion *251*

Lubna Azabal
Changing Times *69*

Obba Babatunde
Material Girls *261*

Lucas Babin
Brick *53*

Lauren Bacall (1924-)
Manderlay *254*

Kevin Bacon (1958-)
Loverboy *247*

Sosie Bacon
Loverboy *247*

Penn Badgley (1986-)
John Tucker Must Die *209*

Carlos Emilio Baez
Apocalypto *12*

Tim Bagley
Employee of the Month *118*

Iris Bahr
Larry the Cable Guy: Health Inspector *227*

David Bailie
Pirates of the Caribbean: Dead Man's Chest *306*

Mireille Bailly
The Child *73*

Diora Baird
The Texas Chainsaw Massacre: The Beginning *387*

Dylan Baker (1958-)
The Matador *260*

Kathy Baker (1950-)
All the King's Men *4*

Simon Baker (1969-)
The Devil Wears Prada *104*
Something New *369*

Sara Kathryn Bakker
End of the Spear *119*

Bob Balaban (1945-)
For Your Consideration *142*
Lady in the Water *223*

Alec Baldwin (1958-)
The Departed *99*
The Good Shepherd *161*
Running with Scissors *331*

Christian Bale (1974-)
The Prestige *313*

Fairuza Balk (1974-)
Don't Come Knocking *106*

Talia Balsam (1960-)
All the King's Men *4*

Maria Bamford (1970-)
Barnyard *(V)* *30*

Antonio Banderas (1960-)
Take the Lead *383*

Elizabeth Banks
Invincible *204*
Slither *365*

Ivana Baquero
Pan's Labyrinth *299*

Abdelkader Bara
Babel *27*

Nabila Baraka
Changing Times *69*

Frances Barber (1958-)
Goal! The Dream Begins *157*

Christian Barbier (1924-)
Army of Shadows *16*

Bridget Barkan
Sherrybaby *358*

Ellen Barkin (1954-)
Trust the Man *400*

Pat Barlow
Nanny McPhee *275*

Hebe Barnes
Nanny McPhee *275*

Zinnia Barnes
Nanny McPhee *275*

Samuel Barnett
The History Boys *179*

Jean-Marc Barr (1960-)
Manderlay *254*

Adriana Barraza
Babel *27*

Jacinda Barrett
The Last Kiss *232*
Poseidon *308*
School for Scoundrels *345*

Drew Barrymore (1975-)
Curious George *(V)* *85*

Justin Bartha
Failure to Launch *127*
Trust the Man *400*

Erinn Bartlett
The Benchwarmers *34*

Gary Basaraba (1959-)
Charlotte's Web *71*

David Alan Basche
United 93 *412*

Dante Basco (1975-)
Take the Lead *383*

Kim Basinger (1953-)
The Sentinel *353*

Angela Bassett (1958-)
Akeelah and the Bee *2*

Linda Bassett
Kinky Boots *220*

Geoffrey Bateman
Manderlay *254*

Jason Bateman (1969-)
The Break-Up *51*

Kathy Bates (1948-)
Charlotte's Web *71*
Failure to Launch *127*

Guiseppe Battiston
Don't Tell *108*

Texas Battle
Final Destination 3 *130*

Vanessa Bauche
The Three Burials of Melquiades Estrada *391*

Chris Bauer
Flags of Our Fathers *135*
The Notorious Bettie Page *286*

Steven Bauer (1956-)
The Lost City *245*

Shane Baumel (1997-)
Over the Hedge *(V)* *295*

Adam Beach (1972-)
Flags of Our Fathers *135*

Kate Beahan
The Return *327*
The Wicker Man *437*

Jennifer Beals (1963-)
The Grudge 2 *169*

Sean Bean (1959-)
Silent Hill *361*

Kuno Becker
Goal! The Dream Begins *157*

David Beckham (1975-)
Goal! The Dream Begins *157*

Kate Beckinsale (1974-)
Click *78*
Underworld: Evolution *410*

Ed Begley, Jr. (1949-)
For Your Consideration *142*

Robert Beitzel
Winter Passing *441*

Richard Bekins
United 93 *412*

Harry Belafonte (1927-)
Bobby *45*

Cassandra Bell
Goal! The Dream Begins *157*

Jamie Bell (1986-)
Flags of Our Fathers *135*

Kristen Bell (1980-)
Pulse *318*

Tobin Bell
Saw III *340*

Camilla Belle (1986-)
The Quiet *325*
When a Stranger Calls *434*

Maria Bello (1967-)
Flicka *138*
Thank You for Smoking *389*
World Trade Center *443*

James Belushi (1954-)
Hoodwinked *(V)* *185*
The Wild *(V)* *439*

Lucas Belvaux
Joyeux Noel *211*

Maurice Benichou
Cache *61*

Annette Bening (1958-)
Running with Scissors *331*

Andre Benjamin
Charlotte's Web *71*
Idlewild *194*

Richard Benjamin (1938-)
Keeping Up with the Steins *216*

Eliza Bennett (1993-)
Nanny McPhee *275*

Jimmy Bennett
Firewall *133*
Poseidon *308*

Lyriq Bent
Saw III *340*

Kenda Benward
The Second Chance *351*

Luke Benward
How to Eat Fried Worms *189*

A.J. Benza
Rocky Balboa *328*

Shelley Berman (1926-)
The Holiday *181*

Gael Garcia Bernal (1978-)
Babel *27*
The King *218*
The Science of Sleep *347*

Elizabeth Berrington
Tristram Shandy: A Cock and Bull Story *398*

Halle Berry (1968-)
X-Men: The Last Stand *447*

Paul Bettany (1971-)
The Da Vinci Code *88*
Firewall *133*

Florrie Betts
Marie Antoinette *257*

Dante "Mos Def" Beze (1973-)
16 Blocks *363*

Abigail Bianca
The Marine *259*

Leslie Bibb (1974-)
Talladega Nights: The Ballad of Ricky Bobby *384*

Jessica Biel (1982-)
The Illusionist *196*

Craig Bierko (1965-)
Scary Movie 4 *344*

Big Boi
See Antwan Andre Patton

Jason Biggs (1978-)
Eight Below *117*

Roy Billing
Aquamarine *14*

Earl Billings
Something New *369*

Peter Billingsley (1971-)
The Break-Up *51*

Rachel Bilson
The Last Kiss *232*

Valerio Binasco
Don't Tell *108*

Juliette Binoche (1964-)
Cache *61*

Morris Birdyellowhead
Apocalypto *12*

Eva Birthistle
Imagine Me & You *197*

Kevin Bishop (1980-)
Russian Dolls *334*

Joachim Bissmeier
Joyeux Noel *211*

Seema Biswas
Water *430*

Jack Black (1969-)
The Holiday *181*
Nacho Libre *273*
Tenacious D in the Pick of Destiny *386*

Lewis Black (1948-)
Accepted *1*
Man of the Year *252*
Unaccompanied Minors *408*

Lucas Black (1982-)
The Fast and the Furious: Tokyo Drift *128*

Julia Blake (1936-)
Aquamarine *14*

JB Blanc
Tristan & Isolde *396*

Rachel Blanchard (1976-)
Snakes on a Plane *366*

Tammy Blanchard (1976-)
The Good Shepherd *161*

Cate Blanchett (1969-)
Babel *27*
The Good German *159*
Notes on a Scandal *284*

Carlos Blanco
Volver *423*

Susan Blommaert
United 93 *412*

Moon Bloodgood
Eight Below *117*

Orlando Bloom (1977-)
Pirates of the Caribbean: Dead Man's Chest *306*

Dylan Blue
Deck the Halls *96*

Emily Blunt
The Devil Wears Prada *104*

Qian Bo
The Promise *315*

Peter Bogdanovich (1939-)
Infamous *200*

Joseph Bologna (1938-)
The Boynton Beach Club *49*
Ice Age: The Meltdown *(V)* *191*

Catharine Bolz
The Groomsmen *167*

Matt Bomer
The Texas Chainsaw Massacre: The Beginning *387*

Alessio Boni
Don't Tell *108*

Dany Boon
Joyeux Noel *211*

Mark Boone, Jr. (1955-)
Lonesome Jim *242*

James Booth (1930-)
Keeping Mum *215*

Paul Borghese
Find Me Guilty *131*

Alex Borstein (1972-)
Little Man *239*

Kate (Catherine) Bosworth (1983-)
Superman Returns *379*

Sam Bottoms (1955-)
Sherrybaby *358*

Sacha Bourdo
The Science of Sleep *347*

Didier Bourdon
A Good Year *164*

Solene Bouten
The Bridesmaid *55*

Bow Wow (1987-)
The Fast and the Furious: Tokyo Drift *128*

Tom Bower
The Hills Have Eyes *178*

David Bowie (1947-)
The Prestige *313*

Darren Boyd
Imagine Me & You *197*

Lynda Boyd
The Fast and the Furious: Tokyo Drift *128*

Peter Boyle (1933-2006)
The Santa Clause 3: The Escape Clause *339*

Jesse Bradford (1979-)
Flags of Our Fathers *135*

Richard Bradford (1937-)
The Lost City *245*

Josef Bradna
Hostel *188*

Terry Bradshaw
Failure to Launch *127*

Zach Braff
The Last Kiss *232*

Bonnie Bramlett
The Guardian *170*

Virgile Bramly
Manderlay *254*

Marlon Brando (1924-2004)
Superman Returns *379*

Andre Braugher (1962-)
Poseidon *308*

Duncan Bravo
Looking for Comedy in the Muslim World *244*

Alex Breckinridge
She's the Man *360*

Abigail Breslin (1996-)
Little Miss Sunshine *240*

Spencer Breslin (1992-)
The Santa Clause 3: The Escape Clause *339*
The Shaggy Dog *357*
Zoom *451*

Jonathan Brewer
Apocalypto *12*

Jordana Brewster (1980-)
Annapolis *10*
The Texas Chainsaw Massacre: The Beginning *387*

Paget Brewster
Unaccompanied Minors *408*

Beau Bridges (1941-)
Charlotte's Web *71*
The Good German *159*

Jeff Bridges (1949-)
Stick It *373*
Tideland *392*

Cameron Bright (1993-)
Running Scared *330*
Thank You for Smoking *389*
Ultraviolet *407*
X-Men: The Last Stand *447*

Ruben Brinkman
Manderlay *254*

Jim Broadbent (1949-)
Art School Confidential *18*

Matthew Broderick (1962-)
Deck the Halls *96*
Strangers with Candy *377*

Adam Brody (1980-)
Thank You for Smoking *389*

Adrien Brody (1973-)
Hollywoodland *183*

Liam Broggy (2000-)
Trust the Man *400*

Shane Brolly
Underworld: Evolution *410*

Albert Brooks (1947-)
Looking for Comedy in the Muslim World *244*

Golden Brooks
Something New *369*

Mehcad Brooks
Glory Road *156*

Pierce Brosnan (1953-)
The Matador *260*

Blair Brown (1948-)
Loverboy *247*
The Sentinel *353*

Clancy Brown (1959-)
The Guardian *170*

Gaye Brown
An American Haunting *8*

Max Brown
Turistas *404*

Rob Brown (1984-)
Take the Lead *383*

Roscoe Lee Browne (1925-)
Garfield: A Tail of Two Kitties *(V)* *154*

Bruce Bruce
Larry the Cable Guy: Health Inspector *227*

Daniel Bruhl (1978-)
Joyeux Noel *211*

Valeria Bruni-Tedeschi
Time to Leave *394*

Zachery Ty Bryan (1981-)
The Fast and the Furious: Tokyo Drift *128*

Joy Bryant
Bobby *45*

Rob Brydon
Tristram Shandy: A Cock and Bull Story *398*

Andrew Bryniarski
The Texas Chainsaw Massacre: The Beginning *387*

Jimmy Buffett (1946-)
Hoot *186*

Lubomir Bukovy
Hostel *188*

Sandra Bullock (1964-)
Infamous *200*
The Lake House *225*
Loverboy *247*

MyAnna Buring
The Descent *101*

Kathy Burke (1964-)
Flushed Away *(V)* *139*

Marylouise Burke
A Prairie Home Companion *311*

Edward Burns (1968-)
The Groomsmen *167*
The Holiday *181*

Heather Burns
The Groomsmen *167*

Ty Burrell (1967-)
Friends with Money *148*

Ellen Burstyn (1932-)
The Fountain *144*
The Wicker Man *437*

Tony Burton
Rocky Balboa *328*

Steve Buscemi (1957-)
Art School Confidential *18*
Charlotte's Web *71*
Monster House *(V)* *268*

Sophia Bush (1982-)
John Tucker Must Die *209*
Stay Alive *371*

Gerard Butler (1969-)
Beowulf & Grendel *35*

Amanda Bynes (1986-)
She's the Man *360*

Dan Byrd
The Hills Have Eyes *178*

Gabriel Byrne (1950-)
Wah-Wah *425*

Rose Byrne (1979-)
Marie Antoinette *257*

Scott Caan (1976-)
Friends with Money *148*

Nicolas Cage (1964-)
The Ant Bully *(V)* *11*
The Wicker Man *437*
World Trade Center *443*

Anne Caillon
Basic Instinct 2 *31*

Michael Caine (1933-)
Children of Men *74*
The Prestige *313*

Paul Calderon
The Sentinel *353*

Bryan Callen
Scary Movie 4 *344*

Adam Campbell
Date Movie *91*

Bruce Campbell (1958-)
The Ant Bully *(V)* *11*

Conchita Campbell
Scary Movie 4 *344*

Isabelle Candelier
A Good Year *164*

Guillaume Canet
Joyeux Noel *211*

Bobby Cannavale (1971-)
The Night Listener *282*
Snakes on a Plane *366*

Dyan Cannon (1937-)
The Boynton Beach Club *49*

Nick Cannon (1980-)
Bobby *45*
Monster House *(V)* *268*

Jose Pablo Cantillo
Crank *83*

Jessica Capshaw (1976-)
The Groomsmen *167*

Nestor Carbonell (1967-)
The Lost City *245*

Linda Cardellini (1975-)
Grandma's Boy *166*

Steven Carell (1963-)
Little Miss Sunshine *240*
Over the Hedge *(V)* *295*

Gia Carides (1964-)
Stick It *373*

Len Cariou (1939-)
The Boynton Beach Club *49*
Flags of Our Fathers *135*

George Carlin (1937-)
Cars *(V)* *63*

Kelly Carlson
The Marine *259*

Robert Carlyle (1961-)
Eragon *121*

Jeff Obafemi Carr
The Second Chance *351*

Kevin Carroll
The Notorious Bettie Page *286*

Madeleine Carroll (1906-87)
When a Stranger Calls *434*

Anna Carteret
Mrs. Palfrey at the Claremont *266*

Roger Casamajor
Pan's Labyrinth *299*

Amira Casar
The Piano Tuner of Earthquakes *303*

Jean-Pierre Cassel (1932-)
Army of Shadows *16*

Seymour Cassel (1935-)
Lonesome Jim *242*

Joanna Cassidy (1944-)
Larry the Cable Guy: Health Inspector *227*

Katie Cassidy (1986-)
Black Christmas *38*
When a Stranger Calls *434*

Michael Cassidy
Zoom *451*

Rafael Castejon (1931-)
The Aura *22*

Dan Castellaneta (1958-)
The Pursuit of Happyness *319*

Keisha Castle-Hughes
The Nativity Story *276*

Diego Catano
Duck Season *113*

Mary Jo Catlett (1938-)
The Benchwarmers *34*

Jessica Cauffiel (1976-)
Hoot *186*

Tom Cavanagh
How to Eat Fried Worms *189*

James (Jim) Caviezel (1968-)
Deja Vu *97*

Henry Cavill
Tristan & Isolde *396*

Fulvio Cecere
John Tucker Must Die *209*

Julio Cesar Cedillo
The Three Burials of Melquiades Estrada *391*

Cedric the Entertainer (1964-)
Charlotte's Web *71*

Pablo Cedron
The Aura *22*

Laura Cellner
Wassup Rockers *429*

John Cena
The Marine *259*

Jorge Cervera
Goal! The Dream Begins *157*

Richard Cetrone
Underworld: Evolution *410*

Ebru Ceylan
Climates *80*

Nuri Bilge Ceylan
Climates *80*

Alain Chabat (1958-)
The Science of Sleep *347*

Lacey Chabert (1982-)
Black Christmas *38*

Alexsei Chadov
Night Watch *283*

Kevin Chamberlin (1963-)
Lucky Number Slevin *249*

Jay Chandrasekhar
Beerfest *32*

Geraldine Chaplin (1944-)
BloodRayne *44*

Dave Chappelle (1973-)
Dave Chappelle's Block Party *92*

Ray Charleson
United 93 *412*

Chevy Chase (1943-)
Zoom *451*

Melody Chase (1968-)
A Scanner Darkly *342*

Edison Chen (1980-)
The Grudge 2 *169*

Kristin Chenoweth
Deck the Halls *96*
The Pink Panther *304*
Running with Scissors *331*
RV *335*

Don Cherry
The Wild *(V)* *439*

Jake Cherry
Night at the Museum *280*

Cecilia Cheung
The Promise *315*

Cindy Cheung
Lady in the Water *223*

Sonny Chiba (1939-)
The Fast and the Furious: Tokyo Drift *128*

Etienne Chicot
The Da Vinci Code *88*

Nicholas Chinlund (1961-)
Ultraviolet *407*

John Cho
American Dreamz *6*

Collin Chou
See Sing Ngai

Jay Chou
Curse of the Golden Flower *86*

Sarita Choudhury (1966-)
Lady in the Water *223*

Ranjit (Chaudry) Chowdhry
Last Holiday *229*

Jesper Christensen
Casino Royale *65*

Eric Christian
The Last Kiss *232*

Dyllan Christopher
Unaccompanied Minors *408*

Bruce Church
See Bruce Bruce

Thomas Haden Church (1960-)
Charlotte's Web *71*
Idiocracy *192*
Over the Hedge *(V)* *295*

Presley Chweneyagae
Tsotsi *401*

Shirl Cieutat
Last Holiday *229*

Greg Cipes
The Wild *(V)* *439*

Blake Clark (1946-)
The Benchwarmers *34*

Patricia Clarkson (1960-)
All the King's Men *4*

Jill Clayburgh (1944-)
Running with Scissors *331*

John Cleese (1939-)
Charlotte's Web *71*

Christian Clemenson (1959-)
United 93 *412*

Aurore Clement
The Bridesmaid *55*

Kristen Cloke (1970-)
Black Christmas *38*

George Clooney (1961-)
The Good German *159*

Glenn Close (1947-)
Hoodwinked (V) *185*

Kim Coates
Silent Hill *361*

Bill Cobbs (1935-)
Night at the Museum *280*

Yohana Cobo
Volver *423*

Rory Cochrane (1972-)
A Scanner Darkly *342*

Shirley Cody
The Second Chance *351*

Scott Coffey (1967-)
Inland Empire (V) *201*

Sacha Baron Cohen (1971-)
Borat: Cultural Learnings of America for Make Benefit Glorious Nation of Kazakhstan *48*
Talladega Nights: The Ballad of Ricky Bobby *384*

Stephen Colbert
Strangers with Candy *377*

Gary Cole (1957-)
Talladega Nights: The Ballad of Ricky Bobby *384*

Anthony Coleman
Blood Diamond *41*

Raphael Coleman
Nanny McPhee *275*

Claudia Coli
Gabrielle *151*

Toni Collette (1972-)
Little Miss Sunshine *240*
The Night Listener *282*

Dean Collins (1990-)
Hoot *186*

Lauren Collins
Take the Lead *383*

Lynn Collins
The Lake House *225*

Stephen Collins (1947-)
Blood Diamond *41*

Stan Collymore
Basic Instinct 2 *31*

Marcus Coloma
Material Girls *261*

Miriam Colon (1945-)
Goal! The Dream Begins *157*

Jennifer Connelly (1970-)
Blood Diamond *41*
Little Children *237*

Bart Conner
Stick It *373*

Billy Connolly (1942-)
Garfield: A Tail of Two Kitties *154*
Open Season (V) *294*

Frances Conroy (1953-)
The Wicker Man *437*

Mark Consuelos
My Super Ex-Girlfriend *270*

Kevin Conway (1942-)
Invincible *204*

Steve Coogan
Marie Antoinette *257*
Night at the Museum *280*
Tristram Shandy: A Cock and Bull Story *398*

Dane Cook
Employee of the Month *118*

Jennifer Coolidge
American Dreamz *6*
Click *78*
Date Movie *91*
For Your Consideration *142*

Bradley Cooper
Failure to Launch *127*

Dominic Cooper
The History Boys *179*

Rob Corddry
Unaccompanied Minors *408*

James Corden
The History Boys *179*

Abbie Cornish
A Good Year *164*
Somersault *367*

Nick Corri
See Jsu Garcia

Kevin Corrigan (1969-)
The Departed *99*
Lonesome Jim *242*

Miranda Cosgrove (1993-)
Keeping Up with the Steins *216*

Ritchie Coster
The Sentinel *353*

Nikolaj Coster-Waldau (1970-)
Firewall *133*

Kevin Costner (1955-)
The Guardian *170*

Marion Cotillard
A Good Year *164*

Christopher Cousins
The Grudge 2 *169*

Allen Covert
Grandma's Boy *166*

Brian Cox (1946-)
Running with Scissors *331*

Courteney Cox (1964-)
Barnyard (V) *30*
Zoom *451*

Tony Cox (1958-)
Date Movie *91*

Richard Coyle
The Libertine *236*

Cylk Cozart
16 Blocks *363*

Daniel Craig (1968-)
Casino Royale *65*
Infamous *200*

Kenneth Cranham (1944-)
A Good Year *164*

Paul Crauchet (1920-)
Army of Shadows *16*

Chace Crawford
The Covenant *81*

Amanda Crew
Final Destination 3 *130*

Terry Crews
The Benchwarmers *34*
Idiocracy *192*

Wendy Crewson (1956-)
The Covenant *81*
Eight Below *117*
The Santa Clause 3: The Escape Clause *339*

Dona Croll
Manderlay *254*

James Cromwell (1940-)
The Queen *323*

Mackenzie Crook
Pirates of the Caribbean: Dead Man's Chest *306*

David Cross (1964-)
Curious George (V) *85*
School for Scoundrels *345*
She's the Man *360*

Joseph Cross
Flags of Our Fathers *135*
Running with Scissors *331*
Strangers with Candy *377*

Russell Crowe (1964-)
A Good Year *164*

Billy Crudup (1968-)
The Good Shepherd *161*
Mission: Impossible III *264*
Trust the Man *400*

Tom Cruise (1962-)
Mission: Impossible III *264*

Jeremy Crutchley
Ask the Dust *19*

Penelope Cruz (1974-)
Volver *423*

Michael Cudlitz
Running Scared *330*

Daniel Cudmore
X-Men: The Last Stand *447*

Rory Culkin (1989-)
Down in the Valley *109*
The Night Listener *282*

John Cullum (1930-)
The Night Listener *282*
The Notorious Bettie Page *286*

Maddy Curley
Stick It *373*

Lynette Curran (1945-)
Somersault *367*

Tony Curran
Beowulf & Grendel *35*
The Good German *159*
Underworld: Evolution *410*

Tim Curry (1946-)
Garfield: A Tail of Two Kitties *(V)* *154*

Jane Curtin (1947-)
The Shaggy Dog *357*

Clifford Curtis (1968-)
The Fountain *144*

Ann Cusack (1961-)
Accepted *1*

Joan Cusack (1962-)
Friends with Money *148*

Sinead Cusack (1948-)
V for Vendetta *419*

Elisha Cuthbert
The Quiet *325*

Henry Czerny (1959-)
The Pink Panther *304*

Gerson Da Cunha
Water *430*

Yaya DaCosta
Take the Lead *383*

Willem Dafoe (1955-)
American Dreamz *6*
Inside Man *202*
Manderlay *254*

Ni Dahong
Curse of the Golden Flower *86*

E.J. Daily
Happy Feet *(V)* *173*

Nadia Dajani
Game 6 *152*

James Dale
The Departed *99*

Kristen Dalton
The Departed *99*

Matt Damon (1970-)
The Departed *99*
The Good Shepherd *161*

Charles Dance (1946-)
Scoop *349*

Hugh Dancy (1975-)
Basic Instinct 2 *31*

Eric Dane
X-Men: The Last Stand *447*

Brittany Daniel (1976-)
Little Man *239*

Albert Daniels
ATL *21*

Alex Daniels (1956-)
The Guardian *170*

Bobby Daniels
The Second Chance *351*

Jeff Daniels (1955-)
Infamous *200*
RV *335*

Blythe Danner (1944-)
The Last Kiss *232*

Paul Franklin Dano (1984-)
The King *218*
Little Miss Sunshine *240*

Peter Dante
Grandma's Boy *166*

James D'Arcy
An American Haunting *8*

Ricardo Darin (1957-)
The Aura *22*

Jack Davenport (1973-)
The Libertine *236*
Pirates of the Caribbean: Dead Man's Chest *306*

Madison Davenport (1996-)
Over the Hedge *(V)* *295*

Seamus Davey-Fitzpatrick
The Omen *292*

Keith David (1954-)
ATL *21*

Jeremy Davies (1969-)
Manderlay *254*

Essie Davis
Charlotte's Web *71*

Hope Davis (1964-)
Infamous *200*
The Matador *260*

Judy Davis (1956-)
The Break-Up *51*
Marie Antoinette *257*

Kristen Davis (1965-)
Deck the Halls *96*
The Shaggy Dog *357*

Lucy Davis
Garfield: A Tail of Two Kitties *154*

Matthew Davis
BloodRayne *44*

Oliver Davis (1993-)
Lucky Number Slevin *249*

Ken Davitian
Borat: Cultural Learnings of America for Make Benefit Glorious Nation of Kazakhstan *48*

Rosario Dawson (1979-)
Clerks II *76*

Jenny Daykin
Nanny McPhee *275*

Isaach de Bankole
Casino Royale *65*
Manderlay *254*

Cecile de France
Russian Dolls *334*

Ana de la Reguera (1977-)
Nacho Libre *273*

Antonio de la Torre
Volver *423*

Frances de la Tour
The History Boys *179*

Derek De Lint (1950-)
When a Stranger Calls *434*

Robert De Niro (1943-)
The Good Shepherd *161*

Alain de Noyencourt
The Science of Sleep *347*

Emilie de Ravin
Brick *53*
The Hills Have Eyes *178*

Samuel de Ryck
The Child *73*

Nathaniel Dean
Somersault *367*

Mark DeCarlo
The Ant Bully *(V)* *11*

Jennifer Decker
Flyboys *140*

Martin Delaney
Beowulf & Grendel *35*

Diane Delano
The Wicker Man *437*

Idalis DeLeon (1966-)
Running Scared *330*

Jorge d'Elia
The Aura *22*

Paul DeMielche
Little Man *239*

Jeffrey DeMunn (1947-)
Hollywoodland *183*

Judi Dench (1934-)
Casino Royale *65*
Notes on a Scandal *284*

Catherine Deneuve (1943-)
Changing Times *69*

David Denman
When a Stranger Calls *434*

Brian Dennehy (1939-)
Everyone's Hero *(V)* *122*

Kat Dennings (1986-)
Big Momma's House 2 *37*
Down in the Valley *109*

Gerard Depardieu (1948-)
Changing Times *69*
Last Holiday *229*

Johnny Depp (1963-)
The Libertine *236*
Pirates of the Caribbean: Dead Man's Chest *306*

Bruce Dern (1936-)
Down in the Valley *109*

Laura Dern (1966-)
Inland Empire *201*

Mark Derwin
Accepted *1*

Emily Deschanel (1978-)
Glory Road *156*

Zooey Deschanel (1980-)
Failure to Launch *127*
Winter Passing *441*

Amanda Detmer (1971-)
You, Me and Dupree *449*

Loretta Devine (1949-)
Dreamgirls *111*

Danny DeVito (1944-)
Deck the Halls *96*

Jenna Dewan (1980-)
Step Up *372*
Take the Lead *383*

Sacha Dhawan
The History Boys *179*

Neil Diamond (1941-)
Keeping Up with the Steins *216*

Cameron Diaz (1972-)
The Holiday *181*

Maria Isabel Diaz
Volver *423*

Leonardo DiCaprio (1974-)
Blood Diamond *41*
The Departed *99*

Andy Dick (1965-)
Employee of the Month *118*
Hoodwinked *(V)* *185*

Kim Dickens (1965-)
Thank You for Smoking *389*

Janice Dickinson
Wassup Rockers *429*

John Diehl (1958-)
Down in the Valley *109*

Vin Diesel (1967-)
The Fast and the Furious: Tokyo Drift *128*
Find Me Guilty *131*

Stephen (Dillon) Dillane
Goal! The Dream Begins *157*

Brooke Dillman
Larry the Cable Guy: Health Inspector *227*

Denny Dillon
United 93 *412*

Kevin Dillon (1965-)
Poseidon *308*

Matt Dillon (1964-)
Factotum *125*
Loverboy *247*
You, Me and Dupree *449*

Paul Dinello
Strangers with Candy *377*

Peter Dinklage
Find Me Guilty *131*
Lassie *228*

Kim Director
Inside Man *202*

Omid Djalili (1965-)
Over the Hedge *(V)* *295*

Debbie Doebereiner
Bubble *57*

Dana Dogaru
The Death of Mr. Lazarescu *94*

Dagmara Dominczyk (1976-)
Trust the Man *400*

Jang Dong-gun
The Promise *315*

Vincent D'Onofrio (1959-)
The Break-Up *51*

Martin Donovan (1957-)
The Quiet *325*
The Sentinel *353*

Ryan Donowho (1980-)
Strangers with Candy *377*

Paul Dooley (1928-)
Cars *(V)* *63*

Stephen Dorff (1973-)
Shadowboxer *355*
World Trade Center *443*

Jamie Dornan
Marie Antoinette *257*

Homie Doroodian
Looking for Comedy in the Muslim World *244*

Michael Douglas (1944-)
The Sentinel *353*
You, Me and Dupree *449*

Brad Dourif (1950-)
Pulse *318*

Ann Dowd
The Notorious Bettie Page *286*

Robert Downey, Jr. (1965-)
Game 6 *152*
A Scanner Darkly *342*
The Shaggy Dog *357*

Billy Drago (1949-)
The Hills Have Eyes *178*

Joyful Drake
Phat Girlz *301*

Richard Dreyfuss (1947-)
Poseidon *308*

Anna Dubrovskaya
Night Watch *283*

Michel Duchaussoy (1938-)
The Bridesmaid *55*

David Duchovny (1960-)
Trust the Man *400*

Lola Duenas
Volver *423*

Haylie Duff (1985-)
Material Girls *261*

Hilary Duff (1987-)
Material Girls *261*

Dennis Dugan (1946-)
The Benchwarmers *34*

Josh Duhamel (1972-)
Turistas *404*

Bill Duke (1943-)
X-Men: The Last Stand *447*

Keir Dullea (1936-)
The Good Shepherd *161*

Pierre-Francois Dumeniaud
The Bridesmaid *55*

Michael Clarke Duncan (1957-)
School for Scoundrels *345*
Talladega Nights: The Ballad of Ricky Bobby *384*

Kevin Dunn (1956-)
All the King's Men *4*
The Black Dahlia *39*

Ryan Dunn (1977-)
Jackass Number Two *207*

Griffin Dunne (1955-)
Game 6 *152*

Kirsten Dunst (1982-)
Marie Antoinette *257*

Romain Duris
Russian Dolls *334*

Daniel Duval
Time to Leave *394*

Robert Duvall (1931-)
Thank You for Smoking *389*

Kieron Dyer
Goal! The Dream Begins *157*

Mio Dzakula
Stick It *373*

Steve Eastin
When a Stranger Calls *434*

Sam Easton
Final Destination 3 *130*

Eriq Ebouaney
The Nativity Story *276*

Aaron Eckhart (1968-)
The Black Dahlia *39*
Thank You for Smoking *389*

Gregg Edelman
Little Children *237*

Joel Edgerton
Kinky Boots *220*

Cory Edwards
Hoodwinked *(V)* *185*

Svetlana Efremova
Stick It *373*

Tamsin Egerton
Keeping Mum *215*

Jerome Ehlers (1958-)
The Marine *259*

Zach Tyler Eisen
See Zach Tyler

Hallie Kate Eisenberg (1992-)
How to Eat Fried Worms *189*

Chiwetel Ejiofor (1976-)
Children of Men *74*
Inside Man *202*
Kinky Boots *220*

Boubker Ait El Caid
Babel *27*

Ron Eldard (1965-)
Freedomland *146*

Carmen Electra (1972-)
Date Movie *91*
Scary Movie 4 *344*

Chris Elliott (1960-)
Scary Movie 4 *344*

Sam Elliott (1944-)
Barnyard *(V)* *30*
Thank You for Smoking *389*

Aunjanue Ellis
Freedomland *146*

Chase Ellison (1993-)
End of the Spear *119*

David Ellison
Flyboys *140*

Idir Elomri
Changing Times *69*

Jabir Elomri
Changing Times *69*

Noah Emmerich
Little Children *237*

Georgia Engel (1948-)
Open Season *(V)* *294*

Dave England
Jackass Number Two *207*

Mike Epps
Something New *369*

R. Lee Ermey (1944-)
The Texas Chainsaw Massacre: The Beginning *387*

Melissa Errico
Loverboy *247*

Mehmet Eryilmaz
Climates *80*

Raul Esparza
Find Me Guilty *131*

Giancarlo Esposito (1958-)
Last Holiday *229*
Sherrybaby *358*

Emilio Estevez (1962-)
Bobby *45*

Mike Estime
Last Holiday *229*

Troy Evans (1948-)
The Black Dahlia *39*

David Fabrizio
Superman Returns *379*

Donald Adeosun Faison (1974-)
Something New *369*

Marianne Faithfull (1946-)
Marie Antoinette *257*

Edie Falco (1954-)
Freedomland *146*
The Quiet *325*

Siobhan Fallon (1972-)
Charlotte's Web *71*

Roger Fan
Annapolis *10*

Dakota Fanning (1994-)
Charlotte's Web *71*

Elle Fanning
Babel *27*

Anna Faris
My Super Ex-Girlfriend *270*
Scary Movie 4 *344*

Vera Farmiga (1973-)
The Departed *99*
Running Scared *330*

Colin Farrell (1976-)
Ask the Dust *19*
Miami Vice *262*

Mia Farrow (1945-)
The Omen *292*

Jon Favreau (1966-)
The Break-Up *51*
Open Season *(V)* *294*

Trevor Fehrman
Clerks II *76*

Tovah Feldshuh (1952-)
Just My Luck *213*
Lady in the Water *223*

Thom Fell
An American Haunting *8*

Shelby Fenner
The Guardian *170*

J. Don Ferguson
The Second Chance *351*

Stacy "Fergie" Ferguson (1975-)
Poseidon *308*

Jodelle Ferland
Silent Hill *361*
Tideland *392*

Vanessa Ferlito
Shadowboxer *355*

Juan Fernandez
The Lost City *245*

Alex Ferns
Joyeux Noel *211*

Will Ferrell (1968-)
Curious George *(V)* *85*
Stranger Than Fiction *375*
Talladega Nights: The Ballad of Ricky Bobby *384*
Winter Passing *441*

Alex Ferris
RV *335*

Pam Ferris (1948-)
Children of Men *74*

William Fichtner (1956-)
Ultraviolet *407*

Joseph Fiennes (1970-)
Running with Scissors *331*

Nathan Fillion (1971-)
Slither *365*

William Finley (1944-)
The Black Dahlia *39*

Albert Finney (1936-)
A Good Year *164*

Angela Finocchiaro
Don't Tell *108*

Colin Firth (1961-)
Nanny McPhee *275*

Jenna Fischer (1974-)
Slither *365*

Ion Fiscuteanu
The Death of Mr. Lazarescu *94*

Laurence Fishburne (1963-)
Akeelah and the Bee *2*
Bobby *45*
Mission: Impossible III *264*

Didier Flamand
Factotum *125*

Tommy Flanagan (1965-)
When a Stranger Calls *434*

Barry Flatman
Saw III *340*

James Fleet
Tristram Shandy: A Cock and Bull Story *398*

Noah Fleiss (1984-)
Brick *53*

Brendan Fletcher (1981-)
RV *335*
Tideland *392*

Josh Flitter
Big Momma's House 2 *37*

Suzanne Flon (1918-)
Joyeux Noel *211*

Neil Flynn (1960-)
Hoot *186*

Dolores Fonzi
The Aura *22*

Harrison Ford (1942-)
Firewall *133*

Frederic Forrest (1938-)
All the King's Men *4*

Aaron Fors
Down in the Valley *109*

Robert Forster (1941-)
Firewall *133*
Lucky Number Slevin *249*

William Forsythe (1955-)
Freedomland *146*

Will Forte
Beerfest *32*

Thierry Fortineau
Gabrielle *151*

Ben Foster (1980-)
X-Men: The Last Stand *447*

Jodie Foster (1963-)
Inside Man *202*

Jon Foster
Stay Alive *371*

Sebastien Foucan
Casino Royale *65*

Edward Fox (1937-)
Lassie *228*

Emilia Fox (1974-)
Keeping Mum *215*

Maj. James Fox
United 93 *412*

Matthew Fox
We Are Marshall *432*

Spencer Fox
The Groomsmen *167*

Zachary Fox
Wah-Wah *425*

Jamie Foxx (1967-)
Dreamgirls *111*
Miami Vice *262*

Jon Francis
See Jon(athan) Gries

James Franco (1978-)
Annapolis *10*
Flyboys *140*
Tristan & Isolde *396*

Deborah Francois
The Child *73*

Morgan Freeman (1937-)
Lucky Number Slevin *249*

Judah Friedlander
Date Movie *91*

Anna Friel (1976-)
Goal! The Dream Begins *157*

Rupert Friend
The Libertine *236*
Mrs. Palfrey at the Claremont *266*

Zhanna Friske
Night Watch *283*

Dean Friss
Black Christmas *38*

Nick Frost
Kinky Boots *220*

Stephen Fry (1957-)
Tristram Shandy: A Cock and Bull Story *398*
V for Vendetta *419*

Takako Fuji
The Grudge 2 *169*

Kurt Fuller (1952-)
Don't Come Knocking *106*
The Pursuit of Happyness *319*

Benno Furmann
Joyeux Noel *211*

M.C. Gainey
Beerfest *32*

Charlotte Gainsbourg (1972-)
The Science of Sleep *347*

Benjy Gaither
Hoodwinked *(V)* *185*

Vincent Gale
Firewall *133*

Bronagh Gallagher
Tristan & Isolde *396*

Patrick Gallagher
Night at the Museum *280*

Carla Gallo
Mission: Impossible III *264*

Nathan Gamble
Babel *27*

Michael Gambon (1940-)
The Good Shepherd *161*
The Omen *292*

The Game (1979-)
Waist Deep *426*

James Gammon (1940-)
Don't Come Knocking *106*

James Gandolfini (1961-)
All the King's Men *4*

Romola Garai (1982-)
Scoop *349*

Andy Garcia (1956-)
The Lost City *245*

Jeff Garcia
Barnyard *(V)* *30*

Jorge Garcia
Deck the Halls *96*

Jsu Garcia (1963-)
The Lost City *245*

Sahara Garey (1991-)
Akeelah and the Bee *2*

Janeane Garofalo (1964-)
The Wild *(V)* *439*

Teri Garr (1949-)
Unaccompanied Minors *408*

Beau Garrett
Turistas *404*

Willie Garson
Zoom *451*

Kyle Gass
Tenacious D in the Pick of Destiny *386*

Michael Gaston
The Notorious Bettie Page *286*

Trish Gates
United 93 *412*

Martina Gedeck
The Good Shepherd *161*

Valerie Geffner
Poster Boy *309*

Sarah Michelle Gellar (1977-)
The Grudge 2 *169*
The Return *327*

Troy Gentile
Tenacious D in the Pick of Destiny *386*

Melissa George (1976-)
Turistas *404*

Brian Geraghty
Bobby *45*
The Guardian *170*
When a Stranger Calls *434*

Peter Gerety (1940-)
Inside Man *202*

Greg Germann (1962-)
Friends with Money *148*

Jami Gertz (1965-)
Keeping Up with the Steins *216*

Ricky Gervais
For Your Consideration *142*
Night at the Museum *280*

Luminata Gheorghiu
The Death of Mr. Lazarescu *94*

Paul Giamatti (1967-)
The Ant Bully *(V)* *11*
The Illusionist *196*
Lady in the Water *223*

Giancarlo Giannini (1942-)
Casino Royale *65*

Holly Gibbs
Nanny McPhee *275*

Tyrese Gibson (1978-)
Annapolis *10*
Waist Deep *426*

Llewella Gideon
Manderlay *254*

Ariadna Gil (1969-)
Pan's Labyrinth *299*

Nancy Giles
Loverboy *247*

Annie Girardot (1931-)
Cache *61*

Alessandro Giuggioli
The Nativity Story *276*

Lola Glaudini
Invincible *204*

Danny Glover (1947-)
Barnyard *(V)* *30*
Dreamgirls *111*
Manderlay *254*
The Shaggy Dog *357*

Julian Glover (1935-)
Scoop *349*

Godfrey
Phat Girlz *301*

Adam Goldberg (1970-)
Deja Vu *97*
Stay Alive *371*

Whoopi Goldberg (1949-)
Everyone's Hero *(V)* *122*

Jeff Goldblum (1952-)
Man of the Year *252*

Sadie Goldstein
Little Children *237*

Sam Golzari
American Dreamz *6*

Diego Eduardo Gomez
Nacho Libre *273*

Cesar Gonzalez
Nacho Libre *273*

Rick Gonzalez
Pulse *318*

Meagan Good
Brick *53*
Waist Deep *426*

Matthew Goode (1978-)
Imagine Me & You *197*

Cuba Gooding, Jr. (1968-)
Shadowboxer *355*

Brian Goodman
Annapolis *10*
The Fast and the Furious: Tokyo Drift *128*

Lucy Gordon
Russian Dolls *334*

Joseph Gordon-Levitt (1981-)
Brick *53*
Shadowboxer *355*

Alexander Gould
How to Eat Fried Worms *189*

Olivier Gourmet
The Child *73*

Heather Graham (1970-)
Bobby *45*

Kelsey Grammer (1954-)
X-Men: The Last Stand *447*

David Marshall Grant (1955-)
The Devil Wears Prada *104*

Hugh Grant (1960-)
American Dreamz *6*

Kate Jennings Grant
When a Stranger Calls *434*

Richard E. Grant (1957-)
Garfield: A Tail of Two Kitties *(V)* *154*

Rodney A. Grant (1959-)
Don't Come Knocking *106*

Rupert Graves (1963-)
V for Vendetta *419*

Macy Gray
Idlewild *194*
Shadowboxer *355*

Noah Gray-Cabey (1995-)
Lady in the Water *223*

Ari Graynor
Game 6 *152*

Eva Green
Casino Royale *65*

Bruce Greenwood (1956-)
Deja Vu *97*
Eight Below *117*

Judy Greer (1971-)
American Dreamz *6*

Clark Gregg (1964-)
Hoot *186*
When a Stranger Calls *434*

Pascal Greggory (1954-)
Gabrielle *151*

Adrian Grenier (1976-)
The Devil Wears Prada *104*

Zach Grenier (1954-)
Pulse *318*

Zena Grey
The Shaggy Dog *357*

Jon(athan) Gries (1957-)
Stick It *373*

Eddie Griffin (1968-)
Date Movie *91*

Nikki Griffin (1978-)
The Fast and the Furious: Tokyo Drift *128*

Rachel Griffiths (1968-)
Step Up *372*

Richard Griffiths (1947-)
The History Boys *179*
Venus *421*

George Grizzard (1928-)
Flags of Our Fathers *135*

Greg Grunberg
Mission: Impossible III *264*

Ignacio Guadalupe
The Three Burials of Melquiades Estrada *391*

Eythor Gudjonsson
Hostel *188*

Gabriel Guedj
Running with Scissors *331*

Christopher Guest
For Your Consideration *142*

Carla Gugino (1971-)
Night at the Museum *280*

Sienna Guillory
Eragon *121*

David Gulpilil (1954-)
The Proposition *316*

Annabelle Gurwitch
The Shaggy Dog *357*

Jack Guzman
End of the Spear *119*

Luis Guzman (1956-)
School for Scoundrels *345*

Maggie Gyllenhaal (1977-)
Monster House *(V)* *268*
Sherrybaby *358*
Stranger Than Fiction *375*
Trust the Man *400*
World Trade Center *443*

Lukas Haas (1976-)
Brick *53*
Material Girls *261*

Julie Hagerty (1955-)
She's the Man *360*

Henry Haggard
The Second Chance *351*

Pat Haggerty
Borat: Cultural Learnings of America for Make Benefit Glorious Nation of Kazakhstan *48*

Kathryn Hahn (1974-)
The Holiday *181*

Tony Hale (1970-)
Larry the Cable Guy: Health Inspector *227*
Stranger Than Fiction *375*

Jackie Earle Haley (1961-)
All the King's Men *4*
Little Children *237*

H. Hunter Hall
Waist Deep *426*

Philip Baker Hall (1931-)
The Matador *260*
The Shaggy Dog *357*

Rebecca Hall
The Prestige *313*

Regina Hall (1971-)
Scary Movie 4 *344*

Victoria Hamilton
Scoop *349*

Mona Hammond
Manderlay *254*

Thierry Hancisse
Gabrielle *151*

Taylor Handley
The Texas Chainsaw Massacre: The Beginning *387*

Tom Hanks (1956-)
The Da Vinci Code *88*

Daryl Hannah (1960-)
Keeping Up with the Steins *216*

Alyson Hannigan (1974-)
Date Movie *91*

Marcia Gay Harden (1959-)
American Dreamz *6*

Robert Hardy (1925-)
Lassie *228*

David Harewood
Blood Diamond *41*

Shalom Harlow (1973-)
Game 6 *152*

Jessica Harmon
Black Christmas *38*

Elisabeth Harnois (1979-)
Strangers with Candy *377*

Woody Harrelson (1962-)
A Prairie Home Companion *311*
A Scanner Darkly *342*

Laura Elena Harring (1964-)
The King *218*

Ed Harris (1949-)
Winter Passing *441*

Jared Harris (1961-)
Lady in the Water *223*
The Notorious Bettie Page *286*

Naomie Harris
Miami Vice *262*
Pirates of the Caribbean: Dead Man's Chest *306*
Tristram Shandy: A Cock and Bull Story *398*

Rachael Harris
For Your Consideration *142*

Tip Harris
ATL *21*

Ian Hart (1964-)
Tristram Shandy: A Cock and Bull Story *398*

Kevin Hart
Scary Movie 4 *344*

Josh Hartnett (1978-)
The Black Dahlia *39*
Lucky Number Slevin *249*

David Hasselhoff (1952-)
Click *78*

Anne Hathaway (1982-)
The Devil Wears Prada *104*
Hoodwinked *(V)* *185*

Cole Hauser (1975-)
The Break-Up *51*

Keeley Hawes (1977-)
Tristram Shandy: A Cock and Bull Story *398*

John Hawkes (1959-)
Miami Vice *262*

Colin Hay
The Wild *(V)* *439*

Salma Hayek (1966-)
Ask the Dust *19*

Anthony Head (1954-)
Imagine Me & You *197*
Scoop *349*

Lena Headey (1976-)
Imagine Me & You *197*

Anthony Heald (1944-)
Accepted *1*
X-Men: The Last Stand *447*

John Heard (1946-)
The Guardian *170*

Heavy D
Step Up *372*

Dan Hedaya (1940-)
Strangers with Candy *377*

Jon Heder
The Benchwarmers *34*
Monster House *(V)* *268*
School for Scoundrels *345*

Garrett Hedlund
Eragon *121*

Kevin Heffernan
Beerfest *32*

Levon Helm (1943-)
The Three Burials of Melquiades Estrada *391*

Katherine Helmond (1934-)
Cars *(V)* *63*

Toby Hemingway
The Covenant *81*

Josh Henderson
Step Up *372*

Martin Henderson (1974-)
Flyboys *140*

Shirley Henderson (1966-)
Marie Antoinette *257*
Tristram Shandy: A Cock and Bull Story *398*

Brad William Henke
Hollywoodland *183*
Sherrybaby *358*

Barry (Shabaka) Henley
Miami Vice *262*

Bonnie Henna
Catch a Fire *67*

Lance Henriksen (1940-)
When a Stranger Calls *(V)* *434*

Gregg Henry (1952-)
The Black Dahlia *39*
Slither *365*
United 93 *412*

Elden (Ratliff) Henson (1977-)
Deja Vu *97*

Taraji P. Henson
Something New *369*

David Herman
Idiocracy *192*

Dalia Hernandez
Apocalypto *12*

Jay Hernandez (1978-)
Hostel *188*
World Trade Center *443*

Adam Herschman
Accepted *1*

Clement Hervieu-Leger
Gabrielle *151*

Jennifer Love Hewitt (1979-)
Garfield: A Tail of Two Kitties *154*

John Benjamin Hickey
Flags of Our Fathers *135*
Infamous *200*

Adam Hicks
How to Eat Fried Worms *189*

Clare Higgins
The Libertine *236*

John Michael Higgins (1962-)
The Break-Up *51*
For Your Consideration *142*

Freddie Highmore
A Good Year *164*

Dule Hill (1974-)
The Guardian *170*

Jonah Hill (1983-)
Accepted *1*

Ciaran Hinds (1953-)
Miami Vice *262*
The Nativity Story *276*

Cheryl Hines
Keeping Up with the Steins *216*
RV *335*

Louise-Anne Hippeau
Time to Leave *394*

Calvin Hobson
The Second Chance *351*

Dustin Hoffman (1937-)
The Lost City *245*
Stranger Than Fiction *375*

Philip Seymour Hoffman (1967-)
Mission: Impossible III *264*
Strangers with Candy *377*

Rick Hoffman
Hostel *188*

Robert Hoffman
She's the Man *360*

Gina Holden
Final Destination 3 *130*

Laurie Holden (1972-)
Silent Hill *361*

Ginny Holder
Manderlay *254*

Tom Hollander (1969-)
A Good Year *164*
The Libertine *236*
Pirates of the Caribbean: Dead Man's Chest *306*

Polly Holliday (1937-)
Stick It *373*

Greg Hollimon
Strangers with Candy *377*

Ian Holm (1931-)
Strangers with Candy *377*

Jennifer Holmes
Hard Candy *175*

Katie Holmes (1978-)
Thank You for Smoking *389*

Chen Hong
The Promise *315*

Samuel Honywood
Nanny McPhee *275*

Ewan Hooper
Kinky Boots *220*

Anthony Hopkins (1937-)
All the King's Men *4*
Bobby *45*
The World's Fastest Indian *445*

Sharon Horgan
Imagine Me & You *197*

Craig Horner
See No Evil *352*

Jane Horrocks (1964-)
Garfield: A Tail of Two Kitties *(V)* *154*

Bob Hoskins (1942-)
Garfield: A Tail of Two Kitties *(V)* *154*
Hollywoodland *183*

Nicholas Hoult
Wah-Wah *425*

Djimon Hounsou (1964-)
Blood Diamond *41*
Eragon *121*

Bryce Dallas Howard (1981-)
Lady in the Water *223*
Manderlay *254*

Clint Howard (1959-)
Curious George *(V)* *85*

Terrence DaShon Howard (1969-)
Idlewild *194*

Brian Howe
The Pursuit of Happyness *319*

Jennifer Hudson
Dreamgirls *111*

Kate Hudson (1979-)
You, Me and Dupree *449*

Oliver Hudson (1976-)
Black Christmas *38*

Geraldine Hughes
Rocky Balboa *328*

Tom Hulce (1953-)
Stranger Than Fiction *375*

Charlie Hunnam (1980-)
Children of Men *74*

Bonnie Hunt (1964-)
Cars *(V)* *63*

Helen Hunt (1963-)
Bobby *45*
A Good Woman *163*

Linda Hunt (1945-)
Stranger Than Fiction *375*

Sam Huntington
Superman Returns *379*

Isabelle Huppert (1955-)
Gabrielle *151*

Rachel Hurd-Wood
An American Haunting *8*

John Hurt (1940-)
Manderlay *254*
The Proposition *316*
V for Vendetta *419*

Mary Beth Hurt (1948-)
Lady in the Water *223*

William Hurt (1950-)
The Good Shepherd *161*
The King *218*

Anjelica Huston (1951-)
Art School Confidential *18*
Material Girls *261*

Danny Huston (1962-)
Children of Men *74*
Marie Antoinette *257*
The Proposition *316*

Josh Hutcherson
RV *335*

Timothy Hutton (1960-)
The Good Shepherd *161*
Last Holiday *229*

Emmanuel Idowu
Manderlay *254*

Rhys Ifans (1968-)
Garfield: A Tail of Two Kitties *(V)* *154*

Tsuyoski Ihara
Letters from Iwo Jima *234*

Celia Imrie (1952-)
Imagine Me & You *197*
Nanny McPhee *275*
Wah-Wah *425*

Francesca Inaudi
Don't Tell *108*

Jeremy Irons (1948-)
Eragon *121*
Inland Empire *201*

Dom Irrera
Barnyard *(V)* *30*

Stanley Irving
Everyone's Hero *(V)* *122*

Bill Irwin (1950-)
Lady in the Water *223*

Steve Irwin
Happy Feet *(V)* *173*

Oscar Isaac
The Nativity Story *276*

Jason Isaacs (1963-)
Friends with Money *148*

Ravil Isyanov
The Good German *159*

Marcel Iures
Goal! The Dream Begins *157*

Zeljko Ivanek (1957-)
Manderlay *254*

Mark Ivanir
The Good Shepherd *161*

Judith Ivey (1951-)
Flags of Our Fathers *135*

Eddie Izzard (1962-)
My Super Ex-Girlfriend *270*
The Wild *(V)* *439*

Hugh Jackman (1968-)
Flushed Away *(V)* *139*
The Fountain *144*
Happy Feet *(V)* *173*
The Prestige *313*
Scoop *349*
X-Men: The Last Stand *447*

Boo Jackson
Imagine Me & You *197*

Cheyenne Jackson
United 93 *412*

Joshua Jackson (1978-)
Bobby *45*

Reggie Jackson (1946-)
The Benchwarmers *34*

Samuel L. Jackson (1948-)
Freedomland *146*
Snakes on a Plane *366*

Derek Jacobi (1938-)
Nanny McPhee *275*
Underworld: Evolution *410*

Glen "Kane" Jacobs (1967-)
See No Evil *352*

Peter Jacobson
Failure to Launch *127*

Brenda James
Slither *365*

Kevin James
Barnyard *(V)* *30*
Monster House *(V)* *268*

Pell James
The King *218*

Petr Janis
Hostel *188*

Allison Janney (1960-)
Over the Hedge *(V)* *295*
Strangers with Candy *377*

Famke Janssen (1964-)
X-Men: The Last Stand *447*

Gabe Jarret (1970-)
Poseidon *308*

Vidula Javalgekar
Water *430*

Ricky Jay (1948-)
The Prestige *313*

Jimmy Jean-Louis
Phat Girlz *301*

Myles Jeffrey
The Ant Bully *(V)* *11*

Carter Jenkins
Keeping Up with the Steins *216*

Alex Jennings
The Queen *323*

Mohan Jhanjiani
Water *430*

Hector Jimenez
Nacho Libre *273*

Chen Jin
Curse of the Golden Flower *86*

Scarlett Johansson (1984-)
The Black Dahlia *39*
A Good Woman *163*
The Prestige *313*
Scoop *349*

Gilbert John
Hard Candy *175*

Aaron Johnson
The Illusionist *196*

Alexz Johnson
Final Destination 3 *130*

Clark Johnson (1954-)
The Sentinel *353*

Kendra C. Johnson
Phat Girlz *301*

Kristen Johnston (1967-)
Strangers with Candy *377*

Sue Johnston
Imagine Me & You *197*

Angelina Jolie (1975-)
The Good Shepherd *161*

Doug Jones
Pan's Labyrinth *299*

Evan Jones
Glory Road *156*

James Earl Jones (1931-)
The Benchwarmers *(V)* *34*
Scary Movie 4 *(V)* *344*

January Jones
The Three Burials of Melquiades Estrada *391*
We Are Marshall *432*

L.Q. Jones (1927-)
A Prairie Home Companion *311*

Nathan Jones
Jet Li's Fearless *208*

Sam Jones, III
Glory Road *156*

Shirley Jones (1934-)
Grandma's Boy *166*

Toby Jones
Infamous *200*

Tommy Lee Jones (1946-)
A Prairie Home Companion *311*
The Three Burials of Melquiades Estrada *391*

Vinnie Jones (1965-)
Garfield: A Tail of Two Kitties *(V)* *154*
She's the Man *360*
X-Men: The Last Stand *447*

Milla Jovovich (1975-)
Ultraviolet *407*

Robert Joy (1951-)
The Hills Have Eyes *178*

Qin Junjie
Curse of the Golden Flower *86*

Jana Kaderabkova
Hostel *188*

Jack Kaeding
Running with Scissors *331*

Shauna Kain
X-Men: The Last Stand *447*

Sung Kang
The Fast and the Furious: Tokyo Drift *128*

John Kapelos (1956-)
Stick It *373*

James Karen (1923-)
The Pursuit of Happyness *319*

Claudia Karvan (1973-)
Aquamarine *14*

Ryo Kase
Letters from Iwo Jima *234*

Kevin Kash
The Groomsmen *167*

John Kavanagh
The Black Dahlia *39*

Julie Kavner (1951-)
Click *78*

Dominic Scott Kay (1996-)
Charlotte's Web *71*
Loverboy *247*

Molly Kayall
The Descent *101*

Michael Keaton (1951-)
Cars *(V)* *63*
Game 6 *152*

Arielle Kebbel
Aquamarine *14*
The Grudge 2 *169*
John Tucker Must Die *209*

Catherine Keener (1961-)
Friends with Money *148*

Matt Keeslar (1972-)
Art School Confidential *18*

Jack Kehler
Invincible *204*

Garrison Keillor
A Prairie Home Companion *311*

Sally Kellerman (1938-)
The Boynton Beach Club *49*

Susan Kellerman
Last Holiday *229*

Nathalie Kelley
The Fast and the Furious: Tokyo Drift *128*

Brett Kelly
Unaccompanied Minors *408*

James Francis Kelly, III
Rocky Balboa *328*

Michael Kelly
Invincible *204*

Teddy Kempner
Manderlay *254*

George Kennedy (1925-)
Don't Come Knocking *106*

Schin A.S. Kerr
Glory Road *156*

Ian Reed Kesler
Poster Boy *309*

Alan Keyes
Borat: Cultural Learnings of America for Make Benefit Glorious Nation of Kazakhstan *48*

Konstantin Khabensky
Night Watch *283*

Malika Khadijah
ATL *21*

Kulbashan Kharbanda
Water *430*

Kid Rock (1971-)
Larry the Cable Guy: Health Inspector *227*

Nicole Kidman (1966-)
Happy Feet *(V)* *173*

Udo Kier (1944-)
BloodRayne *44*
Manderlay *254*

Laura Kightlinger (1969-)
The Shaggy Dog *357*

Rinko Kikuchi (1981-)
Babel *27*

Craig Kilborn (1962-)
The Benchwarmers *34*
The Shaggy Dog *357*

Val Kilmer (1959-)
Deja Vu *97*

Richard Kind (1956-)
The Wild *(V)* *439*

Regina King (1971-)
The Ant Bully *(V)* *11*

Ben Kingsley (1943-)
BloodRayne *44*
Lucky Number Slevin *249*

Greg Kinnear (1963-)
Invincible *204*
Little Miss Sunshine *240*
The Matador *260*

Nazan Kirilmis (1969-)
Climates *80*

James Kirk
She's the Man *360*

Justin Kirk
Ask the Dust *19*

Sami Kirkpatrick
Over the Hedge *(V)* *295*

Mia Kirshner
The Black Dahlia *39*

Keiko Kitagawa
The Fast and the Furious: Tokyo Drift *128*

Taylor Kitsch
The Covenant *81*

Martin Klebba
Pirates of the Caribbean: Dead Man's Chest *306*

Chris Klein (1979-)
American Dreamz *6*

Kevin Kline (1947-)
The Pink Panther *304*
A Prairie Home Companion *311*

Kevin Knapman
Goal! The Dream Begins *157*

Shirley Knight (1937-)
Grandma's Boy *166*

Keira Knightley (1985-)
Pirates of the Caribbean: Dead Man's Chest *306*

Andrew Knott
The History Boys *179*

Beyonce Knowles (1981-)
Dreamgirls *111*
The Pink Panther *304*

Johnny Knoxville (1971-)
Jackass Number Two *207*

Mpho Koaho
Saw III *340*

Boris Kodjoe
Madea's Family Reunion *251*

David Koechner
Barnyard *(V)* *30*
Larry the Cable Guy: Health Inspector *227*
Snakes on a Plane *366*
Thank You for Smoking *389*
Unaccompanied Minors *408*

Jane Krakowski (1966-)
Open Season *(V)* *294*

John Krasinski (1979-)
The Holiday *181*

Alice Krige (1955-)
Silent Hill *361*

Diane Kruger
Joyeux Noel *211*

David Krumholtz (1978-)
Bobby *45*

Marcia Jean Kurtz
Find Me Guilty *131*
Inside Man *202*

Ashton Kutcher (1978-)
Bobby *45*
The Guardian *170*
Open Season *(V)* *294*

Kagiso Kuypers
Blood Diamond *41*

Ryan Kwanten
Flicka *138*

Gosha Kytsenko
Night Watch *283*

Rob LaBelle
RV *335*

Shia LaBeouf (1986-)
Bobby *45*

Tyler Labine
Flyboys *140*

Preston Lacy
Jackass Number Two *207*

Diane Ladd (1939-)
Inland Empire *201*
The World's Fastest Indian *445*

John Lafayette
Loverboy *247*

Emeril Lagasse
Last Holiday *229*

Robin Laing
Joyeux Noel *211*

Maurice LaMarche
Barnyard *(V)* *30*

Lisa Lampanelli
Larry the Cable Guy: Health Inspector *227*

Chus (Maria Jesus) Lampreave (1930-)
Volver *423*

Diane Lane (1965-)
Hollywoodland *183*

Robert Lang
Mrs. Palfrey at the Claremont *266*

Jessica Lange (1949-)
Don't Come Knocking *106*

Frank Langella (1940-)
Superman Returns *379*

Brooke Langton (1970-)
The Benchwarmers *34*

Angela Lansbury (1925-)
Nanny McPhee *275*

Anthony LaPaglia (1959-)
Happy Feet *(V)* *173*

Vincent Laresca (1974-)
The Fast and the Furious: Tokyo Drift *128*

Larry the Cable Guy
Cars *(V)* *63*
Larry the Cable Guy: Health Inspector *227*

Brie Larson
Hoot *186*

Jack Larson
Superman Returns *379*

Ilya Larutenko
Night Watch *283*

Julia Lashae
Last Holiday *229*

Sanaa Lathan (1971-)
Something New *369*

Queen Latifah
Ice Age: The Meltdown *(V)* *191*
Last Holiday *229*
Stranger Than Fiction *375*

Rik Launspach
Manderlay *254*

Dan Lauria (1947-)
Big Momma's House 2 *37*

Avril Lavigne (1984-)
Over the Hedge *(V)* *295*

Jude Law (1972-)
All the King's Men *4*
The Holiday *181*

Christopher Lawford (1955-)
The World's Fastest Indian *445*

Martin Lawrence (1965-)
Big Momma's House 2 *37*
Open Season *(V)* *294*

Byron Lawson
Snakes on a Plane *366*

Bernard Le Coq (1950-)
The Bridesmaid *55*
Cache *61*
Joyeux Noel *211*

Tristan Lake Leabu
Superman Returns *379*

Cloris Leachman (1930-)
Beerfest *32*
Scary Movie 4 *344*

Sharon Leal
Dreamgirls *111*

Denis Leary (1957-)
Ice Age: The Meltdown *(V)* *191*

Jason Lee (1971-)
Clerks II *76*
Monster House *(V)* *268*

Jane Leeves (1962-)
Garfield: A Tail of Two Kitties *(V)* *154*

James LeGros (1962-)
Trust the Man *400*

John Leguizamo (1964-)
The Groomsmen *167*
Ice Age: The Meltdown *(V)* *191*

Kristen Lehman
The Sentinel *353*

Kris Lemche
Final Destination 3 *130*

Steve Lemme (1973-)
Beerfest *32*

Vanessa Lengies
Stick It *373*

Jay Leno (1950-)
Ice Age: The Meltdown *(V)* *191*

Melissa Leo (1960-)
The Three Burials of Melquiades Estrada *391*

Amy Leonard
The Groomsmen *167*

Joshua Leonard
The Shaggy Dog *357*

Louie Leonardo
End of the Spear *119*

Logan Lerman
Hoot *186*

Michael Lerner (1941-)
Poster Boy *309*

Sam Lerner
Monster House *(V)* *268*

Ken Leung
X-Men: The Last Stand *447*

Joanna "JoJo" Levesque (1990-)
Aquamarine *14*
RV *335*

Zachary Levi (1980-)
Big Momma's House 2 *37*

Samm Levine
Pulse *318*

Ted Levine (1958-)
The Hills Have Eyes *178*

Connor Christopher Levins (1999-)
Eight Below *117*

Eugene Levy (1946-)
Curious George *(V)* *85*
For Your Consideration *142*
Over the Hedge *(V)* *295*

Clea Lewis
Ice Age: The Meltdown *(V)* *191*

Gary Lewis
Goal! The Dream Begins *157*
Joyeux Noel *211*

Geoffrey Lewis (1935-)
Down in the Valley *109*

Jenifer Lewis (1957-)
Cars *(V)* *63*
Madea's Family Reunion *251*

Mark Lewis
Beowulf & Grendel *35*

Max Lewis
Notes on a Scandal *284*

Tom Lewis
The Proposition *316*

Gong Li (1965-)
Curse of the Golden Flower *86*
Miami Vice *262*

Jet Li (1963-)
Jet Li's Fearless *208*

Man Li
Curse of the Golden Flower *86*

Alain Libolt
Army of Shadows *16*

Matthew Lillard (1970-)
The Groomsmen *167*

Jennifer Lim
Hostel *188*

Cody Linley
Hoot *186*

Laura Linney (1964-)
Man of the Year *252*

Lucy Liu (1968-)
Lucky Number Slevin *249*

Blake Lively
Accepted *1*

LL Cool J (1968-)
Last Holiday *229*

Suzette Llewellyn
Manderlay *254*

Eric Lloyd (1986-)
The Santa Clause 3: The Escape Clause *339*

Luigi Lo Cascio
Don't Tell *108*

Spencer Locke (1991-)
Monster House *(V)* *268*

Emma Lockhart
Looking for Comedy in the Muslim World *244*

Donal Logue (1966-)
The Groomsmen *167*

Lindsay Lohan (1986-)
Bobby *45*
Just My Luck *213*
A Prairie Home Companion *311*

Alison Lohman (1979-)
Flicka *138*

Kristanna Loken
BloodRayne *44*

Domenick Lombardozzi
Find Me Guilty *131*

Daniel London
Old Joy *291*

Lauren London
ATL *21*

Jackie Long
ATL *21*

Justin Long
Accepted *1*
The Break-Up *51*
Idiocracy *192*

Nia Long (1970-)
Big Momma's House 2 *37*

Eva Longoria
The Sentinel *353*

Tanya Lopert
Changing Times *69*

Sergi Lopez (1965-)
Pan's Labyrinth *299*

Todd Louiso (1970-)
School for Scoundrels *345*
Snakes on a Plane *366*
Thank You for Smoking *389*

Faizon Love
Idlewild *194*
Just My Luck *213*

Deirdre Lovejoy
Step Up *372*

Jon Lovitz (1957-)
The Benchwarmers *34*

Chris Lowe
Black Christmas *38*

Crystal Lowe (1981-)
Final Destination 3 *130*

Rob Lowe (1964-)
Thank You for Smoking *389*

Jessica Lucas
The Covenant *81*

Josh(ua) Lucas (1972-)
Glory Road *156*
Poseidon *308*

Peter J. Lucas
Inland Empire *201*

Luenell (1959-)
Borat: Cultural Learnings of America for Make Benefit Glorious Nation of Kazakhstan *48*

Derek Luke (1974-)
Catch a Fire *67*
Glory Road *156*

Miguel Lunardi
Turistas *404*

Kellan Lutz
Stick It *373*

Will Lyman
Little Children *(V)* *237*

Jane Lynch
For Your Consideration *142*
Talladega Nights: The Ballad of Ricky Bobby *384*

John Lynch (1961-)
Lassie *228*

John Carroll Lynch (1963-)
Looking for Comedy in the Muslim World *244*

Melanie Lynskey (1977-)
Flags of Our Fathers *135*

Tom Lyons
Factotum *125*

Tzi Ma
Akeelah and the Bee *2*

Benu Mabhena
Blood Diamond *41*

Sunny Mabrey
Snakes on a Plane *366*

Kelly Macdonald (1977-)
Lassie *228*
Nanny McPhee *275*
Tristram Shandy: A Cock and Bull Story *398*

Shauna Macdonald
The Descent *101*

Andie MacDowell (1958-)
Barnyard *(V)* *30*

Angus MacFadyen (1964-)
Saw III *340*

Gabriel Macht (1972-)
The Good Shepherd *161*

Allison Mack (1982-)
The Ant Bully *(V)* *11*

J.C. MacKenzie
The Return *327*

Anthony Mackie
Freedomland *146*
We Are Marshall *432*

Steven Mackintosh (1967-)
Underworld: Evolution *410*

Bill Macy (1922-)
The Holiday *181*

William H. Macy (1950-)
Bobby *45*
Everyone's Hero *(V)* *122*
Thank You for Smoking *389*

Rebecca Mader
The Devil Wears Prada *104*

Amy Madigan (1957-)
Winter Passing *441*

Michael Madsen (1959-)
BloodRayne *44*
Scary Movie 4 *344*

Virginia Madsen (1963-)
Firewall *133*
A Prairie Home Companion *311*

Mia Maestro
Poseidon *308*

Mothusi Magano
Tsotsi *401*

Maggie Q (1979-)
Mission: Impossible III *264*

Benoit Magimel (1974-)
The Bridesmaid *55*

Tobey Maguire (1975-)
The Good German *159*

Samantha Mahurin (1999-)
The Prestige *313*

Aissa Maiga
Russian Dolls *334*

Austin Majors
The Ant Bully *(V)* *11*

Lester Makedonsky
Cache *61*

Alexei Maklakov
Night Watch *283*

Israel Makoe
Tsotsi *401*

Rami Malek
Night at the Museum *280*

John Malkovich (1953-)
Art School Confidential *18*
Eragon *121*
The Libertine *236*

Claude Mann
Army of Shadows *16*

Earl Mann
Idiocracy *(V)* *192*

Gabriel Mann
Don't Come Knocking *106*

John Mann
Underworld: Evolution *410*

Robert Mann
Black Christmas *38*

Manorama
Water *430*

Gina Mantegna
Unaccompanied Minors *408*

Charles Maquignon
Manderlay *254*

Kate Mara
We Are Marshall *432*
Zoom *451*

Bam Margera (1979-)
Jackass Number Two *207*

Mark Margolis (1939-)
The Fountain *144*

Miriam Margolyes (1941-)
Flushed Away *(V)* *139*
Happy Feet *(V)* *173*

Julianna Margulies (1966-)
Snakes on a Plane *366*

Jean-Pierre Marielle (1932-)
The Da Vinci Code *88*

Richard "Cheech" Marin (1946-)
Cars *(V)* *63*

Brian Markinson
RV *335*

Rimma Markova
Night Watch *283*

William Marquez
The Lost City *245*

Eddie Marsan
Beowulf & Grendel *35*
The Illusionist *196*
Mission: Impossible III *264*
V for Vendetta *419*

James Marsden (1973-)
Superman Returns *379*
X-Men: The Last Stand *447*

Matthew Marsh
An American Haunting *8*

Garry Marshall (1934-)
Keeping Up with the Steins *216*

Penny Marshall (1947-)
Looking for Comedy in the Muslim World *244*

Andrea Martin (1947-)
Black Christmas *38*

Millicent Martin (1934-)
Mrs. Palfrey at the Claremont *266*

Steve Martin (1945-)
The Pink Panther *304*

Dmitry Martynov
Night Watch *283*

Lauriane Mascaro
Marie Antoinette *257*

Jonathan Mason
Lassie *228*

Anna Massey (1937-)
Mrs. Palfrey at the Claremont *266*

Jerry Mathers (1948-)
Larry the Cable Guy: Health Inspector *227*

Tim Matheson (1947-)
Don't Come Knocking *106*

Marie Matiko
Date Movie *91*

Percy Matsemela
Tsotsi *401*

Carmen Maura (1945-)
Volver *423*

Carlos Maycotte
Nacho Libre *273*

Jefferson Mays
The Notorious Bettie Page *286*

Alphonso McAuley
Glory Road *156*

James McAvoy
The Last King of Scotland *231*

Chi McBride (1961-)
Annapolis *10*

Simon McBurney
Friends with Money *148*
The Last King of Scotland *231*

Debra McCabe
Saw III *340*

Rory McCann
Beowulf & Grendel *35*

Jenny McCarthy (1972-)
John Tucker Must Die *209*

Tom McCarthy
Flags of Our Fathers *135*

Matthew McConaughey (1969-)
Failure to Launch *127*
We Are Marshall *432*

Marion McCorry
The Groomsmen *167*

Helen McCrory
The Queen *323*

Neal McDonough (1966-)
Flags of Our Fathers *135*
The Guardian *170*

Jake McDorman (1986-)
Aquamarine *14*

Frances McDormand (1958-)
Friends with Money *148*

Reba McEntire (1955-)
Charlotte's Web *71*

Ehren McGhehey
Jackass Number Two *207*

Rose McGowan (1975-)
The Black Dahlia *39*

Matt McGrath (1969-)
The Notorious Bettie Page *286*

Tim McGraw
Flicka *138*

Michael McKean (1947-)
For Your Consideration *142*

Lonette McKee (1954-)
ATL *21*

Ian McKellen (1939-)
The Da Vinci Code *88*
Flushed Away *(V)* *139*
X-Men: The Last Stand *447*

Brandon Jay McLaren
She's the Man *360*

Kevin McNally
Pirates of the Caribbean: Dead Man's Chest *306*

Penny McNamee
See No Evil *352*

Ian McNeice (1950-)
The Black Dahlia *39*

Justus E. McQueen
See L.Q. Jones

Peter McRobbie
The Notorious Bettie Page *286*

Ian McShane (1942-)
Scoop *349*
We Are Marshall *432*

Janet McTeer (1962-)
Tideland *392*

Tim Meadows
The Benchwarmers *34*

Anne Meara (1929-)
Night at the Museum *280*

Julio Oscar Mechoso
The Lost City *245*

Gilbert Melki
Changing Times *69*

Eva Mendes (1978-)
Trust the Man *400*

Natalie Mendoza
The Descent *101*

Gonzalo Menendez (1971-)
The Lost City *245*

Vladimir Menshov
Night Watch *283*

Idina Menzel (1971-)
Ask the Dust *19*

Tobias Menzies
Casino Royale *65*

Ryan Merriman (1983-)
Final Destination 3 *130*

Clive Merrison (1945-)
The History Boys *179*

Debra Messing (1968-)
Open Season *(V)* *294*

Johnny Messner
Running Scared *330*

Jesse Metcalfe (1978-)
John Tucker Must Die *209*

Svetlana Metkina
Bobby *45*

Belinda Metz
Eight Below *117*

Paul Meurisse (1912-79)
Army of Shadows *16*

Jason Mewes (1974-)
Clerks II *76*

Breckin Meyer (1974-)
Garfield: A Tail of Two Kitties *154*

Dina Meyer (1969-)
Saw III *340*

Seth Meyers
American Dreamz *6*

Giovanna Mezzogiorno
Don't Tell *108*

Shaun Micallef (1962-)
Aquamarine *14*

Sean Michael
See Sean Michael Afable

Anna Mihalcea
The Bridesmaid *55*

Dash Mihok (1974-)
Hollywoodland *183*

Mads Mikkelsen
Casino Royale *65*

Oliver Milburn
The Descent *101*

Ben Miles
V for Vendetta *419*

Christina Milian (1981-)
Pulse *318*

Tomas Milian (1937-)
The Lost City *245*

Ivana Milicevic
Casino Royale *65*
Running Scared *330*

Jennifer Miller
Lucky Number Slevin *249*

Larry Miller (1953-)
The Ant Bully *(V)* *11*
Keeping Up with the Steins *216*

Rachel Miner
The Black Dahlia *39*

Max Minghella
Art School Confidential *18*

Miou-Miou (1950-)
The Science of Sleep *347*

Daniel Miranda
Duck Season *113*

Maria Mironova (1973-)
Night Watch *283*

Helen Mirren (1946-)
The Queen *323*
Shadowboxer *355*

Dorian Missick
Lucky Number Slevin *249*

Jimi Mistry (1973-)
Blood Diamond *41*

Daryl (Chill) Mitchell
Inside Man *202*

Elizabeth Mitchell (1970-)
Running Scared *330*
The Santa Clause 3: The Escape Clause *339*

Radha Mitchell (1973-)
Silent Hill *361*

Sid Mitchell
Wah-Wah *425*

Katy Mixon
The Quiet *325*

Kim Miyori
The Grudge 2 *169*

Jerry Mofokeng
Tsotsi *401*

Jay Mohr (1970-)
The Groomsmen *167*

Gretchen Mol (1973-)
The Notorious Bettie Page *286*

Alfred Molina (1953-)
The Da Vinci Code *88*

Michelle Monaghan
Mission: Impossible III *264*

Mo'Nique (1968-)
Beerfest *32*
Phat Girlz *301*
Shadowboxer *355*

Sophie Monk
Date Movie *91*

Ricardo Montalban (1920-)
The Ant Bully *(V)* *11*

Flora Montgomery
Basic Instinct 2 *31*

Richard Montoya
Nacho Libre *273*

Demi Moore (1962-)
Bobby *45*

Joel David Moore
Art School Confidential *18*
Grandma's Boy *166*

Julianne Moore (1961-)
Children of Men *74*
Freedomland *146*
Trust the Man *400*

Mandy Moore (1984-)
American Dreamz *6*

Stephan Campbell Moore
A Good Woman *163*
The History Boys *179*

Dylan Moran
Tristram Shandy: A Cock and Bull Story *398*

Jeanne Moreau (1928-)
Time to Leave *394*

Chloe Grace Moretz
Big Momma's House 2 *37*

Tracy Morgan (1968-)
Little Man *239*

David Morrissey (1963-)
Basic Instinct 2 *31*

David Morse (1953-)
Down in the Valley *109*
16 Blocks *363*

Emily Mortimer (1971-)
The Pink Panther *304*

Joe Morton (1947-)
The Night Listener *282*

Samantha Morton (1977-)
Lassie *228*
The Libertine *236*

Mos Def
See Dante "Mos Def" Beze

Mark Moses
Big Momma's House 2 *37*

Benny Moshe
Tsotsi *401*

Jesse Moss
Final Destination 3 *130*

Ebon Moss-Bachrach
The Lake House *225*

Christopher Moynihan
For Your Consideration *142*

Saskia Mulder
The Descent *101*

Graham Mulins
Tristan & Isolde *396*

Peter Mullan (1954-)
Children of Men *74*

Liliana Mumy (1995-)
The Santa Clause 3: The Escape Clause *339*

Frankie Muniz (1985-)
Stay Alive *371*

Lochlyn Munro (1966-)
The Benchwarmers *34*
Little Man *239*

Enrique Murciano (1973-)
The Lost City *245*

Caterina Murino
Casino Royale *65*

Aaron Murphy
The World's Fastest Indian *445*

Brittany Murphy (1977-)
The Groomsmen *167*
Happy Feet *(V)* *173*

Eddie Murphy (1961-)
Dreamgirls *111*

Michael Murphy (1938-)
X-Men: The Last Stand *447*

Bill Murray (1950-)
Garfield: A Tail of Two Kitties *(V)* *154*
The Lost City *245*

Clifton McCabe Murray
She's the Man *360*

Mitchel Musso (1991-)
Monster House *(V)* *268*

Joseph Mydell
Manderlay *254*

Sophia Myles
Art School Confidential *18*
Tristan & Isolde *396*
Underworld: Evolution *410*

Shidou Nakamura
Jet Li's Fearless *208*
Letters from Iwo Jima *234*

Leonardo Nam
The Fast and the Furious: Tokyo Drift *128*

Arthur J. Nascarelli
The Groomsmen *167*
Running Scared *330*

James Naughton (1945-)
The Devil Wears Prada *104*

Kevin Nealon (1953-)
Grandma's Boy *166*

Barbara Nedeljakova
Hostel *188*

Noel Neill (1920-)
Superman Returns *379*

Tim Blake Nelson (1965-)
Hoot *186*

Alex Neuberger
Running Scared *330*

Bebe Neuwirth (1958-)
Game 6 *152*

Chantal Neuwirth
Gabrielle *151*

Laraine Newman (1952-)
Barnyard *(V)* *30*

Paul Newman (1925-)
Cars *(V)* *63*

Ryan Newman (1998-)
Zoom *451*

Lisa Marie Newmyer
A Scanner Darkly *342*

Matt Newton
Poster Boy *309*

Thandie Newton (1972-)
The Pursuit of Happyness *319*

Sing Ngai (1967-)
Jet Li's Fearless *208*

Zenzo Ngqobe
Tsotsi *401*

Austin Nichols (1980-)
Glory Road *156*

Marisol Nichols
Big Momma's House 2 *37*

Jack Nicholson (1937-)
The Departed *99*

Leslie Nielsen (1926-)
Scary Movie 4 *344*

Bill Nighy (1949-)
Flushed Away *(V)* *139*
Notes on a Scandal *284*
Pirates of the Caribbean: Dead Man's Chest *306*
Underworld: Evolution *410*

Mary Nighy
Marie Antoinette *257*

Kazunari Ninomiya
Letters from Iwo Jima *234*

Alessandro Nivola (1972-)
Goal! The Dream Begins *157*

Kenneth Nkosi
Tsotsi *401*

John Noble
Running Scared *330*

Samantha Noble
See No Evil *352*

Amaury Nolasco
The Benchwarmers *34*

Nick Nolte (1941-)
Over the Hedge *(V)* *295*

Nora-Jane Noone
The Descent *101*

Jeffrey Nordling (1962-)
Flicka *138*

Jeremy Northam (1961-)
Tristram Shandy: A Cock and Bull Story *398*

Alex Norton
Pirates of the Caribbean: Dead Man's Chest *306*

Edward Norton (1969-)
Down in the Valley *109*
The Illusionist *196*

Jack Noseworthy (1969-)
Phat Girlz *301*
Poster Boy *309*

Michael Nouri (1945-)
The Boynton Beach Club *49*
Invincible *204*
Last Holiday *229*

Eugenya Obraztsova
Russian Dolls *334*

Kieran O'Brien (1973-)
Goal! The Dream Begins *157*
Tristram Shandy: A Cock and Bull Story *398*

Peter O'Brien (1960-)
The Return *327*

Deirdre O'Connell
Winter Passing *441*

Hester Odgers
Lassie *228*

John F. O'Donohue
The Groomsmen *167*

Steve Oedekerk (1961-)
Barnyard *(V)* *30*

Sandra Oh (1971-)
Hard Candy *175*
The Night Listener *282*

Brian O'Halloran
Clerks II *76*

Catherine O'Hara (1954-)
For Your Consideration *142*
Game 6 *152*
Monster House *(V)* *268*
Over the Hedge *(V)* *295*

David Patrick O'Hara
Tristan & Isolde *396*

Elva Osk Olafsdottir (1964-)
Beowulf & Grendel *35*

Olafur Darri Olafsson
Beowulf & Grendel *35*

William Oldham
Old Joy *291*

Matt O'Leary
Brick *53*

Christian Oliver
The Good German *159*

Eric Christian Olsen
Beerfest *32*

Patrice O'Neal
Scary Movie 4 *344*

Shaquille O'Neal (1972-)
Scary Movie 4 *344*

Julia Ormond (1965-)
Inland Empire *201*

Ed O'Ross (1949-)
Curious George *(V)* *85*

Leland Orser (1960-)
The Good German *159*

John Ortiz
Miami Vice *262*
Take the Lead *383*

Laura Ortiz (1987-)
The Hills Have Eyes *178*

Valery Ortiz (1984-)
Date Movie *91*

Sharon Osbourne
Garfield: A Tail of Two Kitties *(V)* *154*

Patton Oswalt (1969-)
Failure to Launch *127*

Cheri Oteri
The Ant Bully *(V)* *11*

Lorcan O'Toole
Mrs. Palfrey at the Claremont *266*

Peter O'Toole (1932-)
Lassie *228*
Venus *421*

Peter Outerbridge (1966-)
Lucky Number Slevin *249*

Clive Owen (1965-)
Children of Men *74*
Inside Man *202*
The Pink Panther *304*

Can Ozbatur
Climates *80*

Lee Pace
The Good Shepherd *161*
Infamous *200*

Michael J. Pagan
See No Evil *352*

Walter Pagano
Time to Leave *394*

Ellen Page
Hard Candy *175*
X-Men: The Last Stand *447*

Tarah Paige (1982-)
Stick It *373*

Rodolfo Palacios
Apocalypto *12*

Keke Palmer
Akeelah and the Bee *2*
Madea's Family Reunion *251*

Lewis Lemperuer Palmer
Don't Tell *108*

Teresa Palmer (1986-)
The Grudge 2 *169*

Chazz Palminteri (1952-)
Hoodwinked *(V)* *185*
Little Man *239*
Running Scared *330*

Gwyneth Paltrow (1973-)
Infamous *200*
Running with Scissors *331*

Usvaldo Panameno
Wassup Rockers *429*

Archie Panjabi
A Good Year *164*

Joe Pantoliano (1951-)
Larry the Cable Guy: Health Inspector *227*

Anna Paquin (1982-)
X-Men: The Last Stand *447*

Michael Pare (1958-)
BloodRayne *44*

Anthony Ray Parker
The Marine *259*

Jamie Parker
The History Boys *179*

Molly Parker (1971-)
Hollywoodland *183*
The Wicker Man *437*

Sarah Jessica Parker (1965-)
Failure to Launch *127*
Strangers with Candy *377*

Toby Parkes
Keeping Mum *215*

Hunter Parrish
Down in the Valley *109*
RV *335*

David Pasquesi
Strangers with Candy *377*

Vinay Pathak
Water *430*

Robert Patrick (1959-)
Firewall *133*
Flags of Our Fathers *135*
The Marine *259*

Antwan Andre Patton
ATL *21*
Idlewild *194*

Paula Patton
Deja Vu *97*
Idlewild *194*

Jarrad Paul
The Shaggy Dog *357*

Rob Paulsen (1956-)
The Ant Bully *(V)* *11*
Barnyard *(V)* *30*

Sarah Paulson
The Notorious Bettie Page *286*

Sara Paxton
Aquamarine *14*

Guy Pearce (1967-)
The Proposition *316*

Josh Peck
Ice Age: The Meltdown *(V)* *191*

Mizuo Peck
Night at the Museum *280*

Francisco Pedrasa
Wassup Rockers *429*

Simon Pegg
Mission: Impossible III *264*

Luke Pegler
See No Evil *352*

Steve Pemberton
Lassie *228*

Elizabeth Pena (1959-)
The Lost City *245*

Michael Pena
World Trade Center *443*

Austin Pendleton (1940-)
The Notorious Bettie Page *286*

Kal Penn (1977-)
Superman Returns *379*

Sean Penn (1960-)
All the King's Men *4*

Barry Pepper (1970-)
Flags of Our Fathers *135*
The Three Burials of Melquiades Estrada *391*

Piper Perabo (1977-)
Imagine Me & You *197*
The Prestige *313*

Danny Perea
Duck Season *113*

Missy Peregrym (1982-)
Stick It *373*

Nahuel Perez
The Aura *22*

Emily Perkins (1977-)
She's the Man *360*

Millie Perkins (1938-)
The Lost City *245*

Tyler Perry
Madea's Family Reunion *251*

Sean Pertwee (1964-)
Goal! The Dream Begins *157*

Joe Pesci (1943-)
The Good Shepherd *161*

Clarke Peters
Freedomland *146*

Aurelia Petit
The Science of Sleep *347*

Richard Petty
Cars *(V)* *63*

Terry Pheto
Tsotsi *401*

Ryan Phillippe (1974-)
Flags of Our Fathers *135*

Eric Phillips
Hoot *186*

Leslie Phillips (1924-)
Venus *421*

Nathan Phillips
Snakes on a Plane *366*

Jim Piddock
For Your Consideration *142*

Javone Pierce
Manderlay *254*

Wendell Pierce (1962-)
Stay Alive *371*

Olivia Pigeot
Somersault *367*

Tim Pigott-Smith (1946-)
V for Vendetta *419*

Rosamund Pike
The Libertine *236*

Gabe Pimental
Little Man *239*

Chris Pine
Just My Luck *213*

Danny Pino
Flicka *138*

Joe Pistone
The Groomsmen *167*

Brad Pitt (1963-)
Babel *27*

Blake Pittman
Somersault *367*

Jeremy Piven (1965-)
Keeping Up with the Steins *216*

Mary Kay Place (1947-)
Lonesome Jim *242*

Tony Plana (1953-)
Goal! The Dream Begins *157*
The Lost City *245*

Oliver Platt (1960-)
Loverboy *247*

Joan Plowright (1929-)
Curious George *(V)* *85*
Mrs. Palfrey at the Claremont *266*

Christopher Plummer (1927-)
Inside Man *202*
The Lake House *225*

Gerard Plunkett
Eight Below *117*

Kevin Pollak (1958-)
The Santa Clause 3: The Escape Clause *339*

Sarah Polley (1979-)
Beowulf & Grendel *35*
Don't Come Knocking *106*

Carlos Ponce
Just My Luck *213*

Chris Pontius (1974-)
Jackass Number Two *207*

Linden Porco
Little Man *239*

Maria Poroshina
Night Watch *283*

Blanca Portillo
Volver *423*

Natalie Portman (1981-)
V for Vendetta *419*

Richard Portnow (1950-)
Find Me Guilty *131*

Parker Posey (1968-)
For Your Consideration *142*
Superman Returns *379*

Pete Postlethwaite (1945-)
The Omen *292*

Sarah-Jane Potts
Kinky Boots *220*

Melvil Poupaud (1973-)
Time to Leave *394*

Max Prado
The Benchwarmers *34*

Chris Pratt
Strangers with Candy *377*

Harve Presnell (1933-)
Flags of Our Fathers *135*

Megyn Price (1971-)
Larry the Cable Guy: Health Inspector *227*

Jurgen Prochnow (1941-)
Beerfest *32*
The Da Vinci Code *88*

Emily Procter (1968-)
Big Momma's House 2 *37*

Jonathan Pryce (1947-)
Pirates of the Caribbean: Dead Man's Chest *306*

Robert Pugh
Kinky Boots *220*

Don Pugsley
The Good German *159*

Bill Pullman (1953-)
Scary Movie 4 *344*

Leah Purcell
The Proposition *316*
Somersault *367*

Malcolm Purkey
Catch a Fire *67*

Shawn Pyfrom
The Shaggy Dog *357*

Missi Pyle (1973-)
Just My Luck *213*

Cheng Qian
The Promise *315*

Yun Qu
Jet Li's Fearless *208*

Dennis Quaid (1954-)
American Dreamz *6*

Guido Quaroni
Cars *(V)* *63*

Kathleen Quinlan (1952-)
The Hills Have Eyes *178*

Ruben Rabasa (1938-)
The Lost City *245*

Nadem Rachati
Changing Times *69*

Mustapha Rachidi
Babel *27*

Robert Racki
16 Blocks *363*

Damaine Radcliff
Glory Road *156*
Step Up *372*

Mary Lynn Rajskub
Firewall *133*

Dania Ramirez
X-Men: The Last Stand *447*

Efren Ramirez
Crank *83*
Employee of the Month *118*

Harold Ramis (1944-)
The Last Kiss *232*

Haley Ramm (1992-)
X-Men: The Last Stand *447*

Charlotte Rampling (1945-)
Basic Instinct 2 *31*

Laura Ramsey (1982-)
The Covenant *81*
She's the Man *360*

Joe Ranft
Cars *(V)* *63*

David Rasche (1944-)
The Sentinel *353*

John Ratzenberger (1947-)
Cars *(V)* *63*

Raven-Symone
Everyone's Hero *(V)* *122*

Kim Raver (1969-)
Night at the Museum *280*

Rachel Rawlinson
Flushed Away *(V)* *139*

Connie Ray (1956-)
Thank You for Smoking *389*

Lisa Ray
Water *430*

Stephen Rea (1946-)
V for Vendetta *419*

James Rebhorn (1948-)
How to Eat Fried Worms *189*

Robert Redford (1937-)
Charlotte's Web *71*

Jemma Redgrave (1965-)
Lassie *228*

Vanessa Redgrave (1937-)
Venus *421*

Eddie Redmayne
The Good Shepherd *161*

Jason (JR) Reed
Tenacious D in the Pick of Destiny *386*

Norman Reedus (1969-)
The Notorious Bettie Page *286*

Roger Rees (1944-)
Game 6 *152*
Garfield: A Tail of Two Kitties *154*
The Pink Panther *304*
The Prestige *313*

Dana Reeve
Everyone's Hero *(V)* *122*

Keanu Reeves (1964-)
The Lake House *225*
A Scanner Darkly *342*

Alex Reid
The Descent *101*

John C. Reilly (1965-)
A Prairie Home Companion *311*
Talladega Nights: The Ballad of Ricky Bobby *384*

Kelly Reilly
The Libertine *236*
Russian Dolls *334*

Rob Reiner (1945-)
Everyone's Hero *(V)* *122*

Judge Reinhold (1958-)
The Santa Clause 3: The Escape Clause *339*

Jeremie Renier (1981-)
The Child *73*

Jean Reno (1948-)
The Da Vinci Code *88*
Flushed Away *(V)* *139*
Flyboys *140*
The Pink Panther *304*

Simon Rex
Scary Movie 4 *344*

Walter Reyno
The Aura *22*

Ving Rhames (1961-)
Idlewild *194*
Mission: Impossible III *264*

Jonathan Rhys Meyers (1977-)
Mission: Impossible III *264*

Derek Richardson
Hostel *188*

Ian Richardson (1934-)
Joyeux Noel *211*

Kevin M. Richardson
The Wild *(V)* *439*

Miranda Richardson (1958-)
Wah-Wah *425*

LaTanya Richardson Jackson
Freedomland *146*

Shane Richie
Flushed Away *(V)* *139*

Andy Richter (1966-)
Talladega Nights: The Ballad of Ricky Bobby *384*

Ron Rifkin (1939-)
Pulse *318*

Michael Rispoli
Invincible *204*

Bob Ritchie
See Kid Rock

Leonardo Rivera
Volver *423*

Marie Riviere (1956-)
Time to Leave *394*

Linus Roache (1964-)
Find Me Guilty *131*

Jean-Marie Robain (1913-2004)
Army of Shadows *16*

Tim Robbins (1958-)
Catch a Fire *67*
Tenacious D in the Pick of Destiny *386*

Dallas Roberts
Flicka *138*
The Notorious Bettie Page *286*
Winter Passing *441*

Doris Roberts (1930-)
Grandma's Boy *166*
Keeping Up with the Steins *216*

Emma Roberts (1991-)
Aquamarine *14*

Eric Roberts (1956-)
Phat Girlz *301*

Ian Roberts (1966-)
Tsotsi *401*
Wah-Wah *425*

Julia Roberts (1967-)
The Ant Bully *(V)* *11*
Charlotte's Web *71*

Rick Roberts
Man of the Year *252*

Iain Robertson
Basic Instinct 2 *31*

Kathleen Robertson (1973-)
Hollywoodland *183*

Steven Robertson
Joyeux Noel *211*

Keith D. Robinson
Dreamgirls *111*

Wendy Raquel Robinson
Something New *369*

Stefania Rocca (1971-)
Don't Tell *108*

Alex Rocco (1936-)
Find Me Guilty *131*

Manuel Rodal
The Aura *22*

James Roday
Don't Come Knocking *106*

Karel Roden
Running Scared *330*

Elizabeth Rodriguez
Miami Vice *262*

Freddy Rodriguez (1975-)
Bobby *45*
Lady in the Water *223*
Poseidon *308*

Mel Rodriguez
The Three Burials of Melquiades Estrada *391*

Michelle Rodriguez (1978-)
BloodRayne *44*

Paul Rodriguez (1955-)
The World's Fastest Indian *445*

Seth Rogen
You, Me and Dupree *449*

Austin Rogers
How to Eat Fried Worms *189*

Mark Rolston (1952-)
The Departed *99*

Ray Romano (1957-)
Ice Age: The Meltdown *(V)* *191*

Rebecca Romijn (1972-)
X-Men: The Last Stand *447*

Fabrizio Rongione
The Child *73*

Michael Rooker (1956-)
Slither *365*

Mickey Rooney (1920-)
Night at the Museum *280*

Jemima Rooper
The Black Dahlia *39*
Kinky Boots *220*

Stephen (Steve) Root (1951-)
Ice Age: The Meltdown *(V)* *191*
Idiocracy *192*

Rosalia
Wassup Rockers *429*

Anika Noni Rose
Dreamgirls *111*

Darius A. Rose
Nacho Libre *273*

Evan Ross
ATL *21*

Lee Ross
Goal! The Dream Begins *157*

Matt Ross
Last Holiday *229*

Isabella Rossellini (1952-)
Infamous *200*

Emmy Rossum
Poseidon *308*

Tim Roth (1961-)
Don't Come Knocking *106*

Richard Roundtree (1942-)
Brick *53*

Brandon Routh (1979-)
Superman Returns *379*
Jack Rovello
Lonesome Jim *242*
Clive Rowe
Manderlay *254*
Michael Rubenfeld (1979-)
Lucky Number Slevin *249*
Paul Rudd (1969-)
Night at the Museum *280*
Maya Rudolph (1972-)
Idiocracy *192*
A Prairie Home Companion *311*
Mark Ruffalo (1967-)
All the King's Men *4*
Deborah Rush
Strangers with Candy *377*
Grayson Russell
Talladega Nights: The Ballad of Ricky Bobby *384*
Keri Russell (1976-)
Mission: Impossible III *264*
Kurt Russell (1951-)
Poseidon *308*
Lucy Russell
Tristan & Isolde *396*
John A. Russo
The Groomsmen *167*
Amy Ryan
Looking for Comedy in the Muslim World *244*
Winona Ryder (1971-)
A Scanner Darkly *342*
Daryl Sabara (1992-)
Keeping Up with the Steins *216*
Jonathan Sadowski
She's the Man *360*
Melissa Sagemiller
The Guardian *170*
Amir Ali Said
Game 6 *152*
Inside Man *202*
Eva Marie Saint (1924-)
Don't Come Knocking *106*
Superman Returns *379*
Dominique Saldana
Unaccompanied Minors *408*
Luis Rojas Salgado
Wassup Rockers *429*
Abdul Salis
Flyboys *140*
Aleksandr Samojlenko (1964-)
Night Watch *283*
Hiroyuki Sanada
The Promise *315*
Casey Sander
16 Blocks *363*
Will Sanderson (1980-)
BloodRayne *44*
Adam Sandler (1966-)
Click *78*
Michelle Sandler
Tsotsi *401*
Unaccompanied Minors *408*
Thomas Sangster
Nanny McPhee *275*
Tristan & Isolde *396*
Claudio Santamaria
Casino Royale *65*
Carlos Sanz
Crank *83*
Horatio Sanz
School for Scoundrels *345*
Cesar Sarachu
The Piano Tuner of Earthquakes *303*
Sarala
Water *430*
Ines Sastre
The Lost City *245*
Tania Saulnier
Slither *365*
Nadim Sawalha (1935-)
The Nativity Story *276*
Adrian Scarborough
The History Boys *179*
Raynor Scheine
The Sentinel *353*
August Schellenberg
Eight Below *117*
Richard Schickel (1933-)
Ask the Dust *19*
Thomas Schmauser
Joyeux Noel *211*
Rob Schneider (1963-)
The Benchwarmers *34*
Grandma's Boy *166*
David Schofield
Pirates of the Caribbean: Dead Man's Chest *306*
Liev Schreiber (1967-)
The Omen *292*
Carly Schroeder
Firewall *133*
Jennifer Schwalbach Smith (1971-)
Clerks II *76*
Jason Schwartzman (1980-)
Marie Antoinette *257*
Annabella Sciorra (1964-)
Find Me Guilty *131*
Adam Scott
The Matador *260*
The Return *327*
Campbell Scott (1962-)
Loverboy *247*
Seann William Scott (1976-)
Ice Age: The Meltdown *(V)* *191*
Nick Searcy
Flicka *138*
Amy Sedaris (1961-)
Strangers with Candy *377*
Kyra Sedgwick (1965-)
Loverboy *247*
Noah Segan
Brick *53*
Jeremie Segard
The Child *73*
Eric Seigne
The Bridesmaid *55*
Keiko Seiko
Hostel *188*
Rapulana Seiphemo
Tsotsi *401*
Christian Sengewald
Time to Leave *394*
Ivan Sergei (1972-)
The Break-Up *51*
Andy Serkis (1964-)
Flushed Away *(V)* *139*
The Prestige *313*
Assumpta Serna (1957-)
The Piano Tuner of Earthquakes *303*
Michel Serrault (1928-)
Joyeux Noel *211*
John Sessions (1953-)
The Good Shepherd *161*
Chloe Sevigny (1975-)
Manderlay *254*
Rufus Sewell (1967-)
The Holiday *181*
The Illusionist *196*
Tristan & Isolde *396*
Cara Seymour
The Notorious Bettie Page *286*

Mncedisi Shabangu
Catch a Fire *67*

Tony Shalhoub (1953-)
Cars *(V)* *63*

Chuck Shamata
The Sentinel *353*

Garry Shandling (1949-)
Over the Hedge *(V)* *295*
Trust the Man *400*

Michael Shannon
World Trade Center *443*

Molly Shannon (1964-)
Little Man *239*
Marie Antoinette *257*
Scary Movie 4 *344*
Talladega Nights: The Ballad of Ricky Bobby *384*

Vicellous Shannon (1981-)
Annapolis *10*

William Shatner (1931-)
Over the Hedge *(V)* *295*
The Wild *(V)* *439*

Fiona Shaw (1958-)
The Black Dahlia *39*

Vinessa Shaw (1976-)
The Hills Have Eyes *178*

Alia Shawkat
Deck the Halls *96*

Alan Shearer
Glory Road *156*

Harry Shearer (1943-)
For Your Consideration *142*

Charlie Sheen (1965-)
Scary Movie 4 *344*

Martin Sheen (1940-)
Bobby *45*
The Departed *99*

Michael Sheen (1969-)
Blood Diamond *41*
The Queen *323*
Underworld: Evolution *410*

Adrienne Shelly (1966-2006)
Factotum *125*

Marley Shelton (1974-)
American Dreamz *6*
Don't Come Knocking *106*
The Last Kiss *232*

Dax Shepard
Employee of the Month *118*
Idiocracy *192*

Sam Shepard (1943-)
Charlotte's Web *(V)* *71*
Don't Come Knocking *106*
The Return *327*

Quinn Shephard
Unaccompanied Minors *408*

Sheetal Sheth
Looking for Comedy in the Muslim World *244*

Preston Shores
Big Momma's House 2 *37*

Trevor Shores
Big Momma's House 2 *37*

Columbus Short
Accepted *1*

Martin Short (1950-)
The Santa Clause 3: The Escape Clause *339*

Kin Shriner (1953-)
Hoot *186*

M. Night Shyamalan (1970-)
Lady in the Water *223*

Alexander Siddig (1965-)
The Nativity Story *276*

Simone Signoret (1921-85)
Army of Shadows *16*

Ingvar Sigurdsson
Beowulf & Grendel *35*

Ron Silver (1946-)
Find Me Guilty *131*

Sarah Silverman (1970-)
School for Scoundrels *345*

Meera Simhan
Date Movie *91*

Chelan Simmons (1982-)
Final Destination 3 *130*

Henry Simmons
Madea's Family Reunion *251*

J.K. Simmons (1955-)
Thank You for Smoking *389*

Kimora Lee Simmons
Waist Deep *426*

Tyree Simmons
ATL *21*

Ryan Simpkins
Sherrybaby *358*

Andrew Simpson
Notes on a Scandal *284*

Jessica Simpson
Employee of the Month *118*

Jimmi Simpson
Stay Alive *371*

Molly Sims (1973-)
The Benchwarmers *34*

Sylvia Sims
The Queen *323*

Gary Sinise (1955-)
Open Season *(V)* *294*

Stellan Skarsgard (1951-)
Beowulf & Grendel *35*
Pirates of the Caribbean: Dead Man's Chest *306*

Christian Slater (1969-)
Bobby *45*

John Slattery (1963-)
Flags of Our Fathers *135*

Victor Slezak
The Notorious Bettie Page *286*

Ben Sliney
United 93 *412*

Anna Slyusaryova
Night Watch *283*

Amy Smart (1976-)
Crank *83*

Laura Smet (1983-)
The Bridesmaid *55*

Jaden Smith
The Pursuit of Happyness *319*

James Todd Smith
See LL Cool J

K. Smith
Bubble *57*

Kevin Smith (1970-)
Clerks II *76*

Lauren Lee Smith
The Last Kiss *232*

Liz Smith (1925-)
Keeping Mum *215*

Lois Smith (1930-)
Hollywoodland *183*

Maggie Smith (1934-)
Keeping Mum *215*

Michael Bailey Smith
The Hills Have Eyes *178*

Michael W. Smith
The Second Chance *351*

Shawnee Smith (1970-)
Saw III *340*

Tanya Smith
Old Joy *291*

Will Smith (1968-)
The Pursuit of Happyness *319*

Brittany Snow (1986-)
John Tucker Must Die *209*

Leelee Sobieski (1982-)
The Wicker Man *437*

Ian Somerhalder (1978-)
Pulse *318*

Phyllis Somerville
Little Children *237*

Josef Sommer (1934-)
X-Men: The Last Stand *447*

Rich Sommer
The Devil Wears Prada *104*

Chloe Sonnenfeld
RV *335*

Nikki SooHoo (1988-)
Stick It *373*

Bahar Soomekh
Saw III *340*

Nina Sosanya
Manderlay *254*

Shannyn Sossamon (1979-)
The Holiday *181*

Paul Soter (1972-)
Beerfest *32*

Christina Souza
End of the Spear *119*

Sissy Spacek (1949-)
An American Haunting *8*

Kevin Spacey (1959-)
Superman Returns *379*

David Spade (1964-)
The Benchwarmers *34*
Grandma's Boy *166*

Gabriel Spahiu
The Death of Mr. Lazarescu *94*

Joe Spano (1946-)
Hollywoodland *183*

Scott Speedman (1975-)
Underworld: Evolution *410*

Ed Speleers
Eragon *121*

Bruce Spence (1945-)
Aquamarine *14*

Brent Spiner (1949-)
Material Girls *261*

Sylvester Stallone (1946-)
Rocky Balboa *328*

Sebastian Stan
The Covenant *81*

John Standing (1934-)
Lassie *228*

Aaron Stanford
The Hills Have Eyes *178*
X-Men: The Last Stand *447*

Harry Dean Stanton (1926-)
Inland Empire *201*

Robert Stanton
Find Me Guilty *131*

Mike Starr (1950-)
The Black Dahlia *39*

Jason Statham (1972-)
Crank *83*

Imelda Staunton (1956-)
Nanny McPhee *275*

Brian Steele
Underworld: Evolution *410*

Vilia Steele
The Second Chance *351*

Agles Steib
Turistas *404*

Jessica Steinbaum
Wassup Rockers *429*

Bob Stephenson
Friends with Money *148*

Mindy Sterling (1954-)
Ice Age: The Meltdown *(V)* *191*

Jenna Stern (1967-)
16 Blocks *363*

Steve-O
Jackass Number Two *207*

Fisher Stevens (1963-)
Factotum *125*

Sheff Stevens
Poster Boy *309*

Juliet Stevenson (1956-)
Infamous *200*

Patrick Stewart (1940-)
X-Men: The Last Stand *447*

David Ogden Stiers (1942-)
Hoodwinked *(V)* *185*
Lady in the Water *(V)* *223*

Julia Stiles (1981-)
The Omen *292*

Ben Stiller (1965-)
Night at the Museum *280*
School for Scoundrels *345*
Tenacious D in the Pick of Destiny *386*

Erik Stolhanske
Beerfest *32*

Jessica Stone
Loverboy *247*

Joss Stone
Eragon *121*

Sharon Stone (1958-)
Basic Instinct 2 *31*
Bobby *45*

Cara Stoner
End of the Spear *119*

Dirk Storm
See Kevin Nealon

Peter Stormare (1953-)
Nacho Libre *273*

Steven Strait
The Covenant *81*

David Strathairn (1949-)
The Notorious Bettie Page *286*
We Are Marshall *432*

Geoffrey Streatsfield
Kinky Boots *220*

Meryl Streep (1949-)
The Ant Bully *(V)* *11*
The Devil Wears Prada *104*
A Prairie Home Companion *311*

Mark Strong
Tristan & Isolde *396*

Cecilia Suarez
The Three Burials of Melquiades Estrada *391*

Tara Subkoff (1973-)
The Notorious Bettie Page *286*

David Suchet (1946-)
Flushed Away *(V)* *139*

Nicole Sullivan (1970-)
The Ant Bully *(V)* *11*

Betty Sun
Jet Li's Fearless *208*

Daniel Sunjata
The Devil Wears Prada *104*

Ethan Suplee
Art School Confidential *18*
Clerks II *76*

Tammin Sursok (1983-)
Aquamarine *14*

Donald Sutherland (1934-)
An American Haunting *8*
Ask the Dust *19*
Beerfest *32*

Kiefer Sutherland (1966-)
The Sentinel *353*
The Wild *(V)* *439*

Hilary Swank (1974-)
The Black Dahlia *39*

Nick Swardson
Art School Confidential *18*
The Benchwarmers *34*
Grandma's Boy *166*

Patrick Swayze (1952-)
Keeping Mum *215*

Julia Sweeney (1961-)
Don't Come Knocking *106*

Wanda Sykes
Barnyard *(V)* *30*
Clerks II *76*
My Super Ex-Girlfriend *270*
Over the Hedge *(V)* *295*

Magda Szubanski (1961-)
Happy Feet *(V)* *173*

Amber Tamblyn (1983-)
The Grudge 2 *169*

Oga Tanaka
The Grudge 2 *169*

Zoe Tapper
Mrs. Palfrey at the Claremont *266*

Said Tarchani
Babel *27*

Antonio Tarver
Rocky Balboa *328*

Larenz Tate (1975-)
Waist Deep *426*

Channing Tatum
She's the Man *360*
Step Up *372*

Audrey Tautou (1978-)
The Da Vinci Code *88*
Russian Dolls *334*

Georgia Taylor
The History Boys *179*

Jayceon Taylor
See The Game

Lili Taylor (1967-)
Factotum *125*
The Notorious Bettie Page *286*

Noah Taylor (1969-)
The Proposition *316*

Rachael Taylor
See No Evil *352*

Renee Taylor (1935-)
The Boynton Beach Club *49*
Ice Age: The Meltdown *(V)* *191*

Sandra Taylor
Keeping Up with the Steins *216*

Brian Tee
The Fast and the Furious: Tokyo Drift *128*

Juno Temple
Notes on a Scandal *284*

Lew Temple
The Texas Chainsaw Massacre: The Beginning *387*

Jon Tenney (1961-)
Looking for Comedy in the Muslim World *244*

Judy Tenuta
Material Girls *261*

Lee Tergesen (1965-)
The Texas Chainsaw Massacre: The Beginning *387*

Maria Thayer
Accepted *1*
Strangers with Candy *377*

Justin Theroux (1971-)
Inland Empire *201*
Miami Vice *262*
Strangers with Candy *377*

David Thewlis (1963-)
Basic Instinct 2 *31*
The Omen *292*

Jay Thomas (1948-)
The Santa Clause 3: The Escape Clause *339*

Jonathan Thomas
The Second Chance *351*

Kristin Scott Thomas
Keeping Mum *215*

Don Thompson
Slither *365*

Emma Thompson (1959-)
Nanny McPhee *275*
Stranger Than Fiction *375*

Fred Dalton Thompson (1942-)
Looking for Comedy in the Muslim World *244*

Jack Thompson (1940-)
The Good German *159*

Kenan Thompson (1978-)
Snakes on a Plane *366*

Tessa Thompson (1983-)
When a Stranger Calls *434*

Tracie Thoms
The Devil Wears Prada *104*

Erik Thomson
Somersault *367*

Billy Bob Thornton (1955-)
School for Scoundrels *345*

Uma Thurman (1970-)
My Super Ex-Girlfriend *270*

Jennifer Tilly (1963-)
Tideland *392*

Jamie Tirelli
The Groomsmen *167*

Jason J. Tobin
The Fast and the Furious: Tokyo Drift *128*

Stephen Tobolowsky (1951-)
Failure to Launch *127*
Just My Luck *213*

Marisa Tomei (1964-)
Factotum *125*
Loverboy *247*

Lily Tomlin (1939-)
The Ant Bully *(V)* *11*
A Prairie Home Companion *311*

Gordon Tootoosis
Open Season *(V)* *294*

Rip Torn (1931-)
Marie Antoinette *257*
Zoom *451*

Joe Torre
Everyone's Hero *(V)* *122*

Luis Tosar
Miami Vice *262*

Shaun Toub
The Nativity Story *276*

Russell Tovey
The History Boys *179*

Katharine Towne (1978-)
Something New *369*

Stanley Townsend
The Nativity Story *276*

Ugo Soussan Trabelsi
Time to Leave *394*

Michelle Trachtenberg (1985-)
Black Christmas *38*

Danny Trejo (1944-)
Sherrybaby *358*

Raoul Trujillo
Apocalypto *12*

Nicholas Tse
The Promise *315*

Stanley Tucci (1960-)
The Devil Wears Prada *104*
Lucky Number Slevin *249*

Jonathan Tucker (1982-)
Pulse *318*

Alan Tudyk (1971-)
Ice Age: The Meltdown *(V)* *191*

Houston Tumlin (1992-)
Talladega Nights: The Ballad of Ricky Bobby *384*

Robin Tunney (1972-)
Hollywoodland *183*

Paige Turco (1965-)
Invincible *204*

Bree Turner
Just My Luck *213*

Kathleen Turner (1954-)
Monster House *(V)* *268*

Kett Turton
Firewall *133*

John Turturro (1957-)
The Good Shepherd *161*

Aisha Tyler
The Santa Clause 3: The Escape Clause *339*

Liv Tyler (1977-)
Lonesome Jim *242*

Zach Tyler
The Ant Bully *(V)* *11*

Tyrese
See Tyrese Gibson

Cicely Tyson (1933-)
Madea's Family Reunion *251*

Mike Tyson (1966-)
Scary Movie 4 *344*

Galina Tyunina
Night Watch *283*

Mark Umbers (1973-)
A Good Woman *163*

Blair Underwood (1964-)
Madea's Family Reunion *251*
Something New *369*

Deborah Kara Unger (1966-)
Silent Hill *361*

Gabrielle Union (1973-)
Running with Scissors *331*

Misako Uno (1986-)
The Grudge 2 *169*

Brenda Vaccaro (1939-)
The Boynton Beach Club *49*

Wilmer Valderrama
Unaccompanied Minors *408*

Milton Valesquez
Wassup Rockers *429*

Willeke Van Ammelrooy (1944-)
The Lake House *225*

Dick Van Dyke (1925-)
Curious George *(V)* *85*
Night at the Museum *280*

Travis Van Winkle
Accepted *1*

Pierre Vaneck (1931-)
The Science of Sleep *347*

Jacob Vargas
Bobby *45*

Indira Varma
Basic Instinct 2 *31*

Vince Vaughn (1970-)
The Break-Up *51*

Makenzie Vega (1994-)
Just My Luck *213*
X-Men: The Last Stand *447*

Johnny Vegas
The Libertine *236*

Carlos Velasco
Wassup Rockers *429*

Eddie Velasquez
Wassup Rockers *429*

Jonathan Velasquez
Wassup Rockers *429*

Lenny Venito
The Wild *(V)* *439*

Milo Ventimiglia (1977-)
Rocky Balboa *328*

Lino Ventura (1919-87)
Army of Shadows *16*

Maribel Verdu (1970-)
Pan's Labyrinth *299*

Ben Vereen (1946-)
Idlewild *194*

Viktor Verzhbitsky
Night Watch *283*

Ronan Vibert
Tristan & Isolde *396*

Christina Vidal
See No Evil *352*

Steven Vidler (1960-)
See No Evil *352*

Vince Vieluf (1970-)
Firewall *133*

Ronan Vilbert
Beowulf & Grendel *35*

J.R. Villarreal (1992-)
Akeelah and the Bee *2*

Louise Vincent
Gabrielle *151*

Jan Vlasak
Hostel *188*

Mike Vogel
Poseidon *308*

Jon Voight (1938-)
Glory Road *156*

Arnold Vosloo (1962-)
Blood Diamond *41*

Julian Wadham (1958-)
Wah-Wah *425*

Robert Wagner (1930-)
Everyone's Hero *(V)* *122*
Hoot *186*

Donnie Wahlberg (1969-)
Annapolis *10*

Mark Wahlberg (1971-)
The Departed *99*
Invincible *204*

Christopher Walken (1943-)
Click *78*
Man of the Year *252*

Paul Walker (1973-)
Eight Below *117*
Flags of Our Fathers *135*
Running Scared *330*

Peggy Walton Walker
The Second Chance *351*

Basil Wallace
Blood Diamond *41*

Eli Wallach (1915-)
The Holiday *181*

David Walliams
Tristram Shandy: A Cock and Bull Story *398*

Michael Wallis
Cars *(V)* *63*

Dylan Walsh (1963-)
The Lake House *225*

Jessica Walter (1940-)
Unaccompanied Minors *408*

Ashley Walters
Goal! The Dream Begins *157*

Julie Walters (1950-)
Wah-Wah *425*

Patrick Warburton (1964-)
Hoodwinked *(V)* *185*
Open Season *(V)* *294*
The Wild *(V)* *439*

Sela Ward (1957-)
The Guardian *170*

Amelia Warner
Winter Passing *441*

Julie Warner (1965-)
Stick It *373*

Kiersten Warren
Hoot *186*

Marcia Warren
Mrs. Palfrey at the Claremont *266*

David Warshofsky
Running Scared *330*

Denzel Washington (1954-)
Deja Vu *97*
Inside Man *202*

De'Shawn Washington
Step Up *372*

Jascha Washington
Last Holiday *229*

Kerry Washington (1977-)
The Last King of Scotland *231*
Little Man *239*

Ken(saku) Watanabe (1959-)
Letters from Iwo Jima *234*

Emily Watson (1967-)
The Proposition *316*
Wah-Wah *425*

Muse Watson (1948-)
Down in the Valley *109*

Vernee Watson-Johnson
The Ant Bully *(V)* *11*

Naomi Watts (1968-)
Inland Empire *(V)* *201*

Marlon Wayans (1972-)
Little Man *239*

Shawn Wayans (1971-)
Little Man *239*

Jason Weaver
ATL *21*

Sigourney Weaver (1949-)
Infamous *200*

Hugo Weaving (1959-)
Happy Feet *(V)* *173*
V for Vendetta *419*

Robin Weigert
The Good German *159*

Kevin Weisman
Clerks II *76*

Rachel Weisz (1971-)
Eragon *(V)* *121*
The Fountain *144*

Frank Welker (1945-)
The Ant Bully *(V)* *11*
Curious George *(V)* *85*

David Wenham (1965-)
The Proposition *316*

Richmond Werner
Last Holiday *229*

Michael Weston
The Last Kiss *232*

Forest Whitaker (1961-)
Everyone's Hero *(V)* *122*
The Last King of Scotland *231*

Bernard White
American Dreamz *6*

Brian White
Brick *53*

Lillias White
Game 6 *152*

Lynn Whitfield (1953-)
Madea's Family Reunion *251*

Daniel Lawrence Whitney
See Larry the Cable Guy

Jodie Whittaker
Venus *421*

Annie Whittle
The World's Fastest Indian *445*

Connor Widdows
X-Men: The Last Stand *447*

Natasha Wightman
V for Vendetta *419*

Olivia Wilde
Turistas *404*

Misty Wilkins
Bubble *57*

Tom Wilkinson (1948-)
A Good Woman *163*
The Last Kiss *232*

Fred Willard (1939-)
Date Movie *91*
For Your Consideration *142*
Monster House *(V)* *268*

Chris(topher) Williams
The World's Fastest Indian *445*

Harland Williams (1967-)
Employee of the Month *118*

Heathcote Williams (1941-)
Basic Instinct 2 *31*

Malinda Williams (1975-)
Idlewild *194*

Mark Williams (1959-)
Tristram Shandy: A Cock and Bull Story *398*

Olivia Williams (1969-)
X-Men: The Last Stand *447*

Robin Williams (1952-)
Everyone's Hero *(V)* *122*
Happy Feet *(V)* *173*
Man of the Year *252*
Night at the Museum *280*
The Night Listener *282*
RV *335*

Tyler James Williams
Unaccompanied Minors *408*

Tyrell Jackson Williams
Failure to Launch *127*

Kimberly Williams-Paisley
How to Eat Fried Worms *189*
We Are Marshall *432*

Mykelti Williamson (1960-)
ATL *21*
Lucky Number Slevin *249*

Bruce Willis (1955-)
Lucky Number Slevin *249*
Over the Hedge *(V)* *295*
16 Blocks *363*

Anthony H. Wilson
Tristram Shandy: A Cock and Bull Story *398*

Debra Wilson
Scary Movie 4 *344*

Luke Wilson (1971-)
Hoot *186*
Idiocracy *192*
My Super Ex-Girlfriend *270*

Owen Wilson (1968-)
Cars *(V)* *63*
Night at the Museum *280*
You, Me and Dupree *449*

Patrick Wilson (1973-)
Hard Candy *175*
Little Children *237*
Running with Scissors *331*

Rainn Wilson (1968-)
My Super Ex-Girlfriend *270*

Reno Wilson
Crank *83*

Richard Wilson
The Proposition *316*

Thomas F. Wilson (1959-)
Larry the Cable Guy: Health Inspector *227*
Zoom *451*

Penelope Wilton (1946-)
The History Boys *179*

Philip Winchester
Flyboys *140*

Oprah Winfrey (1954-)
Charlotte's Web *71*

Henry Winkler (1945-)
Click *78*

Katheryn Winnick (1978-)
Failure to Launch *127*

Kate Winslet (1975-)
All the King's Men *4*
Flushed Away *(V)* *139*
The Holiday *181*
Little Children *237*

Mary Elizabeth Winstead (1984-)
Black Christmas *38*
Bobby *45*
Final Destination 3 *130*

Ray Winstone (1957-)
The Departed *99*
The Proposition *316*

John Witherspoon
Little Man *239*

Alicia Witt (1975-)
Last Holiday *229*

Frank Witter
Joyeux Noel *211*

Bess Wohl
The Shaggy Dog *357*

Kea Wong
X-Men: The Last Stand *447*

Elijah Wood (1981-)
Bobby *45*
Happy Feet *(V)* *173*

Evan Rachel Wood (1987-)
Down in the Valley *109*
Running with Scissors *331*

Alfre Woodard (1953-)
Something New *369*
Take the Lead *383*

Danny Woodburn
Employee of the Month *118*

Jonathan M. Woodward
The Notorious Bettie Page *286*

Fenella Woolger
Scoop *349*
Wah-Wah *425*

Sam Worthington
Somersault *367*

Jeffrey Wright (1965-)
Casino Royale *65*
Lady in the Water *223*

Yu Xiaowei
The Promise *315*

Xzibit (1974-)
Hoodwinked *(V)* *185*

Raghuvir Yadav
Water *430*

Koji Yakusho (1956-)
Babel *27*

Tony Yalda (1981-)
American Dreamz *6*

Liu Ye
Curse of the Golden Flower *86*

Liu Yeh
The Promise *315*

Dwight Yoakam (1956-)
Crank *83*
The Three Burials of Melquiades Estrada *391*

Dong Yong
Jet Li's Fearless *208*

Arthur Young
When a Stranger Calls *434*

Burt Young (1940-)
Rocky Balboa *328*

Karen Young (1958-)
Factotum *125*

Lee Thompson Young
Akeelah and the Bee *2*

Rudy Youngblood
Apocalypto *12*

Harris Yulin (1937-)
Game 6 *152*

Chow Yun-Fat (1955-)
Curse of the Golden Flower *86*

Grace Zabriskie (1938-)
Inland Empire *201*

Florin Zamfirescu
The Death of Mr. Lazarescu *94*

Billy Zane (1966-)
BloodRayne *44*

David Zayas
16 Blocks *363*

Kevin Zegers (1984-)
Zoom *451*

Nora Zehetner
Brick *53*

Iris Zelaya
Wassup Rockers *429*

Malik Zidi
Changing Times *69*

Jose Zuniga
Mission: Impossible III *264*

Subject Index

Action-Adventure
The Ant Bully *11*
Apocalypto *12*
Beowulf & Grendel *35*
Blood Diamond *41*
Casino Royale *65*
Catch a Fire *67*
Crank *83*
Deja Vu *97*
Eight Below *117*
The Fast and the Furious: Tokyo Drift *128*
Firewall *133*
Flyboys *140*
The Guardian *170*
How to Eat Fried Worms *189*
Last Holiday *229*
Letters from Iwo Jima *234*
The Marine *259*
Miami Vice *262*
Pirates of the Caribbean: Dead Man's Chest *306*
Poseidon *308*
The Promise *315*
The Proposition *316*
Rocky Balboa *328*
Running Scared *330*
The Sentinel *353*
16 Blocks *363*
Superman Returns *379*
The Three Burials of Melquiades Estrada *391*
Ultraviolet *407*
Underworld: Evolution *410*
V for Vendetta *419*
Waist Deep *426*
World Trade Center *443*
X-Men: The Last Stand *447*

Action-Comedy
My Super Ex-Girlfriend *270*

Adapted from a Book
Casino Royale *65*
Gabrielle *151*
A Good Woman *163*
A Scanner Darkly *342*

Adapted from a Fairy Tale
Hoodwinked *185*
Lady in the Water *223*

Adapted from a Game
BloodRayne *44*
Silent Hill *361*

Adapted from a Play
Curse of the Golden Flower *86*
The History Boys *179*
The Libertine *236*

Adapted from a Poem
Beowulf & Grendel *35*

Adapted from a Radio Show
A Prairie Home Companion *311*

Adapted from a Story
Gabrielle *151*
Old Joy *291*

Adapted from an Opera
Crank *83*

Adapted from Comics
Art School Confidential *18*
Garfield: A Tail of Two Kitties *154*
Over the Hedge *295*
Superman Returns *379*
V for Vendetta *419*
Zoom *451*

Adapted from Television
Miami Vice *262*
Strangers with Candy *377*

Adolescence
Down in the Valley *109*
The History Boys *179*

Adoption
Nacho Libre *273*
The Quiet *325*

Africa
Babel *27*
Blood Diamond *41*
Changing Times *69*
Curious George *85*
The Last King of Scotland *231*
Tsotsi *401*
Wah-Wah *425*
The Wild *439*

Aging
The Boynton Beach Club *49*
Changing Times *69*
The Death of Mr. Lazarescu *94*
Don't Come Knocking *106*
Mrs. Palfrey at the Claremont *266*

Rocky Balboa *328*
Venus *421*
The World's Fastest Indian *445*

Airplanes or Air Travel
Flyboys *140*
Snakes on a Plane *366*
Superman Returns *379*
United 93 *412*
We Are Marshall *432*

Alcoholism
Ask the Dust *19*
Factotum *125*
Flags of Our Fathers *135*
The Libertine *236*
Running with Scissors *331*
16 Blocks *363*
Winter Passing *441*

Alien Beings
Superman Returns *379*

American Heartland
Lonesome Jim *242*

American Remakes of Asian Films
The Departed *99*
The Grudge 2 *169*
Pulse *318*

American Remakes of European Films
The Last Kiss *232*

American South
All the King's Men *4*
An American Haunting *8*
Madea's Family Reunion *251*
Manderlay *254*
We Are Marshall *432*

Amnesia
Unknown White Male *413*

Amusement Parks
Final Destination 3 *130*

Angels
Click *78*

Animals
Barnyard *30*
Curious George *85*
Hoodwinked *185*
Hoot *186*
Ice Age: The Meltdown *191*
Open Season *294*
Over the Hedge *295*
The Shaggy Dog *357*
The Wild *439*

Animation & Cartoons
The Ant Bully *11*
Barnyard *30*
Cars *63*
Curious George *85*
Everyone's Hero *122*
Flushed Away *139*
Garfield: A Tail of Two Kitties *154*
Happy Feet *173*
Hoodwinked *185*
Ice Age: The Meltdown *191*
Monster House *268*
Open Season *294*
Over the Hedge *295*
The Wild *439*

Anti-Heroes
16 Blocks *363*
Ultraviolet *407*
V for Vendetta *419*

Anti-War War Films
Joyeux Noel *211*

Apartheid
Catch a Fire *67*

Arctic or Antarctic Regions
Happy Feet *173*
The Santa Clause 3: The Escape Clause *339*
Unaccompanied Minors *408*
Winter Passing *441*

Art or Artists
Art School Confidential *18*
The Da Vinci Code *88*
The Science of Sleep *347*

Assassins or Assassination
Bobby *45*

Australia
The Proposition *316*

Automobiles
Cars *63*
The Fast and the Furious: Tokyo Drift *128*
Who Killed the Electric Car? *435*

Automobiles—Racing
Cars *63*
The Fast and the Furious: Tokyo Drift *128*
Talladega Nights: The Ballad of Ricky Bobby *384*

Babysitting
Babel *27*
When a Stranger Calls *434*

Bachelor Party
Failure to Launch *127*

Baseball
The Benchwarmers *34*
The Break-Up *51*
Everyone's Hero *122*
Game 6 *152*
The King *218*

Basketball
Glory Road *156*
The Heart of the Game *177*
John Tucker Must Die *209*

Beauty Pageants
Little Miss Sunshine *240*

Behind the Scenes
Borat: Cultural Learnings of America for Make Benefit Glorious Nation of Kazakhstan *48*
For Your Consideration *142*
Hollywoodland *183*
Inland Empire *201*

Berlin
The Good German *159*

Biography
Catch a Fire *67*
Jet Li's Fearless *208*
The Notorious Bettie Page *286*
Unknown White Male *413*

Biography: Music
The Devil and Daniel Johnston *102*
The U.S. vs. John Lennon *415*

Biography: Show Business
The Notorious Bettie Page *286*

Birds
Hoot *186*

Black Culture
Akeelah and the Bee *2*
Dave Chappelle's Block Party *92*
Dreamgirls *111*
Glory Road *156*
Idlewild *194*
Last Holiday *229*

Madea's Family Reunion *251*
Manderlay *254*
Phat Girlz *301*
The Pursuit of Happyness *319*
Something New *369*
Waist Deep *426*

Blackmail
The Sentinel *353*

Boats or Ships
Failure to Launch *127*
Flushed Away *139*
Poseidon *308*

Books or Bookstores
Tristram Shandy: A Cock and Bull Story *398*

Boston
The Departed *99*
Game 6 *152*

Boxing
Annapolis *10*
Rocky Balboa *328*

Buddhism
The Covenant *81*

Buses
Wassup Rockers *429*

Business or Industry
Hoot *186*
Material Girls *261*
Who Killed the Electric Car? *435*
Why We Fight *436*

Cannibalism
The Descent *101*
The Hills Have Eyes *178*
The Texas Chainsaw Massacre: The Beginning *387*

Carnivals or Circuses
Final Destination 3 *130*

Cats
Garfield: A Tail of Two Kitties *154*

Central America
Apocalypto *12*

Cheerleaders
John Tucker Must Die *209*

Chicago
The Break-Up *51*
Everyone's Hero *122*
The Lake House *225*
Stranger Than Fiction *375*

Child Abuse
Don't Tell *108*
Running Scared *330*

Childhood
Akeelah and the Bee *2*
The Ant Bully *11*
Cache *61*
Charlotte's Web *71*
Monster House *268*
Pan's Labyrinth *299*
Tideland *392*
Water *430*

Children
Everyone's Hero *122*
Freedomland *146*
Hoot *186*
Nanny McPhee *275*
Sherrybaby *358*
Silent Hill *361*
Unaccompanied Minors *408*

China
Curse of the Golden Flower *86*
Jet Li's Fearless *208*
Mission: Impossible III *264*
The Promise *315*

Christmas
Black Christmas *38*
Deck the Halls *96*
The Holiday *181*
Joyeux Noel *211*
The Santa Clause 3: The Escape Clause *339*
Unaccompanied Minors *408*

Clergymen
The King *218*
The Second Chance *351*

Clothing or Fashion
The Devil Wears Prada *104*
Kinky Boots *220*
Phat Girlz *301*

Coast Guard
The Guardian *170*

Cold War
The Good Shepherd *161*

College
Accepted *1*
Poster Boy *309*
We Are Marshall *432*

Comedy
Accepted *1*
Aquamarine *14*
Art School Confidential *18*
Beerfest *32*
Big Momma's House 2 *37*
The Break-Up *51*
Cars *63*
Click *78*
Date Movie *91*
Duck Season *113*
Failure to Launch *127*
Grandma's Boy *166*
Hoodwinked *185*
Hoot *186*
Imagine Me & You *197*
John Tucker Must Die *209*
Just My Luck *213*
Keeping Mum *215*
Last Holiday *229*
Little Man *239*
Looking for Comedy in the Muslim World *244*
Madea's Family Reunion *251*
Nacho Libre *273*
Nanny McPhee *275*
Night at the Museum *280*
The Pink Panther *304*
School for Scoundrels *345*
Scoop *349*
The Shaggy Dog *357*
Something New *369*
Stick It *373*
Strangers with Candy *377*
Tristram Shandy: A Cock and Bull Story *398*
Wassup Rockers *429*
You, Me and Dupree *449*

Comedy-Drama
Art School Confidential *18*
The Devil Wears Prada *104*
Game 6 *152*
A Good Woman *163*
The Groomsmen *167*
Little Miss Sunshine *240*
Lonesome Jim *242*
Madea's Family Reunion *251*
The Matador *260*
Mrs. Palfrey at the Claremont *266*
A Prairie Home Companion *311*
Russian Dolls *334*
Wassup Rockers *429*

Comedy Performance
Dave Chappelle's Block Party *92*

Coming of Age
Barnyard *30*
Eragon *121*
Keeping Up with the Steins *216*
Running with Scissors *331*
Somersault *367*
Wah-Wah *425*

Computers
Big Momma's House 2 *37*

Concert Films
Awesome! I F***in' Shot That! *23*
Dave Chappelle's Block Party *92*
Neil Young: Heart of Gold *278*

Conspiracies or Conspiracy Theories
The Da Vinci Code *88*
16 Blocks *363*

Contract Killers
Lucky Number Slevin *249*
The Matador *260*
Shadowboxer *355*

Cooking
Last Holiday *229*

Crime or Criminals
Bubble *57*
The Departed *99*
Find Me Guilty *131*
Freedomland *146*
Little Man *239*
The Matador *260*
The Proposition *316*
The Second Chance *351*
16 Blocks *363*
Tsotsi *401*
Waist Deep *426*

Dance
Happy Feet *173*
Step Up *372*
Take the Lead *383*

Deadly Viruses
Ultraviolet *407*

Deafness
Babel *27*
The Quiet *325*

Demons or Wizards
Eragon *121*

Deserts
The Hills Have Eyes *178*
The Three Burials of Melquiades Estrada *391*

Detroit
Dreamgirls *111*

Devils
The Omen *292*

Disaster Films
Poseidon *308*

Divorce
Duck Season *113*
Thank You for Smoking *389*
Wah-Wah *425*

Doctors
Turistas *404*

Doctors or Nurses
The Death of Mr. Lazarescu *94*
The Last King of Scotland *231*
Saw III *340*

Documentary Films
Awesome! I F***in' Shot That! *23*
Dave Chappelle's Block Party *92*
The Devil and Daniel Johnston *102*
The Heart of the Game *177*
An Inconvenient Truth *199*
Neil Young: Heart of Gold *278*
Unknown White Male *413*
The U.S. vs. John Lennon *415*
Who Killed the Electric Car? *435*
Why We Fight *436*
Wordplay *442*

Dogs
Eight Below *117*
Garfield: A Tail of Two Kitties *154*
The Hills Have Eyes *178*
The Lake House *225*
Lassie *228*
The Shaggy Dog *357*

Dragons
Eragon *121*

Drama
Akeelah and the Bee *2*
An American Haunting *8*
Annapolis *10*
Apocalypto *12*
Army of Shadows *16*
Ask the Dust *19*
ATL *21*
Beowulf & Grendel *35*
Bubble *57*
Cache *61*
Changing Times *69*
Climates *80*
Curse of the Golden Flower *86*
The Death of Mr. Lazarescu *94*
Down in the Valley *109*
Eight Below *117*
End of the Spear *119*
The Fast and the Furious: Tokyo Drift *128*
Final Destination 3 *130*
Firewall *133*
Flyboys *140*
Freedomland *146*
Glory Road *156*
Goal! The Dream Begins *157*
The Good German *159*
A Good Woman *163*
Joyeux Noel *211*
The King *218*
The Lake House *225*
The Last Kiss *232*
The Libertine *236*
The Lost City *245*
Loverboy *247*
Manderlay *254*
Marie Antoinette *257*
Mrs. Palfrey at the Claremont *266*
The Nativity Story *276*
The Promise *315*
The Proposition *316*
Running Scared *330*
The Second Chance *351*
16 Blocks *363*
Superman Returns *379*
Take the Lead *383*
The Three Burials of Melquiades Estrada *391*
Tristan & Isolde *396*
Trust the Man *400*
Tsotsi *401*
Venus *421*
Wah-Wah *425*
Waist Deep *426*
Wassup Rockers *429*
Winter Passing *441*
The World's Fastest Indian *445*

Drug Abuse
Running with Scissors *331*
A Scanner Darkly *342*
Tideland *392*

Drugs
Little Miss Sunshine *240*
Sherrybaby *358*
16 Blocks *363*
Tenacious D in the Pick of Destiny *386*

Dystopian Themes
V for Vendetta *419*

Ecology or Environment
Happy Feet *173*

Education or Schooling
Akeelah and the Bee *2*
Art School Confidential *18*
The History Boys *179*
How to Eat Fried Worms *189*

Elevators
Just My Luck *213*
The Shaggy Dog *357*

Engagement
Clerks II *76*
The Illusionist *196*
Mission: Impossible III *264*

Entertainment Industry
American Dreamz *6*
Awesome! I F***in' Shot That! *23*
For Your Consideration *142*
Hollywoodland *183*
Idlewild *194*
Neil Young: Heart of Gold *278*
Tenacious D in the Pick of Destiny *386*

Epic Battles
Beowulf & Grendel *35*
Eragon *121*
Flags of Our Fathers *135*
Joyeux Noel *211*
Letters from Iwo Jima *234*
Night Watch *283*

Escapes
Poseidon *308*
The Wild *439*

Family
Down in the Valley *109*
The King *218*

Family Comedy
Cars *63*
Click *78*
Garfield: A Tail of Two Kitties *154*
Hoot *186*
Ice Age: The Meltdown *191*
Keeping Up with the Steins *216*
Madea's Family Reunion *251*
Nanny McPhee *275*
RV *335*
The Shaggy Dog *357*

Family Drama
An American Haunting *8*
Don't Come Knocking *106*
Flicka *138*
Little Miss Sunshine *240*
Lonesome Jim *242*
The Lost City *245*
Loverboy *247*
The Pursuit of Happyness *319*
Running with Scissors *331*
Time to Leave *394*
Volver *423*
Winter Passing *441*

Family Films
Goal! The Dream Begins *157*
Invincible *204*
The Shaggy Dog *357*

Family Reunions
Madea's Family Reunion *251*
Winter Passing *441*

Fantasy
Aquamarine *14*
Beowulf & Grendel *35*
BloodRayne *44*
Cars *63*
Click *78*
Eragon *121*
Just My Luck *213*
Lady in the Water *223*
The Lake House *225*
Nanny McPhee *275*
Night Watch *283*
Pan's Labyrinth *299*
The Promise *315*
The Science of Sleep *347*
The Shaggy Dog *357*
Superman Returns *379*
Tideland *392*

Farms or Farming
Barnyard *30*
Charlotte's Web *71*

Fascism
Army of Shadows *16*

Fathers
Barnyard *30*
Blood Diamond *41*
Click *78*
Don't Come Knocking *106*
Keeping Up with the Steins *216*
Night at the Museum *280*
The Notorious Bettie Page *286*
Poster Boy *309*
The Pursuit of Happyness *319*
Rocky Balboa *328*
Underworld: Evolution *410*

Female Domestic Employees
Friends with Money *148*
Keeping Mum *215*
The Omen *292*

Female Friends
Aquamarine *14*
Don't Tell *108*
Dreamgirls *111*
Friends with Money *148*
John Tucker Must Die *209*
Notes on a Scandal *284*
Phat Girlz *301*
Water *430*

Femme Fatales
Basic Instinct 2 *31*
The Black Dahlia *39*
The Bridesmaid *55*
Hostel *188*

Film Noir
The Black Dahlia *39*
Brick *53*
Hollywoodland *183*

Filmmaking
Tristram Shandy: A Cock and Bull Story *398*

Firemen
World Trade Center *443*

Flashback
All the King's Men *4*
Black Christmas *38*
Cache *61*
Flags of Our Fathers *135*
The Good Shepherd *161*
A Good Year *164*
Hollywoodland *183*
Jet Li's Fearless *208*
Notes on a Scandal *284*
The Return *327*
Saw III *340*
The Wicker Man *437*

Folklore or Legends
Beowulf & Grendel *35*
Tristan & Isolde *396*

Food
Last Holiday *229*

Food or Food Industry
Larry the Cable Guy: Health Inspector *227*

Football
Invincible *204*
We Are Marshall *432*

Foreign: Argentinean
The Aura *22*

Foreign: Australian
The Proposition *316*
Somersault *367*

Foreign: Belgian
The Child *73*
Joyeux Noel *211*

Foreign: British
Beowulf & Grendel *35*
Casino Royale *65*
Catch a Fire *67*
The Descent *101*
Flushed Away *139*
A Good Woman *163*
The History Boys *179*
Joyeux Noel *211*
Keeping Mum *215*
Kinky Boots *220*
Lassie *228*
The Last King of Scotland *231*
Mrs. Palfrey at the Claremont *266*
Nanny McPhee *275*
Notes on a Scandal *284*
The Piano Tuner of Earthquakes *303*
The Prestige *313*
The Proposition *316*
The Queen *323*
Russian Dolls *334*
Tideland *392*
Tristan & Isolde *396*
Venus *421*
Wah-Wah *425*

Foreign: Canadian
Beowulf & Grendel *35*
Black Christmas *38*
Silent Hill *361*
Slither *365*
Tideland *392*
Water *430*

Foreign: Chinese
Curse of the Golden Flower *86*
Jet Li's Fearless *208*
The Promise *315*

Foreign: Czech
Casino Royale *65*

Foreign: French
Army of Shadows *16*
The Aura *22*
The Bridesmaid *55*
Changing Times *69*
The Child *73*
Climates *80*
Gabrielle *151*
Inland Empire *201*
Joyeux Noel *211*
Lassie *228*
The Piano Tuner of Earthquakes *303*
The Queen *323*
Russian Dolls *334*
The Science of Sleep *347*
Silent Hill *361*
Time to Leave *394*
Wah-Wah *425*

Foreign: German
BloodRayne *44*
Casino Royale *65*
Factotum *125*
Gabrielle *151*
Joyeux Noel *211*
The Last King of Scotland *231*
The Piano Tuner of Earthquakes *303*
Tristan & Isolde *396*

Foreign: Hong Kong
Jet Li's Fearless *208*

Foreign: Icelandic
Beowulf & Grendel *35*

Foreign: Irish
Lassie *228*

Foreign: Italian
Army of Shadows *16*
Don't Tell *108*
Gabrielle *151*
A Good Woman *163*
The Queen *323*
The Science of Sleep *347*

Foreign: Mexican
Pan's Labyrinth *299*

Foreign: New Zealand
The World's Fastest Indian *445*

Foreign: Norwegian
Factotum *125*

Foreign: Polish
Inland Empire *201*

Foreign: Romanian
The Death of Mr. Lazarescu *94*
Joyeux Noel *211*

Foreign: Russian
Night Watch *283*

Foreign: South African
Catch a Fire *67*

Foreign: Spanish
The Aura *22*
A Good Woman *163*
Pan's Labyrinth *299*
Volver *423*

Foreign: Turkish
Climates *80*

Forests or Trees
Hoodwinked *185*
Old Joy *291*
Open Season *294*

Framed
The Sentinel *353*

France
Army of Shadows *16*
Cache *61*
Flyboys *140*
A Good Year *164*
Marie Antoinette *257*

Friends or Friendship
ATL *21*
Charlotte's Web *71*
Clerks II *76*
Duck Season *113*
Flyboys *140*
The Groomsmen *167*
Hoot *186*
Ice Age: The Meltdown *191*
Jackass Number Two *207*
The Last Kiss *232*
The Matador *260*
Old Joy *291*
Russian Dolls *334*

Talladega Nights: The Ballad of Ricky Bobby *384*
Tenacious D in the Pick of Destiny *386*
Venus *421*
You, Me and Dupree *449*

Funerals
The Queen *323*
The Three Burials of Melquiades Estrada *391*

Gambling
Casino Royale *65*

Game Shows
Stay Alive *371*

Games
Wordplay *442*

Gays or Lesbians
The Black Dahlia *39*
The History Boys *179*
Imagine Me & You *197*
Infamous *200*
Little Miss Sunshine *240*
The Night Listener *282*
Poster Boy *309*
Russian Dolls *334*
Time to Leave *394*

Gender Confusion
Kinky Boots *220*
She's the Man *360*

Genetics
X-Men: The Last Stand *447*

Genre Parody
Date Movie *91*
Hoodwinked *185*
Scary Movie 4 *344*

Germany
Beerfest *32*

Ghosts or Spirits
An American Haunting *8*
The Grudge 2 *169*
Pirates of the Caribbean: Dead Man's Chest *306*
Scoop *349*
Silent Hill *361*
Volver *423*

Gifted Children
Loverboy *247*

Great Britain
Children of Men *74*
Garfield: A Tail of Two Kitties *154*
Goal! The Dream Begins *157*
The History Boys *179*
The Holiday *181*
Imagine Me & You *197*
The Libertine *236*
Mrs. Palfrey at the Claremont *266*
Nanny McPhee *275*
The Omen *292*
Scoop *349*
Tristan & Isolde *396*
Tristram Shandy: A Cock and Bull Story *398*

Great Depression
Ask the Dust *19*

Grim Reaper
Final Destination 3 *130*

Gymnastics
Stick It *373*

Handicapped
The Aura *22*

High School
The Quiet *325*
Strangers with Candy *377*

Hispanic Culture
Wassup Rockers *429*

Holidays
Black Christmas *38*

Homeless
The Child *73*
The Pursuit of Happyness *319*

Homosexuality
Imagine Me & You *197*

Honeymoons
A Good Woman *163*

Horror
An American Haunting *8*
Black Christmas *38*
BloodRayne *44*
The Covenant *81*
The Descent *101*
The Grudge 2 *169*
The Hills Have Eyes *178*
Hostel *188*
Monster House *268*
Night Watch *283*
The Omen *292*
Pan's Labyrinth *299*
Pulse *318*
See No Evil *352*
Silent Hill *361*
The Texas Chainsaw Massacre: The Beginning *387*
When a Stranger Calls *434*

Horror Comedy
Scary Movie 4 *344*

Horses
Flicka *138*

Hospitals or Medicine
The Death of Mr. Lazarescu *94*

Hostages
Firewall *133*
Inside Man *202*
The Marine *259*
16 Blocks *363*

Hotels or Motels
Bobby *45*
Mrs. Palfrey at the Claremont *266*
See No Evil *352*

Immigration
Ask the Dust *19*
Children of Men *74*
The Three Burials of Melquiades Estrada *391*

Incest
An American Haunting *8*
Black Christmas *38*
The King *218*

India
Looking for Comedy in the Muslim World *244*
Water *430*

Infants
The Child *73*
Little Man *239*
The Omen *292*
Tsotsi *401*

Insects
Slither *365*

Inteligence Service Agencies
The Good Shepherd *161*

Interracial Affairs
Freedomland *146*
Glory Road *156*
Manderlay *254*
The Second Chance *351*
Shadowboxer *355*
Something New *369*
Wassup Rockers *429*

Interviews
An American Haunting *8*
Catch a Fire *67*

Islam
Looking for Comedy in the Muslim World *244*

Islands
Pirates of the Caribbean: Dead Man's Chest *306*
The Wicker Man *437*

Italy
A Good Woman *163*

Japan
Letters from Iwo Jima *234*

Journalism
Blood Diamond *41*
The Good German *159*
Scoop *349*
Superman Returns *379*

Judaism
Keeping Up with the Steins *216*
The Nativity Story *276*

Jungle Stories
Curious George *85*
End of the Spear *119*
Turistas *404*

Kidnappers or Kidnappings
Mission: Impossible III *264*
Running Scared *330*
The Three Burials of Melquiades Estrada *391*
Tsotsi *401*
Waist Deep *426*

Kings
The Libertine *236*
Tristan & Isolde *396*

Law or Lawyers
Find Me Guilty *131*
The Shaggy Dog *357*

Little People
Little Man *239*

Live Action/Animation Combinations
Garfield: A Tail of Two Kitties *154*
A Scanner Darkly *342*

London
Basic Instinct 2 *31*
Flushed Away *139*
Imagine Me & You *197*
Mrs. Palfrey at the Claremont *266*
Notes on a Scandal *284*
Russian Dolls *334*
Unknown White Male *413*
V for Vendetta *419*
Venus *421*

Loneliness
Changing Times *69*
Lonesome Jim *242*

Lonely Singles
Mrs. Palfrey at the Claremont *266*
Pan's Labyrinth *299*
Somersault *367*

Los Angeles
Akeelah and the Bee *2*
Ask the Dust *19*
Big Momma's House 2 *37*
The Black Dahlia *39*
Crank *83*
Down in the Valley *109*
Friends with Money *148*
Goal! The Dream Begins *157*
Hard Candy *175*
The Holiday *181*
Hollywoodland *183*
Sherrybaby *358*
Something New *369*
Waist Deep *426*
Wassup Rockers *429*

Louisiana
Stay Alive *371*

Mafia
Find Me Guilty *131*
Running Scared *330*

Magic
The Illusionist *196*
Nanny McPhee *275*
The Prestige *313*
Scoop *349*

Marriage
Cache *61*
Changing Times *69*
Click *78*
Friends with Money *148*
Gabrielle *151*
Keeping Mum *215*
The Last Kiss *232*
Marie Antoinette *257*
Notes on a Scandal *284*
Tristan & Isolde *396*
Trust the Man *400*

Martial Arts
Curse of the Golden Flower *86*
Firewall *133*
Jet Li's Fearless *208*
The Promise *315*
Ultraviolet *407*

May-December Romance
Venus *421*

Medieval Era
Tristan & Isolde *396*

Men
School for Scoundrels *345*

Mental Health
Hard Candy *175*
Running with Scissors *331*
Stranger Than Fiction *375*
Tideland *392*

Metamorphosis
Slither *365*

Mexico
Babel *27*
Duck Season *113*
Glory Road *156*
Goal! The Dream Begins *157*
The Matador *260*
Nacho Libre *273*
The Three Burials of Melquiades Estrada *391*

Miami
Miami Vice *262*

Middle East
Looking for Comedy in the Muslim World *244*
The Nativity Story *276*

Midlife Crisis
The Matador *260*

Military: Army
The Good German *159*
Why We Fight *436*

Military: Foreign
Flags of Our Fathers *135*
Letters from Iwo Jima *234*

Military: Marines
Annapolis *10*
Flags of Our Fathers *135*
The Marine *259*

Military: Navy
Annapolis *10*
Flags of Our Fathers *135*
The King *218*

Miners or Mining
Blood Diamond *41*

Minnesota
A Prairie Home Companion *311*

Missing Persons
Freedomland *146*
The Good German *159*
Lucky Number Slevin *249*
The Wicker Man *437*

Missionaries
End of the Spear *119*

Mistaken Identity
The Aura *22*
Big Momma's House 2 *37*
The Departed *99*
Failure to Launch *127*
Garfield: A Tail of Two Kitties *154*
Just My Luck *213*
Little Man *239*
Lucky Number Slevin *249*
Mrs. Palfrey at the Claremont *266*
She's the Man *360*

Modern Shakespeare
She's the Man *360*

Monkeys
Curious George *85*

Monks
The Da Vinci Code *88*
Nacho Libre *273*

Monsters
The Hills Have Eyes *178*
Slither *365*

Moscow
Night Watch *283*

Mothers
Loverboy *247*
Running with Scissors *331*
Silent Hill *361*
Volver *423*

Motorcycles
The World's Fastest Indian *445*

Multiple Personality Disorder
A Scanner Darkly *342*

Museums
Curious George *85*
The Da Vinci Code *88*
Night at the Museum *280*
Tenacious D in the Pick of Destiny *386*

Music: Hip-Hop or Rap
Dave Chappelle's Block Party *92*

Musical
A Prairie Home Companion *311*

Musicals
Dreamgirls *111*
A Prairie Home Companion *311*

Mystery & Suspense
Brick *53*
Bubble *57*
The Da Vinci Code *88*
Freedomland *146*
Hollywoodland *183*
Inland Empire *201*
The Night Listener *282*

Mythology or Legend
Tristan & Isolde *396*

Nashville
Neil Young: Heart of Gold *278*

Native Americans
Flags of Our Fathers *135*

New Jersey
Clerks II *76*
Freedomland *146*

New Orleans
Deja Vu *97*
Last Holiday *229*

New Year's Eve
Poseidon *308*

New York City
Art School Confidential *18*
Curious George *85*
Dave Chappelle's Block Party *92*
The Devil Wears Prada *104*
Everyone's Hero *122*
Game 6 *152*
Inside Man *202*
Just My Luck *213*
Lucky Number Slevin *249*
My Super Ex-Girlfriend *270*
Night at the Museum *280*
School for Scoundrels *345*
16 Blocks *363*
Take the Lead *383*
Trust the Man *400*
Unknown White Male *413*
The Wild *439*
Winter Passing *441*
World Trade Center *443*

New Zealand
The World's Fastest Indian *445*

Newspapers
Superman Returns *379*
Wordplay *442*

Nightclubs
Idlewild *194*
The Lost City *245*

Notable Death Scenes
The Omen *292*

Nuclear Disaster
The Hills Have Eyes *178*

Nuns or Priests
Joyeux Noel *211*
Nacho Libre *273*

Obsessive Love
The Bridesmaid *55*
Changing Times *69*
Loverboy *247*

Oceans or Oceanography
Happy Feet *173*
Poseidon *308*

Opera
Joyeux Noel *211*

Organized Crime
The Departed *99*
Lucky Number Slevin *249*
Manderlay *254*
Running Scared *330*

Pacific Islands
Flags of Our Fathers *135*
Letters from Iwo Jima *234*

Paperboys
The Benchwarmers *34*

Parallel Universe
Inland Empire *201*
Silent Hill *361*

Parenthood
Babel *27*
The Child *73*
Little Children *237*
Sherrybaby *358*
Thank You for Smoking *389*

Paris
Cache *61*
The Da Vinci Code *88*
The Devil Wears Prada *104*
Gabrielle *151*
The Pink Panther *304*
Russian Dolls *334*
The Science of Sleep *347*

Patriotism or Paranoia
The Good Shepherd *161*
Why We Fight *436*

Penguins
Happy Feet *173*
The Wild *439*

Period Piece
Curse of the Golden Flower *86*
The Promise *315*
Tristan & Isolde *396*

Period Piece: 1950s
All the King's Men *4*
End of the Spear *119*
The Good Shepherd *161*
Hollywoodland *183*
The Lost City *245*
The Notorious Bettie Page *286*

Period Piece: 1960s
Bobby *45*
Dreamgirls *111*
Glory Road *156*
The Good Shepherd *161*
Infamous *200*
Wah-Wah *425*
The World's Fastest Indian *445*

Period Piece: 1980s
Catch a Fire *67*
Find Me Guilty *131*
Game 6 *152*
The History Boys *179*
The Pursuit of Happyness *319*

Philosophy or Idealogy
The Fountain *144*

Phones
Black Christmas *38*
When a Stranger Calls *434*

Photography or Photographers
Flags of Our Fathers *135*
Hard Candy *175*
The Notorious Bettie Page *286*
Time to Leave *394*

Pigs
Charlotte's Web *71*

Pirates
Pirates of the Caribbean: Dead Man's Chest *306*

Police
The Black Dahlia *39*
Little Children *237*
Miami Vice *262*
The Wicker Man *437*

Political Campaigns
All the King's Men *4*
Bobby *45*
Man of the Year *252*
Poster Boy *309*

Politics and/or Government
All the King's Men *4*
Children of Men *74*
An Inconvenient Truth *199*
Looking for Comedy in the Muslim World *244*
The Lost City *245*
Man of the Year *252*
Manderlay *254*
The Omen *292*
The Queen *323*
Thank You for Smoking *389*
The U.S. vs. John Lennon *415*
V for Vendetta *419*
Who Killed the Electric Car? *435*
Why We Fight *436*

Pornography or Pornographers
Running Scared *330*

Post-Apocalypse
Ultraviolet *407*

Postwar Era
The Good German *159*

Poverty
The Child *73*
The Pursuit of Happyness *319*

Pregnancy
Children of Men *74*
The Last Kiss *232*
The Nativity Story *276*
The Santa Clause 3: The Escape Clause *339*
Shadowboxer *355*

Presidency
American Dreamz *6*
Man of the Year *252*
The Sentinel *353*

Price of Fame
Dreamgirls *111*

Prison or Jail
Catch a Fire *67*
V for Vendetta *419*

Prostitution
BloodRayne *44*
The Good German *159*
The Matador *260*
Strangers with Candy *377*
Waist Deep *426*
Water *430*

Psychiatry or Psychiatrists
Basic Instinct 2 *31*
Running with Scissors *331*
Stranger Than Fiction *375*

Psychotics or Sociopaths
Down in the Valley *109*
The King *218*
Saw III *340*
See No Evil *352*
When a Stranger Calls *434*

Queens
Tristan & Isolde *396*

Race Against Time
Deja Vu *97*

Radio
The Night Listener *282*
A Prairie Home Companion *311*

Real Estate
A Good Year *164*

Religious Themes
The Da Vinci Code *88*
End of the Spear *119*
Keeping Mum *215*
Looking for Comedy in the Muslim World *244*
The Nativity Story *276*
The Omen *292*
The Second Chance *351*
The Wicker Man *437*

Rescue Missions
Eight Below *117*
The Guardian *170*
Hoot *186*
The Marine *259*
Mission: Impossible III *264*
The Wild *439*
World Trade Center *443*

The Resistance
Army of Shadows *16*

Restored Footage
Army of Shadows *16*

Reunions
The Groomsmen *167*
Keeping Up with the Steins *216*
Old Joy *291*

Revenge
Beowulf & Grendel *35*
BloodRayne *44*
Crank *83*
Hard Candy *175*
John Tucker Must Die *209*
V for Vendetta *419*

Rise from Poverty
Goal! The Dream Begins *157*

Road Trips
Babel *27*
Borat: Cultural Learnings of America for Make Benefit Glorious Nation of Kazakhstan *48*
Don't Come Knocking *106*
Ice Age: The Meltdown *191*
Lassie *228*
Little Miss Sunshine *240*
RV *335*
Tenacious D in the Pick of Destiny *386*
The Three Burials of Melquiades Estrada *391*

Rodents
Flushed Away *139*

Role Reversal
Garfield: A Tail of Two Kitties *154*

Romance
Annapolis *10*
Aquamarine *14*
Ask the Dust *19*
The Black Dahlia *39*
Bubble *57*
Down in the Valley *109*
The Fountain *144*
Hollywoodland *183*
Imagine Me & You *197*
John Tucker Must Die *209*
Loverboy *247*
Nacho Libre *273*
Nanny McPhee *275*
Phat Girlz *301*
The Promise *315*
Russian Dolls *334*
The Science of Sleep *347*
Step Up *372*
Stranger Than Fiction *375*
Superman Returns *379*
Waist Deep *426*

Romantic Comedy
The Boynton Beach Club *49*
The Break-Up *51*
Date Movie *91*
Failure to Launch *127*
A Good Woman *163*
A Good Year *164*
The Holiday *181*
Imagine Me & You *197*
John Tucker Must Die *209*
Just My Luck *213*
Russian Dolls *334*
Something New *369*
You, Me and Dupree *449*

Royalty
Beowulf & Grendel *35*
Curse of the Golden Flower *86*
Eragon *121*
The Fountain *144*
The Illusionist *196*
The King *218*
The Libertine *236*
The Promise *315*
The Queen *323*
Tristan & Isolde *396*

Russia/USSR
BloodRayne *44*
The Death of Mr. Lazarescu *94*
Night Watch *283*
Russian Dolls *334*

Salespeople
Failure to Launch *127*
Last Holiday *229*
Phat Girlz *301*

San Francisco
The Pursuit of Happyness *319*

Satire or Parody
American Dreamz *6*
Date Movie *91*
Idiocracy *192*
Scary Movie 4 *344*
Thank You for Smoking *389*

Science Fiction
Deja Vu *97*
A Scanner Darkly *342*
Superman Returns *379*
Ultraviolet *407*
Zoom *451*

Science or Scientists
Eight Below *117*
An Inconvenient Truth *199*

Scotland
Joyeux Noel *211*

Screwball Comedy
The Break-Up *51*

Seattle
The Heart of the Game *177*

Security Guards
Night at the Museum *280*

Serial Killers
Art School Confidential *18*
The Hills Have Eyes *178*
Scoop *349*
When a Stranger Calls *434*

Sex or Sexuality
Basic Instinct 2 *31*
Hostel *188*
The Notorious Bettie Page *286*
Russian Dolls *334*
Sherrybaby *358*
Somersault *367*

Sexual Abuse
Hard Candy *175*
The Notorious Bettie Page *286*

Skateboarding
Wassup Rockers *429*

Skating
ATL *21*

Slavery
Manderlay *254*
The Promise *315*

Snakes
Snakes on a Plane *366*
The Wild *439*

Soccer
Goal! The Dream Begins *157*
Joyeux Noel *211*
The Pink Panther *304*
She's the Man *360*

South America
End of the Spear *119*
Turistas *404*

Spain
Pan's Labyrinth *299*
Volver *423*

Spies or Espionage
Casino Royale *65*
The Good Shepherd *161*
Mission: Impossible III *264*

Sports
Annapolis *10*
Game 6 *152*

Sports Documentaries
The Heart of the Game *177*

Sports—General
Annapolis *10*
The Benchwarmers *34*
Cars *63*
Game 6 *152*
Glory Road *156*
Goal! The Dream Begins *157*
Invincible *204*
Nacho Libre *273*
Stick It *373*
We Are Marshall *432*
The World's Fastest Indian *445*

Stalkers
Hoot *186*

Stepparents
Pan's Labyrinth *299*
Running Scared *330*
Shadowboxer *355*
Wah-Wah *425*

Suburban Dystopia
Cache *61*
Deck the Halls *96*
Little Children *237*
Little Man *239*
Monster House *268*
Over the Hedge *295*

Suicide
Hollywoodland *183*
Pulse *318*

Super Heroes
My Super Ex-Girlfriend *270*
Superman Returns *379*
X-Men: The Last Stand *447*
Zoom *451*

Survival
The Descent *101*
Eight Below *117*
Flags of Our Fathers *135*
Poseidon *308*
World Trade Center *443*

Swimming
The Guardian *170*

Taxes
Stranger Than Fiction *375*

Teaching or Teachers
Akeelah and the Bee *2*
The History Boys *179*
Take the Lead *383*

Teamwork
Beerfest *32*

Technology
Pulse *318*

Television
American Dreamz *6*

Terrorism
American Dreamz *6*
Children of Men *74*
United 93 *412*
V for Vendetta *419*
World Trade Center *443*

Texas
Glory Road *156*
The King *218*
The Return *327*
The Three Burials of Melquiades Estrada *391*

Thrillers
The Aura *22*
The Bridesmaid *55*
Cache *61*
Hard Candy *175*
The Omen *292*
When a Stranger Calls *434*

Time Travel
Deja Vu *97*
The Lake House *225*

Tokyo
Babel *27*
The Fast and the Furious: Tokyo Drift *128*
The Grudge 2 *169*

Tragedy
Babel *27*
The Prestige *313*

Transvestites or Transsexuals
Big Momma's House 2 *37*
Kinky Boots *220*

True Crime
The Black Dahlia *39*
Hollywoodland *183*

True Stories
An American Haunting *8*
Catch a Fire *67*
Eight Below *117*
End of the Spear *119*
Find Me Guilty *131*

Flyboys *140*
Glory Road *156*
Invincible *204*
Joyeux Noel *211*
Kinky Boots *220*
The Libertine *236*
The Pursuit of Happyness *319*
The Queen *323*
Take the Lead *383*
United 93 *412*
Unknown White Male *413*
We Are Marshall *432*
World Trade Center *443*
The World's Fastest Indian *445*

Vacations
Babel *27*
The Hills Have Eyes *178*
Last Holiday *229*
Phat Girlz *301*
RV *335*

Vampires
BloodRayne *44*
Night Watch *283*
Ultraviolet *407*
Underworld: Evolution *410*

Vigilantes
Hard Candy *175*

Waiters or Waitresses
Ask the Dust *19*
Time to Leave *394*

War: General
Blood Diamond *41*
Tristan & Isolde *396*
Why We Fight *436*

Weddings
The Groomsmen *167*
Imagine Me & You *197*
Nanny McPhee *275*
Pirates of the Caribbean: Dead Man's Chest *306*

Werewolves
Underworld: Evolution *410*

Westerns
Don't Come Knocking *106*
Down in the Valley *109*
A Prairie Home Companion *311*
The Proposition *316*
The Three Burials of Melquiades Estrada *391*

Witchcraft
The Covenant *81*
Nanny McPhee *275*
Silent Hill *361*

Women
The Descent *101*
The Devil Wears Prada *104*
Volver *423*
The Wicker Man *437*

Women of Substance
My Super Ex-Girlfriend *270*

World War I
Flyboys *140*
Joyeux Noel *211*

World War II
Army of Shadows *16*
Flags of Our Fathers *135*
Letters from Iwo Jima *234*

Wrestling
Nacho Libre *273*

Writers
Ask the Dust *19*
Basic Instinct 2 *31*
Factotum *125*
Game 6 *152*
Infamous *200*
Lady in the Water *223*
Mrs. Palfrey at the Claremont *266*
Russian Dolls *334*
Stranger Than Fiction *375*
Winter Passing *441*

Youth Sports
Stick It *373*

Zombies
Slither *365*

Zoos
The Wild *439*

Title Index

This cumulative index is an alphabetical list of all films covered in the volumes of the *Magill's Cinema Annual.* Film titles are indexed on a word-by-word basis, including articles and prepositions. English leading articles (A, An, The) are ignored, as are foreign leading articles (El, Il, La, Las, Le, Les, Los). Acronyms appear alphabetically as if regular words. Common abbreviations in titles file as if they are spelled out. Proper names in titles are alphabetized beginning with the individual's first name. Titles with numbers are alphabetized as if the numbers were spelled out. When numeric titles gather in close proximity to each other, the titles will be arranged in a low-to-high numeric sequence. Films reviewed in this volume are cited in bold with an Arabic number indicating the page number on which the review begins; films reviewed in past volumes are cited with the *Annual* year in which the review was published. Original and alternate titles are cross-referenced to the American release title. Titles of retrospective films are followed by the year, in brackets, of their original release.

A

A corps perdu. *See* Straight for the Heart.

A. I.: Artificial Intelligence 2002

A la Mode (Fausto) 1995

A Lot Like Love 2006

A Ma Soeur. *See* Fat Girl.

A nos amours 1984

Abandon 2003

ABCD 2002

Abgeschminkt! *See* Making Up!.

About a Boy 2003

About Adam 2002

About Last Night... 1986

About Schmidt 2003

Above the Law 1988

Above the Rim 1995

Abre Los Ojos. *See* Open Your Eyes.

Abril Despedacado. *See* Behind the Sun.

Absence of Malice 1981

Absolute Beginners 1986

Absolute Power 1997

Absolution 1988

Abyss, The 1989

Accepted pg. 1

Accidental Tourist, The 1988

Accompanist, The 1993

Accordeur de tremblements de terre, L'. *See* Piano Tuner of Earthquakes, The.

Accused, The 1988

Ace in the Hole [1951] 1986, 1991

Ace Ventura: Pet Detective 1995

Ace Ventura: When Nature Calls 1996

Aces: Iron Eagle III 1992

Acid House, The 2000

Acqua e sapone. *See* Water and Soap.

Across the Tracks 1991

Acting on Impulse 1995

Action Jackson 1988

Actress 1988

Adam Sandler's 8 Crazy Nights 2003

Adam's Rib [1950] 1992

Adaptation 2003

Addams Family, The 1991

Addams Family Values 1993

Addicted to Love 1997

Addiction, The 1995

Addition, L'. *See* Patsy, The.

Adjo, Solidaritet. *See* Farewell Illusion.

Adjuster, The 1992

Adolescente, L' 1982

Adventure of Huck Finn, The 1993

Adventures in Babysitting 1987

Adventures of Baron Munchausen, The 1989

Adventures of Buckaroo Banzai, The 1984

Adventures of Elmo in Grouchland, The 2000

Adventures of Felix, The 2002

Adventures of Ford Fairlane, The 1990

Adventures of Mark Twain, The 1986
Adventures of Milo and Otis, The 1989
Adventures of Pinocchio, The 1996
Adventures of Pluto Nash, The 2003
Adventures of Priscilla, Queen of the Desert, The 1995
Adventures of Rocky and Bullwinkle, The 2001
Adventures of Sebastian Cole, The, 2000
Adventures of Sharkboy and Lavagirl in 3-D, The 2006
Adventures of the American Rabbit, The 1986
Advocate 1995
Aelita 1995
Aeon Flux 2006
Affair of Love, An 2001
Affair of the Necklace, The 2002
Affaire de Femmes, Une. *See* Story of Women.
Affaire de Gout, Un. *See* Matter of Taste, A.
Affengeil 1992
Affliction 1999
Afraid of the Dark 1992
Africa the Serengeti 1995
After Dark, My Sweet 1990
After Hours 1985
After Life 2000
After Midnight 1989
After the Rehearsal 1984
After the Sunset 2005
Afterglow 1979
Against All Odds 1983
Against the Ropes 2005
Age Isn't Everything (Life in the Food Chain) 1995
Age of Innocence, The 1993
Agent Cody Banks 2004
Agent Cody Banks 2: Destination London 2005
Agent on Ice 1986
Agnes Browne 2001
Agnes of God 1985
Aid 1988
Aileen: Life and Death of a Serial Killer 2005
Aileen Wuornos: The Selling of a Serial Killer 1995
Air America 1990
Air Bud 1997
Air Bud: Golden Receiver 1999
Air Force One 1997
Air Up There, The 1995
Airborne 1993
Airheads 1995
Airplane II: The Sequel 1982
Akai Hashi no Shita no Nurui Mizo. *See* Warm Water Under a Red Bridge.
Akeelah and the Bee pg. 2
Akira Kurosawa's Dreams 1990
Al-Jenna-An. *See* Paradise Now.
Aladdin (Corbucci) 1987
Aladdin (Musker & Clements) 1992
Alamo, The 2005
Alamo Bay 1985
Alan and Naomi 1992
Alan Smithee Film, An 1999
Alarmist, The 1999
Alaska 1996
Alberto Express 1992
Albino Alligator 1997
Alchemist, The 1986
Alex & Emma 2004
Alexander 2005
Alfie 2005
Alfred Hitchcock's Bon Voyage & Aventure Malgache. *See* Aventure Malgache.
Ali 2002
Alias Betty 2004
Alice (Allen) 1990
Alice (Svankmajer) 1988
Alice et Martin 2001
Alien Nation 1988
Alien Predator 1987
Alien Resurrection 1997
Alien vs. Predator 2005
Alien^3 1992
Aliens 1986
Alive 1993
Alive and Kicking 1997
All About My Mother 2000
All About the Benjamins 2003
All Dogs Go to Heaven 1989
All Dogs Go to Heaven II 1996
All I Desire [1953] 1987
All I Want for Christmas 1991
All of Me 1984
All or Nothing 2003
All Over Me 1997
All Quiet on the Western Front [1930] 1985
All the King's Men pg. 4
All the Little Animals 2000
All the Pretty Horses 2001
All the Rage. *See* It's the Rage.
All the Real Girls 2004
All the Right Moves 1983
All the Vermeers in New York 1992
All's Fair 1989
All-American High 1987
Allan Quatermain and the Lost City of Gold 1987
Alley Cat 1984
Alligator Eyes 1990
Allnighter, The 1987
Almost an Angel 1990
Almost Famous 2001
Almost Heroes 1999
Almost You 1985
Aloha Summer 1988
Alone. *See* Solas.
Alone in the Dark 2006
Along Came a Spider 2002
Along Came Polly 2005
Alphabet City 1983
Alpine Fire 1987
Altars of the World [1976] 1985
Always (Jaglom) 1985
Always (Spielberg) 1989
Amadeus 1984, 1985
Amanda 1989
Amantes. *See* Lovers.
Amantes del Circul Polar, Los. *See* Lovers of the Arctic Circle, The.
Amants du Pont Neuf, Les 1995

Amateur 1995
Amateur, The 1982
Amazing Grace and Chuck 1987
Amazing Panda Adventure, The 1995
Amazon Women on the Moon 1987
Ambition 1991
Amelie 2002
Amen 2004
America 1986
American Anthem 1986
American Beauty 2000
American Blue Note 1991
American Buffalo 1996
American Chai 2003
American Cyborg: Steel Warrior 1995
American Desi 2002
American Dream 1992
American Dreamer 1984
American Dreamz pg. 6
American Fabulous 1992
American Flyers 1985
American Friends 1993
American Gothic 1988
American Haunting, An pg. 8
American Heart 1993
American History X 1999
American in Paris, An [1951] 1985
American Justice 1986
American Me 1992
American Movie 2000
American Ninja 1984, 1991
American Ninja 1985
American Ninja II 1987
American Ninja III 1989
American Outlaws 2002
American Pie 2000
American Pie 2 2002
American Pop 1981
American President, The 1995
American Psycho 2001
American Rhapsody, An 2002
American Stories 1989
American Splendor 2004
American Summer, An 1991
American Taboo 1984, 1991
American Tail, An 1986
American Tail: Fievel Goes West, An 1991
American Wedding 2004
American Werewolf in London, An 1981
American Werewolf in Paris, An 1997
American Women. *See* The Closer You Get.
America's Sweethearts 2002
Ami de mon amie, L'. *See* Boyfriends and Girlfriends.
Amin: The Rise and Fall 1983
Amistad 1997
Amityville Horror, The 2006
Amityville II: The Possession 1981
Amityville 3-D 1983
Among Giants 2000
Among People 1988
Amongst Friends 1993
Amor brujo, El 1986
Amores Perros 2002
Amos and Andrew 1993
Amour de Swann, Un. *See* Swann in Love.
Anaconda 1997
Analyze That 2003
Analyze This 2000
Anastasia 1997
Anchorman: The Legend of Ron Burgundy 2005
Anchors Aweigh [1945] 1985
And God Created Woman 1988
...And God Spoke 1995
And Life Goes On (Zebdegi Edame Darad) 1995
And Nothing but the Truth 1984
And Now Ladies and Gentlemen 2004
And the Ship Sails On 1984
And You Thought Your Parents Were Weird 1991
And Your Mother Too. *See* Y tu mama tambien.
Andre 1995
Android 1984
Ane qui a bu la lune, L'. *See* Donkey Who Drank the Moon, The.
Angel at My Table, An 1991
Angel Baby 1997
Angel Dust 1987
Angel Dust (Ishii) 1997
Angel Eyes 2002
Angel Heart 1987
Angel 1984
Angel III 1988
Angel Town 1990
Angela's Ashes 2000
Angelo My Love 1983
Angels and Insects 1996
Angels in the Outfield 1995
Anger Management 2004
Angie 1995
Angry Harvest 1986
Anguish 1987
Angus 1995
Angustia. *See* Anguish.
Anima Mundi 1995
Animal, The 2002
Animal Behavior 1989
Animal Factory 2001
Animal Kingdom, The [1932] 1985
Anna 1987
Anna and the King 2000
Anna Karamazova 1995
Annapolis pg. 10
Anne Frank Remembered 1996
Annee des meduses, L' 1987
Annees sandwiches, Les. *See* Sandwich Years, The.
Annie 1982
Annihilators, The 1986
Anniversary Party, The 2002
Another Day in Paradise 2000
Another 48 Hrs. 1990
Another Stakeout 1993
Another State of Mind 1984
Another Time, Another Place 1984
Another Woman 1988
Another You 1991
Anslag, De. *See* Assault, The.
Ant Bully, The pg. 11
Antarctica (Kurahara) 1984

Antarctica (Weiley) 1992
Antigone/Rites of Passion 1991
Antitrust 2002
Antonia and Jane 1991
Antonia's Line 1996
Antwone Fisher 2003
Antz 1999
Any Given Sunday 2000
Any Man's Death 1990
Anything But Love 2004
Anything Else 2004
Anywhere But Here 2000
Apache [1954] 1981
Apartment, The [1960] 1986
Apartment Zero 1988
Apex 1995
Apocalypse Now Redux 2002
Apocalypto pg. 12
Apollo 13 1995
Apostle, The 1997
Apple, The 2000
Appointment with Death 1988
Apprentice to Murder 1988
Apres l'amour. *See* Love After Love.
April Fool's Day 1986
April Is a Deadly Month 1987
Apt Pupil 1999
Aquamarine pg. 14
Arabian Knight, 1995
Arachnophobia 1990
Ararat 2003
Arashi Ga Oka 1988
Arch of Triumph [1948] 1983
Archangel 1995
Architecture of Doom, The 1992
Are We There Yet? 2006
Argent, L' 1984
Aria 1988
Ariel 1990
Arlington Road 2000
Armageddon 1999
Armageddon, The. *See* Warlock.
Armed and Dangerous 1986
Armed Response 1986
Armee des ombres, L'. *See* Army of Shadows.
Army in the Shadows. *See* Army of Shadows.
Army of Darkness 1993
Army of Shadows pg. 16
Around the Bend 2005
Around the World in 80 Days 2005
Arrangement, The [1969] 1985
Aristocrats, The 2006
Arrival, The 1996
Art Blakey 1988
Art Deco Detective 1995
Art of Cinematography, The. *See* Visions of Light.
Art of War, The 2001
Art School Confidential pg. 18
Artemisia 1999
Arthur 1981
Arthur II 1988
Arthur's Hallowed Ground 1986
Article 99 1992
As Good As It Gets 1997
Ashik Kerib 1988
Ask the Dust pg. 19
Aspen Extreme 1993
Assassination 1987
Assassination of Richard Nixon, The 2006
Assassination Tango 2004
Assassins, 1995
Assault, The 1986
Assault of the Killer Bimbos 1988
Assault on Precinct 13 2006
Assignment, The, 1997
Associate, The 1996
Astonished 1989
Astronaut's Wife, The 2000
Asya's Happiness 1988
Asylum 2006
At Close Range 1986
At First Sight 2000
At Play in the Fields of the Lord 1991
Atame. *See* Tie Me Up! Tie Me Down!.
Atanarjuat, the Fast Runner 2002
ATL pg. 21
Atlantic City 1981
Atlantis 1995
Atlantis: The Lost Empire 2002
Atraves da Janela. *See* Through the Window.
Attention Bandits. *See* Warning Bandits.
Au Revoir les Enfants 1987
August 1996
August 32nd on Earth 1999
Aura, The pg. 22
Austin Powers in Goldmember 2003
Austin Powers: International Man of Mystery, 1997
Austin Powers: The Spy Who Shagged Me 2000
Author! Author! 1981
Auto Focus 2003
Autumn in New York 2001
Autumn Tale 2000
Avalon (Anderson) 1988
Avalon (Levinson) 1990
Avanti [1972] 1986
Avengers, The 1999
Avenging Angel 1985
Avenging Force 1986
Aventure Malgache 1995
Aviator, The (Miller) 1985
Aviator, The (Scorsese) 2005
AvP. *See* Alien vs. Predator.
Awakenings 1990
Awesome! I F*in' Shot That!** pg. 23
Awfully Big Adventure, An 1995
Ayn Rand: A Sense of Life 1999
Ayneh. *See* The Mirror.

B

B. Monkey 2000
Ba Mua. *See* Three Seasons.
Baadassss! 2005
Babar 1989
Babe, The 1992
Babe: Pig in the City 1999

Babe, the Gallant Pig, 1995
Babel pg. 27
Babette's Feast 1987
Baby 1985
Baby Boom 1987
Baby Boy 2002
Baby Geniuses 2000
Baby, It's You 1982
Baby's Day Out 1995
Babyfever 1995
Babysitter's Club 1995
Bacheha-Ye aseman. *See* The Children of Heaven.
Bachelor, The 2000
Bachelor Mother [1939] 1986
Bachelor Party 1984
Back Door to Hell [1964] 1995
Back to School 1986
Back to the Beach 1987
Back to the Future 1985
Back to the Future Part II 1989
Back to the Future Part III 1990
Backbeat 1995
Backdraft 1991
Backfire 1987
Backstage 1988
Backstage at the Kirov 1984
Bad Behaviour 1993
Bad Blood 1989
Bad Boy, The 1985
Bad Boys 1982
Bad Boys 1995
Bad Boys 2 2004
Bad Company (Harris) 1995
Bad Company (Schumacher) 2003
Bad Dreams 1988
Bad Education 2005
Bad Girls 1995
Bad Guys 1986
Bad Influence 1990
Bad Lieutenant 1992
Bad Manners 1997
Bad Medicine 1985
Bad Moon 1996
Bad News Bears, The 2006
Bad Santa 2004
Bagdad Cafe 1988
Bail Jumper 1990
Bait 2001
Baja Oklahoma 1988
Bal, Le 1984
Balance, La 1983
Ball of Fire 1987
Ballad of Jack and Rose, The 2006
Ballad of Little Jo, The 1993
Ballad of the Sad Cafe, The 1991
Ballistic: Ecks vs. Sever 2003
Balto 1995
Balzac and the Little Chinese Seamstress 2006
Balzac et la petite tailleuse Chinois *See* Balzac and the Little Chinese Seamstress
Bamba, La 1987
Bambi [1942] 1984
Bamboozled 2001
Band of the Hand 1986
Band Wagon, The [1953] 1981
Bandit Queen 1995
Bandits 1988
Bandits 2002
Bandwagon 1997
Banger Sisters, The 2003
B.A.P.s 1997
Bar Esperanza 1985
Bar Girls 1995
Baraka 1993
Baran 2002
Barb Wire 1996
Barbarian Invasions, The 2004
Barbarians, The 1987
Barbarosa 1982
Barbary Coast [1935] 1983
Barbershop 2003
Barbershop 2: Back in Business 2005
Barcelona 1995
Bare Knuckles. *See* Gladiator.
Barefoot Contessa, The [1954] 1981
Barfly 1987
Bari, Al. *See* Innocent, The.
Barjo 1993
Bark! 2003
Barney's Great Adventure 1999
Barnyard pg. 30
Bartleby 2003
Barton Fink 1991
BASEketball 1999
Bashu, the Little Stranger 1990
Basic 2004
Basic Instinct 1992
Basic Instinct 2 pg. 31
Basileus Quartet 1984
Basket, The 2001
Basket Case II 1990
Basket Case III: The Progeny 1992
Basketball Diaries, The 1995
Basquiat 1996
Bastille 1985
Bat 21 1988
Batman [1989] 1995
Batman and Robin 1997
Batman Begins 2006
Batman Forever 1995
Batman: Mask of the Phantasm 1993
Batman Returns 1992
Bats 2000
Battement d'Aniles du Papillon, Le, *See* Happenstance.
Batteries Not Included 1987
Battle of Shaker Heights, The 2004
Battlefield Earth 2001
Battlestruck 1982
Baule les Pins, La. *See* C'est la vie.
Baxter, The 2006
Be Cool 2006
Beach 1985
Beach, The 2001
Beach Girls, The 1982
Beaches 1988
Bean 1997
Beans of Egypt, Maine, The 1995
Beast, The 1988
Beast in the Heart, The. *See* Don't Tell.
Bear, The (Annaud) 1989
Bear, The (Sarafian) 1984

Beast Within, The 1982
Beastmaster, The 1982
Beastmaster II 1991
Beat, The 1987
Beat Generation-An American Dream, The 1987
Beat Street 1984
Beating Heart, A 1992
Beating of the Butterfly's Wings, The *See* Happenstance.
Beau Mariage, Le 1982
Beau Pere 1981
Beau Travail 2001
Beaumarchais: The Scoundrel 1997
Beautician and the Beast, The 1997
Beautiful 2001
Beautiful Creatures 2002
Beautiful Dreamers 1991
Beautiful Girls 1996
Beautiful Mind 2002
Beautiful People 2001
Beautiful Thing 1996
Beauty and the Beast 1991
Beauty Shop 2006
Beavis and Butt-head Do America 1996
Bebe's Kids 1992
Because of Winn-Dixie 2006
Becky Sharp [1935] 1981
Becoming Colette 1992
Bed and Breakfast 1992
Bed of Roses 1996
Bedazzled 2001
Bedroom Eyes 1986
Bedroom Window, The 1987
Bedtime for Bonzo [1951] 1983
Bee Season 2006
Beefcake 2000
Beerfest pg. 32
Beethoven 1992
Beethoven's Second 1993
Beetlejuice 1988
Before and After 1996
Before Night Falls 2001
Before Sunrise 1995
Before Sunset 2005
Before the Rain 1995
Begotten 1995
Beguiled, The [1971] 1982
Behind Enemy Lines 2002
Behind the Sun 2002
Beijing Bicycle 2003
Being at Home with Claude 1993
Being Human 1995
Being John Malkovich 2000
Being Julia 2005
Belfast, Maine 2001
Believers, The 1987
Belizaire the Cajun 1986
Bella Martha. *See* Mostly Martha.
Belle Epoque 1995
Belle Noiseuse, La 1991
Bellman and True 1988
Bells Are Ringing [1960] 1983
Belly of an Architect 1987
Beloved 2003
Beloved Rogue [1927] 1983
Below 2004
Benchwarmers, The pg. 34
Bend It Like Beckham 2004
Benefit of the Doubt 1993
Bengali Night, The 1988
Benji: Off the Leash! 2005
Benji the Hunted 1987
Benny and Joon 1993
Bent 1997
Beowulf & Grendel pg. 35
Berkeley in the Sixties 1990
Berlin Alexanderplatz 1983
Bernadette 1988
Berry Gordy's The Last Dragon 1985
Bert Rigby, You're a Fool 1989
Beshkempir: The Adopted Son 2000
Besieged 2000
Best Defense 1984
Best Friends 1982
Best in Show 2001
Best Intentions, The 1992
Best Laid Plans 2000
Best Little Whorehouse in Texas, The 1982
Best Man, The 1999
Best Man, The 2000
Best of the Best 1989
Best of the Best II 1993
Best of Times, The 1986
Best of Youth, The 2006
Best Revenge, The 1996
Best Seller 1987
Best Years of Our Lives, The [1946] 1981
Bestia nel cuore, La. *See* Don't Tell.
Betrayal 1983
Betrayed 1988
Betsy's Wedding 1990
Better Luck Tomorrow 2004
Better Off Dead 1985
Better Than Chocolate 2000
Better Than Sex 2002
Betty 1993
Betty Blue 1986
Between the Teeth 1995
Beverly Hillbillies, The 1993
Beverly Hills Brats 1989
Beverly Hills Cop 1984
Beverly Hills Cop II 1987
Beverly Hills Cop III 1995
Beverly Hills Ninja 1997
Bewitched 2006
Beyond Borders 2004
Beyond Rangoon 1995
Beyond Reasonable Doubt 1983
Beyond Silence 1999
Beyond the Limit 1983
Beyond the Mat 2001
Beyond the Rocks 2006
Beyond the Sea 2005
Beyond Therapy 1987
Bhaji on the Beach 1995
Bian Lian. *See* The King of Masks.
Bicentennial Man 2000
Big 1988
Big Bad Mama II 1988
Big Bang, The 1990
Big Blue, The (Besson) 1988
Big Blue, The (Horn) 1988

Big Bounce, The 2005
Big Bully 1996
Big Business 1988
Big Chill, The 1983
Big Daddy 2000
Big Easy, The 1987
Big Fat Liar 2003
Big Fish 2004
Big Girls Don't Cry, They Get Even 1992
Big Green, The 1995
Big Hit, The 1999
Big Kahuna, The 2001
Big Lebowski, The 1999
Big Man on Campus 1989
Big Momma's House 2001
Big Momma's House 2 pg. 37
Big Night 1996
Big One, The 1999
Big Picture, The 1989
Big Shots 1987
Big Squeeze, The 1996
Big Tease, The 2001
Big Time 1988
Big Top Pee-Wee 1988
Big Town, The 1987
Big Trouble (Cassavetes) 1986
Big Trouble (Sonnenfeld) 2003
Big Trouble in Little China 1986
Biker Boyz 2004
Bill and Ted's Bogus Journey 1991
Bill and Ted's Excellent Adventure 1989
Billy Bathgate 1991
Billy Budd [1962] 1981
Billy Elliot 2001
Billy Madison 1995
Billy's Hollywood Screen Kiss 1999
Biloxi Blues 1988
Bin-jip. *See* 3-Iron.
Bingo 1991
BINGO 2000
Bio-Dome 1996
Bird 1988
Bird on a Wire 1990
Birdcage, The 1996
Birdy 1984
Birth 2005
Birth of a Nation, The [1915] 1982, 1992
Birthday Girl 2003
Bitter Moon 1995
Bittere Ernte. *See* Angry Harvest.
Bix (1990) 1995
Bix (1991) 1995
Bizet's Carmen 1984
Black and White 2001
Black Beauty 1995
Black Cat, The (Fulci) 1984
Black Cat (Shin) 1993
Black Cat, White Cat 2000
Black Cauldron, The 1985
Black Christmas pg. 38
Black Dahlia, The pg. 39
Black Dog 1999
Black Harvest 1995
Black Hawk Down 2002
Black Joy 1986
Black Knight 2002
Black Lizard 1995
Black Mask 2000
Black Moon Rising 1986
Black Peter [1964] 1985
Black Rain (Imamura) 1990
Black Rain (Scott) 1989
Black Robe 1991
Black Sheep 1996
Black Stallion Returns, The 1983
Black Widow 1987
Blackboard Jungle [1955] 1986, 1992
Blackout 1988
Blackout. *See* I Like It Like That.
Blade 1999
Blade II 2003
Blade Runner 1982
Blade: Trinity 2005
Blair Witch Project, The 2000
Blame It on Night 1984
Blame It on Rio 1984
Blame It on the Bellboy 1992
Blank Check 1995
Blankman 1995
Blassblaue Frauenschrift, Eine. *See* Woman's Pale Blue Handwriting, A.
Blast 'em 1995
Blast from the Past 2000
Blaze 1989
Bless the Child 2001
Bless Their Little Hearts 1991
Blessures Assassines, Les. *See* Murderous Maids.
Blind Date 1987
Blind Fairies *See* Ignorant Fairies
Blind Fury 1990
Blind Swordsman: Zatoichi, The. *See* Zatoichi.
Blink 1995
Bliss 1986
Bliss 1997
Blob, The 1988
Blood and Concrete 1991
Blood and Wine 1997
Blood Diamond pg. 41
Blood Diner 1987
Blood in Blood Out 1995
Blood, Guts, Bullets and Octane 2001
Blood Money 1988
Blood of Heroes, The 1990
Blood Salvage 1990
Blood Simple 1985
Blood Wedding 1982
Blood Work 2003
Bloodfist 1989
Bloodhounds of Broadway 1989
BloodRayne pg.44
Bloodsport 1988
Bloody Sunday 2003
Blow 2002
Blow Dry 2002
Blow Out 1981
Blown Away 1995
Blue (Jarman) 1995
Blue (Kieslowski) 1993
Blue Car 2004

Blue Chips 1995
Blue City 1986
Blue Crush 2003
Blue Desert 1991
Blue Ice 1995
Blue Iguana, The 1988
Blue in the Face 1995
Blue Kite, The 1995
Blue Monkey 1987
Blue Skies Again 1983
Blue Sky 1995
Blue Steel 1990
Blue Streak 2000
Blue Thunder 1983
Blue Velvet 1986
Blue Villa, The 1995
Bluebeard's Eighth Wife [1938] 1986
Blues Brothers 2000 1999
Blues Lahofesh Hagadol. *See* Late Summer Blues.
Boat, The. *See* Boot, Das.
Boat is Full, The 1982
Boat Trip 2004
Bob le Flambeur [1955] 1983
Bob Marley: Time Will Tell. *See* Time Will Tell.
Bob Roberts 1992
Bobby pg. 45
Bobby Jones: Stroke of Genius 2005
Bodies, Rest, and Motion 1993
Body, The 2002
Body and Soul 1982
Body Chemistry 1990
Body Double 1984
Body Heat 1981
Body Melt 1995
Body of Evidence 1993
Body Parts 1991
Body Rock 1984
Body Shots 2000
Body Slam 1987
Body Snatchers 1995
Bodyguard, The 1992
Bodyguards, The. *See* La Scorta.
Boesman & Lena 2001
Bogus 1996
Boheme, La [1926] 1982
Boiler Room 2001
Boiling Point 1993
Bolero (Derek) 1984
Bolero (Lelouch) 1982
Bollywood/Hollywood 2003
Bom Yeorum Gaeul Gyeoul Geurigo...Bom. *See* Spring, Summer, Autumn, Winter...And Spring.
Bon Plaisir, Le 1984
Bon Voyage 1995
Bon Voyage (Rappenaeau) 2005
Bone Collector, The 2000
Bonfire of the Vanities, The 1990
Bongwater 1999
Bonne Route. *See* Latcho Drom.
Boogeyman 2006
Boogie Nights 1997
Book of Love 1991
Book of Shadows: Blair Witch 2 2001
Boomerang 1992
Boost, The 1988
Boot, Das 1982
Boot Ist Voll, Das. *See* Boat Is Full, The.
Bootmen 2001
Booty Call 1997
Booye Kafoor, Atre Yas. *See* Smell of Camphor, Fragrance of Jasmine.
Bopha! 1993
Borat: Cultural Learnings of America for Make Benefit Glorious Nation of Kazakhstan pg. 48
Border, The 1982
Boricua's Bond 2001
Born American 1986
Born in East L.A. 1987
Born Into Brothels: Calcutta's Red Light Kids 2006
Born on the Fourth of July 1989
Born Romantic 2002
Born to Be Wild 1996
Born to Race 1988
Born Yesterday 1993
Borrowers, The 1999
Borstal Boy 2003
Bose Zellen. *See* Free Radicals.
Bossa Nova 2001
Bostonians, The 1984
Bottle Rocket 1996
Boum, La 1983
Bounce 2001
Bound 1996
Bound and Gagged 1993
Bound by Honor 1993
Bounty, The 1984
Bourne Identity, The 2003
Bourne Supremacy, The 2005
Bowfinger 2000
Box of Moonlight 1997
Boxer, The 1997
Boxer and Death, The 1988
Boxing Helena 1993
Boy in Blue, The 1986
Boy Who Could Fly, The 1986
Boy Who Cried Bitch, The 1991
Boyfriend School, The. *See* Don't Tell Her It's Me.
Boyfriends 1997
Boyfriends and Girlfriends 1988
Boynton Beach Bereavement Club, The. *See* Boynton Beach Club, The.
Boynton Beach Club, The pg. 49
Boys 1996
Boys, The 1985
Boys and Girls 2001
Boys Don't Cry 2000
Boys from Brazil, The [1978] 1985
Boys Next Door, The 1986
Boys on the Side 1995
Boyz N the Hood 1991
Braddock 1988
Brady Bunch Movie, The 1995
Brady's Escape 1984
Brain Damage 1988
Brain Dead 1990
Brain Donors 1995
Brainstorm 1983
Bram Stoker's Dracula 1992

Branches of the Tree, The 1995

Brandon Teena Story, The 2000

Brassed Off 1997

Brat. *See* Brother.

Brave Little Toaster, The 1987

Braveheart 1995

Brazil 1985

Bread and Roses 2002

Bread and Salt 1995

Bread and Tulips 2002

Bread, My Sweet, The 2004

Break of Dawn 1988

Break-Up, The pg. 51

Breakdown 1997

Breakfast Club, The 1985

Breakfast of Champions 2000

Breakfast on Pluto 2006

Breakin' 1984

Breakin' All the Rules 2005

Breaking In 1989

Breaking the Rules 1992

Breaking the Sound Barrier. *See* Sound Barrier, The.

Breaking the Waves 1996

Breakin' II: Electric Boogaloo 1984

Breaking Up 1997

Breath of Life, A 1993

Breathing Room 1996

Breathless 1983

Brenda Starr 1992

Brewster McCloud [1970] 1985

Brewster's Millions 1985

Brian Wilson: I Just Wasn't Made for These Times 1995

Brick pg. 53

Bride, The 1985

Bride and Prejudice 2006

Bride of Chucky 1999

Bride of Re-Animator 1991

Bride of the Wind 2002

Bride with White Hair, The 1995

Bridesmaid, The pg. 55

Bridge of San Luis Rey, The [1929] 1981

Bridge of San Luis Rey, The 2006

Bridge on the River Kwai, The [1957] 1990

Bridges of Madison County, The 1995

Bridget Jones: The Edge of Reason 2005

Bridget Jones's Diary 2002

Brief Encounter [1946] 1990

Brief History of Time, A 1992

Bright Angel 1991

Bright Lights, Big City 1988

Bright Young Things 2005

Brighton Beach Memoirs 1986

Brimstone and Treacle 1982

Bring It On 2001

Bring on the Night 1985

Bringing Down the House 2004

Bringing Out the Dead 2000

Brittania Hospital 1983

Broadcast News 1987

Broadway Damage 1999

Broadway Danny Rose 1984

Brodre. *See* Brothers.

Brokeback Mountain 2006

Brokedown Palace 2000

Broken April. *See* Behind the Sun.

Broken Arrow 1996

Broken Blossoms [1919] 1984

Broken English 1997

Broken Flowers 2006

Broken Hearts Club, The 2001

Broken Lizard's Club Dread. *See* Club Dread.

Broken Rainbow 1985

Broken Vessels 1999

Broken Wings 2005

Bronx Tale, A 1993

Brother (Balabanov) 1999

Brother (Kitano) 2001

Brother Bear 2004

Brother from Another Planet, The 1984

Brother of Sleep 1996

Brotherhood of the Wolf 2003

Brothers 2006

Brothers, The 2002

Brothers Grimm, The 2006

Brother's Keeper 1993

Brother's Kiss, A 1997

Brothers McMullen, The 1995

Brown Bunny, The 2005

Brown Sugar 2003

Browning Version, The 1995

Bruce Almighty 2004

Bruce Lee Story, The. *See* Dragon.

Bu-Su 1988

Bubba Ho-Tep 2004

Bubble pg. 57

Bubble Boy 2002

Buche, La [2000] 2001

Buckminster Fuller: Thinking Out Loud 1996

Buddy 1997

Buddy Boy 2001

Buddy Buddy 1981

Buddy System, The 1984

Buena Vista Social Club, The 2000

Buffalo 66 1999

Buffalo Soldiers 2004

Buffy the Vampire Slayer 1992

Bug's Life, A 1999

Bugsy 1991

Building Bombs 1995

Bull Durham 1988

Bulldog Drummond [1929] 1982

Bulletproof (Carver) 1988

Bulletproof (Dickerson) 1996

Bulletproof Heart 1995

Bulletproof Monk 2004

Bullets Over Broadway 1995

Bullies 1986

Bullshot 1985

Bully 2002

Bulworth 1999

Bum Rap 1988

'Burbs, The 1989

Burglar 1987

Burglar, The 1988

Buried on Sunday 1995

Burke and Wills 1987

Burnin' Love 1987

Burning Secret 1988
Burnt by the Sun 1995
Bushwhacked 1995
Business of Fancydancing, The 2003
Business of Strangers, The 2002
Busted Up 1987
Buster 1988
But I'm a Cheerleader 2001
Butcher Boy, The 1999
Butcher's Wife, The 1991
Butterfield 8 [1960] 1993
Butterflies 1988
Butterfly 2003
Butterfly Effect 2005
Buy and Cell 1988
Buying Time 1989
By Design 1982
By the Sword 1993
Bye Bye Blue Bird 2001
Bye Bye Blues 1990
Bye Bye, Love 1995

C

Cabaret Balkan 2000
Cabeza de Vaca 1992
Cabin Boy 1988
Cabin Fever 2004
Cabinet of Dr. Ramirez, The 1995
Cable Guy, The 1996
Cache pg. 61
Cactus 1986
Caddie [1976] 1982
Caddyshack II 1988
Cadence 1991
Cadillac Man 1990
Cafe Ole 2001
Cafe Society 1997
Cage 1989
Cage aux folles III, La 1986
Cage/Cunningham 1995
Caged Fury 1984
Cal 1984
Calendar 1995
Calendar Girl 1993
Calendar Girls 2004
Calhoun. *See* Nightstick.
Call Me 1988
Calle 54 2002
Caller, The 1987
Calling the Shots 1988
Came a Hot Friday 1985
Cameron's Closet 1989
Camilla 1995
Camille Claudel 1988, 1989
Camorra 1986
Camp 2004
Camp at Thiaroye, The 1990
Camp Nowhere 1995
Campanadas a medianoche. *See* Falstaff.
Campus Man 1987
Can She Bake a Cherry Pie? 1983
Canadian Bacon 1995
Can't Buy Me Love 1987
Can't Hardly Wait 1999
Candy Mountain 1988
Candyman 1992
Candyman II: Farewell to the Flesh 1995
Cannery Row 1982
Cannonball Run II 1984
Canone Inverso. *See* Making Love.
Cape Fear 1991
Capitano, Il 1995
Capote 2006
Captain Corelli's Mandolin 2002
Captain Ron 1992
Captive Hearts 1987
Captive in the Land, A 1995
Captives 1996
Capturing the Friedmans 2004
Car 54, Where Are You? 1995
Carandiru 2005
Caravaggio 1986
Cardinal, The [1963] 1986
Care Bears Adventure in Wonderland, The 1987
Care Bears Movie, The 1985
Care Bears Movie II 1986
Career Girls 1997
Career Opportunities 1991
Careful He Might Hear You 1984
Carlito's Way 1993
Carmen 1983
Carnage 2004
Carne, La 1995
Caro Diario 1995
Carpenter, The 1988
Carpool 1996
Carried Away 1996
Carriers Are Waiting, The 2001
Carrington 1995
Cars pg. 63
Casa de los Babys 2004
Casa in bilico, Una. *See* Tottering Lives.
Casanova 2006
Casino 1995
Casino Royale pg. 65
Casper 1995
Cast Away 2001
Castle, The 2000
Casual Sex? 1988
Casualties of War 1989
Cat on a Hot Tin Roof [1958] 1993
Cat People [1942] 1981, 1982
Catacombs 1988
Catch a Fire pg. 67
Catch Me If You Can 1989
Catch Me If You Can (Spielberg) 2003
Catch That Kid 2005
Catfish in Black Bean Sauce 2001
Cats & Dogs 2002
Cats Don't Dance 1997
Cat's Meow, The 2003
Cattle Annie and Little Britches 1981
Catwoman 2005
Caught 1996
Caught Up 1999
Cave, The 2006
Cave Girl 1985
Caveman's Valentine, The 2002
CB4 1993
Cease Fire 1985
Cecil B. Demented 2001

Celebrity 1999
Celeste 1982
Celestial Clockwork 1996
Cell, The 2001
Cellular 2005
Celluloid Closet, The 1996
Celtic Pride 1996
Cement Garden, The 1995
Cemetery Club, The 1993
Cemetery Man 1996
Center of the Web 1992
Center of the World, The 2002
Center Stage 2001
Central do Brasil. *See* Central Station.
Central Station 1999
Century 1995
Ceravani tanto Amati. *See* We All Loved Each Other So Much.
Cercle Rouge, Le 2004
Ceremonie, La 1996
Certain Fury 1985
Certain Regard, Un. *See* Hotel Terminus.
C'est la vie 1990
Ceux qui m'aiment predont le train. *See* Those Who Love Me Can Take the Train.
Chac 2001
Chain of Desire 1993
Chain Reaction 1996
Chaindance. *See* Common Bonds.
Chained Heat 1983
Chairman of the Board 1999
Challenge, The 1982
Chamber, The 1996
Chambermaid of the Titanic, The 1999
Chameleon Street 1991
Champion [1949] 1991
Champions 1984
Chan Is Missing 1982
Chances Are 1989
Changing Lanes 2003
Changing Times pg. 69
Chantilly Lace 1995
Chaos 2004
Chaos. *See* Ran.
Chaplin 1992
Character 1999
Chariots of Fire 1981
Charlie and the Chocolate Factory 2006
Charlie's Angels 2001
Charlie's Angels: Full Throttle 2004
Charlotte Gray 2003
Charlotte's Web pg. 71
Charm Discret de la Bourgeoisie, Le. *See* The Discreet Charm of the Bourgeoisie.
Chase, The 1995
Chasers 1995
Chasing Amy 1988
Chasing Liberty 2005
Chasing Papi 2004
Chateau, The 2003
Chateau de ma mere, Le. *See* My Mother's Castle.
Chattahoochee 1990
Chattanooga Choo Choo 1984
Cheap Shots 1991
Cheaper by the Dozen 2004
Cheaper by the Dozen 2 2006
Cheatin' Hearts 1993
Check Is in the Mail, The 1986
Checking Out 1989
Cheech & Chong Still Smokin' 1983
Cheech & Chong's The Corsican Brothers 1984
Cheetah 1989
Chef in Love, A 1997
Chelsea Walls 2003
Chere Inconnue. *See* I Sent a Letter to My Love.
Cherish 2003
Cherry Orchard, The 2003
Cherry Pink. *See* Just Looking.
Chevre, La. *See* Goat, The.
Chicago 2003
Chicago Joe and the Showgirl 1990
Chicken Hawk: Men Who Love Boys 1995
Chicken Little 2006
Chicken Run 2001
Chief Zabu 1988
Chihwaseon: Painted Fire 2003
Child, The pg. 73
Child's Play 1988
Child's Play II 1990
Child's Play III 1991
Children of a Lesser God 1986
Children of Heaven, The 2000
Children of Men pg. 74
Children of Nature 1995
Children of the Corn II 1993
Children of the Revolution 1997
Chile, la Memoria Obstinada. *See* Chile, Obstinate Memory.
Chile, Obstinate Memory 1999
Chill Factor 2000
Chimes at Midnight. *See* Falstaff.
China Cry 1990
China Girl 1987
China Moon 1995
China, My Sorrow 1995
China Syndrome, The [1979] 1988
Chinese Box 1999
Chinese Ghost Story II, A 1990
Chinese Ghost Story III, A 1991
Chipmunk Adventure, The 1987
Chocolat (Denis) 1989
Chocolat (Hallstrom) 2001
Chocolate War, The 1988
Choke Canyon 1986
Choose Me 1984, 1985
Chopper 2002
Chopper Chicks in Zombie Town 1991
Chopping Mall 1986
Choristes, Les. *See* Chorus, The.
Chorus, The 2006
Chorus Line, A 1985
Chorus of Disapproval, A 1989
Chosen, The 1982
Christine 1983
Christine F. 1982
Christmas Story, A 1983
Christmas with the Kranks 2005
Christopher Columbus: The Discovery 1992

Chronicles of Narnia: The Lion, the Witch and the Wardrobe, The 2006
Chronicles of Riddick, The 2005
Chronos 1985
Chuck & Buck 2001
Chuck Berry: Hail! Hail! Rock 'n' Roll 1987
C.H.U.D. 1984
Chungking Express 1996
Chunhyang 2001
Chutney Popcorn 2001
Ciao, Professore! 1995
Cider House Rules, The 2000
Cienaga, La 2002
Cinderella Man 2006
Cinderella Story, A 2005
Cinema Paradiso 1989
Cinema Verite: Defining the Moment 2001
Circle, The 2002
Circle of Deceit 1982
Circle of Friends 1995
Circuitry Man 1990
Citizen Ruth 1996
Citta della donne, La. *See* City of Women.
City by the Sea 2003
City Girl, The 1984
City Hall 1996
City Heat 1984
City Limits 1985
City of Angels 1999
City of Ghosts 2004
City of God 2004
City of Hope 1991
City of Industry 1997
City of Joy 1992
City of Lost Children 1996
City of Women 1981
City Slickers 1991
City Slickers II: The Legend of Curly's Gold 1995
City Zero 1995
Civil Action, A, 1999
Civil Brand 2004
Claim, The 2002
Claire of the Moon 1993
Clan of the Cave Bear, The 1986
Clara's Heart 1988
Clash of the Titans 1981
Class 1982
Class Act 1992
Class Action 1991
Class of 1984 1982
Class of 2000 1990
Class of Nuke 'em High 1986
Class of Nuke 'em High Part II 1991
Clay Pigeons 1999
Clean and Sober 1988
Clean Slate 1995
Clean Slate. *See* Coup de torchon.
Clear and Present Danger 1995
Clearcut 1992
Clearing, The 2005
Cleopatra [1963] 1993
Clerks 1995
Clerks II pg. 76
Click pg. 78
Client, The 1995
Cliffhanger 1993
Clifford 1995
Clifford's Really Big Movie 2005
Climate for Killing, A 1995
Climates pg. 80
Cloak and Dagger 1984
Clock, The 1981
Clockers 1995
Clockstoppers 2003
Clockwatchers 1999
Clockwise 1986
Close My Eyes 1991
Close to Eden 1992
Close Your Eyes 2005
Closer 2005
Closer You Get, The 2001
Closet, The 2002
Closet Land 1991
Club Dread 2005
Club Earth. *See* Galactic Gigolo.
Club Paradise 1986
Clue 1985
Clueless 1995
Coach Carter 2006
Cobb 1995
Cobra 1986
Cobra Verde 1988
Coca-Cola Kid, The 1985
Cocaine Wars 1986
Cocktail 1988
Cocoon 1985
Cocoon: The Return 1988
Code 46 2005
Code Inconnu: Recit Incomplet de Divers Voyages. *See* Code Unknown.
Code of Silence 1985
Code Unknown 2003
Coeur en hiver, Un 1993
Coeur qui bat, Un. *See* Beating Heart, A.
Coffee & Cigarettes 2005
Cold Comfort 1989
Cold Comfort Farm 1995
Cold Creek Manor 2004
Cold Feet (Dornhelm) 1989
Cold Feet (Van Dusen) 1984
Cold Fever 1996
Cold Heaven 1992
Cold Moon 1995
Cold Mountain 2004
Cold Steel 1987
Coldblooded 1995
Collateral 2005
Collateral Damage 2003
Colonel Chabert 1995
Colonel Redl 1985
Color Adjustment 1995
Color of Money, The 1986
Color of Night 1995
Color Purple, The 1985
Colorado Territory [1949] 1985
Colors 1988
Colpo di Luna. *See* Moon Shadow.
Combat Shock 1986
Combination Platter 1995
Come and Get It [1936] 1981

Come Back to the Five and Dime Jimmy Dean, Jimmy Dean 1982
Come See the Paradise 1990
Come Undone 2002
Comedian Harmoniest: Six Life Stories, The 1995
Comfort and Joy 1984
Comfort of Strangers, The 1991
Comic Book Confidential 1988
Coming to America 1988
Commandments 1997
Commando 1985
Commando Squad 1987
Comme une image. *See* Look at Me.
Commitments, The 1991
Committed 2001
Common Bonds 1995
Communion 1989
Como Agua Para Chocolate. *See* Like Water for Chocolate.
Company, The 2005
Company Business 1991
Company Man 2002
Company of Strangers, The. *See* Strangers in Good Company.
Company of Wolves, The 1985
Competition [1963] 1985
Complex World 1995
Complot, Le. *See* To Kill a Priest.
Compromising Positions 1985
Con Air 1997
Conan the Barbarian 1982
Conan the Destroyer 1984
Conceiving Ada 2000
Coneheads 1993
Confessions of a Dangerous Mind 2003
Confessions of a Teenage Drama Queen 2005
Confidence 2004
Confidences trop intimes. *See* Intimate Strangers.
Confidentially Yours 1984
Confusion of Genders 2004
Congo 1995
Connie and Carla 2005
Consenting Adults 1992
Conspiracy Theory 1997
Conspirators of Pleasure 1997
Constant Gardener, The 2006
Constantine 2006
Consuming Passions 1988
Contact 1997
Conte d'Automne. *See* Autumn Tale.
Conte de printemps. *See* Tale of Springtime, A.
Conte d'Hiver. *See* A Tale of Winter.
Contender, The 2001
Continental Divide 1981
Control Room 2005
Convent, The 1995
Convicts 1991
Convoyeurs Attendent, Les. *See* The Carriers Are Waiting.
Coogan's Bluff [1968] 1982
Cook, the Thief, His Wife, and Her Lover, The 1990
Cookie 1989
Cookie's Fortune 2000
Cookout, The 2005
Cool as Ice 1991
Cool Dry Place, A 2000
Cool Runnings 1993
Cool World 1992
Cooler, The 2004
Cop 1987
Cop and a Half 1993
Cop Land 1997
Cops and Robbersons 1995
Copycat 1995
Core, The 2004
Corky Romano 2002
Corporation, The 2005
Corpse Bride. *See* Tim Burton's Corpse Bride.
Corrina, Corrina 1995
Corruptor, The 2000
Cosi 1997
Cosi Ridevano. *See* Way We Laughed, The.
Cosmic Eye, The 1986
Cotton Club, The 1984
Couch Trip, The 1988
Count of Monte Cristo, The 2003
Country 1984
Country Bears, The 2003
Country Life 1995
Country of My Skull. *See* In My Country.
Coup de foudre. *See* Entre nous.
Coup de torchon 1982
Coupe de Ville 1990
Courage Mountain 1990
Courage of Lassie [1946] 1993
Courage Under Fire 1996
Courier, The 1988
Cours Toujours. *See* Dad On the Run.
Cousin Bette 1999
Cousin Bobby 1992
Cousins 1989
Covenant, The pg. 81
Cover Girl 1985
Coverup 1988
Cowboy [1958] 1981
Cowboy Way, The 1995
Cowboys Don't Cry 1988
Coyote Ugly 2001
CQ 2003
Crabe Dans la Tete, Un. *See* Soft Shell Man.
Crack House 1989
Crack in the Mirror 1988
Crackdown. *See* To Die Standing.
Crackers 1984
Cradle 2 the Grave 2004
Cradle Will Rock 2000
Craft, The 1996
Crank pg. 83
Crash (Cronenberg) 1997
Crash (Haggis) 2006
Crawlspace 1986
crazy/beautiful 2002
Crazy Family, The 1986
Crazy in Alabama 2000
Crazy Moon 1988
Crazy People 1990
Creator 1985

Creature from the Black Lagoon, The [1954] 1981
Creepozoids 1987
Creepshow 1982
Creepshow II 1987
Crew, The 2001
Crime + Punishment in Suburbia 2001
Crime of Father Amaro, The 2003
Crimes and Misdemeanors 1989
Crimes of Passion 1984
Crimes of the Heart 1986
Criminal 2005
Criminal Law 1988, 1989
Criminal Lovers 2004
Crimson Tide 1995
Crisscross 1992
Critical Care 1997
Critical Condition 1987
Critters 1986
Critters II 1988
Crna macka, beli macor. *See* Black Cat, White Cat.
"Crocodile" Dundee 1986
"Crocodile" Dundee II 1988
"Crocodile" Dundee in Los Angeles 2002
Crocodile Hunter: Collision Course, The 2003
Cronos 1995
Crooked Hearts 1991
Crooklyn 1995
Cross Country 1983
Cross Creek 1983
Cross My Heart 1987
Crossing Delancey 1988
Crossing Guard, The 1995
Crossing the Bridge 1992
Crossover Dreams 1985
Crossroads 1986
Crossroads 2003
Crouching Tiger, Hidden Dragon 2001
Croupier [1997] 2001
Crow: City of Angels, The 1996
Crow, The 1995
Crucible, The 1996
Crude Oasis, The 1995
Cruel Intentions 2000
Cruel Story of Youth [1960] 1984
Crumb 1995
Crush (Maclean) 1993
Crush (McKay) 2003
Crush, The (Shapiro) 1993
Crusoe 1988
Cry Baby Killers, The [1957]
Cry Freedom 1987
Cry in the Dark, A 1988
Cry in the Wild, The 1990
Cry, the Beloved Country 1995
Cry Wolf [1947] 1986
Cry_Wolf 2006
Cry-Baby 1990
Crying Game, The 1992
Crystal Heart 1987
Crystalstone 1988
Cucaracha, La 2000
Cuckoo, The 2004
Cujo 1983
Cup, The 2001
Cup Final 1992
Curdled 1996
Cure, The 1995
Cure in Orange, The 1987
Curious George pg. 85
Curly Sue 1991
Current Events 1990
Curse of the Golden Flower pg. 86
Curse of the Jade Scorpion, The 2002
Curse of the Pink Panther 1983
Cursed 2006
Curtains 1983
Cut and Run 1986
Cutthroat Island 1995
Cutting Edge, The 1992
Cyborg 1989
Cyclo 1996
Cyclone 1987
Cyrano de Bergerac 1990
Czlowiek z Marmuru. *See* Man of Marble.
Czlowiek z Zelaza. *See* Man of Iron.

D

Da 1988
Da Vinci Code, The pg. 89
Dad 1989
Dad On the Run 2002
Daddy and the Muscle Academy 1995
Daddy Day Care 2004
Daddy Nostalgia 1991
Daddy's Boys 1988
Daddy's Dyin' 1990
Dadetown 1996
Daffy Duck's Quackbusters 1988
Dakhtaran-e Khorshid. *See* Daughters of the Sun.
Dakota 1988
Damage 1992
Damned in the U.S.A. 1992
Dance Maker, The 2000
Dance of the Damned 1989
Dance with a Stranger 1985
Dance with Me 1999
Dancer in the Dark 2001
Dancer, Texas Pop. 81 1999
Dancer Upstairs, The 2004
Dancers 1987
Dances with Wolves 1990
Dancing at Lughnasa 1999
Dancing in the Dark 1986
Dangerous Beauty 1999
Dangerous Game (Ferrara) 1995
Dangerous Game (Hopkins) 1988
Dangerous Ground 1997
Dangerous Liaisons 1988
Dangerous Lives of Altar Boys, The 2003
Dangerous Love 1988
Dangerous Minds 1995
Dangerous Moves 1985
Dangerous Woman, A 1993
Dangerously Close 1986
Daniel 1983
Danny Boy 1984
Danny Deckchair 2005

Danny the Dog. *See* Unleashed.
Dante's Peak 1997
Danton 1983
Danzon 1992
Daredevil 2004
Dark Backward, The 1991
Dark Before Dawn 1988
Dark Blue 2004
Dark Blue World 2002
Dark City
Dark Crystal, The 1982
Dark Days 2001
Dark Eyes 1987
Dark Half, The 1993
Dark Obsession 1991
Dark of the Night 1986
Dark Star [1975] 1985
Dark Water 2006
Dark Wind, The 1995
Darkman 1990
Darkness 2005
Darkness, Darkness. *See* South of Reno.
Darkness Falls 2004
D.A.R.Y.L. 1985
Date Movie pg. 91
Date with an Angel 1987
Daughter of the Nile 1988
Daughters of the Dust 1992
Daughters of the Sun 2001
Dauntaun Herozu. *See* Hope and Pain.
Dave 1993
Dave Chappelle's Block Party pg. 92
Dawn of the Dead 2005
Day After Tomorrow, The 2005
Day I Became a Woman, The 2002
Day in October, A 1992
Day of the Dead 1985
Dayereh. *See* Circle, The.
Daylight 1996
Days of Thunder 1990
Days of Wine and Roses [1962] 1988
Daytrippers, The 1997
Dazed and Confused 1993
D.C. Cab 1983
De Eso No Se Habla. *See* I Don't Want to Talk About It.
De-Lovely 2005
De Poolse Bruid. *See* Polish Bride, The.
Dead, The 1987
Dead Again 1991
Dead Alive 1993
Dead Bang 1989
Dead Calm 1989
Dead Heat 1988
Dead Man 1996
Dead Man on Campus 1999
Dead Man Walking 1995
Dead Man's Curve 2000
Dead Men Don't Wear Plaid 1982
Dead of Winter 1987
Dead Poets Society 1989
Dead Pool, The 1988
Dead Presidents 1995
Dead Ringers 1988
Dead Space 1991
Dead Women in Lingerie 1991
Dead Zone, The 1983
Dead-end Drive-in 1986
Deadfall 1995
Deadline 1987
Deadly Eyes 1982
Deadly Friend 1986
Deadly Illusion 1987
Deadly Intent 1988
Deal, The 2006
Deal of the Century 1983
Dealers 1989
Dear American 1987
Dear Diary. *See* Caro Diario.
Dear Frankie 2006
Dear God 1996
Death and the Maiden 1995
Death Becomes Her 1992
Death Before Dishonor 1987
Death of a Soldier 1986
Death of an Angel 1986
Death of Mario Ricci, The 1985
Death of Mr. Lazarescu, The pg. 94
Death to Smoochy 2003
Death Valley 1982
Death Warrant 1990
Death Wish II 1982
Death Wish III 1985
Death Wish IV 1987
Death Wish V: The Face of Death 1995
Deathtrap 1982
Deathstalker 1984
D.E.B.S. 2006
Decade Under the Influence, A 2004
Decalogue, Parts 1 & 2, The [1988] 2001
Decalogue, Parts 3 & 4, The [1988] 2001
Decalogue, Parts 5 & 6, The [1988] 2001
Decalogue, Parts 7 & 8, The [1988] 2001
Decalogue, Parts 9 & 10, The [1988] 2001
Deceived 1991
Deceiver 1999
Deceivers, The 1988
December 1991
Deception 1993
Deck the Halls pg. 96
Decline of the American Empire, The 1986
Decline of Western Civilization Part II, The 1988
Deconstructing Harry 1997
Deep Blue Sea 2000
Deep Cover 1992
Deep Crimson 1997
Deep End, The 2002
Deep End of the Ocean 2000
Deep Impact 1999
Deep in the Heart 1984
Deep Rising 1999
Deepstar Six 1989
Deer Hunter, The 1981
Def by Temptation 1990
Def-Con 4 1985
Def Jam's How to Be a Player 1997

Defending Your Life 1991
Defense Play 1988
Defenseless 1991
Defiant Ones, The [1958] 1992
Defying Gravity 2000
Deja Vu 1999
Deja Vu pg. 97
Delicatessen 1992
Delirious 1991
Deliver Us from Eva 2004
Delta, The 1997
Delta Force, The 1986
Delta Force II 1990
Delta of Venus 1995
Delusion 1991
Demoiselle d'honneur, La. *See* Bridesmaid, The.
Demolition Man 1993
Demonlover 2004
Demons 1986
Demons in the Garden 1984
Den Goda Viljan. *See* Best Intentions, The.
Denise Calls Up 1996
Dennis the Menace 1993
Departed, The pg. 99
Depuis Qu'Otar est Parti. *See* Since Otar Left…
Der Stand der Dinge. *See* State of Things, The.
Der Untergang. *See* Downfall.
Derailed 2006
Dernier Combat, Le 1984
Desa parecidos, Los. *See* Official Story, The.
Descent, The pg. 101
Desert Bloom 1986
Desert Blue 2000
Desert Hearts 1986
Designated Mourner, The 1997
Desire (Salt on Our Skin) 1995
Desire and Hell at Sunset Motel 1992
Desperado 1995
Desperate Hours 1990
Desperate Measures 1999
Desperate Remedies 1995
Desperately Seeking Susan 1985
Destinees Sentimentales. *See* Sentimental Destiny.
Destiny in Space 1995
Destiny Turns on the Radio 1995
Detective 1985
Deterrence 2001
Detour [1946] 1985
Detroit Rock City 2000
Deuce Bigalow: European Gigolo 2006
Duece Bigalow: Male Gigolo 2000
Deuces Wild 2003
Devil and Daniel Johnston, The pg. 102
Devil in a Blue Dress 1995
Devil Wears Prada, The pg. 104
Devil's Advocate, The 1997
Devil's Backbone, The 2002
Devil's Own, The 1997
Devil's Rejects, The 2006
Devotion [1944] 1981
Diabolique 1996
Diagonale du fou. *See* Dangerous Moves.
Dialogues with Madwomen 1995
Diamond Skulls. *See* Dark Obsession.
Diamond's Edge 1990
Diarios de motocicleta. *See* Motorcycle Diaries, The.
Diary of a Hitman 1992
Diary of a Mad Black Woman 2006
Diary of a Mad Old Man 1987
Diary of a Seducer 1997
Dice Rules 1991
Dick 2000
Dick Tracy 1990
Dickie Roberts: Former Child Star 2004
Die Another Day 2003
Die Fetten Jahre sind vorbei. *See* Edukators, The.
Die Hard 1988
Die Hard II 1990
Die Hard with a Vengeance 1995
Die Mommie Die! 2004
Die Story Von Monty Spinneratz. *See* A Rat's Story.
Dieu Est Grand, Je Suis Tout Petite. *See* God Is Great, I'm Not.
Different for Girls 1997
DIG! 2005
Digging to China 1999
Diggstown 1992
Dim Sum 1985
Dimanche a la Campagne, Un. *See* A Sunday in the Country.
Diner 1982
Dinner Game, The 2000
Dinner Rush 2002
Dinosaur 2001
Dinosaur's Story, A. *See* We're Back.
Dirty Cop No Donut 2003
Dirty Dancing 1987
Dirty Dancing: Havana Nights 2005
Dirty Dishes 1983
Dirty Harry [1971] 1982
Dirty Love 2006
Dirty Pretty Things 2004
Dirty Rotten Scoundrels 1988
Dirty Shame, A 2005
Dirty Work 1999
Disappearance of Garcia Lorca, The 1997
Disclosure 1995
Discreet Charm of the Bourgeoisie, The [1972] 2001
Discrete, La 1992
Dish, The 2002
Disney's Teacher's Pet 2005
Disney's The Kid 2001
Disorderlies 1987
Disorganized Crime 1989
Disraeli [1929] 1981
Distant Harmony 1988
Distant Thunder 1988
Distant Voices, Still Lives 1988
Distinguished Gentleman, The 1992
Distribution of Lead, The 1989
Disturbed 1990
Disturbing Behavior 1999
Diva 1982

Divan 2005
Divided Love. *See* Maneuvers.
Divided We Fall 2002
Divine Intervention: A Chronicle of Love and Pain 2004
Divine Secrets of the Ya-Ya Sisterhood, The 2003
Diving In 1990
Divorce, Le 2004
Divorcee, The [1930] 1981
Djomeh 2002
Do or Die 1995
Do the Right Thing 1989
D.O.A. 1988
Doc Hollywood 1991
Doc's Kingdom 1988
Docteur Petiot 1995
Doctor, The 1991
Dr. Agaki 2000
Doctor and the Devils, The 1985
Dr. Bethune 1995
Dr. Butcher, M.D. 1982
Doctor Detroit 1983
Dr. Dolittle 1999
Dr. Dolittle 2 2002
Dr. Giggles 1992
Dr. Jekyll and Ms. Hyde 1995
Dr. Petiot. *See* Docteur Petiot.
Dr. Seuss' How the Grinch Stole Christmas 2001
Dr. Seuss' The Cat in the Hat 2004
Dr. Sleep. *See* Close Your Eyes.
Dr. T and the Women 2001
Doctor Zhivago [1965] 1990
Dodgeball: A True Underdog Story 2005
Dog of Flanders, A 2000
Dog Park 2000
Dogfight 1991
Dogma 2000
Dogville 2005
Doin' Time on Planet Earth 1988
Dolls 1987
Dolls 2006
Dolly Dearest 1992
Dolly In. *See* Travelling Avant.
Dolores Claiborne 1995
Domestic Disturbance 2002
Dominick and Eugene 1988
Dominion: Prequel to the Exorcist 2006
Domino 2006
Don Juan DeMarco 1995
Don Juan, My Love 1991
Dona Herlinda and Her Son 1986
Donkey Who Drank the Moon, The 1988
Donna della luna, La. *See* Woman in the Moon.
Donnie Brasco 1997
Donnie Darko 2003
Don't Be a Menace to South Central While Drinking Your Juice in the Hood 1996
Don't Come Knocking pg. 106
Don't Cry, It's Only Thunder 1982
Don't Move 2006
Don't Say a Word 2002
Don't Tell pg. 108
Don't Tell Her It's Me 1990
Don't Tell Mom the Babysitter's Dead 1991
Don't Tempt Me! *See* No News from God.
Doom 2006
Doom Generation, The 1995
Door in the Floor, The 2005
Door to Door 1984
Doors, The 1991
Dopamine 2004
Dorm That Dripped Blood, The 1983
Dorothy and Alan at Norma Place 1981
Double Dragon 1995
Double Edge 1992
Double Happiness 1995
Double Impact 1991
Double Indemnity [1944] 1981, 1986, 1987
Double Jeopardy 2000
Double Life of Veronique, The 1991
Double Take 2002
Double Team 1997
Double Threat 1993
Double Trouble 1992
Double Vie de Veronique, La. *See* Double Life of Veronique, The.
Doug's First Movie 2000
Down and Out in Beverly Hills 1986
Down by Law 1986
Down in the Delta 1999
Down in the Valley pg. 109
Down Periscope 1996
Down to Earth 2002
Down to You 2001
Down Twisted 1987
Down With Love 2004
Downfall 2006
Downtown 1990
Dracula. *See* Bram Stoker's Dracula.
Dracula: Dead and Loving It 1995
Dracula 2001. *See* Wes Craven Presents: Dracula 2001.
Dragnet 1987
Dragon 1993
Dragon Chow 1988
Dragonfly 2003
Dragonheart 1996
Dragonslayer 1981
Draughtsman's Contract, The 1983
Dream a Little Dream 1989
Dream Demon 1988
Dream for an Insomniac 1999
Dream Lover (Kazan) 1986
Dream Lover (Pakula) 1995
Dream of Light 1995
Dream Team, The 1989
Dream With the Fishes 1997
Dreamcatcher 2004
Dreamchild 1985
Dreamer: Inspired by a True Story 2006
Dreamers, The 2005
Dreamgirls pg. 111
Dreamlife of Angels, The 2000
Dreams. *See* Akira Kurosawa's Dreams.
Dreamscape 1984
Drei Sterne. *See* Mostly Martha.

Dresser, The 1983
Dressmaker, The 1988
Drifter, The 1988
Drifting 1984
Drive 1992
Drive Me Crazy 2000
Driven 2002
Driving Miss Daisy 1989
Drole de Felix. *See* Adventures of Felix, The.
Drop Dead Fred 1991
Drop Dead Gorgeous 2000
DROP Squad 1995
Drop Zone 1995
Drowning by Numbers 1988
Drowning Mona 2001
Drugstore Cowboy 1989
Drumline 2003
Drunks 1997
Dry Cleaning 2000
Dry White Season, A 1989
D3: The Mighty Ducks 1996
Duck Season pg. 113
Ducktales, the Movie 1990
Dude, Where's My Car? 2001
Dudes 1987
Dudley Do-Right 2000
Duel in the Sun [1946] 1982, 1989
Duet for One 1986
Duets 2001
Duolou Tianshi. *See* Fallen Angels.
D.U.I. 1987
Dukes of Hazzard, The 2006
Dulcy [1923] 1981
Duma 2006
Dumb and Dumber 1995
Dumb and Dumberer: When Harry Met Lloyd 2004
Dummy 2004
Dune 1984
Dungeons & Dragons 2001
Dunston Checks In 1996
Duplex 2004
Dust Devil: The Final Cut 1995
Dutch 1991
Dying Gaul, The 2006
Dying Young 1991

E

E la nave va. *See* And the Ship Sails On.
Earth 2001
Earth Girls Are Easy 1989
Earthling, The 1981
East Is East 2001
East is Red, The 1995
East-West 2002
Easy Money 1983
Eat a Bowl of Tea 1989
Eat and Run 1986
Eat Drink Man Woman 1995
Eat the Rich 1988
Eating 1990
Eating Raoul 1982
Ebro Runs Dry, The 1993
Echo Park 1986
Echoes 1983
Echoes of Paradise 1989
Ed 1996
Ed and His Dead Mother 1993
Ed Wood 1995
Eddie 1996
Eddie and the Cruisers 1983
Eddie and the Cruisers II 1989
Eddie Macon's Run 1983
Eddie Murphy Raw 1987
Eden 1999
Edes Emma, Draga Bobe: Vazlatok, Aktok. *See* Sweet Emma, Dear Bobe: Sketches, Nudes.
Edge, The 1997
Edge of Sanity 1989
Edge of Seventeen 2000
Edith and Marcel 1984
Edith's Diary 1986
Ed's Next Move 1996
Edtv 2000
Educating Rita 1983
Education of Little Tree, The 1997
Edukators, The 2006
Edward Scissorhands 1990
Edward II 1992
Efficiency Expert, The 1992
Efter Repetitionen. *See* After the Rehearsal.
Egares, Les. *See* Strayed.
Eiga Joyu. *See* Actress.
8 1/2 Women 2001
Eight Below pg. 117
Eight Days a Week 2000
Eight Heads in a Duffle Bag 1997
Eight Legged Freaks 2003
Eight Men Out 1988
8 Mile 2003
Eight Million Ways to Die 1986
8MM 2000
8 Seconds 1995
8 Women 2003
Eighteen Again 1988
Eighth Day, The 1997
Eighty-Four Charing Cross Road 1987
Eighty-Four Charlie MoPic 1989
Eine Liebe in Deutchland. *See* Love in Germany, A.
Election 2000
Electric Dreams 1984
Elektra 2006
Elephant 2004
Elegant Criminel, L' 1992
Elementary School, The 1995
Eleni 1985
Eleni (2005). *See* Weeping Meadow.
Elf 2004
Eliminators 1986
Elizabeth 1999
Elizabethtown 2006
Ella Enchanted 2005
Elling 2003
Elliot Fauman, Ph.D. 1990
Eloge de l'Amour. *See* In Praise of Love.
Elvira, Mistress of the Dark 1988
Embalmer, The 2004
Emerald Forest, The 1985
Emile 2006
Eminent Domain 1991

Emma 1996

Emmanuelle 5 1987

Emperor Waltz, The [1948] 1986

Emperor's Club, The 2003

Emperor's New Clothes, The 1987

Emperor's New Clothes, The (Taylor) 2003

Emperor's New Groove, The 2001

Emperor's Shadow 2000

Empire of the Sun 1987

Empire Records 1995

Empire Strikes Back, The [1983] 1997

Emploi du Temps, L. *See* Time Out.

Employee of the Month pg. 118

Emporte-Moi. *See* Set Me Free.

Empty Mirror, The 2000

Enchanted April 1992

Enchanted Cottage, The [1945] 1981

Encino Man 1992

Encore. *See* One More.

End of Days 2000

End of Innocence, The 1990

End of Old Times, The 1992

End of the Affair 2000

End of the Line (Glenn) 1987

End of the Line (Russell) 1988

End of the Spear pg. 119

End of Violence, The 1997

Endangered Species 1982

Endurance 2000

Enduring Love 2005

Endgame 1986

Endless Summer II, The 1995

Enemies, A Love Story 1989

Enemy at the Gates 2002

Enemy Mine 1985

Enemy of the State 1999

Enemy Territory 1987

Enfant, L'. *See* Child, The.

English Patient, The 1996

Englishman Who Went Up a Hill But Came Down a Mountain, The 1995

Enid Is Sleeping. *See* Over Her Dead Body.

Enigma (Szwarc) 1983

Enigma (Apted) 2003

Enough 2003

Enron: The Smartest Guys in the Room 2006

Enter the Ninja 1982

Entity, The 1983

Entrapment 2000

Entre nous 1984

Envy 2005

Equilibrium 2003

Equinox 1993

Eragon pg. 121

Eraser 1996

Erendira 1984

Erik the Viking 1989

Erin Brockovich 2001

Ermo 1995

Ernest Goes to Camp 1987

Ernest Goes to Jail 1990

Ernest Rides Again 1993

Ernest Saves Christmas 1988

Ernest Scared Stupid 1991

Eros 2006

Erotique 1995

Escanaba in da Moonlight 2002

Escape Artist, The 1982

Escape from Alcatraz [1979] 1982

Escape from L.A. 1996

Escape from New York 1981

Escape from Safehaven 1989

Escape 2000 1983

Escort, The. *See* Scorta, La.

Especially on Sunday 1993

Esperame en el cielo. *See* Wait for Me in Heaven.

Espinazo de Diablo, El. *See* Devil's Backbone, The.

Est-Ouest. *See* East-West.

Esther Kahn 2003

E.T.: The Extra-Terrestrial 1982

Etat sauvage, L' [1978] 1990

Ete prochain, L'. *See* Next Summer.

Eternal Sunshine of the Spotless Mind 2005

Eternity and a Day 2000

Ethan Frome 1993

Etoile du nord 1983

Eu Tu Eles. *See* Me You Them.

Eulogy 2005

Eulogy of Love. *See* In Praise of Love.

Eureka 1985

Eureka 2002

Europa 1995

Europa, Europa 1991

Eurotrip 2005

Eve of Destruction 1991

Evelyn 2003

Even Cowgirls Get the Blues 1995

Evening Star 1996

Event Horizon 1997

Events Leading Up to My Death, The 1995

Ever After: A Cinderella Story 1999

Everlasting Piece, An 2002

Everlasting Secret Family, The 1989

Every Breath 1995

Every Man for Himself [1979] 1981

Every Time We Say Goodbye 1986

Everybody Wins 1990

Everybody's All-American 1988

Everybody's Famous! 2002

Everybody's Fine 1991

Everyone Says I Love You 1996

Everyone's Hero pg. 122

Everything is Illuminated 2006

Eve's Bayou 1997

Evil Dead, The 1983

Evil Dead II 1987

Evil That Men Do, The 1984

Evil Under the Sun 1982

Evil Woman. *See* Saving Silverman.

Evita 1996

Evolution 2002

Excalibur 1981

Excess Baggage 1997

Exchange Lifeguards 1995

Execution Protocol, The 1995

Executive Decision 1996

eXistenZ 2000

Exit to Eden 1995

Exit Wounds 2002
Exorcism of Emily Rose, The 2006
Exorcist: The Beginning 2005
Exorcist III, The 1990
Exorcist, The [1973] 2001
Exotica 1995
Experience Preferred...but Not Essential 1983
Explorers 1985
Exposed 1983
Extramuros 1995
Extreme Measures 1996
Extreme Ops 2003
Extreme Prejudice 1987
Extremities 1986
Eye for an Eye, An 1996
Eye of God 1997
Eye of the Beholder 2001
Eye of the Needle 1981
Eye of the Tiger 1986
Eyes of Tammy Faye, The 2001
Eyes Wide Shut 2000

F

F/X 1986
F/X II 1991
Fabulous Baker Boys, The 1989
Fabulous Destiny of Amelie Poulain, The. *See* Amelie.
Face/Off 1997
Faces of Women 1987
Facing Windows 2005
Factotum pg. 125
Faculty, The 1999
Fahrenheit 9/11 2005
Failure to Launch pg. 127
Fair Game 1995
Fairytale—A True Story 1997
Faithful 1996
Faithless 2002
Fakebook 1989
Falcon and the Snowman, The 1985
Fall 1997
Fallen 1999
Fallen Angels 1999
Falling, The. *See* Alien Predator.
Falling Down 1993
Falling from Grace 1992
Falling in Love 1984
Falstaff [1966] 1982
Family, The 1988
Family Business 1989
Family Man 2001
Family Prayers 1993
Family Stone, The 2006
Family Thing, A 1996
Famine Within, The 1992
Fan, The 1996
Fandango 1985
Fanny and Alexander 1983
Fanny och Alexander. *See* Fanny and Alexander.
Fantasies [1973] 1982
Fantastic Four 2006
Fantomes des Trois Madeleines, Les. *See* Three Madeleines, The.
Fantome D'henri Langlois, Le. *See* Henri Langlois: The Phantom of the Cinematheque.
Far and Away 1992
Far from Heaven 2003
Far from Home 1989
Far From Home: The Adventures of Yellow Dog 1995
Far North 1988
Far Off Place, A 1993
Far Out Man 1990
Faraway, So Close 1993
Farewell Illusion 1986
Farewell My Concubine 1993
Farewell to the King 1989
Fargo 1996
Farinelli 1995
Farmer and Chase 1997
Fast and the Furious, The 2002
Fast and the Furious: Tokyo Drift, The pg. 128
Fast, Cheap & Out of Control 1997
Fast Food 1989
Fast Food, Fast Women 2002
Fast Forward 1985
Fast Talking 1986
Fast Times at Ridgemont High 1982
Fat Albert 2005
Fat City [1972] 1983
Fat Girl 2002
Fat Guy Goes Nutzoid 1987
Fat Man and Little Boy 1989
Fatal Attraction 1987
Fatal Beauty 1987
Fatal Instinct 1993
Fate Ignoranti. *See* Ignorant Fairies.
Father 1995
Father Hood 1993
Father of the Bride (Minnelli) [1950] 1993
Father of the Bride (Shyer) 1991
Father of the Bride Part II 1995
Fathers and Sons 1992
Father's Day 1997
Fausto. *See* A la Mode.
Favor, The 1995
Favour, the Watch, and the Very Big Fish, The 1992
Fear 1988
Fear 1996
Fear and Loathing in Las Vegas 1999
Fear, Anxiety and Depression 1989
Fear of a Black Hat 1995
Feardotcom 2003
Fearless 1993
Fearless. *See* Jet Li's Fearless.
Feast of July 1995
Federal Hill 1995
Fedora [1978] 1986
Feds 1988
Feed 1992
Feel the Heat 1987
Feeling Minnesota 1996
Felicia's Journey 2000
Felix 1988
Fellini: I'm a Born Liar 2004
Female Perversions 1997
Femme d'a Cote, La. *See* Woman Next Door, The.
Femme de Chambre du Titanic, La. *See* Chambermaid of the Titanic.

Femme de mon pote, La. *See* My Best Friend's Girl.
Femme Fatale 2003
Femme Nikita, La 1991
Femmes de personne 1986
FernGully: The Last Rainforest 1992
Ferris Bueller's Day Off 1986
Festival Express 2005
Festival in Cannes 2003
Feud, The 1990
Fever 1988
Fever Pitch 1985
Fever Pitch 2000
Fever Pitch 2006
Few Days with Me, A 1988
Few Good Men, A 1992
Field, The 1990
Field of Dreams 1989
Fierce Creatures 1997
15 Minutes 2002
Fifth Element, The 1997
50 First Dates 2005
51st State, The. *See* Formula 51.
54 1999
Fifty-Fifty 1993
Fifty-two Pick-up 1986
Fight Club 2000
Fighter 2002
Fighting Back 1982
Fighting Temptations, The 2004
Filles ne Savent pas Nager, Les. *See* Girls Can't Swim.
Fils, Le. *See* Son, The.
Filth and the Fury, The 2001
Fin aout debut septembre. *See* Late August, Early September.
Final Analysis 1992
Final Approach 1991
Final Cut 2005
Final Destination 2001
Final Destination 2 2004
Final Destination 3 pg. 130
Final Fantasy: The Spirits Within 2002
Final Friday, The. *See* Jason Goes to Hell.
Final Option, The 1983
Final Sacrifice, The. *See* Children of the Corn II.
Final Season 1988
Find Me Guilty pg. 131
Finders Keepers 1984
Finding Forrester 2001
Finding Nemo 2004
Finding Neverland 2005
Fine Mess, A 1986
Fine Romance, A 1992
Finestra di Fronte, La. *See* Facing Windows.
Finzan 1995
Fiorile 1995
Fire and Ice (Bakshi) 1983
Fire and Ice (Bogner) 1987
Fire Birds 1990
Fire Down Below 1997
Fire from the Mountain 1987
Fire in Sky 1993
Fire This Time, The 1995
Fire Walk with Me. *See* Twin Peaks: Fire Walk with Me.
Fire with Fire 1986
Firefox 1982
Firehead 1991
Firelight 1999
Firemen's Bell, The [1967] 1985
Firestorm 1999
Firewalker 1986
Firewall pg. 133
Fireworks 1999
Fires of Kuwait 1995
Firm, The 1993
First Blood 1982
First Daughter 2005
First Descent 2006
First Kid 1996
First Knight 1995
First Love, Last Rites 1999
First Monday in October 1981
First Name, Carmen 1984
First Power, The 1990
First Wives Club, The 1996
Firstborn 1984
Fish Called Wanda, A 1988
Fisher King, The 1991
Fistfighter 1989
Fitzcarraldo 1982
Five Corners 1987
Five Days One Summer 1982
Five Graves to Cairo [1943] 1986
Five Heartbeats, The 1991
Five Senses, The 2001
Flags of Our Fathers pg. 135
Flame in My Heart, A 1987
Flaming Star [1960] 1982
Flamingo Kid, The 1984
Flamme dans mon coeur, Une. *See* Flame in My Heart, A.
Flanagan 1985
Flash of Green, A 1985
Flashback 1990
Flashdance 1983
Flashpoint 1984
Flatliners 1990
Flawless 2000
Flaxfield, The 1985
Fled 1996
Fleeing by Night 2004
Flesh and Blood 1985
Flesh and Bone 1993
Flesh Gordon Meets the Cosmic Cheerleaders 1995
Fleshburn 1984
Fletch 1985
Fletch Lives 1989
Flicka pg. 138
Flight of the Innocent 1993
Flight of the Intruder 1991
Flight of the Navigator 1986
Flight of the Phoenix 2005
Flight of the Phoenix, The [1966] 1984
Flight to Fury [1966]
Flightplan 2006
Flintstones, The 1995
Flipper 1996
Flipping 1997
Flirt 1996
Flirting 1992

Flirting with Disaster 1996
Floundering 1995
Flower of Evil, The 2004
Flower of My Secret, The 1996
Flowers in the Attic 1987
Flowing 1985
Flubber 1997
Fluke 1995
Flushed Away pg. 139
Fly, The 1986
Fly II, The 1989
Fly Away Home 1996
Fly by Night 1995
Flyboys pg. 140
Flying Duchman, The 1995
Fog, The 2006
Fog of War: Eleven Lessons from the Life of Robert S. McNamara, The 2005
Folks 1992
Follow the Bitch 1999
Food of the Gods II 1989
Fool for Love 1985
Foolish 2000
Fools of Fortune 1990
Fools Rush In 1997
Footloose 1984
For a Lost Soldier 1993
For Ever Mozart 1997
For Keeps 1988
For Love of the Game 2000
For Love or Money 1993
For Me and My Gal [1942] 1985
For My Sister. *See* Fat Girl.
For Queen and Country 1988, 1989
For Richer or Poorer 1997
For Roseanna 1997
For Sasha 1992
For the Boys 1991
For the Moment 1996
For Your Consideration pg. 142
For Your Eyes Only 1981
Forbidden Choices. *See* Beans of Egypt, Maine, The.
Forbidden Dance, The 1990
Forbidden Quest 1995
Forbidden World 1982
Forced Vengeance 1982
Forces of Nature 2000
Foreign Affair, A [1948] 1986
Foreign Body 1986
Foreign Student 211
Forever 1995
Forever, Lulu 1987
Forever Mary 1991
Forever Young 1992
Forget Paris 1995
Forgotten, The 2005
Formula 51 2003
Forrest Gump 1995
Forsaken, The 2002
Fort Apache [1948] 1983
Fort Apache, the Bronx 1981
Fortress 1993
Fortune Cookie, The [1966] 1986
40 Days and 40 Nights 2003
40 Year Old Virgin, The 2006
48 Hrs. 1982
Foster Daddy, Tora! 1981
Fountain, The pg. 144
Four Adventures of Reinette and Mirabelle 1989
Four Brothers 2006
Four Days in September 1999
Four Feathers, The 2003
Four Friends 1981
4 Little Girls 1997
Four Rooms 1995
Four Seasons, The 1981
Four Weddings and a Funeral 1995
1492: Conquest of Paradise 1992
4th Man, The 1984
Fourth Protocol, The 1987
Fourth War, The 1990
Fox and the Hound, The 1981
Foxfire 1996
Foxtrap 1986
Frailty 2003
Frances 1982
Frank and Ollie 1995
Frank Miller's Sin City. *See* Sin City.
Frankenhooker 1990
Frankenstein. *See* Mary Shelley's Frankenstein.
Frankenstein Unbound. *See* Roger Corman's Frankenstein Unbound.
Frankie and Johnny 1991
Frankie Starlight 1995
Frantic 1988
Fraternity Vacation 1985
Frauds 1995
Freaked 1993
Freaky Friday 2004
Freddie as F.R.O.7 1992
Freddy Got Fingered 2002
Freddy vs. Jason 2004
Freddy's Dead 1991
Free and Easy 1989
Free Enterprise 2000
Free Radicals 2005
Free Ride 1986
Free Willy 1993
Free Willy II: The Adventure Home 1995
Free Willy III: The Rescue 1997
Freedom On My Mind 1995
Freedomland pg. 146
Freejack 1992
Freeway 1988
Freeway 1996
Freeze—Die—Come to Life 1995
French Connection, The [1971] 1982
French Kiss 1995
French Lesson 1986
French Lieutenant's Woman, The 1981
French Twist 1996
Frequency 2001
Fresh 1995
Fresh Horses 1988
Freshman, The 1990
Freud [1962] 1983
Frida 2003
Friday 1995
Friday After Next 2003
Friday Night 2004
Friday Night Lights 2005

Friday the 13th, Part III 1982
Friday the 13th, Part IV 1984
Friday the 13th, Part VI 1986
Friday the 13th Part VII 1988
Friday the 13th Part VIII 1989
Fried Green Tomatoes 1991
Friend of the Deceased, A 1999
Friends & Lovers 2000
Friends with Money pg. 148
Fright Night 1985
Frighteners, The 1996
Fringe Dwellers, The 1987
From Beyond 1986
From Dusk Till Dawn 1996
From Hell 2002
From Hollywood to Deadwood 1988
From Swastikas to Jim Crow 2001
From the Hip 1987
Front, The [1976] 1985
Frosh: Nine Months in a Freshman Dorm 1995
Frozen Assets 1992
Frahlingssinfonie. *See* Spring Symphony.
Fruit Machine, The 1988
Fu-zung cen. *See* Hibiscus Town.
Fucking Amal. *See* Show Me Love.
Fugitive, The 1993
Full Blast 2001
Full Frontal 2003
Full Metal Jacket 1987
Full Monty, The 1997
Full Moon in Paris 1984
Full Moon in the Blue Water 1988
Fun Down There 1989
Fun With Dick and Jane 2006
Funeral, The 1987
Funeral, The (Ferrara) 1996
Funny About Love 1990
Funny Bones 1995
Funny Farm (Clark) 1983
Funny Farm (Hill) 1988
Further Adventures of Tennessee Buck, The 1988

G

Gabbeh 1997
Gabriela 1984
Gabrielle pg. 151
Gaby-A True Story 1987
Gadjo Dilo 1999
Galactic Gigolo 1988
Galaxy Quest 2000
Gallipoli 1981
Gambler, The 2000
Game, The 1997
Game, The 1989
Game 6 pg. 152
Gandhi 1982
Gang-Related 1997
Gangs of New York 2003
Gangster No. 1 2003
Garage Days 2004
Garbage Pail Kids Movie, The 1987
Garbo Talks 1984
Garde a vue 1982
Garden, The 1995
Garden State 2005
Gardens of Stone 1987
Garfield 2005
Garfield: A Tail of Two Kitties pg. 154
Gas Food Lodging 1992
Gate, The 1987
Gate II 1992
Gattaca 1997
Gaudi Afternoon 2002
Gay Divorcee, The [1934] 1981
Gegen die Wand. *See* Head-On.
Genealogies D' Un Crime. *See* Genealogies of a Crime.
Genealogies of a Crime 1999
General, The 1999
General's Daughter, The 2000
Genghis Blues 2000
Gentilezza del tocco, La. *See* Gentle Touch, The.
Gentle Touch, The 1988
Gentlemen Don't Eat Poets 1997
Gentlemen's Agreement [1947] 1989
Genuine Risk 1990
George A. Romero's Land of the Dead 2006
George Balanchine's The Nutcracker 1993
George of the Jungle 1997
George's Island 1991
Georgia 1988
Georgia 1995
Germinal 1993
Geronimo 1993
Gerry 2004
Get Back 1991
Get Bruce! 2000
Get Carter 2001
Get Crazy 1983
Get on the Bus 1996
Get Over It! 2002
Get Real 2000
Get Rich or Die Tryin' 2006
Get Shorty 1995
Getaway, The 1995
Geteilte Liebe. *See* Maneuvers.
Getting Away with Murder 1996
Getting Even 1986
Getting Even With Dad 1995
Getting It Right 1989
Getting to Know You 2001
Gettysburg 1993
Ghare Bhaire. *See* Home and the World, The.
Ghost 1990
Ghost and the Darkness, The 1996
Ghost Dad 1990
Ghost Dog: The Way of the Samurai 2000
Ghost in the Shell II: Innocence 2005
Ghost Ship 2003
Ghosts Can't Do It 1990
Ghosts of Mississippi 1996
Ghosts...of the Civil Dead 1988
Ghost Story 1981
Ghost Town 1988
Ghost World 2002
Ghosts of Mars. *See* John Carpenter's Ghosts of Mars.
Ghostbusters 1984
Ghostbusters II 1989
G.I. Jane 1997

Giant [1956] 1993, 1996
Gift, The (Lang) 1983
Gift, The (Raimi) 2001
Gift From Heaven, A 1995
Gig, The 1986
Gigli 2004
Ginger Ale Afternoon 1989
Ginger and Fred 1986
Ginger Snaps 2002
Gingerbread Man, The 1999
Giornata speciale, Una. *See* Special Day, A.
Giovane Toscanini, II. *See* Young Toscanini.
Girl from Paris, The 2004
Girl in a Swing, The 1988
Girl in the Picture, The 1986
Girl, Interrupted 2000
Girl Next Door, The 2001
Girl Next Door, The (Greenfield) 2005
Girl 6 1996
Girl Talk 1988
Girl with a Pearl Earring 2004
Girl with the Hungry Eyes, The 1995
Girl with the Red Hair, The 1983
Girlfight 2001
Girls Can't Swim 2003
Girls School Screamers 1986
Girls Town 1996
Give My Regards to Broad Street 1984
Giving, The 1992
Gladiator (Herrington) 1992
Gladiator (Scott) 2001
Glamazon: A Different Kind of Girl 1995
Glamour 2002
Glaneurs et la Glaneuse, Les. *See* Gleaners and I, The.
Glass House, The 2002
Glass Menagerie, The 1987
Glass Shield, The 1995
Gleaming the Cube 1989
Gleaners and I, The 2002
Glengarry Glen Ross 1992
Glimmer Man, The 1996
Glitter 2002
Gloire de mon pere, La. *See* My Father's Glory.
Gloomy Sunday 2004
Gloria (Cassavetes) [1980] 1987
Gloria (Lumet) 2000
Glory 1989
Glory Road pg. 156
Go 2000
Go Fish 1995
Go Now 1999
Goal! The Dream Begins pg. 157
Goat, The 1985
Gobots 1986
God Doesn't Believe in Us Anymore 1988
God Is Great, I'm Not 2003
God Is My Witness 1993
God Said "Ha"! 2000
Goddess of 1967, The 2003
Godfather, Part III, The 1990
Gods and Generals 2004
Gods and Monsters 1999
Gods Must Be Crazy, The 1984
Gods Must Be Crazy II, The 1990
God's Will 1989
Godsend 2005
Godzilla 1985 1985
Godzilla 1997
Godzilla 2000 2001
Gohatto. *See* Taboo.
Goin' to Chicago 1991
Going All the Way 1997
Going Berserk 1983
Going Undercover 1988
Goin' South 1978
Gold Diggers: The Secret of Bear Mountain 1995
Golden Bowl, The 2002
Golden Child, The 1986
Golden Gate 1995
Golden Seal 1983
Goldeneye 1995
Gone Fishin' 1997
Gone in Sixty Seconds 2001
Gone With the Wind [1939] 1981, 1982, 1997
Gong fu. *See* Kung Fu Hustle.
Gonza the Spearman 1988
Good Boy! 2004
Good Burger 1997
Good Bye Cruel World 1984
Good Bye, Lenin! 2005
Good Evening, Mr. Wallenberg 1995
Good German, The pg. 159
Good Girl, The 2003
Good Man in Africa, A 1995
Good Marriage, A. *See* Beau Mariage, Le.
Good Morning, Babylon 1987
Good Morning, Vietnam 1987
Good Mother, The 1988
Good Night, and Good Luck 2006
Good Shepherd, The pg. 161
Good Son, The 1993
Good Thief, The 2004
Good Weather, But Stormy Late This Afternoon 1987
Good Will Hunting 1997
Good Woman, A pg. 163
Good Woman of Bangkok, The 1992
Good Work. *See* Beau Travail.
Good Year, A pg. 164
Goodbye, Children. *See* Au Revoir les Enfants.
Goodbye Lover 2000
Goodbye, New York 1985
Goodbye People, The 1986
GoodFellas 1990
Goofy Movie, A 1995
Goonies, The 1985
Gordy 1995
Gorillas in the Mist 1988
Gorky Park 1983
Gorky Triology, The. *See* Among People.
Gosford Park 2002
Gospel 1984
Gospel According to Vic 1986
Gossip 2001
Gossip (Nutley) 2003

Gost 1988
Gotcha! 1985
Gothic 1987
Gothika 2004
Gout des Autres, Le. *See* Taste of Others, The.
Gouttes d'Eau sur Pierres Brulantes. *See* Water Drops on Burning Rocks.
Governess 1999
Goya in Bordeaux 2001
Grace of My Heart 1996
Grace Quigley 1985
Graffiti Bridge 1990
Gran Fiesta, La 1987
Grand Bleu, Le. *See* Big Blue, The (Besson).
Grand Canyon 1991
Grand Canyon: The Hidden Secrets 1987
Grand Chemin, Le. *See* Grand Highway, The.
Grand Highway, The 1988
Grand Illusion, The 2000
Grand Isle 1995
Grande Cocomero, Il. *See* Great Pumpkin, The.
Grandfather, The 2000
Grandma's Boy pg. 166
Grandview, U.S.A. 1984
Grass Harp, The 1996
Gravesend 1997
Graveyard Shift. *See* Stephen King's Graveyard Shift.
Gray's Anatomy 1997
Grease [1978] 1997
Grease II 1982
Great Balls of Fire! 1989
Great Barrier Reef, The 1990
Great Day In Harlem, A 1995
Great Expectations 1999
Great Mouse Detective, The 1986
Great Muppet Caper, The 1981
Great Outdoors, The 1988
Great Pumpkin, The 1993
Great Raid, The 2006
Great Wall, A 1986
Great White Hype, The 1996
Greatest Game Ever Played, The 2006
Greedy 1995
Green Card 1990
Green Desert 2001
Green Mile, The 2000
Greenfingers 2002
Greenhouse, The 1996
Gregory's Girl 1982
Gremlins 1984
Gremlins II 1990
Grey Fox, The 1983
Grey Zone, The 2003
Greystoke 1984
Gridlock'd 1988
Grief 1995
Grievous Bodily Harm 1988
Grifters, The 1990
Grim Prairie Tales 1990
Grind 2004
Gringo 1985
Grizzly Man 2006
Grizzly Mountain 1997
Groomsmen, The pg. 167
Groove 2001
Gross Anatomy 1989
Grosse Fatigue 1995
Grosse Pointe Blank 1997
Ground Zero 1987, 1988
Groundhog Day 1993
Grudge, The 2005
Grudge 2, The pg. 169
Grumpier Old Men 1995
Grumpy Old Men 1993
Grune Wuste. *See* Green Desert.
Guardian, The 1990
Guardian, The pg. 170
Guarding Tess 1995
Guatanamera 1997
Guelwaar 1995
Guerre du Feu, La. *See* Quest for Fire.
Guess Who 2006
Guess Who's Coming to Dinner? [1967] 1992
Guest, The 1984
Guests of Hotel Astoria, The 1989
Guilty as Charged 1992
Guilty as Sin 1993
Guilty by Suspicion 1991
Guinevere 2000
Gummo 1997
Gun in Betty Lou's Handbag, The 1992
Gun Shy 2001
Gunbus. *See* Sky Bandits.
Guncrazy 1993
Gunfighter, The [1950] 1989
Gung Ho 1986
Gunmen 1995
Gunner Palace 2006
Guru, The 2004
Guy Named Joe, A [1943] 1981
Guy Thing, A 2004
Guys, The 2003
Gwendoline 1984
Gyakufunsha Kazoku. *See* Crazy Family, The.
Gymkata 1985

H

H. M. Pulham, Esq. [1941] 1981
Hable con Ella. *See* Talk to Her.
Hackers 1995
Hadesae: The Final Incident 1992
Hadley's Rebellion 1984
Hail Mary 1985
Hairdresser's Husband, The 1992
Hairspray 1988
Haizi wang. *See* King of the Children.
Hak hap. *See* Black Mask
Hak mau. *See* Black Cat.
Half-Baked 1999
Half Moon Street 1986
Half of Heaven 1988
Halfmoon 1996
Hall of Fire [1941] 1986
Halloween III: Season of the Witch 1982
Halloween IV 1988
Halloween V 1989

Halloween VI: the Curse of Michael Myers 1995

Halloween H20 1999

Halloween: Resurrection 2003

Hamburger 1986

Hamburger Hill 1987

Hamlet (Zeffirelli) 1990

Hamlet (Branagh) 1996

Hamlet (Almereyda) 2001

Hammett 1983

Hana-Bi. *See* Fireworks.

Hand That Rocks the Cradle, The 1992

Handful of Dust, A 1988

Handmaid's Tale, The 1990

Hangfire 1991

Hanging Garden, The 1999

Hanging Up 2001

Hangin' with the Homeboys 1991

Hanky Panky 1982

Hanna K. 1983

Hannah and Her Sisters 1986

Hannibal 2002

Hanoi Hilton, The 1987

Hans Christian Andersen's Thumbelina 1995

Hansel and Gretel 1987

Hanussen 1988, 1989

Happenstance 2002

Happily Ever After 1993

Happily Ever After 2006

Happiness 1999

Happy Accidents 2002

Happy End 2001

Happy Endings 2006

Happy Feet pg. 173

Happy '49 1987

Happy Gilmore 1996

Happy Hour 1987

Happy New Year 1987

Happy, Texas 2000

Happy Times 2003

Happy Together 1990

Happy Together 1997

Hard Candy pg. 175

Hard Choices 1986

Hard Core Logo 1999

Hard Eight 1997

Hard Hunted 1995

Hard Promises 1992

Hard Rain 1999

Hard Target 1993

Hard Ticket to Hawaii 1987

Hard Times 1988

Hard to Hold 1984

Hard to Kill 1990

Hard Traveling 1986

Hard Way, The (Badham) 1991

Hard Way, The (Sherman) 1984

Hard Word, The 2004

Hardball 2002

Hardbodies 1984

Hardbodies II 1986

Hardware 1990

Harlem Nights 1989

Harley Davidson and the Marlboro Man 1991

Harmonists, The 2000

Harold & Kumar Go to White Castle 2005

Harriet Craig [1950] 1984

Harriet the Spy 1996

Harrison's Flowers 2003

Harry and Son 1984

Harry and the Hendersons 1987

Harry, He's Here to Help. *See* With a Friend Like Harry.

Harry Potter and the Chamber of Secrets 2003

Harry Potter and the Goblet of Fire 2006

Harry Potter and the Prisoner of Azkaban 2005

Harry Potter and the Sorcerer's Stone 2002

Harry, Un Ami Qui Vous Veut du Bien. *See* With a Friend Like Harry.

Hart's War 2003

Harvard Man 2003

Harvest, The 1995

Hasty Heart, The [1949] 1987

Hatchet Man, The [1932] 1982

Hatouna Mehuheret. *See* Late Marriage.

Haunted Honeymoon 1986

Haunted Mansion, The 2004

Haunted Summer 1988

Haunting, The 2000

Hauru no ugoku shiro. *See* Howl's Moving Castle.

Haute tension. *See* High Tension.

Hav Plenty 1999

Havana 1990

Hawk, The 1995

Hawks 1988

He Got Game 1999

He Liu. *See* River, The.

He Loves Me...He Loves Me Not 2004

He Said, She Said 1991

Head Above Water 1997

Head in the Clouds 2005

Head Office 1986

Head of State 2004

Head On 2000

Head-On 2006

Head Over Heels 2002

Heads or Tails 1983

Hear My Song 1991

Hear No Evil 1993

Hearing Voices 1991

Heart 1987

Heart and Souls 1993

Heart Condition 1990

Heart in Winter, A. *See* Coeur en hiver, Un.

Heart Like a Wheel 1983

Heart of a Stag 1984

Heart of Dixie 1989

Heart of Midnight 1989

Heart of the Game, The pg. 177

Heartaches 1982

Heartbreak Hotel 1988

Heartbreak Kid, The [1972] 1986

Heartbreak Ridge 1986

Heartbreaker 1983

Heartbreakers 2002

Heartburn 1986

Heartland 1981
Hearts in Atlantis 2002
Hearts of Darkness: A Filmmaker's Apocalypse 1992
Hearts of Fire 1987
Heat 1987
Heat (Mann) 1995
Heat and Dust 1984
Heat of Desire 1984
Heathcliff 1986
Heathers 1989
Heatwave 1983
Heaven (Keaton) 1987
Heaven (Tykwer) 2003
Heaven and Earth (Kadokawa) 1991
Heaven and Earth (Stone) 1993
Heaven Help Us 1985
Heaven's Gate 1981
Heaven's Prisoners 1996
Heavenly Bodies 1984
Heavenly Creatures 1995
Heavenly Kid, The 1985
Heavy 1996
Heavyweights 1995
Hecate 1984
Hedwig and the Angry Inch 2002
Heidi Fleiss: Hollywood Madame 1996
Heights 2006
Heist, The 2002
Helas Pour Moi 1995
Held Up 2001
Hell High 1989
Hellbent 1989
Hellbound 1988
Hellboy 2005
Heller Wahn. *See* Sheer Madness.
Hello Again 1987
Hello, Dolly! [1969] 1986
Hello Mary Lou 1987
Hellraiser 1987
Hellraiser III: Hell on Earth 1992
Hellraiser IV: Bloodline 1996
Henna 1991
Henri Langlois: The Phantom of the Cinematheque 2006
Henry 1990
Henry and June 1990
Henry IV 1985
Henry V 1989
Henry Fool 1999
Her Alibi 1989
Her Name Is Lisa 1987
Herbie: Fully Loaded 2006
Hercules 1983
Hercules II 1985
Herdsmen of the Sun 1995
Here Come the Littles 1985
Here On Earth 2001
Here's to Life 2002
Hero 1992
Hero 2004
Hero 2005
Hero and the Terror 1988
He's My Girl 1987
Hey Arnold! The Movie 2003
Hexed 1993
Hibiscus Town 1988
Hidalgo 2005
Hidden. *See* Cache.
Hidden, The 1987
Hidden Agenda 1990
Hidden Hawaii 1995
Hide and Seek 2006
Hideaway 1995
Hideous Kinky 2000
Hiding Out 1987
Hifazaat. *See* In Custody.
High Art 1999
High Crimes 2003
High Fidelity 2001
High Heels 1991
High Heels and Low Lives 2002
High Hopes 1988, 1989
High Lonesome: The Story of Bluegrass Music 258
High Risk 1995
High Road to China 1983
High School High 1996
High Season 1988
High Spirits 1988
High Tension 2006
High Tide 1987
Higher Learning 1995
Highlander 1986
Highlander 2: The Quickening 1991
Highlander 3: The Final Dimension 1995
Highlander: Endgame 2001
Highway Patrolman 1995
Highway 61 1992
Highway to Hell 1992
Hijacking Hollywood
Hijo se la Novia, El. *See* Son of the Bride.
Hi-Lo Country, The 2000
Hilary and Jackie 1999
Hills Have Eyes, The pg. 178
Himmel uber Berlin, Der. *See* Wings of Desire.
Histories d'amerique. *See* American Stories.
History Boys, The pg. 179
History Is Made at Night [1937] 1983
History of Violence, A 2006
Hit, The 1985
Hit and Runway 2002
Hit List 1989
Hit the Dutchman 1995
Hitch 2006
Hitcher, The 1986
Hitchhiker's Guide to the Galaxy, The 2006
Hitman, The 1991
Hocus Pocus 1993
Hoffa 1992
Holcroft Covenant, The 1985
Hold Back the Dawn [1941] 1986
Hold Me, Thrill Me, Kiss Me 1993
Holes 2004
Holiday [1938] 1985
Holiday, The pg. 181
Holiday Inn [1942] 1981
Hollow Man 2001
Hollow Reed 1997

Hollywood Ending 2003
Hollywood Homicide 2004
Hollywood in Trouble 1986
Hollywood Mavericks 1990
Hollywood Shuffle 1987
Hollywood Vice Squad 1986
Hollywoodland pg. 183
Holy Blood. *See* Santa Sangre.
Holy Innocents, The 1985
Holy Man 1999
Holy Smoke 2000
Holy Tongue, The 2002
Hombre [1967] 1983
Home Alone 1990
Home Alone II: Lost in New York 1992
Home Alone III 1997
Home and the World, The 1985
Home at the End of the World, A 2005
Home for the Holidays 1995
Home Free All 1984
Home Fries 1999
Home Is Where the Heart Is 1987
Home of Our Own, A 1993
Home of the Brave 1986
Home on the Range 2005
Home Remedy 1987
Homeboy 1988
Homegrown 1999
Homer and Eddie 1990
Homeward Bound 1993
Homeward Bound II: Lost in San Francisco 1996
Homework 1982
Homicide 1991
Homme et une femme, Un. *See* Man and a Woman, A.
Hondo [1953] 1982
Honey 2004
Honey, I Blew Up the Kid 1992
Honey, I Shrunk the Kids 1989
Honeybunch 1988
Honeymoon Academy 1990
Honeymoon in Vegas 1992
Honeymooners, The 2006
Hong Gaoliang. *See* Red Sorghum.
Honky Tonk Freeway 1981
Honkytonk Man 1982
Honneponnetge. *See* Honeybunch.
Honor Betrayed. *See* Fear.
Honorable Mr. Wong, The. *See* Hatchet Man, The.
Honour of the House 2001
Hoodlum 1997
Hoodwinked pg. 185
Hook 1991
Hoop Dreams 1995
Hoosiers 1986
Hoot pg. 186
Hope and Glory 1987
Hope and Pain 1988
Hope Floats 1999
Horror Show, The 1989
Hors la Vie 1995
Horse of Pride, The 1985
Horse Whisperer, The 1999
Horseman on the Roof, The 1996
Hostage 2006
Hostel pg. 188
Hot Chick, The 2003
Hot Dog...The Movie 1984
Hot Pursuit 1987
Hot Shots! 1991
Hot Shots! Part Deux 1993
Hot Spot, The 1990
Hot to Trot 1988
Hotel Colonial 1987
Hotel De Love 1997
Hotel New Hampshire, The 1984
Hotel Rwanda 2005
Hotel Terminus 1988
Hotshot 1987
Hound of the Baskervilles, The 1981
Hours, The 2003
Hours and Times, The 1992
House 1986
House II 1987
House Arrest 1996
House of Cards 1993
House of D 2006
House of Flying Daggers 2005
House of Fools 2004
House of Games 1987
House of Luk 2001
House of Mirth 2002
House of 1,000 Corpses 2004
House of Sand and Fog 2004
House of the Spirits, The 1995
House of Wax 2006
House of Yes, The 1997
House on Carroll Street, The 1988
House on Haunted Hill 2000
House on Limb, A. *See* Tottering Lives.
House Party 1990
House Party II 1991
House Party III 1995
House Where Evil Dwells, The 1982
Houseboat [1958] 1986
Houseguest 1995
Household Saints 1993
Householder, The 1984
Housekeeper, A 2004
Housekeeper, The 1987
Housekeeping 1987
Housesitter 1992
How I Got into College 1989
How I Killed My Father 2004
How Stella Got Her Groove Back 1999
How to Deal 2004
How to Eat Fried Worms pg. 190
How to Get Ahead in Advertising 1989
How to Get the Man's Foot Outta Your Ass. *See* Baadassss!
How to Lose a Guy in 10 Days 2004
How to Make an American Quilt 1995
How to Make Love to a Negro Without Getting Tired 1990
Howard the Duck 1986
Howard's End 1992
Howling, The 1981
Howling III, The. *See* Marsupials, The.
Howl's Moving Castle 2006

Hsi Yen. *See* Wedding Banquet, The.
Hsimeng Jensheng. *See* Puppetmaster, The.
Hudson Hawk 1991
Hudsucker Proxy, The 1995
Hugh Hefner: Once Upon a Time 1992
Hugo Pool 1997
Huit Femmes. *See* 8 Women.
Hulk 2004
Human Nature 2003
Human Resources 2002
Human Shield, The 1992
Human Stain, The 2004
Humongous 1982
Hunchback of Notre Dame, The 1996
Hungarian Fairy Tale, A 1989
Hunger, The 1983
Hungry Feeling, A 1988
Hunk 1987
Hunt for Red October, The 1990
Hunted, The 1995
Hunted, The 2004
Hunters of the Golden Cobra, The 1984
Huo Yuan Jia. *See* Jet Li's Fearless.
Hurlyburly 1999
Hurricane, The 2000
Hurricane Streets 1999
Husbands and Wives 1992
Hush (Darby) 1999
Hush! (Hashiguchi)
Hustle & Flow 2006
Hyenas 1995
Hypnotic. *See* Close Your Eyes.

I

I Am David 2005
I Am My Own Woman 1995
I Am Sam 2002
I Can't Sleep 1995
I Capture the Castle 2004
I Come in Peace 1990
I Demoni. *See* Demons.
I Don't Buy Kisses Anymore 1992
I Don't Want to Talk About It 1995
I Dreamed of Africa 2001
I Got the Hook-Up 1999
"I Hate Actors!" 1988
I Heart Huckabees 2005
I Know What You Did Last Summer 1997
I Know Where I'm Going [1945] 1982
I Like It Like That 1995
I Love Trouble 1995
I Love You 1982
I Love You, Don't Touch Me 1999
I Love You, I Love You Not 1997
I Love You to Death 1990
I, Madman 1989
I Married a Shadow 1983
I Only Want You to Love Me 1995
I Ought to Be in Pictures 1982
I Remember Mama [1948] 1981
I, Robot 2005
I Sent a Letter to My Love 1981
I Shot Andy Warhol 1996
I Spy 2003
I Stand Alone 2000
I Still Know What You Did Last Summer 1999
I, the Jury 1982
I Think I Do 2000
I Want to Go Home 1989
I Was a Teenage Zombie 1987
I Went Down 1999
I Woke Up Early the Day I Died 2000
Ice Age 2003
Ice Age: The Meltdown pg. 191
Ice Harvest, The 2006
Ice House 1989
Ice Pirates, The 1984
Ice Princess 2006
Ice Rink, The 2001
Ice Runner, The 1993
Ice Storm, The 1997
Iceman 1984
Icicle Thief, The 1990
Ideal Husband, An 2000
Identity 2004
Identity Crisis 1989
Idiocracy pg. 192
Idiots, The [1999] 2001
Idle Hands 2000
Idlewild pg. 194
Iedereen Beroemd! *See* Everybody's Famous!
If Looks Could Kill 1991
If Lucy Fell 1996
If You Could See What I Hear 1982
Igby Goes Down 2003
Ignorant Fairies 2002
Iklimler. *See* Climates.
Ill Testimone dello Sposo. *See* Best Man, The.
I'll Be Home for Christmas 1999
I'll Do Anything 1995
I'll Sleep When I'm Dead 2005
Illtown 1999
Illuminata 2000
Illusionist, The pg. 196
Illustrious Energy 1988
Ils se Marient et Eurent Beaucoup D'Enfants. *See* Happily Ever After.
I'm Dancing as Fast as I Can 1982
I'm Going Home 2003
I'm No Angel [1933] 1984
I'm Not Rappaport 1997
I'm the One That I Want 2001
Imagemaker, The 1986
Imaginary Crimes 1995
Imaginary Heroes 2006
Imagine 1988
Imagine Me & You pg. 197
Immediate Family 1989
Immortal Beloved 1995
Imperative 1985
Importance of Being Earnest, The 1995
Importance of Being Earnest, The (Parker) 2003
Imported Bridegroom, The 1991
Impostor 2003
Impostors 1999
Impromptu 1991

Impulse (Baker) 1984
Impulse (Locke) 1990
In a Shallow Grave 1988
In America 2004
In and Out 1997
In Country 1989
In Crowd, The 2001
In Custody 1995
In Dangerous Company 1988
In Dreams 2000
In Fashion. *See* A la Mode.
In God's Hands 1999
In Good Company 2006
In Her Shoes 2006
In-Laws, The 2004
In Love and War 1997
In My Country 2006
In Our Hands 1983
In Praise of Love 2003
In the Army Now 1995
In the Bedroom 2002
In the Company of Men 1997
In the Cut 2004
In the Heat of Passion 1992
In the Heat of the Night [1967] 1992
In the Land of the Deaf 1995
In the Line of Fire 1993
In the Mirror of Maya Deren 2004
In the Mood 1987
In the Mood for Love 2002
In the Mouth of Madness 1995
In the Name of the Father 1993
In the Realms of the Unreal 2006
In the Shadow of Kilimanjaro 1986
In the Shadow of the Stars 1992
In the Soup 1992
In the Spirit 1990
In This World 2004
In Too Deep 2000
In Weiter Ferne, So Nah! *See* Faraway, So Close.
Inchon 1982
Incident at Oglala 1992
Incident at Raven's Gate 1988
Incognito 1999
Inconvenient Truth, An pg. 199
Incredible Journey, The. *See* Homeward Bound.
Incredibles, The 2005
Incredibly True Adventures of Two Girls in Love, The 1995
Incubus, The 1982
Indecent Proposal 1993
Independence Day 1996
Indian in the Cupboard, The 1995
Indian Runner, The 1991
Indian Summer 1993
Indiana Jones and the Last Crusade 1989
Indiana Jones and the Temple of Doom 1984
Indochine 1992
Inevitable Grace 1995
Infamous pg. 200
Infernal Affairs 2005
Infinity 1991
Infinity (Broderick) 1996
Informer, The [1935] 1986
Inkwell, The 1995
Inland Empire pg. 201
Inland Sea, The 1995
Inner Circle, The 1991
Innerspace 1987
Innocent, The 1988
Innocent, The 1995
Innocent Blood 1992
Innocent Man, An 1989
Innocent Sleep, The 1997
Innocents Abroad 1992
Inside I'm Dancing. *See* Rory O'Shea Was Here.
Inside Man pg. 202
Inside Monkey Zetterland 1993
Insider, The 2000
Insignificance 1985
Insomnia (Skjoldbjaerg) 1999
Insomnia (Nolan) 2003
Inspector Gadget 2000
Instant Karma 1990
Instinct 2000
Intacto 2004
Intermission 2005
Internal Affairs 1990
Interpreter, The 2006
Interrogation, The 1990
Intersection 1995
Interview with the Vampire 1995
Intervista 1993
Intimacy 2002
Intimate Relations 1997
Intimate Strangers 2005
Into the Blue 2006
Into the Night 1985
Into the Sun 1992
Into the West 1993
Intolerable Cruelty 2004
Invaders from Mars 1986
Invasion! *See* Top of the Food Chain.
Invasion of the Body Snatchers [1956] 1982
Invasion U.S.A. 1985
Inventing the Abbotts 1997
Invention of Love 2001
Invincible 2003
Invincible pg. 204
Invisible Circus 2002
Invisible Kid, The 1988
Invitation au voyage 1983
Invitation to the Dance [1956] 1985
I.Q. 1995
Iris 2002
Irma la Douce [1963] 1986
Irma Vep 1997
Iron Eagle 1986
Iron Eagle II 1988
Iron Giant, The 2000
Iron Maze 1991
Iron Triangle, The 1989
Iron Will 1995
Ironweed 1987
Irreconcilable Differences 1984
Irreversible 2004
Ishtar 1987
Island, The 2006
Island of Dr. Moreau, The 1996

Isn't She Great 2001
Istoriya As-Klyachimol. *See* Asya's Happiness.
It Could Happen to You 1995
It Couldn't Happen Here 1988
It Had to Be You 1989
It Happened One Night [1934] 1982
It Happened Tomorrow [1944] 1983
It Runs in the Family 2004
It Takes Two 1988
It Takes Two 1995
Italian for Beginners 2002
Italian Job, The 2004
Italiensk for Begyndere. *See* Italian for Beginners.
It's a Wonderful Life [1946] 1982
It's Alive III 1987
It's All About Love 2005
It's All Gone Pete Tong 2006
It's All True 1993
It's My Party 1996
It's Pat 1995
It's the Rage 2001
Ivan and Abraham 1995
I've Heard the Mermaids Singing 1987

J

Jack 1996
Jack and His Friends 1993
Jack and Sarah 1996
Jack Frost 1999
Jack the Bear 1993
Jackal, The 1997
Jackass Number Two pg. 207
Jacket, The 2006
Jackie Brown 1997
Jackie Chan's First Strike 1997
Jacknife 1989
Jackpot 2002
Jack's Back 1988
Jacob 1988
Jacob's Ladder 1990
Jacquot of Nantes 1993
Jade 1995
Jagged Edge 1985
J'ai epouse une ombre. *See* I Married a Shadow.
Jailhouse Rock [1957] 1986
Jake Speed 1986
Jakob the Liar 2000
James and the Giant Peach 1996
James' Journey to Jerusalem 2005
James Joyce's Women 1985
Jamon, Jamon 1993
Jane Eyre 1996
January Man, The 1989
Japanese Story 2005
Jarhead 2006
Jason Goes to Hell 1993
Jason X 2003
Jason's Lyric 1995
Jawbreaker 2000
Jaws: The Revenge 1987
Jaws 3-D 1983
Jay and Silent Bob Strike Back 2002
Jazzman 1984
Je Rentre a la Maison. *See* I'm Going Home.
Je tu il elle [1974] 1985
Je vous salue, Marie. *See* Hail Mary.
Jean de Florette 1987
Jeanne Dielman, 23 Quai du Commerce, 1080 Bruxelles [1976] 1981
Jeepers Creepers 2002
Jeepers Creepers 2 2004
Jefferson in Paris 1995
Jeffrey 1995
Jekyll and Hyde...Together Again 1982
Jennifer Eight 1992
Jerky Boys 1995
Jerome 2001
Jerry Maguire 1996
Jersey Girl 2005
Jerusalem 1996
Jesus of Montreal 1989
Jesus' Son 2000
Jet Lag 2004
Jet Li's Fearless pg. 208
Jetsons 1990
Jewel of the Nile, The 1985
JFK 1991
Jigsaw Man, The 1984
Jim and Piraterna Blom. *See* Jim and the Pirates.
Jim and the Pirates 1987
Jiminy Glick in Lalawood 2006
Jimmy Hollywood 1995
Jimmy Neutron: Boy Genius 2002
Jimmy the Kid 1983
Jingle All the Way 1996
Jinxed 1982
Jit 1995
Jo-Jo at the Gate of Lions 1995
Jo Jo Dancer, Your Life Is Calling 1986
Joan the Mad. *See* Mad Love.
Jocks 1987
Joe Dirt 2002
Joe Gould's Secret 2001
Joe Somebody 2002
Joe the King 2000
Joe Versus the Volcano 1990
Joe's Apartment 1996
Joey 1985
Joey Takes a Cab 1991
John and the Missus 1987
John Carpenter's Ghosts of Mars 2002
John Carpenter's Vampires 1999
John Grisham's the Rainmaker 1998
John Huston 1988
John Huston and the Dubliners 1987
John Q 2003
John Tucker Must Die pg. 209
Johnny Be Good 1988
Johnny Dangerously 1984
Johnny English 2004
Johnny Handsome 1989
Johnny Mnemonic 1995
Johnny Stecchino 1992
Johnny Suede 1992
johns 1997
Johnson Family Vacation 2005
Joke of Destiny, A 1984
Joseph Conrad's the Secret Agent 1996

Josh and S.A.M. 1993
Joshua Then and Now 1985
Josie and the Pussycats 2002
Journey into Fear [1943] 1985
Journey of August King 1995
Journey of Hope 1991
Journey of Love 1990
Journey of Natty Gann, The 1985
Journey to Spirit Island 1988
Joy Luck Club, The 1993
Joy of Sex 1984
Joy Ride 2002
Joyeux Noel pg. 211
Joysticks 1983
Ju Dou 1991
Juana la Loca. *See* Mad Love.
Judas Kiss 2000
Judas Project, The 1995
Jude 1996
Judge Dredd 1995
Judgement in Berlin 1988
Judgement Night 1993
Judy Berlin 2001
Juice 1992
Julia Has Two Lovers 1991
Julian Po 1997
Julien Donkey-Boy 2000
Jumanji 1995
Jument vapeur, La. *See* Dirty Dishes.
Jump Tomorrow 2002
Jumpin' at the Boneyard 1992
Jumpin' Jack Flash 1986
Jumpin' Night in the Garden of Eden, A 1988
Junebug 2006
Jungle Book, The 1995
Jungle Book 2, The 2004
Jungle Fever 1991
Jungle2Jungle 1997
Junior 1995
Jurassic Park 1993
Jurassic Park III 2002
Juror, The 1996
Jury Duty 1995
Just a Kiss 2003
Just a Little Harmless Sex 2000
Just Another Girl on the I.R.T. 1993
Just Between Friends 1986
Just Cause 1995
Just Friends 2006
Just Like a Woman 1995
Just Like Heaven 2006
Just Looking 2002
Just Married 2004
Just My Luck pg. 213
Just One of the Guys 1985
Just One Time 2002
Just the Ticket 2000
Just the Way You Are 1984
Just Visiting 2002
Just Write 1999
Justice in the Coalfields 1996
Juwanna Mann 2003

K

K-9 1989
K-19: The Widowmaker 2003
K-PAX 2002
Kadisbellan. *See* Slingshot, The.
Kadosh 2001
Kaena: The Prophecy 2005
Kafka 1991
Kalifornia 1993
Kama Sutra: A Tale of Love 1997
Kamikaze Hearts 1995
Kamilla and the Thief 1988
Kandahar 2002
Kandyland 1988
Kangaroo 1987
Kangaroo Jack 2004
Kansas 1988
Kansas City 1996
Karakter. *See* Character.
Karate Kid, The 1984
Karate Kid: Part II, The 1986
Karate Kid: Part III, The 1989
Kate & Leopold 2002
Kazaam 1996
Kazoku. *See* Where Spring Comes Late.
Keep, The 1983
Keep the River On Your Right: A Modern Cannibal Tale 2002
Keeping Mum pg. 215
Keeping the Faith 2001
Keeping Up with the Steins pg. 216
Kerouac, the Movie 1985
Key Exchange 1985
Keys of the Kingdom, The [1944] 1989
Keys to Tulsa 1997
Khuda Gawah. *See* God Is My Witness.
Kickboxer 1989
Kickboxer II 1991
Kicked in the Head 1997
Kicking and Screaming (Baumbach) 1995
Kicking & Screaming 2006
Kid & I, The 2006
Kid Brother, The 1987
Kid Colter 1985
Kid in King Arthur's Court, A 1995
Kid Stays in the Picture, The 2003
Kidnapped 1987
Kids 1995
Kids in the Hall: Brain Candy, The 1996
Kika 1995
Kikujiro 2001
Kill Bill: Vol. 1 2004
Kill Bill: Vol. 2 2005
Kill Me Again 1989
Kill Me Later 2002
Kill-Off, The 1990
Killer Image 1992
Killer Instinct 1995
Killer Klowns from Outer Space 1988
Killer Party 1986
Killing Affair, A 1988
Klling Fields, The 1984
Killing Floor, The 1995
Killing of a Chinese Bookie, The [1976] 1986
Killing Time 1999
Killing Time, The, 1987

Killing Zoe 1995

Killpoint 1984

Kindergarten Cop 1990

Kindred, The 1987

King, The pg. 218

King Arthur 2005

King and I, The 2000

King David 1985

King Is Alive, The 2002

King Is Dancing, The 2002

King James Version 1988

King Kong [1933] 1981

King Kong 2006

King Kong Lives 1986

King Lear 1987

King of Comedy, The 1983

King of Jazz [1930] 1985

King of Masks, The 2000

King of New York 1990

King of the Children 1988

King of the Hill 1993

King Ralph 1991

King Solomon's Mines 1985

Kingdom, Part 2, The 1999

Kingdom, The 1995

Kingdom Come 2002

Kingdom of Heaven 2006

Kingpin 1996

Kings and Queen 2006

King's Ransom 2006

Kinjite 1989

Kinky Boots pg. 220

Kinsey 2005

Kipperbang 1984

Kippur 2001

Kiss Before Dying, A 1991

Kiss Daddy Good Night 1987

Kiss Kiss Bang Bang 2006

Kiss Me a Killer 1991

Kiss Me Goodbye 1982

Kiss Me, Guido 1997

Kiss Me, Stupid [1964] 1986

Kiss of Death 1995

Kiss of the Dragon 2002

Kiss of the Spider Woman 1985

Kiss or Kill 1997

Kiss, The 1988

Kiss the Girls 1997

Kissed 1997

Kissing a Fool 1999

Kissing Jessica Stein 2003

Kitchen Party 1999

Kitchen Stories 2005

Kitchen Toto, The 1987

Kitty and the Bagman 1983

Klynham Summer 1983

Knafayim Shvurot. *See* Broken Wings.

Knight's Tale, A 2002

Knights of the City 1986

Knock Off 1999

Knockaround Guys 2003

Kolya 1997

Korczak 1991

Koyaanisqatsi 1983

Krampack. *See* Nico and Dani.

Krays, The 1990

Krieger und die Kaiserin, Der. *See* Princess and the Warrior, The.

Krippendorf's Tribe 1999

Krotki film o zabijaniu. *See* Thou Shalt Not Kill.

Krull 1983

Krush Groove 1985

K2 1992

Kuffs 1992

Kull The Conqueror 1997

Kundun 1997

Kung Fu Hustle 2006

Kuroi ame. *See* Black Rain.

Kurt and Courtney 1999

L

L. I.. E. 2002

L.627 1995

L.A. Confidential 1997

La Meglio Gioventu. *See* Best of Youth, The.

La Sorgente del fiume. *See* Weeping Meadow.

L.A. Story 1991

La Terre qui pleure. *See* Weeping Meadow.

Laberinto del Fauno, El. *See* Pan's Labyrinth.

Labyrinth 1986

Labyrinth of Passion 1990

Ladder 49 2005

Ladies Club, The 1986

Ladies' Man, The 2001

Ladri di saponette. *See* Icicle Thief, The.

Ladro Di Bambini, Il 1993

Lady and the Duke, The 2003

Lady Beware 1987

Lady Eve, The [1941] 1987

Lady in the Water pg. 223

Lady in White 1988

Lady Jane 1986

Lady Sings the Blues [1972] 1984

Ladybird, Ladybird 1995

Ladybugs 1992

Ladyhawke 1985

Ladykillers, The 2005

Lagaan: Once Upon a Time in India 2003

Lair of the White Worm, The 1988

Laissez-Passer. *See* Safe Conduct.

Lake House, The pg. 225

Lake Placid 2000

Lambada 1990

L'america 1996

Lan Yu 2003

Land and Freedom 1995

Land Before Time, The 1988

Land Girls, The 1999

Land of Faraway 1988

Land of the Dead. *See* George A. Romero's Land of the Dead.

Landlord Blues 1988

Landscape in the Mist 1989

L'Anglaise et le Duc. *See* Lady and the Duke, The.

Lantana 2002

Lara Croft: Tomb Raider 2002

Lara Croft Tomb Raider: The Cradle of Life 2004

Larger Than Life 1996

Larry the Cable Guy: Health Inspector pg. 227

Laserman, The 1988, 1990
Lassie 1995
Lassie pg. 228
Lassie Come Home [1943] 1993
Lassiter 1984
Last Act, The 1992
Last Action Hero 1993
Last American Virgin, The 1982
Last Boy Scout, The 1991
Last Call at Maud's 1993
Last Castle, The 2002
Last Cigarette, The 2000
Last Dance, The 1996
Last Day of Winter, The 1987
Last Days 2006
Last Days of Disco, The 1999
Last Emperor, The 1987
Last Exit to Brooklyn 1990
Last Holiday pg. 229
Last Hunter, The 1984
Last King of Scotland, The pg. 231
Last Kiss, The 2003
Last Kiss, The pg. 232
Last Man Standing 1996
Last Night 1999
Last of England, The 1988
Last of the Dogmen 1995
Last of the Finest, The 1990
Last of the Mohicans, The 1992
Last Orders 2003
Last Party, The 1993
Last Resort 1986
Last Resort 2002
Last Rites 1988
Last Samurai, The 2004
Last Seduction, The 1995
Last September, The 2001
Last Shot, The 2005
Last Starfighter, The 1984
Last Straw, The 1987
Last Supper 1996
Last Temptation of Christ, The 1988
Last Time I Committed Suicide, The 1997
Last Time I Saw Paris, The [1954] 1993
Last Summer in the Hamptons 1995
Last Wedding 2003
Latcho Drom 1995
Late August, Early September 2000
Late Chrysanthemums [1954] 1985
Late for Dinner 1991
Late Marriage 2003
Late Summer Blues 1987
Latin Boys Go to Hell 1997
Latter Days 2005
L'Auberge Espagnole 2004
Laurel Canyon 2004
Law of Desire, The 1987
Law of Enclosures, The 2002
Lawn Dogs 1999
Lawless Heart 2004
Lawnmower Man, The 1992
Lawnmower Man 2: Beyond Cyberspace 1996
Lawrence of Arabia [1962] 1990
Laws of Attraction 2005
Laws of Gravity 1992
Layer Cake 2006
L' Ecole de la chair. *See* School of Flesh, The.
Leading Man, The 1999
League of Extraordinary Gentlemen, The 2004
League of Their Own, A 1992
Lean on Me 1989
Leap of Faith 1992
Leatherface 1990
Leave It to Beaver 1997
Leave to Remain 1988
Leaving Las Vegas 1995
Leaving Normal 1992
Lebedyne ozero. *See* Swan Lake.
Lectrice, La. *See* Reader, The.
Leela 2003
Left Hand Side of the Fridge, The 2002
Legal Eagles 1986
Legally Blonde 2002
Legally Blonde 2: Red, White & Blonde 2004
Legend 1986
Legend of Bagger Vance, The 2001
Legend of Billie Jean, The 1985
Legend of 1900 2000
Legend of Rita, The 2002
Legend of Wolf Mountain, The 1995
Legend of Zorro, The 2006
Legends 1995
Legends of the Fall 1995
Leggenda del Pianista Sull'oceano, La. *See* Legend of 1900.
Lemon Sisters, The 1990
Lemon Sky 1987
Lemony Snicket's A Series of Unfortunate Events 2005
Leo Tolstoy's Anna Karenina 1997
Leolo 1993
Leon the Pig Farmer 1995
Leonard Part VI 1987
Leopard Son, The 1996
Leprechaun 1993
Leprechaun II 1995
Les Patterson Saves the World 1987
Less Than Zero 1987
Let Him Have It 1991
Let It Come Down: The Life of Paul Bowles 2000
Let It Ride 1989
Let's Fall in Love. *See* New York in Short: The Shvitz and Let's Fall in Love.
Let's Get Lost 1988
Let's Spend the Night Together 1983
Lethal Weapon 1987
Lethal Weapon 2 1989
Lethal Weapon 3 1992
Lethal Weapon 4 1999
Letter to Brezhnev 1986
Letters from Iwo Jima pg. 234
Leviathan 1989
Levity 2004
Levy and Goliath 1988
Ley del deseo, La. *See* Law of Desire, The.

Liaison Pornographique, Une. *See* Affair of Love, An.
Liam 2002
Lianna 1983
Liar, Liar 1997
Liar's Moon 1982
Libertine, The pg. 236
Liberty Heights 2000
Licence to Kill 1989
License to Drive 1988
Lie Down With Dogs 1995
Liebestraum 1991
Lies 1986
Life 2000
Life After Love 2002
Life and Nothing But 1989
Life and Times of Allen Ginsberg, The 1995
Life and Times of Judge Roy Bean, The [1972] 1983
Life Aquatic with Steve Zissou, The 2005
Life as a House 2002
Life Classes 1987
Life in the Food Chain. *See* Age Isn't Everything.
Life in the Theater, A 1995
Life Is a Long Quiet River 1990
Life Is Beautiful 1999
Life Is Cheap 1989
Life Is Sweet 1991
Life Less Ordinary, A 1997
Life Lessons. *See* New York Stories.
Life of David Gale, The 2004
Life on a String 1992
Life on the Edge 1995
Life or Something Like It 2003
Life Stinks 1991
Life with Father [1947] 1993
Life with Mikey 1993
Life Without Zoe. *See* New York Stories.
Lifeforce 1985
Lift 2002
Light Ahead, The [1939] 1982
Light It Up 2000
Light Keeps Me Company 2001
Light of Day 1987
Light Sleeper 1992
Lighthorsemen, The 1987
Lightning in a Bottle 2005
Lightning Jack 1995
Lightship, The 1986
Like Father Like Son 1987
Like Mike 2003
Like Water for Chocolate 1993
Lili Marleen 1981
Lilies 1997
Lilies of the Field [1963] 1992
Lillian 1995
Lilo & Stitch 2003
Lily in Love 1985
Limbo 2000
Limey, The 2000
Line One 1988
Lingua del Santo, La. *See* Holy Tongue, The.
Linguini Incident, The 1992
Linie Eins. *See* Line One.
Link 1986
Lion King, The 1995
Lionheart (Lettich) 1991
Lionheart (Shaffner) 1987
Liquid Dreams 1992
Liquid Sky 1983
Lisa 1990
Listen to Me 1989
Listen Up 1990
Little Big League 1995
Little Black Book 2005
Little Buddha 1995
Little Children pg. 237
Little Devil, the 1988
Little Dorrit 1988
Little Drummer Girl, The 1984
Little Giants 1995
Little Indian, Big City 1996
Little Jerk 1985
Little Man pg. 239
Little Man Tate 1991
Little Men 1999
Little Mermaid, The 1989
Little Miss Sunshine pg. 240
Little Monsters 1989
Little Nemo: Adventures in Slumberland 1992
Little Nicky 2001
Little Nikita 1988
Little Noises 1992
Little Odessa 1995
Little Princess, A 1995
Little Rascals, The 1995
Little Secrets 1995
Little Secrets (Treu) 2003
Little Sex, A 1982
Little Shop of Horrors [1960] 1986
Little Stiff, A 1995
Little Sweetheart 1988
Little Thief, The 1989
Little Vampire, The 2001
Little Vegas 1990
Little Vera 1989
Little Voice 1999
Little Women 1995
Little Women [1933] 1982
Live Flesh 1999
Live Nude Girls 1995
Live Virgin 2001
Livin' Large 1991
Living Daylights, The 1987
Living End, The 1992
Living in Oblivion 1995
Living on Tokyo Time 1987
Living Out Loud 1999
Living Proof: HIV and the Pursuit of Happiness 1995
Lizzie McGuire Movie, The 2004
Ljuset Haller Mig Sallskap. *See* Light Keeps Me Company.
Loaded 1996
Local Hero 1983
Lock, Stock, and Two Smoking Barrels 2000
Lock Up 1989
Locusts, The 1997
Lodz Ghetto 1989
Lola 1982

Lola La Loca 1988
Lola Rennt. *See* Run, Lola, Run.
Lolita 1999
London Kills Me 1992
Lone Runner, The 1988
Lone Star 1996
Lone Wolf McQuade 1983
Lonely Guy, The 1984
Lonely Hearts (Cox) 1983
Lonely Hearts (Lane) 1995
Lonely in America 1991
Lonely Lady, The 1983
Lonely Passion of Judith Hearne, The 1987
Lonesome Jim pg. 242
Long Day Closes, The 1993
Long Dimanche de Fiancailles, Un. *See* Very Long Engagement, A.
Long Good Friday, The 1982
Long Gray Line, The [1955] 1981
Long Kiss Goodnight, The 1996
Long Live the Lady! 1988
Long, Long Trailer, The [1954] 1986
Long Lost Friend, The. *See* Apprentice to Murder.
Long Walk Home, The 1990
Long Way Home, The 1999
Long Weekend, The 1990
Longest Yard, The 2006
Longshot, The 1986
Longtime Companion 1990
Look at Me 2006
Look Who's Talking 1989
Look Who's Talking Now 1993
Look Who's Talking Too 1990
Lookin' to Get Out 1982
Looking for Comedy in the Muslim World pg. 244
Looking for Richard 1996
Looney Tunes: Back in Action 2004
Loophole 1986
Loose Cannons 1990
Loose Connections 1988
Loose Screws 1986
L'ora di religione: Il sorriso di mia madre. *See* My Mother's Smile.
Lord of Illusions 1995
Lord of the Flies 1990
Lord of the Rings: The Fellowship of the Rings 2002
Lord of the Rings: The Return of the King 2004
Lord of the Rings: The Two Towers 2003
Lord of War 2006
Lords of Discipline, The 1983
Lords of Dogtown 2006
Lords of the Deep 1989
Lorenzo's Oil 1992
Loser 2001
Losin' It 1983
Losing Isaiah 1995
Loss of Sexual Innocence 2000
Lost and Delirious 2002
Lost and Found 2000
Lost Angels 1989
Lost Boys, The 1987
Lost City, The pg. 245
Lost Highway 1997
Lost in America 1985
Lost in La Mancha 2004
Lost in Siberia 1991
Lost in Space 1999
Lost in Translation 2004
Lost in Yonkers. *See* Neil Simon's Lost in Yonkers.
Lost Moment, The [1947] 1982
Lost Prophet 1995
Lost Souls 2001
Lost Weekend, The [1945] 1986
Lost Words, The 1995
Lost World, The 1997
Lou, Pat, and Joe D 1988
Louis Bluie 1985
Louis Prima: The Wildest 2001
Loulou 1981
Love Actually 2004
Love Affair 1995
Love After Love 1995
Love Always 1997
Love and a .45 1995
Love and Basketball 2001
Love and Death in Long Island 1999
Love and Human Remains 1995
Love and Murder 1991
Love and Other Catastrophes 1997
Love & Sex 2001
Love at Large 1990
Love Child, The 1988
Love Child: A True Story 1982
Love Come Down 2002
Love Crimes 1992
Love Don't Cost a Thing 2004
Love Field 1992
Love in Germany, A 1984
Love in the Afternoon [1957] 1986
Love in the Time of Money 2003
Love Is a Dog from Hell 1988
Love Is the Devil 1999
love jones 1997
Love/Juice 2001
Love Letter, The 2000
Love Letters 1984
Love Liza 2004
Love Potion #9 1992
Love Serenade 1997
Love Song for Bobby Long, A 2006
Love Stinks 2000
Love Story, A. *See* Bound and Gagged.
Love Streams 1984
Love the Hard Way 2004
Love, the Magician. *See* Amor brujo, El.
Love! Valour! Compassion! 1997
Love Walked In 1999
Love Without Pity 1991
Loveless, The 1984, 1986
Lovelines 1984
Lovely & Amazing 2003
Lover, The 1992
Loverboy 1989
Loverboy pg. 247
Lovers 1992
Lovers of the Arctic Circle, The 2000

Lovers on the Bridge 2000
Love's a Bitch. *See* Amores Perros.
Love's Labour's Lost 2001
Loves of a Blonde [1965] 1985
Lovesick 1983
Loving Jezebel 2001
Low Blow 1986
Low Down, The 2002
Low Down Dirty Shame, A 1995
Low Life, The 1996
Lucas 1986
Lucia, Lucia 2004
Lucia y el Sexo. *See* Sex and Lucia.
Lucie Aubrac 2000
Luckiest Man in the World, The 1989
Lucky Break 2003
Lucky Number Slevin pg. 249
Lucky Numbers 2001
L'Ultimo Bacio. *See* Last Kiss, The.
Luminous Motion 2001
Lumumba 2002
Lumumba: Death of a Prophet 1995
Luna Park 1995
Lunatic, The 1992
Lunatics: A Love Story 1992
Lune Froide. *See* Cold Moon.
Lunga vita alla signora! *See* Long Live the Lady!
Lurkers 1988
Lush Life 1995
Lust for Life [1956] 1991
Lust in the Dust 1985
Luther 2004
Luzhin Defence, The 2002

M

M. Butterfly 1993
Ma Femme Est une Actrice. *See* My Wife Is an Actress.
Ma Vie en Rose 1997
Mac 1993
Mac and Me 1988
Macaroni V 1988
MacArthur's Children 1985
Maccheroni. *See* Macaroni.
Machinist, The 2005
Macht der Bilder, Die. *See* Wonderful, Horrible Life of Leni Riefenstahl, The.
Mack the Knife 1990
Macomber Affair, The [1947] 1982
Mad City 1997
Mad Dog and Glory 1993
Mad Dog Coll. *See* Killer Instinct.
Mad Dog Time 1996
Mad Love 1995
Mad Love 2003
Mad Max Beyond Thunderdome 1985
Madagascar 2006
Madagascar Landing. *See* Aventure Malgache.
Madagascar Skin 1996
Madame Bovary 1991
Madame Sata 2004
Madame Sousatzka 1988
Made 2002
Made in America 1993
Made in Heaven 1987
Madea's Family Reunion pg. 251
Madeline 1999
Madhouse 1990
Madman 1983
Madness of King George, The 1995
Madness of Love. *See* Mad Love.
Maelstrom 2001
Mafia! 1999
Magdalene Sisters, The 2004
Magic Hunter 1996
Magic in the Water 1995
Magnolia 2000
Magyar Stories 1988
Mahabharata, The 1990
Maid in Manhattan 2003
Maid to Order 1987
Mail Order Wife 2006
Majestic, The 2002
Major and the Minor, The [1942] 1986
Major League 1989
Major League: Back to the Minors 1999
Major League II 1995
Major League III. *See* Major League: Back to the Minors.
Major Payne 1995
Make Way for Tomorrow [1937] 1981
Making Love (Hiller) 1982
Making Love (Tognazzi) 2002
Making Mr. Right 1987
Making the Grade 1984
Making Up! 1995
Makioka Sisters, The 1985
Mal d'aimer, Le. *See* Malady of Love, The.
Mala education, La. *See* Bad Education
Malady of Love, The 1987
Malcolm 1986
Malcolm X 1992
Malena 2001
Malibu Bikini Shop, The 1987
Malibu's Most Wanted 2004
Malice 1993
Mallrats 1995
Malone 1987
Maltese Falcon, The [1941] 1983
Mama, There's a Man in Your Bed 1990
Mamba 1988
Mambo Italiano 2004
Mambo Kings, The 1992
Man, The 2006
Man and a Woman, A 1986
Man Apart, A 2004
Man Bites Dog 1993
Man Called Sarge, A 1990
Man cheng jin dai huang jin jia. *See* Curse of the Golden Flower.
Man from Elysian Fields, The 2003
Man from Snowy River, The 1982
Man Hunt [1941] 1984
Man I Love, The [1946] 1986
Man in Love, A 1987
Man in the Iron Mask, The 1999
Man in the Moon, The 1991
Man in Uniform, A 1995

Man Inside, The 1990
Man of Iron 1981
Man of Marble [1977] 1981
Man of No Importance, A 1995
Man of the Century 2000
Man of the House (Orr) 1995
Man of the House 2006
Man of the Year 1996
Man of the Year pg. 252
Man on Fire 2005
Man on the Moon 2000
Man on the Train, The 2004
Man Outside 1988
Man Trouble 1992
Man Who Cried, The 2002
Man Who Fell to Earth, The [1975] 1982
Man Who Knew Too Little, The 1997
Man Who Loved Women, The 1983
Man Who Wasn't There, The 1983
Man Who Wasn't There, The 2002
Man Who Would Be King, The [1975] 1983
Man with One Red Shoe, The 1985
Man with Three Coffins, The 1988
Man with Two Brains, The 1983
Man Without a Face, The 1993
Man Without a Past, The 2003
Man Without a World, The 1992
Man, Woman and Child 1983
Manchurian Candidate, The 2005
Manderlay pg. 254
Maneuvers 1988
Mangler, The 1995
Manhattan by Numbers 1995
Manhattan Murder Mystery 1993
Manhattan Project, The 1986
Manhunter 1986
Maniac Cop 1988
Manic 2004
Manifesto 1989
Manito 2004
Mannequin 1987
Mannequin Two 1991
Manny & Lo 1996
Manon des sources. *See* Manon of the Spring.
Manon of the Spring 1987
Man's Best Friend 1993
Mansfield Park 2000
Map of the Human Heart 1993
Mapantsula 1988
Mar Adentro. *See* Sea Inside, The.
March of the Penguins 2006
Marci X 2004
Margaret's Museum 1997
Margarita Happy Hour 2003
Maria Full of Grace 2005
Maria's Lovers 1985
Mariachi, El 1993
Mariages 2003
Marie 1985
Marie Antoinette pg. 257
Marie Baie des Anges. *See* Marie from the Bay Angels.
Marie from the Bay Angels 1999
Marilyn Monroe 1987
Marine, The pg. 259
Marine Life 2001
Marius and Jeannette 1999
Marius et Jeannette: Un Conte de L'Estaque. *See* Marius and Jeannette.
Marked for Death 1990
Marlene 1986
Marooned in Iraq 2004
Marquis 1995
Marriages. *See* Mariages.
Married to It 1993
Married to the Mob 1988
Marrying Man, The 1991
Mars Attacks! 1996
Marsupials, The 1987
Martha and Ethel 1995
Martha and I 1995
Martha, Ruth, and Edie 1988
Martians Go Home 1990
Marusa No Onna. *See* Taxing Woman, A.
Marvin & Tige 1983
Marvin's Room 1996
Mary Reilly 1996
Mary Shelley's Frankenstein 1995
Masala 1993
Mask 1985
Mask, The 1995
Mask of the Phantasm. *See* Batman: Mask of the Phantasm.
Mask of Zorro, The 1999
Masked and Anonymous 2004
Masque of the Red Death 1989
Masquerade 1988
Mass Appeal 1985
Massa'ot James Be'eretz Hakodesh. *See* James' Journey to Jerusalem.
Master and Commander: The Far Side of the World 2004
Master of Disguise 2003
Master of the Crimson Armor. *See* Promise, The.
Masterminds 1997
Masters of the Universe 1987
Matador, The pg. 260
Match Point 2006
Matchmaker, The 1997
Matchstick Men 2004
Material Girls pg. 261
Matewan 1987
Matilda 1996
Matinee 1993
Matrix, The 2000
Matrix Reloaded, The 2004
Matrix Revolutions, The 2004
Matter of Struggle, A 1985
Matter of Taste, A 2002
Maurice 1987
Maverick 1995
Max 2003
Max Dugan Returns 1983
Max Keeble's Big Move 2002
Maxie 1985
Maximum Overdrive 1986
Maximum Risk 1996
May Fools 1990
Maybe Baby 2002
Maybe...Maybe Not 1996
McBain 1991
McHale's Navy 1997

Me and Isaac Newton 2001
Me and My Gal [1932] 1982
Me and the Kid 1993
Me and Veronica 1995
Me and You and Everyone We Know 2006
Me, Myself & Irene 2001
Me Myself I 2001
Me Without You 2003
Me You Them 2002
Mean Creek 2005
Mean Girls 2005
Mean Season, The 1985
Meatballs II 1984
Meatballs III 1987
Meatballs IV 1992
Medallion, The 2004
Medicine Man 1992
Mediterraneo 1992
Meet Joe Black 1999
Meet John Doe [1941] 1982
Meet the Applegates 1991
Meet the Deedles 1999
Meet the Fockers 2005
Meet the Hollowheads 1989
Meet the Parents 2001
Meet Wally Sparks 1997
Meeting Venus 1991
Megaforce 1982
Mein Liebster Feind. *See* My Best Fiend.
Melinda and Melinda 2006
Melvin and Howard 1981
Memento 2002
Memoirs of a Geisha 2006
Memoirs of a Madman 1995
Memoirs of a River 1992
Memoirs of an Invisible Man 1992
Memories of Me 1988
Memphis Belle 1990
Men 1986
Men 1999
Men at Work 1990
Men Don't Leave 1990
Men in Black 1997
Men in Black II 2003
Men in Tights. *See* Robin Hood.
Men of Honor 2001
Men of Respect 1991
Men with Brooms 2003
Men with Guns 1999
Menace II Society 1993
Mȩnage 1986
Men's Club, The 1986
Mephisto 1981
Mercenary Fighters 1988
Merchant of Venice, The 2006
Merci pour le Chocolat 2003
Mercury Rising 1999
Mermaids 1990
Merry Christmas. *See* Joyeux Noel.
Merry Christmas, Mr. Lawrence 1983
Merry War, A 1999
Message in a Bottle 2000
Messenger, The 1987
Messenger: Joan of Arc, The 2000
Messenger of Death 1988
Metallica: Some Kind of Monster 2005
Metalstorm: The Destruction of Jarred-Syn 1983
Metamorphosis: The Alien Factor 1995
Meteor Man, The 1993
Metro 1997
Metroland 2000
Metropolitan 1990
Mexican, The 2002
Mi Vida Loca 1995
Mia Eoniotita ke Mia Mers. *See* Eternity and a Day.
Miami Blues 1990
Miami Rhapsody 1995
Miami Vice pg. 262
Michael 1996
Michael Collins 1996
Mickey Blue Eyes 2000
Micki & Maude 1984
Microcosmos 1996
Midnight (Leisen) 1986
Midnight (Vane) 1989
Midnight Clear, A 1992
Midnight Crossing 1988
Midnight in the Garden of Good and Evil
Midnight Run 1988
Midsummer Night's Sex Comedy, A 1982
Midwinter's Tale, A 1996
Mies Vailla Menneisyytta. *See* Man Without a Past, The.
Mifune 2001
Mighty, The 1999
Mighty Aphrodite 1995
Mighty Ducks, The 1992
Mighty Joe Young 1999
Mighty Morphin Power Rangers: The Movie 1995
Mighty Quinn, The 1989
Mighty Wind, A 2004
Mike's Murder 1984
Mikey and Nicky 1984
Milagro Beanfield War, The 1988
Mildred Pierce [1945] 1986
Miles from Home 1988
Milk and Honey 1989
Milk & Honey 2006
Milk Money 1995
Millennium 1989
Millennium Mambo 2003
Miller's Crossing 1990
Million Dollar Baby 2005
Million Dollar Hotel, The 2002
Million Dollar Mystery 1987
Million to Juan, A 1995
Millions 2006
Mimic 1997
Mina Tannenbaum 1995
Mindhunters 2006
Mindwalk 1991
Ministry of Vengeance 1989
Minner. *See* Men.
Minority Report 2003
Minotaur 1995
Minus Man, The 2000
Mio Viaggio in Italia. *See* My Voyage to Italy.

Miracle 2005
Miracle, The 1991
Miracle Mile 1988, 1989
Miracle on 34th Street 1995
Miracle Woman, The (1931) 1982
Mirror, The 2000
Mirror Has Two Faces, The 1996
Misadventures of Mr. Wilt, The 1990
Mischief 1985
Miserables, The 1995
Miserables, The 1999
Misery 1990
Misfits, The [1961] 1983
Mishima 1985
Misplaced 1995
Misplaced 1989
Miss Congeniality 2001
Miss Congeniality 2: Armed and Fabulous 2006
Miss Firecracker 1989
Miss Mary 1986
Miss Mona 1987
Miss…or Myth? 1987
Missing 1982, 1988
Missing, The 2004
Missing in Action, 1984
Missing in Action II 1985
Mission, The (Joffe) 1986
Mission, The (Sayyad) 1983
Mission: Impossible 1996
Mission: Impossible 2 2001
Mission: Impossible III pg. 264
Mission to Mars 2001
Missionary, The 1982
Mississippi Burning 1988
Mississippi Masala 1992
Mr. and Mrs. Bridge 1990
Mr. & Mrs. Smith 2006
Mr. Baseball 1992
Mr. Death: The Rise and Fall of Fred A. Leuchter, Jr. 2000
Mr. Deeds 2003
Mr. Deeds Goes to Town [1936] 1982
Mr. Destiny 1990
Mr. Frost 1990
Mr. Holland's Opus 1995
Mr. Jealousy 1999
Mister Johnson 1991
Mr. Jones 1993
Mr. Love 1986
Mr. Magoo 1997
Mr. Mom 1983
Mr. Nanny 1993
Mr. Nice Guy 1999
Mr. North 1988
Mr. Payback 1995
Mister Roberts [1955] 1988
Mr. Saturday Night 1992
Mr. Smith Goes to Washington [1939] 1982
Mr. 3000 2005
Mr. Wonderful 1993
Mr. Write 1995
Mr. Wrong 1996
Mistress 1992
Mrs. Brown 1997
Mrs. Dalloway 1999
Mrs. Doubtfire 1993
Mrs. Henderson Presents 2006
Mrs. Palfrey at the Claremont pg. 266
Mrs. Parker and the Vicious Circle 1995
Mrs. Soffel 1984
Mrs. Winterbourne 1996
Misunderstood 1984
Mit Liv som Hund. *See* My Life as a Dog.
Mitad del cielo, La. *See* Half of Heaven.
Mixed Blood 1985
Mixed Nuts 1995
Mo' Better Blues 1990
Mo' Money 1992
Moartea domnului Lazarescu. *See* Death of Mr. Lazarescu, The.
Mobsters 1991
Mod Squad, The 2000
Modern Girls 1986
Modern Romance 1981
Moderns, The 1988
Mogan Do. *See* Infernal Affairs.
Mois d'avril sont meurtriers, Les. *See* April Is a Deadly Month.
Moitie Gauche du Frigo, La. *See* Left Hand Side of the Fridge, The.
Moll Flanders 1996
Molly 2000
Mom and Dad Save the World 1992
Mommie Dearest 1981
Mon bel Amour, Ma Dechirure. *See* My True Love, My Wound.
Mona Lisa 1986
Mona Lisa Smile 2004
Mondays in the Sun 2004
Mondo New York 1988
Mondovino 2006
Money for Nothing 1993
Money Man 1995
Money Pit, The 1986
Money Talks 1997
Money Train 1995
Money Tree, The 1992
Mongolian Tale, A 1997
Monkey Shines 1988
Monkey Trouble 1995
Monkeybone 2002
Monsieur Hire 1990
Monsieur Ibrahim 2004
Monsieur N 2006
Monsignor 1982
Monsoon Wedding 2003
Monster 2004
Monster, The 1996
Monster House pg. 268
Monster in a Box 1992
Monster-in-Law 2006
Monster in the Closet 1987
Monster Squad, The 1987
Monster's Ball 2002
Monsters, Inc. 2002
Montana Run 1992
Montenegro 1981
Month by the Lake, A 1995
Month in the Country, A 1987
Monty Python's The Meaning of Life 1983
Monument Ave. 1999
Moolaade 2005
Moon in the Gutter 1983

Moon Over Broadway 1999
Moon over Parador 1988
Moon Shadow [1995] 2001
Moonlight and Valentino 1995
Moonlight Mile 2003
Moonlighting 1982
Moonstruck 1987
Morgan Stewart's Coming Home 1987
Moriarty. *See* Sherlock Holmes.
Morning After, The 1986
Morning Glory 1993
Morons from Outer Space 1985
Mort de Mario Ricci, La. *See* Death of Mario Ricci, The.
Mortal Kombat 1995
Mortal Kombat II: Annihilation 1997
Mortal Thoughts 1991
Mortuary Academy 1988
Morvern Callar 2003
Mosca addio. *See* Moscow Farewell.
Moscow Farewell 1987
Moscow on the Hudson 1984
Mosquito Coast, The 1986
Most Dangerous Game, The [1932] 1985
Most Fertile Man in Ireland, The 2002
Most Wanted 1997
Mostly Martha 2003
Mother 1996
Mother, The 2005
Mother Lode 1983
Mother Night 1996
Mother Teresa 1986
Mother's Boys 1995
Mothering Heart, The [1913] 1984
Mothman Prophecies, The 2003
Motorama 1993
Motorcycle Diaries, The 2005
Moulin Rouge 2002
Mountain Gorillas 1995
Mountains of Moon 1990
Mountaintop Motel Massacre 1986
Mouse Hunt 1997
Mouth to Mouth 1997
Movers and Shakers 1985
Moving 1988
Moving the Mountain 1995
Moving Violations 1985
Much Ado About Nothing 1993
Mui du du Xanh. *See* Scent of Green Papaya, The.
Mujeres al borde de un ataque de nervios. *See* Women on the Verge of a Nervous Breakdown.
Mulan 1999
Mulholland Drive 2002
Mulholland Falls 1996
Multiplicity 1996
Mumford 2000
Mummy, The 2000
Mummy Returns, The 2002
Munchie 1995
Munchies 1987
Munich 2006
Muppet Christmas Carol, The 1992
Muppets from Space 2000
Muppet Treasure Island 1996
Muppets Take Manhattan, The 1984
Mur, Le. *See* Wall, The.
Murder at 1600 1997
Murder by Numbers 2003
Murder in the First 1995
Murder One 1988
Murderball 2006
Murderous Maids 2003
Muriel's Wedding 1995
Murphy's Law 1986
Murphy's Romance 1985
Muse, The 2000
Muses Orphelines, Les. *See* Orphan Muses, The.
Music Box 1989
Music for the Movies: Bernard Herrmann 1995
Music From Another Room 1999
Music of Chance, The 1993
Music of the Heart 2000
Music Tells You, The 1995
Musime si Pomahat. *See* Divided We Fall.
Musketeer, The 2002
Must Love Dogs 2006
Mustang: The Hidden Kingdom 1995
Musuko. *See* My Sons.
Mutant on the Bounty 1989
Mute Witness 1995
Mutiny on the Bounty [1962] 1984
My African Adventure 1987
My American Cousin 1986
My Apprenticeship. *See* Among People.
My Architect 2005
My Baby's Daddy 2005
My Beautiful Laundrette 1986
My Best Fiend 2000
My Best Friend Is a Vampire 1988
My Best Friend's Girl 1984
My Best Friend's Wedding 1997
My Big Fat Greek Wedding 2003
My Blue Heaven 1990
My Boss's Daughter 2004
My Boyfriend's Back 1993
My Chauffeur 1986
My Cousin Rachel [1952] 1981
My Cousin Vinny 1992
My Crazy Life. *See* Mi Vida Loca.
My Dark Lady 1987
My Demon Lover 1987
My Dinner with Andre 1981
My Family (Mi Familia) 1995
My Father Is Coming 1992
My Father, the Hero 1995
My Father's Angel 2002
My Father's Glory 1991
My Favorite Martian 2000
My Favorite Season 1996
My Favorite Year 1982
My Fellow Americans 1996
My First Mister 2002
My First Wife 1985
My Foolish Heart (1949) 1983
My Giant 1999
My Girl 1991
My Girl II 1995

My Heroes Have Always Been Cowboys 1991
My Left Foot 1989
My Life 1993
My Life and Times with Antonin Artaud 1996
My Life as a Dog [1985] 1987
My Life in Pink. *See* Ma Vie en Rose.
My Life So Far 2000
My Life Without Me 2004
My Life's in Turnaround 1995
My Little Pony 1986
My Mom's a Werewolf 1989
My Mother's Castle 1991
My Mother's Courage
My Mother's Smile 2006
My Name is Joe 2000
My Neighbor Totoro 1993
My New Gun 1992
My New Partner 1985
My Other Husband 1985
My Own Private Idaho 1991
My Reputation [1946] 1984, 1986
My Science Project 1985
My Son the Fanatic 2000
My Sons 1995
My Stepmother Is an Alien 1988
My Summer of Love 2006
My Super Ex-Girlfriend pg. 270
My Sweet Little Village 1986
My True Love, My Wound 1987
My Tutor 1983
My Twentieth Century 1990
My Uncle's Legacy 1990
My Voyage to Italy 2003
My Wife Is an Actress 2003
Mysterious Skin 2006
Mystery, Alaska 2000
Mystery Date 1991
Mystery of Alexina, The 1986
Mystery of Rampo 1995
Mystery of the Wax Museum [1933] 1986
Mystery Men 2000
Mystery Science Theater 3000: The Movie 1996
Mystery Train 1989
Mystic Masseur, The 2003
Mystic Pizza 1988
Mystic River 2004
Myth of Fingerprints, The 1998

N

Nacho Libre pg. 273
Nadine 1987
Nadja 1995
Naked 1993
Naked Cage, The 1986
Naked Gun, The 1988
Naked Gun 2 1/2, The 1991
Naked Gun 33 1/3: The Final Insult 1995
Naked in New York 1995
Naked Lunch 1991
Name of the Rose, The 1986
Nanny McPhee pg. 275
Nanou 1988
Napoleon [1927] 1981
Napoleon 1997
Napoleon Dynamite 2005
Narc 2003
Narrow Margin 1990
Nasty Girl, The 1990
Nate and Hayes 1983
National Lampoon's Christmas Vacation 1989
National Lampoon's Class Reunion 1982
National Lampoon's European Vacation 1985
National Lampoon's Loaded Weapon I 1993
National Lampoon's Senior Trip 1995
National Lampoon's Vacation 1983
National Lampoon's Van Wilder 2003
National Security 2004
National Treasure 2005
National Velvet [1944] 1993
Native Son 1986
Nativity Story, The pg. 276
Natural, The 1984
Natural Born Killers 1995
Navigator, The 1989
Navy SEALs 1990
Near Dark 1987
Nebo nashevo detstva. *See* Sky of Our Childhood, The.
Necessary Roughness 1991
Ned Kelly 2005
Needful Things 1993
Negotiator, The 1999
Neil Simon's Lost in Yonkers 1993
Neil Simon's The Odd Couple 2 1999
Neil Simon's The Slugger's Wife 1985
Neil Young: Heart of Gold pg. 278
Nell 1995
Nell Gwyn [1934] 1983
Nelly & Mr. Arnaud 1996
Nemesis 1993
Nenette et Boni 1997
Neon Bible, The 1995
Nervous Ticks 1995
Net, The 1995
Nettoyoge a Sec. *See* Dry Cleaning.
Never Again 2003
Never Been Kissed 2000
Never Cry Wolf 1983
Never Die Alone 2005
Never Say Never Again 1983
Never Talk to Strangers 1995
Never too Young to Die 1986
Neverending Story, The 1984
Neverending Story II, The 1991
New Adventures of Pippi Longstocking, The 1988
New Age, The 1995
New Babylon, The [1929] 1983
New Eve, The 2001
New Guy, The 2003
New Jack City 1991
New Jersey Drive 1995
New Kids, The 1985
New Life, A 1988
New Nightmare. *See* Wes Craven's New Nightmare.
New Rose Hotel 2000

New World, The 2006
New Year's Day 1989
New York in Short: The Shvitz and Let's Fall in Love 1995
New York Minute 2005
New York, New York [1977] 1983
New York Stories 1989
Newsies 1992
Newton Boys, The 1999
Next Best Thing, The 2001
Next Big Thing, The 2003
Next Friday 2001
Next Karate Kid, The 1995
Next of Kin 1989
Next Stop Greenwich Village [1976] 1984
Next Stop Wonderland 1999
Next Summer 1986
Next Year if All Goes Well 1983
Niagara Falls 1987
Niagara, Niagara 1999
Nice Girls Don't Explode 1987
Nicholas Nickleby 2003
Nick and Jane 1997
Nick of Time 1995
Nico and Dani 2002
Nico Icon 1996
Niezwykla podroz Balthazara Kobera. *See* Tribulations of Balthasar Kober, The.
Night and Day 1995
Night and the City 1992
Night at the Museum pg. 280
Night at the Roxbury, A 1999
Night Crossing 1982
Night Falls on Manhattan 1997
Night Friend 1988
Night Game 1989
Night in Heaven, A 1983
Night in the Life of Jimmy Reardon, A 1988
Night Listener, The pg. 282
'night, Mother 1986
Night of the Comet 1984
Night of the Creeps 1986
Night of the Demons II 1995
Night of the Hunter, The [1955] 1982
Night of the Iguana, The [1964] 1983
Night of the Living Dead 1990
Night of the Pencils, The 1987
Night of the Shooting Stars, The 1983
Night on Earth 1992
Night Patrol 1985
Night Shift 1982
Night Song [1947] 1981
Night Visitor 1989
Night Watch pg. 283
Night We Never Met, The 1993
Nightbreed 1990
Nightcap. *See* Merci pour le Chocolat.
Nightfall 1988
Nightflyers 1987
Nighthawks 1981
Nighthawks II. *See* Strip Jack Naked.
Nightmare at Shadow Woods 1987
Nightmare Before Christmas, The 1993
Nightmare on Elm Street, A 1984
Nightmare on Elm Street: II, A 1985
Nightmare on Elm Street: III, A 1987
Nightmare on Elm Street: IV, A 1988
Nightmare on Elm Street: V, A 1989
Nightmares III 1984
Nightsongs 1991
Nightstick 1987
Nightwatch 1999
Nil by Mouth 1999
9 1/2 Weeks 1986
9 Deaths of the Ninja 1985
Nine Months 1995
Nine Queens 2003
976-EVIL 1989
1918 1985
1969 1988
1990: The Bronx Warriors 1983
1991: The Year Punk Broke 1995
Ninety Days 1986
Ninja Turf 1986
Ninotchka [1939] 1986
Ninth Gate, The 2001
Nixon 1995
No 1999
No Escape 1995
No Fear, No Die 1995
No Holds Barred 1989
No Looking Back 1999
No Man of Her Own [1949] 1986
No Man's Land 1987
No Man's Land 2002
No Mercy 1986
No News from God 2003
No Picnic 1987
No Retreat, No Surrender 1986
No Retreat, No Surrender II 1989
No Secrets 1991
No Small Affair 1984
No Such Thing 2003
No Way Out 1987, 1992
Nobody Loves Me 1996
Nobody's Fool (Benton) 1995
Nobody's Fool (Purcell) 1986
Nobody's Perfect 1990
Noce en Galilee. *See* Wedding in Galilee, A.
Noche de los lapices, La. *See* Night of the Pencils, The.
Nochnoi Dozor. *See* Night Watch.
Noel 2005
Noises Off 1992
Nomads 1986
Non ti muovere. *See* Don't Move.
Nora 2002
Normal Life 1996
Norte, El 1983
North 1995
North Country 2006
North Shore 1987
North Star, The [1943] 1982
Northfork 2004
Nostalgia 1984
Nostradamus 1995
Not Another Teen Movie 2002
Not for Publication 1984

Not of This Earth 1988

Not Quite Paradise 1986

Not Since Casanova 1988

Not Without My Daughter 1991

Notebook, The 2005

Notebook on Cities and Clothes 1992

Notes on a Scandal pg. 284

Nothing but Trouble 1991

Nothing in Common 1986

Nothing Personal 1997

Nothing to Lose 1997

Notorious Bettie Page, The pg. 286

Notte di San Lorenzo, La. *See* Night of the Shooting Stars, The.

Notting Hill 2000

Nouvelle Eve, The. *See* New Eve, The.

November 2006

Novocaine 2002

Now and Then 1995

Nowhere 1997

Nowhere in Africa 2004

Nowhere to Hide 1987

Nowhere to Run 1993

Nueve Reinas. *See* Nine Queens.

Nuit de Varennes, La [1982] 1983, 1984

Nuits Fauves, Les. *See* Savage Nights.

Nuits de la pleine lune, Les. *See* Full Moon In Paris.

Number One with a Bullet 1987

Nuns on the Run 1990

Nurse Betty 2001

Nutcracker Prince, The 1990

Nutcracker, The 1986

Nutcracker, The. *See* George Balanchine's the Nutcracker.

Nuts 1987

Nutty Professor, The 1996

Nutty Professor 2: The Klumps 2001

O

O 2002

O Brother, Where Art Thou? 2001

O' Despair. *See* Long Weekend, The.

Oak, The 1995

Oasis, The 1984

Obecna Skola. *See* Elementary School, The.

Oberst Redl. *See* Colonel Redl.

Object of Beauty, The 1991

Object of My Affection, The 1999

Oblivion 1995

Obsessed 1988

O.C. and Stiggs 1987

Ocean's Eleven 2002

Ocean's Twelve 2005

Oci Ciornie. *See* Dark Eyes.

October Sky 2000

Octopussy 1983

Odd Man Out [1947] 1985

Oedipus Rex 1995

Oedipus Rex [1967] 1984

Oedipus Wrecks. *See* New York Stories.

Of Human Bondage [1946] 1986

Of Love and Shadows 1996

Of Mice and Men 1992

Of Unknown Origin 1983

Off Beat 1986

Off Limits 1988

Off the Menu: The Last Days of Chasen's 1999

Office Killer 1997

Office Party 1989

Office Space 2000

Officer and a Gentleman, An 1982

Official Story, The 1985

Offret. *See* Sacrifice, The.

Oh God, You Devil 1984

O'Hara's Wife 1982

Old Explorers 1991

Old Gringo 1989

Old Joy pg. 291

Old Lady Who Walked in the Sea, The 1995

Old School 2004

Oldboy 2006

Oleanna 1995

Oliver and Company 1988

Oliver Twist 2006

Olivier Olivier 1993

Omen, The pg. 292

On Deadly Ground 1995

On Golden Pond 1981

On Guard! 2004

On the Edge 1986

On the Line 2002

On the Town [1949] 1985

On Valentine's Day 1986

Once Around 1991

Once Bitten 1985

Once More 1988

Once Were Warriors 1995

Once Upon a Crime 1992

Once Upon A Forest 1993

Once Upon a Time in America 1984

Once Upon a Time in Mexico 2004

Once Upon a Time in the Midlands 2004

Once Upon a Time...When We Were Colored 1996

Once We Were Dreamers 1987

One 2001

One, The 2002

One and a Two, A. *See* Yi Yi.

One Crazy Summer 1986

One Day in September 2001

One False Move 1992

One Fine Day 1996

One Flew over the Cuckoo's Nest [1975] 1985, 1991

One from the Heart 1982

One Good Cop 1991

One Hour Photo 2003

101 Dalmatians 1996

101 Reykjavik 2002

102 Dalmatians 2001

187 1997

112th and Central 1993

One Magic Christmas 1985

One More Saturday 1986

One More Tomorrow [1946] 1986

One Nation Under God 1995

One Night at McCool's 2002

One Night Stand 1997

One Tough Cop 1999

One True Thing 1999

Onegin 2000
Onimaru. *See* Arashi Ga Oka.
Only Emptiness Remains 1985
Only the Lonely 1991
Only the Strong 1993
Only the Strong Survive 2004
Only Thrill, The 1999
Only When I Laugh 1981
Only You 1995
Open Doors 1991
Open Range 2004
Open Season pg. 294
Open Water 2005
Open Your Eyes 2000
Opening Night 1988
Opera 1987
Operation Condor 1997
Operation Dumbo Drop 1995
Opportunists, The 2001
Opportunity Knocks 1990
Opposite of Sex, The 1999
Opposite Sex, The 1993
Orange County 2003
Ordeal by Innocence 1985
Order, The 2004
Orgazmo 1999
Original Gangstas 1996
Original Kings of Comedy, The 2001
Original Sin 2002
Orlando 1993
Orphan Muses, The 2002
Orphans 1987
Orphans of the Storm 1984
Osama 2005
Oscar 1991
Oscar & Lucinda 1997
Osmosis Jones 2002
Ososhiki. *See* Funeral, The.
Osterman Weekend, The 1983
Otac Na Sluzbenom Putu. *See* When Father Was Away on Business.
Otello 1986
Othello 1995
Other People's Money 1991
Other Side of Heaven, The 2003
Other Sister, The 2000
Other Voices, Other Rooms 1997
Others, The 2002
Our Lady of the Assassins 2002
Our Relations [1936] 1985
Our Song 2002
Out Cold 1989
Out for Justice 1991
Out in the World. *See* Among People.
Out of Africa 1985
Out of Bounds 1986
Out of Control 1985
Out of Life. *See* Hors la Vie.
Out of Order 1985
Out of Sight 1999
Out of Sync 1995
Out of the Dark 1989
Out of the Past [1947] 1991
Out of Time 2004
Out-of-Towners, The 2000
Out on a Limb 1992
Out to Sea 1997
Outbreak 1995
Outfoxed: Rupert Murdoch's War on Journalism 2005
Outing, The 1987
Outland 1981
Outrageous Fortune 1987
Outside Providence 2000
Outsiders, The 1983
Over Her Dead Body 1995
Over the Edge [1979] 1987
Over the Hedge pg. 295
Over the Hill 1995
Over the Ocean 1995
Over the Top 1987
Overboard 1987
Overexposed 1990
Overseas 1991
Owning Mahowny 2004
Ox, The 1992
Oxford, Blues 1984
Oxygen 2000

P

P.O.W. the Escape 1986
P.S. 2005
Pacific Heights 1990
Pacifier, The 2006
Package, The 1989
Pacte des Loups, Le. *See* Brotherhood of the Wolf.
Pagemaster, The 1995
Paint Job, The 1995
Painted Desert, The 1995
Palais Royale 1988
Pale Rider 1985
Palindromes 2006
Pallbearer, The 1996
Palmetto 1999
Palombella Rossa. *See* Redwood Pigeon.
Palookaville 1996
Panama Deception, The 1992
Pane e Tulipani. *See* Bread and Tulips.
Panic 2001
Panic Room, The 2003
Pan's Labyrinth pg. 299
Panther 1995
Papa's Song 2001
Paparazzi 2005
Paper, The 1995
Paper Hearts 1995
Paper Mask 1991
Paper Wedding, A 1991
Paperback Romance 1997
Paperhouse 1988
Paradise (Donoghue) 1991
Paradise (Gillard) 1982
Paradise Lost 1996
Paradise Now 2006
Paradise Road 1997
Parasite 1982
Parde-ye akhar. *See* Last Act, The.
Parent Trap, The 1999
Parenthood 1989
Parents 1989
Paris Blues [1961] 1992
Paris Is Burning 1991
Paris, Texas 1984
Parsifal 1983
Parsley Days 2001

Parting Glances 1986
Partisans of Vilna 1986
Partners 1982
Party Animal 1985
Party Girl 1995
Party Line 1988
Party Monster 2004
Pascali's Island 1988
Pass the Ammo 1988
Passage, The 1988
Passage to India, A 1984, 1990
Passages 1995
Passed Away 1992
Passenger 57 1992
Passion (Duncan) 2001
Passion (Godard) 1983
Passion d'amore 1984
Passion Fish 1992
Passion in the Desert 1999
Passion of Martin, The 1991
Passion of Mind 2001
Passion of the Christ, The 2005
Passion to Kill, A 1995
Passionada 2003
Pastime 1991
Patch Adams 1999
Patch of Blue, A [1965] 1986
Pathfinder 1990
Paths of Glory [1957] 1991
Patinoire, La. *See* Ice Rink, The.
Patriot, The 2001
Patriot Games 1992
Patsy, The 1985
Patti Rocks 1987
Patty Hearst 1988
Paul Bowles: The Complete Outsider 1995
Paulie 1999
Pauline a la plage. *See* Pauline at the Beach.
Pauline and Paulette 2003
Pauline at the Beach 1983
Paura e amore. *See* Three Sisters.
Pavilion of Women 2002
Pay It Forward 2001
Payback 2000
Paycheck 2004
PCU 1995
Peace, Propaganda & The Promised Land 2006
Peaceful Air of the West 1995
Peacemaker, The 1997
Pearl Harbor 2002
Pebble and the Penguin, The 1995
Pecker 1999
Pee-wee's Big Adventure 1985
Peggy Sue Got Married 1986
Pelican Brief, The 1993
Pelle Erobreren. *See* Pelle the Conqueror.
Pelle the Conquered 1988
Pelle the Conqueror 1987
Penitent, The 1988
Penitentiary II 1982
Penitentiary III 1987
Penn and Teller Get Killed 1989
Pennies from Heaven 1981
People I Know 2004
People on Sunday [1929] 1986
People Under the Stairs, The 1991
People vs. Larry Flynt, The 1996
Pepi, Luci, Bom 1992
Perez Family, The 1995
Perfect 1985
Perfect Candidate, A 1996
Perfect Man, The 2006
Perfect Match, The 1987
Perfect Model, The 1989
Perfect Murder, A 1999
Perfect Murder, The 1988
Perfect Score, The 2005
Perfect Son, The 2002
Perfect Storm, The 2001
Perfect Weapon, The 1991
Perfect World, A 1993
Perfectly Normal 1991
Perhaps Some Other Time 1992
Peril 1985
Peril en la demeure. *See* Peril.
Permanent Midnight 1999
Permanent Record 1988
Personal Best 1982
Personal Choice 1989
Personal Services 1987
Personal Velocity 2003
Personals, The 1983
Persuasion 1995
Pervola, Sporen in die Sneeuw. *See* Tracks in the Snow.
Pest, The 1997
Pet Sematary 1989
Pet Sematary II 1992
Pete Kelly's Blues [1955] 1982
Peter Ibbetson [1935] 1985
Peter Pan 2004
Peter Von Scholten 1987
Peter's Friends 1992
Petit, Con. *See* Little Jerk.
Petite Bande, Le 1984
Petite Veleuse, La. *See* Little Thief, The.
Peyote Road, The 1995
Phantasm II 1988
Phantom, The 1996
Phantom of the Opera, The (Little) 1989
Phantom of the Opera, The (Schumacher) 2005
Phantoms 1999
Phar Lap 1984
Phat Beach 1996
Phat Girlz pg. 301
Phenomenon 1996
Philadelphia 1993
Philadelphia Experiment, The 1984
Philadelphia Experiment II, The 1995
Phobia 1988
Phone Booth 2004
Phorpa. *See* Cup, The.
Physical Evidence 1989
Pi 1999
Piaf 1982
Pianist, The 2003
Pianiste, La. *See* Piano Teacher, The.
Piano, The 1993
Piano Piano Kid 1992

Piano Teacher, The 2003
Piano Tuner of Earthquakes, The pg. 303
Picasso Trigger 1988
Piccolo diavolo, Il. *See* Little Devil, The.
Pick-Up Artist, The 1987
Pickle, The 1993
Picture Bride 1995
Picture Perfect 1997
Picture This: The Life and Times of Peter Bogdanovich in Archer City, Texas 1995
Pie in the Sky 1996
Pieces of April 2004
Pigalle 1995
Piglet's Big Movie 2004
Pigs and Pearls. *See* Montenegro.
Pile ou face. *See* Heads or Tails.
Pillow Book, The 1997
Pimp, The 1987
Pinero 2002
Pink Cadillac 1989
Pink Flamingos [1972] 1997
Pink Floyd the Wall 1982
Pink Nights 1991
Pink Panther, The pg. 304
Pinocchio 2003
Pinocchio and the Emperor of the Night 1987
Pipe Dream 2003
Pirate, The [1948] 1985
Pirate Movie, The 1982
Pirates of Penzance, The 1983
Pirates of the Caribbean: Dead Man's Chest pg. 306
Pirates of the Caribbean: The Curse of the Black Pearl 2004
Pit and the Pendulum, The 1991
Pitch Black 2001
Pitch Black 2: Chronicles of Riddick. *See* Chronicles of Riddick, The.
Pixote 1981
Pizza Man 1991
Pizzicata 2000
Placard, Le. *See* Closet, The.
Place in the Sun, A [1951] 1993
Place in the World, A 1995
Places in the Heart 1984
Plague, The 1995
Plague Sower, The. *See* Breath of Life, A.
Plain Clothes 1988
Plan B 1997
Planes, Trains and Automobiles 1987
Planet of the Apes 2002
Platform 2004
Platoon Leader 1988
Play It to the Bone 2001
Play Misty for Me [1971] 1985
Playboys, The 1992
Player, The 1992
Players Club, The 1999
Playing by Heart 1999
Playing for Keeps 1986
Playing God 1997
Pleasantville 1999
Pledge, The 2002
Plenty 1985
Plot Against Harry, The 1990
Plouffe, Les 1985
Ploughman's Lunch, The 1984
Plump Fiction 1999
Plunkett and Macleane 2000
Pocahontas 1995
Poetic Justice 1993
Point Break 1991
Point of No Return 1993
Pointsman, The 1988
Poison 1991
Poison Ivy 1992
Pokayaniye. *See* Repentance.
Pola X 2001
Polar Express, The 2005
Police 1986
Police Academy 1984
Police Academy II 1985
Police Academy III 1986
Police Academy IV 1987
Police Academy V 1988
Police Academy VI 1989
Polish Bride, The 2000
Polish Wedding 1999
Pollock 2001
Poltergeist 1982
Poltergeist II 1986
Poltergeist III 1988
Pomme, La. *See* Apple, The.
Pompatus of Love, The 1996
Ponette 1997
Pontiac Moon 1995
Pooh's Heffalump Movie 2006
Poolhall Junkies 2004
Pootie Tang 2002
Popcorn 1991
Pope Must Die, The 1991
Pope of Greenwich Village, The 1984
Porgy and Bess [1959] 1992
Porky's 1982
Porky's II: The Next Day 1983
Pornographic Affair, An. *See* Affair of Love, An.
Porte aperte. *See* Open Doors.
Portrait Chinois 2000
Portrait of a Lady, The 1996
Poseidon pg. 308
Positive I.D. 1987
Posse 1993
Possession 2003
Possible Worlds 2001
Post Coitum 1999
Post Coitum, Animal Triste. *See* Post Coitum.
Postcards from America 1995
Postcards from the Edge 1990
Poster Boy pg. 309
Postman, The (Radford) 1995
Postman, The (Costner) 1997
Postman Always Rings Twice, The 1981
Pound Puppies and the Legend of Big Paw 1988
Poupees russes, Les. *See* Russian Dolls.
Poussi re d'ange. *See* Angel Dust.
Powaqqatsi 1988
Powder 1995
Power 1986

Power, The 1984

Power of One, The 1992

Powwow Highway 1988

Practical Magic 1999

Prairie Home Companion, A pg. 311

Prancer 1989

Prayer for the Dying, A 1987

Prayer of the Rollerboys 1991

Preacher's Wife, The 1996

Predator 1987

Predator II 1990

Prefontaine 1997

Prelude to a Kiss 1992

Prenom, Carmen. *See* First Name, Carmen.

Presidio, The 1988

Presque Rien. *See* Come Undone.

Prestige, The pg. 313

Presumed Innocent 1990

Pret-a-Porter. *See* Ready to Wear.

Pretty Baby [1978] 1984

Pretty in Pink 1986

Pretty Persuasion 2006

Pretty Woman 1990

Prettykill 1987

Prey for Rock and Roll 2004

Priatiel Pakoinika. *See* Friend of the Deceased, A.

Price Above Rubies, A 1999

Price of Glory 2001

Price of Milk 2002

Prick Up Your Ears 1987

Pride and Prejudice 2006

Priest 1995

Priest of Love 1981

Primal Fear 1996

Primary Colors 1999

Primary Motive 1995

Prime 2006

Prince and Me, The 2005

Prince of Darkness 1987

Prince of Egypt, The 1999

Prince of Pennsylvania, The 1988

Prince of the City 1981

Prince of Tides, The 1991

Princess Academy, The 1987

Princess and the Goblin, The 1995

Princess and the Warrior, The 2002

Princess Bride, The 1987

Princess Caraboo 1995

Princess Diaries, The 2002

Princess Diaries 2, The 2005

Principal, The 1987

Principio da Incerteza, O. *See* Uncertainty Principle, The.

Prison 1988

Prisoner of the Mountain

Prisoners of the Sun 1991

Private Function, A 1985

Private Investigations 1987

Private Life of Sherlock Holmes, The [1970] 1986

Private Parts 1997

Private School 1983

Private Worlds [1935] 1982

Prize Winner of Defiance, Ohio, The 2006

Prizzi's Honor 1985

Problem Child 1990

Problem Child II 1991

Producers, The 2006

Professional, The 1995

Program, The 1993

Programmed to Kill 1987

Project Greenlight's Stolen Summer. *See* Stolen Summer.

Project X 1987

Prom Night II. *See* Hello Mary Lou.

Promesse, La 1997

Promise, The 1995

Promise, The pg. 315

Promised Land 1988

Promised Life, The 2005

Proof (Moorhouse) 1992

Proof 2006

Proof of Life 2001

Prophecy, The 1995

Proposition, The 1999

Proposition, The pg. 316

Proprietor, The 1996

Prospero's Books 1991

Protocol 1984

Przesluchanie. *See* Interrogation, The.

Psych-Out [1968] 1995

Psycho (Hitchcock) [1960] 1981

Psycho (Van Sant) 1999

Psycho II 1983

Psycho III 1986

Psycho Beach Party 2001

Puberty Blues 1983

Public Access 1995

Public Eye, The 1992

Puerto Rican Mambo (Not a Musical), The 1995

Pulp Fiction 1995

Pulse pg. 318

Pump Up the Volume 1990

Pumping Iron II 1985

Pumpkin 2003

Pumpkinhead 1988

Punch-Drunk Love 2003

Punchline 1988

Punisher, The 2005

Puppet Masters, The 1995

Puppetmaster, The 1995

Puppetoon Movie 1987

Puppies [1957] 1985

Pure Country 1992

Pure Luck 1991

Purgatory 1989

Purple Haze 1983

Purple Hearts 1984

Purple Noon [1960] 1996

Purple People Eaters, The 1988

Purple Rain 1984

Purple Rose of Cairo, The 1985

Pursuit of Happyness, The pg. 320

Pushing Tin 2000

Pyromaniac's Love Story, A 1995

Q

Q & A 1990

Qianxi Mambo. *See* Millennium mambo.

Qimsong. *See* Emperor's Shadow, The.

Qiu Ju Da Guansi. *See* Story of Qiu Ju, The.

Quarrel, The 1992
Quartet 1981
Quatre Aventures de Reinette et Mirabelle. *See* Four Adventures of Reinette and Mirabelle.
Queen, The pg. 323
Queen City Rocker 1987
Queen Margot 1995
Queen of Diamonds 1995
Queen of Hearts 1989
Queen of the Damned 2003
Queens Logic 1991
Quelques Jours avec moi. *See* Few Days with Me, A.
Querelle 1983
Quest, The 1996
Quest for Camelot 1999
Quest for Fire 1982
Question of Silence, The 1984
Quick and the Dead, The 1995
Quick Change 1990
Quiet, The pg. 325
Quiet American, The 2003
Quiet Earth, The 1985
Quiet Man, The [1952] 1981
Quiet Room, The 1997
Quigley Down Under 1990
Quills 2001
Quitting 2003
Quiz Show 1995

R

Rabbit-Proof Fence 2003
Race for Glory 1989
Race the Sun 1996
Rachel Papers, The 1989
Rachel River 1987
Racing Stripes 2006
Racing with the Moon 1984
Radio 2004
Radio Days 1987
Radio Flyer 1992
Radioland Murders 1995
Radium City 1987
Rage: Carrie 2 2000
Rage in Harlem, A 1991
Rage of Honor 1987
Raggedy Man 1981
Raggedy Rawney, The 1988
Raging Angels 1995
Raging Fury. *See* Hell High.
Ragtime 1981
Raiders of the Lost Ark 1981
Rain 2003
Rain. *See* Baran.
Rain Killer, The 1990
Rain Man 1988
Rain Without Thunder 1993
Rainbow Brite and the Star Stealer 1985
Rainbow, The 1989
Raining Stones 1995
Raintree County [1957] 1993
Rainy Day Friends 1985
Raise the Red Lantern 1992
Raise Your Voice 2005
Raisin in the Sun, A [1961] 1992
Raising Arizona 1987
Raising Cain 1992
Raising Helen 2005
Raising Victor Vargas 2004
Rambling Rose 1991
Rambo: First Blood Part II 1985
Rambo III 1988
Ramona 1995
Rampage 1987, 1992
Ran 1985
Random Hearts 2000
Ransom 1996
Rapa Nui 1995
Rapid Fire 1992
Rappin' 1985
Rapture, The 1991
Raspad 1992
Rasputin [1975] 1985
Rat Race 2002
Ratboy 1986
Rat's Tale, A 1999
Ratcatcher 2001
Rate It X 1986
Ravenous 2000
Raw Deal 1986
Rawhead Rex 1987
Ray 2005
Rayon vert, Le. *See* Summer.
Razorback 1985
Razor's Edge, The 1984
Re-Animator 1985
Read My Lips 2003
Reader, The 1988, 1989
Ready to Rumble 2001
Ready to Wear 1995
Real Blonde, The 1999
Real Genius 1985
Real McCoy, The 1993
Real Men 1987
Real Women Have Curves 2003
Reality Bites 1995
Rear Window [1954] 2001
Reason to Believe, A 1995
Rebel 1986
Rebound 2006
Reckless 1984
Reckless 1995
Reckless Kelly 1995
Reckoning, The 2005
Recruit, The 2004
Recruits 1986
Red 1995
Red Corner 1997
Red Dawn 1984
Red Dragon 2003
Red Eye 2006
Red Firecracker, Green Firecracker 1995
Red Heat 1988
Red Planet 2001
Red Rock West 1995
Red Scorpion 1989
Red Sonja 1985
Red Sorghum 1988
Red Surf 1990
Red Violin, The 1999
Redl Ezredes. *See* Colonel Redl.
Reds 1981
Redwood Pigeon 1995

Reefer and the Model 1988
Ref, The 1995
Reflecting Skin, The 1991
Reform School Girls 1986
Regarding Henry 1991
Regeneration 1999
Reign of Fire 2003
Reindeer Games 2001
Reine Margot, La. *See* Queen Margot.
Rejuvenator, The 1988
Relax, It's Just Sex 2000
Relentless 1989
Relic, The 1997
Religion Hour, The. *See* My Mother's Smile.
Remains of the Day, The 1993
Remember the Titans 2001
Remo Williams 1985
Renaissance Man 1995
Rendez-vous 1988
Rendezvous in Paris 1996
Renegades 1989
Rent 2006
Rent-a-Cop 1988
Rent Control 1984
Rented Lips 1988
Repentance 1987
Replacement Killers, The 1999
Replacements, The 2001
Repo Man 1984
Repossessed 1990
Requiem for a Dream 2001
Requiem for Dominic 1991
Rescue, The 1988
Rescuers Down Under, The 1990
Reservoir Dogs 1992
Resident Alien: Quentin Crisp in America 1992
Resident Evil 2003
Resident Evil: Apocalypse 2005
Respiro 2004
Ressources Humaines. *See* Human Resources.
Restless Natives 1986
Restoration 1995
Resurrected, The 1995
Retour de Martin Guerre, Le. *See* Return of Martin Guerre, The.
Return, The pg. 327
Return of Horror High 1987
Return of Martin Guerre, The 1983
Return of Superfly, The 1990
Return of the Jedi 1983, 1997
Return of the Living Dead, The 1985
Return of the Living Dead II 1988
Return of the Living Dead III 1993
Return of the Musketeers, The 1989
Return of the Secaucus 7 1982
Return of the Soldier, The 1983
Return of the Swamp Thing, The 1989
Return to Me 2001
Return to Never Land 2003
Return to Oz 1985
Return to Paradise 1999
Return to Snowy River 1988
Return to the Blue Lagoon 1991
Reuben, Reuben 1983
Revenge 1990
Revenge of the Nerds 1984
Revenge of the Nerds II 1987
Revenge of the Ninja 1983
Reversal of Fortune 1990
Revolution 1985
Revolution! 1995
Revolution #9 2004
Rhapsody in August 1991
Rhinestone 1984
Rhyme & Reason 1998
Rhythm Thief 1995
Rich and Famous 1981
Rich Girl 1991
Rich in Love 1993
Rich Man's Wife 1996
Richard III 1995
Richard Pryor Here and Now 1983
Richard's Things 1981
Richie Rich 1995
Ricochet 1991
Riddle of the Sands, The 1984
Ride 1999
Ride in the Whirlwind 1966
Ride to Wounded Knee 1995
Ride with the Devil 2000
Ridicule 1996
Riding Giants 2005
Riding in Cars with Boys 2002
Riding the Edge 1989
Rien ne va plus. *See* Swindle, The.
Riff-Raff 1993
Right Hand Man, The 1987
Right Stuff, The 1983
Rikky and Pete 1988
Rimini Rimini 1987
Ring, The 2003
Ring Two, The 2006
Ringer, The 2006
Ringmaster 1999
Riot in Cell Block 11 [1954] 1982
Ripe 1997
Ripoux, Les. *See* My New Partner.
Rising Sun 1993
Risk 1995
Risky Business 1983
Rita, Sue and Bob Too 1987
River, The (Rydell) 1984
River, The (Tsai) 2002
River of Death 1993
River Rat, The 1984
River Runs Through It, A 1992
River Wild, The 1995
Riverbend 1989
River's Edge 1987
Road Home, The 2002
Road House 1989
Road to El Dorado, The 2001
Road to Perdition 2003
Road to Wellville, The 1995
Road Trip 2001
Road Warrior, The 1982
Roadside Prophets 1992
Rob Roy 1995
Robert A. Heinlein's The Puppet Masters. *See* Puppet Masters, The.
Robin Hood 1991
Robin Hood: Men In Tights 1993

Robocop 1987
Robocop II 1990
Robocop III 1993
Robot Jox 1990
Robot Stories 2005
Robots 2006
Rock, The 1996
Rock-a-Doodle 1992
Rock 'n Roll Meller. *See* Hellbent.
Rock Hudson's Home Movies 1995
Rock School 2006
Rock Star 2002
Rock the Boat 2000
Rocket Gibraltar 1988
Rocket Man 1997
Rocketeer, The 1991
Rocky III 1982
Rocky IV 1985
Rocky V 1990
Rocky Balboa pg. 328
Roger and Me 1989
Roger Corman's Frankenstein Unbound 1990
Roger Dodger 2003
Roi Danse, Le. *See* King Is Dancing, The.
Rois et reine. *See* Kings and Queen.
Rok spokojnego slonca. *See* Year of the Quiet Sun, A.
Roll Bounce 2006
Rollerball 2003
Rollercoaster 2001
Rolling Stones at the Max 1991
Roman Holiday [1953] 1989
Romance 2000
Romance of Book and Sword, The 1987
Romancing the Stone 1984
Romantic Comedy 1983
Romeo 1989
Romeo and Julia 1992
Romeo is Bleeding 1995
Romeo Must Die 2001
Romper Stomper 1993
Romuald et Juliette. *See* Mama, There's a Man in Your Bed.
Romy & Michelle's High School Reunion 1997
Ronin 1999
Rooftops 1989
Rookie, The 1990
Rookie, The 2003
Rookie of the Year 1993
Room with a View, A 1986
Roommates 1995
Rory O'Shea Was Here 2006
Rosa Luxemburg 1987
Rosalie Goes Shopping 1990
Rosary Murders, The 1987
Rose Garden, The 1989
Rosencrantz and Guildenstern Are Dead 1991
Rosewood 1997
Rosie 2000
Rouge of the North 1988
Rough Cut 1982
Rough Magic
Roughly Speaking [1945] 1982
'Round Midnight 1986
Rounders 1999
Rover Dangerfield 1991
Row of Crows, A. *See* Climate for Killing, A.
Roxanne 1987
Roy Rogers: King of the Cowboys 1995
Royal Tenenbaums, The 2002
Royal Wedding [1951] 1985
Rubin and Ed 1992
Ruby 1992
Ruby in Paradise 1993
Rude Awakening 1989
Rudy 1993
Rudyard Kipling's the Second Jungle Book 1997
Rugrats Go Wild! 2004
Rugrats in Paris: The Movie 2001
Rugrats Movie, The 1999
Rules of Attraction, The 2003
Rules of Engagement 2001
Rumba, La. *See* Rumba, The.
Rumba, The 1987
Rumble Fish 1983
Rumble in the Bronx 1996
Rumor Has It... 2006
Rumpelstiltskin 1987
Run 1991
Run Lola Run 2000
Run of the Country, The 1995
Runaway Bride 2000
Runaway Jury 2004
Runaway Train 1985
Rundown, The 2004
Runestone, The 1992
Running Brave 1983
Running Free 2001
Running Hot 1984
Running Man, The 1987
Running on Empty 1988
Running Scared 1986
Running Scared pg. 330
Running with Scissors pg. 331
Rupert's Land 2001
Rush 1991
Rush Hour 1999
Rush Hour 2 2002
Rushmore 1999
Russia House, The 1990
Russian Dolls pg. 334
Russia's Wonder Children 2001
Russkies 1987
Russlands Wunderkinder. *See* Russia's Wonder Children.
Rustler's Rhapsody 1985
Rustling of Leaves, A 1990
Ruthless People 1986
RV pg. 335
Ryan's Daughter [1970] 1990

S

S.F.W. 1995
Sabrina [1954] 1986
Sabrina 1995
Sacrifice, The 1986
Saddest Music in the World, The 2005
Sade 2004
Safe 1995

Safe Conduct 2003
Safe Journey. *See* Latcho Drom.
Safe Passage 1995
Safety of Objects, The 2003
Sahara 2006
Sahara (McLaglen) 1984
St. Elmo's Fire 1985
Saint, The 1997
Saint Clara 1997
Saint of Fort Washington, The 1993
Saison des Hommes, La. *See* Season of Men, The.
Salaam Bombay! 1988
Salmer fra Kjokkenet. *See* Kitchen Stories.
Salmonberries 1995
Salome's Last Dance 1988
Salsa 1988
Salt of the Earth [1954] 1986
Salt on Our Skin. *See* Desire.
Salton Sea, The 2003
Saltwater 2002
Salvador 1986
Sam and Sarah 1991
Samantha 1995
Sam's Son 1984
Samba Traore 1995
Same Old Song 2000
Sammy and Rosie Get Laid 1987
Sandlot, The 1993
Sandwich Years, The 1988
Sang for Martin, En. *See* Song for Martin, A.
Sans toit ni loi. *See* Vagabond.
Santa Claus 1985
Santa Clause, The 1995
Santa Clause 2, The 2003
Santa Clause 3: The Escape Clause, The pg. 339
Santa Fe 1988
Santa Sangre 1990
Sara 1995
Saraband 2006
Sarafina! 1992
Satan 1995
Satisfaction 1988
Saturday Night at the Palace 1987
Saturday Night, Sunday Morning: The Travels of Gatemouth Moore 1995
Sauve qui peut (La Vie). *See* Every Man for Himself.
Savage Beach 1989
Savage Island 1985
Savage Nights 1995
Savannah Smiles 1983
Save the Last Dance 2002
Save the Tiger [1973] 1988
Saved! 2005
Saving Grace (Young) 1986
Saving Grace (Cole) 2001
Saving Private Ryan 1999
Saving Silverman 2002
Savior 1999
Saw 2005
Saw III pg. 340
Saw II 2006
Say Anything 1989
Say It Isn't So 2002
Say Yes 1986
Scandal 1989
Scandalous 1984
Scanner Darkly, A pg. 342
Scanners III: The Takeover 1995
Scarface 1983
Scarlet Letter, The [1926] 1982, 1984
Scarlet Letter, The 1995
Scarlet Street [1946] 1982
Scary Movie 2001
Scary Movie 2 2002
Scary Movie 3 2004
Scary Movie 4 pg. 344
Scavengers 1988
Scenes from a Mall 1991
Scenes from the Class Struggle in Beverly Hills 1989
Scent of a Woman 1992
Scent of Green Papaya, The (Mui du du Xanh) 1995
Scherzo del destino agguato dietro l'angelo come un brigante di strada. *See* Joke of Destiny, A.
Schindler's List 1993
Schizo 2006
Schizopolis 1997
School Daze 1988
School for Scoundrels pg. 345
School of Flesh, 432
School of Rock 2004
School Spirit 1985
School Ties 1992
Schtonk 1995
Schultze Gets the Blues 2006
Science des reves, La. *See* Science of Sleep, The.
Science of Sleep, The pg. 347
Scissors 1991
Scooby-Doo 2003
Scooby-Doo 2: Monsters Unleashed 2005
Scoop pg. 349
Scorchers 1995
Score, The 2002
Scorpion 1986
Scorpion King, The 2003
Scorta, La 1995
Scotland, PA 2003
Scout, The 1995
Scream 1996
Scream 2 1997
Scream 3 2001
Scream of Stone 1995
Screamers 1996
Screwed 2001
Scrooged 1988
Sea Inside, The 2005
Sea of Love 1989
Sea Wolves, The 1982
Seabiscuit 2004
Search and Destroy 1995
Search for Signs of Intelligent Life in the Universe, The 1991
Searching for Bobby Fischer 1993
Season of Dreams 1987
Season of Fear 1989
Season of Men, The 2003
Seasons 1995
Second Best 1995
Second Chance, The pg. 351

Second Sight 1989
Second Skin 2003
Second Thoughts 1983
Secondhand Lions 2004
Secret Admirer 1985
Secret Garden, The 1993
Secret Life of Walter Mitty, The [1947] 1985
Secret Lives of Dentists, The 2004
Secret Love, Hidden Faces. *See* Ju Dou.
Secret of My Success, The 1987
Secret of NIMH, The 1982
Secret of Roan Inish, The 1995
Secret of the Sword, The 1985
Secret Places 1985
Secret Policeman's Third Ball, The 1987
Secret Window 2005
Secretary 2003
Secrets 1984
Secrets & Lies 1996
Seduction, The 1982
See No Evil pg. 352
See No Evil, Hear No Evil 1989
See Spot Run 2002
See You in the Morning 1989
Seed of Chucky 2005
Seeing Other People 2005
Segunda Piel. *See* Second Skin.
Selena 1998
Self Made Hero, A 1998
S'en Fout la Mort. *See* No Fear, No Die.
Sender, The 1982
Sensations 1988
Sense and Sensibility 1995
Sense of Freedom, A 1985
Senseless 1999
Sentimental Destiny 2002
Sentinel, The pg. 353
Separate Lies 2006
Separate Vacations 1986
Seppan 1988
September 1987
Serendipity 2002
Serenity 2006
Sgt. Bilko 1996
Serial Mom 1995
Series 7: The Contenders 2002
Serpent and the Rainbow, The 1988
Servants of Twilight, The 1995
Serving Sara 2003
Sesame Street Presents: Follow That Bird 1985
Session 9 2002
Set It Off 1996
Set Me Free 2001
Seto uchi shonen yakyudan. *See* MacArthur's Children.
Seunlau Ngaklau. *See* Time and Tide.
Seven 1995
Seven Hours to Judgement 1988
Seven Men from Now [1956] 1987
Seven Minutes in Heaven 1986
Seven Women, Seven Sins 1987
Seven Year Itch, The [1955] 1986
Seven Years in Tibet 1998
Seventh Coin, The 1993
Seventh Sign, The 1988
Severance 1989
Sex and Lucia 2003
Sex, Drugs, and Democracy 1995
Sex, Drugs, Rock and Roll 1991
sex, lies and videotape 1989
Sex: The Annabel Chong Story 2001
Sexbomb 1989
Sexy Beast 2002
Shades of Doubt 1995
Shadey 1987
Shadow, The 1995
Shadow Army, The. *See* Army of Shadows.
Shadow Conspiracy, The
Shadow Dancing 1988
Shadow Magic 2002
Shadow of the Raven 1990
Shadow of the Vampire 2001
Shadow of the Wolf 1993
Shadowboxer pg. 355
Shadowlands 1993
Shadows and Fog 1992
Shadrach 1999
Shaft 2001
Shag 1988
Shaggy Dog, The pg. 357
Shakedown 1988
Shakes the Clown 1992
Shakespeare in Love 1999
Shaking the Tree 1992
Shall We Dance? 1997
Shall We Dance? 2005
Shallow Grave 1995
Shallow Hal 2002
Shame 1988
Shanghai Knights 2004
Shanghai Noon 2001
Shanghai Surprise 1986
Shanghai Triad 1995
Shaolin Soccer 2005
Shape of Things, The 2004
Shark Tale 2005
Sharky's Machine 1981
Sharma and Beyond 1986
Shatterbrain. *See* Resurrected, The.
Shattered 1991
Shattered Glass 2004
Shaun of the Dead 2005
Shaunglong Hui. *See* Twin Dragons.
Shawshank Redemption, The 1995
She Hate Me 2005
She Must Be Seeing Things 1987
Sherrybaby pg. 358
She-Devil 1989
Sheena 1984
Sheer Madness 1985
Shelf Life 1995
Sheltering Sky, The 1990
Sherlock Holmes [1922] 1982
Sherman's March 1986
She's All That 2000
She's De Lovely. *See* De-Lovely.
She's Gotta Have It 1986
She's Having a Baby 1988
She's Out of Control 1989
She's So Lovely 1997
She's the Man pg. 360

She's the One 1996

Shiloh 2: Shiloh Season 2000

Shimian Maifu. *See* House of Flying Daggers.

Shine 1996

Shining, The [1980]

Shining Through 1992

Shipping News, The 2002

Shipwrecked 1991

Shiqisuide Danche. *See* Beijing Bicycle.

Shirley Valentine 1989

Shiza. *See* Shizo.

Shoah 1985

Shock to the System, A 1990

Shocker 1989

Shoot the Moon 1982

Shoot to Kill 1988

Shooting, The [1966] 1995

Shooting Fish 1999

Shooting Party, The 1985

Shootist, The [1976] 1982

Shopgirl 2006

Short Circuit 1986

Short Circuit II 1988

Short Cuts 1993

Short Film About Love, A 1995

Short Time 1990

Shot, The 1996

Shout 1991

Show, The 1995

Show Me Love 2000

Show of Force, A 1990

Showdown in Little Tokyo 1991

Shower, The 2001

Showgirls 1995

Showtime 2003

Shrek 2002

Shrek 2 2005

Shrimp on the Barbie, The 1990

Shvitz, The. *See* New York in Short: The Shvitz and Let's Fall in Love.

Shy People 1987

Siberiade 1982

Sibling Rivalry 1990

Sicilian, The 1987

Sick: The Life and Death of Bob Flanagan, Supermasochist 1997

Sid and Nancy 1986

Side Out 1990

Sidekicks 1993

Sidewalk Stories 1989

Sidewalks of New York, The 2002

Sideways 2005

Siege, The 1999

Siesta 1987

Sign o' the Times 1987

Sign of the Cross, The [1932] 1984

Signal Seven 1986

Signs 2003

Signs & Wonders 2002

Signs of Life 1989

Silence, The 2001

Silence After the Shot, The. *See* Legend of Rita, The.

Silence at Bethany, The 1988

Silence of the Lambs, The 1991

Silencer, The 1995

Silent Fall 1995

Silent Hill pg. 361

Silent Madness, The 1984

Silent Night 1988

Silent Night, Deadly Night 1984

Silent Night, Deadly Night II 1987

Silent Night, Deadly Night III 1989

Silent Rage 1982

Silent Tongue 1995

Silent Touch, The 1995

Silent Victim 1995

Silk Road, The 1992

Silkwood 1983

Silver City (Sayles) 2005

Silver City (Turkiewicz) 1985

Silverado 1985

Simon Birch 1999

Simon Magnus 2002

Simon the Magician 2001

Simone 2003

Simpatico 2000

Simple Men 1992

Simple Plan, A 1999

Simple Twist of Fate, A 1995

Simple Wish, A 1997

Simply Irresistible 2000

Sin City 2006

Sin Noticias de Dios. *See* No News from God.

Sinbad: Legend of the Seven Seas 2004

Since Otar Left 2005

Sincerely Charlotte 1986

Sinful Life, A 1989

Sing 1989

Singin' in the Rain [1952] 1985

Singing Detective, The 2004

Singing the Blues in Red 1988

Single White Female 1992

Singles 1992

Sioux City 1995

Sirens 1995

Sister Act 1992

Sister Act II 1993

Sister, My Sister 1995

Sister, Sister 1987

Sisterhood of the Traveling Pants, The 2006

Sisters. *See* Some Girls.

Sitcom 2000

Siu lam juk kau. *See* Shaolin Soccer.

Siulam Chukkau. *See* Shaolin Soccer.

Six Days, Seven Nights 1999

Six Days, Six Nights 1995

Six Degrees of Separation 1993

Six Pack 1982

Six-String Samurai 1999

Six Ways to Sunday 2000

Six Weeks 1982

16 Blocks pg. 363

Sixteen Candles 1984

Sixteen Days of Glory 1986

Sixth Day, The 2001

Sixth Man, The 1997

Sixth Sense, The 2000

Sixty Glorious Years [1938] 1983

'68 1987

Skeleton Key, The 2006

Ski Country 1984

Ski Patrol 1990
Skin Deep 1989
Skins 2003
Skipped Parts 2002
Skulls, The 2001
Sky Bandits 1986
Sky Blue 2006
Sky Captain and the World of Tomorrow 2005
Sky High 2006
Sky of Our Childhood, The 1988
Skyline 1984
Slacker 1991
Slackers 2003
Slam 1997
Slam Dance 1987
Slap Shot [1977] 1981
Slapstick 1984
Slate, Wyn, and Me 1987
Slave Coast. *See* Cobra Verde.
Slave Girls from Beyond Infinity 1987
Slaves of New York 1989
Slaves to the Underground 1997
Slayground 1984
SLC Punk 2000
Sleazy Uncle, The 1991
Sleep With Me 1995
Sleepers 1996
Sleeping with the Enemy 1991
Sleepless in Seattle 1993
Sleepover 2005
Sleepwalkers. *See* Stephen King's Sleepwalkers.
Sleepy Hollow 2000
Sleepy Time Gal, The 2002
Sliding Doors 1999
Sling Blade 1996
Slingshot, The 1995
Slipping Down Life, A 2005
Slither pg. 365
Sliver 1993
Slugs 1988
Slums of Beverly Hills 1999
Small Faces 1996
Small Soldiers 1999
Small Time Crooks 2001
Small Wonders 1996
Smash Palace 1982
Smell of Camphor, Fragrance of Jasmine 2001
Smile Like Yours, A 1997
Smiling Fish and Goat on Fire 2001
Smilla's Sense of Snow 1997
Smithereens 1982, 1985
Smoke 1995
Smoke Signals 1999
Smokey and the Bandit, Part 3 1983
Smoking/No Smoking [1995] 2001
Smooth Talk 1985
Smurfs and the Magic Flute, The 1983
Snake Eyes 1999
Snake Eyes. *See* Dangerous Game.
Snakes on a Plane pg. 366
Snapper, The 1993
Snatch 2002
Sneakers 1992
Sniper 1993
Snow Day 2001
Snow Dogs 2003
Snow Falling in Cedars 2000
Snows of Kilimanjaro, The [1952] 1982
S.O.B. 1981
So I Married an Axe Murderer 1993
Soapdish 1991
Sobibor, October 14, 1943, 4 p.m. 2002
Society 1992
Sofie 1993
Soft Fruit 2001
Soft Shell Man 2003
Softly Softly 1985
Sokhout. *See* Silence, The.
Sol del Membrillo, El. *See* Dream of Light.
Solarbabies 1986
Solaris 2003
Solas 2001
Soldier 1999
Soldier, The 1982
Soldier's Daughter Never Cries, A 1999
Soldier's Story, A 1984
Soldier's Tale, A 1988
Solid Gold Cadillac, The [1956] 1984
Solo 1996
Solomon and Gaenor 2001
Some Girls 1988
Some Kind of Hero 1982
Some Kind of Wonderful 1987
Some Like It Hot [1959] 1986, 1988
Some Mother's Son 1996
Someone Else's America 1996
Someone Like You 2002
Someone to Love 1987, 1988
Someone to Watch Over Me 1987
Somersault pg. 367
Something New pg. 369
Something to Do with the Wall 1995
Something to Talk About 1995
Something Wicked This Way Comes 1983
Something Wild 1986
Something Within Me 1995
Something's Gotta Give 2004
Sommersby 1993
Son, The 2003
Son of Darkness: To Die For II 1995
Son of the Bride 2003
Son of the Mask 2006
Son of the Pink Panther 1993
Son-in-Law 1993
Sonatine 1999
Song for Martin 2003
Songcatcher 2001
Songwriter 1984
Sonny 2003
Sonny Boy 1990
Sons 1989
Sons of Steel 1988
Son's Room, The 2002
Sontagsbarn. *See* Sunday's Children.
Sophie's Choice 1982
Sorority Babes in the Slimeball Bowl-o-Rama 1988

Sorority Boys 2003
Sorority House Massacre 1987
Sotto Sotto. *See* Softly Softly.
Soul Food 1997
Soul Man 1986
Soul Plane 2005
Soul Survivors 2002
Sound Barrier, The [1952] 1984, 1990
Sound of Thunder, A 2006
Sour Grapes 1999
Source, The 2000
Soursweet 1988
Sous le Sable. *See* Under the Sand.
Sous le Soleil de Satan. *See* Under the Sun of Satan.
Sous Sol 1997
South Central 1992
South of Reno 1987
South Park: Bigger, Longer & Uncut 2000
Southern Comfort 1981
Souvenir 1988
Space Cowboys 2001
Space Jam 1996
Spaceballs 1987
Spacecamp 1986
Spaced Invaders 1990
Spacehunter: Adventures in the Forbidden Zone 1983
Spalding Gray's Monster in a Box. *See* Monster in a Box.
Spanglish 2005
Spanish Prisoner, The 1999
Spanking the Monkey 1995
Spartacus [1960] 1991
Spartan 2005
Spawn 1997
Speaking in Strings 2000
Speaking Parts 1990
Special Day, A 1984
Special Effects 1986
Specialist, The 1995
Species 1995
Species 2 1999
Specter of the Rose [1946] 1982
Speechless 1995
Speed 1995
Speed 2: Cruise Control 1997
Speed Zone 1989
Spellbinder 1988
Spellbound [1945] 1989
Sphere 1999
Spice World 1999
Spices 1989
Spider 2004
Spider-Man 2003
Spider-Man 2 2005
Spies like Us 1985
Spike of Bensonhurst 1988
Spirit of '76, The 1991
Spirit of St. Louis, The [1957] 1986
Spirit: Stallion of the Cimarron 2003
Spirited Away 2004
Spitfire Grill, The 1996
Splash 1984
Splendor 2000
Split 1991
Split Decisions 1988
Split Image 1982
Split Second 1992
Splitting Heirs 1993
Sponge Bob Square Pants Movie, The 2005
Spoorloos. *See* Vanishing, The.
Spring Break 1983
Spring Forward [2000] 2001
Spring, Summer, Autumn, Winter...And Spring 2005
Spring Symphony 1986
Sprung 1997
Spun 2004
Spy Game 2002
Spy Hard 1996
Spy Kids 2002
Spy Kids 2: The Island of Lost Dreams 2003
Spy Kids 3-D: Game Over 2004
Squanto: A Warrior's Tale 1995
Square Dance 1987
Squeeze 1997
Squeeze, The 1987
Squid and the Whale, The 2006
Stacking. *See* Season of Dreams.
Stage Beauty 2005
Stakeout 1987
Stakeout II. *See* Another Stakeout.
Stalag 17 [1953] 1986
Stand and Deliver 1988
Stand by Me 1986
Stander 2005
Standing in the Shadows of Motown 2003
Stanley and Iris 1990
Stanley Kubrick: A Life in Pictures 2002
Stanno tutti bene. *See* Everybody's Fine.
Stanza de Figlio, La. *See* Son's Room, The.
Star Chamber, The 1983
Star 80 1983
Star Is Born, A [1954] 1983, 1985
Star Kid 1999
Star Maker, The 1996
Star Maps 1997
Star Trek II: The Wrath of Khan 1982
Star Trek III: The Search for Spock 1984
Star Trek IV:The Voyage Home 1986
Star Trek V: The Final Frontier 1989
Star Trek VI: The Undiscovered Country 1991
Star Trek: First Contact 1996
Star Trek: Generations 1995
Star Trek: Insurrection 1999
Star Trek: Nemesis 2003
Star Trek: The Motion Picture [1979] 1986
Star Wars: Episode I—The Phantom Menace 2000
Star Wars: Episode II—Attack of the Clones 2003
Star Wars: Episode III—Revenge of the Sith 2006
Star Wars: Episode IV—A New Hope [1977] 1997
Starchaser 1985
Stardom 2001

Stardust Memories [1980] 1984
Stargate 1995
Starman 1984
Stars and Bars 1988
Stars Fell on Henrietta, The 1995
Starship Troopers 1997
Starsky & Hutch 2005
Starstruck 1982
Startup.com 2002
State and Main 2001
State of Grace 1990
State of Things, The 1983
Statement, The 2004
Stateside 2005
Station, The 1992
Station Agent, The 2004
Stay 2006
Stay Alive pg. 371
Stay Tuned 1992
Staying Alive 1983
Staying Together 1989
Steal America 1992
Steal Big, Steal Little 1995
Stealing Beauty 1996
Stealing Harvard 2003
Stealing Heaven 1988
Stealing Home 1988
Stealth 2006
Steamboy 2006
Steaming 1986
Steel 1997
Steel Magnolias 1989
Steele Justice 1987
Stella 1990
Stella Dallas [1937] 1987
Step Into Liquid 2004
Step Up pg. 372
Stepfather, The 1987
Stepfather II 1989
Stepford Wives, The 2005
Stephen King's Cat's Eye 1985
Stephen King's Children of the Corn 1984
Stephen King's Graveyard Shift 1990
Stephen King's Silver Bullet 1985
Stephen King's Sleepwalkers 1992
Stephen King's The Night Flier 1999
Stephen King's Thinner 1996
Stepmom 1999
Stepping Out 1991
Stick 1985
Stick, The 1988
Stick It pg. 373
Sticky Fingers 1988
Stigmata 2000
Still Crazy 1999
Still of the Night 1982
Stille Nach Dem Schuss, Die. *See* Legend of Rita, The.
Sting II, The 1983
Stir Crazy [1980] 1992
Stir of Echoes 2000
Stitches 1985
Stolen Life, A [1946] 1986
Stolen Summer 2003
Stone Boy, The 1984
Stone Cold 1991
Stone Reader 2004
Stonewall 1996
Stop Making Sense 1984
Stop! Or My Mom Will Shoot 1992
Stories from the Kronen 1995
Stormy Monday 1988
Story of Qiu Ju, The 1993
Story of the Weeping Camel, The 2005
Story of Us, The 2000
Story of Women 1989
Story of Xinghau, The 1995
Storytelling 2003
Storyville 1992
Straight for the Heart 1990
Straight Out of Brooklyn 1991
Straight Story, The 2000
Straight Talk 1992
Straight to Hell 1987
Strange Brew 1983
Strange Days 1995
Strange Invaders 1983
Strange Love of Martha Ivers, The [1946] 1991
Stranger, The 1987
Stranger Among Us, A 1992
Stranger Is Watching, A 1982
Stranger Than Fiction pg. 375
Stranger than Paradise 1984, 1986
Stranger's Kiss 1984
Strangers in Good Company 1991
Strangers with Candy pg. 377
Strapless 1990
Strawberry and Chocolate 1995
Strayed 2005
Streamers 1983
Street Fighter 1995
Street Smart 1987
Street Story 1989
Street Trash 1987
Street Wars 1995
Streets 1990
Streets of Fire 1984
Streets of Gold 1986
Streetwalkin' 1985
Streetwise 1985
Strictly Ballroom 1993
Strictly Business 1991
Strictly Propaganda 1995
Strike It Rich 1990
Striking Distance 1993
Strip Jack Naked (Nighthawks II) 1995
Stripes 1981
Stripped to Kill 1987
Stripped to Kill 2 1989
Stripper 1986
Striptease 1996
Stroker Ace 1983
Stryker 1983
Stuart Little 2000
Stuart Little 2 2003
Stuart Saves His Family 1995
Stuck On You 2004
Student Confidential 1987
Stuff, The 1985
Stupids, The 1996
Substance of Fire, The 1996
Substitute, The 1996

Suburbans, The 2000
Suburban Commando 1991
Suburbia 1984
subUrbia 1997
Subway 1985
Subway to the Stars 1988
Such a Long Journey 2001
Sudden Death 1985
Sudden Death 1995
Sudden Impact 1983
Sudden Manhattan 1997
Suddenly, Last Summer [1959] 1993
Suddenly Naked 2002
Sugar & Spice 2002
Sugar Cane Alley 1984
Sugar Hill 1995
Sugar Town 2000
Sugarbaby 1985
Suicide Kings 1999
Suitors, The 1989
Sullivan's Pavilion 1987
Sum of All Fears, The 2003
Sum of Us, The 1995
Summer 1986
Summer Camp Nightmare 1987
Summer Catch 2002
Summer Heat 1987
Summer House, The 1993
Summer Lovers 1982
Summer Night with Greek Profile, Almond Eyes, and Scent of Basil 1987
Summer of Sam 2000
Summer Rental 1985
Summer School 1987
Summer Stock [1950] 1985
Summer Story, A 1988
Summertime [1955] 1990
Sunchaser 1996
Sunday 1997
Sunday in the Country, A 1984
Sunday's Child 1989
Sunday's Children 1995
Sunset 1988
Sunset Boulevard [1950] 1986
Sunset Park 1996
Sunshine 2001
Sunshine State 2003
Super, The 1991
Super Mario Bros. 1993
Super Size Me 2005
Supercop 1997
Superfantagenio. *See* Aladdin.
Supergirl 1984
Superman II 1981
Superman III 1983
Superman IV 1987
Superman Returns pg. 379
Supernova 2001
Superstar 1991
Superstar 2000
Sur 1988
Sur Mes Levres. *See* Read My Lips.
Sure Fire 1993
Sure Thing, The 1985
Surf II 1984
Surf Nazis Must Die 1987
Surf Ninjas 1993
Surrender 1987
Survival Quest 1990
Surviving Christmas 2005
Surviving the Game 1995
Surviving Picasso 1996
Survivors, The 1983
Suspect 1987
Suspect Zero 2005
Suspended Animation 2004
Suspicious River 2002
Suture 1995
Swamp, The. *See* Cienaga, La.
Swamp Thing 1982
Swan Lake 1991
Swan Princess, The 1995
Swann in Love 1984
S.W.A.T. 2004
Sweet and Lowdown 2000
Sweet Country 1987
Sweet Dreams 1985
Sweet Emma, Dear Bobe: Sketches, Nudes 1995
Sweet Hearts Dance 1988
Sweet Hereafter, The 1997
Sweet Home Alabama 2003
Sweet Liberty 1986
Sweet Lorraine 1987
Sweet Nothing 1996
Sweet November 2002
Sweet Revenge 1987
Sweet Sixteen 1984
Sweet Sixteen 2004
Sweet Talker 1991
Sweetest Thing, The 2003
Sweetie 1990
Sweetwater 1988
Swept Away 2003
Swept from the Sea 1999
Swimfan 2003
Swimming Pool 2004
Swimming to Cambodia 1987
Swimming Upstream 2006
Swimming With Sharks 1995
Swindle, The 2000
Swing Kids 1993
Swing Shift 1984
Swingers 1996
Switch 1991
Switchback 1997
Switching Channels 1988
Swoon 1992
Sword and the Sorcerer, The 1982
Swordfish 2002
Swordsman III. *See* East is Red, The.
Sylvester V 1987
Sylvia 1985
Sylvia 2004
Syriana 2006

T

Table for Five 1983
Taboo 2001
Tacones lejanos. *See* High Heels.
Tadpole 2003
Tadpole and the Whale 1988
Tag 1982
Tai-pan 1986

Tailor of Panama, The 2002
Take a Letter, Darling [1942] 1984
Take the Lead pg. 383
Take Two 1988
Taking Care of Business 1990
Taking Lives 2005
Taking of Beverly Hills, The 1991
Taking Off [1971] 1985
Taking Sides 2004
Tale of Ruby Rose, The 1987
Tale of Springtime, A 1992
Tale of Winter, A 1995
Talented Mr. Ripley, The 2000
Tales from the Crypt: Bordello of Blood 1996
Tales from the Crypt Presents Demon Knight 1995
Tales from the Darkside 1990
Tales from the Hood 1995
Tales of Ordinary Madness 1983
Talk 1995
Talk of Angels 1999
Talk Radio 1988
Talk to Her 2003
Talkin' Dirty After Dark 1991
Tall Guy, The 1990
Tall Tale: The Unbelievable Adventures of Pecos Bill 1995
Talladega Nights: The Ballad of Ricky Bobby pg. 384
Talons of the Eagle 1995
Talvisota 1989
Taming of the Shrew, The [1967] 1993
Tampopo 1987
Tango and Cash 1989
Tango Bar 1988, 1989
Tango Lesson, The 1998
Tank 1984
Tank Girl 1995
Tao of Steve, The 2001
Tap 1989
Tape 2002
Tapeheads 1988
Taps 1981
Target 1985
Target 1996
Tarnation 2005
Tarzan 2000
Tarzan and the Lost City 1999
Tasogare Seibei. *See* Twilight Samurai, The.
Taste of Others, The 2002
Tatie Danielle 1991
Taxi 2005
Taxi Blues 1991
Taxi nach Kairo. *See* Taxi to Cairo.
Taxi to Cairo 1988
Taxi to the Toilet. *See* Taxi Zum Klo.
Taxi Zum Klo 1981
Taxing Woman, A 1988
Taxing Woman's Return, A 1989
Tea in the Harem 1986
Tea With Mussolini 2000
Teachers 1984
Teacher's Pet: The Movie. *See* Disney's Teacher's Pet.
Teaching Mrs. Tingle 2000
Team America: World Police 2005
Tears of the Sun 2004
Ted and Venus 1991
Teen Witch 1989
Teen Wolf 1985
Teenage Mutant Ninja Turtles 1990
Teenage Mutant Ninja Turtles II 1991
Teenage Mutant Ninja Turtles III 1993
Telephone, The 1988
Telling Lies in America 1997
Temp, The 1993
Tempest 1982
Temporada de patos. *See* Duck Season.
Temps qui changent, Les. *See* Changing Times.
Temps qui reste, Les. *See* Time to Leave.
Temps Retrouve. *See* Time Regained.
Temptress Moon 1997
Ten 2004
Ten Things I Hate About You 2000
10 to Midnight 1983
Tenacious D in the Pick of Destiny pg. 386
Tender Mercies 1983
Tenebrae. *See* Unsane.
Tenue de soiree. *See* Menage.
Tequila Sunrise 1988
Terminal, The 2005
Terminal Bliss 1992
Terminal Velocity 1995
Terminator, The 1984
Terminator 2 1991
Terminator 3: Rise of the Machines 2004
Termini Station 1991
Terminus. *See* End of the Line.
Terms of Endearment 1983
Terror Within, The 1989
Terrorvision 1986
Tess 1981
Test of Love 1985
Testament 1983
Testimony 1987
Tetsuo: The Iron Man 1992
Tex 1982, 1987
Texas Chainsaw Massacre, The (Nispel) 2004
Texas Chainsaw Massacre, Part II, The 1986
Texas Chainsaw Massacre: The Beginning, The pg. 387
Texas Comedy Massacre, The 1988
Texas Rangers 2003
Texas Tenor: The Illinois Jacquet Story 1995
Texasville 1990
Thank You and Good Night 1992
Thank You for Smoking pg. 389
That Championship Season 1982
That Darn Cat 1997
That Night 1993
That Old Feeling 1997
That Sinking Feeling 1984
That Thing You Do! 1996
That Was Then...This Is Now 1985
That's Entertainment! III 1995
That's Life! 1986, 1988

The au harem d'Archi Ahmed, Le. *See* Tea in the Harem.

Thelma and Louise 1991

Thelonious Monk 1988

Theory of Flight, The 1999

There Goes My Baby 1995

There Goes the Neighborhood 1995

There's Nothing Out There 1992

There's Something About Mary 1999

Theremin: An Electronic Odyssey 1995

They All Laughed 1981

They Call Me Bruce 1982

They Drive by Night [1940] 1982

They Live 1988

They Live by Night [1949] 1981

They Might Be Giants [1971] 1982

They Still Call Me Bruce 1987

They Won't Believe Me [1947] 1987

They're Playing with Fire 1984

Thiassos, O. *See* Traveling Players, The.

Thief 1981

Thief, The 1999

Thief of Hearts 1984

Thieves 1996

Thin Blue Line, The 1988

Thin Line Between Love and Hate, A 1996

Thin Red Line, The 1999

Thing, The 1982

Thing Called Love, The 1995

Things Are Tough All Over 1982

Things Change 1988

Things to Do in Denver When You're Dead 1995

Think Big 1990

Third World Cop 2001

Thirteen 2004

Thirteen Conversations About One Thing 2003

Thirteen Days 2001

Thirteen Ghosts 2003

13 Going On 30 2005

Thirtieth Floor, The 2000

Thirtieth Warrior, The 2000

Thirty Two Short Films About Glenn Gould 1995

Thirty-five Up 1992

37, 2 le Matin. *See* Betty Blue.

Thirty-six Fillette 1988

This Boy's Life 1993

This Is Elvis 1981

This is My Father 2000

This is My Life 1992

This Is Spinal Tap 1984

This World, Then the Fireworks 1997

Thomas and the Magic Railroad 2001

Thomas Crown Affair, The 2000

Thomas in Love 2002

Those Who Love Me Can Take the Train 2000

Thou Shalt Not Kill 1988

Thousand Acres, A 1997

Thousand Pieces of Gold 1991

Thrashin' 1986

Three Amigos 1986

Three Brothers 1982

Three Burials of Melquiades Estrada, The pg. 391

Three...Extremes 2006

3:15 1986

Three for the Road 1987

Three Fugitives 1989

3-Iron 2006

Three Kinds of Heat 1987

Three Kings 2000

Three Lives & Only One Death 1996

Three Madeleines, The 2001

Three Men and a Baby 1987

Three Men and a Cradle 1986

Three Men and a Little Lady 1990

Three Musketeers, The 1993

Three Ninjas Kick Back 1995

Three Ninjas 1992

Three O'Clock High 1987

Three of Hearts 1993

Three Seasons 2000

Three Sisters 1988

3 Strikes 2001

3000 Miles to Graceland 2002

Three to Get Ready 1988

Three to Tango 2000

Three Wishes 1995

Threesome 1995

Threshold 1983

Through the Eyes of the Children. *See* 112th and Central.

Through the Olive Trees 1995

Through the Wire 1990

Through the Window 2001

Throw Momma from the Train 1987

Thumbelina. *See* Hans Christian Andersen's Thumbelina.

Thumbsucker 2006

Thunder Alley 1986

Thunderbirds 2005

Thunderheart 1992

THX 1138 [1971] 1984

Thy Kingdom Come...Thy Will Be Done 1988

Tian di ying xiong. *See* Warriors of Heaven and Earth.

Tian Yu. *See* Xiu Xiu: The Sent Down Girl.

Tideland pg. 392

Tie Me Up! Tie Me Down! 1990

Tie That Binds, The 1995

Tieta of Agreste 2000

Tiger Warsaw 1988

Tigerland 2002

Tiger's Tale, A 1987

Tigger Movie, The 2001

Tightrope 1984

Til' There Was You 1997

Till Human Voices Wake Us 2004

Tillsammans. *See* Together.

Tim Burton's Corpse Bride 2006

Time After Time 1983

Time and Tide 2002

Time Bandits 1981

Time Code 2001

Time for Drunken Horses, A 2001

Time Indefinite 1995

Time Machine, The (Pal) [1960] 1983

Time Machine, The (Wells) 2003
Time of Destiny, A 1988
Time of Favor 2002
Time of the Gypsies 1990
Time Out 2003
Time Regained 2001
Time to Die, A 1991
Time to Kill, A 1996
Time to Leave pg. 394
Time Will Tell 1992
Timebomb 1992
Timecop 1995
Timeline 2004
Timerider 1983
Timothy Leary's Dead 1997
Tin Cup 1996
Tin Men 1987
Titan A.E. 2001
Titanic 1997
Tito and Me 1993
Titus 2000
To Be or Not to Be 1983
To Begin Again. *See* Volver a empezar.
To Die For 1989
To Die For 1995
To Die Standing (Crackdown) 1995
To Gillian on Her 37th Birthday 1996
To Kill a Mockingbird [1962] 1989
To Kill a Priest 1988
To Live 1995
To Live and Die in L.A. 1985, 1986
To Protect Mother Earth 1990
To Render a Life 1995
To Return. *See* Volver.
To Sir with Love [1967] 1992
To Sleep with Anger 1990
To Wong Foo, Thanks for Everything! Julie Newmar 1995
Todo Sobre Mi Madre. *See* All About My Mother.
Together 2002
Together 2004
Tokyo Pop 1988
Tokyo-Ga 1985
Tom and Huck 1995
Tom and Jerry 1993
Tom & Viv 1995
Tomb Raider. *See* Lara Croft: Tomb Raider.
Tomboy 1985
Tombstone 1993
Tomcats 2002
Tommy Boy 1995
Tomorrow [1972] 1983
Tomorrow Never Dies 1997
Tomorrow's a Killer. *See* Prettykill.
Too Beautiful for You 1990
Too Hot to Handle [1938] 1983
Too Much 1987
Too Much Sleep 2002
Too Much Sun 1991
Too Outrageous! 1987
Too Scared to Scream 1985
Too Soon to Love [1960]
Tootsie 1982
Top Dog 1995
Top Gun 1986
Top of the Food Chain 2002
Top Secret 1984
Topio stin omichi. *See* Landscape in the Mist.
Topsy-Turvy 2000
Tora-San Goes to Viena 1989
Torajiro Kamone Uta. *See* Foster Daddy, Tora!
Torch Song Trilogy 1988
Torment 1986
Torn Apart 1990
Torn Curtain [1966] 1984
Torque 2005
Torrents of Spring 1990
Tortilla Soup 2002
Total Eclipse 1995
Total Recall 1990
Totally F***ed Up 1995
Toto le heros. *See* Toto the Hero.
Toto the Hero 1992
Tottering Lives 1988
Touch 1997
Touch and Go 1986
Touch of a Stranger 1990
Touch of Evil [1958] 1999
Touch of Larceny, A [1959] 1986
Touch the Sound 2006
Touching the Void 2005
Tough Enough 1983
Tough Guys 1986
Tough Guys Don't Dance 1987
Tougher than Leather 1988
Touki-Bouki 1995
Tous les matins du monde 1992
Toward the Within 1995
Town and Country 2002
Town is Quiet, The 2002
Toxic Avenger, The 1986
Toxic Avenger, Part II, The 1989
Toxic Avenger, Part III, The 1989
Toy, The 1982
Toy Soldiers (Fisher) 1984
Toy Soldiers (Petrie) 1991
Toy Story 1995
Toy Story 2 2000
Toys 1992
Trace, The 1984
Traces of Red 1992
Track 1988
Tracks in the Snow 1986
Trade Winds [1939] 1982
Trading Hearts 1988
Trading Mom 1995
Trading Places 1983
Traffic 2001
Tragedia di un umo ridiculo. *See* Tragedy of a Ridiculous Man.
Tragedy of a Ridiculous Man 1982
Trail of the Lonesome Pine, The. *See* Waiting for the Moon.
Trail of the Pink Panther 1982
Train de Vie. *See* Train of Life.
Train of Life 2000
Training Day 2002
Trainspotting 1996
Trancers 1985
Transamerica 2006
Transformers, The 1986
Transporter 2 2006

Transylvania 6-5000 1985
Trapped 2003
Trapped in Paradise 1995
Traps 1995
Traveling Players, The [1974] 1990
Traveller 1997
Travelling Avant 1987
Travelling North 1987
Traviata, La 1982
Tre fratelli. *See* Three Brothers.
Treasure Island 2001
Treasure of the Four Crowns 1983
Treasure of the Sierra Madre, The [1948] 1983
Treasure Planet 2003
Trees Lounge 1996
Trekkies 2000
Tremors 1990
Trenchcoat 1983
Trespass 1992
Trial, The 1995
Trial and Error 1997
Trial by Jury 1995
Tribulations of Balthasar Kober, The 1988
Trick 2000
Trick or Treat 1986
Trigger Effect, The 1996
Trilogia: To Livadi pou dakryzei. *See* Weeping Meadow.
Trilogy: After the Life, The 2005
Trilogy: An Amazing Couple, The 2005
Trilogy: On the Run, The 2005
Trilogy: The Weeping Meadow. *See* Weeping Meadow.
Trip to Bountiful, A [1953] 1982
Trip to Bountiful, The 1985
Triplets of Belleville, The 2004
Trippin' 2000
Tristan & Isolde pg. 396
Tristram Shandy: A Cock and Bull Story pg. 398
Triumph of Love, The 2003
Triumph of the Spirit 1989
Trixie 2001
Trmavomodry Svet. *See* Dark Blue World.
Trois Couleurs: Blanc. *See* White.
Trois Couleurs: Bleu. *See* Blue.
Trois Couleurs: Rouge. *See* Red.
Trois Hommes et un couffin. *See* Three Men and a Cradle.
Trojan Eddie 1997
Troll 1986
Trolosa. *See* Faithless.
TRON 1982
Troop Beverly Hills 1989
Trop belle pour toi. *See* Too Beautiful for You.
Tropical Rainforest 1992
Trouble at the Royal Rose. *See* Trouble with Spies, The.
Trouble Bound 1995
Trouble in Mind 1985
Trouble with Dick, The 1987
Trouble with Spies, The 1987
Troubles We've Seen: A History of Journalism in Wartime, The 2006
Troublesome Creek: A Midwestern 1997
Trout, The 1983
Troy 2005
Truce, The 1999
True Believer 1989
True Blood 1989
True Colors 1991
True Confessions 1981
True Crime 2000
True Heart Susie [1919] 1984
True Identity 1991
True Lies 1995
True Love 1989
True Romance 1993
True Stories 1986
Truite, La. *See* Trout, The.
Truly, Madly, Deeply 1991
Truman Show, The 1999
Trumpet of the Swan, The 2002
Trust 1991
Trust Me 1989
Trust the Man pg. 400
Trusting Beatrice 1993
Truth About Cats & Dogs, The 1996
Truth About Charlie, The 2003
Truth or Consequences: N.M., 1997
Truth or Dare 1991
Tsotsi pg. 401
Tuck Everlasting 2003
Tucker 1988
Tuff Turf 1985
Tully 2004
Tumbleweeds 2000
Tune, The 1992
Tune in Tomorrow... 1990
Tunel, El. *See* Tunnel, The.
Tunnel, The 1988
Turandot Project, The 2002
Turbo: A Power Rangers Movie, 1997
Turbulence, 1997
Turistas pg. 404
Turk 182 1985
Turn It Up 2001
Turner and Hooch 1989
Turning Paige 2003
Turtle Beach 1995
Turtle Diary 1985, 1986
Turtles are Back...In Time, The. *See* Teenage Mutant Ninja Turtles III.
Tuxedo, The 2003
Twelfth Night 1996
Twelve Monkeys 1995
Twelve O'Clock High [1949] 1989
Twenty Bucks 1993
20 Dates 2000
25th Hour 2003
24 Hour Party People 2003
24 Hours. *See* Trapped.
21 Grams 2004
TwentyFourSeven 1999
24 Hour Woman 2000
28 Days 2001
28 Days Later 2004
28 Up 1985
2046 2006
Twenty-ninth Street 1991

Twenty-one 1991
Twice Dead 1988
Twice in a Lifetime 1985
Twice upon a Time 1983
Twilight 1999
Twilight of the Cockroaches 1990
Twilight of the Ice Nymphs 1999
Twilight Samurai, The 2005
Twilight Zone: The Movie 1983
Twin Dragons 2000
Twin Falls Idaho 2000
Twin Peaks: Fire Walk with Me 1992
Twin Town 1997
Twins 1988
Twist 1993
Twist and Shout 1986
Twisted 2005
Twisted Justice 1990
Twisted Obsession 1990
Twister 1990
Twister 1996
Two Bits 1995
Two Brothers 2005
Two Can Play That Game 2002
2 Days in the Valley 1996
Two Evil Eyes 1991
Two Family House 2001
2 Fast 2 Furious 2004
Two for the Money 2006
Two Girls and a Guy 1999
200 Cigarettes 2000
Two If By Sea 1996
Two Jakes, The 1990
Two Moon Junction 1988
Two Much 1996
Two Ninas 2002
Two of a Kind 1983
Two Small Bodies 1995
2010 1984
Two Weeks Notice 2003
Twogether 1995
Tycoon 2004

U

U-571 2001
UFOria 1986
Ugly, The 1999
UHF 1989
Ulee's Gold 1997
Ultraviolet pg. 407
Ulysses' Gaze 1995
Un Air de Famille 1999
Unaccompanied Minors pg. 408
Unbearable Lightness of Being, The 1988
Unbelievable Truth, The 1990
Unborn, The 1991
Unbreakable 2001
Uncertainty Principle, The 2003
Uncle Buck 1989
Uncommon Valor 1983
Unconquering the Last Frontier 2002
Undead 2006
Under Cover 1987
Under Fire 1983
Under Hellgate Bridge 2002
Under Siege 1992
Under Siege II: Dark Territory 1995
Under Solen. *See* Under the Sun.
Under Suspicion (Moore) 1992
Under Suspicion (Hopkins) 2001
Under Suspicion. *See* Garde a vue.
Under the Boardwalk 1988
Under the Cherry Moon 1986
Under the City's Skin. *See* Under the Skin of the City.
Under the Donim Tree 1996
Under the Sand 2002
Under the Skin 1999
Under the Skin of the City 2003
Under the Sun 2002
Under the Sun of Satan 1987
Under the Tuscan Sun 2004
Under the Volcano III 1984
Underclassman 2006
Undercover Blues 1993
Undercover Brother 2003
Underground 1999
Underneath, The 1995
Undertow (Red) 1995
Undertow (Green) 2005
Underworld 1997
Underworld (Wiseman) 2004
Underworld: Evolution pg. 410
Undisputed 2003
Unfaithful (Lyne) 2003
Unfaithful, The [1947] 1985
Unfaithfully Yours 1984
Unfinished Business 1986
Unfinished Life, An 2006
Unfinished Piece for Piano Player, An [1977] 1982
Unforgettable 1996
Unforgiven 1992
Ungfruin Goda Og Husid. *See* Honour of the House.
Unheard Music, The 1986
Unholy, The 1988
Unhook the Stars 1996
Union Square 2005
United 93 pg. 412
United States of Leland 2005
Universal Soldier 1992
Universal Soldier: The Return 2000
Unknown White Male pg. 413
Unlawful Entry 1992
Unleashed 2006
Unsane 1987
Unstrung Heroes 1995
Untamed Heart 1993
Until September 1984
Until the End of the World 1991
Untouchables, The 1987
Unzipped 1995
Up at the Villa 2001
Up Close & Personal 1996
Up for Grabs 2006
Up the Creek 1984
Upside of Anger, The 2006
Uptown Girls 2004
Uranus 1991
Urban Legend 1999
Urban Legends: Final Cut 2001
Urbania 2001
Ursula 1987
U.S. Marshals 1999

U.S. vs. John Lennon, The pg. 415
Used People 1992
Usual Suspects, The 1995
Utu 1984
U-Turn 1997
U2: Rattle and Hum 1988

V

V for Vendetta pg. 419
V. I. Warshawski 1991
V lyudyakh. *See* Among People.
Va Savoir 2002
Vagabond 1986
Valentin 2005
Valentina 1983
Valentine 2002
Valentino Returns 1989
Valiant 2006
Valley Girl 1983
Valmont 1989
Vamp 1986
Vampire in Brooklyn 1995
Vampire's Kiss 1989
Van, The 1997
Van Gogh 1992
Van Helsing 2005
Vanilla Sky 2002
Vanishing, The (Sluizer) 1988
Vanishing, The (Sluizer) 1993
Vanity Fair 2005
Vanya on 42nd Street 1995
Varsity Blues 2000
Vasectomy 1986
Vegas in Space 1993
Vegas Vacation 1997
Veillees d'armes. *See* Troubles We've Seen, The: A History of Journalism in Wartime.
Velocity of Gary, The 2000
Velvet Goldmine 1999
Vendetta 1986
Venice/Venice 1992
Venom 1982
Venus pg. 421
Venus Beauty Institute 2001
Vera Drake 2005
Verdict, The 1982
Vermont is for Lovers 1995
Verne Miller 1987
Veronica Guerin 2004
Veronika Voss 1982
Very Annie Mary 2003
Very Long Engagement, A 2005
Vertical Limit 2001
Vertical Ray of the Sun, The 2002
Vertigo [1958] 1996
Very Bad Things 1999
Very Brady Sequel, A 1996
Very Thought of You, The 2000
Vesnicko ma strediskova. *See* My Sweet Little Village.
Veuve de Saint-Pierre, La. *See* Widow of Saint-Pierre, The.
Via Appia 1991
Viaggio d'amore. *See* Journey of Love.
Vibes 1988
Vice Squad 1982
Vice Versa 1988
Victim [1961] 1984
Victor/Victoria 1982
Victory 1981
Videodrome 1983
Vie Apres l'Amour, La. *See* Life After Love.
Vie continue, La 1982
Vie de Boheme, La 1995
Vie est rien d'autre, La. *See* Life and Nothing But.
Vie est un long fleuve tranquille, La. *See* Life Is a Long Quiet River.
Vie Promise, La. *See* Promised Life, The.
Vierde Man, De. *See* 4th Man, The.
View from the Top 2004
View to a Kill, A 1985
Village, The 2005
Village of the Damned 1995
Ville est Tranquille, La. *See* Town is Quiet, The.
Vincent and Theo 1990
Violets Are Blue 1986
Violins Came with the Americans, The 1987
Violon Rouge, Le. *See* Red Violin, The.
Viper 1988
Virgen de los Sicanos, La. *See* Our Lady of the Assassins.
Virgin Queen of St. Francis High, The 1987
Virgin Suicides, The 2001
Virtuosity 1995
Virus 2000
Vision Quest 1985
Visions of Light 1993
Visions of the Spirit 1988
Visit, The 2002
Visiting Hours 1982
Visitor, The. *See* Ghost.
Vital Signs 1990
Volcano 1997
Volere, Volare 1992
Volunteers 1985
Volver pg. 423
Volver a empezar 1982
Vor. *See* Thief, The.
Voyager 1992
Voyages 2002
Voyeur 1995
Vroom 1988
Vulture, The 1985
Vzlomshik. *See* Burglar, The.

W

Waco: The Rules of Engagement 1997
Wag the Dog 1997
Wagner 1983
Wagons East! 1995
Wah-Wah pg. 425
Waist Deep pg. 426
Wait for Me in Heaven 1990
Wait Until Spring, Bandini 1990
Waiting... 2006
Waiting for Gavrilov 1983
Waiting for Guffman 1997
Waiting for the Light 1990
Waiting for the Moon 1987
Waiting to Exhale 1995

Waitress 1982
Waking Life 2002
Waking Ned Devine 1999
Waking the Dead 2001
Walk in the Clouds, A 1995
Walk Like a Man 1987
Walk on the Moon, A 1987
Walk on the Moon, A (Goldwyn) 2000
Walk the Line 2006
Walk to Remember, A 2003
Walker 1987
Walking and Talking 1996
Walking After Midnight 1988
Walking Dead, The 1995
Walking Tall 2005
Wall, The 1986
Wall Street 1987
Wallace & Gromit: The Curse of the Were-Rabbit 2006
Waltz Across Texas 1983
Wandafuru raifu. *See* After Life.
Wannsee Conference, The 1987
Wannseekonferenz, Die. *See* Wannsee Conference, The.
Wanted: Dead or Alive 1987
War 1988
War, The 1995
War Against the Indians 1995
War and Love 1985
War at Home, The 1997
War of the Buttons 1995
War of the Roses, The 1989
War of the Worlds 2006
War Party 1988
War Room, The 1993
War Tapes, The pg. 427
War Zone, The 2000
WarGames 1983
Warlock 1989, 1990
Warlock: The Armageddon 1993
Warm Nights on a Slow Moving Train 1987
Warm Summer Rain 1989
Warm Water Under a Red Bridge 2002
Warning Bandits 1987
Warning Sign 1985
Warrior Queen 1987
Warriors of Heaven and Earth 2005
Warriors of Virtue 1997
Wash, The 1988
Washington Heights 2004
Washington Square 1997
Wassup Rockers pg. 429
Watch It 1993
Watcher, The 2001
Watchers 1988
Water 1986
Water pg. 430
Water and Soap 1985
Water Drops on Burning Rocks 2001
Waterboy, The 1999
Waterdance, The 1992
Waterland 1992
Waterloo Bridge [1940] 1981
Waterworld 1995
Wavelength 1983
Waxwork 1988
Way Down East [1920] 1984
Way of the Gun, The 2001
Way We Laughed, The 2002
Way We Were, The [1973] 1981
waydowntown 2001
Wayne's World 1992
Wayne's World II 1993
We All Loved Each Other So Much 1984
We Are Marshall pg. 432
We Don't Live Here Anymore 2005
We Never Die 1993
We of the Never Never 1983
We the Living 1988
We Think the World of You 1988
We Were Soldiers 2003
Weather Man, The 2006
Weather Underground, The 2004
Wedding, A [1978] 1982
Wedding Banquet, The 1993
Wedding Bell Blues 1997
Wedding Crashers 2006
Wedding Date, The 2006
Wedding Gift, The 1995
Wedding in Galilee, A 1987
Wedding Planner, The 2002
Wedding Singer, The 1999
Weeds 1987
Weekend at Bernie's 1989
Weekend at Bernie's II 1993
Weekend Pass 1984
Weekend Warriors 1986
Weekend with Barbara und Ingrid, A 1995
Weeping Meadow 2006
Weight of Water, The 2003
Weininger's Last Night 1995
Weird Science 1985
Welcome Home 1989
Welcome Home, Roxy Carmichael 1990
Welcome in Vienna 1988
Welcome to Collinwood 2003
Welcome to Mooseport 2005
Welcome to the Dollhouse 1996
Welcome to Sarajevo 1997
Welcome to Woop Woop 1999
Wendigo 2003
We're Back 1993
We're No Angels [1955] (Curtiz) 1982
We're No Angels (Jordan) 1989
We're Talkin' Serious Merry 1992
Wes Craven Presents: Dracula 2000 2001
Wes Craven Presents: They 2003
Wes Craven's New Nightmare 1995
West Beirut 2000
West Beyrouth. *See* West Beirut.
Western 1999
Wet and Wild Summer. *See* Exchange Lifeguards.
Wet Hot American Summer 2002
Wetherby 1985
Whale Rider 2004
Whales of August, The 1987
What a Girl Wants 2004
What About Bob? 1991

What Dreams May Come 1999
What Happened to Kerouse? 1986
What Happened Was... 1995
What Lies Beneath 2001
What Planet Are You From? 2001
What the (Bleep) Do We Know? 2005
What Time Is It There? 2002
What Women Want 2001
Whatever 1999
Whatever It Takes (Demchuk) 1986
Whatever It Takes (Raynr) 2001
What's Cooking? 2001
What's Eating Gilbert Grape 1993
What's Love Got To Do With It 1993
What's the Worst That Could Happen? 2002
When a Man Loves a Woman 1995
When a Stranger Calls pg. 434
When Brendan Met Trudy 2002
When Father Was Away on Business 1985
When Harry Met Sally 1989
When Love Comes 2000
When Nature Calls 1985
When Night is Falling 1995
When the Cat's Away 1997
When the Party's Over 1993
When the Whales Came 1989
When the Wind Blows 1987
When We Were Kings 1997
When Will I Be Loved 2005
Where Angels Fear to Tread 1992
Where Are the Children? 1986
Where Spring Comes Late 1988
Where the Boys are '84 1984
Where the Day Takes You 1992
Where the Green Ants Dream 1985
Where the Heart Is (Boorman) 1990
Where the Heart Is (Williams) 2001
Where the Heart Roams 1987
Where the Money Is 2001
Where the Outback Ends 1988
Where the River Runs Black 1986
Where The Rivers Flow North 1995
Where the Truth Lies 2006
Wherever You Are 1988
While You Were Sleeping 1995
Whispers in the Dark 1992
Whistle Blower, The 1987
White 1995
White Badge 1995
White Balloon, The 1996
White Boys 2000
White Chicks 2005
White Countess, The 2006
White Dog 1995
White Fang 1991
White Fang II: Myth of the White Wolf 1995
White Girl, The 1990
White Hunter, Black Heart 1990
White Man's Burden 1995
White Men Can't Jump 1992
White Mischief 1988
White Nights 1985
White Noise 2006
White of the Eye 1987, 1988
White Oleander 2003
White Palace 1990
White Rose, The 1983
White Sands 1992
White Sister, The [1923] 1982
White Squall 1996
White Trash 1992
White Winter Heat 1987
Who Framed Roger Rabbit 1988
Who Killed the Electric Car? pg. 435
Who Killed Vincent Chin? 1988
Who Knows? *See* Va Savoir.
Who Shot Pat? 1992
Whole Nine Yards, The 2001
Whole Ten Yards, The 2005
Whole Wide World, The 1997
Whoopee Boys, The 1986
Whore 1991
Who's Afraid of Virginia Wolf? [1966] 1993
Who's Harry Crumb? 1989
Who's That Girl 1987
Who's the Man? 1993
Whose Life Is It Anyway? 1981
Why Do Fools Fall In Love 1999
Why Has Bodhi-Dharma Left for the East? 1995
Why Me? 1990
Why We Fight pg. 436
Wicked Lady, The 1983
Wicked Stepmother 1989
Wicker Man, The [1974] 1985
Wicker Man, The pg. 437
Wicker Park 2005
Wide Awake 1999
Wide Sargasso Sea 1993
Widow of Saint-Pierre, The 2002
Widows' Peak 1995
Wife, The 1996
Wigstock: the Movie 1995
Wilbur Wants to Kill Himself 2005
Wild, The pg. 439
Wild America 1997
Wild at Heart 1990
Wild Bill 1995
Wild Bunch, The [1969] 1995
Wild Duck, The 1985
Wild Geese II 1985
Wild Hearts Can't Be Broken 1991
Wild Horses 1984
Wild Life, The 1984
Wild Man Blues 1999
Wild Orchid 1990
Wild Orchid II: Two Shades of Blue 1992
Wild Pair, The 1987
Wild Parrots of Telegraph Hill, The 2006
Wild Reeds 1995
Wild Thing 1987
Wild Things 1999
Wild Thornberrrys Movie, The 2003
Wild West 1993
Wild Wild West 2000
Wildcats 1986
Wilde 1999
Wilder Napalm 1993
Wildfire 1988

Willard 2004
William Shakespeare's A Midsummer's Night Dream 2000
William Shakespeare's Romeo & Juliet 1996
William Shakespeare's The Merchant of Venice. *See* Merchant of Venice, The.
Willow 1988
Wilt. *See* Misadventures of Mr. Wilt, The.
Wimbledon 2005
Win a Date with Tad Hamilton 2005
Wind 1992
Wind, The [1928] 1984
Wind in the Willows, The 1997
Wind Will Carry Us, The 2001
Window Shopping 1995
Window to Paris 1995
Windtalkers 2003
Windy City 1984
Wing Commanders 2000
Winged Migration 2004
Wings of Desire 1988
Wings of the Dove 1997
Winner, The 1997
Winners, The 2000
Winners Take All 1987
Winslow Boy, The 2000
Winter Guest, The 1997
Winter Meeting [1948] 1986
Winter of Our Dreams 1982
Winter Passing pg. 441
Winter People 1989
Winter Solstice 2006
Winter Tan, A 1988
Winter War, The. *See* Talvison.
Wiping the Tears of Seven Generations 1995
Wired 1989
Wired to Kill 1986
Wirey Spindell 2001
Wisdom 1986
Wise Guys 1986
Wisecracks 1992
Wish You Were Here 1987
Wishmaster 1997
Witchboard 1987
Witches, The 1990
Witches of Eastwick, The 1987
With a Friend Like Harry 2002
With Friends Like These... 2006
With Honors 1995
With Love to the Person Next to Me 1987
Withnail and I 1987
Without a Clue 1988
Without a Paddle 2005
Without a Trace 1983
Without Evidence 1996
Without Limits 1999
Without You I'm Nothing 1990
Witness 1985
Witness for the Prosecution 1986
Witness to a Killing 1987
Wittgenstein 1995
Wizard, The 1989
Wizard of Loneliness, The 1988
Wizard of Oz, The [1939], 1999
Wo De Fu Qin Mu Qin. *See* Road Home, The.
Wo Die Gruenen Ameisen Traeumen. *See* Where the Green Ants Dream.
Wo Hu Zang Long. *See* Crouching Tiger, Hidden Dragon.
Wolf 1995
Wolfen 1981
Woman, Her Men, and Her Futon, A 1992
Woman in Flames, A 1984
Woman in Red, The 1984
Woman in the Moon 1988
Woman in the Window, The [1944] 1982
Woman Next Door, The 1982
Woman on the Beach, The [1947] 1982
Woman's Pale Blue Handwriting, A 1988
Woman's Tale, A 1991
Wombling Free [1979] 1984
Women on the Verge of a Nervous Breakdown 1988
Women's Affair 1988
Wonder Boys 2001
Wonderful Days. *See* Sky Blue.
Wonderful, Horrible Life of Leni Riefenstahl, The 1995
Wonderland (Saville) 1989
Wonderland (Winterbottom) 2001
Wonderland (Cox) 2004
Woo 1999
Wood, The 2000
Woodsman, The 2005
Woodstock 1995
Wordplay pg. 442
Working Girl 1988
Working Girls 1987
World According to Garp, The 1982
World and Time Enough 1996
World Apart, A 1988
World Gone Wild 1988
World Is Not Enough, The 2000
World of Henry Orient, The [1964] 1983
World Trade Center pg. 443
World Traveler 2003
World's Fastest Indian, The pg. 445
Worth Winning 1989
Wraith, The 1986
Wrestling Ernest Hemingway 1993
Wrong Couples, The 1987
Wrong Guys, The 1988
Wrong Is Right 1982
Wrong Man, The 1995
Wrong Turn 2004
Wrongfully Accused 1999
Wu ji. *See* Promise, The.
Wu jian dao. *See* Infernal Affairs.
Wyatt Earp 1995

X

X. *See* Malcolm X.
X-Files, The 1999
X-Men, The 2001
X-Men: The Last Stand pg. 447
X2: X-Men United 2004
Xero. *See* Home Remedy.

Xiao cai feng. *See* Balzac and the Little Chinese Seamstress.
Xica [1976] 1982
Xica da Silva. *See* Xica.
Xingfu Shiguang. *See* Happy Times.
Xiu Xiu, The Sent Down Girl 2000
Xizao. *See* Shower, The.
XX/XY 2004
XXX 2003
XXX: State of the Union 2006

Y

Y tu mama tambien 2003
Yaaba 1990
Yards, The 2001
Yari No Gonza Kasane Katabira. *See* Gonza the Spearman.
Yatgo Ho Yan. *See* Mr. Nice Guy.
Year My Voice Broke, The 1987, 1988
Year of Comet 1992
Year of Living Dangerously, The 1983
Year of the Dragon 1985
Year of the Gun 1991
Year of the Horse 1997
Year of the Quiet Sun, A 1986
Yearling, The [1946] 1989
Yellowbeard 1983
Yen Family 1988, 1990
Yentl 1983
Yes 2006
Yes, Giorgio 1982
Yesterday. *See* Quitting.
Yi Yi 2001
Ying xiong. *See* Hero.
Yol 1982
Yor: The Hunter from the Future 1983
You Can Count on Me 2001
You Can't Hurry Love 1988
You Got Served 2005
You, Me and Dupree pg. 449
You So Crazy 1995
You Talkin' to Me? 1987
You Toscanini 1988
Young Adam 2005
Young Dr. Kildare [1938] 1985
Young Doctors in Love 1982
Young Einstein 1988
Young Guns 1988
Young Guns II 1990
Young Poisoner's Handbook, The 1996
Young Sherlock Holmes 1985
Young Soul Rebels 1991
Youngblood 1986
Your Friends & Neighbors 1999
Yours, Mine & Ours 2006
You've Got Mail 1999
Yu-Gi-Oh! The Movie 2005

Z

Zappa 1984
Zapped! 1982
Zathura 2006
Zatoichi 2005
Zebdegi Edame Darad. *See* And Life Goes On.
Zebrahead 1992
Zegen. *See* Pimp, The.
Zelary 2005
Zelig 1983
Zelly and Me 1988
Zentropa 1992
Zero Degrees Kelvin 1996
Zero Effect 1999
Zero Patience 1995
Zeus and Roxanne 1997
Zhou Yu's Train 2005
Zir-e Poust-e Shahr. *See* Under the Skin of the City.
Zjoek 1987
Zombie and the Ghost Train 1995
Zombie High 1987
Zoolander 2002
Zoom pg. 451
Zoot Suit 1981
Zuotian. *See* Quitting.
Zus & Zo 2004